The Social Science Encyclopedia

The Social Science Encyclopedia, first published in 1985 to acclaim from social scientists, librarians and students, was thoroughly revised in 1996, when reviewers began to describe it as a classic. This third edition has been radically recast. Over half the entries are new or have been entirely rewritten, and most of the balance have been substantially revised.

Written by an international team of contributors, the *Encyclopedia* offers a global perspective on the key issues with the social sciences. Some 500 entries cover a variety of enduring and newly vital areas of study and research methods. Experts review theoretical debates from neo-evolutionism and rational choice theory to poststructuralism, and address the great questions that cut across the social sciences. What is the influence of genes on behaviour? What is the nature of consciousness and cognition? What are the causes of poverty and wealth? What are the roots of conflict, wars, revolutions and genocidal violence?

This authoritative reference work is aimed at anyone with a serious interest in contemporary academic thinking about the individual in society.

Adam Kuper is an anthropologist, author of many books, regular broadcaster and contributor to the *TLS* and the *London Review of Books*. He is a Fellow of the British Academy.

Jessica Kuper retired in 2002 as senior commissioning editor in the social sciences at Cambridge University Press.

The Social Science Encyclopedia

Third edition

Edited by Adam Kuper
and Jessica Kuper

VOLUME II
L-Z

Routledge
Taylor & Francis Group

LONDON AND NEW YORK

First edition published in 1985
Second edition published in 1996
Third edition published in 2004
by Routledge
2 Park Square, Milton Park Abingdon, Oxon, OX14 4RN
Simultaneously published in the USA and Canada
by Routledge
270 Madison Ave., New York, NY 10016

Routledge is an imprint of the Taylor & Francis Group

© 2004 Routledge
Typeset in Times by Taylor & Francis Books, Ltd
Printed and bound in Great Britain by TJ International Ltd, Padstow,
Cornwall.

British Library Cataloguing in Publication Data
A catalogue record for this book is available from the British Library

Library of Congress Cataloging in Publication Data
A catalog record for this title has been requested.

ISBN 0–415–32096–8 (set)
ISBN 0–415–34774–2 (Volume I)
ISBN 0–415–34775–0 (Volume II)

Contents

Illustrations

The Social Science Encyclopedia

Third edition

VOLUME II
L–Z

L

LABELLING THEORY

Labelling theory has made a key contribution to the analysis of crime and deviance by turning away from the study of the presumed 'deviant' (like the criminal or the drug user) and focusing instead upon reactions to deviance. The publication of Becker's influential *Outsiders* in 1963 helped the theory achieve prominence. In this study, ostensibly of drugs, Becker provides the canonical statement:

> deviance is *not* a quality of the act the person commits, but rather a consequence of the application by others of rules and sanctions to an 'offender'. The deviant is one to whom that label has successfuly been applied; deviant behaviour is behaviour that people so label.

In the critical and counter-cultural days of the mid-1960s, labelling theory was seen as the harbinger of radical new approaches. It focused upon the power of groups to define deviance. It championed the rights of groups designated deviant. It often celebrated the lifestyles of 'deviants' who had been inhumanely labelled. And it led to arguments for decriminalization, decarceration, destigmatization, deprofessionalization and demedicalization. Associated with the Society for the Study of Social Problems in the USA, it led to the growth of the National Deviancy Conference in Britain (Taylor and Taylor 1973).

In its most explicit form, labelling theory suggested that societal reactions, far from merely being responses to deviance, may often be causal in producing deviants. As Lemert (1967), another founder, argued, the idea that 'social control leads to deviance' is a 'potentially richer premise for studying deviance'. An earlier formulation of this position by Tannenbaum (1938) suggested that the very 'process of making the criminal is a process of tagging, defining, identifying, segregating, describing, emphasising, making conscious and self conscious; it becomes a way of stimulating, suggesting, emphasising, evoking the very traits that are complained of'.

In a more general form labelling theory argued for a reconceptualization of the entire field of deviance enquiry; instead of assuming definitions of deviance as objectively given and focusing thereafter on explaining the deviant, this approach recommended looking at deviance as subjectively problematic, relativistic and changing. In this general form, labelling theory suggests four key questions.

The first examines the nature of the societal reaction, problematizing the very categories associated with deviance. This means looking, for instance, at the labels used by various social control agents – such as the police or the courts – in recognizing and defining 'deviants'. It leads to research on the perceptions held of 'delinquents' by court officials (Emerson 1969), stereotypes of mentally ill people held by psychiatrists (Scheff 1966) or the role of the media in depicting social problems (Cohen and Young 1975). The focus hence is shifted from deviant being to deviant construct and stereotyping is a major concern.

A second question is causal, asking why certain groups get stigmatized, criminalized or defined as sick. Usually, this involves historical questions – asking about the ways in which legislation came into being to define marijuana as criminal, the ways in which the category of 'the homosexual' was invented in the nineteenth century, or how notions of 'madness' entered civilization. Research also asks how groups and organizations come to create their own categories of deviance – in courtrooms, in the mass media, in classrooms or at home.

A third question examines the conditions by which deviants are selected for processing – the 'screening' process. Not only are the decisions of formal control agents examined (e.g. how police apprehend delinquents), but so too is the role of more informal definers, such as those of the family or friends who may protect or reject 'deviants' (Goffman 1961a, 1961b).

A final and perhaps most common question concerns the impact of sanctions and labels on deviants. Sanctions could, for instance, deter crime, but labelling theorists usually argue that labelling may well exacerbate, amplify or even cause crime and deviance. Labelling may initiate deviant careers, generate deviant subcultures, and sometimes the overreach of the criminal law into areas of victimless crimes may create more problems than solved (Schur 1963). Finally, it is also concerned with the wider impact of labelling on the culture – the creation of a moral order, boundaries and the good.

Despite its enormous popularity and influence, labelling theory has been heavily criticized (Taylor et al. 1973; Plummer 1979). It neglects a concern with the causes of deviance. It is too social psychological – neglecting wider concerns of power, structure and history – being too individualistic, subjective and relativistic. It is vague and lacks an objective foundation. From the left, it is accused of being insufficiently critical of the state; from the right, it is seen as 'too soft' on criminals, too willing to side with the underdog, and too subversive.

Although labelling theory is always cited as one of the major sociological theories of crime and deviance, the original research and controvesies that surrounded it during the 1970s have largely abated. It now lives on in two major traditions: moral panic theory, and social constructionism.

Moral panic theory was developed by Becker, Cohen and Young. The focus here becomes the exaggerated responses of control agencies (largely the media) in stirring up concern and anxiety. It has been applied to many areas such as excessive concern over drug use, child abuse and Satanism. In many cases, it is not always clear whether the concern of the media is

justified (cf. Jenkins 1992; Critcher 2003). The theory of social constructionism is an approach in sociology which argues that 'conditions must be brought to people's notice in order to become social problems' (Best 1990: 11). Closely allied to Becker's notion of moral enterprise, it looks at the ways individuals, groups and societies come to label certain phenomena as problems and how others then respond to such claims. Joel Best for instance has traced the 'rhetoric and concern about child victims', whilst Joseph Gusfield (1981) has traced the drink-driving problem. Broadly, there is seen to be a 'social problems market-place' in which people struggle to own social problems: these theories continue to examine the rhetorics, the claims and the power struggles behind such defintional processes. Donileen Loseke has written the classic text on this position (2003 [1999]).

In sum: labelling theory highlights societal reactions to crime and deviance. It has a long history but becomes particularly prominent in the 1960s and 1970s. Since that time, and after a number of critiques, the theory has become something of an orthodoxy. Currently, the theory of moral panics and the theory of social constructionism have become its modern day reincarnations.

KEN PLUMMER
UNIVERSITY OF ESSEX

References

Becker, H.S. (1963) *Outsiders: Studies in the Sociology of Deviance*, New York.
Best, J. (1990) *Threatened Children: Rhetoric and Concern about Child Victims*, Chicago.
Cohen, S. (2002 [1970]) *Folk Devils and Moral Panics*, 3rd edn, London.
Cohen, S. and Young, J. (1975) *The Manufacture of News*, London.
Critcher, C. (2003) *Moral Panics and the Media*, Buckingham.
Emerson, R. (1969) *Judging Delinquents*, Chicago.
Goffman, E. (1961a) *Stigma*, Harmondsworth.
—— (1961b) *Asylums*, Harmondsworth.
Gusfield, J.R. (1981) *The Culture of Public Problems: Drinking-Driving and the Symbolic Order*, Chicago.
Jenkins, P. (1992) *Intimate Enemies: Moral Panics in Contemporary Great Britain*, New York.
Lemert, E. (1967) *Human Deviance, Social Problems and Social Control*, Englewood Cliffs, NJ.
Loseke, D. (2003 [1999]) *Thinking about Social Problems: An Introduction to Constructionist Perspectives*, 2nd edn, New York.
Plummer, K. (1979) 'Misunderstanding labelling per-

spectives', in D. Downes and P. Rock (eds) *Deviant Interpretations*, Oxford.

Scheff, T.J. (1966) *Being Mentally Ill*, London.

Schur, E. (1963) *Crimes without Victims*, Englewood Cliffs, NJ.

Tannenbaum, F. (1938) *Crime and the Community*, Cincinnati, OH.

Taylor, I. and Taylor, L. (1973) *Politics and Deviance*, Harmondsworth.

Taylor, I., Walton, P. and Young, J. (1973) *The New Criminology*, London.

SEE ALSO: crime and delinquency; deviance; homosexualities; prejudice; social exclusion; stereotypes; stigma

LABOUR MARKET ANALYSIS

Since before Adam Smith, labour markets have been known to differ greatly from other markets. Workers cannot be separated from the services they provide, and their motivation and beliefs critically affect how they work. Labour is not exchanged on a labour market: instead, people contract to supply labour in a form to be specified in detail (and within certain limits) only after they have been hired. The employment relationship is often of considerable duration. In 1998, the percentage of workers with their current firms for 10 years or more was: UK, 32 per cent; USA, 26 per cent; Germany, 38 per cent; and Japan, 43 per cent (Auer and Cazes 2000). As many workers change firms only occasionally, it is clear that many employment problems are the result of a complex mix of market and organizational causes. Which of these we believe is the predominant cause will condition whether we start from price theory, stressing the analogy with other markets, and the 'competitive hypothesis', as would most neo-classical economists, or from a more organizational or institutional approach. To explore the differences between these I shall look at labour allocation and work incentives.

The majority, 'neo-classical', tradition emphasizes competition and flexible prices, believing that these will, in the long run, provide the best overall outcomes for the greatest number. Because firms compete for workers, those with dangerous or unpleasant working conditions have to pay more to attract them. If they need workers with particular skills, then, by offering higher wages, they provide an incentive for people to undertake the necessary training. The price mechanism works better than government

educational planning based on surveys of skill needs because it forces firms to say not only what skills they would like, but also how much they would be worth to them. In the context of unemployment, with flexible wages and no restrictions on laying workers off, firms would hire extra labour until workers no longer thought the wages offered worthwhile.

Faced with bad working conditions, skill shortages or unemployment, neo-classical economists would generally look first for failures of, or obstacles to, the price mechanism. Is it better to seek to improve dangerous or unhealthy working conditions by means of government regulation, which is costly to run and is often easily evaded, or to rely on the price mechanism? The latter means that employers have to pay more to attract workers, and so have a financial incentive to invest in technology to improve conditions. If accident rates remain high, is it because employers enjoy monopsonistic power in their local labour markets, or because of some perversity in the price mechanism? For example, employers may fear that if they are the first to invest in safer equipment they will attract the most accident-prone workers (Elliott 1991).

If an industry faces persistent problems of skill shortages, are the incentives for people to train right? Do the rewards for skilled jobs adequately compensate for the outlays involved? Are employers failing to get any return on training they provide because workers are leaving once their training is complete? If the skills are transferable, should the trainees bear most of the cost, perhaps as low trainee allowances? In the case of unemployment among low-skilled workers, are minimum-wage laws or collective agreements setting pay levels that make it uneconomic to employ them – 'pricing them out of jobs'?

Treating wages as if they were market prices, and labour as a freely traded commodity, arguably comes closest to reality when looking at the markets for casual labour, where job durations are typically rather short, and for craft and professional occupations where skills are transferable between firms.

In recent years, this 'competitive hypothesis' has come under challenge from three directions, all of which place more emphasis on firms' human resource policies, and on the institutions that underpin interfirm co-operation in collective activities such as training. The first concerns the growing interest in the persistence of low-skilled and low-paid work in labour markets. In 1995, Card and Krueger relaunched the analytical interest in these labour markets by challenging the received wisdom that raising minimum wages would always mean less jobs. Employer monopsony power had always been accepted as a theoretical possibility in isolated communities where a single employer might dominate a company town. However, the increased mobility with the automobile, and the growing distances people were willing to travel to work left this as a curiosity. To explain the empirical evidence they observed, that increased minimum wages often did not result in lower employment, Card and Krueger developed a simple 'dynamic monopsony' model in which employers could choose between two alternative human resource strategies. They could pay good wages and run a fully staffed operation. Alternatively, they could seek to pay as little as possible and endure high labour turnover and persistent unfilled vacancies. In a competitive labour market, the latter strategy might not be viable. However, if employers face a captive labour market, and many of their employees fear losing their jobs, then they can pressurize them to work harder to cover the unfilled vacancies without extra pay. Although company towns may be a feature of the past, the uneven distribution of domestic responsibilities in many households means that women are often restricted in the distance they can travel to work, and hence limited in their choice of potential employers. Subsequent work on low pay, for example by the OECD (1998) and by Manning (2003), has provided further support for Card and Krueger's re-evaluation of the competitive hypothesis.

A second challenge arises when looking at relations within the enterprise, and when looking at the institutions that characterize modern labour markets such as trade unions and training organizations. Many job changes occur within firms, through promotions and job reassignments, as indeed do interregional job moves (about 40 per cent of such moves in the UK in the late 1980s). It has been common to contrast the allocation of labour between firms, on 'external' or 'local' labour markets, with that within the firm, on 'internal' labour markets (ILMs). Whereas the former involves movement between firms, or between unemployment and jobs, the latter involves movement between jobs or employment locations within firms.

Whether wages act in the same way on ILMs as they are reputed to do on local labour markets is hotly debated (e.g. Rosenberg 1989). Some argue that the force of competition among workers is weak compared with intergroup power relations, and once workers have been hired, management's primary task is to organize and motivate staff, not negotiate market prices.

The reasons why firms develop ILMs, and hence their overall significance for economic theory, are also under debate. Building on price theory, the neo-classical approach seeks to explain ILMs as a response to certain kinds of failure in the market system. For example, ILMs may develop in firms where the necessary skills are lacking on their local labour markets, or firms may develop ILMs to encourage workers to take a long-term interest in their firm's success. In the first case, many firms have their own unique production methods, or a particular style of service, and then develop their own training programmes linking these to job progression, thus creating an ILM (Doeringer and Piore 1971). In the second case, because workers have much better knowledge of their work and the production process than management, they have a strong incentive to manipulate information in order to negotiate a more favourable effort-bargain, but which reduces productivity. By creating an ILM, the employer gives workers a long-term stake in their firm's success so that they will wish to raise productivity (Williamson 1975). In both explanations, the ILM remains nested within the general framework of price theory.

An alternative, 'institutionalist' view of ILMs treats them as the normal pattern for firms to adopt unless there already exists a structure of occupational markets for qualified labour (OLMs). Interfirm markets for labour with transferable skills are in fact like public goods and so depend upon a high degree of co-operation among employers to control 'free-rider' behaviour. Without this support, they are inherently unstable (Marsden 1986; Crouch 1995). Although in theory the trainee should bear the cost of wholly transferable training (Becker 1975), there are strong theoretical and practical reasons why employers commonly bear much of the cost.

The 'cost-sharing' mechanisms predicted by Becker tend to break down for a number of reasons. Relying on low trainee pay rates limits investments in transferable skills to what working-class families can afford to subsidize. Adult skilled workers may be leery of low trainee rates, fearing that trainees could be exploited as a form of cheap, substitute labour, and therefore seek either to restrict numbers, or to raise trainee pay rates. Employers may not be able to enforce apprenticeship contracts and recoup their training costs – the cause of its decline in the USA.

Hence, employers have an incentive to cut their own training expenditures and to 'poach' skilled labour from their competitors. This increases the costs for employers who continue to train, and thus further encourages poaching. Out of the resulting vicious circle the OLM atrophies and breaks up, and firms resort to ILM practices in order to be sure to capture the returns on their investment in skill formation.

Yet despite these problems, we observe many large OLMs for occupational skills in Germany, in parts of UK industry, and in many countries in the artisan sector and professional services. Their survival has depended largely upon a strong institutional infrastructure capable of controlling free-rider activities by employers, and of reassuring skilled workers that cost-sharing would not lead to their being substituted by cheap apprentice labour. In Germany, the local chambers of industry and commerce, to which all local employers have to belong, provide powerful channels for peer group pressures against free-riding, and strong supervisory powers exercised by the works councils, supported by the unions, have ensured that apprentices get their full training. In the absence of such structures, firms will generally adopt ILM strategies.

Thus to contrast the two approaches on labour allocation, neo-classical economists generally look for blockages in the price mechanism as potential causes of many of the serious labour market problems, and commonly identify institutional factors as one of the prime culprits. The institutionalist approach treats the institutional framework as a precondition for an effective price mechanism. Thus, in the case of skills training, the former stresses the need for low trainee rates of pay and high rewards for skilled workers, whereas the latter stresses the need to create the institutional structures under which adult workers will accept the cost-sharing solution, and employers will refrain from poaching (Marsden and Ryan 1990).

Turning to incentives within the firm, a revolution has taken place in economic thinking on wages, giving rise to the new 'Economics of Personnel'. Many economists within the neo-classical mainstream have abandoned the idea that the market sets a single rate of pay for a given job as irrelevant to many jobs. Instead, they have argued that workers are attracted to jobs by the whole package of benefits on offer, be they short-term employment at a fixed wage or the prospect of career employment and salary progression. Employers adopt one or other model depending on the kind of worker they wish to recruit. Thus fast-food firms might have relatively simple incentive structures with a rate for the job, whereas retail banks might offer complex structures with career jobs, age or performance incremental pay scales, and so on, depending on the kind of recruit they want.

Employers are also concerned about the quality of performance their staff provide (see Akerlof and Yellen 1986, and the textbook by Baron and Kreps 1999). In many types of jobs, substandard performance by the employee does not become apparent for some time. By providing career employment, the employer has time to monitor performance, and to sanction good or bad results. Employees might be encouraged to stay by taking a starting salary below the value of their output in the expectation that, later in their career, they would be paid in excess of it. By offering such profiles, employers can attract employees who are looking for a long-term job. In addition, the penalty of dismissal for poor performance increases with seniority (since alternative jobs in other firms would not pay them for skills and experience specific to their previous employer) so the incentive to perform well increases. Some other theories look at how different kinds of salary and promotion systems encourage good rather than perfunctory performance. Competition for promotion can be organized as a 'tournament' to ensure high performance, thus top salaries may reflect less the value of the work done by top managers than that of those competing for the top jobs (see, for example, Lazear 1998). Another theory looks at pay as involving a 'partial gift exchange' with reciprocity whereby employers offer better than average career conditions to their staff, and, in return, employees feel that they should reciprocate by giving better performance (Akerlof and Yellen 1986).

These theories focus mainly upon performance and incentives for individual firms, and there is minimal reference to supporting institutional structures. The need for the latter becomes apparent when we consider what is needed in order to promote co-operative exchange within the workplace. It can be argued that co-operative exchange leads to high productivity because it encourages flexible working and information sharing. Such practices are hard to obtain in many organizations because they affect small-group power relations (Brown 1973). Since co-operation usually involves one party placing itself in a weak position *vis-à-vis* others (for example by sharing information it controls) it exposes itself to exploitation. Therefore, parties will not normally adopt a co-operative stance unless they are confident the others will do likewise. The rise of 'lean production' and the increasing awareness of the greater job flexibility to be found in German and Japanese workplaces, as compared with the job demarcation rules until recently common in Britain or the seniority rules common in the USA, have brought these issues to centre stage (Womack *et al.* 1990).

Game theory stresses the difficulty of obtaining stable co-operative exchange unless there is some kind of trust, and thus some kind of framework to support it (Dasgupta 1988). Two important conditions should be met: the parties need to know something about the motivations and intentions of the others, and they need some framework of guarantees to give them redress, and to enable them to exchange information so that genuine cases when *force majeure* prevents reciprocity can be distinguished from simple opportunism. Concrete examples of such frameworks can be found in the current practice of German co-determination, and in the relations between large Japanese firms, enterprise unions and their federations (Aoki 1988, 2001).

In recent years, the concept of *employment system* has gained currency as a framework for relating the microlevel employment relationship with firms' human resource management, and with labour market institutions (Katz and Darbishire 2000; Marsden 1999). These are of four main types, which are obtained by combining two basic organizational principles. The first concerns whether the employment systems accommodate ILM or OLM patterns. These define jobs either from the point of view of the firm's production technology, or from that of workers' occupational skills. The different methods of skill formation associated with each of these have a profound influence on firms' human resource management policies, and also on the bases for union organization depending on whether unions seek to regulate jobs within firms, or occupations that span labour markets. The second principle concerns the definition and regulation of employees' work obligations. As mentioned in the opening paragraph, employees' agreement to let management direct their work extends only within certain limits. These may be defined in terms of the individual tasks comprising their jobs, as under traditional 'taylorist' job design, or they may be determined by the function to which they contribute, as is common in Japanese concepts of work design (Marsden 1999). When workers' jobs are clearly defined by their tasks, work patterns may be somewhat rigid, but they can operate at quite low levels of mutual trust. In contrast, when jobs are defined in relation to functions in the work system, they can be very flexible, but there is a high requirement on workplace trust and co-operation. An adversarial bargaining style works well with the first, but a more 'problem-solving' approach to conflict resolution is needed for the second. By virtue of the complementarities between the different levels of employment relations, the job, company HR policy and labour market regulation, one can expect whole sectors, and sometimes even whole economies, to be dominated by a particular type of employment system, a feature that has been observed in the growing volume of international comparative research on labour market organization.

The balance between market competitive pressures on the one hand, and organizational and institutional influences on the other, is partly a theoretical and partly an empirical question. To some extent, also, both sets of processes are complementary. For example, markets cannot function without contracts or some kind of mutual understanding, and even the most hermetic ILMs have to recruit at some points from the outside, and have to provide workers with sufficient rewards to retain them. Competition is also a source of institutional innovation in labour markets, as we have seen with the spread of employment systems based on functional patterns of work organization.

DAVID MARSDEN
LONDON SCHOOL OF ECONOMICS
AND POLITICAL SCIENCE

References

Akerlof, G. and Yellen, J. (eds) (1986) *Efficiency Wage Models of the Labour Market*, Cambridge, UK.

Aoki, M. (1988) *Information, Incentives, and Bargaining in the Japanese Economy*, Cambridge, UK.

—— (2001) *Toward a Comparative Institutional Analysis*, Cambridge, MA.

Auer, P. and Cazes, S. (2000) 'The resilience of the long-term employment relationship: Evidence from the industrialised countries', *International Labour Review* 139(4): 379–408.

Baron, J. and Kreps, D. (1999) *Strategic Human Resources: Frameworks for General Managers*, New York.

Becker, G.S. (1975) *Human Capital: A Theoretical and Empirical Analysis, with Special Reference to Education*, Chicago.

Brown, W.E. (1973) *Piecework Bargaining*, London.

Card, D. and Krueger, A. (1995) *Myth and Measurement: The New Economics of the Minimum Wage*, Princeton, NJ.

Crouch, C. (1995) 'Organised interests as resources or as constraint: Rival logics of vocational training policy', in C. Crouch and F. Traxler (eds) *Organised Industrial Relations in Europe: What Future?* Avebury.

Dasgupta, P. (1988) 'Trust as a commodity', in D. Gambetta (ed.) *Trust: Making and Breaking Cooperative Relations*, Oxford.

Doeringer, P.B. and Piore, M.J. (1971) *International Labor Markets and Manpower Analysis*, Lexington, MA.

Elliott, R.F. (1991) *Labor Economics: A Comparative Text*, New York.

Katz, H. and Darbishire, O. (2000) *Converging Divergencies: Worldwide Changes in Employment Systems*, Ithaca, NY.

Lazear, E.P. (1998) *Personnel Economics for Managers*, New York.

Manning, A. (2003) *Monopsony in Motion: Imperfect Competition in Labor Markets*, Princeton, NJ.

Marsden, D.W. (1986) *The End of Economic Man? Custom and Competition in Labour Markets*, Brighton.

—— (1999) *A Theory of Employment Systems: Microfoundations of Societal Diversity*, Oxford.

Marsden, D.W. and Ryan, P. (1990) 'Institutional aspects of youth employment and training policy in Britain', *British Journal of Industrial Relations* 28(3).

OECD (1998) *Employment Outlook 1998*, OECD, Paris

Rosenberg, S. (ed.) (1989) *The State and the Labor Market*, New York.

Williamson, O.E. (1975) *Markets and Hierarchies: Analysis and Antitrust Implications*, New York.

Womack, J., Jones, D.T. and Roos, D. (1990) *The Machine that Changed the World*, New York.

SEE ALSO: employment and unemployment; supply-side economics; trade unions

LACAN, JACQUES (1901–81)

Of all the psychoanalysts who elaborated Freud's theory of mental functioning and his innovative treatment method during the twentieth century, Jacques Lacan is without question the most controversial. He has been deified by some as the only true successor to the Freudian throne, and vilified by others as a theoretical nonsense-monger and clinical charlatan. Nevertheless, Lacanian psychoanalysis constitutes a genuine alternative to the mainstream neo-Freudian and Kleinian approaches, and Lacanian concepts have been widely used by researchers in the social sciences and the humanities.

Lacan was born in Paris on 13 April 1901 in a middle-class Roman-Catholic family. After training as a medical doctor, he specialized in psychiatry, completing a doctoral dissertation on paranoia in 1932 (Lacan 1975 [1932]). During the 1920s Lacan discovered the work of Sigmund Freud and started exploring psychoanalysis, encouraged by the intellectual and artistic experiments of the surrealist movement. Shortly before the outbreak of the Second World War, and after completing his training analysis with Rudolph Loewenstein, Lacan was adopted as a full member of the Paris Psychoanalytic Society (SPP), which enabled him to start a private practice. In 1953, Lacan's employment of the so-called 'variable-length session', as opposed to the standard '50-minute hour', became controversial, and triggered an institutional rift in the French psychoanalytic community (Miller 1976). Ten years later, the same issue led to Lacan being expelled from the International Psychoanalytic Association (IPA) and in June 1964 he created his own school, the *Ecole freudienne de Paris* (now the *Ecole de la Cause freudienne*) (Miller 1977). Although his ideas became increasingly complex and difficult, if not obscure, Lacan's audience grew exponentially during the 1960s and 1970s. By the time of his death in 1981 his influence as a teacher, writer and clinician was so immense that some of his terms (the real, the symbolic and the imaginary, for example) had already entered the language, much like Freud's notion of the Oedipus complex.

Theoretically, Lacan always claimed that his work entailed nothing more than a 'return to Freud' (Lacan 2002 [1955]), warranted by what he perceived to be the dubious deviations from Freud's original inspiration within the post-

Freudian literature. In the face of the accusations of mystification levelled against Lacan's interpretation of Freud, he himself argued that he was the only psychoanalyst working within an orthodox Freudian framework. Even when he advocated the marriage of Freudian theory with the principles of structuralist linguistics, as developed by Ferdinand de Saussure and Roman Jakobson (Lacan 2002 [1957]), Lacan believed that this was a project of cross-fertilization fully in accordance with the founder's ambition. In his reading of Freud, *The Interpretation of Dreams* (Freud 1900) revolves entirely around linguistic operations, and so does the clinical practice of psychoanalysis.

Because of Lacan's longstanding allegiance to the structuralist paradigm, his name is often mentioned alongside that of other 'structuralist' scholars such as Claude Lévi-Strauss, Roland Barthes and Louis Althusser. Yet from the mid-1960s Lacan progressively distanced himself from structuralism, with its insistence on the formative power of language. In 1972 he confessed in his seminar (in the presence of the great structuralist linguist, Jakobson) that his take on psychoanalysis favoured 'linguistricks' (*linguisterie*) rather than linguistics (Lacan 1998 [1972–3]: 15). This did not imply that he embraced the 'poststructuralist' theories of Michel Foucault and Jacques Derrida. Rather he began to reflect on some of his own conceptual categories, especially those destined to reach out into a space beyond the boundaries of language, such as *the real*, *jouissance* and the object *a*. In moving away from structuralism, Lacan also abandoned the ambition with which he had begun in the 1960s of transforming psychoanalysis into a structuralist science (Lacan 1977 [1964]). He now also explored the possibility of enriching psychoanalytic knowledge with the mathematical operations of topology and the theory of knots. During the mid-1970s Lacan enjoyed treating his audience to exceedingly complex manipulations of the figure of the 'Borromean knot', demonstrating its special features on the blackboard and often substituting this type of writing and drawing for the purportedly more ambiguous production of speech.

Lacan made innumerable contributions to the field of psychoanalysis, most of which have, however, not been taken up by analysts outside Lacan's own school, and some of which provoked opposition within the Lacanian community itself. On a theoretical level, Lacan introduced a range of new ideas (the mirror stage, the desire of the analyst, the split subject, the theory of the four discourses, etc.), all of which were meant to rationalize and formalize the practice of psychoanalysis. Technically, he invented the 'variable-length session' and reworked Freud's principles of transference handling and interpretation. Scorning the way in which psychoanalysts were trained within the IPA, Lacan organized his own School around the so-called 'procedure of the pass', which no doubt constitutes his most significant institutional innovation (Lacan 1982 [1974]).

Like Lacan's ideas themselves, the editorial policies underpinning the publication of his texts have been subjected to serious criticism, and much of his work is not yet available in published form, even in the original French. For the Anglophone reader it is not always easy to grasp the impact of Lacan's contributions. This is due in part to the stylistic difficulty of his texts, but also to the fact that only six of the twenty-eight volumes of Lacan's seminars are currently available in an official English translation, and his *Ecrits*, a 900-page collection of papers spanning a 20-year period to 1966, has been published in English only in a much truncated version (Lacan 2002).

DANY NOBUS
BRUNEL UNIVERSITY

References

Freud, S. (1900) 'The interpretation of dreams', in *The Standard Edition of the Complete Psychological Works of Sigmund Freud*, Vols 4–5, London.
Lacan, J. (1975 [1932]) 'De la psychose paranoïaque dans ses rapports avec la personnalité', in *De la psychose paranoïaque dans ses rapports avec la personnalité, suivi de premiers écrits sur la paranoïa*, Paris, pp. 13–362.
—— (1977 [1964]) *The Four Fundamental Concepts of Psychoanalysis*, ed. J.-A. Miller, London.
—— (1982 [1974]) 'Note italienne', *Ornicar?* 25: 7–10.
—— (1998 [1972–3]) *The Seminar. Book XX: On Feminine Sexuality, the Limits of Love and Knowledge (Encore)*, ed. J.-A. Miller, New York.
—— (2002) *Ecrits: A Selection*, New York.
—— (2002 [1955]) 'The Freudian thing, or the meaning of the return to Freud in psychoanalysis', in *Ecrits: A Selection*, New York, pp. 107–37.
—— (2002 [1957]) 'The instance of the letter in the unconscious or reason since Freud', in *Ecrits: A Selection*, New York, pp. 138–68.
Miller, J.-A. (1976) *La Scission de 1953 – La communauté psychanalytique en France 1*, Paris.

—— (1977) *L'Excommunication – La communauté psychanalytique en France 2*, Paris.

Further reading

Bowie, M. (1991) *Lacan*, London.
Evans, D. (1996) *An Introductory Dictionary of Lacanian Psychoanalysis*, London.
Fink, B. (1997) *A Clinical Introduction to Lacanian Psychoanalysis: Theory and Technique*, Cambridge, MA.
Macey, D. (1988) *Lacan in Contexts*, London.
Nobus, D. (2000) *Jacques Lacan and the Freudian Practice of Psychoanalysis*, London.
Roudinesco, E. (1997 [1993]) *Jacques Lacan*, New York.
Schneiderman, S. (1983) *Jacques Lacan: The Death of an Intellectual Hero*, Cambridge, MA.

SEE ALSO: Freud; psychoanalysis; structuralism; poststructuralism

LANDSCAPE

Landscape in conventional usage is a spatial concept, denoting an area of land whose coherence sets it apart from surrounding territory. Its medieval origins as a legal term in Germanic languages relate to the areal extent of customary law governing a community's authority over land (as, for example, over the cultivated lands of a group of parishes or townships). Its parallels in the Romance languages (*pays, paesaggio, paisaje*) have a similar derivation. The suffix *scape* relates to the words ship and shape, implying community or fellowship organization and human design of space (Olwig 2002). Since the later sixteenth century, however, landscape and its parallels in other European languages have accreted a strongly visual and graphic dimension, largely from their connections with survey and perspective pictorial images (landscape painting). The coherence and design of a landscape is now assumed to derive from its visual framing and composition. From being a term of art, landscape evolved to denote actual scenery, spaces that either have the qualities of a painting, or that are viewed aesthetically. Landscape gardening, which extended the aesthetic qualities of the garden beyond its traditional enclosure, played a role in this semiotic transformation. This meaning of landscape has been further extended to refer to any area, aesthetically pleasing or otherwise, but it retains both strong visual reference and a close connection to cultivated land, rather than urbanized or maritime spaces, to which the

derivative terms townscape and seascape are applied. 'Wilderness' may be referred to as landscape when its visual qualities are being emphasized.

Among the social sciences, geography has paid greatest attention to landscape, although the discipline of landscape architecture has in recent years extended its concern from design to more theoretical consideration of its object (Corner 1999; Groth and Bressi 1997). Drawing on German geographical precedents, the geographer Carl Sauer and his students at Berkeley used landscape as a central concept in studies of human transformation of the natural world and its characteristic cultural expressions in particular regions (Leighly 1963). The cultural landscape was an empirical datum for assessing the changes wrought by material culture on a pre-existing natural landscape, through such activities as cultivation, domestication, land drainage and forest clearance (Thomas 1956). This ecological emphasis of landscape study remains vital in environmental and cultural heritage conservation of traditional agrarian landscapes, especially in continental Europe (Palang 2003). The study of landscape as an expression of culture was extended to more contemporary and vernacular scenes by J.B. Jackson, founder of the journal *Landscape*, whose writings sought to explore changing US popular culture through such elements as the highway strip, the front yard and the shopping mall (Jackson 1984; Meinig 1979).

Since the mid-1980s increased academic emphasis has been placed on the cultural politics of landscape, with the recognition that landscape represents a way of seeing and representing space with close historical and conceptual connections to power (Bender 1994; Cosgrove and Daniels 1988). Landscape thus often serves to naturalize and thereby mask unequal social relations (Daniels 1989). The historical connections between landscape, mapping and property ownership have been explored (Cosgrove 1996), as have the roles of landscape representations in constructing, sustaining and contesting the identities of communities and places at different scales. Iconic landscapes such as Niagara Falls (McKinsey 1985), Constable's Suffolk (Daniels 1992), Western Ireland or the Canadian shield (Unwin 1998) play a significant role in the construction of national identity. Literary and artistic representations of landscape are today given as much attention as actual material landscapes. Conservation of heritage landscapes for social and economic purposes, and contemporary architecture's shift away from narrow focus upon individual buildings towards the broader spatial context (or landscape) of building projects, are among the practical concerns that have brought landscape more centrally into the field of policy and planning. As a mediating concept of nature and culture, landscape's theoretical significance continues to grow.

DENIS COSGROVE
UNIVERSITY OF CALIFORNIA AT LOS ANGELES

References

Bender, B. (ed.) (1994) *Landscape: Politics and Perspectives*, London.
Corner, J. (1999) *Recovering Landscape: Essays in Contemporary Landscape Architecture*, Princeton.
Cosgrove, D. (1996) *Social Formation and Symbolic Landscape*, Madison, WI.
Cosgrove, D. and Daniels, S.J. (1988) *The Iconography of Landscape*, Cambridge, UK.
Daniels, S. (1989) 'Marxism, culture and the duplicity of landscape', in R. Peet and N. Thrift (eds) *New Models in Geography*, London, pp. 176–200.
—— (1992) *Fields of Vision: Landscape and National Identity in England and the United States*, London.
Groth, P. and Bressi, T. (1997) *Understanding Ordinary Landscape*, New Haven and London.
Jackson, J.B. (1984) *Discovering the Vernacular Landscape*, New Haven, CT.
Leighly, J. (1963) *Land and Life: Selections from the Writings of Carl Orhvin Satter*, Berkeley, CA.
McKinsey, E. (1985) *Niagara Falls. Icon of the American Sublime*, Cambridge, UK.
Meinig, D. (1979) *The Interpretation of Ordinary Landscapes*, Oxford.
Olwig, K. (2002) *Landscape, Nature and the Body Politic: From Britain's Renaissance to America's New World*, Madison, WI.
Palang, H. (2003) *Landscape Interfaces: Cultural Heritage and Landscape Ecology*, Dordrecht.
Thomas, W.L. (1956) *Man's Role in Changing the Face of the Earth*, Chicago.
Unwin, T. (1998) *A European Geography*, London.

SEE ALSO: cartography; cultural geography; spatial analysis

LANGUAGE

Language is the most human of all human abilities. It may be the defining characteristic of *Homo sapiens*. Wherever humans exist, language exists. Although no one knows the precise number of languages in the world, something in the order of 6,000 to 6,600 is a good estimate, the exact number depending on one's definition of language versus dialect. (For the layman, the term 'dialect' connotes a substandard deformation of a standard language or, sometimes, an unwritten language spoken by a small tribal group. As a technical linguistic term, 'dialect' simply refers to any socially or geographically recognizable variant of a language, e.g. Standard US English, Oxbridge English, Australian English, Indian English, Appalachian English, cockney and black vernacular English are all 'dialects of English'.) Considering that the world is populated by billions of people, the number of distinct languages is actually rather small. In addition, a large portion of the world's population speaks only a small handful of these thousands of languages: Chinese (Mandarin), English, Spanish, Portuguese, Russian, Arabic, Hindi and Indonesian/Malay count among the extra-large languages with hundreds of millions of speakers. English can rightfully be considered the world's most widespread language, especially when one takes into account second-language users, but it is not the language with the most speakers. Mandarin Chinese, with close to a billion speakers, can claim this first spot.

Although some 6,000+ distinct languages exist, most of them can be grouped into families of related languages in the same way that different plants and animals can be grouped into species, genera and families. There are a few isolates, such as Basque and Hadza (Tanzania), but these are rare. Better-known families are Indo-European, to which English belongs, Sino-Tibetan (East Asia), Athabaskan (North America) and Niger-Congo (Africa south of the Sahara). Lower-level families such as Bantu and Semitic are easily recognizable, whereas historically much deeper and larger superfamilies such as Nostratic (Europe, Northern Asia, the Caucasus and the Middle East) and Amerind (almost all native languages of the New World from southern Canada to Patagonia) are more tenuous groupings that are subject to ongoing debate.

At first sight, the world's languages show remarkable and seemingly unlimited variation in appearance and structure. Apache, Chinese, Hebrew, !Kung, Lapp, Mohawk, Mongolian, Russian, Thai, Uzbek, Warlpiri and Zulu seem very different from one other in almost every respect. Yet, despite these surface differences, all human languages are governed by universal properties and constraints. This fundamental notion can be traced back to thirteenth-century observations by Roger Bacon; but in modern times it owes its recognition and scholarly impact to the ideas of Noam Chomsky, the dominant linguist and innovative thinker about language in the second half of the twentieth century.

A basic postulate held by all linguists, and taught in every introductory linguistics course, is that human languages are all equally complex. This is probably not literally true; certainly it has never been shown to be so. What does seem to be true is that there are no so-called primitive languages in the sense that all human languages are essentially equally capable of expression. If one can express a proposition in one language, the same thought can be expressed in another, although the form and manner of expression may differ considerably. The expressive potential of languages shows up in the remarkable elasticity of their lexicons. The vocabulary of every language is a living organism that is always in the process of being enriched to include new words for new things or concepts. Vocabulary expansion is accomplished through a variety of means such as borrowing words from another language, e.g. *pizza* (from Italian) or *hadj* (from Arabic), combining words to form compounds, e.g. *skyscraper* or *pickpocket*, blending words together, e.g. *smog* from *smoke* and *fog* or *motel* from *motor* and *hotel*, coining new words, a common practice of manufacturers of new products as exemplified by *aspirin*, *kleenex* and *bandaid*, or using acronyms as single words, e.g. *radar* from *radio detecting and ranging* or *AIDS* from *acquired immune deficiency syndrome*. Abbreviated forms of longer words or phrases may also become lexicalized, as exemplified by *ad* for *advertisement* or *bra* for *brassière*, and proper names may be used as common terms, such as *champagne*, from the *Champagne* region in France (although the French object strongly to this generic usage or 'genericide') or *sandwich*, named from the fourth Earl of Sandwich, who, it is reported, ate his food between slices of bread so that he need not take time off from gambling to eat in normal fashion. These examples are all from English, but all languages can expand vocabularies in similar fashion, as is shown by compounds such as *cure-dent* (toothpick) in French, *Panzerkraftwagen* (armoured car) in German, *farar-hula* (civilian, lit. white cap) in Hausa (Nigeria), or *heneba* (prince, lit. son of chief) in Akan (Ghana).

A universal characteristic of languages is that the form/sound of vocabulary items has no natural real-world connection to its referent or meaning. Most languages have a few items such as 'mama' or 'meow' that are onomatopoetic, i.e. there is supposedly some direct connection between the sound and the meaning, but the essence of human language is a system composed of totally arbitrary signs whose meaning is assigned only by convention and history. For example, the word meaning 'house' is *house* in English, *maison* in French, *casa* in Spanish, *dom* in Russian, *gida* in Hausa and *nyumba* in Swahili. In none of these languages, or any of the thousands of other languages of the world, is the pronunciation of the word any more indicative of the meaning 'house' than in any of the others.

All human languages utilize a finite set of discrete sounds like 's', 'm', 't', 'a' and 'i', which can be defined by a finite set of phonetic properties or features. In addition to consonants and vowels, accent (as in English) or tone (as in Yoruba) are common properties of the phonological inventory of languages. Some sounds, e.g. the clicks of !Kung and Xhosa, and other Southern African languages, are non-existent elsewhere in the world, but most languages draw on the same finite universal set of phonological units.

The sound segments combine to form syllables that in term form meaningful units like *cat*, *play*, *common* or *-ess* (as in *princess*) called *morphemes*. Some words consist of just one morpheme; others are complex morphological units in which simple morphemes combine to form words like *cats*, *replay*, *uncommonly* or *princess*. Each language has specific constraints on word formation. In English one can add *un-* as a prefix to negate the meaning of word, as in *unlikely* or *unfortunate*, but one cannot add it at the end as a suffix, i.e. *likelyun* and *fortunateun* are not words in English. Nor can one add it to all words even as a prefix: note the non-existence of *uncat* and *unplay*.

Just as in word formation, there are constraints or grammatical rules that determine how words can be combined to form sentences. *The cat is on the mat* means something different from *The mat is on the cat*, and *cat the on is mat the* means nothing because the words are not combined according to the syntactic rules of English.

The syntactic rules in every language are similar in kind although they may differ in specific constraints. Thus, in English, adjectives typically precede the nouns they modify (as in *the red house*) whereas in French they usually follow (as in *la maison rouge*). But in all languages these rules of syntax include a principle of productivity and recursion that permits the generation of an infinite set of phrases and sentences. We know that this is so since any speaker of any language can produce and understand sentences never spoken or heard previously. This recursive aspect is also revealed by the fact that, in principle, there is no longest sentence in any language: one can keep adding additional words or phrases or conjoin sentences with words like *and* or *but* or relative clauses, such as *The cat is on the mat and the mat is on the floor*, or *The cat is on the mat that is on the floor*, or *The cat is on the mat and the mat is on the floor and the floor is made of wood that comes from the forest in the north of the country near the border that separates Maine from Canada.*

Speakers of a language know these rules. The system of knowledge that underlies the ability to speak and understand the infinite set of sentences constitutes the *mental grammar* of a language that is acquired by a child and is accessed and used in speaking and understanding. This underlying linguistic knowledge is not identical to the functional processes used in speaking and understanding. In actual linguistic performance, speakers access this mental grammar along with other non-linguistic systems (motor, perceptual, cognitive) in order to create and understand speech. This difference between the knowledge of language (the grammar) and linguistic performance accounts for why in principle language is boundless and sentences may be infinitely long, whereas in performance, where memory and other physical limitations come into play, each sentence is finite and the total number of sentences produced and understood in any one lifetime is finite.

The universality of language and of the grammars that underlie all languages suggests that the human brain is uniquely suited for the acquisition and use of language. This view is receiving increasing support from research on child language acquisition and from neurological studies of language disorders such as aphasia. No one now questions the position put forth by Paul Broca in 1861 that language is specifically related to the left hemisphere. Furthermore, there is converging evidence that focal damage to the left cerebral hemisphere does not lead to an across-the-board reduction in language ability, and that lesions in different locations in the left brain are quite selective and remarkably consistent in the manner in which they undermine language. This selectivity reflects the different parts of the grammar. Access to and processing of the phonology (sound system), the lexicon (inventory of morphemes and words), the syntax (rules of sentence formation) and the semantics (rules for the interpretation of meanings) can all be selectively impaired. There is also strong evidence showing that the language faculty is independent of other mental and cognitive faculties. That is, language not only appears to be unique to the human species but also does not appear to be dependent on general intelligence. Severely retarded individuals can learn language, whereas persons with brain lesions may lose language abilities and still retain other cognitive abilities.

An aspect of language about which we know little but which is currently the subject of exciting and promising research is the origin of language. In the mid-nineteenth century, the question of language origin was viewed as so speculative and amateurish that the leading linguists of the day banned further debate on the subject. With recent developments in cognitive science and human palaeontology and genetics, the subject has had a rebirth. The best way to provide a picture of where things now stand with regard to research on the origin of language is to focus on questions rather than answers (where consensus is still sorely lacking). Was language created once (monogenesis) – the majority view – or did different groups of early humans independently create language (polygenesis)? When did this happen? Estimates range wildly from as early as 150,000–200,000 BP (coinciding with the appearance of *Homo sapiens sapiens*), to barely 50,000 years ago (a date that is probably much too recent). Did the language faculty appear suddenly almost full blown from rich mental capacities already in existence or did language first appear in very rudimentary form only to reach its current elaborate grammar through a long evolutionary process involving adaptive selection? Assuming an African origin for modern humans, what is the connection between the uniquely human capacity for language and the successful spread of modern man out of Africa some 60,000 years ago to the four corners of the world?

In the final analysis, the origin and spread of

language is not an esoteric historical question, but rather is a core question that will help us understand the striking feature of the 6,000 or so languages of the world that we know today, namely that they are incredibly, and often surprisingly, different from one another, and yet, when one probes deeply enough, they all seem to come from a common mould.

VICTORIA A. FROMKIN
FORMERLY UNIVERSITY OF CALIFORNIA
AT LOS ANGELES
PAUL NEWMAN
INDIANA UNIVERSITY

Further reading

Chomsky, N. (1975) *Reflections on Language*, New York.
—— (1986) *Knowledge of Language: Its Nature, Origins, and Use*, New York.
Crystal, D. (1997) *The Cambridge Encyclopedia of Language*, 2nd edn, Cambridge, UK.
Garry, J. and Rubino, C. (eds) (2001) *Facts about the World's Languages: An Encyclopedia of the World's Major Languages, Past and Present*, New York.
Pinker, S. and Bloom, P. (1990) 'Natural language and natural selection (with commentaries)', *Behavioral and Brain Sciences* 13: 707–84.

SEE ALSO: first-language acquisition; language and culture; linguistics; sociolinguistics

LANGUAGE AND CULTURE

Language is related to culture in three major ways: (1) language itself is a part of culture; (2) every language provides an index of the culture with which it is most intimately associated; (3) every language becomes symbolic of the culture with which it is most intimately associated. As the above partitioning indicates, we are concerned simultaneously with language as a general human capacity and with specific languages intimately and traditionally associated only with a subset of cultures.

Language as a part of culture

Most human behaviours are language-embedded, thus language is an inevitable part of culture. Ceremonies, rituals, songs, stories, spells, curses, prayers and laws (not to mention conversations, jokes, gossip, requests, commands and instructions) are all speech acts or speech events. Additionally, such complex cultural arenas as socialization, education, barter and negotiation are also entirely awash in language. Language is, therefore, not only part of culture but also a major and crucial part thereof. All those who seek fully to enter into and understand a given culture must, accordingly, master its language, for only through that language can they possibly participate in and experience the culture. Language shift, or loss of a culture's intimately and traditionally associated language, is indicative of extensive culture change, at the very least, and possibly of cultural dislocation and destruction, although a sense of continuous cultural identity may, nevertheless, persist, at a conscious or unconscious attitudinal level.

At the attitudinal level the relationship between language and culture is a recursive one, i.e. not only is there a relationship in that language is part of every culture, but also in that the attitudes of the users of the language towards it, positive, negative or neutral, also come to shape both the uses of, the overt actions towards and, ultimately, even the very nature of a particular language in a particular culture.

Language as an index of culture

The role of language as an index of culture is a by-product (at a more abstract level) of its role as part of culture. Languages reveal the ways of thinking or of organizing experience that are common in their associated cultures. Of course, languages provide lexical terms for the bulk of the artefacts, concerns, values and behaviours recognized by their associated cultures. Above and beyond such obvious indexing, languages also reveal the native clusters or typologies into which subsets of referents are commonly categorized or grouped. Colours, illnesses, kinship relationships, foods, plants, body parts and animal species are all culture-bound typologies and their culturally established systematic qualities are revealed by their associated culture-bound languages. This is not to say that speakers of particular languages are inescapably forced to recognize only the categories encoded in their particular mother tongues. Cultures everywhere consider their own traditionally associated language to be superior than those of surrounding cultures due to its 'having a word for' or being 'able to distinguish between X and Y' lacking elsewhere. Such language-bound restrictions upon cultures (and vice versa) can be counteracted, at least in part, via cross-cultural and cross-linguistic experience, including exposure to mathematical and scientific languages that provide different categories from those encountered in individual cultures and their associated mother tongues.

Language as symbolic of culture

Language is the most elaborate symbol system of humankind. It is no wonder, therefore, that particular languages become symbolic of the particular ethnocultures in which they are embedded and which they index. This is not only a case of a part standing for the whole (as when Yiddish stereotypically stands for or evokes Eastern European-derived ultra-Orthodox Jewish culture when we hear it spoken or even mentioned), but also a case of the part becoming a rallying symbol for (or against) the whole and, in some cases, becoming a cause (or a target) in and of itself. Language movements and language conflicts utilize languages as symbols that will mobilize populations to defend (or attack) and to foster (or reject) the cultures and establishments associated with them. Language-and-culture myths simultaneously tout the perfection of one's own traditionally associated language and at the same time support language planning so that the same traditionally associated language can be rendered more adequate for the discharge of functions related to modernity and modern power-statuses. Corpus-planning always has a hidden status-planning agenda that is aimed at conserving cultural specificity even while fostering transcultural statuses.

JOSHUA A. FISHMAN
EMERITUS, YESHIVA UNIVERSITY

Further reading

Cooper, R.L. and Spolsky, B. (eds) (1991) *The Influence of Language on Culture and Thought*, Berlin.

Dutton, T. (1992) *Culture Change, Language Change*, Canberra.

Fishman, J.A. (1996) *In Praise of the Beloved Language: A Comparative Analysis of Positive Ethnolinguistic Consciousness*, Berlin.

Gumperz, J.J. and Levinson, S.C. (eds) (1996) *Rethinking Linguistic Relativity*, Cambridge.

Muhlhausler, P. and Harre, R. (1990) *Pronouns and People: The Linguistic Construction of Personal Identity*, Oxford.

Preston, D. (ed.) (1999) *Handbook of Perceptual Dialectology*, Vol. 1, Amsterdam.

Urban, G. (1991) *A Discourse-Centered Approach to Culture*, Austin, TX.

SEE ALSO: language; sociolinguistics

LAW

Law seeks to work in the world. This simple description goes a long way towards capturing the meaning of law as a social institution. Law seeks to order, change and give meaning to the society of which it is a part. It deploys various tools – rules and regulations, rewards and incentives, threats and promises – in order to accomplish these meaning-giving, ordering, changing tasks. The tools that law uses as well as the tasks that it performs are historically contingent and culturally specific, varying often dramatically from time to time and place to place. Law is embedded in, even as it helps to constitute, different cultural traditions.

Yet increasingly in the twenty-first century, law pervades much of the political lives of citizens in many different nations, and it provides a forum in which the distinctive temper of a culture may find expression. In the USA and Europe it plays a major, though variable, role in articulating values and dealing with conflict. While the role of law has never been more substantial or controversial in those places (Kagan 2001), in countries from Argentina and Brazil to South Africa and those of Eastern Europe, people are seeking to develop their own versions of the rule of law as a means of ordering their societies.

The pervasiveness of law reflects human tendencies to engage in normative argument as a regular part of social interaction and to interpret social action in the language of right and wrong. Law, however, is more than a branch of applied ethics: in many cultures, the concept of legal legitimacy is associated not only with the adequacy or normative appeal of legal commands, but also with elaborate rhetorical practices and traditions of reading and interpreting. Finally, law finds its most vivid expression when moral argument and interpretation result in the application of force. While law depends on persuasion, inducements and voluntary compliance, force (or its possible application) remains the critical tool for legal enforcement (Sarat 2001).

Thinking about law in this way draws attention to the various domains in which law performs. The language of enactment and performance directs attention to text as well as context, role and action, without privileging the word over the world or the world over the word. Here we might think about the performative qualities of language, the way certain linguistic acts bring states of being into existence. We might be drawn to the human actions that go into giving a performance, thinking not only about texts and language, but staging, symbolization, relation to audience. We might think about law as a domain for exploring the desires that performances seek to satisfy and the pleasures that legal performances provide. Judges interpreting a statute must take into account their audience, anticipating its likely reactions, staging their decisions in such a way as to enable particular connections between the law's pronouncement and the pleasures that audience members may be expected to derive from the performance of law.

Two contrasting ways of thinking about the work that law does in the world might be termed the 'instrumental' and the 'constitutive' (Trubek 1984; Sarat and Kearns 1993). They differ from each other largely in what they take to be the principal means by which law works: whether (roughly) by imposing external sanctions and inducements or by shaping internal meanings and creating new statuses.

One of the views, instrumentalism, posits a relatively sharp distinction between various kinds of legal standards, on the one hand, and various kinds of non-legal human activities, on the other. It then explores the effects of the former on the latter. By contrast, the constitutive perspective contends that social life is so bound up with law that the relevant category for the scholar is not the external one of causality (as the reference to effects would suggest) but the internal one of meaning (Gordon 1984). In bold outline, the constitutive view suggests that law works in the world from the inside out, by providing the principal categories in terms of which social life is made to seem largely natural, normal, cohesive and coherent.

Instrumentalism

Instrumentalism conceives of law as a tool for sustaining or changing aspects of social life. However it does its work, law's job is effectively to regulate the activities of legal subjects, the things they do or abstain from doing. The effectiveness of legal regulation might be directly observable in the behaviour of persons (e.g. driving faster on the interstate after speed limits were raised from 55 to 65 m.p.h.) or it might be only indirectly detectible (e.g. the increased confidence in banks following the creation of FDIC) by inferring beliefs from practices. The point is that instrumentalists need not share any particular view about the kinds of intervening mechanisms deployed by law to shape or sustain various social arrangements (Ackerman 1984). The crucial thing is this: instrumentalists are centrally interested in law's effectiveness (roughly, in the extent to which a law is observed or not observed, followed or violated, used or ignored), rather than in the effects of law, more broadly conceived.

The distinction between effects and effectiveness might initially seem suspect since it is impossible to determine a law's effectiveness without knowing its effects, or some of them. But the appended phrase, 'or some of them', makes all the difference. To the extent that instrumentalists view laws as tools, and, more specifically as tools for promoting previously identified purposes, the relevant effects are just those that advance or imperil these intended outcomes. These (and only these) are the effects that matter, determining the effectiveness of a law and so its instrumental value (Feeley 1976).

Historically, instrumentalists have not only begun their enquiry from the perspective of legal materials, they have favored some legal materials (namely, rules) over others, focusing on the way these particular carriers of legal direction are used, violated or ignored. Rules tend to compartmentalize social phenomena and to operate on those aspects of social life that are most amenable to this kind of all-or-nothing normative ordering (Hart 1961). The effect is to make a law's immediate consequences more apparent. On the other hand, scholarship that correspondingly centres on rules is all the more likely to absorb their logic and, like the rules themselves, to detach the regulated activities from their full social setting.

Legal rules are treated as tools used to facilitate the accomplishment of various ends, goals or purposes whose origins tend to be treated by instrumentalists as being substantially independent of law itself (Silbey and Bitner 1982). Law mirrors society. Changes in law tend to follow social changes, and are often intended to do no more than to make those changes permanent (Friedman 1975). Legal rules are used to maintain, reproduce and alter the everyday in conscious, rational and planned ways.

Perhaps the key to the instrumentalist understanding is the belief that there is a fairly firm division between the legal and the social. Law is treated as an important influence on society, while being situated somehow outside of it. As Gordon has observed, writers in this tradition

> divide the world into two spheres, one social and one legal. Society is the primary realm of social experience. It is 'real life': What's immediately and truly important to people... goes on there....'Law' or 'the legal system', on the other hand, is a distinctly secondary body of phenomena. It is a specialized realm of state and professional activity that is called into being by the primary social world in order to serve that world's needs. Law is auxiliary – an excrescence on social life, even if sometimes a useful excrescence.
>
> (1984: 60)

Law, then, is pictured as a residual category whose role in the everyday is episodic, artificial and often disruptive.

Understood this way the key question about law is when can legislation or judicial decisions reliably be counted on to guide behaviour or produce social changes in expected or desired ways (Rosenberg 1993)? To answer this question scholars begin by identifying the goals of legal policy and move to assess its success or failure by comparing those goals with the results produced. Where, as is almost invariably the case, the results do not match the goals, attention typically shifts to the factors that might explain the supposed gap between law on the books and law in action. By understanding the causes of observed discrepancies, hope is kept alive of reducing or eliminating such gaps in the future and thus increasing law's effectiveness.

The constitutive perspective

While instrumentalism conceives of law as largely external to the social practices it regulates, no instrumentalist would deny that law occasionally constructs new practices, if not from whole cloth, then from unfamiliar weaves. The idea of ownership and the status of tenant, for instance, while not utterly unrelated to prior notions of possession and longstanding occu-

pancy, import new rights, meanings and roles. Such laws might be said not merely to regulate what was already in place, but to bring into being something new, to constitute new relations and meanings.

From this perspective, law permeates social life, and has effects on it, in ways that the instrumental view tends to overlook (Engel and Munger 2003). Law-thought and legal relations (or emanations from such thought and relations) dominate self-understanding and one's understanding of one's relations to others. Citizens are not, as instrumentalists suggest, merely pushed and pulled by laws that impinge on us, as it were from the outside. Rather, they internalize the meanings and representations of law. As a consequence, law's 'demands' tend to seem natural and necessary, and hardly like demands at all. According to the constitutive perspective, law has 'colonized our souls', making us internalize its demands at the same time that it reinforces the illusion of independence from law.

In *Local Knowledge*, Clifford Geertz suggested that

> law, rather than a mere technical add-on to a morally (or immorally) finished society, is, along of course with a whole range of other cultural realities...an active part of it.... Law...is, in a word, constructive; in another constitutive; in a third, formational....Law, with its power to place particular things that happen...in a general frame in such a way that rules for the principled management of them seem to arise naturally from the essentials of their character, is rather more than a reflection of received wisdom or a technology of dispute-settlement.
>
> (1983: 218 and 230)

Meaning is perhaps the key word in the vocabulary of those who speak about law in constitutive terms.

> Our gaze focuses on meaning, on the ways... (people) make sense of what they do – practically, morally, expressively...juridically – by setting it within larger frames of signification, and how they keep those larger frames in place or try to, by organizing what they do in terms of them.
>
> (Geertz 1983: 232)

So conceived, law is inseparable from the interests, goals and understandings that shape or comprise social life. Law is part of the everyday world, contributing powerfully to the apparently stable, taken-for-granted quality of that world and to the generally shared sense that as things *are*, so *must* they be.

To acknowledge that law has this kind of meaning-making power is to accept that some social practices are not logically separable from the laws that shape them. Arguably, marriage is such a practice, assuming for the moment that what distinguishes this social practice from similar bonds of affection of indefinite duration is that it can be instituted, and terminated, only with the law's blessings. A different and more diffuse example of law's constructive powers might be the general similarities between legal and non-legal practices regarding the ascription of praise and blame. Thus, even where people are not familiar in detail with legal rules and doctrines, their habits of mind and social practices will tend to be highly legal in character. To the extent that legal regulations do more than merely modify conduct but also alter the way persons view themselves and conceive of their relations with one another, then the distinction between instrumentalist and constitutive perspectives tends to collapse. Perhaps, then, the distinction is a matter of degree, but the central contrasts – between external and internal influences, and between sanctions and meaning – are still sufficiently powerful to keep alive the distinction between instrumental and constitutive views of law.

To say, as defenders of the constitutive view do, that law is a continuous part of social practice means several things: first, law is *internal* to the constitution of those practices, linked by meaning to the affairs it controls; second, and correlatively, that law operates largely by influencing modes of thought rather than by determining conduct in any specific case (Hunt 1990). From the constitutive perspective, law enters social practices and is, indeed, 'imbricated' in them, by shaping consciousness, by making law's concepts and commands seem, if not invisible, then perfectly natural and benign.

Getting beyond 'the law-first perspective'

Instrumental and constitutive approaches to law share a common commitment to what might be called 'the law-first perspective'. They both start with law. However, to understand law we need, in one sense, to turn away from it, from its rules, doctrines, precedents and professional accoutrements, and attend to events or practices that seem, on the face of things, removed from law, or at least not dominated by law at the outset. As Silbey puts it, law 'is located in concrete and particular circumstances where the relations of ends and means are governed by situational rather than abstract or general criteria' (1985: 15). By beginning with such circumstances, it is possible to see that law encompasses more than its official stuff, that motives, needs, emotions, anxieties, aspirations that are not entirely fixed by legal meanings or by legal forces operate throughout without totally losing their identity to law. In fact, it is law that regularly buckles, and is resisted, or reinterpreted, or distorted.

If there is a single defect common to the constitutive and instrumental perspectives in legal scholarship, it is the unargued postulate that law's story can be told in terms of the effects of legal doctrine or practices on a relatively stable, placid, non-legal Other. But, in fact, the Other that law seeks to affect has its own normative direction and momentum, even when it is obliged to accommodate law's presence. It is unlikely, then, that law's influence can accurately be portrayed in a static tale of fixed effects or displaced meanings. If the world in which law seeks to work is a normatively resourceful place, then a more plausible conjecture is that law's story will be an ongoing one. It will have more the feel of a narrative account than the law-like presentations we have come to expect from empirically minded social scientists. On the other hand, such accounts will be decidedly empirical in character, if by this one means they will be grounded in extensive observations, rigorously assembled – and imaginatively 'read', of course.

In all of this, it is as dangerous to overstate the penetration of law into the world as to underestimate its presence. While both law and norms work to produce order, to relegate relations to the realm of the taken-for-granted, neither is nor can be completely successful. The way people use or ignore law is itself a sign of their resistance to the constitutive effects of law. The constitutive power of law with the characteristic habits, skills and cultures that it enables always provides room for challenge and opposition even as it imposes constraints. Such challenge and opposition is itself manifest in the ways people use or ignore the legal facilities available to them.

Instrumental and constitutive approaches have, to this point in time, largely talked past each other. Their different views of law are a result of differences in theory and method. If they are going to talk to each other, and if we are to understand law, we cannot choose abstractly one or another of these theories and methods. Law plays a constitutive role in the world, yet it is also available as a tool to people as they seek to maintain or alter their daily lives. While it is a mistake to claim that law is absent in those instances where people eschew legal forms or resolve disputes without recourse to law, so too it is a mistake to claim that law's presence is only ideological. Law works in the world as both constituent and instrument.

AUSTIN SARAT
AMHERST COLLEGE

References

Ackerman, B. (1984) *Reconstructing American Law*, Cambridge, MA.

Engel, D. and Munger, F. (2003) *Rights of Inclusion: Law and Identity in the Life Stories of Americans With Disabilities*, Chicago.

Feeley, M. (1976) 'The concept of law in social science: A critique and notes on an expanded view', *Law and Society Review* 10(497).

Friedman, L. (1975) *The Legal System: A Social Science Perspective*, New York.

Geertz, C. (1983) *Local Knowledge: Further Essays in Interpretive Anthropology*, New York.

Gordon, R. (1984) 'Critical legal histories', *Stanford Law Review* 36(57–125).

Hart, H.L.A. (1961) *The Concept of Law*, Oxford.

Hunt, A. (1990) 'Rights and social movements: Counter-hegemonic strategies', *Journal of Law and Society* 17(310).

Kagan, R. (2001) *Adversarial Legalism: The American Way of Law*, Cambridge, MA.

Rosenberg, G. (1993) *The Hollow Hope: Can Courts Bring about Social Change?*, Chicago.

Sarat, A. (2001) *When the State Kills: Capital Punishment and the American Tradition*, Princeton, NJ.

Sarat, A. and Kearns, T.R. (eds) (1993) *Law in Everyday Life*, Ann Arbor, MI.

Silbey, S. (1985) 'Ideals and practices in the study of law', *Legal Studies Forum* 9(15).

Silbey, S. and Bitner, E. (1982) 'The availability of law', *Law and Policy Quarterly* 4(399).

Trubek, D. (1984) 'Where the action is: Critical legal studies and empiricism', *Stanford Law Review* 36(575).

Further reading

Ewick, P. and Silbey, S. (1998) *The Common Place of Law: Stories from Everyday Life*, Chicago.

Felman, S. (2003) *The Juridical Unconscious: Trials and Traumas in the Twentieth Century*, Cambridge, MA.

Greenhouse, C., Yngvesson, B. and Engel, D. (1994) *Law and Community in Three American Towns*, Ithaca, NY.

Kahn, P. (1999) *The Cultural Study of Law: Reconstructing Legal Scholarship*, Chicago.

Valverde, M. (2003) *Law's Dream of a Common Knowledge*, Princeton, NJ.

SEE ALSO: judicial process; sociolegal studies

LAW OF RETURNS

The law of returns is a set of abstract generalizations about the relationship between inputs and outputs around which earlier economists structured important parts of their analysis. Ricardo was one of the important early users of the law, and he made assumptions about returns in production central to his theory. Both the close of his model and his theory of distribution depended upon the existence of diminishing returns in agriculture. Ricardo (1817) argued that as more and more labour was added to land, the intensive and extensive margins would decrease, creating rent for the more productive land and reducing output per unit of labour.

Malthus also used this 'law' as a foundation for his predictions that while the population would grow geometrically, the food supply would grow only arithmetically (Malthus 1993 [1798]). His argument was that because land was fixed, diminishing returns would eventually set in, leading him to conclude that the world population would eventually be faced with starvation. (In later editions of his famous population essay he recognized that his predictions were not coming true and modified his argument accordingly.)

The law of returns played a smaller role in Adam Smith's analysis. Smith discussed a variety of possibilities for returns, including the possibility of increasing returns, which could occur in manufacturing as the market was expanded (Smith 1776; Eltis 1993 [1975]). Senior expanded upon these ideas and made diminishing returns in agriculture and increasing returns in industry two of his four elementary propositions upon which the foundations of economics as a science is based (Senior 1838).

Marshall further developed these ideas about returns in his *Principles* and talked about particular industries as being increasing or decreasing returns industries (Marshall 1920). His classification was criticized both by John Clapham (1922), who saw much of the discussion as creating empty economic boxes that empirically could not be filled in, and by Piero Sraffa (1926), who saw diminishing returns as not applying to perfect competition, since it was not clear in many cases if any factor was fixed. These criticisms led both to a decrease of appeals to the 'law' and to clarifications of its implications.

Today a general law of returns is not presented in the principles of economics textbooks, and is little discussed in the profession. Textbook discussions of production functions focus rather on issues of returns to scale and marginal returns. Economies of scale refer to what happens to output when all inputs are increased by equal amounts. If output increases by the same percentage, there are constant returns to scale. If output increases by less than that percentage, there are decreasing returns to scale. Finally, if output increases by the same percentage, there are constant returns to scale. Marginal returns refers to what happens to increases in output when one input is continually increased while other inputs are held constant.

The remaining vestige of the law of returns that shows up in standard textbooks is the law of diminishing marginal returns. This holds that the additional output produced by further inputs eventually will diminish progressively. This 'law of diminishing marginal returns' underlies the explanation of the upward-sloping short-run supply curve, which assumes that one variable is fixed and one variable is flexible.

Many logical conundrums can be devised with reference to these laws. For example, some have argued that decreasing returns to scale are impossible, since a person can always continue to do the same thing over and over again. That argument, however, is based on a specific definition of input, and is dependent on the assumption that the contribution of the individual overseeing and monitoring production can be increased along with other inputs, which is probably not what those who argued for the existence of decreasing returns to scale had in mind.

Textbook discussions of diminishing marginal returns are more a pedagogical exercise than they are a discussion of useful laws, since in the real world inputs are generally more or less variable. The law of diminishing returns is therefore more a logical proposition, which is sometimes specified in texts as the flower-pot law. (If more and more seeds are planted in a flower-pot, eventually they will not have enough soil in which to grow.) In the real world, however, the law of diminishing marginal returns seldom plays a central role in the production decisions made by firms. Such decisions are generally more concerned with longer-run considerations. When firms make these decisions it is often not clear what is the fixed factor: capital is often more variable than labour. Problems of expansion present themselves rather as monitoring problems.

Even in agriculture, where the law of diminishing marginal returns seems to be a logical truism, it has not been empirically relevant, because the law assumes a given technology. Technological change has continually overwhelmed any diminishing marginal returns in agriculture. Output per unit of land has continually increased, negating the dire predictions of Malthus.

More recent work on returns in production has focused on dynamic issues, in which path dependencies, histories and dynamic feedbacks play a central role; and multidimensional issues of production, in which interrelationships among the production of various outputs are central (Romer 1986, 1987, 1990; Arthur 1994). Dynamic and multiproduct interrelationships can create falling costs, but they do not represent returns to scale, or returns to a production process with a fixed input. They are time- and production-dependent returns, which can only be expressed in a dynamic or multi-output context. Thus, the static categorization of types of returns into scale and fixed-inputs returns needs to be supplemented by categories of dynamic and multiple-product returns. The correct analytical specification of laws of return requires the consideration of more complicated dynamic interrelationships between inputs and outputs. It is difficult to make general empirical statements about returns in production.

The issues of dynamic returns and multiproduct interdependencies, the difficulty of differentiating types of returns, and the problems in the way of defining inputs and outputs have relegated the law of returns to a historical curiosity with little relevance to modern discussions of production in economics.

DAVID COLANDER
MIDDLEBURY COLLEGE

References

Arthur, B.W. (1994) *Increasing Returns and Path Dependence in the Economy*, Ann Arbor, MI.
Clapham, J.H. (1922) 'Of empty boxes', *Economic Journal* 32: 305–14.
Eltis, W. (1993 [1975]) 'Adam Smith's theory of economic growth', reprinted in *Classical Economics, Public Expenditure and Growth*, Aldershot, UK.
Malthus, T. (1993 [1798]) *An Essay on the Principle of Population*, ed. G. Gilbert. Oxford.
Marshall, A. (1920) *Principles of Economics*, London.
Ricardo, D. (1817) *On the Principles of Political Economy and Taxation*, London.
Romer, P. (1986) 'Increasing returns and long run growth'. *Journal of Political Economy* 94: 1,002–37.
—— (1987) 'Growth based on increasing returns due to specialization', *American Economic Review* 77(2): 56–62.
—— (1990) 'Endogenous technological change', *Journal of Political Economy* 98: 71–102.
Senior, N. (1838) *An Outline of the Science of Political Economy*, New York.
Smith, A. (1776) *An Inquiry into the Nature and Causes of the Wealth of Nations*, Edinburgh.
Sraffa, P. (1926) 'The laws of returns under competitive conditions', *Economic Journal* 36 (December): 536–50.

Further reading

Krugman, P. (1979) 'Increasing returns, monopolistic competition, and international trade', *Journal of International Economics* 4 (November): 469–79.
Young, A. (1928) 'Increasing returns and economic progress', *Economic Journal* (December): 527–42.

SEE ALSO: factors of production; production and cost frontiers

LEADERSHIP

Leadership is the process of influencing people in a way that enhances their contribution to the achievement of group goals. It typically involves one person having a positive impact on the behaviour of many others. As a central feature of effective organizations and societies, it is the most researched topic in the field of organizational behaviour. It has also been the focus of intense academic and public debate for over 2,000 years.

The literature on leadership is concerned above all with the factors that enable the plans of an individual to be translated into the actions of a collectivity. 'How is it that one person's vision becomes other people's mission?' Traditionally, answers have been framed in terms of individual qualities that individuals do or do not have, but increasingly leadership is seen as a group process that centres on a social psychological relationship between leaders and followers.

Classical answers to this question, which continue to have popular appeal, pointed to the central role played by the leader's personality. According to Plato (1993 [380 BCE]), leaders were people who were born with a range of traits that set them apart from the general populace – for example, quickness of learning, courage and broadness of vision. Subsequent research extended the list of attributes considerably, so that, in an influential review, Stogdill (1948) was able to identify twenty-nine personal dimensions that various researchers had associated with successful leadership. These ranged from age, height and physique to co-operativeness, flexibility and persistence.

However, research indicated that personal attributes were very unreliable predictors of leadership. Some effective leaders are young, others are old. Some are flexible, others are inflexible. And so on. In response, researchers in the 1950s attempted to identify leaders on the basis of their behaviour rather than their character. Again, this strategy met with very mixed results, but it did help to identify two forms of activity that appear to be widely implicated in leadership: 'consideration' and 'initiation of structure' (Bowers and Seashore 1966). A number of studies around this time converged on the view that leadership could be manifest in two ways: by building positive relationships, and by defining appropriate tasks and goals.

It nevertheless proved hard to predict whether any given individual would behave in either or both of these ways, and so would be an effective leader. In response, researchers developed contextual approaches to leadership that placed more emphasis on the situations in which leaders operated. Radical formulations suggested that context was everything, and that the character of the individual counted for nothing. More nuanced formulations, termed contingency models, suggested that successful leadership is a product of the match or fit between the personality of the leader and features of the situations in which he or she operates.

The most influential of these contingency models is probably Fiedler's (1964) *least preferred co-worker* model. This argues that leaders can be distinguished in terms of their disposition towards their least preferred co-worker (LPC), and that context can be differentiated in terms of (1) the quality of leader–member relations, (2) the degree to which the task is structured, and (3) the leader's position power. High LPC leaders (ones with a positive view of their LPC) are predicted to be most effective in conditions where either (a) relations are good, structure is high and the leader's position is strong, or (b) relations are bad, structure is low and the leader's position is either weak or strong. Stated crudely, 'hard' (i.e. low LPC) leaders are predicted to do well when conditions are all very favourable or all very unfavourable, but 'soft' (i.e. high LPC) leaders are predicted to do well when conditions are more mixed.

Contingency theories vary considerably in the attributes of the leader and the characteristics of the situation that they consider important. Nonetheless, they remain the most widely embraced class of leadership theory. In particular, they are a very popular component of management and personal development courses which attempt to (1) classify individuals as having a particular leadership style and (2) train them to identify (or create) situations in which this style will be effective.

However, there are some serious empirical and theoretical problems with contingency theories. Most significantly, they are commonly faulted for being reductionistic in their attempts to distil a complex and synergetic 'whole' down to a limited subset of component 'parts'. The fact that these elements are conceptualized as static and fixed is a further difficulty. There is evidence, for example, that the character of effective leaders is fluid and responsive to context rather than invariant, and is therefore not amenable to measurement using standard psychometric personality inventories (see Haslam and Platow 2001).

Disenchantment with contingency models is reflected in at least four distinct theoretical movements that have been the focus of research in the last few decades. The transactional approach, most closely associated with the work of Hollander (1964), argues that any analysis of leadership needs to be complemented by an examination of the role that *followership* plays in validating and empowering any leader. According to this view, leadership emerges from a process of social exchange. Followers work to enact a leader's commands only when they believe that the leader is doing something for them in return. This analysis suggests that followers will only obey the novel orders of a leader if he or she has built up 'idiosyncrasy credits' based on demonstrated service to the group. That is why followers are more likely to support a leader if he or she is elected rather than appointed, and if he or she emerges from within the group rather than being imposed on it from outside.

A major objection to this approach is that it reduces a higher-order experience to a cost–benefit analysis. When it is most effective, followership appears to embody more than the logic of 'you scratch my back and I'll scratch yours'. Recognition of this fact has led to a re-emphasis by tranformational theorists of the importance of leader charisma in facilitating acts of citizenship, loyalty and service to the group (Burns 1978). However, as with earlier personality approaches, it proves extremely difficult, if not impossible, to specify a priori which attributes actually contribute to charisma. There appear, for example, to be few personal characteristics that people like Mahatma Gandhi, Adolf Hitler, Princess Diana and Nelson Mandela have in common, and which separate them from less charismatic mortals.

This observation has led researchers such as Meindl (1993) to argue that leadership has much less to do with the properties of leaders in the abstract than with the favourability of the general environment within which they operate. Supporting this view, studies show that when groups progress from failure to success their leaders are often perceived to be highly charismatic, even if their personality and behaviour is identical to that of a leader whose group has gone from success to failure, and who is perceived to be extremely uncharismatic. Extending this line of reasoning, research on leader categorization theory has argued that leadership is grounded not in the creative behaviour of leaders but in the attributions that followers make (Lord and Maher 1991). According to this view, effective leadership revolves around being perceived as a good leader by living up to followers' stereotypic expectations of what leadership in a given domain should involve (e.g. business leaders should be well dressed, political leaders should have strong convictions).

All of these departures from contingency approaches have served to stimulate productive and vigorous lines of research. However, in recent years, an increasingly influential approach that has attempted to integrate and extend their various critical themes has been developed by social identity and self-categorization theorists (Turner and Haslam 2001). Central to this work is an argument that leadership is made possible by a social identity (a common sense of 'us-ness') that leaders and followers share. Leadership flows from the capacity of individuals to embody the contextually determined character of the group, and leaders are 'entrepreneurs of identity' in the sense that their influence derives from an ability to create and embody a positive and distinct sense of 'who we are' (Reicher and Hopkins 2004).

Studies that support the social identity approach show, for example, that leaders are seen to be more representative of a group and as more charismatic – and are more likely to encourage acts of followership – to the extent that they are seen to represent a position that positively distinguishes their group from other groups with which it is compared at a particular point in time (i.e. in a way that makes 'us' look better than 'them'; Haslam and Platow 2001). These ideas are currently being expanded upon in work that reconnects the analysis of leadership with broader questions of social influence, social categorization and identity development and mobilization (Haslam 2004).

S. ALEXANDER HASLAM
UNIVERSITY OF EXETER

References

Bowers, D.G. and Seashore, S.E. (1966) 'Predicting organizational effectiveness with a four-factor theory of leadership', *Administrative Science Quarterly* 11: 238–63.

Burns, J.M. (1978) *Leadership*, New York.

Fiedler, F.E. (1964) 'A contingency model of leader effectiveness', in L. Berkowitz (ed.) *Advances in Experimental Social Psychology*, Vol. 1, New York, pp. 149–90.

Haslam, S.A. (2004) *Psychology in Organizations: The Social Identity Approach*, 2nd edn, London.

Haslam, S.A. and Platow, M.J. (2001) 'Your wish is my command: How a leader's vision becomes a follower's task', in M.A. Hogg and D.J. Terry (eds) *Social Identity Processes in Organizational Contexts*, Philadelphia, PA, pp. 213–28.

Hollander, E.P. (1964) *Leaders, Groups, and Influence*, New York.

Lord, R.G. and Maher, K.J. (1991) *Leadership and Information Processing: Linking Perceptions and Performance*, London.

Meindl, J.R. (1993) 'Reinventing leadership: A radical, social psychological approach', in J.K. Murnigham (ed.) *Social Psychology in Organizations: Advances in Theory and Research*, Englewood Cliffs, NJ, pp. 89–118.

Plato (1993 [380 BCE]) *The Republic*, Oxford.

Reicher, S.D. and Hopkins, N. (2004) 'On the science of the art of leadership', in D. van Knippenberg and M.A. Hogg (eds) *Leadership, Power and Identity*, London.

Stogdill, R.M. (1948) 'Personality factors associated with leadership: A survey of the literature', *Journal of Psychology* 25: 35–71.

Turner, J.C. and Haslam, S.A. (2001) 'Social identity, organizations and leadership', in M.E. Turner (ed.) *Groups at Work: Advances in Theory and Research*, Hillsdale, NJ, pp. 25–65.

SEE ALSO: authority; entrepreneurship; group dynamics; legitimacy; Machiavelli; political psychology; power

LEGITIMACY

The concept of legitimacy as it is used in the social sciences and political and legal theory is complex and multidimensional. It always includes two important defining characteristics: the idea of rules or procedures that, when followed appropriately, authorize a right to rule; and the notion that there is some basis in belief (such as ideology, express or tacit consent, or sacred conviction), shared by the ruler and the ruled, that justifies a form of rule. These two characteristics suggest a distinction between procedural and substantive legitimacy. The former indicates that observing the rules and decision processes is always important when considering the legitimacy of an order. The latter characteristic points to the importance of accountability and the justification of the exercise of authority or power when judging the legitimacy of an order. When the order is a complex nation-state, particularly one that is new or in transition, judgements and assessments are often as much about *il*legitimacy as legitimacy.

The discussion of legitimacy has an ancient pedigree. Questions about the moral worth or rightness of different forms of rule were present at the very beginning of systematic thinking about human communities. In *The Politics*, for instance, Aristotle held that some constitutions were 'right' (those promoting the common interest of citizens), while others were 'perverted' (those serving only the particular interest of rulers), a distinction grounded in a teleological metaphysics. However, classical theory lacked a language and precise terminology for legitimacy, relying instead on general conceptions of order and lawfulness. Explicit conceptions of legitimacy and legitimation were an invention of modern thought and especially social contract theory, represented best in Rousseau's promise in the *Social Contract* to demonstrate how political authority could be rendered 'legitimate'. His theoretical answer – authority becomes legitimate because we consent to it – and his defence of a popular 'general will' served as both an epitaph for the Aristotelian tradition and a warning about the contestability of legitimacy in the modern age. This shift from a metaphysical to a voluntaristic account prepared the way for the contribution of Max Weber, the most important modern theorist of legitimacy.

All modern theory starts from the assumption that legitimacy has to do with the quality of authoritativeness, lawfulness, bindingness or rightness attached to an order. A government or state is considered 'legitimate' if it possesses the 'right to rule'. Unfortunately, the definition begs the most crucial question: in what does 'right' consist, and how can its existence and meaning be determined? Generally speaking, this question has been answered in two ways. One school of thought has argued with Weber (1968 [1922]) that 'It is only the probability of orientation to the subjective *belief* in the validity of an order which constitutes the valid order itself.' According to this view, 'right' reduces to belief in the appropriateness of an existing order and the 'right to rule'. The presence of objective, external or universal standards for judging rightness grounded in natural law, reason or some other transhistorical principle is typically rejected as philosophically impossible and sociologically naïve. In his sociology of legitimacy, Weber attempted to guard against the relativistic consequences of such a conception by identifying four *reasons* for ascribing legitimacy to any social order: tradition, affect, value-rationality and legality (or instrumental, purposive rationality). This classification then served as the basis for his famous analysis of the three ideal types of

'legitimate domination' (*legitime Herrschaft*): traditional, charismatic and legal-rational.

Since the appearance of Weber's work scholars have continued to debate the logic, meaning and application of his views. Some have sharply criticized the sociological approach for subverting a significant distinction between legitimate and illegitimate forms of rule; for failing to distinguish legitimacy from legality; and for confusing important distinctions among belief elicited through coercion, habit or rational choice. The sense in which Weber may be guilty of these charges is also a matter of dispute. Underlying these criticisms from the second school of thought is the conviction, expressed particularly in the work of Jürgen Habermas, that a satisfactory theory of legitimacy must be philosophically grounded in such a way as to render possible a 'rational judgement' about the 'right to rule'. For Habermas (1975 [1973], 1984 [1981]), grounds have been sought in a complex 'consensus theory of truth', where 'truth' signifies 'warranted assertability' under conditions of *ideal* 'communicative competence'.

Whether Habermas or others sharing his assumptions have provided a coherent grounding for the theory of legitimacy remains a disputed issue. One difficulty with their attempt is that it comes at an awkward time, philosophically considered, for under the influence of particular interpretations of Nietzsche, Heidegger, Dewey and Wittgenstein, several contemporary thinkers have mounted a serious challenge to the project of identifying foundations of knowledge that can be used to achieve definitive criteria for rationality or 'truth'. Prominent examples include Rorty's 'pragmatism', Lyotard's 'postmodernism' and Foucault's 'genealogical critique of knowledge'. If such challenges succeed, then it becomes difficult to imagine any viable alternative to the Weberian typological approach.

In light of such an impasse in philosophy, since the mid-1970s work on legitimacy in the social sciences and the law has proceeded generally in three directions. First, social scientists attracted to empirical investigation have either worked towards testing hypotheses about legitimation in experimental settings, or they have dropped the term legitimacy altogether, hoping to avoid troubling normative issues while searching for measurable levels of 'regime support'. In this view it is simply observable loyalty or obedience to a regime, whatever its sources or reasons, which counts as the indicator of legitimacy.

Second, some scholars have focused attention on *il*legitimacy or *de*legitimation, arguing that the real problems of the modern state lie with its essential lack of legitimacy, as illustrated most dramatically by the collapse of the former Soviet Union and Yugoslavia, and events in Europe after 1989. When a state fails, how can the legitimacy of the successor regime be established? The appearance of new states or nation-states in transition to democracy in Central and Eastern Europe, Asia and the Middle East, and Africa has raised this question about legitimation in an especially urgent way. But so has the emergence of rogue states in violation of international norms, states sequestering armed movements, or failed states whose territory has been appropriated by organized groups with their own political or criminal agendas. In these last instances the novel argument has been advanced that a legally constituted sovereign state may lack legitimacy because it has violated widely accepted international norms, such as protection of basic human rights – a claim that can serve as a justification for intervention.

Third, a number of social scientists have begun to investigate state structure and policy, and in particular the relationship between the state and civil society, in an effort to understand the factors conditioning the legitimacy of a constitution or a particular regime. While a state-centred view is sometimes labelled Weberian and a state/civil society framework neo-Marxist, there is little reason to believe that they cannot be combined in a unified approach. Scholars can investigate strategies used by the state (particularly in the domains of security, science, technology, communication, health and education) to shore up declining belief in its right to rule, as well as the sources of legitimation emergent in the group processes composing civil society that condition a public's degree and kind of support for existing political institutions and governmental policies.

Important questions about legitimacy can be raised at many institutional levels – in relation to the international system, the state and nation-state, and the forces emergent in the social order. Whatever conclusions emerge from the different directions enquiry has taken, contemporary developments and complexities within the modern nation-state and the international system suggest that the problem of legitimacy will remain centrally important in the political world for decades to come, and for that reason in the social sciences and political and legal theory as well.

LAWRENCE A. SCAFF
WAYNE STATE UNIVERSITY, DETROIT

References

Habermas, J. (1975 [1973]) *Legitimation Crisis*, Boston, MA.
—— (1984 [1981]) *The Theory of Communicative Action*, 2 vols, Boston, MA.
Weber, M. (1968 [1922]) *Economy and Society*, New York.

Further reading

Barker, R. (1990) *Political Legitimacy and the State*, Oxford.
Barnard, F. (2001) *Democratic Legitimacy*, Montreal.
Beetham, D. (1991) *The Legitimation of Power*, London.
Connolly, W. (ed.) (1984) *Legitimacy and the State*, Oxford.
Roth, B. (1999) *Governmental Illegitimacy in International Law*, New York and London.

SEE ALSO: authority; leadership; power

LÉVI-STRAUSS, CLAUDE (1908–)

Claude Lévi-Strauss was born in Brussels, of French parents. After attending the Lycée Janson de Sailly in Paris he studied at the Faculty of Law in Paris, where he obtained his licence, and at the Sorbonne, where he received his teacher's qualification in philosophy (*agrégation*) in 1931. After teaching for two years at the lycées of Mont-de-Marsan and Laon, he was appointed to the French university mission in Brazil, serving as professor at the University of São Paulo from 1935 to 1938. Between 1935 and 1939 he organized and directed several ethnographic expeditions in the Mato Grosso and the Amazon. Returning to France on the eve of the war, he was mobilized. After the armistice, in June 1940, he succeeded in reaching the USA, where he taught at the New School for Social Research in New York. Volunteering for the Free French forces, he was attached to the French scientific mission in the USA and founded with H. Focillon, J. Maritain, J. Perrin and others the École Libre des Hautes Études in New York, of which he became secretary-general. In 1945 he was appointed cultural counsellor of the French

Embassy to the USA but resigned in 1948 in order to devote himself to his scientific work.

Lévi-Strauss's doctoral thesis, submitted at the Sorbonne, was made up of his first two studies, *La Vie familiale et sociale des Indiens Nambikwara* (1948) and *Les Structures élémentaires de la parenté* (1949) (*The Elementary Structures of Kinship*, 1969). In 1949 he became deputy director of the Musée de l'Homme, and later director of studies at the École Pratique des Hautes Études, chair of the comparative religion of non-literate peoples, in succession to Maurice Leenhardt. In 1959 he was appointed to the Collège de France, establishing a chair in social anthropology. He taught there until his retirement in 1982.

The name of Claude Lévi-Strauss has become linked indissolubly with what later came to be called 'structural anthropology'. Reading his first articles, such as 'Structural analysis in linguistics and anthropology' (1963 [1945]), one is struck by the clarity with which from the first he formulated the basic principles of structuralism. As the title of the essay suggests, he found his inspiration in the linguistics of Saussure and above all in the phonological method developed by Trubetzkoy and by Jakobson (with whom he was associated in New York during the Second World War). He drew from them rules of procedure: concentrate not on conscious phenomena but on their unconscious infrastructure; do not attribute an independent value to the elements of a system but rather a positional meaning, that is to say, the value of the elements is dependent upon the relations that combine and oppose them, and these relations must be the foundation of the analysis; recognize at the same time that these relations also have a merely positional significance within a system of correlations whose structure must be extracted.

Lévi-Strauss applied this method first to the study of kinship systems, demonstrating their formal analogy with phonetic systems. His article of 1945 paid especial attention to the problem of the avunculate, sketching some of the central themes of his *Elementary Structures*, which he was then elaborating. These included the central role of marriage exchange, which implies a prohibition on incest (of which exchange is, in a sense, the other, positive, side of the coin). Marriage exchange is the condition of kinship: 'Kinship is allowed to establish and perpetuate itself only through specific forms of marriage.'

He also stressed the social character of kinship, which has to do not with 'what it retains from nature', but rather with 'the essential way in which it diverges from nature' (1963 [1945]). Finally, Lévi-Strauss proposed the definition of kinship systems, and of social systems more generally, as systems of symbols.

Another influence that is also apparent, and that Lévi-Strauss has always acknowledged, is the work of Marcel Mauss. His sympathy for the thought of Mauss is apparent when he compares the method of analysis in Mauss's *Essai sur le don* with the approach of structural linguistics, or when, in the same essay, he charges anthropology with the task of studying 'the unconscious mental structures which one may discern by investigating the institutions, or better still the language', and which render intelligible the variety and apparent disorder of appearances (Lévi-Strauss 1983 [1950]).

This was the goal which had been set by the author of *The Elementary Structures of Kinship*:

> The diversity of the historical and geographical modalities of the rules of kinship and marriage have appeared to us to exhaust all possible methods for ensuring the integration of biological families within the social group. We have thus established that superficially complicated and arbitrary rules may be reduced to a small number. There are only three possible elementary kinship structures; these three structures are constructed by means of two forms of exchange; and these two forms of exchange themselves depend upon a single differential characteristic, namely the harmonic or disharmonic character of the regime considered. Ultimately, the whole imposing apparatus of prescriptions and prohibitions could be reconstructed *a priori* from one question, and one alone: in the society concerned, what is the relationship between the rule of residence and the rule of descent?
>
> (1969 [1949]: 493)

Furthermore, these kinship structures rest upon universal mental structures: the force of the rule as a rule, the notion of reciprocity and the symbolic character of the gift.

Lévi-Strauss returned to deal with one unanswered question 15 years later, in *The Raw and the Cooked* (1970 [1964]). Are these kinship structures really primary, or do they rather represent 'the reflections in men's minds of certain social demands that had been objectified in institutions'? Are they the effect of what one might term an external logic? His *Mythologiques*, of which this was the first volume, put this functionalist hypothesis out of court, demonstrating that in mythology, which, in contrast to kinship, 'has no obvious practical function...is not directly linked with a different kind of reality', processes of the same order were to be found. Whether systems were actually 'lived', in the course of social life, or like the myths, simply conceived in an apparently spontaneous and arbitrary manner, they led back to the same sources, which one might legitimately describe as 'mental'. This answer had in fact been given earlier, in *Le Totémisme aujourd'hui* (*Totemism*, ([1962] 1973) and *La Pensée sauvage* (*The Savage Mind*, 1966), the latter book asserting, in opposition to Lévy-Bruhl's notion of a 'prelogical mentality', that 'savage' forms of thinking are to be found in us all, providing a shared basis that is domesticated by our various cultures.

The issue was whether the structuralist method applied only to kinship structures, and moreover only to those Lévi-Strauss termed 'elementary', which are not universal, even among those societies that traditionally are called traditional. The re-examination of totemism demonstrated how successfully this method could be applied to the symbolic systems with the aid of which people structure their representations of the world. The analysis of myths demonstrated, further, that the method not only worked for closed systems, like kinship systems, but also applied to open systems, or at least to systems whose closure could not be immediately established and whose interpretation could be developed only in the manner of a 'nebula' in the absence of 'the general appearance of a stable and well-defined structure' (*The Raw and the Cooked*).

In his last lectures at the Collège de France, between 1976 and 1982, Lévi-Strauss took up problems of kinship once more, but moved on from the systems based on unilineal descent and preferential alliance, concerning which he had developed his theory of elementary structures in 1949. He now investigated societies whose fundamental grouping brought together 'either cognates and agnates, or else cognates and maternal kin', and which he termed the 'house', borrowing a term that was used in medieval Europe. These

studies are described in his book, *Paroles données* (1984). Here he demonstrates that structuralism is by no means disqualified from the study of 'a type of institution which transcends the traditional categories of ethnological theory, combining descent and residence, exogamy and endogamy, filiation and alliance, patriliny and matriliny', and can analyse the complex matrimonial strategies that simultaneously or in succession employ principles 'which elsewhere are mutually exclusive'. What is the best alliance? Should one seek a spouse in the vicinity, or far away? These are the questions that dominate the myths. But they are not posed by savages alone. At a conference held in 1983 Lévi-Strauss cited materials from Blanche de Castille, Saint-Simon and the peasant populations of Japan, Africa, Polynesia and Madagascar to show that 'between societies which are called "complex" and those which are wrongly termed "primitive" or "archaic", the distance is less great than one might think'.

It is therefore mistaken to criticize anthropologists, certainly if they are structuralists, for ignoring history and considering the societies that they study as though they were static, despite the fact that, like our own, they exist in time, even if they may not situate themselves in time in the same fashion. This criticism rests upon a misunderstanding that Lévi-Strauss, however, tried to forestall very early. It is significant that it was in 1949 – the year in which his *Elementary Structures* appeared – that he published an essay with a title – 'History and ethnology' – that he was to use again for his conference paper in 1983. In his article of 1949 he emphasized that the difference between the two disciplines was a consequence of their very complementarity, 'history organizing its data with reference to conscious characterizations, ethnology with reference to the unconscious conditions of social life'. In 1983, taking into account what has come to be called the *'nouvelle histoire'*, this complementarity is restated, but at another level. In fact

it was through their contact with ethnology that the historians recognized the importance of those obscure and partly submerged facets of life in society. In return, as a consequence of the renewal of its field of study and its methods, history, under the name of historical anthropology, has become a source of considerable assistance to ethnologists.

Thus anthropology and history can serve each other, at least if historians do not concern themselves only with the succession of kings and queens, with wars, with treaties and with the conscious motives of actors, but study customs, beliefs and all that which is covered by the vague term *mentalité*, in a given society at a given time, especially if the anthropologist recognizes that the past of so-called complex societies increases 'the number of social experiments which are available for the better knowledge of man'.

It is true that in his inaugural lecture at the Collège de France in 1960 Lévi-Strauss opposed 'cold' societies – those that chose to ignore their historical aspect, and that anthropologists had traditionally preferred to study – and 'hot' societies – those that, on the contrary, valued their historicity and that were of especial interest to historians. Nevertheless, this opposition did not put in question the historicity of one or other type of society, but rather their attitude to their respective pasts. Every society presents a double aspect: structural and historical. But while one aspect might be especially favoured, this does not lead to the disappearance of the other. And, in truth, the cold societies do not deny the past: they wish to repeat it. For their part, hot societies cannot totally deny their 'coldness': the history that they value is theirs only by virtue of a certain continuity that guarantees their identity. This explains the paradox that the very peoples who are most concerned with their history see themselves through stereotypes. And recognizing, or desiring, a history does not prevent them from thinking of others, and especially their neighbours, in a static mode. One might instance the set fashion in which, for example, the French and the English represent each other. Thus structuralism does not put history in question, but rather an idea of history that is so common: the idea that history can concern itself only with flux, and that change is never-ending. Yet although nature does not, apparently, make jumps, history does not seem to be able to avoid them. Certainly one might interest oneself in the moments of transition. One might equally interest oneself in the intervening periods, and is history not in essence constituted by such periods? The times within which different states of society succeed each other are not less discontinuous than the space within which societies contemporary in time but equally different, often ignorant of each other, share a border. It matters little whether the distancing – which appears to ethnologists to be the condition of their research, since it is 'the other' as such that is the object of their research – is temporal or spatial.

Obviously it is not necessary to accept the notion of a possible fusion between anthropology, as conceived by Lévi-Strauss, and history. Historians strive to surmount discontinuity, their goal being to establish genealogical connections between one social state and another. Anthropologists, on the contrary, try to profit from discontinuity, by discovering, among distinct societies (without concerning themselves as to whether or not they figure in the same genealogical tree), homologies that attest to the reality of a shared foundation for humanity. Lévi-Strauss has always striven to recognize this 'original logic' beneath a diversity of expressions that have often been judged to be absurd, explicable only by positing the priority of affect over intellect, but which are 'a direct expression of the structure of the mind...and not an inert product of the action of the environment on an amorphous consciousness' (*Totemism*, 1962).

If one might talk of a Kantian aspect to structuralism (and Lévi-Strauss has never denied it), one should note that its course inverts that of Kant in two ways. First, instead of positing a transcendental subject, it tries to detach, from the variety of concrete systems of representations, collective modes of thought. Second, from among these systems it selects those that diverge most from ours. Kantianism without a transcendental subject thus, although the ambition of discovering in this way 'a fundamental and communal matrix of constraints', or in other words invariants, would seem nevertheless at the least to evoke its shade.

Such an enterprise appears to dispose of subjectivity, or at least to put it within parentheses, and this has indeed been one of the reproaches directed at structuralism: that it does not deal with man as a subject. There is a misapprehension here. As Lévi-Strauss, indeed, remarked in his 'Introduction à l'oeuvre de Marcel Mauss' (1983 [1950]):

Every society different from ours is an object; every group in our society, apart from our own, is an object; indeed, each usage, even of our own group, which we do not share, is an object. Yet this unlimited series of objects, which together constitute the object of the ethnographer, whatever its historical or geographical features, is still, in the end, defined in relation to himself. However objective in analysis, he must in the end achieve a subjective reintegration of them.

Again, in the same text: 'In the last analysis, the ethnological problem is a problem of communication.' That is to say, communication between subjects, between 'the Melanesian of whatever island', as Mauss put it, 'and the person who observes him, listens to him...and interprets him'. A similar point was made in *La Pensée sauvage*, published 12 years later, which ended with a consideration of the convergence between the laws of 'savage thought' and modern theories of information, that is, of the transmission and reception of messages. Thus the subject is not neglected or denied, but (while avoiding a solipsism that would obviously be the negation of anthropology) one might say that there is always a plurality of subjects, without which indeed the problem of communication would not present itself, and it is their relations that are significant. This remains a constant principle of Lévi-Strauss's structuralism: it is the relations that matter, not the terms.

That is also the principle which has guided this brief review. It has been concerned less with the analysis of texts, each considered in itself, than with their relations – from a point of view as much synchronic as diachronic – the aim being to abstract the invariant features of a body of work that is at once complete yet always open.

JEAN POUILLON
PARIS

References

Lévi-Strauss, C. (1963 [1958]) 'Introduction: History and ethnology', in *Structural Anthropology*, New York.
—— (1963 [1945]) 'Structural analysis in linguistics and anthropology', in *Structural Anthropology*, New York.
—— (1966 [1962]) *The Savage Mind*, Chicago.
—— (1969 [1949]) *The Elementary Structures of Kinship*, London.
—— (1970 [1964]) *The Raw and the Cooked*, London.
—— (1973 [1962]) *Totemism*, Boston and London.
—— (1983 [1950]) *Introduction to Marcel Mauss*, London.
—— (1984) *Paroles données*, Paris.

Further reading

Eribon, D. (1991) *Conversations with Claude Lévi-Strauss*, Chicago.
Johnson, C. (2003) *Claude Lévi-Strauss: The Formative Years*, Cambridge, UK.
Lévi-Strauss, C. (1961 [1955]) *A World on the Wane*, New York.
—— (1963 [1949]) 'History and ethnology', in *Structural Anthropology*, New York.
—— (1963 [1958]) *Structural Anthropology*, New York.
—— (1972 [1966]) *From Honey to Ashes*, London.
—— (1978 [1968]) *The Origin of Table Manners*, London.
—— (1981 [1971]) *The Naked Man*, London.
—— (1977) 'The scope of anthropology', *Structural Anthropology* 2.
—— (1987 [1983]) *A View from Afar*, London.
Pace, D. (1983) *Claude Lévi-Strauss: The Bearer of Ashes*, London.

SEE ALSO: structuralism

LIBERALISM

Although it is the predominant political ideology in the West, liberalism is a protean doctrine whose meaning can perhaps be conveyed only by the use of adjectives that describe its particular nuances. The two most familiar are social liberalism and economic liberalism.

The various liberalisms, nevertheless, derive from various interpretations of the morally appropriate relationship between the individual and the state, or organized community. Liberalism has traditionally presupposed that the individual is logically prior to society and that political forms should respect this by allocating a protected sphere within which the person should be free to pursue self-determined goals. It rests upon a belief in a pluralism of purposes such that none is entitled to special privilege, and claims that law and state should preserve an institutional framework of equal justice. It is therefore indissolubly connected to a form of constitutionalism that limits political authority.

Liberals vary in the extent to which they acknowledge the role of reason in human affairs. However, liberalism has always rejected conservative claims that traditional institutional arrangements are entitled to allegiance in advance of a consideration of the value they might have in the protection of individual self-fulfilment. There is also an implicit universalism in liberalism in that it proclaims a moral validity independently of particular historical and social circumstances.

This purported validity is derived normally from either a utilitarian calculation of the advantages that accrue from individual self-determination or from a purely moral perspective that rests on the inviolability of the person.

John Locke (1690) was perhaps the originator of modern liberalism with his argument that government was bound by natural law and that its function was limited to the protection of individual rights, especially the entitlement to property that derived from individual appropriation, subject to moral law. Furthermore, his liberalism included a right to disobedience if government transgressed the boundaries of individualism specified by morality. Despite this, Lockean liberalism could be said to be embedded in the English common law tradition, which was maturing in the seventeenth century.

However, the modern development of liberalism owes more to the influence of the Enlightenment on European thought. This produced a much more rationalistic version that explicitly subjected all received social arrangements to the test of an abstract reason, uncontaminated by traditional practices. From Voltaire onwards French liberalism in particular was inherently distrustful of experience and supposed that liberty-enhancing institutions were to be designed from first principles. It was a form of liberalism that came to be significantly different from the cautious empiricism of David Hume and Adam Smith, who were distinctive in identifying liberty with the spontaneous growth of market institutions and their associated legal framework. This leaves a small role for government since the 'invisible hand' of the exchange system was thought to generate the public good out of the self-regarding actions of private agents (Smith 1776).

From the early nineteenth century, liberalism began to be associated explicitly with *laissez-faire* economics and utilitarianism, and its moral dimensions were limited to the promotion of happiness. However, Jeremy Bentham (1789), while still claiming that individuals were the units of social evaluation (for him collective entities such as the state and society were 'fictions' that were constructed out of the motivations of discrete, pleasure-seeking agents), maintained that there was a role for political direction in the creation of an artificial harmony of interests. This, theoretically, allowed an expanded role for the state. But throughout the

century the natural processes of the market in the allocation of resources and in the determination of income became the key features of liberalism. The growth of free trade and the limiting of government to the provision of defence, law and order, and other essential public goods, were practices associated exclusively with liberalism. The doctrine was also understood as the means for achieving universal peace, as well as prosperity. John Stuart Mill, although he thought of himself as a liberal utilitarian, was exceptional in stressing the moral value of individuality and in his *On Liberty* (1859) was as concerned to argue for freedom as a contribution to the development of the personality as well as for its role in wealth creation. The latter was, in fact, understated.

In the early twentieth century, liberalism began to take on a much more social orientation and the state was charged with the duty of providing conditions for the fulfilment of the good life. Under the influence of writers such as L.T. Hobhouse (1911), British liberal doctrine became associated with the rise of the welfare state. This could still claim to be individualistic in that the state was not understood to embody collective values irreducible to those of private agents, or as the source of a morality that could claim an unquestioned loyalty from citizens, but certainly the role of the state in creation of a more equal society became integral to liberalism. Economic liberty, the protection of property rights and the inviolability of contract faded into the background. The great theorists of economic intervention, such as Keynes (1936), could all claim to be liberal, despite their rejection of the *traditional* liberal doctrine that a free market is automatically self-correcting. The creation of the general interest was now the direct responsibility of liberal governments.

In the contemporary world, liberalism has shed much of its earlier utilitarianism. This is largely because of its embrace of the theory of social justice. Thus Rawls (1971) argues that justice is the first virtue of society and its demands must be met (normally) before conditions of economic well-being become relevant to the evaluation of government policy. The doctrine remains rationalistic and critical of received institutions. Using the contractarian method, Rawls asks individuals which principles of social and economic organization they would adopt if they were ignorant of their present circumstances and the value of their particular talents. In addition to choosing the traditional liberal values of equality before the law and free expression, Rawls argues that rational agents would opt for a redistributive rule that would permit inequality only in so far as that is needed to ensure the greatest benefit to the least advantaged. This is seen to be consistent with rational self-interest since an individual may turn out to be the least advantaged in the conditions of the real world.

This approach has come to be definitive of late twentieth-century liberalism (especially in the USA). It is Kantian in foundation since it stresses the inviolability and separateness of persons. Individual interests cannot be conflated into a social utility function since this would put the ends of society in a privileged position. It is also 'neutral' about conceptions of the good. Ways of life are matters of individual determination, since for the state to favour any one would be to assume a moral knowledge that it cannot have. It would also involve the unequal treatment of people. It is permitted only to promote the primary goods, those encompassing the conditions of basic well-being, liberty, equality of opportunity and self-respect, and must eschew any ideas of perfectionism. In its original formulation it was heavily universalistic, since individuals are deliberately abstracted from any communal affiliations and asked to deliberate over moral rules that are applicable to all agents. The doctrine is heavily egalitarian because it denies the moral validity of, not merely inherited wealth, but also the advantages that accrue from the distribution of natural assets (skills and talents that are socially valuable). Nobody deserves their talents; they are the product of the random processes of nature. The original liberal notion of self-ownership is explicitly rejected. The earnings derived from natural assets constitute a common pool that is available for redistribution according to the principles of social justice. The only concession to the liberal utilitarian's notion of efficiency is that some inequality is required to ensure that the talented use their skills so that everybody (including the least advantaged) benefits. The final link between this liberalism and economic liberalism is broken with Rawls's claim that his system is consistent with either capitalist or socialist ownership of the means of production.

This is not specifically a natural rights doctrine because Rawls and his followers do not utilize a notion of individual claims prior to society, but its moral metaphysic provides liberalism with intellectual armoury to be used against positive law (legislation). The legalistic social liberals, especially Ronald Dworkin (1977), have been active in claiming rights against the state. These individual rights (though they do not include economic freedoms) take priority over communal interests or the will of the majority. This version of liberalism has prospered in the USA precisely because the written constitution there gives the judiciary considerable interpretative authority over the content of liberal rights.

Economic liberalism has undergone a minor revival since the mid-1970s. Here the emphasis has been either on individual rights to property, which social liberalism's egalitarianism severely attenuates, or on the alleged economic incoherence of liberal redistributivism. Thus Nozick (1974), in a revised version of Locke's doctrine, argues that individuals have rights to their natural talents and to the products of voluntary exchange and inheritance. For the state to intervene to create an egalitarian order would be to violate these rights and to use individuals (in a non-Kantian manner) as mere means to the ends of society. The state is limited to the enforcement of legitimately acquired property rights, to the protection of freedom of contract and to the correction of past wrongs.

Friedrich von Hayek (1976) takes a more economic view. For him there is no distinction between production and distribution: any redistribution of resources must have a feedback effect (through reduced incentives) on productive possibilities so that society as a whole is worse off. To entrust the state with redistributive powers is to pose serious threats to liberty and the rule of law. Justice is really a type of constitutionalism that forbids the state imposing various outcomes (particular patterns of income and wealth) on a natural market process. Furthermore, Hayek maintains that in a pluralistic, liberal society there is no agreement about the morality of distribution. For example, there is no theory of desert that can secure universal assent and any interference with the verdict of an anonymous market is a threat to the liberal order. Hayek's liberalism is firmly tied to market economics and the doctrine of the rule of law. What is surprising is his claim that these arrangements will emerge spontaneously if people are left some liberty. The role of reason in the evaluation of social order is seriously diminished.

Whatever their disagreements about economics, modern liberals are united at least in their opposition to that kind of conservatism that locates the identity of the individual within given social orders which are immune from rational criticism. The individual is accorded a peculiar kind of sovereignty that is resistant to the claims of community. Methodologically, almost all liberals doubt the explanatory value of collectivist or holistic theories. They also reject the moral implications that such models may have. Similarly, while not denying the legitimacy of democratic procedures, liberals are not willing to endanger the sanctity of the individual by unconstrained majority rule.

NORMAN BARRY
UNIVERSITY OF BUCKINGHAM

References

Bentham, J. (1789) *An Introduction to the Principles of Morals and Legislation*, London.
Dworkin, R.M. (1977) *Taking Rights Seriously*, London.
Hayek, F.A. von (1976) *The Mirage of Social Justice*, London.
Hobhouse, L.T. (1911) *Liberalism*, London.
Keynes, J.M. (1936) *The General Theory of Employment, Interest and Money*, London.
Locke, J. (1690) *Two Treatises of Government*, London.
Mill, J.S. (1859) *On Liberty*, London.
Nozick, R. (1974) *Anarchy, State and Utopia*, New York.
Rawls, J. (1971) *A Theory of Justice*, Cambridge, MA.
Smith, A. (1776) *An Enquiry into the Nature and Causes of the Wealth of Nations*, London.

SEE ALSO: Bentham; freedom; Hayek; Locke; Mill

LIBERTARIANISM

Libertarianism is usually understood as a theory of the morally permissible use of non-consensual force. It holds that agents initially fully own themselves and have moral powers to acquire private property rights in external things. It judges non-consensual force against a person permissible only when it is necessary to prevent that person from violating someone's rights or to impose rectification for such violation (e.g. compensation or punishment). Libertarianism judges it impermissible to use force against an innocent person merely to advance some impersonal good, to benefit that person (paternalism), to benefit others, or even to prevent third parties from violating the rights of others. These limits on the use of force radically limit the legitimate powers of government.

Libertarianism holds that agents are, at least initially, *full self-owners*. This means that they own themselves in just the same way that they can fully own inanimate objects. This full private ownership of a person or thing includes (1) *full-control rights* over its *use*, (2) a *full immunity to the non-consensual loss* of any of the rights of ownership, as long as one does not violate the rights of others, (3) a *full power to transfer* these rights to others (by sale, rental, gift or loan), and (4) a *full right to compensation* if someone violates these rights. The property rights in question are *moral* rights, and may not be legally recognized.

Something like self-ownership is arguably needed to recognize the fact there are some things (e.g. various forms of physical contact) that may not be done to a person without his or her consent, but which may be done with that consent. One might, however, endorse full-*control* self-ownership without endorsing the other rights of full self-ownership.

Three main objections to full self-ownership are the following. (1) Because it holds that agents have not only the right to control the use of their person, but also the right to *transfer* that right (e.g. by sale or gift) to others, voluntary enslavement is permitted. (2) Full self-ownership entails that individuals have no enforceable obligations, except by voluntary agreement, to perform actions that help the needy. (3) Full self-ownership rules out forced service (e.g. draft into the military) even when such service is needed to provide public goods. Libertarians typically defend voluntary slavery on the ground (roughly) that the right to *exercise* one's autonomy is more fundamental than the *protection or promotion* of one's autonomy. Libertarians typically defend the lack of an enforceable duty to help the needy or to provide public goods on the ground that such duties involve a kind of partial involuntary slavery.

So far, we have considered agent self-ownership. In addition to agents, there are three other relevant kinds of objects in the world: (1) non-agent beings with moral standing (e.g. children and animals), (2) artefacts (things with no moral standing that were created by agents), and (3) natural resources (things with no moral standing and that were not created by agents, e.g. unimproved land, oil and air). Libertarianism is committed to full self-ownership for agents, but it can take different positions on the ownership of the remaining three kinds of object. In particular, there is an important distinction between *right-libertarianism* and *left-libertarianism*, depending on the stance taken on how natural resources can be owned.

Right-libertarianism – the traditional form of libertarianism – holds that natural resources are initially unowned and typically may be appropriated without the consent of, or significant payment to, others. It holds, for example, that whoever first discovers, first mixes his or her labour with, or first claims a natural resource owns that resource provided, perhaps, that certain minimal conditions are satisfied. *Radical right-libertarians* – such as Rothbard (1978, 1982) – hold that that there are no constraining conditions. Natural resources are simply up for grabs. *Lockean right-libertarians* – such as Nozick (1974) – on the other hand, hold that appropriation is legitimate only if 'enough and as good' (the Lockean proviso, specified by Locke (1960 [1690]) is left for others. Lockean right-libertarians interpret the Lockean proviso in welfarist terms: no one should be made worse off in some sense by the appropriation. This can be further interpreted in different ways: Is it the specific act of appropriation that should make no one worse off, or is it the general practice of appropriation of natural resources that should make no one worse off? However that is answered, what is the appropriate baseline: non-appropriation (no private property of natural resources), the most efficient (in some specified sense) form of property rights (which may be limited in various ways), or something else? By definition, right-libertarianism interprets the Lockean proviso either as inapplicable or as imposing minimal conditions.

Left-libertarianism, by contrast, holds that natural resources are owned by the members of society in some egalitarian sense, so that appropriation is legitimate only with their consent, or with a significant payment to them. According to one version of left-libertarianism, natural resources are *jointly owned* in the sense that authorization to use, or to appropriate, is given through some specified collective decision-making process (e.g. by majority or unanimous decision). A problem with this approach is that collective approval may be impossible or extremely difficult to obtain. Furthermore, even where it is not difficult to obtain, it is unclear why one shouldn't be permitted to use, or appropriate, natural resources as long as one compensates others for the full value of such use or appropriation. Few left-libertarians endorse joint ownership of natural resources.

The most well-developed, and best-known, form of left-libertarianism is *Georgist libertarianism* – as developed, for example, by George (1879) and Steiner (1994). It holds that agents may appropriate unappropriated natural resources as long as they pay for the competitive value (based on supply and demand) of the rights they claim. Given the existence of multiple generations, the most plausible version of this approach arguably requires that rights over natural resources be *rented* (as opposed to purchased) at the competitive rent value (so as to ensure that for *each* generation the total payment equals current competitive value). Both George and Steiner defend the view that the fund so generated should be divided equally among all (i.e. that each person is entitled to an equal share of the value of natural resources). Other views, however, are possible. One is that the funds should be allocated to promote effective equality of opportunity for a good life (and thus give more to those who have less valuable opportunities).

Georgist left-libertarianism – even the version that allocates the rent fund to promote effectively equality of opportunity – does not guarantee that people have effectively equal opportunities to have a good life. The rents from rights over natural resources may not be sufficient for that purpose. Otsuka (2003) defends a version of left-libertarianism that does guarantee equal opportunities for a good life. He argues that individuals may unilaterally appropriate natural resources to the extent that it is compatible with everyone having an equal opportunity for a good life. To the extent a person appropriates more than such a share (which will be relatively small for those who are relatively well endowed), he or she owes others compensation for their decreased opportunities for a good life.

Libertarianism can be understood as a basic principle or as a derivative one. We have been understanding libertarianism to be a basic moral principle (e.g. based on natural rights). It is possible, however, to defend libertarianism as a derivative principle. Rule utilitarianism could lead to libertarian principles, as could rule contractarianism (e.g. Narveson 1988).

PETER VALLENTYNE
UNIVERSITY OF MISSOURI

References

George, H. (1879) *Progress and Poverty*, 5th edn, New York.
Locke, J. (1960 [1690]) *Two Treatises of Government*, New York.
Narveson, J. (1988) *The Libertarian Idea*, Philadelphia.
Nozick, R. (1974) *Anarchy, State and Utopia*, New York.
Otsuka, M. (2003) *Libertarianism without Inequality*, Oxford.
Rothbard, M. (1978) *For a New Liberty: The Libertarian Manifesto*, rev. edn, New York.
—— (1982) *The Ethics of Liberty*, Atlantic Highlands.
Steiner, H. (1994) *An Essay on Rights*, Cambridge, MA.

Further reading

Barnett, R. (1998) *The Structure of Liberty: Justice and the Rule of Law*, Oxford.
Cohen, G.A. (1995) *Self-Ownership, Freedom, and Equality*, Cambridge.
Grunebaum, J. (1987) *Private Ownership*, New York.
Hayek, F.A. (1960) *The Constitution of Liberty*, Chicago.
Hospers, J. (1971) *Libertarianism*, Los Angeles.
Lomasky, L. (1987) *Persons, Rights, and the Moral Community*, New York.
Machan, T. (ed.) (1974) *The Libertarian Alternative: Essays in Social and Political Philosophy*, Chicago.
—— (ed.) (1982) *The Libertarian Reader*, Totowa.
Paul, J. (ed.) (1982) *Reading Nozick: Essays on Anarchy, State, and Utopia*, Oxford.
Simmons, J.A. (1992) *The Lockean Theory of Rights*, Princeton, NJ.
Sreenivasan, G. (1995) *The Limits of Lockean Rights in Property*, New York.
Vallentyne, P. and Steiner, H. (eds) (2000) *Left Libertarianism and Its Critics: The Contemporary Debate*, New York.
—— (eds) (2000) *The Origins of Left Libertarianism: An Anthology of Historical Writings*, New York.

SEE ALSO: anarchism; Locke

LIFE HISTORY

Life histories, if properly conceived, are fundamental units of analysis in the social sciences. A life history may be defined as the sequence of events and experiences in a life from birth to death, set, ideally, in relation to social, cultural and historical contexts. Life histories can be studied not only with the 'life history method' of having a respondent recount the story of his or her life, but also with the full range of social scientific and historical methods, including archival research, participant observation, experimental methods and prospective longitudinal research. Given their potential to link psychological structures and processes with particular social, cultural and historical contexts, life histories are of interest to a variety of disciplines.

Within the social sciences, it is possible to identify roughly three periods in the study of life histories. (1) From approximately 1920 to the Second World War there was a substantial and growing interest in life histories, associated with the rise of personality psychology, and also with a more general public and academic interest in oral histories and the study of personal documents (Allport 1942; Langness and Frank 1981). (2) Following the Second World War, and on to the late 1960s, interest in life history studies declined, while greater attention was given to more structured quantitative and experimental methods. (3) Since the 1970s, there has been an enormous outpouring of work in the study of individual lives; this is associated with developments in fields such as life history research in psychopathology (Roff and Ricks 1970), the study of adult development (Levinson *et al.* 1978), sociological studies of the life course (Elder 1974), oral history and life stories (Bertaux 1981), personality psychology (Alexander 1990; Barenbaum and Winter 2003; McAdams and Ochberg 1988; Rabin *et al.* 1990), psychobiography (Erikson 1975; Runyan 1982, 1997), and narrative psychology (Josselson *et al.* 2002).

The debate about the value of studying individual life histories is interwoven with evolving conceptions within psychology about what counts as 'scientific'. The study of life histories has often been spurned in favour of quantitative and experimental studies, but the value of narrative, contextualist and historical forms of research, which study unique sequences of events, is now increasingly acknowledged. In consequence, life histories are more readily seen as a legitimate form of social scientific enquiry. Studies of individual life histories are most appropriately evaluated not in terms of how useful they may be for testing causal generalizations (a criterion most appropriate for experimental studies), but rather for their ability to present and interpret information about the life of a single individual. Such studies can usefully be evaluated through a 'quasi-judicial' methodology (Bromley 1977), analogous to procedures in courts of law, where evidence, inferences and interpretations are presented and critically assessed by those with competing interests and points of view, who can challenge alternative accounts.

The discipline of psychology has long struggled with the study of individual lives, but it is reasonable to think that the study of individual life histories is a necessary complement to the study of group differences, or to the search for generalizations about human behaviour and mentality.

WILLIAM MCKINLEY RUNYAN
UNIVERSITY OF CALIFORNIA, BERKELEY

References

Alexander, I.E. (1990) *Personology: Method and Content in Personality Assessment and Psychobiography*, Durham, NC.

Allport, G.W. (1942) *The Use of Personal Documents in Psychological Science*, New York.

Barenbaum, N. and Winter, D. (2003) 'Personality', in D.K. Freedheim (ed.) *Handbook of Psychology*, Vol. 1, Hoboken, NJ.

Bertaux, D. (ed.) (1981) *Biography and Society: The Life History Approach in the Social Sciences*, Beverly Hills, CA.

Bromley, D.B. (1977) *Personality Description in Ordinary Language*, New York.

Elder, G.H., Jr (1974) *Children of the Great Depression*, Chicago.

Erikson, E.H. (1975) *Life History and the Historical Moment*, New York.

Josselson, R., Lieblich, A. and McAdams, D. (eds) (2002) *Up Close and Personal: The Teaching and Learning of Narrative Research*, Washington, DC.

Langness, L.L. and Frank, G. (1981) *Lives: An Anthropological Approach to Biography*, Novato, CA.

Levinson, D. with Darrow, C.N., Klein, E.B., Levinson, M.H. and, McKee, B. (1978) *The Seasons of a Man's Life*, New York.

McAdams, C. and Ochberg, R. (eds) (1988) *Psychobiography and Life Narratives*, Durham, NC.

Rabin, A., Zucker, R., Emmons, R. and Frank, S. (eds) (1990) *Studying Persons and Lives*, New York.

Roff, M. and Ricks, D. (eds) (1970) *Life History Research in Psychopathology*, Vol. 1, Minneapolis, MN.

Runyan, W.M. (1982) *Life Histories and Psychobiography: Explorations in Theory and Method*, New York.

—— (1997) 'Studying lives: Psychobiography and the conceptual structure of personality psychology', in R. Hogan, J. Johnson and S. Briggs (eds) *Handbook of Personality Psychology*, New York, pp. 41–69.

Further reading

http://www.narrativepsych.com.
http://www.psychobiography.com.

SEE ALSO: case study; life-span development; oral history; personality

LIFE-SPAN DEVELOPMENT

Life-span development refers both to continuity and to systematic change over the course of a lifetime, from conception until death. It is not so much a theory as an approach to considering and studying human development, one that emphasizes context. Context includes the individual life-cycle, but may also involve the family life-cycle and the effects of gender, race, ethnicity, socioeconomic status, religion, culture, cohort, time in history and a variety of other social factors, as well as biological influences. Given this holistic view, life-span development is multi-disciplinary and interdisciplinary in nature.

Within psychology, some theorists and researchers focus on the biological and physical domains, others on cognitive areas, and still others on the emotional and social aspects of development. Development may be perceived as being continuous and cumulative (as with increases in height) or as being discontinuous with qualitative shifts (e.g. with different cognitive skills developing in stages, as per Piaget's theory, 1930 [1923]). Traditional developmental psychologists tended to concentrate on describing common patterns of development in infancy and childhood, as well as in adolescence to a certain extent, with an emphasis on the impact of 'nature' (e.g. Gesell 1933; Hall 1904). In principle, however, no one particular age period (nor domain) is viewed as being more significant than any other in life-span development studies, nor is any age period or area of development considered, in and of itself, separate from others. In the past few decades, those adopting this approach have extended their study to include adult development and ageing, although until recently relatively little attention has been devoted to the mid-life period (see Staudinger and Bluck 2001). By taking a wider and more contextual view, differences found in certain domains that were once viewed as losses may now be recognized as adaptive changes and even advances (e.g. adults who do not respond as expected to Piagetian childhood tasks may not have regressed cognitively, but may be displaying more highly developed 'postformal operational' thought processes, according to Baltes 1987).

Erikson (1950) proposed one of the first and most comprehensive theories of personality development. The first five stages that he set out parallel the childhood and adolescent stages in Freud's (1938) developmental theory, but Erikson also characterized stages in young adulthood, maturity and old age, each marked by specific developmental crises or conflicts. Significant issues arise at certain ages, but those same issues may be faced again at other times, and resolved differently. The resolution of each crisis depends, in part, on the resolutions of earlier crises. Erikson also recognized the influence of the environment, emphasizing the ways in which the individual's social roles and interactions vary across the life-span. Unlike Freud, who believed that personality was set by age 5 or 6, Erikson believed that new personality strengths or 'virtues' could be gained during each of the eight stages of the life-cycle. For instance, in later life, if one resolves the 'ego integrity versus despair' crisis relatively positively (depending upon the resolutions in the previous seven stages), then one may develop 'wisdom'.

Regardless of domain, certain assumptions tend to be inherent in the life-span developmental approach. Development is viewed as an active, lifelong process of adaptation, with both gains and losses (Baltes *et al.* 1998). Studies made from the life-span development perspective typically emphasize plasticity, multidimensionality, multi-directionality, multiple contexts and multiple causality. That is, aspects of development are modifiable and involve various domains, and each may exhibit a different pattern of change and/or stability, and be affected by a variety of specific factors. These principles are clearly illustrated in the research literature on intelligence across the life-span (e.g. Schaie 1996), which suggests that intelligence may consist of various abilities, innate or acquired, each of which may follow its own particular developmental trajectory, with losses in some cognitive areas being compensated by gains in other areas.

Within the life-span development perspective, some influences are referred to as normative age-graded (e.g. average age of puberty) and these have been the focus of much developmental psychology theory and research. (Refer to Annenberg's 2001 interactive website for an interesting and informative summary of normative physical, cognitive and psychosocial developments from infancy through childhood, adolescence, adulthood and later life: http://learner.org/discoveringpsychology/development/index.html.) Theorists also consider the effects of normative history-graded influences on human development (e.g. the impact of living in the USA during the terrorist attacks of 11 September 2001). In addition, there are non-normative or idiosyncratic events that are not common to a whole age group or cohort (e.g. winning the lottery). These latter influences contribute to individual variation in development, especially in adulthood. In fact, as age-related norms continue to change and the timing of social events and roles become less predictable (e.g. going to college), non-normative experiences may increase in significance. Neugarten (1979) went so far as to claim that we are becoming an 'age irrelevant' society.

Age does, however, remain the major variable of interest in life-span development research. This type of research seeks to describe, explain and predict what changes (or remains the same) with age. Important methodological issues include the definition of particular age groups, the equivalence and validity of concepts and measurement tools across age groups, and whether age changes or only age group differences are measured. While developmental research proposes to measure changes with age, there may be confounding variables that influence the findings and mask true developmental patterns. That is, many studies are cross-sectional, comparing individuals of different ages at one point in time. When differences are found, the conclusion is often that the variable changes with age. However, no actual changes were measured, only differences between groups, which might be due to other factors, such as cohort effects. For example, cognitive differences between young and older adults may be due to cohort differences in education level, rather than due to the effects of age, *per se*. Longitudinal research designs, on the other hand, do measure changes, as individuals are studied over time. However, the results are limited to only one cohort, there are often high (and selective) attrition rates, and the age effects may be confounded by other events that have occurred between the times of measurement. Sequential designs have been developed and used to disentangle these various effects, by combining aspects of cross-sectional, longitudinal and other research designs (Schaie 1996). This type of developmental research is very informative, but the cost in terms of time, money and commitment may be prohibitive (see Clark-Plaskie and Lachman 1999 for a detailed example of life-span research designs and issues in sense of control perceptions).

MARGARET CLARK-PLASKIE
EMPIRE STATE COLLEGE

References

Annenberg/CPB (2001) 'Discovering psychology series: Life-span development', http://learner.org/discoveringpsychology/development/index.html.

Baltes, P.B. (1987) 'Theoretical propositions of life-span developmental psychology: On the dynamics between growth and decline', *Developmental Psychology* 23: 611–26.

Baltes, P.B., Lindenberger, U. and Staudinger, U.M. (1998) 'Life-span theory in developmental psychology', in R.M. Lerner (ed.) *Handbook of Child Psychology*, 5th edn, New York, pp. 1,029–143.

Clark-Plaskie, M. and Lachman, M.E. (1999) 'The sense of control in midlife', in S. Willis and J.D. Reid (eds) *Life in the Middle*, New York, pp. 181–208.

Erikson, E. (1950) *Childhood and Society*, New York.

Freud, S. (1938) *The Basic Writings of Sigmund Freud*, New York.

Gesell, A. (1933) 'Maturation and patterning of behavior', in C. Murchison (ed.) *A Handbook of Child Psychology*, Worcester, MA.

Hall, G.S. (1904) *Adolescence*, New York.

Neugarten, B.L. (1979) 'Time, age, and the life cycle', *American Journal of Psychiatry* 136: 887–94.

Piaget, J. (1930 [1923]) *The Child's Conception of the World*, New York.

Schaie, K.W. (1996) *Intellectual Development in Adulthood: The Seattle Longitudinal Study*, Cambridge.

Staudinger, U.M. and Bluck, S. (2001) 'A view on midlife development from life-span theory', in M. Lachman (ed.) *Handbook on Midlife Development*, New York, pp. 3–39.

SEE ALSO: developmental psychology; life history; life tables and survival analysis; rites of passage

LIFE TABLES AND SURVIVAL ANALYSIS

Demographers' interests in mortality and cohort attrition come together in the life table, which provides a statistical description of the shrinking over time of a cohort of individuals, as they die. (The French, with a certain perverse pessimism, call this a 'death table'.) The life table itself is composed of a number of columns showing the values of the different life table functions at each age, starting from birth. Basic columns show mortality rates at each age, and probabilities of dying between one birthday and the next. Another column, the stationary or life table population, shows the numbers of people there would be at each age if deaths occurred according to the life table, fertility exactly balanced mortality, and if there was no migration. Another column, the expectation of life, shows the average number of years left to be lived by people who survive to a particular birthday. Perhaps the most important column shows the number of people out of the original cohort who survive to each birthday, its value at 'exact' age 0 (that is, the zeroth birthday, or birth) being the scaled size of the original birth cohort. When the size of the original birth cohort is unity, this function gives the probability of surviving to a particular birthday, and is known as the survivorship function or survival function.

The simplest life table to conceptualize is the cohort life table, a birth cohort being registered and then followed until all its members die. The life table is progressively constructed by relating to the number of individuals who survive to a particular birthday the number of deaths that occur during the following year, or period of years, until the next designated birthday. The method is generally impracticable for a human population, however, since the process of calculation, like the process of extinction of the cohort, takes about a century.

An alternative approach is to calculate a period life table based on the mortality rates of a particular year or calendar period. Such life tables are routinely produced by national statistical offices. The mortality rates are obtained by relating counts of deaths at particular ages, as obtained from vital statistics, to estimates of the population alive at those ages, as derived from a population enumeration. The cohort to which the life table refers is synthetic, in the sense that the rates are not derived from the experience of an actual cohort, nor would any real cohort necessarily have experienced the mortality rates measured over the calendar period in question. In industrialized countries, for example, the people who contribute to mortality rates at the oldest ages are survivors of much harsher conditions than are experienced by the infants and children. Thus the period life table is a model because it shows not the experience of a real cohort, but the implications of a particular schedule of mortality.

The standard-period life table has many applications. Its mortality rates are input to population projections. It provides summary statistics, such as expectation of life at birth, which national governments use as indicators of population health; such statistics are tracked from year to year, and unexpected movements attract attention. Cross-national comparisons of life tables lead to a ranking of countries according to the favourability of their mortality experience.

There are many variants of the standard-period life table. The most obvious is that life tables are almost invariably calculated separately by sex, since men generally suffer higher mortality than women. In addition, if similar discriminating information is provided on both death certificates and census schedules, then separate mortality rates, and hence life tables, can be calculated according, for example, to occupation, ethnicity or marital status. Also, cause-specific life tables can be calculated from mortality rates according to cause of death. Finally, multiple-decrement life tables can be calculated that show simultaneous cohort attrition from a number of causes.

Any cohort, however defined, suffers attrition. In the 1970s, demographers began to apply the mechanics of the cohort life table to other than birth cohorts, and to events other than death. People married during a particular calendar period, for example, form a marriage cohort and, once married, might divorce; likewise, women who have borne a second child might bear a third. Further, depending on the particular cohort under examination, and the event that removes people from observation, the unit of time may be not just a year, but a month or even a day. Such applications, which are typically based on data from large specially designed population surveys, are known by the more general term of survival analysis, where 'survival' refers to the avoidance of the event of interest, whether it be divorce for a marriage cohort, or a third birth for women with two children.

Just as with applications of conventional-period life tables, the observer may wish to compare the 'survival' experience of different subcohorts. When samples are sufficiently large and the desired comparisons fairly simple, statistical tests can be applied to determine whether differences between the patterns of attrition in each subcohort are attributable to chance alone. More generally, however, demographers employ modelling procedures that were made possible by a statistical breakthrough in the early 1970s that showed how to combine life tables with techniques of multivariate regression.

GIGI SANTOW
SYDNEY

Further reading

Cox, D.R. and Oakes, D. (1984) *Analysis of Survival Data*, London.
Kalbfleisch, J.D. and Prentice. R.L. (1980) *The Statistical Analysis of Failure Time Data*, New York.
Keyfitz, N. (1968) *Introduction to the Mathematics of Population*, Reading, MA.
Shryock, H.S., Siegel, J.S. and Associates (1973) *The Methods and Materials of Demography*, Washington, DC.

SEE ALSO: event–history analysis; life-span development; morbidity

LINGUISTICS

Linguistics is the scientific study of language. While the roots of modern linguistics lie in the grammatical traditions of ancient India, classical antiquity and Arabic civilizations, modern linguistics as an academic discipline is typically traced to early nineteenth-century Germany with the rise of the German university system. Linguistics is characteristically divided into the study of language from a diachronic perspective and the study of language from a synchronic perspective. Diachronic linguistics focuses on the historical processes that affect languages over time and on the classification of languages into families. Synchronic linguistics concentrates on the description and analysis of (mainly) spoken language as it is used by its speakers. In the nineteenth century, linguistics was centred on diachronic study. The major achievements of nineteenth-century linguistics included the development of a methodology for establishing genetic relations among languages, the discovery of historical sound laws and the reconstruction of earlier stages of languages, the so-called proto-languages. Under the methodology that was developed (and still generally accepted), a genetic relationship among languages can be established if systematic sound correspondences are attested amongst them. While certain language families and their internal relationships have become well established such as that of the Indo-European language family, the relationships of other language families are less well established. One present-day controversy concerns the relationship among the Indian languages of the Americas, that is, the issue of to what extent the Native American languages are related to one another. Whereas some scholars have posited over a hundred separate unrelated language families for the Americas, Joseph Greenberg (1987) has proposed that these families can be reduced to three superfamilies. Other controversial classifications include various attempts to relate the Indo-European language family to other large language families (such as the Altaic or Afro-Asiatic), but these attempts have been subjected to significant criticism.

An important early contributor to the development of synchronic language study was Wilhelm von Humboldt (1767–1835) who emphasized the importance of describing languages and doing typological comparison among languages. Humboldt is probably best known for popularizing the division of languages into isolating, agglutinative and inflectional, which describes languages by the degree and type of affixation. An isolating language has little, if any, affixation (e.g. prefixation and suffixation). An agglutinating language exhibits a great deal of affixation and may even incorporate a sentence into a single word. (Such languages are called polysynthetic or incorporating.) Inflectional languages indicate certain meanings and relationships by affixation (e.g. case endings on nouns that indicate whether the noun is the subject or object of the sentence) or by internal changes in the form of words (e.g. English sing/sang/sung). This classification should not be viewed as absolute since one language may exhibit more than one type. For example, the English possessive may be expressed inflectionally by the suffix 's' as in 'Janet's hat', or in a more isolating manner as in 'the hat of Janet' where no affix appears. Humboldt's focus on synchronic language study did not have widespread influence in his own day. The rise of synchronic linguistics in the twentieth century can be traced to the work on non-Western languages undertaken by Franz Boas (1858–1942) and his students and colleagues at Columbia University. The key to the Boasian approach to linguistics was the insistence that each language be described in its own terms and not according to a preset Latin or Germanic model.

Synchronic linguistics as now conceived has a considerable number of subfields. A large body of work has been dedicated to the analysis of language structure. This includes the three primary areas of syntax (sentence structure), morphology (word structure) and phonology (sound structure). Since Noam Chomsky's *Syntactic Structures* (1957) initiated a new school of transformational generative grammar, a primary goal of syntactic research has been to account for the fact that all languages allow for an infinite number of sentences and to account for the similarities and differences found among languages with respect to the variety of sentence types. As an example, there has been much research on the properties of reflexive sentences. In the sentence 'John wanted the doctor to examine himself', the reflexive word 'himself' can refer only to the doctor. However, in the Japanese rendition of the same sentence, the corresponding reflexive word is ambiguous as to whether it refers to the doctor or John. The identity of the referent of the English reflexive is thus bounded by the clause in which it is located while that of the Japanese reflexive is not. Research in morphology has revolved around issues of word-formation, specifically concerning the properties manifested by affixes when they attach to words to form new words (e.g. read/readable). Typically, a specific affix may only go on words of a certain part of speech and then there may be other restrictions on its combination. For example, the English superlative suffix -est only attaches to adjectives that are two syllables or less, as is evidenced by the comparison of *smart–smartest* with *intelligent–most intelligent* (not *intelligentest*). Phonology, which deals with the description and distribution of sounds (i.e. consonants and vowels), and, in some cases, tone and accent, has been a focus of synchronic linguistics for the past century. A large body of recent work on phonology centres on the role of the syllable in sound patterning and on the effect this has on the location of word stress. One finding is that in many languages a heavy syllable (i.e. a syllable ending in a consonant or possessing a long vowel) is more likely to be stressed than a light one (i.e. a syllable ending in a short vowel), as can be seen by the difference in the location of stress in the English words *Canada* and *veranda* where, in the latter word, stress is on the syllable that ends in a consonant. Other areas of research with respect to language structure include semantics (the study of meaning) and phonetics (the study of how sounds are made physiologically and their acoustic properties).

Within the different subfields of synchronic linguistics, research either tends to examine the details of specific languages or it tends to be typological. Typological work investigates a specific phenomenon in many languages with the aim of finding the attested variation with respect to that phenomenon and to find correlations between that phenomenon and other properties. Universal properties of languages may then be postulated. As an example of syntactic typology, a major division among languages concerns whether the basic word order is Subject–Verb–Object [SVO] (as in English), Verb–Subject–Object [VSO] (as in Standard Arabic), or Subject–Object–Verb [SOV] (as in Japanese). Researchers have discovered that this distinction is correlated with other syntactic properties such as whether the preposition occurs before the noun phrase (as in English or Arabic), or after the noun phrase (as in Japanese).

Synchronic linguistics focuses on issues of theoretical concern (e.g. developing theories that account for observations such as the relation between word stress and syllable weight, or on why there is a difference in reflexives as to whether they are clause-bound). However, many linguists continue to devote their energy to describing languages by writing grammars and dictionaries. Currently, there is a particular attention to languages that are endangered. Scholars have observed that a large number of the world's languages (approximately 6,000) do not have many speakers and many of those languages are not being learned by younger people because of the influence of dominant languages with more speakers. An example of this would be the influence that English has had in North America and that Spanish and Portuguese have had in Latin America on the declining number of Native American languages that are still in daily use.

A major area of linguistic research that bridges diachronic and synchronic linguistics is the immense area of sociolinguistics that examines variation in language and language use according to such factors as gender, social class, age, ethnicity, level of formality and geographical region. These factors may influence various aspects of language structure or language use. As an example, whether or not the sound 'r' is pronounced at the end of syllables in the English of the northeast coast of the USA may be largely dependent on the social class of the individual and on the level of formality of the social interaction. The study of sociolinguistics is often important for diachronic studies because certain styles may preserve older forms of the language that are no longer in common use, or because they may be symptoms of a language change in progress.

Finally, because of the centrality of language for many disciplines, one finds that linguistics is constantly expanding to encompass other subfields. Examples include psycholinguistics, computational linguistics, forsenic linguistics, (first) language acquisition and second language learning.

STUART DAVIS
INDIANA UNIVERSITY

References

Greenberg, J. (1987) *Language in the Americas*, Stanford, CA.

Further reading

Andresen, J.T. (1990) *Linguistics in America 1769–1924: A Critical History*, London.
Chomsky, N. (1988) *Language and Problems of Knowledge: The Managua Lectures*, Cambridge, MA.
Darnell, R. (1998) *And Along Came Boas: Continuity and Revolution in American Anthropology*, Philadelphia, PA.
Greenberg, J. (ed.) (1978) *Universals of Human Language*, 4 vols, Stanford, CA.
Labov, W. (2001) *Principles of Linguistic Change: Social Factors*, Oxford.
Newmeyer, F. (1986) *Linguistic Theory in America*, 2nd edn, Orlando, FL.
Robins, R.H. (1979) *A Short History of Linguistics*, 2nd edn, New York.

LIQUIDITY

Liquidity is, to quote Kenneth Boulding, 'a quality of assets which … is not a very clear or easily measurable concept' (1955): all economists know what it is but few would want to define it. Nevertheless, a definition is necessary and, for most uses, the definition must allow it to be measured.

While liquidity usually refers to a 'quality of assets', it may also apply to markets or agents (i.e. individuals or firms). However, in these applications it remains the quality of the assets traded in the market, or owned by the agent, which determines their liquidity.

Two measurable definitions of liquidity stand out. Lippman and McCall (1986) discuss 'notions' of liquidity, which keeps their technical analysis in touch with more down-to-earth ideas. Their notions are that money is perfectly liquid; an illiquid asset cannot be sold; an asset is more liquid if it is traded in a market with a large number of participants; and liquidity depends on the desire of the holder to sell. They then include these notions in a model in which the seller maximizes the expected present value of the money received from the sale, and liquidity is measured by the *expected time taken to sell the asset*. The present value increases with the selling price, but decreases with the expected delay until the transaction.

Grossman and Miller (1988) measure liquidity in terms of '*immediacy*', that is, the ability of an asset to be sold immediately. In financial markets, immediacy is supplied by 'market-makers' – intermediaries who declare a price at which they themselves are prepared to buy so that sellers can sell immediately at that price. The market-makers then search for another buyer to take the assets at a higher price, the price difference being the intermediary's reward for providing liquidity, or immediacy. Liquidity increases with the number of market-makers. Financial markets can be contrasted with the housing market in this respect. Intermediaries in the latter tend not to buy houses themselves; their concern is to ensure that potential buyers are aware that a house is for sale; for this they charge a commission. Consequently, this market, with few market-makers, is not very liquid.

While a lot of research in this area is concerned with the liquidity of tradeable assets such as equities, the liquidity of non-tradeable assets has also attracted attention recently. The principal non-tradeable asset is the humble bank account that, by and large, most people regard as just as liquid as cash. This becomes interesting when we consider that most of the loans that we receive from banks are far from liquid, and we should be somewhat alarmed if banks started to reduce their loans to us in the same way that we reduce our loans (i.e. deposits) to them. So we make short-term, liquid loans to the banks, and they use the same money to make long-term

illiquid loans to us. If the banks did not exist, those wishing to lend money would find themselves at odds with those wanting to borrow it: the lender wants his loan to be liquid, but the borrower wants it to be illiquid. Somehow the banks transform the illiquid loan into a liquid deposit: a process known as liquidity transformation. This does of course entail some risk, since if all the depositors want their money back at the same time, the bank will be unable to recall enough of its loans to meet the depositors' demands. Furthermore, since the depositors know this, they have an incentive to monitor the bank's deposit withdrawals, and remove their money if it looks as though other depositors are removing theirs; this is the source of bank runs. Such runs can be very serious: for example, Milton Friedman (1963) blames the Great Depression on the inability of US banks to withstand several waves of bank runs that arose in the early 1930s.

Two of the leading researchers in the field (Douglas Diamond and Philip Dybvig 1983) summarize this rather neatly as, 'Illiquidity of assets provides the rationale for both the existence of banks and for their vulnerability to runs.' In a later paper, Diamond (1997) brings the issues of asset market liquidity and bank deposit liquidity together in a single model, and issues a warning to the banks, i.e. that as we see markets become more liquid, we shall also see the banking sector contract.

DAVID BARR
IMPERIAL COLLEGE, LONDON

References

Boulding, K.E. (1955) *Economic Analysis*, 3rd edn, New York.
Diamond, D.W. (1997) 'Liquidity, banks and markets', *Journal of Political Economy* (October).
Diamond, D.W. and Dybvig, P.H. (1983) 'Bank runs, deposit insurance, and liquidity', *Journal of Political Economy* (June).
Friedman, M., with A.J. Schwartz (1963) *A Monetary History of the United States, 1867–1960*, Princeton, NJ.
Grossman, S.J. and Miller, M.H. (1988) 'Liquidity and market structure', *Journal of Finance* (July).
Lippman, S.A. and McCall, J.J. (1986) 'An operational measure of liquidity', *American Economic Review* (March).

SEE ALSO: monetary policy; money

LITERACY

In the mid-1960s the place and meaning of the concept and the fact of literacy in the social sciences was a simple and secure one. Tied closely to the liberal, post-Enlightenment synthesis of modernization theory, literacy was seen as a central variable among that complex of factors that distinguished modern, developed or developing, and advanced societies *and* individuals, from the lesser developed areas and persons of the world. Literacy, moreover, was typically conceptualized more as an independent variable than a dependent factor. Support for this set of propositions was drawn, on the one hand, from a set of once commonsensical assumptions and expectations, rooted in a special view of the nature of (historical) development that emphasized the linearity and certainty of progress, and, on the other hand, from a number of aggregate macro-level ecological correlations that saw literacy levels relatively highly associated with many of the other indicators of social development, ranging from fertility rates to measures of economic development. Although literacy itself was at best vaguely defined and variously measured, a diffuse positivism and functionalism undergirded the prominence accorded to it in many formulations. But despite strong assumptions, there were surprisingly few empirical or critical studies. Important questions were few: expectations of literacy's key contribution to social and economic development, political democratization and participant citizenship, widening awareness and identification, seizure of opportunities, and action orientations dominated. As such, promotion of literacy often featured as a central element in plans for the development of underdeveloped areas, especially by North American and Western European social scientists, governments and foundations.

Such an understanding no longer maintains its hegemony. In fact, no central theory governs expectations about the roles and meanings of literacy, and its very nature has itself become problematic and arouses contention and increasingly critical attention. From its formerly secure status as critical independent variable, literacy is now conceptualized more as a dependent factor; the linearity of its contributions is also debated. Ironically, as the status – so to speak – of literacy as an independently determinative variable, necessary if not always sufficient, has declined, its

place on the agenda of social science research and discussion has risen. There are lessons in that transformation.

Many sources account for this change. Among them are the discovery of the limits of modernization theory and the theoretical synthesis on which it was based; greater awareness of the differences (and different effects) among literacy, schooling and education – terms too often used interchangeably and confused conceptually; recognition of the problematic nature of literacy, and the conceptual and empirical difficulties that the subject represents. For example, by the 1960s, the severe problems of measuring literacy – comparing measures and resulting rates for different places and periods, and assessing associations and contributions – were frequently noted; a variety of measures and definitions, with a trend towards their inflation, proliferated. Whether literacy's impacts were attitudinal and ideational, cognitive, skill-linked, concrete or more abstract, all-pervasive or more selective, sparked further discussion and weakened common bases of understanding. In addition, the conservative functions and consequences of literacy and, indeed, certain 'non-effects' received renewed attention. Empirical studies became more sensitive to weak and contradictory findings; discussions of literacy 'gaps' and time 'lags' in association with other expected aspects and concomitants of development punctuated the literature. International attention increased: from the twin sources of UNESCO's calls for action and analysis and path-breaking national literacy campaigns in the Third World. The discovery of persisting *il*literacy in the advanced societies led to the identification of *il*literacy, and sometimes literacy, too, as a social problem, and a late twentieth-century threat to national security, economic productivity, national welfare and the promise of democratic life. Rapid changes in communications technology, especially of non-print and non-alphabetic forms (in contrast to the traditional bases of literacy), not only led to sometimes frenzied questions about the 'future' and 'decline' of literacy and print, but also stimulated more questions about definitions, measures and levels of individual and national skills requisite for survival and advancement in late modern societies. Whereas literacy was seldom deemed *un*important or non-consequential, or *il*literacy *not* an obstacle or liability, its precise contributions and impacts could no longer be assumed.

The challenge of a number of revisionist 'critical theories' was also important. So too was the development of a historical analysis of literacy and illiteracy, much of which aimed specifically at testing the literacy–modernization linkages. In a number of careful, often statistical, studies, historians throughout the world sharply qualified traditional expectations of a series of direct connections tying rising levels of literacy to developments in societies, economies, polities and cultures. This is one area in which historians and social scientists have had much of importance to contribute to one another. In part, historians discovered relatively high levels of literacy in advance of 'modernization'; they simultaneously located important 'take-offs' prior to mass or even moderately high literacy rates. Literacy's linkages to the spread of modern attitudes and its relationship to individual advancement have been questioned. Notions of stages or threshold levels have also been criticized. Many macrolevel correlations seem to break down in disaggregated testing.

There are, however, a number of critical points at which historical and social scientific analyses reflect one another conceptually and empirically. These include the nature of literacy as a *dependent* variable; its dependence on *context*; the *limits* of universal impacts and generalized consequences (which have major implications for literacy's place in social science theories); the epistemological complications of *defining and measuring* literacy levels at the societal plane or literacy abilities at the individual level; the weakness of the traditional literacy–illiteracy *dichotomy*; and the fact that changes in literacy levels may often *follow from*, rather than precede, basic social, economic, political or cultural transformations. Literacy, increasingly, is connected to the larger network of communicative competencies (the oral, for example), not contrasted dichotomously and developmentally from them; it is also conceptualized more as a *continuous, widely varying, and nonlinear* attribute. Its importance as shaper of attitudes and as a symbol and symbolic influence stands beside, in partial independence from, its role in cognitive and skill determination. To speak of literacy in the abstract is now considered hazardous, if not quite meaningless. Today, notions of many or multiple literacies, rather than one or a few, signal both our increasing understanding and the persisting ideological, conceptual and empirical complications. Literacies range from alphabetic, numeric, scientific, geographical and corporeal to emotional, cultural, civic and critical among a great many more that are touted. Among this research especially compelling are questions of pedagogy and learning (diSessa 2000; Selfe 1999; Welch 1999)

Among the most critical of contemporary research approaches to literacy is the emerging social psychology of literacy. Scribner and Cole (1981) document the limits of literacy by itself and the theoretical assumptions that link it universally to higher forms of thought and practice; they point towards a formulation of literacy as *practice and context* determined and determining. This has stimulated more research among cognitive psychologists. Anthropological studies have moved towards ethnographies of literacy in use and non-use (Barton and Hamilton 1998; Heath 1983). Historical studies continue their path-breaking relevance (Graff 1987 [1979], 1987; Furet and Ozouf 1977; Harris 1989; Houston 2002; Vincent 2000). By contrast, the sociology and economics of literacy find their theoretical presuppositions and empirical methods challenged and seek new paradigms (Arnove and Graff 1987; Brandt 2001). The future of literacy studies is a challenging and unusually important one.

HARVEY J. GRAFF
UNIVERSITY OF TEXAS, SAN ANTONIO

References

Arnove, R.F. and Graff, H.J. (eds) (1987) *National Literacy Campaigns in Historical and Comparative Perspective*, Oxford.

Barton, D. and Hamilton, M. (1998) *Local Literacies: Reading and Writing in One Community*, London.

Brandt, D. (2001) *Literacy in American Lives*, Cambridge, UK.

diSessa, A. (2000) *Changing Minds: Computers, Learning, and Literacy*, Cambridge, MA.

Furet, F. and Ozouf, J. (1977) *Lire et écrire: l'alphabétisation des français de Calvin à Jules Ferry*, 2 vols, Paris [English translation of Vol. 1, Cambridge, 1983].

Graff, H.J. (1987) *The Legacies of Literacy: Continuities and Contradictions in Western Society and Culture*, Bloomington, IN.

—— (1987 [1979]) *The Literacy Myth: Literacy and Social Structure in the Nineteenth Century City*, New Brunswick, NJ.

Harris, W. (1989) *Ancient Literacy*, Cambridge, MA.

Heath, S.B. (1983) *Ways with Words*, Cambridge, UK.
Houston, R. (2002) *Literacy in Early Modern Europe*, London.
Scribner, S. and Cole, M. (1981) *The Psychology of Literacy*, Cambridge, MA.
Selfe, C. (1999) *Technology and Literacy in the 21st Century*, Carbondale, IL.
Vincent, D. (2000) *The Rise of Mass Literacy: Reading and Writing in Modern Europe*, Oxford.
Welch, K. (1999) *Electric Rhetoric: Classical Rhetoric, Oralism, and a New Literacy*, Cambridge, MA.

Further reading

Brandt, D. (2001) *Literacy in American Lives*, Cambridge.
Cope, B. and Kalantzis, M. (eds) (2000) *Multiliteracies: Literacy Learning and the Design of Social Futures*, London.
Cushman, E., Kintgen, E., Kroll, B. and Rose, M. (eds) (2001) *Literacy: A Critical Sourcebook*, New York.
Finnegan, R. (1988) *Literacy and Orality*, Oxford.
Goody, J. (ed.) (1968) *Literacy in Traditional Societies*, Cambridge, UK.
Graff, H.J. (1995) *The Labyrinths of Literacy: Reflections on Past and Present*, Pittsburgh, PA.
Kaestle, C., Moore, H., Stedman, L., Tinsley, K. and Trollinger, W., Jr (1991) *Literacy in the United States: Readers and Reading Since 1880*, New Haven, CT.
Lankshear, C. and McLaren, P. (eds) (1993) *Critical Literacy: Politics, Praxis, and the Postmodern*, Albany, NY.
Street, B. (ed.) (1993) *Cross-Cultural Approaches to Literacy*, Cambridge, UK.

LOCKE, JOHN (1632–1704)

John Locke was born in 1632 at Wrington in Somerset. In 1652 he entered Christ Church College, Oxford, where he received his MA in 1658. In that same year he was elected student of Christ Church; in 1660 he became lecturer in Greek, lecturer in rhetoric in 1662 and censor of moral philosophy in 1664. From 1667 to 1681 Locke was physician and secretary to Anthony Ashley Cooper, Lord Ashley (later First Earl of Shaftesbury). He was elected fellow of the Royal Society in 1668, and was secretary to the Lords Proprietors of Carolina from 1668 to 1675. In 1684 he was deprived of his appointment to Christ Church by royal decree. He lived in Holland from 1683 to 1689, was Commissioner on the Board of Trade from 1696 to 1700, and died at Otes (Oates) in the parish of High Laver, Essex, in 1704.

Locke's *Essay Concerning Human Understanding* (1690) made a major contribution to psychology and to philosophical psychology. That work offered the outlines of a genetic epistemology, and a theory of learning. Locke's interest in children is reflected not only in his pedagogical work, *Some Thoughts Concerning Education* (1693), but in many passages of the *Essay* where he traced the development of awareness in children. The oft-quoted metaphor used by Locke to characterize the mind as a blank tablet should not blind us to the fact that the Lockean mind comes equipped with faculties, that the child has specific 'tempers' or character traits which the educator must learn to work with, and that human nature for Locke has basic self-preserving tendencies to avoid pain and seek pleasure. These tendencies were even called by Locke 'innate practical principles'. The innate claim that his psychology rejected was for truths (moral and intellectual) and specific ideational contents.

Much of the *Essay* is occupied with discussing how we acquire certain ideas, with showing how a combination of physical and physiological processes stimulate and work with a large number of mental operations (for example joining, separating, considering, abstracting, generalizing) to produce the ideas of particular sense qualities and many complex notions, such as power, existence, unity. One such complex notion is the idea of self or person.

The account of the idea of self – or rather, *my* idea of *my* self, for Locke's account of this notion is a first-person account – emerges out of a discussion of the question, 'Does the soul always think?' That question had been answered in the affirmative by Descartes. For Locke, not only was it empirically false that the soul always thinks, but also that question suggested wrongly that something in me (my soul), not me, thinks. *I* am the agent of my actions and the possessor of my thoughts. Moreover, all thinking is reflexive; when I think, I am aware that I am thinking, no matter what form that thinking takes (sensing, willing, believing, doubting or remembering). It is the awareness of my act of thinking that also functions in awareness of self. Consciousness appropriates both thoughts and actions. The self or person for Locke consists in that set of thoughts and actions which I appropriate and for which I take responsibility through my consciousness.

Appropriation is a fundamental activity for Locke. I appropriate my thoughts and actions to form my concept of self. The *Essay* details the appropriation by each of us of ideas and knowledge. Education is also an appropriation of information, but more importantly of habits of good conduct. Education is a socializing process. It takes place usually within the family, with a tutor (for Locke writes about the education of a gentleman's son). But the account of the socialization process extends to Locke's political writings, *Two Treatises of Government* (1690), where he discusses the family, duties that parents have to their children and to each other (a marriage contract is part of his account of the family), and the rights and duties of citizens in a political society. The appropriation of land, possessions and eventually money by the activities of the person constitutes an early stage in Locke's account of the movement from the state of nature to a civil (political) society.

The political society, as the prepolitical state of nature, is grounded in law and order; order is respect and responsibility to each other and ultimately to God whose law of nature prescribes these duties. Locke's law of nature is a Christianized version of that tradition. The individual laws that he cites on occasion prescribe and proscribe the actions sanctioned or denied by the liberal religion of his day. These laws differed little in content from those innate moral truths Locke attacked; it was not the truths he rejects, only the claim that they were innate. Locke's society is fairly slanted in favour of the individual: preservation of the person, privacy of property, tacit assent, the right of dissent. At the same time, the pressures towards conformity and the force of majority opinion are also strong. The structure of his civil society, with its checks and balances, its separation of powers, its grounding on the law of nature, is designed to achieve a balance between the rights and needs of the individual and the need for security and order. His views on toleration (which were expressed in a series of tracts), while directed mainly against religious intolerance, match well with his insistence that government does not have the right to prescribe rites, rituals, dress and other practices in religion. Locke's toleration did not, however, extend to unbelief, to atheism.

The methodology for acquiring knowledge recommended by Locke and illustrated in his *Essay* stressed careful observation. Both in the physical sciences and in learning about ourselves and others, it was the 'plain, historical method' (that is, experience and observation) that holds the promise of accurate knowledge, or sound probability. Knowledge was not limited to demonstrative, deductive processes. Truth claims were always open to revision through further reports and observations. These concepts of knowledge and this experiential method were extended by Locke to what was later termed (for example by Hume) 'the science of man' or 'of human nature'. His detailed attention to his own thought processes enabled him to map the wide variety of mental operations and to begin the development of a cognitive psychology. His interest in children, throughout his life, led to observations and descriptions of their behaviour. He had many friends who had children, and lived for several years on different occasions with families who had several young children. The *Essay* uses some of these observations as the basis for a brief genetic learning theory, and his *Some Thoughts* contains many remarks and recommendations for raising children based upon his first-hand experience with children in their natural environment.

Locke's social theory grew out of his reading and (more importantly) out of these habits of observing people in daily life. In his travels in France and Holland, he often recorded details of activities and practices, religious, academic and ordinary. Where direct observation was not possible, he used the new travel literature for reports on other societies, other customs and habits. He had his own biases and preferences, to be sure, but with his dedication to reason and rationality, he seldom allowed emotions to affect his observation or his conclusions. He was an articulate representative of the Royal Society's attitudes in the sciences, including what we know as the social sciences.

JOHN W. YOLTON
RUTGERS UNIVERSITY

References

Locke, J. (1690) *Essay Concerning Human Understanding*, London.
—— (1690) *Two Treastises of Government*, London.
—— (1693) *Some Thoughts Concerning Education*, London.

Further reading

Aaron, R.I. (1971) *John Locke*, 3rd edn, Oxford.
Ayers, M.R. (1999) *Locke*, London.
Colman, J. (1983) *John Locke's Moral Philosophy*, Edinburgh.

Cranston, M. (1957) *John Locke: A Biography*, New York.

Dunn, J. (1969) *The Political Thought of John Locke*, Cambridge, UK.

—— (2003) *Locke: A Very Short Introduction*, Oxford.

Locke, J. (1689) *Epistola de Tolerantia*, Gouda.

—— (1689) *Letter Concerning Toleration*, London.

—— (1690) *A Second Letter Concerning Toleration*, London.

—— (1692) *A Third Letter for Toleration*, London.

—— (1692) *Some Considerations of the Consequences of the Lowering of Interest and Raising the Value of Money*, London.

—— (1695) *Further Considerations Concerning Raising the Value of Money*, London.

—— (1695) *Short Observations on a Printed Paper, Intituled 'For Encouraging the Coining Silver Money in England, and After, for Keeping it Here'*, London.

—— (1695) *The Reasonableness of Christianity, as Delivered in the Scriptures*, London.

—— (1697) *A Letter to Edward Lord Bishop of Worcester*, London.

—— (1714) *Works*, 3 vols, London.

Tully, J. (1980) *A Discourse on Property: John Locke and his Adversaries*, Cambridge, UK.

Yolton, J.W. (1956) *John Locke and the Way of Ideas*, Oxford.

—— (1970) *Locke and the Compass of Human Understanding*, Cambridge, UK.

SEE ALSO: liberalism; libertarianism; social contract

M

MACHIAVELLI, NICCOLÒ (1469–1527)

Machiavelli had a political baptism of fire. Italy was in a state of war at the end of the fifteenth century. The French and Spanish kingdoms, the republican cities, the Pope's Swiss guards and the *condottieri* formed and broke alliances as they struggled to win and to control territories. Within Florence, the Dominican Savonarola preached reform, both spiritual and political. He was burned at the stake on the *piazza della signoria* in 1498, a few days before Machiavelli was given his first administrative appointment, as a secretary of the Florentine chancery. A man of the Renaissance, a contemporary of Michelangelo and of Leonardo da Vinci, Machiavelli was first and foremost the eyewitness of the unsettled history of his time, and it is this that constitutes the background of his political thought.

He received a typical bourgeois education. Based on the study of Latin texts, it was designed to lead to an administrative or legal career, and although his social origins prevented him from becoming a diplomat, Machiavelli played a central role in Florence's military and diplomatic life until 1512, when the Republic of Florence was abolished. The Medici, who now governed the city, excluded him from public life.

Machiavelli developed theories on politics and also on military questions, subjects that often intermingle in his works. The *Art of War*, the only work published during his lifetime (1520), was a European bestseller. His other writings were published in 1532, after his death. Each is representative of an established literary genre in which political thought was formulated in the fifteenth and sixteenth centuries. *The Prince* imitates and at the same time subverts an established genre, known as the 'mirror of the prince', designed for the instruction of princes. The *History of Florence* and the *Discourses* are typical examples of the way in which Renaissance political thought was expressed in the form of historical writings. All of these works were written on Machiavelli's initiative, except for the *History*, which was commissioned by Cardinal Jules Medici in 1520.

It is a mistake to oppose *The Prince* (written in 1513–14) and the *Discourses* (begun in 1513 and probably finished in 1518), as some commentators have done, as if one was written by the adviser of the tyrants, and the other by a lover of the republican regime. Even though they were not published during Machiavelli's lifetime, they were soon known in Florence. Machiavelli himself made partial readings of the *Discourses* in the *Orti Oricellari*, at gatherings to which a Florentine aristocratic family, the Rucellai, invited writers and thinkers to discuss literature and politics. The *Art of War*, written as a dialogue, shows what this kind of private discussion, free from public censorship, may have been like.

Machiavelli does not deal with the question of what would be the best political system or form of government. Instead he asks how the rulers of a city could establish a stable and long-lasting regime, one that takes account of the particular circumstances of the city's foundation, its history and its customs. The key character in *The Prince*, *il principe*, has to achieve power, and then retain it. The first part of the book is based on the analysis of the various means to win power. Only occasionally does Machiavelli propose very general principles, for example that the prince should depend only on himself, and have his own army. Much of his advice is, rather, context-dependent. He then considers the ways in which a prince may hold on to newly won or inherited power. In the long run, no prince can depend on the use of force alone. He should always suspect the personal ambitions of members of the elite, the *grandi*, and so he must ensure that the common people respect him and even fear him, but do not hate him. To this end, he must make a display of the virtues most appreciated by the people (mercy, fidelity, humanity, religious faith, integrity).

The prince needs to forget his own being in order to think of himself purely in terms of his image, and he must adapt his manners to constantly changing historical conditions. He should surround himself with good advisers, yet make up his mind alone. In order to keep his power he must be ready to be bad and even cruel, but has always to act in a calculated way, so that his cruelty does not engender hatred. (The difficulty in living up to these requirements suggests that *The Prince* presents an ideal and imaginary figure.)

The *Discourses* also deal with the question of a stable and long-lasting government, but in an utterly different context. The reader is invited to follow the turbulent history of the Roman Republic. The idea that every city is composed of conflicting groups is the cornerstone of Machiavelli's analysis in this treatise. The *grandi* desire to dominate and command, while the masses, the *popolo*, wish neither to be dominated nor to be commanded. In a city accustomed to princely domination, the *popolo* expect the prince to protect them against the *grandi*. In Rome things were different, for reasons that go back to the time of its foundation. The fact that the Senate required the military involvement of the masses, or plebs, but without granting them a political role, triggered protest and the demand for institutional representation, resulting in the creation of the tribunes in 479 BCE. The result was a never-ending struggle between *popolo* and *grandi*. To Machiavelli, this antagonism was the basis of liberty, as the plebs constrained the Senate to promote greater equality, and to submit the *grandi* to the rule of law. However, as time passed the Republic lost its vigour. Roman citizens began to neglect the public good, a process Machiavelli described as corruption and that he regarded as inevitable

Machiavelli's interest in the history of the Roman Republic is related to his reflections about Florence. This city seems to meet some essential requirements for political freedom (a feeling of civil equality was widespread among its citizens and there seemed to be a real desire to be free), and yet Florence failed to establish a long-lasting and stable republic. However, Rome, thought of as a paradigm for liberty, is not a model to be imitated. Florence could not follow Rome's way to freedom, because it did not share its main characteristics, which flowed from the way in which it had been founded, its history and its religion and way of life. What the history of Rome provided was a tool with the help of which it was possible to understand Florence's failure and to propose a course of action that fitted its circumstances. Machiavelli's critical analysis of his time is rooted in history, and comparative history provides the basis of his political thought.

MARIE GAILLE-NIKODIMOV
CNRS, LYON

Further reading

Fleischer, M. (ed.) (1972) *Machiavelli and the Nature of Political Thought*, New York.
Pocock, J.G.A. (1975) *The Machiavellian Moment. Florentine Political Thought and the Atlantic Republican Tradition*, Princeton, NJ.
Skinner, Q. (1981) *Machiavelli*, Oxford.
Strauss, L. (1978) *Thoughts on Machiavelli*, Chicago.
Vatter, M.E. (2000) *Between Form and Event: Machiavelli's Theory of Political Freedom*, Amsterdam.

MACROECONOMIC POLICY

Government policy that is intended to influence the behaviour of the economy as a whole, in particular the level of economic activity, unemployment and the rate of inflation, is called *macroeconomic*. This is in contrast with *microeconomic* policy directed towards the development or efficiency of particular industries, regions, activities or markets. One of the main attractions of macroeconomic policy, it can be argued, is that it enables the government to point the economy as a whole in the right direction without interfering with the proper functioning of the market system.

Traditionally the goals of macroeconomic policy have been full employment and price stability. The stability of output from year to year, avoiding rapid booms or deep recessions, is an additional objective. The growth rate of output in the longer term, however, is commonly believed to depend on a quite different set of factors, such as technology, training and incentives, which fall rather within the domain of 'supply-side' or microeconomic policy. In an open economy, either the balance of payments position or the behaviour of the exchange rate in the foreign exchange market can be seen as a separate objective of macroeconomic policy, or else as a constraint on its operation.

The instruments of macroeconomic policy are both monetary and fiscal. Monetary policy is operated by the central bank, for example the US Federal Reserve Board or the Bank of England. The stringency of policy can be measured either by the level of real interest rates (that is nominal interest rates *minus* the rate of inflation) or by the growth of the money supply (variously defined). One advantage of monetary policy as a means of influencing the economy is that, unlike fiscal policy, it can be reviewed and changed almost continuously in the light of new information.

The instruments of fiscal policy are taxation and public spending, controlled by the government or federal administration subject to the important proviso of legislative support. Different taxes and expenditures affect the economy in different ways, but by 'fiscal policy' in the present context we mean the effect of the budget as a whole on the level of aggregate demand in the economy. Except in a dire emergency fiscal policies are usually changed only once a year. Their use for managing the economy is also limited by the need for prudence in the management of the public accounts themselves.

The idea that monetary and fiscal policies could, and should, be used to manage aggregate demand in the economy emerged from the experience of the Great Depression of the 1930s. Following the Second World War, the use of public borrowing and interest rates to stabilize the economy was accepted as a principle of policy, as the ideas of Maynard Keynes converted most of the economics profession. There was then a period of about 20 years when full employment was maintained, and inflation held at a tolerable level, in most of the advanced industrial countries. It is open to question, nevertheless, whether this so-called 'Golden Age' was the result of skill in the operation of macroeconomic policies. It may be, rather, that the belief

of business and consumers that governments could underwrite economic stability created the confidence that sustained demand. By the late 1960s, policy, although maybe no less skillful, was far less successful.

Economists themselves began to lose faith in the effectiveness of Keynesian demand management. In the 1970s and 1980s there was a neo-classical or monetarist counter-revolution, originating in Chicago and led by Milton Friedman. One underlying issue in this debate concerned the relationship between the two goals of full employment and price stability. It might be possible, by cutting taxes or cutting interest rates, to increase employment in the short run without adding much to inflation straight away; however, in the longer term the neo-classical argument was that the situation would be reversed, with unemployment back at its 'natural' level and nothing to show for the expansionary policy except a burst of higher inflation.

An extensive literature on the theory of macroeconomic policy first appeared in the 1960s, drawing on control engineering. The economy could be represented by a mathematical model in which the main behavioural relationships at the aggregate level were each described by a dynamic equation. The response of target variables to the use of policy instruments could be estimated, and feedback rules devised that would minimize the impact of external shocks such as increases in the price of imports. From the 1970s, this mechanistic approach to policy design was modified to take account of expectations, both in the specification of models and in the design of policy rules. If the use of policy instruments follows any logical rule then it will be understood and anticipated by those whose behaviour it is intended to control. This suggests that the creation of the right kind of expectations is itself an integral part of policy design. Taken to the limit, this could suggest that policy will achieve its aims if, and only if, it is believed that it will do so – that any policy regime is viable provided that it commands sufficient confidence.

In recent decades attention has concentrated on the design of credible regimes in which the monetary and fiscal authorities commit themselves to follow certain preannounced policy rules. A central bank for example may commit itself to vary interest rates or the growth of the money supply so as to keep the rate of inflation within a predetermined band. A finance ministry may set itself defined objectives for government borrowing or the relation of the national debt to national income. There is a general perception that politicians will be tempted to break such promises so as to gain popularity, by cutting taxes or interest rates, especially when seeking re-election. To avoid such suspicion, they can increase their credibility by giving greater independence to central banks or by entering into international agreements. The formation of a monetary union, as in the 'euro area', removes the responsibility for monetary policy from individual member states almost entirely, and also limits considerably their freedom of manœuvre in respect of fiscal policy.

It might seem that the design of monetary or fiscal policy is now something quite different from macroeconomic policy as it was developed 50 or so years ago. It might even be questioned whether the same term can now be used to describe it. Nevertheless, the actual conduct of policy, by the Federal Reserve, the Bank of England or the European Central Bank, month by month and year by year, still requires the same process of assessment, forecasting how the economy will develop if interest rates are unchanged and then estimating what change in interest rates would be needed to bring the forecast rate of inflation into line with a target. Moreover, governments still seem ready to take the credit when the economy performs well, and to be blamed when it does not – just as if they were in control of it.

ANDREW BRITTON
NATIONAL INSTITUTE OF ECONOMIC
AND SOCIAL RESEARCH, LONDON

Further reading

Britton, A.J.C. (1991) *Macroeconomic Policy in Britain 1974–1987*, Cambridge, UK.
—— (2001) *Monetary Regimes of the Twentieth Century*, Cambridge, UK.
Dornbusch, R. and Fischer, S. (1987) *Macroeconomics*, New York.
Friedman, M. (1968) 'The role of monetary policy', *American Economic Review* (March).
Keynes, J.M. (1936) *The General Theory of Employment, Interest and Money*, London.
Miles, D and Scott, A (2002) *Macroeconomics – Understanding the Wealth of Nations*, New York.

SEE ALSO: econometrics; employment and unemployment; inflation and deflation; macroeconomic theory; public goods; stagflation

MACROECONOMIC THEORY

The term 'macroeconomics' was coined by Ragnar Frisch in 1933 to apply to the study of the relationships between broad economic aggregates such as national income, inflation, aggregate unemployment, the balance of payments and so on. It can be contrasted with the study of individual decision-making units in the economy such as households, workers and firms, which is generally known as microeconomics. It is no coincidence that the 1930s also saw the development of Keynesian economic theory, landmarked by *The General Theory of Employment, Interest and Money* (Keynes 1936) and the founding of the Econometric Society whose aim was to advance 'economic theory in its relation to statistics and mathematics'. Prior to this period, no explicit distinction was made between microeconomic and macroeconomic theory, although many classical analyses, such as Hume's specie-flow mechanism, or earlier studies of the relationship between the balance of trade and national wealth by mercantilists such as Mun, were couched in what are now recognizably macroeconomic terms. The real fillip to the development of macroeconomic theory, however, was the rise of Keynesian economics – the so-called Keynesian revolution. Classical economists such as Smith and Hume and neo-classical economists such as Marshall and Pigou saw the world in equilibrium terms where quantities flowed and prices moved as if in a large, well-oiled machine: 'it is impossible to heap up money, more than any fluid, beyond its proper level' (Hume 1752). In the long run, the classical or neo-classical view was that everything would, indeed, reach its 'proper level'. Thus, faced with the large-scale and chronic unemployment of the interwar years, an acceptable classical response to the question, 'What is the solution to the unemployment problem?' might have been 'a reduction in the population' – presumably brought about by conscripts to the army of unemployed falling below a subsistence level of income. While this would clearly be a very long-term solution, the retort would have been that unemployment is a very long-term problem: thus, Keynes's famous dictum that 'in the long run, we are all dead'. Keynesian macroeconomic theory argued that economies could go into 'underemployment equilibrium' and may require government intervention, particularly in the form of public spending, in order to move towards a full-employment equilibrium.

Another important school of macroeconomic theory, which is essentially classical in its outlook, is monetarism, of which the University of Chicago has traditionally been thought of as the intellectual home. The essential differences between Keynesian and monetarist macroeconomic theory can be sketched as follows. At its most fundamental level, macroeconomics can be thought of as dealing with the interactions of five aggregate markets: the goods market, the money market, the bond market, the foreign exchange market and the labour market. Monetarists focus on only the second of these markets and are typically concerned with the supply of and demand for money. This is because a number of assumptions are implicitly made with respect to supply and demand in the various markets. The foreign exchange market is assumed to clear (supply is equal to demand) because the exchange rate is flexible. The wage rate is assumed to adjust so that there is no involuntary unemployment – everyone who wants to work at the going wage rate will find a job – so that the labour market clears. Similarly, goods prices are assumed to be flexible so that the goods market clears. This leaves only the bond market and the money market. But an important principle of economics, known as Walras's law, states that if n-1 markets of an n-market system clear, then the nth must clear also (this is essentially the same as solving a simultaneous equation system). Thus, given the foregoing assumptions, the bond market can be ignored and equilibrium conditions in the entire macroeconomy can be characterized by equilibrium conditions in the money market alone. Typically, Keynesian macroeconomic theory will deny one or more of these underlying assumptions. For example, if, because of long-term labour contracts, wages are rigid, then there may be fewer vacancies than the number of people looking for work at the going wage rate – the labour market will not clear and there will be involuntary unemployment.

The high tide of Keynesian macroeconomic theory, in the 1950s and 1960s, was the counterpart to the apparent success of Keynesian macroeconomic policy, particularly in the USA and the UK. Rising unemployment and inflation towards the end of the 1960s and into the early 1970s, however, generated a further crisis in macroeconomic theory, culminating in a monetarist counter-revolution. Indeed, by the time that Richard Nixon, in 1969, declared, 'we are all Keynesians now', the tide had probably already turned. Milton Friedman, the High Priest of monetarism, had already given his inaugural lecture to the American Economic Association (Friedman 1968) in which he outlined his theory of the 'expectations-augmented Phillips curve', which appeared to explain the coexistence of inflation and unemployment in monetarist terms. Like the classical economists, monetarists assume that there is an equilibrium or natural rate of employment. According to this view, government can only increase employment beyond this level, say, by an expansionary monetary policy, by fooling workers into underestimating the level of inflation. Thus, if the government increases the money supply and prices begin to rise, to the extent that workers underestimate next period's inflation rate, they will set their wage demands too low. Thus, in the next period, labour will appear cheap to producers and more workers will be taken on and the aggregate level of employment will rise. When inflation expectations catch up, however, workers will raise their wage claims accordingly, the real or price-adjusted wage rate will go back to its old level, and the economy returns to the natural rate of employment – albeit at a higher inflation rate.

In the 1970s, a third school of macroeconomic theory emerged, known as the New Classical School, and associated primarily with economists such as Robert Lucas and Thomas Sargent, then both at the University of Minnesota. New classical economists developed further the monetarist assertion that monetary policy is only effective in the short run into the key assertion that it is almost always ineffectual. They did this by taking the monetarist apparatus and grafting on the additional assumption of 'rational expectations'. According to the rational expectations hypothesis, agents' expectations of future macroeconomic variables are essentially the same as the true mathematical expectation based on all of the available information. Thus, in the example given above, agents would realize that the money supply has been increased and, using all of the available information, would form their best estimate of next period's price level. This is not to say that they would have perfect foresight, but that their best estimate is as likely to be an overestimate as an underestimate, since if they consistently underestimated price movements they would rationally revise their method of estimation. Thus, on average, agents' forecasts will be correct – wage increases will on average match price increases brought about by an expansionary monetary policy, the price-adjusted wage rate will stay the same, and the level of unemployment will not move. If traditional monetarism allowed a role for activist monetary policy only to the extent that agents could be fooled, new classical theory argued that it was extremely difficult to fool them. The rational expectations revolution of the 1970s fuelled a major industry in academic macroeconomics. Although there are many who would disagree, it is probably true to say that New Classical macroeconomics has now run its course, largely as a result of a general loss of faith in the assumption of rational expectations – itself occasioned by numerous empirical studies that reject the hypothesis in a number of contexts – and increasing evidence of the stickiness of wages and prices.

Where does this leave macroeconomic theory? To a large extent in a state of crisis. As the foregoing discussion should make clear, schools of macroeconomic theory may be broadly classified according to whether monetary 'non-neutralities' (i.e. the effects of monetary policy on real aggregate variables such as output and employment) arise for informational reasons – as in equilibrium schools of thought such as monetarist, New Classical or, more recently, real business cycle theory (see, e.g., Lucas 1987) or for other reasons such as price or wage rigidity, as in Keynesian macroeconomic theory. Because of a general loss of faith in the ability of econometrics to discriminate between alternative views of macroeconomics – not least because of their observational equivalence under certain conditions (Sargent 1976) – the ultimate preference for one macroeconomic theory over another probably has more to do with the economist's faith in a certain underlying view of the world rather than anything else. Thus, real business-cycle theorists continue to analyse dynamic models in which prices are flexible and economic agents are rational optimizers, while the primary task of the 'New Keynesian Economics' 'is to explain why changes in the aggregate price level are sticky' (Gordon 1990). Given that different macroeconomic policy prescriptions are forthcoming from each class of theory – typically interventionist for Keynesian or New Keynesian theory, non-inter-

ventionist for equilibrium theorists – the choice may lie as much in the domain of political ideology as in that of economic theory.

MARK TAYLOR
UNIVERSITY OF LIVERPOOL

References

Friedman, M. (1968) 'The role of monetary policy', *American Economic Review* 58.
Gordon, R.J. (1990) 'What is New Keynesian Economics?', *Journal of Economic Literature* 28.
Hume, D. (1752) 'On the balance of trade', in D. Rotwein (ed.) *Essays Moral, Political, and Literary*, London.
Keynes, J.M. (1936) *The General Theory of Employment, Interest and Money*, London.
Lucas, R.E., Jr (1987) *Models of Business Cycles*, Oxford.
Sargent, Thomas J. (1976) 'On the observational equivalence of natural and unnatural theories of macroeconomics', *Journal of Political Economy* 84.

SEE ALSO: classical economics; Keynesian economics; macroeconomic policy; microeconomics; public goods; rational expectations; supply-side economics

MALINOWSKI, BRONISLAW KASPER (1884–1942)

Malinowski had a profound influence on British social anthropology through his innovative methods of field research, his wide-ranging theoretical writings, his inspired teaching and his entrepreneurial promotion of a revitalized discipline. His Trobriand corpus remains the most comprehensive and widely read in world ethnography.

Born in Cracow, Malinowski studied mathematics, physics and philosophy at the Jagiellonian University. His doctoral thesis on the positivist epistemology of Mach and Avenarius foreshadowed his later formulations on 'functionalism', the methodological doctrine with which his name is associated.

After studying chemistry and psychology at Leipzig, Malinowski's interests turned decisively to anthropology, and in 1910 he became a student of ethnology under Seligman and Westermarck at the London School of Economics (LSE). He soon aspired to be 'Anthropology's Conrad'. Malinowski was in Australia when the First World War was declared in Europe but despite his status as an enemy alien he was permitted to do fieldwork in eastern Papua. It was during three expeditions between 1914 and 1918 that he reaped the ethnographic benefits of 'living right among the natives' and mastering their language. Intensive fieldwork involving participant observation was henceforth to become the hallmark of British anthropology, though Malinowski's posthumously published field diaries (1967) exploded his own myth of easy rapport and helped to precipitate the crisis of conscience that afflicted anthropology in the 1970s.

Returning to England in 1920 with his Australian bride, Malinowski began full-time teaching at the LSE in 1924, and was appointed to a professorship in 1927. He did much of his writing at his villa in the Italian Tyrol, but travelled widely in Europe, Africa and the USA. It was while on sabbatical in 1938 that the Second World War broke out in Europe, and he was advised to remain in the USA. In 1940 and 1941 he conducted fieldwork in Mexico, and just before his sudden death in 1942 he was appointed to a permanent professorship at Yale.

Aided by his sometime rival Radcliffe-Brown, Malinowski generated the most significant paradigm shift in British anthropology since its creation in the mid-nineteenth century: from the speculatively prehistorical study of cultural traits as 'survivals' (whether in an evolutionist or diffusionist mode) to the empirical, synchronic study of social 'institutions' within living, functioning cultures. This shift was marked by the collection and synthesis of new kinds of data by increasingly professional academic investigators. Malinowski's lengthy, 'heroic' immersion in an exotic society was thus the culmination of a trend, and prolonged fieldwork thereafter became a rite of passage for entry into the profession.

Malinowski's theoretical contributions to anthropology lay in fields as disparate as the family, psychoanalysis, mythology, law, economic anthropology and pragmatic linguistic theory. Yet the key to understanding any culture, he taught, lay in the interrelation of its constituent 'institutions'; thus his demand for the empirical observation of social behaviour in concrete cultural contexts. His most compelling Trobriand works in this vein concerned the ceremonial exchange of the *Kula* (1922); kinship, sex and marriage (1929); and gardening, land tenure and the language of magic (1935). Although his literary romanticism exoticized their culture, Malinowski demystified the Trobrianders themselves: his exemplary 'Savages' were pragmatic, self-motivated, rational human beings.

The allure of Malinowski's sociological functionalism (and a timely turn to practical anthropology) won him generous Rockefeller funding for his students' fieldwork in Africa. As a prescription for gathering rich data, functionalism clearly worked. However, the schematized form in which Malinowski developed his biologically based cultural functionalism (1944a) did not outlive him.

Malinowski was a charismatic and challenging teacher – loved or loathed – who trained a generation of postgraduates in his famous Socratic seminar. Established in key academic posts in Britain and elsewhere, his students gave the discipline its distinctive intellectual profile until the 1960s.

As a publicist and polemicist, Malinowski wrote, lectured and broadcast on many social issues of his day. A romantic positivist, a scientific humanist, a linguistically gifted cosmopolitan and a political liberal, he passionately opposed totalitarianism (1944b) and was gratified when his books were burned by the Nazis. In the 1980s, re-evaluation by Polish scholars of his earliest work restored Malinowski's reputation in his homeland and placed him in the mainstream of European modernism.

MICHAEL W. YOUNG
AUSTRALIAN NATIONAL UNIVERSITY

References

Malinowski, B. (1922) *Argonauts of the Western Pacific*, London.
—— (1929) *The Sexual Life of Savages*, London.
—— (1935) *Coral Gardens and Their Magic*, 2 vols, London.
—— (1944a) *A Scientific Theory of Culture*, Chapel Hill, NC.
—— (1944b) *Freedom and Civilization*, New York.
—— (1967) *A Diary in the Strict Sense of the Term*, London.

Further reading

Ellen, R., Gellner, E., Kubica, G. and Mucha, J. (eds) (1988) *Malinowski between Two Worlds*, Cambridge, UK.
Firth, R. (ed.) (1957) *Man and Culture*, London.
Stocking, G.W. (1983) 'The ethnographer's magic', in G.W. Stocking (ed.) *Observers Observed*, Madison, WI.
—— (1995) *After Tylor: British Social Anthropology 1888–1951*, Madison, WI, Ch. 6.

Thornton, R. and Skalnik, P. (eds) (1992) *The Early Writings of Bronislaw Malinowski*, Cambridge, UK.
Young, M.W. (2004) *Malinowski: Odyssey of an Anthropologist*, New Haven, CT.

SEE ALSO: ethnography; social anthropology

MALTHUS, THOMAS ROBERT (1766–1834)

Thomas Robert Malthus, cleric, moral scientist and economist, was born near Guildford, Surrey. He entered Jesus College, Cambridge, in 1784, graduated in mathematics as Ninth Wrangler in 1788 and was a non-resident fellow of his college from 1793 until his marriage in 1804. Originally destined for a career in the Church of England, he became curate of Okewood in Surrey in 1796, and rector of Walesby in Lincolnshire in 1803; but from 1805 until his death he served as professor of history and political economy at Haileybury College, then recently founded by the East India Company for the education of its cadets.

The source of Malthus's reputation as a political economist lay in his *Essay on the Principle of Population* published in 1798, but this essay was originally written to refute the 'perfectibilist' social philosophies of such writers as Godwin and Condorcet, and as such was developed within the context of an essentially Christian moral philosophy, as was all of Malthus's writing. At the core of Malthus's argument was his theory that

> Population, when unchecked, increases in a geometrical ratio. Subsistence increases only in an arithmetical ratio....By that law of our nature which makes food necessary to the life of man, the effects of these two unequal powers must be kept equal. This implies a strong and constantly operating check on population from the difficulty of subsistence.

In the first edition of his *Essay*, Malthus identified the checks to population as either preventive (keeping new population from growing up) or positive (cutting down existing population); hence followed the bleak conclusion 'that the superior power of population cannot be checked without producing misery or vice'. In the second, much enlarged, edition (1803) he extended the category of preventive checks to include 'moral restraint', thus admitting the possibility of population being contained without either misery or vice as necessary consequences. Even when thus modified, Malthus's population principle seemed to impose narrow limits to the possibilities of economic growth and social improvement, although he himself did not so intend it. Idealists and reformers consequently railed against the implications of the theory, but his fellow economists accepted both its premises and its logic, and for most of the nineteenth century it remained one of the classical 'principles of political economy'.

His population principle was not Malthus's only contribution to economic thought: he was among the first to state (in 1815) the theory of rent as a surplus generally associated with the name of his friend and contemporary, David Ricardo. Both were followers of Adam Smith but Malthus's development of Smith's system differed significantly from Ricardo's, notably in his use of supply and demand analysis in the theory of value as against Ricardo's emphasis on labour-quantities, and his explanation of the 'historical fall' of profits in terms of competition of capitals rather than by the 'necessity of resort to inferior soils' that Ricardo stressed.

Malthus and Ricardo debated at length 'the possibility of a general glut' of commodities. Ricardo argued for the validity of Say's Law, that 'supply creates its own demand', while Malthus asserted the possibility of oversaving (and overinvestment) creating an excess supply. Ricardo's apparently watertight logic won acceptance for Say's Law for over a century, until Keynes in 1933 drew attention to Malthus's use of the principle of 'effective demand' and contended that 'the whole problem of the balance between Saving and Investment had been posed' in the Preface to his *Principles of Political Economy* in 1820. Economists tend to see Malthus's *Principles* not so much as containing a notable foreshadowing of Keynes's theory of employment as presenting, albeit through a glass darkly, a subtle and complex analysis of the conditions required to initiate and maintain balanced growth in a market economy.

R.D. COLLISON BLACK
QUEEN'S UNIVERSITY BELFAST

References

Keynes, J.M. (1933) *Essays in Biography*, London.

Malthus, T.R. (1798) *An Essay on the Principle of Population*, 2nd edn 1803, 6th edn 1826, London.
—— (1820) *The Principles of Political Economy, Considered with a View to Their Practical Application*, 2nd edn 1836, London.

Further reading

James, P. (1979) *Population Malthus, His Life and Times*, London.
Sraffa, P. (ed.) (1951–2) *Works and Correspondence of David Ricardo*, Vol. 2, Cambridge, UK, pp. 308, 312; Vol. 8, pp. 257, 285, 300–1; Vol 9, pp. 9–11, 15–17, 19–27.
Winch, D. (1987) *Malthus*, Oxford.

SEE ALSO: demography; population and resources; population projections

MARGINAL ANALYSIS

Broadly speaking, marginal analysis is any application of differential calculus to economics. It is applicable whenever the relevant commodities and the economic processes of production and consumption are divisible, at least approximately. It is the foundation, *inter alia*, of modern value theory for markets in which prices balance the optimizing decisions of the various agents in an economy. In this, the equilibrating prices and the quantities traded are determined 'on the margin'. This nineteenth-century insight removed difficulties such as Adam Smith's paradox of value, e.g. the cheapness of water that is essential to life versus the expensiveness of diamonds that are merely decorative: it is not the utility gained from the total consumption of a commodity that determines its value, but the utility gained from the last unit consumed – 'the tail wags the dog', as Paul Samuelson puts it. Another widespread use of differential calculus is in sensitivity analysis. This can involve examining the dependence of both the value and the solution of a particular economizing activity on its conditioning parameters; an example is the Hicks–Slutsky description of household demand. It can also be a study of a Pareto-optimum or of an equilibrium: an example is the comparative statics of macroeconomic equilibrium/disequilibrium solutions that is the core of stabilization theory. Later developments, e.g. growth theory, led to the use of calculus techniques ranging from differential equations to those of dynamic optimization.

Mathematically, every marginal concept is the derivative of some function. In a particular problem, some functions are given, and others constitute the solution. When a problem is set up as a system of equations $E(x,-) = 0$ for the decision variables a.k.a. basic variables x, its solution $x^*(-)$ is a function of the problem's parameters a.k.a. free variables, $-$. By using the Implicit Function Theorem, the derivatives of the solution with respect to the parameters can then be given as $Dx^* = -(DxE)-1D\alpha E$ (evaluated at $x^*(-)$). This is known as sensitivity analysis of the solution or comparative statics (although the problem may well be one of 'dynamics'). The equation system ($E = 0$) may be a market equilibrium condition; or it may be Lagrange's characterization of a constrained optimum point by a system of first-order conditions (FOCs) on x and auxiliary variables – known as Lagrange multipliers, which can be thought of as price penalties for breaking the constraints. For optimization of $f(x,-)$ over x subject to $h(x,-) = 0$, given $-$ and the functions f and h, the FOCs are: $h(x,-) = 0$ *and* $-xf(x,-) - D\alpha h(x,-) = 0$. Derivatives of the given functions are thus used to formulate optimality conditions. For example, derivatives of production and utility functions, which describe technologies and consumer preferences, can be used to formulate the equalities of relative prices to marginal rates of substitution or transformation as conditions for profit or utility maximization. In terms of the Lagrangean, defined as
$L(-,x,-) = f(x,-) - \alpha h(x,\alpha)$, the main FOC is $=_xL(\alpha,x,\alpha) = 0$. It follows that the marginal optimal value equals the corresponding *partial* derivative of the Lagrangean (evaluated at the optimal solution together with the supporting multiplier) – i.e. the derivatives of $V(\alpha)$, which is by definition $f(x^*(\alpha),\alpha)$, are $\alpha V(\alpha) = \alpha_\alpha L(\alpha^*(\alpha),x^*(\alpha),\alpha) = \alpha_\alpha f(x^*(-),-) - {}^*(\alpha)D\alpha h(x^*(\alpha),\alpha)$. This is the General Envelope Theorem. Its particular cases include, or imply, Roy's Identity (giving consumer demand in terms of the indirect utility function), the Hotelling–Shephard Lemmas (giving producer supply or input demand in terms of the profit or cost functions), the Wong–Viner Envelope Theorem (equating short-run marginal costs and long-run marginal costs, though under very restrictive assumptions), and the marginal interpretation of Lagrange multipliers (i.e. $V(\alpha) = \lambda^*(\alpha)$ when the constraint has the form $h(x) = \alpha$ and the maximand f is independent of α).

These relationships can be used in various ways. For example, they serve as sources of econometric information about value functions, i.e. they are used to estimate the true value functions such as the indirect utility, profit or cost from empirical data on both prices and quantities. This is usually done by assuming a special functional form and estimating its defining parameters (which are, of course, entirely different from the optimization problem's parameters). When the 'given functions' of an optimization problem *are* actually known, there are other uses for these relationships. For example, in short-run profit maximization, the marginal values of the fixed inputs k can be calculated simply as the supporting multipliers, r^*, for the constraints of the form $g(x) \leqslant k$ – i.e. when the fixed inputs impose capacity constraints on the output bundle x (or, in other words, when the ks are additive a.k.a. ordinary or 'right-hand side' parameters). The imputed values r^* can then be used to solve long-run problems of investment and pricing. Remarkably, the Lagrangean method gives a way of calculating the marginal values even when there is no explicit formula for the optimal value.

In convex optimization, Lagrange multipliers are themselves an optimal solution – to what is called the dual problem – and this gives them another characterization. Also, the dual may be mathematically simpler than the original (primal) problem, and this can be exploited in solving both problems.

With the development of mathematical programming in the 1940s came the recognition that economic theory is beset with problems of non-differentiability, and that smooth calculus alone is an inadequate tool for rigorous analysis. Tjalling Koopmans introduced geometrical techniques using the convexity properties of consumer preferences and production technologies to overcome these difficulties. This work was hailed by Gerard Debreu as freeing 'economics from its traditions of differential calculus and compromises with logic'. The radical change of approach that followed brought economic theory within the pale of formal mathematics and led to better understanding and results of greater generality. However, the absence of calculus techniques in high theory limits the range and applicability of its results. Such shortcomings are now being addressed using the mathematical theory of generalized multivalued derivatives. Subdifferentiation, in particular, is now a fully developed calculus for convex optimization problems, and

the smooth-calculus results so useful for earlier developments, e.g. the envelope theorem, have been extended to subdifferentiable functions. As a consequence, longstanding problems are being solved, and better scientific results are coming into the subject.

ANTHONY HORSLEY
LONDON SCHOOL OF ECONOMICS
AND POLITICAL SCIENCE

Further reading

Debreu, G. (1959) *Theory of Value*, New York.
Koopmans, T.C. (1957) *Three Essays on the State of Economic Science*, New York.
Samuelson, P.A. (1971) *Foundations of Economic Analysis*, Cambridge, MA.
Takayama, A. (1985) *Mathematical Economics*, Cambridge, UK.

SEE ALSO: maximization

MARKETS

Markets are institutions that enable exchange of goods and services to take place between buyers and sellers. They play a central role in allocating resources and distributing income in most modern economies. More generally, the market mechanism can be thought of as a process by which the decisions taken by different agents in the economy – individuals' decisions about consumption of alternative goods, firms' decisions about what and how much to produce, workers' decisions about work, and so on – are all co-ordinated through adjustments in prices.

Markets and efficiency

The market mechanism has several important advantages. It co-ordinates decentralized decisions by a very large number of economic agents without the need for conscious control. It provides strong incentives and disciplines producers against wasteful use of resources. It conveys information about constantly changing market conditions and allows for flexibility in decision-making. Finally, it does not usually lead to excessive concentration of economic power.

In a 'perfectly competitive' market, sellers sell a homogeneous product; both buyers and sellers are price-takers, i.e. each agent perceives him or herself as so small relative to the market as a whole that his or her decisions have no effect on the market price or the behaviour of the other agents; buyers have perfect information on prices; and there are no restrictions on entry and exit in the long run.

Economists have established two important welfare properties of perfectly competitive markets. First, in the absence of externalities (see below) and under certain conditions that ensure that an equilibrium exists, perfectly competitive markets achieve an efficient allocation of resources, in the sense that it is impossible to make any individual better off without simultaneously making someone else worse off. Second, again under certain conditions that have to do with the kind of preferences consumers have and the kind of technological constraints firms face, any desired efficient allocation of resources can be achieved for some initial distribution of lump-sum income. Thus to change the distribution of resources in society, one need only redistribute lump-sum income and let the price mechanism operate freely to achieve efficiency.

Market failure

The large majority of product and labour markets are not perfectly competitive, however. In fact, many product markets, especially for manufactured products, are oligopolistic, i.e. the number of firms is relatively small and/or there are a few firms with large market shares. In these circumstances, each firm has some market power, in the sense that it can affect the market price and this price is higher than marginal cost. Furthermore, each firm recognizes that its decisions will affect the decisions of other firms in the market, which leads to strategic interaction between firms. Firms in oligopolistic markets often produce differentiated products and compete not only on price, but also on several other dimensions, such as product quality and characteristics, advertising, location, pre-sale and after-sale services, and so on. Unlike perfectly competitive firms, oligopolistic firms may enjoy positive net profits – these are sometimes substantial, but more often they are restricted by free entry. Since price in oligopoly is set above marginal cost, production is lower than the socially optimal level and resources are not allocated efficiently.

Imperfect competition is an important source of inefficiency in a market economy. Imperfect competition in product markets cannot be avoided, however, because there are many industries in which the minimum scale for efficient operation of firms is simply too large relative to the size of the market to support many competing firms. Moreover, a firm may possess market power because it is efficient or innovative, and some degree of market power may be desirable in order to provide incentives to invest and innovate. The aim of government policy is not therefore to achieve a state of perfect competition, but to ensure that competition between firms is 'effective', i.e. firms do not collude or otherwise abuse their market power and there are no barriers to entry. In situations where effective competition is difficult or impossible because firms possess a lot of market power and are likely to abuse it, the direct regulation of firms becomes necessary. This is typically the case in industries whose technological characteristics are such that average industry cost is minimized when a single firm or very few firms serve the whole market.

A second source of inefficiency in a market economy is the existence of 'public goods', i.e. goods that are non-rival (so that the fact that one person is enjoying the good does not prevent another person from enjoying it) and non-excludable (so that a person cannot be made to pay for the good by being excluded from enjoying it if he or she does not pay). Examples of public goods are national defence and law and order. In the absence of government intervention, the market provides a lower than optimal amount of public goods because of the free-rider problem, i.e. the incentive for individuals to understate their willingness to pay for these goods.

A third source of market failure is the existence of externalities. An externality arises whenever consumption or production by one person or firm directly affects consumption or production by another person or firm. For example, pollution is a negative externality, while education may give rise to positive externalities. A firm that produces a product through a pollution-intensive technology does not take into account the effect of pollution on the welfare of others when deciding how much to produce, what technology to use, and so on. In the absence of government intervention, the market will provide a larger than optimal amount of goods and services with negative externalities and a lower than optimal amount of goods and services with positive externalities. There are a number of ways that the government can deal with externalities. These include taxing or subsidizing certain activities; imposing standards or quantity restrictions; or creating a market for the externality (for instance in the case of pollution, by introducing tradeable pollution permits).

A fourth important source of market failure is missing markets (such as for certain types of insurance) and incomplete or asymmetric information. Incomplete information may lead to private choices by individuals that do not represent their best interests. This is part of the reason why governments set health, safety and quality standards, and it also helps to justify government intervention in health care and education.

Government intervention in a market economy can be justified for all the reasons described above, but also for distributional reasons. Markets cannot be relied upon to produce the distribution of income, wealth, skills, health care, and so on, which a society finds desirable. Because redistribution of lump-sum income is difficult in practice, redistribution occurs primarily through taxes and subsidies that also affect the incentives and economic decisions of individuals and firms. This implies that there is often a trade-off between economic efficiency and income redistribution, although there is probably no simple relationship at the macroeconomic level between the degree of inequality and long-run economic growth.

Markets versus governments

Although government intervention can often improve on market outcomes, it does not always do so. First, governments are often not sufficiently well informed, or they are not as well informed as private agents, about various parameters that affect optimal economic decisions. Second, politicians and civil servants have their own objectives, monetary or non-monetary (such as job security or getting re-elected), and they are not necessarily aiming to minimize economic inefficiencies or achieve a more desirable distribution of income when designing and implementing economic policies. Third, government intervention often implies significant administrative costs and inefficiencies caused by weak or distorted incentives and lack of proper monitoring. Fourth, government involvement creates opportunities for rent-seeking activities and lobbying by various special interest groups; this implies a waste of resources and is also likely to distort policy outcomes. In debates about the proper role of

government, therefore, the relevant comparison is often between an imperfect market outcome and an imperfect government intervention.

Government intervention in the market can take many forms: taxes and subsidies, imposition of standards, competition policy, regulation, franchising (i.e. selling the right to serve a market for a certain period to a private firm) and government provision of goods and services. The case for government provision is considerably weaker than the case for other kinds of government intervention in the market. Nevertheless, it may be justified under certain circumstances or for certain kinds of goods and services. In particular, government provision may be superior to provision by private firms when there are significant opportunities for cost reduction in the production process that lead either to the deterioration of quality beyond what is socially desirable or to unequal access to the good or service, *and* quality or universal access cannot be easily observed and specified in a contract between the government and a private firm. Otherwise private ownership or government ownership with contracts to the private sector for the provision of the good or service (with or without regulation) might be better alternatives.

GEORGE SYMEONIDIS
UNIVERSITY OF ESSEX

Further reading

Blank, R. (2000) 'When can public policy makers rely on private markets? The effective provision of social services', *Economic Journal* 110: C34–C49.

Helm, D. (1986) 'The assessment: The economic borders of the state', *Oxford Review of Economic Policy* 2(2): i–xxiv.

Inman, R.P. (1987) 'Markets, governments, and the "new" political economy', in A.J. Auerbach and M.S. Feldstein (eds) *Handbook of Public Economics*, Vol. 2, Amsterdam.

Salanié, B. (2000) *Microeconomics of Market Failures*, Cambridge, MA.

Shleifer, A. (1998) 'State versus private ownership', *Journal of Economic Perspectives* 12(4): 133–50.

Spulber, D.F. (ed.) (2002) *Famous Fables of Economics: Myths of Market Failure*, Oxford.

Stiglitz, J.E. (1994) *Whither Socialism*, Cambridge, MA.

Varian, H. (2002) *Intermediate Microeconomics: A Modern Approach*, 6th edn, New York.

SEE ALSO: asymmetric information; auctions; bargaining; capital, credit and money markets; competition; exchange; monopoly; prices, theory of; regulation; transaction costs

MARRIAGE

Historically and cross-culturally marriage has taken many different forms. Anthropologists especially devoted much energy to specifying these forms and analysing the economic and social characteristics that generated distinct marriage systems. Frequently marriage was examined from a jural perspective with emphasis placed on the rights and responsibilities that marriage generated, not only between husbands and wives but also between their kin (Fortes 1962). Within this framework, matters such as control of sexuality, the legitimacy of children, the economic stability of households and the control and transmission of property were central.

The relationship between economic transformation and the form that marriage takes has also been the focus of much attention within the social sciences. In particular, sociologists have long been interested in the ways in which marriage was patterned by industrialization. The principal argument, put forcefully by writers like Goode (1963) and Stone (1979), is that the introduction of wage labour effectively breaks the control that the wider kin group, and especially parents, can exert over the younger generation's marital behaviour. Where individual welfare and lifestyles are dependent on resources generated through productive property controlled by other kin, marriage systems will tend to reflect collective rather than individual concerns. However, as wage labour increasingly dominates within the economic system, so individuals are freed from their dependence on inherited property and more able to exert their own will over marriage issues, including, of course, choice of spouse.

It is within this context that romantic love and compatibility come to dominate cultural images of the essential character of marriage. Within contemporary 'marital blueprints' (Cancian 1987), in the industrialized world at least, emotional satisfaction, intimacy and personal fulfilment are emphasized as both the rationale for marriage and the criteria of its success (Jamieson 1998). At an ideological level, it is love – the largely untheorized, supposedly special romantic and sexual attraction between two individuals – that is prioritized within marriage discourses. Indeed Giddens (1992), among others, has argued that the social and economic conditions of late modernity have further boosted the cultural significance of intimacy and romantic love through freeing sexual expression from reproduction. It is within this context that the current historically high levels of marital separation and divorce need to be understood: the more that emotional intimacy and personal fulfilment are seen as the *sine qua non* of marriage, the less acceptance there is of relationships where such feelings are absent.

Inherent in these views of marriage is the notion that it is a relationship increasingly characterized by equality. However, as feminist scholarship has consistently demonstrated, marriage continues to be marked by a high division of labour and an unequal distribution of resources. In this, marriage reflects the inequalities that exist outside the domestic arena. In particular, despite changes in employment practices, in most marriages wives continue to carry the primary responsibility for domestic organization and childcare. This is now commonly combined with some form of paid work, but the gendered hierarchies of employment (for a discussion of this in Britain, see Crompton 1997) usually result in women earning significantly less than their male partners, for whom employment is prioritized. The social organization of childcare also continues to be highly gendered, even if many fathers do play a more active part than in the past. In the early and arguably key phase of a marriage, the birth of children encourages a more tightly bound division of labour (Allan and Crow 2001), usually with negative consequences for women's social and economic participation.

If the interaction of labour market differentials and women's socialization as nurturers and carers results in a clear division of responsibility in marriage, it also has an impact on the allocation of resources between wives and husbands. Although obtaining appropriate data is not as straightforward as it might seem, the evidence from different countries indicates that men routinely have higher levels of personal expenditure than their female partners, more control over major decisions and higher priority given to their work and leisure projects. Given the differential character of their primary responsibilities, they also have somewhat more freedom over their use of time, especially, though not only, when there are children in the household. Although a range of other social, cultural and economic factors clearly impinge on this, women's leisure participation is often more constrained than that of their male partners by the disjointed and piecemeal nature of their domestic responsibilities, the need to combine this with involvement in paid work and their lesser access to money for personal expenditure. Research, as well as media attention, has also continued to demonstrate the significant role that marital violence plays in sustaining male control and privilege in some marriages (Johnson and Ferraro 2000).

The claim that marriage is being undermined with modernity is a common one. The high levels of separation and divorce occurring in different industrial societies are one reason for this. So too, though, are the significant changes that have arisen in patterns of cohabitation, that is sexual and domestic unions that have not been legally sanctioned. However, while cohabitation has become far more common and much less stigmatized since the mid-1970s than previously, its consequences for marriage are more difficult to calculate (Lewis 2001). For many, cohabitation serves as an alternative form of engagement rather than an alternative to marriage; in Britain, as elsewhere, the majority of marrying couples now live together prior to their wedding (Haskey 2001). On the other hand, cohabiting couples are increasingly likely to have children, while overall fertility rates are in decline. Currently a quarter of all births in the UK are to cohabiting couples (Kiernan and Smith 2003). Nevertheless, it remains an open question whether significant numbers of people will choose cohabitation rather than marriage as a form of union throughout their life course. Single-sex marriage is another issue that has created considerable controversy in the early twenty-first century. It has been legalized in a number of European countries and, since 2003, in Massachusetts. However, thirty-seven states in the USA have passed legislation since 1996 which requires that marriage must be between a man and a woman (see Merin 2002).

GRAHAM ALLAN
KEELE UNIVERSITY

References

Allan, G. and Crow, G. (2001) *Families, Households and Society*, London.
Cancian, F. (1987) *Love in America*, Cambridge, UK.
Crompton, R. (1997) *Women and Work in Modern Britain*, Oxford.
Fortes, M. (ed.) (1962) *Marriage in Tribal Societies*, Cambridge, UK.
Giddens, A. (1992) *The Transformation of Intimacy*, Cambridge, UK.
Goode, W.J. (1963) *World Revolution and Family Patterns*, New York.
Haskey, J. (2001) 'Cohabitation in Britain', *Population Trends* 103.
Jamieson, L. (1998) *Intimacy*, Cambridge, UK.
Johnson, M and Ferraro, K. (2000) 'Research on domestic violence in the 1990s', *Journal of Marriage and the Family* 62.
Kiernan, K. and Smith, K. (2003) 'Unmarried parenthood: New insights from the Millennium Cohort Study', *Population Trends* 114.
Lewis, J. (2001) *The End of Marriage?* Cheltenham.
Merin, Y. (2002) *Equality for Same Sex Couples*, Chicago.
Stone, L. (1979) *The Family, Sex and Marriage in England 1500–1800*, Harmondsworth.

SEE ALSO: division of labour by sex; divorce; family; kinship

MARSHALL, ALFRED (1842–1924)

The British economist Alfred Marshall was one of the dominant figures in his subject during the late nineteenth and early twentieth centuries. His 1890 masterwork, the *Principles of Economics*, introduced many of the tools and concepts that economists use in price theory even today. The book also presented an influential synthesis of received theories of value and distribution.

Marshall was born on 26 July 1842 in Bermondsey, London, his father William being at the time a clerk at the Bank of England. Alfred was educated at Merchant Taylors' School, revealing there his aptitude for mathematics. Somewhat against his father's wishes, he entered St John's College, Cambridge, to embark on the mathematics tripos, graduating in 1865 as Second Wrangler. He was then elected to a fellowship at St John's. Soon abandoning mathematics for ethics and psychology, his growing interest in social questions led him to economics, which by 1870 he had chosen as his life's work. He took a prominent part in the teaching for the moral sciences tripos until leaving Cambridge in 1877 on marriage to his one-time student, Mary Paley.

Although Marshall published little, these early years were the formative ones for his economic views. He mastered the classical tradition of A. Smith, D. Ricardo and J.S. Mill, and was encouraged towards a mathematical approach by early acquaintance with the works of A.A. Cournot and J.H. von Thünen. Priority for the marginal revolution of the early 1870s clearly goes to W.S. Jevons, L. Walras and C. Menger, but Marshall had been working on similar lines before 1870. However, his attitude towards these new developments remained somewhat grudging, and he was always reluctant to publish merely theoretical exercises. More general influences significant in this early period were those of H. Sidgwick (perhaps more personal than intellectual), H. Spencer and G.W.F. Hegel. The last two, in tune with the spirit of the age, led Marshall towards an organic or biological view of society. He found the early socialist writers emotionally appealing, but unrealistic in their views as to evolutionary possibilities for human nature. Somewhat later, he saw merit in the programme of the German Historical School of Economics, but deplored its anti-theoretical stance. It was from these and other varied sources, including energetic factual enquiry, that he distilled and long pondered his subtle, complex and eclectic approach to economic questions.

Marshall returned to Cambridge in 1885, from exile in Bristol and Oxford, as professor of political economy and the acknowledged leader of British economists. He had already commenced work on his *Principles*. His first two significant publications had appeared in 1879. One was a selection of theoretical chapters from a never-completed book on foreign trade, printed by Sidgwick for private circulation under the title *The Pure Theory of Foreign Trade: The Pure Theory of Domestic Values*. These superb chapters did much to establish Marshall's reputation among British economists. The other was an ostensible primer, the *Economics of Industry*, co-authored by his wife, which foreshadowed many of the ideas of the *Principles*. It was this work that first brought Marshall's views to the attention of foreign economists.

Marshall lived in Cambridge for the rest of his life, resigning his chair in 1908 to devote all his energies to writing. The years were externally uneventful and dominated by the internal struggle to give vent and adequate expression to his vast store of knowledge. The first volume of what was intended as a two-volume work on *Principles of Economics* appeared in 1890 and cemented his international reputation. Although this first volume went through eight editions, little progress was made with the second volume, which had been intended to cover money, business fluctuations, international trade, labour and

industrial organization. Among the famous concepts introduced in the *Principles*, as it soon came to be known, were consumer surplus, long- and short-period analysis, the representative firm and external economies. The elucidation and criticism of these and related concepts were to occupy English-speaking economists for many years.

In 1903, under the influence of the tariff agitation, Marshall embarked on a tract for the times on national industries and international trade. This too grew vastly in his hands and, when it eventually appeared in 1919, *Industry and Trade* realized his earlier intentions only incompletely. The book's tone, historical and descriptive rather than theoretical, has made it better known among economic historians than among economists. The years that remained were devoted to a last-ditch effort to salvage some of his unpublished earlier work. Some important early contributions to the theories of money and international trade at last saw the light in *Money, Credit and Commerce* in 1923, but the book remains an unsatisfactory pastiche. Marshall died on 13 July 1924 at the age of 81 having failed to do much that he had wished, yet still having achieved greatness.

During his years as professor, Marshall was instrumental in establishing the specialized study of his subject at Cambridge, which eventually became a leading centre for economic study and research. As teacher and adviser he inspired his students with his own high and unselfish ambitions for his subject. Among the several students who were to attain professional prominence and influence, A.C. Pigou and J.M. Keynes should especially be mentioned. Nationally, Marshall was a public figure and played an important role in government inquiries and in the professionalization of economics in Britain. Internationally, he was cosmopolitan in outlook and kept close contact with economists and economic events abroad.

Marshall was anxious to influence events and deeply concerned for the future of Britain, and especially of its poorer and less privileged citizens. Yet he preferred to remain above the fray of current controversy, whether scientific or concerned with policy, trusting that constructive work and patient study would provide the surer if slower route towards the desired goals. His desire for historical continuity and the avoidance of controversy led him frequently to underplay the novelty of his ideas and to exaggerate their closeness to those of his classical forebears.

JOHN K. WHITAKER
UNIVERSITY OF VIRGINIA

Further reading

Groenewegen, P. (1995) *A Soaring Eagle: Alfred Marshall 1842–1924*, Aldershot and Brookfield, VT.
Guillebaud, C.W. (ed.) (1965) *Marshall's Principles of Economics, Variorum Edition*, London.
Pigou, A.C. (ed.) (1925) *Memorials of Alfred Marshall*, London.
Whitaker, J.K. (ed.) (1975) *The Early Economic Writings of Alfred Marshall, 1867–1890*, London.
—— (ed.) (1996) *The Correspondence of Alfred Marshall, Economist*, Cambridge.

SEE ALSO: classical economics; neo-classical economics

MARX, KARL HEINRICH (1818–83)

Marx was a German social scientist and revolutionary, whose analysis of capitalist society laid the theoretical basis for the political movement bearing his name. Marx's main contribution lies in his emphasis on the role of the economic factor – the changing way in which people have reproduced their means of subsistence – in shaping the course of history. This perspective has had a considerable influence on the whole range of social sciences.

Karl Heinrich Marx was born in the town of Trier in the Moselle district of the Prussian Rhineland on 5 May 1818. He came from a long line of rabbis on both his father's and his mother's sides. His father, a respected lawyer in Trier, had accepted baptism as a Protestant in order to be able to pursue his career. The atmosphere of Marx's home was permeated by the Enlightenment, and he assimilated a certain amount of romantic and early socialist ideas from Baron von Westphalen – to whose daughter, Jenny, he became engaged in 1835 and later married. In the same year he left the local gymnasium, or high school, and enrolled at the University of Bonn. He transferred the following year to the University of Berlin, where he soon embraced the dominant philosophy of Hegelianism. Intending to become a university teacher, Marx obtained his doctorate in 1841 with a thesis on post-Aristotelian Greek philosophy.

From 1837 Marx had been deeply involved in the Young Hegelian movement. This group espoused a radical critique of Christianity and, by implication, a liberal opposition to the Prussian autocracy. Finding a university career closed to him by the Prussian government, Marx moved into journalism. In October 1842 he became editor, in Cologne, of the influential *Rheinische Zeitung*, a liberal newspaper backed by Rhenish industrialists. Marx's incisive articles, particularly on economic questions, induced the government to close the paper, and he decided to emigrate to France.

Paris was then the centre of socialist thought and on his arrival at the end of 1843, Marx rapidly made contact with organized groups of *émigré* German workers and with various sects of French socialists. He also edited the shortlived *Deutsch-französische Jahrbücher*, which was intended to form a bridge between nascent French socialism and the ideas of the German radical Hegelians. It was also in Paris that Marx first formed his lifelong partnership with Friedrich Engels. During the first few months of his stay in Paris, Marx rapidly became a convinced communist and set down his views in a series of manuscripts known as the *Ökonomisch-philosophische Manuskripte* (*Economic and Philosophic Manuscripts of 1844*). Here he outlined a humanist conception of communism, influenced by the philosophy of Ludwig Feuerbach and based on a contrast between the alienated nature of labour under capitalism and a communist society in which human beings freely developed their nature in co-operative production. For the first time there appeared together, if not yet united, what Engels described as the three constituent elements in Marx's thought – German idealist philosophy, French socialism and English economics. It is above all these *Manuscripts* that (in the West at least) reoriented many people's interpretation of Marx – to the extent of their even being considered as his major work. They were not published until the early 1930s and did not attract public attention until after the Second World War; certain facets of the *Manuscripts* were soon assimilated to the existentialism and humanism then so much in vogue, and presented an altogether more attractive basis for non-Stalinist socialism than textbooks on dialectical materialism.

Seen in their proper perspective, these *Manuscripts* were in fact no more than a starting-point for Marx – an initial, exuberant outpouring of ideas to be taken up and developed in subsequent economic writings, particularly in the *Grundrisse* (1857–8) and in *Das Kapital* (1867). In these later works the themes of the '1844 Manuscripts' would certainly be pursued more systematically, in greater detail and against a much more solid economic and historical background, but the central inspiration or vision was to remain unaltered: humankind's alienation in capitalist society, and the possibility of emancipation – of people controlling their own destiny through communism.

Because of his political journalism, Marx was expelled from Paris at the end of 1844. He moved (with Engels) to Brussels, where he stayed for the next 3 years. He visited England, then the most advanced industrial country in the world, where Engels's family had cotton-spinning interests in Manchester. While in Brussels, Marx devoted himself to an intensive study of history. This he set out in a manuscript known as *The German Ideology* (also published posthumously); its basic thesis was that 'the nature of individuals depends on the material conditions determining their production'. Marx traced the history of the various modes of production and predicted the collapse of the present one – capitalism – and its replacement by communism.

At the same time that he was engaged in this theoretical work, Marx became involved in political activity and in writing polemics (as in *Misère de la Philosophie* (1847) (*The Poverty of Philosophy*) against what he considered to be the unduly idealistic socialism of Pierre Joseph Proudhon. He joined the Communist League, an organization of German *émigré* workers with its centre in London, for which he and Engels became the major theoreticians. At a conference of the league in London at the end of 1847, Marx and Engels were commissioned to write a *Manifest der kommunistischen Partei* (1848) (*Manifesto of the Communist Party*), a declaration that was to become the most succinct expression of their views. Scarcely was the *Manifesto* published when the 1848 wave of revolutions broke in Europe.

Early in 1848, Marx moved back to Paris, where the revolution had first erupted. He then went on to Germany where he founded, again in Cologne, the *Neue Rheinische Zeitung*. This widely influential newspaper supported a radical democratic line against the Prussian autocracy. Marx devoted his main energies to its editorship, since the Communist League had been virtually disbanded. With the ebbing of the revolutionary tide, however, Marx's paper was suppressed. He sought refuge in London in May 1849, beginning the 'long, sleepless night of exile' that was to last for the rest of his life.

On settling in London, Marx grew optimistic about the imminence of a fresh revolutionary outbreak in Europe, and he rejoined the rejuvenated Communist League. He wrote two lengthy pamphlets on the 1848 revolution in France and its aftermath, entitled *Die Klassenkämpfe in Frankreich 1848 bis 1850* (1850) (*The Class Struggles in France*) and *Der achzehnte Brumaire des Louis Bonaparte* (1852) (*The Eighteenth Brumaire of Louis Bonaparte*). But he soon became convinced that 'a new revolution is possible only in consequence of a new crisis', and devoted himself to the study of political economy to determine the causes and conditions of this crisis.

During the first half of the 1850s the Marx family lived in three-room lodgings in the Soho district of London and experienced considerable poverty. The Marxes already had four children on their arrival in London, and two more were soon born. Of these, only three survived the Soho period. Marx's major source of income at this time (and later) was Engels, who was drawing a steadily increasing income from his father's cotton business in Manchester. This was supplemented by weekly articles he wrote as foreign correspondent for the *New York Daily Tribune*. Legacies in the late 1850s and early 1860s eased Marx's financial position somewhat, but it was not until 1869 that he had a sufficient and assured income settled on him by Engels.

Not surprisingly, Marx's major work on political economy made slow progress. By 1857–8 he had produced a mammoth 800-page manuscript – a rough draft of a work that he intended should deal with capital, landed property, wage-labour, the state, foreign trade and the world market. This manuscript, known as *Grundrisse* (*Outlines*), was not published until 1941. In the early 1860s he broke off his work to compose three large volumes, entitled *Theorien über den Mehrwert* (1861–3) (*Theories of Surplus Value*), which discussed his predecessors in political economy, particularly Adam Smith and David Ricardo.

It was not until 1867 that Marx was able to publish the first results of his work in Volume 1 of *Das Kapital*, devoted to a study of the capitalist process of production. Here he elaborated his version of the labour theory of value, and his conception of surplus value and exploitation that would ultimately lead to a falling rate of profit and the collapse of capitalism. Volumes 2 and 3 were largely finished in the 1860s, but Marx worked on the manuscripts for the rest of his life. They were published posthumously by Engels. In his major work, Marx's declared aim was to analyse 'the birth, life and death of a given social organism and its replacement by another, superior order'. In order to achieve this aim, Marx took over the concepts of the 'classical' economists that were still the generally accepted tool of economic analysis, and used them to draw very different conclusions. Ricardo had made a distinction between use-value and exchange-value. The exchange-value of an object was something separate from its price and consisted of the amount of labour embodied in the objects of production, though Ricardo thought that the price in fact tended to approximate to the exchange-value. Thus – in contradistinction to later analyses – the value of an object was determined by the circumstances of production rather than those of demand. Marx took over these concepts, but, in his attempt to show that capitalism was not static but a historically relative system of class exploitation, supplemented Ricardo's views by introducing the idea of surplus-value. Surplus-value was defined as the difference between the value of the products of labour and the cost of producing that labour-power, that is, the labourer's subsistence; for the exchange-value of labour-power was equal to the amount of labour necessary to reproduce that labour-power and this was normally much lower than the exchange-value of the products of that labour-power.

The theoretical part of Volume 1 divides very easily into three sections. The first section is a rewriting of the *Zur Kritik der politischen Ökonomie* (1859) (*Critique of Political Economy*) and analyses commodities, in the sense of external objects that satisfy human needs, and their value. Marx established two sorts of value – use-value, or the utility of something, and exchange-value, which was determined by the amount of labour incorporated in the object. Labour was also of a two-fold nature according to whether it created use-values or exchange-values. Because 'the exchange-values of commodities must be capable of being expressed in terms of something common to them all', and the only

thing they shared was labour, then labour must be the source of value. But since evidently some people worked faster or more skilfully than others, this labour must be a sort of average 'socially necessary' labour time. There followed a difficult section on the form of value, and the first chapter ended with an account of commodities as exchange values, which he described as the 'fetishism of commodities' in a passage that recalls the account of alienation in the *Pariser Manuskripte* (1844) (*Paris Manuscripts*) and (even more) the *Note on James Mill* (1844). 'In order', said Marx here,

> to find an analogy, we must have recourse to the mist-enveloped regions of the religious world. In that world the productions of the human brain appear as independent beings endowed with life, and entering into relation both with one another and the human race. So it is in the world of commodities with the products of men's hands.

The section ended with a chapter on exchange and an account of money as the means for the circulation of commodities, the material expression for their values and the universal measure of value.

The second section was a small one on the transformation of money into capital. Before the capitalist era, people had sold commodities for money in order to buy more commodities. In the capitalist era, instead of selling to buy, people had bought to sell dearer: they had bought commodities with their money in order, by means of those commodities, to increase their money.

In the third section Marx introduced his key notion of surplus-value, the idea that Engels characterized as Marx's principal 'discovery' in economics. Marx made a distinction between *constant* capital, which was 'that part of capital which is represented by the means of production, by the raw material, auxiliary material and instruments of labour, and does not, in the process of production, undergo any quantitative alteration of value', and *variable* capital. Of this Marx said:

> That part of capital, represented by labour power, does, in the process of production, undergo an alteration of value. It both reproduces the equivalent of its own value, and also produces an excess, a surplus value, which

may itself vary, may be more or less according to the circumstances.

This variation was the rate of surplus-value around which the struggle between workers and capitalists centred. The essential point was that the capitalist got the worker to work longer than was merely sufficient to embody in the product the value of the labour power: if the labour power of workers (roughly what it cost to keep them alive and fit) was £4 a day and workers could embody £4 of value in the product on which they were working in 8 hours, then, if they worked 10 hours, the last 2 hours would yield surplus-value – in this case £1.

Thus surplus-value could arise only from variable capital, not from constant capital, as labour alone created value. Put very simply, Marx's reason for thinking that the rate of profit would decrease was that, with the introduction of machinery, labour time would become less and thus yield less surplus-value. Of course, machinery would increase production and colonial markets would absorb some of the surplus, but these were only palliatives and an eventual crisis was inevitable. These first nine chapters were complemented by a masterly historical account of the genesis of capitalism that illustrates better than any other writing Marx's approach and method. Marx particularly made pioneering use of official statistical information that came to be available from the middle of the nineteenth century onwards.

Meanwhile, Marx devoted much time and energy to the First International – to whose General Council he was elected on its foundation in 1864. This was one of the reasons he was so delayed in his work on *Das Kapital*. He was particularly active in preparing for the annual congresses of the International and in leading the struggle against the anarchist wing of the International led by Mikhail Bakunin. Although Marx won this contest, the transfer of the seat of the General Council from London to New York in 1872 – a move that Marx supported – led to the swift decline of the International. The most important political event during the existence of the International was the Paris Commune of 1871, when the citizens of Paris, in the aftermath of the Franco-Prussian war, rebelled against their government and held the city for 2 months. On the bloody suppression of this rebellion, Marx wrote one of his most famous pamphlets –

entitled *Address on the Civil War in France* (1871) – which was an enthusiastic defence of the activities and aims of the Commune.

During the last decade of his life Marx's health declined considerably, and he was incapable of the sustained efforts of creative synthesis that had so obviously characterized his previous work. Nevertheless, he managed to comment substantially on contemporary politics in Germany and Russia. In Germany he opposed, in his *Randglossen zum Programm der deutschen Arbeiterpartei* (1875) (*Critique of the Gotha Programme*), the tendency of his followers Wilhelm Leibknecht and August Bebel to compromise with the state socialism of Ferdinand Lassalle in the interest of a united socialist party. In Russia, in correspondence with Vera Sassoulitch, he contemplated the possibility of Russia's bypassing the capitalist stage of development and building communism on the basis of the common ownership of land characteristic of the village council or *mir*. Marx, however, was increasingly dogged by ill health, and he regularly travelled to European spas and even to Algeria in search of recuperation. The deaths of his eldest daughter and of his wife clouded the last years of his life, and he died in London on 13 March 1883.

The influence of Marx, so narrow during his lifetime, expanded enormously after his death. This influence was at first evident in the growth of the Social Democratic Party in Germany, but reached worldwide dimensions following the success of the Bolsheviks in Russia in 1917. Paradoxically, although the main thrust of Marx's thought was to anticipate that a proletarian revolution would inaugurate the transition to socialism in advanced industrial countries, Marxism was most successful in developing in Third World countries, such as Russia or China. Since the problems of these countries are primarily agrarian and the initial development of an industrial base, they are necessarily far removed from what were Marx's immediate concerns: for him, the collapse of Soviet communism would have been a source neither of surprise nor of dismay. On a more general level, over the whole range of the social sciences, Marx's materialist conception of history and his analysis of capitalist society have made him probably the most influential figure of the twentieth century.

DAVID MCLELLAN
GOLDSMITHS' COLLEGE, UNIVERSITY OF LONDON

Further reading

Avineri, S. (1968) *The Social and Political Thought of Karl Marx*, Cambridge, UK.

Cohen, G. (1978) *Karl Marx's Theory of History: A Defence*, Oxford.

Engels, F., 'Introduction', in K. Marx (1875) *Critique of the Gotha Programme* [numerous English-language editions].

McLellan, D. (1974) *Karl Marx: His Life and Thought*, New York.

Marx, K. (2001) *Selected Writings*, ed. D. McLellan, 2nd edn, Oxford.

—— (1844) *Economic and Philosophic Manuscripts* [numerous English-language editions for Marx's works].

—— (1844) *Paris Manuscripts*.

—— (1844) *Note on James Mill*.

—— (1845–6) *The German Ideology*.

—— (1847) *The Poverty of Philosophy*.

—— (1850) *The Class Struggles in France*.

—— (1852) *The Eighteenth Brumaire of Louis Bonaparte*.

—— (1857–8) *Grundrisse*.

—— (1859) *Critique of Political Economy*.

—— (1861–3) *Theories of Surplus Value*.

—— (1867) *Das Kapital*.

Marx, K. and Engels, F. (1848) *Manifesto of the Communist Party*.

Ollman, B. (1971) *Alienation, Marx's Conception of Man in Capitalist Society*, Cambridge, UK.

Peffer, R. (1990) *Marxism, Morality and Social Justice*, Princeton, NJ.

Plamenatz, J. (1975) *Karl Marx's Philosophy of Man*, Oxford.

Torrance, J. (1995) *Karl Marx's Theory of Ideas*, Cambridge.

White, J. (1996) *Karl Marx and the Origins of Dialectical Materialism*, Basingstoke.

SEE ALSO: communism; Marxian economics; Marx's theory of history and society; Marxist history; socialism

MARX'S THEORY OF HISTORY AND SOCIETY

Marx's general sociohistorical theory, often known as the materialist conception of history or historical materialism, seeks, in the words of Engels:

> the ultimate cause and the great moving power of all important historic events in the economic development of society, in the changes in the modes of production and exchange, and in the consequent division of society into distinct classes, and in the struggles of these classes against one another.

Marx first elaborated his theory, which became the guiding thread of his subsequent studies, in *Die Deutsche Ideologie* (*The German Ideology*) of 1845–6. A famous, but very compact, statement of it appears in Marx's Preface to *Zur Kritik der politischen Ökonomie* (1859) (*A Contribution to the Critique of Political Economy*).

There Marx contends that the economic structure of society, constituted by its relations of production, is the real foundation of society. It is the basis 'on which rises a legal and political superstructure and to which correspond definite forms of social consciousness'. On the other hand, society's relations of production themselves 'correspond to a definite stage of development of [society's] material productive forces'. In this manner 'the mode of production of material life conditions the social, political and intellectual life process in general'. As society's productive forces develop, they clash with existing production relations, which now fetter their growth. 'Then begins an epoch of social revolution' as this contradiction rifts society and as people become, in a more or less ideological form, 'conscious of this conflict and fight it out'. This conflict is resolved in favour of the productive forces, and new, higher relations of production, whose material preconditions have 'matured in the womb of the old society itself', emerge that better accommodate the continued growth of society's productive capacity. The bourgeois mode of production represents the most recent of several progressive epochs in the economic formation of society, but it is the last antagonistic form of production. With its demise the prehistory of humanity will come to a close.

According to Marx, the expansion of the productive forces (that is, of the means of production and of the skill and expertise of human labour power) determines society's relations of production because, as he wrote to Annenkov, 'Men never relinquish what they have won.' In order to retain 'the fruits of civilization' they will change their way of producing to accommodate the acquired productive forces and facilitate their continued advance. The relations of production, though, influence the momentum and qualitative direction of the development of the productive forces; capitalism in particular is distinguished by its tendency to raise society to a productive level undreamt of before. Still, Marx's materialist conception assigns explanatory primacy to the development of the productive forces, envisioning, for instance, the emergence of capitalism as a response to the level of the productive forces existing at the time of its origin.

The development of society's productive capacity thus determines the main contours of its socioeconomic evolution, while the various economic structures that result shape, in turn, society's legal and political institutions, or superstructure. Which other social institutions are properly part of the superstructure is a matter of debate, but Marx certainly thought that all the various spheres and realms of society reflect the dominant mode of production and that the general consciousness of an epoch is shaped by the nature of its productive system. The Marxist theory of ideology contends that certain ideas originate or are widespread because they sanction existing social relations or promote particular class interests. The economy's determination of legal and political forms, however, tends to be relatively direct, whereas its influence over other social realms, culture and consciousness generally is more attenuated and nuanced.

Because a superstructure is needed to organize and stabilize society, the economic structure brings about those institutions that are best suited to it. Law, in particular, is necessary to 'sanction the existing order' and grant it 'independence from mere chance and arbitrariness'. This function itself gives the legal realm some autonomy, because the existing relations of production are represented and legitimated in an abstract, codified form, which in turn fosters the ideological illusion that the law is entirely autonomous with respect to the economic structure. In addition, under capitalism the 'fictio juris of a contract' between free agents conceals the real nature of production, in particular, the 'invisible threads' that bind wage-labour to capital and lead to its exploitation. In precapitalist societies, for example in feudalism, tradition and custom perform a similar legitimizing and stabilizing function, and may also win a degree of autonomy from the economic realm. There the social relations of production are entangled with the relations of personal domination that characterize the other spheres of feudal life, thus obscuring their true nature.

In the social organization of production, people stand in different relations to the forces and products of production, and in any given mode of production these relations will be of certain characteristic sorts. One's economic position, as that is understood in terms of the existing social production relations, gives one certain material interests in common with others and determines one's class. Hence follow the familiar definitions of the bourgeoisie and proletariat by reference to the purchase and sale, respectively, of labour power (and the underlying ownership or non-ownership of the means of production).

A central thesis of Marx is that class position, so defined, determines the characteristic consciousness or world-view of its members. For example, Marx's discussion of the Legitimists and Orleanists in *Der achzehnte Brumaire des Louis Bonaparte* (1852) (*The Eighteenth Brumaire of Louis Bonaparte*) emphasizes that on the basis of its socioeconomic position each class creates 'an entire superstructure of distinct and peculiarly formed sentiments, illusions, modes of thought and views of life'. The differing material interests of classes divide them and lead to their struggle. Classes differ in the extent to which their members recognize themselves to be a class, so that antagonisms between classes may not be discerned by the participants, or may be understood only in a mystified or ideological manner.

The ultimate success or failure of a class is determined by its relation to the advance of the productive forces. In the words of *The German Ideology*, 'The conditions under which definite productive forces can be applied are the conditions of the rule of a definite class of society.' That class which has the capacity and the incentive to introduce or preserve the relations of production required to accommodate the advance of the productive forces has its hegemony ensured. Marx's theory views class rule, hitherto, as both inevitable and necessary to force the productivity of the direct producers beyond the subsistence level. The productive progress brought by capitalism, however, eliminates both the feasibility of, and the historical rationale for, class rule. Because the state is primarily the vehicle by which a class secures its rule, it will wither away in postclass society.

Marx's 'Preface' designates the Asiatic, ancient, feudal and modern bourgeois modes of production as the major epochs in humanity's advance, but these mark the general stages of socioeconomic evolution as a whole – not the steps that history obliges every nation without exception to climb. In a famous letter of November 1877, Marx characteristically denied propounding 'any historic-philosophic theory of the *marche générale* imposed by fate upon every people', but this oft-quoted remark does not amount to a rejection of historical determinism. Although Marx's theory permits countries to lag behind or even skip steps, their course must still be accounted for within the overarching pattern of socioeconomic evolution, and that development is due to the productive forces. Marx could consistently believe in a necessary, productive-force-determined evolution of history without holding that every social group is preordained to follow the same course. In addition, it seems likely that Marx would have been willing to revise his list of historical stages (or at least the prefeudal ones) because he paid relatively little attention to humanity's early modes of production. Modification of Marx's schema, as well as of his analysis of capitalism (and the projected transition to socialism), is in principle compatible with his basic theory of society and history.

It should be borne in mind that Marx's theory does not pretend to explain every last detail of history and society. Certain social and cultural phenomena are beyond its explanatory range, and from its broad purview many historical events, and certainly the specific forms they take, are accidental. Nor does the theory seek to explain fully and scientifically individual behaviour, though it attempts to situate that behaviour within its sociohistorical confines. In so far as there are ineluctable tendencies in history, these result from, not despite, the choices of individuals.

Marx's ideas have had an influence on the social sciences, the significance of which it is hard to exaggerate. Not only has his work inspired, to various extents, countless writers, but even those who reject Marx frequently find themselves obliged to define their own thought in relation to his. Despite the perennial attractions of Marx's approach and the fertility of his insights, controversy continues over the basic concepts and theorems of his theory, the relative importance of its various components and the specific features that characterize his sociohistorical methodology. Given Marx's far-reaching claims and the lack of an interpretative consensus, a conclusive assessment of the viability of his general theory of society and history is exceedingly difficult.

WILLIAM H. SHAW
SAN JOSÉ STATE UNIVERSITY, CALIFORNIA

Further reading

Cohen, G.A. (2000) *Karl Marx's Theory of History: A Defence*, expanded edn, Oxford.
Elster, J. (1985) *Making Sense of Marx*, Cambridge, UK.
Marx, K. (1845–6) *The German Ideology* [numerous editions; available as ebook Microsoft Reader].
—— (1852) *The Eighteenth Brumaire of Louis Bonaparte* [numerous English-language editions].
—— (1859) *A Contribution to the Critique of Political Economy* [numerous English-language editions].
Shaw, W.H. (1978) *Marx's Theory of History*, Stanford, CA.
Wetherly, P. (ed.) (1992) *Marx's Theory of History: The Contemporary Debate*, Aldershot, UK.
Wood, A. (1981) *Karl Marx*, London.

SEE ALSO: alienation; class, social; hegemony; Marx; Marxian economics; Marxist history

MARXIAN ECONOMICS

The cornerstones of Marxian economics were first presented in Karl Marx's *Capital*. They have since been debated, refined and extended by succeeding generations of Marxian economists, philosophers and social theorists, thus forming the rich and varied tradition that today is referred to as Marxian economics.

As a 'critique of political economy' (the subtitle of *Capital*), Marxian economics represents a critique both of mainstream economics and of capitalism, the economic and social system celebrated within mainstream economics. It thus constitutes a decisive break from the methods and propositions put forward by orthodox economists, from Adam Smith to Paul Samuelson, and presents a far-reaching indictment of exploitation and the other features that have characterized capitalist development, from the nineteenth century to the present day.

Marxian economics presumes, and points in the direction of, communal alternatives to the capitalist organization of economy and society. This is its Utopian moment – imagining the possibility of community, not individual, involvement in and control over the class aspects of the economy. But it does not contain a specific scheme or blueprint for such alternatives. Still, Marxian economics has often been used to analyse and criticize the socialist systems that have been constructed in the name of Marxism, in the Soviet Union and elsewhere, during the 150 years since *Capital* was first published.

The key to understanding *Capital* and the history of Marxian economics is to see them as interventions into a field of economics (or, as it was known in the eighteenth and nineteenth centuries, political economy) that has been defined and developed by others. Marx studied the works of the classical political economists such as Adam Smith and David Ricardo (during the famous years in the British Museum) and, on the basis of his critical reading (the notes of which comprise the so-called fourth volume of *Capital*, *Theories of Surplus Value*), took up and challenged many of their basic concepts and methods. Latter-day Marxian economists have done the same with the works of succeeding schools of thought, including neo-classical and Keynesian economics.

One example of this critical approach pertains to the idea of the commodity. Throughout the long history of mainstream economic analysis, commodity exchange has been considered as an essential aspect of human nature, i.e. human beings are assumed to have a natural propensity to buy and sell the goods they have produced. Moreover, the 'wealth of nations' (what today is called gross domestic product and various other aggregate measures) is conceptualized and measured as the sum of those commodities, such that the total value of incomes earned in the production of those goods is equal to the money spent on acquiring them. For Marxists, there is nothing natural about commodity exchange. The widespread circulation of the products of labour in markets is a relatively recent historical invention, which is based on the initial emergence and subsequent reproduction of a whole host of economic, cultural and political conditions. In addition, according to Marxian economists, capitalist commodities contain a 'surplus-value', an extra value produced by workers for which no equivalent value has been paid by capitalists. Therefore, the growth of capitalist wealth is accompanied by the growth of unpaid, or surplus, labour.

A second example is the falling rate of profit (Cullenberg 1994). Classical political economists were concerned that capitalism was beset by a tendency for the rate of profit to fall, and thus for capitalist economies to enter into crisis. This tendency was variously ascribed to an increase in the stock of capital and intensified competition among capitalists (Smith) or a gradual decline in the productivity of agricultural labour and a subsequent increase in wages and land rent (Ricardo). Marxist economists have criticized both theories, arguing that if capitalism exhibits a tendency for the rate of profit to fall it is due to an increase (not a decline) in the productivity of labour and that capitalism also contains various countervailing tendencies (which lead to increases in the rate of profit). The success of capitalism, not its failure, is therefore responsible for the contradictory tendencies of the rate of profit both to fall and to rise.

Marxian economics thus offers different answers to the questions posed by mainstream economic theory. It also asks entirely different questions. Instead of starting from an essential human nature, it embeds the individual in history and society. Rather than assuming equilibrium in markets and social harmony, it focuses on crisis and class exploitation. Moving outside the terms of debate defined by private and state-regulated forms of capitalism, Marxian economics is oriented by the possibility of ending all forms of capitalist exploitation (Resnick and Wolff 1987).

The concepts and method of Marxian economics are developed across the three volumes of *Capital*. Volume I, 'a critical analysis of capitalist production', presents the initial definitions of the basic concepts that together make up a distinctly Marxian theory of labour value: use-value and exchange-value (the social usefulness of the object and its value in exchange, which form the two-fold nature of the commodity), commodity fetishism (a Marxian theory of commodity-exchanging economic agents), money (the universal equivalent), value (the amount of labour embodied in the commodity during the course of production), the existence of labour power as a commodity (the buying and selling of individuals' ability to work), surplus-value (the extra value created by capitalist labourers, for which they are not compensated), capital (the value of labour power as well as that of raw materials and machinery) and the accumulation of capital (the use of surplus-value to purchase more capital, one of the conditions of existence of capitalism). The result is a conception of a capitalist commodity as follows:

$$w = c + v + s$$

where, using traditional notion, w is the commodity's value, c is constant capital (the value of the raw materials and means of production that are transferred to the commodity), v is variable capital (the amount paid to labourers, equal to the value of their labour power) and s is surplus-value (the unpaid labour of the workers who produced the commodities). This is the basis of the contentious Marxian claim that the direct producers are exploited within capitalism: they create value ($v + s$), part of which (s) is appropriated by capitalists for literally doing nothing.

The analysis of Volume I is carried out on the assumption that the value of a capitalist commodity is realized when it is sold on the market. In Volume II, the focus shifts to 'the process of circulation of capital', the ways in which the value of capitalist commodities enters into and circulates through markets, especially on an aggregate level. In a precursor to the kinds of macroeconomic concerns later emphasized by John Maynard Keynes, Marx introduces the flow of commodity value (through various stages – money-capital, productive-capital, commodity-capital), the element of historical time and various reproduction schema (broken down into two groups of industries or departments, wage goods and capital goods). The purpose is to demonstrate how dependent capitalism is on the precarious balance of flows of value between and among sectors throughout the economy.

According to the economist Ernest Mandel, 'if the first volume of *Capital* is the most famous and widely read, and if the second is the unknown one, the third is the most controversial'. Marx's analysis of 'the process of capitalist production as a whole' in Volume III combines the results of the preceding volumes in order to discuss such phenomena as capitalist competition (within and across industries), the formation of an average rate of profit, the role of commodity-capitalists and money-capitalists (i.e. capitalists other than those directly involved in the production of commodities, and who receive a portion of the surplus-value appropriated from workers), land rent and income distribution. One of the results is that, contrary to the assumption of Volume I, capitalist commodities will in general not exchange at their values but, instead, at their 'prices of production'.

If one considers the three volumes together, the picture of capitalism that emerges is anything but simple: the existence of commodities involves both production and markets (including consumption). The economy is 'overdetermined' by (it conditions and is conditioned by) the rest of society. The appropriation of surplus-value (by capitalists from direct producers) and its distribution (to still others, including the state, other capitalists and so on in order to secure some of the conditions of existence of capitalism) imply a complex class structure. The contradictory tendencies of capitalism create the possibility of both crises, solutions to such crises and movements beyond capitalism.

Beginning with the elements presented in *Capital*, and utilizing still other texts (especially the *Grundrisse*, the notebooks that prepared the way for the later work, as well as *A Contribution to the Critique of Political Economy* and *Wages, Price, and Profit*) generations of scholars have debated, revised and further elaborated the method and concepts of Marxian economic theory.

Alongside analyses of the labour process and industrial factories, Marxian economics has investigated such varied sites and practices as households, the state, multinational corporations, domestic service, self-employment, the informal sector and the sex industry. It has been extended to the international arena, with specifically Marxian notions of imperialism, foreign trade, structural adjustment, transnational finance and investment, and globalization.

Methodologically, Marxian economists have followed two major traditions of interpretation: modernism and postmodernism. Modernist Marxian economics has been characterized by its emphasis on laws of motion, cause-and-effect relations, a realist ontology and the epistemologies of conventional social science. Postmodern versions of Marxian economics highlight other elements: contingency and decentring, non-deterministic causation, discursive construction and postpositivist theories of knowledge (Ruccio and Amariglio 2003).

These conceptual extensions and methodological discussions, combined with the persistent problems evident in both mainstream economics and contemporary capitalism, signify the continued vitality and relevance of Marxian economics.

DAVID F. RUCCIO
UNIVERSITY OF NOTRE DAME

References

Cullenberg, S. (1994) *The Falling Rate of Profit: Recasting the Marxian Debate*, London.

Mandel, E. (1936) 'Introduction', in K. Marx, *Capital*, New York.

Marx, K. (1952 [1865]) *Wages, Price, and Profit*, Moscow.

—— (1973 [1953]) *Grundrisse: Foundations of the Critique of Political Economy*, London.

—— (1977 [1867]) *Capital: A Critique of Political Economy*, 3 vols, New York.

—— (1987 [1859]) 'Preface to a contribution to the critique of political economy', in *Marx–Engels Collected Works*, Vol. 29, New York, pp. 257–65.

Resnick, S.A. and Wolff, R.D. (1987) *Knowledge and Class: A Marxian Critique of Political Economy*, Chicago

Ruccio, D.F. and Amariglio, J. (2003) *Postmodern Moments in Modern Economics*, Princeton, NJ.

SEE ALSO: Marx; Marx's theory of history and society

MARXIST HISTORY

When Karl Marx referred to his system as 'historical materialism' he was signalling his indebtedness to two important intellectual traditions. The first was to the French Enlightenment with its emphasis on the determination of social attitudes and behaviour by material forces such as climate and the economy: intended initially to undermine established religious ways of thinking, this became the basis of a more positive method of systematic economic analysis. The second was to the German reaction against the Enlightenment, with its emphasis on the value of all modes of thought when understood within their original historical contexts: intended initially to defend inherited religious ways of thinking, this became the basis of a more general method of sympathetic cultural understanding. Though many later historians first encountered economic determinism and cultural historicism through the writings of Marx, these approaches did not originate with him and even their combination into historical materialism had been anticipated by Scottish Enlightenment thinkers such as Adam Smith who had developed their own accounts of the stages of social development. Marx himself was well aware of this and in his famous letter to Weydemeyer rejected any claim to have discovered the existence of classes and class struggle in history, and emphasized that his own contribution was to show that 'the class struggle necessarily leads to the dictatorship of the proletariat' (1852). Thus while Marx has become the best-known purveyor of historical materialism, the specifically Marxist element within this was his

argument that, just as feudalism had unintentionally given rise to the bourgeoisie and its revolutionary transformation of society, so the economic development of capitalism would necessarily give rise to a united proletariat and its revolutionary expropriation of the means of production from the bourgeoisie.

For 50 years after his death in 1883, Marxist historical work was largely restricted to the writings of left-wing activists attempting to justify their political strategies by compiling material on the recent economic development of capitalism. However, the interwar depression and the rise of fascism, combined with the apparent success of socialism in the Soviet Union, made Marxism more plausible in the West and it began to pass into the mainstream of historical debate, particularly through the work of Maurice Dobb and Ernest Labrousse. Dobb was a Cambridge economist who became involved in history through his pioneering work on the Russian economy under the Soviet regime. More importantly, Dobb's (1946) essays on the economic development of capitalism set the agenda for research into the transition from feudalism to capitalism and into the economic formation of the modern working class, which was to guide the next generation of British Marxist historians. Labrousse was a historian at the Sorbonne whose studies of economic cycles in eighteenth-century France were intended to uncover the precise material causes of the outbreak of the Revolution of 1789 (Labrousse 1943). More importantly, his pioneering application of sophisticated quantitative methods had a significant influence on the shift towards more rigorous demographic and econometric history among the next generation of French historians around the journal *Annales*.

The period after the Second World War therefore saw flourishing schools of Marxist historians in the Western universities, focusing mainly on the analysis of the material structures underlying political developments. Important work on the origins of the English Revolution in the seventeenth century, on the development of the British labour movement in the nineteenth century, and on the economic and social history of the French *départements* in the early-modern and modern periods has since faced major challenges but has made a permanent contribution to the establishment of a more problem-oriented approach in place of the older narrative style of historical writing. This is best understood as part of a wider movement towards economic history that had equally important roots in radical-liberal work on the British Industrial Revolution beginning with Arnold Toynbee (1884), and in democratic work on material factors in US history beginning with the 'frontier thesis' of Frederick Jackson Turner (1893). Moreover, even at the moment of its apparent triumph, Marxist history was increasingly subject to internal tensions, particularly following the Soviet invasion of Hungary in 1956. This embarrassing failure of the major socialist regime raised questions about the political teleology that had underpinned the Marxist approach to history, and led to a re-examination of the confident economic determinism and a re-emphasis on the elements of cultural historicism in Marx's writings. This was particularly marked in Britain, with its strong native tradition of ethical and idealist socialism; one of the most influential contributions was Edward Thompson's (1963) study of the early nineteenth-century English working class. This emphasized political and religious traditions as much as economic structures, and interpreted them in their own terms rather than with the advantage of hindsight, producing the famous manifesto about rescuing even those who had followed backward-looking or Utopian ideas 'from the enormous condescension of posterity'. While undoubtedly leading to fresh insights into the experiences of ordinary people, this kind of work also launched Marxist history into an attempt to reconcile economic determinism and political agency, class structure and the autonomy of culture, within which it began to lose its coherence as a system.

The next great depression in the 1970s and 1980s then undermined rather than reinforced Marxism, as Western labour movements suffered reverses at the hands of reactionary regimes and the Soviet Union was completely discredited as a viable political alternative to liberal democracy. Those historians in the Marxist tradition who were still concerned with concrete historical analysis moved away from the old teleological framework through the deconstruction of key materialist categories such as class, and the inclusion of the impact of state activity within their range of social forces. As a result, their work became increasingly reabsorbed into the liberal mainstream. Those historians in the Marxist tradition who attempted to maintain a distinctive unifying focus tended to emphasize the determining impact of language on consciousness, and, where this went beyond a suggestive new approach to popular movements and became the basis of a critical approach to historical method, it sheared away not only the old materialist teleology but also any falsifiable approach to the analysis of cultural contexts. Ironically, then, many of those historians who still professed loyalty to the critical heritage of Marx began to propose an increasingly ungrounded version of historicism.

ALASTAIR J. READ
UNIVERSITY OF CAMBRIDGE

References

Dobb, M. (1946) *Studies in the Development of Capitalism*, London.
Labrousse, C.E. (1943) *La Crise de l'économie française à la fin de l'Ancien Régime*, Paris.
Marx, K. (1852) 'Marx to Weydemeyer, 5 March 1852', in K. Marx and F. Engels, *Collected Works*, Vol. 39, London.
Thompson, E.P. (1963) *The Making of the English Working Class*, London.
Toynbee, A. (1884) *Lectures on the Industrial Revolution of the Eighteenth Century in England*, London.
Turner, F.J. (1893) 'The significance of the frontier in American history', *Report of the American Historical Society*, Washington, DC.

Further reading

Hobsbawm, E. (1978) 'The Historians' Group of the Communist Party', in M. Cornforth (ed.) *Rebels and Their Causes*, London.
Prost, A. (1992) 'What has happened to French social history?' *Historical Journal* 35.

SEE ALSO: Marx; Marx's theory of history and society

MASS MEDIA

The term 'mass media' (plural of medium) refers collectively to various organized means of public communication. The main separate mass media are: printed books, newspapers and periodicals; radio; film, video and television; the Internet in some of its uses. Taken together they can be considered as a social institution with certain roles in society and governed by certain expectations, conventions, rules and regulations. The mass media are primarily concerned with the production and distribution of knowledge in the widest sense of the word, and have a number of salient characteristics, including the use of relatively advanced technology for the (mass) production and dissemination of messages; the systematic organization and social regulation of this work; and the direction of messages at potentially large audiences who are unknown to the sender and free to attend or not. The mass-media institution is essentially open, operating in the public sphere to provide regular channels of communication for messages of a kind determined by what is culturally and technically possible, socially permitted and in demand by a large enough number of individuals.

It is usual to date the beginnings of mass media from the first recognizably modern newspaper, in the early seventeenth century, which in turn was a new application of the technology of printing, already in use for over 150 years for the multiple reproduction of book manuscripts. The audiovisual and electronic forms that have subsequently been developed, mainly since the end of the nineteenth century, have caused existing media to adapt and have enlarged the total reach of media, as well as extended the diversity of their social functions.

This history of media development is, nevertheless, more than a record of technical advance and of increasing scale of operation. It was a social innovation as much as a technological invention, and turning points in media history are marked, if not caused, by major social changes. The history of the newspaper, still the archetypal as well as the first, mass medium, illustrates the point very well. Its development was linked to the emergence of the bourgeois (urban-business-professional) class, which it served in cultural, political and commercial activities. It became an essential instrument in subsequent economic and political struggles, a necessary condition for economic liberalism, constitutional democracy and, perhaps, also, revolution and bureaucratic centralism. Its development thus reflects not only political and economic forces but also major social and cultural changes. The latter include urbanization; rising living standards and the growth of leisure; and the emergence of forms of society that are, variously, democratic, highly organized, bureaucratic, nationalistic and committed to gradual change. Consideration of newer media, especially film, radio and television, and including the Internet, would not greatly modify this assessment. These media have not greatly widened the range of functions already performed by the newspaper as advertiser, entertainer and forum for the expression of opinion and culture.

During the early period of media development commentators were struck by the immense popular appeal of the new media and by the power that they might exert in society. Beyond that, views divided sharply on whether to welcome or regret the new instruments of culture and information, and a division between pessimists and optimists has been an enduring feature of assessments of mass media, starting to fade only as the inevitability and complexity of the media are accepted. The pessimistic view stems partly from the pejorative connotations of the term 'mass', which includes the notions of vast scale, anonymity, impersonality, uniformity, lack of regulation and mindlessness. At the extreme, the media were regarded, sometimes by conservative and radical critics alike, as instruments for manipulation, a threat to existing cultural and spiritual values, and to democracy. But optimists saw the mass media as a powerful means of disseminating information, education and culture to the previously excluded classes and of making feasible a genuine participatory democracy. By the 1930s some circumstantial evidence and enough theory supported both sides, but there was little systematic investigation.

The relationship between the mass media and the society in which they operate has always been controversial and uncertain. On the one hand, they can be considered as simply the means by which free expression and exchange of information and ideas can be attained. As such, it is not very appropriate to speak of the role or obligation of the media, except as services to would-be communicators and audiences. This view is upheld by established rights to press or media freedom and individual rights to free expression. On the other hand, most mass media are operated as large-scale, centralized, commercial enterprises and they both claim and are attributed a good deal of power and influence in society. Moreover, as noted, none of the major institutions of society including commerce, government, law or politics could operate effectively without the mass media. Leaving aside the question of harmful effects, from this point of view the media are too important to be left entirely without regulation or guidance. In practice, societies have developed complex forms of governance in which law, policy, custom and regulation as well as informal pressures help to ensure that essential roles are fulfilled. The use of media has become so integrated into the practices of organized social life that close and formal direction or control is not needed. Nevertheless, the question has been increasingly asked as to whether the media have acquired too much power to be left without control or accountability, given their unique capacity to reach the public directly and shape the impressions that the public acquires of 'social reality'. This is as much to do with the good they are capable of as well as the harm they can cause. It is also argued that other social institutions have become too dependent on the media.

If the mass media play an essential part in mediating a wide range of relationships within societies, they have also come to be seen as playing a comparable part in mediating relations between nation-states and world blocs. The flow of information and culture by way of mass media does much to establish and confirm patterns of perception, of hostility and attraction and also the relations of economic dependence and latent conflict between the different worlds of East and West, North and South. While mass media still largely consist of separate national systems, the increasing internationalization of networks and content is now interesting researchers.

The history of mass media has so far been fairly short and very eventful, but it already seems on the point of a new and significant departure that may change the essential character of mass communication. The most important developments are of smaller-scale, point-to-point and potentially interactive media, employing cable, satellite or computer technology. The Internet is the prime case. It is likely that there will be a continuing move away from centralized and uniform media of distribution towards a more abundant and functionally diversified provision of messages based on receiver demand. The boundaries between mass communication and the emerging new forms of information transfer are likely to become even more blurred in what is being hailed as an emerging 'information society'. Nevertheless, the issues that shaped early debates about mass media are still relevant in the new conditions, especially those that concern the contribution of mass communication to equality or inequality, order or change, unity or fragmentation. Because of their public functions, nationally and internationally, traditional mass media are unlikely to be replaced by the new media, except in so far as the latter become more like the old media.

DENIS MCQUAIL
UNIVERSITY OF SOUTHAMPTON

Further reading

Curran, J. and Gurevitch, M. (eds) (1996) *Mass Media and Society*, London.
McQuail, D. (2000) *Mass Communication Theory: An Introduction*, 4th edn, London.

SEE ALSO: globalization; information society; McLuhan; media effects; media and politics; popular culture

MATERIAL CULTURE

Material culture is an important source of evidence across the social sciences and humanities. It can be narrowly defined as the study of the material products of human manufacturing processes or, as George Kubler (1962) argues, more euphoniously, as 'the history of things'. As well as focusing on art and artefacts it usually encompasses the study of the technological processes involved in the manufacture of the objects and the conceptual systems within which they are embedded. It can also include the human construction of the environment as a cultural and economic landscape, since artefacts are instrumental in economic processes and landscapes are transformed through human action. In the social sciences, artefacts are viewed as part of culture and integral to the processes of social reproduction. They cannot be understood in isolation from the broader social and cultural contexts within which they exist.

In nineteenth-century anthropology, material objects were included with other cultural traits in the models of evolutionary theorists such as Pitt-Rivers, Tylor and Haddon. Material culture was taken to be an index of the level of social and cultural development of particular societies, and typological analyses established formal sequences that were assumed to demonstrate the evolution of societies from simple to complex forms. Diffusionist theorists, who were concerned to trace the origins of ideas, also used material culture as a major source of evidence. Probably because of its use as evidence in evolutionary and diffusionist theory, and its association with 'speculative history', material culture was largely neglected by British anthropology for the first half of the twentieth century. As a consequence the study of material culture was missing from the fieldwork revolution that began to transform anthropology at the turn of the century, when interest shifted to studying contemporary societies in their own right as functioning wholes. In the USA the situation was more complex. Material culture was an integral part of culture-area theory and the ecological evolutionary anthropology of White and Steward. Moreover, US archaeology maintained theoretical interest in material culture at a time when it was largely neglected in the rest of the discipline. From the 1960s onwards it was in the branches of ethnoarchaeology, 'new' archaeology and behavioural archaeology (Gould and Schiffer 1981) that much research into contemporary material culture was pursued.

The 1960s saw a general renewal of interest in the subject, stimulated by the growth of symbolic anthropology and the interest of archaeologists in the material culture of contemporary societies as a source of data for archaeological interpretation. Moreover, with the demise of functionalism and the move to a more historically informed theoretical framework, material culture came into its own again as a source of information that could add a time dimension to research (see Appadurai 1986). The separation of material culture from other social and cultural data is now recognized to be arbitrary, and objects have been reintegrated within social theory. This has had a dual effect: the opening up of a previously neglected body of data that provides insight into social processes, and a better understanding of the artefacts themselves. Material culture has been increasingly used as a source of evidence by social historians, psychologists and exponents of cultural studies. Research in material culture has contributed in particular to the literature on exchange, processes of value creation (Munn 1986) and to an understanding of processes of consumption.

The analytic core of research into material culture remains the explanation or interrogation of the form of material objects. Artefacts are uniquely material in nature: they can be recorded in detail and people can be questioned about their form. But the objective is, in part, to uncover through analysis the ideational systems that underlie the production and consumption of artefacts, to abstract from the surface concrete-

ness of their form by connecting them to history and relating them to the diversity of social processes. Analysis has often been framed in terms of semiotics or meaning (see Hodder 1989). It is, however, important to take a broad perspective on meaning that can relate the instrumental functions of an object to other dimensions of its value that may include such factors as aesthetics, style, symbolism and economics.

The concept of objectification has proved useful in the study of material culture. Material objects can be viewed as objectifications of the systems of knowledge, methods of production and division of labour used in their manufacture, and as objectifications of the values that are represented in patterns of consumption and contexts of use. This positioning of objects at the fulcrum of a process linking production with consumption has made them a fruitful subject for analysis. The analysis of material culture provides information on value creation, on the expression of individual identity and on the motivations underlying consumer behaviour. Increasingly material culture is being used as a source of information in the study of complex societies and global patterns and processes (Miller 1987).

As in the nineteenth century, social scientists are once again viewing material culture as important evidence for historical and global processes, but they have adopted new and very different theoretical perspectives. While there is still interest in material culture objects as indices of cultural boundaries and markers of social categories, researchers have become equally concerned with transformations in the value and meaning of objects as they move from context to context, either as part of local exchange systems or global trading processes (Thomas 1991). Material objects frequently outlast their maker; thus they are both sources of evidence about previous lifeways and objects to be reflected on by the generations who succeed their makers. As time progresses, artefacts often get caught up in ideological process and find themselves incorporated in new contexts that were never envisioned by their original manufacturers. The study of material culture encompasses the analysis of ideological restructurings, whether in the form of present-day heritage industry or in the process of the reinterpretation of rock art over the generations and its consequences on the production of later paintings. Material culture not only creates potential for but also constrains human action, and it is subject to human agency; people make meaningful objects but they can also change the meaning of objects. The important place the analysis of material culture has gained in contemporary anthropology has been reflected in the establishment of the *Journal of Material Culture*, which is devoted specifically to the subdiscipline.

HOWARD MORPHY
AUSTRALIAN NATIONAL UNIVERSITY

References

Appadurai, A. (ed.) (1986) *The Social Life of Things*, Cambridge, UK.
Gould, R. and Schiffer, M. (1981) *Modern Material Culture Studies: The Archaeology of Us*, New York.
Hodder, I. (1989) *The Meaning of Things: Material Culture and Symbolic Expression*, London.
Kubler, G. (1962) *The Shape of Time*, New Haven, CT.
Miller, D. (1987) *Material Culture and Mass Consumption*, Oxford.
Munn, N.M. (1986) *Fame of Gawa*, Cambridge, UK.
Thomas, N. (1991) *Entangled Objects: Exchange, Material Culture and Colonialism in the Pacific*, Cambridge, MA.

MATHEMATICAL MODELS

As mathematics is a powerful, flexible language and models are representations, mathematical models are representations framed in mathematical terms. The motivating force for using mathematical models is the need for clarity and precision. A good metaphor for a mathematical model is a map. A map is a simple device for representing a complex geographical locality. Much of the richness of the locality is removed in the representation but enough remains for it to be recognized. Whether the map is a good one depends not only on its properties but also on the use to which it is put. If you want to get through a city quickly, a simple map of the arterial routes suffices. For a walking tour of a city centre, a detailed map of the city centre is enough, and if you are hiking in open country a geological survey map works fine. Essentially, a model must make substantive sense, be technically adequate and have sufficient realism to make it useful.

Discussions of mathematical models are frequently co-ordinated by at least two of the following distinctions. One differentiates process models from structural models, the second deter-

ministic models from probabilistic ('stochastic') models, and the third differentiates models using discrete variables from those using continuous variables. In principle, an eight-cell table can be constructed using these three criteria and each cell filled with mathematical models sharing the criteria defining the cell.

Models of processes explicitly attempt to model change and provide an understanding of the mechanisms of change. Frequently used tools include differential equations and difference equations. Models of structure attempt to represent and understand the structure of social relations. Frequently used mathematical tools include graph theory and matrix algebra; also algebras such as groups, semi-groups and lattices find applications in these structural analyses, as well as category theory and algebraic topology.

Stochastic models are used to model processes whose outcomes are governed by a probabilistic mechanism(s). Many types of stochastic models are available to social scientists (see Bartholomew 1982). Deterministic models eschew stochastic mechanisms in favour of deterministic mechanisms and relations (see Epstein 1997). The process models of social change can be deterministic or stochastic. The structural models tend to be deterministic. Discrete models use variables that can take only one of the small number of states, whereas continuous models use variables that are, or can be, treated usefully as if they are continuous. For the process models, a further distinction can be made concerning the representation of time: it, too, can be taken as discrete or continuous.

Mathematical models have wide-ranging applications throughout the social sciences. A modeller selects a mathematical model well suited for a substantive problem where knowledge of alternative model candidates and selection of the most fruitful one(s) is critical. Mathematical modellers tend to draw on mathematics already developed using models formulated in other disciplines. This is unproblematic when the model captures the crucial theoretical aspects, and critical empirical components, of the substantive problem. Indeed, mathematical models draw their power from being devoid of substantive content: a mathematical model can be used fruitfully in different areas of one field and in many different fields. Seldom have mathematics been invented because of social science needs, which contrasts with the physical science tradition exemplified by the invention of the differential-integral calculus by Newton and Leibniz. Exceptions include game theory, decision theory and some areas of artificial intelligence research. So much for models, but what is a good model?

Good models must be adequate in all components of its methodology. The Theory–Model–Data triangle provides a way of discussing this. There are three pairs of mappings – between theory and model; between model and data; and between theory and data – and all are important (although different model builders may place differential emphasis on them).

The theory–model linkage is concerned with expressing a clear link between a theory and its representation in a mathematical model. The theory has to map into the model with little distortion or loss. Deductively, there is a mathematical formalization of the theory while, inductively, this can be a formal generalization of the theory. The mathematical model then has to be useful. Useful, here, means the machinery of the mathematical system has to be mobilized to derive mathematical results. These results can be mapped to the theory and to the data. Deductively, the model maps to the (empirical) data by specifying, or predicting, empirical outcomes. The model is truly predictive if it makes predictions that can be checked empirically. Sometimes models are not predictive in this sense. Instead they lead to the construction of descriptions based on data. Also deductively, the mathematical results (theorems) map to the theory by specifying the theoretical implications of the derivations through the mappings linking theory and model.

When the empirical predictions and specifications stemming from the model are confronted with data, several outcomes are possible. First, the predictions made on the basis of the theory and the model may be borne out providing support for the model. The results are filtered back through the mappings and interpreted substantively. Second, if a model calls only for empirical descriptions, these by themselves are not, at face value, too important. However, they must make sense when interpreted theoretically. Third, the model may lead to predictions that are disconfirmed, calling the model (and theory) into question. The model builder then has to establish if the model should be rebuilt or discarded. Further, this decision has other important impli-

cations: measurements must be good and sound empirical evidence is decisive.

The frequently made distinction between mathematical models and statistical analysis is a very blurred one. First, formal approaches often incorporate error specification (a theory of error) – which other approaches generally do not. This informs estimation. Second, the properties of the statistical tools are stated and established mathematically. Finally, new mathematical models and their uses generate new estimation problems and new statistical questions.

Space precludes discussion of the rest of the Theory–Model–Data triangle but each does constrain the others. The theory, the model and the data have to make sense and be consistent with one another.

The charge is often made that mathematical models overlook much of the richness and texture of social life. They do, and this is a virtue (which is not to say that the richness and texture are irrelevant). The claim that social phenomena are incredibly complex and that this complexity cannot be captured via mathematical models need not detain us. While the basic laws of physics are simple, for example Newton's laws of motion, they generate behaviours that are, and appear to observers as, very complex. Note also that complex mathematical formulae are generated from simple start points. A direct attempt to model complexity, for example, to predict the exact trajectory of a snowflake in a storm or a leaf in a wind, would appear bizarre and fruitless. Yet in the social sciences there are many attempts to model, in one way or another, the surface phenomena of human life. Given a distinction between noise and true signals, the modeller and the critic need to evaluate the model on the basis of (good) measurement of signals rather than of noise. While empirical evidence is decisive, not all measurements count. That social behaviour is complex cannot be denied, but the principles governing this behaviour need not be complex. They may even permit a mathematical description (which does not mean we have slavishly to follow the mathematical antics of the natural sciences – or even use the same mathematics). In this context, computer simulation models are used fruitfully.

Using simulation models offers a link between mathematical models and substantive phenomena. Social process rules can be embedded in computer code to generate social systems based on these rules. Simple rules can generate complex phenomena. For an extensive introduction to the use of simulation methods, see Gilbert and Troitzsch (1999). Hummon and Fararo (1995) discuss 'computational sociology' in terms of the use of computational methods in the context of formal and substantive modelling. When explicit mathematical models are used, the intent frequently is to establish analytical solutions given the model. When models become too complex for there to be analytic solutions, simulation methods can be very useful.

It does not follow that all social scientists should use mathematics, only that some do. While mathematical models are used quite frequently, only a minority of social scientists create and use them. Yet, even so, we can point to a powerful drive towards mathematical expression of and solutions to disciplinary, and, more strongly, interdisciplinary problems. Social science publications like the *Journal of Mathematical Sociology* and the *Journal of Mathematical Psychology* find counterparts among the natural sciences in the *Journal of Mathematical Physics* and *Mathematical Geology*. Of course, neither set validates the other. There are many publications without 'mathematics' in their title but that, nevertheless, carry a heavy mathematical imprint. These include *Psychometrika*, *Sociological Methodology*, *Social Networks*, *Geographical Analysis*, *Econometrica* and *Environment and Planning* (both Series A and B). Within all of these journals good mathematical social science can be found. What is less clear is whether all of this activity stems from an intrinsic need for the use of mathematics in a discipline or a crude imitation between fields. For genuine advance, it seems clear that a focus on significant problems is needed. Social network analysis provides one such focus, especially the evolution of social networks (see contributions in the collection edited by Doreian and Stokman 1997). There are many other such potential foci – all that is required is a good substantive problem.

PATRICK DOREIAN
UNIVERSITY OF PITTSBURGH

References

Bartholomew, D.J. (1982) *Stochastic Models for Social Processes*, 3rd edn, New York.
Doreian, P. and Stokman, F.N. (eds) (1997) *Evolution of Social Networks*, New York.
Epstein, J.M. (1997) *Nonlinear Dynamics, Mathematical Biology and Social Science*, Reading, MA.
Gilbert, N. and Troitzsch, K.G. (1999) *Simulation for the Social Scientist*, Buckingham.
Hummon, N.P. and Fararo, T.J. (1995) 'The emergence of computational sociology', *Journal of Mathematical Sociology* 20: 79–87.

Further reading

Edling, C.R. (2002) 'Mathematics in sociology', *Annual Review of Sociology* 28: 197–220.

SEE ALSO: networks, social; statistical reasoning

MAXIMIZATION

According to an oft-quoted view, economics is about 'doing the best one can in a situation of scarcity'. Many, if not most, problems in economics fall under this heading. For example, consumers are assumed to choose the best bundle of commodities out of the range possible given their income constraints. The government is assumed to choose its policies to do the best it can for society as a whole, again given the constraints it faces. Such optimization may be said to be at the heart of economic analysis. The mathematical counterpart of this essentially economic problem is the maximization of an objective function subject to constraints on the choice variables.

The general maximization problem may be written as

$$\text{Max}_{\underline{x}}\ W\ (\underline{x}) \text{ subject to } \underline{x} \in X$$

where $W\ (\cdot)$ is the objective function, $\underline{x}$ is the vector of control (or choice) variables. These are shown to be restricted to the set X, which therefore specifies the constraints of the problem. The *economics* of the problem lies in the specification of the objective function $W\ (\cdot)$ and the constraint set $\underline{X}$. However, once these are specified, we still have to solve the problem in order to derive further economic results of interest. This is where the mathematical theory of maximization comes in.

If $\underline{x}^*$ satisfies

$$W\ (\underline{x}^*) \geq W\ (\underline{x}) \text{ for all } \underline{x} \in X$$

then $\underline{x}^*$ is said to be a *global* solution to the problem. On the other hand, if the inequality holds only for $\underline{x}$ in a neighbourhood of $\underline{x}^*$, then

$\underline{x}^*$ is said to be a *local* solution to the problem. The *Weierstrass theorem* in mathematics says that, if the set X is compact and non-empty, and if the objective function $W(\underline{x})$ is continuous on X, then a global solution exists for the above problem. Most economic problems satisfy these conditions. However, can we say more about the nature of the solution $\underline{x}^*$? The answer is that we can, if we define the set $\underline{X}$ in greater detail.

For many economic problems the constraint set $\underline{X}$ can be specified implicitly as a series of inequalities that the control variable has to satisfy. Consider, therefore, the problem

$$\text{Max } W(\underline{x}) \text{ subject to } \underline{g}(\underline{x}) \text{ ø } \underline{b}; \underline{x} \text{ ù } Q$$

where $\underline{x}$ is a $n \times 1$ vector. The $\underline{b}$ and the $m \times 1$ vector of functions g define the constraints on $\underline{x}$. Consider now the following function

$$(\underline{x}, \underline{\lambda}) = W(\underline{x}) + \underline{\lambda} \cdot (\underline{b} - \underline{g}(\underline{x}))$$

where λ is a $m \times 1$ vector of non-negative auxiliary variables. The m elements of λ are known as Lagrange multipliers and $+ (\underline{x}, \underline{\lambda})$ is known as the Lagrangian of the problem. The *Kuhn–Tucker theorem* in non-linear programming then provides the conditions that characterize the solution to the problem. These conditions are

$$\frac{\partial}{\partial \underline{x}}(\underline{x}^*, \underline{\lambda}^*) \text{ ø } Q; \frac{\partial (\underline{x}^*, \underline{\lambda}^*)}{\partial \underline{x}} \cdot \underline{x}^* = O; \underline{x}^* \text{ ù } O$$

$$\frac{\partial}{\partial \lambda}(\underline{x}^*, \underline{\lambda}^*) \text{ ù } O; \underline{\lambda}^* \cdot \frac{\partial}{\partial \underline{\lambda}} \cdot (\underline{x}^*, \underline{\lambda}^*) = O; \underline{\lambda}^* \text{ ù } O.$$

The first part of the Kuhn–Tucker theorem says that if there exist $\underline{x}^*$, $\underline{\lambda}^*$ satisfying the above conditions, then $\underline{x}^*$ is a solution to the problem. The second part says that if $W(\cdot)$ is concave, $g(\cdot)$ are convex and there is some point $\hat{\underline{x}}$ for which the constraint is satisfied with strict inequality, then, for there to be a solution to the problem, there must exist $\underline{\lambda}^*$ such that $\underline{x}^*$, $\underline{\lambda}^*$ satisfy the Kuhn–Tucker conditions.

The Kuhn–Tucker conditions provide the basis for characterizing the optimum in most economic models. For example, if $\underline{x}^*$ ù Q, then we must have that

$$\frac{\partial}{\partial \underline{x}}(\underline{x}^*, \underline{\lambda}^*) = Q;$$

or

$$\frac{\partial W(\underline{x}^*)}{\partial x_i} = \lambda^* \cdot \frac{\partial g^*(\underline{x}^*)}{\partial \underline{x}_i} \text{ for } i = 1, 2, ..., n.$$

In the case where the problem is the consumer's problem of choosing quantities x_i to maximize the utility function $U(\underline{x})$ subject to a single budget constraint

$$\sum_{i=1}^{n} p_i x_i \text{ ø } y$$

these conditions become

$$\frac{\partial U(\underline{x}^*)}{\partial x_i} = \lambda p_i \ i = 1, 2, ..., n.$$

or

$$\frac{\partial U(\underline{x}^*)}{\partial x_i} = \frac{\partial U(\underline{x}^*)}{\partial x_j} = \frac{p_i}{p_j}$$

that is, the marginal rate of substitution between any pair of goods must equal the price ratio of those two goods. Similar conditions can be derived and interpreted for other problems. In fact the $\underline{\lambda}^*$ have interpretation in terms of shadow prices that tell us the values to the agent of releasing each constraint at the margin.

S.M. RAVI KANBUR
CORNELL UNIVERSITY

Further reading

Baumol, W. (1965) *Economic Theory and Operations Analysis*, 2nd edn, Englewood Cliffs, NJ.

Dixit, A.K. (1975) *Optimization in Economic Theory*, London.

Intriligator, M.D. (1971) *Mathematical Optimization and Economic Theory*, Englewood Cliffs, NJ.

Sundaram, R.K. (1996) *A First Course in Optimization Theory*, Cambridge, UK.

SEE ALSO: marginal analysis; optimization

MCLUHAN, MARSHALL (1910–80)

McLuhan was for a time one of the most cited authors in the field of study of mass communication, following the publication of his two main books, *The Gutenberg Galaxy* (1962) and *Understanding Media* (1964). Moreover, he was probably as well known outside the circle of academic media specialists as within it. After a fairly conventional career as a teacher of literature, he became a spinner of innovative theory and a publicist for his ideas about the consequences for culture and society of changes in communication technology – from writing to print and from print to electronic media. Although his assessment of television happened to be especially topical in the 1960s, he was also continuing a North American (perhaps especially Canadian) tradition of interest in technology, communication and the new. He owed the inspiration for his central thesis to a forerunner and colleague at the University of Toronto, the economic historian Harold J. Innis, who had traced the connection between changes in communication technology in the ancient and medieval world, and changing forms of political and social power. Innis argued that each medium had a bias towards a certain kind of application, message and effect, and thus, eventually, a bias towards a certain kind of society. A similar version of (rather soft) communication determinism was elaborated by McLuhan, with particular stress on the difference between the pictorial medium of television, which involves the spectator imaginatively and sensorily, and the medium of print, with its linear, sequential logic and its bias towards rationalism and individualism. A central element in his theory concerns the way in which we experience and understand 'reality'. He referred to media as 'extensions of man' and included under this heading almost all objects and forms that embody meaning. His ideas stimulated the development of a school devoted to 'medium theory', represented for instance in the work of Joshua Meyrowitz (see Meyrowitz 1985).

McLuhan's dicta are often best remembered summarily by his own catchphrase 'the medium is the message'. He was a controversial figure and it is impossible in a few words to strike an adequate balance in assessing his work. On the positive side were a lively imagination; a striking and aphoristic turn of phrase; an ability to cross academic boundaries and synthesize his eclectic finds. Furthermore, he seems to have exerted charm as a person and influence as a teacher. The principal entry on the debit side is that he lacked any discernible system of thought or adherence to an established tradition of research method, so that his many ideas are often both questionable and untestable. Whichever side one takes, he did call attention to the need to have an understanding of the means and vehicles of communication at an opportune moment and in a way that could not be ignored. In respect of his own message, the manner of delivery may well

have been more significant than the content. His central ideas have remained relevant as forms and technologies of communication have continued to evolve. He anticipated much subsequent debate about communication and 'globalization'. His approach had more in keeping with later postmodernism than with then-contemporary rationalism and scientism (reflecting the linearity of print culture). Most significant, perhaps, is that his thesis has been revived with reference to new computer-based media and the Internet, and possibly with more justification than in the case of television.

DENIS MCQUAIL
UNIVERSITY OF SOUTHAMPTON

References

McLuhan, M. (1962) *The Gutenberg Galaxy*, London.
—— (1964) *Understanding Media*, London.
Meyrowitz, J. (1985) *No Sense of Place*, New York.

Further reading

McLuhan, E. and Zingone, F. (1995) *Essential McLuhan*, New York.

SEE ALSO: mass media

MEDIA AND POLITICS

In all technologically advanced countries, the media have become a central political arena. Their most obvious importance lies in the huge audiences they reach, and the way these audiences transcend and cut across other social divisions and political constituencies. Just as importantly, the massive presence of the media acts as a force for disclosure from official institutions, and so has transformed political processes and created tensions surrounding the control of information and impressions.

The development of the media has always been intertwined with aspirations for democracy and struggles for political control (Keane 1991). The press had a deeply ambiguous history, chequered with political patronage, official subservience and expedient compromises. The news was reported with both fear and favour, as independent journalistic functions emerged uncertainly and erratically within what were primarily political instruments. But whether under state despotism, party patronage or under more solidly commercial bases, with the growth of the press barons in the nineteenth and early twentieth centuries, newspapers never manifested any golden age of journalistic purity. There have always been charges that the press appealed to 'baser' instincts, just as earlier forms of personal information exchange centred on salacious gossip (Stephens 1988) and that it indulged in sensationalism and wilful distortion.

The outcome from all these idiosyncrasies and expediencies was the invention of a qualitatively new institution, one devoted to disclosure and dependent on audience acceptance with its own priorities, incentives and constraints, whose growth was fanned by the competition for market share and/or political influence. One institutional dynamic was towards an ever increasing conception of what it could and should make public and to do so in ways that had the greatest audience appeal. Such imperatives made the media's route to their current political centrality inevitable.

Access to the media is now a key political resource. Efforts to influence media content and to counteract the attempts at media manipulation by opponents are an important battleground in many political conflicts. While media analysts have hesitated in pronouncing upon the political impacts of media, political participants certainly act as if the media have great power. From the time, when in their very different ways, Franklin Roosevelt and the German Nazis recognized the importance of radio, political leaders and activists from all parts of the spectrum have devoted great energy to influencing or controlling the media. Some terrorist groups have demanded media access among their demands, while others have planned their actions to achieve maximum international media exposure. Coup leaders typically commandeer broadcasting stations as one of their early targets, based upon an appreciation of establishing the appearance of control and the elimination of opportunities for counter-mobilization. Leaders in liberal democracies have sizeable staffs and resources devoted to achieving the most favourable media coverage.

The grievances of disaffected groups with a political system typically now include dissatisfaction with the media and its treatment of them. Disadvantaged groups and embattled leaders commonly blame the media as one key reason for their problems. However, discontents with the media are not limited to the politically disadvantaged. The performance of the media has attracted a variety of powerful but contrasting critiques. Dissatisfactions cross the political spectrum, provoking ideological critiques from both left and right. More embracingly, broadcasting, in particular, has been blamed for a cheapening of political discourse (Postman 1986); for the dominance of entertainment over political priorities; for the sale of political influence through advertising; and for being cognitively disabling and increasing popular political alienation.

However, the views of the critics are as contentious and problematic as the performance of the media. The power of the media to control public thinking has proved more limited than some feared. Many of the claims about media influence confuse visibility with power. Reassuringly, efforts at media manipulation by political leaders have met with mixed success. The collapse of communist regimes in Eastern Europe demonstrated that not even a generation of media control could secure them legitimacy from the populace.

The problems with claims about unidirectional ideological effects of the media go beyond the frequent difficulties of demarcating criteria and the transparent biases of the observers. Solely textual approaches to news, casting it in terms of myth or ideology, fail to capture its impact as a central institution, whose functioning affects the actions and relationships of key political participants. The media have been the focus of new complexes of political activity, including the growth of 'spin doctors' and other 'minders'. An institution devoted to disclosure sets up tensions, and is ripe for unintended consequences and many-sided conflicts. The suicide of British defence scientist, David Kelly, after being named as the source of a BBC story about the Government 'sexing up' intelligence reports to make Britain's participation in the 2003 Iraq War more politically palatable, was a stark demonstration of the intensity of such controversies.

Especially but not only in liberal democracies, the media's impact upon the processes of policymaking and the operation of other political institutions has been many-sided (Tiffen 1989). It has increased the government's speed of response. Prominence in the news has often influenced the priorities of political decision-making, media attention imparting 'heat as well as light' (Sigal 1973) upon issue agendas. When media attention changes the timing of decisions, their content and effectiveness may also change. Most fundamentally, news has enlarged the scope of information available to the public. It has broadened the geographical range of the world with which they are regularly acquainted and deepened their knowledge of their own societies and politics. An often overlooked consequence is that policy-making, or at the least the presentation of policies, is more constrained towards options that are publicly acceptable.

In these ways, the political significance of the media is far more profound and pervasive than the occasional deliberate exercise of power by those who occupy strategic positions in it – proprietors, editors, journalists or advertisers. Moreover the attribution of manipulative manœuvres to such media figures, when based solely upon external readings of content, often lack any grasp of the internal constraints and motivations.

Each new advent in media has been greeted by great hopes and fears. These are often to do with aspects of the quality of cultural and political life, not easily subjected to measurement. Nevertheless false forecasts have clearly abounded. Moreover, despite the importance of political influences on media developments, they typically unfold in ways not foreseen by media policymakers or would-be controllers. Media history bears ample testimony to the limited prescience of both policy-makers and their critics. Despite the difficulties of predicting future developments, two current trends promise to be of increasing political importance – the multiplicity of media outlets and trends towards internationalization.

The enormously increased technological capacity to deliver numerous channels to households, via satellites, cable and terrestrial services, has coincided with a trend, through most Western countries and in newly democratized polities, towards deregulation as a general policy stance. This has been particularly manifested in media and telecommunications policies, even though market rhetoric, centring on the consumer sovereignty brought by open competition, has rarely fitted media developments very well. The huge start-up costs, the desirable economies of scale in supply, production and distribution, and the logic of advertising strategies, all seem to lend themselves to oligopoly.

Many countries have allowed new commercial broadcasters to enter, at the same time as the finance available for public-service broadcasters has been squeezed. Most obviously the increased outlets will increase consumer choice, but the end of the process and its political implications are hard to foresee. Some say broadcasting will give way, at least in niche markets, to narrowcasting. The traditional democratic concern with massification is already being supplemented by a concern with fragmentation.

The second and partly related trend is an increase in media capacities to transmit information around the globe instantaneously. This is a central part of the growing political importance of transnational forces, and the increasing influence of international influences upon domestic politics. The media were one element, for example, in the international opinion that helped to buttress domestically reformist leaders like Gorbachev and Yeltsin, and one thread in the way international actions and support contributed to the success of the African National Congress and the relatively peaceful transition from apartheid in South Africa.

Increasingly, the audiences for news are becoming international, with consequences for the conduct of foreign policy and the control strategies of national regimes. The massive presence of the Western media probably prevented a bloodier regime crackdown during the fall of the Marcos regime in the Philippines in 1986. Chinese protesters deliberately appealed to the Western media in attempting to change domestic power balances during the protests that culminated in the 1989 Tiananmen Square massacres. All international conflicts are now accompanied by controversies over the media's coverage of them. Very different pictures of the Iraqi war were presented in Fox News and al Jazeera.

At the same time, trends have made the international flow of news and information even more unbalanced, the control of technology and commercial capacity has become more concentrated, the forces for international integration have in some important ways eroded national sovereignty, and the presence of Western advertising and programming will have unknown cultural effects upon new audiences.

The safest prediction is that the history of the media will continue to be ambiguous, with double-edged implications for many political ideals, and in an equally complicated and contentious but dynamic future, politics and the media will continue to develop inextricably bound to each other.

RODNEY TIFFEN
UNIVERSITY OF SYDNEY

References

Keane, J. (1991) *The Media and Democracy*, London.
Postman, N. (1986) *Amusing Ourselves to Death: Public Discourse in the Age of Entertainment*, London.
Sigal, L. (1973) *Reporters and Officials*, Lexington, MA.
Stephens, M. (1988) *A History of News: From the Drum to the Satellite*, New York.
Tiffen, R. (1989) *News and Power*, Sydney.

Further reading

McNair, B. (2000) *Journalism and Democracy: An Evaluation of the Political Public Sphere*, London.
Moeller, S.D. (1999) *Compassion Fatigue. How the Media Sell Disease, Famine, War and Death*, New York.
Norris, P. (2000) *A Virtuous Circle. Political Communication in Postindustrial Societies*, Cambridge.
Street, J. (2001) *Mass Media, Politics and Democracy*, London
Tumber, H. (ed.) (1999) *News. A Reader*, Oxford.

SEE ALSO: mass media; media effects; public sphere

MEDIA EFFECTS

The rise of mass media (press, film, radio, television, etc.) during the twentieth century has been accompanied by continuous claims and counter-claims concerning their effects. The term 'effects' refers to two essentially different things: the potential to inform and influence according to the wishes of mass-media senders, and the many, often unintended, consequences for individuals and societies that may have followed the extensive availability and use of mass media. Belief in the power and effects of media in both senses is founded on certain distinctive features of the new technologies for mass communication, especially their enormous capacity to carry information, sounds, images and ideas of all kinds; the possibility of reaching very large proportions of a national (and now a global) population almost simultaneously or in a very short time; the apparent capacity to overcome old barriers to communication, not only those of time and space, but also those of culture, age and economic differences; and the evidently great attraction of mass media to nearly everyone.

The potential of far-reaching effects of the two kinds mentioned is without question great and real. It is confirmed by everyday experience and simple observation of a world in which distant events are often common knowledge instantly, styles and fashions disseminated by the media are encountered in much the same form across the globe, and the routine of daily life is nearly everywhere patterned by the ubiquitous and rather similar television screen, radio and newspaper. Furthermore, an additional witness to the power of media can readily be found in the vast sums that are spent by advertisers and by propagandists of all kinds on mass media.

The first period of scientific investigation of mass media undertaken between the mid-1930s and the late 1950s resulted in a much more modest estimate of media effects than was previously assumed, even a new myth of media powerlessness. The earlier stimulus–response model of influence was replaced by a model of indirect influence, according to which the media were seen to be subject to mechanisms of selective attention, perception and response, such that any effects would be more likely to reinforce existing tendencies than to cause any major change. Further, the working of media was seen to be subordinate to the existing patterns of social and personal influence, and consequently not well conceived of as an external influence. While the evidence reassured many critics and discomfited prophets of doom, it seemed to lead to no slackening of efforts to use media, in ever more subtle ways, for political and commercial ends. Since the 1960s there has been further development in the assessment of mass-media effects in the direction of a renewed belief in their potency.

The earlier research, despite its reassuring message, left open the possibility that media effects could be considerable under certain conditions: first, where there exists a monopoly or uniformity of message content; second, where the messages seem to concern matters beyond immediate experience or direct relevance; and, third, where there is a cumulation over a long period of time of similar messages. Research attention accordingly shifted from the search for direct, short-time effects on individuals and towards the following: structures of ownership and control of media; patterns of ideology or culture in messages and texts; professional and organizational contexts in which media knowledge is manufactured. Assessing the influence of mass media, experts emphasize what people learn from the media, focusing on cognitive effects in the widest sense. We may learn from the media what is normal or approved, what is right or wrong, what to expect as an individual, group or class, and how we should view other groups or nations. Aside from the nature and magnitude of media effects on people, it is impossible to doubt the enormous dependence of individuals, institutions and society as a whole on mass media for a wide range of information and cultural services.

It can be said with some confidence that the mass media have, in general, the following main kinds of effects in significant measure. They provide us with much of our information about our near and extended environment; they influence our habits of consumption; they provide models and examples (positive or negative) that guide our development and behaviour; they help us to relax; they help us to participate in and relate more effectively to our social group and environment. At another level, it is also clear that the mass media now facilitate and influence the working of major social institutions, such as those of politics, government, the justice system and business. A longer-term and more general effect of mass media is the influence they exert on culture, whether this is taken to mean social habits and practices, symbolic goods produced and consumed, values, language use or cultural identifications (to nation, locality, social group, etc.).

In respect of these different kinds of media effects (individual, institutional or cultural), there is some consensus on the general direction of the effects that can be expected. In relation to individual information, opinions and behaviour, it is probable that people are influenced according to the dominant emphasis and direction in the media to which they are most exposed. Whatever receives most attention and is portrayed in a positive light by trusted or liked sources is, other things being equal, likely to lead to effects in line with the content of the media message. In respect of institutions, it begins to look as if the media, when taken up for institutional purposes, do serve these ends quite well, but they also have a significant effect on the institutions themselves as they adapt their activities to the potential and the demands of the media. In respect of culture, the media tend to promote the homogeneity of culture nationally and internationally (the phenomenon of cultural 'globalization'). Another feature is the rise of a new form of media culture that is an outcome of technology, a new class of cultural producers, and a new industrial and commercial system.

This conventional wisdom concerning the effects of the mass media is often invoked as a general truth, largely because it is tried and tested, and fits much everyday observation. It is only part of the story, however. It does not explain why there is so much dispute, debate and continued searching for harder evidence to back the general hypotheses formulated. The main reasons for uncertainty are as follows. Both intended and unintended effects of mass media can be perceived as either good or bad, and there are often vested interests in claiming or denying one or the other; mass media can rarely be separated out and measured as a single causal factor, except in the most simple laboratory conditions; effects are far from unidirectional and are rarely predictable except in the most general terms; there are many and varied individual, social and cultural barriers to media effects; the mass media are also continually changing, as new technologies change the potential and as the societal context changes.

In respect of individuals, the main area of dispute has concerned the potential for mass media to encourage the imitation or learning (especially by young people) of aggressive, anti-social or undesirable values and behaviour. This charge by critics of the media has been answered by some controls on content, inconclusive research and by claims that the mass media teach many more pro-social than anti-social messages. In general, they do seem to be on the side of the established order (a point of objection for another group of critics). Advertising and political communication are the institutional forms that have been subjected to most scrutiny. This has produced somewhat contradictory assessments, as have studies of possible media effects in other spheres. On the one hand, research has failed to prove their effectiveness very clearly. On the other hand, they are blamed for a variety of ills, including manipulation of consumers, and the fostering of political cynicism. A self-fulfilling prophecy can often be discerned, since perceptions of media potency are influential even when reliable evidence of media effects is missing or contradictory. The potential for mass communication to integrate society and homogenize culture has also to be weighed against the view that mass media can have isolating and atomizing effects on social life, through encouraging privatization and individual consumerism. The media may offer a new global media culture to all, but they also undermine and weaken traditional and particular cultures. In most of these disputes, the standards of evidence required to settle questions of media effects cannot be attained by social research, even if the parties in dispute would be ready to listen.

In any case, it is clear (although only fragmentarily demonstrable) that mass media do normally have inconsistent and even contradictory effects, which depend on the circumstances of context and place. At the root of this observation is the crucial fact (which has often been demonstrated) that effects are produced by people themselves, individually and in institutions, in interaction with media but not by the media directly. This applies whether the effects are considered as information, behaviour, opinions or expressions of value. A one-sided media-centric view of social and cultural change has tended for too long to dominate discussion of media effects, although it has been clearly rejected by current theory and research. In the new era of more interactive media it is even more important to consider the role of the recipient of media as well as that of the communicator. The expression 'media effects' is itself misleading, although it will have to continue to serve as a signpost for a much more complex phenomenon.

DENIS MCQUAIL
UNIVERSITY OF SOUTHAMPTON

Further reading

Bryant, J. and Zillmann, D. (eds) (2002) *Media Effects*, Mahwah, NJ.
Comstock, G., Chaffee, S., Katzman, N., McCombs, M. and Roberts, D. (1978) *Television and Human Behavior*, New York.
McQuail, D. (2000) *Mass Communication Theory*, 4th edn, London.
Perse, E. (2001) *Media Effects and Society*, Mahaw, NJ.

SEE ALSO: mass media; media and politics

MEDICAL ANTHROPOLOGY

It is not possible to find a definitive text or even adequately to summarize the most popular and populous subdiscipline of anthropology in the USA and most rapidly growing elsewhere. Articles in the *Medical Anthropology Quarterly*, published by the American Anthropological Association, tend to ignore foreign writing. (For European perspectives, see Diasio 1999.)

The reactions of people in other societies and cultures to the occurrence of disorders centred on the body have always interested anthropologists and physicians, and the many who practise in the combined fields. W.H.R. Rivers was interested in the native response to disease, as was the US psychiatrist, Caudill (1958), whose *The Psychiatric Hospital as a Small Society* remains a classic. Most assumed that physical disease was a natural occurrence, existing independently of specific cultural beliefs. Thus when Victor Turner (1964) was commissioned by the Rhodes–Livingstone Museum to study Lunda medicines, both he and his sponsors assumed that while healing practice would be culturally variable, the diseases to which it was a response would be fixed. Turner himself was apologetic lest his lack of medical knowledge hindered his recognition of which 'real' diseases were being treated, and Janzen (1978) later enlisted a physician to avoid similar embarrassment. Another physician, Fabrega, recognized that the perception of disease entities and the measures taken against them might be seen as parts of other systems of more or less consistent thought rather than merely defying conventional Western wisdom (Fabrega and Silver 1973). This last, of course, owed much to Arab ideas reaching Europe through Spain as did some aspects of medical thought in the Americas. Local practices could therefore be analysed and described as ethnomedicine in their own right rather than seen as an inadequate, perhaps magico-religious, stage on the way to one true definitive, scientific understanding. While Frake (1961) and his successors were able to perceive system in relatively unchallenged and unitary, pristine, if complex form, scholars like Leslie (1977) in India and Kleinman (1978) in China were faced with complicated situations in which vast numbers of people seemed able to live with, and within, apparently incompatible systems of belief about bodily ills and how to heal them. This, like the second-wave pattern of new age imported complementary-medicine alternatives that share the names, if not the exact practices, of their cultural origin, seems to be achieved without apparent feelings of cognitive discomfort. 'Medical pluralism', as it came to be known, was similarly observed in Africa, where, despite political ambivalence (Comaroff 1981; McCullough 1983), Western medicine was partially embraced at the same time as longer existing, but seemingly inconsistent, views were developed instead of being abandoned.

The persistence of such pluralism, however, did cause discomfort to anthropologists about the adequacy of their own theories. In the English-speaking world a series of conferences in the early 1970s, also participated in by African, Antipodean, Asian and European scholars (see Loudon 1976), initiated a theoretical rethinking that is still vigorously in progress and which increasingly draws, in addition to anthropology, on contributions from, among others, philosophy, sociology, literary criticism, history and social studies of science and technology (see, e.g., Good 1994; Lindenbaum and Lock 1993; Mol 2003). This has involved, sometimes in uneasy partnership, even within the same person, both medically qualified and lay scholars recognizing the validity of different interpretations of the same set of perceived deviations from a norm of physical health and well-being. Kleinman (1978) called these diverse perceptions *explanatory models*. He identified those who held them as variously using (relatively unsystematized) popular, folk and professional discourses to arrive at models that might be centred broadly either on views of the nature of physical bodily experience (*disease*) and/or on subjective experience of suffering (*illness*).

Others, influenced by ethnography and current ideas in medical sociology, emphasized, in addition to disease and illness, a separate category of *sickness* (Young 1982). This last was defined either as social causation (in the continuing tradition of Virchow and eighteenth-century public health) or as cultural performance – building on Turner's (1982) later work – or as a combination of the two. First, this was intended to enable escape from the danger fallen into by incautious, biomedically committed but anthropologically unsophisticated, readings, which represented illness and disease as merely a contrast in perceptions between an objective, true and realist medical analysis and a subjective, false and imaginary patient view; knowledge was contrasted with mere belief. Second, it allowed for the possibility even, and perhaps especially, in

industrial society that the parameters of sickness might be seen as including not only technological, social and politico-economic factors before, but also, after the event, ritual and instrumental elements of culturally legitimate healing processes. These might be as diverse as exorcism of spirits and hospitalization or the wearing of amulets, the prescription, denial and use of drugs or the incorporation of heart pacemakers or hip prostheses.

By the mid-1980s, two trends seemed to be dominating understanding of bodily disorder in its social and cultural context. The first was associated with the developing radical critique (mainly outside anthropology) of the political economy and social organization of biological medicine (termed 'biomedicine'), which was centred round the concept of sickness. The second focused not so much on illness as such, as on the cultural process by which it was given meaning by sufferers and their helpers (Hahn 1983). Here the crucial concept was *suffering*, from whatever physical or other cause it had arisen.

While these intellectual debates were in train in the USA, much useful ethnography was being carried out and published (see, e.g., Bastos 1999 and Whiteford et al. 2000), and professionalization was in process. A Society for Medical Anthropology had been formed within the American Anthropological Association and flourished to the extent of producing a newsletter and then transforming it into a fully fledged journal. The first article in this *Medical Anthropology Quarterly* was by Scheper Hughes and Lock (1987) and pointed out that the emperor had all too many clothes. So much focus had been placed either phenomenologically, on how disorder was suffered, or critically, on how it was created, that the physical body that endured the ills had all but disappeared from view behind a screen of European philosophies. The authors sought to remedy this by drawing from more ethnographically situated theories of Mauss, Mary Douglas and other symbolic anthropologists about the body social; from history and sociology about the body politic and social control; and, above all, by drawing from non-Western philosophy, Western phenomenological writings, non-biomedical and minority biomedical views, and feminist thought, in order to formulate a counter-theory to the dualistic thinking about the body and its ills that (they argued) had dominated much Western culture at least since Descartes.

Their article, and the discussions of which it formed the centre, served to reflect and to crystallize a much more widespread tendency to see sickness in terms of personal agency. The description of biological disease had been transcended, if not replaced, by the situated praxis of embodied persons in misfortune. In their theory and in their practice, medical anthropologists had come to argue that their concern with the multiple aspects of failure in the lived body had led them back from a biomedically dominated applied empiricism at the periphery of social and cultural anthropology to the centre of a more general anthropological discipline. Misfortune is seen as causing persons to question their cultural ability to produce and reproduce their social being and personal identity – a threat to ontological security. Its analysis helps to make possible for all, including those charged with the care and cure of the sick, self-understanding of the most life-changing aspects of shared human consciousness.

RONALD FRANKENBERG
BRUNEL UNIVERSITY

References

Bastos, C. (1999) *Global Responses to AIDS: Science in Emergency*, Bloomington, IN.

Caudill, W.A. (1958) *The Psychiatric Hospital as a Small Society*, Cambridge, MA.

Comaroff, J. (1981) 'Healing and cultural transformation: The Tswana of Southern Africa', *Social Science and Medicine* 15B(3).

Diasio, N. (1999) *La Science impure: anthropologie et médecine en France, Grande Bretagne, Italie, Pays Bas*, Paris.

Fabrega, H. and Silver, D. (1973) *Illness and Shamanistic Healing in Zinacantan: An Ethnomedical Analysis*, Stanford, CA.

Frake, C.O. (1961) 'The diagnosis of disease among the Subanum of Mindanao', *American Anthropologist* 63.

Good, B.J. (1994) *Medicine, Rationality and Experience: An Anthropological Perspective*, Cambridge, UK.

Hahn, R. (1983) 'Rethinking "illness and disease"', *Contributions to Asian Studies* 18.

Janzen, J.M. (1978) *The Quest for Therapy in Lower Zaïre*, Berkeley, CA.

Kleinman, A. (1978) 'Concepts and a model for the comparison of medical systems as cultural systems (see also commentary by Alan Thomas)', in C. Leslie (ed.) *Theoretical Foundations for the Comparative Study of Medical Systems, Social Science and Medicine* (special issue) 12B.

Leslie, C.M (1977) 'Pluralism and integration in the Indian and Chinese medical system', in D. Landy (ed.) *Culture, Disease, and Healing: Studies in Medical Anthropology*, London and New York, pp. 511–17.

Lindenbaum, S. and Lock, M. (eds) (1993) *Knowledge, Power and Practice: The Anthropology of Medicine and Everyday Life*, Berkeley, CA.

Loudon, J. (ed.) (1976) *Social Anthropology and Medicine*, London.

McCullough, J. (1983) *Black Soul, White Artifact: Fanon's Clinical Psychology and Social Theory*, Cambridge, UK.

Mol, A. (2003) *The Body Multiple: Ontology in Medical Practice*, Durham, NC, and London.

Scheper Hughes, N. and Lock, M. (1987) 'The mindful body: A prolegomenon to future work in medical anthropology', *Medical Anthropology Quarterly* 1.

Turner, V. (1964) *Lunda Medicine and the Treatment of Disease*, Rhodes–Livingstone Museum Occasional Paper no. 15, Livingstone, Northern Rhodesia.

—— (1982) *From Ritual to Theatre: The Human Seriousness of Play*, New York.

Whiteford, L.M. and Manderson, L. (eds) (2000) *Global Health Policy, Local Realities: The Fallacy of the Level Playing Field*, Boulder, CO.

Young, A. (1982) 'Anthropologies of illness and sickness', *Annual Review of Anthropology* 11.

SEE ALSO: medical sociology; public health; transcultural psychiatry

MEDICAL SOCIOLOGY

Medical sociology is concerned with the broad preserve of medicine in modern society. Since its emergence in the 1950s, the subject has expanded rapidly, making it one of the largest (if not the largest) specialized areas of sociology. This growth is partly due to the realization that many of the problems confronting modern health care are essentially social in nature; however, it also reflects the growing interest of medicine itself in the social aspects of illness, particularly in relation to psychiatry, paediatrics, general practice (or family medicine), geriatrics and public health. The patronage of medicine has provided the wherewithal for much academic expansion in the form of appointments, an extended teaching role and ease of access for research funds and settings. But medical sociology has had to pay a price for this alliance (and reliance) on medicine in terms of a distortion of emphasis in the problems, methods and theories judged appropriate for the discipline.

Medical sociology first emerged as a distinct area of study in the 1950s. The first specialist journal in the field, the *Journal of Health and*

Human Behaviour (later the *Journal of Health and Social Behaviour*), was launched in 1960. In these early years, despite the ascendancy of structural-functionalism, medical, psychological and psychosocial perspectives predominated. The new postwar interest in social epidemiology, for example, which sought to identify the role of social factors in the causation of disease, was pursued by both interested physicians and sociologists. Early studies showed the influence of social structure, in particular of social class, in the aetiology of both psychiatric and organic disease, though identification of specific social mechanisms proved more difficult.

The failure to establish the intervening variables between social structure and disease led many sociologists to explore aetiology at the level of individual stress. Although more the province of the psychologist, stress was seen to offer the possibility of bridging the gap between the social and the biological, especially when refined to encompass life events and notions of loss. In early studies, research tended to concentrate on those illnesses, such as psychiatric disturbances, which seemingly lacked biological correlates, and so could not be explained wholly in biological terms. However, the net has widened considerably to embrace organic diseases with supposed biological causes, as it is recognized that this does not preclude an often important role for social factors in either establishing susceptibility or in actually triggering the onset.

The interest in social factors in illness, together with the contemporary discovery (through morbidity surveys conducted by both sociologists and physicians) of a symptom iceberg in the community, led to another important area in the early development of medical sociology, namely illness behaviour. Given that symptoms were so prevalent in the community, the traditional medical model, which viewed symptoms as a simple stimulus to seek help, seemed inappropriate. More complex answers were needed to questions as to why people consulted the doctor, and studies explored the particular patterns of behaviour and reactions to stress and illness that affected the decision to seek medical help.

If social epidemiology and illness behaviour were subjects that emerged at the interface between medical sociology and medicine, other research topics such as 'labelling' and the sociology of the professions were obviously more closely drawn from general sociology. 'Labelling theory' and the notion of 'stigma' were applied at an early stage to particular diagnostic groups, such as physically handicapped and mentally ill people. The medical profession itself provided an archetypal occupational organization for those sociologists intent on exploring the role of professions in the occupational division of labour.

While such issues in general sociology were taken up in medical sociology, they tended to be explored in a medico-centric way. The medical profession, with its supposed esoteric knowledge, and altruistic code of service, was seen as an ideal for the aspiring paramedical occupations. If there is one contemporary slogan that sums up the early years of the subdiscipline, it is the difference between sociology *in* medicine and sociology *of* medicine, though arguably the latter was by far the weaker partner. Even so, by 1967 the field of medical sociology was sufficiently well expanded for the appearance of another journal, *Social Science and Medicine*, which in its title steered a neutral course between the conflicting claims of the two medical sociologies.

If it were possible to identify a year or a particular text as marking a watershed in medical sociology, there might well be agreement that the publication of Freidson's *Profession of Medicine* in 1970 was a significant event. It offered a synthesis of earlier studies on professions, labelling, medical organization, patient perceptions and so on, and it was to be marked out as a key text in establishing the formal identity of medical sociology. At the same time, as its subtitle – 'a study of the sociology of applied knowledge' – implied, Freidson indicated a new direction for the discipline. At root, both illness *and* disease were social constructs, reflections of social organization, professional interests, power relations and so on. Freidson's achievement was to liberate medical sociology from the confines of medically defined categories, whether it was in the profession's beneficent view of itself, or in the supposed biological and objective nature of illness. He opened up patient experience and medical knowledge to more penetrating and systematic analysis.

During the 1970s and 1980s, health care delivery and health policy were subjected to a more critical theoretical approach, particularly from sociologists of a Marxist persuasion, who argued the case for fully resourced and equitable state provision. However, in the 1990s the triumph of the market (on both sides of the Atlantic) as a means of distributing health care drove the sociologist of health care on to unfamiliar territory. The state still (and increasingly so in the USA) underwrites the resources, but 'controlled markets' are meant to provide the necessary consumer choice and competition. Yet, despite the rhetoric on what policy is, or should be, sociologists are discovering from more local and grounded studies that 'health policy-in-action' is a more negotiated and precarious process than official accounts might lead one to suppose.

Interest in the detail of social life has also found expression in patients' experience of illness. Formerly studied only as an adjunct of illness behaviour, patients' views of illness are now investigated in their own right. Medical theories of illness may claim coherence and validity, but it seems that patients' explanatory frameworks may also be sophisticated. Borrowing from medical anthropology, sociologists view patients as needing to know the answer to the questions 'Why me?' 'Why now?' and 'Why this (illness)?' In following up such questions, qualitative methodologies have come to dominate empirical work with patients.

The corollary of the acceptance that patients' theories of illness are as meaningful as medical ones is a recognition that medical knowledge itself can be the object of critical sociological enquiry. Only since the end of the eighteenth century has medicine reduced illness to an intracorporal pathological lesion, a fact which indicates that medical knowledge is both culturally and historically located. Medical knowledge may be explored not as a form of superior scientific truth, but as a means available to controlled, alienated or depoliticized people in the conduct of their lives. Equally, it can be argued that medical knowledge and practice play a crucial role in fabricating the analysable and calculable body of modern society.

The title of a new journal, *Sociology of Health and Illness*, first published in 1979, perhaps reflected more accurately the widening interests of this branch of sociology than the term 'medical sociology'. Nevertheless, the ties with medicine remain. Many medical sociologists are employed by medical institutions or on medically defined tasks. Indeed, many of them are directly concerned to ameliorate patient suffering, not least through the rapidly expanding field of

health services research. Medicine, however, is a fickle ally. The promise of the sociology–medicine alliance that was so crucial in establishing the discipline in the 1970s is under threat as medicine's biological underpinning is reinvigorated by the New Genetics. The challenge now is whether medical sociology should embrace the new biology, or rather treat it as simply another manifestation of a social world. As ever, medical sociology occupies an uneasy space between major disciplines.

DAVID ARMSTRONG
KING'S COLLEGE, UNIVERSITY OF LONDON

Reference

Freidson, E. (1970) *Profession of Medicine: A Study of the Sociology of Applied Knowledge*, New York.

Further reading

Bloom, S.W. (2002) *The Word as Scalpel: A History of Medical Sociology*, Oxford.
Brown, P. (ed.) (2000) *Perspectives in Medical Sociology*, Long Grove, IL.
Cockerham, W.C. (2003) *Medical Sociology*, 9th edn, Upper Saddle River, NJ.
Fitzpatrick, R., Hinton, J., Newman, S., Scambler, G. and Thompson, J. (1984) *The Experience of Illness*, London.
Foucault, M. (1963) *The Birth of the Clinic: An Archaeology of Medical Perception*, London.
Goffman, E. (1961) *Asylums: Essays on the Social Situation of Mental Patients and Other Inmates*, Harmondsworth.
Kleinman, A., Eisenberg, J. and Good, B. (1978) 'Culture, illness and cure', *Annals of Internal Medicine* 88.
Starr, P. (1982) *The Social Transformation of American Medicine*, New York.

SEE ALSO: body; epidemiology; genomics; health economics; medical anthropology; medicine, history of; morbidity; public health

MEDICINE, HISTORY OF

Doctors have long been conscious of traditions of the past. One of the Hippocratic treatises (third century BCE) was entitled *Ancient Medicine*, and the veneration long accorded to Hippocrates, Galen and other ancient medical writers guaranteed a steady stream of editions of classical authors well into the seventeenth century. From the eighteenth century, historical surveys of medicine began to be produced by doctors such as John Freind, Daniel Leclerc and Kurt Sprengel.

Physicians seeking membership in the Royal College of Physicians of London were still expected to be literate in the literature of antiquity until the mid-nineteenth century, but the growth of science within medicine, the development of national traditions within Europe and places where European influences dominated, and the increased use of the vernacular in teaching and writing gradually raised awareness of the present at the expense of the past, rendering the ancients genuinely *historical* figures.

In late nineteenth-century Germany, the history of medicine was energetically pursued by a number of doctors and philologists, and Institutes for the History of Medicine were established in several universities, most importantly in Leipzig, where Karl Sudhoff held the chair from 1905 to 1925. Henry Sigerist, Owsei Temkin and Erwin Ackerknecht all worked in Leipzig before emigrating to the USA, from the late 1920s. Whereas the history of medicine had previously been viewed as part of cultural or intellectual history, Sigerist brought to his scholarship a vision of the wider social forces that have always shaped notions of health and disease, and the doctor–patient encounter. As director of the Institute of the History of Medicine at Johns Hopkins University from 1932, Sigerist helped create a small professional discipline in his adopted country, and encouraged doctors to take seriously the study of their profession's past.

By the 1950s, medical history was being taught within a few medical schools in the USA, Germany, Spain and several other countries, and most professional medical historians came to the subject from a medical background. At the same time, parallel developments in the history of science helped foster a wider scholarly community. Most historians were comfortable operating within the ordinary conventions of 'Whiggism' (Herbert Butterfield's phrase), in which the study of medical history revealed the gradual triumph of truth over error, and science over superstition.

Since the 1960s, the practice of medical history has changed. From being a subject pursued largely by doctors for doctors, it has become the concern of scholars from many disciplines, including (*inter alia*) economic and social history, historical demography, sociology and anthropology. This has meant that the centre of gravity of academic history of medicine has shifted from the medical schools to social sciences departments.

Allied to this has been the greater range of sources brought to the discipline. Traditionally, medical historians concentrated on the great names and famous achievements of the past. Medical historians are now as likely to be interested in health as in the history of disease and discovery, to be concerned with the ordinary and mundane as with the elite, to write about the patient as the doctor. To this end, new kinds of printed and manuscript sources as well as artefacts have been put to the service of medical history. These include such materials as self-help manuals and advice books, diaries and personal papers of ordinary doctors as well as sufferers, the administrative and financial records of medical institutions, case books and iconographical material, legal records and theological tracts. Once health is included in the discipline's brief, the terrain becomes very wide.

The medical history being written today is more probing than of old. It has challenged comfortable notions of inevitable progress and disinterested professional behaviour. Several topics have been actively pursued. Following Michel Foucault's pioneering work in the 1960s, the history of psychiatry has attracted much attention. Historians have argued that definitions of mental disorder are historically contingent and psychiatry itself has been an agent of social control. Fringe and alternative practitioners have been rescued from historical oblivion. Tropical medicine has been revealed to be a tool of empire. Women, both as healers and as sufferers, have been minutely scrutinized. The politics of health and welfare have been analysed.

To accommodate these kinds of enquiries, a number of new journals and societies have been established. These have supplemented rather than replaced more traditional outlets and associations, and tensions between doctors and historians occasionally surface. The social history of medicine has been accused of having left the medicine out. Nevertheless, the subject has expanded and become more confident, even in an era of widespread academic retrenchment.

W.F. BYNUM
WELLCOME INSTITUTE FOR
THE HISTORY OF MEDICINE

Further reading

Brieger, G.H. (1980) 'The history of medicine', in P.J. Durbin (ed.) *A Guide to the Culture of Science, Technology and Medicine*, New York.

—— (1993) 'The historiography of medicine', in W.F. Bynum and R. Porter (eds) *Companion Encyclopedia of the History of Medicine*, London.

Porter, R. and Wear, A. (eds) (1987) *Problems and Methods in the History of Medicine*, London.

Webster, C. (1983) 'The historiography of medicine', in P. Corsi and P. Weindling (eds) *Information Sources in the History of Science and Medicine*, London.

SEE ALSO: medical sociology

MEMES

'Meme' is a word coined by Richard Dawkins (1976) to identify cultural traits with the ability to replicate themselves. By now, the word 'meme' has gained sufficient currency to be included in the *Oxford English Dictionary*, where they are defined as 'an element of a culture that may be considered to be passed on by non-genetic means, especially imitation'. The idea that social learning involves the replication of particles of information separates memetics from other positions on the nature of cultural evolution, which either argue that the social transmission of information is unimportant (e.g. evolutionary psychology, sociobiology), or that it need not involve information replication (e.g. gene-culture coevolutionary theory) (Laland and Brown 2002). The fact that memes are supposed to vary, be inherited and suffer from selection pressures makes them, potentially at least, the foundation of an evolutionary theory of cultural change. Further, memes are evolutionary agents believed to be interested in preserving themselves. For a memeticist, not only are cultural traits identifiable as individualized units, or memes, but also they have the power to cause, in some way, their own duplication. This means that memes can be responsible for the persistence of cultural traits that do not directly favour the biological fitness of the group in which those traits find themselves.

Dawkins originally thought that memes could encompass behaviours, artefacts or mental contents as varied as 'tunes, ideas, catch-phrases, clothes fashions, ways of making pots or building arches' (Dawkins 1976). However, he later argued that only mental information had the ability to duplicate itself (Dawkins 1982).

Although Dawkins originally intended memes to serve primarily as a counterfoil to genes as an alternative example of how a replicator might work (Dawkins 1989), a minor industry has been devoted to explicating the role of memes in the human way of life (Blackmore 1999; Dennett 1995; Aunger 2000, 2002). At the same time, very little empirical work has been inspired by the meme idea, and even some of its primary proponents doubt that memetics can ever become a proper science (Dennett 1995). An exception to the general lack of empirical utility of the meme idea is seen in studies of how birdsongs evolve over time and space. Lynch (1996), for example, showed that the frequency of various vocal elements in chaffinch songs ('memes') has systematically changed in ways predictable from selective evolutionary forces working on bird populations.

Social scientists have been wary of extending this kind of approach to humans. This is partly because memetics is intended to be a Darwinian, rather than Lamarckian, theory of cultural evolution. In this respect, memeticists deny that cultural novelties are intentionally directed at solving particular problems, or that people modify cultural traits in ways that can then be directly learned by others (an instance of the inheritance of 'acquired' variation). Critics argue that ignoring human rationality and intentionality, and hence the meaningfulness of human behaviour, destroys the legitimacy of the memetic project (e.g. Kuper 2001). At the same time, there is no theoretical reason to suppose that just because culture evolves it must be founded on evolution in a replicator. Biological evolution may be grounded in the replication of a biological entity, genes, but this does not imply that every evolutionary process must be – Darwinism is a more general framework, involving simply the variation, selection and retention of information (Cziko 1997).

Memetics is beset by a variety of other problems, large and small. One of the more crucial problems is that the standard model of meme selection is tautological: successful memes are defined only by the fact that they persist over time, rather than because they have an independent quality that causes them to flourish over specified alternatives (e.g. Blackmore 1999). A non-tautological model of meme selection is put forward by Aunger (2002), based on evidence about mental representation and the management of information from neuroscience. But his claims remain untested.

One of the smaller problems with memes is that memetic mutation rates may be orders of magnitude higher than for genes (Dawkins 1976; Dennett 1995). But models show that memes may even change every time they are reproduced without invalidating the central claim that memes serve as the foundation of evolutionary lineages (Henrich and Boyd 2002).

A more significant complaint is that memetics does not articulate well with theory in psychology about the way in which social learning occurs. The view that memes are 'mind viruses', capable of diffusing through populations of host victims at will, seems to deny that brains have significant sophistication at filtering the information they imbibe from their surroundings.

A related problem derives from the fact that memeticists typically identify imitation as the replication mechanism used by memes. The suggestion is that if imitation is defined as the ability to copy behaviour or ideas by observing them, then surely the product of that observation must be replicated information. However, even if social transmission is a process in which information might be duplicated, it does not follow that the information itself is responsible. Other processes – such as common mental mechanisms for inferring mental or cultural content from sensory stimuli – could lead to the same result. The fact that humans have sophisticated social learning abilities does not prove the existence of memes.

If evidence for the replication of information through social communication is not empirically validated, then the idea that memes exist should be abandoned. Scientists will then no longer have any reason to refer to memes in their explanations of sociocultural phenomena. This would still represent a contribution to science, since it would eliminate one hypothesis for how culture works. But scientists would then be left with the interesting prospect of having to develop an evolutionary theory of cultural change that does not depend on the replication of bits of information. Meanwhile, the meme concept continues to inspire discourse in a variety of disciplines, from history to computer science, and to populate the popular media.

ROBERT AUNGER
UNIVERSITY COLLEGE LONDON

References

Aunger, R. (ed.) (2000) *Darwinizing Culture: The Status of Memetics as a Science*. Oxford.
—— (2002) *The Electric Meme: A New Theory of How We Think*, New York.
Blackmore, S. (1999) *The Meme Machine*, Oxford.
Cziko, G. (1997) *Without Miracles: Universal Selection Theory and the Second Darwinian Revolution*, Cambridge, MA.
Dawkins, R. (1976) *The Selfish Gene*, Oxford.
—— (1982) *The Extended Phenotype*, Oxford.
—— (1989) *The Selfish Gene*, 2nd edn, Oxford.
Dennett, D. (1995) *Darwin's Dangerous Idea*, London.
Henrich, J. and Boyd, R. (2002) 'Why cultural evolution does not require replication of representations', *Culture and Cognition* 2: 87–112.
Kuper, A. (2000) 'If memes are the answer, what is the question?' in R. Aunger (ed.) *Darwinizing Culture: The Status of Memetics as a Science*, Oxford, pp. 175–88.
Laland, K. and Brown, G. (2002) *Sense and Nonsense: Evolutionary Perspectives on Human Behaviour*, Oxford.
Lynch, A. (1996) 'The population memetics of birdsong', in D.E. Kroodsma and E.H. Miller (eds) *Ecology and Evolution of Acoustic Communication in Birds*, Ithaca.

Further reading

Aunger, R. (in press) 'Three roads to cultural recurrence', in Dan Sperber (ed.) *The Epidemiology of Ideas*, Chicago.

MEMORY

The study of human memory investigates the reception and encoding of information and the later influence of retained information upon behaviour, either in the processes of remembering and recognizing, or in other more indirect ways. A useful distinction, generally accepted in the area and originally made more than 100 years ago by William James (1890), is that between *primary* and *secondary* memory. Primary memory refers to short-term retention whereas secondary memory refers to long-term retention. Both these broad domains of human memory have been extensively investigated since James's original proposal; they can be divided into a number of discrete types of memory, some of which are associated with distinct brain areas and others of which are distinguished by different types of knowledge and memory processes. Two major advances in the last 20 years have been the application of this understanding of human memory to neuropsychological disorders and to consciousness and memory.

The concept of primary memory encompasses the very brief retention of literal aspects of an event as well as the somewhat more durable retention of information in *working memory*. Temporary fast-decaying and easily overwritten sensory memory stores such as *iconic* and *echoic* memory retain perceptual and auditory information, respectively, in a literal manner for periods measured in fractions of a second. These sensory memory stores facilitate, for example, the smooth perception of films and unbroken perception of sequences of utterances and music. However, the human brain rapidly extracts information from sensory memory stores and recodes it into appropriate forms for retention in working memory, where it can be retained for a period of a few minutes, or longer if it is frequently rehearsed. For example, speech-based auditory information is recoded into phonological form for immediate output (as in repetition) or for further processing in terms of meaning. A structure called the *phonological loop* is thought to mediate this recoding; this structure has been identified as critical in the acquisition of language and vocabulary by children. Patients who have suffered damage to the phonological loop through brain injury, that is, in strokes, viral diseases and through head injury, although still capable of producing speech, can no longer process novel speech input. For example, they cannot learn new languages.

In contrast the concept of secondary memory refers to long-term storage over periods of hours, months, years, decades and even a lifetime. Long-term memory is the terminus of information flow through the memory system and consists of a massively complex and extensive system of durable retention. Three classes of knowledge are often distinguished in long-term memory. First, *procedural memory* refers to knowledge that cannot be brought into consciousness but which underlies and supports the retention and execution of skilled and practised behaviour. For example, many people can whistle, ride a bicycle or sign their name, but no one can introspect upon this; these skills are known only by being performed. In the later stages of degenerative brain diseases such as Alzheimer's disease, striking impairments of procedural memory are often evident. Second, *semantic memory* refers to facts and knowledge about the world. This knowledge can be consciously retrieved and stated. People know *a tiger is a cat*, *a robin is a bird* or *London is the capital of England*, and can answer many additional questions about such facts. Interestingly, in some cases of brain injury the ability to make such judgements can be selectively lost. For instance, some brain-injured patients lose the ability to make correct semantic judgements about living things while retaining an ability to make comparatively normal judgements about artefacts. For other patients this pattern is reversed. Taken together, these sorts of findings suggest that the representation of semantic knowledge in the brain may be highly structured. Third, *episodic* or *autobiographical memory* refers to memory for experienced episodes and events. In amnesia this type of memory may become impaired so that although patients' ability to recall memories from the period before their injury or illness remains intact, their ability to create or encode new memories is totally lost. Such patients have intact short-term working memories and so can perform some everyday tasks and hold short conversations, but as they are unable to create new memories they remain unaware of tasks that have been completed and conversations that have been conducted, even when these occurred only a few minutes previously.

Perhaps the most intriguing and certainly the most hopeful finding is that amnesic patients who cannot create new autobiographical memories can none the less acquire new information. For instance, amnesic patients shown a list of words and some minutes or hours later asked to recall the list not only may fail to recall any words but may even fail to recall that they were shown any words. However, if instead of recall the patient is asked to make some response that does not entail explicit remembering then strong evidence of the retention of the original word list can be demonstrated. So powerful is this implicit learning or memory that amnesic patients have, for example, been taught to operate computers (when this was something they did not do prior to their injury), and, with appropriate social and memorial supports, some amnesic people have been able to return to work. The reality of implicitly remembering has now been extensively investigated in non-brain-damaged individuals where it is sometimes referred to as *fluency*. This captures the nature of implicitly remembering as, typically, some current task is speeded and made more fluent when it features items processed in an earlier episode, even though these are not consciously recalled at the time. Consider how quickly and fluently you can now read the word 'neuropsychological'.

Current understanding of human memory based on theories developed in the psychological laboratory is now providing important insights into memory dysfunctions following brain injury and age-related memory changes. The current research initiative into conscious and non-conscious aspects of memory promises to expand this understanding in important directions.

MARTIN A. CONWAY
UNIVERSITY OF BRISTOL

Further reading

Baddeley, A.D. (1990) *Human Memory: Theory and Practice*, Hove.
Collins, A.F., Gathercole, S.E., Conway, M.A. and Morris, P.E. (eds) (1993) *Theories of Memory*, Hove.
James, W. (1890) *Principles of Psychology*, Vol. 1, New York.
Parkin, A.J. (1993) *Memory: Phenomena, Experiment, and Theory*, Oxford.

SEE ALSO: ageing; cognitive neuropsychology; cognitive psychology; mental imagery; thinking

MEMORY, SOCIAL

The concept of social memory was defined in the early twentieth century by the French sociologist Maurice Halbwachs (1877–1945). A loyal disciple of Emile Durkheim, Halbwachs undertook the task of defining and analysing memory as a 'social fact'. His theoretical loyalty to the Durkheimian school, which developed by way of a reaction against the ideas of his initial master, the philosopher Henri Bergson, led him to advance a theory of 'collective memory' that has much in common with Durkheim's notion of 'collective consciousness'. His goal was to demonstrate that memory was not a product of an inner consciousness, but a cognitive skill acquired in a social setting, the product of the human capacity for social interaction. Individual memories can only unfold, like language, in the context of social interactions and in relation to collective idioms, images and ideas. Equally, collective memory, though structured by rules of social organization and cultural expression, can only be present in the individual mind (Halbwachs 1925, 1992 [1950]).

Halbwachs discussed forms and expressions

taken by the collective memory among artists, among the working class, in religious beliefs and in family life. His essay, 'The legendary topography of the gospels in the Holy Land' (in Halbwachs 1992 [1950]), introduced the dimension of space in the analysis of memory, which had conventionally been treated only in relation to time.

After a long period of neglect, Halbwachs's pioneering studies were taken up in the 1970s and 1980s, initially by social historians associated with the Parisian *Annales* School, who were attempting to study popular perceptions of the large movements of history, which Braudel had termed the *longue durée* (Le Goff 1996 [1986]; Nora 1996–8 [1984–92]; Valensi and Wachtel 1991). Drawing on Halbwachs's intellectual heritage, these historians insisted on the methodological value of oral history and autobiography. Personal testimonies and narratives were granted a legitimate status as sources of historical research. Halbwachs's influence was also apparent in the appreciation that collective memories may be of interest to scholars even if they are historically unreliable (Yerushalmi 1982).

Social and cultural anthropologists later drew particular attention to the interplay between collective memory and identity (e.g. Bahloul 1996). For anthropologists, too, the notion of social memory stimulated methodological initiatives. Life histories and personal narratives were given new attention, and narratives were now viewed by ethnographers as strategies of empowerment, resistance and history-making (e.g. Herzfeld 1991). Following the collapse of the Berlin Wall, anthropologists showed how Eastern European peoples began to draw upon restored sources of memory to support strategies of political and ideological decolonization (Verdery 1996). Other scholars studied expressions of collective memory to help them to understand the vernacular perception of colonial domination, the aftermath of decolonization and the experience of migration (Bahloul 1996). A number of studies drew attention to the ways in which collective memory may manipulate time so as to generate either oblivion or silence, especially when it relates to traumatic past (Lapierre 1989).

Social memory is now generally treated as the source of often invented traditions, which may be a resource for the legitimation of a social or political status (Hobsbawm and Ranger 1983). Many studies emphasize the objectified forms of collective memory, as it is inscribed in material culture, in monuments or in private artefacts. Connerton has drawn attention to the ritual structure of memory performance, in both national secular commemorations and in religious services (1989).

Sturken has analysed the history and the form of the Vietnam Veterans' Memorial in Washington, DC, and revealed the ways in which the monument is not only the product of collective memory, but also itself creates new forms of remembrance, endowed with a range of cultural and political meanings, and generates fresh representations of war, victory and mourning (Sturken 1991).

JOËLLE BAHLOUL
INDIANA UNIVERSITY

References

Bahloul, J. (1996) *The Architecture of Memory*, Cambridge, UK.
Connerton, P. (1989) *How Societies Remember*, Cambridge, UK.
Halbwachs, M. (1925) *Les Cadres sociaux de la mémoire*, Paris.
—— (1992 [1950]) *On Collective Memory*, Chicago.
Herzfeld, M. (1991) *A Place in History: Social and Monumental Time in a Cretan Town*, Princeton, NJ.
Hobsbawm, E. and Ranger, T. (eds) (1983) *The Invention of Tradition*, Cambridge, UK.
Lapierre, N. (1989) *Le Silence de la mémoire*, Paris.
Le Goff, J. (1996 [1986]) *History and Memory*, New York.
Nora, P. (1996–8 [1984–92]) *Realms of Memory*, New York.
Sturken, M. (1991) 'The wall, the screen, and the image: The Vietnam veterans' memorial', *Representations* 35: 118–42.
Valensi, L. and Wachtel, N. (1991) *Jewish Memories*, Berkeley, CA.
Verdery, K. (1996) *What Was Socialism and What Comes Next?* Princeton, NJ.
Yerushalmi, H.Y. (1982) *Zakhor: Jewish History and Jewish Memory*, Seattle.

Further reading

Casey, E.S. (1987) *Remembering: A Phenomenological Study*, Bloomington, IN.
Küchler, S. and Melion, W. (eds) (1991) *Images of Memory: On Remembering and Representation*, Washington, DC.
Lowenthal, D. (1985) *The Past Is a Foreign Country*, Cambridge, UK.
Nora, P. (ed.) (2001) *Rethinking France*, Chicago.
Yates, F. (1969) *The Art of Memory*, New York.

SEE ALSO: Annales School; oral history

MENTAL HEALTH

The concepts of mental health and illness have come to play a central role in the way that Western societies understand and regulate themselves. In the process, they have undergone a series of transformations. The view of mental disorders as 'illness' or 'disease' gained currency during the rise of the psychiatric profession in the mid-nineteenth century. It did not imply that all such disorders had a physical cause, for psychiatry recognized 'functional' as well as 'organic' types of mental illness. (In the early nineteenth century, indeed, asylum doctors often interpreted mental illness in terms of a breakdown of reason or morality, and the favoured way of dealing with it was called 'moral treatment'.) Nevertheless, the concepts of mental illness and health resembled their physical counterparts in one respect: they constituted a clear dichotomy.

From the beginning of the twentieth century the organization of mental health care – and with it the concept of mental health itself – changed drastically. New forms of treatment, such as psychoanalysis, were developed to replace incarceration, with the aim of intervening before disturbances became totally disabling. New professions (e.g. psychotherapy, social work and clinical psychology) came into being. Inspired by the dramatic results that hygienic measures had achieved in the fight against disease, the Mental Hygiene Movement in the USA set out to find the psychic equivalents of clean drinking water and good drainage. In the wake of these developments, mental health and illness lost their 'all-or-nothing' character and came to be regarded simply as two poles of a continuum, with an infinite number of gradations in between.

During the twentieth century three further developments took place. First, the range of conditions that can potentially be classified as mental illness expanded dramatically to include almost every kind of failure to cope or deviation from normality: from drug abuse to broken marriages, from eating disorders to religious fundamentalism. Second, mental health professionals (like their counterparts in physical medicine) have devoted more attention to the healthy end of the continuum, i.e. to the 'normal' population and the way it lives. Third, all traces of moral content have gradually been expunged from the concepts of illness and health; in keeping with the positivist ideals of most psychiatrists and psychologists, the aim has been to provide a non-judgemental, scientifically objective account of human problems.

With these changes, the concept of mental health acquired a crucial influence on the way that human problems are formulated and dealt with, and the associated professions have expanded greatly in power and numbers. Kittrie (1971) refers to 'the therapeutic state', Castel *et al.* (1982) to the 'psychiatric society'.

The last two decades of the twentieth century saw a renewed emphasis on biochemical approaches to mental illness. Research in this area has been increasingly concerned with the effects of psychotropic drugs, and is often financed by the companies that market these drugs. At the same time, the greatly increased demand for mental health services has led to increased attention to their efficiency and financial management. 'Managed care' favoured standardized methods that could achieve demonstrable, quick results, and this provided a further boost to the pharmacological approach.

One more development at the end of the twentieth century deserves mention: the increased attention for the relevance of cultural differences in mental health. At a global level, there has been a recognition that theories and methods developed in Western mental health care might not be applicable without modification to non-Western countries (Kleinman and Cohen 1997). The same considerations apply in modern multicultural societies, where services have to be provided for groups varying greatly in social position and cultural background. The rise of 'transcultural psychiatry' (e.g. Kleinman 1980) has provided a steadily increasing challenge to established views on mental health.

Modern perspectives on mental health

Social scientists have approached mental health in two main ways. Some ally themselves with psychiatry and carry out epidemiological research on the connection between mental illness and the social environment. Classic studies in this vein are those of Hollingshead and Redlich (1958), who found an increased incidence of mental illness in lower social classes, and Brown and Harris (1978), who identified pre-disposing and precipitating factors in women's depression.

Others, however, adopt a more critical stance. Some see the mental health professions as a vast apparatus of social control: these writers, following Szasz (1961), regard mental illness as a myth – a smokescreen for repressive interventions in people's personal lives. This critique came to the fore in the 1960s in the work of Goffman (1961), Scheff (1966) and the 'anti-psychiatrists'. However, the idea that psychiatry simply 'medicalizes' deviance never gained widespread acceptance. Such a notion seems warranted if one thinks of forcibly sedated prisoners, political activists or schoolchildren; but it runs into problems when treatment is actively sought by people anxious to get rid of their symptoms. Indeed, it is precisely when people appear to have no control over their behaviour and when it fails to make sense that the concept of mental illness is invoked (Ingleby 1982).

In the late 1970s a different critical approach to the mental health professions came to the fore. Foucault (1980) and his followers emphasized that power in the modern state is typically 'productive', not 'repressive': the discourses of psychiatry and psychology actively help people formulate their projects and their problems. They are not ideological *distortions* of reality: they help to *produce* reality itself. The sociologist De Swaan (Brinkgreve *et al.* 1979) coined the term 'proto-professionalization' to describe the way that lay-people avidly internalize the viewpoint of professionals. However central the concept of mental health may be to the management of social problems, we cannot regard it as something imposed from above.

This, however, does not imply that there is no room for criticism. First, though modern professionals are more often seen as friendly partners than as police officers, they have considerable power in shaping the way that we make sense of our world. Writers such as Lasch (1977) have questioned whether we are wise to entrust such power to them. Second, the aura of moral neutrality which professionals cultivate is misleading; their views always contain an implicit normative commitment to certain ideals. Feminists, in particular, have shown up the patriarchal assumptions underlying supposedly objective analyses of women's psychological problems. Third, though the medical model may be much more complex and sophisticated than it was in the 1890s, it still takes the individual as its unit of analysis. If problems – such as those of young mothers, elderly people, migrants, homeless or unemployed people – are routinely reduced to personal ones, it is extremely hard to reconstruct them as collective ones. Although critical approaches to mental health have not figured prominently in social science since the 1970s, such a crucial and contentious concept is unlikely to escape attention indefinitely.

DAVID INGLEBY
UTRECHT UNIVERSITY

References

Brinkgreve, C., Onland, J. and De Swaan, A. (1979) *De opkomst van het Psychotherapeutisch Bedrijf* [*The Rise of the Psychotherapy Industry*], Utrecht.

Brown, G. and Harris, T. (1978) *Social Origins of Depression*, London.

Castel, F., Castel, R. and Lovell, A. (1982) *The Psychiatric Society*, New York.

Foucault, M. (1980) 'Truth and power', in *Power/ Knowledge: Selected Interviews and Other Writings 1972–1977*, Hassocks.

Goffman, E. (1961) *Asylums: Essays on the Social Situation of Mental Patients and Other Inmates*, New York.

Hollingshead, A.B. and Redlich, F.C. (1958) *Social Class and Mental Illness*, New York.

Ingleby, D. (1982) 'The social construction of mental illness', in A. Treacher and P. Wright (eds) *The Problem of Medical Knowledge: Examining the Social Construction of Medicine*, Edinburgh.

Kittrie, N. (1971) *The Right to be Different*, Baltimore, MD.

Kleinman, A. (1980) *Patients and Healers in the Context of Culture: An Exploration of the Borderland between Anthropology, Medicine and Psychiatry*, Berkeley, CA.

Kleinman, A. and Cohen, A. (1997) 'Psychiatry's global challenge', *Scientific American* (March): 74–7.

Lasch, C. (1977) *Haven in a Heartless World: The Family Besieged*, New York.

Scheff, T. (1966) *Being Mentally Ill: A Sociological Theory*, London.

Szasz, T. (1961) *The Myth of Mental Illness*, New York.

Further reading

Ingleby, D. (ed.) (2004) *Critical Psychiatry: The Politics of Mental Health*, 2nd edn, London.

SEE ALSO: DSM-IV; social problems; transcultural psychiatry

MENTAL IMAGERY

The term 'mental imagery' is used in two ways. It refers to a subjective experience, 'seeing with the mind's eye', 'hearing with the mind's ear' and so on. It is also used to refer to a specific way in which information is represented and processed, which happens to produce such experiences. In this latter sense, a mental image is a perceptual representation that is stored briefly in short-term memory. Most research is concerned with image representations. Imagery can be studied with a variety of techniques, which range from behavioural observations (e.g. the time required to use images in certain ways, or the effects of imagery on accuracy) to neuropsychological assessments (e.g. deficits following brain damage, or brain areas that are activated during imagery). Visual imagery has been the topic of most research.

Purposes of imagery

Imagery has at least seven functions. First, it plays a role in some forms of reasoning and problem-solving by allowing one to predict the outcome of a specific action; for example one can look in a crowded cupboard and see how to rearrange the contents to make space for another box (Finke 1989). Second, one can use imagery to reason about abstract concepts by visualizing symbols, such as graphs or Venn diagrams. Third, imagery can help one to comprehend verbal descriptions of specific situations. Fourth, imagery is used when one recalls visual or spatial information that has not been verbally coded; for example consider how you try to recall what was on your dinner table last night. Fifth, imagery can help one to memorize information; for example memory for pairs of words increases substantially if one visualizes the named objects as if they were interacting in some way (see, e.g., Bower 1972; Paivio 1971). Sixth, imagery can be used to help one improve skills; by visualizing oneself practising an action, one can calibrate the stored information that directs that action. Finally, when subjects were asked to record their images on an hourly basis, they reported that most imagery occurred in daydreams (Kosslyn *et al.* 1990). However, the subjects reported that even such aimless imagery sometimes reminded them of an important oversight or gave them an idea.

Imagery relies on many of the same neural mechanisms that are used in like-modality perception (Kosslyn *et al.* 2001). Visual images not only interfere with visual perception more than with auditory perception (and vice versa for auditory images), but also can be confused for actual stimuli (Craver-Lemley and Reeves 1987; Finke 1989; Johnson and Raye 1981). Some visual illusions also occur in imagery (e.g. Berbaum and Chung 1981); brain damage that disrupts perception also tends to disrupt imagery in the same way (Farah 1988). However, the two abilities are not identical, as witnessed by the fact that brain damage can sometimes affect them separately (Kosslyn 1994). Brain-scanning techniques have revealed that very similar parts of the brain are activated during visual imagery and visual perception. Indeed, it appears that visual memories are sorted in an abstract form, and at least some images are reconstructed in parts of the brain that are topographically organized; these images actually depict information. Other types of images, however, may not be picture-like in this way. This, though, is an area of controversy (Roland and Gulyas 1994; Kosslyn and Thompson 2003).

Imagery processing

Once images are formed, they can 'stand in' for actual objects in many ways. One can scan over imaged objects, rotate them, 'zoom in' on them, fold them and so on; in all cases, the more processing (scanning, rotating, zooming, etc.) that is required, the more time is required (Kosslyn 1994; Shepard and Cooper 1982).

Images occur when input is retained briefly or when one activates stored information to generate an image. An image of a single shape apparently is generated by the same mechanisms that prime one to see a specific object during perception, but in imagery this priming is so strong that the pattern is reconstructed. If one needs a detailed image, additional parts are added, one at a time, into the image (see Kosslyn *et al.* 1988). The processes used to add parts are complex, and draw on mechanisms in both cerebral hemispheres. Counter to the common wisdom, imagery is not a right-hemisphere process (for a review, see Kosslyn 1994).

STEPHEN M. KOSSLYN
HARVARD UNIVERSITY

References

Berbaum, K. and Chung, C.S. (1981) 'Muller–Lyer illusion induced by imagination', *Journal of Mental Imagery* 5.

Bower, G.H. (1972) 'Mental imagery and associative learning', in L. Gregg (ed.) *Cognition in Learning and Memory*, New York.
Craver-Lemley, C. and Reeves, A. (1987) 'Visual imagery selectively reduces vernier acuity', *Perception* 16(5).
Farah, M.H. (1988) 'Is visual imagery really visual? Overlooked evidence from neuropsychology', *Psychological Review* 95.
Finke, R.A. (1989) *Principles of Mental Imagery*, Cambridge, MA.
Johnson, M.K. and Raye, C.L. (1981) 'Reality monitoring', *Psychological Review* 88.
Kosslyn, S.M. (1994) *Image and Brain: The Resolution of the Imagery Debate*, Cambridge, MA.
Kosslyn, S.M., Cave, C.B., Provost, D. and Von Gierke, S. (1988) 'Sequential processes in image generation', *Cognitive Psychology* 20.
Kosslyn, S.M., Ganis, G. and Thompson, W.L. (2001) 'Neural foundations of imagery', *Nature Reviews Neuroscience* 2: 635–42.
Kosslyn, S.M., Segar, C., Pani, J. and Hillger, L.A. (1990) 'When is imagery used? A diary study', *Journal of Mental Imagery* 14.
Kosslyn, S.M., and Thompson, W.L. (2003) 'When is early visual cortex activated during visual mental imagery?' *Psychological Bulletin*, 129(5): 723–46.
Paivio, A. (1971) *Imagery and Verbal Processes*, New York.
Roland, P.E. and Gulyas, B. (1994) 'Visual imagery and visual representation', *Trends in Neurosciences* 17 [including commentaries].
Shepard, R.N. and Cooper, L.A. (1982) *Mental Images and their Transformations*, Cambridge, MA.

Further reading

Paivio, A. (1986) *Mental Representations*, New York.
Tippett, L. (1992) 'The generation of visual images: A review of neuropsychological research and theory', *Psychological Bulletin* 112.
Tye, M. (1991) *The Imagery Debate*, Cambridge, MA.

SEE ALSO: sensation and perception; vision

METHODS OF SOCIAL RESEARCH

The term 'method' is widely used in social enquiry. A great range of research writing and teaching is provided in the social sciences under such titles as *Research Methods* (Burgess 1993), *Methods of Social Research* (Stacey 1969), *Social Research Methods* (Bryman 2001), *Sociological Research Methods* (Bulmer 1984), *Survey Methods in Social Investigation* (Moser and Kalton 1971), *A Methodology for Social Research* (Sjoberg and Nett 1968) and *Methods of Social Study* (Webb and Webb 1932). As a consequence, some clarification is required on the different terms that are used to discuss work on research methodology and research methods, given that both these terms are ambiguous and lack clarity. Some of the key terms that are used in discussions of methodology include *general methodology*, which is associated with the principles guiding an empirical enquiry; *research strategy* or *research procedure*, which refer to the way in which a particular study is designed and conducted; *research process*, which denotes the interrelationship between the activities that occur within a project and the principles and procedures that are used; and *research techniques or methods*, referring to specific fact-finding operations that yield social data. These issues are of equal importance in all forms of social research, and need to be considered in relation to each other. Techniques and methods of investigation should not therefore be seen in isolation. They must be linked to the substantive problems that the researcher wishes to investigate. The research problem in an investigation determines the methods of investigation that are to be used. The methods that are used are also linked to the philosophical and epistemological issues that a project raises, and to the social processes that occur within a project. Issues relating to the research process may lead to the modification of the methods that are used. Within the social sciences there are a range of methods that can be used, and it is the task of researchers to select which are most appropriate for their studies so that reliable and valid data are collected.

The choice of research methods that are available to social scientists has been well summarized by de Vaus (1996) in terms of experimental methods, survey methods and case-study methods. To these approaches we must add documentary and historical methods. There is a range of different styles of investigation based on experiments, surveys, case studies (including ethnography) and documentary and historical methods that include the use of written texts as well as non-text materials. The researcher may use a combination of the different approaches available in order to deal with issues concerned with validity through methodological triangulation (the use of different methods, theories, investigators and data) (Denzin 1970).

Investigators who use different approaches to social research may use similar methods. Interviews, questionnaires, observation and documents are appropriate in many forms of social research. The distinguishing feature of research

projects is the way in which the data are collected using these different approaches, and in turn the way in which analysis takes place. Interviews may be structured with specific questions, which include closed (fixed choice) as well as open-ended responses, or unstructured where similar topics are raised through an interview agenda. Structured interviews often involve the use of interview schedules that are completed by an interviewer, while unstructured interviews are frequently tape-recorded and subsequently transcribed (Burgess 1984, 1993; Hammersley and Atkinson 1995).

Observation includes systematic observation that includes the use of particular schedules such as Flanders Interaction Analysis (Croll 1986), or may be closer to participant observation as used in many anthropological and some sociological studies (Burgess 1984). The collection of documentary evidence may take a variety of forms including written material, oral histories (collected by interview) and photographic and visual evidence (Scott 1990).

Some writers discuss social research in terms of opposing styles of investigations, and make comparisons to highlight the differences between them. However, researchers will get little benefit by engaging in arguments about the superiority of one technique as opposed to another. Instead, there is a need to focus on research problems using as wide a range of methods of research as are available. Indeed, Mitchell (1977) has highlighted the similarities involved in surveys and case-study (ethnographic) research.

While researchers perform an important role in the conduct of social surveys, they play a greater part in ethnographic studies where they are central to data collection. In each case, the researcher has to consider the use of different methods in relation to the particular project. However, researchers also need a knowledge of the key methods associated with the principal styles of social investigation.

(1) *Experiments* measure the effects of manipulating one variable on another. Usually, samples are taken from known populations and are allocated to different experimental conditions. Such an approach usually involves hypothesis testing. The problems that such an approach can deal with include internal validity, that is, the extent to which a study establishes that a factor or variable has caused the effect that is found, and external validity, that is, the degree to which

findings can be generalized from a sample to a population. Researchers have also developed the quasi-experiment that has been designed to apply the principles associated with experimental work in laboratories to field situations so that comparisons are made between different groups within the field.

(2) *The survey* is probably the most common method of social investigation that is used in social research. It is often associated with the use of a questionnaire or a formal interview. Such schedules are developed, piloted and finalized before a study is actually conducted. Accordingly, questionnaire design, attitude measurement and question wording are important aspects associated with social surveys that may take the form of face-to-face interviews, postal surveys or telephone interviews. Much of the work associated with the conduct of surveys includes the careful design of the questionnaire, the training of survey interviewers, the preparation of the interview schedule and the administration of the research instrument, which has to be coded and analysed. The use of technology increasingly plays a role in the development of such approaches including computer-based interviewing and data analysis using statistical packages.

(3) *Ethnographic case* studies may involve the use of observation, and, more particularly, participant observation, together with unstructured interviews and conversations. The ethnographer is involved in using participatory techniques in order to understand the social situation in which those who are studied are involved. In particular, observation of people *in situ* forms a large part of this approach, in conjunction with conversational style interviews. Participant observers usually take a role in a particular setting that has resulted in a topology of researcher roles: complete participant, participant as observer, observer as participant, and complete observer. While these roles never exist in their pure form, they do provide an important framework for the ethnographer to use in a field setting. The methods used by the ethnographer to record data are particularly important, for fieldnotes and interview transcripts constitute the data that are subsequently coded and analysed. New technology plays a major role with software programs being used to assist in the preparation and analysis of ethnographic data (Bryman and Burgess 1994) but it still requires researchers to develop and use their research imagination – for this there is no substitute.

(4) *Documents* are produced in all organizations; they are therefore a major source of evidence for the social researcher. They can take a variety of forms and are often classified as primary source material or secondary source material. A distinction can be made between ready-made documents that are automatically available to a researcher, and specially commissioned documents where researchers invite the participants in their study to produce material (perhaps in the form of a diary) that is kept over a short period of time. Interest has been growing in oral-historical approaches, which are very similar to interview-based studies and have links with ethnographic and survey-based approaches of investigation. Increasing use is also being made of non-textual documentary materials, with visual evidence including photographs, film and videos playing an increasing role (Prosser 1998). New technology again becomes an important resource that the social researcher can use (Scott 1990).

(5) *Mixed methods*: there is a tendency to subdivide the different approaches that have been used in social investigation. However, there are considerable links and overlaps between the different methods of investigation, so much so that some writers have talked about the importance of triangulation or multimethod strategies of investigation (Bryman 2001; Burgess 1984; Denzin 1970; Pole and Lampard 2002). In this respect, researchers need to evaluate the range of methodological tools that can be brought to bear upon the particular problem that they have to investigate. Ethnographic methods can be linked together with survey investigation and with documentary and historical methods, given that they may complement each other, with surveys prefacing fieldwork and informing fieldwork activity. Alternatively, fieldwork activity may generate concepts and questions that are then utilized within the framework of questionnaire design. Two key questions about the data that are collected demand consideration, namely, are they reliable? Are they valid? These are the fundamental issues that researchers must address about any method of social investigation.

ROBERT G. BURGESS
UNIVERSITY OF LEICESTER

References

Bryman, A. (2001) *Social Research Methods*, London.
Bryman, A. and Burgess, R.G. (eds) (1994) *Analysing Qualitative Data*, London.
Bulmer, M. (ed.) (1984) *Sociological Research Methods*, 2nd edn, London.
Burgess, R.G. (1984) *In the Field*, London.
—— (1993) *Research Methods*, London.
Croll, P. (1986) *Systematic Classroom Observation*, Lewes.
Denzin, N. (1970) *The Research Act*, Chicago.
de Vaus, D.A. (1996) *Surveys in Social Research*, 4th edn, London.
Hammersley, M. and Atkinson, P. (1995) *Ethnography: Principles into Practice*, 2nd edn, London.
Mitchell, C. (1977) 'The logic and methods of sociological enquiry', in P. Worsley (ed.) *Introducing Sociology*, Harmondsworth.
Moser, C.A. and Kalton, G.K. (1971) *Survey Methods in Social Investigation*, 2nd edn, London.
Pole, C.J. and Lampard, R. (2002) *Practical Social Investigation: Qualitative and Quantitative Methods*, London.
Prosser, J. (ed.) (1998) *Image-Based Research: A Sourcebook for Qualitative Researchers*, London.
Scott, J. (1990) *A Document of Record*, Oxford.
Sjoberg, G. and Nett, R. (1968) *A Methodology for Social Research*, New York.
Stacey, M. (1969) *Methods of Social Research*, Oxford.
Webb, S. and Webb, B. (1932) *Methods of Social Study*, London.

Further reading

Burgess, R.G. (ed.) (1988–2001) *Studies in Qualitative Research*, 6 vols, London.
Denzin, N.K and Lincoln, Y.S (2000) *Handbook of Qualitative Research*, 2nd edn, Thousand Oaks, CA.
Hughes, C. (2002) *Key Concepts in Feminist Theory and Research*, London.
Reinharz, S. (1992) *Feminist Methods in Social Research*, New York.
Robson, C. (1993) *Real World Research*, Oxford.
Smith, H.W. (1975) *Strategies of Social Research: The Methodological Imagination*, Englewood Cliffs, NJ.
Yin, R. (1989) *Case Study Research*, Beverly Hills, CA.

MICROECONOMICS

Microeconomics is that portion of economic theory concerned with the economic behaviour of individual units in the economy, and the factors determining the prices and quantities exchanged for particular goods and services. It can be contrasted with macroeconomics, which is concerned with the determination of values for aggregates for the economy. For example, microeconomics examines the determination of the price of wheat, or the relative prices of wheat and steel, or employment in the steel industry, while macroeconomics deals with the determination of the level of employment in a particular economy, or with the level of prices of all commodities. Although this distinction between two areas of economic analysis is useful for many purposes, and economic theory textbooks are usually devoted either to microeconomics (also known as 'price theory') or to macroeconomics, it should not be taken to imply that these two levels of analysis are independent. Microquestions, such as those concerning the relative prices produced in competitive and monopolistic industries, cannot be answered without reference to the level of aggregate demand in the economy, while macroeconomics is built on microfoundations that specify the nature of competition in different industries, for example competitive or oligopolistic.

The development of microeconomics as a distinct area was part of the marginal or neo-classical approach that came to dominate economic theory after the 1970s. In contrast to classical economics, which was concerned with the economic growth of nations due to the growth of their productive resources, and which explained the relative prices of goods on the basis of the 'objective' conditions of their costs of production, neo-classical theory turned its attention to the efficient allocation of given resources (under the implicit assumption of full employment) and to the 'subjective' determination of individual prices based on marginal utility.

The topics dealt with by microeconomic analysis are often presented under the following six headings: theory of consumer behaviour; theory of exchange; theory of production and cost; theory of the firm; theory of distribution; and welfare economics. The common theme underlying these topics is the attempt of individual actors to achieve an optimal position, given the values of the parameters constraining their choices. Consumers try to maximize satisfaction (or utility), given their tastes, incomes and prices of all goods; firms try to maximize profits, and this means, among other things, that any rate of output is produced at least cost. The conditions for maximization are expressed in terms of marginal equalities. For example, for profit maximization a firm's rate of output should be such that marginal revenue is equal to marginal cost. In traditional approaches to microeconomics it is assumed that the self-seeking actions of individual units result in equilibrium positions where, given the values of the parameters, all participants are making the best of the situations facing them. They can be concerned either with partial equilibrium analysis (developed by Marshall) that concentrates on the determination of equilibrium values in a particular industry, assuming that the values in other industries are determined independently of these particular values, or with general equilibrium analysis (developed by Leon Walras), which provides full scope for the interdependence of all sectors of the economy, and deals with the simultaneous determination of all prices and quantities in the system. This generality is obtained at some cost, with the treatment being formal and mathematical, and important aspects of economic processes that occupy time are ignored. Contemporary microeconomics is particularly concerned with the strategic analysis of markets in conditions of imperfect competition, where information is incomplete and unreliable, and under various regimes ranging from monopoly through high regulation to something approaching a free market.

A. ASIMAKOPULOS
formerly MCGILL UNIVERSITY

Further reading

Mansfield, E. and Yohe, G.W. (2000) *Microeconomics: Theory and Applications*, New York.
Wolfstetter, E. (2002) *Topics in Microeconomics*, Cambridge, UK.

SEE ALSO: asymmetric information; auctions; bargaining; consumer behaviour; econometrics; firm, theory of; markets; maximization; prices, theory of

MIGRATION

Population shifts are a central feature of premodern history. The DNA 'architecture' revealed by the human genome project conclusively situates the common origin of humankind in Africa. Humans were subsequently dispersed by the disintegration of the continents or by relocation. Flight from natural disasters, adverse climatic changes and competition from other species or communities were common causes of movement. Hunting and gathering, and, when pastoral societies developed, the search for better pasture, were other forms of early migration. Ancient civilizations – notably the Egyptian, Inca, Meso-

potamian, Indus and Zhou – were often dependent on subordinating neighbouring peoples by force of arms and dragooning them over long distances to work to build the monuments and structures like the pyramids, temples and canal systems.

In his comprehensive account, Hoerder (2002) suggests that as early as the eleventh century interdependencies and interconnections occurred at a level of complexity that can merit the adjectives 'long-distance' or 'global' migration. The webs of commerce and knowledge, together with their accompanying forms of migration (undertaken by explorers, merchants, pilgrims, journeymen, warriors and colonizers), served to link previously separated cultures and regions. This early form of what might be termed 'proto-globalization' challenges Wallerstein's argument (1974) that it was only in the sixteenth century that the opening sequences of globalization occurred.

Although there remains considerable debate about when precisely the period of 'modernity' commences, it is evident that a new phase of long-distance migration was closely associated with the increased intensity and scope of trade, the growth of manufacturing industries, regimented forms of agricultural production and the accelerated pace of urbanization. Transatlantic slavery is the most dramatic example of migration in the modern period. The establishment of sugar, rubber and coffee plantations in the Caribbean and Latin America, and cotton production in the southern states of the USA, demanded large cohorts of unfree workers. As local populations died from European diseases or could not be persuaded to work in the harsh conditions that prevailed, West Africans were forcibly seized and transported, often with the connivance of local slave traders. When slavery ended (in 1834 in the British colonies) indentured labour from India, with smaller numbers from Japan and China, became the main sources of plantation labour. Indentured workers were generally contracted for 7 years, with the option of returning to their countries of origin. The majority of workers stayed and formed the basis of the Indian populations of Fiji, Mauritius, South Africa, Trinidad and Guyana, and the Japanese populations of Brazil and Peru.

Indentureship and transatlantic slavery were so embedded in the history of European capitalism and the emergence of the USA as a dominant power, that it is easy to overlook other contemporaneous regional circuits of migration – for example in the Indian subcontinent, the Islamic world, the Baltic–North Sea area, across the Sahara and from island to island in the Pacific. These migration 'webs' arose for many reasons – including military conquest, exploration, fleeing from oppression or disaster, engaging in trade or undertaking a spiritual quest. However, commencing in the mid-nineteenth century, most long-distance migration was determined by colonization and the search for work. Perhaps the most far-reaching examples of settler migration took place when the European powers burst out of their confines in the sixteenth century and established colonies of settlement in the New World, Asia, Australasia, and North and South Africa. These settlements were distinctive in that the local people (Inuit, Native American, 'Indios', Khoisan, Maori, Carib or Aborigine) were displaced from their hold on the land and the newcomers proclaimed their own autochthonous status. With considerable insouciance they constructed political institutions and assigned land, civic privileges and property to themselves as if the countries they invaded were theirs by right of occupation.

Labour migrants were rarely in so fortunate a position, at least initially. To be sure, many who came to the USA in the period 1880–1914 to work in the new mass industries were able eventually to achieve independent proprietorship, assets and property. Equally, however, many labour migrants were held back by continuing poverty, bad wages or restrictions on settlement. All over the world, poorer peasants were 'pushed' off the land as large farmers and landlords consolidated their holdings, often by force of arms. Neophyte workers were 'pulled' into the towns and cities as mining companies and factory owners required labour for stripping out the earth's resources and provided goods for mass consumption and export. Their conditions of work were often so adverse that many early socialists saw such migrant workers as ripe for revolutionary action, a political aspiration that was rarely realized.

Why people move

The dynamics that activate the flows of labour migrants are (as in the passage above) frequently depicted in the language of 'push' and 'pull'.

However, as the contributors in Cohen's (1996) reader on migration theories demonstrate, we must be careful not to exaggerate the degree of choice on offer. Labour migrants usually do not operate with a rational, calculative model of the world in which they weigh options and possibilities in the free labour market. Opportunities are tightly constrained and structured by such factors as rural emiseration, employment and housing prospects, transport costs, international law, migration policies (of sending and receiving states), the recruitment practices of agencies and employers, and the need for documentation like passports, visas and work certificates (or the money to pay illegal recruiters).

This argument can be writ large by suggesting that there is complex interplay between individual motivations, collective household strategies and the underlying structural causes of migration. Why particular individuals or households decide to make themselves part of a more general movement or to resist the possibility of migration is not always apparent: indeed one largely underexplored theme is to answer the question 'Why do people stay?' When we focus on those who move, researchers have often found that family and household strategies are evolved to determine the order of movement, the number persuaded to leave and the preferred destinations of migrant members. These strategies can serve to balance the risks facing the household with its continuing possibilities of income, security and reproduction in its current location.

While it is generally true that an individual's resolve to migrate cannot be separated from the local, institutional and global context in which that decision was reached, this applies with particular force to 'compelled' or 'flight' migration, where mass displacements and population flows are occasioned by events outside the individual's control – wars, 'ethnic cleansing', natural disasters, pogroms and the like. One effect of the civil strife and the swirl of populations in the post-Cold War period after 1989 has been that it is increasingly difficult to differentiate between 'economic migrants' and 'political refugees'. People move because they dread political persecution and because their means of livelihood and their dignity have been stripped away from them. They leave because their whole world has been shaken by a series of sickening seismic shocks, the full effects of which they can barely comprehend, let alone measure and predict. They move because they have to, or because they fear for the future.

Contemporary migration

While events on the ground are often confusing and ambiguous, destination states remain determined to try to maintain and even sharpen the distinction between political refugees (who they may have to admit given their international responsibilities and treaty obligations) and economic migrants who they wish, in general, to exclude. Despite states' attempts to restrict, control, manage and select immigrants of all kinds, seen at a global level, migration of all sorts has rapidly increased in the last two decades of the twentieth century and continues into the new millennium. At least seven types are evident:

- Notwithstanding strong controls by Western industrial states, *legal labour migration* either continues in less obvious ways or flows to other areas – it has not come to a halt. Dealing with Asia alone, Castles and Miller (1998) estimated that by the mid-1990s there were about 3 million Asians legally employed outside their own countries within Asia, and another 3 million employed in other continents, notably in the Gulf States.
- Though impossible to estimate with precision, *illegal or undocumented labour migration* has more than taken the place of those stopped at the frontier. The Mexican–US frontier has remained leaky while a notable new migration space for illegal workers has opened up in South Africa, where the abolition of post-apartheid controls on internal movement has exposed the incapacity of the state to control inwards movements from the surrounding region. Undocumented labour is now taking two predominant forms: (1) overstaying and (2) deliberate illegal entry. While the former largely remains a matter of individual entrepreneurship, there is increasing evidence of the organization of illegal entry. Large sums of money change hands, entry certificates and visas are forged, and border guards are bribed. One frequent feature that perpetuates illegal entry is the complicity of employers who wish to exploit the vulnerability of illegal workers.
- The number of *refugees and displacees* is also difficult to estimate because of varying statistical criteria, but in 2003 the United Nations High Commission for Refugees listed nearly 18 million 'persons of concern'. The expression 'persons of concern' covers asylum seekers, internal displacees and a narrower legal definition of the 'refugee' arising from the 1951 Geneva Convention. In paraphrase, a (Convention) refugee is someone who is fleeing from a real threat of persecution in their country of origin on the grounds of their background or their political opinions. Displacees do not cross international frontiers but are expelled by warlords and local bosses in areas like the newly emerging polities of the former Soviet Union and the broken-backed postcolonial states of Africa.
- Many earlier studies of migration dealt with *women migrants* as a residual category, as those 'left behind'. Where they crossed a border, women have generally been treated as dependent or family members. Numerically and sociologically we have entered a new phase of female migration. This movement is in response to the demand for women in the global service economy. Some of this is in the sex industry, where hostesses, entertainers, etc. are required in very significant numbers in countries like Japan. A somewhat more respectable version of the trade is in the 'mail order bride' trade – dominated by the Philippines. The Philippines also is market leader for domestic labour and exports tens of thousands of female domestic workers each year. To the brides and the domestics we must add waitresses, casual staff in fast food outlets, cleaners, nurses (particularly geriatric nurses), secretaries, hotel reception staff and stewardesses, many of whom are supplied from abroad. By the mid-1990s 1.5 million Asian women were working abroad.
- Also 'hidden from history', but in a very different way, are a large group of *highly skilled international transients* like accountants, computer experts, entrepreneurs, lawyers, academics, doctors, business managers, construction engineers and consultants. Some are freelance consultants, but most work for international companies trying to complete contracts, initiate business deals or develop branch plants in the country of destination. This group of migrants has variously been called 'skilled transients', 'sojourners' or 'denizens' (in the sense of a privileged foreigner). They do not have extensive civic rights in the new countries they work in. They do not, for

example, have the vote, cannot draw on social security systems and do not have rights of permanent residence. However, they do not really need these facilities and privileges. If they want to vote they can exercise their vote by post. Their companies insure them, often pay for privileged education for their children, provide generous pensions and subsidize family visits. Others operate in the cracks between tourism, self-employment and agency work.

- Unlike the earlier group, there is also a significant group of *skilled workers* who are offered permanent settlement and access to citizenship by admitting states. There is now no country that unreservedly welcomes immigrants of all sorts. Indeed for the last century there have been formal and informal restrictions on immigration. However, a number of countries institutionalized a more rational system of bidding for particular migrants. The two countries that have perfected the system of 'immigration shopping' are Canada and Australia. They have linked their economic development, manpower and immigration departments structurally and are intent on finding selected migrants to fill slots in the labour market. If dentists are needed in Manitoba an immigration vacancy will be created, just as radiographers going to Tasmania are welcomed. (Without going into the points systems in detail, what importing countries ideally require are skills, youth, cultural fit, good health, education and lack of dependants.) Equally welcomed are permanent 'business' or 'entrepreneurial' migrants who bring investments and often jobs with them.

- While I have concentrated on international migration it is worth remembering that *internal migration* is very much greater in volume though generally less politically contentious. However, there is at least one case of internal migration, China, which has global implications. In China, where up to 30 million people are on the move annually, the sheer scale of the movement has already generated apartheid-type internal passport controls on entry to the industrial cities of the south and this in turn has important implications for human rights. Step migration on this scale from rural area to small town, to big city, is also likely ultimately to result in considerable international migration.

Conclusion

Migration is not only about the movement of people. It can also generate enormous shifts at the subjective, social and cultural levels. As a consequence of population mobility, cultural and linguistic diversity is omnipresent, and the capacity to communicate with others and to understand their cultures is available, at least potentially, to many. Travel and migration have led to the necessity of cheek-by-jowl relationships between diverse peoples at work or at street corners, and in markets, neighbourhoods, schools and recreational areas. With globalization, mass migration and the awareness of inequality, developing a functional cosmopolitanism is now becoming a matter of everyday survival for many workers, labour migrants and refugees. Equally, at a social or more intimate personal level many individuals now seem to be more than ever prone to articulate complex affiliations, meaningful attachments and multiple allegiances to issues, people, places and traditions that lie beyond the boundaries of their resident nation-state. This holds especially for migrants, members of ethnic diasporas and other transnational communities. This development has profound implications for how we understand traditional social scientific notions like 'community', 'ethnicity', 'nation' or 'society'.

ROBIN COHEN
UNIVERSITY OF WARWICK

References

Castles, S. and Miller, M. (1998) *The Age of Migration: International Population Movements in the Modern World*, 2nd edn, Basingstoke.
Cohen, R. (ed.) (1996) *Theories of Migration*, Cheltenham.
Hoerder, D. (2002) *Cultures in Contact: World Migrations in the Second Millennium*, Durham, NC.
Wallerstein, I. (1974) *The Modern World System*, New York.

Further reading

Chaliand, G. and Rageau, J.-P. (1995) *The Penguin Atlas of Diasporas*, New York.
Cohen, R. (ed.) (1995) *The Cambridge Survey of World Migration*, Cambridge, UK.
Vertorec, S. and Cohen, R. (eds) (1999) *Migration, Diasporas and Transnationalism*, Cheltenham.

SEE ALSO: globalization; population projections; vital statistics

MILITARY REGIMES

Military regimes are those whose primary political office holders are soldiers, and whose central pillar of support is the military institution itself. It is a regime ushered into power, driven, propped up and dominated by military interests. This simple definition allows us to differentiate these kind of regimes from others that may be similar. For example, in some instances, formal positions of political authority are occupied entirely by civilians, while informal power is wielded by a military that sits behind the throne. As influential as the armed forces may be, they do not constitute a regime, because non-uniformed personnel run the government. In other cases, officers may play a central role in governance, but serve at the pleasure of a strong, civilian political party, as in communist systems or non-communist, single-party systems. These too cannot be considered military regimes.

Even within the confines of our definition, there is considerable room for variation. Military regimes differ in their causes, ideology, organization and purpose. Almost all military regimes get to power via military coups. But why they seize power is a different matter. Explanations for military intervention are almost as numerous as the interventions themselves. Here is an inventory of just some of the reasons given: satisfying professional needs, filling a political vacuum, ending a political stalemate, replacing incompetent or corrupt civilians, confronting non-performing institutions, suppressing an explosion of societal demands, reversing economic deterioration, ending systemic violence and political instability, quelling internal subversion, guerrillas, terrorism, populism, communism, militant unionism, suppressing ethnic and tribal clashes, ridding the military of threats to its own survival, ending budgetary deprivation, and eliminating threats to private property. It is important to distinguish between the military's own post-coup rationales, and the underlying reasons for what they do. Typically, new military leaders will find fault with the civilians they had just replaced, blaming them and their policies for practically all the ills that had befallen the nation. Certainly, one cannot dismiss the notion that political leaders make catastrophic mistakes that prove fatal to the democracy. But quite often the problems that bring on coups are deeply embedded and systemic, lying beyond the quick fixes of any politician. The military's self-serving rationales for intervention may not adequately unveil the underlying causal explanations for coups.

Of those underlying causes, there are two basic categories: those that originate within the military institution itself, and those that originate outside of it. Often times, the real motive for military intervention can be traced back to the military's own professional needs and political beliefs. Their core objective is to preserve if not enlarge their coercive might, against foreign or domestic foes. To do so, they must maintain standards of material well-being and organizational control, including budgets, living conditions, equipment, discipline, cohesion and *esprit de corps* within the ranks. Any civilian government that stands in their way of fulfilling these needs could become the victim of a coup. Beyond that, armies are guided by their own understandings of the political world around them. These understandings are moulded by experiences, myths, traditions, perceptions and doctrines. Soldiers may believe that their historically defined and indeed legitimate role in a society is to serve as political arbiters, deciding who should be allowed to participate and who shouldn't, or who should rule and who shouldn't. The military may also define for themselves what is in the best interests of national security, 'see' threats to security that others don't, or exaggerate the harm those threats could cause.

Non-military explanations for military coups begin with society. It is the masses, social classes, economic sectors or political organizations that share vital links and interests with the armed forces, which motivate soldiers to seize power. Sometimes soldiers are conservative, seizing power to advance the middle-class objective of protecting economic gains from the 'threat' posed by the lower classes. Or, they may align with the very rich and powerful landed elites or business/financial classes to further their interests. On rarer occasions, the military has been a progressive force, siding with the workers, peasants or the poor. Whoever sponsors the military, one thing is clear: military coups usually do not succeed unless there is some significant social backing for them.

Once in power, militaries organize their regimes in different ways. The classic structure is that of the military junta that seizes control of the executive branch, shuts down the legislative and judicial arms of government, cancels elections and prohibits political party activity. Yet some militaries want to legitimate themselves by staging elections that are tightly controlled and that limit participation to those parties they deem acceptable. They will reopen legislatures under constrained conditions; executive power will dominate and there will be no meaningful checks and balances. Naturally, such limits rob the regime of the very legitimacy it had hoped to create. But the military has always had a low tolerance for dissent, and simply cannot risk granting too much authority to those who may disagree with them.

Military regimes also vary according to how institutionalized they are. At one end of the spectrum are those characterized by a complete fusion of military and governmental roles. Here, the military *is* the government. All branches of the armed services get cabinet appointments, staff ministries and help to make the day-to-day policy decisions. Authority is decentralized among the service branches, and decision-making is done collectively. Some civilians may be hired, but they serve completely at the pleasure of military superiors, do not affiliate with or represent the interests of political parties or interest groups, and are often technocratic in orientation. At the other end are the more personalistic (sometimes referred to as sultanistic) dictatorships, dominated by a military strong man. The armed forces are still the foundation for the regime, but immerse themselves less in governance. Authority is concentrated in the hands of a single dictator who calls the shots, and who has licence to form his own cabinet (often comprised of civilians) and formulate his own policies. And yet the military institution is never too far away. What discretion is granted to the strong man can be withheld should he fail to defend the interests of the military institution.

There is no ideal blueprint for organizing military regimes. Each has its own strengths and weaknesses. The more institutionalized models have the advantage of keeping the military very close to insure its views are heard and respected, and its interests protected. Yet the very proximity of the profession to the centres of power can serve not only as an institutional check but also as a bureaucratic drag on governmental deliberations. It can also politicize the ranks, as officers are forced to take sides in contentious policy disputes. These disputes can lead to institutional divisions, pitting officer against officer, army against navy or senior against junior ranked personnel. By concentrating so much authority in so few hands sultanistic regimes can dispense with institutional checks and balances, and avoid bureaucratic encumbrances, thus allowing for speedier decisions. But success hinges on the personal cunning and survival of the leader and the Achilles' heel of these regimes is that they are too dependent on one man. Should the sultan fall prey to serious miscalculation, illness or death, so too goes the regime, either because no one with his ability has arisen to positions of high enough rank, or because succession rules have not been worked out. These faults notwithstanding, scholars have found that personalistic military regimes have endured considerably longer than the alternatives.

Of course, not all military regimes intend to stay in power for the long term. It all depends on the purpose for which these regimes were created. Some regimes have short-term horizons. They seize power temporarily to resolve a crisis, restore political calm or remove a government not to its liking, followed shortly by a call for new elections. The military are intent on returning to barracks as quickly as possible, either because they have no interest in governance, do not believe it is their historic duty or because they are concerned about the potential harm it could cause them professionally.

Others have longer-term horizons. Having lost all confidence in the ability of elected leaders to resolve the nation's problems, and convinced they can do a better job, these officers intend on ruling indefinitely, with no goal of, let alone timetable for, democratic restoration. Sometimes, they wish to rule for long periods of time simply in order to preserve the privileges of those (including themselves) who enjoy the economic, social and political status quo. Running what amounts to a protection racket, they offer security to the economic elites in exchange for their support. Other times they are more messianic, on a mission to create a future they believe no one else can be relied upon to ensure. In those cases, they are convinced that the nation's problems are deeply rooted, and cannot be resolved without a fundamental, sometimes radical transformation of the polity, the economy and social class relations. In pursuit of those ends, military regimes have been known to be brutally repressive, bent on 'cleansing' the society of groups, movements and ideas that may conflict with their long-term plans.

Military regimes can rely on repression for long periods of time. However, without a concomitant effort to build political coalitions of support many will falter.

Whatever goodwill they may have earned initially will be squandered, and a resentful public will press for the return of their political freedoms. At that point, some military regimes will press on, but most will give way to power-sharing with civilians, full-fledged democracy or some other political formula agreeable to those who have lost their tolerance for military rule.

DAVID PION-BERLIN
UNIVERSITY OF CALIFORNIA, RIVERSIDE

Further reading

Alagappa, M. (ed.) (2001) *Coercion and Governance: The Declining Political Role of the Military in Asia*, Stanford, CA.
Decalo, S. (1976) *Coups and Army Rule in Africa: Studies in Military Style*, New Haven, CT.
Finer, S.E. (1988) *The Man on Horseback: The Role of the Military in Politics*, Boulder, CO.
Pinkney, R. (1990) *Right-Wing Military Government*, Boston.
Remmer, K. (1991) *Military Rule in Latin America*, Boulder, CO.

MILL, JOHN STUART (1806–73)

John Stuart Mill, the classic exponent of liberalism, was brought up in utilitarian principles by his father, James Mill, a close friend and associate of Bentham. His rigorous childhood education, described in his *Autobiography* (1873), involved a brilliant and precocious mastery of classical languages by the age of 7. For most of his working life he was a clerk at India House in London, though briefly a Member of Parliament. After a long association, he married Harriet Taylor whom he always claimed as his inspiration and intellectual partner. On their marriage, in protest against the legal situation of women at the time, he wrote a formal renunciation of the property and similar rights bestowed on him as a husband.

Mill was a many-sided thinker and writer – a philosopher, social scientist and humanist. Among the subjects he treated were politics, ethics, logic and scientific method. He also wrote on the position of women (*The Subjection of Women*, 1859), constitutional reform (*Considerations on Representative Government*, 1861) and economics (*Principles of Political Economy*, 1848).

In *Utilitarianism* (1861) Mill expounded and defended the principle that the tendency of actions to promote happiness or its reverse is the standard of right and wrong. His version of utilitarianism was from a logical point of view possibly flawed, but from a moral point of view enhanced, by the notion that some forms of happiness are more worthwhile than others. *On Liberty* (1859) is the classic argument for the claims of the individual against the state, and in it Mill makes an impassioned defence of the principles of liberty and toleration. Isaiah Berlin (1969) writes of Mill that 'the highest values for him…were individual liberty, variety, and justice'. This is sometimes seen as inconsistent with his basic utilitarianism, but Mill believed that principles like liberty and justice were themselves important social instruments for utility. This follows from his view of human nature, and in particular from his belief that self-determination and the exercise of choice are themselves part of a higher concept of happiness, and that 'collective mediocrity' is a recipe for social stagnation and permanent cultural and economic arrest. Writing on toleration, Mill argued in favour of liberty of thought, speech and association, as well as for freedom to cultivate whatever lifestyle one chooses, subject only to the constraint of not harming others. It is often disputed whether there are any actions that do not affect other people in some way, but the distinction between other-regarding and self-regarding actions – the postulation of a public realm and a private realm – is an essential element of liberalism.

Mill applied these principles to education, defending a liberal and secular education. He considered compulsory education not an invasion of liberty but essential to it. However, he believed strongly that there should not be a 'state monopoly of education' but that state education should be one amongst a number of competing systems.

In *A System of Logic, Ratiocinative and Deductive* (1843), Mill defended a classical view of induction as empirical generalization, and held that this can supply a model for both logical deduction and scientific method. In some respects this may be seen as a classic version of British empiricism, and indeed Mill was an empiricist in the sense that he believed truth, including mathematical truth, was to be established by observation rather than intuition; however, because he was prepared to accept the uniformity of nature as a basic postulate, his account does not have the sceptical consequences that this position might otherwise seem to involve. Mill extended his discussion of methodology to cover the application of experimental method to social science and set out to provide 'a general science of man in society'. His argument is to be found in Book VI of A System of Logic, which has been called the most important contribution to the making of modern sociology until Durkheim's Rules of Sociological Method (1950 [1895]).

While some of his immediate successors saw Mill as the unfortunate propounder of views that are inherently irreconcilable, a number of modern commentators have offered a revisionist interpretation of Mill as a consistent thinker. This position was taken at one time by John Gray (1983), who argued that Mill's active rather than passive conception of happiness necessarily involves a social setting in which liberty and toleration are the norm. Later, however, Gray attacked his own revisionist interpretation – an interpretation shared also by, for example, Ryan (1987) and Berger (1984) – arguing that Mill's Victorian faith in progress obscured from him the truth that the empirical assumption that liberty will contribute to happiness is either unsupported or false. This breaking of the link between happiness and liberty, Gray suggests, together with the collapse of classical utilitarianism that results from recognizing the ultimate incommensurability of pleasures of various kinds, is fatal to any form of liberalism. The revision of revisionism should not be taken, however, as anything more than a sign of the perennial interest of Mill's ideas, and Mill, more than any of his critics, would no doubt see this as another opportunity to insist that no truth should ever be allowed to become a dead dogma, even the truth of liberalism itself.

BRENDA ALMOND
UNIVERSITY OF HULL

References

Berger, F. (1984) Happiness, Justice and Freedom: The Moral and Political Philosophy of John Stuart Mill, Berkeley, CA.
Berlin, I. (1969) 'John Stuart Mill and the ends of life', in Four Essays on Liberty, Oxford.
Durkheim, E. (1950 [1895]) The Rules of Sociological Method, London.
Gray, J. (1983) Mill on Liberty: A Defence, London.
Ryan, A. (1987) The Philosophy of John Stuart Mill, 2nd edn, London.

Further reading

Capalddi, N. (2004) John Stuart Mill: A Biography, Cambridge, UK.
Skorupski, J. (1989) John Stuart Mill, London.
Ten, C.L. (1980) Mill on Liberty, Oxford.

SEE ALSO: globalization; vital statistics

MIND

'Mind' is derived from old Teutonic gamundi, meaning to think, remember, intend. These various senses are apparent in current phrases such as to bear in mind, remind, give one's mind to, make up or change one's mind. Most verbal forms are now obsolete or dialectal but remain in such phrases as 'never mind' or 'mind how you go' in the sense of attend. Traditionally 'mind' has been used to refer collectively to mental abilities such as perceiving, imagining, remembering, thinking, believing, feeling, desiring, deciding and intending. Sometimes an agent is implied: 'Mind is the mysterious something which feels and thinks' (Mill 1843); sometimes not: 'What we call mind is nothing but a heap or collection of different perceptions, united together by certain relations' (Hume 2000 [1739–40]).

In classical Greece, questions about the mind were interwoven with those about the soul or spirit, as was the case in medieval Europe, where theological concerns predominated. Plato's tripartite division of the mind into cognitive, conative and affective functions lasted at least until the nineteenth century. Numerous classifications of mental faculties were offered in the eighteenth and nineteenth centuries. Although these were generally speculative and non-explanatory, they laid the ground for later work in psychometrics and cortical localization of function, and subsequently modularity (Fodor 1983) and neuropsychology.

Diverse criteria have been offered for distinguishing the mental from the physical (Feigl 1958) but there are problems associated with many of them. According to the first, mental phenomena are private whereas physical phenomena are public. Descartes (1953 [1641]) claimed that physical bodies were spatially extended and subject to deterministic laws, whereas minds were non-spatial and free. Brentano (1995 [1874]) suggested intentionality as characteristic of the mental: perceiving, thinking and desiring imply objects that may have no objective existence. Other philosophers have pointed to the qualitative features of conscious experiences (so-called 'qualia'), which seem irreducible to physical properties, as definitive of the mental. Attempts have also been made to distinguish mental and physical in terms of different logics, for example intensional and extensional (Chisholm 1967) or linguistic conventions (Ryle 1949).

Traditionally the mind has been identified with conscious experience: 'Consciousness...is the condition or accompaniment of every mental operation' (Fleming 1858); 'No proposition can be said to be in the Mind which it was never conscious of' (Locke 1690). However, this proposition is patently false. Neurophysiologists and clinicians in the nineteenth century recognized different levels of functioning in the nervous system and acknowledged unconscious mental activity, although the idea has a much more venerable history dating back at least to classical Greek times. William James (1890) pointed out that it is only the perchings and not the flights of thought that are available to consciousness. The majority of mental processes take place outside awareness – for instance large parts of perception, retrieval, skills and creative thinking. This fact is made even more obvious by consideration of such phenomena as hypnosis, subliminal perception, learning without awareness, split personality and blind-sight (a clinical condition in which patients with damage to the occipital lobes may report no experience of seeing and yet be able to make correct discriminations in a forced choice situation).

If mind is characterized as the system that governs behaviour rather than being identified with the contents of consciousness, then the way is open for more mechanistic approaches to its study. With the rise of cognitive psychology, the most popular framework has been the computer metaphor, premised on a functionalist philosophy: what characterizes the mental is its functional organization rather than its material constitution. According to the computational model of mind, mental activity is computation, and mental processes are operations performed on representations and can be modelled by the manipulation of abstract symbols according to formal rules in a digital computer. The computational model has been criticized as being both behaviouristic and dualistic (Russell 1984). Functionalism cannot provide a satisfactory analysis of qualitative differences in experience; and mental processes are considered to be independent of any particular physical realization. It has been doubted whether the context-free, formal manipulation of abstract symbols can deal adequately with meaning and reference (Searle 1980). Orthodox artificial intelligence underemphasizes the dynamic interaction with the environment and ignores the developmental and biological dimensions of mental life.

A more biologically realistic alternative has regained popularity: neural networks, which employ connectionist principles and exhibit parallel distributed processing. They show such features as context address-ability and resistance to local damage, and account well for many psychological phenomena such as pattern recognition, learning and memory. They have also enabled fruitful links to be established with neuro-physiological research.

The mind can be modelled by a hierarchy of multiple parallel processors, enabling speed and flexibility, with interaction and dependencies within and between levels. At the lowest level they govern sensory and motor interactions with the external world. At the highest level overall goals are monitored. Some of the modules may be fairly general in function; the majority are probably relatively specialized. The evidence suggests a broad division of labour between those specialized for verbal processing and those specialized for spatial processing. A small subset of results, but not the inner workings, are available to consciousness in a limited-capacity serial processor that interrelates products of parallel processors. The system can construct models of the external world (including one of itself), which influence its input and output. The contents of the mind appear to be images, propositions, models and procedures for carrying out actions. It is clear that 'mind' is a term that is too vague to be useful. The tools are now available for the detailed specification of its function, which will require the combined efforts of work in artificial intelligence, experimental psychology and neuroscience.

ELIZABETH R. VALENTINE
ROYAL HOLLOWAY COLLEGE,
UNIVERSITY OF LONDON

References

Brentano, F. (1995 [1874]) *Psychology from an Empirical Standpoint*, London.

Chisholm, R.M. (1967) 'Intentionality', in P. Edwards (ed.) *The Encyclopaedia of Philosophy*, Vol. 4, New York.

Descartes, R. (1953 [1641]) *Discourse on Method*, London.

Feigl, H. (1958) 'The "mental" and the "physical"', in H. Feigl, M. Scriven and G. Maxwell (eds) *Concepts, Theories and the Mind–Body Problem*, Minneapolis, MN.

Fleming, W. (1858) *The Vocabulary of Philosophy*, London.

Fodor, J.A. (1983) *The Modularity of Mind*, Cambridge, MA.

Hume, D. (2000 [1739–40]) *A Treatise of Human Nature*, eds D. and M. Norton, Oxford.

James, W. (1890) *Principles of Psychology*, New York.

Locke, J. (1690) *Essay Concerning Human Understanding*, London.

Mill, J.S. (1843) *A System of Logic*, London.

Russell, J. (1984) *Explaining Mental Life*, London.

Ryle, G. (1949) *The Concept of Mind*, Chicago.

Searle, J.R. (1980) 'Minds, brains and programs', *Behavioral and Brain Sciences* 3.

Further reading

Clark, A. (1995) *Associative Engines: Connectionism, Concepts and Representational Change*, Cambridge, MA.

Gregory, R.L. and Zangwill, O.L. (eds) (1998) *The Oxford Companion to the Mind*, Oxford.

Johnson-Laird, P.N. (1983) *Mental Models: Toward a Cognitive Science of Language, Inference, and Consciousness*, Cambridge, UK.

Valentine, E.R. (1992) *Conceptual Issues in Psychology*, 2nd edn, London.

SEE ALSO: artificial intelligence; consciousness

MIXED ECONOMY

A purely private right to a resource may be said to exist when an individual can select any use for that resource including the option of sale. This may be contrasted with other specifications of property rights like communal access to roads, state ownership of railways or, indeed, when any privately owned resource is subject to restrictions in the range of its use. The degree to which purely private rights prevail in an economy would reflect the degree to which an economy is mixed, but a precise measure has yet to be devised.

There are two broad ways of thinking about the mixed economy. One is to ask how and why the public sector has increased its share of property rights. The other way is to ask why the economy should be mixed, and this was the main focus of debate in the postwar period up to about the late 1960s. It was a debate partly about aims, but perhaps more about whether certain economic and social aims are better achieved by non-private rights to resources. In this sense, the mixed economy is the outcome of policies consciously espoused by parties, supported by a majority of voters and executed by governments. To understand the post-1945 growth of the public sector, one needs, in this light, first to emphasize the effect of the interwar years of large-scale unemployment. For many people, the low income levels and social tragedies seemed damning evidence of the inefficiencies and injustices of capitalism, to be remedied in part by public ownership of the means of production. Doubts that resources would be efficiently allocated in such a system disappeared for some by the demonstration that public ownership was consistent with the use of a price system. The efficient allocation of resources that was theoretically obtainable in a perfectly competitive world was obtainable also by public firms adjusting output levels to the point where prices equalled marginal costs, but with the key difference that, with capital publicly owned, profits accrued to the nation rather than to a select few. Similarly, the Keynesian demonstration that unemployment could be an equilibrium feature of capitalism pointed to an enhanced role for the state. While an expansion of private investment would have beneficial effects on income and employment levels comparable to increased public spending, Keynes had stressed the role of pessimistic expectations in preventing a sufficiently low level of interest rates or in inhibiting a business investment expansion independently of interest rate levels.

In the decades after 1950, these arguments gradually lost some of their force. Rising living standards in economies where over 60 per cent of GDP still emanated from the private sector, financial losses in public enterprises, waiting-lists for certain public services together with some embryonic doubts, especially by US economists, about whether government deficit manipulation was actually the source of full employment, undermined some of the support for government economic activity. That support was, however, largely sustained, at least intellectually, by several strands of earlier thought receiving increased emphasis. It is clear, for example, that the analysis of public goods has a wider applicability than law, order and defence. In so far as the issue is one of spill-over effects in consumption and production, then, in a world of continuing urbanization, government corrective action for transport congestion, air pollution and safety regulation seemed vital. In a similar technical vein, while public ownership was no longer seen as the best vehicle for improving income distribution, a strand in the early support for such government intervention was to prevent private monopolistic exploitation of economies of scale common in fuel, transport and general infrastructure development. The arguments for public provision of education, health and even housing had never relied solely on the issue of income distribution; rather there were questions about the access to information, to capital markets and to the speed with which the price system could deal fairly with shortages. Finally, though perhaps least convincingly, the differential growth experience of the post-1945 economies entered the economist's agenda in the 1960s with government again seen as an important catalyst.

There has, however, always been the view that the above is a misconception both of how the private competitive system works and how public ownership works. Private monopoly in the field is quite consistent with competition for the field so that auction bidding for franchises for refuse collection, electricity supply and such services could eliminate monopoly profits. How, second, will private decision-makers react to the existence of spill-over effects? If there are net gains to be exploited by public action on the height of chimneys or on river pollution by up-stream firms, how can we be sure that private decision-makers have not already entered economic dealings to their joint satisfaction? And if the argument is that, especially with large groups, there are transaction costs in private exchange relations, so also are there costs to the government in acquiring information, casting doubt on whether its solution will be any better. More generally, why should the analysis of utility-maximizing behaviour stop at the door of the public sector?

Civil servants, public industry managers and politicians are the relevant decision-makers. In the Austrian tradition the cost of an activity is the value of the alternative forgone by the decision-maker, not by some vague entity like the state. In summary, there is no guarantee on this line of thought that government action will yield a superior solution to the private-sector solution with all its warts (see, e.g., Demsetz 1982). Such doubts mounted in the 1970s and 1980s, fuelled in part by the increasing growth of government and the part this might have played as the source of monetary expansion in the late 1960s and early 1970s. By the mid-1970s, moreover, Keynesianism as a theoretical framework for analysing unemployment and inflation was under strong attack, precisely because of its deficient analysis of the microbehaviour of agents in the economy. By the 1990s a commitment to private enterprise and competitive markets had been embedded in bodies like the World Bank and the European Union.

While such debates on policy have been continually supported by positive studies of how economic systems work, they have not fully confronted the basic question of why the public sector has grown. Indeed, much of the debate has treated the state as an autonomous force, as something separate from the features of the rest of the economy. Doubts about such a characterization should arise when it is recognized that the pre-nineteenth-century, early modern European absolutist states had interventionist bureaucracies and armies where the attenuation of private rights, if we could only measure it, might bear comparison to modern state sectors. Many Marxists would certainly want to locate the characterization of the modern state in the capitalist mode of production, in the sense of the state being another form of monopoly capital or a collective form to secure for capitalism what private capital on its own cannot secure – legal system, control of trade unions and so on. An alternative longer-term view is that the industrialization which started in the late eighteenth century meant a rapidly increasing division of labour, thereby enhancing the role of transaction costs and the supply of organized interest groups. The same forces that have advanced the middle-man, the white-collar worker and those engaged in banking, accounting, law, insurance, property and trade, are also important in prompting the provision of transaction cost-reducing services by government, that is, basic transportation, justice, police, fire, defence, postal services, licensing, quality inspection and measurement standards. The attenuation of purely private rights usually requires group or collective action; there are in-built disincentives to such action that, in democracies, take a long time to overcome. It was in the latter part of the nineteenth century that the significant changes became observable. Over the years from 1869 to 1970 the percentage of the US labour force in government grew from 3.5 per cent to 18.1 per cent, matching rises from 7.8 per cent to 19.1 per cent in retail trade, 0.4 per cent to 4.0 per cent in finance, insurance and real estate, and 11.1 per cent to 17.4 per cent in other services.

In the last quarter of the twentieth century, two strong but contrasting pressures affected the size of government. Continuing concern that free enterprise was rough on those at the bottom of the income pile and did not deliver optimal amounts of health and education made for rising expenditures on social services. On the other hand more and more services financed by government were being contracted out. This was not simply a matter of the privatization of transport, telecommunications and energy. It was a fundamental change in the structure of economies, the rise of services, which reached dramatic proportions by the end of the century. In all sectors of advanced economies, the increased sophistication of final products and processes, ranging from CDs, videos, restaurants, pharmaceuticals and electronics, occasioned a rise in the number of personnel in supporting activities like research and development, computing, accounting, legal services, management consultancy. Some was provided in-house but more and more was supplied by independent specialist firms supplying services to industry and agriculture whose own products had a rising service content. Such activities were also splintering out from government with much more franchising, subcontracting, buying-in of services, all of which was greatly facilitated by the growth of information technology. By 1995 the service sector (including government but excluding housing) accounted for 78.9 per cent of the labour force in the USA, 74.1 per cent in the UK, 71.0 per cent in France and 62.6 per cent in West Germany. By 1989 the service sector in the USA accounted for 85 per cent of accumulated investment in information technology and in the UK the total capital stock

in business and financial services exceeded that in the rest of the economy (excluding dwellings). Hence, on the one hand the size of government was being reduced as activities were contracted out. On the other hand, expenditure on social services was pushing in the other direction. After 1945, public expenditure (including transfer payments) accounted for a consistently rising proportion of GDP in most countries, reaching, for example, 38.9 per cent in the UK by 1964. Despite all the political noise in the 1970s and 1980s about reducing the size of government, no long-term decline occurred. By 1993 it had reached 46.8 per cent.

ROBERT MILLWARD
UNIVERSITY OF MANCHESTER

Reference

Demsetz, H. (1982) *Economic, Legal and Political Dimensions of Competition*, Amsterdam.

Further reading

Haynes, M. and Thompson, S. (2000) 'Productivity, employment and the "IT paradox": Evidence for financial services', in R. Barrell, G. Mason and M. O'Mahony (eds) *Productivity, Innovation and Economic Performance*, Cambridge, pp. 93–116.
Lange, O. (1936) 'On the economic theory of socialism', *Review of Economic Studies* 4.
Lord Roll of Ipsden (ed.) (1982) *The Mixed Economy*, London.
Millward, R. (2004) 'The rise of the service economy', in R. Floud and P. Johnson (eds) *The Economic History of Britain since 1700: Volume III: 1939–2000*, Cambridge.
North, D.C. and Wallis, J.J. (1982) 'American government expenditures: A historical perspective', *American Economic Association: Papers and Proceedings* 72(2): 336–40.
Olson, M. (1982) *The Rise and Decline of Nations*, New Haven, CT.

SEE ALSO: markets; nationalization; planning, economic; public goods; regulation

MODERNIZATION

Modernization theory emerged out of a conjunction of historical forces and ideas after the end of the Second World War. The historical forces included the long collapse of the European and British colonial empires, which began after the First World War and was more or less completed by the 1950s, and resulted in the emergence of new nation-states in Africa, the Middle East and

Asia. Other factors also included the emergence of the USA as a world power, the situations in Latin America and Southeast Asia, and the Soviet Union with its own imperializing ambitions, portraying itself as the counter-model to capitalism (So 1990).

However, the constellation of ideas that embodied modernization theory was more complex and interesting than its ideological representation might otherwise suggest. Historically it belonged to the theoretical reflections in the new discipline of sociology concerned with the formation of modern societies in contrast to those classified as traditional ones. The processes that were viewed as central to the complexity and dynamism of modern societies were markets and patterns and images of mass consumption, industrialization and the increasing division of labour. Apart from these 'material' processes there were other factors including secularization, mass education, the separation between civil society and the state, and the formation of liberal democracy as the conduit through which social power circulated.

These processes became viewed as normal ones for modern societies in terms of the paradigm of social evolution that emerged in the nineteenth century and came to dominate twentieth-century sociology, including functionalism and systems theory from Durkheim, to Parsons, to Marxism. There was an assumption that societies moved on a historical trajectory based on these dynamic processes, and those that did not were viewed as backward or underdeveloped. Modernization was viewed as a positively transforming process that was irreversible (Parsons 1971; Black 1966).

The development of nation-states in Africa, Asia and the Middle East drew on these assumptions and threw them into relief. The adoption of a particular model of modernization by the elites of newly formed nation-states occurred in the context of external, and wider and more encompassing, geopolitical forms of power. This external context entailed that forms of dependency emerged as the newly formed nation-states were linked into capitalist markets. In this context, economic modernization was viewed as paramount and occurred in the forms of loans and infrastructural development, which was linked to the specialization of particular forms of commodity production. It was assumed that this commodity specialization and infrastructural and technical development would provide the 'spurt' required for economic 'take-off' and self-sustained growth that would occur in successive stages and result in a mature capitalist society oriented to mass consumption (Rostow 1990; So 1990).

However, Gunder Frank and other dependency theorists argue that this form of economic modernization is a power relation of capitalist financial centres over peripheral or semi-peripheral ones. This capitalist power relation organized the peripheral countries to produce commodities geared towards consumption at the centre. Specialized commodity production had the effect of not only tying these commodities, and the particular division of labour within the labour market that this commodity production entailed, to cycles within the globalizing capitalist world economy, but also disrupting cycles of traditional commodity production. The combined effect of each of these processes has been increases in poverty, unemployment and national debt (Gunder Frank 1969, 1984; So 1990).

In addition to their condition of dependence and underdevelopment, Wallerstein argued that these nation-states are spatially integrated into the long history of a capitalist system that is more than just a centre–periphery arrangement. For Wallerstein and world-systems theorists, the long history of capitalism encompasses the sixteenth century of European expansion and settlement, British colonial dominance in the nineteenth century, a period of instability from approximately 1870 until the middle of the mid-twentieth century encompassing both World Wars, and the postwar period at least up until 1989. Viewed from a world-systems perspective, nation-states, and especially the more recently formed ones, belong to this longer five-phase history of colonialism. This history is nothing but the continuous history of capitalism. The post-colonial experience is a more recent phase in its longer history (Wallerstein 1996, 1979, 1989; Bergesen 1980).

Both dependency and world-systems theory contested the evolutionary and developmentalist assumptions that were built into conventional social theory, and by so doing introduced spatial and long-term power relations into it. Moreover, both perspectives contributed to a theoretical and substantive sensitization to regional and national particularities. However, within dependency and world-systems perspective, this sensibility was circumscribed, as the national and regional particularities, themselves, were subsumed by, and subordinated to, the logic of a global economic system.

Recent arguments concerning globalization in the wake of the post-1989 world have continued the legacy of both modernization and world-systems theories, especially, with an even greater emphasis on the unequal, colonizing and integrating capacity of capitalism at the levels of not only the economy, but also of culture and politics, making the nation-state obsolete.

However, a critique of contemporary modernization theory as globalization can begin from observations that came from the long history of capitalism, observations that emphasize civilizational rather than only economic encounters (Wallerstein 1984). The result of this critique has been an analysis that has concentrated on a three-fold combination and intersection of the long histories of regions and cultures, the specificity of modernizing impulses, and conflicts at junctures of both of these forces, the result of which are multiple modernities. One particular juncture has been the continuing (re-)formation of nations in which wars of independence give way to often violently articulated competing claims for participating in, shaping or contesting the particular model of modernization being pursued by the predominant elite.

This perspective is typified by the work of, among others, Schmuel Eisenstadt and Johann P. Arnason. In their work, each deploys an image of tension between conflict and integration *within* modernity itself, *between* all of its different dimensions, and *between* these dimensions and the civilizational backdrops against which these modernities develop. In this way, credence is given to the specific characteristics of regional and civilizational identities and geographies, and the way in which tensions and conflicts are constitutive of these (Eisenstadt 2002, 2003; Arnason 1996, 1997, 2002).

These tensions have entailed that the appropriation of occidental institutional patterns, ways of thinking and acting, and the human self-images that accompany these – for example of being rational, free, a national or a capitalist – has neither been immediate nor straightforward. Rather, a continuous selection, reinterpretation and reformulation of traditions and modernities has occurred that has given rise to new political and institutional arrangements and cultural programmes that have their own antinomies and

tensions, in which conceptions of collective identity, including negative and positive conceptions of others, including the West, are constantly reconstructed (Eisenstadt 2002).

JOHN RUNDELL
UNIVERSITY OF MELBOURNE

References

Arnason, J.P. (1996) *Nation and Modernity*, Arhus, Denmark.
—— (1997) *Social Theory and Japanese Experience: The Dual Civilization*, New York.
—— (2002) 'The multiplication of modernity', in Eliezer Ben-Rafael with Yitzhak Sternberg (eds) *Identity, Culture and Globalization*, Leiden.
Bergesen, A. (1980) *Studies in the Modern World System*, New York.
Black, C.E. (1966) *The Dynamics of Modernisation*, New York.
Eisenstadt, S. (2002) 'The civilizations of the Americas: The crystallization of distinct modernities', *Comparative Sociology* 1(1) s. 43–61.
—— (2003) *Comparative Civilizations and Multiple Modernities*, Vols 1 and 2, Leiden.
Gunder Frank, A. (1969) *Capitalism and Underdevelopment: Historical Studies of Chile and Brazil*, New York.
—— (1984) *Essays on Dependence and Reformism*, London.
Parsons, T. (1971) *The System of Modern Societies*, New Jersey.
Rostow, W.W. (1990) *The Stages of Economic Growth: A Non-Communist Manifesto*, 3rd edn, Cambridge.
So, A.Y. (1990) *Social Change and Development*, London.
Wallerstein, I. (1979) *The Capitalist World Economy*, Cambridge.
—— (1984) *The Politics of the World Economy: The States, the Movements and the Civilizations*, Cambridge.
—— (1989) *The Modern World System*, New York.
Wallerstein, I. with T.K. Hopkins (1996) *The Age of Transition: Trajectory of the World-System, 1945–2025*, London.

Further reading

Rundell, J. (1997) 'Beyond crisis beyond novelty: The tensions of modernity', *New Formations* 31 (spring/summer).

SEE ALSO: economic development; underdevelopment

MONETARY POLICY

Monetary policy refers to the setting of interest rates to achieve certain economic goals, usually the control of inflation or some measure of real activity. Control means short-term stabilization and/or the achievement of some target level over the longer term. The key issues concern the way in which the policy should be implemented, the choice of goals and the authorities that should be empowered to take these decisions.

The main *instrument* of monetary policy is the rate of interest charged by the central bank on the money that it provides to the banking system. Whatever the policy goal, day-to-day policy decisions are often taken with reference to an *intermediate target* or *indicator*, such as the exchange rate or the rate of monetary growth.

The money supply itself is not an instrument of monetary policy as the central bank cannot exercise direct control over it. It can, however, exercise indirect control through its control of the rate that it charges to the banking system. At the heart of this system is a group of banks who keep deposit accounts at the central bank. The balances on these accounts, together with cash, constitute the monetary base. In the course of each business day, individuals and firms withdraw money from each of these banks and keep it as cash, or deposit it with the other banks. Towards the end of each day, the accumulation of these transactions leaves some banks owing money to others – money that must be delivered by the end of the day. The debtors usually obtain the necessary money by borrowing it from other banks through the interbank market. Occasionally, however, some of them will find by the close of business that they have not been able to borrow sufficient funds to cover their obligations. They must then turn to the central bank that, as *lender of last resort*, can supply money by buying some of the bank's assets (often Treasury Bills) or providing an overdraft. The interest rate on these funds will influence the rate that the banks charge on their loans to customers and the amount they are willing to lend.

Central banks may attempt to implement monetary policy through *open market operations*, that is, their purchase or sale of financial assets, usually government bonds. Each sale takes money out of the economy and deprives the banking system of some of the funds it will need later in the day to settle its internal debts, that is, the whole system will be short of funds. This ensures that some banks will have to get funds from the central bank, which will allow the latter to force interest rates up if it so wishes. However, the central bank cannot refuse to make the funds available unless it is willing to let one or more banks become insolvent. Thus it is not possible for the bank to practise *monetary base control*, although it can of course use the monetary base as an intermediate target and adjust its lending rates accordingly.

Arguments about the goals of monetary policy became heated after the publication of Keynes's *General Theory* in 1936. Previously most economists had held the classical view that the level of economic activity could not be influenced by policy actions and that the target for monetary policy should be prices or inflation. Keynes took the opposite view and recommended management of aggregate demand as a means of stabilizing the economy. Keynesians, but not necessarily Keynes himself, also held the view that fiscal, rather than monetary, policy was the most effective demand management tool.

By the 1960s the battle appeared to have been won by the short-term activity stabilizers, and the opposition, by then labelled monetarists, were a dwindling band. However, the experiences of the 1970s began a move towards a long-term inflation goal. The issue turned on whether the economy is self-righting or not. The very essence of Keynesianism is that it is not, or at least not before we shall all be dead.

The monetarists, by now holed-up in Chicago and a few lonely outposts in England, attacked this view on two fronts: first, that it was in fact monetary policy which would have the greater effect on demand; and, second, that the economy would always settle to a natural rate of activity and policy-makers should attend to improving this natural rate rather than interfering with the market forces that lead the economy towards it. They also added the somewhat inflammatory opinion that the authorities were not competent to adjust demand at the right time. By taking this view, they condemned demand management by both monetary and fiscal policy, but were particularly agitated by the prospect of demand managers using the powerful monetary policy incompetently. Far better, they argued, to take such a potent weapon out of the hands of the managers and assign it to the long-term goal of low inflation by setting a fixed target for the rate of monetary growth.

Nestling between the two great pillars of the mechanics of monetary policy and the structure of the economy is an awkward little subject known as the 'transmission mechanism', by which changes in monetary policy come to affect output and jobs. Views on this changed enormously in the 1970s and 1980s. Previously, it had been thought that monetary policy changes simply caused people and firms to demand more, or less, domestically produced output, or to switch between domestic goods and imports if the policy action moved the exchange rate. Subsequently, it was argued that their behaviour would be influenced by both actual and *expected* policy, and that for a change in monetary policy to have an effect on activity it would have to come as a surprise. For example, if firms knew in advance that the authorities were going to relax monetary policy in an attempt to increase output beyond the natural rate, they would increase their prices in advance. To achieve a temporary increase in output the expansion would have to be greater than expected. To achieve a long-term expansion a sequence of accelerating monetary growth surprises would be necessary, with an accompanying acceleration of inflation.

Theoretical models were developed to analyse these expectational effects, culminating in the *rational expectations hypothesis*, which provided weapons for both sides. First, it was claimed that intelligent individuals could predict all the actions of a rational monetary authority, that is, that policy surprises were impossible. The activists countered that even expected policy can be effective if firms typically set prices before they become aware of future policy actions. Conversely, if the authorities are known to be committed to full employment, wage bargainers have little to fear in pressing for large pay increases because they know that if firms cannot afford them, and start laying off labour, the authorities will increase the level of demand so that they can increase prices to raise the money to meet the enlarged wage bill. Thus stabilization policy creates an *inflationary bias*. Furthermore, active policy makes it difficult for firms to distinguish between those increases in shop prices which indicate that their share of the natural rate of demand has increased, and those which reflect policy actions that will eventually lead to all prices increasing with no long-term demand change. Thus active monetary policy can reduce the efficiency of prices as a signalling mechanism.

The policy game also creates a difficulty for the implementation of a passive long-term inflation target, however. The optimal long-term strategy is to announce that low inflation will be maintained through thick and thin. However, should a recession emerge, the optimal short-term response of a government concerned about its election prospects might be to increase demand by a monetary relaxation. Thus the optimal long-term policy is not consistent with both the short-term objectives of the government and the events that may emerge over time, a problem known as *time inconsistency*.

This lack of *policy credibility* can be overcome by establishing a reputation for riding out recessions without a policy response. Alternatively, the time inconsistency can be removed by changing the objectives of the decision-makers – possibly by changing the decision-makers themselves, by handing the responsibility to an institution charged with keeping inflation down and with no interest in winning elections. The natural choice for this is, of course, the central bank. The successful anti-inflation performance of the relatively independent Bundesbank in the 1980s and 1990s offered strong support for this choice and was a key factor in the 1990 decision to make the European Central Bank independent of European governments.

Since the early 1990s several countries have chosen to follow the independent central bank route, and the low and stable levels of inflation since the mid-1990s can be attributed, in the main, to this choice. But this has led to a new problem. If a central bank is instructed to keep inflation below a certain level (2.5 per cent is fairly typical) or face some unpleasant consequences, the bank will have an incentive to push inflation as far below the target as possible, which may easily result in deflation. Deflation can be at least as damaging as inflation. For example, consider a firm that sets its wages in line with current output prices, but then finds that these prices fall during the year. Clearly the firm may struggle to meet its costs. Recent events in Japan provide an illustration both of how damaging deflation can be, and how difficult it can be to escape it. The difficulty arises because low inflation is usually accompanied by low interest rates, which limits the banks' ability to relate the economy by cutting its rates, since these will eventually reach zero and can go no further. The solution appears to lie in the setting of *symmetrical inflation targets*: these penalize the bank as much for undershooting its target as for overshooting it. At present very few independent central banks have such targets: notable exceptions being the Bank of England and the Bank of New Zealand. The European Central Bank, however, does not have a symmetrical target, and is charged with running its anti-inflation policy with consideration given to general economic conditions, which sounds remarkably similar to the objective of a government concerned that recession may damage its election chances.

DAVID BARR
IMPERIAL COLLEGE, LONDON

Reference

Keynes, J.M. (1936) *The General Theory of Employment, Interest and Money*, London.

Further reading

Blanchard, O.J. and Fischer, S. (1989) *Lectures on Macroeconomics*, Cambridge, MA.
Goodhart, C.A.E. (1984) *Monetary Theory and Practice*, Basingstoke.

SEE ALSO: liquidity; macroeconomic policy; money; money, quantity theory of; supply-side economics

MONEY

The ordinary person knows what money is: it is what he or she reckons prices in, makes contracts in and uses to buy things with. While money has taken many different concrete forms, both across societies and over time, its defining feature is general acceptability: people are always glad to take it, whether they intend to keep it for a time as a form of saving or to spend it.

The economist, looking at money from a macroeconomic perspective, sees these two possibilities of disposal as two of the functions of money: money as a medium of exchange, which facilitates the circulation of goods and services, and money as a store of value, which allows its holder to postpone specific expenditure decisions. The latter possibility leaves producers uncertain about future demands for their goods.

In a financially sophisticated society, other assets are close substitutes for money in both these functions. Assets may be ranked by the ease and speed with which they can be converted into money quickly without significant loss of value. The closer substitutes are called liquid assets. Money is unique, however, in being the asset

acceptable as the final means of payment: one may use, say, a credit card ('plastic money') as the medium of exchange, but one discharges the debt thus incurred with one of the assets that counts as money.

At any point in time in any society there are several assets that discharge the functions of money. Copper coins coexisted with gold or silver coins to cover small transactions, just as coins and notes coexist with bank deposits in modern economies. Paper notes and bank deposits were once innovations, and thought of as money-substitutes. Over time, as public confidence in new forms of money develops, a practical definition of money will come to include those new assets. Central banks report data on several more or less inclusive aggregates of monetary assets.

Government has done much to establish the general acceptability of particular assets. The sovereign's head on coins was designed to testify to their metallic content. As privately issued forms of money such as bank deposits have usurped coin as the dominant form of money, the precondition for acceptability has been confidence in the convertibility of deposits into state-issued money – notes and coin. This convertibility came to be supported by central banks providing state money as lenders of last resort to avoid bank crises and failures.

The criterion of general acceptability underscores the social foundation of money, but no single monetary asset is acceptable in all transactions, The use of particular forms of money in the payment of wages both reflects and enhances, in a self-reinforcing manner, acceptability based on social consensus. But acceptability would not be forthcoming without the support of state-enforced laws of contract. The state may also declare what is legal tender and what it will accept in payment of taxes (Wray 1998).

The polarity of social consensus and the power of the state have been manifest in recent years concerning the new currency for the European Union. Some governments declared the euro the new currency while others allowed a popular vote (and the euro was rejected). In settled monetary systems there is a mutuality of state and social support of money, in contrast to the dichotomy debated by philosophers of money (see Frankel 1977).

The role ascribed to money differs dramatically between schools of thought in economics.

To neo-classical economists, whose methodology is individualistic and based on certain and full knowledge, money is just an intermediary in exchange, something that is a technical improvement on barter but which has no effect on the relations between the 'real' objects being traded. Money is a veil. The alternative vision is to see money as a pervasive and non-neutral force in the economy. The *locus classicus* of this point of view is Keynes's *General Theory*. The two points of view are well explored in Smithin (2000).

VICTORIA CHICK
UNIVERSITY COLLEGE LONDON

References

Frankel, S.H. (1977) *Money: Two Philosophies*, Oxford.
Keynes, J.M. (1936) *The General Theory of Employment, Interest and Money*, London.
Smithin, J. (ed.) (2000) *What is Money?* London.
Wray, L.R. (1998) *Understanding Modern Money: The Key to Full Employment and Price Stability*, Cheltenham.

Further reading

Davidson, P. (2003) *Financial Markets, Money and the Real World*, Cheltenham.
Smithin, J. (2003) *Controversies in Monetary Economics*, 2nd edn, Cheltenham.

SEE ALSO: capital, credit and money markets; gold standard; Keynesian economics; liquidity; monetary policy; money, quantity theory of

MONEY, QUANTITY THEORY OF

The quantity theory of money is the proposition that there is a causal connection between the quantity of money and the general level of prices. The connection was well established by the middle of the seventeenth century: 'It is a common saying that plenty or scarcity of money makes all things dear or good cheap' (Mun 1928 [1664]). A modern version is 'Inflation is too much money chasing too few goods.' In its strongest version, not only is money the cause of price changes but also prices are supposed to change in proportion to the monetary change, in the long run. Discussion of the relation between money and prices began as shrewd observation of the effect of influxes of precious metals.

The doctrine that prices would eventually rise equiproportionately with the quantity of money, leaving the purchasing power of money unchanged (the 'neutrality of money'), was started by John Locke (1923 [1691]). His purpose was to refute the mercantilist equation of money with national wealth by showing that money's value varied inversely with its quantity. His reasoning was based on an abstract comparison of the same economy with two different stocks of money (allowing for the velocity of money's circulation). Hume (1955 [1752]) asserted that proportionality applied in the long run to actual variations in the amount of money in real-world economies, a doctrine that cannot be supported by Locke's comparative-static method. No appropriate reasoning was offered by Hume or anyone since, though it is a widely accepted article of faith among neo-classical economists.

Hume's treatment of the short-run effects of monetary changes was, in contrast, good theory – indeed the first *explanation* of the relation between money and prices. (In present-day language he explained the transmission mechanism.) An increase of money (from abroad, in exchange for exports) encourages greater output and employment, without, at first, any increase in wages. If workers become scarce, wages will increase (though Hume remarks that the manufacturer will also expect greater productivity). At first, prices of wage-goods are stable and production rises to meet demand. But gradually all prices rise until the situation prior to the monetary increase is restored in terms of purchasing power. The line of reasoning put forward by Milton Friedman (1969) is strikingly similar.

Thornton (1939 [1802]), Tooke (1844) and Fullarton (1844) challenged the central quantity-theory idea that the money supply was the primary causal force, in recognizing the role of the demand for credit in generating bank money. J.S. Mill (1857), too, dealt with non-metallic, credit money (bank notes, cheques). The older theorists allowed for hoarding, which would dampen the effect on prices. Hoarding is plausible in the case of precious metals, but credit money has no alternative use, making hoarding more difficult to justify. Credit money also gives rise to the possibility that purchases could be made without possessing money at all.

Bank liabilities took a long time to be recognized as money. Irving Fisher (1911) postulated a different velocity of circulation for currency and bank-deposit money in his version of the quantity theory, and even in 1930 Keynes writes of 'money proper' meaning coin and notes issued by the monetary authorities.

The quantity theory developed in Cambridge, England (starting with Marshall 1975 [1871], 1926 [1888–9]), was based on the concept of a demand for money chiefly for transactions needs. Expected expenditure levels, for which money balances were required, were indicated by one's income and wealth, subject to an interest rate incentive.

Friedman (1956) also holds that the quantity theory is a theory of the demand for money. Although he begins from the other end of the spectrum of money's functions, namely that money is an asset to be held, he contrives in the end to arrive at a formulation similar to transactions-based quantity theory. His theory implies that an exogenous change in money will affect aggregate money-income, but the division between price and quantity less definite than it was in Hume. The quantity theory is a cornerstone of modern monetarist thought.

Keynes, although originally an adherent of the quantity theory (1923), broke with it in 1936 by providing a rationale for substantial hoarding of money when interest rates were expected to rise, in order to avoid capital losses.

The problem of credit raised by Thornton, Mill and others is not amenable to analysis in the demand-for-money framework. It is being addressed by post-Keynesian work on endogenous money (Desai 1987) and is seen as a counterweight to the quantity theory.

VICTORIA CHICK
UNIVERSITY COLLEGE LONDON

References

Desai, M.J. (1987) 'Endogenous and exogenous money', in J. Eatwell, M. Milgate and P. Newman (eds) *The New Palgrave: A Dictionary of Economics*, London.

Fisher, I. (1911) *The Purchasing Power of Money*, New York.

Friedman, M. (1956) 'The quantity theory of money – a restatement', in M. Friedman (ed.) *Studies in the Quantity Theory of Money*, Chicago.

—— (1969) 'The role of monetary policy', *American Economic Review* 58.

Fullarton, J. (1844) *On the Regulation of Currencies*, London.

Hume, D. (1955 [1752]) *Of Money*, in E. Rotwein (ed.) [David Hume's] *Writings on Economics*, London.

Keynes, J.M. (1923) *A Tract on Monetary Reform*, London.

—— (1930) *A Treatise on Money*, 2 vols, London.

—— (1936) *The General Theory of Employment, Interest and Money*, London.

Locke, J. (1923 [1691]) *Some Considerations of the Lowering of Interest and Raising the Value of Money, Works of John Locke*, Vol. 5, London.

Marshall, A. (1926 [1888–9]) 'Evidence to the Gold and Silver Commission', in J.M. Keynes (ed.) *Official Papers of Alfred Marshall*, London.

—— (1975 [1871]) 'Money', in J. Whittaker (ed.) *The Early Economic Writings of Alfred Marshall*, 2 vols, London.

Mill, J.S. (1857) *Principles of Political Economy*, 2 vols, London.

Mun, T. (1928 [1664]) *England's Treasure by Foreign Trade*, Oxford.

Thornton, H. (1939 [1802]) *An Enquiry into the Nature and Effects of the Paper Credit of Great Britain*, New York.

Tooke, T. (1844) *An Inquiry into the Currency Principle*, London.

Further reading

Blaug, M., Eltis, W., O'Brian, D., Patinkin, D., Skidelsky, R. and Wood, G.E. (1995) *The Quantity Theory of Money: From Locke to Keynes and Friedman*, Cheltenham.

Laidler, D.E.W. (1991) *The Golden Age of the Quantity Theory: The Development of Neoclassical Monetary Economics: 1870–1914*, Oxford.

Marshall, A. (1923) *Money, Credit and Commerce*, London.

Mayer, T. (1978) 'The structure of monetarism', in T. Mayer (ed.) *The Structure of Monetarism*, New York.

SEE ALSO: Friedman; Keynes; monetary policy; money

MONOPOLY

A firm or individual (the monopolist) has a monopoly over the provision of a good or service when there is no alternative provider. The monopolist can select a combination of price and sales from all the market possibilities represented by the demand curve. There are two factors that limit the monopolist's power to extract profit by increasing price. First, if the product is not a necessity for them, consumers could reject the product and buy other goods; second, if there are close substitutes, for example different brands of the same kind of good, then the consumer can select one of these competing brands. Essentially the more the type of good is a necessity, and the less similar are alternative brands or products, the lower the fall in sales for a given price rise and the greater the monopolist's power to make profit (Chamberlin 1933; Robinson 1933).

Advertising tends to increase perceptions of product differences, and increase brand loyalty. This may also prevent competitors from entering the market and thus preserve future monopoly power (Schmalensee 1978).

There are two main reasons why economic welfare may be reduced by the existence of monopoly. First, monopoly power allows price to be set above marginal cost. Thus further (unsupplied) units would cost less than the amount somebody would be willing to pay. The absence of these unsupplied units is an allocative inefficiency caused by the firm's desire to keep prices high. Second, without sufficient competition from other suppliers and with imperfect control by the firm's owners, costs may be inefficiently high. To offset these adverse factors, the firm's monopoly may allow greater economies of scale (in the limit there are cases of 'natural' monopoly where multiple suppliers of, say, piped water would be obviously inefficient) (Schmalensee and Willig 1989; Williamson 1968).

Whether any particular monopoly requires regulation to safeguard the consumers' interests is a matter for anti-trust policy (Scherer and Ross 1990). Regulation may take the form of prevention (by refusing permission for mergers), breaking up existing monopolies, price controls or restrictions on allowable profit. However, all monopoly regulation suffers from the fact that the monopolists know more about their markets than the regulator (asymmetric information). If monopoly rents are unavoidable then the distribution of costs and benefits can be changed by setting up an auction for the monopoly right: at the limit competition for the monopoly will transfer all the benefit to the government or other ultimate owner. Also, many activities may be divided into natural monopoly activities (e.g. distributing electricity) and others (e.g. producing electricity). Hence the size of the monopoly activity can be reduced by defining its boundaries.

Monopolists may not be private profit-maximizing firms, but rather state firms pursuing other objectives. Then the welfare arguments have to be reassessed. Also, monopolies (and monopoly power) may be the necessary outcome of the need for dynamic incentives. Thus a patent granted to an invention yields a monopoly to the inventor. Without such patent protection, the investment necessary to produce the invention may not occur. Thus some kinds of monopoly may be inevitable in order to yield appropriate incentives to obtain dynamic efficiency of economic growth through technical innovation.

Finally, monopoly has a natural inverse termed monopsony: only one buyer in a market. Analysis is very similar and examples include the state buying road construction and defence projects.

NORMAN IRELAND
UNIVERSITY OF WARWICK

References

Chamberlin, E. (1933) *The Theory of Monopolistic Competition*, Cambridge, MA.
Robinson, J. (1933) *The Economics of Imperfect Competition*, London.
Scherer, F.M. and Ross, D. (1990) *Industrial Market Structure and Economic Performance*, Boston, MA.
Schmalensee, R. (1978) 'Entry deterrence in the ready to eat breakfast cereal industry', *Bell Journal of Economics* 9.
Schmalensee, R. and Willig, R.D. (1989) *Handbook of Industrial Organization*, Amsterdam.
Williamson, O. (1968) 'Economics as an anti-trust defence: The welfare trade-offs', *American Economic Review* 58.

SEE ALSO: competition; markets; regulation

MORBIDITY

In literature the term 'morbidity' describes a gloomy state of mind. In the social sciences it refers to health experience, more specifically to episodes of sickness. At any given time a population contains a certain number of sick people. They may be reckoned either in terms of the number of diseases and injuries they suffer or according to the amount of sickness time they experience. Those issues – sickness, its incidence and its duration – define the study of morbidity. As a subject of study, morbidity addresses the quality of life, seeking to learn why sicknesses occur and what effects they have on individuals and society. Mortality studies address the possibility of prolonging life. Life expectancy at birth is often employed as a gauge of the success of mortality policies. In morbidity studies, the aim is rather to diminish the number of sickness episodes and to reduce the amount of sickness time that individuals and populations experience. Whereas life expectancy is an estimate of how long members of a population can be expected to live, a counterpart, health expectancy, estimates what portion of that lifetime will be spent in good health and what portion in bad health.

By the 1960s mortality was declining across the world. For Western Europe, where the history is known in detail, that decline began in the late eighteenth century, a time when infectious diseases were commonplace. Since that time the risk of dying at any given age has diminished, and life expectancy has increased from about 30 or 35 years at birth to more than 75 years. Although in the past scholars often assumed that morbidity must have closely approximated mortality during the health transition, research into health experience suggests the contrary. At each age the likelihood of death has declined sharply, but the likelihood of falling sick – of initiating a new episode of disease or injury – has declined at a more gradual pace and along a different course. In other words, the likelihood of dying from any given sickness has changed over time, both for individual diseases and for all the ailments that people deem to be sickness. The lethality of diseases declined and humankind gained more control over the causes and risk factors associated with disease and injury. But the average duration of sickness episodes remained stable or increased. Thus health expectancy has not kept pace with the increase in life expectancy.

Several reasons have been advanced for the different trajectories of sickness time and of survival. First, less progress has been made in the control of non-communicable diseases, yet they are generally more lethal and last longer than the commonplace communicable diseases of the past. In the past people were sick more often, but on average their sicknesses were much shorter than those of the late twentieth century. Second, a theory called heterogeneous frailty explains rising sickness time by pointing to changes in population composition. 'New survivors', those individuals who lived longer as mortality declined, appear to have suffered more sickness. Third, medicine has enjoyed notable success at deferring the resolution of long sicknesses, especially in adults. Finally, cultural factors may have promoted a broader definition of sickness by the society and the individual.

Over the life course health experiences differ sharply among individuals and between men and women. Some people are often sick while others claim never to have been sick a day in their lives. These differences reflect varying attitudes that govern whether a particular experience should be counted as sickness. They also reflect differences in exposure to disease and injury risks, and perhaps also differences in the degree to which prior health experience continues to influence subsequent health. Many diseases leave lasting effects after recovery, and the same is true of commonplace experiences (exposure to solar radiation) and behaviours (cigarette smoking). Those 'insults' appear to accumulate at differential rates. Health experience later in life, and the timing of death, may be due not only to differences in individuals that are present at birth, which is what the theory of heterogeneous frailty suggests, but also to differences acquired over the life course. In the past and the present alike women report more sicknesses than men, but live longer.

In developed countries the leading problems for morbidity policy deal with the prevention of protracted sicknesses, including the increasingly elongated final episode of sickness that results in death. Costs of treating sickness have increased in recent decades at a pace faster than most other costs, resulting in a health sector that persistently eats up a growing share of resources. For developing countries the problems in this area are more complex. Especially in Africa and Asia acute infectious diseases, respiratory infections and chronic degenerative diseases all threaten, demanding a more varied and costly set of health policies. Yet most countries in those regions have meagre resources to spend on health. The task of research in the social sciences on morbidity is to treat sickness itself as an effect, and to search for the means to reduce its burden on the individual and society.

JAMES C. RILEY
INDIANA UNIVERSITY

Further reading

Belanger, A., Martel, L., Berthelot, J.M. and Wilkins, R. (2002) 'Gender differences in disability-free life expectancy for selected risk factors and chronic conditions in Canada', *Journal of Women and Aging* 14.

Murray, C.J.L. and Lopez, A.D. (1996) *The Global Burden of Disease*, Geneva.

Palloni, A., Pinto-Alnurre, G. and Pelaez, M. (2002) 'Demographic and health conditions of ageing in Latin America and the Caribbean', *International Journal of Epidemiology* 31.

Riley, J.C. (1998) 'Mortality and morbidity: Trends and determinants', *World Health Statistics Quarterly* 51 (2–4) (special issue): 177–90.

SEE ALSO: epidemiology; fertility; life tables and survival analysis; mortality; public health; vital statistics

MORTALITY

Individuals are born and die only once but populations experience a series of births and deaths of individuals. Social scientists study the rate of mortality, the social and economic determinants of mortality rates, and the ways in which societies deal with the death of an individual. The simplest summary measure of mortality is the crude death rate or CDR (the number of deaths per year per thousand population). It measures the effect of mortality on the population growth rate. However, the CDR is affected by the age distribution in the population. Populations in which there are a large proportion of children tend to have lower CDRs. Therefore, it is not useful for comparing mortality levels in populations with different levels of fertility or different levels of migration, both of which affect the age distribution.

More refined comparisons use age-specific death rates (annual deaths per thousand in an age group). A related measure is the infant mortality rate (IMR). The IMR for a year is the number of infant deaths (deaths before the first birthday) during the year per 1,000 live births during the same year. For a cohort of live births, the IMR is the proportion who die before their first birthday. The IMR varies from a low of about 5 to over 300 per 1,000. The IMR is often used as an indicator of mortality in the whole population since estimates of infant mortality are available for many populations that lack reliable estimates of adult mortality.

A life table characterizes mortality in a period of years by showing what would happen to a group of newborns (a hypothetical cohort) if the current age-specific death rates at each age did not change during their lifetime. The expectation of life at birth or life expectancy (e_0) is the average age at death in a life table. In general, e_0 is not the most common age at death for the hypothetical cohort. For example, in the USA in 2000 the life expectancy was 76.9 years. However, the life table suggests that only about 24 per cent of a hypothetical cohort would die when they were between ages 70 and 79 whereas 51 per cent would die over age 80 (Miniño et al.

2002). The value of e_0 is pulled down by the small number of individuals who die at very young ages.

Mortality has declined rapidly since the 1830s in European populations and more recently in the rest of the world. Most of the decline resulted from reductions in deaths to infectious and parasitic diseases. Although modern medical advances such as antibiotics and vaccines have been important in declines in developing countries, they have been less important in the mortality declines in populations of European origin. Mortality rates to such infectious diseases as tuberculosis, diphtheria, measles, diarrhoeas and pneumonia declined drastically before the development of effective medical measures to prevent or treat these diseases (Omran 1980). Most of these declines can be attributed to changes in nutrition, basic public health interventions such as improved water and sanitation, and changes in personal behaviours such as basic cleanliness and child-feeding practices. There is substantial variation among mortality declines in low-income countries. For example, China has experienced a very rapid decline in mortality to communicable diseases. On the other hand, life expectancy declined between the early 1970s and the 1990s in some areas of Eastern Europe, the former Soviet Union (especially among males) and parts of Southern and Eastern Africa (United Nations 2000).

In many low-income countries, the outlook for continued mortality declines is threatened by the increasing prevalence of HIV/AIDS. In 2002 there were an estimated 42 million individuals living with HIV/AIDS and there were about 3 million AIDS deaths. Africa has been especially hard hit with 29 million living cases and about 2.4 million AIDS deaths in 2002 (United Nations Programme on HIV/AIDS 2002). In some countries in Southern Africa, a third of all adults are infected. A few African countries may have declines in life expectancy of as much as 15 years as a result of AIDS. The high prevalence of HIV/AIDS is also associated with high rates of widowhood and orphanhood, and has serious implications for social and economic structure.

There is no evidence that the declines in mortality are coming to an end in high-income countries. Past predictions of 'maximum achievable' values for life expectancy have often been surpassed within a few years and mortality rates at the oldest ages continue to decline rapidly (including the rate for centenarians) (Oeppen and Vaupel 2002). Declining mortality rates will increase the number of years that future recipients of Social Security and pension funds will collect benefits (Lee 2000). This has serious implications for the future of these programmes. The effect of declining mortality on future medical expenses for the elderly may not be as large. It is likely that future declines in mortality will be accompanied by improved health (Lubitz et al. 2003).

The mortality declines have encouraged changes in social structures (United Nations 1982). For example, in high-mortality populations there are high proportions widowed and orphaned. These societies generally have strong social mechanisms for ensuring the welfare of widows and orphans. These often include rapid remarriage of widows or a sharing of the financial responsibility for children among the father's or the mother's brothers. In societies with low mortality, these mechanisms become less important and the support of elderly parents during a potentially long period of low economic productivity becomes a more significant problem.

The age distribution of a population is an important factor in shaping social structure, but mortality does not play the major role in this. In particular, the proportion of the population that is over 65 is largely determined by fertility rates that affect the ratio of the number of children to the number of persons of childbearing age. However, recent mortality declines have increased the proportion of the 'old' (over 65) who are among the 'oldest old' (over 85) to about 12 per cent.

The age distribution of dying persons is also important. In a typical high-mortality country about 15 per cent of the population and 40 per cent of the deaths are under age 5. In the USA in 2000 only 6.9 per cent of the population and 1.2 per cent of the deaths were under age 5. Most deaths in the USA are over age 75 (57 per cent) compared to only 11 per cent of the deaths in a typical high-mortality population. This distribution has implications for cultural attitudes towards life and death. For example, in some high-mortality societies children are not given a name until they have survived the first few weeks of life.

There is increasing interest in determining the extent to which ageing is determined by genes. Data from Danish twins suggest genetic differences explain about 25 per cent of the variation in life-span among survivors to adulthood (Herskind et al. 1996). One version of the gene for apolipoprotein-E (APOE), the e4 type or 'allele', is associated with increased risk of both heart disease and Alzheimer's disease. Since these are both common causes of death, e4 is also associated with increased mortality risks over age 50 (Ewbank 2002). Since the effect of APOE works through very specific causes of death it is considered a 'frailty' gene rather than a 'longevity' gene (Gerdes et al. 2000). There may be longevity genes that have alleles associated with variations in so many aspects of health that they can be said to affect the rate of 'ageing'.

In all populations, mortality and morbidity (illness and functional limitations) vary with indicators of social status such as education, income and occupation. In the USA, race/ethnicity and measures of social and economic status are associated with substantial differences in mortality and disability (Geronimus et al. 2001). The mechanisms through which social factors affect health differ across populations. They include differences in nutrition, housing, access to and use of health services, and such behavioural differences as child-feeding practices, smoking and alcohol consumption (United Nations 1982).

DOUGLAS C. EWBANK
UNIVERSITY OF PENNSYLVANIA

References

Ewbank, D.C. (2002) 'Mortality differences by APOE genotype estimated from demographic synthesis', Genetic Epidemiology 22(2).

Gerdes, L.U., Jeune, B., Ranberg, K.A., Nybo, H. and Vaupel, J.W. (2000) 'Estimation of apolipoprotein-E genotype-specific relative mortality from the distribution of genotypes in centenarians and middle-aged men: Apolipoprotein-E is a "frailty gene" not a "longevity gene"', Genetic Epidemiology 19(3).

Geronimus, A.T., Bound, J., Waidmann, T.A., Cohen, C.G. and Steffick, D. (2001) 'Inequality in life expectancy, functional status, and active life expectancy across selected black and white populations in the United States', Demography 38(2).

Herskind, A.M., McGue, M., Holm, N.V., Sörensen, T.I.A., Harvald, B. and Vaupel, J.W. (1996) 'The heritability of longevity: A population-based study of 2872 Danish twin pairs born 1870–1900', Human Genetics 97(3).

Lee, R. (2000) 'Long-term population projections and the US Social Security System', Population and Development Review 26(1).

Lubitz, J., Liming, C., Kramarow, E. and Lentzner, H.

(2003) 'Health, life expectancy, and health care spending among the elderly', *New England Journal of Medicine* 349(11).

Miniño, A.M., Arias, E., Kochanek, K.D., Murphy, S.L. and Smith, B.L. (2002) 'Deaths: final data for 2000', *National Vital Statistics Report* 50(15), Hyattsville, MD: National Center for Health Statistics.

Oeppen, J. and Vaupel, J.W. (2002) 'Broken limits to life expectancy', *Science* 296(5,570).

Omran, A.R. (1980) 'Epidemiologic transition in the US', *Population Bulletin* 32.

United Nations (1982) *Levels and Trends of Mortality Since 1950*, Department of International Economic and Social Affairs (ST/ESA/SER.A/74), New York.

—— (2000) *World Population Monitoring 1998: Health and Mortality: Selected Aspects*, Department of Economic and Social Affairs, Population Division (ST/ESA/SER.A/174), New York.

United Nations Programme on HIV/AIDS (2002) 'AIDS epidemic update', Geneva: UNAIDS [updates available from http://www.unaids.org].

Further reading

Christensen, D. (2001) 'Making sense of centenarians', *Science News* 159(10).

Gribble, J. and Preston, S. (eds) (1993) *The Epidemiological Transition: Policy and Planning Implications for Developing Countries*, Washington, DC.

Martin, L. and Soldo, B. (eds) (1997) *Racial and Ethnic Differences in the Health of Older Americans*, Washington, DC.

Piot, P., Bartos, M., Ghys, P.D., Walker, N. and Schwartländer, B. (2001) 'The global impact of HIV/AIDS', *Nature* 410(6,831).

Wachter, K.W. and Finch, C.E. (eds) (1997) *Between Zeus and the Salmon: The Biodemography of Longevity*, Washington, DC.

SEE ALSO: epidemiology; fertility; life tables and survival analysis; morbidity; public health; vital statistics

MULTICULTURALISM

A latecomer to the social sciences vocabulary, the term 'multiculturalism' is misleading if the '-ism' is taken at face value. The word evokes a vision of society freed from discrimination on ethnic or racist, religious or national criteria, in short, a vision of equality across, or perhaps regardless of, 'cultural' differences. Yet the singular suffix '-ism' hides a vast variety of usages that range from bottom-up projects to top-down policies and from mass media and marketing hypes to highly specialized academic debates. Moreover, they are formulated differently in different nation-states, as will be evident from even the briefest historical review.

The word first arose in Canadian public debates of the mid-1960s when bottom-up activists, top-down policy-makers and liberal scholars faced the same triad of problems: the rights to autonomy of indigenous peoples or 'first nations' with particular territorial claims, the 'cultural' rights to political secession of language-based nationalists in Québec, and the civil and cultural rights of the more recent immigrants. By the 1970s, the term gained ground in the USA where some voices narrowed it down to an issue of 'race' and others broadened it out to include 'lifestyle'. While the 'first nations' and 'race' usages spread to Latin America, the Western European policy and academic debates came to focus on 'immigration', and Eastern European debates had to face the dilemmas of ethnicity as opposed to nationality, ethnonationalism as opposed to civic nationalism (Tishkov 1997). Although the entire range of problem definitions is equally recognizable in the former Third World, too, there has been remarkably little comparative work (Ackermann 1997).

To explore a foundation for the newcomer term, it may be useful to recall some basics first. In its most general sense, the latecomer word describes the oldest condition of any politically organized society coexisting with any other: dealing with cultural difference and diversity in one social space, however defined, be it 'the other bank of the river' or 'my children's school'. The ethnographic record of anthropologists is full (though all too often in footnotes) of bi- and trilingual overlaps between culturally distinct populations, and it is brimful with culturally defined minorities coexisting and interacting with culturally distinguished majorities or hegemonies. In that general sense, then, multicultural coexistence is as old as the principle of exchange. The forms of such exchanges may range from the mere toleration of cultural 'others' through the creation of interdependence and sometimes niche-economies to a hegemonic project of fusing formerly distinct cultures by a process of *métissage*, *mestisaje*, hybridization or creolization, usually supervised by seemingly self-evident ethnic or religious elites. What seems new about multiculturalism is thus a very recent set of problems, and it is closely connected to the late-modern crisis of the ex-colonialist or postcolonial nation-state as a credible 'imagined community' (Anderson 1983).

The nation-state was once expected to transcend pre-established patterns of ethnic, dynastic, religious or other 'cultural' loyalties and identifications. Whether one examines the First, Second or Third World, however, there is hardly a nation-state that has overcome its record of civic inequality and social and cultural exclusion, and none that has implemented its foundation charter: to ensure universal exchange in a market of resources and ideas equally open to all residents on equal terms. These observations clearly jar with the widespread claim to 'democratic' governance, be it based on equality of citizenship, individual social mobility or even both of these supported by welfare state policies. The rise of multiculturalism as a programmatic vision is thus directly connected with the crisis of credibility of the late-modern nation-state.

Given the enormous variety of people and peoples, parties and pundits all campaigning under the flag of multiculturalism, one could be forgiven for seeking refuge in a taxonomy of 'schools'. Textbook distinctions range from 'conservative' via 'corporate' and 'liberal' to 'critical' multiculturalisms. Useful as such a taxonomy might be, it is also highly questionable. If 'conservative multiculturalism' seeks the assimilation of cultural differences into what it calls the majority culture, then it is a contradiction in terms and should simply be called neo-nationalism. If 'corporate multiculturalism' accords different group rights to different 'cultural communities', then it must ask itself whether it wants a cross-culturally pluralist society or a 'plural society' (Furnivall 1948), the discredited colonial project of making peace by apartheid and keeping apartheid at peace. 'Liberal multiculturalism' may seek the social integration of cultural minorities on the principle of equal individual citizenship, but it all too often ignores repressive power structures, cultural hierarchies and hegemonic practices. Just these, however, define the agenda from 'revolutionary' to 'critical' multiculturalism (McLaren 1997; Anthias 2001). Categorizations by 'school', however, tend to create a proliferation of further categories, while most societies exhibit a multitude of mutually contradictory and even self-contradictory processes that straddle all scholastic taxonomies.

To see some order behind the semantic chaos, one may perhaps reduce it to four main currents. Viewed as a set of bottom-up projects or top-down policies, multiculturalism can be invoked as an emancipatory set of practices or as a communitarian one. Viewed as a school of thought, multiculturalism can be argued as either an essentialist (self-appellation: 'realist') or a pluralist (invective: 'constructivist') theory of culture. Historically, it is best to start with multiculturalism as a set of projects and policies, for the academic usages and redefinitions have often responded to the public usages of the word.

Viewed as an emancipatory set of projects or policies, multiculturalism was put on the map by protagonists who had seen the difficulties of a civil rights project to emancipate ethnic or religious minorities into effective citizenship and who therefore demanded collective cultural rights. Despite the resistance of nation-state political elites, there were successes in replacing nationalist and ethnocentric school curricula with 'multicultural curricula' and sometimes successes with initiating policies of 'affirmative action', 'positive discrimination' or 'ethnic targeting'. All of these initiatives helped to remedy old-established patterns of systemic oppression, civil inequality and daily discrimination and exclusion. These projects and policies were thus largely a good thing, except when driven to excess.

In polarized nation-states, especially the USA, 'multicultural education' was hijacked by protagonists of exclusivist 'ethnic studies' who seemed merely to reciprocate the ethnocentrism of whites with a 'Black Athena'-style ethnocentrism of their own (Bernal 1991). At the same time, even well-intentioned policies of 'affirmative action' were faced with widespread resentment against the growth of 'identity politics'. The populist reactions against this 'cult of ethnicity' (Schlesinger 1992) were sometimes extreme in their naïvety and their faith in an all-encompassing civil religion, but more discerning critics, too, questioned the efficacy of multiculturalist policies. Thus, Wilson (1987) convinced even progressive policy-makers that top-down policies of 'affirmative action' could not achieve the emancipation of 'the truly disadvantaged', after Rothschild (1981) had analysed the seemingly irresistible movement of 'ethnopolitics' as a double-edged ideology 'mobilizing ethnicity...into political leverage for altering or reinforcing...systems of structured inequality between and among ethnic categories'. In this process, ethnopolitics 'stresses, ideologizes, reifies, modifies, and sometimes virtually re-creates the putatively distinctive and unique cultural heritages of the ethnic groups that it mobilizes' (Rothschild 1981: 2–3). Both the policy and the theoretical critiques seemed to agree that multiculturalist policies falsely rephrased issues of social justice and civic equality as issues of ethnic or 'cultural' identifications (Barry 2000).

Admittedly, multicultural projects and policies fared better in Canada and Britain, Western Europe and parts of Australia and Asia. There, multicultural policies continue to be enforced by constitutional commitments and sometimes legal reforms. In other nation-states, too, one may observe a spread of legal pluralism, a longstanding demand of many multiculturalists, though this has been largely confined to matters of family law and remains a far cry from the political philosophers' calls for value pluralism and anti-foundationalism (Young 1990). Multiculturalism continues to function as a set of projects and policies, but it continues also to face a number of inherent dilemmas: it stresses collective rights for collectivitites ('cultures', 'minorities') that are notoriously hard to define and bound; it often appears to value differences above the liberal orthodoxy of universal civil equality; and it is easily hijacked by activist elites or nation-state elites, both of which may prefer to exaggerate and manipulate differences rather than to accommodate or overcome them. Moreover, multicultural policies often face extreme reactions from neo-nationalist circles reinventing an outdated ethnonationalism, and the very word 'multicultural' can even be reduced to an offensive banality by commercial exploitations such as 'ethnomarketing' (Costa and Bamossy 1995; Gilroy 2000).

Why, then, this scepticism vis-à-vis, or perhaps hiatus within, the multicultural programme as either bottom-up project or top-down policy? The question opens up the second field of contention, a theoretical one: if multiculturalism is a school of thought about culture, then it must answer three questions: What is culture? How can culture give rise to rights? And which cultures are to be granted which rights?

Despite their very different starting-points, the most influential liberal theorists, Kymlicka (1989) and Taylor (1992), can both be seen to trace collective cultural rights from the accepted liberal version of recognizing individual rights to representation, self-determination and/or recognition. While Kymlicka's culture concept is broadly based on ethnicity, Taylor's focuses on criteria of 'authenticity'. Both, however, have to face the same impasse: the harder one tries to deduce 'cultural group' rights from the well-enshrined liberal starting-point of individual rights – be they rights to self-esteem, civic equality or recognition – the more one has to fall back on the most uncomfortable choice of all: namely, to select some 'cultures' worthy of more recognition from other 'cultures' deserving less recognition (Kymlicka 1995: 76; Taylor 1994: 72). The price of liberalism, so it appears from both their arguments, is a selective endorsement of communitarianism, that is, a selective granting of collective 'cultural' rights to selected 'societal cultures' (Kymlicka) or 'cultural communities' (Taylor). Pragmatically, this may be all that can be done; yet analytically, the selection of worthier cultures from less worthy ones has always been anathema to all liberal scholars. Intent on avoiding the temptations of reifying or essentializing the concept of culture, as liberal thinkers have always been, the price of multiculturalism as a political philosophy appears to be pigeon-holing people first in order to give them rights later.

Could one then think of multiculturalism as a postessentialist project, policy or school of thought? The literature offers two approaches here: one questions the nature of culture, the other questions the nature of citizenship. Questioning the nature of culture means disowning the liberal fiction of individuals acting in full and predictable harmony with their purported cultural identities. Culture, so it is argued here, is not constitutive of a person's identity, but merely contributive. Working in this vein, Turner (1993) offered the first anthropological critique of what he called 'difference multiculturalism'; Bhabha (1994) offered a postmodernist critique that emphasized the inherently flexible, multifaceted and indeed necessarily hybrid character of culture in the abstract as well as any 'one culture' in the (misplacedly) concrete sense of the word. Providing a bridge between this school of thought and the alternative, Walzer (1987, 1997) rightly raised questions about the ethical angle of multicultural coexistence, as also about the quotidian realities and subjective experiences of an ethically satisfying communication with cultural others who must retain the right to articulate their difference.

The alternative approach works by rethinking citizenship as both a concept (Young 1990) and as a processual practice (Schiffauer et al. 2003).

Developing the classic idea of 'social citizenship' (Marshall 1965), Young (1990) developed the concept of a situationally and contextually 'differentiated citizenship', and thereby sparked off numerous interdisciplinary efforts to reformulate the 'old' language of equal citizenship so that it could accommodate the 'new' language of multiculturalism. Young's seminal ideas also influenced the more recent feminist debates about multiculturalism (Okin 1999; Nash and Marre 2001) that stress the inherently gendered character of multiculturalist approaches if collective rights are based on a falsely reified concept of culture.

Rethinking citizenship as a learnt practice, Schiffauer *et al.* (2003) drew attention to the processes of 'civil enculturation'. Citizenship, so it is argued, is not to be understood as a static status or even as an agreement on *what* to argue for the common good; rather, it describes a process of socialization that inculcates a set of conventions and competences on *how* to argue for the common good. Remarkably, these conventions remain highly nation-state specific even when different nation-states seem to face 'the same' multicultural problem.

To review these debates, rather than imposing a conclusion upon them, multiculturalism has come a long way, both in practice and in theory, from a naïve understanding of 'cultures' as self-evident collectivities intrinsically entitled to definable collective rights granted by one or another elite. Speaking of practice, emancipatory projects and policies can turn into communitarian ones at the flick of a rhetorical or legalistic switch. Speaking of theory, even classically liberal schools of thought can turn from a well-intentioned programme of recognizing and valuing cultural differences into an unintended exercise in reifying and essentializing 'other people's cultures' and even the culture concept itself.

The differences have sometimes been exaggerated to the point of dogmatic hype. The competition for political, economic and cultural resources bears the Cain's mark of cultural discrimination almost everywhere, yet emancipatory projects and policies were accused all too readily of the (merely intellectual) sin of essentializing culture. The essentialists attacked in this way rightly called themselves 'realists' and blamed their opponents for being mere 'constructivists', as exemplified by Bader's (2001) critique of Baumann (1996, 1999). Culture, so one might

conclude from the controversies among multiculturalists, appears to involve two mutually contradictory dimensions all the time. On the one hand, it lends itself to reification: it offers normative agreements, if not precisely on *what* one should argue or do, then certainly on *how* one should argue or act; it inculcates these conventions by complex and subtle processes of enculturation; and it sanctions deviance by a repertoire of measures from informal social control to systematic violence. On the other hand, culture is not a photocopy machine turning out human clones, and there is nothing to be gained, therefore, from reducing people, or for that matter citizens, to mono-dimensional dupes of their assumed 'cultural identity'.

So far as multiculturalism is concerned as an '-ism', the dilemma may perhaps be phrased in starker terms: is it to be a form of 'many-cultures-ism' or a 'cultural multi-ism'? An essentialist or 'realist' approach to culture and cultures may be beneficial in liberating social competition from the shackles of cultural prejudice and exclusion. The risk, however, is that it will reduce multiculturalism to a patronizing and potentially ethnicist 'many-cultures-ism'. At the same time, a self-professedly 'culture-blind' liberalism emerges equally scarred from these debates. Liberalism, too, is 'a fighting creed' (Taylor 1994: 62), and, empirically, civil rights and civic equality have never been achieved anywhere without a decisive, and powerfully sanctioned, delegitimation of old-established patterns of discrimination decreed on putatively 'cultural' grounds. The idea of a 'cultural multi-ism' has a few things to learn, perhaps, from the basics alluded to at the outset: the longstanding human practice of exchanging across boundaries that at one moment are reified as ethnic, religious or cultural barriers and at the next moment are relativized by a cross-cutting interest and a situational redefinition. Both Young (1990) and Gutmann (1999) have intimated this as a vision of every human acting, and being understood to act, as a multifaceted multicultural microcosm in situational interaction with others. Lest this sound too splendid, we do, of course, still need political, economic and other opportunity structures to enable such interaction to proceed regardless of all our cultural boundary work.

GERD BAUMANN
UNIVERSITY OF AMSTERDAM

References

Ackermann, A. (1997) *Ethnic Identity by Design or by Default? A Comparative Study of Multiculturalism in Singapore and Frankfurt am Main*, Frankfurt.

Anderson, B. (1983) *Imagined Communities: Reflections on the Origin and Spread of Nationalism*, London.

Anthias, F. (2001) 'New hybridities, old concepts: The limits of culture', *Ethnic and Racial Studies* 24(4): 619–41.

Bader, V. (2001) 'Culture and identity: Contesting constructivism', *Ethnicities* 1(2): 251–85.

Barry, B. (2000) *Culture and Equality*, Cambridge.

Baumann, G. (1996) *Contesting Culture. Discourses of Identity in Multi-ethnic London*, Cambridge.

—— (1999) *The Multicultural Riddle. Re-Thinking National, Ethnic and Religious Identities*, New York.

Bernal, M. (1991) *Black Athena: The Afroasiatic Roots of Classical Civilization, II: The Archaeological and Documentary Evidence*, London.

Bhabha, H. (1994) *The Location of Culture*, London.

Costa, J.A. and Bamossy, G.J. (eds) (1995) *Marketing in a Multicultural World: Ethnicity, Nationalism, and Cultural Identity*, London.

Furvivall, J.S. (1948) *Colonial Policy and Practice*, London.

Gilroy, P. (2000) *Between Camps. Race, Identity and Nationalism at the End of the Colour Line*, London.

Gutmann, A. (1999) *Democratic Education*, Princeton, NJ.

Kymlicka, W. (1989) *Liberalism, Community, and Culture*, Oxford.

—— (1995) *Multicultural Citizenship*, Oxford.

McLaren, P. (1997) *Revolutionary Multiculturalism – Pedagogics of Dissent for the New Millennium*, Boulder, CO.

Marshall, T.H. (1965) *Class, Citizenship, and Social Development: Essays*, Garden City, NY.

Nash, M. and Marre, D. (eds) (2001) *Multiculturalismos y genero*, Barcelona.

Okin, S.M. (1999) *Is Multiculturalism Bad for Women?* Princeton, NJ.

Rothschild, J. (1981) *Ethnopolitics: A Conceptual Framework*, New York.

Schiffauer, W., Baumann, G., Kastoryano, R. and Vertovec, S. (eds) (2003) *Civil Enculturation. Nation-State, Schools, and Ethnic Difference in Four European Countries*, Oxford.

Schlesinger, A., Jr (1992) *The Disuniting of America: Reflections on a Multicultural Society*, New York.

Taylor, C. (1992) *Multiculturalism and the Politics of Recognition*, Princeton, NJ.

—— (1994) 'The politics of recognition', in A. Gutmann (ed.) *Multiculturalism: Examining the Politics of Recognition*, Princeton, NJ, pp. 25–74.

Tishkov, V. (1997) *Ethnicity, Nationalism and Conflict in and after the Soviet Union: The Mind Aflame*, London.

Turner, T. (1993) 'Anthropology and multiculturalism: What is anthropology that multiculturalists should be mindful of?' *Cultural Anthropology* 8: 411–29.

Walzer, M. (1987) *Interpretation and Social Criticism*, Cambridge, MA.

—— (1997) *On Toleration*, New Haven, CT.

Wilson, W.J. (1987) *The Truly Disadvantaged: The Inner City, the Underclass, and Public Policy*, Chicago.

Young, I.M. (1990) *Justice and the Politics of Difference*, Princeton, NJ.

SEE ALSO: culture; ethnic politics; ethnicity; human rights; identity; postcolonialism

MULTINATIONAL ENTERPRISES

A multinational enterprise owns and controls productive activities located in more than one country. It owns the outputs of these activities even though it may not own the assets used: these may be hired locally in each country. The multinational does not necessarily transfer capital abroad; finance can often be obtained locally as well. The multinational is thus, first, an international producer, and only second a foreign investor.

The activities of the multinational enterprise form an integrated system; they are not usually a mere portfolio of unrelated operations. The rationale for integration is that managerial control within the enterprise co-ordinates the activities more profitably than would arm's length contractual relations (Buckley and Casson 1991).

The antecedents of the modern multinational enterprise are found in the late nineteenth century, in British direct investments in the colonies, and in the merger movement in the USA from which the modern corporation evolved. In the interwar period, multinational operations focused upon backwards integration into minerals (especially oil). Horizontal integration was effected through international cartels rather than multinational firms. After the Second World War, many US enterprises began to produce in Western Europe, particularly in high-technology industries producing differentiated products. They transferred new US technology to Europe, together with improved management and accounting practices, and the experience of selling to a multicultural market of the kind that was developing within the European Community. In the 1970s European firms began to produce in the USA on a larger scale than before, often in the same industries in which US firms were producing in Europe. At the same time, Japanese firms began to produce abroad on a large scale in low-wage Southeast Asian countries, particularly in low technology industries such as textiles.

The value added by some of the world's largest multinationals now exceeds the gross national products of some of the smaller countries in which they produce. However, there are increasing numbers of very small multinational firms: not all multinationals conform to the popular image of the giant corporation.

Multinational operations provide firms with a number of benefits in addition to the operating economies afforded by integration. Intermediate products transferred between the parent company and its overseas subsidiaries – or between one subsidiary and another – can be valued at transfer prices that differ from those prevailing in arm's length trade. The transfer prices can be set so as to minimize *ad valorem* tariff payments, in order to reallocate profits to subsidiaries in low-tax countries, and to allow the enterprise to bypass exchange controls by disguising capital transfers as income. Transfer prices are particularly hard for fiscal authorities to detect when the resources transferred are inherently difficult to value: this is particularly true of payments for technology and management services that are very common in firms in high-technology industries. Reliable evidence on transfer pricing is difficult to obtain, though there are some proven instances of it.

Multinational operations also give the enterprise access to privileged information through membership of producers' associations in different countries, and enable it to co-ordinate internationally the lobbying of government for favourable changes in the regulatory environment. Multinationals are often accused of enlisting the support of powerful governments in the pursuit of their interests in foreign countries, though once again reliable evidence is difficult to obtain. The United Nations actively monitors the behaviour of multinationals through its Centre on Transnational Corporations.

MARK CASSON
UNIVERSITY OF READING

Reference

Buckley, P.J. and Casson, M.C. (1991) *The Future of the Multinational Enterprise*, 2nd edn, London.

Further reading

Buckley, P.J. and Casson, M.C. (1980) *Economic Theory of the Multinational Enterprise: Selected Papers*, London.
Dunning, J.H. (1992) *Multinational Enterprises and the Global Economy*, Wokingham.
Rugman, A.M. and Brewer, T.L. (eds) (2001) *The Oxford Handbook of International Business*, Oxford.

SEE ALSO: corporate enterprise; globalization; international trade

N

NATIONAL ACCOUNTS

National accounts are essential for understanding the structure and performance of an economy. They provide an objective basis by which the level and progress of the wealth of nations can be measured (Shaikh and Tonak 1994).

The term national accounts refers both to a database and to an empirical framework. As a database, these accounts provide a quantitative description of a nation's economic income and output. As an empirical framework, they serve as a double-entry macroeconomic accounting system. Gross domestic product (GDP), one of the most commonly used output statistics of the national accounts database, can therefore be estimated and checked in two different ways.

Conventional systems of national accounts include the United Nations System of National Accounts (UN/SNA); country or region-specific accounts, such as the US National Income and Product Accounts (NIPA), or the European System of Accounts (ESA); and various forms of input–output tables (I–O) and flow accounts (including capital finance and flow-of-funds).

The main focus of national accounting systems is production. Although the primary aim is to measure the creation and use of new national wealth, national accounts may be supplemented by data on financial flows in the economy (capital and flow-of-funds accounts), or by data that link production and financial flows to the corresponding stocks (national balance sheets).

The history of national accounts

In the seventeenth century, William Petty in England and Sieur de Boisguillebert in France made pioneering estimates of national wealth. The Physiocrats believed that only the agricultural sector was truly productive, but in the eighteenth century Adam Smith included other sectors, such as manufacturing, in his estimates. However, his definition of what is productive was based on the distinction between productive and unproductive labour, for which materiality was the main criterion. Because Smith considered only productive activities to be wealth producing, the relative share of productive and unproductive labour obviously became a determining factor for the accumulation of national wealth. Smith's criterion for distinguishing productive labour was challenged and modified by Marx, but he retained Smith's emphasis on productive employment as a significant factor in determining national output. Beginning with the Material Product System in the Soviet Union, some socialist countries introduced alternative formulations of national accounts based on the theories about productive labour of Marx and, especially, Smith.

The first relatively comprehensive estimates of a nation's income and output were only made after the Great Depression, and these estimates became more sophisticated following the publication of John Maynard Keynes's *General Theory* in 1936. The groundbreaking work on national income by Simon Kuznets in the USA and Richard Stone in the UK earned them Nobel Prizes in 1971 and 1984, respectively.

For neo-classical economic theory, what counted when it came to production was the marketability of a product. Anything that was marketable was considered to be the outcome of production. Measures of national product therefore shifted from what has been termed the 'restricted production' definition of the classical economists to a 'comprehensive production' definition favoured by neo-classical economists (Studenski 1958: 12). Some commentators have pointed to the ideological convenience of a definition of production that treats all market activities as productive (Shaikh and Tonak 1994). In any case, criticisms have been levelled both at the limited scope of these conventional measures, and at their use of marketability as the sole criterion. This has led to the formulation of alternatives to the measures of gross domestic product (GDP) or gross national product (GNP).

GDP and GNP

The key statistical category in national accounts is GDP. This is the total *market* value of all *final* goods and services produced in an economy in a specified *period*, usually one year. GDP is therefore a *flow* concept, always associated with a time interval. Formerly, measures of GNP were often preferred. GNP includes the income (or business profits) generated by the citizens of the nation abroad. GDP includes all income generated within the borders of a nation, without taking into consideration the national origin of individuals (or firms).

Since the structure of national accounts is based on double-entry accounting, GDP may be calculated in two ways: either through the expenditures made, or the incomes generated. The contemporary formulations of the expenditure and the income sides are fully consistent with Keynes's view of macroeconomic activities. To arrive at an estimate of GDP on the expenditure side, consumption (C), investment (I), government expenditures (G) and net exports (X-M) are added together. On the income side, GDP is estimated by adding compensation of employees, rents, interest, proprietors' income and profit (which together constitute *national income*), depreciation, indirect business taxes (netted of subsidies), business transfers and net factor payments to the rest of the world. Estimating GNP from GDP only requires adding net factor income, i.e. the income from foreign domestic factor sources *minus* foreign factor income generated domestically. Table 3 is an illustration of this arithmetic based on the recent data from the USA.

The main categories of expenditure indicate the way in which national output is allocated to various purposes. The income side gives a general sense of national (functional) income distribution. Such national accounts play an important role in macroeconomic policy-making and implementation. The measure of GDP per capita has also been widely used as a measure of economic well-being. The publicity given to these figures has profound political and cultural implications.

Alternative national accounts

The explicit focus of conventional national accounts on marketed activities has been the

Table 3 Gross domestic product (billions of dollars) – USA, 2002

Expenditures		Incomes	
Consumption	7,303.7	Compensation of employees	5,969.5
Gross investment	1,593.2	Proprietors' income	756.5
Government expenditures	1,972.9	Rental income	142.4
Net exports	−423.6	Corporate profits	787.4
		Net interest	684.2
		Indirect business tax	800.4
		Business transfers	44.1
		Less: subsidies	32.5
		Depreciation	1,393.5
		Net factor payments	9.6
		Statistical discrepancy	−183.9
Gross domestic product	10,446.2	Gross domestic product	10,446.2

Source: US Department of Commerce, Bureau of Economic Analysis (http://www.bea.doc.gov/bea/dn/selected.htm).

subject of criticism for many years. A variety of alternatives have been proposed, many of which may be classified as *extended* accounts. Extended accounts include unmarketed economic activities, including household work and illegal sources of income (Eisner 1988). Another approach takes account of environmental degradation and natural resource depletion (Daly and Cobb 1989).

A second group of alternative estimates is based on unease about the widespread use of GDP per capita figures as an indicator of well-being. Two influential new measures are the Human Development Index (HDI) developed by the United Nations Development Programme, and the Genuine Progress Index (GPI) developed by Redefining Progress. HDI measures a country's level of development. It is a summary composite number that combines measures of three broad areas: longevity (measured by life expectancy at birth), knowledge (literacy and enrolment rates) and standard of living (measured by GDP per capita adjusted for purchasing price parity). By including two important aspects of human development, i.e. longevity and knowledge, in addition to GDP per capita, HDI redirects public attention to broader disparities between countries. Table 4 gives an idea of how such an inclusion (based on a broader notion of development) shuffles the ranking of the twenty wealthiest countries.

GPI, originally estimated for the USA (other estimations have been attempted in Germany and the UK), is another composite index based on significant adjustments of the official statistics, including the basic categories of national accounts such as consumption. When adjustments are made to take into consideration income distribution, unpaid housework, community work, pollution, resource depletion, loss of leisure, etc., the impression of the overall well-being

Table 4 GDP per capita (purchasing power parity US $) versus HDI of the top twenty countries in 2001

	HDI Rank	GDP per capita	GDP index	HDI	GDP per capita rank minus HDI rank
1	Norway	29,620	0.95	0.944	4
2	Iceland	29,990	0.95	0.942	2
3	Sweden	24,180	0.92	0.941	15
4	Australia	25,370	0.92	0.939	8
5	The Netherlands	27,190	0.94	0.938	3
6	Belgium	25,520	0.92	0.937	5
7	USA	34,320	0.97	0.937	−5
8	Canada	27,130	0.94	0.937	1
9	Japan	25,130	0.92	0.932	5
10	Switzerland	28,100	0.94	0.932	−3
11	Denmark	29,000	0.95	0.930	−5
12	Ireland	32,410	0.96	0.930	−9
13	UK	24,160	0.92	0.930	6
14	Finland	24,430	0.92	0.930	3
15	Luxembourg	53,780	1.00	0.930	−14
16	Austria	26,730	0.93	0.929	−6
17	France	23,990	0.91	0.925	3
18	Germany	25,350	0.92	0.921	−5
19	Spain	20,150	0.89	0.918	5
20	New Zealand	19,160	0.88	0.917	8

Source: *Human Development Report, 2003* (http://www.undp.org/hdr2003/).

Table 5 The US GDP per capita versus GPI (1992 chained dollars)

	GDP per capita	GPI per capita
1950	10,581.8	5,319.4
1955	12,059.8	6,582.3
1960	12,525.0	6.804.8
1965	14,827.9	7.786.9
1970	16,569.5	8,721.2
1975	17,937.9	8,770.7
1980	20,310.3	8,731.6
1985	22,374.8	8,535.8
1990	24,600.3	7,910.6
1997	27,163.0	6,521.1

Source: Redefining Progress (http://www.rprogress.org/projects/gpi/).

of a nation may be very different from that conveyed by GDP figures. Table 5 shows the marked difference between the two indicators in the case of the USA. It will be seen that GDP per capita figures steadily increased in the USA from 1950, while GPI per capita declined after the mid-1980s.

E. AHMET TONAK
SIMON'S ROCK COLLEGE OF BARD

References

Daly, H.E. and Cobb, J.B. (1989) *For the Common Good: Redirecting the Economy toward Community, the Environment, and the Sustainable Future*, Boston.

Eisner, R. (1988) 'The total incomes system of accounts', *Journal of Economic Literature* 26: 1,611–84.

Shaikh, A. and Tonak, E.A. (1994) *Measuring the Wealth of Nations: The Political Economy of National Accounts*, New York.

Studenski, P. (1958) *The Income of Nations*, New York.

SEE ALSO: accounting; balance of payments; informal/shadow economy

NATIONALISM

The term 'nationalism' is used loosely in a number of different ways, to refer to a large range of phenomena (cultural, political, psychological, social). Sometimes the term 'nationalism' refers to the process of forming or maintaining nation-states (otherwise called 'nation-building'); sometimes it refers to the psychological feeling or identification with a particular national community; sometimes, to the aspiration to be self-determining; and, sometimes, to pride in the culture, language and symbolism associated with the nation (Hutchinson and Smith 1994: 3). The range of phenomena encompassed by the term 'nationalism' makes it imperative for students of nationalism to define the term carefully. One attempt at a very narrow definition, which identifies a 'core' to nationalism, is Ernest Gellner's claim that nationalism is primarily a political principle, which holds that the political and national unit should be congruent (Gellner 1983: 1). This has the advantage of conceptual clarity, indeed simplicity, but it also entails that every nationalist movement seeks separation or independence. In fact, however, many self-described nationalists do not demand independent statehood. They are content with other forms of recognition, within existing multinational states. A more inclusive, and yet faithful to ordinary language, definition of nationalism views it as a political ideology, centred on the idea that there is moral significance attached to membership in a nation, and in the continued (in the past and into the future) existence of the nation. On that basis, nationalists argue for political rights to protect the nation's continued existence, and express its identity.

The term 'nation' is also contested. Although it is very difficult to enumerate a list of characteristics that is shared by all examples of what we would normally regard as national communities, there is general agreement on certain clarifications of the concept of the 'nation'. There is a well-established distinction between nations, states and ethnic groups (Connor 1994: 90–117). These three concepts – state, nation and ethnic group – are closely interrelated, since (1) ethnic groups have the potential to become nationally mobilized; (2) many nations aspire to be politically self-governing (aspire to have states); and (3) states like to characterize their body politic as being a 'nation', for this implies that they have a common political identity. It is, however, important to distinguish them carefully. Ethnic groups (like nations) are social groups, characterized by myths of common descent, some common culture and mutual recognition, and complex rituals regarding boundary-maintenance. However, they are not coextensive with nations because they lack the political self-consciousness that is usually associated with national communities. What is distinctive about nations is the way in which they frame their aspirations or understand themselves as an actual or potential political community. Nations are not coextensive with states. This confusion (between states and nations) still pervades the literature especially in 'international relations'. It is embedded in terms such as 'United Nations', which is really an organization of sovereign states. Some states have more than one recognized nation (they are viewed as a 'compact' between two founding 'nations', as is Canada for example); some nations have more than one state (e.g. North and South Korea, West and East Germany prior to 1989); and some nations (e.g. Kurdish and Palestinian nations) do not have their own states, although many of their members aspire to this.

Debate on what constitutes a nation mainly revolves around the balance between subjective and objective elements. Most theorists agree that a subjective identification with a historic territory or homeland and with conationals is a necessary condition for shared nationality. This subjective component is based on objective elements – the various ties of shared language or religion or culture or public life that helps to make members identify with one another as a community. David Miller has usefully defined a nation as 'a community (1) constituted by shared beliefs and mutual commitments, (2) extended in history, (3) active in character, (4) connected to a particular territory, and (5) marked off from other communities by its distinct public culture' (Miller 1995: 27). These objective conditions are very general, and could be constituted in different ways by different communities.

Primordialism versus modernism in the history of nationalism

A prominent debate among theorists of nationalism concerns the primordial versus modernist character of nationalism. Primordialists, it is contended, view nationalism as rooted in ancient hatreds, and national conflicts as immutable and enduring. Modernists, by contrast, emphasize that nations are socially constructed, and link nationalism with broad historical forces in the modern period.

One prominent version of modernism is put forward by Gellner who contends that national

forms of identity became prominent and politically relevant in the modern period due to important economic and social forces. For Gellner, and others, they are linked with industrialization, and the social and bureaucratic changes that accompany industrialization (or precede it, in the case of states aspiring to be industrialized).

In Gellner's formulation of the argument, there are clear stages of economic and social organization (Gellner 1983). In the feudal period right up to the latter half of the eighteenth century, in some parts of Europe, and persisting in more remote areas much later than this, Europe was composed predominantly of agro-literate (feudal) empires, which were characterized by rigidly hierarchical social stratification. Peasants were tied to the land by dependency, force and ignorance; craftsmen and merchants predominated in the town; the clerical class monopolized literacy and numeracy; and the aristocracy, originally a military caste, came later to monopolize land holdings and to be loosely related (by oaths of fealty) to the monarch. Linguistic and cultural diversity was functional, because it reinforced the social hierarchies on which the system was based. In an industrialized society, by contrast, the economy is crucially dependent on standardized modes of communication and cultural practices, and people's life chances are shaped by the language in which they communicate, as well as other cultural forms of interaction. Culture is profoundly politicized, mainly because the state is heavily involved in the reproduction of language and culture. Anderson's *Imagined Communities* builds on this basic idea by suggesting that the boundaries of national identity have been shaped by the vernacular reading of communities that were created through print capitalism (Anderson 1993).

Unfortunately, this type of account offers us very little prescriptive guidance on how these identities should be regarded by the state. For one thing, the fact that they are socially constructed does not mean that these identities are easy to deconstruct, or that they should be treated less seriously. Indeed, in many cases, by identifying the very real advantages (in terms of life chances) of being a majority group in the state, and the almost inescapable logic, in the modern context, of identifying oneself in this way, many of these modernist accounts can support arguments that recognize the centrality of national forms of identity, at least as long as the state and the economy bear any resemblance to the modern one.

As an academic debate, the one between so-called primordialists and modernists has not been a particularly fruitful one. One problem is that, although primordialist sentiments are common enough in ordinary discourse and low-brow journalism, it is difficult to find an academic exponent of 'primordialism'. Even the frequently cited passage from Clifford Geertz's work, held up as an example of 'primordialism', in fact only contended that it is the agent's belief in their primordial attachments that drives conflict, but nowhere says that these attachments are in fact primordial in the sense of immutable (Geertz 1994; Fearon and Laitin 1999). Anthony Smith's work on the ethnic origins of nations did of course emphasize the premodern element out of which nations and nationalism were forged. He does not, however, view these nations, or national identities, as immutable, nor is this view inconsistent with the view that the modern context gives them a special political significance (Smith 1983).

Types of nations and nationalisms

In the nineteenth century, nationalism was regarded as a progressive and liberal force, associated with the unification of a number of backward regions into the republic of Italy, and anti-imperial movements in Russia and Central Europe. Most nationalists were also liberals, and vice versa; both nationalists and liberals were organizing against the illiberal, anti-democratic regimes of Tsarist Russia and the Austro-Hungarian empire.

In the twentieth century, and especially since the Second World War, nationalism has been associated with racism, tribalism, xenophobia, chauvinism and violence. These contending visions of nationalism – one, associated with liberalism and democracy, the other, which is associated with xenophobia and ethnic exclusiveness – have typically been discussed in terms of a distinction between 'types' of nationalism. Civic nationalism, which is generally associated with France and the USA, is the doctrine that all people in the state are members of the nation. This form of nationalism is not based on race or ethnic descent, and is open and inclusive. Ethnic nationalism is the doctrine that membership in the nation is confined to people in the same ethnic group. It is generally associated with German nationalism, and is often described as illiberal, defensive and exclusive.

There are many different variations on this basic distinction: Hans Kohn characterizes the distinction in terms of 'Western' and 'Eastern' types of nationalism (Yack 1995). The basic idea is that there is an important normative distinction between these different types, and a different dynamic associated with nationalist movements, depending on the 'type' of nationalism that they are organized to promote. Crudely stated, civic 'Western' nationalism is good; 'Eastern' ethnic nationalism is bad.

The civic–ethnic distinction captures something important in any normative assessment of nationalism. It is important that membership in the nation is potentially open to all, and inclusive of all, so that no one or no group feels excluded and marginalized. However, the civic–ethnic distinction is of limited usefulness, because it ignores the cultural dimension and the related potential for marginalization implicit in both types of nationalism.

All states make decisions on cultural matters that are bound to be contentious. They have to make decisions on what language(s) the courts, bureaucracy, organs of government, schools and so on will operate in, whether a particular statue should be erected, whether a particular kind of parade should be permitted, what symbols should be adopted in the state. This is true of civic nations, such as France and the USA. While everyone in the territory is conceived of as a member of the nation, the nation involves certain cultural characteristics, e.g. France creates Frenchmen, it teaches the French language, French history, French literature, and so on. While these requirements are potentially open to all, there is also a potential for marginalization and alienation of minorities who do not identify with the state or with the majority cultural/linguistic group on the territory (Kymlicka 1995; McGarry and O'Leary 1993).

The distinction between civic and ethnic nations fails to capture the cultural bias of civic states. If we distinguish between civic and ethnic nationalism on the grounds that 'ethnic nationalism' employs racial categories, and depends on ethnic descent, whereas civic nationalism does not, then, we find that almost all nationalisms are 'civic' and very few are 'ethnic'. The 'ethnic nationalism' category would be underpopulated.

On the other hand, if we describe the distinction between civic and ethnic nationalism in terms of civic nationalism being political, and ethnic nationalism involving the promotion of culture, or the expression of a particular culture, then almost all nationalisms become ethnic and very few are civic (Brubaker 1998).

Nationalist movements

The beginnings of nationalism may be traced to Europe in the latter half of the eighteenth century. Many historians identify the period from 1775 to 1807 (which includes the 1775 partition of Poland, the 1776 Declaration of Independence, the French Revolution and Fichte's 1807 Address to the German Nation) as pivotal in the development of nationalist movements and ideology. The French Revolution certainly signalled the break-up of feudalism, and replaced loyalty to the king with loyalty to the patrie (fatherland). The creation of a National Assembly, and the united and unitary state with common laws and institutions, realized the nation-state ideal. The aggressive and militarily successful French Republic then became a model for the creation of other political communities in Europe and Latin America. French armies also facilitated the spread of nationalism to other countries. Nationalism involved both the break-up of multinational empires and the incorporation of independent city-states and principalities into nation-states. In 1848, rebellions on behalf of national independence broke out all over Europe: amongst Poles, whose territory was divided between Russia, Germany and Austria; by Czechs, Italians and Hungarians, agitating against the Austrian (Hapsburg) monarchy; and by Serbs, Croats, Slovenes and Romanians, living in Habsburg lands, and in the Balkan peninsula under the Ottoman Empire. In 1861, the Italian peoples were united; in 1871, the German peoples were united (Seton-Watson 1977).

When the USA entered the First World War, President Woodrow Wilson declared that the nationalist aspirations of the various peoples in Europe were a central issue in the conflict. In his famous Fourteen Points speech of 1919, he endorsed the principle of national self-determination. After the First World War, numerous states were carved out of the remains of the Austro-Hungarian, Russian and Ottoman empires: Poland, Czechoslovakia, the Kingdom of the Serbs, Croats and Slovenes, Estonia, Latvia, Lithuania, and Finland. Beyond Europe, Ataturk reorganized modern Turkey along nationalist lines in the post-First World War period, and Japan, which had already successfully defeated Russia in the 1905 war, and had independently become organized along national lines, served as an inspiration for the nation-state ideal in Asia.

Nationalist ideology fell into disfavour after the Second World War. Because of the incorporation of nationalist symbols and rhetoric into the fascist ideologies of the Third Reich and Mussolini's Italy, nationalism was widely associated in Europe with xenophobia and ethnic exclusiveness. At the same time, however, nationalist ideals – of self-government, popular sovereignty and freedom from external domination – became incorporated into the movement for decolonization in Asia and Africa. It became widely accepted that it is not sufficient for a government to make rules and dispense justice with a minimum of brutality and coercion. The government must also be one that the people, who are subject to its rule, think of as, in some sense, their own.

Nationalist movements have not abated since the demise of the overseas empires (Keating 1996). Most states in the world are not (nationally) homogeneous, and many of these face movements within them for national self-determination. The multinational states of the Soviet Union, Yugoslavia, Czechoslovakia and Ethiopia have collapsed along national lines, and nationalism continues to be a force for political instability, as many of the successor states are themselves comprised of a number of actual (or potential) national groups (McGarry 1998). There are secessionist struggles, justified on nationalist grounds, in all areas of the globe: in developed regions (e.g. Quebec, Catalonia, the Spanish Basque country, Israel/Palestine) and in developing countries (e.g. Sudan, Kashmir in India, Sri Lanka, Indonesia and the Kurdish regions of Iraq and Turkey).

Problems with nationalism

A common objection to nationalism is that its core idea – that we should give preference to fellow nationals and to our own national traditions and institutions – is incompatible with the moral conception that actions are to be governed by principles that give equal consideration to all people who are affected by an action. Because nationalists advocate a form of partiality, its critics contend that it is like racism. Racists and nationalists alike are said to treat the in-group (the national group/the racial group) differently from the way they treat outsiders, and to refuse to give equal weight to the interests of all citizens. There is, however, a competing view of ethics, which suggests that our communal attachments and relationships themselves give rise to ethical obligations (Scheffler 2001). The family is the clearest example of an unchosen associative relationship, which is generally thought to give rise to obligations. The ethical issue, then, can be reformulated as follows: is national partiality an unacceptable form of partiality (and so like racism), or is it an entirely legitimate and acceptable form of partiality (and so like the family)?

One of the ways to decide on the acceptability or unacceptability of national partiality is to assess the consequences of nationalist sentiment and national movements. Nationalist movements typically result in two kinds of projects: nation-building projects, which involve the creation of a unified identity as members of a common political project, and national self-determination projects, which involve aspirations of national groups to be self-governing or to enjoy political autonomy, including secession (Moore 2001).

The central problem with nation-building projects is that, in many cases, they are not completely neutral among different identities. They often involve the promotion of the majority identity, with the result that minority groups feel that their identity is denied or not recognized. Nation-building policies, paradoxically, may lead to the alienation of groups of people who do not share the majority group's culture or identity, and who perceive that the political project is the vehicle for the expression of the majority identity (McGarry and O'Leary 1993).

National self-determination projects are often criticized on the grounds that they lead to intrastate and interstate (often called 'international') instability. Robert Lansing, then Secretary of State under President Woodrow Wilson, famously complained that national self-determination is bound to be the basis of impossible demands, which will raise hopes that cannot be realized, and cost thousands of lives (Emerson 1971). The most significant aspect of Lansing's fear was that it grossly underestimated the consequences of nationalist violence.

In many cases, nationalist aspirations (for self-determination, or secession) are denied, and this leads to a violent struggle and to a cycle of minority marginalization and distrust. This cycle of distrust is fuelled by perceptions among the majority group that members of the secessionist or nationalist minority are 'traitors' to the state, and hence not to be trusted.

MARGARET MOORE
QUEEN'S UNIVERSITY, CANADA

References

Anderson, B. (1993) *Imagined Communities: Reflections on the Origins and Spread of Nationalism*, London and New York.

Brubaker, R. (1998) 'Myths and misconceptions in the study of nationalism', in M. Moore (ed.) *National Self-Determination and Secession*, Oxford, pp. 322–65.

Connor, W. (1994) 'Terminological chaos (a nation is a nation, is a state, is an ethnic group, is a...)', in *Ethnonationalism. The Quest for Understanding*, Princeton, NJ.

Emerson, R. (1971) 'Self-determination', *American Journal of International Law* 65(3).

Fearon, J. and Laitin, D. (1999) 'Violence and the social construction of ethnic identities', unpublished manuscript, 22 January 1999 version.

Geertz, C. (1994) 'Primordial and civic ties', in J. Hutchinson and A. Smith (eds) *Nationalism*, Oxford.

Gellner, E. (1983) *Nations and Nationalism*, Ithaca, NY.

Hutchinson, J. and Smith, A.D. (eds) (1994) *Nationalism*, Oxford.

Keating, M. (1996) *Nations against the State: The New Politics of Nationalism in Quebec, Catalonia and Scotland*, Basingstoke.

Kymlicka, W. (1995) *Multicultural Citizenship*, Oxford.

McGarry, J. (1998) 'Orphans of secession', in M. Moore (ed.) *National Self-Determination and Secession*, Oxford.

McGarry, J. and O'Leary, B. (1993) *The Politics of Ethnic Conflict Regulation*, London.

Miller, D. (1995) *On Nationality*, Oxford.

Moore, M. (2001) *The Ethics of Nationalism*, Oxford.

Scheffler, S. (2001) *Boundaries and Allegiances. Problems of Justice and Responsibility in Liberal Thought*, Oxford.

Seton-Watson, H. (1977) *Nations and States: An Enquiry into the Origins of Nations and the Politics of Nationalism*, London.

Smith, A.D. (1983) *The Ethnic Origins of Nations*, Oxford.

Yack, B. (1995) 'The myth of the civic nation', *Critical Review* 10(2): 193–211.

Further reading

Brubaker, R. (1992) *Citizenship and Nationhood in France and Germany*, Cambridge, MA.

Hobsbawm, E.J. (1990) *Nations and Nationalism since 1780*, Cambridge, UK.

Horowitz, D.L. (1985) *Ethnic Groups in Conflict*, Berkeley, CA.

Renan, E. (1939) 'What is a nation?' in Z. Zimmern (ed.) *Modern Political Doctrines*, London.

SEE ALSO: ethnic politics; fascism; secession; state

NATIONALIZATION

The last quarter of the twentieth century witnessed wholesale privatization of public-sector industries – railways, telecommunications, post, electricity, gas and water supplies as well as coal mining and parts of manufacturing. The pattern was set by the UK in the 1980s and spread to Western Europe and the Third World. It was part of a wider process of deregulation that started early in the USA. The advocates of privatization pointed to poor economic performance of the nationalized industries, 1945–79, which was certainly true as far as financial results were concerned, if not for broader measures of efficiency. This has prompted new research on the origins of nationalization. In the nineteenth and early twentieth centuries, sectors like railways in Germany, Sweden and Italy, gas and electricity supplies in Scandinavia, the telegraph, telephone and water supply almost everywhere were municipalized or nationalized either to raise revenue in cash-hungry councils facing mounting public health programmes or to supply services that had strategic significance for governments but were hopelessly unprofitable, even with subsidies. Socialism as a driving force seems to have been more important in the decade after 1945 and accounted for some of the less successful examples of government entrepreneurship in manufacturing.

At the heart of the term nationalization is the act of converting a privately owned resource into one owned by the central government (or local government in the case of 'municipalization'). One might then ask how the use and development of the resource and the economic organization of production may be predicted to change. Instead of exploring this issue, many economists in the period *c.*1950–70 in both Europe and North America took an essentially prescriptive stance. 'What advice can one give about the use of the resources?' they asked, invariably on the presumption that the managers, civil servants and ministers are disinterested recipients of that advice. Since no one would want to deny that resources should be used efficiently, economists translated their own concept of efficiency into guidelines of behaviour. Publicly owned industries should, as a first approximation, set user prices and extend the use of resources up to the point where the marginal cost of output equals price. The rationale for this is that no gains could then be made by switching resource usage in or out of the industry, since consumer valuation of the marginal dose of resources is just equal to its valuation in other activities. The implications of such a rule are quite striking, suggesting, for example, different electricity tariffs for different times of day, high fares and tariffs for transport, gas and electricity to high-cost rural areas, low fares and freight rates for bulky, long-distance rail journeys. Much work has been undertaken, especially in relation to state enterprises like Électricité de France, on the detailed implementation of these policy proposals, in terms of identifying short- and long-run marginal costs, demand elasticities and timestream aspects of investment projects. While many economists have not felt that the price at marginal cost rule should be modified to take into account questions of income distribution – on the grounds that the tax system is the way to handle that – they have not advocated the simple rule when spill-over effects exist or when information flows have been regarded as deficient. Health and education are therefore viewed as areas raising other considerations.

The forgotten question about how the use of resources would actually change under public ownership re-emerged in the 1970s, partly as a product of the growing influence of a persistent element in US economic thinking – the study of institutional behaviour – and partly because the economists' policy prescriptions were either ignored or found too difficult to implement. The restriction of a private interest to the end of promoting a public interest can be achieved in a variety of ways. Such regulation has a long history in Europe, embracing areas like the factory inspectorate and the control of private railway and fuel companies in the interwar period. The shift in the immediate post-1945 period to public ownership of strategic industries was itself partly a reflection of the siege mentality of the 1930s and 1940s. The main thrust of 'positive' theories has come from US thinking on the property rights characteristics of public firms. For example, one approach stresses that citizen-owners can dispose of their rights in publicly owned activities only by engaging in high-cost activities like migration or concerted political action. This is contrasted with private ownership, where each owner has the unilateral ability to buy and sell shares, an act viewed as a capitalization of the expected results of current management action. A significant wedge between owner and management therefore arises in public firms, the nearest approximation to which for private firms is the cost to owners of monitoring management behaviour. In the former case the wedge permits scope for discretionary behaviour by civil servants, management and politicians. The precise outcome in each public firm would depend on the way in which property rights are specified and the constraints on the various parties in the pursuit of their own utility-maximizing position. But the broad expectation is that productivity will be lower and unit costs higher in public than in private firms. Testing such theories is difficult, for when public firms have product monopolies there is no contemporaneous private firm to act as benchmark, and in the absence of monopoly one has to separate the effects of competition from the effects of ownership. In nineteenth-century Europe, municipal and private firms coexisted in gas, electricity and water supply, as well as tramways and light railways, and detailed studies suggest there was little difference in efficiency between the municipal and private sectors. For the twentieth century, the USA, with its mixture of publicly owned firms (municipal rather than national) and private firms, some of which are regulated, provided another rich data source. The evidence for the USA on productivity and unit costs shows a very varied pattern, with public firms coming out better in electricity supply, private firms in refuse collection and water supply, and with no clear-cut differences in transport. Pricing structures in public firms seem unambiguously to be less closely geared to the supply costs of particular activities, though whether this is due to electoral influences, empire building or a disinterested pursuit of fairness is not yet clear.

ROBERT MILLWARD
UNIVERSITY OF MANCHESTER

Further reading

Chester, N. (1975) *The Nationalisation of British Industry 1945–51*, London.

Millward, R. and Parker, D. (1983) 'Public and private enterprise: Relative behaviour and efficiency', in R. Millward and M.T. Sumner (eds) *Public Sector Economics*, London.

Toninelli, P.A. (ed.) (2000) *The Rise and Fall of State Owned Enterprise in the Western World*, Cambridge.

SEE ALSO: mixed economy; privatization; public goods; regulation

NEO-CLASSICAL ECONOMICS

The term 'neo-classical economics' refers to the enhanced version of classical economics that was promoted and developed in the late nineteenth century, primarily by Alfred Marshall and Leon Walras. The most familiar versions were developed in the twentieth century by John Hicks (1946 [1939]) and Paul Samuelson (1983 [1947]). Despite what neo-classical might usually imply, neo-classical economics differs from the classical only in matters of emphasis and focus. Unlike classical methods of explaining the state of any economy in terms of seemingly mysterious forces like the 'invisible hand', neo-classical economics tries to provide a complete explanation by focusing on the actual mechanisms that lead to the explained state.

The pure world that neo-classical economists attempt to explain consists of independently minded individuals making decisions that can be completely rationalized in terms of aims and means, interacting with one another only by means of market competition, and all the while being limited only by the constraints provided by nature. It is important to note what is omitted from this world-view. There is no necessary role for social institutions such as churches or governments, except those that can be explicitly explained as the consequences of individual market choices. Likewise, there is no role for authorities. The individual or the decision-making unit such as a firm always knows what is best for him, her or it.

In the neo-classical world, whenever individuals are not satisfied with current affairs (say, not consuming enough bread), they allegedly enter the market and compete with other buyers by bidding up the price (of bread), thereby creating an incentive for at least one producer to sell to them rather than anyone else. This process of increasing the going market price raises the average selling price and thereby indicates to producers that more is wanted, and to other buyers that they should consider cheaper substitutes (for bread). If a sufficient amount of time is allowed for all such market activity to be worked out, eventually all individuals will be satisfied relative to what they can afford (to afford any more may mean that they would have had to work more than what they considered optimal). The market process is worked out to a point where one individual can gain only by causing others to lose and thereby leaving them unsatisfied. In other words, in the long run everyone is happy relative to their own personal aims and to their natural givens (for example to their inherited resources or skills).

Since the 1930s, formal analyses of this very special neo-classical world have frequently demonstrated that any attempt to interfere with its preconceived free-market mechanism – either by manipulating prices or by restricting market trading – can only lead to a world where some people are not being allowed to choose what they want and thus lead to a non-optimal state of affairs. Nevertheless, it has often been pointed out by critics, such as John Maynard Keynes, that the amount of time necessary for the market activity to be worked out is unrealistic. Other critics, such as Thorstein Veblen, merely claimed that the neo-classical world was fundamentally unrealistic as some individuals do not act independently, and thus there is no guarantee, even if there were enough time, that everyone will be satisfied. While there are a few exceptions, most neo-classical economists have been concerned with either the formal analytics of the special neo-classical world or the applicability of its many formal theorems to everyday world problems.

Few of the economists who focus on the analytical aspects of economic theory are actually attempting to answer their critics. Rather, most neo-classical economic theorists have been concerned with other equally important questions. Can we really confidently rely on a world-view that allows only independent decision-making and only free competition? How can one specify the details of the formal neo-classical world so as to justify such confidence? Critics still question the sufficiency of any purely competitive, individualist world and ask whether other details are

necessary. Does this world require that there be numerous individuals participating as buyers and as sellers? Does it require an infinity of time for the long run and thus by doing it so render an impossible world? While the necessity of such additional conditions remains somewhat in doubt, a few logically sufficient views of a world of individual decision-makers have been worked out in great, yet tedious, detail.

Since, by methodological commitment, all events are ultimately to be explained in neo-classical economics as being the logical consequences of individual decision-making guided by market events, the elements of individual decision-making have had to yield to extensive formal analysis. Unfortunately, despite the many impressive displays of mathematical agility and prowess, not much has been accomplished beyond what can be learned from any elementary calculus textbook. Every individual is thought to be maximizing with respect to some particular quantitative aim (for example utility, profit or net income) while facing specified natural constraints (such as technical knowledge or capabilities, or personal skills). It follows, then, whenever utility (the quantity representing the level of satisfaction achieved by consuming the purchased goods) is maximized, the formal relationship between the quantity of any good and the utility (the 'utility function') must be one where, over the relevant range of choice, each additional unit of the good must add slightly less to the total utility than did any previous unit. This is termed 'diminishing marginal utility' and it (or some multidimensional version such as 'diminishing marginal rates of substitution') is a necessary condition for each individual's utility function. Why any individual's marginal utility is diminishing has never been adequately explained using economics principles alone. It can be asserted only that it is a necessary condition for the viability of any neo-classical world. Similar analysis has been provided for the other aims that individuals might have (such as profit, wealth, welfare), although virtually all other aims can be reduced to the analytics of utility maximization (see Samuelson 1983 [1947]).

Other neo-classical economists have been trying indirectly to answer the critics by showing that, even without assurances that the neo-classical world is realistic or possible, it can be used to provide detailed explanations of current economic events. Countless academic articles have been written that demonstrate the robustness of neo-classical theories. All are of a form that implies that any desirable economic event must be the logical consequence of the aims and choices of individuals, and any undesirable event must be the result of unforeseen natural events or the consequence of interference in the market by well-meaning governments or corporations. So far, few critics have been convinced by the tedious formalities or even by the number of allegedly successful demonstrations.

LAWRENCE A. BOLAND
SIMON FRASER UNIVERSITY, CANADA

References

Hicks, J. (1946 [1939]) *Value and Capital*, 2nd edn, Oxford.
Samuelson, P. (1983 [1947]) *Foundations of Economic Analysis*, New York.

Further reading

Boland, L. (2003) *The Foundations of Economic Method: A Popperian Perspective*, 2nd edn, London.

SEE ALSO: classical economics; macroeconomic theory; Marshall; microeconomics; prices, theory of

NETWORKS, SOCIAL

A social network can best be considered as any articulated pattern of connections in the social relations of individuals, groups and other collectivities. Social networks are often thought of as being constituted only by interpersonal relations, such as those of friendship, kinship and neighbourhood, but the methodology of social network analysis applies far more generally, and not only to interpersonal relations but also to economic, political, religious, legal or other types of social relations.

Social network analysis is not a particular theory of social relations. Nor does it rest upon any particular theory. Although it rests upon theoretical assumptions about the character of social relations, there is no substantive 'network theory' that can be applied to diverse areas. While it plays a role in the development of theories concerning social networks, social network analysis itself is method and not a theory. What it offers is a general mathematical method

for describing the structures exhibited by networks of social relations.

Simmel and other social theorists had invoked the metaphor of the 'web' or 'fabric' of social life, but it was in the 1930s that certain social scientists began to take these metaphors more seriously as ways of understanding 'social structure'. From these textile metaphors, aimed at understanding the 'interweaving' and 'interlocking' relations through which social actions were organized, the metaphor of the 'social network' emerged, originally being developed, in a nontechnical form, in social psychology and in social anthropology. Jacob Moreno in social psychology and Radcliffe-Brown in anthropology began to employ this idea. Moreno's training was in psychotherapy and he worked particularly with young children. After he left Vienna and settled in the USA he undertook a series of investigations into friendship patterns among schoolchildren, aiming to explore the psychological consequences of different types of group relations. He invented the device of the 'sociogram' to represent these relations diagrammatically: individual children were represented as points and their friendship choices as lines, with arrows showing the direction of the choice. This work evolved into the new discipline of 'sociometry' and, from there, into 'group dynamics'. Moreno's idea of representing a social network as a sociogram was used early on by George Lundberg to model community relations.

Radcliffe-Brown saw the possibility of pursuing the network metaphor in rigorous mathematical work. His ideas were taken up by W. Lloyd Warner in his research into US communities and, in particular, in the experimental studies undertaken with Elton Mayo at the Hawthorne electrical plant in Chicago. In these Hawthorne Experiments, the informal social relations of work groups were, once again, mapped in diagrammatic form, the social network diagrams looking strikingly similar to the electrical network diagrams that abounded in the factory. Warner's community studies pioneered the use of matrix algebra to represent large networks, and such ideas as the 'clique' made their first appearance as ways of understanding the formation of cohesive groupings within a social network.

Until the 1950s, however, no distinct methodology of social network analysis existed, and the ideas remained largely metaphorical and programmatic. A beginning was made in the formalization of the network metaphor in the work of George Homans (1951), who tried to synthesize the results of anthropological and small-group research, later recasting these ideas in the framework of exchange theory. Homans used rudimentary methods of matrix rearrangement to disclose the group structure. If individuals are represented by the rows of a matrix and events or organizations by its columns, he argued, it is possible to represent the relationship of an individual to an event or organization by the cell where the row and column intersect. The pattern of entries (1s and 0s) in the cells of the matrix therefore represents the density and pattern of interaction and contains identical information to that in the sociograms. Homans's method of rearrangement consisted of a very simple manual shuffling of rows and columns until a sharp separation of subgroups appeared. These relatively distinct subgroups, he argued, are the cliques into which the network is formed.

The greatest strides in social network analysis were made, however, by the British social anthropologists John Barnes, Elizabeth Bott and Clyde Mitchell, who were all associated, to varying degrees, with Max Gluckman's department at Manchester University. Particularly important was Siegfried Nadel, who explicitly took up Radcliffe-Brown's advocacy of formal methods and devised methods for modelling positions and roles in social structures. Nadel's pioneering work (1957) gave voice to the earlier works by Barnes, Bott, and Mitchell. Barnes (1954) explicitly used the network idea in reporting his fieldwork in a Norwegian fishing village. Bott (1957) analysed kinship and friendship networks of married couples in London. Mitchell undertook and supervised research on urban social networks in Central Africa that was subsequently published in an influential volume (Mitchell 1969). In the work of Mitchell, such ideas as 'density', 'durability' and 'reachability' were used to analyse the structure of social networks in formal terms. Of particular importance was Ronald Frankenberg's (1966) use of this work to synthesize a large number of British community studies in terms of a 'morphological continuum' running from the purely rural to the more complex urban and suburban social networks.

The major breakthrough in social network analysis occurred in the USA during the 1960s, when a number of sociologists associated with Harrison White at Harvard began to use the sophisticated mathematics made possible by advances in computing techniques to examine social networks. Many of these early studies concerned interlocking directorships in business, but they ranged over such areas as the search for work and the search for illegal abortions (Wellman and Berkowitz 1988). Through their example, social network analysis was institutionalized as a research specialism. The development of computer technology and the ready availability of computers has allowed formal network techniques to be more widely employed in numerous areas, and a number of standard packages are now available. Despite this proliferation of formal and quantitative techniques, however, much qualitative research on social networks is still undertaken.

The basis of many ideas in network analysis is the mathematical theory of graphs, though ideas from algebraic topology, multidimensional scaling, correspondence analysis and statistics are also employed. Fundamental to the method is the idea of a social network as comprising 'points' connected by 'lines', and the pattern of lines connecting the points can be represented in a matrix ready for mathematical processing. While visual inspection of sociograms can be a great help for small networks, larger networks have generally required less direct forms of representation. In recent years, however, Linton Freeman has employed a number of visualization methods that can be used with larger data sets and can handle change over time. These computer-based methods allow the on-screen representation of three-dimensional sociograms and their manipulation in real time.

The principal measures that have been used in social network analysis are those of density, centrality, components, cliques, blocks and various ideas of social distance. The idea of density, for example, refers to the proportion of all possible relations that actually exist in a network and so is the most direct measure of its cohesion. The ideas of components and cliques point to the various ways in which dense networks may, nevertheless, be fragmented or disjointed into more or less distinct subnetworks that may have an independent capacity for action and may lower the solidarity of the network as a whole. Centrality concerns the strategic positions of any one point in relation to the overall pattern of connections and the flow of influence, support or power that the network involves: it highlights the 'stars', the 'isolates', and the 'intermediaries', as well as the overall centralization of the network. More and more techniques are now becoming available to handle what is often referred to as 'two-mode' data. A simple network of connections among individuals consists of 'one-mode' data, but a network in which, say, individuals are connected to organizations consists of 'two-mode' data. Some of the most intriguing work in technical network analysis at the moment is concerned with devising measures of distance and centrality in such networks. The basic techniques and measures of social network analysis are discussed in Scott (2000) and more fully in Wasserman and Faust (1993). Many of the key contributions have been brought together in Scott (2002), and recent advances are reviewed in Carrington *et al.* (2004).

JOHN SCOTT
UNIVERSITY OF ESSEX

References

Barnes, J.A. (1954) 'Class and committee in a Norwegian island parish', *Human Relations* 7.
Bott, E. (1957) *Family and Social Network*, London.
Carrington, P.J., Scott, J. and Wasserman, S. (eds) (2004) *Models and Methods in Social Network Analysis*, New York.
Frankenberg, R. (1966) *Communities in Britain*, London.
Homans, G. (1951) *The Human Group*, London.
Mitchell, J.C. (ed.) (1969) *Social Networks in Urban Situations*, Manchester.
Nadel, S.F. (1957) *The Theory of Social Structure*, Glencoe, IL.
Scott, J. (2000) *Social Network Analysis: A Handbook*, 2nd edn, London.
—— (ed.) (2002) *Social Networks: Critical Concepts in Sociology*, 4 vols, London.
Wasserman, S. and Faust, K. (1993) *Social Network Analysis: Methods and Applications*, New York.
Wellman, B. and Berkowitz, S.D. (eds) (1988) *Social Structures*, Cambridge, UK.

SEE ALSO: mathematical models

NEURAL NETWORKS

Neural networks are a diverse set of abstract structures (see Arbib 1998, or Levine 2000, 2002, for review). Some are primarily designed to simulate functioning of real brains. Others are composed of interacting subsystems that represent cognitive entities, such as words or concepts, but may bear little relationship to known brain structures. Still others are designed for engineering or computer applications requiring 'intelligent' functions (e.g. data classification, visual pattern recognition or robotics). These subclasses of neural networks overlap extensively and often have similar architectures. This essay discusses neural networks that fit in the first two categories, that is, networks designed to simulate either brain interactions or cognitive processes or both.

Psychology and cognitive neuroscience have been gradually reaching this point of quantifiability since the late 1960s. Of course, there is a time-honoured tradition of using statistics in psychological data analysis. Yet statistics can provide some types of answers and not others. It can tell us of the existence of a behavioural or cognitive effect, such as a difference in some measurable variable between two groups of people or animals, or a causal relationship between two variables. However, statistics cannot tell us much about underlying mechanisms that might be responsible for the effect's or relationship's occurrence. To understand mechanisms, a different set of quantitative methods is required: one that deals with interactions among elements and subsystems. This is where neural networks come in.

Probably the best definition of neural networks to date, though a very imperfect one, occurs in a 1988 study commissioned by the US Defense Advanced Research Projects Agency (DARPA):

a neural network is a system composed of many simple processing elements operating in parallel whose function is determined by network structure, connection strengths, and the processing performed at computing elements or nodes....Neural network architectures are inspired by the architecture of biological nervous systems, which use many simple processing elements operating in parallel.

More recently, the notion of biological neurons as 'simple processing elements' has been challenged as researchers have discovered the complexity of subthreshold electrical interactions among the thousands of dendrites of a single neuron and of biochemical interactions among transmitters and receptors involving various messenger compounds. Neural networks encompass networks with realistic dendritic interactions as well as those with formal, simpler neurons.

As neural networks have evolved, network models have added more detail about simulated brain areas. This is partly due to the greater availability of behaviourally relevant biological data via advances such as PET and fMRI brain imaging. This also means that different 'schools' of neural network modelling have partially converged and developed somewhat similar data-driven models.

Another trend is that models have covered an expanded range of psychological data. In the 1970s, network modelling was most advanced in the area of visual perception, and next most advanced in serial learning and short-term memory. The early and middle 1980s saw the growth of models in animal learning and conditioning. The late 1980s and early 1990s saw early models of high-level cognition and its breakdown in various mental disorders. All these areas are still active, and in the last 5 years some models have appeared in social psychology. The network tools available, and the knowledge of cognitive neuroscience, are now sophisticated enough that all areas of psychology – cognitive, behavioural, physiological, social, developmental and clinical – are amenable to neural network modelling.

Computational modelling has increasingly become a part of the research enterprise in cognitive and behavioural aspects of neuroscience. Neural network modelling is sometimes a partner to experimental work in neuroscience and psychology, but the development of theories that can predict experimental results in cognitive neuroscience has been gradual and uneven. Knowledge of the brain has proceeded 'from the outside in', so the relationship between theory and experiment is more firmly established in the study of sensory (especially visual) and motor systems than it is in the study of high-order mental processes and cognitive-emotional interactions.

The mathematics used in computational models of neural networks varies widely. The most successful neural network models utilize the mathematics of *dynamical systems*. This is the study of the dynamics over time among any number of interacting variables, by means of differential equations or updating rules for algebraic equations. Dynamical systems have been applied to understanding systems in the physical, biological and social sciences over the last century (Abraham *et al.* 1992). The field is sometimes also called chaos theory, although chaos is

only one of many phenomena that can occur in a dynamical system. Since these systems are usually complex and non-linear, they will typically include more than one *attractor*, or state, that the system can reach over long periods of time.

No one neural network can be taken to be representative of the heterogeneous collection of network architectures and theories that now cover a wide range of brain regions and mental functions. However, the network of Figure 8, developed by Raizada and Grossberg (2001) to model two interacting visual processes (attention and perceptual grouping), illustrates current trends in constructing biologically relevant neural networks.

The model in Figure 8 is based on interactions among the *lateral geniculate nucleus*, the way station between the retina and visual cortex, and two processing stages in the visual cortex itself, called *V1* and *V2*. Like all of primate cerebral cortex, V1 and V2 consist of six layers. Raizada and Grossberg argue that this layer structure and its interactions are important for perception. Connections between these cortical areas are partly bottom-up, partly top-down, partly horizontal, and employ both excitation and inhibition. These facilitate the ability to make perceptual groupings, such as groupings along boundaries of visual objects, depend on the entire visual context and not just the objects being grouped. Such context dependence enables such effects as 'pop out' of visual targets surrounded by other objects that are dissimilar either in orientation, shape or texture. Context dependence is achieved by means of neural interactions whereby responses of neurons depend not only on stimuli within their receptive fields but also on stimuli surrounding those fields. In particular the model repeatedly uses the *on-centre off-surround* architecture whereby network nodes representing visual features (locations or orientations) compete via mutual inhibition with nodes representing nearby features. This has often been used in perceptual models to enhance contrasts and suppress irrelevant inputs.

The interactions in the network of Figure 8 are set to parameter values that enable top-down attentional signals to amplify ongoing cortical activity but not to generate activity on their own. This is done so that one does not hallucinate seeing objects when thinking about them. Also, attention-facilitated grouping of objects allows for illusory contours to develop in configurations

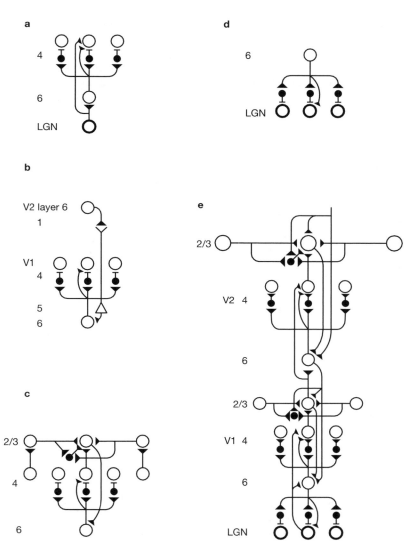

Figure 8 V1/V2 model based on known cortical connections

Source: Reprinted with permission from Raizada and Grossberg (2001)

Notes: At each cortical layer, visual locations are represented along rows. (a) Lateral geniculate nucleus (LGN) provides bottom-up activation both directly into layer 4 and indirectly via layer 6 and the 664 on-centre off-surround path. (b) *Folded feedback* carries attentional signals from higher cortex into layer 4 of V1, via the 664 path. Corticocortical feedback axons tend to originate in layer 6 of the higher area and terminate in the lower cortex's layer 1, then excite apical dendrites of layer 5 pyramidal cells that project to layer 6. The feedback is then 'folded' back up by passing through the 664 on-centre off-surround path. (c) Connecting 664 to the layer 2/3 grouping circuit: like-oriented layer 4 cells with opposite contrast polarities compete (not shown) before generating outputs that converge onto layer 2/3. Groupings that form within layer 2/3 also send activation into the folded feedback path, to enhance their own positions in layer 4 via the 664 on-centre, and suppress input to other groupings via the 664 off-surround. (d) Top-down feedback from V1 layer 6 to LGN also has an on-centre off-surround. On-centre feedback selectively enhances LGN cells that are consistent with the activation they cause, and off-surround contributes to length-sensitive responses that facilitate grouping perpendicular to line ends. (e) The whole circuit. V2 repeats V1 patterns at a larger spatial scale. Horizontal layer 2/3 connections have a longer range in V2, allowing groupings between more widely spaced stimuli. V1 layer 2/3 projects to V2 layers 6 and 4. Higher cortical areas send feedback to V2 that ultimately reaches layer 6.

involving two objects of like orientation (such as in 'pac-man' figures) that are separated along continuous lines. Illusory contours are a by-product of a visual mechanism designed to fill in 'blind spots' such as those caused by blood vessels.

The detailed example is given from vision because that is the area in which neural network modelling is most advanced and most predictive of data. However, similar types of neural network modelling have appeared in almost every branch of cognitive neuroscience. There have been brain-region-based models, for example, of Pavlovian conditioning data in monkeys and rodents. Network models have also appeared of the performance of brain-damaged patients versus normals on tests used by clinical neuropsychologists. Such tests include the Wisconsin Card Sorting Test, where the subject must classify cards by colour, shape or number of designs on the face, and the rule changes in the middle of the task. Another test that has been modelled is the Iowa Gambling Task, where subjects are given play money and must choose between four decks of cards, two of which yield more gains in the short run but net losses in the long run, while the other two yield smaller short-term gains but good long-term payoffs.

As in the Raizada–Grossberg network combining attention and grouping, the designs of all these networks are often inspired by the need to satisfy paradoxical requirements. These are examples of what Grossberg (2000) called the *complementary brain*. This means that many of the brain's functions can be defined as satisfying two complementary sets of evolutionary requirements. For example, we need to be open to learning new information without forgetting some important information that we learned previously: Grossberg called this the *stability–plasticity dilemma*. He listed other complementary requirements in mental functioning, covering diverse mental processes including conditioning (the need to process cognitive information and also to be sensitive to motivational feedback) and visual perception (the need to define boundaries and also to define features between the boundaries).

The 'complementary brain' can be generalized still further to social interactions. For example, we are hard-wired both to preserve our own interests and to bond co-operatively with others of our species. This leads us to complementary needs because the bonding requires us at times to temporarily sacrifice our own self-interest to help someone else we care about.

Cognitive neuroscience is making inroads into these difficult social issues (see Cacioppo *et al.* 2002) and other issues involving interaction between emotion and high-order cognition. As these areas develop further, neural networks will be used increasingly to generate experimental predictions about cognitive-emotional interactions as they have begun to do in the areas of perception, motor control and conditioning. Such modelling helps unify a heterogeneous database that includes, for example, single-neuron recording studies, animal lesion studies, human brain imaging studies and clinical observations.

DANIEL S. LEVINE
UNIVERSITY OF TEXAS AT ARLINGTON

References

Abraham, F.D. (with R.H. Abraham and C.D. Shaw) (1992) *A Visual Introduction to Dynamical Systems Theory for Psychology*, Santa Cruz, CA.

Arbib, M.A. (ed.) (1998) *The Handbook of Brain Theory and Neural Networks*, 2nd edn, Cambridge, MA.

Cacioppo, J.T., Taylor, S.E. and Schacter, D.L. (eds) (2002) *Foundations in Social Neuroscience*, Cambridge, MA.

DARPA (1988) *DARPA Neural Network Study*, Alexandria, VA.

Grossberg, S. (2000) 'The complementary brain: Unifying brain dynamics and modularity', *Trends in Cognitive Sciences* 4: 233–46.

Levine, D.S. (2000) *Introduction to Neural and Cognitive Modeling*, 2nd edn, Mahwah, NJ.

—— (2002) 'Neural network modeling', in J. Wixted *et al.* (eds) *Stevens' Handbook of Experimental Psychology*, Vol. 4 (Methodology), pp. 223–69.

Raizada, R.D.S. and Grossberg, S. (2001) 'Context-sensitive binding by the laminar circuits of V1 and V2: A unified model of perceptual grouping, attention, and orientation contrast', *Visual Cognition* 8: 431–66.

SEE ALSO: cognitive neuropsychology; connectionism

NON-VERBAL COMMUNICATION

The term 'non-verbal communication' can refer to communication through touch or smell, through various kinds of artefacts such as masks and clothes, or to formalized systems such as semaphore. Sometimes it has been used to include vocal features such as intonation, stress, speech rate, accent and loudness, although this is more contentious. In addition, it can refer to different forms of body movement: to facial expression, gaze, pupil size, posture, gesture and interpersonal distance. Because the term non-verbal is a definition only by exclusion, the features it can include are virtually limitless.

For communication to occur, non-verbal behaviour does not have to be intended as such. A person's intentions may not always be clear. Non-verbal communication may take place even against the express intentions of the communicator. A member of a lecture audience might well try hard to appear attentive, but still be incapable of suppressing the occasional yawn. To the speaker, the listener may still communicate boredom, despite the best intentions not to do so! Communication can also take place without conscious awareness, in the sense that neither encoder nor decoder can specify the non-verbal cues through which a message is transmitted. People may be left with the feeling that someone was upset or angry without being able to identify exactly what cues were responsible for that impression. Non-verbal communication can also be idiosyncratic. Hand gestures, for example, may take their meaning from their visual resemblance to objects or actions that they seek to depict, or from the way in which they are used in conjunction with speech.

There is now a substantive research literature on non-verbal communication, extending back over several decades. In this tradition, non-verbal behaviour is typically contrasted with speech, its forte the communication of emotion and interpersonal relationships. But there is another viewpoint. Given the close interconnectedness of non-verbal behaviour and speech, their separation may be highly artificial. In particular, hand and facial gestures may be treated as visible acts that communicate meanings, and arguably should be treated as part of natural language (Bavelas and Chovil 2000).

The most influential contemporary perspective on the non-verbal communication of emotion is still undoubtedly the neurocultural model of facial expression. According to Ekman (1972), there are at least six fundamental emotions associated with innate facial expressions, which can be modified through the learning of what are called 'display rules'. Display rules are norms that guide the expression of emotion in different social contexts, and they vary both within and between cultures. The neurocultural model is based on a distinction between two principal types of facial expression: those that are spontaneous, and those that are under voluntary control. A great deal of neuropsychological evidence is consistent with this proposal (Rinn 1991). The model is also supported by cross-cultural experiments which show that observers from both literate and preliterate cultures can identify at least six different emotions (anger, fear, surprise, disgust, happiness and sadness) from photographed facial expressions (Ekman 1972). There may also be a seventh universal emotion, that of contempt (Ekman and Friesen 1986).

The neurocultural model was widely accepted for about 20 years, but in the last decade it has been seriously called into question. It has been established that the language used to describe emotion is by no means universal. Neither the words for so-called basic emotions such as anger or sadness, nor even the word for emotion itself, is found in every culture (Russell 1991). Furthermore, Ekman's cross-cultural experiments rely on a forced-choice methodology that obliges people to identify photographed facial expressions from just six or seven categories of emotion. This technique may well overestimate universality by producing an artificially high level of agreement (Russell 1991). Nevertheless, even when raters are given an additional option to the effect that 'none of these terms are correct' together with additional emotion labels (alarmed, bored, excited), they still tend to select Ekman's basic emotion categories (Frank and Stennett 2001).

Because non-verbal cues are important to the communication of emotions, they have been regarded as central to interpersonal relationships. Indeed, when participants in one study were requested to describe their own intimate experiences, they often actually defined intimacy in terms of non-verbal behaviour. One individual wrote that 'a touch of the hand…the meeting of our eyes, conveyed our intimacy better than a thousand words' (Register and Henley 1992). Moreover, non-verbal cues are not only significant within a relationship. They can also provide important signals about relatedness to an outside observer. It has been shown, for instance, that observers can accurately identify important information about an unseen conversational partner from the non-verbal behaviour of one participant alone. Even very young children can tell whether their mother is conversing with a friend or a stranger. Adult observers are also able to identify the gender of the unseen conversational partner, and whether or not the person was of the same age as the other conversationalist.

Non-verbal communication has often been regarded as a kind of language of emotion and interpersonal relationships, but it is also closely related to speech. It is often used, for example, to accompany vocal stress. In the case of spoken English, speech is typically produced in groups of words, averaging about five in length, where there is one primary vocal stress, conveyed principally through changes in pitch, loudness and rhythm. Movements of all parts of the body, particularly hand gestures and head movements, are closely synchronized with vocal stress. Such movements can convey a variety of meanings. Head movements, for example, may signal a great deal more than just 'yes' or 'no' (McClave 2000). Vigorous shakes of the head may accompany emphatic words such as 'a lot', 'great' or 'really'. A wide sweep of the head may be used to indicate inclusiveness accompanying such words as 'everyone' or 'everything'. When a person starts to quote directly from someone else's speech, a shift in head orientation may slightly precede or directly accompany the quotation. Such non-verbal behaviour can be seen as integral to the spoken message, and has figuratively been referred to as 'mixed syntax'.

Body movement nevertheless has very different properties from speech: it is visual, and may indeed be highly visible; it is usually silent; and it is also a form of bodily action. This can make it extremely useful for particular communication tasks (Kendon 1985). We can catch or hold people's attention with flamboyant gestures. We can stress important words or phrases with a movement of the head, a raised eyebrow or an emphatic gesture. Just as a picture may be worth a thousand words, so miming an action may have much greater impact or simply be more informative than a long verbal description. Some things are too delicate to put into words, but you may be able to say it all with an appropriate gesture or facial expression.

Indeed, body movement is arguably as fundamental as speech for the representation of meaning (Kendon 1985). The use of hand gestures has been shown to develop simultaneously with speech in children, and to dissolve together with speech in aphasia (McNeill 1985). Speech and gesture can be seen to interact with one another in creating meaning: not only does gesture clarify the meaning of speech, but speech can also clarify the meaning of the gesture. In short, body movement may be seen not just as an alternative to speech, but as an additional resource, as part of a multichannel system of communication that allows the skilled speaker further options with which to convey meaning.

Research on non-verbal communication has considerable practical significance. The proposal that social behaviour should be regarded as a skill has been very influential (Argyle and Kendon 1967), for it can be taught, learned and improved through what has now become known as communication skills training (CST). CST often includes instruction in non-verbal communication, and has been used to improve performance in many different contexts, including employment interviews, therapy with psychiatric patients, intercultural communication and occupational training with groups such as teachers, doctors, nurses and policemen (Bull 2002). The practical significance of studying non-verbal communication goes well beyond such formal training procedures. Even the very act of carrying out research and disseminating results, by highlighting the fine details of social interaction, makes it easier for people to change their behaviour, if they so desire (Bull 2002).

In summary, the relatively short history of scientific research on non-verbal communication has produced two main traditions. According to the first, its particular importance lies in communicating emotion, and the emphasis of research is on its use within interpersonal relationships. The other approach insists that non-verbal behaviour is so closely synchronized with speech that it should be regarded as part of natural language. From this latter perspective, the study of non-verbal communication should arguably eventually disappear, to be replaced by a message model in which auditory and visual elements of face-to-face communication are treated as an integrated whole.

PETER BULL
UNIVERSITY OF YORK, UK

References

Argyle, M. and Kendon, A. (1967) 'The experimental analysis of social performance', in L. Berkowitz (ed.)

Advances in Experimental Social Psychology, Vol. 3, London.

Bavelas, J.B and Chovil, N. (2000) 'Visible acts of meeting: An integrated message model of language in face-to-face dialogue', *Journal of Language and Social Psychology* 19.

Bull, P. (2002) *Communication under the Microscope: The Theory and Practice of Microanalysis*, London, especially Ch. 2, 'Nonverbal communication', pp. 24–53.

Ekman, P. (1972) 'Universal and cultural differences in facial expressions of emotion', in J.R. Cole (ed.) *Nebraska Symposium on Motivation 1971*, Lincoln, NB.

Ekman, P. and Friesen, W.V. (1986) 'A new pancultural facial expression of emotion', *Motivation and Emotion* 10.

Frank, M.G. and Stennett, J. (2001) 'The forced-choice paradigm and the perception of facial expressions of emotion', *Journal of Personality and Social Psychology* 80.

Kendon, A. (1985) 'Some uses of gesture', in O. Tannen and M. Saville-Troike (eds) *Perspectives on Silence*, Norwood, NJ.

McClave, E.Z. (2000) 'Linguistic functions of head movements in the context of speech', *Journal of Pragmatics* 32.

McNeill, D. (1985) 'So you think gestures are nonverbal?' *Psychological Review* 92.

Register, L.M. and Henley, T.B. (1992) 'The phenomenology of intimacy', *Journal of Social and Personal Relationships* 9.

Rinn, W.E. (1991) 'Neuropsychology of facial expression', in R.S. Feldman and B. Rime (eds) *Fundamentals of Nonverbal Behaviour*, Cambridge.

Russell, J.A. (1991) 'Culture and the categorization of emotions', *Psychological Bulletin* 110.

Further reading

Knapp, M.L. and Hall, J. (1997) *Nonverbal Communication in Human Interaction*, 4th edn, Orlando, Fl.

SEE ALSO: emotion

O

OPTIMIZATION

Economics focuses on situations in which individuals have objectives, but where their choices of possible actions to attain those objectives are subject to constraints. When an economic agent is attempting to achieve his or her goals in the most rational manner possible, given the constraints he or she faces, he or she is said to be *optimizing*.

The assumption that agents optimize is a cornerstone of the standard paradigm of economic theory. A firm's objective might be to obtain the largest profits, the greatest market share or the lowest incidence of defective products possible. The constraints that the firm faces are typically resource and market constraints. Resource constraints include limits to how much output the firm can produce given the land, labour and the physical, human and financial capital it has available. It also faces constraints that arise from the market conditions under which it operates, such as the amount of demand for its products, the number and strength of its competitors, the wages prevailing in the labour market and the prices it must pay to its suppliers.

For an individual consumer, the objective is to obtain the highest utility of consumption possible, subject to budgetary constraints. Where a consumer is seeking to maximize his or her utility subject to a budget constraint, he or she is said to be optimizing his or her consumption decision.

Optimality may also be defined at the level of a group, or a society as a whole. Intuitively, if there is no way for a society to be made better off than it is already, it may be said to be at an optimum. However, such a definition is not precise, as it sidesteps the question of how a society, or a group as a whole, rather than an individual, can be made better off. The welfare of a society must be defined as some function of the welfare of its individual members, and there are many ways that each individual can be weighted in comparison to others. To provide an unambiguous standard, the generally accepted notion in economics of optimality at the societal level is Pareto-optimality. An outcome is Pareto-optimal if it has the property that no one member of society can be made better off without making another member worse off. If an individual could be made better off without harming any other person, the level of welfare in society would improve by in fact making him or her better off, no matter what weights are accorded to any particular individuals. Notice that optimality at the societal level is not necessarily associated with a particular allocation of income among individuals. Under the concept of Pareto-optimality, the transfer of money from one member of society to another does not necessarily increase the welfare of the society, even if it makes the distribution of incomes more equal.

Optimization on the part of each individual may lead to a Pareto-optimal outcome for a group. As Adam Smith first noted, when every individual follows his or her optimal strategy, competitive markets produce an optimal social outcome. In a competitive market, firms optimize if they sell whenever the market price more than covers their marginal cost. Rational consumers optimize by making a purchase whenever an item has a value that is greater for them than its price. Taken together with the principle that the price should be at a level where supply equals demand, the rationality of buyers and sellers implies a market equilibrium. Except for cases in which the good traded in the market creates an externality, this equilibrium is Pareto-optimal.

In other circumstances, however, individual optimization does not produce the best possible outcome for a group. Consider, for example, the incentives present in an industry cartel. Normally the optimal decision for any firm is to set a price that undercuts all other firms, to gain market share. However, for a group consisting of all of the firms in the industry, the best strategy would be for all firms to agree to charge the same high price. Another example of a clash between individual and group optimization occurs in team production. Suppose that the output of a team of workers rises as all its individual members put in extra effort. The problem is that effort is costly: an individual incurs negative utility when he or she expends effort. The optimal strategy for any individual worker may therefore be to do as little work as possible, and to enjoy a free ride on the back of the effort of others.

The choice of which mathematical technique should be used to solve optimization problems depends on the structure of the problem under consideration, but all of the techniques have some common features (see Takayama 1994). An objective function is specified, which either always takes on higher values for better outcomes (such as a function representing a firm's profits), or always takes on lower values for better outcomes (for example a firm's cost function). Obtaining the best outcome possible is therefore equivalent either to maximizing or minimizing the value of the objective function. The objective function may represent the incentives available to an individual or to a group, but it must depend on at least one variable that the decision-maker controls. (For example, the profit function of a firm may vary depending on the quantity of goods it offers for sale, or the price it charges.) Any constraint that limits the options of the optimizing individual has to be specified. The decision-maker then selects the values of the variables presented to him or her so as to maximize the objective function, subject to the constraints.

When the set of possible strategies can be thought of as a continuous variable, as when a firm chooses a price to charge for its product, or when a consumer decides on how much to buy of a divisible good (such as petrol, for example), calculus is typically used to find the optimal choice. (More precisely, the application of calculus requires the objective function to be differentiable.) The first-order conditions define the conditions necessary for an optimum, and therefore indicate candidate solutions. The second-order conditions determine whether a solution to the first-order condition is a maximum or a minimum, and whether the candidate solution is a local (the best value only over a range of possible choices) or a global optimum (the best value among all possible choices).

Calculus cannot be applied in some cases, as when the choice of decision variable is restricted to discrete values, or when the objective function is not differentiable. In such situations, mathematical programming methods are typically used. In economics, these usually have the structure of linear or integer programming problems (see Franklin 1980). One example of an optimization problem in which linear programming is employed is the transportation problem. The cost of transporting goods from multiple suppliers in different locations to a number of destinations is to be minimized, subject to the constraint that demand in every location is satisfied. Another example is the assignment problem, as for example when a company is allocating offices to employees in a new office building. The problem here is to assign units of a commodity to individuals in such a way that the value to the group is maximized.

Special mathematical models are required for the solution of dynamic optimization problems, which are common in economics. These problems have the structure that an optimal decision sequence must be found, and the property that a choice made at a certain point in time affects the future decision environment. For example, in a model of optimal economic growth, the individual agents who make up a society must make a sequence of decisions at different points in time (Cass 1965). The decisions consist of choices of allocations of resources between current consumption and investment that yields future consumption. If time can be thought of as discrete, that is, as being made up of distinct periods (days, months or years for example), dynamic programming techniques are applied to calculate optimal sequences of decisions (Sargent 1987). If time is better represented as a continuous flow, as is the case in a financial market, where decisions can be made and reacted to in real time, optimal control, using the calculus of variations, is commonly employed. The optimization task involves finding a function specifying the optimal decision at any point in time.

Experimental research with human subjects has explored in detail the actual decisions that people make in economic settings. The data emerging from this research have led to two criticisms of the standard assumption of optimization in economics. The first discrepancy has to do with the nature of the objective function that people seek to optimize. Standard economic theory assumes that agents are maximizing their own individual payoff in a manner that is unaffected by the payoffs others receive, and that they do not take into account what the people with whom they are dealing did in the past. However, experiments show that agents do sometimes take into account the consequences that their decisions will have for the benefits that go to others. In some contexts, altruism, a willingness to sacrifice some personal gain in order to increase the payoff made to relatively low earners, is observed. Envy, the willingness to give up extra income to reduce the gain of another person, who earns more than they do, is also a common behaviour. Furthermore, reciprocal behaviour is common among subjects in economic experiments. Agents often sacrifice some of their own earnings in order to reward generous behaviour and to punish selfish behaviour (see Fehr and Gaechter 2000).

The second discrepancy between standard models of optimization and the actual decisions that human beings make is due to the presence of bounded rationality in decision-making. When a decision task is complex, people can have great difficulty finding optima. However, even in simple decision situations, various anomalous choices suggest that individuals often exhibit systematic deviations from optimal decision-making. One such anomalous pattern is the preference reversal phenomenon. Suppose an individual is asked whether he or she prefers lottery A or lottery B. Lottery A yields a payoff of 5 with probability 0.8 and zero otherwise. Lottery B yields a payoff of 21 with probability 0.2 and zero otherwise. When asked which of the lotteries they prefer, many individuals choose A, but when asked which one they would pay more for, the same individuals choose B. One of the responses must be less than optimal, because A cannot be preferred to B while B is simultaneously preferred to A. Another example is the existence of violations of the conjunction rule.

Which of the following is more likely: (1) a man has a heart attack; (2) a man is under 55 and has a heart attack; (3) a man smokes and has a heart attack; and (4) a man is over 55 and has a heart attack? Although (1) is the correct response since it occurs in at least every case that any one of the other alternatives occur, many people select (3) or (4) as the most likely (see Camerer 1995 for a discussion of these and other anomalies in individual-choice behaviour). Decision-making biases of this kind clearly interfere with the ability of agents to make optimal decisions.

CHARLES NOUSSAIR
EMORY UNIVERSITY

References

Camerer, C. (1995) 'Individual decision making', in J. Kagel and A. Roth (eds) *The Handbook of Experimental Economics*, Princeton, NJ.

Cass, D. (1965) 'Optimal growth in an aggregative model of capital accumulation', *Review of Economic Studies* 32(3): 233–40.

Fehr, E. and Gaechter, S. (2000) 'Fairness and retaliation: The economics of reciprocity', *Journal of Economic Perspectives* 14(1): 159–81.

Franklin, J. (1980) *Methods of Mathematical Programming: Linear and Non-Linear Programming, Fixed-Point Theorems*, Heidelberg, Germany.

Sargent, T. (1987) *Dynamic Macroeconomic Theory*, Cambridge, MA.

Takayama, A. (1994) *Analytical Methods in Economics*, New York.

SEE ALSO: consumer behaviour; decision-making; economic man; maximization; Pareto efficiency; rational choice (action) theory

ORAL HISTORY

Oral history is the recording and interpretation of spoken testimonies about an individual's past. In contrast to oral tradition, it is more often concerned with experiences in the recent past than with the transmission of memories across generations (Henige 1982).

A variety of theories and methods fall within this rubric. Oral testimonies may be used to give a detailed account of an individual life (a 'life history' or 'personal narrative') or to facilitate historical reconstruction and the analysis of social change ('cross-analysis') (Bertaux 1981; Lummis 1987; P. Thompson 1988).

The life history method was pioneered by the Chicago School in studies of immigrant experience, youth culture, and crime and deviance

(Plummer 1983). Life history interviews are usually semi-structured or unstructured. They aim, as Malinowski (1922) put it, 'to grasp the native's point of view, his relation to life, to realise his vision of the world'.

Cross-analyses based on oral testimony typically use larger samples with more structured interviews. An influential UK example is Paul Thompson's (1993) study of social structure and social change in Edwardian Britain. Begun in 1968, this project gathered personal recollections from a representative sample (based on the 1911 census) of 500 people. In practice, despite these disparate foundations, techniques of cross-analysis and life history are often used together.

Oral testimony is one of the oldest and most widely used forms of historical evidence. It is the main form of historical record in non-literate societies, and was commonly used in European historical research before the mid-nineteenth century (for example in the work of the French historian Jules Michelet (1847)). As the influence of positivism grew, however, oral sources were increasingly viewed with suspicion on grounds of reliability (Henige 1982; P. Thompson 1988).

During the postwar period, oral history underwent a revival in Europe and the USA with the emergence of social history. The generation and preservation of oral sources was central to this history from below, with its concern to recover the experiences of those who had been marginalized from historical records. Oral history in this recovery mode remains a vitally important way of gathering evidence about non-elite social groups, who are often the subjects of legal, parliamentary or other official records, but for whom there is little evidence in their own words. Oral history of this kind has been undertaken on areas such as women and work (Davidoff and Westover 1986; Roberts 1984), local and occupational history (Samuel 1975; White 1980), rural history (Blythe 1977; Ewart-Evans 1975), childhood (Humphries 1981; T. Thompson 1981) and family history (Hareven 1982). A perceived strength of this kind of oral history is its capacity to elicit evidence both of past events and the individual's feelings about them.

Critics and advocates of oral history have debated the merits of this recovery mode. Its chronological scope will always be limited, given that evidence is usually confined to living memory. Sceptics also argue that the method is teleological, as narrators inevitably represent the past in terms of present concerns. Document-led historians have above all expressed concern about its reliability, given that there can be as much as 70 years between the experience and narration of an event. Oral historians have responded by pointing out that long-term memory remains accurate, and that written sources such as court records or eyewitness accounts are in any case often transcribed oral accounts (P. Thompson 1988).

With the emergence of cultural history during the 1980s and 1990s, advocates of oral history have criticized the recovery mode on the opposite grounds. Rather than seeking equivalence across documentary and oral sources, they emphasize the distinctiveness of speech as a mode of representing the past (Tonkin 1992). Rather than suppressing the effects of memory, they highlight the ways in which people may misremember, elide dates or suppress memories. Psychological or affective truths – which may well contradict historical ones – become objects of analysis (Samuel and Thompson 1990). For example, Alessandro Portelli (1991) has compared written accounts of the death of an activist in Terni, an Italian steelworks town, with the oral accounts of ex-communists. Underscoring their need to keep radical traditions alive, Terni's communists had revised the date and occasion of the death so that it coincided with a high-point in local labour militancy.

Portelli's work reflects a broader shift towards exploring the symbolic and subjective dimensions of oral testimony. Collective memories may be analysed, as in Portelli's study or Luisa Passerini's (1987) work on interwar Italian fascism. Alternatively, individual or family myths may be interpreted in terms of the psychic functions they serve (Fraser 1984; Samuel and Thompson 1990). A stress on language and narrative forms is common to these approaches. Cadences and patterns of speech, pauses and silences, and the interactions between interviewer and interviewee are seen as objects of analysis rather than obstacles to recall. Testimonies are interpreted as present cultural artefacts rather than as unmediated reflections of past experience.

More recent oral history work thus stresses the particular qualities of spoken testimonies such as retrospection, memory and a symbiotic relationship between source and interpreter. The interpretative focus has shifted from the past as lived to the past as represented. This has resulted in a more interdisciplinary approach to oral history, which now includes not only social history and sociology, but also feminist studies (especially Gluck and Patai 1991), psychoanalysis, literary studies, anthropology and cultural studies.

MICHAEL ROPER
UNIVERSITY OF ESSEX

References

Bertaux, D. (ed.) (1981) *Biography and Society: The Life History Approach in the Social Sciences*, London.

Blythe, R. (1977) *Akenfield: Portrait of an English Village*, Harmondsworth.

Davidoff, L. and Westover, B. (eds) (1986) *Our Work, Our Lives: Women's History and Women's Work*, London.

Ewart-Evans, G. (1975) *Where Beards Wag All: The Days That We Have Seen*, London.

Fraser, R. (1984) *In Search of a Past*, London.

Gluck, S.B. and Patai, D. (1991) *Women's Words: The Feminist Practice of Oral History*, New York.

Hareven, T. (1982) *Family Time and Industrial Time*, New York.

Henige, D. (1982) *Oral Historiography*, London.

Humphries, S. (1981) *Hooligans or Rebels?* Oxford.

Lummis, T. (1987) *Listening to History: The Authenticity of Oral Evidence*, London.

Malinowski, B. (1922) *Argonauts of the Western Pacific*, London.

Michelet, J. (1847) *Histoire de la Révolution Française*, Vol. 2, Paris, p. 530.

Passerini, L. (1987) *Fascism in Popular Memory: The Cultural Experience of the Turin Working-Class*, Cambridge, UK.

Plummer, K. (1983) *Documents of Life: An Introduction to the Problems and Literature of a Humanistic Method*, London.

Portelli, A. (1991) *The Death of Luigi Trastulli and Other Stories: Form and Meaning in Oral History*, New York.

Roberts, E. (1984) *A Woman's Place: An Oral History of Working Class Women 1890–1940*, Oxford.

Samuel, R. (1975) 'Quarry roughs: Life and labour in Headingham Quarry, 1860–1920', in *Village Life and Labour*, London.

Samuel, R. and Thompson, P. (eds) (1990) *The Myths We Live By*, London.

Thompson, P. (1988) *The Voice of the Past: Oral History*, 2nd edn, Oxford.

—— (1993) *The Edwardians: The Remaking of British Society*, 2nd edn, London.

Thompson, T. (1981) *Edwardian Childhoods*, London.

Tonkin, E. (1992) *Narrating Our Pasts: The Social Construction of Oral History*, Cambridge, UK.

White, J. (1980) *Rothschild Buildings: Life in an East London Tenement Block 1887–1920*, London.

SEE ALSO: cultural history; folklore; life history

ORIENTALISM

Orientalism is the extension and application to social science of the work of the literary and cultural critic Edward Said, particularly the understandings developed by the academic discipline called oriental studies. His *Orientalism* (1978) describes how Westerners have understood the Middle East, classically called the Orient. As a generic term, orientalism refers to distortions in the perception and analysis of alien societies that resemble the distortions that Said discerns in oriental studies. These distortions, critics say, are found frequently in anthropology (see Clifford 1988; Fabian 1983).

One distortion is exaggerating 'the difference between the familiar (Europe, the West, "us") and the strange (the Orient, the East, "them")' (Said 1978: 43). This is found in writing that focuses on the exotic in the societies it describes. More subtly, it is found in theories or models that compare the West and the alien and that portray the alien as little more than a mirror-image of the Western. Examples include the comparison of hierarchical (India) and egalitarian (Western) societies (e.g. Dumont 1970, 1977) and the comparison of gift (Melanesian) and commodity (Western) societies (e.g. Gregory 1982).

A second distortion is treating a society as though it is an unchanging expression of some basic essence or genius, a distortion sometimes called 'essentialism'. Here, social and cultural practices and institutions are portrayed or understood as being 'what they are *because* they are what they are for all time, for ontological reasons that no empirical matter can either dislodge or alter' (Said 1978: 70). This refers particularly to those who seek to discern a stable and coherent social order that somehow simply inheres in the society being described as part of its essence. Closely related to this is a third distortion, portraying and analysing a society as though it is radically separated from the West. This occurs especially when writers ignore points of contact between the society and the West, and so ignore the colonial relations that may have existed between the two societies, as it also ignores Western intrusions in that society. These are ignored because they do not reflect what is taken to be the true essence of the society involved.

Although many condemn orientalism, it may be inescapable. Groups commonly distinguish themselves from others by casting those others as exotic in some way, and there is no reason to expect that Western writers, or any other, are exempt from this tendency. To compare two societies or sets of people, after all, is almost necessarily to stress their differences and slight their similarities, and to construe them in terms of fundamental attributes or essences.

JAMES G. CARRIER
OXFORD BROOKES AND INDIANA UNIVERSITIES

References

Clifford, J. (1988) *The Predicament of Culture: Twentieth-Century Ethnography, Literature, and Art*, Cambridge, MA.
Dumont, L. (1970) *Homo Hierarchicus: The Caste System and its Implications*, London.
—— (1977) *From Mandeville to Marx: The Genesis and Triumph of Economic Ideology*, Chicago.
Fabian, J. (1983) *Time and the Other: How Anthropology Makes Its Object*, New York.
Gregory, C.A. (1982) *Gifts and Commodities*, London.
Said, E. (1978) *Orientalism*, Harmondsworth.

P

PARAPSYCHOLOGY

Strictly speaking, parapsychology refers only to the study of psychokinesis (PK) and extrasensory perception (ESP). *Psychokinesis* (literally *mind movement*) refers to the ability physically to affect objects or events by mental influence alone, known popularly as 'mind over matter'. *Extrasensory perception* refers to three different phenomena: *telepathy*, which is direct communication between two minds without the use of the known sensory channels; *clairvoyance*, which is awareness of objects and events at a distant location, without the use of the known sensory channels or logical inference; and *precognition*, which is knowledge of events before they happen, other than by logical inference. In practice, however, the term parapsychology is often used more widely to refer to the study of any paranormal events (i.e. events that cannot be explained in terms of the known laws of science). This wider definition would include such areas as astrology, the Bermuda triangle, biorhythm theory, firewalking, ghosts, Kirlian photography, UFOs (unidentified flying objects), unusual life-forms (for example the yeti) and so on.

Although reports of paranormal events crop up all over the world, and over a long historical period, widespread interest in the subject in the modern Western world was sparked by the birth of spiritualism. In 1848, the Fox sisters, 11-year-old Kate and 13-year-old Margaret, in the small New York town of Hydesville, reported hearing a rapping sound in their home. It was claimed that these sounds were messages from the dead and thus the spiritualist movement was born. Within a relatively short period, seances were popular across both the USA and Europe, and the range of phenomena produced at such events had gone beyond simple rapping. They included levitation, ectoplasmic manifestations, spirit voices and so on. Many great scientists became interested in such phenomena leading to the formation in Britain of the Society for Psychical Research (SPR) in 1882. The American Society for Psychical Research (ASPR) was founded in 1885. It was hoped at the time that the study of mediums and their abilities might provide proof that the soul survives after death, but convincing proof was never forthcoming. Many mediums were caught red-handed in the act of cheating, but this by no means persuaded their supporters, including some of the finest scientists of the time, that all of the effects produced by such mediums were fraudulent. Even the confession by Margaret Fox in 1888 that the apparent rapping which had given rise to spiritualism 40 years earlier was nothing more than the noise produced by her 'cracking' her toes did little to shake the conviction of true believers.

Eventually, however, the need for more controlled testing of paranormal claims was recognized. A milestone in parapsychological investigation was the establishment in 1935 by Joseph Banks Rhine of the Parapsychology Laboratory at Duke University. Rhine, with the assistance of his wife Louisa and other colleagues, introduced quantitative studies rather than relying upon anecdotal evidence. He carried out studies of PK, in which subjects would attempt to influence the roll of a dice, and studies of ESP using a special pack of cards, known as a Zener pack. Each set of twenty-five cards contained five of each type of symbol (plus sign, square, circle, wavy line, and star). By chance alone, one would expect a subject to get about five correct if asked to guess the sequence of cards in a shuffled deck. Rhine's early research appeared to demonstrate that subjects could perform on both ESP and PK tasks at a level far higher than could be explained simply on the basis of chance expectation. However, his early work was criticized on both methodological and statistical grounds. When controls were tightened in response to such criticisms, significant results, although still produced, were harder to obtain. Since this pioneering research, however, the experimental sophistication of parapsychologists has increased tremendously. Two techniques that have been used widely are remote viewing (in which a 'sender' visiting a randomly selected remote site attempts to project mental impressions of the site back to a 'receiver') and the *ganzfeld* procedure (in which a sender attempts to transmit information telepathically to a receiver, the latter being under conditions of perceptual deprivation).

Critics of parapsychology remain unconvinced by the evidence produced. There is no doubt that many of the claimed phenomena subsumed under the wider definition of parapsychology are not genuine. For example, hundreds of empirical investigations of the claims of traditional astrology show conclusively that it lacks any validity, and neither Kirlian photography nor firewalking, contrary to popular belief, require any psychic explanation. Furthermore, the claims regarding PK and ESP at the core of parapsychology have not been proven to the satisfaction of the wider scientific community. Critics continue to highlight methodological and statistical problems in the area, pointing out that such extraordinary claims require a very high standard of evidence. After all, if parapsychological claims are true, the rest of science will require major revision. A further problem is the ever-present possibility of fraud. It is salutary to consider the case of S.G. Soal, a British investigator whose work in the 1940s was hailed by parapsychologists as providing incontrovertible evidence for the reality of telepathy. In the 1970s, however, it was shown conclusively that there were anomalies in the data set. Soal's results were apparently fraudulently obtained, although this was demonstrated only after several decades and might easily have never come to light. The single most damaging criticism of parapsychology, however, is that even after over a century of organized scientific research, and despite claims to the contrary, parapsychologists have been unable to specify the conditions that would be required for a reliably reproducible paranormal effect. Until this is achieved, critics will remain understandably reluctant to accept the reality of the paranormal.

CHRISTOPHER FRENCH
GOLDSMITHS' COLLEGE, UNIVERSITY OF LONDON

Further reading

Alcock, J., Burns, J. and Freeman, A. (eds) (2003) *Psi Wars: Getting to Grips with the Paranormal*, Exeter, UK, and Charlottesville, VA.
Irwin, H.J. (1999) *An Introduction to Parapsychology*, 3rd edn, Jefferson, NC, and London.
Stein, G. (ed.) (1996) *The Encyclopedia of the Paranormal*, Amherst, NY.

PARETO EFFICIENCY

Pareto efficiency is a concept used by economists to define the efficient organization of an economy. Roughly speaking, it requires not only that production should be organized in an efficient manner, but also that this production should be distributed efficiently among consumers. In formal terms, an allocation of resources, which specifies not only what is produced with the basic resources available to the economy, but also how that production is distributed among consumers, is Pareto efficient if the following holds: there is no other feasible allocation in which no individual is worse off and at least one individual is strictly better off than in the initial allocation (equivalently, it is impossible to make someone better off without simultaneously making at least one individual worse off). Here, 'feasible' refers to what can be produced given the available resources and technology.

The Italian sociologist and economist, Vilfredo Pareto (1848–1923), was the first to use this definition of efficiency, although Edgeworth had earlier employed the same idea without apparently realizing its general applicability. Pareto efficiency is too weak to be equated with optimality in any meaningful sense, and consequently the term has gradually replaced the misleading 'Pareto-optimality' in usage. The weakness of the concept stems from the fact that it has nothing to say about distributional issues. To put the matter at its starkest, imagine an economy with a fixed amount of a single type of good, say apples. Suppose that all the apples are allocated to a particular individual, who likes to have as many apples as possible, and everyone else gets nothing. This allocation is Pareto efficient as any other allocation will make our individual worse off, but it is certainly not optimum in any reasonable sense. This weakness, however, is also the reason why it is *the* accepted definition of efficiency within orthodox theory. It is held to be value-free because its application requires no opinion as to the relative merits of different welfare distributions. Moreover, its use requires relatively weak information about individual welfare: it is only necessary to know how individuals rank alternative allocations; neither cardinal information about intensities of preferences nor interpersonal comparabilty of individual welfare is required.

The concept plays a central role in modern welfare economics. A key result is the so-called first theorem of welfare economics, which asserts that a competitive market economy will under mild conditions lead to a Pareto efficient allocation of resources. This theorem is the formalization in a precise mathematical sense of Adam Smith's 'invisible hand', whereby a society of individuals, each behaving in a self-seeking manner, results in an outcome that is to the common good in some sense. Pareto attempted unsuccessfully to establish this result; it was left to a later generation of theorists to come up with a satisfactory derivation.

JONATHAN THOMAS
UNIVERSITY OF WARWICK

References

Edgeworth, F.Y. (1881) *Mathematical Psychics*, London.

Pareto, V. (1897) *Cours d'économie politique*, Vol. 2, Lausanne.

Smith, A. (1981 [1776]) *An Inquiry into the Nature and Causes of the Wealth of Nations*, eds R.H. Campbell, A.S. Skinner and W.B. Todd, New York.

Further reading

Little, I.M.D. (1950) *A Critique of Welfare Economics*, Oxford.

Sen, A.K. (1979) 'Personal utilities and public judgements: Or what's wrong with welfare economics?' *Economic Journal* 89.

SEE ALSO: efficiency (economic); optimization; social choice; welfare economics

PARSONS, TALCOTT (1902–79)

Talcott Parsons, the son of a Congregational minister in Colorado, became the most important US sociological theorist. He studied biology and philosophy at Amherst College and then did graduate work in social science at the London School of Economics and at Heidelberg. In 1927, he joined the Harvard economics department and in 1931 switched to the sociology department, which had just been created. He became chairman of the sociology department in 1944 and then chairman of the newly formed department of social relations in 1946, a position he retained until 1956. He officially retired in 1973 but continued writing until his death (in Munich) in 1979. He sought to formulate a theoretically informed comprehensive classification scheme for all social action. Identifying sociocultural forces as the dominant ones shaping human activity, he assigned sociology the role of integrating the analyses of psychology, politics and economics into a science of human action. Sociology also had the role of providing other social sciences with their boundary assumptions (such as specifying what market imperfections exist).

Parsons's first book, *The Structure of Social Action* (1937), assesses the legacy to sociology of Marshall, Pareto, Durkheim and Weber. These thinkers, Parsons argues, converged from different directions on a common solution to the problem of why society is not characterized by a Hobbesian war of all against all. According to Parsons, their solution is that people share common values and norms. Parsons's subsequent work, particularly *The Social System* (1951), *Towards a General Theory of Action* (1951) and *Family, Socialization and Interaction Process* (1955), develops the importance of the integration of a shared normative structure into people's need-dispositions for making social order possible. Social order rests on institutionalized actions. An action is institutionalized when following a social norm both brings favourable responses from others and is satisfying in itself. Although the concern with people being socialized into a society's structure gives a conservative flavour to Parsons's thought, Parsons's frame of reference for the problem of order is accepted widely. However, the framework's status is in dispute. Some see it as foundational for sociology, while others argue it is an untestable conceptual frame and that the real questions are the specific conditions that generate particular social orders. Questions also arise over how domination and self-interested actions are to be integrated into the analysis of social order.

Parsons argues that for a social structure to persist, four functions must be performed. These are adaptation, goal-attainment, integration and pattern-maintenance or tension-management. Societies tend to differentiate functionally to produce separate institutions specializing in each of these functions. The economy is adaptive, the polity specializes in goal-attainment, the stratification system is integrative, while education and religion are both concerned with pattern-maintenance. The most important social change in human history has been a gradual evolution of more functionally differentiated societies. For the evolution of a more differentiated structure to be successful, there must be adaptive upgrading, inclusion and value generalization. The increased specialization produced by functional differentiation makes adaptive upgrading possible. Inclusion refers to processes (such as extension of the franchise) that produce commitment by people to the new more specialized structures. Finally, values must be generalized or stated more abstractly in order to legitimize a wider range of activities.

Parsons sees money, power, influence and commitment as generalized symbolic media that mediate the interchanges among the differentiated sectors of society. Power is defined as the capacity to achieve results. He develops an analysis of power based on it being the political system's equivalent of money. Force is the equivalent of the gold backing of a currency – it provides a back-up to power, but if it has to be resorted to frequently then the political system is breaking down. This approach to power directs attention to how as societies, institutions and organizations change, so also does their ability to achieve results. Power can increase: it is not a zero-sum concept. Critics attack this approach as directing attention away from power as domination and control of some by others.

Many of Parsons's specific analyses have proved highly influential. Particularly noteworthy are his analysis of illness as legitimized deviance; of McCarthyism as a response to strains in US society resulting from the USA assuming the responsibilities of being a world power; of the pressures in US society pushing towards full citizenship for black Americans; and of secularization as a result of increasing functional differentiation.

Parsons's influence on American sociology is immense. His *The Structure of Social Action* was the first major English-language presentation of the works of Weber and Durkheim, and helped make their ideas central to US sociology's heritage. Many of Parsons's specific analyses and concepts are widely accepted, though few people accept his overall position. In the 1940s and 1950s, he was the dominant US theorist. In the 1960s his ideas came under increasing attack for being incapable of dealing with change. Since then, this criticism has come to be seen as simplistic. His work is being examined increasingly in terms of the solutions it offers to various dilemmas about how to theorize about society. While questions abound about the adequacy and logical status of his solution to the problem of order, his approach is adopted explicitly or implicitly by many sociologists.

KEN MENZIES
UNIVERSITY OF GUELPH, CANADA

Further reading

Barber, B. and Gerhardt, U. (eds) (1999) *Agenda for Sociology: Classic Sources and Current Uses of Talcott Parsons's Work*, Baden-Baden.
Hamilton, P. (1983) *Talcott Parsons*, London.
—— (ed.) (1992) *Talcott Parsons: Critical Assessments*, 4 vols, London.

PARTIES, POLITICAL

Scholars who have specialized in the study of political parties have found it difficult to agree on a definition of the term. The oldest definition, which emerged in the nineteenth century, may still be the best one: political parties are organizations that try to win public office in electoral competition with one or more similar organizations. The problem with this definition is that it excludes three kinds of organizations that are also usually referred to as parties: first, those that are too small to have a realistic chance to win public office, especially executive office, but that do nominate candidates and participate in election campaigns; second, revolutionary parties that aim to abolish competitive elections; and, third, the governing groups in totalitarian and other authoritarian one-party states. However, the inclusion of these three additional categories makes the definition overly broad. This difficulty may be solved partly by distinguishing two very different types of parties: the governing parties in one-party states and the competitive parties in two-party and multiparty democracies or near-democracies (that is, countries that are not fully democratic but that do allow free electoral competition).

The principal problem that remains is how to draw a distinction, in two-party and multiparty systems, between political parties and interest groups. Interest groups may sometimes also nominate candidates for public office without *ipso facto* changing their character from interest group to political party. Hence two further criteria have been proposed. One concerns the breadth of the interests represented by parties and interest groups. The typical function of interest groups is to articulate interests, whereas political parties serve the broader function of 'aggregating' the articulated interests (Almond 1960). This distinction is obviously one of degree rather than of a sharp dividing line. It also applies more clearly to two-party systems with broadly aggregative parties than to multiparty situations.

The second criterion, suggested by Blondel (1995), entails a combination of the kinds of goals that parties and interest groups pursue and the types of membership that they have. Interest groups tend to have either a promotional or protective character. Promotional associations tend to advance specific points of view (such as environmentalism or the abolition of capital punishment) and are in principle open to all citizens. Protective associations (such as trade unions or veterans' associations) defend certain groups of people; their membership is therefore more limited, but their goals are broader and may extend over the entire range of public policy issues. Political parties can now be distinguished from both promotional and protective groups: their goals are general (like those of protective associations), but their membership is open (like that of promotional groups). The borderline cases are single-issue parties, which resemble promotional groups, and cultural or ethnic minority parties, which are similar to protective groups.

Parties can be classified according to three principal dimensions. The first is their form of organization, which distinguishes between mass and cadre parties. Mass parties have relatively many formal members and are centralized, disciplined and highly oligarchical; cadre parties have a much smaller formal membership and lower degrees of centralization, discipline and oligarchy. The second is the parties' programmes, which may be ideological or pragmatic, and which may reflect a leftist, centrist or rightist outlook. The third is the parties' supporters, who may be mainly working class or mainly middle class, or may be defined in terms other than the socioeconomic spectrum, such as religion and ethnicity.

Duverger (1963) has shown that these dimensions are empirically related: socialists and other parties of the left tend to be based on working-class support, and are often ideological mass parties; conservative and centre parties tend to be supported more by middle-class voters, and are pragmatic cadre parties. The link between party organizations and programmes in Western democracies was stronger in the period before the Second World War than in the postwar era. The general postwar trend has been for parties to assume the character of mass parties but also to become more pragmatic. The relationship between programmes and supporters has also grown somewhat weaker, but it is still true that the parties of the left tend to be supported by working-class voters to a greater extent than the parties of the right. Social class is a good predictor of party choice in virtually all democracies, but in religiously or linguistically divided countries voting behaviour is more strongly determined by religion and language (Lijphart 1979).

The way in which a political party operates in a democracy depends not only on its own characteristics but also on its interaction with other parties. In this respect, the literature on political parties has emphasized the difference between two-party and multiparty systems. Here another definitional problem arises. How should we determine the number of parties in a party system? For instance, Britain is usually said to have a two-party system, although no fewer than nine different parties were elected to the House of Commons in the 2001 election. The usual practice is to count only the large and important parties and to ignore the small parties. But how large does a party have to be in order to be included in the count?

Sartori (1976) has proposed that only those parties should be counted that have either coalition potential or blackmail potential. A party possesses coalition potential if it has participated in cabinet coalitions (or in one-party cabinets) or if it is regarded as a possible coalition partner by the other major parties. A party without coalition potential may have blackmail potential: it may be ideologically unacceptable as a coalition partner, because the other parties regard it as too extreme, but it may be so large that it still exerts considerable influence. Sartori's counting rules therefore appear to be based on the two variables of size and ideological compatibility, but it should be pointed out that the size factor is the crucial one. A very small party with only a few parliamentary seats may be quite moderate and ideologically acceptable, but it will generally not have coalition potential simply because the support it can give to a cabinet is not sufficiently substantial. Hence the parties that Sartori counts are mainly the larger ones, regardless of their ideological compatibility. Moreover, although size is the dominant factor, he does not use it to make further distinctions among larger and smaller parties: they are all counted equally.

Blondel (1995) has tried to use both the number of parties and their relative sizes in classifying party systems. His four categories are two-party systems, two-and-a-half party systems, multiparty systems with a dominant party, and multiparty systems without a dominant party. Two-party systems, like those of Britain and (until 1996) New Zealand, are dominated by two large parties, although a few small parties may also have seats in parliament. A two-and-a-half party system consists of two large parties and one that, although considerably smaller, does have coalition potential and does play a significant role, such as the German Free Democrats and the Irish Labour Party. Multiparty systems have more than two-and-a-half significant parties. These may or may not include a dominant party. Examples of the former are the Liberal Democrats in the Japanese multiparty system and the Social Democrats in the Scandinavian countries. The French Fourth Republic offers a good example of a multiparty system without a dominant party.

The concepts of a dominant party and a half party serve the useful function of distinguishing between parties of different sizes, but they only offer a rough measurement. A more precise index is the effective number of parties (Taagepera and Shugart 1989). It is calculated according to a simple formula that takes the exact share of parliamentary seats of each party into consideration. For a pure two-party system with two equally strong parties, the effective number of parties is 2.0. If the two parties are highly unequal in size – for instance if they have 65 and 35 per cent of the seats – the effective number of parties is 1.8. This is in agreement with the view that such a party system deviates from a pure two-party system in the direction of a one-party system. If there are three parties of equal strength, the index is 3.0. In a two-and-a-half party system in which the parliamentary seats are distributed in a 45:43:12 ratio, the effective number of parties is exactly 2.5.

Party systems have a strong empirical relationship with electoral systems and with cabinet coalitions and cabinet stability (Lijphart 1999). Among the countries that were continuously democratic from the end of the Second World War until 1996, the average effective number of parties in the four democracies with plurality methods of election (Canada, New Zealand, the UK and the USA) was 2.2 during this period; in fourteen, mainly West European, countries with proportional representation, the average effective number of parties was 3.9, almost twice as many. Moreover, as the effective number of parties increases, the probability that a coalition cabinet will be formed also increases, but the longevity of cabinets decreases.

AREND LIJPHART
UNIVERSITY OF CALIFORNIA, SAN DIEGO

References

Almond, G.A. (1960) 'Introduction: A functional approach to comparative politics', in G.A. Almond and J.S. Coleman (eds) *The Politics of the Developing Areas*, Princeton, NJ.

Blondel, J. (1995) *Comparative Government*, 2nd edn, New York.

Duverger, M. (1963) *Political Parties: Their Organisation and Activity in the Modern State*, trans. B. North and R. North, New York.

Lijphart, A. (1979) 'Religious vs. linguistic vs. class voting: The "crucial experiment" of comparing Belgium, Canada, South Africa, and Switzerland', *American Political Science Review* 73.

—— (1999) *Patterns of Democracy: Government Forms and Performance in Thirty-Six Countries*, New Haven, CT.

Sartori, G. (1976) *Parties and Party Systems: A Framework for Analysis*, Vol. 1, Cambridge, UK.

Taagepera, R. and Shugart, M.S. (1989) *Seats and Votes: The Effects and Determinants of Electoral Systems*, New Haven, CT.

Further reading

Budge, I. and Keman, H. (1990) *Parties and Democracy: Coalition Formation and Government Functioning in Twenty States*, Oxford.

Diamond, L. and Gunther, R. (2001) *Political Parties and Democracy*, Baltimore.

Janda, K. (1980) *Political Parties: A Cross-National Survey*, New York.

Klingemann, H.-D., Hofferbert, R.I. and Budge, I. (1994) *Parties, Policies, and Democracy*, Boulder, CO.

Laver, M. and Hunt, W.B. (1992) *Policy and Party Competition*, New York.

Lijphart, A. (1994) *Electoral Systems and Party Systems: A Study of Twenty-Seven Democracies, 1945–1990*, Oxford.

Lipset, S.M. and Rokkan, S. (eds) (1967) *Party Systems and Voter Alignments: Cross-National Perspectives*, New York.

Strøm, K. (1995) 'Political parties', in S.M. Lipset (ed.) *The Encyclopedia of Democracy*, Vol. 3, Washington, DC.

Von Beyme, K. (1985) *Political Parties in Western Democracies*, New York.

SEE ALSO: democracy; elections; representation, political; voting

PARTITION

Dictionaries guide us to treat partition and division as synonyms. In the social sciences partition is correspondingly used to refer to the division of a country into separate areas of government. But this usage fails to differentiate partitions from secessions, or from decolonizations and the withdrawal of occupying powers from territories that they had incorporated into their political systems. To capture the cases that people invariably discuss as examples of a political partition, partition may be defined as an externally proposed and imposed fresh border cut through at least one community's national homeland, creating at least two separate political units under different sovereigns or authorities.

A partition creates new boundaries. The freshness, that is the novelty, and hence the perceived artificiality of the cut, is protested at the time and subsequently. Critics invariably describe it with medical metaphors: as an operation, an amputation, dismemberment or a vivisection. A partition proposal is generally developed outside the homeland – though it may have local advocates,

or resigned collaborators. They are necessarily regarded by at least one 'loser' as an imposition, a violation of the homeland.

Partition must be distinguished from two strategies intended to eliminate ethnonational differences. One is *downsizing* by a political centre, whether imperial or not. If a state quits a territory, but leaves its prior provincial borders untouched, then that is not a partition. It is decolonization, dereliction or withdrawal. The second is the *recognition of a secession* by a political centre. Secession is not something states do; it is an action of regions, or provinces, or member-states of a federation. By contrast, partition is something that states do, something they may execute against a seceding region, against a national liberation movement, or in the course of downsizing.

Types

We may distinguish two types of partition:

1 *mononational partitions*, i.e. divisions of relatively homogeneous nations, such as the Germans, the Koreans and the Vietnamese during the Cold War; and

2 *multinational partitions*, i.e. divisions of ethnically, religiously or nationally heterogeneous polities, e.g. of Ireland, Hungary, Poland, Kurdistan, Palestine or India.

Mononational partitions gave rise to schizophrenic entities, which claim to be the true embodiment of the nation, and that seek reunification in their own image, e.g. in Germany the capitalist liberal democratic west eventually prevailed; in Vietnam the communist north. Mononational partitions are preserved if the original separation is strongly supported by great or neighbouring powers, e.g. the USA forcefully blocked the military unification of Korea and Vietnam, and the USSR vetoed the reunification of Germany until the Gorbachev era. In nationalists' eyes, mononational partitions are regarded as abominations, artificial and unsustainable. They have proven unstable. Multinational partition, by contrast, divides one or more national homelands within a heterogeneous polity. The reversibility of such partitions is less certain than those of mononational partitions.

A second important distinction is between partitions that create new international borders, and those that do not. *Internal partitions* involve territorial engineering to organize one or more ethnonational groups, and to disorganize others. Such strategies need not lead to changes in the existing sovereign border. *External partitions*, by contrast, involve a transformation of the existing sovereign border, and the modification of previous jurisdictions.

One consequence of this definitional approach follows. In the twentieth century there were far fewer external multinational partitions than secessions and decolonizations. Only the following cases of external multinational partitions may reasonably count after 1945: Cyprus (1974); India (1947–8: which included the partitions of Bengal and Punjab, and that led in 1948–9 to the *de facto* partition of Kashmir) and Palestine (1947–9). Efforts to partition Croatia and Bosnia Herzegovina during the wars of the Yugoslavian succession were defeated. These, however, are not the only twentieth-century cases. International settlements and revolutions after the First World War and the Second World War saw the partitions of multinational empires, including national homelands within those empires, e.g. the dismemberment of the Austro-Hungarian, Tsarist and Ottoman empires led to the partitions of Hungary, Ukraine, and Kurdistan.

Arguments for and against partitions of pluralist territories

Comparative case studies of partition suggest that arguments in its favour rely on some variant of the proposition that it is the most realistic available form of conflict-resolution in the circumstances, and that in its absence worse will follow, including genocide or large-scale ethnic expulsions. The promise is also usually held out that after partition there will be a reduction in violence and conflict-recurrence, and that the new more homogenized polities will have better prospects of stable democratization. Proponents of partition may also advocate procedures to promote the involvement of the 'affected parties' in order to achieve as much consent as possible. They try to establish rules and see roles for commissions in appraising the claims for appropriate boundaries. Paternalist advocates of partition, in contrast, assume that local agreement is unlikely in the absence of a war, and support the intervention of a powerful third party.

All these arguments have been heavily criticized (cf. McGarry and Moore 1997; Rothchild 1997; Sambanis 2000). The main counter-arguments are as follows:

1   The affected parties – politicians and the relevant publics – are most unlikely to agree unanimously, and even if representative politicians did concur, it is most unlikely that all the adversely affected people will agree, even if they are offered significant compensation.

2   Any partition is likely to be rejected by the affected nationalists, precisely because they sever their nations.

3   Partition can only be truly morally compelling with additional unargued premises, viz. the undesirability, infeasibility or insecurity of efforts to establish binational or multinational federal, consociational or confederal arrangements.

4   There is evidence that partitions are perverse, achieving the exact opposite of what they intend. They increase conflict. They cause conflict that accompanies the partition, and such conflict is consistently worse than that which preceded it (Sambanis 2000).

5   Critics maintain that partitions are unlikely to produce ethnically homogeneous states. Postpartition India and Pakistan are multi-ethnic. Postpartition Israel was left with a significant Arab minority – and soon had waves of new Jewish refugees of diverse ethnic formation. Northern Ireland was left with a unionist/cultural Protestant: nationalist/cultural Catholic ratio of 67:33, which has since shifted to 60:40, and is now moving to 55:45. Partition, in short, cannot be enough for rigorous homogenizers. In the absence of successful cleansing, partition does not provide the clean, homogenizing break promised by its exponents.

6   Partitions cause significant economic disruption, and not just because they may be accompanied by communal conflict and warfare, and sudden flows of refugees. They disturb established monetary and exchange networks, increase transactions costs, enhance the likelihood of protectionism and provide incentives for smuggling and other border-related criminal activity. They lead to the depreciation of significant capital investments in transport, as roads, railways and

canals have their original functions terminated or significantly damaged, and to losses
that may flow from failure to co-operate in
agriculture, water management, and energy
production and distribution (Moriarty
1994). Democratization may be adversely
affected: The Turkish Republic of Northern
Cyprus, Pakistan, Northern Ireland and
Israel/Palestine are not obvious advertise-
ments for state- and democracy-building
(see Leff 1999; Schaeffer 1999).

Partitions of heterogeneous polities are always
imposed on at least some section of one ethnonational community, usually a minority, and always
involve outsiders. They always cause violence,
and encourage attempts at ethnic expulsions.
They do not normally terminate conflict, and
may elevate it to the interstate level. They are
partially chaotic, and always have unintended
consequences because politicians cannot control
their repercussions. They always involve some
non-transparent negotiations. Procedural partitions face almost insuperable difficulties, while
boundary commissions face serious difficulties in
specifying their terms of reference, and leave
wide discretion to legal interpretations not foreseen by those who create them. Partitions without ethnic cleansing will lead to 'orphaned'
minorities, who lack the clout they once had.
They usually create irredentists and encourage
new secessionists, and new controversies over the
right of return, and are likely to create unexpected boundary and recognition disputes. These
considerations, regrettably, do not stop people
from proposing them.

BRENDAN O'LEARY
UNIVERSITY OF PENNSYLVANIA

References

Leff, C. (1999) 'Democratization and disintegration in
multinational states: The breakup of the Communist
federations', *World Politics* 51(2): 205–35.
McGarry, J. and Moore, M. (1997) 'The problems with
partition', *Politics and the Life Sciences* (September).
Moriarty, M. (1994) 'The cost of partition', *International Review of Applied Economics* 8.
Rothchild, D. (1997) 'Secession is a last resort', *Politics
and the Life Sciences* 16(2): 270–2.
Sambanis, N. (2000) 'Partition as a solution to ethnic
war: An empirical critique of the theoretical literature', *World Politics* 52 (July): 437–83.
Schaeffer, R.K. (1999) *Severed States: Dilemmas of
Democracy in a Divided World*, New York.

Further reading

Christie, C.J. (1992) 'Partition, separatism and national
identity: A reassessment', *The Political Quarterly*
63(1): 68–78.
Fraser, T.G. (1984) *Partition in Ireland, India, and
Palestine: Theory and Practice*, New York.
Lake, D. and Rothchild, D. (1998) 'Spreading fear: The
genesis of transnational ethnic conflict', in D. Lake
and D. Rothchild (eds) *The International Spread of
Ethnic Conflict: Fear, Diffusion, and Escalation*,
Princeton, NJ, pp. 3–32.
O'Leary, B. and McGarry, J. (1995) 'Regulating nations
and ethnic communities', in A. Breton, G. Galeotti,
P. Salmon and R. Wintrobe (eds) *Nationalism and
Rationality*, Cambridge, UK, pp. 245–89.

SEE ALSO: consociation; ethnic politics;
federalism and federation; genocide; imperialism;
nationalism; secession; state

PASTORALISM

Pastoralism is a form of livelihood based upon
the management of herds of domestic animals,
including, in the Old World, cattle, sheep, goats,
horses, camels, yak and reindeer, and in the New
World, llamas and alpacas. It is well adapted to
semi-arid, mountainous or subarctic environments that are unsuited to agriculture. However,
most pastoralists either cultivate a little themselves, or obtain part of their food from agricultural neighbours in exchange for animal produce.
Not much is known about the historical origins
of pastoralism, but in most parts of the world it
has probably arisen as a by-product of agricultural intensification. Only in the Eurasian subarctic and possibly in the Peruvian Andes did
pastoral economies follow directly on the hunting of wild herds of the same species.

Pastoralists are commonly supposed to be
nomadic. Though the grazing requirements of
their herds often necessitate frequent shifts of
location, the nature and extent of this movement
varies considerably from one region to another.
Sometimes it takes the form of a regular seasonal
migration, but in other cases the movement
appears most irregular, though in fact it is
conditioned by the erratic incidence of local
rainfall. Some pastoralists spend much of their
lives in settled communities, or move in order to
combine the husbandry of flocks and herds with
that of crops or orchards. Since domestic animals
may provide not only food and raw materials,
but also a means of transport, many pastoral
peoples are heavily involved in long-distance

trade. Their nomadic movement may also have political significance, as a strategy to escape domination by an encompassing state organization. People who move about are hard to tax and administer, and for this reason central governments have always had an interest in the settlement of nomads.

Most pastoral societies are markedly egalitarian. Local groups or camps are fluid in composition, and disputes are solved by the parties going their separate ways. However, the recognition of living animals as movable, self-reproducing property opens up possibilities not only for their accumulation but also for their functioning as a medium of exchange. The transfer of animals from household to household as gifts, loans or marriage payments serves to cement enduring social relations. The possession of animal property further structures relations within, as well as between, domestic groups, allowing men to control their juniors who stand to inherit, and who may need animals in order to marry with bridewealth. Relations between men and women depend critically on whether women can own animals or can only mediate transactions of animal wealth between men.

Pastoral peoples are among the most vulnerable in the modern world. In the past they have often held the key to power in the regions they traversed, by virtue of their military superiority and control over trade. Their presence is now generally considered an embarrassment by the administrations of the territories they inhabit. Restrictions on movement, enforced settlement and commercialization have undermined traditional strategies of security, so that occasional ecological crises – previously endured – have turned into human disasters of catastrophic proportions.

TIM INGOLD
UNIVERSITY OF ABERDEEN

Further reading

Chang, C. and Coster, H.A. (eds) (1994) *Pastoralism at the Periphery*, Phoenix, AZ.
Galaty, J.G. and Johnson, D. (eds) (1990) *The World of Pastoralism: Herding Systems in Comparative Perspective*, London.
Ingold, T. (1980) *Hunters, Pastoralists and Ranchers*, Cambridge, UK.
Khazanov, A.M. (1984) *Nomads and the Outside World*, Cambridge, UK.

SEE ALSO: hunters and gatherers

PATRIARCHY

Patriarchy, literally meaning the rule of the father, is a term that has been widely used in a range of contrasting accounts which seek to describe or explain the conditions of male superiority over women. What is not always understood is that the different uses of the term reflect differing understandings of the relationship between nature and culture in the organization of social life.

The modern history of this term starts with the lawyer Henry Maine's *Ancient Law* (1861), which argued that 'The patriarchal family was the fundamental and universal unit of society' (Coward 1983: 18). Like many of his contemporaries, Maine defined human society as society with law, and saw legality as being historically founded on the authority that fathers exercised over their families.

Maine was quickly challenged by evolutionary theorists (influenced by Darwin), especially Bachofen (1968 [1861]), McLennan (1865) and Morgan (1877), who claimed that modern society developed through a succession of stages from nature to culture. This contradicted Maine's view that human organization had been fully social from its beginnings.

According to the evolutionists, the earliest stage of human organization was matriarchy based on biological links between mother and child rather than social links with the father (patriarchy), which was a later and more advanced stage.

The idea of patriarchy as a vital developmental stage can be seen in the social theory of Marx, Engels and Weber, and in the psychoanalytic theory constructed by Freud. Engels's (1884) writing focused on the connection between private property, the patriarchal family and the origins of female oppression. Patriarchal household heads controlled women as the reproducers of children.

Thus, in the tradition of Morgan, Engels saw women's social position, unlike men's, as structured by their physical nature. Engels's account provided the framework for Marxist feminist critiques of patriarchy. However, a continuing tension developed between Marxist historical materialism, which insisted that a change in class relations would free women of their oppression, and the implications of Engels's biologically based account, which inadvertently introduced the possibility that it would not.

Attempts to resolve this contradiction not only include the development of dual-systems theory (e.g. Barrett 1988; Delphy 1970–7; Eisenstein 1979; Rubin 1975), but also have led some Marxist feminists to reject the use of the term patriarchy altogether.

Whereas the Marxist approach argues that material structures determine relations between men and women, radical feminists (e.g. Daly 1978; Dworkin 1981; Millett 1971; Rich 1979) reverse the equation. For them, patriarchal values structure relations between the sexes and these inequalities of gender become paradigmatic of all other social inequalities and are not reducible to any other causes. However, although this view of patriarchy is a social explanation of gender oppression, it also tends, despite itself, to take for granted a natural distinction between men and women due to its central focus on an antagonistic gender dichotomy.

In these debates, the question that was constantly being asked was both whether the oppression of women was universal and whether it was natural.

Because of its cross-cultural perspective, anthropology had always potentially offered a critique of assumptions that relations between men and women are everywhere the same. However, it was not until the 1970s that the discipline began to engage with feminist perspectives (e.g. Ortner 1974; Reiter 1974; Rosaldo and Lamphere 1974) and began to shift its focus away from kinship and towards gender. Drawing on ethnographic evidence from outside Europe, anthropologists increasingly suggested that the apparently obvious biological differences between men and women did not necessarily account for, or directly explain, the very many different ways in which relationships between the sexes can be envisaged and enacted. Non-Western societies do not necessarily make a strong dichotomous distinction between male and female based in biology, nor oppose nature to culture (e.g. Atkinson and Errington 1990; MacCormack and Strathern 1980). The concept of patriarchal domination may therefore seriously misrepresent the complexity of sexual relations and gendered identity, both outside and within the West. From the mid-1980s, anthropologists therefore moved away from the question of the causes of patriarchy to a comparative ethnogra-

phy of the different components of gendered identities, including, for example, race.

FENELLA CANNELL
LONDON SCHOOL OF ECONOMICS
AND POLITICAL SCIENCE
SARAH GREEN
UNIVERSITY OF MANCHESTER

References

Atkinson, J.M. and Errington, S. (eds) (1990) *Power, Difference and Gender in Island Southeast Asia*, Stanford, CA.

Bachofen, J.J. (1968 [1861]) *Myth, Religion and Mother-Right*, London.

Barrett, M. (1988) *Women's Oppression Today: The Marxist–Feminist Encounter*, London.

Coward, R. (1983) *Patriarchal Precedents: Sexuality and Social Relations*, London.

Daly, M. (1978) *Gyn-ecology: The Metaethics of Radical Feminism*, Boston, MA.

Delphy, C. (1970–7) *The Main Enemy*, London.

Dworkin, A. (1981) *Pornography: Men Possessing Women*, New York.

Eisenstein, Z. (ed.) (1979) *Capitalist Patriarchy and the Case for Socialist Feminism*, New York.

Engels, F. (1884) *The Origins of the Family, Private Property and the State, in the Light of the Researches of Lewis H. Morgan*, London.

MacCormack, C. and Strathern, M. (eds) (1980) *Nature, Culture and Gender*, Cambridge, UK.

McLennan, D. (1865) *Primitive Marriage*, London.

Maine, H. (1861) *Ancient Law*, London.

Millett, K. (1971) *Sexual Politics*, New York.

Morgan, L.H. (1877) *Ancient Society*, New York.

Ortner, S.B. (1974) 'Is female to male as nature is to culture?' in M.Z. Rosaldo and L. Lamphere (eds) *Woman, Culture and Society*, Stanford, CA.

Reiter, R.R. (ed.) (1974) *Toward an Anthropology of Women*, London.

Rich, A. (1979) *On Lies, Secrets and Silence*, New York.

Rosaldo, M.Z. and Lamphere, L. (eds) (1974) *Woman, Culture and Society*, Stanford, CA.

Rubin, G. (1975) 'The traffic in women', in R. Reiter (ed.) *Toward an Anthropology of Women*, London.

SEE ALSO: feminist theory; gender, sociology of; women; women's studies

PEACE STUDIES

As an identifiable field of study, peace studies has its origins in the period between the two world wars, especially in the work of Lewis Fry Richardson in Britain and Quincy Wright in the USA. Much of the early work was in reaction to the intense human destruction of the First World

War and therefore focused on understanding the causes of war.

The development of the Cold War in the 1950s stimulated a fresh surge of interest in the study of peace, with the establishment of the Center for Research on Conflict Resolution at the University of Michigan and the International Peace Research Institute in Oslo (PRIO). The Stockholm International Peace Research Institute (SIPRI) was established shortly afterwards. Michigan's *Journal of Conflict Resolution* and PRIO's *Journal of Peace Research* became the main outlets for academic contributions to the field.

For 20 years from the mid-1950s, the main concern of peace studies was with applying social science disciplines, such as political science, sociology and economics, to major problems of international conflict, principally those of the Cold War. This was considered to be in marked contrast to traditional strategic studies and international relations, which were regarded by peace researchers as relying too heavily on law, history and military strategy.

Peace studies also fostered attempts to visualize a truly peaceful society, extending the idea of peace to mean more than the absence of war. Could societies with deep social and economic divisions achieve such a condition of 'negative peace'? Peace researchers now began to analyse the socioeconomic conditions under which a harmonious order was possible.

In the early 1970s, the problems of newly independent, formerly colonial states began to attract attention, in part as a consequence of the controversy in the USA over the Vietnam War, and in general North–South issues became a major focus of research. Other studies and initiatives concerned the enduring conflicts in the Middle East and Northern Ireland, and, increasingly, issues of environmental security. There was still, however, a strong concern with the militarism of the Cold War and a continuing commitment to the study and practice of mediation and other forms of conflict resolution, research that was often supported by individuals and charitable trusts associated with the Society of Friends (Quakers) in the USA and Britain.

Heightened Cold War tensions in the early 1980s stimulated fresh interest in peace studies. Specialist degree courses were now provided in a number of Western universities. At the same time, peace studies came under sustained attack from academics and politicians, especially in the USA and Britain. At a time of intense East–West confrontation, peace studies was considered to be a subversive activity, to be equated with appeasement. With the collapse of the Soviet Union and the ending of the Cold War at the end of the 1980s, the attacks on peace studies decreased and the subject found wider academic favour. As the post-Cold War world began to evolve not into a more peaceful international order, but rather a complex disorder of frequent ethnic, nationalist and resource-led conflicts, the need for a serious intellectual focus on issues of peace, conflict and violence became more readily apparent. In this context, some of the main strands of peace studies since the late 1950s appeared to be acquiring a new salience, including in particular concerns about militarization, the potential of North–South conflicts, and the related issues of peacekeeping, mediation and conflict resolution. There is also the new and urgent question, whether globalization brings with it new threats to human security. A noteworthy development in peace studies is its expansion in Africa and Latin America, which has stimulated a fresh emphasis on local and regional studies in conflict resolution and conflict prevention. Scholars from the South also tend to offer analyses of international conflict trends that aspire to be more global than the Eurocentric models that had previously been dominant.

PAUL ROGERS
UNIVERSITY OF BRADFORD

Further reading

Jeong, H.-W. (1999) *The New Agenda for Peace Research*, Aldershot, UK.

Kurtz, L. (ed.) (1999) *Encyclopaedia of Violence, Peace and Conflict*, Oxford.

Mack, A. (1991) 'Objectives and methods of peace research', in T. Woodhouse (ed.) *Peacemaking in a Troubled World*, Oxford.

SEE ALSO: conflict resolution; international institutions; international relations; war studies

PENOLOGY

Penology is the study of penalties (from the Greek Ποινή, penalty), although in its broadest sense it is also concerned with the consequences and merits of attempting to deal with various kinds of conduct by criminal prohibition ('criminalizing'). It includes not only the study of penal codes of law, but also the investigation of ways in which penal codes are applied by courts in practice, and the manner in which each type of penal measure is applied by courts in practice ('sentencing'), and the manner in which each type of sentence is applied. For example, even when a penal code appears to oblige courts to pronounce a sentence (such as imprisonment for life), there are ways of avoiding this (such as convicting the offender of manslaughter instead of murder). Most penal systems also provide legal devices by which the full penalty is not exacted. Fines can be partially remitted. Time in prison can be – and usually is – reduced by parole (conditional or unconditional) or, more rarely, by an amnesty. Penologists study all such expedients, and the reasoning used by courts, probation officers, administrators and others to discriminate between offenders for such purposes. One reason is the belief that certain types of offenders are more likely than others to respond to certain types of penalty or training. Another is the decision that this or that offender is so dangerous that he or she must be given a special sentence that curtails his or her freedom for longer than would otherwise be normal.

An important task of penologists is to provide answers to the question 'How effective is this (or that) measure?' Effectiveness is usually assessed by reconvictions or rearrests. The latter is more accurate where sophisticated offenders are concerned because of their skill in deceiving courts. Follow-ups must be long enough to include a substantial period for which the offender has been free (of prison, probation or hospital): two years at least, and longer in the case of sexual offenders, because their offences are less likely to lead to rearrest or reconviction. It is not easy to be sure that apparent 'desistance' has really occurred, or whether, if it has, it is the effect of the sentence or merely of the offender's remorse, shame or – most likely – changed circumstances. So follow-up researchers must be content with *comparing* apparent desistance rates. Moreover, since desistance is so often the result of something other than the sentence, large samples are needed to establish confidence in findings. Even then researchers must not forget that sentencers are not usually willing to assign offenders randomly to different measures, as medical researchers can, but base their sentences on assumptions about effectiveness, public sentiment and so on. (A few random allocation experiments have been

achieved, in special circumstances: see Farrington 1983.) In consequence, statistical devices have to be employed, for example by separating samples into subgroups believed to have different desistance rates. The more previous convictions (or arrests) in an offender's record, the more likely he or she is to be reconvicted. Other personal data can also improve the accuracy of the prediction. When such precautions are taken, apparent differences between the effectiveness of different sentences are greatly reduced. The percentage of cases in which a sentence's choice of measure achieves genuine desistance must therefore be rather small. This must not be misunderstood as the 'Nothing Works' doctrine. It is more likely that in most cases the kind of sentence handed out will not determine whether an offender desists.

Corrective effectiveness is not the only consideration of those who pronounce sentence. Prevention by incapacitation is another. Incapacitation may take the form of disqualification (from driving, or from the practice of certain professions), detention (in prison or mental hospital), deportation, or surgical or chemical castration. The more severe measures are controversial, chiefly because the probability that a given offender will repeat his or her offence seldom approaches certainty, and is usually well below 50 per cent (Walker 1996).

Sentencers and penal policy-makers also have in mind the reactions of the public. Some penalties are valued as general deterrents. The effectiveness of general deterrents has been exaggerated, for example by supporters of capital punishment; but the statistical evidence suggests that *so far as homicide is concerned* potential murderers who think before they act are as likely to be deterred by 'life' as by death. The effect of the death penalty on other types of crime, such as drug-dealing, has not been systematically studied in countries that use it. Whatever the penalty, however, its deterrent effectiveness depends to a great extent on people's own estimates of the probability of detection or conviction. For some this seems to be immaterial because they tend to commit impulsive or compulsive crimes (von Hirsch *et al.* 1999).

A subject for more recent attention has been people's reactions to sentencing policies or specific sentences. Common findings are that uninformed people overestimate the severity of sentences, and that they are likely to consider a specific sentence as too lenient. However, their views tend to change when they are told what circumstances the sentencer took into account.

Another subject with which penologists have concerned themselves is offenders' rights and welfare, including protection against excessive stigma. 'Labelling theory' suggests that stigma is one of the facts that militate against desistance.

As for the aims of sentencing, English judges, long before Durkheim, have contributed the belief that penalties have an important symbolic function, declaring publicly the moral disapproval with which most people regard harmful offences. Some have even said that an important task of sentencers is to lead public opinion, although this seems to exaggerate public respect for sentencers (Walker and Marsh 1984). More tenable is the view that sentencers believe that they are *reflecting* public opinion.

Jurisprudential views about the proper aims of punishment are also influential (Walker 1995). Scepticism about the effectiveness of corrective and deterrent measures, together with the controversial use of very long detention in the name of prevention or therapy (especially for the mentally disordered), has revived the traditional Kantian emphasis on the need for penalties to reflect the culpability and therefore the deserts of the offender. Another revival has been the notion of 'restorative justice', involving compensation or restitution by offenders (Braithwaite 2001). Although obviously not a practicable solution in all circumstances, this appeals, like the Kantian approach, to moral sentiments.

These developments have been encouraged by pessimism about correction. Yet arguments based on principles often have to give way before economic pressures, which compel politicians and administrators to count the cost of penalties, especially imprisonment.

NIGEL WALKER
UNIVERSITY OF CAMBRIDGE

References

Braithwaite, J. (2001) *Restorative Justice and Responsive Regulation*, New York.
Farrington, D.P.F. (1983) 'Randomised experiments on crime and justice', in M. Tonry and N. Morris (eds) *Crime and Justice*, Vol. 4, Chicago.
Von Hirsch, A., Bottoms, A., Burney, E. and Wikstrom, P.O. (1999) *Criminal Deterrence and Sentencing Severity*, Oxford.
Walker, N. (1995) *Why Punish?* Oxford.
—— (ed.) (1996) *Dangerous People*, London.
Walker, N. and Marsh, C. (1984) 'Do sentences affect public disapproval?' *British Journal of Criminology* 24(1): 27ff.

Further reading

Garland, D. (1990) *Punishment and Modern Society*, Chicago.
Tonry, M. and Petersilia, J. (1999) *Prisons*, in *Crime and Justice*, Vol. 26, Chicago.

SEE ALSO: crime and delinquency; criminology; social control

PERSON

The sociological concept of the person embodies a complex and fruitful insight. First, all societies have some general ideas about the constitution of individual human beings and of the reasons they act as they do. All societies, in other words, have their own view of human psychology. Second, in all societies these psychological ideas are inextricably woven together with moral evaluations about what people should and should not do, especially to each other. All societies, that is, have a system of morality and law. This bundle of ideas and values, this combination of a psychology and a morality, comprises a society's concept of the person. Societies differ greatly in their concepts of the person, as shown by anthropologists, historians and sociologists studying a broad variety of cultures and periods of history.

Both the importance of the notion of person, and its historical and cultural mutability, were first recognized at the beginning of the twentieth century by Durkheim and his collaborator Mauss (Durkheim and Mauss 1967 [1903]; Mauss 1985 [1938]). They wrote of 'person' as a category of thought, by which they meant that it is a fundamental and inescapable constituent of human cognition, a framework without which thought itself would be impossible, like the categories of time and space. On this view it is inconceivable that any society could be without some concept of person, since such ideas render each of us mentally intelligible and morally accountable to others, thereby creating human societies as opposed to random collections of autistic individuals. Durkheim and Mauss laid down that the concept of the person differs sharply from the concept of individual human beings in their biological, or their purely idiosyncratic, constitution. Personhood is concerned with the moral nature of people, with their accountability and responsibility within society, with their capacities to achieve such accountability and responsibility, and therefore with the fundamental sense in which human beings are, in their thought and feeling, creatures of their society and its past.

The mutability of notions of the person from time to time and place to place makes the concept a splendid tool for comparative cultural and social analysis. Societies may differ, for example, in their concept of who is qualified for personhood: among the Lugbara of Uganda and some other African societies, men but not women are considered to have the necessary capacity for moral judgement and self-control to make them fully responsible members of society. Hence men but not women are – or can become, since judgement is considered to increase with age until death – full persons, and these conceptions have important implications for the way that society is organized and for the distribution of political and economic obligations and opportunities. In most North Atlantic societies, on the other hand, personhood is bestowed very early, with birth or even before, on people of both sexes. But whereas the Lugbara concept of personhood stresses responsibility to others, the North Atlantic tendency is to stress the rights of persons to individual goods – for example to the pursuit of individual happiness. North Atlantic personhood therefore accompanies a very different form of economic and political life, one in which the very notions of social responsibility and of social groups beyond the individual may be little developed or problematical.

MICHAEL CARRITHERS
UNIVERSITY OF DURHAM

References

Durkheim, E. and Mauss, M. (1967 [1903]) *Primitive Classification*, Chicago.
Mauss, M. (1985 [1938]) 'A category of the human mind: The notion of person', *The Notion of Self*, in M. Carrithers, S. Collins and S. Lukes (eds) *The Category of the Person: Anthropology, History, Philosophy*, Cambridge, UK, pp. 1–25.

Further reading

Carrithers, M., Collins, S. and Lukes, S. (1985) *The Category of the Person: Anthropology, History, Philosophy*, Cambridge.

SEE ALSO: identity; individualism; role; self-concept

PERSONALITY

Personality (from the Latin *persona*, an actor's mask) is an ill-defined concept embracing the entire constellation of psychological characteristics that differentiate people from one another. There is no consensus on its precise definition: in 1937 Gordon W. Allport quoted more than fifty distinct definitions, and the list has grown considerably since then. The underlying assumptions common to all definitions are that people have more or less stable patterns of behaviour across certain situations, and that these behaviour patterns differ from one person to the next. Whereas most areas of psychological research are concerned with universal aspects of behaviour and mental experience, the study of personality focuses specifically on individual differences.

The earliest personality theory of note, uncertainly attributed to Hippocrates (*c.*400 BCE) or Galen (*c.*AD 170) and widely accepted throughout the Middle Ages, is the doctrine of the four temperaments. People were classified into four personality types according to the balance of humours or fluids in their bodies. People were thought to be more or less sanguine (optimistic), melancholic (depressive), choleric (short-tempered) or phlegmatic (unemotional) according to the balance in their bodies of blood (*sanguis*), black bile (*melaina chole*), yellow bile (*chole*) and phlegm (*phlegma*). The physiological basis of this theory collapsed during the Renaissance with advances in biological knowledge, but the underlying typology survived in some modern personality theories.

The first systematic investigation of individual differences using modern empirical methods was Francis Galton's study of intelligence in England in 1884, based on tests of sensory discrimination that turned out to be poorly related to general intelligence. The first standardized measure of intelligence, based on tests of reasoning and scored according to age norms, was developed by the French psychologists Alfred Binet and Theodore Simon in 1905, and it stimulated research into other kinds of individual differences. Work on intelligence continued to flourish independently and is still (illogically) excluded from most academic discussions of personality.

The simplest personality theories focus on single traits or characteristics. Among the most extensively researched of the single-trait theories are those concerned with authoritarianism, field dependence and locus of control.

Authoritarianism is a personality characteristic associated with anti-Semitism, ethnocentrism, and political and economic conservatism, first identified in 1950 by Adorno and several co-authors of a monumental study entitled *The Authoritarian Personality*. It is usually measured with a version of the F scale, a questionnaire designed by Adorno and his colleagues to measure rigid adherence to conventional middle-class values, a submissive and uncritical attitude towards authority figures, a dislike of subjectivity and imagination, a belief in supernatural determinants of human fate, a preoccupation with strong/weak, leader/follower relationships, a distrustful and misanthropic attitude towards people in general, a tendency to project unconscious impulses on to others, and an exaggerated concern with other sexual matters.

Field dependence is a personality trait, first identified by Witkin in 1949, associated with the way in which people perceive themselves in relation to the environment. A field-dependent person is strongly influenced by the environment and tends to assimilate information non-selectively; a field-independent person, in contrast, is more reliant on internally generated cues and more discriminating in the use of external information. The trait was originally investigated with the rod-and-frame test, in which the respondent, seated in a darkened room, tries to adjust a luminous rod to the vertical position within a tilted rectangular frame. Field-dependent people are unduly influenced by the tilted frame, whereas field-independent people are more able to discount the frame and concentrate on internal gravitational cues in judging the vertical. Researchers later developed more convenient measures of field dependence, notably the paper-and-pencil embedded-figures test, which involves the identification of simple geometric figures embedded in larger, more complex diagrams. Scores on these tests are predictive of behaviour across a wide range of situations. Witkin and Goodenough (1977) concluded from the voluminous published research that field-independent people are especially adept at certain forms of logical thinking, tend to gravitate towards occupations such as engineering, architecture, science teaching and experimental psychology, and are often regarded by others as ambitious, inconsiderate and opportunistic. Field-dependent people excel at interpersonal relations and are generally considered to be popular, friendly, warm and sensitive; they are most usefully employed in such occupations as social work, elementary school teaching and clinical psychology. Field dependence generally declines with age, and women are more field dependent, on average, than men.

Locus of control is a personality trait first described by Phares (1957) and incorporated by Rotter (1966) into his social learning theory. It indicates the degree to which people consider their lives to be under their own personal control. It is measured on a continuum from *internal* to *external* by means of questionnaires constructed by Rotter and others. People whose locus of control is internal tend to believe that they are largely responsible for their own destinies, whereas those whose locus is external tend to attribute their successes and failures to the influence of other people and uncontrollable chance events. According to Rotter (1966) and his followers, a person's locus of control affects the way that person will perceive most situations and influences behaviour in predictable ways. Research has consistently shown that people whose locus of control is internal, as compared to those whose locus is external, are more likely to adopt health-promoting activities such as weight-watching, giving up smoking, visiting dentists regularly and taking exercise; they are relatively resistant to social influence and persuasion, and are generally better adjusted and less anxious than those whose locus of control is external. Mental disorders such as schizophrenia and depression are generally associated with external locus of control.

More ambitious multitrait theories of personality are intended to account for human personality as a whole rather than just one aspect of it. Their aim is to identify the constellation of fundamental traits that constitute the structure of personality, and to explain differences between people according to their location on these dimensions. Allport and Odbert (1936) found 4,500 words denoting personality traits in a standard English dictionary, after eliminating synonyms. The first task of any multitrait theory is to identify the most important of these, taking into account the considerable overlap between them. A statistical technique designed for this purpose, called factor analysis, reduces the measured correlations between a large number of traits to a relatively small number of dimensions or factors. These primary factors, which will generally be found to correlate with one another, can then be reduced to a still smaller number of higher-order factors. This is analogous to reducing the multitude of distinguishable shades of colour to the three dimensions of hue, saturation and brightness, which suffice to explain all the differences. Influential multitrait theories have been proposed by Raymond B. Cattell, who has concentrated mainly on primary factors, and Hans J. Eysenck, who preferred higher-order factors, and a consensus eventually emerged in favour of what came to be called the Big Five personality factors.

Cattell's theory (Cattell and Kline 1977), which he outlined in the 1940s and elaborated over the succeeding decades, is based on 171 traits that are intended to encompass the entire sphere of personality. They represent the list of dictionary traits and the addition of a handful of technical terms. Factor analytic studies of ratings and questionnaires reduced the list to sixteen primary factors or source traits, measured by a standardized paper-and-pencil test called the Sixteen Personality Factor (16PF) questionnaire. They include easily recognizable characteristics such as intelligence, excitability, submissiveness/dominance and forthrightness/shrewdness, together with several others for which Cattell invented neologisms, such as sizia, threcta and zeppia.

An important aspect of personality in Cattell's theory, in addition to the temperament and ability factors that determine *how* people behave, is the analysis of motivational factors determining *why* they behave as they do. According to the theory, the ultimate sources of motivation, called ergs, are biologically based and culturally universal factors such as food-seeking, mating, gregariousness and acquisitiveness. The means by which they are satisfied are called sentiments; these are culturally variable and include such activities as sport, religion and work. Five ergs and five sentiments are measured by the Motivational Analysis Test (MAT). Factor analysis has revealed three basic dimensions of motivation, corresponding roughly to Freud's id, ego and superego. If a person is motivated to read a particular book, for example, this may be because of impulsive desire (id interest), rational choice (ego interest) or a sense of obligation (superego interest).

Eysenck's (1967) theory, which he developed steadily from the 1940s until his death in 1997, is simpler than Cattell's, partly because it is based on higher-order factors. The three major factors or dimensions of personality in this theory are extraversion (E), neuroticism (N) and psychoticism (P). They are measured by standardized scales such as the Eysenck Personality Questionnaire (EPQ). Traits associated with the extraversion factor are sociability, friendliness, enjoyment of excitement, talkativeness, impulsiveness, cheerfulness, activity and spontaneity. Traits associated with neuroticism include worrying, moodiness, tenseness, nervousness and anxiety. Psychoticism involves feelings of persecution, irrational thinking, a liking for very strong physical sensations, inhumane cruelty and lack of empathy. According to Eysenck's theory, the location of a person on these three independent factors explains a great deal about that person's everyday behaviour. The theory also accounts for psychological disorders. Low E, high N and low P, for example, is suggestive of obsessional neurosis; high E, high N and low P points to hysteria; low E, low N and high P is characteristic of schizophrenia; and so on. Most people, of course, fall somewhere between the extremes on all three scales. Eysenck believed the three factors to be biologically based and largely hereditary, and he has devoted a great deal of attention to their possible locations in the brain and central nervous system.

A consensus emerged towards the end of the 1980s that five dimensions or factors are required to capture all aspects of personality. The Big Five, as they came to be called, are usually labelled agreeableness, conscientiousness, extraversion, neuroticism and openness to experience or intellect (Goldberg 1993). In this approach, agreeableness is characterized by traits such as kindness, generosity, warmth, unselfishness and trust; conscientiousness by organization, thoroughness, reliability and practicality; and openness to experience or intellect by imagination, curiosity and creativity. Extraversion and neuroticism are defined as in Eysenck's theory, and psychoticism is not regarded as a dimension of normal personality. The Big Five personality factors are usually measured by a standardized scale called the NEO Five-Factor Inventory

(NEO-FFI), developed by Costa and McCrae in 1992.

The most important controversy in the field of personality, initiated by Mischel (1968), centres on the issue of consistency. Mischel summarized an impressive array of evidence that seemed to cast doubt on one of the underlying assumptions of all personality theories – that people display more or less stable patterns of behaviour across situations. He drew particular attention to the low correlations between personality test scores and behaviour, and concluded that behaviour can be more reliably predicted from past behaviour than from personality test scores. This suggestion implies that behaviour is merely predictive of itself, and that theories of personality are futile, at least for predicting behaviour. Mischel (1968) recommended that personality research should be abandoned in favour of the investigation of situational factors that influence behaviour.

The situationist (or contextualist) critique of personality generated a considerable amount of debate and research, much of it appearing to refute Mischel's arguments and evidence. The debate is unresolved, but the views of most authorities since the mid-1970s have tended towards interactionism. According to this view, human behaviour is dependent partly on internal personality factors, partly on external situational factors and partly on interactions (in the statistical sense) between personality and situational factors.

ANDREW M. COLMAN
UNIVERSITY OF LEICESTER

References

Adorno, T.W., Frenkel-Brunswik, E., Levinson, D.J. and Sanford, R.N. (1950) *The Authoritarian Personality*, New York.

Allport, G.W. (1937) *Personality: A Psychological Interpretation*, New York.

Allport, G.W. and Odbert, H.S. (1936) 'Trait-names; a psycholexical study', *Psychological Monographs* 47 (whole no. 211).

Cattell, R.B. and Kline, P. (1977) *The Scientific Analysis of Personality and Motivation*, London.

Eysenck, H.J. (1967) *The Biological Basis of Personality*, Springfield, IL.

Goldberg, L.R. (1993) 'The structure of phenotypic personality traits', *American Psychologist* 48.

Mischel, W. (1968) *Personality and Assessment*, New York.

Phares, E.J. (1957) 'Expectancy changes in skill and chance situations', *Journal of Abnormal and Social Psychology* 54.

Rotter, J.B. (1966) 'Generalized expectancies for internal versus external control of reinforcement', *Psychological Monographs* 80(609).

Witkin, H.A. and Goodenough, D.R. (1977) 'Field dependence and interpersonal behavior', *Psychological Bulletin* 84.

Further reading

Engler, B. (2003) *Personality Theories: An Introduction*, 6th edn, Boston, MA.

Hall, C.S., Lindzey, G. and Campbell, J.B. (1998) *Theories of Personality*, 4th edn, New York.

Pervin, L.A. (2003) *The Science of Personality*, 2nd edn, New York.

SEE ALSO: personality assessment

PERSONALITY ASSESSMENT

Personality describes the ways in which people behave – not how well they can perform ('abilities'), their feelings ('moods') or their motivations. Clinicians sometimes try to see the world from an individual's point of view, attempting to understand the patient's hopes, fears, needs, expectations, experiences, etc., and special techniques, such as the Repertory Grid and Q-sort, have been designed to assist clinicians and researchers to do this. However this is time-consuming to perform, and in real life one often wants to compare individuals rather than to understand what makes a person unique. For example, one may want to decide which fifty individuals out of thousands of applicants are temperamentally best-suited to be trained as astronauts.

Most modern researchers view personality in terms of a number of traits. These are characteristics (e.g. anxiety, sociability) that everyone has to a greater or lesser extent. In order to assess a person's personality it is necessary to establish the number and nature of these traits, and then to devise ways of measuring them. A statistical technique called factor analysis has been widely used to determine the number and nature of the main personality traits. The number is somewhat smaller than used to be thought. Hans Eysenck's research suggests that there are three main traits. These are Extroversion (sociable, optimistic), Neuroticism (nervous, anxious) and Psychoticism (tough-minded, cold and uncaring). Costa and McCrae's research suggests five factors: Extroversion, Neuroticism, Openness to Experience, Conscientiousness and Agreeableness. These traits are usually assessed using the Eysenck Personality Questionnaire (revised) and the

NEO-PI(R). These are substantial questionnaires. The respondent indicates how well each of 100+ statements – e.g. 'I easily lose my temper' – describe them. A factor analysis conducted by the test designer shows which items measure each trait, and the responses are then scored to reflect this. For example, if someone agrees they have a short temper, a point is added to their Neuroticism score. If they disagree that they enjoy studying alone, this will add a point to their Extroversion score. By summing these responses each person is given a score on each trait.

To interpret the meaning of these scores it is necessary to establish norms (average scores that tell us how people usually perform). The questionnaires are therefore administered to large, random samples of the population, and the number of people who obtain each score is determined. One can then use these norms to determine – for example – that only 1 per cent of the population scores more than 23 out of 30 on Neuroticism, whereas 90 per cent score between 10 and 20. Someone with a score of 24 would therefore be regarded as highly neurotic, while someone with a score of 9 would be more emotionally stable than average.

There is debate about whether a simple questionnaire can adequately assess all these traits. For example, research shows that two quite different groups of people obtain low scores on Neuroticism questionnaires. Some are genuinely emotionally stable individuals. Others simply feel that they *should* try to behave calmly and analytically, effectively denying or repressing their emotions. It transpires that these two groups of people perform quite differently at some cognitive tasks. Clearly, therefore, a simple Neuroticism scale is of limited use when used in isolation. Supplementary analyses may be needed to distinguish between the repressors and genuine low-neurotics.

There are several well-known problems that apply to all questionnaires. In the case of ability tests, a person can only solve the items correctly if they have a high level of ability. In contrast, there is no guarantee that the answers given to the items in a personality questionnaire provide reliable guides to personality. A person may not have enough insight into themselves to provide accurate answers to particular questions. Someone may simply not recognize, for instance, that they have a much fiercer temper than is normal. Respondents may also be uncertain about the meaning of some items. If one feels intense irritation but does not show it, does this mean that one has a 'temper'? Also, respondents may consciously decide to give socially desirable responses to items. (Few people would choose to admit to being mean or having no sense of humour.) If the questionnaire is being given as part of a selection procedure (e.g. for employment) then respondents may well deliberately try to portray themselves as well-adjusted team-players. So whilst scores on personality questionnaires show respectable correlations with other variables (e.g. biological, genetic markers) when used with co-operative volunteers such as students, it is not always obvious that they are effective when used as part of a personnel selection procedure. Some tests include scales to detect 'faking good' in an attempt to reduce this problem.

Three other approaches to personality assessment are sometimes used. The first involves rating behaviour in a range of real-life situations. People are followed around by trained raters who note how they behave in their everyday lives. However, it is difficult to design a rating scale that can be applied to people who have very different lifestyles; the presence of a rater may itself influence behaviour; and this method is time-consuming and expensive.

Objective tests assess behaviour in a standard setting. The person who is being assessed either does not know what aspects of their performance are being measured, or is physically unable to alter their response. For example, one could administer any questionnaire measuring attitudes and then score only the extent to which individuals use the extreme points of the 5-point rating scale. Their actual attitudes would be of no interest. Or one could measure a person's muscle tension when watching a stress-inducing film. Unfortunately, there has been only one attempt to develop a large battery of objective tests to measure the main personality traits (Cattell's 'objective-analytic test battery'), but later research shows that these objective tests simply do not measure the traits that they were designed to assess.

Projective tests (q.v.) used to be a popular method of assessing personality. People are typically shown pictures that are capable of being interpreted in many different ways, and asked to describe what is happening. However, there is little evidence that 'experts' who score these responses agree with each other, or that the scores reflect personality. They have now been abandoned by all but a few die-hards.

COLIN COOPER
QUEEN'S UNIVERSITY BELFAST

Further reading

John, O.P. and Srivastava, S. (1999) 'The big-five trait taxonomy', in L.A. Pervin and O.P. John (eds) *Handbook of Personality: Theory and Research*, 2nd edn, New York, pp. 139–53.
Kline, P. (2000) *The Handbook of Psychological Testing*, 2nd edn, London.
Wiggins, J.S. and Pincus, A.L. (1992) 'Personality: Structure and assessment', *Annual Review of Psychology* 43: 473–504.

SEE ALSO: personality; projective tests

PHENOMENOLOGY

Although the terms 'phenomenon' and 'phenomenology' had been used earlier, by Kant and Hegel, for example, it was Edmund Husserl (1859–1938) who founded the philosophical movement that bears this name. Its main concern is to provide philosophy with a foundation that will enable it to be a pure and autonomous discipline free from all presuppositions. Its method is essentially descriptive, and its aims are to uncover the fundamental structures of intentionality, consciousness and the human life world (*Lebenswelt*). The idea of the 'life world' of 'lived experience' that is always 'taken for granted', even by the empirical sciences, is one of the main concepts of phenomenology that has interested many social scientists, including psychologists and psychiatrists, as well as political thinkers. An essential feature of all versions of phenomenology that is of interest to many social scientists is its anti-naturalism. This is to be understood as an opposition to the uncritical importation of the methods and concepts of the natural sciences but not as hostility to science as such. Nevertheless, critics have argued that when phenomenological concepts are transferred from their original domain to the context of social science, their meaning is often radically transformed. In addition, an added complication in assessing the contribution of phenomenology to the human sciences is encountered when one considers that, since Husserl, this movement has lost whatever unity it might once have claimed for itself. The term 'phenomenology' has been used in a great variety of contexts and it is probably wise to consider it as referring more to a general attitude rather than to any particular substantive philosophical doctrine.

Phenomenological ideas have had a marked influence upon a significant number of sociologists who have been critical of many of the generally and uncritically accepted philosophical assumptions underlying the practice of their discipline. The key figure in the transition from pure phenomenology to modern sociology is undoubtedly Alfred Schütz (1899–1959). Schütz, with a background in law and social science, and personally acquainted with Husserl, arrived in the USA from Austria in 1939. Here he greatly influenced successive generations of philosophers and social scientists, including economists, at the New School for Social Research in New York. In his major work, translated as *The Phenomenology of the Social World* (1967 [1932]), Schütz examines Max Weber's ideas about the methodology of the social or cultural sciences. Central to Weber's account is the view that these sciences are concerned with an 'interpretive understanding' of human 'social action'. Although this is essentially correct, in Schütz's opinion Weber's ideas require further clarification that is best achieved through a phenomenological analysis of the structure of social reality and of the interpretation of that reality.

Schütz's ideas are clearly set out (although his position remains unchanged) in his *Collected Papers* (3 vols, 1962–6). A central argument is that

the thought objects constructed by the social scientist refer to and are founded upon the thought objects constructed by the common sense thought of man living his everyday life among his fellow-men. Thus the constructs used by the social scientist are, so to speak, constructs of the second degree, namely constructs of the constructs made by the actors on the social scene, whose behaviour the scientist observes and tries to explain in accordance with the procedural rules of his science.

The relationship between social scientists and their subject matter is totally unlike that between natural scientists and their subject matter. The social world is an interpreted world, and the facts of the social sciences are interpreted facts. According to Schütz, this essential characteristic of social reality provides social science with its central problem: attempting to construct objective accounts of a subjective reality. This account is, in many ways, similar to that put forward by philosophers, such as Peter Winch, influenced by the work of Ludwig Wittgenstein (Winch 1958). It is also, therefore, not surprising that Schütz found himself criticizing the excessive system-building and generalizing pretensions of US social theory as represented by the work of Talcott Parsons.

In modern sociology, the use of Schütz's ideas has taken several directions, but common to all is an effort to clarify the philosophical and methodological foundations of sociological knowledge. The foundational statements of these different trends are to be found in P. Berger and T. Luckmann's *The Social Construction of Reality* (1966), which is primarily concerned with how a phenomenological approach can redirect the traditional sociology of knowledge towards an investigation of the taken-for-granted world of common-sense knowledge; in A.V. Cicourel's *Method and Measurement in Sociology* (1964), a critique of the research methods of conventional social science, which fails to recognize the implicit use of common-sense knowledge; and in H. Garfinkel's *Studies in Ethnomethodology* (1967), the most radical use of phenomenological ideas resulting in fundamental scepticism of the achievements of conventional social science.

Inevitably, all who claim to be working within the broadly defined phenomenological tradition have radicalized or reinterpreted many of the original ideas of phenomenology. Most phenomenological sociologists have concentrated upon relatively small-scale problems, such as discourse analysis, and have been sceptical of the achievements of mainstream sociology and its concern with the macroanalysis of social structures. In part, this can be traced back to Schütz's analysis of Weber's work in which he discusses his methodological essays without considering his important studies in the fields of comparative religion and politics, but it also mirrors the underlying difficulties that the phenomenological project has faced in attempting to develop an understanding of the nature of the sciences, both natural and social.

From its earliest beginnings phenomenology has developed in different directions and it has adapted to different national intellectual traditions. For example, Alfred Schütz himself was influenced considerably by the US pragmatist movement. Husserl's successor to his chair at Freiburg, Martin Heidegger, developed an original version of existential phenomenology in his *Being and Time* (1997 [1927]). This work has had a profound influence upon successive generations of social and political thinkers. Social and political philosophers such as Hannah Arendt, Jean-Paul Sartre and Maurice Merleau-Ponty have all been influenced and inspired by aspects of this version of phenomenology. A central development, initiated by Heidegger, was the development of the phenomenological method in the direction of hermeneutics as demonstrated in the important work of Hans-Georg Gadamer, *Truth and Method* (1975 [1960]).

Phenomenology is no exception to the general rule that no philosophy exists in a cultural and political vacuum. Husserl's work exhibits an awareness of living in an age of crisis, both intellectual and political. His *Philosophy and the Crisis of European Man* (1965 [1935]) discusses the threat to European civilization implicit in the acceptance of scientific and philosophical naturalism. Notwithstanding these anxieties, Husserl remained committed to the preservation of the ideals of the Enlightenment. Heidegger, who, unlike Husserl, was deeply influenced by Nietzsche, took his version of existential phenomenology in a profoundly anti-Enlightenment direction. Heidegger's stress upon the historicity, the threat of 'technology', the finitude of human existence and the limits of reason has been one of the deepest intellectual sources of the 'postmodernist' current in contemporary social and political thought. Philosophers concerned with the human sciences such as Michel Foucault and Jacques Derrida in France and Richard Rorty, Charles Taylor and Herbert Dreyfus in North America have developed their own distinctive theories to a large degree from a dialogue with phenomenological themes. However, the fact of Heidegger's support for the Nazi regime is a problem that will not go away. The difficult question here is that of the nature of the inner relationship, if any, between his political conduct and his philosophy.

The influence of phenomenological themes can also be witnessed in the way in which Jürgen Habermas, a defender of the Enlightenment tradition, as well as a critic of Heidegger and his influence upon contemporary political thinkers, has adapted Husserl's concept of 'the life world' and its 'colonization' in his development of a political theory that has its main roots in the early work of the critical theorists of the Frankfurt School (Habermas 1984 [1981]).

An important development arising from the application of the phenomenological method to the problems of the human sciences is the recognition of the linguistic character of human social existence. This can be seen, in contrasting ways, in the work of Habermas and Gadamer. Whereas Gadamer stresses the historical and limiting embeddedness of human conduct within particular traditions, Habermas, in opposition, while accepting much of the anti-naturalism of Husserl, appeals to the ideas of non-phenomenological thinkers as diverse as Marx and Kant to avoid what he considers to be the unnecessarily conservative implications of this version of hermeneutic phenomenology.

PETER LASSMAN
UNIVERSITY OF BIRMINGHAM

References

Berger, P. and Luckmann, T. (1966) *The Social Construction of Reality*, New York.
Cicourel, A.V. (1964) *Method and Measurement in Sociology*, New York.
Gadamer, H.-G. (1975 [1960]) *Truth and Method*, New York.
Garfinkel, H. (1967) *Studies in Ethnomethodology*, Englewood Cliffs, NJ.
Habermas, J. (1984 [1981]) *The Theory of Communicative Action*, London.
Heidegger, M. (1997 [1927]) *Being and Time*, Albany, NY.
Husserl, E. (1965 [1935]) *Philosophy and the Crisis of European Man*, New York.
Schütz, A. (1967 [1932]) *The Phenomenology of the Social World*, Chicago.
Winch, P. (1958) *The Idea of a Social Science and Its Relation to Philosophy*, Oxford.

Further reading

Dreyfus, H. (1992) *What Computers Still Can't Do: A Critique of Artificial Reason*, Boston.
Garfinkel, H. (2002) *Ethnomethodology's Program: Working Out Durkheim's Aphorism*, Lanham, MD.
Langsdorf, L. and Watson, S.H. (eds) (1998) *Reinterpreting the Political: Continental Philosophy and Political Theory*, Albany, NY.
Luckmann, T. (ed.) (1978) *Phenomenology and Sociology*, London.
Moran, D and Mooney, T. (eds) (2002) *The Phenomenology Reader*, London.
Picevic, E. (1970) *Husserl and Phenomenology*, London.
Wagner, H.R. (ed.) (1970) *Alfred Schutz: On Phenomenology and Social Relations*, Chicago.

SEE ALSO: ethnomethodology; Habermas; philosophy of the social sciences

PHILOSOPHY OF THE SOCIAL SCIENCES

Philosophy of the social sciences comprises the study of the aims and methods of the social sciences (sociology, anthropology, political science, psychology, economics; borderline cases are history, geography, demography and linguistics); it constitutes a subspeciality within philosophy of science – the study of the aims and methods of science in general. Standard anthologies organize their material around such questions as the following. Are natural things fundamentally different from social things? Must then the sciences of social things use different methods from the sciences of natural things? Are then sciences of the social at all possible? Alternatively, are social things mere aggregates? Do social things mix facts and values? Are values a social product? From this list it is apparent that the subject is engaged with traditional philosophical concerns – ontological, epistemological and normative.

Rarely is there a perfect fit between a subject as defined by academic bureaucracy and what its practitioners actually do. And transcendental arguments to the effect that the subject is an impossibility cannot but complicate an encyclopedia article. All frameworks for presenting philosophy of the social sciences have their limitations. An Aristotelian matrix approach, dividing the subject up into orderly categories and concepts, would conceal unruly and disorderly elements. The historical approach risks identifying the subject with present preoccupations. The kinship approach, tracing all present elements to a common ancestor, risks merging and simplifying descent. The map-making approach, trying to give an overall picture, has to ignore continental drift. What follows is a tentative metaphysical sketch map, supplemented by a little history. If the result is a trifle untidy the reader should be aware that this is because the terrain itself is mountainous, misty in places and we are forced to map from sea level, without radar.

Nature and convention

The phrase 'philosophy of the social sciences' suggests that there is scientific study of the social (denied by phenomenologists and some followers of Wittgenstein, see below), and that the aims and methods of such study may differ from those of science in general (denied by the logical positivists and others, see below). The distinction between the natural and the social, between nature and convention, is deeply rooted in Western thinking. It was not always so, but it is the notion of impersonal nature that is recent. Humankind used to take itself as the measure of all things and explained nature anthropomorphically; one result of the scientific revolution (in post-Renaissance Western Europe) was to overthrow anthropomorphism, to depersonalize nature and explain it by postulating orderly and law-like processes unfolding mechanically. Such was the flush of seventeenth- and eighteenth-century enthusiasm for the new science that even humanity itself was to be treated as part of nature, or as 'a machine': its aims and its desires as motive forces – or motives for short – and its actions as movements, including social movements and social revolutions akin to the revolving of the heavens (Gellner 1964; Agassi 1977).

The euphoria dissipated over such problems as how to maximize the creation of wealth; how to realize moral and political aims in social institutions; how to prevent suicide. These seemed to demand, if not anthropomorphism, then, at least, laws of human convention. If nature is taken to be those aspects of things that are more or less given, governed by laws and motive forces that we cannot alter, then convention covers all forms of orderliness that are not constant from place to place and time to time, and that are humanly alterable. This division of our environment into unchanging and changing parts affects our efforts to explain it. It makes it our first task when facing a problem to decide to what extent it belongs to nature or to convention – usually a far from uncontroversial allocation.

The well-established sciences of nature loom over all discussion of what is natural and what is conventional. And this metaphysical issue gets a methodological twist as follows: it is widely held that the rise and success of natural science is to be explained as the application of a particular method, the empirical method. Thus, if a problem is identified as natural, the methods of the natural sciences are appropriate, but, having been successful with nature, perhaps those methods are also appropriate for problems of convention. To the ancient Greeks this might have seemed absurd. But as European society under industrialization changed from *Gemeinschaft* to *Gesellschaft*, more systematic thought had to be given to altering current conventions and making them work better. As social thought grew in cognitive power and practical importance, debates about the boundary between nature and convention, and hence the appropriate methods with which to approach convention, took on a life of their own. Some philosophers of social science, greatly exercised over questions of method, are unaware that they debate a disguised metaphysical issue. One example of this is those who advocate the empirical method because they hold that nature is real and observable, whereas conventions are abstract unobservables (Kaufmann 1944). A relic of this thinking is the individualism/holism dispute over what is more and what is less real among conventions. One party, the individualists, holds that only individual human beings are real and larger-scale social entities are aggregates that can be, for explanatory purposes, reduced to theories about individuals. The other party, the holists, questions the reality of individuals when they can be explained as creatures of society. Although there is some purely philosophical debate of such issues, under the influence of positivism they are usually joined in methodological form: Which is more empirically observable – the individual or the whole? A convincing case can be made for either side. This is not the case when the debate is recast as one over methodology (see below).

Awkwardly cutting across all attempts to map this field are Marxist variants of each set of issues. Marx could be said to hold that there was only nature, not convention, and that his dialectical materialism should be seen as part of natural science. The cross-cutting occurs because Marxists will not permit him to be treated as just one of a succession of social scientists; as a result almost every issue in the philosophy of the social sciences is duplicated within Marxism, but in a manner that exaggerates the importance of Marx.

725 PHILOSOPHY OF THE SOCIAL SCIENCES

Positivism and its legacy

Empiricist methodology always had its a priorist opponents, but the triumph of Newton's physics over Descartes was taken to be a triumph of empiricism over a priorism. Despite Kant's valiant attempt at reconciliation, a priorist methodologies have grown increasingly estranged from science. Simmel (1950), Durkheim (1938 [1895]) and Weber (1949) all wrote their classics on the aims and methods of the social sciences when the anti-science tendencies in German academic philosophy were at their peak. Both empiricism and a priorism inform their work.

Militant empiricism reached its apogee in the logical positivism movement that began in the 1920s. All cognition was appropriated into science, the success of which was attributed to the use of the empirical method. Theories not empirically verifiable were declared non-scientific and merely metaphysical. The battle line the positivists drew in social studies was, 'Could the social sciences live up to their name by producing verifiable theories?' If so, then the unity and identity of science and cognition could be upheld. It was from this programme for incorporating the social sciences into unified science that the academic subject of philosophy of the social sciences was born. The primary interests of the logical positivists were in the natural sciences, but their predilection to focus on logic, economics, statistics, Marx, psychoanalysis and linguistics ensured that attempts were made to give a positivist account of each that would secure its place in unified science. In face of this challenge the a priorists took some time to regroup. Some retreated to the rather unpromising ground of Marxism (the Frankfurt School), which they tried to Hegelianize and a priorize (Frisby 1976). Others drew on various combinations of phenomenology, hermeneutics and the later Wittgenstein.

So long as logical positivism flourished within philosophy (down to the early 1960s), intense debates took place over the degree to which the empirical method could be utilized in what were now unself-consciously called 'the social sciences'. The limits of mathematical and quantitative methods and simplicity were explored, as was the problem of whether facts could be separated from values. To admit that social phenomena resisted measurement and quantification, and that they were permeated by values,

would undermine the verifiable empirical basis of the social sciences. The literature generated in these debates is the core of the first courses and textbooks of philosophy of the social sciences (Brodbeck 1968; Krimerman 1969).

Meanwhile, the regrouped opponents of logical positivism engaged with the same problems. However, they considered the limits of empiricism to be much more severe, and the problem of values to be much more pervasive, than did the logical positivists. Indeed the limits of empiricism were held to be the limits of natural science. The conscious, self-conscious, meaning-generating and reflexive activities of human beings were a totally different order of thing, demanding a totally different approach. That approach involved historical imagination (*Verstehen*), which requires the scrutiny of texts (hermeneutics) and some phenomenological rather than any empirical method (Turner and Roth 2003; Dallmayr and McCarthy 1977; Natanson 1963; Schütz 1962). Textualist studies have flourished since the mid-1980s (Clifford and Marcus 1986), often blended with historical rethinking (Geertz 1988).

Dispute about method hid dispute about aims. If social things were unlike natural things then possibly attempting to explain and predict them was inappropriate. Followers of the later Wittgenstein went even further than the continental a priorists to develop transcendental arguments against the very possibility of a science of the social. Winch (1958), Louch (1966), Taylor (1985, 1989) and Searle (1995), despite differences, converge on the idea that what makes social things social are the meaning-generating activities of human beings that show themselves in rules of behaviour. Language, for example, is not random noises but patterns that make sense. Clearly linguistic rules are not natural; rather they are activities that define and constitute human life together. We cannot then explain human conduct in the way that we offer mechanical causal explanation in natural science, but only by mastering from the inside the rules in use and their degrees of freedom. People do social things for reasons, not in obedience to laws. The ever-growing literature on Winch, on Searle, on whether reasons are causes and on so-called collective intentions can be traced through *The Philosopher's Index* and the quarterly *Philosophy of the Social Sciences*.

Methodological differences, rationality, relativism

The logical positivists and their opponents agree in translating metaphysical and epistemological issues into methodology. They also agree on the pivotal role played for method by the possibility of human intervention, in particular those interventions that are unintended consequences of social thought altering people's behaviour. (Popper (1945) labels this the Oedipus effect, while Merton (1957) labels it the self-fulfilling prophecy.) Both Marxists and conservatives like to play down the desirable or effective scope for intervention in society, but this argument traps them with their own theories. What is the purpose of theorizing about society if the best we can do to improve it is to let it alone? Moreover, how is that view to be sustained when adequate theorizing itself improves society? One reaction to this is to attribute a privileged status to theorizing, to see it as somehow underdetermined by the general processes of society. Efforts were made first by Marx and Durkheim, and then, under the label 'sociology of knowledge', by Mannheim, to connect forms of putative cognition with social forms, class interest and the like, meanwhile exempting from such determination natural science and such theorizing itself (Mannheim 1936 [1929]). The 'strong programme' of the sociology of knowledge – first proposed by Merton, although he attributes it to Mannheim – revokes the exemption for natural science (Bloor 1976). This is supported by the idea that reality, especially what people take reality to be, is itself a social construction – an idea that may be ascribed to the school of phenomenology but which goes specifically to Berger and Luckmann (1966). This issue, however, gets debated directly rather than methodologically, with the marshalling of comparative evidence to show how reality can be constructed very differently in different times and places. (Radical psychological theorists – labelling theory, so-called – extended the argument to the boundary between normal and abnormal psychological states, suggesting that psychopathology too is a matter of convention.) Much of the evidence came from anthropology, which had described societies where world-views, counting, the very categories of language and hence of reality, were different from ours. Reality seemed socially relative. Winch (1964) extended his ear-lier work in this direction, arguing that Evans-Pritchard's (1937) classic study of Azande witchcraft was conceptually confused in assessing the reality of magic by the standards of science. Battle was joined by the anthropologist Horton, who upheld the validity of such comparisons (Horton and Finnegan 1973). He thus followed Gellner, the leading critic of the various sociological idealisms (Gellner 1992; Horton 1993).

Anthropology also stimulated the so-called rationality debate, another treatment of the issue of relativism. The search for a characterization of what constituted human rationality stemmed from Aristotle's suggestion that it was rationality that set the human animal apart from other animals. Rationality was for long taken to mean reasoning, ratiocination and logic. Mill (1843) took it for granted that logic was the laws of the human mind. Anthropologists had once held that uncivilized peoples lacked the ability to reason, were incapable, even, of coherent speech. In the twentieth century they reversed themselves and found 'primitive' peoples to be as rational as, if not in some ways more rational than, us. Yet societies without science and full of superstition were, by positivist standards, not rational. Relativists countered that standards of rationality were embodied in differing social arrangements and hence differed. Absolutists argued that a necessary minimum for rationality – logic – was a necessary minimum for social life to function at all, therefore no extant societies lacked rationality. Still others tried to model degrees of rationality (Elster 1983; Jarvie 1984; Wilson 1970).

As logical positivism petered out in philosophy in the 1960s, it lingered on in the social sciences. Political science and psychology experienced in the 1950s the behavioural revolution (hence 'behavioural sciences'), in which positivist notions of aims and methods came to dominate. They are also to be found in rational choice and decision theory, and in the extensions of economic analysis to social life in general (Becker 1976, 1997). In sociology and social anthropology the early positivism and empiricism of Durkheim had been blended in the 1940s into structural-functionalism, a way of going about thinking about society that, despite serious logical flaws (Gellner 1973), for a time survived as the mainstream account of aims and methods. Although there was much debate over functionalism, it was endorsed as a method, perhaps because, stemming from a richer positivism, the extreme naturalism and inductivism of logical positivism rarely infected the work of sociologists and anthropologists – even if, sometimes, they echoed the rhetoric (Jarvie 1964). Eventually, however, culturalism and even postmodernism engulfed social studies (Kuper 1999). Philosophers of the social sciences have been strong critics of this trend (Gellner 1992; Root 1993; Harris 1992; Fay 1996).

Already in the 1940s there had been intervention in the debates about the aims and methods of the social sciences from another quarter. An economist, Hayek (1952), and an anti-positivist philosopher, Popper (1957), in articles that became new classics as books, argued that social scientists harboured mistaken views about the natural sciences. Hayek stressed that in science there were elements of a priori model building; Popper said that scientific method was trial and error. They thus criticized the identification of science with the positivist description of it. Both attacked the search for historical laws. Positivism was declared caricature and labelled 'scientism', then diagnosed as underlying Marxism and a priorism as well.

Drawing primarily on the example of neo-classical economics, Hayek and Popper argued that the test of methods was results: by that test the freedom economists exercised to invent simplified models and work out their implications before complicating the models with real-world additions was one used generally in common sense and professional social thought. Their work was part of a vigorous methodological debate within economics stemming from Robbins (1932) and Hutchison (1938), later pressed further by Friedman (1953), Klappholz and Agassi (1959), and others (Blaug 1992; Caldwell 1993). Alas, to the other social sciences economics is like mathematics to the non-scientist: a basic subject everyone knows they should be conversant with, and about which they feel guilty because they are not. Moreover, there is ambivalence: economics has high status, yet whether economic theories are testable has been repeatedly questioned and still is. Hence debates in economics about model-building, rationality, realistic assumptions, whether theories should aim at truth or predictive success, and the value of mathematization are scarcely referred to in discussions of the aims and methods of the other social sciences (Boland 1997). This is especially poignant because the debates within economics presuppose that eco-nomic behaviour is conventional and hence that the methods of economics are different from those of natural science.

The very important claim that positivists, Marxists and anti-science a priorists all held false images of science had little impact. Hayek and Popper's argument that more nuanced accounts of method would allow the social sciences to belong to unified science was ignored. Instead, their most controverted point was an ontological one. First, do humans act rationally – do they act at all? In opposition to the Hegelian tendency in Marx to reify abstractions and endow them with causal force (relations of production, classes and so on), Hayek and Popper sidestepped ontology (but see Gilbert 1989; Jarvie 1972) and proposed the principle of rational action or methodological individualism as more fruitful and in better conformity to the actual practice of the social sciences. This was the principle to attribute aims only to individuals and not to social wholes. Social institutions, they held, were real, but they were built, sustained and given aims only by individuals. A lively and extended debate continues (Udehn 2001).

To a large extent Popper and Hayek did not carry the day, as positivist and behaviourist and holistic social science flourished through the 1960s. Early in that decade an essay on the history of science was published that was destined finally to purge logical positivism from the social sciences. In common with Popper, Hayek and the positivists, it upheld the unity of science, while explicitly patronizing the social sciences as underdeveloped. Its author, a physicist, was a self-taught historian utterly innocent of any of the social sciences except history. The book was *The Structure of Scientific Revolutions*, the author, Thomas Kuhn (Fuller 2000; Barnes 1982; Kuhn 1962).

Kuhn argued that what distinguished a science from a prescience or a non-science was its domination by a paradigm, that is, a recognized piece of work that people copy in method, style and substance. Such paradigms are fully in place when they are incorporated in current textbooks and imposed on novices. Noticing the incessant warring about fundamentals in the social sciences, the existence of rival textbooks, Kuhn could not but characterize them as presciences. There is thus some irony in the way that social scientists seized on Kuhn's ideas and reversed them, arguing that since the social sciences have textbooks they have paradigms, therefore they are sciences. But Kuhn specifically says there must be agreement among the leadership of a field on a single paradigm if work in that field is to count as scientific. Conclusion: there are as many social sciences, or branches of the social sciences, as there are paradigmatic works, e.g. once we declare that Freud and Piaget do not contest child psychology but that there are two fields, genetic psychology and developmental psychology, a prescientific field is transformed into two paradigm-dominated scientific fields.

Kuhn's critics argued that there are textbooks of pseudo-science (astrology), non-science (theology) and doubtful cases (psychoanalysis). More telling, Kuhn provides a legitimation-procedure for the boundary-drawing of academic bureaucrats who wish to conceal debate, controversy and confusion, and give the impression of the orderly march of progress in 'fields', 'subjects', 'areas' and so on. Yet the categories of natural and conventional, not to mention physical, chemical, biological or mathematical, may themselves stem from problems and hotly debated theories (Hattiangadi 1978–9).

A more relativist reading of Kuhn is that no special aims or methods characterize natural science, which is a subject much like any other, distinguishable if at all by its social status. Hence comparison with the social sciences was an empirical matter *for the social sciences* and the 'strong programme' of the sociology of knowledge vindicated itself (Bloor 1976). Whether the results point to identity or contrast, they belong to the sociology of knowledge, which thus is the truly comprehensive discipline. Social studies of science, then, under whatever rubric, have implications in all directions, in sociology as well as philosophy, in meta-theory as well as theory (Fuller 2000).

I.C. JARVIE
YORK UNIVERSITY, CANADA

References

Agassi, J. (1977) *Towards a Rational Philosophical Anthropology*, The Hague.
Barnes, B. (1982) *T.S. Kuhn and Social Science*, London.
Becker, G. (1976) *The Economic Approach to Human Behavior*, Chicago.
—— (1997) *The Economics of Life*, New York.
Berger, P. and Luckmann, T. (1966) *The Social Construction of Reality*, New York.

Blaug, M. (1992) *The Methodology of Economics*, 2nd edn, London.
Bloor, D. (1976) *Knowledge and Social Imagery*, London (2nd edn, Chicago, 1991).
Boland, L.A. (1997) *Critical Economic Methodology: A Personal Odyssey*, London.
Brodbeck, M. (ed.) (1968) *Readings in the Philosophy of the Social Sciences*, New York.
Caldwell, B. (1993) *The Philosophy and Methodology of Economics*, Brookfield, VT.
Clifford, J. and Marcus, G.E. (eds) (1986) *Writing Culture: The Poetics and Politics of Ethnography*, Berkeley, CA.
Dallmayr, F. and McCarthy, T. (1977) *Understanding Social Inquiry*, Washington, DC.
Durkheim, E. (1938 [1895]) *Rules of Sociological Method*, Glencoe, IL.
Elster, J. (1983) *Sour Grapes*, Cambridge, UK.
Evans-Pritchard, E.E. (1937) *Witchcraft, Oracles and Magic among the Azande*, Oxford.
Fay, B. (1996) *Contemporary Philosophy of the Social Sciences*, Oxford.
Friedman, M. (1953) *Essays in Positive Economics*, Chicago.
Frisby, D. (ed.) (1976) *The Positivist Dispute in German Sociology*, London.
Fuller, S. (2000) *Thomas Kuhn: A Philosophical History for Our Times*, Cambridge, MA.
Geertz, C. (1988) *Works and Lives: The Anthropologist as Author*, Oxford.
Gellner, E. (1964) 'French 18th century materialism', reprinted in his *The Devil in Modern Philosophy*, London, 1974.
—— (1973) *Cause and Meaning in the Social Sciences*, London.
—— (1992) *Postmodernism, Reason and Religion*, London.
Gilbert, M. (1989) *On Social Facts*, London.
Harris, J.F. (1992) *Against Relativism: A Philosophical Defense of Method*, LaSalle, IL.
Hattiangadi, J.N. (1978–9) 'The structure of problems: I and II', *Philosophy of the Social Sciences* 8(9).
Hayek, F.A. (1952) *The Counter-Revolution of Science*, Glencoe, IL.
Horton, R. (1993) *Patterns of Thought in Africa and the West*, Cambridge, UK.
Horton, R. and Finnegan, R. (eds) (1973) *Modes of Thought*, London.
Hutchison, T.W. (1938) *The Significance and Basic Postulates of Economic Theory*, London.
Jarvie, I.C. (1964) *The Revolution in Anthropology*, London.
—— (1972) *Concepts and Society*, London.
—— (1984) *Rationality and Relativism*, London.
Kaufmann, F. (1944) *Methodology of the Social Sciences*, Oxford.
Klappholz, K. and Agassi, J. (1959) 'Methodological prescriptions in economics', *Economica* 26.
Krimerman, L. (ed.) (1969) *The Nature and Scope of Social Science: A Critical Anthology*, New York.
Kuhn, T.S. (1962) *The Structure of Scientific Revolutions*, Chicago.
Kuper, A. (1999) *Culture: The Anthropologists' Account*, Cambridge, MA.

Louch, A.R. (1966) *Explanation and Social Action*, Berkeley, CA.

Mannheim, K. (1936 [1929]) *Ideology and Utopia*, London (original edn, *Ideologie und Utopie*, Bonn).

Merton, R. (1957) *Social Theory and Social Structure*, Glencoe, IL.

Mill, J.S. (1843) *A System of Logic*, London.

Natanson, M. (ed.) (1963) *Philosophy of the Social Sciences: A Reader*, New York.

Popper, K.R. (1945) *The Open Society and Its Enemies*, London.

—— (1957) *The Poverty of Historicism*, London.

Robbins, L. (1932) *Essay on the Nature and Significance of Economic Science*, London.

Root, M. (1993) *Philosophy of Social Science*, Oxford.

Schütz, A. (1962) *Collected Papers*, Vol. 1: *The Problem of Social Reality*, The Hague.

Searle, J. (1995) *The Construction of Social Reality*, New York.

Simmel, G. (1950) *The Sociology of Georg Simmel*, ed. K.H. Wolff, Glencoe, IL.

Taylor, C. (1985) *Philosophy and the Human Sciences*, Cambridge, UK.

—— (1989) *Sources of the Self: The Making of Modern Identity*, Cambridge, MA.

Turner, S. and Roth, P. (2003) *The Blackwell Guide to the Philosophy of the Social Sciences*, Oxford.

Udehn, L. (2001) *Methodological Individualism: Background, History, Meaning*, London.

Weber, M. (1949) *Methodology of the Social Sciences*, ed. E. Shils, Glencoe, IL.

Wilson, B. (ed.) (1970) *Rationality*, Oxford.

Winch, P. (1958) *The Idea of a Social Science*, London.

—— (1964) 'Understanding a primitive society', *American Philosophical Quarterly* 1.

Further reading

Bloor, D. (1997) *Wittgenstein, Rules and Institutions*, London.

Borger, R. and Cioffi, F. (1970) *Explanation in the Behavioural Sciences*, Cambridge, UK.

Brown, R. (1963) *Explanation in Social Science*, London.

Bunge, M. (1996) *Finding Philosophy in Social Science*, New Haven, CT.

Collin, F. (1997) *Social Reality*, London.

Durkheim, E. (1915 [1912]) *Elementary Forms of the Religious Life*, London.

Emmet, D. and MacIntyre, A. (1970) *Sociological Theory and Philosophical Analysis*, London.

Gellner, E. (1975) *Legitimation of Belief*, Cambridge, UK.

—— (1985) *Relativism and the Social Sciences*, Cambridge, UK.

Giddens, A. (1976) *New Rules of Sociological Method*, New York.

Hands, D.W. (2001) *Reflection without Rules: Economic Methodology and Contemporary Science*, Cambridge, UK.

Hollis, M. (1994) *The Philosophy of Social Sciences: An Introduction*, Cambridge, UK.

Hollis, M. and Lukes, S. (eds) (1982) *Rationality and Relativism*, Oxford.

Hookway, C. and Pettit, P. (eds) (1978) *Action and Interpretation*, Cambridge, UK.

Little, D. (1998) *Microfoundations, Method and Causation: On the Philosophy of the Social Sciences*, New Brunswick, NJ.

Martin, M. (1999) *Verstehen*, New Brunswick, NJ.

Martin, M. and McIntyre, L. (1994) *Readings in the Philosophy of Social Science*, Cambridge, MA.

Simmel, G. (1980) *Essays on Interpretation in Social Science*, Totowa, NJ.

Skinner, Q. (ed.) (1985) *The Return of Grand Theory in the Human Sciences*, Cambridge, UK.

SEE ALSO: phenomenology; positivism; reason, rationality and rationalism; relativism

PHYSIOLOGICAL PSYCHOLOGY

In his classic textbook, Grossman (1967) described physiological psychology as the study of 'physiological and chemical processes (and their anatomical substrates) that intervene between the arrival of sensory signals in the central nervous system and the elaboration of appropriate responses to them'. This could potentially include the brain mechanisms underlying all our simple and complex cognitive, emotional and motivational processes; the brain mechanisms themselves could range from activity of single neurons to the involvement of major brain structures. The term 'physiological' might be stretched to cover all aspects of cellular processes in the body, especially hormones (the endocrine system) and genetics.

Physiological psychology could trace its roots to pioneering figures in the nineteenth century, and by the 1960s it had emerged as an enterprise at the interface of biology, physiology, neurology and psychology. Many of its practitioners emerged from non-psychological backgrounds in the biological or medical sciences. Nevertheless, common interests can be identified, certainly up to the 1970s. The key research areas were sensory and motor functions of the cerebral cortex; motivational states, including sleep and arousal, hunger, thirst and temperature control; emotion; and memory and learning. However, what is striking about all the texts of the period is the absence of data from studies on humans. In Morgan (1965) forty pages out of 500 are given over to human brain disorders and 'psychochemistry'. In Grossman (1967) there is nothing specific on human brain function.

The reason for this was the need for physiological psychology to distinguish itself from the neurological tradition in medicine. Studies of the brain-damaged human have provided essential data for the understanding of brain function, but from the nineteenth century this was seen as the province of the medically trained clinical neurologist. As physiological psychology developed during the twentieth century, it evolved its own methods and traditions, central to which was the use of non-human animals for experiments, particularly on the effects of systematic lesions (brain damage) and electrical stimulation. The behaviours investigated were, of course, restricted to the repertoires of the animals used, in particular to the ubiquitous laboratory rat. Hence the focus on sensory and motor processes, and motivational systems such as hunger and thirst. If emotion was studied, it was likely to consist of intense states such as fear and aggression, easily identifiable in animals. Even higher cognitive processes such as memory and learning would be restricted to learning tasks appropriate to the animal under investigation. The increasing use of primates did make some of the behaviours studied easier to generalize to the human condition, but a clear distinction remained between physiological psychology and the explicit study of the human brain.

During this period, radical developments occurred that altered the nature of physiological psychology. The 1960s saw the beginnings of technological developments that are ongoing and that have revolutionized brain research. As one example, synaptic neurotransmission using neurotransmitters was only discovered in the brain in the 1950s. Ten years later, pharmacological techniques had developed to the point where acetylcholine, dopamine, noradrenaline and serotonin had been identified as neurotransmitters, and there were detailed models of how they were involved in normal and abnormal behaviour. By the 1970s this field of *psychopharmacology* was established in its own right, with specialized professional societies, research journals and textbooks. The same developments can be seen in other areas formerly the province of physiological psychology. For instance, studying interactions between hormones, the nervous system and behaviour has now evolved into *psychoneuroendocrinology*.

At the same time, cognitive neuropsychology was taking its first strides. The systematic psychological study in humans of complex cognitive processes such as attention, perception and memory (cognitive psychology) began in the late 1950s with Broadbent's pioneering work on selective attention. During the 1960s the field developed rapidly and incorporated impairments in cognitive processes (amnesia, problems with face recognition, etc.) following brain damage in humans, an area that became known as *cognitive neuropsychology*. Drawing also on studies of intact and brain-damaged participants, new models of human cognition and emotion have been developed. There has been much less recourse to animal studies of brain function.

However, the most influential development in brain research since 1970 has been the introduction of brain-scanning techniques, such as MRI, fMRI, PET, MEG, etc. These allow us to study the brain in living *human* participants as they perform psychological tests. Functions are being localized to brain areas with increasing precision and detail, particularly in the fields of sensory, perceptual and motor processes, cognition and emotion. Behavioural topics that were once the province of physiological psychology are increasingly being incorporated into the general area of *neuroscience*, which is itself now divided into *cognitive neuroscience, affective (emotional) neuroscience*, etc.

Modern textbooks on physiological psychology still have 'traditional' chapters that emphasize animal-based research and cover the nature and functions of the neuron, the organization of the nervous system, sensory and motor processes, and mechanisms of basic physiological processes such as hunger and thirst. However, coverage of higher-level cognitive and emotional functions has changed dramatically. The study of learning and memory now focuses on human amnesic states, although there is still room for important animal-based work on neuronal mechanisms of memory. The accumulation of findings from psychopharmacology and scanning studies into the 'abnormal' brain means that most texts now have substantial entries on, for instance, schizophrenia, depression and anxiety. However, it should also be emphasized that findings from scanning studies have also supported correspondences between brain anatomy in humans and that of experimental animals (Albright *et al.* 2000), validating the continued use of animals in brain research.

The very term 'physiological psychology' is rarely used these days. Textbooks and review articles are more likely to use terms like 'Biopsychology', Physiology of Behaviour' or 'Biological Psychology' in their titles, perhaps reflecting a sense that the study of the biological underpinnings of behaviour is no longer a unified enterprise, whose practitioners are in general agreement on the demarcation lines between physiological psychology, neurology, cognitive neuropsychology, etc. Anyone now researching human brain function, be they psychologist, neurologist or psychiatrist, is more likely to refer to themselves as a *neuroscientist*, perhaps modified by a descriptor such as *cognitive*.

This is not to say that the traditional topic areas and methods of physiological psychology have disappeared. Research on neuronal function, brain mechanisms of hunger and thirst, the cellular basis of learning and memory, etc., are still heavily dependent on controlled studies in animals. Entire research areas such as the study of drugs, neurotransmitters and behaviour (*psychopharmacology*) still rely heavily on animal experimentation. More recent but highly significant areas of research include interactions between molecular genetics and behaviour, such as the use of genetically modified mice to model Alzheimer's disease.

It could be argued that the disappearance of the term 'physiological psychology' reflects the health of the field rather than any decline. Physiological psychology developed at a time when systematic experimentation on the human brain was largely impossible outside the specialized field of clinical neurology. We are now in a position where a course in biopsychology can be substantially based on data from human studies. Moreover, every topic covered in the classic textbooks of the 1960s is now a full research specialization in its own right. Whole books are devoted to the behavioural functions of single brain structures, or to the role of a particular neurotransmitter. No single researcher can hope to stay abreast of developments much beyond his or her own speciality. As knowledge increases so does the awareness that distinctions between physiological or biopsychology, neuropsychology, clinical neurology, etc., are increasingly artificial. Hence the popularity of generic terms such as 'neuroscientist'. The study of the biological bases of behaviour has expanded exponentially over the last 30 years. It has built on the foundations of classic physiological psychology, but technical developments have allowed radical advances both in traditional areas and in completely new directions such as pharmacology and genetics.

SIMON GREEN
BIRKBECK COLLEGE, UNIVERSITY OF LONDON

References

Albright, T.D., Kandel, E.R. and Posner, M.I. (2000) 'Cognitive neuroscience', *Current Opinion in Neurobiology* 10(5): 612–24.
Grossman, S.P. (1967) *A Textbook of Physiological Psychology*, New York.
Morgan, C.T. (1965) *Physiological Psychology*, 3rd edn, New York.

SEE ALSO: cognitive neuropsychology; instinct

PIAGET, JEAN (1896–1980)

Jean Piaget, the Swiss psychologist, biologist and philosopher, was professor of experimental psychology at the University of Geneva (1940–71) and of developmental psychology at the Sorbonne in Paris (1952–63). As a psychologist, Piaget was influenced by Freud, Janet, J.M. Baldwin and Claparède. Piaget's theories and experiments, which he published in innumerable books and articles, place him among the foremost psychologists of the century.

Piaget's lifelong quest was for the origins of knowledge. Trained as a biologist, and initially influenced by Bergson's evolutionary philosophy, he sought to explain the conditions of knowledge by studying its genesis. Evolutionary theory, the developmental psychology of children's intelligence, and the history of science were to provide the scientific underpinnings of this epistemological project.

In his early work (1923–36), Piaget tried to gain insight into children's logic by studying their verbally expressed thought. Using a free method of interrogation, the 'clinical method', Piaget investigated children's reasoning about everyday phenomena, causality and moral problems. A leading idea expressed in Piaget's early books is that of egocentrism in early childhood and its gradual replacement by socialized, and therefore logical, thinking. Young children's egocentrism is revealed in their incapacity to differentiate between their own point of view and that of another. Neither experience nor the influence of adults are sufficient grounds for the attainment of logical thinking. Instead, Piaget explained the abandonment of egocentrism by the child's desire and need to communicate with children of the same age.

In the late 1920s and early 1930s Piaget made extensive observations of his own children as babies and elaborated his theory of sensorimotor intelligence in infancy. Contrary to contemporary conceptions, he considered babies as actively and spontaneously oriented towards their environment. As they 'assimilate' things to their action patterns, they at the same time have to 'accommodate' these patterns to the exigencies of the external world. In this process of interaction with the environment the child's innate reflexes and patterns of behaviour are altered, differentiated and mutually co-ordinated. The organization of action patterns gives rise to a 'logic of actions'. In his account of the development of the object concept, Piaget states that initially children do not appear to recognize a world existing independently of their actions upon it. A baby playing with a toy does not search for it when it is covered; according to Piaget, it ceases to exist for the baby. The concept of an independently existing world is gradually constructed during infancy and is attained only at about 18 months when the child becomes capable of representing things mentally.

The existence of a logic in action, demonstrated in the baby studies, made Piaget revise his earlier theories of the origins of logical thinking in early and middle childhood. Logical operations are prepared in sensorimotor intelligence and the former are the result of internalization of the latter. The attainment of logical thinking, therefore, is not the result of verbal interactions with other children, but of the child's reconstruction of the action logic on a new, mental plane. Piaget now viewed cognitive development as resulting in stages, characterized by a dynamic equilibrium between the child's cognitive structures and the environment. Development is the result of a process of equilibration, in which equilibria of a progressively more stable kind are sought and attained. Piaget distinguished three stages: the sensorimotor stage (0–18 months), the stage of concrete operations (about 7–11 years) and the stage of formal operations (from about 11 years). In each of these three stages children's thinking is characterized by its own kind of logic: an action logic in the sensorimotor stage, a logic applied to concrete situations in the concrete operational stage, and a logic applied to statements of a symbolic or verbal kind in the formal operational stage.

In the period between the sensorimotor and the concrete operational stage (which Piaget called the pre-operational period) the child's thinking lacks the possibility to carry out operations, that is, reversible mental actions. Piaget and his collaborators demonstrated in many simple yet elegant experiments the transition from pre-operational to concrete thinking about concepts such as number, velocity, space and physical causality. In these experiments they no longer restricted themselves to verbal interaction, but introduced materials that the child could manipulate. In the famous conservation task, the child must judge whether the amount of fluid poured into a glass of different proportions changes or does not change. Pre-operational children are characteristically misled by the perceptual appearance of the situation. Only concrete operational children can reverse the transfer in thought and give the correct answer.

From 1950 onwards Piaget produced his great epistemological studies, in which he rejected empiricism and rationalism. Consequently he opposed behaviourism, maturational theories of development and nativist ideas in Gestalt psychology. The newborn child is neither a *tabula rasa*, ready to receive the impression of the environment, nor endowed with a priori knowledge about the world. Piaget showed himself a pupil of Kant by assuming that our knowledge of the world is mediated by cognitive structures. But, unlike Kant, he did not consider these as fundamental ideas given at birth: he showed them to be the products of a lengthy process of construction in the interaction of subject and environment. He therefore coined his epistemology a *genetic* epistemology.

The aim of genetic epistemology is to reconstruct the development of knowledge from its most elementary biological forms up to its highest achievements, scientific thinking included. Psychology has a place in this project, in so far as it studies the development of biological structures in the human baby into sensorimotor and operational intelligence. But the enterprise is essentially a biological one, as the development of intelligence is conceived of as an extension of biological adaptation. Intelligence is the specific product in humans of the same biological principles applying to all living nature: adaptation resulting in structural reorganizations and in equilibria of increasing stability.

Piaget saw psychology as a necessary but

limited part of his epistemology; and he always regretted the exclusive interest in the psychological component of his work. In the International Centre for Genetic Epistemology, which he founded at the University of Geneva in 1955 and to which he attracted specialists in all fields of study, he stimulated the interdisciplinary study of epistemology. But the acclaim for his epistemological ideas was never more than a shadow of the universal enthusiasm for the *psychologist* Piaget.

Piaget's influence on developmental psychology can hardly be overestimated. His ideas were seen as a help in supplanting behaviouristic and psychoanalytic theories in psychology. He set the margins for discussions in cognitive developmental psychology from the 1960s up to the present time. But his ideas and methods have always been the object of sharp criticism. Many developmental psychologists think that Piaget underrated the cognitive capacities of young children, and he is reproached for neglecting in his later studies the social context of development in favour of an isolated epistemic subject. Therefore, many now go beyond the mature Piaget and find inspiration in his early works.

ED ELBERS
UNIVERSITY OF UTRECHT

Further reading

Boden, M. (1979) *Piaget*, London.
Ducret, J.-J. (1984) *Jean Piaget*, Geneva.
Flavell, J.H. (1963) *The Developmental Psychology of Jean Piaget*, Princeton, NJ.
Gruber, H.E. and Vonèche, J.J. (eds) (1977) *The Essential Piaget: An Interpretive Reference and Guide*, London.
Piaget, J. (1926 [1923]) *The Language and Thought of the Child*, London.
—— (1932 [1932]) *The Moral Judgment of the Child*, London.
—— (1952 [1936]) *The Origin of Intelligence in the Child*, London.
—— (1950) *Introduction à l'épistémologie génétique*, 3 vols, Paris.
—— (1971 [1967]) *Biology and Knowledge*, London.
—— (1976 [1974]) *The Grasp of Consciousness*, London.
—— (1977 [1975]) *The Development of Thought: Equilibration of Cognitive Structures*, Oxford.
Piaget, J. and Inhelder, B. (1956 [1948]) *The Child's Conception of Space*, London.
—— (1964 [1959]) *The Early Growth of Logic in the Child*, London.
—— (1969 [1966]) *The Psychology of the Child*, London.
Rotman, B. (1977) *Jean Piaget: Psychologist of the Real*, Hassocks.
Sutherland, P. (1992) *Cognitive Development Today: Piaget and His Critics*, London.

SEE ALSO: developmental psychology

PLACE

A place is an area in which people live together, and thus a key concept in geographical analysis. Much modern social science has emphasized compositional rather than contextual theories of social organization and life (Thrift 1983): people have been categorized according to who they are rather than where they come from, and sociological categories such as class and status have taken precedence over the geographical category of place. Since the mid-1980s, however, the importance of the contextual has been realized (Agnew and Duncan 1989): people are socialized as members of groups that are constituted in places, and the nature of those groups can vary from place to place.

A major impetus to this reincorporation of place within social science was given by Giddens's (1984) promotion of structuration theory, in which locale is a key concept. A locale is a setting for interaction, and since much interaction requires the individuals involved to be co-present in time and space, most locales are necessarily places. Locales, which may vary in their spatial and temporal extent, are thus crucial arenas within which interaction occurs and group identity develops. (Increasingly, of course, 'placeless' interpersonal interaction is being facilitated through the Internet and other technologies, and the future importance of co-location in many social, cultural, political and even economic processes is a topic of considerable interest and suggestion.)

Giddens drew considerably on the work of a Swedish geographer, Torsten Hägerstrand (1982), whose contextual theory of time geography asserts that projects involving interpersonal interaction can only be realized if the parties involved are co-present in a place. Whether this is possible depends on three constraints being overcome: capability constraints (Can an individual reach a certain place at a given time?); coupling constraints (Can all of the individuals concerned be in the place at the same time?); and authority constraints (Do all of the individuals involved have access to the place at the required time?). Operation of these constraints defines the possibilities for project realization. Each individual's biography is a constrained trajectory through time and space: where trajectories intersect, so interaction is enabled and biographies potentially changed. A place's contents – who is there, when – vary, therefore: when one is in a place, and who with, are major influences on individual and group socialization and behaviour.

Others have produced similar arguments. In her seminal *Spatial Divisions of Labour*, for example, Massey (1995 [1984]) argues that the geography of industrial restructuring can be understood only if the context of the places within which it occurs is appreciated: the nature of social relations varies between places, with some consequently being much more attractive to investors than others. This has stimulated a substantial body of research in which place is usually treated as synonymous with locality: differences between localities in their economic, social, cultural and political structures have been sought as means of understanding how they differ and what this implies for future change (as, for example, with the 1984–5 miners' strike in Great Britain: Johnston 1991).

The importance of a place's characteristics to its economic future is growing because of the increased mobility of two of the major factors of production, capital and labour: places have to attract and retain investments and people, with those involved in their management operating accordingly. This has generated interest in the creation and selling of places among business and political groups, who may combine in a local alliance in order to promote 'their place' and compete with others (Harvey 1985; Reynolds 1994). Local interest groups realize the importance of creating a positive image of 'their place', which may involve both restructuring social relations and substantial investment in the built environment in order to effect the right conditions for attracting capital investment. The changing geography of uneven development, at a variety of spatial scales, is thus closely linked to the success and failure of the politics of place.

For some authors the importance of place (locality, locale) in the processes of socialization and restructuring illustrates the validity of arguments for postmodernism, which prioritizes difference, as do some feminist and other approaches that stress 'positionality': Jackson notes that 'both movements challenge us to consider from where we speak and whose voices

are sanctioned' (1992: 211). Within geography, the renewed interest in places – as created locales within which social relationships are produced and reproduced – has stimulated what is termed a 'cultural turn' in the discipline; alongside it, there has been a 'spatial turn' in some humanities and social science disciplines, as the importance of space and place to their subject matter has been realized (Crang and Thrift 2000).

R.J. JOHNSTON
UNIVERSITY OF BRISTOL

References

Agnew, J. and Duncan, J.S. (eds) (1989) *The Power of Place: Bringing Together Geographical and Sociological Imaginations*, Boston, MA.

Crang, M. and Thrift, N.J. (eds) (2000) *Thinking Space*, London.

Giddens, A. (1984) *The Constitution of Society*, Cambridge, UK.

Hägerstrand, T. (1982) 'Diorama, path and project', *Tijdschrift voor Economische en Sociale Geografie* 73.

Harvey, D. (1985) 'The geopolitics of capitalism', in D. Gregory and J. Urry (eds) *Social Relations and Spatial Structures*, London.

Jackson, P. (1992) 'Changing ourselves: A geography of position', in R.J. Johnston (ed.) *The Challenge for Geography – A Changing World: A Changing Discipline*, Oxford.

Johnston, R.J. (1991) *A Question of Place: Exploring the Practice of Human Geography*, Oxford.

Massey, D. (1995 [1984]) *Spatial Divisions of Labour: Social Structures and the Geography of Production*, 2nd edn, London.

Reynolds, D.R. (1994) 'Political geography; The power of place and the spatiality of politics', *Progress in Human Geography* 19.

Thrift, N.J. (1983) 'On the determination of social action in space and time', *Society and Space: Environment and Planning D* 1.

Further reading

Duncan, S. and Savage, M. (1991) *New Perspectives on the Locality Debate*, London.

Johnston, R.J. (1991) *A Question of Place: Exploring the Practice of Human Geography*, Oxford.

SEE ALSO: region

PLANNING, ECONOMIC

Economic planning is the use of a systematic alternative method of allocating economic resources either to replace or supplement the market mechanism. Its main justification is when the market mechanism fails to supply the right signals to decision-makers. This may be because economies of scale render the atomistic market mechanism ineffective, or because the market is incapable of taking into account the long-run needs of the economy. The state may possess knowledge that the market does not, whether about general economic uncertainties, the preferences of the community as a whole, or the longer-run future. Alternatively, the state may simply reject the validity of the individual preferences that underlie the market system. Critics of planning have focused on the insuperable quantities of information that must be processed if the entire economy is to be organized by one body, and the undemocratic implications of the state's overruling individuals' choices. National economic planning fell into disrepute in the 1980s as a result of the perceived inability of the planned economies of the Soviet Union and Eastern Europe to adapt to changing technological and international competitive conditions. The term 'planning' has a degree of ambiguity: it can mean attempting to control the economy from the centre or the attempt to provide common forecasts for investors to work to, which would not necessarily be for one unique scenario.

In reality, no single system is ever wholly planned and controlled from the centre. Even in the USSR consumer goods were not administratively distributed; enterprise managers actually had considerable scope for negotiations with GOSPLAN and there was informal trade and sometimes barter between enterprises. The state tried to influence firms using incentive schemes, but managers could manipulate data to maximize bonuses. The Soviet state could not handle the vast amount of information that it would have needed to direct everything, even if there had been no inherent uncertainty.

Before 1989 many proposals were made for reforming planning in the USSR and Eastern Europe (most of which had copied the Soviet model after 1945) in order to replace the coercive element by fully incentive-based systems, but with very little success. A major problem with such reforms was that, where the prices were set wrongly, a partially decentralized system may be even worse than a centrally planned one as managers follow the logic of bonuses rather than real market forces. It was also felt that the logic of 'planning' made it hard to enforce the threat of bankruptcy, widely perceived as necessary to ensure the full play of market forces, and so most

of the former socialist countries opted for a rapid transition to a wholly market economy after 1989. The Chinese economy was the major exception where a state-owned sector coexists with a very rapidly growing private and locally controlled sector, which largely escapes state control and that by the early 1990s had overtaken the state sector in size. Cuba and North Korea remained traditional bureaucratically planned economies.

In the West, economic planning was very much a wartime phenomenon. The Second World War saw the successful use of planning to achieve war priorities in the UK and USA. After 1945 some idea of planning was advocated by many in the West, using incentives or just forecasts as a way of combining the coordinating powers of both the market and the plan. But actual attempts at planning displayed a lack of coherence between policy instruments, and between the instruments and the desired objectives. State intervention in many countries and periods has often been very *ad hoc* and did not always deserve the name 'planning'. 'Indicative' planning was attempted in France: here the planners forecast the best available growth path for the economy and tried to influence people's expectations and investments to create a self-fulfilling prophecy. French planning had some real success before 1965, but it has faded since then. In practice it always involved far less coherence and more direct (but not always co-ordinated) intervention than the term indicative planning implies. The Commissariat Général du Plan remains in place as a government think tank. A misunderstanding of French experience led to the abortive UK National Plan (1965–70); too much weight was placed on the idea that an optimistic plan could be self-fulfilling, raising investment and growth by raising expectations.

After 1989 the former socialist countries rejected any kind of planning on the grounds that, although the market system might bring them some problems of adjustment, their economies were so distorted that no one, and especially not the discredited state planners, was likely to do better than the trial and error process of market forces. But critics, such as Stiglitz, argue that socialist 'planning' has been replaced by a 'market fundamentalism' with a naïvely idealized vision of the market's ability to give people the right signals.

Economic planning may be carried out at a lower level than the national economy. There is regional and sectoral planning, which may or may not be made consistent with national planning. Large corporations also engage in planning, and there have been suggestions that the planning activities of large corporations can be building blocks for the creation of national plans. Sceptics point out that corporate plans are usually speculative scenarios rather than fully worked out operational programmes.

Less developed countries have often engaged in 'development planning'. This has rarely attempted to follow a strictly centralized model, if only because agriculture does not lend itself well to central control and because the political and bureaucratic preconditions are such as to make it very hard to manage. Too often 'planning' just meant a large and inefficient state-owned sector and regulations restricting new private investment. India still retains a Planning Commission, whose function is to establish a framework for medium-term government economic strategy. But a key element of the 10th Plan for 2003–7 is the development of a coherent policy to build up the private sector

Considerable debate reigns over how far the successful industrializing countries of Asia, first Japan, then Taiwan and above all Korea, relied on market forces rather than on a form of planning through state influence over the banking system. Wade argues that the Korean state together with its conglomerates or 'Chaebols' more or less created a comparative advantage in electronics by deliberately fostering interfirm co-ordination and scale economies. But even those who believe state planning helped Korea in the past are unsure if it would work now. Increasingly, developing countries are seeing the key development strategy as the creation of a favourable investment climate in very general terms, rather than to predict or control new investment. The need for institutions that ensure the best possible flow of economic information is sometimes overlooked in this context, but it is unlikely to involve full-blown economic planning agencies.

A plan with a single forecast or a rigid set of objectives makes no sense in an uncertain world, but some form of multiscenario forecasting at a higher level than the firm may be able to help decision-makers. The European Commission has occasionally attempted to organize such exer-cises, of which perhaps the most striking concerned the attempt to alert economic actors to the potential significance of the '1992' Internal Market plan and to induce changes in expectations and behaviour. But during the 1980s a consensus built up that private capital markets were uniquely qualified to process and generate economically valuable information about future investment and financial prospects.

The recent crises that have occurred in various financial markets have undermined the strongest version of the argument that capital markets are 'efficient' in the sense of accurately reflecting all known information at a point in time and ensuring the optimal allocation of investment. The recent huge swings up and down of share values, and the dot.com boom and bust, suggest that we cannot assume that private investors have perfect foresight in their allocation of investment. On the other hand, in a world of high uncertainty and rapid technological change it is not obvious that forecasting by public agencies can do any better, let alone any collective planning of productive investment. If we lived in a world where all economic actors were able to form 'rational expectations' about the economic future at all times this would be the end of the story, but there is clearly still room in all economies for collective thinking and consultation about the future, and for medium-term economic policy strategies that try to ensure coherence across time and across issues. Whether we have a single agency to do it, and call this 'planning' is another matter.

PETER HOLMES
UNIVERSITY OF SUSSEX

Further reading

http://planningcommission.nic.in.
http://www.plan.gouv.fr/.
Stiglitz, J.E. (1995) *Whither Socialism?* Cambridge, MA.
Wade, R. (1990) *Governing the Economy*, Princeton, NJ.
World Bank (1996) *World Development Report: From Plan to Market*, Oxford.

SEE ALSO: mixed economy; forecasting and prediction

PLATO (C.427–C.348 BCE)

Plato (the name may have originated as a

nickname) was of long-established aristocratic Athenian stock, and born (c.427 BCE) into a deeply political extended family at a time of the most extreme upheaval known to classical Athens or indeed classical Greece generally: the Peloponnesian War (431–404) so brilliantly analysed by his older contemporary and fellow-citizen Thucydides. Thucydides was formally exiled by the Athenian democracy; Plato in effect went into self-imposed internal exile, disgusted – so says the possibly authentic Seventh Letter ascribed to him – first by the behaviour of relatives such as Critias and Charmides, who played leading roles respectively in the junta later known as the Thirty Tyrants and in the associated gang of ten who ruled the Peiraieus (404–403), and then by the Athenian democracy's judicial murder (as he saw it and portrayed it in the *Apology* and other works) of his revered mentor Socrates. Though refusing from his early twenties until his death at about 80 to play any active, public part in the, in fact, relatively moderate Athenian democracy, he and many of his more prominent ex-pupils remained politically engaged as intellectuals and philosophers; and that he should have attempted a philosophical conversion of a Sicilian absolute ruler in 367, or that his final work was entitled *Laws*, hardly came as surprises, even if some of the details of these flawed enterprises certainly were.

All Plato's twenty or so published works are extant, and all are cast in the elaborately literary dialogue form that Plato, influenced both by the theatre and by public and sometimes publicly adjudicated disputes among would-be teachers of wisdom, brought to a pitch of perfection. Plato never figures as a character in his dialogues (though his two elder brothers and other relatives do), so as the better to be present in them throughout. Scholars agree in general on a broad tripartite classification of the unquestionably authentic works – into early (*Apology*, *Crito*, for instance), middle (*Gorgias*, *Republic*) and late (*Timaeus*, *Theaetetus*, *Laws*) periods – but cannot agree altogether either on the authenticity of all the attributed works or on their absolute or relative chronology. This last is important, as his ideas on such fundamental elements of his thought as the theory of forms or conceptions of an ideal polity evolved over his 50 or more years of intellectual activity and literary composition. The institute for advanced study that he established in the 380s in a sacred grove to the north of central Athens has added a name to our vocabulary: the Academy. It long outlived its Founder, although it too inevitably evolved over the eight centuries or so of its existence.

The early dialogues mostly portray a vigorously middle-aged Socrates in his role as self-proclaimed 'gadfly' of the Athenians, challenging a series of generally well-meaning but unsophisticated upper-class Athenians over their conception of virtue and individual virtues, and engaging with them provocatively at a level of analysis deeper than they had ever thought to operate on. When asked to define abstract notions such as courage (*Laches*), piety (*Euthyphro*) or moderation (*Charmides* – surely an ironic choice) – Socrates's interlocutors instead provide specific instances of brave, pious or temperate behaviour. Socrates, by proving to them that such acts would not be considered virtuous in all circumstances, demonstrates that they have failed to meet his challenge of primary definition.

In the *Republic* (a misleading translation of a Greek word, *politeia*, which meant something more like 'political arrangements'), a mature work of his middle period, Plato conspicuously raised the stakes by pitting Socrates at first against a leading Sophist, Thrasymachus of Chalcedon (just opposite modern Istanbul, ancient Byzantium, on the Asiatic side of the Bosporus). The Sophists were not a school, more an intellectual movement, and one that Plato through his Socrates was especially keen to resist, not least because the real Socrates was widely perceived to be nothing more than a Sophist himself. Their unconventionality often took the form, if only for debating purposes, of an extreme relativism, and it was entirely in character that Plato's Thrasymachus should have argued – or rather asserted – that values and virtues have no intrinsic definitions but are defined situationally by the relevant ruling class as what is in their opinion in their own best interests. Against such relativism Plato's Socrates – and perhaps therefore Plato himself, at least up to a very considerable point – advocated a theory of Forms or Ideas, drawing a radical distinction between a world of ultimate, abstract reality accessible in full only to a select band of super-intelligent elite persons and the ever-changing and second-best world of ordinary sense-data accessible to all, but for the most part falsely perceived. The Form of the Good, or Virtue itself, was the attainable goal of the true Platonic philosopher alone.

If there is any truth to the claim that 'The legacy of Greece to Western philosophy is Western philosophy' (B. Williams), then Plato has a better claim than any ancient Greek to having been that legacy's progenitor, especially as regards philosophical analysis and epistemology. Plato, as a true intellectual, privileged the theoretical life of a philosopher and teacher above all others. His contributions to social thought as we would now define it lie mainly in the fields of moral and political philosophy, psychology and educational theory. These cannot be divorced from his cosmology and theology, however, and any understanding of his political and social outlook must take full measure of his determined, principled widening of the gap between body and spirit (Greek *psykhê*, which both before and after Plato had a strongly corporeal, material component as well as a purely spiritual one).

This gap performed two kinds of work, at once sociological and epistemological. On the one hand, it formalized a psychological split between lower and higher elements in the personality and linked this to a justification of social hierarchy. On the other, through the claim that virtue was a kind of knowledge it offered solutions to logical problems raised by earlier philosophers and provided a foundation for belief in the immortality of the soul. Thus was Plato enabled to preserve an essential core of religious belief from the Sophistical criticisms that had been directed against all religious belief and practice, and – not incidentally – to defend Socrates posthumously against the (successful) charge that he had 'introduced new gods and not duly recognized the gods that the city recognized'.

The most widely read of all Plato's works is surely the *Republic*, but it is very hard to know how to read it most appropriately. The long central section, following the demolition of Thrasymachus's opening definition of justice and its attempted reformulations, and preceding the concluding tirade against any form of mimetic art, whether verbal or pictorial, consists of the establishment in words by Socrates and his interlocutors of an ideal city known tautologously as Callipolis ('Beautiful City'). But is this a 'model' (*paradeigma*) laid up in heaven to be an object of theoretical contemplation and only

indirectly a source of practical political wisdom, or is it rather a blueprint for the construction of a Platonic city here on earth, a city in which Platonic philosophers will rule virtuously in accordance with their privileged knowledge of the Form of the Good (Virtue)? Plato's Socrates playfully offers both interpretations without seriously settling the issue.

In Plato's final work, the hugely long and long-winded *Laws*, we find the old philosopher grappling with detailed problems of law-drafting in an apparently far more pragmatic spirit than that evinced in either the *Republic* or the intermediary and mediating *Statesman*. There is, for example, a notable absence from the ideal city of Magnesia on Crete – here elaborately constructed on papyrus by the three interlocutors (a Spartan, a Cretan and a surrogate Plato) – of the three class divisions that in the *Republic* were modelled on divisions of the soul. This is one of the several major differences that raise the issue of whether the *Laws* is to be seen as complementing the *Republic*, or rather as revising or superseding it. Both works, too, evoke in their acutest form the issue of Plato's own political allegiances: crudely, and anachronistically, was he some sort of proto-fascist, or – to go to the opposite extreme – was he rather some peculiar form of ancient democrat (given that *dêmokratia*, literally 'people-power', was in ancient Greece both face-to-face and in-your-face)? The following views, as expressed most memorably in the *Republic*, and not repudiated in the *Laws*, would seem to tilt the balance firmly towards at any rate a non-democratic Plato.

Since coming closer to the world of Ideas or Forms was for Plato both the highest aim of human life and the standard by which all kinds of knowledge are judged, it followed that human societies should be directed by philosophers or by laws formulated by philosophers. The human personality was taken to be divided into three elements: intelligence, *amour propre* (*thumos*) and the physical appetites. Education aims to train the first to dominate the other two. *Thumos* refers to a set of qualities regarded somewhat ambivalently in Plato's culture. It was the basis of the human pursuit of prestige and honour, and thus – like the appetites – beneficial when exercised in moderation but dangerous when obsessive. Too eager a pursuit of honour, however, led to tyranny or to a tendency to take offence for no reason. Thus there was a popular basis for the view that even ambition for what the ordinary person in the street considered the supreme good had to be controlled. This point was particularly important for Plato, because his belief that the good society was a society ruled by good and wise men meant that the essential problem of political organization was to prevent the ruling elite from becoming corrupted.

Because a philosophical education involved training in subjects such as astronomy and mathematics for which not all had equal interest or aptitude, and because philosophers had to detach themselves from activities and preoccupations likely to strengthen the influence of their *thumos* and bodily appetites, the hierarchy of faculties in the *psykhê* led to a hierarchy of groups in the ideal city. Properly educated philosophers would have supreme authority, semieducated watch-dogs would act as a military and police force on their behalf, and those who supplied the economic needs of the city would have the lowest status of all. Education was to be carefully adjusted to the reproduction of the system; the lower class were to be trained to obedience and persuaded by a political myth that their status was due to natural causes; poets should represent only socially commendable behaviour; knowledge of alternative forms of society was to be carefully suppressed, except in the case of selected members of the ruling elite.

Such views led in the twentieth century to attacks on Plato as a proto-fascist. In the *Laws* the more extreme proposals of the *Republic* (in particular the abolition of private property and the family for the philosopher rulers) were dropped. Return to law as a source of authority was, however, a capitulation to the rigid type of definition of virtue that Socrates had attacked (see the *Statesman*). Plato died without finding a way through or round this aporia.

PAUL CARTLEDGE
UNIVERSITY OF CAMBRIDGE

Reference

Williams, B. (1981) 'Philosophy', in M.I. Finley (ed.) *The Legacy of Ancient Greece. A New Appraisal*, Oxford.

Further reading

Bambrough, R. (ed.) (1967) *Plato, Popper and Politics*, Cambridge.

Bobonich, C. (2003) *Plato's Utopia Recast. His Later Ethics and Politics*, Oxford.
Davies, J.K. (1971) *Athenian Propertied Families, 600–300 BC*, Oxford.
Dover, K.J. (1974) *Greek Popular Morality in the Time of Plato and Aristotle*, Oxford.
Gouldner, A.W. (1965) *Enter Plato: Classical Greece and the Origins of Social Theory*, New York.
Kraut, R. (ed.) (1992) *The Cambridge Companion to Plato*, Cambridge, UK.
Lane, M.S. (2000) 'Socrates and Plato: An introduction', in C. Rowe and M. Schofield (eds) *The Cambridge History of Greek and Roman Political Thought*, Cambridge, UK, Ch. 8.
—— (2002) *Plato's Progeny. How Plato and Socrates Still Captivate the Modern Mind*, London.
Popper, K. (1945) *The Open Society and Its Enemies*, London.
Rowe, C. (2000) 'The *Politicus* and other dialogues', in C. Rowe and M. Schofield (eds) *The Cambridge History of Greek and Roman Political Thought*, Cambridge, UK, Ch. 11.
Rowe, C. and Schofield, M. (eds) (2000) *The Cambridge History of Greek and Roman Political Thought*, Cambridge, UK.
Schofield, M. (2000a) 'Approaching the *Republic*', in C. Rowe and M. Schofield (eds) *The Cambridge History of Greek and Roman Political Thought*, Cambridge, UK, Ch. 10.
—— (2000b) 'Plato and practical politics', in C. Rowe and M. Schofield (eds) *The Cambridge History of Greek and Roman Political Thought*, Cambridge, UK, Ch. 13.
Stalley, R.F. (1983) *An Introduction to Plato's Laws*, Oxford.
Wood, E.M. and Wood, N. (1978) *Class Ideology and Ancient Political Theory: Socrates, Plato and Aristotle in Social Context*, Oxford.

POLICE AND POLICING

The idea of the police must be distinguished from the broader concept of policing, although in contemporary societies the two are commonly assimilated. Police refers to a specific kind of social institution, while policing implies a process with particular social functions. Police are not found in every society, and police organizations and personnel can take a variety of forms. It is arguable, however, that policing of some kind is a universal requirement of any social order, and may be carried out by a number of different institutional arrangements and social processes.

Policing connotes a set of activities *directed* at preserving the security of a particular social order. That order may variously be seen as resting upon a basic consensus of interests, or a manifest (and/or latent) conflict of interests between groups differentially placed in a hierarchy of power and privilege, or perhaps a complex intertwining of the two. As one analyst has put it, the police function may involve parking tickets *and* class repression (Marenin 1983). Whether particular policing activities actually succeed in securing social order is a moot point, as is the relationship between policing and other elements of social control.

Policing is a specific subset of social control processes. It must be distinguished from the broader elements of the creation of social order (for example socialization and the creation and reproduction of cultural and ethical standards), as well as from institutions for adjudication and punishment of deviance.

Policing may be defined as surveillance coupled with the threat of the initiation of sanctions for any deviance that may be discovered thereby. The most familiar system of this kind is the one implied by the modern sense of police: this connotes a formal organization concerned primarily with regular uniform patrol of public space together with *post hoc* investigation of reported or discovered crime or disorder. However, policing can be accomplished by a diverse array of people and techniques, of which the modern idea of policing is only one. Policing may be carried out by professional state employees with an omnibus policing mandate – the archetypal modern concept of *the* police (which itself can take a variety of forms) or by state agencies with other primary purposes, such as the Atomic Energy Authority, Customs and Excise, parks and transport constabularies, and other 'hybrid' bodies. Policing may also be done by professional employees of specialist private police agencies or by in-house security personnel hired by an organization whose main business is not policing.

Policing functions may also be performed by citizens in a voluntary capacity within state organizations, like the British Special Constabulary; in association with the state police, like Neighbourhood Watch schemes; or in volunteer bodies, which are not under any state auspices. Sometimes such volunteer policing may be in tension with the state, like the Guardian Angels, and the various forms of vigilantism that have flourished in many times and places.

Policing may be carried out by state bodies with other primary functions (like the British Army in Northern Ireland), or by employees (state or private) with other primary roles (like caretakers, shop assistants or porters). Policing may also be done by non-human processes: surveillance technology, architecture or the security aspects of particular natural or built environments. All these strategies of policing are prevalent now as in the past, although it is only the state agency with the specific mandate of policing that is popularly understood by the label police (South 1988; Jones and Newburn 1998; Johnston 2000; Reiner 2000a, 'Introduction'; Johnston and Shearing 2003).

Until modern times policing functions were carried out primarily as a by-product of other social relationships and by citizen volunteers or private employees. Anthropological studies have shown how many preliterate societies have existed without any formalized system of policing. Specialized policing institutions emerge only in relatively complex societies (Schwartz and Miller 1964). This is not merely a reflex of a burgeoning division of labour. Policing may originate in collective and communal processes of social control, but specialized police forces develop together with social inequality and hierarchy. They are means for the emergence and protection of more centralized state systems. The development of specialized police 'is linked to economic specialisation and differential access to resources that occur in the transition from a kinship- to a class-dominated society' (Robinson and Scaglion 1987: 109; Robinson *et al.* 1994). In contemporary societies the police become the agency specialized in the handling of the state's distinctive capacity: the monopoly of legitimate force (Bittner 1974).

There are varying explanations for the creation of specialized police agencies in modern societies. Different countries have experienced divergent historical routes, and interpretations of the rise of the police will vary between different theoretical and political positions (Reiner 2000a: Chs 1–2). Anglo-American police ideology postulates a fundamental distinction between continental European police systems, which originate overtly as instruments of state control, and the British system, which is represented as a necessary adjustment of ancient forms of communal self-policing in the face of the exigencies of industrialization. More recent historical and comparative research has exposed the oversimplification of this orthodox perspective. The British, US and other common-law systems of police may not have originated as direct and explicit tools of the state, but their emergence and development is closely related to shifting structures of state control and class conflict (Emsley 1996; Miller 1999). The supposedly community-based British model was in any case for home consumption only. A more militaristic and coercive state-controlled system of policing was always exported to colonial situations (Brogden 1987).

Since the mid-1960s a substantial body of research on police organization and practice has developed, primarily in Britain and North America, but increasingly elsewhere as well; this is now a major branch of criminology (Reiner 2000b; Bowling and Foster 2002). The main source of police research was the growing awareness that the popular conception of the police as simply a law-enforcement agency was misleading in two ways. From the outset police research showed that the police performed a variety of order-maintenance and social service functions apart from dealing with crime and criminals (Banton 1964; Punch 1979). Moreover, in performing their various tasks the police exercised considerable discretion and regularly deviated from the rule of law (Holdaway 1983; Manning 1997; Skolnick 1966; Dixon 1997). The recognition of police discretion raised the questions – for research, policy and politics – of how it was exercised in practice, its relationship to legal and social justice, and how it could be made accountable (Lustgarten 1986; McConville et al. 1991; Reiner and Spencer 1993; Walker 2000).

The development of police research has coincided with a period in which growing concern about rising crime and about police malpractice has kept law and order at the centre of political controversy. Police forces have grown in powers and resources as a consequence. However, the apparent failure of crime rates to respond to increased police capacity has called into question the actual and potential effectiveness of the police as a crime-control mechanism. Researchers have shown that there is little scope for reducing crime by increasing police deployment (Clarke and Hough 1984; Morgan and Newburn 1997), although innovative tactics may have a modest impact (Sherman 1992; Jordan 1998). Despite this evidence, since the early 1990s British governments have launched a sweeping and highly controversial package of reforms on the premise that managerial reorganization on pri-

vate-sector businesslike lines can inject a higher level of efficiency that can make the police effective in dealing with crime (Reiner and Spencer 1993).

It is becoming increasingly apparent, however, that the police by themselves can play only a limited role in managing the problems of crime. Crime control involves a more complex mix of policing strategies involving the police in partnership with citizens, private security, and technological and environmental crime prevention methods, as the 1998 *Crime and Disorder Act* recognizes. Above all, it requires social and economic policies that can tackle the roots of crime and reinvigorate informal social control processes. The police are becoming once more a part of a more complex web of policing processes.

R. REINER
LONDON SCHOOL OF ECONOMICS
AND POLITICAL SCIENCE

References

Banton, M. (1964) *The Policeman in the Community*, London.

Bittner, E. (1974) 'Florence Nightingale in pursuit of Willie Sutton: A theory of the police', in H. Jacob (ed.) *The Potential for Reform of Criminal Justice*, Beverly Hills, CA.

Bowling, B. and Foster, J. (2002) 'Policing and the police', in M.Maguire, R.Morgan and R. Reiner (eds) *The Oxford Handbook of Criminology*, 3rd edn, Oxford.

Brogden, M. (1987) 'The emergence of the police: The colonial dimension', *British Journal of Criminology* 27(1).

Clarke, R. and Hough, M. (1984) *Crime and Police Effectiveness*, London.

Dixon, D. (1997) *Law in Policing*, Oxford.

Emsley, C. (1996) *The English Police: A Political and Social History*, 2nd edn, London.

Holdaway, S. (1983) *Inside the British Police*, Oxford.

Johnston, L. (2000) *Policing Britain: Risk, Security and Governance*, London.

Johnston, L. and Shearing, C. (2003) *Governing Security: Explorations in Policing and Justice*, London.

Jones, T. and Newburn, T. (1998) *Private Security and Public Policing*, Oxford.

Jordan, P. (1998) 'Effective policing strategies for reducing crime', in P. Goldblatt and C. Lewis (eds) *Reducing Offending*, Home Office Research Study 187, London.

Lustgarten, L. (1986) *The Governance of the Police*, London.

McConville, M., Sanders, A. and Leng, R. (1991) *The Case for the Prosecution: Police Suspects and the Construction of Criminality*, London.

Manning, P. (1997) *Police Work: The Social Organisation of Policing*, 2nd edn, Cambridge, MA.

Marenin, O. (1983) 'Parking tickets and class repression: The concept of policing in critical theories of criminal justice', *Contemporary Crises* 6(2).

Miller, W. (1999) *Cops and Bobbies*, 2nd edn, Columbus, OH.

Morgan, R. and Newburn, T. (1997) *The Future of Policing*, Oxford.

Punch, M. (1979) 'The secret social service', in S. Holdaway (ed.) *The British Police*, London.

Reiner, R. (2000a) *The Politics of the Police*, 3rd edn, Oxford.

—— (2000b) 'Police research', in R. King and E. Wincup (eds) *Doing Research on Crime and Justice*, Oxford.

Reiner, R. and Spencer, S. (eds) (1993) *Accountable Policing: Effectiveness, Empowerment and Equity*, London.

Robinson, C. and Scaglion, R. (1987) 'The origin and evolution of the police function in society', *Law and Society Review* 21(1).

Robinson, C., Scaglion, R. and Olivero, M. (1994) *Police in Contradiction: The Evolution of the Police Function in Society*, Westport, CT.

Schwartz, R.D. and Miller, J.C. (1964) 'Legal evolution and societal complexity', *American Journal of Sociology* 70(1).

Sherman, L. (1992) 'Attacking crime: Police and crime control', in M. Tonry and N. Morris (eds) *Modern Policing*, Chicago.

Skolnick, J. (1966) *Justice without Trial*, New York.

South, N. (1988) *Policing for Profit*, London.

Walker, N. (2000) *Policing in a Changing Constitutional Order*, London.

Further reading

Shearing, C. and Stenning, P. (eds) (1987) *Private Policing*, Beverly Hills, CA.

SEE ALSO: crime and delinquency; criminology; social control

POLITICAL ANTHROPOLOGY

The anthropology of politics is essentially an ethnographic discipline. It grows not by reasoning and exposition but by the accumulation of details about government, power and resistance. It derives its rigour from ethnography, theory and critique. Its ethnographic roots lie in Morgan's *The League of the Iroquois* (1851) but it was not until the 1940s with African field research wedded to structural-functional theory and a critique of evolutionary models that it became established as a major subfield within anthropology. Until the 1960s most ethnographic field research was carried out in Third World territories or among native peoples or ethnic minorities in the USA, India, Australia and South Africa. Rarely did anthropologists study state power structures (Vincent 1990).

During the Cold War, the intelligence and military interventions and the proxy wars of the USSR and the USA transformed the postcolonial societies in which political anthropologists worked. Field research could be dangerous (Reyna and Downs 1997). Armies mutinied, elected governments were overthrown, corruption was rife, and warlords, drug smuggling and the arms trade became the subject of political ethnographies. The situation described by E.E. Evans-Pritchard in his classic ethnography of the Nuer (Evans-Pritchard 1940) was transformed in the postindependence Sudan, where the south became a war zone that witnessed the targeting of civilian populations (especially women and children), struggles over oil resources, human rights infringements, and the militarization of Nuer and Dinka, who were armed by outside powers (Hutchinson 1996).

The fall of the Berlin Wall shifted the attention of anthropologists to political issues within the former USSR and to the explicit study of US global interests. Together with an analysis of neoliberalism in the contemporary global political arena, the Enlightenment discourse came in for criticism (Comaroff and Comaroff 1999). The distinction between 'civil society' and 'political society' (governance) appears particularly troublesome at a time when a politicized 'global civil society' is emerging. Other Enlightenment principles, such as cosmopolitanism, equality, citizenship, individual rights, the sanctity of private property, progress, popular sovereignty and the common good, have also come under review. This has opened up promising directions for grounded analyses of global politics and critiques of global political agendas (imperial, commercial and humanitarian).

Twenty-first-century political anthropology engages with such problematic global phenomena as AIDS, poverty, democracy, development, displacement, refugees, protest movements, failing states, non-governmental organizations (NGOs), the politics of organ merchandizing, and the militarization of culture. Retaining political anthropology's focus on process and agency, Aihwa Ong has explored ethnographically 'the cultural logics of globalization', emphasizing the role played by capitalism, neo-liberalism, transnationality and flexible citizenship (Ong 1999).

Recent political ethnographies address topics ranging from infrapolitical sovereignty in Siberia (Hann 2002) to the use of the labels 'mafias' in Sicily, Russia and Eastern Europe (Schneider and Schneider 2003), bringing readers up to date on the current state of play in different parts of the world of Bailey's classic political drama of stratagems and spoils (Bailey 1980). The moral positions and personal inclinations of the ethnographers have also become the focus of theorizing, and critique (Gledhill 2000).

JOAN VINCENT
BARNARD COLLEGE,
COLUMBIA UNIVERSITY

References

Bailey, F. (1980) *Stratagems and Spoils: A Social Anthropology of Politics*, Oxford.
Comaroff, J.L. and Comaroff, J. (1999) 'Introduction', *Civil Society and the Political Imagination*, Chicago.
Evans-Pritchard, E.E. (1940) *The Nuer: A Description of the Modes of Livelihood and Political Institutions of a Nilotic People*, Oxford.
Gledhill, J. (2000) *Power and Its Disguises: Anthropological Perspective on Politics*, London.
Hann, C.M. (ed.) (2002) *Postsocialism: Ideals, Ideologies and Practices in Eurasia*, London.
Hutchinson, S.E. (1996) *Nuer Dilemmas: Coping with Money, War, and the State*, Berkeley, CA.
Ong, A. (1999) *Flexible Citizenship: The Cultural Logics of Transnationality*, Durham, NC, and London.
Reyna, S. and Downs, R. (eds) (1997) *Deadly Developments: Capitalism, States and War*, Amsterdam.
Schneider, J. and Schneider, P. (2003) *Reversible Destiny: Mafia, Antimafia and Their Struggle for Palermo*, Berkeley, CA.
Vincent, J. (1990) *Anthropology of Politics: Visions, Traditions and Trends*, Arizona.

Further reading

Nugent, D. and Vincent, J. (eds) (2004) *A Companion to the Anthropology of Politics*, Oxford.

SEE ALSO: colonialism; imperialism; state, origins of; tribe

POLITICAL CULTURE

The term 'political culture' has entered everyday language; as a concept, it enjoyed a new lease of life in the social sciences from the 1980s onwards. The author of one of the most systematic explorations of the notion of political culture has suggested that 'the enduring nature of its appeal in the face of a large body of criticism' derives partly from 'a dissatisfaction both with an account of politics that ignores the issues of meanings and culture, and with an account of culture that ignores issues of politics and power' (Welch 1993).

Although some of the themes evoked by the concept of political culture were not unknown to classical political thought, the term political culture appears to have been first used by Herder (Barnard 1969), and its elaboration and development as a concept of modern political science dates from the 1950s (especially Almond 1956). Substantive empirical research organized around the concept began to appear in the 1960s (see e.g. Almond and Verba 1963; Pye and Verba 1965). These early applications of the concept were linked to questionable theories of political development, but the value of an understanding of political culture in no way depends upon its incorporation in a particular type of developmental, structure-functionalist or systems analysis.

While the concept of political culture had a generally lower salience in the 1970s than in the 1960s, it began to attract in that decade greater attention than hitherto from students of communist systems. A number of them identified as a vital issue, of both theoretical and practical importance, the degree of consonance or dissonance between, on the one hand, the values and political doctrine being promulgated through the official agencies of political socialization by the communist power-holders and, on the other, the values and fundamental political beliefs to be found among the mass of the people (Brown 1984; Brown and Gray 1977; White 1979). It had been argued that communist states represented particularly successful cases of political socialization from above. Thus, for example, Huntington and Dominguez (1975) suggested that 'the most dramatically successful case of planned political cultural change is probably the Soviet Union' and that communist systems had been an exception to a more general rule that conscious, mobilizational efforts to change political cultures had fared poorly (Greenstein and Polsby 1975). Studies of political culture in the European communist countries called into question, however, the success there of official political socialization. A variety of sources of evidence were drawn upon by researchers, for in most communist countries, relevant survey data were either unavailable or unreliable and overt political behaviour could also be misleading. Conformist political actions did not necessarily imply the internalization of Marxist–Leninist norms in highly authoritarian regimes where the penalties for political non-conformity were severe.

The collapse of most communist systems by the beginning of the 1990s, while not providing conclusive evidence regarding popular values and beliefs in the late 1970s, tended to lend support to those who emphasized the relative failure of communist political socialization efforts. Writing in 1983 – some years before the communist regimes in Russia and Eastern Europe came to an end following a process of peaceful change – Gabriel Almond (1989) went so far as to see communism as 'a test of political culture theory' and concluded:

> What the scholarship of comparative communism has been telling us is that political cultures are not easily transformed. A sophisticated political movement ready to manipulate, penetrate, organize, indoctrinate and coerce and given an opportunity to do so for a generation or longer ends up as much or more transformed than transforming.

Political culture has been defined in a variety of different ways and several distinctive approaches to the study of it may be identified. So far as definitions are concerned, they can be classified into two broad categories: those that confine the scope of political culture to the subjective orientation of nations, social groups or individuals to politics; and those that broaden the concept to include patterns of political behaviour. Most political scientists have favoured the more restrictive category. Representative definitions in this first group include those that see political culture as 'the system of empirical beliefs, expressive symbols and values which defines the situation in which political action takes place' (Verba 1965), or as 'the subjective perception of history and politics, the fundamental beliefs and values, the foci of identification and loyalty, and the political knowledge and expectations which are the product of the specific historical experience of nations and groups' (Brown 1977).

An example of a broader definition is that which views political culture as 'the attitudinal and behavioural matrix within which the political system is located' (White 1979). Scholars who prefer this second, broader type of definition of the concept have suggested that in characterizing political culture in subjective or psychological terms, 'political scientists have parted company with the great majority of anthropologists' (Tucker 1973). That view appears, however, not only to downplay the great diversity of definitions of culture among anthropologists but also to overlook a growing body of work within social and cultural anthropology. As Ladislav Holy (1979) put it: 'New insights into the working of social systems have been achieved in anthropology through following the implications of an analytical distinction between the conceptual and cognitive world of the actors and the realm of events and transactions in which they engage.' Definitions matter less than the use to which the concept of political culture is put and the extent to which its employment helps to illuminate important aspects of political life. In 1990, an entire series of books entitled 'Political Cultures' was launched under the general editorship of the late Aaron Wildavsky. Its starting-point was that 'political cultures broadly describe people who share values, beliefs, and preferences legitimating different ways of life', but it stressed an 'openness to a variety of approaches to the study of political cultures'. The volume which launched the series (Thompson et al. 1990) draws extensively on the pioneering work of the anthropologist Mary Douglas. In contrast to the studies conducted in the 1960s, the authors emphasize the variety of political cultures to be found within each country and move the focus of attention from differences between nations to differences within nations. Having set out the case for 'the social construction of nature', Thompson et al. argue that if 'the boundaries between the political and the nonpolitical are socially constructed, then the study of political culture must assume a central place' in the discipline of political science.

This approach is consonant with the work of Welch (1993), who draws upon phenomenological social theory in claiming that 'the social environment through which people move is constituted and made meaningful by them'. Denying the 'givenness' of any part of that environment, he criticizes much of the existing body of work on political culture. 'Culture,' Welch (1993) suggests, 'is not a set of givens of which political culture is a subset; it is a process, and "political culture" refers to that process in its political aspects.'

Among the many debates that surround the concept of political culture is an emerging one on the value of survey research as a way of eliciting and understanding political cultures. Some of the newer writing, which draws heavily on the insights of anthropology (see, e.g., Welch 1993), sees survey research as at best of marginal value as an aid to interpreting political cultures, while other scholars – in a more sociological tradition – emphasize the dangers of the subjective views of the social scientist being projected on to the social actors studied in the absence of well-grounded surveys. An influential example of essentially non-quantitative cultural analysis is the work of Harrison and Huntington (2000), while studies of political culture in postcommunist Europe have taken full and interesting advantage of the new opportunities to conduct rigorous survey research (e.g. Pollack *et al.* 2003). Increasingly, a valuable body of interpretative work on political culture is being built up, albeit from a variety of definitional and methodological starting-points.

ARCHIE BROWN
UNIVERSITY OF OXFORD

References

Almond, G.A. (1956) 'Comparative political systems', *Journal of Politics* 18.
—— (1983) 'Communism and political culture theory', *Comparative Politics* 13.
—— (1989) *Communism and Political Culture Theory. A Discipline Divided*, Newbury Park, CA.
Almond, G.A. and Verba, S. (eds) (1963) *The Civic Culture: Political Attitudes and Democracy in Five Nations*, Princeton, NJ.
Barnard, F.M. (1969) 'Culture and political development: Herder's suggestive insights', *American Political Science Review* 62.
Brown, A. (1977) 'Introduction', in A. Brown and J. Gray, *Political Culture and Political Change in Communist States*, London.
—— (1984) *Political Culture and Communist Studies*, London.
Brown, A. and Gray, J. (1977) *Political Culture and Political Change in Communist States*, London.
Greenstein, F.I. and Polsby, N.W. (eds) (1975) *Macropolitical Theory*, Vol. 3 of *Handbook of Political Science*, Reading, MA.
Harrison, L.E. and Huntington, S.P. (2000) *Culture Matters: How Values Shape Human Progress*, New York.
Holy, L. (1979) 'Changing norms in matrilineal societies: The case of Toka inheritance', in D. Riches (ed.) *The Conceptualization and Explanation of Processes of Social Change*, Belfast.
Huntington, S. and Dominguez, J.I. (1975) 'Political development', in F.I. Greenstein and N.W. Polsby (eds) *Macropolitical Theory*, Vol. 3 of *Handbook of Political Science*, Reading, MA.
Pollack, D., Jacobs, J., Müller, O. and Pickel, G. (2003) *Political Culture in Post-Communist Europe: Attitudes in New Democracies*, Aldershot.
Pye, L.W. and Verba, S. (eds) (1965) *Political Culture and Political Development*, Princeton, NJ.
Thompson, M., Ellis, R. and Wildavsky, A. (1990) *Cultural Theory*, Boulder, CO.
Tucker, R.C. (1973) 'Culture, political culture and communist society', *Political Science Quarterly* 88.
Verba, S. (1965) 'Conclusion: Comparative political culture', in L.W. Pye and S. Verba (eds) *Political Culture and Political Development*, Princeton, NJ.
Welch, S. (1993) *The Concept of Political Culture*, London.
White, S. (1979) *Political Culture and Soviet Politics*, London.

Further reading

Douglas, M. (1975) *Implicit Meanings: Essays in Anthropology*, London.
—— (1982) *In the Active Voice*, London.

SEE ALSO: culture

POLITICAL ECONOMY

Since the eighteenth century, many kinds of scholarship have contended for the title 'political economy', including Marxist analysis, dependency theory, and the rational or 'public choice' approach derived from economics. However, the field of political economy is dominated today by rational choice theory. To be sure, important works of political economy continue to be produced that are empirically based and do not employ rational choice explicitly, such as Putnam (2000) or Przeworski *et al.* (2000). And the political economy of industrial systems and of international relations remain largely (though not entirely) outside this model. But there is no rival paradigm, leaving only the rational choice approach still standing, if a little wobbly, as the bell rings in the twenty-first century.

Modern political economy was born of an attempt to bring together issues and theories in economics and political science. In economics, Samuelson (1954) introduced the theory of public goods in the study of government expenditure. Public goods (e.g. defence) have the property that consumption by one person does not mean that someone else cannot consume the same good.

Markets do not provide these goods efficiently, if at all. Other cases for government intervention include externalities, and cases of differential information between buyers and sellers. These market failures provided a normative case for government provision, but gave no clue as to how governments would actually behave. Economics needed a positive theory of government behaviour. In political science, on the other hand, there were and are many interesting empirical studies of various political systems, but in the absence of a broad-based theory there was no way to reach generalizations or conclusions.

There was also a growing acceptance that the methods of economics were largely independent of the subject matter studied and could be applied to problems in law, psychology, sociology, politics or anthropology, as well as to economic markets for goods and services. Partly as a result of these new applications of economic reasoning, it came to be realized that many of the traditional critiques of economics were misguided. The application of rational choice theory does not commit one to the idea that people are necessarily selfish, interested only in money, driven only to consume market goods and services, capable of lightning fast calculation, or perfectly informed, as is suggested in some caricatures of economic theory.

The founding works were Downs (1957), Schumpeter (1976 [1943]), and Buchanan and Tullock (1962). According to these theorists, politicians maximize votes, or the probability of being (re-)elected to office. The basic force that leads politicians to consider the interests of citizens is the competition among political parties. Rousseau's conception of democracy as a system that implemented the will of the people, however defined, was replaced by the definition of democracy as effective competition for public office, a definition that has become widely accepted.

However, the first generation of research carried out from this perspective appeared to produce a number of anomalies. To illustrate, consider the 'pure' theory of voting, which eschews institutions such as political parties, etc., and asks what the effects of different voting rules are on the decisions of an abstract collectivity (a jurisdiction, committee, town hall meeting, etc.). If the issue space is one-dimensional (left–right) and certain other conditions are met, the result is the median voter theorem. Applied to political systems, this means that the different political parties will converge on the same platform, one that represents the preferences of the median voter. Some polities approximate this result most of the time. Others do not. Moreover, this result is extremely fragile theoretically: as soon as the conditions are relaxed, e.g. if there are multiple dimensions, or many political parties, the result is the so-called 'impossibility theorem', from which it follows that essentially anything can happen. Yet another problem is the so-called 'voting paradox' (if people are rational and selfish, why would they bother to vote?).

The first generation of public choice theorists were also typically very critical of the power of the state. They produced a stream of research showing that regulation was bad, most government programmes were inefficient, governments were too big, and so on. For example, the government was said to be inefficient because its expansion is driven by interest groups, and each interest group pays only a share of the costs but gets the entire benefit of government programmes tailored for it. Niskanen (1971) argued that government departments were too large as a consequence of bureaucratic strategies for maximizing divisional budgets. However, these propositions did not stand up if rational choice theory was systematically applied. To take one example, even if the polity is thought of as being made up only of interest groups, each seeking a selfish benefit for their group, competition should guarantee that relatively efficient programmes will tend to win out. The reason is that economic gains and losses enter the political calculus so that, for instance, the greater the net losses from a government policy or programme, the more political pressure will be applied to replace it. In consequence, economically efficient policies will tend to be selected (Becker 1983).

The second generation of public choice researchers ascribed this anti-government bias to a denial of the rationality of actors and the competitiveness of the political system. They insisted that the assumptions about full rationality and competition with which economists approached the private sector should be carried over into the analysis of the public sector. It was argued, for instance, that politicians would seldom be foolish enough to allow themselves to be exploited by the bureaucracy. Moreover, competition among bureaucrats would expose the information distortions that bureaucrats use to get a larger budget, rival politicians would seek to inform voters, and the citizenry would not allow institutions to persist that were systematically flawed. And so on. (See Wittman 1995 for a systematic exposition.)

The second generation also paid greater attention to the structure of politics and government, and borrowed more heavily from political science and sociology. Just as individual maximization in private markets is subject to the laws governing contracts and exchange, so rational choice in politics is constrained by political and social institutions. It therefore matters whether the polity is a unitary state or a federation, what laws govern campaign finance, how the media are owned and regulated, etc.

There was also a fresh interest in ideology. Some argued that politicians and political parties are not driven only by the prospect of office, but may also be motivated by the desire to implement certain policies that they hold dear (see, e.g., Alesina and Rosenthal 1995). The political structure itself demands that candidates express such preferences. A candidate for president or prime minister must first become the leader of the party, and the preferences of party activists are by nature farther from the centre than those of the general population. Party competition with this structure results in some polarization, in which the parties offer distinct platforms to the voters rather than converge at the median. These factors also generate the so-called 'political business cycle', in which governing politicians seek to manage the economy so that unemployment hits a trough just before the next election.

Other research stressed that the divergence of the major political parties is constrained in most political systems. The new theory of probabilistic voting showed that seemingly small changes in the assumptions can restore the median voter theorem even with multiple dimensions. (For example, assume that a voter is more likely to vote for a candidate, the closer the candidate's position is to the voter's, rather than that a voter will with certainty vote for the candidate whose position is closest to his.) And the median outcome has been shown to be relevant even for multiparty systems. (See Mueller 2003 for a survey.)

Another new development was the introduction of leaders and social interactions into the model, with the aim of explaining the voting paradox (Uhlaner 1989). Participation in political and social movements has also been studied. The guiding assumption here is that any citizen is more likely to act if he or she believes that others are also planning to participate. According to Chong (1991), for example, the belief that the movement would succeed was particularly important in stimulating participation in the US Civil Rights movement. On this way of thinking, the problem that leaders of social movements face is not, as Olson (1965) had suggested, that they have to provide selective private incentives to individuals in order to motivate them to participate. Rather, the dilemma is how to persuade people that others will participate in such numbers that it is in the individual's interest to join them. Models like this have also been used to analyse the late twentieth-century revolutions in Iran and Eastern Europe.

The rational choice paradigm has also been newly applied to some new and important questions. One of these is the behaviour of dictatorships. Can one understand the actions of Stalin, Hitler or Saddam Hussein on the premise that they were not rational? Or does power and the overriding desire to remain in office provide a better starting-point (Wintrobe 1998)? Another new development is the study of political campaigning, including the circumstances under which political campaigning tends to be informative rather than persuasive, how much campaign contributions influence the positions of politicians (see Mueller 2003), and how competitiveness in the media influences political competition (Besley and Burgess 2000). The workings of legislatures have also been examined: how congressmen make deals with each other, how they control regulatory agencies and bureaucracies, and their relationship with the president and the judiciary in a US style system (Weingast and Marshall 1988). And the rise of nationalism and extremism has also been investigated. For example, Breton *et al.* (2002) use public-choice theory to ask how much democracy contains, produces or accommodates extremist pressures. Public-choice theory has become mainstream, and while it has undergone considerable modifications in the process, there is no turning back.

RONALD WINTROBE
UNIVERSITY OF WESTERN ONTARIO

References

Alesina, A. and Rosenthal, H. (1995) *Partisan Politics, Divided Government and the Economy*, New York.

Becker, G. (1983) 'A theory of competition among groups for political influence', *Quarterly Journal of Economics* 98: 371–400.

Besley, T. and Burgess, R. (2000) *The Political Economy of Government Responsiveness: Theory and Evidence from India*, London.

Breton, A., Galeotti, G., Salmon, P. and Wintrobe, R. (eds) (2002) *Political Extremism and Rationality*, New York.

Buchanan, J.M. and Tullock, G. (1962) *The Calculus of Consent*, Ann Arbor, MI.

Chong, D. (1991) *Collective Action and the Civil Rights Movement*, Chicago.

Downs, A. (1957) *An Economic Theory of Democracy*, New York.

Mueller, D. (2003) *Public Choice III*, New York.

Niskanen, W. (1971) *Bureaucracy and Representative Government*, Chicago.

Olson, M. (1965) *The Logic of Collective Action*, Cambridge, MA.

Przeworski, A., Alvarez, M.E., Cheibub, J.A. and Limongi, F. (2000) *Democracy and Development: Political Institutions and Well-Being in the World 1950–1990*, New York.

Putnam, R. (2000) *Bowling Alone: The Collapse and Revival of American Community*, New York.

Samuelson, P. (1954) 'The pure theory of public expenditure', *Review of Economics and Statistics* 36: 387–9.

Schumpeter, J. (1976 [1943]) *Capitalism, Socialism and Democracy*, London.

Uhlaner, C. (1989) 'Rational turnout: The neglected role of groups', *American Journal of Political Science* 3: 390–422.

Weingast, B.R. and Marshall, W. (1988) 'The industrial organization of congress, or why legislatures, like firms, are not organized as markets', *Journal of Political Economy* 96(1): 132–63.

Wintrobe, R. (1998) *The Political Economy of Dictatorship*, New York.

Wittman, D.A. (1995) *The Myth of Democratic Failure: Why Political Institutions Are Efficient*, Chicago.

SEE ALSO: public choice; rational choice (action) theory; voting

POLITICAL PSYCHOLOGY

Political psychology is concerned with the interrelationships between psychological and political processes. The field draws on diverse disciplinary sources including cultural and psychological anthropology, economic psychology, sociology and, most particularly, psychology and political science. The major theoretical influences from psychology have been psychoanalytic theory, personality theory, social and developmental psychology, and increasingly cognitive psychology. On the political science side, political psychologists have drawn mainly on studies of public psychology and behaviour, political leadership and decision-making, and analyses of political conflict both within and between nations.

Methodologically, also, this is an eclectic field, its techniques commonly including intensive case studies, survey methods and small-group experimentation, some of which are obviously more appropriate than others for particular research questions. A study of a specific president, foreign minister or other leader and their views or judgements might focus on the individual and draw on personality theory. However, a study of how a particular body reaches collective decisions cannot depend on theories of individual psychology alone. Methodologically, studies of public opinion must sample a broadly representative range of respondents, and cannot rely on individual in-depth interviews.

Studies in political psychology must also be sensitive to levels of analysis and contextual issues. Whether studies focus on an individual leader, small or larger groups, or larger collective processes, each is embedded in complex psychological and material contexts that must be considered. Leaders, for example, may choose a course of action consonant with their own psychologies, but they must also take into account a variety of other considerations. Or to take another example, governmental decision-making groups may make very productive use of good decision procedures, but outcomes in the real world will depend on circumstances that go well beyond the adequacy of the procedures they used to reach their decisions.

In short, the processes and substantive areas studied in political psychology are varied and complex. It is therefore not surprising that no one theoretical or methodological paradigm has emerged for the entire field. However, as a maturing field, political psychology is characterized by an increasing degree of theoretical specification: of the origins and developmental paths of the political psychology dynamics it uncovers, of the nature of the dynamics themselves, and finally of the contextual forces that sustain or inhibit these dynamics. Modern political psychology treats individual and group psychology as a variable, not a given.

While the field does not have one major paradigm, there is an emergent consensus on four basic frames of understanding: the developmental, the dynamic, the contextual and the importance of composite theory. The first approaches political behaviour by examining the ways that the past has helped shape the present. The second examines political behaviour as stemming from multiple, not single, psychological and political factors, while the third examines the situational factors that either inhibit or facilitate the political behaviours in question. Lastly, composite theory stresses the application of dual or multiple theoretical frames to address specific substantive areas.

Composite theory is clearly necessary given the field's subject matter. Studies of how children acquire politically relevant dispositions depend on concepts and models that must be integrated from developmental psychology, psychoanalytic theory and, depending on the particular focus of the study, cognitive psychology. Studies of political decision-making, in addition to understanding the actual issues that must be decided, must draw on knowledge of groups processes, cognitive psychology, and in the case of the leader his or her own psychology and judgement.

Like other social science fields, political psychology is embedded in its historical and political contexts. The justly famous Authoritarian Personality studies of the 1930s asked how and why seemingly intelligent, educated and cultured people could be drawn to demagogues espousing racist ideologies. The nuclear standoff between the former Soviet Union and the USA gave rise to a generation of studies on the prevention of war and the psychology of deterrence. And the imperial presidencies of Lyndon Johnson and Richard Nixon, and the one-term presidencies of Jimmy Carter, Gerald Ford and George H.W. Bush stimulated theoretical and substantive research on the psychology of successful presidential performance.

STANLEY A. RENSHON
THE CITY UNIVERSITY OF NEW YORK

Further reading

Barber, J.D. (1993) *Presidential Character: Predicting Performance in the White House*, Englewood Cliffs, NJ.

George, A.L. (1980) *Presidential Decision Making in Foreign Policy: The Effective Use of Information and Advice*, Boulder, CO.

Jervis, R. (1976) *Perception and Misperception in International Politics*, Princeton, NJ.

Lasswell, H.D. (1948) *Power and Personality*, New York.

Renshon, S.A. (1998) *The Psychological Assessment of Presidential Candidates*, New York.

—— (ed.) (2001) *One America? Political Leadership, National Identity and the Dilemmas of Diversity*, Washington, DC.

Sears, D.O., Huddy, L. and Jervis, R. (eds) (2003) *The Oxford Handbook of Political Psychology*, New York.

SEE ALSO: leadership

POLITICAL SCIENCE

Political science is an academic discipline, devoted to the systematic description, explanation, analysis and evaluation of politics and power. Political science might be more accurately labelled 'politology', as indeed it is in some European countries, both because some of its practitioners reject the idea that their discipline is like that of the natural sciences and because the subject does not have one unified body of theory or paradigm (unlike some of the natural sciences).

The historical antecedents of the discipline are most apparent in the works of Western political philosophers in a canonical tradition stretching from Plato's *Republic* through to Machiavelli's *The Prince* and Hobbes's *Leviathan*. However, political science has also evolved from numerous other forms of ancient and medieval enquiry, especially history, political economy and jurisprudence. The ambition to create a science of politics is an old one, at least as old as Aristotle's *Politics*, but agreement on its scope, methods and results remains elusive.

The scope of the contemporary discipline of political science is extensive. The major subfields of enquiry include political thought, political theory, political history, political institutions, comparative political analysis, public administration, public policy, rational choice, political sociology, international relations, and theories of the state.

Political thought

The classics of Western political thought, the accumulated body of texts and writings of great philosophers, still frame the intellectual education of many students of political science. The canon of great Western thinkers includes texts from the ancient world such as the writings of Plato and Aristotle, from the medieval and early modern period the works of Aquinas, Augustine, Hobbes, Locke, Rousseau and Montesquieu, and finally the books of modern writers like Kant, Hegel, Marx, Tocqueville and John Stuart Mill.

This canon has, however, been regularly attacked as ethnocentric, because it ignores the philosophical traditions of non-occidental countries. It is additionally criticized as sexist because it is a canon of male writers who make contestable assumptions about men and women (Okin 1980; Pateman 1988); it is also condemned as biased towards liberal political assumptions. Finally, the canon is rejected by those who claim that a mature science should supersede its origins, and that therefore the study of political thought should be left to historians. In response, defenders of the study of political thought sometimes claim that the thoughts of the great thinkers have often transcended their times, and for that matter their geographical, ethnic and sexual origins. Moreover they claim that ancient, medieval and early modern political thought shared three common preoccupations, which are still live issues among political scientists: first, explaining the nature of the state and what makes a state legitimate and worthy of obedience; second, explaining the nature of justice and the role or otherwise of politics in securing justice; and, third, explaining and speculating about the nature of a good political system.

Interpreters of political thought have always differed over the reasons they advance for continuing to pay detailed attention to classical texts. Some believe that the classics contain permanent truths, although they dispute which particular authors and texts contain them. They think it is the duty of educators to transmit these truths to subsequent generations, and regard much empirical political science as a betrayal of 'the great tradition'. A similar group of thinkers, influenced by Leo Strauss, maintain that the classics contain timeless truths but that they are accessible only to a civilized elite. By contrast other historians of political thought, while agreeing that the classics address timeless questions, maintain that the canon is more important for the questions it raises than the answers it provides; it is a starting-point rather than a set of lessons. For example, consider the abstract question, raised in diverse forms by Hobbes, Locke and Rousseau, 'Would rational persons in a state of nature agree to establish a state, and if so of what type?' This question helps clarify the conceptions of human nature assumed in political thought as well as the nature of political obligation, political legitimacy and the state. Others, influenced by Quentin Skinner, argue that the classics, far from being timeless, are texts addressed to the authors' contemporaries, and that the authors were engaged in political arguments of specific relevance to their own times. For them the task of political thought is to recover the original meanings and contexts of classical discourses, often by focusing on forgotten and marginal writers. This contextualist and historicist approach is criticized for assuming radical discontinuities in the meaning and accessibility of texts, and for implying that we have to do the impossible – become contemporaries of the authors of great texts in order to understand them. Moreover, this approach is hoist by its own petard: critics ask 'Which contemporary political controversies are such historians addressing when they offer readings of canonical texts?'

Political theory

Contemporary political philosophers have appropriated the title of 'political theorists' for themselves, although other political scientists insist that they engage in positive political theory proper, that is, the search for regularities in and deductive propositions about politics and power. The best way to appreciate this controversy is to realize that self-styled political theorists are usually normative in orientation and that their political theory has evolved from the history of political thought.

Much contemporary Anglo-American theory (i.e. political theory written in the English language) has a deductive and analytical flavour – reflecting the rising ascendancy of rational choice within this field. It addresses, often with mathematical and logical rigour, many of the themes raised in the classics. Political theorists partly see their task as that of conceptual clarification, explicating the possibly contradictory meanings of key concepts, like democracy, liberty, equality, law, legitimacy and rights. However, their major concern is with normative questions, such as 'What is justice?' This is an issue most famously tackled in our times by John Rawls's (1971) book *A Theory of Justice*. In this text Rawls revived the idea of the social contract made famous by

Hobbes, Locke and Rousseau, to ask what principles of justice would be adopted by rational individuals behind a 'veil of ignorance' in which they would not know what positions in society they themselves would subsequently occupy. Rawls's answer, much disputed, is that rational individuals would embrace (in the following order of importance) the principles of equal liberties for all, the meritocratic principle of equality of opportunity, and the 'difference principle' justifying inequalities in income and resources only if they better the condition of the worst off. These conclusions and the methods by which they are derived are the subject of an enormous critical literature. Seminal work in this area has now extended beyond justice within a given state and within a given generation to issues of distributive justice across generations and across the world.

Political history

Some political scientists describe themselves first and foremost as political historians – albeit with a bias towards contemporary history. They believe that the task of political science is to offer retrodictive explanations rather than predictions, and are critical of mere historians whom they accuse of being methodologically unself-conscious, overly descriptive and naïve believers in the idea that truth lies in the governmental archives.

Political historians tend, crudely speaking, to be divided into two camps. Students of 'high politics' study elite decision-makers; they believe that the personalities and machinations of key elites shape history and cannot be subsumed away as mere by-products of other causes. They also generally believe that self-aggrandizement and self-interest account for most elite behaviour. Exponents of high politics are sometimes denigrated by their colleagues in the profession as mere biographers. By contrast, exponents of 'low politics', or history from below, believe that mass political behaviour provides the key to explaining major political episodes, such as revolutions. For them the charisma, plots or blunders of political leaders are less important than major changes in the values, interests and actions of collectivities, and in charting the importance of such phenomena they make use of the methodological techniques common across the social sciences.

Political institutions

It was the study of political institutions, especially the roles of constitutions, executives, legislatures, judiciaries, bureaucracies, political parties and electoral systems, which first prompted the formal establishment of political science departments in many universities in liberal states at the end of the nineteenth century. The concerns of the first institutionalists were often indistinguishable from those of constitutional or public lawyers: mapping the formal and procedural consequences of political institutions. Contemporary political scientists still spend much of their time monitoring, evaluating and hypothesizing about the origins, development and consequences of political institutions, such as plurality-rule electoral systems or quasi-governmental organizations. The bulk of them are interested primarily in tracing the origins and developments of institutions, and providing 'thick' or 'phenomenological' (what it's really like) descriptions of these institutions, normally of the countries in which they reside. Some of their less tolerant colleagues claim they engage in thick description simply because they are thick rather than proper political scientists. Such critics are sceptical of the activities of their colleagues who are simply area specialists or knowledgeable about government or public administration in one country: they may provide essential data for political science, but they are not themselves scientific practitioners.

Comparative politics

These critics maintain that a comparative focus provides the only way to be genuinely social scientific. In their view political science is concerned with establishing universal laws or 'theories of the middle range', that is, generalizations that can provide rigorous and tested, albeit time-bound, explanations of political phenomena. In its narrowest form, comparative political institutions has developed as a discipline that compares constitutions, executives, legislatures and judiciaries – either within or across states – with a view to explaining differences in the way in which political issues are processed and resolved. Such work can deal with narrow questions – such as the repercussions of having bureaucracies staffed by those with a legal training as opposed to some other educational or professional background – or more broad-ranging matters – such as the repercussions of having a separation of powers or a parliamentary system of government. Analysis also extends to the comparison of federations, consociations, militaries, political parties, electoral systems and systems of interest-representation. In its wider form, *comparative political analysis*, political scientists use general concepts that are not country-specific and are committed to positivist methods of enquiry.

Comparative political analysis developed as part of the behaviourist movement in the social sciences that criticized the formalistic and legalistic nature of institutional political science of the 1950s and 1960s. It sought to test and quantify propositions about mass and elite political behaviour, arguing that constitutional, legal and formal analyses frequently had little substantiated empirical support. The behavioural revolution was accompanied by rigorous quantitative research on electoral systems and electoral behaviour, the functioning of political parties and party systems, the role of interest groups, and the making of public policy, with the emphasis on studies of decision-making. The antithesis between formal institutionalists and quantitative political scientists has mostly been overcome; modern empirical political scientists normally embrace methods and insights from both approaches.

The marriage between institutionalism and the use of modern empirical techniques (like survey research and statistical testing) is perhaps most fruitfully revealed in the testing of cross-national generalizations. Arend Lijphart's (1984) *Democracies: Patterns of Majoritarian and Consensual Government in Twenty One Democracies* is an exemplary work of comparative political analysis, indicating the fundamental consequences of choosing either majoritarian or consensual political institutions in democracies. Rein Taagepeera and Mathew Shugart's (1989) study of *Seats and Votes: The Effects and Determinants of Electoral Systems* is another example of rigorous positivist political science that has formalized and improved our knowledge of the workings of electoral systems, while Weaver and Rockman's (1993) edited text *Do Institutions Matter?* demonstrates the resurgence of interest in assessing exactly how institutions shape policy-making in democratic states.

Two broad differences in methods employed by comparativists are well illustrated in the study of democratization: one school of thought seeks to provide global predictive explanations of democratization on the bases of simple indices of development or the distribution of power-resources (e.g. Vanhanen 1990), while another engages in comparative historical investigations of a more limited range of cases to provide more multidimensional and descriptively rich accounts of patterns of democratization (e.g. Moore 1966). A similar division in methods applies to students of revolutions. Comparative political analysis is also concerned to explain variations in the origins and repercussions of ethnic and national conflict, and the ways in which they are managed by states (see, e.g., Gurr 1993; Horowitz 1985; Lijphart 1977; McGarry and O'Leary 1993).

Public administration and public policy

These are empirical and normative branches of political science that overlap with law and economics. Whereas public administration focuses on the institutional arrangements for the provision of public services, and historically has been concerned with ensuring responsible and equitable administration, public policy specialists analyse the formation and implementation of policies, and address the normative and empirical merit of arguments used to justify policies.

The most vigorous intellectual debates in public administration presently centre on 'public management', the allegedly 'new public management', and the validity of rational choice interpretations of the workings of political institutions, especially public bureaucracies (Dunleavy 1991).

Neither public administration nor public policy have one dominant approach: exponents of pluralism, behaviourism, rational choice, Marxism and feminism are to be found engaged in debate with institutionalists who derive their inspiration from the work of the political sociologist Max Weber. These diverse frames of reference do, however, structure most policy advocacy in Western liberal democracies (Bobrow and Dryzek 1987).

Conventional public policy analysis, especially in the USA, is of a quantitative bent, and is influenced by those with expertise in economics, decision analysis and social policy. The subject matter of this subdiscipline is the formulation, implementation and evaluation of public policies. Technical public policy analysts are well versed in cost–benefit, risk–benefit and sensitivity analysis as well as the more standard social scientific modelling and statistical techniques. The positivist and managerialist orientation of these analysts has been criticized by authors like Giandomenico Majone (1991) who maintain that arguments about policy can only rarely be satisfied by 'hard science'. Most of the time policy advocacy works through persuasion in the absence of determinate evidence, and so some conclude that democracies should be structured to ensure that persuasion is open and competitive, and that rhetoric in the best sense be openly encouraged in democratic fora – rather than having a policy process shrouded by 'decisionistic' technocrats with illegitimate claims to expertise (Majone 1991).

Public policy specialists examine who has the power to put policy proposals on the agenda, for example voters, interest groups, ethnic groups, professional organizations, dominant classes, political parties, mass media (this is the field of policy formulation); how policies are made (the study of decision-making) and executed by elected and unelected officials (the study of implementation); and whether public policies are effective and desirable (the field of evaluation). The distinction between area specialists, who focus on public policies in one country or one set of institutions (such as the European Union), and specialists in comparative public policy, who seek to be social scientists intent on establishing regularities, is characteristic of the field. In comparative public policy attempts are made to explain policy divergences and policy convergences both within and across states. Specialists in this field ask and attempt to answer questions such as 'Does it matter which political parties are in power in explaining policy outcomes?' This has led to intensive investigation of whether the presence of left-wing or right-wing parties in government makes any difference to policy outcomes (and if so by how much?), for example in the domain of taxation or social welfare provision.

Political economy

An increasing number of political scientists work at the boundaries of politics and economics. Some believe that theories of political behaviour, just like theories of economic behaviour, should start from simple assumptions about human beings and should construct predictions about their behaviour from these assumptions. For exponents of rational choice, the test of a good theory is its predictive power rather than the incontestable truth of its assumptions. Their critics claim that exponents of rational choice share with economists the belief that human beings are simply overgrown pigs, insatiably pursuing their avaricious self-interest. Exponents of rational choice generally make the assumption that human beings are rational and self-interested agents. They build testable hypotheses on the assumption that voters wish to maximize their utility, that politicians are pure office-seekers who wish to maximize the votes they can win at elections, and that utility-maximizing bureaucrats seek to maximize their departmental budgets. Such thinking has generated an extensive literature, for example on the political economy of the business cycle, in which theorists try to predict how politicians manipulate economic instruments to cement or create political support (e.g. Tufte 1978), and theories of regulation, in which analysts seek to predict which industries will be regulated by government (see the discussion in Hood 1994).

More generally political economists look for rent-seeking explanations of political and economic phenomena. They ask the questions 'Who benefits?' and 'Who pays?' in seeking to explain political outcomes. Rational choice investigations of domestic political economy are complemented by students of international political economy who seek to integrate the disciplines of politics and economics in research on international organizations like GATT, NAFTA and the European Union, as well as more general studies of the political economy of protectionism and free trade.

Confusingly, the label political economy is also used by political scientists working within the Marxist tradition. They generally accept the propositions of historical materialism and explain policy outcomes as responses to the imperatives of capital accumulation, class struggle and crisis-containment. They deploy Marxist theories of the state in their analyses of liberal democracies, and theories of imperialism and underdevelopment in their studies of the states of the ex-colonial world.

Political sociology is an important interdisciplinary interface of sociology and political science, which has evolved since the 1950s. Political sociologists reject the firm distinction between the political and the social, and stress the high degree of interaction between the two, which traditional approaches to both sociology and political science underemphasized. Political sociology draws upon arguments developed from the works of the most famous classical sociologists, notably Max Weber (particularly his writings on rationalization, bureaucratization and the sociology of domination), Emile Durkheim (especially his discussions of collective identifications and norms) and Karl Marx (especially his writings on state and class).

Political sociology's original focus upon the relationship between social structure (mainly economic class) and political behaviour (mainly voting) has expanded considerably since the mid-1960s to include all aspects of power relations between and within social groups. Debate in this field is often between those who treat political institutions as largely autonomous from social structural determination, those who believe that political institutions are largely reducible to social structural determination, and those who view the distinction between the political and social as fluid and indeterminate. The latter are presently dominant. For example, theorists of political and social movements like Charles Tilly distinguish between the polity, where formal political influence is concentrated, and the external society, but regard the processes of mobilizing resources in pursuit or defence of interests as essentially similar for both challengers and members of the polity – in line with pluralist conceptions of the state and society.

Another division within political sociology is between those who espouse functionalist theories, which treat conflict as an aberration from a normal state of equilibrium, and approaches of a Marxist or pluralist origin, which view conflict as a continuous and ubiquitous feature of politics.

Subjects studied in political sociology include the influence of childhood socialization on political beliefs; the importance of sex, ethnicity, religion and class in shaping and explaining political beliefs and preferences (especially voting preferences); the influence of the mass media in politics; and the definition and consequences of political culture.

International relations

The relations between states are the subject of international relations, which is a misleading title for the subdiscipline of political science that focuses on trans-state and interstate relations in diplomacy, economic transactions, and war and peace. The origins of international relations lie in the works of theologians, who addressed arguments as to when and how war was just, of early modern jurists, like Grotius, Pufendorf and Vattel, who sought to establish that there was a law of nations coequal to the domestic law of states, and of political philosophers, like Rousseau and Kant, who addressed the possibility of moral conduct in war and the need for a stable and just international order.

Practitioners of international relations focus on a diverse array of subjects – international organizations, international political economy, war studies, peace studies and foreign policy analysis – but normatively are divided into two principal schools of thought, that of idealists and realists. The former believe that states can and should conduct their affairs according to law and morality, and that functional co-operation across state boundaries establishes the bases for moral conduct. Realists, by contrast, believe that states are fundamentally amoral in their foreign policy; relations between states are governed by interests rather than goodness; peace is the result of a balance of power between states rather than normative order and functional co-operation. Methodologically, international relations has followed the rest of political science, adopting behavioural and quantitative approaches in the 1950s and 1960s, and being subject to fragmentation since the 1970s as diverse pluralist, Marxist, structuralist, rational choice and feminist critics of disciplinary orthodoxies have vied with one another.

Theories of the state

Many would concur that the subject matter of theories of the state provide the most unified focus for contemporary political theory, political thought, public administration, public policy, political sociology and international relations. Given that the political world is constituted by states, and is likely to remain so for the foreseeable future, this is not surprising.

Defining the concept of the state is a matter of some controversy. On organizational definitions the state is a special type of government that must exercise sovereign authority over a specified territory and population, and have that sovereignty recognized by other states. Internally a state must be the formal source of law, the monopolist of civil force and the ultimate extractor of taxation; externally it must, in principle, be capable of autonomous diplomacy if not war-making. On this organizational understanding states vary in the extent to which they are effectively internally and externally sovereign, centralized, bureaucratized, co-ordinated and subject to the control and direction of their citizens.

If states form the subject matter of political science, the question arises as to how long they have been in existence. It is widely argued that the modern state emerged in late medieval Europe through the supersession of feudal polities. It remains a moot point whether the ancient empires of the Mediterranean, the Middle East, India, China or pre-Columbian America should be described as states, given that features such as sovereignty, centralization, territoriality and bureaucratization were either non-existent or underdeveloped in such political systems. The most frequent argument is to maintain a sharp distinction between the city-states, feudal polities and empires of agrarian societies and the states and empires of commercial and industrial societies – with their more extensive capabilities to control and penetrate their societies.

Although states vary considerably in their origins and forms, almost all of them, leaving aside a few residual traditional monarchies, seek to legitimize themselves as emanations of their peoples, and they do so in two ways, which can be reinforcing or contradictory. On the one hand they claim to be expressions of popular or democratic sovereignty (even dictators now make this claim); on the other hand they usually claim to be the state of a nation, an emanation of the self-determination of the people of X. These two claims explain some of the dynamics of modern states: competition for definition and control of the state centres on claims to represent the popular will, while competition for definition and control of the territorial boundaries of the state centres on claims to represent the national will. These processes are reflected in the sometimes reinforcing and sometimes contradictory activities of state-building and nation-building, and their opposites, state-fragmentation and nationalist secession.

Much contemporary political science has focused on the organization of the state in liberal democracies, in part responding to the growth of state activities in the capitalist democracies of the West, which in the twentieth century have seen the state's functions expand beyond a minimal core (defence, order and law-making, and protection of the dominant religion) to include extensive economic and social management and regulation. Five distinct schools of thought on the empirical workings of the democratic state are evident in modern political science: pluralism, Marxism, rational choice, elite theory (sometimes called neo-statism or new institutionalism) and neo-pluralism. Some claim to have developed novel feminist and green theories of the state, though these claims are disputed, and such work for the present at least is much less extensively developed.

Each of these bodies of thought is divided about the extent to which the democratic state is controlled by its citizens and their voluntary organizations (Dunleavy and O'Leary 1987). Simplifying matters, three answers address this issue: there are those who think that states are controlled by their societies (or at least the most powerful in their societies); there are those who think that states are sufficiently autonomous to redirect and reshape the pressures placed upon them by their societies (or the most powerful in their societies); and finally there are those who think that states are so autonomous that they can act directly against the pressures emanating from their societies (or the most powerful in their societies).

The present and future of the discipline

Political science is therefore both a multidisciplinary and multitheoretical subject. It is a vibrant field of enquiry, and is not likely to disappear unless politics is abolished, a possibility that most of the profession happily regard as impossible. The classical preoccupations of political philosophers and historians remain, and political science departments generally resisted the siren voices of irrationalist postmodernism. This disciplinary conservatism does not of course mean political conservatism. Political scientists vary considerably in their ideological orientations, while remaining committed to reason and dispassionate analysis; indeed they often see their role as 'speaking truth to power'. While some worry that the discipline is in danger of dividing into warring sects (Almond 1989), others see the lack of paradigmatic closure as beneficial for the subject, and they observe throughout the world comparative and empirical political analysts busying themselves in research on democracy, democratization, the prerequisites of legitimate and effective states, and the prospects for justice and conflict-resolution in the new international order – tasks that require little justification.

BRENDAN O'LEARY
UNIVERSITY OF PENNSYLVANIA

References

Almond, G. (1989) *A Discipline Divided: Schools and Sects in Political Science*, London.
Bobrow, D.B. and Dryzek, J.S. (1987) *Policy Analysis by Design*, Pittsburgh, PA.
Dunleavy, P. (1991) *Democracy, Bureaucracy and Public Choice: Economic Explanations in Political Science*, Brighton.
Dunleavy, P. and O'Leary, B. (1987) *Theories of the State: The Politics of Liberal Democracy*, London.
Gurr, T.R. (1993) *Minorities at Risk: A Global View of Ethnopolitical Conflicts*, Washington, DC.
Hood, C. (1994) *Explaining Economic Policy Reversals*, Buckingham.
Horowitz, D. (1985) *Ethnic Groups in Conflict*, Berkeley, CA.
Lijphart, A. (1977) *Democracy in Plural Societies: A Comparative Exploration*, New Haven, CT.
—— (1984) *Democracies: Patterns of Majoritarian and Consensual Government in Twenty One Democracies*, New Haven, CT.
McGarry, J. and O'Leary, B. (eds) (1993) *The Politics of Ethnic Conflict Regulation*, London.
Majone, G. (1991) *Evidence, Argument and Persuasion in the Policy Process*, New Haven, CT.
Moore, B. (1966) *The Social Origins of Dictatorship and Democracy: Lord and Peasant in the Making of the Modern World*, Harmondsworth.
Okin, S.M. (1980) *Women in Western Political Thought*, London.
Pateman, C. (1988) *The Sexual Contract*, Cambridge, UK.
Rawls, J. (1971) *A Theory of Justice*, Cambridge, MA.
Taagepeera, R. and Shugart, M. (1989) *Seats and Votes: The Effects and Determinants of Electoral Systems*, New Haven, CT.
Tufte, E. (1978) *Political Control of the Economy*, Princeton, NJ.
Vanhanen, T. (1990) *The Process of Democratisation: A Comparative Study of 147 States*, New York.
Weaver, R.K. and Rockman, B. (eds) (1993) *Do Institutions Matter? Government Capabilities in the United States and Abroad*, Washington, DC.

Further reading

Bottomore, T. (1992) *Political Sociology*, London.
Dahl, R. (1984) *Modern Political Analysis*, Englewood Cliffs, NJ.
Katznelson, I. and Milner, H. (eds) (2002) *Political Science: The State of the Discipline III*, New York.
Marsh, D. and Stoker, G. (eds) (2002) *Theory and Methods in Political Science*, London.

POLITICAL THEORY

Political theory is an enterprise with a long and distinguished ancestry. Once our forebears had ceased to regard their social and political institutions simply as hallowed by tradition, and began to ask why they took the form that they did, and whether they might not be improved, political theory was born. What things should be allowed by law and what forbidden? Who should rule, and how far should the ruled accept an obligation to obey? What is justice, among individuals and in society? These questions and others like them inevitably arise whenever people begin to reflect critically on their practices and institutions, and political theory tries to answer them in a systematic way. Its methods have been drawn at different times from different disciplines: philosophy, theology, law, history and, more recently, the social sciences. So not only have political theories varied in their practical stance – ranging from, at one extreme, wholesale defences of the existing social and political order to, at the other, manifestos for revolutionary change – but also they have rested on different beliefs about how we should go about answering questions like those above. Some theories have started from a conception of human nature, and asked what political and social arrangements would best fulfil the needs and interests of human beings. Others have interpreted existing institutions as part of an overall pattern of historical development – either as the culmination of that pattern, or as a transient stage destined to be replaced by something higher. Others again have begun by asking what kind of knowledge is possible in political matters, and gone on to defend institutional arrangements that give power to people in proportion to their capacity to use it for the good of society as a whole.

In the twentieth century these methodological issues came to the fore, propelled especially by the impact of positivism. Older political theories, from Plato and Aristotle down to Marx and Mill, sought to combine in a seamless whole an understanding of the existing social and political world with proposals for conserving or changing it. Central to positivism, however, was the claim that there could be no logical connection between empirical propositions describing the world as it is and normative propositions telling us how we ought to act. Acceptance of this claim implies that political theory as traditionally understood rested on a mistake. The mistake was to run together explanations of social and political relationships with recommendations about how those relationships should be conducted in future.

Positivism is no longer the dominant force that it once was in philosophy and the social sciences, but one of its legacies has been that the label 'political theory' is now often applied to three forms of theorizing – empirical, formal and normative – whose aims are somewhat different.

First, *empirical political theory* is a term commonly used to refer to the theoretical parts of political science. Political scientists are interested in describing and explaining particular political events, but they are also interested in developing broader explanatory theories that draw together a wide range of phenomena under a single umbrella. They have, for instance, tried to explain in general terms why revolutions occur, or what conditions are required to make stable democratic government possible. The issues that are considered are often similar to those addressed in the older tradition of political theory, but much greater use is typically made of quantitative evidence to test theoretical claims. Thus someone seeking to produce a theory about the causes of revolution would characteristically begin by looking for correlations between the outbreak of revolutions and other phenomena such as the extent of economic inequality in the societies under consideration.

Second, *formal political theory* is a burgeoning field that overlaps considerably with 'social choice theory', 'public choice theory', etc. It borrows from economics the idea of rational actors pursuing their goals under certain institutional constraints, and then attempts to model political systems as if they were made up of such actors in various roles – politicians, bureaucrats, voters, etc. Given rational actors and a set of procedural rules, what will the final configuration of the system be? Two major applications are to collective decision procedures and to party competition in a representative democracy. In the first case, the theorist postulates a population, each of whom has his or her own preferences as between a number of policies, and looks at how these preferences will be amalgamated into a 'collective choice' by various decision rules (such as majority voting). One well-known result of these investigations is Arrow's (1963) theorem, according to which *no* decision rule can simultaneously meet a number of reasonable-sounding conditions (such as that if each person taken separately prefers x to y, the decision procedure should also choose x in preference to y). In the second case, the theorist again assumes a population with given policy preferences, and looks at how parties will behave under a democratic electoral system on the assumption that each party's aim is to win the election and each voter's aim is to secure policies that correspond as closely as possible to his or her preferences. This application was originally developed by Antony Downs (1957) and has since been considerably elaborated.

Third, *normative political theory* remains closest in spirit to the traditional enterprise, in so far as it is directly concerned with the justification of political institutions and policies. It aims to lay down principles of authority, liberty, justice and so forth, and then to specify what kind of social order would most adequately fulfil these principles. There is, however, deep disagreement among normative theorists about what kind of justification is possible here.

At one extreme stand those who adhere to some form of value-subjectivism. Ultimate political principles simply express the personal standpoint of those who espouse them and are incapable of further justification. The task of political theory is on this view two-fold: it consists partly in clarifying the basic principles themselves – removing conceptual ambiguity, giving the principles a more formal statement – and partly in showing what they imply in practice. Thus some people may declare that the freedom of the individual is their fundamental political value, but this in itself does not settle whether such a person should be in favour (say) of a nightwatchman state or an interventionist welfare state. The theorist's job, on this view, is to explore what the idea of freedom means, and then to apply it to practical issues, such as whether redistributive taxation reduces the freedom of the wealthy, or increases the freedom of the poor, or does both. But if other people were to sidestep the argument by declaring that individual freedom had no value for them in the first place, the political theorist would have nothing further to say in reply.

At the other end of the spectrum stand those who adhere to some form of foundationalism, the view that it is possible to find objective grounds to support basic political principles. Prominent here have been various different versions of contractarian political theory. Contractarian theorists hold that there is a set of basic political principles that all rational people would agree to given appropriate conditions. The most influential example has been John Rawls's (1971) theory of justice, which understands justice as the principles that rational individuals would choose to be governed by in an 'original position' in which they were ignorant of their personal characteristics, their ideals of the good life and their social position. Somewhat similar in spirit is Jürgen Habermas's (1984) claim that legitimate norms are those that would be agreed to in an 'ideal speech situation' from which coercion and domination are absent and in which the participants have to persuade one another by the force of argument alone.

Not all foundationalists are contractarians. The other main option is naturalism, where a normative theory is supported by appeal to human needs and interests that are claimed to be universal. Some contemporary naturalists, such as Masters (1989), appeal to sociobiology and argue that our social and political institutions must be appropriate to our genetically given human nature. Others, such as MacIntyre (1981), are neo-Aristotelians who argue that the best social order is one that fosters to the greatest extent distinctively human capacities, such as powers of reason and virtue.

The main difficulty faced by foundationalists is that of responding to human variety, whether this is expressed in cultural differences between societies or in cultural cleavages within societies, along lines of class, gender, ethnicity and so forth. If human beings differ from one another in radical ways – in beliefs, in basic values, in identities – how can we claim that under suitable conditions of abstraction they would all agree to the same political principles, or that they share basic needs and interests that could be used to justify a determinate set of political arrangements? Foundationalists are accused, by postmodernists and others, of an unsustainable universalism that flattens out observable differences between human beings.

This line of thought leads political theory back to value-subjectivism. There is, however, a third possibility, which may be called an interpretative approach to political theory. Here it is claimed that societies are founded upon certain shared understandings that it is political theory's task to draw out and convert into explicit principles. These understandings are contained in a society's language, its conventions and practices; they vary from one society to the next, but in any given context they are relatively determinate and relatively stable. Thus the US Constitution, for example, interpreted over time, provides a rich source of common understandings on which the political theorist can draw, whereas in the UK the absence of a written constitution means that shared understandings take a different form, and have to be found in parliamentary debates, in public opinion and so forth. Among the most influential of contemporary political theorists favouring an interpretative approach are Charles Taylor (1985) and Michael Walzer (1983).

The interpretative approach to political theory raises the question of how political theories are related to the world-views of ordinary men and women: the pictures of the social world that we all carry with us and use to make sense of everyday political events. In particular, how does political theory differ from ideology, understood as a more or less systematic and action-guiding framework for understanding the social world? The answer is that political theories invariably have an ideological content, but to a greater or lesser extent succeed in scrutinizing and testing those assumptions that ideologies take for granted. Thus liberal ideology might take it for granted that existing social inequalities reflected differences in individual merit, whereas a political theory of a liberal stripe would need both to scrutinize the idea of merit itself – in virtue of what should one person be considered more meritorious than another? – and to look for evidence that there was indeed a relationship between personal merit so defined and the possession of social advantages.

To distinguish itself from mere ideology, political theory must make use both of formal analysis and of the empirical evidence collected by the social sciences. This suggests that the distinction between empirical, formal and normative theory referred to earlier cannot be an absolute one. Rather we should distinguish between forms of political theory that are driven by an interest in explanation and those that are driven by an interest in justification. The distinction cannot be absolute because, on the one hand, normative theories make empirical assumptions about the kind of social order that will result if certain principles are acted upon; while, on the other hand, explanatory theories always rest upon judgements about which phenomena are significant enough to warrant our attempts to explain them (we try to develop theories of democracy or theories of revolution because we regard these as important phenomena, whether we approve of them or disapprove). Thus political theory continues to occupy an essential place in contemporary social science, and the idea, once touted, that it might disappear altogether now seems faintly ridiculous. As Isaiah Berlin (1962) remarked,

> So long as rational curiosity exists – a desire for justification and explanation in terms of motives and reasons, and not only of causes or functional correlations or statistical probabilities – political theory will not wholly perish from the earth, however many of its rivals, such as sociology, philosophical analysis, social psychology, political science, economics, jurisprudence, semantics, may claim to have dispelled its imaginary realm.

DAVID MILLER
UNIVERSITY OF OXFORD

References

Arrow, K. (1963) *Social Choice and Individual Values*, New Haven, CT.
Berlin, I. (1962) 'Does political theory still exist?', in P. Laslett and W.G. Runciman (eds) *Philosophy, Politics and Society*, Vol. 2, Oxford.
Downs, A. (1957) *An Economic Theory of Democracy*, New York.
Habermas, J. (1984) *The Theory of Communicative Action*, Vol. 1, Boston, MA.
MacIntyre, A. (1981) *After Virtue*, London.
Masters, R. (1989) *The Nature of Politics*, New Haven, CT.
Rawls, J. (1971) *A Theory of Justice*, Cambridge, MA.
Taylor, C. (1985) *Philosophy and the Human Sciences: Philosophical Papers 2*, Cambridge, UK.
Walzer, M. (1983) *Spheres of Justice*, Oxford.

Further reading

Barry, B. (1990) *Political Argument*, 2nd edn, Hemel Hempstead.
Gaus, G. (2000) *Political Concepts and Political Theories*, Boulder, CO.
Goodin, R. and Pettit, L. (eds) (1993) *A Companion to Contemporary Political Philosophy*, Oxford.
Kymlicka, W. (2002) *Contemporary Political Philosophy*, 2nd edn, Oxford.
Miller, D. and Siedentop, L. (eds) (1983) *The Nature of Political Theory*, Oxford.
Plant, R. (1991) *Modern Political Thought*, Oxford.
Runciman, W.G. (1969) *Social Science and Political Theory*, Cambridge, UK.
Swift, A. (2001) *Political Philosophy: A Beginners' Guide for Students and Politicians*, Cambridge, UK.

POPULAR CULTURE

The importance of popular culture as a field of enquiry has been increasingly recognized in the last three decades as a result of simultaneous shifts of emphasis in anthropology, sociology, history and literary studies. Increased awareness within anthropology of the heterogeneity and non-unanimity of cultural representations, together with an increasing focus on meaning and interpretation rather than system and structure; an interest, in history and sociology, in the 'view from below'; a shift in criticism from evaluative studies of a literary canon to a more neutral analysis of textual construction: all these have served to move popular culture nearer to the centre of contemporary scholarship (Mukerji and Schudson 1991). This general interest across the disciplines has been accompanied by the rise of a new, hybrid, interdisciplinary field, cultural studies, wholly devoted to the study of popular culture.

The idea of popular culture as a field available to study and documentation took shape in the late eighteenth century, at a time when many rural folk customs were beginning to disappear with industrialization and urbanization. J.G. Herder pioneered the idea of folk culture as a national heritage to be collected and preserved, and this was reinforced by European romantic writers and scholars who sought an authentic soil in which to plant new varieties of cultural nationalism. It was only towards the end of the nineteenth century, however, that folklore studies, influenced by early anthropological science, became institutionalized as a recognized field in universities (Burke 1978). If the industrial revolution precipitated the first wave of interest in people's culture, a second revolution – that of communications technology, from the early twentieth century onwards – gave rise to the study of popular and mass culture as we now know it.

The influential Frankfurt School, dominated by Adorno and Horkheimer in the interwar years, took a pessimistic view of mass culture as the technocratic manipulation of passive consumers in the context of increasingly totalitarian states. Though much of their analysis has now been superseded, the debate about the effects of mass culture still rumbles on (Strinati 1995). In the last 20 years, the most significant recent development in Euro-American cultural studies has been a conscious reversal of the Frankfurt School approach, shifting the focus from manipulative media technocrats to the active and subversive consumer who appropriates and refashions media genres to suit his or her own tastes and needs. The new emphasis on consumption exists in fruitful tension with the older preoccupation with production and distribution; the consumer in a sense becomes a producer.

'Popular' is a notoriously slippery and contested term. Its content depends on what other term/s it is being contrasted with, for it is always a relational or residual category. It is generally agreed that for the term to have meaning, some form of social stratification must be present, for 'popular' culture is always identified in contrast to the culture associated with some other social stratum (high, courtly, aristocratic, bourgeois, elite, canonical, etc.). In addition to this vertical distinction, one influential definition proposed a three-stage historical model: *folk* culture prevailed until the industrial revolution, when it was superseded, in the cities, by a working-class *popular* culture characterized by live performance (e.g. music hall) and then, following the revolution in communications technology, by modern electronically-mediated *mass* culture (Hall and Whannel 1964). Historians, however, have tended to include preindustrial 'folk' culture under the heading 'popular', while many proponents of cultural/communication studies have treated popular as synonymous with 'mass', maintaining that popular culture came into existence only after the industrial revolution or even after the communications revolution. Though a base-line definition of 'popular' would be 'produced and/or consumed by the common people', historians have shown that popular culture cannot be neatly matched to a bounded social class; cultural fields are always porous and characterized by circulation across social boundaries (Chartier 1987), and until the eighteenth century in Europe it would be more accurate to

postulate a common culture shared by upper and lower classes alike, with a literate high culture accessible only to the upper class superimposed (Burke 1978). The gradual self-separation of the bourgeoisie from common culture, which became by default associated only with the lower classes – seen in Europe in the seventeenth and eighteenth centuries – has also been attested for nineteenth- and early twentieth-century India (Kumar 1988). It may be that this process of separation is now being undone: some have argued that a characteristic of postmodernity is that the high/low distinction has also been eroded, and replaced with a market-place of competing forms that consumers select according to personal taste rather than class or educational background.

The concept of the 'popular' is not only protean in its definitions, it is also highly charged politically and emotionally, and can be used both positively and pejoratively. The boundaries between popular and not-popular are themselves sites of struggle and contestation. An additional distinction was introduced by Latin American theorists in the 1970s, between 'people's' art that arises spontaneously from amongst the people but is contaminated by false consciousness, and 'truly popular' art that is the outcome of ideological enlightenment, often precipitated by radical cadres. In sites where culture was mobilized in protracted liberation struggles – such as the anti-apartheid struggle in South Africa in the 1970s and 1980s – the study of popular culture tended to take the form of a rigorous separation of the radical 'popular' from the reactionary or complicit 'people's'.

The study of popular culture is inherently interdisciplinary. At its broadest, popular culture has been taken to include all lived experience including work practices, family life, etc., and the full range of the humanities and social sciences has been relevant in its exploration. But though it has attracted some positivist approaches (as in the sociology of print, most notably exemplified by Robert Escarpit), the overwhelming tendency has been to explore popular culture texts or practices as forms of communication. This emphasis on symbolic and signifying practices means that the central instances of popular culture have tended to be genres that can be studied as 'texts' (popular music and fiction, television programmes, radio, video, the press, graffiti) or forms of behaviour that can most readily be understood as having a symbolic or signifying dimension (such as football, dance styles, clothing and hairstyle, food, shopping, etc.), and the predominant mode of analysis has been semiotic.

The Euro-American tradition of cultural studies has focused mainly on contemporary or recent forms, and has included non-Western cultures mainly in the framework either of multiculturalism *within* the West, or of 'globalization'. This perspective has had a stimulating effect because of its presumption that all cultures are interconnected and participate in a broad global mass culture, but has also had the perhaps unintentional effect of putting all the emphasis on international culture flows – principally though not exclusively US in origin – and on local importations and adaptations of these, rather than on the often deep-rooted and idiosyncratic local popular traditions. While it is true that most areas of the globe have been touched in one way or another by US mass culture, and some areas have enthusiastically embraced it, detailed work on Latin American, South Asian and African popular cultures shows that much more has to be taken into account. The historical trajectory and present-day nature of modernity in these areas was shaped by factors such as the survival of feudal or clientelist social forms within emergent capitalism; urbanization that in some areas, e.g. West Africa, was precipitated more by commerce and administration than by industrialization; and the populism of states using mass media to constitute a modern nation out of disparate congeries of ethnically and culturally diverse peoples. Popular culture, correspondingly, took forms that did not fit the predominant Euro-American model. It was characterized by the continued vitality of 'traditional' or 'tribal' cultures, and the local generation of numerous hybrid, modern genres that are not imported, though they are vitally linked to global culture (Rowe and Schelling 1991; Chakrabarty 1989; Fabian 1978; Barber 1997). This means that the predominant definitions and assumptions of popular culture studies in Europe and the USA are having to be rethought in order to move towards a truly global comparative study of popular culture.

Are generalizations about the form and content of popular culture possible? The literature does suggest a number of recurrent and pervasive themes: among them the volatility and vitality of popular culture genres; their roots in, or recourse to, orality; their heterogeneity, arising from generative modes of assemblage, incorporation and recycling ('bricolage'); the primacy of an emotional and moralizing tendency; and their hidden or overt political topicality. Though the search for signs of resistance and rebellion in every popular genre has by now been abandoned, the idea of the popular as a site in which hegemony may be both established and subverted has remained a key orientation. Other features often attributed to popular culture in general turn out on further inspection not to hold good: for example the idea that popular culture is typically simple, concrete, explicit, univocal, full of action, lacking in irony and reflection. This is true of many genres, but one only has to listen to the enormously popular Brazilian singers Gilberto Gil and Caetano Veloso to realize that popular lyrics can be complex, allusive and hauntingly beautiful poetry; while in Ghana it is noteworthy that the more democratic and widely disseminated form of highlife music, played on the acoustic guitar, had lyrics that were more complex formally and thematically than the lyrics of the big-band highlife patronized by the elites.

KARIN BARBER
UNIVERSITY OF BIRMINGHAM

References

Barber, K. (ed.) (1997) *Readings in African Popular Culture*, London.
Burke, P. (1978) *Popular Culture in Early Modern Europe*, London.
Chakrabarty, D. (1989) *Rethinking Working-Class History: Bengal 1890–1940*, Princeton, NJ.
Chartier, R. (1987) *The Cultural Uses of Print in Early Modern France*, Princeton, NJ.
Fabian, J. (1978) 'Popular culture in Africa: Findings and conjectures', *Africa* 48: 315–34.
Hall, S. and Whannel, P. (1964) *The Popular Arts*, London.
Kumar, N. (1988) *The Artisans of Banaras: Popular Culture and Identity, 1880–1986*, Princeton, NJ.
Mukerji, C. and Schudson, M. (eds) (1991) *Rethinking Popular Culture: Contemporary Perspectives in Cultural Studies*, Berkeley, CA.
Rowe, W. and Schelling, V. (1991) *Memory and Modernity: Popular Culture in Latin America*, London.
Strinati, D. (1995) *An Introduction to Theories of Popular Culture*, London.

SEE ALSO: culture; folklore; mass media; sport, sociology of

POPULATION AND RESOURCES

The relationships of population size and growth to resources have been subject to intense debate and substantial confusion. Much of the debate centres on the *scarcity* of resources and whether they are running out, or being used up too fast, as a result of rapid population growth. Several insights are germane to analysing this issue.

First, for resources that are traded in well-functioning markets, the price of the resource is the best single assessment of its scarcity. Scarcity should *not* be measured simply by the amount of resources remaining or yet to be discovered, but rather by reference to demand or value to end-users. A resource with tiny supply and no demand is not scarce; a resource with substantial supply and huge demand may well be scarce.

Second, by the price measure, and based on historical evidence of relatively constant or declining real prices over time, most non-renewable resources are not particularly scarce, nor are they becoming increasingly scarce. Expansion of supply and/or curtailments of demand have been more than sufficient to maintain a long-run balance of resources *vis-à-vis* their use. Changes in demand and supply for resources have been heavily influenced by new discoveries, changes in technology resulting in reduced use of relatively scarce resources, and the capacity of consumers and producers to make appropriate substitutions of relatively abundant for relatively scarce resources.

Third, historically the major cause of an expanded demand for resources has not been rapid population growth, but rather rises in income. Prosperous countries, where population growth is slow, consume an inordinate amount of resources. In the future, as Third-World countries become more prosperous and given their predictably large populations resulting from rapid population growth in recent and future decades, upwards pressures on resource prices will become considerably stronger. This resource scarcity will be increasingly costly to circumvent.

Fourth, overuse of resources due to population or income pressures is most likely to occur where market prices do not adequately reflect true present and future scarcity, and where governments are unable or unwilling to provide appropriate and offsetting regulations. Forests, fisheries, clean air, clean water and even common land represent areas where markets and prices can fail to allocate resources well. This is because property rights are in some settings difficult to establish, monitor and enforce. After all, one cannot sell something that one does not own for a price; thus prices are not available to signal scarcity in such cases. Moreover, the true demand or value of some resources is quite uncertain. An important example is the value that individuals and/or societies place on the existence of plant and animal species, and on biological diversity. While population pressures are not the primary cause of overuse of resources where markets and government policies are deficient, population pressures are indeed an exacerbating cause, and sometimes an important one.

Very little is known operationally about the optimal size of population *vis-à-vis* resources, although there is much discussion about sustainable population levels. Estimates of the earth's carrying capacity for various important resources (mainly land and water for food production) vary from 5 billion to 30 billion people. Estimates of the capacity of biological and ecological systems to regenerate, or be sustainable on a long-term basis, are equally vague. Current predictions are for a world population of 9 billion to 12 billion by the end of the twenty-first century. Whether this population size will be sustainable – whether it will preserve over time a reasonable stock of resources for future generations – is not known with any degree of certainty.

ALLEN C. KELLEY
DUKE UNIVERSITY

Further reading

Marquette, C.M. and Bilsborrow, R. (1994) 'Population and the environment in developing countries: Literature survey and research bibliography', UN Document ESA/P/WP. 123, 16 February, New York.

Panayotou, T. (1993) *Green Markets: The Economics of Sustainable Development*, San Francisco, CA.

Simon, J.L. (1996) *The Ultimate Resource 2*, Princeton, NJ.

United Nations (2001) *World Population Monitoring 2001: Population, Environment and Development*, New York.

SEE ALSO: conservation; energy; environment, sociology of; environmental economics

POPULATION GENETICS

For much of its history population genetics worked in relative isolation, often asking and attempting to answer its own questions about the evolutionary process. What are the basic rules of natural selection that apply to the sort of inheritance systems found in the natural world? But from a period that many viewed as static and uninspired just a few years ago, population genetics has recently emerged as one of the elite of biomedical disciplines. Population geneticists are now the darlings of the international seminar circuit. This is because population genetics is crucial to current efforts to make efficient use of the wealth of new information generated by the genome project and related endeavours.

Associated with this renaissance has been a clear change in mission. Population genetics today is not the discipline it was. It looks similar. Many of the tools are the same, and the conceptual foundations have not changed since the development of the field in the early twentieth century. However, there has been a striking change in its overarching goals. It is not too much to say that the primary focus of population genetics now is as a service discipline, called upon principally to address questions from other fields, for example concerning the demographic history of humans, or the medical significance of human genetic variation. This is not to say that the traditional population genetics questions are now answered, or are no longer of interest. Rather, the focus has shifted to other questions.

Population genetics emerged from the effort to reconcile evolution by natural selection with the discrete inheritance patterns described first by Gregor Mendel. The first insight delivered by this new discipline is now known as Hardy–Weinberg equilibrium, and it is the starting-point for all undergraduate courses in population genetics. Hardy–Weinberg equilibrium is a mathematical demonstration that the rules of genetic inheritance as described by Gregor Mendel do not, themselves, change the amount of genetic variation in the population. This finding overcame an important difficulty with the theory of evolution by natural selection when it still depended upon an earlier model of inheritance, called blending inheritance. If genetic differences between people were due, at a fundamental level, to a quantitative variable, then the inheritance process would itself reduce variation in the population. This argument has been famously represented as combining different colours. Imagine a population of red and white individuals. Under a model of blending inheritance, everyone eventually winds up pink, and there are no genetic differences between individuals. Since the theory of evolution by natural selection requires genetic differences, evolution stops. The mathematical description of how Mendel's rules influence the proportion of discrete elements of inheritance (that is, different allelic forms of genes) was the first population genetic result, and it came to characterize the whole field, so that population genetics is usually defined as the science that describes how evolutionary forces change the frequencies of alleles in populations over time. In the case of Hardy–Weinberg equilibrium the only factor considered is Mendelian inheritance itself, and the answer is that this inheritance system does not change the frequencies of types.

The next major contribution was due to the gifted and opinionated British geneticist R.A. Fisher. He was the first to show that the particulate inheritance envisioned by Gregor Mendel is consistent with the observations of his contemporaries who were interested in quantitative aspects of variation in natural populations. These researchers had perceived a problem with the Mendelian view, because they observed that genetic variation was continuous. How could continuous variation result from the particulars responsible for inheritance as described by Mendel? Fisher showed that under reasonable assumptions, the particulate inheritance imagined by Mendel could lead to the patterns of variation described by the quantitative geneticists, who were known at the time as biometricians.

From these beginnings, until recent times, the main thrust of population genetics was to understand general rules of the evolutionary process. The field did have applied aspects throughout its history, including, for example, quantitative and ecological genetics. But the leading population geneticists were generally more concerned with questions that arose within the field itself. How important are chance effects in evolutionary change? Does selection always increase the average fitness of a population? How does the nature of the genetic control of the trait (e.g. one gene or two genes) influence its evolution? Attention has now shifted, however. This is because population genetics had evolved techniques well suited to relating genetic variation to variation at the level of the individual. If could therefore answer questions such as whether particular individuals are likely to get certain diseases, and predict how they might respond to treatment. For this reason, population genetics has become central to understanding how human genetic variation influences disease and health.

The field of population genetics has never been a stranger to controversy. At various times, ideas from population genetics have been used to promote extreme social agendas. For example, models that predict the standing load of genetic mutations in the population have been used to raise concerns about the relaxation of selection due to medical advances, and the possible consequent deterioration of the human gene pool. Others have claimed that correlations in intelligence among relatives implies genetic control of intelligence, and have argued that human intelligence would deteriorate if less intelligent members of society produce more offspring than the more intelligent members. Indeed, many of the founders of population and human genetics, such as Francis Galton and R.A. Fisher, were intimately involved in the eugenics movement. Although it is by now generally appreciated that the eugenic arguments were profoundly misguided, population genetics has become enmeshed in other controversies, such as those related to the nature of human genetic variation. For example, a recent California state ballot that would outlaw the governmental use of race in most settings cited claims in the scientific literature that racial groups differ very little from one another genetically. These claims of racial similarity are, however, hotly contested in the scientific literature, some scientists arguing that the major races do indeed have important genetic differences. It should be appreciated that all the geneticists who participate in this debate accept that the differences among races are slight relative to the differences among individuals within races. This is a central conclusion drawn from years of human population genetics research, and is now beyond dispute. But there remains disagreement about the nature of the small proportion of human genetic variation that is correlated with the geographical origin of peoples. Some take the view that the genetic differences among people related to their geographical origin can be adequately represented by traditional racial labels, while others argue the racial labels are misleading and inadequate descriptions of regional patterns of human genetic variation. These questions have not only medical significance. As many have emphasized, they are also relevant to how people view themselves and

for their relationships to one another. It does not seem that the new, applied, mission of population genetics will free it from controversy.

DAVID B. GOLDSTEIN
UNIVERSITY COLLEGE LONDON

Further reading

Cavalli-Sforza, L.L., Menozzi, P. and Piazza, A. (1994) *The History and Geography of Human Genes*, Princeton, NJ.
Halliburton, R. (2003) *Introduction to Population Genetics*, New York.
Hartl, D.L. and Clark, A.G. (1997) *Principles of Population Genetics*, 3rd edn, Sunderland, MA.
Provine, W.B. (1971) *The Origins of Theoretical Population Genetics*, Chicago.

SEE ALSO: genetics and behaviour; genomics; human evolution; race

POPULATION HISTORY

Modern human beings have been on earth for around 150 thousand years, beginning with small numbers in East Africa. By 2000 there were just over 6 billion people living or less than 6 per cent of the 106 billion calculated to have ever lived. In one sense, our conquest of the planet has been a recent event, with a six-fold multiplication in population over the last century and a half, and an anticipated further increase of probably no more than 50 per cent. Coale (1974) drew on a range of historical estimates to posit that the global population, consisting solely of hunter-gatherers, had reached perhaps 8 million by 8000 BCE when 97 per cent of our historical time-span to the present had passed. The invention and spread of agriculture allowed denser settlement so that numbers may have reached 300 million by the beginning of our era.

The estimation of population numbers for the world and its major components has excited increasing interest. The calculations depend on complete population counts or censuses that were not available even for much of Europe, North America and Australasia until the second half of the nineteenth century and for most of Africa before the second half of the twentieth century. No estimate was possible at all until most parts of the world were known to each other as a result of the sixteenth-century voyages of discovery and overland expeditions from Europe to Asia.

The first estimates came in this period from priests, mostly Jesuit and Italian, who had been associated with the missioning of East Asia. They correctly concluded that most of the world's population at the time lived in Europe, India, China and Japan (probably at least three-quarters did so), and employed comparative rural settlement densities and city sizes to make reasonable guesses. Those closely connected with these attempts, which continue to be influential up to the present day, included (with dates of important population estimates) Giovanni Botero (1596), Martino Martini (1655) and Giovanni Battista Riccioli (1661). The latter arrived at a total of 1 billion, approximately double the present estimate for the mid-seventeenth century partly because of huge overestimates for the little-known populations of the Americas and Oceania. Modern demography largely owes its origin to the new scientific attitudes in England during the latter half of the seventeenth century, and in this atmosphere Gregory King produced in 1696 a more modest, and undoubtedly more accurate, figure of 700 million (in a manuscript, not to be published for another one hundred years).

More recent estimates of historic global population size and trend have drawn heavily on numerous sources located by the eighteenth-century German theologian, statistician and demographer, Johann Peter Süssmilch, in works published in mid-century that sought to demonstrate a divine pattern in demographic phenomena. The nineteenth-century work was largely done by Karl Friedrich Dieterici and his colleagues at the Prussian Statistical Office, Berlin, and by German geographers at the University of Gotha. These sources were augmented in the twentieth century by George Knibbs, Australian Chief Statistician, in 1917 in a volume on the mathematical theory of population and in 1932 by the US statistician and demographer, Walter Willcox, in a volume published by the National Bureau of Economic Research.

All more recent works stands on that of Willcox and much merely modifies his estimates. That forming what has been called 'the mid-century consensus' included work by the British biologist and social scientist, Alexander Carr-Saunders (1936), a revision by Willcox in 1940, and the American who had directed the United Nations Population Division, John Durand (1967). These were given further authority by inclusion in the two major United Nations'

studies of *The Determinants and Consequences of Population Trends* (1953, 1973). Subsequent estimates have included those of Colin Clark (1967), Jean-Noël Biraben (1979), Colin McEvedy and Richard Jones (1978), and Angus Maddison (2001). Estimates for the twentieth century have been strongly influenced by compilations in the first half of the century in the League of Nations *Statistical Year Books* and in the second half in the United Nations' *Demographic Year Books*. In their estimates of past population, Willcox and Carr-Saunders started at 1650 while Durand (1967) argued that sources were too insecure to go back earlier than 1750. Nevertheless, Clark (1967), Durand (1974), Biraben (1979) and Maddison (2001) have now produced estimates back for 2,000 years while McEvedy and Jones (1978) have gone back millennia earlier.

The historical estimates

None of the estimates is really independent. All draw on each other although most suggest modifications for specific regions or periods. All, also, are strongly influenced by nineteenth- and twentieth-century census figures. However, not even recent figures are completely secure. Durand, in a tradition established by the United Nations projections of future populations, produced low, medium and high estimates for past populations. The uncertainty of such estimates is shown even for relatively recent dates: according to Durand's high, medium and low estimates, the world first attained 1 billion people – demographically a significant occurrence – around 1760, 1810 or 1830 respectively. Table 6 shows the range of twentieth-century estimates.

There is approximate, but far from exact, agreement on the dimensions of population growth, although it remains possible that the truth lies outside ranges given in Table 6. The global population may have been around 8 million 10,000 years ago, 250 million 2,000 years ago, and a little higher 1,000 years ago. The first billion was probably reached in the early nineteenth century, the second billion in the 1930s, and the sixth billion in late 1999.

A major problem with many of the estimates is a circularity in the argument. Estimated population growth rates are often employed to calculate population numbers, while these numbers may then be used to calculate growth rates. The

Table 6 Estimates of world population, 0–AD 2000 (millions)

Period	Year	Range		Sources	
		High	Low	High	Low
Historic	0	297	169	Durand (1974)	McEvedy and Jones (1978)
	1000	310	253	Durand (1974)	Biraben (1979)
	1500	484	423	Durand (1974)	McEvedy and Jones (1978)
	1700	680	603	Biraben (1979)	McEvedy and Jones (1978); Maddison (2001)
		United Nations (2001)	Maddison (2001)		
Recent	1950	2,519	2,512		
	2000	6,071	5,908 [1998]		

Source: Clark (1967), Durand (1974), McEvedy and Jones (1978), Biraben (1979), Maddison (2001), United Nations (2001). See Maddison (2001) for detailed references.

Table 7 Estimates of world population and continental distribution, 0–AD 2050 (in millions and percentage distribution)

		0	1500	1950	2000	2050*
World population (millions)		231	438	2,519	6,057	8,919
Continental distribution (%)						
	Europe	14	20	22	12	5
	Asia and Pacific	76	65	56	61	57
	Africa	7	11	9	13	26
	Americas	3	4	13	14	12

Note: * United Nations 2002 Medium Projection.

interest in population growth rates often derives from the desire to show regional growth or the increase in European population as evidence of economic growth and particularly of the commercial revolution of the sixteenth to eighteenth centuries and of the subsequent Industrial Revolution and the creation of a global economy. This is particularly the case in the work of Willcox and Maddison. The latter employed his population figures to estimate real national and per capita income growth over the last 2,000 years.

The sixteenth- and seventeenth-century population estimates were vitiated by overestimating the populations of the Americas and Oceania (where it was believed a populous great south continent was to be found). Until the second half of the twentieth century Africa's historical population was overestimated, being thought to have been stationary at around 100 million for cen-

turies and incapable of growth. Table 7 presents world population and its continental distribution according to the most recent published estimates (Maddison 2001; United Nations 2001).

Clearly, the changes in the coming 50 years will in some aspects be greater than in the two previous millennia. Because of very low fertility (with birth rates below death rates) Europe's population is likely to fall both relatively and absolutely (from 728 to 632 million) while Africa's population will increase disproportionately (from 796 to 1,803 million).

JOHN C. CALDWELL
AUSTRALIAN NATIONAL UNIVERSITY

References

Biraben, J.-N. (1979) 'Essai sur l'évolution du nombre des hommes', *Population* 1 (January/February): 13–24.

Clark, C. (1967) *Population Growth and Land Use*, New York.

Coale, A.J. (1974) 'The history of the human population', *Scientific American* 231(3): 41–51.

Durand, J. (1967) 'The Modern Expansion of World Population', in *Proceedings of the American Philosophical Society*, Philadelphia, 117, Number 3.5.136–159.

—— (1974) *Historical Estimate of World Population*, Philadelphia, PA.

McEvedy, C. and Jones, R. (1978) *Atlas of World Population History*, London.

Maddison, A. (2001) *The World Economy: A Millennial Perspective*, Paris.

United Nations (2001) *World Population Prospects: The 2000 Revision*, New York.

Further reading

Caldwell, J.C. and Schindlmayr, T. (2002) 'Historical population estimates: Unraveling the consensus', *Population and Development Review* 28(2): 183–204.

SEE ALSO: demographic transition; population projections

POPULATION PROJECTIONS

Population projections are calculations that illustrate the development of populations when certain assumptions are made about the course of future population growth. Projections can be made for the country as a whole, for major geographical or political subdivisions of a country, or for particular classes of a population. The assumptions of the projection may mirror patterns of growth observed in the past, may be based on an extrapolation of past trends, or may be conjectural, speculative or illustrative. The length of the projection period may vary from a few years to many decades, depending on the needs being served, the population in question and the availability of resources.

Several procedures for projecting populations can be distinguished. A total population can be projected forwards in time by means of a balancing equation, whereby future population size is estimated by adding to previously enumerated population changes over the intervening period due to natural increase (births less deaths) and net migration. The method demands a satisfactory initial population count and reliable estimates of the components of population growth, and is warranted only for fairly short projection periods.

A slightly different approach can be taken by projecting an initial population by reference to a rate of annual increase under the assumption of a mathematical model for the form of population growth. The most commonly used model is that of exponential growth. The technique also permits calculations of a population's doubling time, or the rate of growth that must have been operating to produce a particular population size after a certain number of years. Variants of the method incorporate other patterns of growth, such as the logistic, but have the common feature that future population size is estimated without regard to the components of growth.

If a population's age structure is not constant, because of past fluctuations in vital rates or age-selective migration, it is greatly preferable to extrapolate from a known age structure on the basis of age-specific fertility and mortality rates. This is known as the component method of population projection, and is performed in several steps. The first is to calculate the survivors of the initial population on the basis of an assumed or underlying life table, and the second is to calculate the children born and surviving over the projection period. Thus, for example, with a projection period of 5 years, one would calculate the survivors of people initially aged 0–4 years, 5–9 years and so on, to give the numbers aged 5–9, 10–14 and so on, in the projected population, and then apply age-specific fertility rates to women in the childbearing years to derive the number of children whose survivors will go to make up the 0–4 age group in the projected population. A final refinement might be to adjust for known or assumed rates of immigration and emigration.

Demographers are perhaps best known for making population projections. Nevertheless, there is a major historical difference of opinion within the profession as to the role of the demographer in this regard, and even as to the function of a projection. According to Brass (1974), 'the forecasting of future populations would seem to many people the main practical justification for the science of demography'. Opposing this view Grebenik (1974) declared that 'it is perhaps salutary to remind ourselves that there is only one feature that all demographic predictions have had in common, and that is that they have all been falsified by events'. We can go some way towards reconciling these points of view by distinguishing, as does Keyfitz (1972), between a prediction of what will actually happen in the future, and a projection, which is merely the numerical consequence of a series of assumptions. A projection is bound to be correct (barring arithmetic error), while a single forecast is nearly certain to be invalidated by subsequent events. For example, a forecast might be based on current mortality that is subject to change, or on an assumed future level of mortality that proves to have been incorrect.

Whatever limitations or qualifications that demographers place on their projections, they cannot prevent their being used as forecasts. The most useful forecasts are therefore accompanied by measures of uncertainty; the case for these is made cogently by Keilman *et al.* (2002). The production of such probabilistic forecasts, which are comparatively recent in the history of the development of projection methodology, represents a major advance in population forecasting and goes some way towards resolving the concerns quoted earlier.

MICHAEL BRACHER
SYDNEY

References

Brass, W. (1974) 'Perspectives in population prediction: Illustrated by the statistics of England and Wales (with discussion)', *Journal of the Royal Statistical Society A* 137(4).

Grebenik, E. (1974) 'Discussion', in W. Brass, *Journal of the Royal Statistical Society A* 137(4).

Keilman, N., Pham, D.Q. and Hetland, A. (2002) 'Why population forecasting should be probabilistic – illustrated by the case of Norway', *Demographic Research* 6, article 15, http://www.demographic-research.org/Volumes/Vol6/15/.

Keyfitz, N. (1972) 'On future population', *Journal of the American Statistical Association* 67.

Further reading

Dorn, H. F. (1950) 'Pitfalls in population forecasts and projections', *Journal of the American Statistical Association* 45.

Hajnal, J. (1955) 'The prospects for population forecasts', *Journal of the American Statistical Association* 50.

Lutz, W. (ed.) (1996) *The Future Population of the World: What Can We Assume Today?* London.

Shyrock, H.S., Siegal, J.S. and associates (1973) *The Methods and Material of Demography*, Washington, DC.

SEE ALSO: fertility; migration; mortality; vital statistics

POPULISM

Populism is one of the least precise terms in the vocabulary of social science. The political phenomena to which it refers are extraordinarily diverse, with few connecting links. Only one feature is shared by all so-called populists, namely a rhetoric of appeals to 'the people' understood in a variety of senses. However, a distinction can be drawn between two broad families of populisms, each of them internally differentiated: populism as a form of radical movement based on or oriented towards rural grievances, and populism as a style of politics.

Populism as rural radicalism has three variants, which overlap to some extent but also show sharp differences:

First, there are radical farmers' movements, of which the paradigm case is the US People's Party of the 1890s. This movement, whose adherents coined the label Populist, grew out of the economic grievances of farmers in the western and southern states, and for a time appeared to threaten the US two-party system. The Populists, whose manifesto declared 'We seek to restore the government of the Republic to the hands of "the plain people"', demanded a variety of reforms, including monetary inflation by increased coinage of silver.

Second, there are movements of radical intellectuals aiming at agrarian socialism and romanticizing the peasantry. The model here is *Narodnichestvo* (Populism), a phase of the nineteenth-century Russian revolutionary movement during which disaffected intellectuals went to the people to try to provoke them to revolution. At the height of the movement in 1874, thousands of young people flocked to the countryside to preach the gospel of agrarian socialism. They believed that since communal cultivation of land still survived in the Russian village, a new socialist society could be constructed upon this rural foundation once the state was destroyed. When the peasantry proved unresponsive, some of the *Narodniki* took to terrorism instead.

Third, there are spontaneous grassroots peasant movements, aimed at control of the land and freedom from elite domination. There is no acknowledged paradigm movement, but examples include the Zapatistas in the Mexican Revolution and the peasant parties of Eastern Europe after the First World War. Third World revolutionary movements with a peasant base, such as Maoism, may be regarded as a fusion of Marxism with populism. Agrarian populism is often thought to be characteristic of developing countries, and has been plausibly linked to the strains of economic and social modernization.

Populism as a political style includes a variety of diverse phenomena:

First, populist dictatorship includes cases in which a charismatic leader appeals beyond conventional politicians to the masses, and gains unconstitutional power by giving them 'bread and circuses'. Juan Peron, who (with the help of his wife Eva) built up a loyal popular following in Argentina in the 1940s, is an obvious case.

Second, populist democracy is hostile to representation and seeks to keep as much power as possible in the hands of the people. Its characteristic institutional devices are the popular referendum on legislation passed by a representative assembly; popular initiative, whereby voters can bypass the assembly and initiate legislation to be voted on in a referendum; and the recall, whereby representatives can be forced by dissatisfied constituents to undergo an extra election before the end of their term of office. Some populists are attracted by the opportunities offered by modern technology for the electorate to offer instant judgements on political issues.

Third, 'reactionary populism' describes politicians who play to the prejudices of the masses in democratic countries against what are taken to be the more enlightened views of the political elite. Politicians who gain popularity by playing on ethnic hostilities or right-wing views about law and order are particularly liable to the charge of populism in this sense.

Finally, 'politicians' populism' is the style of politicians who avoid ideological commitments and claim to speak for the whole people rather than for any faction, and of catch-all people's parties that are short on principles, eclectic in their policies and prepared to accept all comers.

These populist political styles may be combined but do not necessarily occur together. Similarly, agrarian populists may use some populist political styles, as in the case of the US Populists of the 1890s.

When used to describe a political style, the term populist is usually derogatory. However, as democratization spreads, opportunities for political populism grow with it, because these political styles exploit the gap between democratic theory and practice. There is an unavoidable tension between democracy as a form of state and democracy's legitimizing principle, the sovereignty of the people. Populists mobilize support by appealing through past democratic institutions and politicians to the people they are supposed to represent. In doing so they make use of the ambiguities of the notion, 'people'. In English, this can refer to 'the united people', that is, the nation as a whole as opposed to squabbling factions; the 'common people', as opposed to the rich and powerful; 'ordinary people', as opposed to professional politicians; and 'our people', as opposed to foreigners or ethnic minorities. Populist politicians often use these ambiguities to appeal to a number of different constituencies simultaneously.

As political populists incline to a demagogic style and frequently mobilize support by playing on nationalist or ethnic hostilities, there are affinities with some versions of fascism. However, political populism can be distinguished from fascism in the strict sense by its characteristic lack of ideological commitments.

MARGARET CANOVAN
UNIVERSITY OF KEELE

Further reading

Berlet, C. and Lyons, M.N. (2000) *Right-wing Popularism in America: Too Close for Comfort*, New York.
Canovan, M. (1981) *Populism*, New York.
Ionescu, G. and Gellner, E. (eds) (1969) *Populism: Its Meanings and National Characteristics*, London.
Trautman, K.G. (ed.) (1997) *The New Populist Reader*, Oxford.

SEE ALSO: democracy; fascism; radicalism

POSITIVISM

The explicit postulates of logical positivism are not accepted by most practising social scientists. Nonetheless, there remains an amorphous and implicit self-consciousness, a self-perception, that pervades contemporary social science practice, which may be called the 'positivist persuasion'. Its heyday in the social sciences was in the mid-twentieth century, but it has continued to guide social science into the present.

The major postulates of this persuasion are:

First, a radical break exists between empirical observations and non-empirical statements. This seems like a simple and rather commonsensical position, but it is actually a fundamental, specifically intellectual principle that has enormous ramifications.

Second, because of this assumed break between

general statements and observations, more general intellectual issues – philosophical or metaphysical – are not fundamentally significant for the practice of an empirically oriented discipline.

Third, this elimination of the non-empirical (purely intellectual) reference is taken to be the distinguishing feature of the natural sciences, and it is believed that any objective study of society must follow suit.

Finally, questions that are of a theoretical or general nature can be dealt with correctly only in relation to empirical observations. There are three important corollaries of this fourth point. The first has to do with the formulation of scientific theories. Positivists argue that theories should build upon generalizations, which are in turn based upon observation. The second concerns conflict between theories. According to positivists, theoretical disputes must be resolved by empirical tests. They cannot be settled by conceptual arguments. It follows, and this is the third corollary, that if theoretical conflicts cannot be resolved by an empirical test, then they fall outside the realm of properly scientific discourse.

For the positivist, therefore, the development of the social sciences is thought of as in principle progressive, as linear and cumulative. The division of labour in the social sciences, the segmentation or internal differentiation of a scientific field, is viewed as the product of specialization rather than the result of generalized, non-empirical disagreement. It is taken to be the result of focusing on different aspects of empirical reality rather than as a sign of fundamental disagreement between scientists who seek to explain the same element of empirical reality in different ways.

The ramifications of these beliefs about social science were and continue to be enormous. They have had an impoverishing effect on the social scientific imagination, in both its empirical and theoretical modes. By unduly emphasizing the observational and verificational dimensions of empirical practice, positivist doctrine severely constrains the range of empirical analysis. The fear of speculation imposes an often exaggerated reliance on techniques within the social sciences, so that studies aspire to achieve an illusory precision or are content to produce often superficial correlations. Energy is devoted to methodological rather than conceptual innovation, for the scientific challenge is increasingly understood to be the achievement of ever more pure forms of observational expression. The avoidance of generalization contributes in turn to the atomization of social scientific knowledge. Finally, but perhaps most significantly, the positivist doctrine has caused a widespread failure of nerve in theoretical sociology.

What might an alternative position look like? Clearly, even in postwar US social science, alternatives were put forward. What was usually proposed was some kind of humanistic alternative to scientific study: humanistic geography, sociology, political science, psychology and even the humanistic narrative approach in contrast to the analytic approach in history. These humanist alternatives had in common their anti-scientific stances, a position that was held to imply the following: a focus on people rather than external forces; an emphasis on emotions and morality rather than instrumental calculation; interpretative rather than quantitative methods; the ideological commitment to a moral society, i.e. one that resists the twin dangers of technology and positivist science. In the European tradition this sharp dichotomy was supposedly formalized by Dilthey in his distinction between *Geisteswissenschaften* and *Naturwissenschaften*, between hermeneutics and science. In its most radical form, the hermeneutical position argues that the uniquely subjective topic of the 'human studies' makes generalizations impossible; in more moderate form, it argues that even if some generalizations are possible, our effort must aim only at understanding rather than explanation, thus allowing causal analysis to be monopolized by natural science.

These mid-century forms of humanistic or hermeneutical alternatives to positivism erred by accepting positivism as an accurate characterization of natural science. The clear-cut nature of the distinctions drawn by humanist authors of the 1940s and 1950s now seem almost quaint in their acceptance of the confidence, power and self-supporting epistemology of 'big science'. Postempiricist philosophy, history and sociology of science, which developed from the mid-1960s, has conclusively demonstrated that the positivist persuasion was wrong, not just about the usefulness of natural science as a guide to social science, but about natural science itself. From the wide range of this discussion there are certain basic points upon which most of the participants in this movement are agreed. These are the fundamental postulates of the 'postpositivist persuasion', and they all point to the rehabilitation of the theoretical.

First, all scientific data are theoretically informed. The fact/theory distinction is not concrete, does not exist in nature, but is analytic. Calling statements observational is a manner of speech. We use some theories to provide us with the 'hard facts', while we allow others the privilege of tentatively explaining them.

Second, empirical commitments are not based solely on empirical evidence. The principled rejection of evidence is often the very bedrock upon which the continuity of a theoretical science depends.

Third, the elaboration of general scientific theory is normally dogmatic rather than sceptical. Theoretical formulation does not proceed, as Popper would have it, according to the law of the fiercest struggle for survival: it does not adopt a purely sceptical attitude to generalizations, limiting itself only to falsifiable positions. To the contrary, when a general theoretical position is confronted with contradictory empirical evidence that cannot be simply ignored (which is often the first response), it proceeds to develop *ad hoc* hypotheses and residual categories that allow these anomalous phenomena to be 'explained' in a manner that does not surrender a theory's more general formulations.

Finally, fundamental shifts in scientific belief will occur only when empirical challenges are matched by the availability of alternative theoretical commitments. This background of theoretical change may be invisible, as empirical data give the *appearance* of being concrete (as representing external reality) rather than analytic (representing thought as well). But this appearance is misleading. The struggle between general theoretical positions is among the most powerful energizers of empirical research.

These insights had the potential to take social studies beyond the humanism versus science dichotomy, but they have not had this effect. Since the liminal moment of the 1960s when postpositivism swept through social theory, the philosophy of science, anthropology and sociology, several alternative research programmes have developed. Yet, while compelling in their own right, these have had the collective effect of merely establishing new versions of the humanism versus science dilemma. Ironically, this binary opposition allows positivism to continue to flourish in social science.

In cultural anthropology, the turn towards interpretation initiated by Clifford Geertz was developed by the next generation into a full-blown relativism. Anthropology was conceived in opposition to science. Under the aegis of postmodern social and literary theory, the wincing regrets of a discipline once connected with colonialism were sublimated into a sceptical epistemology. The scientific frameworks of Western thought were deemed incapable of producing ethically adequate knowledge of other cultures. Anthropologists refrained from offering truth-claims that could be contested outside cultural difference. The favoured method of anthropology, ethnography, was detached from scientific claims about culture, and instead situated inside modernist literary ambitions or the critical and materialist political economy of globalization. This pointed to moral and political critique as the primary task of 'cultural studies'.

The invention and explosion of cultural studies can be traced to the moment in postpositivism when the writings of Michel Foucault were introduced to wide acclaim in US social sciences and humanities. As cultural studies emerged from various theoretical traditions, including the psychoanalytical and neo-Marxist, the heritage of interpretive methodology became harnessed to what were taken to be the central and overriding themes of Foucault's work: the power/knowledge connection, the critique of science and rationality, and the disciplinary nature of modern Western institutions. While a good deal of exceptional empirical research has emerged in cultural studies, the general belief that Foucault's work provides an entirely new and all-encompassing critical framework for social research has had several undesirable consequences. First, his critique of science as a social institution has been taken as a warning against using scientific norms of evidence and argument in both empirical and theoretical studies. The nihilistic strands of his implicit epistemology allow knowledge claims to be made in all sorts of different ways, according to rules that are never specified, in order to avoid 'disciplining' what should be fundamentally 'unruly' knowledge. Second, despite the deeply empirical intent of Foucault's life work, the flight from science has led some of his followers to argue that the main priority of social research should be political and moral critique. If and when data sources are engaged, their interpretation is most often guided by a priori political commitments. US cultural studies has often been driven by the pragmatic question of why leftist thought has failed to influence mainstream politics and social life. Public values and symbolic forms are accordingly treated either as supports of power or as sources for resistance to hegemony.

This problematic understanding of interpretation is shared by the reorientation of critical theory promoted by Jürgen Habermas and his associates. Though often directly opposed to the developments within poststructuralism, critical theory shares with Foucauldian cultural studies the formal commitment to an a priori political position as the fundamental guide to interpretations of social reality. Merely descriptive interpretation was taken to be at once impossible and politically reprehensible. The argument was made that social science must deal, first and foremost, with normative questions, concerning the possibility of communal self-determination through open public debate. This turn towards normative considerations – the imbuing of all observations and arguments with moral judgements – was justified by claiming that practical reason was everywhere the same, because it was produced by the universal conditions of human communication.

All three of these movements within social science took their first impetus from the postpositivist moment. However, despite their sophistication and interest, they have rearticulated the 'humanist' or moral alternative to positivism presented during the latter's heyday in social science. And they have been counter-productive. By insisting on making moral judgements while at the same time proclaiming moral and cognitive relativism, they have actually reinvigorated the positivist persuasion in social science, encouraged the pursuit of other chimeras, such as 'social realism', or reinforced intellectual boundaries. Within sociology, for example, the resistance to generalized theoretical debate has remained in place, even within research paradigms that have moved away from abstracted empiricism and misguided quantification. For example, the movement known as neo-institutionalism incorporates culture as an explanatory element of institutions, but does not engage the problems of indeterminacy and interpretation that this should entail. The result is the addition of a new variable to a paradigm that maintains a generally positivist orientation to explaining social life.

Taking the purportedly anti-theoretical nature of the central texts of microsociology as justification for eschewing theory construction, sociological ethnography recognizes itself as interpretive but remains determinedly empiricist in its orientation to qualitative data. The burgeoning field of the sociology of culture has tended to define itself as the 'sociology of' a specific domain – of beliefs, conceptual toolkits, or recorded culture – in contrast with a 'cultural sociology' that mandates the reorientation of social enquiry in a postpositivist way.

What might such a truly postpositivist social science look like? It will have to fulfil two general requirements. First, it has to be reflexively theoretical, that is, able not only to acknowledge but to consider carefully and debate its own presuppositions. While it is no longer clear whether universal theories of human societies, human nature or human rationality are possible, desirable or even ethically defensible, to take this to mean the end of universalizing theory is incorrect. That even the most extreme forms of relativism implicitly acknowledge that human thought and action is embedded in structures of understanding both general and inaccessible to its immediate grasp reveals the need for conceptual debate and reflexive discussion at the most abstract levels of thought. Second, postpositivist social science has to be methodologically sophisticated, that is, able to integrate the interpretation of meaning, the politics of knowledge, and a healthy historicism and cultural relativism with general scientific norms of evidence, adequate explanation and model construction. Though philosophical justification via dogmatic reference to the unchanging nature of scientific rationality is no longer a possibility, the project of specifying certain precepts for intersubjectively valid knowledge in social science has only just begun.

That such a development of postpositivism might be possible is demonstrated by many exemplars of social scientific research that have been stimulated by the theoretical revolutions of the 1960s. Powerful explanations of social processes have been advanced, in cultural history, social movement theory and comparative-historical sociology. The explanations that are provided appear, often, to be adequate at the level both of theory and meaning. The scholars engaged in this work practise universalism, as a self-conscious and self-critical commitment to objectivity. While 'objectivity' and 'truth' may not be metaphysically guaranteed, their existence as social ideals can have beneficial consequences when pursued in a postpositivist way.

That a comprehensible postpositivist paradigm for social research has not yet emerged is due to the continuing separation of theory and empirical research. This separation is not entirely the fault of abstracted empiricism. Contemporary social theory has too often clung on to the classical positivist view that theory and observations should not be mixed up. A true postpositivism would recognize that the many deeply interpretive and highly discursive debates within social and cultural theory should not be seen as 'pure metaphysics' any more than scientific research should be seen as 'pure observation'. Rather, interpretive debates in theory should be seen as attempts to turn metaphysical presumptions and assumptions into workable presuppositions whose implications for empirical research can be spelled out and investigated in a rigorous manner.

Paradoxically, positivism in contemporary social science has had one valid function, that of shadowing practices that lose sight of the goal of producing valid empirical research and true abstract knowledge. Postpositivism has shown that the scientific mind has taken manifold forms depending on time and place, and that it has been able to reform itself in the face of extremely difficult obstacles. As the social sciences continue to search for self-understanding, we trust that this resourcefulness will continue to be demonstrated.

JEFFREY C. ALEXANDER
ISAAC REED
YALE UNIVERSITY

Further reading

Alexander, J.C. (1983) *Theoretical Logic in Sociology*, 4 vols, London.
Bohman, J. (1991) *The New Philosophy of Social Science: Problems of Indeterminacy*, Cambridge, UK.
Frisby, D. (ed.) (1976) *The Positivist Dispute in German Sociology*, London.
Giddens, A. (ed.) (1974) *Positivism and Sociology*, London.
Habermas, J. (1988) *On the Logic of the Social Sciences*, Cambridge.
Halfpenny, P. (1982) *Positivism and Sociology*, London.
Keat, R. and Urry, J. (1975) *Social Theory as Science*, London.
Marcus, G. and Fischer, M. (1986) *Anthropology as Cultural Critique*, Chicago.

SEE ALSO: philosophy of the social sciences; science, sociology of

POSTCOLONIALISM

Generally understood as a critique of colonialism in all its facets – textual, figural, spatial, historical, political and economic – postcolonial theory stands in a curiously belated relation to the politics of decolonization. The great movements of liberation from European colonialism occurred between the 1940s and 1960s, flanked by the declaration of Indian Independence in 1947 and the decolonization of Algeria in 1962. True to its guilty prefix, however, postcolonialism only crystallized as an academic discipline in the early 1970s and 1980s, achieving its distinctive signature with the publication of Edward Said's *Orientalism* (1978) and Salman Rushdie's *Midnight's Children* (1981): the former a severe critical indictment of Western attitudes towards the non-West, the latter a rambunctious fictional imprecation of anti-colonial nationalism. If different in genre, both Said's study and Rushdie's novel successfully epitomize postcolonialism as the discursive purveyor of a peculiarly postmodern idiom, suspicious of the totalizing civilizational polarities of 'West' and 'East' that framed the colonial encounter, and yet susceptible to the multicultural, bilingual and polyvocal mixing of identities that followed in its wake. Frequently condemned, much like the discipline they accidentally inaugurated, for their distance from and elision of 'real' anti-colonial politics, these writers do, indeed, suffer from an elitist and metropolitan perspective, far removed in time and timbre from the rigours of decolonization. At the same time, if lacking street credibility, they capture in different ways a unique moment of collaboration between 'Third World' politics and 'First World' theory or philosophy; successfully sealing an influential compact between the elusive traditions of Western and non-Western self-critique. This ideological partnership is arguably at the heart of postcolonialism, and one facilitated by a series of subtle theoretical and political shifts set in motion by the end of the 1970s with the rise in fashion, specifically within the Anglo-American academy, of poststructuralist soul-searching.

Following the disillusionments of the 1968 revolution, French philosophy under the guardianship of thinkers such as Jean-François Lyotard, Michel Foucault and Jacques Derrida, embarked upon an energetic exhumation of a longstanding tradition of Western anti-humanism, travelling from the philosophical iconoclasm of Friedrich Nietzsche through Max Weber and Martin Heidegger to the thought of Theodor Adorno and Max Horkheimer. These thinkers variously excoriated the dark side of 'modernity', allegedly manifest in the violence at the core of Western epistemology and in the destructive power underscoring the triumphal progress of Western rationality. Following this example contemporary poststructuralism embarked upon a renewed deconstruction of Western institutions, pointing its elegant and accusing fingers at the inevitable exclusions, in the name of law, knowledge, reason, health, upon which the liberal gains of the Enlightenment have long been predicated. Fulsome in their critique of sexism, homophobia, racism and fascism, however, poststructuralism proper never quite named colonialism as a culprit in the excesses of modernity. Nonetheless it created sufficient breach within the apparently impenetrable façade of Western self-representation through which the secrets of imperialism could now be clearly observed and subjected to cross-examination. It was thus a distinctly poststructuralist invitation that opened the way for, among others, Edward Said's exposé of the imperial structures of attitude and reference sustaining the Western canon; for Gayatri Spivak's sustained disavowal of the shibboleth of Western humanism; and for Homi Bhabha's therapeutic nagging at the seamy underside of Enlightenment rationality (Said 1993; Spivak 1987, 1999; Bhabha 1994). Much like their poststructuralist collaborators, postcolonial critics set to work, in the incipient stages of their discipline, at the job of demystifying the West, undermining, in so doing, all pietistic claims of the imperial civilizing mission.

This was not by any means the first time that the West had been taken to task by an anti-colonial prosecution. Mahatma Gandhi's *Hind Swaraj* (1909) anticipates the methods of postcolonialism in its polemical censure of the negative side-effects produced by Western civilization. The writings of Frantz Fanon, the Martiniquian theorist of the Algerian revolution, likewise, refuse to concede any ground to the European myths of progress and humanism (Fanon 1990). But where these earlier writers found in cultural or anti-colonial nationalism a limited but necessary counter to the forces of imperialism, contemporary postcolonialism is predominantly allergic to any politics even vaguely redolent of 'fundamentalism' or 'essentialism'. This distinguishing bias against cultural nationalism, 'tribalism' and nativism is borne of a peculiarly poststructuralist habit of mind wherein modes of resistance based on oppositionality or reversal are believed simply to replicate or reproduce, in different clothing, the very form of oppression from which liberation is sought. Hence most postcolonial theorists seem to agree that anti-colonial nationalisms invariably turned the structures of imperialism against vulnerable indigenous groups such as women, tribals, lower castes and the poor generally; colonizing from within all those unhoused at the crowded margins of Third-World societies (Chatterjee 1993).

If theoretically overdetermined by poststructuralism, postcolonialism's disciplinary aversion to nationalism has also been fuelled in large part by the genuine failure of so many postcolonial nation-states to distribute equitably the privileges of independence. By the 1970s the postcolonial world, once valorized for its cultural defiance and revolutionary energies, appeared tragically in the grip of economic stagnation, dictatorial regimes and violent separatism. Provoking a mood of disenchantment in the liberal West, these negative mutations in Third World politics also became the subject of a creative critique of elitist anti-colonial nationalism led by postcolonial 'leftist' intellectuals. Of these theorists perhaps none have influenced postcolonial theory more powerfully than a small group of South Asian historians who called themselves the Subaltern Studies Collective. Emerging in the mid-1980s, members of this circle engaged in an effort to disclose the story of 'minor' or 'subjugated' non-nationalist forms of anti-colonial counteraction in India. The basic methodological principles followed by these historians were announced in Ranajit Guha's *Elementary Aspects of Peasant Insurgency in Colonial India* (1983), which argued that a closer examination of peasant culture in rural India liberated the idea of anti-colonial politics or protest from its historic association with nationalism. Such culture, accordingly, made it possible to imagine the needs, aspirations and complaints of all those who for reasons of religion, class, caste and gender were not accommodated within the carefully policed space of the postcolonial nation-state. Wary of the structural and ideological continuities between the colonial and nationalist elite, Subaltern Studies cleared a small but important space within historiography for the plural and heterogeneous politics of peasant insurgency, so bringing the forgotten imperatives of Marxism to bear upon the poststructuralist content of postcolonial thought.

In this period socialism also entered into productive alliance with postcolonialism under the aegis of British 'New Left' theory. During the late 1980s, faced by Margaret Thatcher's co-option of the old working class, the left patch-worked an altogether new constituency out of Britain's female, unskilled, unemployed, black and migrant subclass. Committed to a politics of multiculturalism, New Left thinking released into postcolonial polemic the dynamism of a politicized migrant population equally resistant to the possessive claims of the culturalist anti-colonial nation as also to the exclusions of conservative and racist neo-imperial nationalisms. Of the many theorists engaged in this overhauling of the traditional left Stuart Hall led the charge on behalf of ethnic minorities subject to forms of internal colonialism within mainstream Britain (Hall 1988). His manifesto for the supercession of 'race' over 'class' as a category for postcolonial socialist analysis found an articulate champion in Paul Gilroy, whose landmark study, *There Ain't No Black in the Union Jack* (1987), pointed to the imperial residue still in circulation within the exclusionary tactics of First World immigration policy.

Over time the disparate figures of South Asia's 'subaltern peasant' and Britain's 'diasporic migrant' have become the privileged and ubiquitous icons of postcolonialism, confounding the polarizing consequences of the colonial encounter through a double vision simultaneously local and global. Increasingly, however, postcolonial theorists have come to favour a global perspective over its local counterpart, arguing that the binaries 'West' and 'non-West' can only be dismantled through a scrupulous cosmopolitanism or internationalism, unmindful of imperial and nationalist borders and war zones (Breckenridge *et al.* 2000). If compelling, this search for a common political language or agenda runs the risk of occluding the very principles of cultural

difference and particularity from which anti-colonial politics first gained nourishment. In a world order where globalization is the authorizing language of a new and insidious Empire, postcolonialism needs to pursue the rhetoric of cosmopolitanism with caution. Otherwise, as its numerous antagonists argue, much like the cultural nationalisms that it condemns it too may find itself replicating or reproducing the ideological structures to which it claims to be resistant. Contemporary Anglo-American imperialism, Michael Hardt and Antonio Negri claim in *Empire* (2000), shares an unsettling vocabulary with postcolonialism, extending its sovereignty precisely by undermining the categories of the nation, race and ethnicity, and by promoting a rhetoric of hybridity, transnationalism and border crossing. In these circumstances the survival of postcolonialism as an ethical and intellectual doctrine depends heavily upon the creativity of its practitioners, specifically on their ability to construe coalitional forms of transnational solidarity alert to the cultural, economic, religious, political and geographical particularity of all participants.

LEELA GANDHI
LA TROBE UNIVERSITY, AUSTRALIA

References

Bhabha, H. (1994) *The Location of Culture*, London.
Breckenridge, C.A., Pollock, S., Bhabha, H.K. and Chakrabarty, D. (eds) (2000) Special Issue on Cosmopolitanism, *Public Culture* 12(3).
Chatterjee, P. (1993) *The Nation and Its Fragments: Colonial and Postcolonial Histories*, Princeton, NJ.
Fanon, F. (1990) *The Wretched of the Earth*, 3rd edn, trans. Constance Farrington, Harmondsworth.
Gandhi, M.K. (1938 [1909]) *Hind Swaraj*, reprint, Ahemadabad.
Gilroy, P. (1987). *There Ain't No Black in the Union Jack: The Cultural Politics of 'Race' and Nation*, London.
Guha, R. (1983) *Elementary Aspects of Peasant Insurgency in Colonial India*, Oxford.
Hall, S. (1988) *The Hard Road to Renewal: Thatcherism and the Crisis of the Left*, London and New York.
Hardt, M. and Negri, A. (2000) *Empire*, Cambridge, MA, and London.
Rushdie, S. (1982) *Midnight's Children*, 2nd edn, London.
Said, E. (1991 [1978]) *Orientalism: Western Conceptions of the Orient*, 3rd edn, Harmondsworth.
—— (1993) *Culture and Imperialism*, London.
Spivak, G. (1987) *In Other Worlds: Essays in Cultural Politics*, London and New York.
—— (1999) *A Critique of Postcolonial Reason: Toward*

a History of the Vanishing Present, Cambridge, MA, and London.

Further reading

Gandhi, L. (1998) *Postcolonial Theory: A Critical Introduction*, New York.
Loomba, A. (1998) *Colonialism/Postcolonialism*, London and New York.
Moore-Gilbert, B. (1997) *Postcolonial Theory: Contexts, Practices, Politics*, London.
Young, R.J.C. (2001) *Postcolonialism: An Historical Introduction*, Oxford.

SEE ALSO: colonialism; imperialism; multiculturalism; postculturalism

POSTINDUSTRIAL SOCIETY

The term 'postindustrial society' seems to have originated with Arthur Penty, a Guild Socialist and follower of William Morris, at the end of the nineteenth century. Penty looked forward to a 'postindustrial state' based on the small craft workshop and decentralized units of government. The concept was not taken up again until the 1950s, when it was given an entirely new twist. It owes its present meaning largely to the writings of the Harvard sociologist, Daniel Bell.

In numerous works, especially *The Coming of Post-Industrial Society* (1973), Bell has argued that modern industrial societies are entering into a new phase of their evolution, a postindustrial phase. Postindustrial society is as different from classic industrial society as the latter was from preindustrial agrarian society. It is concerned with the production of services rather than goods, the majority of its workforce is in white-collar rather than manual occupations, and many of these workers are professional, managerial or technical employees. The old working class is disappearing, and with it many of the class conflicts of industrial society. New alignments, based on status and consumption, are supplanting those based on work and production.

Postindustrial society is a highly educated society; indeed, knowledge is its central resource, but knowledge in a special sense. Industrial society ran on practical knowledge, the knowledge that comes from doing rather than from pure research. Its representative figures are inventors like Watt and Edison. Postindustrial society depends on theoretical knowledge, the knowledge that is developed in universities and research institutes. It not only looks to theoreti-cal knowledge for many of its characteristic industries, such as the chemical and aeronautical industries, but increasingly puts a good part of its national resources into developing such knowledge, in the form of support for higher education and research and development activities. This shift of emphasis is reflected in the growth in importance of the 'knowledge class' – scientists and professionals – and of 'knowledge institutions', such as universities. These will eventually displace businesspeople and business organizations as the ruling complex in society.

Bell's account of postindustrial society has been the most influential. It is based largely on generalization from US experience, but many European sociologists have found sufficient similarities in their own societies to concur: for instance Alain Touraine in *The Post-Industrial Society* (1971), although he stressed more than Bell that conflicts in the new society will be as severe as in the old. Bell's ideas have been particularly acceptable to futurologists of both West and East, who have made the concept of postindustrial society central to their thinking. In Eastern Europe, postindustrialism has usually been given a Marxist gloss, as a 'higher stage' on the way to full socialism, but, with that necessary qualification, East European reception of the postindustrial idea has been remarkably warm.

How plausible is the postindustrial concept? Many of the changes that Bell notes in the economy and the occupational structure are undoubtedly occurring. Industrial societies are to a large extent now white-collar, service societies. But that is largely because they have exported their manufacturing sectors to the countries of the Third World, without in any way giving up their control. Multinational corporations have their headquarters in the cities of the 'postindustrial' world, but set up their plants and recruit their workforce in the industrialized world, for obvious reasons of cheapness and political convenience. Hence postindustrial societies contain and continue the ethic and social purpose of industrialism, which in many cases overwhelms the striving towards the newer postindustrial ethic of social responsibility and professional commitment. The same feature is clear in the area to which great importance is attributed, white-collar and professional work. We may be (almost) all professionals now, but much professional work has been 'industrialized' by bureaucratization and the application of computer technology, thus making professional workers increasingly like the proletarians of industrial society. The bulk of research in universities and the R&D (research and development) departments of industry and government is devoted to extensions and refinements of existing products and processes, such as newer car designs or higher-definition television sets. Additionally, research is directed towards newer and more efficient ways of waging war (defence and space research) or controlling the population (much applied social science). In neither case can we discern a new social principle at work, such as would signal the coming of a new social order.

In recent years, largely under the stimulus of the writings of Ivan Illich and E.F. Schumacher, a new concept of postindustrialism has grown. In many ways this harks back to the original usage of the term by Penty. It picks out the features of modern society that genuinely suggest a movement *beyond* industrialism, rather than, as with Bell, a continuation of it. Although nostalgia for preindustrial life plays some part in this reformulation, the more serious thinkers look to the most advanced sectors of modern technology and organization to supply the building-blocks of the new society. They are especially impressed by the capacity of modern technology to abolish work: work, that is, as paid employment. Left to itself, this process can take the disastrous shape of mass unemployment and a reversion to the social conflicts of the 1930s. But they see also an opportunity that can be seized, given the political will. Work in the highly rationalized formal economy can be reduced to a minimum and shared out equally. From the wages for such work, together with some form of minimum-income guarantee, we can purchase the 'appropriate' or 'intermediate' technology needed to deliver a good deal of the goods and services we require. Work can largely be organized in the informal economy around a revived local domestic or communal economy. If such a future society contains in it the elements of a preindustrial way of life, reversing some of the tendencies towards centralization and large-scale bureaucratic organization inherent in industrialism, it is no less postindustrial for that.

In the 1980s Daniel Bell returned to the theme of the postindustrial society, which he now more firmly identified as 'the information society'. Under this banner the concept has been given a new lease of life, as witnessed by a flourishing literature on the subject. Many of the changes discussed by Bell have now also been incorporated in theories of 'postmodernity'.

KRISHAN KUMAR
UNIVERSITY OF VIRGINIA

Further reading

Frankel, B. (1987) *The Post-Industrial Utopians*, Cambridge.
Kumar, K. (1995) *From Post-Industrial to Post-Modern Society*, Oxford.
Rose, M.A. (1991) *The Post-Modern and the Post-Industrial*, Cambridge.
Webster, F. (1995) *Theories of the Information Society*, London.

SEE ALSO: futurology; information society

POSTMODERNISM

The term 'postmodernism' (and 'postmodern') has been used variably to refer to what are interpreted as major changes in the way the contemporary world can and ought to be represented. The term, introduced from architecture and art criticism, which then passed into philosophy and literary studies, has now become something of a commonplace in the social sciences. In architecture, where it first gained currency, postmodernism referred to an active break with the principal tenets of modern architecture and the emergence of new combinations of older styles, the return of concrete as opposed to abstract forms, the active use of kitsch and pastiche. In a renowned programmatic statement, the French philosopher J.-F. Lyotard (1984 [1979]) announced the demise of the great paradigm of scientific rationality and the return of multiple wisdoms, cultures, a relativism of knowledges. Richard Rorty (1980), another early representative of philosophical postmodernism, stressed the impossibility of scientific models of progress and argued for 'edifying conversation' among paradigms rather than cumulative development. The early discussion in the social sciences was very much intertwined with the more general philosophical discussions and was especially focused on Habermas's (1981) critique of Lyotard, Bell (1973) and others, and the ensuing debate between proponents of postmodernism versus modernism. For Habermas (1987), postmodernism was a dangerously conservative rejection of the incomplete modern project, a capitulation to the apparent failure of the emancipatory content of that project. For Lyotard (1984 [1979]) it was a liberation from the straitjacket of rationalist purity of the master discourses of a totalitarian modernity.

The onslaught on hegemonic discourses has occurred across the whole of the social fabric. In anthropology, 'ethnographic authority' came under attack in the 1980s and was to be replaced by more dialogical approaches (Clifford 1988). More extreme, perhaps more consistent, versions of the attack on anthropological authority (Tyler 1990) questioned the very adequacy of written language to represent 'the other'. The attack on general scientific paradigms has been a central issue in sociology and other social sciences, but it has remained more varied and perhaps more general than in anthropology, where the question of authority and voice are central methodological issues. In sociology, especially cultural sociology, the issue of postmodernism has come increasingly to focus on a characterization of contemporary Western societies, i.e. 'the postmodern condition'. This is evident in work by Lash and Urry (1987), Mingione (1991), Vattimo (1987), Baudrillard (1970, 1972, 1978), Featherstone (1991), and others whose approaches are often quite opposed to one another in spite of rather strong similarities with regard to the nature of the conditions they describe. Literary theorists and the growing field of cultural studies have had a significant place in many of these discussions (e.g. Jameson 1991). Numerous sets of oppositions have been used to characterize the difference between postmodernism and modernism. Among the most common are the following:

Modernism	Postmodernism
scientific knowledge	wisdom (cultural knowledge)
grand theory	relative cultural corpuses
universalism	particularism
monovocality	polyvocality
symbolic meaning	simulacra
coherence	pastiche
holism	fragmentation
history	histories
rational ego	libidinal self
intellectual	tactile

We should distinguish between the terms postmodern and postmodernism. The former might be said to refer to a social and cultural condition, whereas the latter refers to a mode of thought, strategy or style. Very much of the discussion during the 1980s concerned the pros and cons of postmodernism as an intellectual position. Subsequently the discussion moved towards an attempt at interpreting the social conditions themselves. There are numerous interpretations of the 'postmodern condition'. For some it is an aspect of what Bell (1973) referred to as postindustrialization, the movement from mass industrial towards information-based technology and the emergence of an information society in which control of communication was to become central. For Bell (1976) the postmodern is a product of modernism itself, the effect of the destruction of meaning, of morality, of authoritative structures, leading ultimately to 'pornotopia'. Baudrillard's interpretation of the advent of information technology argues that symbolic meaning is disappearing, being replaced by a plethora of floating signifiers where the social is reduced to simulacra. The latter interpretation represents a world devoid of meaning in which there is little hope in the future, whereas for other approaches (e.g. Lyotard) the postmodern is the advent of a non-hegemonic political and intellectual strategy. It is not always easy to separate political identity from analysis in the discussions of the postmodern. Advocates of postmodernism have openly attacked modernism as a hegemonic discourse, a structure of control and domination in which discipline was instated by way of rationality itself. For Jameson (1991) and others, postmodernism is characterized, instead, as the 'cultural logic of late capitalism', a dissolution of modernism related to the breakdown of meaning structures, itself a product of disintegration of the modern 'Oedipal' self with a centre of authority and capable of symbolic practice. The result resembles Baudrillard's vision of superficiality and pastiche, but the explanation is explicitly Marxist, as opposed to the former's use of notions of consumer society and information society. Attempts to come to grips with the social transformations underlying the apparent decline of modernity are represented by Lash and Urry (1987) and Harvey (1990). For Lash and Urry (1987) the decline of modernity is part of a general process of disorganization of capitalism, a fragmentation of formerly hierarchical processes leading to various forms of social disorder, and a demand for flexibility. For Harvey (1990) the major process involved is the time–space compression produced by an increasingly rapid process of capitalist reproduction on a global scale. Vattimo (1987), in another important analysis of the degeneration of modernity, has tried to link postmodernism to the decline of Western hegemony and the emergence of multiple political voices in the centre itself. This interpretation is very close to Friedman's view of postmodernity as a label for the cultural aspect of the decline of hegemony itself, the fragmentation of a formerly homogeneous/ranked universe, both social and representational (Friedman 1988, 1992, 1994).

It could be argued that what is often designated as postmodernism is an aspect of the fragmentation of the global system. Here there is a link between the decentralization of capital accumulation, the decline of Western hegemony, the decline of modernism as a strategic identity of self-development, and the emergence of multivocality, multiculturalism and of indigenous, Fourth World movements. There is an interesting parallel among different sets of fragmentations: the fragmentation of knowledge into separate relative fields, the disintegration of the evolutionary scheme of social types into a plethora of different cultures that have been interpreted as incommensurable with respect to one another, the real 'ethnification' of the nation-state, both as a result of regionalization and immigration, the apparent rise of so-called narcissistic disorders that might be indicative of the dissolution of individual ego structures. The individual is also subject to changes in conditions of existence that in their turn alter practices of identification and meaning construal. This is the key to understanding the relation between economic and social processes, and cultural phenomena characteristic of postmodernity.

Postmodernism has had special significance for anthropology. This can be accounted for in terms of the special place of anthropology in Western identity and its various discourses. Anthropology is that field which represents 'the others' of the world to the centre. These others have been part and parcel of our identification of the world and thus our self-identity. Whether evolutionist or relativist, anthropology has provided a scheme within which we could place ourselves. This was largely dependent upon the ability to represent the populations of the periphery in unproblematic terms. The attack on ethnographic authority began to undermine the capacity to represent. The anthropologist could no longer 'read' or

simply represent in any other way. This hierarchical practice would have to be replaced by a more sensitive relation to our 'object', so that instead of translating 'them' into a homogeneous text we would have a multivocal representation of their reality. In numerous collections of articles (Clifford and Marcus 1986; Marcus and Fisher 1986), the question of authority, voice and text were discussed at length. While the initial work was very much self-centred on problems of the ethnographer it is also the case that Clifford, and later Marcus, were aware of the larger context of the shift from a homogeneous/neatly ranked and hegemonic world order to a situation of increasing fragmentation. Marcus explicitly speaks of the need to grasp the ethnographic realities of the world-system, and it is clear that the purely methodological critiques of representativity in ethnography are critical for the field today. The re-evaluation of ethnographic method, especially as applied to contemporary heterogenous and multilayered realities, may not have been the goal of postmodernist critiques, but it may prove to be their major contribution. The analysis of the contemporary world in anthropological terms has not, however, played a salient role in these discussions. Oblique reference to the decline of the colonial power structures is mere background material for the focus on voice and text that so preoccupies anthropologists of the postmodern. To the extent that anthropologists have begun to study the postmodern world rather than concentrating on postmodernist implications for method and questions of representation, they have taken to analysing various aspects of the changing global situation: the formation of diaspora cultures and multicultural contexts, the politics of identity, processes of social disintegration, 'balkanization', changing forms of consumption, etc. These studies might not have anything in particular to do with postmodernity as such. But in their concern with understanding contemporary situations in global terms and with doing ethnography that is concrete and multivocal, as is required by studies geared to revealing the complexity of these situations, they can be said to be contributing to an anthropology of the postmodern situation. There is thus a certain convergence here in the social sciences: an anthropology increasingly focused on the disjointed present, a sociology focusing on the social conditions involved in what appears to be a decline or at least radical transformation of modernity, a political science focused increasingly on aspects of multi-culturalism, problems of democracy in the Second and Third Worlds, and the relation between culture and power (Apter 1993; Bayart 1993 [1989]; Young 1993). It is likely that this orientation to an understanding of a world undergoing vastly changing power relations and their cultural consequences shall eventually replace or fill in the categories that are currently referred to as postmodernity and postmodernism.

JONATHAN FRIEDMAN
ECOLE DES HAUTES ETUDES
EN SCIENCES SOCIALES, PARIS

References

Apter, A. (1993) *Democracy, Violence and Emancipatory Movements: Notes for a Theory of Inversionary Discourse*, Geneva.
Baudrillard, J. (1983 [1978]) *In the Shadow of the Silent Majorities*, New York.
—— (1998 [1970]) *The Consumer Society: Myths and Structures*, London.
Baudrillard, J. and Levin, C. (1981 [1972]) *For a Critique of the Political Economy of the Sign*, New York.
Bayart, F. (1993 [1989]) *The State in Africa: The Politics of the Belly*, New York.
Bell, D. (1973) *The Coming of Post-Industrial Society*, New York.
—— (1976) *The Cultural Contradictions of Capitalism*, London.
Clifford, J. (1988) *The Predicament of Culture: Twentieth Century Ethnography*, Cambridge, MA.
Clifford, J. and Marcus, G. (eds) (1986) *Writing Culture: The Poetics and Politics of Ethnography*, Berkeley, CA.
Featherstone, M. (1991) *Consumer Culture and Postmodernism*, London.
Friedman, J. (1988) 'Cultural logics of the global system', *Theory, Culture and Society* 5(2–3).
—— (1992) 'Narcissism, roots and postmodernity', in S. Lash and J. Friedman (eds) *Modernity and Identity*, Oxford.
—— (1994) *Cultural Identity and Global Process*, London.
Habermas, J. (1981) 'Modernity versus postmodernity', *New German Critique* 22.
—— (1987) *The Philosophical Discourses of Modernity*, Cambridge, MA.
Harvey, D. (1990) *The Condition of Postmodernity*, Oxford.
Jameson, F. (1991) *Postmodernism, or the Cultural Logic of Late Capitalism*, London.
Lash, S. and Urry, J. (1987) *The End of Organized Capitalism*, Oxford.
Lyotard, J.-F. (1984 [1979]) *The Postmodern Condition: A Report on Knowledge*, Minneapolis, MN.
Marcus, G. and Fisher, M. (1986) *Anthropology as Cultural Critique: An Experimental Movement in the Social Sciences*, Chicago.
Mingione, E. (1991) *Fragmented Societies*, Oxford.
Rorty, R. (1980) *Philosophy and the Mirror of Nature*, Oxford.
Tyler, S. (1990) *The Unspeakable: Discourse, Dialogue and Rhetoric in the Postmodern World*, Madison, WI.
Vattimo, G. (1987) *La Fin de la modernité: nihilisme et herméneutique dans la culture postmoderne*, Paris.
Young, C. (ed.) (1993) *The Rising Tide of Cultural Pluralism: The Nation State at Bay?* Madison, WI.

SEE ALSO: globalization; Habermas; information society; postindustrial society; poststructuralism

POSTSTRUCTURALISM

Poststructuralism inherits from structuralism the conviction that our knowledge of ourselves and the world is the effect of structures that are not obvious or even perceptible to us. But it breaks with structuralism's assumption that these structures are both universal and binary, insisting on *difference* as the key to such understanding as is available.

Poststructuralism begins from an account of meaning. On the basis that the distinctions it is possible to make in one language do not always find precise equivalents in another, the work of Ferdinand de Saussure indicated that meaning was not the origin of language, but its effect (1974 [1916]). Meaning is not given either in the world or in our heads, but is produced by the differences between signifiers (words and phrases, or their symbolic analogues, visual, logical, mathematical or scientific). The implication is that we have no access to free-standing concepts, pure intelligibility or foundational, metaphysical truths. On the contrary, what we know exists in its inscription, as a result of the signifying differences we learn in culture. Language is thus not transparent to a fact or an idea, understood as having an independent existence behind or beyond it, and knowledges are in consequence culturally and historically relative. This should not, of course, be taken to imply that the world does not exist, but only that it does not determine what we (think we) know about it.

The structuralist anthropology of Claude Lévi-Strauss, in quest of the universal values linking diverse cultures, shared a tendency of Western thought to cement difference as opposition between antithetical alternatives (1966 [1962]). On the basis that binary oppositions are seductive, but ultimately reductionist, and drawing on Saussure's account of meaning, poststructuralism reinscribes difference as the critical term. Jacques Derrida's *Of Grammatology* (1997 [1967]) still stands as the classic poststructuralist analysis of the impossibility of foundationalism and the unsustainable character of binary oppositions. There Derrida demonstrated the inevitable intrusion of the defining opposite into the self-same. If with Saussure we understand a meaning by reference to its differentiating other, the trace of that alterity necessarily enters into our understanding of the meaning itself. He included in his analysis Lévi-Strauss's own inadvertent ethnocentrism, displayed in the idealization of the tribal innocence that the anthropologist opposed directly to Western corruption. *Of Grammatology* also draws attention to Saussure's phonocentrism, his reproduction, in spite of himself, of the traditional privilege accorded to speech, conventionally treated as pure, immediate and direct, in contrast to writing, which is commonly regarded as secondary, fallen. Derrida shows that neither Lévi-Strauss nor Saussure manages to sustain the purity each attributes to the privileged term of the antithesis.

Opinion varies on whether it is legitimate to classify as poststructuralist other influential figures who constituted Derrida's immediate context, including Roland Barthes, Jacques Lacan, Louis Althusser and Michel Foucault. The conclusion we reach on this issue probably depends on the features of their work we choose to emphasize.

Roland Barthes, for instance, began as a structuralist literary critic, but registered increasing unease about the irony that Saussure's theory of meaning as differential had been appropriated on behalf of a quest for universal patterns. His *Mythologies* (1993 [1957]) acknowledged in its title the eminence of Lévi-Strauss as the structuralist mythographer of the day, but repudiated the concept of universality, wittily unveiling the cultural specificity of our own Western myths, where history masquerades as timeless nature and the changeable human being is misrepresented as 'Eternal Man'. In *S/Z* (1975 [1970]), silently registering Derrida's intervention, Barthes parodied structuralist criticism, subjecting a short story to detailed analysis in the light of five codes designed to comprehend its meaning. The textual analysis repeatedly gives way, however, to apparently anarchic digressions, isolated on the page and independently numbered. These interpolations offer wide-ranging reflections prompted by the text but are quite unable to be contained within the self-imposed restriction of the codes.

Lacan reread Freud for a post-Saussurean generation, arguing in his *Écrits* (1977 [1967]), as well as a succession of annual seminars from 1953–4 onwards (and still in the process of publication), that the unconscious was best understood in terms of an absent imperative, refused admission into language and culture. The existence of this other motivating force, independent of the conscious mind and often in conflict with it, has the effect of differentiating human beings from themselves. In so far as we are not what we believe ourselves to be, and are driven by desires for which we have no name, our self-image as subjects in possession of the objects of our knowledge, or in quest of the objects of our conscious wishes, is always and inevitably a misrecognition.

Althusser, meanwhile, reread Marx in the light of both Saussure and Lacan to differentiate between the levels that interact in the social formation. Althusser's Marxism plays down the economic determinism of previous accounts. Instead, politics, on the one hand, and ideology, on the other, also exert their own pressures from a position of 'relative autonomy', and may even conflict with the economy and with each other (1969 [1965]). His account of ideology stresses its unconscious character: what we think we know, the 'obvious', is ideologically constructed and historically produced. Ideology has the effect of constituting subjects who misrecognize their place in the process of production and 'work by themselves' to further its interests, mistakenly regarded as their own (1971).

Foucault, conversely, developed a history of knowledge-as-power that took direct issue with Marxism. If there is a poststructuralist element in his work, it resides above all in the differential account of history as crucially discontinuous. What might be read as progress or increasing liberalization is reinterpreted as a series of refinements of power that have, Foucault argues, the effect of subjecting us still further to disciplines that mask the power relations they construct.

Calling into question, as it does, the sovereignty of the human subject as the origin of meaning and history, poststructuralism is easily misread as a form of determinism. If we are not absolutely self-defining and self-determining, so the argument goes, we must be incapable of agency. But poststructuralism characteristically deconstructs such binary oppositions: in practice, the stress on difference always presents the subject with alternative perspectives, knowledges and political options. Moreover, poststructuralists commonly align themselves with resistance to oppression. Lacan argues that psychoanalytic health depends on the pursuit of unconscious desire (if only we could identify it), in defiance of the conventional ethics imposed by the tyrannical demands of civilization (1992 [1959]); Althusser takes for granted a framework of class struggle and the possibility of a heroic refusal to obey the ruling ideology; Foucault's protagonists are a succession of criminals, suicides and sexual misfits who resist their own subjection (1977 [1975], 1979 [1976]).

The term 'resistance' in postwar French culture carries the full force of the underground struggle against the German occupation. This was a generation that had seen at first hand the consequences of illegitimate power, and the difficulty, as well as the necessity, of opposing it. At the same time, these poststructuralists were also motivated to find ways of accounting for French wartime collaboration, and, beyond that, for the susceptibility of civilized Germany to genocidal values.

In view of its emphasis on resistance, poststructuralism was not incompatible with contemporary political movements in the 1960s and 1970s. Derrida has written sympathetically of feminism (1979 [1976], 1982) and anti-racism (1998 [1996]). Foucault famously distinguished between homoerotic practices and the construction of the homosexual as a perverse personality. This identification, he argued, took place in the eighteenth century, and thus belonged to history and culture, not nature (1979 [1976]). The politics of difference promotes sexual and racial diversity.

Poststructuralist analysis has repercussions in Jean-François Lyotard's postmodern emphasis on dissension as the motor of thought (1984 [1979]), as well as his account of the differend, an incommensurability between positions that means no shared framework is available to resolve the differences between them. The differend implies a politics of struggle for a justice that cannot be definitively identified or attained (1988 [1983]). Ironically, Lyotard's work also

reverts (with a difference, of course) to the starting-point of poststructuralism in its emphasis on social interaction as ultimately a matter of language. To speak, he insists, is to fight, even when our opponent is no more than the language itself (1984 [1979]).

CATHERINE BELSEY
CARDIFF UNIVERSITY

References

Althusser, L. (1969 [1965]) *For Marx*, Harmondsworth.
—— (1971) *Lenin and Philosophy and Other Essays*, London.
Barthes, R. (1975 [1970]) *S/Z*, London.
—— (1993 [1957]) *Mythologies*, London.
Derrida, J. (1979 [1976]) *Spurs: Nietzsche's Styles*, Chicago.
—— (1982) 'Choreographies', *Diacritics* 12: 66–76.
—— (1997 [1967]) *Of Grammatology*, Baltimore, MD.
—— (1998 [1996]) *Monolingualism of the Other, or, the Prosthesis of Origin*, Stanford, CA.
Foucault, M. (1977 [1975]) *Discipline and Punish*, Harmondsworth.
—— (1979 [1976]) *The History of Sexuality, Volume 1*, London.
Lacan, J. (1977 [1967]) *Écrits*, London.
—— (1992 [1959]) *The Ethics of Psychoanalysis*, London.
Lévi-Strauss, C. (1966 [1962]) *The Savage Mind*, London.
Lyotard, J.-F. (1984 [1979]) *The Postmodern Condition: A Report on Knowledge*, Minneapolis, MN.
—— (1988 [1983]) *The Differend: Phrases in Dispute*, Minneapolis, MN.
Saussure, F. de (1974 [1916]) *Course in General Linguistics*, London.

SEE ALSO: Derrida; Foucault; Lacan; Lévi-Strauss; Saussure; structuralism

POVERTY

When people lack or are denied the income and other resources, including the use of assets and receipt of goods and services in kind equivalent to income, to obtain the conditions of life – that is, the diets, material goods, amenities, standards and services – to enable them to play the roles, participate in the relationships and follow the customary behaviour that is expected of them by virtue of their membership of society they can be said to be in poverty. They are deprived because of their poverty. The key to understanding is the definition and measurement of the two variables that can be shown to be closely related – 'income' and 'deprivation'. The determination of a poverty line cannot be justified merely by the arbitrary selection of a low level or percentage of average or median income. Only scientific criteria independent of income can justify where the poverty line should be drawn. The multiplicity and severity of different types of deprivation can constitute those criteria. The aim of investigation is therefore to define a threshold of income below which people are found to be increasingly deprived. The two measures are not easily decided. The relevant measure of 'income' should include the value of assets and income in kind that can be treated as equivalent to income – 'resources' sometimes being used to denote this wider interpretation. Second, the measure of multiple deprivation must be decided from evidence about each and every sphere of human activity – again not being arbitrarily chosen spheres – at work where the means largely determining position in several spheres of activity are earned; at home, in neighbourhood and family; in travel, and in a range of social and individual activities outside work and home or neighbourhood in performing a variety of roles in fulfilment of social obligations. The degree of material and social deprivation relative to income is the 'relative deprivation' method of ascertaining the threshold of income for households of different composition ordinarily required to surmount poverty so that conclusions can be reached about trends in poverty in and across different countries (Townsend 1979: 31; 1993: 33–6). In the twenty-first century this approach can allow a scientific and international consensus to be finally reached about the concept and its uses.

There are historical antecedents that have to be traced and qualifications that have to be made in reaching the conclusion above. The understanding and relief of poverty has been a major preoccupation of human beings for many centuries. In England various laws to regulate and maintain the poor were enacted before the time of Elizabeth I (Lambarde 1579) and the first recorded body of 'Commissioners for the Poor' started work in 1630 (HM 1630). Attempts were made both to assess conditions throughout England and to trace corresponding conditions across Europe (see for example Eden 1797; Himmelfarb 1984; and Woolf 1987). In the late eighteenth century, governments and ruling groups grudgingly came to feel obliged to define the needs of the poor in relation to the income of the poor. In Britain and much of Europe those in charge of small areas like parishes developed forms of indoor and outdoor relief for the poor long before the Industrial Revolution. Economies newly based on manufacturing industry and a wage system posed new problems of estimating and regulating the amounts to be received by the poor outside as well as inside Poor Law institutions. The costs of maintaining institutions and their inmates had given concern to ruling groups and in the formulation of a new scheme to manage the poor from 1834 in Britain. The principle of 'less eligibility' played a crucial part in the thinking both of politicians and those undertaking scientific enquiries.

> The first and most essential of all conditions, a principle which we find universally admitted, even by those whose practice is at variance with it, is, that [the pauper's] situation on the whole shall not be made really or apparently so eligible as the situation of the independent labourer of the lowest class.
>
> (Report from His Majesty's Commissioners 1834: 228)

The rate-payers wanted the costs of maintaining the able-bodied and non-able-bodied poor to be kept as low as possible. Those in charge of the economy and many employers wanted the poor to be prepared to accept the lowest wage rates on offer. The history of poverty has not been one of dispassionate search for the precise amount of resources required to surmount deprived conditions of life but one of continuing struggle between dispassionate investigation and the prejudiced certainties of those who have accumulated valuable fixed interests. Compromises were reached both about necessary income and the extent of appropriate investigation. Sometimes limited relief was provided in bread and other benefits in kind, and sometimes in cash, or a mixture of cash and bread, especially for the non-institutionalized poor. Need, and therefore the benefits to meet need, depended on perceptions of how many of the poor were 'deserving'. But with the Enlightenment and the evolution of the modern industrial state there were demands for the rationalization of the methods and amounts of relief that were customary.

For such reasons governments and administrators became concerned to define the minimum needs of institutional inmates and of the able-bodied poor outside institutions. They sought justification for their decisions from independent scientific enquiries. The early work of nutritionists in Germany, the USA and Britain was addressed to such questions. In Germany, for example, there was the work of Kuczynski and Zuntz (see Leibfried 1982; and see also Hoffmann and Leibfried 1980; and Leibfried and Tennstedt 1985). In the USA historical work by Aronson (1984) also revealed the powerful influence of such early nutritionists. The scale and variety of nutrients to maintain life became an important area of public enquiry. A new stage of relatively scientific work on poverty had arrived.

From the 1880s to the present day three alternative conceptions of poverty evolved as a basis for international and comparative work. They depended principally on the ideas of subsistence, basic needs and relative deprivation. In Britain the 'subsistence' standard developed in two stages, first in conjunction with the work of nutritionists by means of surveys carried out by entrepreneurs like Rowntree (1901 and 1918) and then in the war years 1939–45 by means of a report on social security drawn up by Sir William, later Lord, Beveridge (Beveridge Report 1942). Formerly, under the old Poor Laws, the needs of the poor had been measured in terms of quantities of bread or bread-flour or the cash equivalent, and in some parishes allowances for the addition of other necessities had become common practice (see Report from His Majesty's Commissioners 1834: 22). Now, as a result of work prompted by the nutritionists, families were defined to be in poverty when their incomes were not 'sufficient to obtain the minimum necessaries for the maintenance of merely physical efficiency' (Rowntree 1901: 86). A family was treated as being in poverty if its income minus rent fell short of the poverty line. Although allowance was made in the income for clothing, fuel and some other items this allowance was very small and food accounted for much the greatest share of subsistence.

The investigations of Rowntree, Bowley and others during the 1890s and the early decades of the twentieth century influenced scientific practice and international and national policies for the rest of the century. Examples are the statistical measures adopted to describe social conditions, at first within individual countries but later with wide application by international agencies like the World Bank. Beveridge's particular interpretation of 'subsistence' was carried over into the postwar years after 1945 as a means of justifying the low rates of national assistance and national insurance that were then adopted. The idea of subsistence was freely exported to member states of the former British Empire. Thus, the wages of blacks in South Africa were partly legitimated by the 'poverty datum line' (Pillay 1973; Maasdorp and Humphreys 1975). In framing development plans, former colonized territories like India and Malaysia drew heavily on the subsistence conceptualization (India 1978; Malaysia 1986). In the USA 'subsistence' remains the linchpin, even if today elaborately formulated, of the Government's measures of poverty (US Department of Health, Education and Welfare 1976; Fisher 1998; Citro and Michael 1995).

The use of 'subsistence' to define poverty came to be heavily criticized (Rein 1970; Townsend 1979). The chief criticism was that within that approach human needs are interpreted as being predominantly physical needs – that is, for food, shelter and clothing – rather than as social needs. On the contrary, it was argued, people are not simply individual organisms requiring replacement of sources of physical energy. They are social beings expected to perform socially demanding roles as workers, citizens, parents, partners, neighbours and friends (Lister 1990). Moreover, they are not simply consumers of physical goods but producers of those goods and are also expected to act out different roles in their various social associations. They are dependent on collectively provided utilities and facilities. These needs apply universally and not merely in the rich industrial societies. But physical needs also turn out upon examination to be subject to rapid change because of changes in patterns of activity and production and consumption. They are not, after all, fixed or unvarying. Even the amount and kind as well as the cost of the food that is eaten depends on the roles people play and the dietary customs they observe socially. So, in the final analysis, material needs turn out to be socially determined in different ways.

By the 1970s a second formulation – of 'basic needs' – began to exert wide influence. Basic needs were said to include two elements: first, certain minimum requirements of a family for private consumption (adequate food, shelter and clothing, as well as certain household furniture and equipment); and, second, essential services provided by and for the community at large, such as safe drinking water, sanitation, public transport and health, education and cultural facilities (ILO 1976: 24–5; and see also ILO 1977). Particularly in rural areas, basic needs were also extended to land, agricultural tools and access to farming.

The concept of 'basic needs' played a prominent part in a succession of national plans fostered by the big powers and by international agencies (see, for example, Ghai *et al*. 1977 and 1979) and in international reports (see, for example, UNESCO 1978; and Brandt 1980). Evidently the term is an extension of the subsistence concept. In addition to material needs for individual physical survival and efficiency are the facilities and services (for health care, sanitation and education) required by local communities and populations as a whole.

The attractions of the 'subsistence' concept included its limited scope and therefore limited implications for policy and political action. It seemed easier to restrict the meaning of poverty to material and physical needs than also to the non-fulfilment of social roles, given the overriding emphasis on individualism within the revival of neo-classical economics and liberal-pluralism. The attraction of the 'basic needs' concept, on the other hand, has been the emphasis on establishing at least some of the preconditions for community survival and prosperity in all countries. However, the more that social aspects of needs come to be acknowledged, the more it becomes necessary to accept the relativity of need to the world's as well as to national resources, because as time passes these are increasingly found to be under the control of transnational companies and international agencies. The more the concept of poverty is restricted to physical goods and facilities the easier it is to argue that the growth of material wealth nationally is enough to deal with the phenomenon, and that a complex combination of growth, redistribution and reorganization of trading and other institutional relationships, and the reconstitution of traditional with new social associations, is unnecessary.

In the late twentieth century social scientists turned, for such reasons, to a third, more comprehensive and rigorous, social formulation of the meaning of poverty: that of relative deprivation (Townsend 1979, 1985 and 1993;

Chow 1982; Bokor 1984; Mack and Lansley 1984; Ferge and Miller 1987; Desai and Shah 1988; Luttgens and Perelman 1988; Saunders and Whiteford 1989; Lister 1991; Scott 1994; Nolan and Whelan 1996; Øyen *et al*. 1996). Some of the authors of this research came to appreciate that people's subjective reports on their conditions and experiences correlated reasonably well with painstaking objective observation, and offered a short-cut, which was nonetheless reliable, to those methods of research, which were undoubtedly expensive and time-consuming (see especially Gordon *et al*. 2000). Although 'subjective' and 'objective' poverty are of course distinct in principle they overlap in detailed exposition. Methods of enquiry often assume a continuum between the two and points on that continuum can be chosen for particular scrutiny and the extraction of information.

'Relativity' applies to both resources and to material and social conditions. Societies are passing through such rapid change that a poverty standard devised at some historical date in the past is difficult to justify in new conditions. People living in the present are not subject to the laws and obligations as well as customs that applied to a previous era. Globalization is remorselessly interrelating peoples and their standards of living at the same time as inequalities are growing in most countries. There are, therefore, major objections to merely updating any historical benchmark of poverty by some index of prices. Over many years the 'relativity' of meanings of poverty has been recognized in part if not comprehensively. Adam Smith, for example, recognized the ways in which 'necessities' were defined by custom in the early part of the nineteenth century. He gave an instance of the labourer's need to wear a shirt (Smith 1776).

Neither is it enough to describe poverty as a condition applying to those whose disposable income is low relative to others. This is to fail to distinguish conceptually between inequality and poverty. Poverty may best be understood as applying not just to those who are victims of a maldistribution of resources but, more exactly, to those whose resources do not allow them to fulfil the elaborate social demands and customs that are placed upon citizens of that society in the first place. This is a criterion that lends itself to scientific observation of deprivation, measurement and analysis.

The driving motivation for putting forward poverty as 'relative deprivation' could be said to be scientific and international. There are respects in which the 'subsistence' concept minimizes the range and depth of human need just as the 'basic needs' concept is restricted primarily to the physical facilities of the communities of the Third World. As with any formulation, there are problems in defining poverty operationally. Under the 'relative deprivation' approach a threshold of income is conceived, according to size and type of family, below which withdrawal or exclusion from active membership of society becomes disproportionately accentuated. Whether that threshold exists depends on the scientific evidence that can be marshalled on its behalf and whether sociological and economic approaches may be reconciled (for an introduction to the controversy see Townsend 1979: Ch. 6; Desai and Shah 1988; Desai 1986; Sen 1983 and 1985; Townsend 1985 and 1993: Ch. 6). Reconciliation is some distance away. In 2003 calls were made for a new conceptual advance. Despite the influence of Sen's contributions to development studies for two decades his ideas on capabilities had 'not penetrated into the mainstream of poverty analysis among economists' (Kanbur 2003). There are forms of impoverishment, for example through social exclusion, when individual capabilities to overcome poverty are not at issue. Those capabilities are also identified as originating within the individual rather than with groups or nations collectively or determined externally. Capabilities are also different from perceptions. Perceptions offer a valuable correction sometimes to independent investigation and analysis of behaviour and living conditions.

While subjective judgements and reports by cross-sections of population may offer a short-cut to representative calculations about poverty (for example Gordon *et al.* 2000; Nolan and Whelan 1996; Mack and Lansley 1984), elaborate objective observation of behaviour and material and social conditions remains the necessary and fundamental task. Detailed and comprehensive scientific observation can demonstrate both the extent and severity of non-participation among those with low incomes and meagre other resources, because people lead different roles during their lives and may have complex patterns of association.

Attempts by the international financial organi-zations, such as the World Bank and the International Monetary Fund, and also by regional associations, like the European Union, to define poverty operationally have turned out to be short-term expedients rather than of continuing value. Thus the World Bank adopted a rule of thumb measure of $370 per year per person at 1985 prices (the 'dollar a day' poverty line) for all the poorest developing countries. This was temporarily convenient as a crude indicator but was not subsequently converted either into the measure said to be necessary by the Bank in 1990, nor into the kind of measure that is fully cross-national and hence scientifically reliable (Townsend and Gordon 2002: 358–64).

A consensus on approaches to poverty was in fact reached after the Copenhagen World Summit for Social Development in 1995 in the 'Declaration and Programme for Action' signed by 117 countries (UN 1995). In planning to defeat poverty governments agreed to issue frequent reports on the extent of poverty in their own territories to be based on measures of both 'absolute' and 'overall' poverty. This has the potentiality to cut through the problem created by the current pursuit of different regional measures of poverty and act as a bridge for comparable investigations in countries at different levels of development. This will provide genuine measures of the scale of extreme and overall poverty in the world and of the success or failure of different policies in alleviating poverty. Consistency of meaning across all societies has become the top scientific issue of the twenty-first century. Reports on poverty in poor countries during the late twentieth century were more critical, and theoretically more convincing and radical, than those about poverty in rich countries. Ideological self-deception about the absence of poverty was a marked feature of a number of rich societies after 1939–45. But the process of social polarization in most countries in combination with globalization suggests that the supposed absence or extremely small extent of poverty in a number of those countries had been a convenient illusion that could be maintained no longer. The tendency to restrict meanings of poverty to particular regions of the world has undermined the power of the concept. Divergencies of meaning have produced, or reflected, divergencies in the methodologies of measurement, modes of explanation and strategies of amelioration. As new work on child poverty has shown, empirical data for all countries can now be marshalled consistently in relation to multiple forms of material and social deprivation (Gordon et al. 2000).

PETER TOWNSEND
LONDON SCHOOL OF ECONOMICS
AND POLITICAL SCIENCE

References

Aronson, N. (1984) *The Making of the US Bureau of Labor Statistics Family Budget Series: Relativism and the Rhetoric of Subsistence*, Evanston, IL.

Beveridge Report (1942) *Social Insurance and Allied Services*, London.

Bokor, A. (1984) 'Deprivation; dimensions and indices', in R. Andor and T. Kolosi (eds) *Stratification and Inequality*, Budapest.

Brandt, W. (1980) *North–South: A Programme for Survival*, London.

Chow, N.W.S. (1982) *Poverty in an Affluent City: A Report of a Survey of Low Income Families in Hong Kong*, Hong Kong.

Citro, C.F. and Michael, R.T. (eds) (1995) *Measuring Poverty: A New Approach, Panel on Poverty and Family Assistance*, Washington, DC.

Desai, M. (1986) 'On defining the poverty threshold', in P. Golding (ed.) *Excluding the Poor*, London.

Desai, M. and Shah, A. (1988) *An Econometric Approach to the Measurement of Poverty*, Oxford.

Eden, F.M. (1797) *The State of the Poor: Or an History of the Labouring Classes in England from the Conquest to the Present Period*, 3 vols, London.

Ferge, Z. and Miller, S.M. (eds) (1987) *The Dynamics of Deprivation: A Cross-National Study*, London.

Fisher, G.M. (1998) 'Setting American standards of poverty: A look back', *Focus*, 19(2).

Ghai, D., Godfrey, M. and Lisk, F. (1979) *Planning for Basic Needs in Kenya*, Geneva.

Ghai, D.P., Khan, A.R., Lee, E.L.H. and Alfthan, T. (1977) *The Basic Needs Approach to Development: Some Issues Regarding Concepts and Methodology*, Geneva.

Gordon, D., Adelman, L., Ashworth, K., Bradshaw, J., Levitas, R., Middleton, S., Pantazis, C., Patsios, D., Payne, S., Townsend, P. and Williams, J. (2000) *Poverty and Social Exclusion in Britain*, York.

Himmelfarb, G. (1984) *The Idea of Poverty: England in the Early Industrial Age*, London.

HM (1630) *Orders for the Relief of the Poor*, London.

Hoffmann, A. and Leibfried, S. (1980) *Regularities in the History of Subsistence Scales – 100 Years of Tradition and the Deutscher Verein*, Bremen.

India (1978) *Five Year Plan 1978–83*, Delhi.

International Labour Office (ILO) (1976) *Employment Growth and Basic Needs: A One-World Problem*, Geneva.

—— (1977) *Meeting Basic Needs: Strategies for Eradicating Mass Poverty and Unemployment*, Geneva.

Kanbur, R. (2003) *Conceptual Challenges in Poverty and Inequality: One Development Economist's Perspective*, Helsinki.

Lambarde, W. (1579) *Eirenarchaor of the Office of the Justice of the Peace (Laws Relating to the Poor, Rogues and Vagabonds before the Elizabethan Poor Laws)*, London.

Leibfried, S. (1982) 'Existenzminimum und Fursorge-Richtsatze in der Weimarer Republik', *Jahrbuch der Sozialarbeit* 4.

Leibfried, S. and Tennstedt, F. (eds) (1985) *Regulating Poverty and the Splitting of the German Welfare State*, Frankfurt/Main.

Lister, R. (1990) *The Exclusive Society: Citizenship and the Poor*, London.

—— (1991) 'Concepts of poverty', *Social Studies Review* 6: 192–5.

Luttgens, A. and Perelman, S. (1988) *Comparing Measures of Poverty and Relative Deprivation: An Example for Belgium*, European Society for Population Economics, Mannheim.

Maasdorp, G. and Humphreys, A.S.V. (eds) (1975) *From Shanty Town to Township: An Economic Study of African Poverty and Rehousing in a South African City*, Cape Town.

Mack, J. and Lansley, S. (1984) *Poor Britain*, London.

Malaysia (1986) *Fifth Malaysia Plan 1986–1990*, Kuala Lumpur.

Nolan, B. and Whelan, C.J. (1996) *Resources, Deprivation and Poverty*, Oxford.

Øyen, E., Miller, S.M. and Samad, S.A. (eds) (1996) *Poverty: A Global Review*, Oslo.

Pillay, P.N. (1973) *Poverty Datum Line Study among Africans in Durban*, Katmandu, Nepal.

Rein, M. (1970) 'Problems in the definition and measurement of poverty', in P. Townsend (ed.) *The Concept of Poverty*, London, pp. 46–63.

Report from His Majesty's Commissioners (1834) *Inquiry into the Administration and Practical Operation of the Poor Laws*, London.

Rowntree, B.S. (1901) *Poverty: A Study of Town Life*, London.

—— (1918) *The Human Needs of Labour*, London.

Saunders, P. and Whiteford, P. (1989) *Measuring Poverty: A Review of the Issues*, Canberra.

Scott, J. (1994) *Poverty and Wealth: Citizenship, Deprivation and Privilege*, London.

Sen, A. (1983) 'Poor relatively speaking', *Oxford Economic Papers* 35: 153–69.

—— (1985) 'A reply', *Oxford Economic Papers* 37: 669–76.

Smith, A. (1776) *An Inquiry into the Natural Causes of the Wealth of Nations*, Edinburgh.

Townsend, P. (1979) *Poverty in the United Kingdom*, London.

—— (1985) 'A sociological approach to the measurement of poverty – a rejoinder to Professor Amartya Sen', *Oxford Economic Papers* 37: 659–68.

—— (1993) *The International Analysis of Poverty*, New York.

Townsend, P. and Gordon, D. (2002) *World Poverty: New Policies to Defeat an Old Enemy*, Bristol.

UN (1995) *The Copenhagen Declaration and Programme for Action: The World Summit for Social Development, 6–12 March 1995*, New York.

UNESCO (1978) *Study in Depth on the Concept of Basic Human Needs in Relation to Various Ways of*

Life and Its Possible Implications for the Action of the Organisations, Paris.

US Department of Health, Education and Welfare (1976) *The Measure of Poverty, a Report to Congress as Mandated by the Education Amendments of 1974*, Washington, DC.

Woolf, S. (1987) *The Poor in Western Europe in the Eighteenth and Nineteenth Centuries*, London.

World Bank (1990) *World Development Report 1990: Poverty*, Washington, DC.

Further reading

Atkinson, A. (1989) *Poverty and Social Security*, London.

Drewnowski, J. and Scott, W. (1966) *The Level of Living Index*, Report No. 4, Geneva.

George, V. (1989) *Wealth, Poverty and Starvation*, London.

Gordon, D. and Townsend, P. (eds) (2001) *Breadline Europe: The Measurement of Poverty*, Bristol.

Scott, J. (1994) *Poverty and Wealth: Citizenship, Deprivation and Privilege*, London.

Sen, A. (1988) *Poverty and Famines: An Essay in Entitlement and Deprivation*, London.

SEE ALSO: basic needs; deprivation and relative deprivation; social exclusion; welfare economics

POWER

Definitions of power are numerous. In so far as there is a commonly accepted formulation, power is understood as the ability to bring about intended consequences. Attempts to specify the concept more tightly have been fraught with disagreements, and even this broad-brush characterization is open to objection – theorists who talk of the 'power structure' or 'class power' do not, for the most part, ascribe intentions to such 'agents'.

Within the social sciences, different disciplinary and theoretical interests have led to a variety of approaches to the study of power. Some perspectives emphasize different bases of power (for example wealth, status, knowledge, charisma and authority), different forms of power (such as influence, coercion, manipulation, force and control) and different ends of power (such as individual or community ends, political and economic outcomes, and stable social and political orders). Each approach tends to emphasize different aspects of the concept, according to its theoretical and practical interests. Definitions of power have also been deeply implicated in debates in social and political theory on the essentially conflicting or consensual nature of

social and political order. Further disagreements concern whether power is a zero-sum or positive-sum concept (Mills 1956; Parsons 1960); whether it properly refers to a property of an agent (or system) or to a relationship between agents (or systems) (Arendt 1970; Lukes 1974; Parsons 1963); if it can be a potential or a resource (Barry 1975; Wrong 1979); if it is reflexive or irreflexive, transitive or intransitive (Cartwright 1959); and over whether it can describe only a property of, or relationship between, individual agents, rather than also being used to describe systems, structures or institutions (Lukes 1978; Parsons 1963; Poulantzas 1979; Barry 1975; Dowding 1996). Furthermore, there is disagreement over whether power necessarily rests on coercion (Cartwright 1959) or if it can equally rest on shared values and beliefs (Beetham 1991; Giddens 1977; Arendt 1970; Parsons 1963). It is also unclear how such disputes can be rationally resolved, since it has been argued that power is a theory-dependent term and that there are few, if any, convincing meta-theoretical grounds for resolving disputes between competing theoretical paradigms (Gray 1983; Lukes 1974; Morriss 2002 [1987]).

In the 1950s discussions of power were dominated by the conflicting perspectives offered by power elite theories, which stressed power as a form of domination exercised by one group over another against a background of a fundamental conflicts of interests (Mills 1956; Weber 1978 [1922]), and structural-functionalism, which saw power as the 'generalized capacity of a social system to get things done in the interests of collective goals' (Parsons 1960). Where Parsons emphasized power as a systems property, as a capacity to achieve ends, Mills viewed power as a relationship in which one side prevailed over the other, establishing systematic patterns of domination. Parsons understands power as the capacity to secure outcomes, and he emphasizes in particular the capacity to mobilize collective commitments as a means of achieving collective ends. Different systems have different amounts of power – different capacities to secure their ends – because they are differentially able to mobilize the commitments and values of their members in the pursuit of collective goals. This 'power to (achieve outcomes)' or 'outcome power' need not be concerned with collective commitments – there is no reason why individuals cannot have this form of power – but for both Arendt and

Parsons the more theoretically interesting political questions concern ways in which collectivities can be mobilized and harnessed to collective values. This structural-functionalist perspective has been further developed in the work of the German sociologist Nicolas Luhmann (1979).

The primary focus of debate from the 1960s, however, became Mills's Weberian account of the power elite in US society. Mills, in contrast to Parsons, saw power in terms of being able to get people to do what they would not otherwise do, where they do not want to do what they are made to do. This is 'power over' rather than 'power to' (although clearly if you have power over B then you have the power to do certain things), and it switches the focus from A's power *to* achieve certain ends (Russell 1938; Wrong 1979) to A's power *over* B. The focus is on who prevails in conflict, who dominates and who is subordinated to the wishes and interests of others. Where 'power to' in Parsons's hands could be maximized when there was complete agreement on and commitment to shared ends and values, 'power over' is concerned with situations in which the interests and concerns of individuals are conflicting and in which some individuals or groups are able to impose their will on others (earning it the alternative title of 'social power'; Dowding 1996).

Mills's theory of a power elite prevailing over the citizens of US society was attacked by pluralists who rejected his assumption that some group or elite necessarily dominates any community. Rather, they argued, power is exercised by voluntary groups representing coalitions of interests that are often united for a single issue and that vary considerably in their permanence (Dahl 1957, 1961; Polsby 1963). Using detailed empirical studies of decision-making in local communities, the pluralists presented a view of US society as 'fragmented into congeries of small special-interest groups with incompletely overlapping memberships, widely differing power bases, and a multitude of techniques for exercising influence on decisions salient to them' (Polsby 1963). Their perspective was rooted in a commitment to the study of observable decision-making, in that it rejected talk of power in relation to non-decisions (Merelman 1968; Wolfinger 1971), the mobilization of bias, or to such disputable entities as 'real interests'. With a marked preference for studying only cases of observable conflict, the pluralists could find little

evidence of systematic forms of domination within US communities. This focus on observable decision-making subsequently attracted extensive criticism from neo-elite and conflict theorists (Bachrach and Baratz 1970; Connolly 1974; Lukes 1974), who accused pluralists of failing to recognize that conflict is frequently managed in such a way that the public decision-making processes mask the real struggles and exercises of power in communities. Both the selection and formulation of issues for public debate and the mobilization of bias within the community should be recognized as involving the exercise of power. Lukes (1974) further extended the analysis of power to include cases where A affects B contrary to B's real interests – where B's interests may not be empirically obtainable in the form of held and expressed preferences, but where they can be stated in terms of the preferences B would hold when B exercises autonomous judgement. If we grant that there are cases where A's power is such that he is able to get B to do what he wants by structuring B's situation and manipulating the information available to B, and does so to such an extent that B comes to believe that she also wants what A wants, then we need some counter-factual claims about what B *would* want (when uninfluenced by A) to assess how far A is in fact exercising power over B. Where A's conduct with respect to B is unobservable, or lies in the past but still shapes B's decision-making, we may have no empirical evidence of conflicting interests between A and B yet certain types of outcome nonetheless invite questions about the interests of the parties, even when their expressed preferences deny conflict (see, e.g., Gaventa 1980). Radical theorists of power have also engaged with structural-Marxist accounts of class power over questions of whether it makes sense to talk of power without reference to agency (Lukes 1974; Poulantzas 1973, 1979). Although these debates dominated discussions of power in social and political theory in the 1970s and 1980s, they have become increasingly marginal following the considerable theoretical developments made concerning power by exchange and rational choice theorists (Barry 1975; Dowding 1996). They have also been undermined by further criticisms of stratification theories of power developed from the extremely influential, if rather elusive, contribution of Foucault's post-structuralism (see below, Foucault 1980, 1982; McNay 1994).

Note that the focus on 'power over' is often associated with what Morriss (2002 [1987]) refers to as 'the exercise fallacy' – that is, it encourages an identification of A's power with what A gets other people to do, rather with the relatively enduring capacities that A has to bring about things or to get people to do. When A exercises power over B, A gets B to do one of the things A can get B to do; his power is not identical with what he gets B to do, but refers to what he can, in the broadest sense, bring about. Of course, there are theorists, as we shall see, who wholly resist the idea that power can be understood as a dispositional property – a relatively enduring capacity – and embrace the exercise fallacy (treating power as what A in fact gets B to do), but there are grounds for resisting that view.

Having the power to get B to do something that B would not otherwise do may encompass a wide range of actions. It may involve mobilizing commitments or activating obligations, and it is common to refer to such compliance as secured through authority. We may also be able to get B to do something by changing B's interpretation of a situation and of the possibilities open to B – using various means ranging from influence and persuasion to manipulation. Or we may achieve our will through physical restraint, or force. Finally, we may use threats and throffers (a combination of threat and offer – making someone an offer they can't refuse) in order to secure B's compliance – that is, we may coerce B (Nozick 1969). In each case, A gets B to do something A wants that B would not otherwise do, although each uses different resources (agreements, information, strength, or the control of resources that B either wants or wants to avoid), and each evidences a different mode of compliance (consent, belief, physical compliance or rational choice).

In broad terms, the concept of power captures a type of causality in the social sciences, but it cannot be reduced to those causal relationships since it includes the ability or capacity to bring about such effects. So it is concerned not just with what happens, but with what people are in a position to bring about. Hence the importance of counter-factual analysis to accounts of power – to know what someone could bring about it is not enough to know what they did bring about. This position has been refined by rational choice theory to model the power of agents in bargaining situations in terms of their ability to deploy resources to secure their ends over others, and the costs they must incur to do so, relative to the costs incurred by those over whom they prevail. Barry's seminal contribution (1975) offers a sophisticated range of ways of understanding power in these terms but presents a powerful case for looking less at what A is in a position to pay to get, and more at what A could get at low cost. To be concerned with what someone can bring about at low cost is to a considerable extent an index of the security A enjoys relative to others. To be unable to get anyone to do anything except at very high cost is an index of powerlessness and is also likely to be an index of the ease with which others can impose their will on you, even if they have no special interest in doing so at this particular point in time (as such it is also an index of liberty and its lack). The greater the range and depth of compliance one can command at low cost, the greater one's power – and the greater the vulnerability of others. Barry has subsequently used similar theoretical tools to develop (1980a, 1980b) an account of specifically political power in which he contrasts power with the gains that can be secured through luck and the ability decisively to act where one's position gives pivotal power.

An analysis of politics in terms of luck rather than power runs against the general tenor of elite theory, although neither Barry's account, nor the extensions offered by Dowding (1996), need require this move. Barry's primary interest is in the pivotal positions that people turn out to have, serendipitously, by virtue of the preferences that other players have and because of the order in which the commitments or decisions of each player are announced. Dowding does extend the analysis to discuss systematic luck, which threatens to be an oxymoron. Nonetheless, one example might be that capitalists can avoid the costs of collective action to protect themselves from potentially hostile governments simply because if they each act as rational maximizers, governments who are concerned to protect economic growth and stability will be forced to sustain economic conditions that are favourable to them. As Dowding notes, capitalists are powerful (because of what they individually control), but they are also lucky (because of their strategic situation and because they do not need to engage in collective action to ensure that their interests predominate).

Macro-social theorists who see the structural patterns of advantage and disadvantage that exist within social orders as offering the basis for general theories of social power are resistant to the idea that it is possible to reduce their theories to the micro-foundations, such as those offered by Barry, of the choices of individual agents (see Coleman 1990 on macro- and micro-theories). But there is no doubt that doing so allows a more systematic theorizing of who is able to bring about what, against whose resistance and at what relative cost, and that doing so can also help to explain how relative advantage in starting-point can result in the ability to improve upon that relative advantage. For rational choice theorists, the fact that the societies tend to have outcomes that are inegalitarian and reproduce poverty and disadvantage for substantial proportions of their populations, while securing for a relative few a disproportionate share of resources and better life chances, does not justify automatically attributing these differentials to the ability of some to exercise power over and impose such distributions on others. In any situation of conflict or exchange the varying types and quantities of resource (financial, cultural, social and so on) with which different participants start may help predict the outcome of that exchange (although luck may also play a large part), but that does not warrant us attributing power to those background conditions themselves, since they are not themselves capable of exercising agency. And in so far as they are subject to agency (and many are not – no agent controls capitalism itself), this too can be explained and understood in terms of the choices and agency of individuals.

Moreover, in the hands of its most subtle practitioners there is nothing in a rational choice approach that is intrinsically hostile to recognizing many of the elements that critical theorists have identified in their criticisms of the early pluralists. It does not rule out recognizing the differential ability of agents to manipulate the background conditions to bargaining, as when a group is able to control the formation of the agenda. Nor, in principle, does it rule out the related recognition that not all preferences may be expressed in a decision process. However, the concept of counterfactual real interests, whose identification has no basis in the expressed preferences of agents, is treated with considerable suspicion, as are accounts of complete ideological control (with at least some of the suspicion arising from the difficulties rational choice theorists have in coping with endogenous preference change). But the treatment is suspicious rather than wholly dismissive. There is recognition that context can shape interests, and recent literature has helped explore some of the issues associated with preference suppression, preference falsification and adaptive preference change (see Kuran 1995). Indeed, work from radical social theorists has also seen a renewed attention to the view that much of what they wish to claim may be captured in the distinction between what people say and what they think (Scott 1990). Nonetheless, it remains extremely difficult, both empirically and theoretically, to identify appropriate criteria for distinguishing between autonomous and heteronymous preferences (and between heteronymous preferences that are the effect of context, and those that are the effect of either the direct or mediated intentional agency of others). Taking expressed preferences has the advantage of methodological simplicity and congruence with the dependent actor's interpretation. However, taking 'repressed' and counterfactual preferences can certainly be justified on occasion and can frequently provide a more persuasive account of the complexities of social life and of the multiple ways in which people's interests are shaped by their context and by their interaction with others so that conflict is pre-emptively settled. That said, any such account is under pressure to ground claims about real interests – and they tend to do so by departing from a want-regarding conception of interests to one that makes some judgement about what a rational agent, suitably situated, would prefer (where the appeal to rationality often invokes an ideal-regarding element). Among critical social theorists (such as Lukes), the appeal to autonomous, rational preferences has sometimes been coupled with an assumption that such preferences are essentially consensual – that one builds the consensual resolution of conflict into an account of what interests individuals can reasonably claim are owed the respect of their fellow citizens. But this means that the standard for real interests is being set by a context in which there is, by definition, no conflict. Which means that we are effectively using the term power to describe our deviation from Utopia (see the critique by Gray 1983).

For all the gains of this more analytical approach, a number of major issues remain.

One of the concerns of radical social theorists was to link the idea of power with that of responsibility (Connolly 1974; Lukes 1974). That is, the point of demonstrating that A exercised power over B was in part to identify A as responsible for B's outcomes. This normative project was always deeply flawed, not least in the equivocation between responsibility as a matter of causal agency and moral responsibility. Of course there is a case for saying that a mining company has some responsibility for the poor health and low living standards of the miners working for it, in so far as the company is causally responsible for that state of affairs. But, as Zola showed in *Germinal*, there are serious issues about who really has power in this state of affairs, and the issue of power (who is able to prevail against whom) does not automatically settle the issue of moral responsibility. If companies must compete to survive and must maximize profits to attract shareholders, and if they cannot do either without low wages and poor conditions, is it they who exercise power, or is this just a situation so structured that the attribution of causal and moral responsibility must simply part company? Furthermore, in any zero-sum conflict, where either A or B wins, it is difficult to regard the winner as having moral responsibility for B's fate: either A or B gets the job; A performs better than B, so A gets the job. Is A responsible for B's not getting the job? If an employer has one job and must choose between A and B must he take moral responsibility for B's fate if he gives A the job? Of course, some types of outcome are linked to moral responsibility: if I act negligently with respect to cleanliness in my food-processing plant then I have some moral responsibility for the harmful outcomes. But not every consequence of my actions is something I either intend or can otherwise be held responsible for – as in the pricing decisions made by businessmen that can profoundly affect individuals in ways they could not have foreseen – or even if we could have foreseen them, they are such that we cannot be expected to accord them weight in our decision-making. It is not difficult to sympathize with Lukes's and Connolly's decision to accept that the unintended consequences of action by those with power need to be considered so as to 'capture conceptually some of the most subtle and oppressive ways in which the actions of some can contribute to the limits and troubles faced by others' (Connolly 1974), but they run together causal and moral responsibility too quickly since it is clear that simply defining the unintended effects of A's actions as an integral element of A's power must lead us to doubt the attribution of moral responsibility (the causal chains of actions are such that had I not done C then B would not have done X, but that causal chain does not mean that I exercise power over B with respect to X). Implicitly recognizing this, both equivocate over how far unintended effects can be admitted, and they place weight on A's negligence with regard to B's interests, and on counterfactual conditionals to the effect that A could have done otherwise or could have recognized the consequences of his actions, but there are simply insurmountable problems in attributing responsibility to an agent for all the consequences of his or her action, just as not everything that results from my action really should be thought of as a function of my power (Reeve 1982). Finally, if we were to accept the case for linking power with moral responsibility and were to follow Barry's account of power in terms of what A has the ability to bring about at low cost, then we would have to regard A as morally responsible for both what he does bring about *and* for what he could have brought about or have avoided. There is some case for this, but it seems preferable to decouple what A has the power to do, and for what he is morally responsible.

A further issue concerns the way in which theories of political power have tended to assume that we should understand the state's power in terms of its monopoly of coercive force and its centralized exercise of sovereignty over its subjects. On this view there is a tendency to think of state power as a central capacity that imposes order on potentially competing elements in society. Moreover, it is not difficult to see the attraction of linking an account of economic and social structures to this perspective to produce an integrated account of the way in which societies are structured and ruled by an elite who combine the different strands of class and political power in their hands. This view, however, has been challenged not only by rational choice theorists but also in the work of the French political philosopher and historian Michel Foucault.

Foucault's work prior to 1970 focused on the analysis of discursive formations – patterns of statements, knowledge claims, and rules of evidence, extrapolation and inference – which he treats as constructing the objects of knowledge. In his early work on madness, the development of medicine, and the emergence of the human sciences, he sees sanity and insanity, standards of health and disease and standards of normality and pathology, not as natural or inherent, but as product of the intellectual and practical apparatuses that the medical and human sciences bring to bear in constructing their objects of study and practice (Foucault 1964 [1961], 1969 [1968], 1970 [1966], 1977 [1963]). A major development in his work is signalled in his 1970 lecture in which he claimed that he had come to see that his previous work implicitly revolved around the concept of power – that these discursive frameworks were not simply fields of intellectual and practical enquiry, but were infused with power, which works in conjunction with the development of these knowledges (Foucault 1971). In his next major work, on the birth of the prison (Foucault 1980 [1975], 1977 [1975]), he provided an account of the changing ways in which crime and the criminal are constructed, offering a powerfully evoked account of the transition from the use of execution and torture to demonstrate the power of the state in the public sphere, to the incarceration and panoptic surveillance of the prisoner. It was coupled with an attack on the developing alliance of the state and the social sciences in the development of a 'carceral' society. Rather than the treatment of prisoners and the insane being seen as the fruit of enlightenment and the development of a more humane and civilized society, Foucault represents the nineteenth and twentieth centuries as increasingly an 'iron cage' – not of Weberian bureaucracy, but of administrative, penal, medical and governmental regulation, dovetailing with the application of the human sciences in the normalization of the population under the watchful eye of the state. Moreover, where Weber sees bureaucracy as having at least some instrumentally rational core, Foucault 'genealogies' demonstrate the extent to which the intellectual foundations of our 'knowledge' are rooted in the arbitrary play of power relations and represent the unholy alliance of power and knowledge in the institution of a pattern of dominance throughout the social order.

When pressed for the exact understanding of power with which he works, Foucault's position is hard to pin down. He is insistent that much

political theory misconstrues power as linked to sovereignty, and as a form of dominance that issues from the state. In contrast, he presents power as essentially dispersed and fragmented ('power is everywhere; not because it embraces everything, but because it comes from everywhere'; Foucault 1978 [1976]), except when coupled with claims to truth and knowledge. In this sense he is also arguing for an account of power that reduces it to micro-foundations. Yet his position is often confusing because he resists the view that these micro-foundations can be understood in terms of capability, agency and intention. In his earliest comments on power he presented it not as something the agent exercises, but as a set of relations and forces within and through which the subject is constituted. Later discussions are more conventional, but they retain the insistence that power is not to be thought of as a resource or capacity, but as an active force overcoming resistance. In this he seems wholeheartedly to embrace Morriss's 'exercise fallacy' while simultaneously denying individual agency and intent. One reason for this is that Foucault is concerned with '*pouvoir*' – that is, with the action that determines an outcome – not with '*puissance*' – the capacity to do something (Aron 1986; Morriss 2002 [1987]). The fact that the English language lacks the words to mark this distinction (leading to some very clumsy translations of Foucault's work) tends to obscure the implicit commitment represented by Foucault's unwillingness to speak of *puissance*. His poststructuralism is nowhere more evident than in his desire to reduce the power of the state, of class or of capital, to a micro-account of relations and networks of force and resistance, while simultaneously treating the process of power and resistance as constitutive of the field of individual agency and intention, rather than as their outcome. The difficulty with this position is that its conception of power is so distinctive, and so rooted in his broader theoretical claims, that it is difficult to connect with the great majority of writing on power, and difficult to gain a critical purchase on. Among the many things he says about power there are some striking claims – not least, his willingness to connect the will to truth with power and his view that that power is a productive, not just a repressive, force – but it remains extraordinarily hard to extract from his writing a theory of power that is intelligible within the broader terms of debate on the concept in contemporary social science. Critics differ rather dramatically on whose loss this is! The theoretical and practical pressures that exist at the boundaries of the many different interpretations of power often go to the heart of the nature of political and social science, and this does much to account for the concept's messiness. Few positions are wholly without appeal, and different perspectives offer different gains. Although meta-theoretical grounds for arbitration between competing conceptions of power seem largely absent, we can make a few comments on this issue. Narrow, behavioural definitions of power may serve specific model- and theory-building interests, but they inevitably provide a much-simplified analysis of social order and interaction. However, more encompassing definitions risk collapsing into confusion. Thus, while there are good theoretical grounds for moving beyond stated preferences to some notion of reflective preferences – so as, for example, to give a fuller account of B's dependence – we need to watch that we register that the respect in which A is responsible for what B does when B is coerced, might in turn be moderated when the analysis broadens the scope of the impact of A on B from those things that A intends that B should do as a result of his intervention. Indeed, depending on how we construe the relevant counterfactuals, we might deny that agents are liable for many of the effects of their actions, and while we may want a social theory to register this broader range of effects, we are clearly not dealing with power in quite the same way as when A intentionally gets B to do something B would not otherwise do, and where what B does is what A wants him to do, and where B does what A wants him to do because of the threat or offer that A makes B. Political, economic and social life may be deeply conflict ridden, and some groups may systematically lose out, but it might not be true that those who tend to win intend to disadvantage any individual in particular, or that they could avoid harming others without allowing others to harm them (as in Hobbes's state of nature). Also, although we are free to use different definitions of power (such as the three dimensions identified by Lukes 1974), we should recognize that each definition satisfies different interests, produces different results and allows different conclusions, and we need to take great care to avoid confusing their results. Finally, we should recognize that

although definitions of power are theory-dependent, they can be criticized in terms of the coherence of the theory, its use of empirical data, and the plausibility of its commitments to positions in the philosophies of mind and action.

MARK PHILP
UNIVERSITY OF OXFORD

References

Arendt, H. (1970) *On Violence*, London.
Aron, R. (1986) 'Macht, power, puissance: Democratic prose or demoniacal poetry', in S. Lukes (ed.) *Power*, Oxford.
Bachrach, P. and Baratz, M.S. (1970) *Power and Poverty, Theory and Practice*, Oxford.
Barry, B. (1975) 'Power: An economic analysis', in B. Barry (ed.) *Power and Political Theory*, London.
—— (1980a) 'Is It better to be powerful or lucky? Part 1', *Political Studies* 28(2): 183–94.
—— (1980b) 'Is It better to be powerful or lucky? Part 2', *Political Studies* 28(3): 338–52.
Beetham, D. (1991) *The Legitimacy of Power*, New Brunswick, NJ.
Cartwright, D. (1959) 'A field theoretical conception of power', in D. Cartwright (ed.) *Studies in Social Power*, Ann Arbor, MI.
Coleman, J. (1990) *Foundations of Social Theory*, Cambridge, MA.
Connolly, W. (1974) *The Terms of Political Discourse*, Lexington, MA.
Dahl, R. (1957) 'The concept of power', *Behavioral Science* 2.
—— (1961) *Who Governs? Democracy and Power in an American City*, New Haven, CT.
Dowding, K. (1996) *Power*, Buckingham.
Foucault, M. (1964 [1961]) *Madness and Civilization*, London.
—— (1969 [1968]) *The Archaeology of Knowledge*, London.
—— (1970 [1966]) *The Order of Things: An Archaeology of the Human Sciences*, New York.
—— (1971) *L'Ordre du discourse*, Paris.
—— (1977 [1975]) *Discipline and Punish: The Birth of the Prison*, New York.
—— (1977 [1963]) *The Birth of the Clinic*, New York.
—— (1978 [1976]) *The History of Sexuality: Volume 1*, New York.
—— (1980 [1975]) *Discipline and Punish*, London.
—— (1980) *Power/Knowledge: Selected Interviews and Other Writings, 1972–1977*, Brighton.
—— (1982) 'The subject and power', in H. Dreyfus and P. Rabinow (eds) *Michel Foucault: Beyond Structuralism and Hermeneutics*, Brighton.
Gaventa, J. (1980) *Power and Powerlessness: Quiescence and Rebellion in an Appalachian Valley*, Oxford.
Giddens, A. (1977) '"Power" in the writings of Talcott Parsons', in *Studies in Social and Political Theory*, London.
Gray, J.N. (1983) 'Political power, social theory, and

essential contestability', in D. Miller and L. Siedentop (eds) *The Nature of Political Theory*, Oxford.

Kuran, T. (1995) *Private Truths and Public Lies: The Social Consequences of Preference Falsification*, Cambridge, MA.

Luhmann, N. (1979) *Trust and Power*, London.

Lukes, S. (1974) *Power: A Radical View*, London.

—— (1978) 'Power and authority', in T. Bottomore and R. Nisbet (eds) *A History of Sociological Analysis*, London.

McNay, L. (1994) *Foucault: A Critical Introduction*, Oxford.

Merelman, R.M. (1968) 'On the neo-élitist critique of community power', *American Political Science Review* 62.

Mills, C.W. (1956) *The Power Elite*, London.

Morriss, P. (2002 [1987]) *Power: A Philosophical Analysis*, 2nd edn, Manchester.

Nozick, R. (1969) 'Coercion', in S. Morgenbesser, P. Suppes and M. White (eds) *Philosophy, Science and Method: Essays in Honor of Ernest Nagel*, New York.

Parsons, T. (1960) 'The distribution of power in American society', in *Structure and Process in Modern Societies*, Glencoe, IL.

—— (1963) 'On the concept of political power', *Proceedings of the American Philosophical Society* 107.

Polsby, N. (1963) *Community Power and Political Theory*, New Haven, CT.

Poulantzas, N. (1973) *Political Power and Social Classes*, London.

—— (1979) *State, Power, Socialism*, London.

Reeve, A. (1982) 'Power without responsibility', *Political Studies* 3.

Russell, B. (1938) *Power*, London.

Scott, J.C. (1990) *Domination and the Arts of Resistance: Hidden Transcripts*, New Haven.

Weber, M. (1978 [1922]) *Economy and Society*, Berkeley, CA.

Wolfinger, R.E. (1971) 'Nondecisions and the study of local politics', *American Political Science Review* 65.

Wrong, D. (1979) *Power: Its Forms, Bases and Uses*, Oxford.

Further reading

Lukes, S. (ed.) (1986) *Power*, Oxford.

Rogers, M.F. (1980) 'Goffman on power, hierarchy and status', in J. Ditton (ed.) *The View from Goffman*, London.

White, D.M. (1972) 'The problem of power', *British Journal of Political Science* 2.

SEE ALSO: authority; leadership; legitimacy; social control

PRAGMATICS

Pragmatics is often defined as the study of language use, and contrasted with semantics, the study of sentence meaning. In a narrower sense, pragmatics is the study of how linguistic properties and contextual factors interact in the interpretation of utterances, enabling hearers to bridge the gap between sentence meaning and speaker's meaning.

A major influence has been the philosopher H.P. Grice, whose *William James Lectures* at Harvard in 1967 (Grice 1989) are fundamental. Grice argued that many aspects of utterance interpretation traditionally regarded as conventional, or semantic, could be more explanatorily treated as conversational, or pragmatic. For Grice, the crucial feature of pragmatic interpretation is its *inferential* nature: the hearer is seen as constructing and evaluating a hypothesis about the speaker's meaning, based, on the one hand, on the meaning of the sentence uttered, and, on the other, on background or contextual assumptions and general communicative principles that speakers are normally expected to observe. Aspects of the speaker's meaning inferred on the basis of contextual assumptions and communicative principles are called *implicatures*.

Most recent work in pragmatics takes the inferential nature of utterance interpretation for granted. Controversy exists, however, about the nature and number of communicative principles involved. Grice treated communication as both rational and co-operative, and proposed a Co-Operative Principle and maxims of truthfulness, informativeness, relevance and clarity that he saw as universal. The universality of his maxims has been questioned. It is sometimes claimed that different cultures have different principles or maxims (see e.g. Keenan 1979). An alternative view is that pragmatic variation results from differences in the content or organization of contextual assumptions rather than in the principles of communication themselves.

The view that co-operation is essential to communication is retained by neo-Gricean pragmatists such as Horn (1984) and Levinson (2000), who use reformulated versions of the maxims to account for a range of *generalized* implicatures, which are described by Grice as carried in all normal contexts, and contrasted with more radically context-dependent *particularized* implicatures. An alternative approach is taken by relevance theory (Sperber and Wilson 1995), which argues that the key to communication lies in more basic facts about human cognition, that co-operation is not essential to communication, and that particularized and generalized implicatures are understood in just the same way.

According to relevance theory, the human cognitive system automatically allocates attention to information that seems relevant. Any act of communication demands the audience's attention; as a result, it creates an expectation of relevance. In interpreting an utterance or other act of communication, a rational hearer should choose the interpretation that best satisfies this expectation. Relevance theorists claim that no other principles of communication are needed. In this way, they reject Grice's Co-Operative Principle and maxims while retaining his central insights about the inferential nature of communication and the importance of speaker intentions.

For survey and discussion of current approaches to pragmatics, see Horn and Ward (2004). Grice's collected papers on pragmatics are published in Grice (1989). For a recent relevance-theoretic account, see Carston (2002).

DEIRDRE WILSON
UNIVERSITY COLLEGE LONDON

References

Carston, R. (2002) *Thoughts and Utterances: The Pragmatics of Explicit Communication*, Oxford.
Grice, H.P. (1989) *Studies in the Way of Words*, Cambridge, MA.
Horn, L. (1984) 'Towards a new taxonomy for pragmatic inference: Q- and R-based implicature', in D. Schiffrin (ed.) *Meaning, Form, and Use in Context*, Washington, DC.
Horn, L. and Ward, G. (2004) *Blackwell's Handbook of Pragmatics*, Oxford.
Keenan, E. (1979) 'The universality of conversational postulates', *Language in Society 5*.
Levinson, S. (2000) *Presumptive Meanings*, Cambridge, MA.
Sperber, D. and Wilson, D. (1995) *Relevance: Communication and Cognition*, 2nd edn, Oxford.

SEE ALSO: discourse analysis; semantics; sociolinguistics; symbolic interactionism

PREJUDICE

In the literal sense of the word, prejudice means prejudgement. Prejudiced individuals are people who have made up their minds about a certain topic before assessing the relevant information. This sense of prejudgement has formed an important part of the social psychological concept of prejudice. In addition, social psychologists have tended to use the term prejudice to refer to particular sorts of prejudgements. Although logically it is possible to be prejudiced in *favour* of a group or person, psychologists tend to reserve the term for judgements that are unreasonably negative evaluations *against* a social group. Thus racist, anti-Semitic and sexist attitudes would all be considered prime examples of prejudice. The prejudiced person is seen as someone who has prejudged a whole group unfavourably and who is likely to be biased against individual members of that group simply because of their group membership. Prejudiced beliefs are assumed to be erroneous or likely to lead the believer into making erroneous judgements. Moreover, they are seen as being resistant to change, for prejudiced people will reject evidence that does not confirm their beliefs.

Social psychologists have argued that the prejudiced person's error derives, in part, from a tendency to think about social groups in terms of stereotypes. In one of the first psychological investigations of stereotypes, Katz and Braly (1933) found that white US college students had a widespread tendency to ascribe clichéd descriptions, or stereotypes, to social groups. Blacks would be classed as 'superstitious' and 'lazy'; Jews as 'mercenary' and 'grasping'; Turks as 'cruel' and 'treacherous', and so on. By thinking in terms of such stereotypes, prejudiced people not only entertain unfavourable views about groups as a whole, but also exaggerate the percentage of individuals who might happen to possess the stereotyped trait.

Some psychologists have suggested that prejudiced people might possess a particular sort of personality type that leads them to think in rigid stereotypes. In a classic study, Adorno *et al.* (1950) argued that people with 'authoritarian personalities' are motivated by an intolerance of ambiguity. Authoritarians experience the world in hierarchical terms, using conventional stereotypes to demean so-called 'inferior' out-groups. There is some evidence that contemporary right-wingers in the USA, especially those sharing the views of the Christian right, may show a tendency towards authoritarian characteristics, including prejudices against foreigners, criminals and homosexuals (Altemeyer 1988).

There is a fundamental problem with explaining prejudice in terms of personality types. In most populations authoritarian personalities represent a minority, comprising between 10 or 15 per cent of the total population. However, racist, sexist and xenophobic prejudices can be much more widespread. They can form part of the 'common sense' that is generally accepted in racist, patriarchal or nationalist societies. Thus, the majority of the population may generally accept stereotypes about minorities and therefore such stereotypes can be seen to serve ideological, rather than personality, functions (Pickering 2001).

In recent years, many social psychologists have concentrated upon examining what Henri Tajfel (1981) called the 'cognitive aspects of prejudice', rather than exploring the emotional dynamics of prejudice. This cognitive research has studied the presence of 'normal' patterns of thinking in prejudice. Psychologists have shown how people might use stereotyped assumptions to make sense of the social world, especially if they need to make judgements quickly or routinely. Experiments have illustrated the extent to which people tend to search for evidence that confirms their presuppositions and to ignore contradictory evidence. For example, a person, who views a particular group as lazy, will often unconsciously interpret any ambiguous behaviour on the part of a group member as conforming to the stereotype of laziness. Similarly, the behaviour of the hard-working group member may pass unnoticed, or be discounted as 'exceptional'. In this way, the cognitive processes of thinking often psychologically protect stereotypes against disconfirmation (Brown 1996).

This is one reason why prejudices are so hard to break down. Mere contact with out-group members is no guarantee that erroneous prejudices will be discarded. Sometimes intergroup contact can increase prejudice because it can provide opportunities for in-group members to interpret the behaviour of out-group members in ways that confirm their own prior group stereotypes. Nevertheless, intergroup contact in certain conditions, such as that between equal groups sharing common goals, can lessen prejudices (Pettigrew 1998). In general, the cognitive approach to studying prejudice has suggested that prejudiced thinking does not represent an abnormal type of cognition. The drawback of this approach, however, is that it has difficulty in explaining the dynamics of extreme prejudice (Billig 2002).

There has been growing recognition that pre-judiced thinking may not be as cognitively simple as earlier investigators had assumed. In particular, people can express prejudices without making unqualified statements about *all* Jews, *all* blacks, or *all* women, etc. In fact, prejudiced persons often protect their stereotypes by admitting exceptions. For these reasons, a number of social psychologists have been paying close attention to the discourse that is used to formulate prejudiced views. In fact, some investigators claim that prejudice is above all a discursive phenomenon, for stereotypes are judgements that are phrased in language (van Dijk 1993; Wetherell and Potter 1993). Discourse studies have revealed the subtleties of prejudice. In contemporary Western societies, there is a general acceptance that prejudice is wrong. Many speakers, wishing to avoid being seen as prejudiced, will not use blatant stereotyping to the same extent that, for example, the subjects in the Katz and Braly study did. Instead, speakers will adopt complex discursive strategies to make negative evaluations of minority groups, disclaiming their own prejudice, while simultaneously expressing stereotyped views. Phrases such as 'I'm not prejudiced but...' are typically used to preface condemnatory remarks against out-groups. Such disclaimers illustrate how the notion of prejudice has itself become very part of the discourse of prejudice. In consequence, many contemporary investigators concentrate on deconstructing the rhetorical moves in contemporary discourses of immigration, sexist practice, nationalism, etc., rather than ascribing motives to the speakers of those discourses (Billig 2003).

MICHAEL BILLIG
LOUGHBOROUGH UNIVERSITY

References

Adorno, T.W., Frenkel-Brunswik, E., Levinson, D.J. and Sanford, R.N. (1950) *The Authoritarian Personality*, New York.

Altemeyer, B. (1988) *Enemies of Freedom: Understanding Right-Wing Authoritarianism*, San Francisco.

Billig, M. (2002) 'Henri Tajfel's "Cognitive Aspects of Prejudice" and the psychology of bigotry', *British Journal of Social Psychology* 41.

—— (2003) 'Political rhetoric', in D.O. Sears, L. Huddie and R. Jervis (eds) *Oxford Handbook of Political Psychology*, New York.

Brown, R. (1996) *Prejudice*, Oxford.

Katz, D. and Braly, K. (1933) 'Racial stereotypes of one hundred college students', *Journal of Abnormal and Social Psychology* 28: 280–90.

Pettigrew, T.F. (1998) 'Intergroup contact theory', *Annual Review of Psychology* 49.

Pickering, M. (2001) *Stereotyping*, London.

Tajfel, H. (1981) *Human Groups and Social Categories*, Cambridge, UK.

van Dijk, T.A. (1993) *Elite Discourses and Racism*, Newbury Park, CA.

Wetherell, M. and Potter, J. (1993) *Mapping the Language of Racism*, London.

SEE ALSO: attitudes; labelling theory; racism; stereotypes; stigma

PRICES, THEORY OF

The theory of prices lies at the heart of neo-classical economics. Its twin components of optimization and equilibrium form the basis of much of modern economic analysis. Not surprisingly, then, the theory of prices is also a showcase for economic analysis – reflecting its strength but also exposing its weaknesses.

The neo-classical theory of prices considers a stylized economy consisting of consumers and producers, and the set of commodities that is consumed and produced. The object of the theory is to analyse the determination of the prices of these commodities. Given a set of prices, one for each commodity, consumers are assumed to decide on their consumption pattern in order to maximize a utility function representing their tastes between the different commodities. They are assumed to take prices as parametric and to choose commodity demands and factor supplies in order to maximize utility, subject to a budget constraint which says that expenditure (on commodities consumed) cannot exceed income (from selling factors, which are included in the list of commodities). Producers also take prices as parametric, but they maximize profits (revenue from selling commodities minus costs of purchasing factors of production), subject to technological constraints, these profits being distributed back to consumers. Consumers' commodity demands and factor supplies can be seen as functions of the parametric prices and producers' commodity supplies, and factor demands can also be seen as functions of these prices. Given these functions, derived from utility maximization and from profit maximization, we can ask the following question: Does there exist a set of *equilibrium* commodity and factor prices, such that all markets clear, that is, the aggregate demand for each commodity and each factor equals aggregate supply?

If such a set of prices existed and if the economy tended towards these prices, then the above theory of prices (that they are determined in a manner so as to balance supply and demand) would have relevance. The existence question was settled in the early postwar period, culminating in the work of Debreu (1959) – for which he was awarded the Nobel Prize in economics. Mathematically, the problem is one of finding a solution to a set of non-linear equations in the price vector. The major mathematical theorem that is invoked is the *fixed-point theorem*, which says that any continuous map from a compact convex set into itself has a fixed point, that is, there is an element such that that element is mapped back into itself. The requirement that prices lie in a compact convex set is met if we notice that the entire system described above is homogeneous of degree zero in prices: scaling all prices by a given number leaves all decisions unaltered. For example, doubling all commodity and factor prices would not alter the optimal combinations of commodity supplies and factor demands: the profit at the old combinations would merely be doubled. Consumers' profit income would, therefore, double, as would their factor incomes and expenditures on commodities; the pattern of consumption and factor supply would be the same as it was before. Given such homogeneity of the system, we can in effect restrict prices to be such that they add up to unity. This, together with the fact that they are not allowed to be negative, restricts the price vector to lie in the unit simplex, which is a compact, convex set.

The next key requirement is that of continuity: we need individual demand and supply functions to be continuous in the prices that form their arguments. Continuity, along with the other assumptions of the fixed-point theorem, guarantees existence of an equilibrium set of prices. But what guarantees continuity? Since the demand and supply curves are derived from the maximization decisions of producers and consumers, the answer must lie in the objective functions and in the constraints of these problems. In fact, it is convexity of individual indifference curves that guarantees continuity of commodity demands and factor supplies as functions of the price vector. A similar analysis would apply to production technology, profit maximization and the continuity of the resulting supply functions.

If the equilibrium price vector exists, then we have a theory of prices, a theory that relies on the role of prices as co-ordinating the independent demand and supply decisions of individuals, which are based in turn on quite independent optimization. But will the equilibrium price vector be attained? For this we need to consider *dynamics*, how the economy moves when it is out of equilibrium. The simple way of thinking about this is to consider what happens in a given market when the price is such that supply exceeds demand. Then, it is argued, there will be a downwards pressure on prices as the excess supply makes itself felt. Similarly, when price is such that demand exceeds supply, the price will rise and reduce this gap. The limit of this process, occurring in all markets simultaneously, will be to move the price vector to its equilibrium pattern. The 'invisible hand' of Adam Smith leads the market to a state of rest.

If the above account were acceptable, then we would have a theory of the determination of prices: the forces of supply and demand would move the economy towards a price such that all markets clear. There are, however, at least two flies in the ointment. First, recall the assumption of price-taking behaviour, which formed the logical basis for deriving supply and demand curves. As Arrow once remarked, 'If everybody is a price taker, then who changes the price?' Second, if a market does not clear at the going price, some agents will be rationed: they will not be able either to purchase what they wish to purchase or to sell what they wish to sell. It then seems plausible that they will recalculate their demands on the basis of these new constraints, which, again, destroys the earlier basis for calculation of supply and demand curves.

Orthodox theory has invented the fiction of an 'auctioneer' who performs the twin tasks of adjusting prices in response to disequilibrium, along with the fiction that no trade can take place out of equilibrium, in order to overcome the above problems. But this is no more than a device to maintain the formal structure of the theory. Once the artificial construct of the auctioneer is removed, the theory breaks down. Since the theory cannot guarantee convergence to equilibrium prices within its own logical framework, it is a theory of prices only in so far as the economy is in equilibrium. This is fine for

the theory, but supply and demand equilibrium has certain features that are directly at variance with observed reality – involuntary unemployment, for example. Since supply of labour equals demand for labour in equilibrium, and the theory of prices only permits considerations of supply and demand equilibrium, the theory that claims to account for the determination of prices cannot account for the phenomenon of unemployment. These features were stressed by Malinvaud (1977).

The orthodox theory of prices outlined here can and has been extended to cover time, by use of the device of 'dated goods'. A commodity is now defined in terms of its consumption characteristics as well as in terms of its location in time. The number of goods is thus increased by a factor equal to the number of time periods considered in the analysis. Markets are supposed to exist *now* for all future goods, and an equilibrium set of prices is determined in exactly the same way as before. A similar device is used to introduce uncertainty. Uncertainty is captured in terms of a probability distribution over which 'state of nature' will rule at a given point in time. Goods are then distinguished according to the time and the state of nature in which they are consumed: an umbrella today if the sun shines is a different good from an umbrella today if it rains, and each of these is, in turn, different from an umbrella tomorrow if it rains, and so on. Once again, markets are assumed to exist *now* for these future contingent commodities, and prices for these goods are determined by equilibrium of demand and supply. It is, of course, a major requirement of the theory that these markets for state-contingent goods exist now. If they do not, then equilibrium may not exist, as shown, for example, by Hart (1975).

To summarize, the modern neo-classical theory of prices attempts to provide a rigorous basis for Adam Smith's claim that an 'invisible hand' leads markets to a situation in which the optimizing decisions of agents are rendered consistent with each other. The modern theory demonstrates precisely the conditions under which this must be true. In doing so in a formal and rigorous way, it shows how implausible it is that equilibrium, even if it exists, will be obtained. Of course, in conducting this analysis, the modern theory neglects institutional features of actual economics – the analysis is in an abstract setting. But it seems unlikely that if the validation of the co-ordinating role of markets is questionable in the abstract setting, it will be any more plausible once the institutional constraints have been introduced.

S.M. RAVI KANBUR
CORNELL UNIVERSITY

References

Debreu, G. (1959) *Theory of Value*, New Haven, CT.
Hart, O. (1975) 'On the optimality of equilibrium when the market structure is incomplete', *Journal of Economic Theory* 11: 418–43.
Malinvaud, E. (1977) *The Theory of Unemployment Reconsidered*, Oxford.

Further reading

Brunnermeier, M.K. (2001) *Asset Pricing under Asymmetric Information*, Oxford.
Ruggles, N. and Ruggles, R. (1999) *Pricing Systems, Indexes and Price Behavior*, Cheltenham, UK.

SEE ALSO: markets; microeconomics; neo-classical economics

PRIMITIVE SOCIETY

The term 'primitive' is derived from the Latin *primitivus*, meaning the first or earliest of its kind. A form of this word is used in various European languages to refer to the first or early form of an institution (e.g. the primitive Church, meaning the early Christian Church). It may also describe a present condition resembling the ancient form. In a related sense, the term may be applied to the aboriginal inhabitants of a place, or to the original ancestors of a population. With the development of evolutionary theory, the designation 'primitive' came to be used alongside the already established terms 'savage' and 'barbarian' to describe early human populations and their customs, or to refer to contemporary populations and institutions that were thought to hark back to a primitive stage of development. It was now assumed that all human peoples and societies shared a point of origin, and, further, that some contemporary peoples and societies had made only slight progress from that common starting-point.

Some seventeenth-century thinkers had suggested that contemporary 'savages' represented the earlier stage of modern society, but it was with the Enlightenment that secular universal histories appeared that assumed an inevitable progression from an original state of savagery through various stages until the achievement of the highest human condition, which was civilization. A four stage theory of development was advanced by Turgot in 1750 and developed by the writers of the Scottish Enlightenment. These stages were defined with reference to the dominant economic modes: hunting, pastoralism, farming and commerce. It was assumed that political and moral arrangements were dependent on these economic forms, or at least that they progressed together. Some of these writers drew on ethnographic information about tropical societies to illustrate the way of life of earlier societies, Ferguson (1966 [1767]), for instance, writing that 'it is in their present condition, that we are to behold, as in a mirror, the features of our own progenitors'.

In the generation that followed the publication of the *Origin of Species* in 1859, debates on the primitive condition of human society were greatly influenced by Darwinian theory, but there were evident continuities with the universal histories of the Scottish Enlightenment, and the faith that human history was a record of rational advances. E.B. Tylor's *Researches into the Early History of Mankind and the Development of Civilization* (1865) promoted the view that there had been a progressive development in social institutions and in knowledge and techniques, and he emphasized the contrasts between what he termed primitive and civilized modes of thought, and the development from magical and religious thinking to science.

Victorian anthropologists agreed that the most primitive human societies were based on kinship. Each primitive society was originally an organic whole. It then split into two or more identical segments, each of which traced its ancestry to a single founder. Women and goods were held communally by the men of each group, and marriage took the form of regular exchanges between them. Each group worshipped its own ancestral spirits. Only after a very long period of savagery and a great revolution – the greatest in human history, according to Henry Maine (1861) – had kinship groups at last been replaced by territorial associations as the basis of society. This revolution was accompanied by the invention of private property, and the emergence of individual marriage and the family.

These theories are now thoroughly discredited. Our knowledge of ethnography and archaeology has developed enormously over the past century. Can we now define a type of primitive society, to which the most ancient human societies approximated? Is it represented to some degree by certain modern societies of hunter-gatherers?

Biologically modern human beings first emerged in Africa some 130,000–150,000 years ago and established themselves first in Asia and then in Europe about 50,000 years ago. These populations experienced a common burst of rapid cultural development about 20,000 years ago. The societies they formed were small in scale. People lived by hunting and gathering. Despite the simplicity of the technology there was considerable regional differentiation, and there is evidence that extensive trading networks developed in some regions. Burial practices seem to indicate the beginnings of social stratification, but nothing further can be said with any certainty about their public institutions. Nor does the archaeological evidence allow firm conclusions to be drawn about the division of labour by sex and about domestic arrangements, although there is evidence that households were formed around domestic hearths. There is no direct evidence as to religious beliefs, although some archaeologists have made tentative deductions from the cave art associated with some of these sites.

There is a long tradition of research that would treat living populations – sometimes referred to as 'primitive contemporaries' – as equivalent to the societies of the Upper Palaeolithic, formed by the first modern humans in Europe. However, there are four compelling empirical reasons against adopting this approach. The first has already been noted: since we do not know what (for example) Upper Palaeolithic societies were like, we cannot say which modern societies resemble them.

The second problem is that technology, or even mode of subsistence, is an unreliable predictor of social, political and even economic institutions. It is difficult to make any generalization about all contemporary hunter-gatherers, or small-scale farmers, or herders. Most contemporary foragers do live in small-scale local communities and deploy simple technologies, though some Inuit communities, for example, used modern technologies for centuries, and established large and complex local communities, while continuing to depend on foraging. However, even the hunter-gatherers whose technologies are still apparently traditional and simple vary greatly in ideology, in organization and in their relationships with neighbours.

The third objection is that the main long-term variations in cultural tradition appear to be regional. The Kalahari hunter-gatherers, or San, for example, have more in common on most measures with the Khoi herders of Southern Africa than with the Hadza of Tanzania or the Pygmies of the Ituri forest in the Congo, who also lived until recently largely by foraging. If regional cultural traditions are historically deep, and shape the ways of life of peoples with very different technologies, then we should pay more attention to regional cultural history than to cross-cultural typologies and hypothetical stages of evolution.

The fourth objection is that there are no isolated modern communities of foragers, or herders. The conditions under which such people live are completely different from those that governed the lives of their (or our) ancestors in the distant past. Upper Palaeolithic hunters and gatherers lived in a world of hunters. Modern communities of foragers do not. When they were first studied by ethnographers, all so-called 'primitive people' were subjects of colonial or settler states. All now live as citizens of modern states. They have also all, without exception, been engaged for many generations in social and economic relationships with neighbours who live very differently. The consequence is that peoples such as the Kalahari Bushmen, Congo Pygmies or Inuit are all adapted socially and culturally to the economic, cultural and political pressures exerted upon them by their neighbours. According to one strand of contemporary thinking, the organization and ideology of foragers must be understood largely as the product of their relations with the larger societies in which they are embedded (Wilmsen 1989). Some hunter-gatherers have been driven to depend on foraging after living for long periods by farming or herding. All this suggests that the way of life of modern hunters or herders may be a poor guide to that of hunters and herders who lived thousands of years ago.

There is also a theoretical objection to the notion of primitive society, which has to do with the idea of evolution that it deploys, usually rather loosely. Theorists of primitive society may make rhetorical claims to the Darwinian legacy, but their assumptions of unilineal progress are foreign to Darwinian thinking, which emphasizes the effects of local circumstances. ('I believe in no fixed law of development', Darwin wrote.) In general, proponents of 'primitive society' assume that all human societies – or, taking a very long view, the human population as a whole, with insignificant local exceptions – passed through a series of similar social and cultural stages. Primitive societies, living or dead, correspond in significant ways to the societies that existed at some unstated period in the distant past, when everyone lived in the same way, worshipped the same gods, married by the same rules, voted in the same sorts of leaders, and obeyed the same laws. They then experienced similar revolutionary transformations, in a set sequence. There is no empirical foundation for this fantasy, and no theoretical justification for it in Darwinian theory. Similar objections hold against ideas of 'primitive mentality'.

The idea of primitive society

The idea of a primitive society has no firm scientific basis. Why then has it persisted for so long? It could be used to justify colonial and imperial policies, but this was not simply an ideological weapon of imperialism. The idea of a primitive society also appealed to many radical philosophers, such as Marx, who wished to believe that history dictated a necessary progressive course from a baseline shared by all. Romantics, in the tradition of Rousseau, could construct an image of society less destructive, more noble, better attuned to nature, than our own.

Statements about the nature of primitive society are best understood as the necessary complement to the idea of civilization. It is the mirror image of the way in which modern Europeans or North Americans imagine their own society. The speculations of science fiction create alternative worlds, situated in the future, in order to comment on our own circumstances. Similarly, the pseudo-scientific idea of primitive society throws the most valued achievements of modernity into imaginative relief. It constructs an imagined counterpart to our image of ourselves. But the notion of what constitutes the modern, or civilized, condition is not stable, and so the literature on primitive society presents a variety of competing views of what the opposite of a civilized society would be like.

ADAM KUPER
BRUNEL UNIVERSITY

References

Ferguson, A. (1966 [1767]) *An Essay on the History of Civil Society*, ed. D. Forbes, Edinburgh.
Maine, H. (1861) *Ancient Law*, London.
Tylor, E.B. (1865) *Researches into the Early History of Mankind and the Development of Civilization*, London.
Wilmsen, E. (1989) *Land Filled with Flies: A Political Economy of the Kalahari*, Chicago.

Further reading

Boas, F. (1911) *The Mind of Primitive Man*, New York.
Kuper, A. (1988) *The Invention of Primitive Society: The Persistence of an Illusion*, London.
Lowie, R. (1920) *Primitive Society*, New York.
Stocking, G. (1987) *Victorian Anthropology*, New York.

SEE ALSO: hunters and gatherers; state, origins of; tribe

PRISONERS' DILEMMA

The 'prisoners' dilemma' (PD) is the most famous 'toy game' in game theory. Game theory was invented by von Neumann and Morgenstern (1944) in order to examine human strategic interaction. Toy games illustrate general classes of problems, and the prisoners' dilemma models a form of collective-action problem. The name 'Prisoners' Dilemma' derives from a story by Albert Tucker. The police are certain that two suspects together committed a major crime, but do not have sufficient evidence to convict. The suspects are separated and offered a deal. If one confesses allowing the police to convict the other, the police will argue for leniency for the confessor. If both confess, both will receive reduced sentences. If neither confesses, then the police will convict them both of a minor crime on trumped-up charges.

The following matrix can represent the PD game:

| | | Prisoner J | |
		Co-operate	Defect
Prisoner	Co-operate	2,2	4,1
K	Defect	1,4	3,3

The two players, J and K, each have one of two strategies: they can either co-operate with each other, or they can defect from such co-operation (and confess to the police). We read the payoffs in the matrix, with K's first and J's second, and each player prefers payoff 1 to 2, 2 to 3 and 3 to

4. By inspecting the matrix one can see that the defect strategy *dominates* the co-operate strategy since *no matter what the other player chooses* each player prefers defecting to co-operating (1 is preferred to 2 and 3 is preferred to 4). Yet when both choose to defect they each receive their third-most-preferred payoff (3) to their second-most-preferred payoff (2). Universal co-operation is universally preferred to universal defection, but universal co-operation is individually unstable (it is dominated) and individually inaccessible (it requires the co-operation of the other).

The game can represent numerous social and political situations such as the decision to join a trade union, whether or not to drop litter, or the decision of nations to co-operate in free trade. In many PD applications there are more than two players, which complicates the analysis and, depending on other conditions, may allow sub-groups to co-operate to mutual advantage. Many people feel the need to challenge the standard analysis of the game since they feel the prisoners could co-operate with each other, and, after all, trade unions have formed, we do not always drop litter, and nations have reached free-trade agreements. However, solutions to collective-action problems should not be confused with the problem itself. Sometimes coercion helps overcome collective-action problems, and sometimes private-good side-payments help people to co-operate. Furthermore, repeated interaction allows co-operative solutions to develop. The standard analysis is correct and our intuitions over the simple PD go astray since in real life we rarely, if ever, face a one-off PD. Rather we interact with each other time and again.

Robert Axelrod (1984) popularized the Tit-for-Tat strategy in repeated PD games. Tit for Tat is a strategy where a player will co-operate once for each round that the other player co-operates and defect once for each defection. The strategy is simple but effective since it allows players to co-operate to gain mutual advantage but does not allow a player to be exploited in the long-term. In fact the so-called folk theorem of PD-like games shows that with suitable future discounting of the payoffs (that is one values future payoffs slightly less the further in the future they are) any finite sequence of outcomes (both co-operating, both defecting, or one defecting and one co-operating) is rational in an infinitely repeated game. This is illustrated in Figure 9.

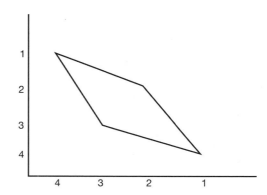

Figure 9 Graphical representation of folk theorem payoffs

The payoffs to each player are given on the two axes. Since each of the four outcomes is feasible, the long-term payoff is constrained within the diamond shape. The average payoff is therefore anywhere inside the diamond shape. One may intuitively understand the folk theorem, if one sees that one may continue for a while to co-operate with a defector if one thinks one can persuade him to co-operate, but may also exploit someone who seems willing to be exploited. If both fear exploitation both will defect, but if both can learn to co-operate that outcome might be stable for finite periods as both gain from that co-operation.

If it seemed that the simple PD shows that rational individuals will not co-operate with each other, then it might appear that the folk theorem of the repeated PD shows that 'anything can happen'. From an unintuitive definite prediction we get no prediction. This may not seem to be a forward step in analysing social life, but what the folk theorem might show is that we need to look at the precise mechanisms and institutions that lead to one set of outcomes rather than another. It points us to understanding how rational players learn to co-operate, or not, given the structure of the situation they face.

KEITH DOWDING
LONDON SCHOOL OF ECONOMICS
AND POLITICAL SCIENCE

References

Axelrod, R. (1984) *The Evolution of Cooperation*, New York.
von Neumann, J. and Morgenstern, O. (1944) *Theory of Games and Economic Behavior*, Princeton, NJ.

Further reading

Binmore, K. (1992) *Fun and Games: A Text on Game Theory*, Lexington, KY.

Gintis, H. (2000) *Game Theory Evolving*, Princeton, NJ.

Heap, S.H., Hollis, M., Lyons, B., Sugden, R. and Weale, A. (1992) *The Theory of Choice: A Critical Guide*, Oxford.

Poundstone, W. (1992) *Prisoner's Dilemma*, New York.

SEE ALSO: collective action; game theory; rational choice (action) theory

PRIVACY

One of the supposed virtues of liberal democracy is its protection of privacy. From its roots in the late eighteenth-century 'democratic revolutions' to its institutionalization in the various declarations on human rights now in existence, privacy is mooted as a principle that can be used to defend us from the state and over-powerful corporations, thereby protecting our liberties. Both socially and politically, privacy has thus become a crucial yardstick by which the nature of a society and its polity might be measured. For liberals and many on the political left, the democratic society is the one with an entrenched defence of privacy, understood in commonsensical terms as 'the right to be left alone' or in more legalistic jargon as 'decisional autonomy'.

The idea that 'privacy' is a political virtue came about with the rise of capitalism, the consolidation of the state and the gradual emergence of liberal democracy. Under feudalism a range of bodies had been the carriers of 'publicness' – the Church, the prince, the nobility. With the breakdown of feudalism these powers disintegrated into private elements on the one hand and public ones on the other. 'Private' came to imply exclusion from the sphere of the state apparatus, referring to an individual without public office or official position. 'Public' came to refer to the state that had developed under absolutism into an entity having an objective existence independent of the 'private' person of the ruler. 'The public' thus came to refer to the 'public authority' and contrasted with everything 'private', while private persons could be contrasted with 'public persons' such as those in authority. At the same time, however, and in a development capturing some of the tension surrounding the public–private distinction, 'the public' also gradually came to refer to the collection of otherwise private individuals, understood as together forming a public; hence the term 'public opinion'.

The bourgeois revolutions of the late eighteenth century, and especially the language of individual rights within which they were framed, contributed enormously to the process whereby privacy became central to the language of political discourse. The idea was strongly taken up by liberalism in its attempt to defend individuals from both extensive state power and what they called the tyranny of the majority, to the extent that privacy came to form one of the central planks of liberal ideology. Alexis de Tocqueville's analysis of democracy in the USA aimed to show that as political society expands so the sphere of private life contracts, and the Americans had therefore got it right in trying to restrict political society. Similarly, John Stuart Mill's defence of liberty rests on the idea that political communities should aim to prevent interference by law in the details of private life. As liberalism gradually won the battle for the idea of democracy, wrenching democracy away from the socialist and communist connotations it once had, part of the reading it imposed was that 'democracy' implied privacy for individuals. This then became a way to 'measure' the liberties allowed by all regimes: 'non-democratic' or 'totalitarian' regimes were tested and criticized for the extent to which they infringed the kind of right to privacy supposedly cherished in 'free' societies. It has also become a way of trying to make sense of the social and political implications of new technologies such as security cameras, mobile phone records, credit card records, itemized receipts from shopping trips, fingerprinting and DNA testing – all of which are said to threaten privacy.

This liberal understanding of privacy has become almost the common sense of political discourse. It has been especially entrenched in the legal, political and ideological systems of Western liberal democracies. Article 12 of The Universal Declaration of Human Rights (1948), for example, holds that 'no one shall be subjected to arbitrary interference with his privacy, family, home or correspondence'. But it is important to note how significant a historical and ideological transformation was effected by liberalism in this defence of privacy. Prior to the emergence of liberalism, privacy had been a negative state – the state of 'privation'. For the ancient Greeks, those experiencing privacy were being *deprived*. Specifically, they were being deprived of *public participation* in the affairs of the state. To live an entirely private life meant for the Greeks living a life deprived of something essential to a truly human life: of being seen and heard by others, of having a public relationship with them through the intermediary of a common world of things, and thus of participating in an attempt to help shape the social and political world for the better. The privation of privacy lies accordingly in the absence of others.

The historical point is important because a significant political debate also hangs on it. One should not get too carried away by high-profile victories for 'public' figures who have been successful in preventing, for example, unauthorized photographs of their wedding or holiday being shown. Most of us will never be in a position to be concerned about whether national newspapers are going to show pictures of us on the beach wearing skimpy swimwear. While such cases may have a certain sociological interest, for example in raising the question of the extent to which 'public' figures should have 'private' lives, in themselves they have little to do with the question of privacy as it affects the bulk of the population on an everyday basis. And this question is distinctly political.

That can be seen in the critique of privacy from both the political left and right. The far right has tended to argue that only those who have something to conceal gain from asserting the right to privacy. The fascist doctrine that there should be nothing outside the state and that everything must be for the state implies the abolition of private life. The position held by some on the left is more complex and sophisticated. One argument is that privacy is a bourgeois concept in that it does little more than demand certain *individual* liberties. Privacy as an idea is related to the rise of individualism, and there is a well-known argument that individualism as a theory and the idea of the person as an individual have their origins in the rise of capitalism. In other words, the rise of the idea of privacy was an ideological offshoot of the rise of capital. Some writers push this point even further and argue that the defence of privacy went hand in hand historically with the defence of capital: aiming to give the individual protection, 'privacy' made an ideological contribution at the same time to the consolidation of the power of capital. The greatest defence of capital ever written, Adam Smith's *Wealth of Nations* (1776), rests heavily on the idea that wealth accumulation is first and foremost a private business that the state should not try to police. It is for this reason that one of the most common uses of 'private' is in its conjunction with 'property'.

A second dimension to the left critique of privacy is to point to its limitations in controlling state power. On these grounds the key term in article 12 of The Universal Declaration of Human Rights cited above is 'arbitrary interference'. As much as article 12 appears to *defend* privacy it also appears to *permit* its interference so long as a state can claim that the interference is necessary rather than arbitrary. The mechanism by which states claim such necessity is usually 'national security'. States therefore retain an ideological mechanism for overriding any right to privacy. This can be illustrated by the example of Britain in the first few years of the twenty-first century, when the state was moving slowly to integrate a right to privacy into British law while at the same time it aimed to log and store for 7 years every phone call made in Britain, built a 25 million pound email surveillance centre at MI5, issued the highest ever number of warrants for telephone tapping and mail opening, and pushed through the Terrorism Act enabling state agencies to place under surveillance (on the grounds of national security) virtually any politically active or interested citizen. This one-step-forwards one-step-backwards approach to privacy suggests that the central tensions surrounding the concept will not go away. It might also suggest that privacy has severe limitations when used as a mechanism for defending us from state power.

MARK NEOCLEOUS
BRUNEL UNIVERSITY

Further reading

D'Entreves, M.P. and Vogel, U. (eds) (2000) *Public and Private*, London.
Kumar, K. and Alexander, J. (eds) (1997) *Public and Private in Thought and Practice*, Chicago.
Moore, B., Jr (1984) *Privacy: Studies in Social and Cultural History*, New York.
Neocleous, M. (2002) 'Privacy, secrecy, idiocy', *Social Research* 69(1).
Schoeman, F. (ed.) (1984) *Philosophical Dimensions of Privacy*, Cambridge, UK.

SEE ALSO: public sphere

PRIVATIZATION

Strictly speaking privatization refers to the transfer of assets owned by the state to some form of private ownership, although it has been used more widely to denote any transfer of economic activity to the private sector, such as 'contracting out' of hospital cleaning and joint ventures using private capital. The focus here is on the narrower (ownership) definition, but many of the arguments apply equally to the wider usage.

The word privatization, as well as the concept, came to prominence in the 1980s. The previous term had been 'denationalization', which indicates both the nature of the process and the extent to which it was a reaction against earlier nationalization. However, this is only one of several reasons for the rise of privatization, both economic and political.

The basic economic argument is an efficiency one. Traditional theory has always favoured the competitive market solution to the problem of economic organization, but it also recognizes that the presence of monopoly may undermine this conclusion; this is especially true of 'natural monopolies', such as those in the energy, transport and communications sectors, where competition is not practicable. The choice between public and private ownership then comes down to a decision as to whether the benefits of private ownership in terms of greater incentives for economic efficiency and freedom from interference by civil servants and politicians outweigh the benefits of public ownership in terms of controlling a monopoly. For 30 years after the Second World War the consensus favoured public ownership; since the late 1970s many of the arguments for state ownership have faded from view as the *Zeitgeist* of the 1980s led to a preference for private ownership and market solutions in general.

Thus one aim of privatization has been the promotion of wider share ownership. A more immediate factor, hinted at above, was the perceived failure of nationalization. Also the natural monopoly argument for public ownership was weakened by technical change in some industries, and by the realization that it applied only to parts of others.

Finally there are financial objectives. The simplest is that privatization is a way of raising money for the government, permitting a reduction in other sources such as taxation. Also the industries are then able to use the normal capital markets for their investment needs. In some cases this is reinforced by national accounting conventions: in the UK, nationalized industry borrowing has traditionally been included in the public-sector borrowing requirement, and reducing this has at times been a major target of government policy.

Clearly not all the objectives on this list are mutually compatible: the more competition is introduced, for example, the lower the proceeds of a privatization are likely to be. The weights given to different objectives will be reflected in the method of privatization used. The most conspicuous has been the public flotation, where the industry is converted into a corporation and shares are then sold to the public. Alternatives include debt-financed management buy-outs, in which the firm is sold to its existing management, and trade sales to another private company.

Judging the success or otherwise of privatization is complicated by the need to disentangle the effects of the change of ownership from those of changes in the level of competition, and often in technology, which occurred at the same time. However, criticism has generally been strongest where monopolies were privatized without the introduction of any real competition, and where shares were heavily underpriced.

By definition privatization cannot continue indefinitely; eventually the supply of state-owned assets must run out. In the UK, for example, the majority had been sold by the mid-1990s. Worldwide, however, the policy seems set for a long run. The collapse of communism, and the opening up of much of Eastern Europe after 1989, led many countries there to see privatization as a fast route to a market economy, as well as attracting capital from the West. The policy has also had some support in developing countries, although the balance of the arguments there can be different. Often the share of investment accounted for by public enterprise is very high, and its role in national planning means that privatization is not seen as an attractive option. However, it is seen as attractive by the World Bank and the IMF, and countries receiving financial support from these bodies come under strong pressure to move towards a market economy, including privatization (a general policy approach often referred to as the 'Washington consensus'). How successful this is likely to be is often questioned, particularly by those who favour the New Institutional Economics approach and its emphasis on the importance of the institutional setting and its social impact for the success of any policy.

STEPHEN TROTTER
UNIVERSITY OF HULL

Further reading

Abu Shair, O.J.A.R. (1997) *Privatization and Development*, Basingstoke.
Armstrong, M., Cowan, S. and Vickers, J. (1994) *Regulatory Reform: Economic Analysis and British Experience*, Cambridge, MA.
Bishop, M., Kay, J. and Mayer, C. (1994) *Privatization and Economic Performance*, Oxford.
Cook, P., Kirkpatrick, C. and Nixson, F. (1998) *Privatization, Enterprise Development and Economic Reform: Experiences of Developing and Transitional Economies*, Cheltenham.
Jackson, P.M. and Price, C.M. (1994) *Privatisation and Regulation: A Review of the Issues*, London.
Kalyuzhnova, Y. and Andreff, W. (2003) *Privatisation and Structural Change in Transition Economies*, Basingstoke.

SEE ALSO: mixed economy; nationalization; regulation

PROBLEM-SOLVING

Although 'problems' come in many guises, a generally accepted definition is that 'a problem arises when a living organism has a goal but does not know how this goal is to be reached' (Duncker 1945: 1). Other general points (Gilhooly 1996; Green and Gilhooly 2003) are that: problems typically have three major components, viz. a starting state of affairs, a goal state to be reached and a set of possible actions for transforming the starting state into the goal state; problems can be relatively well- or ill-defined and can vary in the degree to which they require extensive prior knowledge or not. Solving problems is a major function of thought and has long been researched in cognitive psychology. Since the information-processing approach to cognitive psychology became theoretically dominant in the early 1960s, thinking has generally been regarded as a serial symbol manipulation process that makes use of a very limited working memory, supported by an extensive long-term memory. This approach has been fruitful and, by emphasizing both analysis and organization, largely avoids the dangers of elementarism and vagueness that had beset the earlier behaviourist and Gestalt approaches respectively. Although connectionist approaches, which postulate considerable parallel processing among a large number of simple elements, were put forward as latter-day versions of Gestalt theory (Holyoak and Spellman 1993), little detailed work has been carried out on this project (except in the special case of analogical reasoning, e.g. Holyoak and Hummel 2001). Most research on problem-solving is still in the now classical tradition of serial symbol processing. Much research on problem-solving has focused on move problems and reasoning problems.

Move problems

In this class of well-defined tasks, objects or quantities have to be manipulated (in reality or symbolically) in order to change some given starting configuration into a goal configuration. Normally, the available moves or actions are specified for the would-be solver at the start. Move problems may or may not involve an adversary. Non-adversary move puzzles have been extensively investigated. 'Search' is seen as a key process in problem-solving. During search, alternative sequences of action must be conceived and checked for promise. A number of studies of search in problem-solving have used the Tower of London task. This problem requires participants to first plan out how to move a set of coloured same-sized discs arranged over three pegs from a starting pattern to a target pattern by moving only one disc at a time. Gilhooly, Phillips *et al.* (1999) studied individuals thinking aloud while solving the Tower of London problem. Their results suggest that working-memory limitations tend to shape search patterns so that typically one action is selected from those available at each step. Search builds up a limited length of sequence before returning to the start state and re-exploring. (This process of searching depth first to a certain limit, then backing up and systematically searching all branches of the search tree to the depth limit is known as 'progressive deepening'.) The general strategy used was means–ends analysis, which led to search patterns focused on finding moves that would reduce differences between the current state and the goal state. Similar results indicating very focused mental search have also arisen from studies of similar 'move' tasks, such as the Tower of Hanoi (Davies 2000).

The importance of prior experience with the problem area in heavily knowledge-dependent problems clearly emerged in the study of adversary move problems. De Groot (1965) found that both amateur and grandmaster chess players searched mentally to similar extents when asked to choose the best next move in a given board position, but the grandmasters always came up with a better move. A series of studies have shown that master-level players are able to remember realistic game situations more easily than randomly arranged chess boards. This is not true of novice players. These results indicated that master-level players have developed a very extensive network of familiar patterns in terms of which they can efficiently encode new positions (Chase and Simon 1973). The role of recognition of familiar patterns in expert problem-solving has also been demonstrated in studies of real-life time-critical problem-solving, e.g. among fire-fighters, critical care nurses and pilots (Klein 1999).

Reasoning problems

Reasoning problems have been the focus of considerable attention. Deductive reasoning involves drawing necessary consequences from given premises. Inductive reasoning involves assessing the likely truth of hypotheses in the light of evidence. In the deductive area, the syllogism has been a favourite experimental task. The somewhat venerable 'atmosphere' hypothesis, according to which the presence of particulars or negatives in the premises colours the conclusions reached (Woodworth and Sells 1935), still seems to be *descriptively* useful in summarizing error patterns (Begg and Denny 1969), although the explanation for these patterns remains controversial, for the following reasons.

The arguments of Henle (1962) for human rationality, which stressed the discrepancies between experimenters' and participants' interpretations of syllogistic tasks, have been very influential. Phenomena that are not accounted for by the atmosphere hypothesis have been uncovered, for example Johnson-Laird's finding that the figure of the premises affects the nature of the conclusion drawn. Johnson-Laird (1983, 1993) was able to account for this 'figural bias' effect and for other fine-grain results with a computer simulation that embodied his very influential 'theory of reasoning' as a process of working with *mental models* of the situations described by the premises. Poor performance is explained by failure of the participant to consider all possible mental models that could be consistent with the premises. More difficult problems tend to have more alternative models to be considered. Wetherick (1989; Wetherick and Gilhooly 1990) has proposed a simpler explanation in terms of a matching bias where participants match their conclusion to the logical form of the last possible premise in the argument. Gilhooly, Logie et al. (1999, 2002) have found that, as with the move problems discussed above, solving syllogisms involves use of working memory when information in the premises has to be combined mentally.

Inductive reasoning has been intensively studied, especially in the contexts of concept learning and Wason's four-card task. In the case of concept learning, Bruner et al. (1956) noticed a reluctance among their participants to attempt falsification of current hypotheses, and this apparent 'set' for verification was the starting-point for a long series of studies by Wason (1966) and others using the four-card task. In this task, participants have to say which cards need to be turned over to test a conditional rule relating the showing and the not-showing faces of the cards. For example, the rule might be 'if there is an "A" on one side there is a "4" on the other side'. Given cards showing A, B, 4 and 7, which need be turned over? (Answer: A and 7.) Most participants do not choose the potentially falsifying '7' card. This result was interpreted by Wason as showing 'verification bias'. A number of subsequent studies found improved performance if the materials were thematic rather than abstract (Manktelow and Evans 1979). Facilitation was also found if the rules were of dubious truth-value (Pollard and Evans 1981) or if certain ambiguities in the standard task were clarified (Smalley 1974). Evans (1980) proposed that most responses to the standard abstract form of the task are due to an unconscious, non-rational, 'matching bias'. Supporting evidence comes from the high success rates found with negative 'if–then' rules, coupled with zero transfer to positive rules. In the case of thematic versions of the rule, better performance seems to be due to the elicitation of a 'familiar reasoning schema' for 'permissions', which maps on to the conditional rule (Cheng and Holyoak 1985). In many cases where the four-card task is easy, participants are essentially trying to detect when rules for taking benefits have been broken, e.g. when the cards represent drinkers and on one side is the person's age and on the other what is being consumed (alcoholic or not) with a rule about drinking age. A possibly surprising suggestion by Cosmides (1989; Fiddick *et al.* 2000) is that evolutionary pressures have led to the development of innate 'cheat-detecting' processes that are activated by social contract situations in which benefits are obtained on the basis of a cost. As Cosmides's theory would predict, four-card tasks representing situations in which cheating is possible are generally found easy. At present, the evolutionary theory of reasoning about cheats is interesting but by no means without competition (e.g. Oaksford and Chater 1996).

Conclusion

Overall, the results of research on problem-solving in the areas of move problems and reasoning are broadly consistent with the standard information-processing assumptions of serial processing, limited working memory and vast long-term memory. Perhaps not surprisingly, data from studies of daydreaming and creative thinking suggest, however, that more complex models will be required to explain thought in general (Gilhooly 1996) than seem required for the special case of problem-solving.

K.J. GILHOOLY
UNIVERSITY OF PAISLEY

References

Begg, I and Denny, J.P. (1969) 'Empirical reconciliation of atmosphere and conversion interpretations of syllogistic reasoning errors', *Journal of Experimental Psychology* 81.

Bruner, J.S., Goodnow, J.J. and Austin, G.A. (1956) *A Study of Thinking*, New York.

Chase, W.G. and Simon, H.A. (1973) 'Perception in chess', *Cognitive Psychology* 4.

Cheng, P.W. and Holyoak, K.J. (1985) 'Pragmatic reasoning schema', *Cognitive Psychology* 17.

Cosmides, L. (1989) 'The logic of social exchange: Has natural selection shaped how humans reason? Studies with the Wason selection task', *Cognition* 31.

Davies, S.P. (2000) 'Move evaluation as a predictor and moderator of success in solutions to well-structured problems', *Quarterly Journal of Experimental Psychology* 53A.

De Groot, A.D. (1965) *Thought and Choice in Chess*, The Hague.

Duncker, K. (1945) 'On problem solving', *Psychological Monographs* 58.

Evans, J. St B.T. (1980) 'Current issues in the psychology of reasoning', *British Journal of Psychology* 71.

Fiddick, L., Cosmides, L. and Tooby, J. (2000) 'No interpretation without representation: The role of domain-specific representations in the Wason selection task', *Cognition* 77.

Gilhooly, K.J. (1996) *Thinking: Directed, Undirected and Creative*, 3nd edn, London.

Gilhooly, K.J., Logie, R.H. and Wynn, V. (1999) 'Syllogistic reasoning tasks, working memory and skill', *European Journal of Cognitive Psychology* 11.

Gilhooly, K.J., Phillips, L.H., Wynn, V., Logie, R.H. and Della Sala, S. (1999) 'Planning processes and age in the 5 disk Tower of London task', *Thinking and Reasoning* 5.

Gilhooly, K.J., Logie, R.H. and Wynn, V. (2002) 'Syllogistic reasoning tasks and working memory: Evidence from sequential presentation of premises', *Current Psychology* 21

Green, A. and Gilhooly, K.J. (2003) 'Problem solving', in N. Braisby, G.Pike and M. Le Voi (eds) *Cognitive Psychology*, Oxford.

Henle, M. (1962) 'On the relation between logic and thinking', *Psychological Review* 69.

Holyoak, K.J. and Hummel, J.E. (2001) 'Toward an understanding of analogy within a biological symbol system', in D. Gentner, K.J. Holyoak and B.N. Kokinov (eds) *The Analogical Mind: Perspectives from Cognitive Science*, Cambridge, MA.

Holyoak, K.T. and Spellman, B.A. (1993) 'Thinking', *Annual Review of Psychology* 44.

Johnson-Laird, P.N. (1983) *Mental Models*, Cambridge, UK.

—— (1993) *Human and Machine Thinking*, Hillsdale, NJ.

Klein, G. (1999) *Sources of Power: How People Make Decisions*, Cambridge, MA.

Manktelow, K.K. and Evans, J. St B.T. (1979) 'Facilitation of reasoning by realism: Effect or non-effect?' *British Journal of Psychology* 70.

Oaksford, M. and Chater, N. (1996) 'Rational explanation of the selection task', *Psychological Review* 103.

Pollard, P. and Evans, J. St B.T. (1981) 'The effects of prior beliefs in reasoning: An associational interpretation', *British Journal of Psychology* 72.

Smalley, N.S. (1974) 'Evaluating a rule against possible instances', *British Journal of Psychology* 65.

Wason, P.C. (1966) 'Reasoning', in B. Foss (ed.) *New Horizons in Psychology* 1, Harmondsworth.

Wetherick, N.E. (1989) 'Psychology and syllogistic reasoning', *Philosophical Psychology* 2.

Wetherick, N.E. and Gilhooly, K.J. (1990) 'Syllogistic reasoning: Effects of premise order', in K.J. Gilhooly, M.T.G. Keane, R.H. Logie and G. Erdos (eds) *Lines of Thinking*, Vol. 1, Chichester.

Woodworth, R.S. and Sells, S.B. (1935) 'An atmosphere effect in formal syllogistic reasoning', *Journal of Experimental Psychology* 18.

Further reading

Baron, J. (2000) *Thinking and Deciding*, 3rd edn, Cambridge, UK.

Manktelow, K. (1999) *Reasoning and Thinking*, Hove, UK.

Wason, P.C. and Shapiro, D. (1971) 'Natural and contrived experience in a reasoning problem', *Quarterly Journal of Experimental Psychology* 23.

SEE ALSO: thinking

PRODUCTION AND COST FRONTIERS

Production functions and cost frontiers are the cornerstones of the economic analysis of production. A *production frontier* is a mathematical relationship that captures the essential features of the technology by means of which an organization transforms resources such as land, labour and capital into an index of goods or services such as steel or education. It is the economist's distillation of the salient information contained in the engineer's blueprints. Mathematically, let y denote the quantity of a single output produced by the quantities of inputs denoted $(x_1,\ldots, x_n)$. Then the production frontier $f(x_1,\ldots, x_n)$ describes the *maximum* quantity of output that can be obtained from the input combination $(x_1,\ldots, x_n)$, given the technology in use, and so $y \leqslant f(x_1,\ldots, x_n)$. The production frontier is a non-decreasing and quasi-concave function of $(x_1,\ldots, x_n)$. Several important features of the structure of the technology are captured by the shape of the production frontier. Relationships among inputs include the degree of substitutability or complementarity among pairs of inputs, as well as the ability to aggregate groups of inputs into a shorter list of input aggregates. Relationships between output and the inputs include the elasticities of $f(x_1,\ldots, x_n)$ with respect to each input. The sum of these elasticities, the scale elasticity, provides a measure of economies of scale. Finally, the technical efficiency with which inputs are utilized to produce output is expressed in ratio form as $TE = y/f(x_1,\ldots, x_n) \leqslant 1$.

Each of these features has implications for the shape of the cost frontier, which is intimately related to the production frontier. A cost frontier is also a mathematical relationship, one that relates the expenses an organization incurs to the quantity of output it produces, and to the unit prices it pays for the inputs it employs in the production process. Mathematically, let E denote the expense an organization incurs in the production of output quantity y when it pays unit prices $(p_1,\ldots, p_n)$ for the inputs it employs. Then the cost frontier $c(y, p_1,\ldots, p_n)$ describes the *minimum* expenditure required to produce output quantity y when input unit prices are $(p_1,\ldots, p_n)$, given the technology in use, and so $E \geqslant c(y, p_1,\ldots, p_n)$. A cost frontier is a non-decreasing function of y, and a non-decreasing, linearly homogeneous and concave function of $(p_1,\ldots, p_n)$. However, the degrees to which minimum cost varies with a change in the quantity of output produced or in any input price depends on the features describing the structure of production technology. For example, the reciprocal of the elasticity of $c(y, p_1,\ldots, p_n)$ with respect to output provides a measure of scale economies. The existence of scale economies enables maximum output to expand more rapidly than input usage increases, thereby causing minimum cost to increase less rapidly than output expands. Scale economies thus create a technological incentive for large-scale production, and by analogous reasoning scale diseconomies create a technological deterrent to large-scale production. For another example, if a pair of inputs are close substitutes in production, and if the unit price of one of the inputs increases, the resulting increase in minimum cost is less than if the two inputs were poor substitutes, or complements. Finally, if waste in the organization causes actual output to fall short of maximum possible output, or if inputs are misallocated in light of their respective unit prices, then actual cost exceeds minimum cost; both technical and allocative inefficiency are costly. The cost efficiency of production is also expressed in ratio form as $CE = c(y, p_1,\ldots, p_n)/E \leqslant 1$, and CE decomposes into technical and allocative components.

As these examples suggest, under fairly general conditions the shape of the cost frontier is a mirror image of the shape of the production frontier. Thus the cost frontier and the production frontier generally provide equivalent information concerning the structure of production technology. This equivalence relationship between production frontiers and cost frontiers is known as 'duality', and it states that one of the two frontiers has certain features if, and only if, the other has certain features. Such a duality relationship is based on the mathematics of convex sets and their supporting hyperplanes, and it has a number of important economic implications. Since the production frontier and the cost frontier are based on different data, duality enables us to employ either frontier as the basis of an economic analysis of production, depending on data availability and without fear of obtaining conflicting inferences.

The main advantage of duality is that it greatly simplifies comparative statics analysis, the prediction of output supply and input demand responses to changes in output and input prices. The properties of output supply and input demand equations may be inferred from the properties of $f(x_1,\ldots, x_n)$ through the solution of a constrained optimization problem. However, it is much easier to exploit duality to derive output supply and input demand equations directly from $c(y,p_1,\ldots, p_n)$ through a process of differentiation. Since $c(y,p_1,\ldots, p_n)$ satisfies certain properties, the differentiation procedure ensures that output supply and input demand equations satisfy related properties. The derivation of input demand equations from the cost frontier is known as Shephard's (1953) lemma. Related analysis aimed at investigating the nature of scale economies, the degree of input substitutability or complementarity, or the extent and nature of productive inefficiency, can be conducted using the production frontier or, again more easily, using the cost frontier.

If the time period under consideration is sufficiently short, then the assumption of a given, unchanging technology is valid. The longer-term effects of technical progress, or the adaptation of existing superior technology, can be introduced into the analysis. Technical progress increases the maximum output that can be obtained from a given collection of inputs, or reduces input requirements for a given amount of output. Consequently in the presence of unchanging input prices technical progress reduces the minimum cost that must be incurred to produce a given quantity of output. This phenomenon is merely an extension to the time dimension of the duality relationship that links production frontiers and cost frontiers; technical progress shifts $f(x_1,\ldots, x_n)$ up and shifts $c(y,p_1,\ldots, p_n)$ down. Of particular empirical interest are the magnitude of technical progress and its cost-reducing effects, and the possible labour-saving bias of technical progress and its employment effects that are transmitted from the production frontier, to the cost frontier and then to the demand equation for labour.

Production and cost frontiers can be constructed from empirical data, using either econometric techniques or mathematical programming techniques. In this case the economic concept of a frontier corresponds to the popular notion of 'best practice'. Best-practice frontiers are increasingly used in target setting and performance monitoring in the public sector, and in the regulation of utilities. In both instances the objective is to induce cost-minimizing behaviour, and to force the organization to share the gains with consumers by constraining product or service prices.

C.A. KNOX LOVELL
UNIVERSITY OF GEORGIA

Reference

Shephard, R. (1953) *Cost and Production Functions*, Princeton, NJ.

Further reading

Chambers, R. (1988) *Applied Production Analysis: A Dual Approach*, Cambridge, UK.
Danre, R., Grosskopf, S. and Lovell, C.A.K. (1994) *Production Frontiers*, Cambridge, UK.
Färe, R. and Primont, D. (1995) *Multi-Output Production and Duality*, Boston.
Frisch, R. (1965) *Theory of Production*, Chicago.
Fuss, M. and McFadden, D. (eds) (1978) *Production Economics: A Dual Approach to Theory and Applications*, 2 vols, Amsterdam.
Johansen, L. (1972) *Production Functions*, Amsterdam.
Kumbhakar, S. and Lovell, C.A.K. (2000) *Stochastic Frontier Analysis*, Cambridge, UK.
Shephard, R. (1970) *Theory of Cost and Production Functions*, Princeton, NJ.

SEE ALSO: economies of scale; factors of production; law of returns; productivity

PRODUCTIVITY

Productivity represents a relationship between the inputs used in a productive process and the output they generate. It is increases in productivity that make possible growth in income per head. A considerable amount of work has gone into an analysis of the historic growth process in the Western world, in an attempt to unravel the extent to which the growth in output has been achieved through growth in productivity rather than through increases in inputs. Thus Kendrick

(1961) looked at the USA, Denison (1967) tried to analyse the reasons for different growth rates in different countries, and Matthews et al. (1982) analysed the growth process in the UK. Since the oil crises of 1973–4, growth rates in many Western countries have slowed down. Attempts to find explanations for what, to a casual observer, seems to be a reduction in productivity growth are found in Denison (1979) and Matthews (1982).

The essence of productivity analysis is a production function of the type $\gamma = f(K, L)$ where K, L are inputs of capital and labour respectively and γ is output. A simple notion of productivity growth would be one in which productivity grows in the same way as manna appears from heaven. Thus one may find the production function is in fact $\gamma = e^{al}f(K, L)$. Here output grows at the rate a, even though there need be no increase in the measured inputs. In his analyses Denison (1979) attempted to decompose this growth in productivity into changes arising from sources such as education, economies of scale, advances in knowledge and so on. Courbis (1969) presented a clear framework showing how the index number problems of productivity measurement fit into a general scheme of index numbers.

The above production led to attempts to analyse neutral progress as that which is capital and labour saving in equal proportions. If there are constant returns to scale, the above production can be written as $\gamma = f(e^{al}K, e^{al}L)$, which represents Hicks's (1965) neutral technical progress. But the above approach does not take account of the fact that capital is a produced good. Rymes (1972, 1983) argued that Harrod (1961) produced a more suitable framework in order to allow for this. In such a framework one comes close to arguing that all increases in productivity are attributable to increases in labour productivity. Finally, Bruno and Sachs (1982) made the obvious point that capital and labour are not only inputs to production. Any analysis that fails to take account of changes in raw material inputs may give misleading results.

MARTIN WEALE
NATIONAL INSTITUTE OF ECONOMIC
AND SOCIAL RESEARCH, LONDON

References

Bruno, M. and Sachs, J. (1982) 'Input price shocks and the slowdown in economic growth: The case of UK manufacturing', *Review of Economic Studies* 49: 679–705.

Courbis, R. (1969) 'Comptabilité nationale à prix constants et à productivité constante', *Review of Income and Wealth* 15(1): 33–76.

Denison, E.F. (1967) *Why Growth Rates Differ*, Washington, DC.

—— (1979) *Accounting for Slower Growth: The United States in the 1970s*, Washington, DC.

Harrod, R.F. (1961) 'The neutrality of improvements', *Economic Journal* 71 (June): 300–4.

Hicks, J.R. (1965) *Capital and Growth*, Oxford.

Kendrick, J.W. (1961) 'Productivity trends in the United States', *National Bureau for Economic Research*, New York.

Matthews, R.C.O. (ed.) (1982) *Slower Growth in the Western World*, London.

Matthews, R.C.O., Feinstein, C.H. and Odling-Smee, J.C. (1982) *British Economic Growth, 1856–1973*, Oxford.

Rymes, T.K. (1972) 'The measurement of capital and total factor productivity in the context of the Cambridge theory of capital', *Review of Income and Wealth* 18(1): 79–108.

—— (1983) 'More on the measurement of total factor productivity', *Review of Income and Wealth* 29(3): 297–316.

SEE ALSO: economies of scale; factors of production; production and cost frontiers; research and development (R&D)

PROFIT

In terms of business accounting, gross profit is the difference between total sales revenue and expenditure on wages and salaries, rents and raw materials, and any other outlays incurred in the day-to-day operation of the firm. Net profit is gross profit net of money costs, such as interest payable on loans and depreciation allowance. After deduction of tax, profit may be distributed among the firm's owners or retained to contribute to reserve and investment funds.

In economics, profit is also regarded as revenue net of cost, but the costs concerned include imputed costs, as well as expenditures on inputs to the production process. A distinction is drawn between normal and supernormal (or excess) profit. Normal profit is regarded as the income accruing to the entrepreneur. It is the return that the entrepreneur must receive to cover the opportunity costs of the inputs employed. If actual profits are less than normal profits, then entrepreneurs will be able to switch their resources to a more profitable activity. The imputed costs, referred to above, are, therefore, the opportunity costs, namely the returns that could be earned by employing or hiring out the entrepreneur's assets to gain maximum pecuniary gain. Supernormal profits are profits earned in excess of normal profits. In competitive markets these should be zero, in the long run, but in markets with elements of monopoly (or oligopoly) they may be non-zero, hence they are often called monopolistic profits. In pure, perfectly or imperfectly competitive markets, excess profits can be made in the short run but, given the assumption of freedom of entry into the market, these will not persist in the long run. Similarly, less than normal profits may be earned in competitive markets, in the short run, provided that variable costs are being covered, but the assumption of freedom of exit will ensure that normal profits are made in the long run. A major factor leading to the persistence of excess profits in the long run, in monopolistic markets, is therefore the existence of barriers to entry to the market.

Profit has been variously regarded as the wages paid to the entrepreneur; as the rent paid for specialist knowledge possessed by the entrepreneur; as the interest on the entrepreneur's capital; as recompense for risk taking; as payment for management skills; and, by Marx (see below), as surplus value expropriated by capitalists from workers.

In connection with modern firms, the view that profit is the return to entrepreneurial risk taking is complicated by the fact that the ownership of the firm is often divorced from its control. In the simple case of an entrepreneur who is both owner and manager of the firm, this return to risk view is attractive. In a limited company, however, the problem arises that it is not easy to see how the risk is divided between the shareholders, who receive the distributed profits, and the management, which may be regarded as essentially salaried employees. The matter is further confused when some of the management holds shares, in the form of directorships, and when the management is responsive to the wishes of shareholders, expressed at shareholders' meetings. It is also to be noted that not all risks need be borne by the firm, since many of them can be converted into a known cost through insurance.

F.H. Knight (1971) distinguished between risk and uncertainty. Risk entails events that occur with known probability and that can be insured against, in principle. Uncertainty occurs due to a change in the environment and entails unforeseeable events. These could include technological innovations. The existence of uncertainty creates an environment in which, even in competitive markets, excess profits may be made in the short run. In the long run, when the change is understood, profits will return to normal. If the world is such that change is continually creating unforeseen events, or 'shocks', then there will always be newly created profitable opportunities. Change will be signalled by movements in the market price or in quantities, such as sales or inventories, and the firm must decide how to respond to such changes in order to take advantage of profitable opportunities. In order to do this the firm must form expectations of future changes and respond rapidly once prices or quantities deviate from expectations. In the case of fundamental innovations, where no market previously existed (e.g. the creation of 'the Internet'), there may be 'first mover' advantages (profits) to be gained from early entry into the new market before competition builds up. Patents can often be secured to assure such advantages for a fixed period in order to encourage innovation. In a competitive market, a firm that waits until the change is fully understood will have missed the profitable opportunity, since others will have taken it up already. Lucas (1977) has developed a theory of the business cycle based on responses, in pursuit of profit, to price changes in the presence of rationally formed expectations.

Marx (1898) took a very different view of profit and its source. He argued that labour was only paid wages sufficient to maintain its labouring power. Normal profit then resulted from selling the product at its real value, which included surplus value resulting from unpaid labour. The whole of the expropriated surplus value or profit is not necessarily pocketed by the employing capitalist, however. The landlord may take one part, namely rent, and the money-lending or finance capitalist may claim a portion of surplus value, in the form of interest. The surplus value remaining in the hands of the employing capitalist may then be called industrial or commercial profit. Profit is not derived from land or capital as such, but is due to the fact that ownership of these factors enables capitalists to extract surplus value from workers. Clearly this view has had to be modified by Marxian theorists in the light of increasing ownership of capital, through direct or indirect shareholding, by workers.

ANDY MULLINEUX
UNIVERSITY OF BIRMINGHAM

References

Knight, F.H. (1971) *Risk, Uncertainty and Profits*, Chicago.
Lucas, R.E. (1977) 'Understanding business cycles', in R.E. Lucas (1981) *Studies in Business Cycle Theory*, Oxford.
Marx, K. (1898) *Wages, Prices and Profit*, London.

SEE ALSO: accounting; business cycles; investment; maximization

PROJECTIVE TESTS

Projective tests are based on the premise that personality, motivation and/or mood (rather than past experience, mental abilities or chance) influence how we interpret potentially ambiguous objects. In practice these are usually pictures – for example a drawing involving several people; an inkblot; or a severely blurred photograph or sketch, which may resemble people viewed through a thick fog. The key thing is that each picture should be ambiguous, and that it is not at all obvious what is 'really' there, or what precisely is taking place. These techniques were popular with psychiatrists in the first half of the twentieth century, examples of widely cited tests being the Rorschach inkblots, the Thematic Apperception Test and the Object Relations Technique. People are usually shown a standard set of up to twenty pictures, and asked to say what they think is going on in each picture, and perhaps also what they think may have happened in the past, who the characters are, how they feel, and what may happen next. Some modern techniques, such as the Apperceptive Perception Test, ask participants to fill in some multiple-choice items to describe each picture. Other tests may ask people to draw something, as in the 'House Tree Person' test where a house, a tree and a person are sketched.

The theory underlying these tests is that people will interpret the ambiguities in the pictures in line with their own personality, needs, drives, etc. Each test has a scoring system that attempts to encode the responses that are made to each picture (e.g. the extent to which a person reports movement, or focuses on a small detail of the picture whilst ignoring the rest) and an interpretation protocol that relates these scores to personality or psychopathology. Those who wish to use these tests usually have to undergo a long apprenticeship, so complicated are the scoring and interpretation procedures.

Projective tests suffer from so many methodological problems that they are now rarely used. The first weakness is that they are not usually tied to any mainstream theory of personality. Although the idea of projection appeals to those with a psychoanalytic bent, few projective tests set out to assess any of the important concepts of any mainstream psychoanalytic theory (e.g. strength of Oedipal fixation). Without an underlying theory, how can we know how to score the test? Is it significant that a person focuses on one area of an inkblot, or draws a house without chimney pots? Second, there is little consensus about how to score responses. At least three different systems exist for scoring the Rorschach inkblots. Third, the reliability of scoring is woefully low. When two different psychologists are shown a person's responses, they usually come to different conclusions. Finally, there is little or no hard evidence that responses to projective tests are influenced by personality – let alone evidence that such relationships are so substantial that tests may be used to *measure* personality.

COLIN COOPER
QUEEN'S UNIVERSITY BELFAST

Further reading

Eysenck, H.J. (1959) 'Review of the Rorschach inkblots', in O.K. Buros (ed.) *Fifth Mental Measurement Yearbook*, New Jersey.
Semeonoff, B. (1976) *Projective Techniques*, London.

SEE ALSO: fantasy; personality assessment

PSYCHOANALYSIS

It is now almost a century since psychoanalysis emerged under the direction of a single man, Sigmund Freud. Freud founded psychoanalysis in late nineteenth-century Vienna as both a therapeutic practice and a theory of the human mind. Therapeutically, psychoanalysis is perhaps best known as the 'talking cure' – a slogan used to describe the magical power of language to relieve mental suffering. The nub of the talking cure is known as 'free association'. The patient says to the analyst everything that comes to mind, no matter how trivial or unpleasant. This gives the analyst access to the patient's imagined desires and histories, which may then be interpreted and reconstructed within a clinical session. The aim of psychoanalysis as a clinical practice is to uncover the hidden passions and conflicts that support neurosis, in order to relieve the patient of his or her distressing symptoms.

Theoretically, psychoanalysis is rooted in a set of dynamic models concerning psychical life. The unconscious, repression, sexual drives, narcissism, denial, displacement: these are the core dimensions of the Freudian account of selfhood. For Freud, the human subject is not something that exists independently of sexuality, libidinal enjoyment, fantasy or the social and patriarchal codes of modern culture. In fact, the human subject of Enlightenment reason – that unified, stable and integrative entity – is deconstructed by psychoanalysis as a fantasy that is itself secretly libidinal. Knowledge, for Freud as for Schopenhauer and Nietzsche, is internal to the world of desire. In the light of Freudian psychoanalysis, a whole series of contemporary ideological oppositions – the intellect and emotion, commerce and pleasure, masculinity and femininity, rationality and irrationality – are potentially open to displacement.

While previously poets and philosophers such as Goethe, Schiller and Nietzsche looked at the nature of unconscious passion in terms of the aesthetic, Freud looks at its implications for human sexuality and psychical life. Freud's originality is to be found in his critical analysis of the unconscious as *repressed*. One of the most substantial findings of Freud is that there are psychical phenomena that are not available to consciousness, but which nevertheless exert a determining influence on everyday life. In his celebrated metapsychological essay 'The unconscious' (1914), Freud argues that the human subject is not immediately available to itself, that consciousness is not the expression of some core of continuous selfhood. On the contrary, the human subject for Freud is a *split* subject, torn between consciousness of self and the underlying forces of repressed desire. For Freud, examination of the language of his patients revealed that there is a profound turbulence of passion behind all draftings of self-identity, a radical *otherness* that is internal to the subject itself.

In developmental terms, Freud traces the psychic effects of our early dependence on others – usually our parents – in terms of our biologically fixed needs. The infant, Freud says, is incapable of surviving itself without the provision of care, warmth and nourishment from others. However – and this is fundamental in Freud – human need always outstrips the biological, linked as it is to the attaining of pleasure. Freud's exemplary case is the small child sucking milk from its mother's breast. After the infant's biological need for nourishment is satisfied, there is the emergence of a certain pleasure in sucking itself, and this for Freud is the core of unconscious sexuality. Freud's psychoanalysis thus radicalizes the links between sexuality and subjectivity. From this angle, sexuality is not some preordained, unitary biological force that springs into existence fully formed at birth. Rather, sexuality is *created*, not prepackaged. For Freud, sexuality is 'polymorphously perverse', an extreme flexibility as concerns the sexual drive and its objects. Sexual subjectivity emerges as a precarious and contingent organization of libidinal pleasures, a subjectivity carried on within the tangled frame of infantile sexuality.

Clinical and theoretical developments in psychoanalysis since Freud's day have significantly recast the notion of the self, as well as the broader connections between individual experience and society. Roughly speaking, attention has shifted from the intrapsychic world of the self to the interpersonal sphere, to relations between self and other. That is to say, post-Freudian theory focuses on the emotional relations between human subjects rather than the inner world of the individual self alone. From this intersubjective angle, the dynamics of emotional conflict appear in a new light. Psychic conflict and pathology are no longer understood as merely rooted in sexual repression and the denial of passion, as in the classical view of psychoanalysis. Rather, repressive emotional disorders are traced to various pathologies that underlie human relationships, primarily the complex way that interpersonal relationships can distort psychic life, selfhood and gender. Much of the impetus for this conceptual shift of focus has come from the failure of classical psychoanalysis to comprehend the sufferings of the modern clinical patient. In the post-Freudian period, the clinical picture of typical analysands has been not one of individuals suffering from disturbances in sexual repression and self-control, but rather that of individuals experiencing a profound emotional poverty in relations with others, coupled with a more general estrangement from the self.

These changes within psychoanalysis are registered in the US post-Freudian tradition and the British school of object relations theory in very different ways. Both traditions of thought share the view that classical Freudian metapsychology is unable adequately to comprehend the nature of human motivation, problems of selfhood and contemporary difficulties in living. They also share a common emphasis upon interpersonal processes in theorizing problems of selfhood and relationship difficulties. Yet there are also fundamental differences between these psychoanalytic traditions. The US post-Freudian tradition divides into two schools of thought: (1) ego psychology and (2) the interpersonal (or culturalist) model of psychoanalysis. Ego psychology is generally concerned with the genesis, development and adaptive capacities of the ego. The key figures in this school of psychoanalytic thought include Anna Freud, Heinz Hartmann, Ernest Kris, R.M. Lowenstein, Erik H. Erikson and David Rapaport. The interpersonal tradition in psychoanalysis shares this focus on the rational capacities of selfhood, but also emphasizes the place of social and cultural conditions in its constitution. The key figures in this theoretical tradition include Erich Fromm, Harry Stack Sullivan, Karen Horney and Clara Thompson. The British school of object relations theory, by contrast, focuses on the dynamics and structures of intersubjectivity itself, tracing the complex emotional links between the self and other people. The central figures in this school of psychoanalytic thought include W.R.D. Fairbairn, Harry Guntrip, Melanie Klein, D.W. Winnicott, John Bowlby and Michael Balint.

Winnicott's work has been especially influential in this context. Following Freud, Winnicott emphasizes that the newly born infant has to develop a sense of self from an original state of 'unintegration'. This struggle of the self for an individuated existence characteristically centres on the quality of object relation between child and mother. For Winnicott, the emergence of true and authentic selfhood is tied to a state of 'primary maternal preoccupation'. Through such preoccupation, the mother offers a special sort of presence, or devotion, which allows the child to experience itself as omnipotent and self-identical.

The mother thus objectively provides support for connection with external reality, while at that moment the child is free to create a 'representational world'.

If all goes well during this process of maternal devotion, or what Winnicott calls 'good enough mothering', the small infant is able to develop a sense of independence in line with the exercise of his or her ego functions. In this connection, Winnicott suggests that it is vital for the mother not only to be responsive to her infant's needs, but also to establish a kind of non-intrusive presence, a presence that allows the child freely to create, imagine and desire. By offering non-demanding support, the mother leads the child to a positive experience of aloneness, thereby establishing a basis for 'going-on-being' in the world. Winnicott describes this as the child's move into 'transitional space'. The emergence of a stable core of selfhood, according to Winnicott, depends on establishing the kind of relationship that is at once liberating and supportive, creative and dependent, defined and formless. For it is within this interplay of integration and separation that Winnicott locates the roots of authentic selfhood, creativity and the process of symbolization, as well as social relations and culture. It is precisely from this angle that Winnicott draws his infamous distinction between the 'true self', a person capable of creative living, and the 'false self', a person unable to establish stable emotional relations with others. For Winnicott, the 'false self' is fashioned out of the loss of maternal sensitivity, as the small infant tries desperately to make some emotional connection with the mother by abandoning its own wishes and incorporating her demands, desires and feelings. It is as if the child, unable adequately to express inner needs and emotional longings, turns defensively against itself by internalizing the attitudes and reactions of others. Pathologies of selfhood thus screen authentic human strivings, and this, for Winnicott, is the essence of the 'false self' as it operates 'to hide the true Self, which it does by compliance with environmental demands' (1965: 147).

In Winnicott's version of object relations theory, then, other persons play an essentially facilitating role in the construction of the self. It is only if the mother, and later significant-others, are unable to provide a supportive, non-intrusive environment that a debilitating fragmentation of the self arises. What Winnicott's model of development can be said to overlook, however, is the intensity of unconscious passion and emotional fracturing, which for Melanie Klein functions in the form of fantasy. What is involved in the fantasy world of the individual, says Klein, is a kind of continual shuttling of inner and outer worlds, from which a sense of self emerges as an outcrop of unconscious 'internal objects'. The self for Klein is originally caught up in, and dispersed within, a world of 'part-objects' – for example fantasies about the maternal breast. Adopting Freud's scandalous concept of the death drive, Klein puts aggression and destructiveness at the heart of psychic functioning. She contends that the tendency towards destruction is transferred or projected to the earliest 'part-objects', from which the mother (or more accurately, at this point, the breast) is, in turn, experienced as dangerous or persecuting. Such anxieties are in fact so terrifying, in Klein's view, that the infant must 'split' mother into good and bad objects, thereby displacing the pain of destructive unconscious fantasy. This splitting of the world into good and bad is what Klein terms the 'paranoid-schizoid' position. In order to get beyond these schizoid poles of paranoid displacing and projective idealizing, the infant has to integrate split representations (and the conflictive feelings that underlay them) and thereby accept that the mother is an independent and separate person. Klein argues that the main stumbling block in this respect is the child's fear that it has injured the loved object permanently, due to the infant's violent fantasies concerning the maternal body. To transcend this, it is necessary for the infant to 'make reparation' through the experience of guilt and ambivalence – a process that Klein terms the 'depressive' position. The negotiation of depressive feelings in the Kleinian framework carries a positive value, from which the creative and stable self emerges.

Many psychoanalytic theorists have identified loss as central to self-constitution. Indeed the connections between loss and identity have been underwritten throughout the history of psychoanalysis, and yet the interpretation of identity-formation that has most profoundly influenced contemporary psychoanalysis is that elaborated by the French analyst Jacques Lacan. Lacan's rereading of Freud, through the lens of structuralist linguistics and poststructuralist theories of discourse, has provided a crucial point of reference for the analysis of the *arising of the subject* in and through language, and especially of the intersubjective structuring of desire.

For Freud, the human infant begins life in a symbiotic relation to its mother's body. The infant, at the start of life, makes no psychical distinction between self and other, itself and the outside world. Lacan calls this psychic experience the 'imaginary order'. The imaginary for Lacan is a prelinguistic, pre-Oedipal order in which desire slides around an endless array of maternal part-objects – such as breasts, lips, gaze, skin and the like. According to Lacan, however, this imaginary experience of wholeness is broken apart once the infant recognizes itself as having an identity separate from maternal, imaginary space. This primordial moment of separation is experienced by the infant as a devastating loss; a loss so painful that it results in a *primary repression* of the pre-Oedipal connection to the maternal sphere, a repression that founds the unconscious. Once severed from primary identification with the pre-Oedipal mother, the infant is projected into the realm of language, the differences internal to signification that Lacan calls the 'symbolic order'. The symbolic in Lacan's theory is that plane of received social meanings, logic and differentiation. Symbolization and language permit the subject to represent desire to itself and to others. Yet the representation of desire, says Lacan, is always stained by a scar of imaginary, maternal identification. As speaking subjects, our discourse is always marked by a lack, the repressed unconscious. 'The unconscious,' says Lacan, 'is the discourse of the Other.'

Lacan discusses the imaginary tribulations of self-constitution via a consideration of Freud's theory of narcissism. In 'The mirror stage as formative of the function of the I' (1977), Lacan contends that the infant apprehends a sense of bodily unity through the recognition of its image in a mirror. However, this reflecting mirror image is not at all what it seems. Lacan says that what the mirror produces is a 'mirage of coherence': an alienating *misrecognition*. In short, the mirror *lies*. It leads the infant to imagine itself as stable and unified, when in fact its psychical space is fragmented, its physical movements unco-ordinated. The reflecting mirror leads the infant into an unfettered realm of narcissism, underpinned by hate and aggression, given the unbridgeable gap between ideal and actuality. This imaginary drafting of the self, says Lacan, 'situates the agency of the ego, before its social determination, in a fictional direction' (1977: 2).

The imaginary can thus be described as a kind of archaic realm of distorted mirror images, a spatial world of indistinction between self and other, from which primary narcissism and aggressivity are drawn as key building blocks in the formation of identity. These concerns are being further developed and explored in neo-Lacanian and post-Lacanian psychoanalysis, especially in the work of French analysts such as Julia Kristeva and Luce Irigaray.

ANTHONY ELLIOTT
UNIVERSITY OF THE WEST OF ENGLAND

References

Freud, S. (1935–74) *The Standard Edition of the Complete Psychological Works of Sigmund Freud*, London.
Klein, M. (1988) *Love, Guilt and Reparation and Other Works 1921–1945*, London.
Lacan, J. (1977) *Ecrits: A Selection*, London.
Winnicott, D.W. (1965) *The Maturational Process and the Facilitating Environment*, London.

Further reading

Elliott, A. (2002) *Psychoanalytic Theory: An Introduction*, Durham, NC.
Laplanche, J. and Pontalis, J.B. (1980) *The Language of Psychoanalysis*, London.
Segal, H. (1986) *Introduction to the Work of Melanie Klein*, London.

SEE ALSO: Freud; Lacan; unconscious

PSYCHOLOGICAL ANTHROPOLOGY

Psychological anthropology is an area of anthropological theory focusing on intersections of mind, culture and society. Because of anthropology's traditional definition of culture as shared, collective and public, psychological anthropology's interest in the personal often placed it within the margins of the field as a whole. It has been shaped particularly by interdisciplinary conversations between anthropology and other disciplines concerned with culture and psychology (Schwartz *et al.* 1992). Historically, psychological anthropology's fieldwork-based approach and emphasis upon naturalistic data brought it into more sustained conversation with psychoanalysis and linguistics than with experimental psychology. In more recent years, the development of

cognitive and biological approaches in academic psychology produced new convergences between anthropology and cognitive science (Holland and Quinn 1987) as well as the emerging area of cultural psychology (Bruner 1990; Stigler *et al.* 1990; Wertsch *et al.* 1995).

The antecedents of psychological anthropology may be found in the earlier field of 'culture and personality', which emerged in mid-twentieth-century US anthropology. Associated most prominently with the work of Franz Boas's students Margaret Mead and Ruth Benedict, the field was influenced by interdisciplinary scholars in anthropology, psychology and linguistics, including Edward Sapir (1949), A.I. Hallowell (1955) and Gregory Bateson (1972). The long-term goal of culture and personality researchers was to develop a science of culture capable of identifying causal links between psychological processes and social and cultural forms.

Informed by Freudian theory, the major questions posed by the culture and personality school asked how individuals learn, adhere to and/or resist dominant beliefs and ideologies. In focusing on tensions between the individual and society, the field studied both the effects of culture on the person as well as the psychological underpinnings of collective norms, beliefs and practices. Culture and personality theory sought to represent cultural patterns of behaviour in terms of modal personality types, often assessed with projective tests and other psychological methods. During the Second World War, culture and personality theorists worked to develop models of the national character of distant enemies. Ruth Benedict's classic study of Japanese character, *The Chrysanthemum and the Sword* (1946), was a product of these efforts.

Historically, anthropologists working in this area used psychological theories and methods to study relations between cultural approaches to childrearing, personality formations and specific types of cultural belief and practice. Psychoanalytic theory, for example, has been applied to the interpretation of religious beliefs in terms of prevailing psychological processes. In work extending over several decades John and Beatrice Whiting and their students developed a systematic framework for the comparative study of socialization practices. Their work sought to identify the effects of culturally prescribed childrearing practices on human development (Whiting and Whiting 1975). Other approaches utilized more 'person-centred methods', including life history interviewing, to explore the cultural shaping of identity, emotion and experience (Levy 1973).

As the field grappled with problems of validity that plagued the assessment of personality and emotion across cultures, global studies of entire cultures were superseded by more circumscribed research on specific modes of thought, feeling and action. More recent research has shown interest in linguistic and cognitive processes (D'Andrade 1995), the self and ethnopsychology (Shweder and LeVine 1984), and the politics of emotion and the body (Schwartz et al. 1992).

The focus of interpretive anthropology in the 1960s and 1970s on problems of translation and representation, together with poststructural critiques of the culture concept, complicated and subverted concepts of both 'culture' and 'psychology' as coherent and separate spheres of investigation. Instead of assuming the universal applicability of standard psychological concepts and methods, current studies examine the relevance of models of emotion and person across cultures. Similar to A.I. Hallowell's (1955) studies of the cultural construction of the self among the Ojibwa, research explores the terms and functions of local psychologies or 'ethnopsychologies'. In this regard, the entire field of cultural anthropology has become more psychological, spawning a large number of person-centred ethnographies concerned with the social and semiotic processes that shape subjectivity and emotional meaning.

Comparative studies of concepts of person and emotion in diverse languages show a wide range of intra- and intercultural variation, as well as areas of cross-cultural convergence. As ethnographic studies of emotion multiplied, so did awareness of the semantic complexities of emotion language across cultures (Wierzbicka 1992). Once regarded as the province of psychology concerned with the inner dynamics of the mind, emotions and subjectivity are now studied in a wide range of ethnographic and linguistic research examining emotional meaning in ordinary talk and interaction (Lutz and Abu-Lughod 1990).

Questions about the cultural specificity of English-language expressions for mind and emotion inevitably raised questions about the limits of academic psychology as ethnopsychology. The reflexive turn of psychological anthropology has produced a number of studies of the implicit models of academic and clinical psychology, including categories of psychiatric disorder. Thus, O'Nell's study (1996) of depression in a Native American community not only traces the historical and cultural roots of depressive experience in that community, but also identifies limitations in psychiatric assessment techniques more suited to Western concepts of the person than Native American sensibilities. Tanya Luhrmann's ethnographic study of US psychiatry (2000) argues that psychiatric discourse reflects two countervailing models of the mind – one person-centred and one brain-centred – which in turn have systematic effects upon diagnostic and treatment decisions.

As images of culture as shared, normative and fixed have been displaced by culture as contested, variable and emergent, research in psychological anthropology has focused on the social practices that constitute self and emotion, often in the fine-grained negotiations of everyday life (Desjarlais and O'Nell 1999). Psychological anthropology increasingly attends to the social and historical contexts within which cultural subjectivities are formed, focusing on the politics of self and emotion in a variety of social spaces, whether involving gender relations, the role of the state, or globalization. Attention to relations of power that frame emotional meaning, and to the political effects of emotional language, has led to more research on pressing social issues such as violence in all its forms, from spouse abuse to genocidal warfare (Das 2000; Hinton 2002).

GEOFFREY M. WHITE
UNIVERSITY OF HAWAI'I, HONOLULU

References

Bateson, G. (1972) *Steps to an Ecology of Mind*, San Francisco, CA.

Benedict, R. (1946) *The Chrysanthemum and the Sword*, New York.

Bruner, J. (1990) *Acts of Meaning*, Cambridge, MA.

D'Andrade, R.G. (1995) *The Development of Cognitive Anthropology*, Cambridge, UK.

Das, V. (2000) *Violence and Subjectivity*, Berkeley, CA.

Desjarlais, R. and O'Nell, T. (eds) (1999) *The Pragmatic Turn in Psychological Anthropology*, special issue of *Ethos* 27(4).

Hallowell, A.I. (1955) *Culture and Experience*, Philadelphia, PA.

Hinton, A.L. (2002) *Annihilating Difference: The Anthropology of Genocide*, Berkeley, CA.

Holland, D. and Quinn, N. (eds) (1987) *Cultural Models in Language and Thought*, Cambridge, UK.

Levy, R. (1973) *The Tahitians: Mind and Experience in the Society Islands*, Chicago.

Luhrmann, T.M. (2000) *Of Two Minds: The Growing Disorder in American Psychiatry*, New York.

Lutz, C. and Abu-Lughod, L. (eds) (1990) *Language and the Politics of Emotion*, Cambridge, UK.

O'Nell, T.D. (1996) *Disciplined Hearts: History, Identity, and Depression in an American Indian Community*, Berkeley, CA.

Sapir, D. (1949) *Selected Writings in Language, Culture and Personality*, Berkeley, CA.

Schwartz, T., White, G. and Lutz, C. (eds) (1992) *New Directions in Psychological Anthropology*, Cambridge, UK.

Shweder, R. and LeVine, R. (eds) (1984) *Culture Theory: Essays on Mind, Self, and Emotion*, Cambridge, UK.

Stigler, J., Shweder, R. and Herdt, G. (eds) (1990) *Cultural Psychology: Essays on Comparative Human Development*, Cambridge, UK.

Wertsch, J., del Rio, P. and Alvarez, A. (1995) *Sociocultural Studies of Mind*, New York.

Whiting, B.B. and Whiting, J.W.M. (1975) *Children of Six Cultures: A Psychocultural Analysis*, Cambridge, MA.

Wierzbicka, A. (1992) *Semantics, Culture, and Cognition*, Oxford.

SEE ALSO: cultural anthropology; transcultural psychiatry

PSYCHOLOGY

Psychology is the study of the nature, functions and phenomena of behaviour and mental experience. A definition along these lines is acceptable to most psychologists but does not command universal agreement, because the discipline tends to be interpreted differently from different theoretical perspectives, and no unified theory of psychology has emerged. According to the origins of the word, psychology is discourse about the soul – from the Greek words *psyche* (soul) and *logos* (word, discourse or reason). General dictionaries often interpret *discourse* loosely as 'study' and *soul* as 'mind', yielding a seemingly natural definition of psychology as the study of the mind. This is inadequate, however, because psychology is concerned not only with internal mental experiences but also with physical behaviour, in both humans and animals. Furthermore, many of the behavioural phenomena that are of central importance in psychology are not directly associated with mental experiences, typical examples being various reflexes and brain mechanisms. Some psychologists therefore prefer to define psychology simply as the study of behaviour, or the science of behaviour, but these

definitions raise further problems. Although psychological research is necessarily based on observations of behaviour, the researcher's interest often centres on the unobservable mental experiences underlying the behaviour rather than the behaviour itself. For example, the rapid eye movements that are observed in studies of dreaming are of little intrinsic interest, but they are psychologically significant because we know that they accompany mental experiences of dreaming.

There is general agreement that behaviour and mental experience are governed by principles that we can discover and understand through research, but opinions differ about the questions that we should ask and the research methods that we should use to answer them. One of the reasons for these differences is the scope of academic psychology's subject matter, which is unmatched in breadth and diversity by any other major discipline. In addition, psychology encompasses not only academic research but also several branches of applied psychology and associated professions, including clinical and counselling psychology; educational psychology; industrial, occupational and organizational psychology; forensic and criminological psychology; and health psychology. While academic research is confined mainly to universities and research establishments, applied psychological research and professional practice take place in hospitals and clinics, counselling agencies, commercial and industrial companies, prisons and correctional institutions, government departments and private practices.

The growth of professional psychology has led to widespread confusion between psychology and various cognate disciplines, practices and professions. In particular, psychiatry and psychoanalysis are often mistaken for psychology. Psychiatry is a branch of medicine concerned with the treatment of mental disorders. Psychiatrists are medical practitioners who have chosen to specialize in psychiatry. Psychologists are not medically qualified, and most are not primarily concerned with mental disorders, although professional clinical psychologists work closely with psychiatrists in psychiatric hospitals and elsewhere treating mentally disordered patients. More confusingly still, psychoanalysts also treat people with problems of adjustment and mental disorders, but they are not necessarily qualified in either psychology or psychiatry. Psychoanalysis includes several methods of psychotherapy based on theories of mental structure and function developed by the Austrian neurologist Sigmund Freud (1856–1939) and his followers, notably his daughter Anna Freud (1895–1982), the Austrian-born British psychoanalyst Melanie Klein (1882–1960) and the Swiss psychoanalyst Carl Gustav Jung (1875–1961). Freudian, Kleinian, Jungian and other psychoanalysts are accredited by their own professional bodies after undergoing extended training analyses. Psychoanalysis and psychiatry are entirely independent of psychology and its associated professions, although there are areas of overlap and mutual influence.

Historical background

Psychology has existed as an independent discipline for less than a century and a half, but psychological speculations, practices and research can be traced back to the records of ancient civilizations. To give just two examples, there is documentary evidence of the practice of hypnosis in ancient Egypt (Ellenberger 1970), and according to *The Histories* of Herodotus (1972 [429 BCE], part 1, book 2, paragraph 2), the pharaoh Psammetichus I (664–610 BCE) performed a crudely controlled psychological experiment to determine whether human beings have an inborn capacity for speech.

The first systematic psychological investigations were carried out in ancient Greece by the pre-Socratic philosophers of the sixth and fifth centuries BCE, before the concept of an individual soul had been conceived. Thales of Miletus (*c*.624–*c*.545 BCE) and his followers were the first to understand that the brain plays an important role in mental experience, and, in particular, that our eyes cannot see and our ears cannot hear on their own, without some form of internal representation of the light or sound patterns, because internal representation is required before any interpretation can begin. This insight paved the way for the scientific study of sensation and perception. In about 350 BCE Aristotle, in his treatise *De Anima* (Concerning the Soul), put forward the doctrine that every living body possesses an individual soul that gives it life. He classified souls in order of merit, from the lowest, the merely nutritive and reproductive souls of plants, through the sensitive souls of animals – sensitive by virtue of possessing the five classical senses of vision, hearing,

smell, taste and touch that Aristotle adumbrated – to the highest, the uniquely rational souls of human beings.

From about AD 400, for over a thousand years, the intellectual life of Europe was dominated by a form of Christian theology in which the individual soul played a central role, but religious dogma encouraged people to concentrate on saving their souls rather than studying them. Little of psychological significance emerged from the Dark Ages (up to about AD 1000) and later Middle Ages, with a few notable exceptions, such as the *Confessions* of St Augustine of Hippo (354–430), containing the earliest psychological analysis of the stream of consciousness.

The first important postmedieval thinker was the French philosopher René Descartes (1596–1650). He was also the first to wrestle with a major problem arising from the fact that mental experiences, including thoughts, sensations and emotions, belong to a separate, immaterial domain of existence from physical behaviour and bodily processes. The problem, later called the mind–body problem, was that of explaining how a physical cause can have a mental effect, as when stepping on a flame with a naked foot causes pain, and conversely how an immaterial mental cause, such as a thought or a desire, can move a limb in the physical domain. Descartes believed the human body to be a machine that operates according to ordinary physical laws. His deep problem was how the material and immaterial domains interact, and modern discussions of consciousness in psychology still debate focus on variations of this problem (see Dennett 1991).

In the late seventeenth century, after the introduction of the microscope and relaxation of the Church's objection to post-mortem examinations, knowledge of anatomy and physiology gradually accumulated, and the eighteenth century was marked by a rationalistic outlook that encouraged systematic empirical studies of the brain and nervous system. In 1780 the Italian physiologist Luigi Galvani (1737–98) discovered that the severed leg of a frog moves when an electrical current is passed through it. This provided the first clue that the nervous system is driven by electrical impulses, a fundamental discovery from which the physiology of the nervous system began to unfold.

During the early decades of the nineteenth century, the prevailing currents of philosophy and biology eventually converged towards the emergence of an independent discipline of psychology. In 1846, the physiologist Ernst Heinrich Weber (1795–1878) published experimental evidence relating the psychological magnitude of sensations to the physical intensity of stimuli, and in 1860 the philosopher-mystic Gustav Theodor Fechner (1801–87) enunciated a fundamental psychophysical law relating sensation to stimulus intensity that laid the foundations of modern psychophysics. But Weber regarded psychophysics as a contribution to physiology, and Fechner regarded it as a clarification of the mind–body problem and thus a contribution to philosophy. It fell to the German physiologist Wilhelm Max Wundt (1832–1920) to establish psychology as a new and separate discipline in its own right. He began the preface of his *Grundzüge der physiologischen Psychologie* (Principles of Physiological Psychology, 1873) with the sentence: 'The book that I herewith offer to the public attempts to mark out a new domain of science', and in 1879 he founded the world's first dedicated psychological laboratory, the *Institut für experimentelle Psychologie* in Leipzig.

What emerges from this brief historical summary is that psychology has existed as an independent discipline only since 1873 (or perhaps 1879, the date preferred by most historians of psychology), but its roots go much deeper. Although it is a relatively young discipline, and the various branches of applied psychology are even younger, psychological thought has been in evidence throughout recorded history. That is what the German psychologist Hermann Ebbinghaus meant by his cryptic and widely misunderstood remark that 'psychology has a long past but a short history' (1922 [1908]: 1). For more information about the history of psychology, see Freedheim (2003).

Subject matter

The oldest area of psychological research is the study of sensation and perception. Sensation is the 'raw' experience resulting from stimulation of a sense organ, and perception is the interpretation of sensation in relation to its presumed external stimulus, following information processing and interpretation. Although this distinction was first made in the eighteenth century and is entrenched in modern psychology, it has become increasingly difficult to defend in the light of advancing understanding of perception. Taking vision as an example, we now know that a great deal of information processing takes place in the retina of the eye, as soon as light reaches the visual receptors, therefore 'raw' visual sensation without any information processing is impossible. Research into sensation and perception deals with such topics as shape perception, colour perception, movement perception, depth perception, hearing, sound localization, the chemical senses (taste and smell), the skin and body senses, psychophysics and perceptual illusions (see Schiffman 2001).

Another important area of psychological research focuses on biological aspects of behaviour, including behaviour genetics, studies of the brain and nervous system, states of consciousness including sleep and dreaming, and the psychological effects of drugs (see Carlson 2002). Neuropsychology is the study of disorders of the brain and nervous system, and their effects on behaviour and mental experience. Significant developments in the neurosciences and genetics from the late twentieth century onwards have led to rapid advances in some of these fields. In particular, non-invasive methods of brain imaging have generated new information about how the brain works. Functional magnetic resonance imaging (fMRI) provides a real-time dynamic picture of activity in specific brain regions during mental activities, and it has greatly facilitated brain research.

One of the most active areas of psychological research is cognitive psychology, the study of information processing, including memory, attention, imagery, language, thinking and problemsolving (see Eysenck and Keane 2000). The hybrid field of cognitive neuropsychology occupies the interface between cognitive psychology and neuropsychology, and is concerned with impaired cognitive functioning in brain-damaged patients, and implications for normal functioning. For example, competing theories of reading can be tested by studying errors made by braindamaged patients. It turns out that people with a certain type of reading impairment, usually called surface dyslexia, can read only by translating each letter into its corresponding sound and have great difficulty reading words with irregular spellings, such as *yacht*. On the other hand, people with deep dyslexia or phonological dyslexia can read only by whole-word recognition and cannot easily translate letters into sounds.

They have great difficulty reading simple non-words such as *lak*, and they also make characteristic semantic errors, such as misreading the word *dinner* as 'food'. This shows that at least two quite distinct mechanisms are involved in reading, and that different forms of dyslexia are caused by different types of neurological impairment.

In psychology, learning is interpreted as any change in behaviour brought about by experience, and all mental and behavioural characteristics that are not wholly innate are learned in this sense. An active area of research focuses on learning and skills (see Schwartz *et al.* 2001). The basic principles of learning are similar in human and non-human species, and research in this area is often performed on rats, pigeons and other animals. A simple but important form of learning, called classical conditioning, was discovered around the turn of the century by the Russian physiologist Ivan Petrovich Pavlov. Pavlov found that a stimulus that does not ordinarily cause a dog to salivate, such as the sound of a bell, if repeatedly presented just before a small amount of dried meat powder is squirted into the dog's mouth, will eventually elicit salivation on its own. A slightly different mechanism, called instrumental or operant conditioning, was discovered in the 1930s by the US psychologist Burrhus F. Skinner, who argued that it explained all learned behaviour. It is based on the law of effect, according to which any behaviour that is rewarded will tend to be repeated, and it formed the linch-pin of the behaviourist movement that dominated psychology in the 1940s and 1950s.

Research into motivation and emotion is devoted to studying the psychological processes that energize or drive behaviour and the affective mental states that accompany or follow certain experiences (see Reeve 2000). Emotional states often have motivational effects, and the two are also linked through sharing brain structures, notably the limbic system on the inner surface of the temporal lobes surrounding the brainstem. Sources of motivation include the physiological drives of hunger, thirst and sex, and various forms of social motivation, such as the need for achievement and the need for affiliation. The US psychologists Paul Ekman and Wallace Friesen (1971) identified six 'primary' emotions – happiness, sadness, disgust, fear, anger and surprise – associated with facial expressions that appear to be innate. The evidence for innateness is that these expressions appear soon after birth, even in congenitally blind and deaf infants who could not have learned them from others, and are expressed and interpreted similarly even in isolated cultures. Research into emotion has also been influenced by the surprisingly tenacious cognitive-appraisal theory of the US psychologist Stanley Schachter (1964), according to which physiological arousal forms the basis of every emotion, the specific emotion depending only on the person's interpretation of the cause of the arousal.

Research into personality and intelligence is devoted to trying to delineate and explain the ways in which people differ psychologically from one another (see Sternberg and Ruzgis 1994). Personality differences have been studied extensively, and by the late 1980s a consensus had emerged that just five factors constitute the fundamental dimensions of human personality. The so-called Big Five are extraversion (characterized by traits such as sociability and assertiveness), agreeableness (kindness, generosity), conscientiousness (thoroughness, reliability), neuroticism (nervousness, moodiness) and openness to experience or intellect (imagination, creativity). Differences in intelligence have been studied ever since the French psychologists Alfred Binet and Théodore Simon constructed the first standardized IQ test in 1905. IQ tests measure general intelligence, but there is some controversy over whether intelligence is a unitary attribute. Research has consistently shown that people who are good at some kinds of thinking and problem-solving tend to be good at others, and vice versa, but different people have different intellectual strengths and weaknesses, and some psychologists therefore prefer to think in terms of multiple intelligences or abilities. In the early 1990s, research began into a previously neglected ability called emotional intelligence, encompassing the capacity to monitor one's own and other people's emotions, to discriminate between different emotions and label them appropriately, and to use emotional information to guide thinking and behaviour.

Developmental psychology is concerned with psychological attributes of infants, older children, adolescents, adults and old people, and more generally with psychological changes across the life-span (see Berk 2004). Research into cognitive development has been strongly influenced by the work of the Swiss psychologist Jean

Piaget, who showed that thinking develops through a series of predictable stages. At first, infants manifest egocentrism, neglecting to differentiate subjective from objective aspects of experience and failing to understand that objects temporarily hidden from view continue to exist. Children below about 7 years of age, before the stage of concrete operations, are usually unable to master internal representations of physical objects and to solve problems involving conservation, such as understanding that the number of objects in a group stays the same if they are rearranged, or that a quantity of liquid stays the same if it is poured into a differently shaped jug. Only during the stage of formal operations, from about 12 years, do children generally become proficient at manipulating abstract concepts as well as mental representations of physical objects.

Social psychology is devoted to social behaviour in all its forms, including social attitudes, compliance, conformity, obedience to authority and attribution processes (see Brehm *et al.* 2002). Attitudes are evaluative responses to other people, objects or abstract ideas. Sophisticated techniques have been developed for measuring them, and a great deal is now known about attitude change and persuasion. The persuasive influence of a message depends on certain well-documented characteristics of the source, message, recipient and channel of communication (face-to-face communication, films, television, radio, Internet, telephone, print media). Conformity, compliance and obedience to authority are distinct but related social influence processes. Conformity involves yielding to social pressure in the absence of any explicit request to yield; compliance is yielding to explicit requests from another person or other people; obedience is yielding to orders or instructions from someone in a position of authority. Attribution theory seeks to explain how people perceive, infer and ascribe causes to their own and other people's behaviour. Research has established that we tend to attribute another person's behaviour to internal dispositional causes rather than external situational causes if the behaviour seems different from how other people would behave in the same situation but characteristic of that person's behaviour in similar and dissimilar situations in the past. If the behaviour seems similar to that of others in the same situation but uncharacteristic of the particular person's past behaviour in similar and different situations, then we are likely to attribute it to external causes. Social psychology also exists as a field of research in sociology, where many of the same phenomena are studied but there tends to be more emphasis on non-experimental approaches.

Abnormal psychology is concerned with the classification, aetiology (causation), diagnosis, treatment and prevention of mental disorders and disabilities, and it underpins the profession of clinical psychology. The classes of mental disorders in the internationally recognized *Diagnostic and Statistical Manual of Mental Disorders* of the American Psychiatric Association (1994) include the following, among others: schizophrenia and other psychotic disorders (including paranoid schizophrenia); mood disorders (including depression and mania); anxiety disorders (including obsessive-compulsive disorder, posttraumatic stress disorder and the phobic disorders); sexual disorders (including the sexual dysfunctions); eating disorders (including anorexia nervosa and bulimia nervosa); personality disorders (including antisocial personality disorder); and disorders of infancy and childhood (including autistic disorder, attention-deficit/hyperactivity disorder and mental retardation).

The fundamental aim of basic psychological research is to understand and explain behaviour and mental experience, but the various branches of applied psychology are driven by more practical aims. They are concerned with applications of psychology to problems of everyday life. Applied psychology relies partly on basic research and partly on applied research specifically designed to answer practical questions. In clinical psychology, the research findings are applied to the treatment and management of mental disorders. In educational psychology, research into problems of learning, adjustment and behaviour is applied to providing practical help to teachers, parents and children with learning or behaviour problems. In industrial, occupational and organizational psychology, research is applied to improving the well-being and efficiency of working people. In forensic and criminological psychology, the goals are to deal more effectively with crime and punishment.

Research methods

The breadth of psychology's subject matter is matched by a wide diversity of research methods, including experiments, quasi-experiments, correlational methods, case studies and passive-observational studies. Controlled experimentation is often regarded as the most powerful method, because it allows hypotheses about cause–effect relationships to be tested rigorously. Its defining features are manipulation of a conjectured cause, called the independent variable, and control of extraneous variables that might also influence the behaviour under investigation, called the dependent variable. Control of extraneous variables is usually achieved by random allocation of research participants or subjects to groups that are treated identically apart from the manipulation of the independent variable. This ensures that pre-existing differences between participants and other extraneous variables are distributed according to the laws of probability, enabling statistical methods to be used to evaluate any observed effect for its significance in relation to chance. A typical example of a simple experiment is a study of eyewitness testimony (Loftus 1979) in which participants viewed a video recording of two cars colliding. Half the participants were randomly assigned to a treatment condition in which they were asked how fast the cars were going when they 'smashed into each other', and the rest were asked how fast the cars were going when they 'hit each other'. Participants in the first group estimated the speed to be 7 miles per hour faster, on average, than those in the second, and a week later, 32 per cent of those exposed to the word *smashed* had developed false memories of broken glass in the video, compared to only 14 per cent of those exposed to the word *hit*.

Many legitimate research problems do not lend themselves to experimental research, because independent variables cannot be manipulated or extraneous variables controlled, and in such cases other research methods are used. Various quasi-experimental designs are used to answer questions about cause–effect relationships without full manipulation or control. Correlational research focuses on the relationship between variables, such as extraversion and cigarette smoking, birth order and self-esteem, or gender and verbal ability. Case studies, involving detailed investigations of individuals, are especially common in clinical psychology. Passive-observational studies are sometimes used to record human or animal behaviour without influencing it. Passive-observational and other non-experimental research sometimes yields data that are not susceptible to statistical analysis. In social psychology, in particular, qualitative research methods based on analysis of purely verbal data are increasingly popular. For more information on research methods in psychology, see Graziano and Raulin (2004).

Emerging issues

Psychology is constantly evolving, and new areas of research and professional practice continue to emerge. For example, a new interdisciplinary research field called social cognitive neuroscience was launched at a conference in Los Angeles in 2001. It is devoted to studying behaviour and mental experience at the social, cognitive and neural levels, focusing on brain mechanisms underlying social and cognitive processes. Research in social cognitive neuroscience typically involves brain imaging and neuropsychological methods to investigate social psychological phenomena, with cognitive psychology bridging the neural and the social levels of analysis.

Cognitive science, an interdisciplinary enterprise embracing cognitive psychology, anthropology, computer science, artificial intelligence, linguistics and philosophy, has introduced new ways of studying language, learning, perception, thinking, problem-solving and above all knowledge representation. Within this field, neural networks have attracted a great deal of research attention since the 1980s. Neural networks are theoretical (or occasionally actual) systems of interconnected artificial nerve cells constituting a neurocomputer designed to simulate the operation of the human brain. Many connectionists (neural network theorists) believe that mental experiences arise from the interaction of many interconnected computing units, each in a specified state of activation, and each having the capacity to affect others by either excitatory or inhibitory connections, the entire system being activated by a stimulus that affects a subset of the units, activation then propagating through the network until an equilibrium state of minimum energy is attained.

Developments within the various branches of applied psychology include the emergence of new fields of research and professional practice. Within the broader area of forensic and criminological psychology, investigative psychology is an emerging field in which psychological principles are applied to the investigation of crimes and the apprehension of criminals. It includes criminal profiling, in which the behaviour and circumstances associated with serious crimes are studied in an effort to identify the probable characteristics of perpetrators, especially serial murders or rapists. Within the general area of health psychology, there has been rapid growth in psychoendocrinology, devoted to the study of the interactions between hormones, behaviour and mental experience, and psychoneuroimmunology, focusing on the interactions between psychological phenomena, the nervous system and the immune system, including especially effects of psychological stress on immune responses.

ANDREW M. COLMAN
UNIVERSITY OF LEICESTER

References

American Psychiatric Association (1994) *Diagnostic and Statistical Manual of Mental Disorders*, 4th edn, Washington, DC.
Berk, L.E. (2004) *Development through the Lifespan*, 3rd edn, Boston, MA.
Brehm, S.S., Kassin, S.M. and Fein, S. (2002) *Social Psychology*, 5th edn, Boston, MA.
Carlson, N.R. (2002) *Foundations of Physiological Psychology*, 5th edn, Boston, MA.
Dennett, D.C. (1991) *Consciousness Explained*, Boston, MA.
Ebbinghaus, H. (1922 [1908]) *Summary of Psychology*, London.
Ekman, P. and Friesen, W. (1971) 'Constants across cultures in the face and emotions', *Journal of Personality and Social Psychology* 17.
Ellenberger, H.F. (1970) *The Discovery of the Unconscious: The History and Evolution of Dynamic Psychiatry*, New York.
Eysenck, M.W. and Keane, M. (2000) *Cognitive Psychology: A Student's Handbook*, 4th edn, Hove, UK.
Freedheim, D.K. (ed.) (2003) *Handbook of Psychology, Volume 1, History of Psychology* [E-book], New York.
Graziano, A.M. and Raulin, M.L. (2004) *Research Methods: A Process of Inquiry*, 5th edn, Boston, MA.
Herodotus (1972) *The Histories*, Harmondsworth.
Loftus, E.F. (1979) *Eyewitness Testimony*, Cambridge, MA.
Reeve, J. (2000) *Understanding Emotion and Motivation*, 3rd edn, New York.
Schachter, S. (1964) 'Interactions of cognitive and physiological determinants of emotional state', in L. Festinger (ed.) *Advances in Experimental Social Psychology*, Vol. 1, New York, pp. 49–80.
Schiffman, H.R. (2001) *Sensation and Perception: An Integrated Approach*, 5th edn, New York.
Schwartz, B., Wasserman, E.A. and Robbins, S.J.

(2001) *Psychology of Learning and Behavior*, 5th edn, New York.
Sternberg, R.J. and Ruzgis, P. (eds) (1994) *Personality and Intelligence*, Cambridge, UK.

Further reading

Colman, A.M. (1999) *What is Psychology?* 3rd edn, London.
Goldberg, L.R. (1991) 'The structure of phenotypic personality traits', *American Psychologist* 48.
Myers, D.G. (2003) *Psychology*, 7th edn, New York.
Sternberg, R.J. (2001) *Psychology: In Search of the Human Mind*, 3rd edn, Belmont, CA.

PUBLIC ADMINISTRATION

In what is probably still the most thoughtful and comprehensive work on the subject, Dunsire (1973) identified no fewer than fifteen main meanings for the term administration. Given that the number of alternative definitions of public is also not small, it is hardly surprising that the field of public administration suffers identity problems. The development of public administration as a field of study (and, in parallel, as a field of practice) has been subject to constant incursions and borrowings. Public administration has long been disputed territory and its scholars (public administrationists) have frequently agonized over their intellectual parentage and prospects. Yet what the field may have lost through lack of a coherent identity it has – at least in the view of its enthusiasts – more than made up for by the richness of its polyglot theoretical baggage.

One standard text condenses the various meanings of public administration into just three: first, the activity of public servants; second, the structure of executive government; and, third, the systematic study of the first two (Greenwood and Wilson 1989). We are naturally most concerned with the third of these meanings, but the nature of the field of study cannot be adequately comprehended without an appreciation of the continuous and close proximity of the practice of public administration, both as the day-to-day doings of countless public officials and the patterning and repatterning of a wide variety of state institutions. The development of the academic field has mirrored the growth of 'big government', a growth that took off in many European and North American states in the mid or late nineteenth century and continued (with occasional pauses) until the early 1980s.

As a proto-social science, separate from the older study of the law, public administration can cite a number of distinguished ancestors. Frederick William I of Prussia (1713–40) created university chairs in 'cameralistics' or 'council studies', hoping to ensure a supply of adequately trained public officials. Napoleon Bonaparte developed a distinct and forceful system of state administration and a scientific training for elite civil servants and army officers. At least half of Jeremy Bentham's great Constitutional Code is concerned with the structures and procedures of government departments (Bowring 1843), and J.S. Mill theorized extensively on the ways in which administrative structures could influence administrative behaviours (Lerner 1961). However, the best-known name in the early elaboration of administrative theory is probably that of Woodrow Wilson. In 1887, Wilson (later to become President of the USA) published a seminal paper entitled 'The study of administration'. Wilson argued that politics and administration could and should be separated from each other, and that administration could then be analysed and implemented in a wholly scientific manner. 'If I see a murderous fellow sharpening a knife cleverly,' he observed, 'I can borrow his way of sharpening the knife without borrowing his probable intention to commit murder' (Wilson 1887: 220). In a strikingly analogous way, contemporary politicians frequently argue that modern business methods may be imported to the public sector without also introducing the more inequitable and rapacious practices of the commercial world. Both the possibility and the desirability of such a separation remain the subjects of intense dispute.

Public administration scholars have always borrowed theories and approaches from larger and more prestigious academic neighbours. Law was probably the first of these, and it continues to contribute a particular concern with the correctness of procedures and with the accountability of public administrators to the appropriate public authorities. How are those who wield the resources and authority of the state to be held to account? How are those citizens who may have suffered at the hands of incompetent or corrupt officials to obtain redress? Where, and how, should administrative discretion be exercised?

Since the 1920s, political studies, organization theory and management science have each in turn become more influential. The study of politics has had a particularly profound influence. Until recently, public administration scholars would most probably be located in university departments of government, politics or political science. Public administrationists from this background have tended to concentrate on 'higher' questions of the relationships between politicians and top civil servants; of the role civil servants could or should play in the policy-making process; of how public institutions could be structured so as to make them responsive to the objectives of politicians yet efficient, fair and free from partisan bias. (A good example is Self 1972.)

Organization theory is itself a relatively recent field of study, not without its own boundary disputes. Since the 1940s, however, it has generated many theories, concepts and taxonomies that have been gratefully taken up by public administrationists. Herbert Simon's (1947) analysis of the limits to rational decision-making in organizational contexts was exceptionally fruitful. From the mid-1960s onwards a less elegant but nevertheless influential body of theory grew up around a series of research projects investigating the relationships between an organization's performance, its internal structures and the contingencies in its environment (Donaldson 2001).

Most recently, public administration has come under the influence of management studies. Management studies has expanded hugely in terms of publications and student numbers, and public administration programmes in US and British universities have been absorbed within schools of management and business studies. This assimilation of public administration within the generic study of management was not unconnected with the contemporary political fashion for adopting private-sector 'business methods'. Management studies tended initially to restrict itself to important but relatively mundane issues such as management information systems, operational logistics, recruitment policies, different approaches to planning and so on. By the mid-1980s, however, public administration was exposed to a much more ambitious managerial rhetoric of 'cultural change'. Some governments began to make extensive use of privatization, and brought in management consultants to advise on bureaucratic reform. Wide recourse was had to private-sector techniques within the public sector. There seemed to be a substantial shifting of the public/private boundary and/or a fundamental restructuring of many public institutions. This was the 'New Public Management', or NPM, a set of doctrines and associated practices that became dominant in the USA, the UK and Australasia, and influential in many other countries (Pollitt 2003).

The future of public administration as a distinct field of study is not easy to predict. It is possible that it will disappear completely into the generic study of management, or that it will fragment into policy sectors (health care management; environmental management and so on). On the other hand, political scientists are interested once more in the actual implementation of political programmes and policies. If it survives as a separate academic entity, the discipline may continue to eke out its existence on the margins of academically more prestigious and popular subjects, defining itself in terms of the nature of its concerns and its substantive territory of interest rather than by laying claim to any unique conceptual or theoretical vocabulary. The field may also continue to develop along somewhat different trajectories in different countries.

To portray public administration in this way is not meant to belittle its importance. Public administrationists, under whichever labels they have toiled, have helped us to make sense of the many and contrasting ways in which governments and their agents daily allocate and transfer huge sums of money, process millions of citizens through a myriad of transactions, embark upon vast infrastructural projects, issue numerous licences, permits, refusals, fines and guidelines, and employ a sizeable proportion of the workforce in most modern economies. This is not a trivial endeavour.

CHRISTOPHER POLLITT
ERASMUS UNIVERSITY, ROTTERDAM

References

Bowring, J. (ed.) (1843) *The Works of Jeremy Bentham*, 10 vols, Edinburgh.
Donaldson, L. (2001) *The Contingency Theory of Organizations*, Thousand Oaks, CA.
Dunsire, A. (1973) *Administration: The Word and the Science*, London.
Greenwood, J. and Wilson, D. (1989) *Public Administration in Britain Today*, 2nd edn, London.
Lerner, M. (ed.) (1961) *Essential Works of John Stuart Mill*, New York.
Pollitt, C. (2003) *The Essential Public Manager*, Buckingham.
Self, P. (1972) *Administrative Theories and Politics*, London.
Simon, H. (1947) *Administrative Behavior: A Study of Decision-Making Processes in Administrative Organization*, New York.
Wilson, W. (1887) 'The study of administration', *Political Science Quarterly* 2.

SEE ALSO: bureaucracy

PUBLIC CHOICE

Public choice, or the economic theory of politics, is the application of the economist's way of thinking to politics. It studies those areas in which economic and political forces interact, and is one of the few successful interdisciplinary topics. The behaviour of the individual is taken to be rational, an assumption that political scientists and sociologists have also found to be fruitful.

While the term public choice was coined in the late 1960s, the type of politico-economic analysis has a long history. Condorcet was the first to recognize the existence of a voting paradox: in a system of majority voting, the individual preferences cannot generally be aggregated into a social decision without logical inconsistencies. Italian and Scandinavian public finance scholars have also explicitly dealt with political processes, in particular in the presence of public goods. Another forerunner is Schumpeter, who regarded the competition between parties as the essence of democracy.

There are four areas that are central to public choice.

First, *preference aggregation*: Condorcet's finding of a voting paradox has been generalized to all possible methods of aggregating individual preferences. The impossibility result remains in force, in particular when many issue-dimensions are allowed for.

Second, *party competition*: under quite general conditions, the competition of two vote-maximizing parties leads to an equilibrium: both parties offer the same policies in the median of the distribution of voters' preferences. The programmes proposed differ substantially when there are more than two parties competing, and when they can form coalitions.

Third, *interest groups*: the product of the activity of a pressure group is a public good, because even those not participating in its finance may benefit from it. Consequently, economic interests are in general not organized. An exception is when the group is small, when members only receive a private good from the organization, or when it is enforced by government decree.

Fourth, *public bureaucracy*: due to its monopoly power in the supply of public services, the public administrations tend to extend government activity beyond the level desired by the population.

In recent years, the theories developed have been empirically tested on a wide scale. The demand for publicly provided goods and services has been econometrically estimated for a great variety of goods, periods and countries. An important empirical application is *politico-economic models* that explicitly study the interaction of the economic and political sectors. A vote-maximizing government, which has to take into account the trade-off between inflation and unemployment, willingly produces a political business cycle. More inclusive politico-economic models have been constructed and empirically tested for various representative democracies: economic conditions such as unemployment, inflation and growth influence the government's re-election requirement, which induces in turn the government to manipulate the economy to secure re-election.

Viewing government as an endogenous part of a politico-economic system has far-reaching consequences for the theory of economic policy. The traditional idea of government maximizing the welfare of society has to be replaced by an emphasis on the consensual choice of the appropriate rules and institutions.

BRUNO S. FREY
UNIVERSITY OF ZURICH

Further reading

Frey, B.S. (1978) *Modern Political Economy*, Oxford.
Mueller, D. (2003) *Public Choice III*, Cambridge, UK.

SEE ALSO: interest groups and lobbying; political economy; public goods; supply-side economics; voting

PUBLIC GOODS

Public goods are characterized by non-excludability (individuals not paying for the good cannot be excluded) and by non-rivalry in con-sumption (that is, it does not cost anything when, in addition, other persons consume the good). The supply of a public good is Pareto-optimal (efficient) if the sum of the marginal utilities (or the sum of the marginal willingness to pay) of the persons benefiting equals the marginal cost of supply. This efficiency condition differs from the one of the polar opposite, private goods, where marginal utility has to equal marginal cost of supply.

The basic problem of public goods is that the prospective consumers have no incentive to reveal their preferences for such a good and are thus not ready to contribute towards financing the provision of the good. In the extreme case this incentive to act as 'free rider' leads to no supply of the public good at all, although everyone would potentially benefit from its provision.

Public goods is one of the few theoretical concepts in modern economics often used by other social sciences. One of the most important applications is to the problem of organizing economic interests. Pressure groups largely provide a public good because all persons and firms sharing these interests benefit from the activity. For that reason, there is little or no incentive to join. The (pure) public goods conditions apply, however, only when the interests are shared by a large number of persons or firms, for example by consumers and taxpayers, and when there are no exclusive benefits offered to members only.

The incentive to act as a free rider in a market setting may (partly) be overcome by resorting to the political process. The direct use of simple majority voting does not guarantee that the resulting public-good supply is Pareto-optimal. This is only the case if median voters (who throw the decisive vote) have a 'tax price' equal to their marginal willingness to pay. This will rarely be the case. In a representative democracy the competition between two parties leads under ideal conditions to the same outcome for public-goods supply as simple majority voting. With more than two parties and/or imperfect political competition, the resulting public-goods supply cannot in general be determined. Public goods should not be identified with public provision: some public goods are privately provided, and there are many non-public goods that are politically provided.

Decision-making procedures have been devised that solve the free-rider problem. These preference-revealing mechanisms result in no one gaining by understating his or her preference for the public good. However, these proposals are difficult to understand by the participants and violate the principle of anonymity of voting.

In laboratory experiments, it appears that individuals are ready to contribute to the cost of providing a public good to some extent, even in the large number setting. Ethical considerations seem to play a significant role in the public-goods context; many people appear to have moral qualms about behaving as free riders.

BRUNO S. FREY
UNIVERSITY OF ZURICH

Further reading

Cornes, R. and Sandler, T. (1996) *The Theory of Externalities, Public Goods and Club Goods*, Cambridge, UK, and New York.
Kaul, I., Grunberg, I. and Stern, M.-A. (eds) (1999) *Global Public Goods: International Cooperation in the 21st Century*, New York and Oxford.

SEE ALSO: macroeconomic policy; macroeconomic theory; mixed economy; nationalization; public choice

PUBLIC HEALTH

Public health is often regarded as being a part of general health care, but there are real and important differences, because public health is mainly concerned with the health of populations as distinct from the illness of individuals. Fostering healthy environments, marketing healthy lifestyles, educating people about healthy choices, protecting people from harm, screening for disease, controlling infections, legislating against harmful practices, etc., are all public health activities. These initiatives do not relate to individuals particularly, and tend not to be responses to illness, except in the case of an epidemic. This means that in most important respects, particularly in the relevant applied sciences, public health is different from therapeutic medicine, although the aims are the same: to save people from unnecessary suffering from disease. The essential biology is, of course, also the same, but the salient social context is always very different. Public health aims to prevent disease or illness. The role of clinical medicine is to treat it. Public health therefore needs to be more political because it seeks to change aspects

of social, political and economic processes in order to minimize health risks. Its appropriate application is nonetheless scientifically varied and highly complex.

Should public health be organized as a distinct field, apart from clinical medicine, recognizing the true differences and concentrating more on the social, environmental and community-based aspects of public health? Should public health concentrate more on health and less on the illness being prevented? Such moves will remain difficult while public health remains largely the responsibility of the health (care) sector, and so cannot easily operate in other sectors.

To regard public health policies as a part of health care is to limit its potential effectiveness. This is because public health provision is not in general demand led, and it must necessarily include the active participation of the healthy, most of whom will not be engaging with the established health care sector. Health care, in contrast, *is* demand led (i.e. consequent upon illness or lack of well-being), and health care provision is usually perceived to be underfunded, since demand is unlimited. If it is viewed as part of the established provision of health care for the sick, public health will always remain on the margin, since it seems less urgent than the immediate needs of ill people. Recognition of its importance for the health gain of populations tends to be underestimated. However, the effective prevention of avoidable chronic disease requires that public health policies are strongly supported, and allowed to operate across sectors.

In his recent review for the UK Treasury, Wanless (2002) linked health care policy in the longer term to choices for effective public health strategies now. The implementation now of effective public health policies will result in lower demand for health care later on. Starkly put, the choice is between carrying on with the current weak public health, poor population health and expensive health services, or moving to a strong public health regime that should deliver better general health, and so would allow the health services to concentrate more on treating unavoidable illness and the elderly. It is estimated that given an effective public health strategy, and a more engaged health policy, Britain's National Health Service might spend £30 billion less per year on treatment by 2022 (at today's prices) than it spends today. While the consequences of more effective public health are notoriously difficult to predict, it is known, for example, that more than 30 per cent of premature coronary heart disease and a similar proportion of cancers are preventable in principle. (In the UK, social class 1 men under the age of 70 have reduced their CHD mortality to very low levels (McPherson *et al.* 2002).) These figures assume modest and readily achievable changes in real prevailing choices, and address only two of the commonest causes of premature ill health and death.

It must be recognized, however, that the effects of public health policies are measured in decades, because of the time that it takes for most chronic disease to become clinically manifest. Cutting down on fast foods, salt or cigarettes, for example, has minimal consequence (even if dramatically achievable) in population terms in the first couple of decades, particularly if they occur among the young. Forty years is the average lag between effect and benefit among young people (with exceptions, such as personal accidents, looming quite large).

Thomas McKeown (1979), among others, has pointed out that in the early twentieth century, public health science, largely concerned with controlling infectious diseases, was far in advance of personal medical care. Subsequent changes in medical training have reversed the position. The specialist practice of public health is currently divided and weak. Public health science is arguably in much the same state as clinical science was in the 1950s, and urgently needs to develop its evidence base, its applications and its training programmes. Finding out what works will itself often take decades, and successful strategies are often specific to particular settings (McPherson 2001). Exponents need special training, for they must be highly skilled in a complex and, in the case of public health, uniquely broad knowledge base, coming largely from epidemiology. In the UK, though not in the USA, public health specialist practice has been developed as a medical speciality, and has come to be defined in relation to other medical specialities (Lewis 1991).

What is required is rather an autonomous identity for public health specialists. Some governments are showing awareness of the issues (see, e.g., Department of Health 1999, 2001), and significant changes in the organization of public health practice are taking place (Beagle-

hole 2003), despite resistance from some politicians, and even from established specialists.

KLIM MCPHERSON
OXFORD UNIVERSITY

References

Beaglehole, R. (ed.) (2003) *Global Public Health: A New Era*, Oxford.

Department of Health (1999) *Saving Lives: Our Healthier Nation*, London.

—— (2001) *The Report of the CMO's Project to Strengthen the Public Health Function*, London.

Lewis, J. (1991) 'The public's health: Philosophy and practice in the twentieth century', in R.M. Acheson and E. Fee (eds) *A History of Education in Public Health*, Oxford.

McKeown, T. (1979) *The Role of Medicine: Dream, Mirage, or Nemesis?* 2nd edn, Princeton, NJ.

McPherson, K. (2001) 'Are disease prevention initiatives working?' *Lancet* 357 1,790–2.

McPherson, K., Brittton, A. and Causer, L. (2002) *Coronary Heart Disease: Estimating the Impact of Changes in Risk Factors*, London.

Wanless, D. (2002) *Securing Our Future Health: Taking a Long-Term View*, London.

Further reading

Davey, B., Gray, A. and Seale, C. (2001) *Health and Disease: A Reader*, Milton Keynes.

SEE ALSO: epidemiology; morbidity; mortality

PUBLIC OPINION POLLS

Opinion polls are a form of sample survey. The term may be used to describe any survey designed to measure social and political attitudes, but it is most commonly applied to surveys of voting intention and political attitudes conducted on behalf of the mass media.

The first attempts to gauge the balance of public opinion were made in the nineteenth-century USA, but this was before the advent of sampling theory. Before the 1930s most polls were undertaken directly by newspapers themselves, the most famous for the *Literary Digest*. These relied on mail questionnaires sent to samples drawn from known population listings such as telephone directories or car registration lists.

The first professional polling organization independent of the media was not established until 1935, when George Gallup established the American Institute of Public Opinion. Its methods received early vindication when it correctly forecast Roosevelt's triumph over Landon in the 1936 presidential election. The *Literary Digest* poll, in contrast, put Landon ahead: telephone and car owners proved to be unrepresentative of the country as a whole. The following year Gallup's methods were imported into Great Britain by Henry Durant.

Gallup's methods rested on the foundation of 'random sampling theory'. Developed by statisticians at the turn of the century, its premise is that by selecting and interviewing a small sample of voters (provided that all voters have had an equal chance of being selected), the result of a poll will on average faithfully reflect the distribution of opinion within the electorate as a whole. Further, the poll's range of possible sampling error can be calculated, provided always that the sample to be interviewed has been selected at random from the known population.

But by no means are all modern polls based on the application of random sampling theory. For example, until the mid-1990s at least in Great Britain most opinion polls (like most market research but not most social surveys) were undertaken using 'quota sampling'. Instead of being allocated specific names or addresses to interview, interviewers were instead requested to contact a certain number of people with a given combination of characteristics such as age, gender and social class. These quotas were set to ensure that the total numbers of persons interviewed in each quota category reflects their known distribution in the population as a whole. While it lacked the statistical underpinning of random sampling, quota sampling was defended on the grounds that in practice it seems to work as well. For instance, pre-election polls using the method usually proved to be reasonably close to the actual outcome.

In some countries such as France and Germany, the publication of opinion poll results in the period immediately before polling day is banned. But elsewhere, as in Britain and the USA, opinion polls are themselves a major feature of the media coverage of campaigns up to and including the final day. Indeed, reports of the results of opinion polls are often the most common lead story in British newspapers at election times.

The prominence of opinion polls in modern elections has, however, been accompanied by several high-profile failures. The first such failure was in the US presidential election of 1948, when all the polls suggested wrongly that Harry Truman would lose against Thomas Dewey. This encouraged US pollsters to improve their methods and in particular to ensure that they interviewed closer to election day itself. Similarly, in the British general election of 1970 all but one of the polls anticipated Labour's re-election to office, an error that was also blamed on concluding interviewing too early, so missing an alleged late swing of popular support from Labour to the Conservatives.

The most recent embarrassment for the polls was in Britain's 1992 general election, when the polls suggested right until the last day that Labour were ahead of the Conservatives. This error could not be accounted for simply by a late swing of public opinion. Rather it raised substantial doubts about the accuracy and effectiveness of the practice of quota sampling and left the market-research industry in a state of methodological flux.

The methodology of opinion polls is also influenced by changes in technology. Following the demise of the *Literary Digest* poll, polls were traditionally undertaken by interviewing people face-to-face in their own homes or, in the case of some quota samples, in the street. But the spread of telephone ownership to near saturation point in some countries such as the USA, Canada and parts of Northern Europe resulted in an increasing use of telephone interviews. Amongst the advantages of telephone interviewing are its greater speed and spread. Its introduction has also facilitated a return to more truly random methods of sampling through the use of random digit dialling. But it has disadvantages too, notably its lower levels of response from potential respondents and, still in many countries, the unevenness of telephone ownership within the population. Both these factors can lead to biases in the resulting sample.

The most recent technological change to affect the industry is the advent of the Internet, which holds out the promise of not only even greater speed than telephone surveys but also lower cost. But even in countries with relatively high Internet penetration, such as the USA, a significant and socially distinctive set of the population do not have access. Moreover, no list of electronic mail addresses from which a random sample could be drawn is available for the general population. Internet polling companies have attempted to overcome these problems by recruiting panels of potential respondents, which can then be used to create socially representative samples, and by ensuring that their final samples are appropriately weighted.

Opinion polls do not deal only with the subject of voting intention and they are certainly not confined to election periods. They address a range of topical questions, attempting to inject the public's voice into current debates, whether about social, moral, political or economic issues. They also serve the purpose of monitoring the course of public opinion on such matters as the popularity of governments and party leaders, the images of parties, the salience of particular social or political problems, evaluations of the economy and so on.

The crafting of such questions requires considerable skill to ensure that they are comprehensible to all respondents and not biased towards one viewpoint or another. Even the most carefully drafted questions may, however, produce misleading or spuriously precise answers, often suggesting a sense of certainty among the public about an issue that, in reality, most people know or care little about. Nonetheless, the strength of polls lies in their ability to bring greater levels of accuracy than would otherwise be available to the description of the ebbs and flows of public opinion. Even using as few as around 1,000 interviews, the polls sometimes manage to read the mood of the whole adult population of a country (or even of several countries, as in the case of the European Union's regular Eurobarometer survey) on a range of social and political issues of the day.

JOHN CURTICE
UNIVERSITY OF STRATHCLYDE
ROGER JOWELL
SOCIAL AND COMMUNITY PLANNING RESEARCH
AND CITY UNIVERSITY, LONDON

Further reading

Couper, M.P. (2000) 'Web surveys: A review of issues and approaches', *Public Opinion Quarterly* 64.
Jowell, R., Hedges, B., Lynn, P. and Heath, A. (1993) 'The 1992 British election: The failure of the polls', *Public Opinion Quarterly* 57.
Moon, N. (1999) *Opinion Polls: History, Theory and Practice*, Manchester.
Roll, C.W., Jr and Cantril, A.H. (1972) *Polls: Their Use and Misuse in Politics*, New York.
The Opinion Polls and the 1992 General Election: A Report to the MRS (1994) London.
Worcester, R.M. (1991) *British Public Opinion: A Guide to the History and Methodology of Political Opinion Polling*, Oxford.

SEE ALSO: focus groups; questionnaires; sample surveys

PUBLIC SPHERE

The concept of the public sphere is used most commonly to refer to the realm of public discourse and debate, a realm in which individuals can discuss issues of common concern. The public sphere is generally contrasted with the private domains of personal relations and of privatized economic activity.

One of the most important accounts of the public sphere was provided by Jürgen Habermas in his classic work *The Structural Transformation of the Public Sphere* (1989 [1962]). Habermas traced the development of the public sphere (Öffentlichkeit) from ancient Greece to the present. He argued that, in seventeenth- and eighteenth-century Europe, a distinctive type of public sphere began to emerge. This 'bourgeois public sphere' consisted of private individuals who gathered together in public places, like salons and coffee houses, to discuss the key issues of the day. These discussions were stimulated by the rise of the periodical press, which flourished in England and other parts of Europe in the late seventeenth and eighteenth centuries. The bourgeois public sphere was not part of the state but was, on the contrary, a sphere in which the activities of state authorities could be confronted and criticized through reasoned argument and debate.

The development of the bourgeois public sphere had important consequences for the institutional form of modern states. By being called before the forum of the public, Parliament became increasingly open to scrutiny; and the political role of the freedom of speech was formally recognized in the constitutional arrangements of many modern states. But Habermas argued that, as a distinctive type of public domain, the bourgeois public sphere gradually declined in significance. Many salons and coffee houses eventually disappeared, and the periodical press became part of a range of media institutions that were increasingly organized on a commercial basis. The commercialization of the press altered its character: the press gradually ceased to be a forum of reasoned debate and became more and more concerned with the pursuit of profit and the cultivation of images.

Habermas's argument concerning the transformation of the public sphere has been criticized on historical grounds (Calhoun 1992), and in terms of its relevance to the social and political conditions of the late twentieth century (Thompson 1991). But the concept of the public sphere remains an important reference point for thinkers who are interested in the development of forms of political organization that are independent of state power. It also remains a vital notion for theorists who are concerned with the impact of communication media in the modern world. The concept emphasizes the importance of open argument and debate – whether conducted in the media or in a shared locale – as a means of forming public opinion and resolving controversial political issues.

JOHN B. THOMPSON
UNIVERSITY OF CAMBRIDGE

References

Calhoun, C. (ed.) (1992) *Habermas and the Public Sphere*, Cambridge, MA.

Habermas, J. (1989 [1962]) *The Structural Transformation of the Public Sphere: An Inquiry into a Category of Bourgeois Society*, Cambridge, UK.

Thompson, J.B. (1991) *Ideology and Modern Culture: Critical Social Theory in the Era of Mass Communication*, Cambridge, UK.

Further reading

Keane, J. (1991) *The Media and Democracy*, Cambridge, UK.

Landes, J. (1988) *Women and the Public Sphere in the Age of the French Revolution*, Ithaca, NY.

Sennett, R. (1974) *The Fall of Public Man*, Cambridge, UK.

SEE ALSO: Habermas, Jürgen; intellectuals; media and politics; privacy

Q

QUEER THEORY

Queer theory is a predominantly North American, humanities-based approach that aims to subvert all traditional categories linked with gender and sexuality (especially gay, lesbian, bisexual and transgender and heterosexual categories). It developed towards the end of the 1980s, and can be seen as linked to poststructuralism, postmodernism, multiculturalism and lesbian and gay studies. Some might even claim a genealogy back to certain strands of anarchistic thought. Whilst the ideas of Michel Foucault certainly loom large (with his talk of 'regimes of truth' and 'discursive explosions'), the roots of queer theory (if not the term) are usually seen to lie in the work of Eve Kasofsky Sedgwick and Judith Butler (Turner 2000). The former argued in *The Epistemology of the Closet* that

> many of the major nodes of thought and knowledge in twentieth century Western culture as a whole are structured – indeed fractured – by a chronic, now endemic crisis of homo/heterosexual definition, indicatively male, dating from the end of the nineteenth century...any understanding of any aspect of modern Western culture must be, not merely incomplete, but damaged in its central substance to the degree that it does not incorporate a critical analysis of modern homo/heterosexual definition.
>
> (Sedgwick 1994 [1990]: 1)

'Queer' deconstructs discourses and creates a greater openness and fluidity by suggesting that very few people really fit into the straitjackets of our contemporary gender and sexual categories. It hence becomes a stark attack on 'normal business in the academy' (Warner 1993: 25), challenging the thoroughly gendered mode of thinking behind much academic work. As such it remains an intensely political project.

Alexander Doty suggests at least six different meanings for the term. Sometimes it is used simply as a synonym for lesbian, gay, bisexual, transgender (LGBT). Sometimes it is an 'umbrella term' that puts together a range of so-called 'non-straight positions'. Sometimes it simply describes any non-normative expression of gender (which could include 'straight'). Sometimes it is used to describe 'non-straight things' not clearly signposted as lesbian, gay, etc., but which bring with them a possibility for such a reading even if incoherently. Sometimes it locates the 'non-straight work, positions, pleasures and readings of people who don't share the same sexual orientation as the text they are producing or responding to'. Taking it even further, Doty then suggests it may be a particular form of cultural readership and textual coding that creates spaces not contained within conventional categories like gay, straight, transgendered. Interestingly, what all his meanings have in common is that they are in some way descriptive of *texts* and they are in some way linked to (usually transgressing) categories of *gender and sexuality* (Doty 2000: 6–7).

Queer theory highlights the analysis of texts. A first instance of this was Sedgwick's *Between Men* (1985) where she looked at a number of key literary works (from Dickens to Tennyson) and reread them as driven by homosexuality, homosociality and homophobia. Whilst patriarchy might condemn the former, it positively valorizes the latter (Sedgwick 1985). Following from this, all manner of literature, media and cultural forms have been analysed this way. Amongst the many texts analysed, there have been queer readings of Diderot's *The Nun*, Wilde's *The Importance of Being Earnest*; operas, musicals, television comedies (such as lesbian readings of the sitcoms *I Love Lucy* or *The Golden Girls*). As well as many films – from queer readings of *Rebel without a Cause* and *The Wizard of Oz* to *Pulp Fiction* and *Buffy, the Vampire Slayer* (e.g. Doty 1993, 2000). Indeed, almost no text can escape the eyes of the queer theorist.

Responses to queer theory have been mixed. It would not be too unfair to say that outside the world of queer theorists in the world of 'straight academia', it has been more or less ignored and has had minimal impact. It is comparatively rare in mainstream literary analysis or social theory for queer to be taken seriously. This has had the unfortunate consequence of largely ghettoizing the whole approach. Ironically, those who may most need to understand the working of the heterosexual–homosexual binary divide in their work can hence ignore it (and they usually do); whilst those who least need to understand it, actively work to deconstruct terms that really describe themselves.

Queer theory also poses the paradox of being inside the academy whilst wanting to be outside of it. Queer theory must explicitly challenge any kind of closure or settlement of ideas and so any attempts at definition or codification must be a non-starter. It also shows the real paradox of this mode of thinking. It cannot establish anything; it must always move on; it must deconstruct *ad nauseam*. And yet, at the same time, it often brings a sense of academic elitism as yet more new categories are invented.

The term itself has also been seen as provocative: a pejorative and stigmatizing word from the past is reclaimed by that very stigmatized grouping and renegotiated its meaning – as such it has a distinct generational overtone. Older gays and lesbians feel much less comfortable with it and it serves as a generational marker. More than this: there are very many from within the lesbian, gay, bisexual and transgender movement (LGBT as it is currently clumsily called) who also reject its tendency to deconstruct the very idea of gay and lesbian identity – hence abolishing a field of study and politics when it has only just got going. Sheila Jeffreys (2003) is particularly scathing, seeing the whole queer movement as a serious threat to the gains of radical lesbians in the late twentieth century. By losing the cate-gories of women and men in a fog of (largely masculine) queer deconstruction, it becomes impossible to see the roots of women's subordination to men.

KEN PLUMMER
UNIVERSITY OF ESSEX

References

Doty, A. (1993) *Making it Perfectly Queer*, Minnesota.
—— (2000) *Flaming Classics: Queering the Film Canon*, London.
Jeffreys, S. (2003) *Unpacking Queer Politics*, Oxford.
Sedgwick, E.K. (1985) *Between Men: English Literature and Male Homosocial Desire*, New York.
—— (1994 [1990]) *The Epistemology of the Closet*, London.
Turner, W.B. (2000) *A Genealogy of Queer Theory*, Philadelphia.
Warner, M. (1993) *Fear of a Queer Planet: Queer Politics and Social Theory*, Minneapolis.

Further reading

Edwards, T. (1998) 'Queer fears: Against the cultural turn', *Sexualities* 1(4) (November): 471–84.
Halberstam, J. (1998) *Female Masculinity*, Duke University Press, Durham, NC.
Roseneil, S. (2003) 'The heterosexual/homosexual binary', in *Handbook of Lesbian and Gay Studies*, London, pp. 27–43.
Seidman, S. (ed.) (1996) *Queer Theory/Sociology*, Oxford.
Sullivan, N. (2003) *A Critical Introduction to Queer Theory*, Edinburgh.

SEE ALSO: gender, sociology of; homosexualities; sexual behaviour

QUESTIONNAIRES

Questionnaires pose questions in a structured and standardized fashion, a format lending itself to sample surveys as well as to diagnostic psychological tests and many administrative tasks. 'Structure' here refers to questions appearing *not* in haphazard order. Items in a questionnaire unfold either in a fixed sequence or according to some systematic rule such as alternating versions or even outright randomization, so long as the sequence is coded. A well-designed questionnaire usually has a logic to its structure. Blocks of items may be arranged according to a flow of topics or question formats. A questionnaire might, for example, commence with experiences from the respondent's childhood, proceeding through time to the present. It is a rule of good questionnaire design to begin with a question having high interest to respondents, and one that most people are eligible to answer. Sociodemographic or 'face-sheet' items often appear towards the end of a questionnaire to minimize damage later on, both because their interest-appeal may be low and because some such questions (especially about income) may be intrusive, eroding subsequent co-operation. Complexities of the respondent's life experience may be accommodated using 'skip' instructions. For example, questions regarding current occupation typically begin with a labour force status filter to ascertain whether the respondent is now working, is looking for work, or is outside the labour force as a student, homemaker or retiree. Those not currently in paid work would be asked to skip beyond the questions about occupation, to resume with the next relevant item. 'Standardization' as referred to above means that every item is asked either with unvarying wording and answer format or with systematic, planned variation in which a record is kept of which respondents answer which version of each question.

The word 'questionnaire' implies self-enumeration. Questionnaires can be distributed by hand (for example in a classroom), through the mail, via the Internet or through arrangements such as the 'drop-off', where a fieldworker leaves the questionnaire for householders to complete by themselves, with provision either for mailing the completed form back to the research office or for a return house-call and pick-up by the fieldworker. A questionnaire administered by a fieldworker, in a face-to-face interview or over the telephone, is generally termed a 'schedule'.

Many of the same rules for design apply equally to self-completed questionnaires and fieldworker-administered interview schedules. Both have been profoundly affected by developments over the past two decades in computer survey software. Researchers using interview schedules in 'CATI' or 'CAPI' (computer-assisted telephone/personal interview) form have since the 1980s been able to enrich studies by having skip instructions automatic and non-visible, by recalling to the screen information given earlier (even in an earlier wave of a panel study), by setting up experiments within a survey in which the order of questions is varied (with the computer remembering the order), and by randomizing the order

of checklist responses, to mention just some of the possibilities. It is the Web questionnaire, however, which has brought the self-enumerated mode into the computer age. A Web questionnaire can include 'sound bites', pictures and other graphics, even film clips, and colours can be varied section by section.

The self-enumerated format of questionnaires makes it especially important to explore variations in wording, answer format, question order, etc., for no fieldworker is present to help interpret ambiguous instructions or phrasings. Along with the Internet, 'desktop publishing' has been a boon for designers of questionnaires, opening up new lines of methodological research. Can comprehension be improved by expanding the contrast in fonts, by allowing more or less white space per page, by liberal use of italics and bolded text? Dillman's (2000) second edition of his widely known 1978 text gives many examples of the possibilities.

For all the expanding possibilities of scientific investigation into optimal design through controlled experimentation, an element of common sense and trial-and-error remains integral to good questionnaire construction. As Payne (1951) said in his classic text, over 50 years ago, there is an *Art of Asking Questions*. Questionnaire designers must constantly consider such issues as whether to offer questions in open-ended or closed-response format, for medium-is-the-message effects occur. Sometimes, no matter how much a response checklist is informed by pretesting in open format, open and closed questions fail to produce identical frequency distributions. The write-in entries from open questions keep research nearer to the respondent's own frame of reference. The preset checklist in a closed question, however, may help clarify a question. The one format is not intrinsically superior to the other, except in so far as closed questions require less labour expense at the data-processing stage. Questions in 'agree-disagree' or 'yes-no' form have an appealing simplicity, but may oversimplify, along with leading respondents into a 'yea-saying' mindset. The more extended closed-answer formats such as the Likert Scale may be preferable, where several adverbs describe a hierarchy of sentiments around dimensions such as agreement, favourability or frequency. Should respondents, then, be offered two choices on attitude questions, three, the Likert five or the 'magical number' (Miller 1956) seven? Should 'no opinion' or 'don't know' be offered as response options? These decisions must be made with reference to the topic at hand, the sophistication of the respondents, comparability with prior research, and perhaps the 'house effect' preferences of different survey organizations.

Cynics may claim that, depending on how key questions are worded, a questionnaire can be used to show almost anything. Researchers have long realized that question wording, layout and answer format may affect results. The best defences against such problems are, first, an attitude of seeking the truth rather than confirmation of preconceptions, followed by an orientation towards carefully pilot testing draft questions, using techniques such as the 'cognitive interview' to help gauge how respondents interpret items, and liberal use of the experimental method so that results from alternative question wordings and formats can be compared across randomly selected subsets within a sample. In this manner, the intrinsic tendency for questionnaire design to influence results moves from a source of error to a source of variance, to be included in models alongside other explanatory variables.

JOHN GOYDER
UNIVERSITY OF WATERLOO

References

Dillman, D.A. (2000) *Mail and Internet Surveys: The Tailored Design Method*, 2nd edn, New York.

Miller, G.A. (1956) 'The magical number seven, plus or minus two: Some limits on our capacity for processing information', *Psychological Review* 63.

Payne, S.L. (1951) *The Art of Asking Questions*, Princeton, NJ.

Further reading

Converse, J.M. (1984) 'Strong arguments and weak evidence: The open/closed questioning controversy of the 1940s', *Public Opinion Quarterly* 48.

Foddy, W. (1993) *Constructing Questions for Interviews and Questionnaires: Theory and Practice in Social Research*, Cambridge, UK.

Schuman, H. and Presser, S. (1981) *Questions and Answers in Attitude Surveys: Experiments on Question Form, Wording, and Context*, San Diego, CA.

Sirken, M.G. (1999) *Cognition and Survey Research*, New York.

SEE ALSO: public opinion polls; sample surveys

R

RACE

Race is a fundamental division of the human species, roughly equivalent to the zoological subspecies. It does not exist in nature. Those who have maintained the biological reality of human races have notably failed to agree on their number, defining characteristics or origins. The reason is that the actual patterns of human biological diversity undermine the concept of race (Montagu 1964). The concept of race rests upon two fallacies. First, there is the expectation that the gene pool of bounded groups distinguish them sharply from other groups. This is contradicted by the facts. Second, 'race' is defined on the basis of the shared possession of a common specific essence by all members of a defined group or category, who thus embody the group's attributes. This is an example of a fallacy known to philosophers as essentialism (Zack 2002).

The life of the race concept

The idea that the human species could be subdivided into a small number of relatively homogeneous units (which does not necessarily entail seeing them as being of unequal worth, but often does) emerged first during the Enlightenment, as a consequence of the unique social, economic and political forces then at play.

Prior to that time, human diversity had been seen in purely local terms. The ancient Greeks, for example, recognized that the Scythians to the north were fairer, and the Ethiopians to the south were darker, but this did not lead them to think there were a few basic kinds of people. Travellers' accounts, from Pliny the Elder's *Natural History* in the first century through the *Travels of Sir John Mandeville* in the fourteenth century, spoke of headless peoples, one-legged peoples, one-eyed peoples, etc., without a concept of broad geographical homogeneity.

In 1684, however, a French adventurer and physician named François Bernier published the first suggestion on record that the human species could be effectively and naturally subdivided along geographical lines (Hannaford 1996). He was unsure whether the indigenous peoples of Africa comprised one group or two, but he juxtaposed them against the peoples of Europe, West Asia and America (as a single group); the peoples of East Asia; and the Lapps (Saami) of Scandinavia. Bernier's approach was adopted by the great Swedish naturalist Carl Linnaeus, whose most famous work, *The System of Nature*, revolutionized biology by placing classification at its core. Even in its first edition (1735), Linnaeus classified humans among the 'Anthropomorpha' (along with monkeys and sloths), and divided them into four continental groups, incorporating the famous colour-coding as well: white Europeans, red Americans, dark (later, yellow) Asians and black Africans. By the tenth edition (1758), which modern taxonomy adopts as its reference point, Linnaeus had augmented his colour-coded geographical subspecies with terse descriptions: physical, mental and cultural. Thus, *Homo sapiens Europaeus albus* had long, flowing blond hair and blue eyes, a sanguine personality, wore tight-fitting clothes and was governed by law. By contrast, *Homo sapiens Americanus rufus* had thick, straight black hair, a choleric personality, painted himself with fine red lines and was governed by custom (Bendyshe 1865).

After Linnaeus, the proper way to do biology was to begin by classifying. The heir to Linnaeus's work on the human species was Johann

Friedrich Blumenbach, who jettisoned Linnaeus's non-biological traits, and made the skull and face the defining features of races. Blumenbach travelled more extensively than Linnaeus and was struck by the continuity of human form, and by the arbitrariness of subdivision; nevertheless, he proceeded to follow Linnaeus by classifying humans into subspecies. Oddly, where Linnaeus had put forth the blond, blue-eyed Northern European as archetype of the group, Blumenbach admired most the skulls of peoples from the Caucasus, in Southeastern Europe, and thus called this group Caucasian. There seems to have been little discussion about which was the most appropriate avatar of the peoples of Europe.

By the end of the eighteenth century, the word 'race', which had previously had a colloquial meaning equivalent to stock or lineage, came to be synonymous with the Linnaean subspecies (Hudson 1996). Thus, two uses of the term became common – an older, informal usage designating any human group with a name, and a newer, formal taxonomic usage, validated by science. When used together, they created a situation in which there were 'races within races'. By the middle of the twentieth century, physical anthropologists had appropriated to themselves the formal scientific use of race, and were dismissing the older use, which had produced talk of the races of Jews, gypsies and Aryans (Brace 1982; Marks 1995).

Pre-Darwinian scholars, operating within the formal structures of the Great Chain of Being, commonly regarded non-European races as lower, and specifically more ape-like – although the precise meaning of such a comparison was nuanced in the absence of a concept of evolution. The emergence of Darwinism actually brought little change in perceptions of human diversity. Lacking a fossil record of human evolution, early Darwinians such as Ernst Haeckel simply capitalized on a pre-existing imagery linking the non-European races to the apes as evidence for the ascent of the human species.

Intertwined with the idea of the number and provenance of the human races was the question of their ancestries – unitary (monogenesis) or separate (polygenesis). Most pre-Darwinian scholars acknowledged that the criterion of interbreeding sufficed to established humans as a single species with a single origin, which was certainly compatible with Scripture and yet implied a microevolutionary process able to generate diverse modern human appearances from Adam and Eve. The contrary view – that different races actually comprise different species – surfaced around the time of the American Civil War, in works by the physician Josiah Nott and diplomat George Gliddon (Stanton 1960; Haller 1970), and the zoologist Louis Agassiz (Lurie 1954), and around the Civil Rights movement a century later, promoted by the US anthropologist Carleton Coon and the English geneticist R.R. Ruggles Gates (Marks 2000; Jackson 2001). Calling Africans and Europeans different species, or otherwise overstating their differences and divergent histories, was readily perceived as scientifically contrived apologetics for the perpetuation of large-scale injustices, and only found a narrow, if ardent, following.

However, an internal critique of the formal taxonomic use of the term 'race' was emerging as well. As early as the 1930s, biologist Julian Huxley and anthropologist Alfred Cort Haddon (1936) were arguing for a lexical substitution of 'ethnic group' for the politically tainted 'race'. Huxley himself (1938) had coined the term 'cline' to describe a geographical gradient of the features of a variable species, and, by 1941, the Anglo-American anthropologist Ashley Montagu was questioning the very reality of race as a structuring principle of human variation (Barkan 1993).

Patterns of human variation

Contemporary anthropology and genetics sees five patterns in the biological structure of the human species that, taken together, undermine and discredit the classical notion of race as subspecies.

Human variation is clinal, not racial

The most basic aspect of human variation is what had been implicitly acknowledged by the ancient world: that groups of people physically blend into their neighbours (Livingstone 1962). Why should it be the case that local populations resemble one another and the boundary between presumptive major human groups is so difficult to establish? Modern anthropology points to two causes. First, natural selection adapts populations to their local circumstances, thus adaptive physical features should vary gradually along with environments (Jablonski and Chaplin 2000), and, second, people interbreed with their neighbours, so connecting them genetically. In consequence, people differ biologically across the globe, but that difference is structured locally: people are similar to those nearby and different from those far away.

Human variation is polymorphic, not polytypic

Every population has taller and shorter people, quicker and slower, stronger and weaker, more agile and more clumsy, more articulate and less articulate, more introverted and less introverted, etc. It was the major contribution of population genetics, however, to be able to quantify this variation, and to partition it meaningfully. It is now established that of the detectable genetic variation in the human species, about 85 per cent is found within populations; 5–10 per cent is found between local populations; and 5–10 per cent is found between continental mega-populations (Lewontin 1972; Barbujani et al. 1997; Rosenberg et al. 2002). While this does not in and of itself refute the existence of races, it does show that the genetic variation upon which they would be necessarily predicated makes up only a tiny fraction of the total genetic variation found in our species.

Humans are depauperate in genetic variation

While humans seem remarkably diverse, the bulk of the diversity we perceive is cultural. Humans vary significantly in a relatively few features of the face and body. Once again, geneticists are able to quantify this observation meaningfully. If we compare a segment of DNA across a large sample of humans, we find considerably less variation among the human samples than we find in an assortment of chimpanzees or gorillas (Kaessmann et al. 2001). And yet the humans live all over the world, while the chimpanzees and gorillas live only in semi-isolated refugia in equatorial Africa. The amount of genetic variation we can detect across chimpanzee subspecies is comparable to the amount of genetic variation we detect between humans and Neandertals, a bit of whose DNA has been preserved well enough to be studied (Krings et al. 1999). There is consequently no zoological justification for identifying subspecies among living humans.

All peoples comprise genetic subsets of Africans

When we examine the DNA sequence variation of humans partitioned continentally, we find more variation, more divergent variation, and more ancient variants among Africans than among Europeans or Asians. While the overall extent of genetic diversity in a population may have other causes, such as strong selection or population size, the overall pattern is one of Africa providing the founding gene pool for the rest of the human species (Merriwether et al. 1991; Tishkoff et al. 1996).

Race is inherited culturally, not biologically

Perhaps the most counter-intuitive fact about race is that it is fundamentally a cognitive, not a natural, category. This can be demonstrated in several ways. First, the common racial juxtaposition of Africans against Europeans creates a problem at the boundary – the Near East – where the peoples of East Africa are more similar to the nearby peoples of the Arabian Peninsula than they are to the peoples of Western or Southern Africa. Second, there is no evidence that these peoples are less 'pure' than anyone else, as people seem to have been living in that area for as long as *Homo sapiens sapiens* has been on earth. Contrasting only people from the farthest regions (Northern Europe, West Africa, East Asia) compares not the purest, but simply the most geographically distant and divergent. Third, in contrast to the fractional and probabilistic nature of biological heredity, race tends to be inherited in a qualitative, all-or-nothing fashion. While many US censuses had categories for 'mulatto', 'quadroon' and 'octoroon' – reflecting crude proportion of African ancestry – a person in any of those categories was nevertheless barred from marrying a 'white' in a majority of states, a crime called miscegenation. In essence, seven white great-grandparents were not sufficient to make one 'white', but one black great-grandparent could make one 'black'. And, fourth, racial categories are identities whose composition and classification change with the politics of the place and era. The racial categories 'coloured' and 'black' were synonymous in the USA. In South Africa, however, the law discriminated between people classified as 'black' and 'coloured', and they were not officially supposed to intermarry. The British census features the racial categories 'Indian,' 'Pakistani' and 'Bangladeshi' but these are absent from the US census – where 'Indian', of course, means something rather different. In the USA, however, 'Hispanic' is a recognized identity that appears in few other national censuses. States tally groups that have political salience. Censuses do not, however, apply some established scientific classification of human subspecies, if only because none such classification exists (Lee 1993).

The future of human classification

The twentieth century saw a distinction drawn between race (a presumptively natural group) and ethnicity (a presumptively constructed social identity). The value of this distinction lies in calling attention to the creative and complex ways in which human beings categorize themselves, sometimes in parallel with biological or geographical criteria, and sometimes not. Even when the criteria incorporate biological distinctions, they may be accompanied by political inequalities and social prejudices that are not derived from the biological differences themselves, but which simply exploit the biological features to mark the unfavoured group.

We now recognize, however, that just as race is not an objective, natural category, nor is ethnicity not an entirely subjective, cognitive category. To some extent both terms are giving ground to 'population'. Where 'race' most commonly refers to an aggregated continental group, 'population' designates a more geographically localized group of people, a more biologically 'real' entity – even if demographically labile. And since a population is often geographically localized, it should not be surprising that people of a common ethnicity often share physical features, in addition to the obviously culturally based physical similarities, such as body language and decoration.

Although we recognize that race is historically and culturally constructed, we must acknowledge that ideas about race constitute a political and social force that may, and often does, affect many aspects of a human life. Racism exists independently of the reality of races, in the same way that religion exists independently of the reality of God. The particular issue at hand is the poor match between categories of political salience and the distribution of biological variation in the human species.

As more people designate themselves as being of 'mixed race' (which only recently became a formal category on US censuses), we can envision the progressive blurring of racial categories. However, it is likely that people will always self-identify with one or more ethnicities, as they serve to orient us socially and impart meaning to our lives, embodying particular identities (Smedley 1999). Thus, the categories – 'Hispanic' and 'Arab' (based formally on linguistic criteria), and 'indigenous' or 'Native' (based on geography, economics and/or ancestry) – have become politically significant identities in recent years, and thus quasi-racial categories (Kuper 2003), while those like 'Jewish' and 'Irish' are no longer considered such (Brodkin 1999; Ignatiev 1996). The human drive to classify ourselves and others stays with us, but the categories into which we classify people evolve.

JONATHAN MARKS
UNIVERSITY OF NORTH CAROLINA
AT CHARLOTTE

References

Barbujani, G., Magagni, A., Minch, E. and Cavalli-Sforza, L.L. (1997) 'An apportionment of human DNA diversity', *Proceedings of the National Academy of Sciences, USA* 94.

Barkan, E.A. (1993) *The Retreat of Scientific Racism*, New York.

Bendyshe, T. (1865) 'The history of anthropology', *Memoirs of the Anthropological Society of London* 1.

Brace, C.L. (1982) 'The roots of the race concept in American physical anthropology', in F. Spencer (ed.) *A History of American Physical Anthropology, 1930–1980*, New York.

Brodkin, K. (1999) *How Jews Became White Folks and What That Says about Race in America*, Piscataway, NJ.

Haller, J.S., Jr (1970) 'The species problem: Nineteenth-century concepts of racial inferiority in the origin of man controversy', *American Anthropologist* 72.

Hannaford, I. (1996) *Race: The History of an Idea in the West*, Baltimore.

Hudson, N. (1996) 'From "nation" to "race": The origin of racial classification in eighteenth-century thought', *Eighteenth-Century Studies* 29.

Huxley, J.S. (1938) 'Clines: An auxiliary taxonomic principle', *Nature* 142.

Huxley, J. and Haddon, A.C. (1936) *We Europeans*, New York.

Ignatiev, N. (1996) *How the Irish Became White*, New York.

Jablonski, N. and Chaplin, G. (2000) 'The evolution of human skin coloration', *Journal of Human Evolution* 39.

Jackson, J.J., Jr (2001) 'In ways unacademical': The

reception of Carleton S. Coon's *The Origin of Races*', *Journal of the History of Biology* 34.

Kaessmann, H., Wiebe, V. and Paabo, S. (2001) 'Great ape DNA sequences reveal a reduced diversity and an expansion in humans', *Nature Genetics* 27.

Krings, M., Geisert, H., Schmitz, R.W., Krainitzki, H. and Pääbo, S. (1999) 'DNA sequence of the mitochondrial hypervariable region II from the neandertal type specimen', *Proceedings of the National Academy of Sciences, USA* 96.

Kuper, A. (2003) 'The return of the native', *Current Anthropology* 44.

Lee, S.M. (1993) 'Racial classifications in the US census: 1890–1990', *Ethnic and Racial Studies* 16.

Lewontin, R.C. (1972) 'The apportionment of human diversity', *Evolutionary Biology* 6.

Livingstone, F.B. (1962) 'On the non-existence of human races', *Current Anthropology* 3.

Lurie, E. (1954) 'Louis Agassiz and the races of man', *Isis* 45.

Marks, J. (1995) *Human Biodiversity: Genes, Race, and History*, New York.

—— (2000) 'Human biodiversity as a central theme of biological anthropology: Then and now', *Kroeber Anthropological Society Papers* 84.

Merriwether, D.A., Clark, A.G., Ballinger, S.W., Schurr, T.G., Soodyall, H., Jenkins, T., Sherry, S.T. and Wallace, D.C. (1991) 'The structure of human mitochondrial DNA variation', *Journal of Molecular Evolution* 33.

Montagu, A. (1964) *Man's Most Dangerous Myth: The Fallacy of Race*, 4th edn, Cleveland.

Rosenberg, N.A., Pritchard, J.K., Weber, J.L., Cann, H.M., Kidd, K.K., Zhivotovsky, L.A. and Feldman, M.W. (2002) 'Genetic structure of human populations', *Science* 298.

Smedley, A. (1999) '"Race" and the construction of human identity', *American Anthropologist* 100.

Stanton, W.R. (1960) *The Leopard's Spots: Scientific Attitudes toward Race in America, 1815–59*, Chicago.

Tishkoff, S., Dietzsch, E., Speed, W., Pakstis, A.J., Kidd, J., Cheung, K., Bonne-Tamir, B., Santachiara-Benerecetti, A., Moral, P., Krings, M., Paabo, S., Watson, E., Risch, N., Jenkins, T. and Kidd, K. (1996) 'Global patterns of linkage disequilibrium at the CD4 locus and modern human origins', *Science* 271.

Zack, N. (2002) *Philosophy of Science and Race*, New York.

Further reading

Montagu, A. (1941) 'The concept of race in the human species in the light of genetics', *Journal of Heredity* 32.

SEE ALSO: genetics and behaviour; population genetics; racism

RACISM

Racism, the idea that there is a direct correspondence between a group's values, behaviour and attitudes, and its physical features, is one of the major social problems confronting contemporary societies. Racism is also a relatively new idea: its birth can be traced to the European colonization of much of the world, the rise and development of European capitalism, and the development of the European and US slave trade. These events made it possible for colour and race to become pivotal links in the relations between Europeans, Americans and the people of Africa, Asia, Latin America and Australia. Though belief in the idea of the link between race and behaviour has never been proven, the tenaciousness of ideas supporting this connection has been elevated to a status of folk truth among the general population in many, if not most, countries (Williams 1990). Indeed, if the assertion of such a relationship were the only defining aspect of racism, its impact might be less damaging, though no less unacceptable. Instead, a more pernicious feature of racism entails the belief that some groups, those of a certain hue, with less power and low status, are inferior; others, of another hue, with greater power and high status, are deemed superior.

Racism is a highly complex and multifaceted concept and can be delineated into several areas, but it might be important to differentiate racism from ethnocentrism, a concept with which it is often confused and used, unfortunately, interchangeably. For example, Jones (1981) begins his critique of racism by distinguishing the two terms. Ethnocentrism entails the acceptance of the belief that individuals and groups seek to interpret events and situations, and to evaluate the actions, behaviour and values of other individuals and groups from their particular cultural perspectives. This view simply assumes that all insider values are 'acceptable', 'right' and 'good'; conversely, all outsider values are 'unacceptable', 'wrong' and 'bad'. What distinguishes ethnocentrism from racism is that in the former, there is no attempt to base insider/outsider differences along racial or colour lines. Oliver C. Cox (1948) makes a similar point in his study of class, caste and colour: studies of early civilizations and empires demonstrated that ethnocentrism was clearly evident; the ethnocentrism focused solely on language and culture. That is, one was civilized if one understood the language and culture of the insider, but a barbarian if one did not. The early Greek idea of dividing the world into these two spheres, the civilized or the barbarian, was typical.

The Social Darwinism of the nineteenth century (Hofstadter 1955; Ryan 1981) laid the foundation for what is called 'ideological racism'. The logic is as follows: nature rewards groups that win the struggle for existence; strong groups, the winners, have won the right to control and, hence, decide the fate of the losers, the weaker groups. Those groups that lose in the struggle against other groups, by dint of this loss, confirm their weakness and inferiority. Since this ideology emerged simultaneously with the rise of European imperialism and the colonization of the continents, and gave credence to these events, and because the people and races being colonized and conquered were Africans, Asians and Native Americans, the close relationship between race, colour and ideas of superiority or inferiority was viewed by Europeans and Americans as having been confirmed.

As the European and American political, economic and cultural powers became more deeply entrenched in what DuBois called the 'coloured world', other attempts were made to justify the ever-increasing racial inequality. One new doctrine may be called 'scientific racism'. This racism entailed the use of 'scientific techniques', to sanction the belief in European and US racial superiority. The first technique was the use of 'objective' IQ tests, and their results, to confirm the high position of Europeans and the low positions of all other races in what its proponents called a racial hierarchy. Almost simultaneously with the use of 'scientific tests' was the use of brain size to prove inferiority or superiority. Those who believed in racial inequality were, thus, eager to use the lofty name of science to support their efforts to dominate and control other races and continents. In one of his studies, Pierre Van Den Berghe (1964) cut to the heart of the racist logic when he stated that despite all talk of inferiority or superiority, groups dominate other groups because only by doing so can they ensure and enforce inequality. But it can be said that this enforced inequality has yet a more ulterior motive that is even more central to the idea of racism: to isolate, penalize, ostracize and push the pariah group outside of the normal and ongoing social, political, economic and cultural discourse so that the pariah group will, in fact, be 'made' inferior.

During the 1960s when race and racism were crucial themes, Stokely Carmichael and Charles Hamilton (1967) coined the term 'institutional racism', using it in conjunction with 'individual racism' to differentiate the overwhelming importance of the former over the latter. An individual may be a racist and choose to discriminate against another individual or a group. This individual act is in contrast to institutional racism in which organizational networks linked to rules, procedures and guidelines make it difficult for members of one group to affiliate institutionally. In this case, it is not so much the individual who discriminates though individuals may do so as supervisors and managers for the company. In institutional racism, institutional rules and procedures that have been established on the basis of the qualifications and standards of the group in power serve to keep all other groups out, though this may not have been the intent of the original rules, procedures and guidelines. In fact, individuals employed in racist institutions may attest to their own lack of racism while proclaiming that they too are trapped and imprisoned by the laws, rules and procedures. There are other instances, however, when institutions willingly and knowingly discriminate. Since the mid-1980s, for example, the US Government has uncovered extensive patterns of institutional racism in housing, employment, education and banking, generally directed against racial minorities. Turner et al. (1984) presented a concise history of the interlocking networks that provide power and force to the racism which permeates institutions. One of the glaring consequences of the intensity of the traditional patterns of institutional racism has been the extent to which white Americans, and whites in South Africa and Britain, have been the recipients of massive affirmative action programmes in which they, whites, had a monopoly on jobs, incomes and bureaucratic positions, while those not white were removed from the competitive field. We have just recently begun to understand the extent to which centuries of affirmative action for whites have consigned minorities to a secondary role in economics, politics, education and other areas of social life.

In the USA, some attention has focused on the idea of 'reverse racism'. Racism in any form, practised by any group, should be challenged and contested, but the idea that minorities in the USA now have sufficient power to injure the interests of the majority group is not consistent with the facts. In all areas of living (political, economic, educational, etc.) whites continue to have a huge monopoly. When one looks closely at the data provided by those who claim that reverse racism is alive and real, one generally sees anecdotal evidence in which much of the information used is obtained third or fourth hand, that is, a friend of a friend said his friend did not get a job or lost a job to a black. When these anecdotal sketches are used, the minority who gets the job or the promotion is invariably less qualified, very incompetent, etc. In the USA, a member of a minority group who is a racist may insult a member of the majority, but in no area of US life are minorities, who may be racists, in a position to control institutionally or determine the opportunity structure for the majority. When majorities are racists, and when they control the major institutions, as described by Turner *et al.* (1984), they can and do control the opportunity structure for minority people.

Since the 1960s when racial analysis became a major issue in social relations, ample data have been collected verifying the negative consequences of racism for minority groups. Generally, these negative consequences resonate around the theme of powerlessness in all areas. In the 1980s some sociologists began to focus on the impact of racism on whites (Dennis 1981). This new twist on the consequences of racism shifts the focus somewhat, for it suggests that racism is not merely something that happens to the oppressed; rather there are social, emotional and ethical issues for the majority culture that controls the institutions which constitute the continuing source of racism. Attention has also been devoted to the idea that racism may be a more consciously directed act and idea than previously assumed. In the 1981 study (Dennis 1981), it was revealed that many parents did, in fact, socialize their children to be racists; racial training did not occur by chance. Children are guided in their racial training by adults, mainly parents (Dennis 1981, 1994). However, during their teen years, even the children from the most racist families tend to move away from the positions of parents and to assert their own views of other groups based on their relationship with these groups at school, work or in various social circles.

In the mid-1990s, the abolition of apartheid in South Africa will certainly alter the racial history in that country. But we now know, based on history in the USA and Britain, that the abolition of racially restrictive laws will not end all semblance of racism. Though much of the myth of race resides in institutional arrangements, another large part resides in patterns of racial thinking and the ideological orientation of individuals and groups in the society. Laws restricting discrimination may be effective to some degree, and groups may be frightened enough by the price they might pay for discriminating, yet ideological racism, enshrined in the deeply held racial myths in a society, may survive among the population in many forms. This then is the test for nations that contain diverse racial groups and which have had a history of racial domination and conflict: how to ensure individual and group equity; how to ensure that group cultural and racial differences be viewed as objective social and biological realities without the accompanying invidious distinctions.

RUTLEDGE M. DENNIS
GEORGE MASON UNIVERSITY

References

Carmichael, S. and Hamilton, C. (1967) *Black Power*, New York.

Cox, O.C. (1948) *Caste, Class and Race*, New York.

Dennis, R. (1981) 'Socialization and racism: The white experience', in B. Bowser and R. Hunt (eds) *Impacts of Racism on White Americans*, Newbury Park, CA.

—— (1994) 'The racial socialization of white youth', in B. Bowser and R. Hunt (eds) *Impacts of Racism on White Americans*, 2nd edn, Newbury Park, CA.

Hofstadter, R. (1955) *Social Darwinism in American Thought, 1860–1915*, Boston, MA.

Jones, J. (1981) 'The concept of racism and its changing reality', in B. Bowser and R. Hunt (eds) *Impacts of Racism on White Americans*, Newbury Park, CA.

Ryan, W. (1981) *Equality*, New York.

Turner, J., Singleton, R. and Musick, D. (1984) *Oppression*, Chicago.

Van Den Berghe, P. (1964) *Caneville*, Middletown, CT.

Williams, R. (1990) *Hierarchial Structures and Social Values: The Creation of Black and Irish Identities in the United States*, Cambridge, UK.

SEE ALSO: affirmative action; multiculturalism; prejudice; race; stereotypes

RADICALISM

Though social theories and philosophical analyses may be termed radical, the primary modern usage of the word radicalism is to designate basic or extreme political challenges to established order. The term (with an uppercase R) came into use in the late eighteenth and early nineteenth centuries to refer to an elite political faction that sought parliamentary and other rationalizing reforms, and became a key root of the Liberal Party in England. Almost immediately, a lowercase usage developed to describe all sorts of political orientations that shared either an analysis of current troubles claiming to go to their roots, or a programme deduced from first principles. Under pressure of the French Revolution and various English popular agitations, attention came increasingly to focus on actual mobilizations – radical actions – rather than merely radical ideas.

Social scientists are still divided in the extent of their emphasis on the importance of rationalistic analyses (for example Marxist class consciousness) compared to other more directly social sources of radical actions. There are two conventional views among the latter group. One, now nearly discredited, holds that social atomization and marginalization dispose those cut off from the social mainstream to engage in protests that reveal more of their psychological troubles than any serious programme for social change. The other stresses the underlying interests that a common position in relation to some external factor, such as markets or means of production, gives to individuals. Both positions are challenged by empirical findings that a great deal of organization and internal cohesion are necessary to radical collective action. Common objective interests are not necessarily enough to produce concerted action. Activists can hope to achieve this coalescence through further organizational efforts, and they often see trade unions and similar organizations as way-stations on the road to class organization.

Traditional communities, however, have been the basis of more radical movements than class or any other abstract bonds and formal organizations. The popular radical movements (as opposed to elite radicals) of early industrial Britain acted on radical social roots in reaction to the disruptions of the Industrial Revolution. Though the members of these communities often lacked sophisticated radical analyses, they had visions profoundly at odds with conditions around them. Perhaps even more importantly, they had the social strength in their communal relations to carry out concerted action against great odds for long periods of time; few compromise positions were open to them, unlike the members of the modern working class. These sorts of social

foundations continue to be central to radical movements around the world. Peasants and other traditional farmers along with artisans and craft workers form the mainstay of these radical movements.

Social revolutions, the most radical of actual political transformations, certainly have many causes besides anti-governmental radical movements. A state structure weakened by external conflicts or internal disunity may, for example, be essential to the success of a revolutionary movement. Where revolutions succeed, and transform societies rather than only change regimes, two sorts of radical groups have generally been involved. On the one hand, there has usually been a tightly organized, forward-looking, relatively sophisticated group of revolutionaries. On the other hand, there has also generally been a broad mass of protesters and rebels acting on the basis of strong local communities and traditional grievances. The latter are essential to making the revolution happen, to destabilizing the state. The former, however, are much better positioned to seize power during the transformation.

At least in the contemporary world of states and other large-scale abstract social organizations, there is a paradox to radicalism (which may of course be of the 'right' as well as the 'left'). Most radicalism is based on local bonds and tradition, yet, when successful, it both disrupts tradition and displaces power towards the centre of society and its large-scale systems of control. This is true even of radical movements aimed at less extreme goals than revolutions. The US Civil Rights movement could succeed in ending local intolerance and oppression only by forcing an increase of central state power and its penetration into local life. But it could not at the same time make local communities democratic and preserve their autonomy as free realms of direct participation.

CRAIG CALHOUN
NEW YORK UNIVERSITY AND PRESIDENT OF THE
SOCIAL SCIENCE RESEARCH COUNCIL, NEW YORK

Further reading

Calhoun, C. (1983) 'The radicalism of tradition', *American Journal of Sociology* 88.
McCarthy, T.P. and McMillan, J.C. (eds) (2003) *The Radical Reader: A Documentary History of the American Radical Tradition*, New York.

Moore, B., Jr (1979) *Injustice: The Social Bases of Obedience and Revolt*, White Plains, NY.

Varon, J. (2004) *Bringing the War Home: The Weather Underground, the Red Army Faction, and Revolutionary Violence in the Sixties and Seventies*, Berkeley, CA.

SEE ALSO: fascism; populism; revolutions; social movements

RATIONAL CHOICE (ACTION) THEORY

Rational choice (or action) theory (RCT) suggests precepts as to how agents (individuals or collectivities) make decisions and take action. Like all theories it is supported by explicitly adopted simplifications. The term is now used to refer to both the 'standard' theory and various developments (bounded rationality, satisficing and prospect theory), which derive from the standard theory. RCT underpins most of economic theory but is much less widely accepted in the other major social sciences. Economics itself is, however, currently experiencing a contested intellectual shift towards the developments just mentioned. Many advocates of RCT believe it provides a unifying theoretical framework, which may be applied across all the social sciences. As such RCT can be construed as either a strictly axiomatic theory (e.g. Savage's axiomatization of expected-utility theory (EUT)), or in a much more informal manner (particularly in political science and sociology).

The standard model pictures the agent as being capable of choosing the 'best' way to act in a given (often subjectively perceived) situation, after having assessed the consequences of all the available (feasible) opportunities. It enables the social scientist to pinpoint, from the standpoint of an agent, the optimal course of action. Whether or not the agent's own standpoint departs from an 'objective' (i.e. the social scientist's) standpoint is usually conceived in terms of the information available to the agent. So formulated the theory could, retrospectively, always locate at least one best course of action. Further constraints are normally incorporated in order to obviate this possibility. Thus it is assumed that the processes of assessing the feasible opportunities and of computing the preferences across them are independent of each other. This implies that (information constant) preferences do not fluctuate in an *ad hoc* manner across alternative decision situations.

Rationality is also often used to cover the idea of making valid inferences from the information available. It is standard to distinguish decision-making (action) under certainty, risk and uncertainty. In the standard model, which supports EUT, the agent is assumed to be capable both of deterministically assessing the consequences of each course of action and of placing a preference or (with additional formal assumptions) an exogenously derived real-valued utility (value) over all the consequences. These induce a complete preference ranking over the opportunities. In practice, however, EUT is often modelled as if the agent is unsure of the consequences of different courses of action.

An exogenous 'space of states of the world' (S) (beyond the control of the agent) and a function taking the combination of all states and feasible alternatives onto the (utility/value bearing) consequences are also assumed. Lack of certainty on the agent's behalf is introduced by his or her *prior* probabilistic (objective or subjective/risk or uncertainty) beliefs relating to our set S. Changing information is then usually handled by a Bayesian updating procedure. In this way EUT and Bayesian inference became the (formal) building blocks of standard RCT. Risk-aversion, or alternatively a taste for taking risks, can be incorporated into the model. It is by relaxing some of these demanding assumptions that the non-standard versions of the theory have evolved. Contrary to the view of many critics, the standard model does not imply an assumption that actors are motivated only by self-regard, self-interest or 'material' considerations. However, most economists do start with such assumptions. Other social scientists often take a broader view, also seeking to find an (endogenous) theory of preference/utility formation.

RCT is used as an analytical framework in both parametric and strategic situations. In the former, the agent makes a decision about a course of action where the situation is fixed (and more or less understood). In the latter, the situation involves an estimation by the agent about what course of action other agents will (have in the past, or are currently, or will in the future) adopt. Such situations are usually analysed using game theory, in which the leading solution is a Nash equilibrium (or some refinement thereof). Game theory now lies at the heart of much theorizing in all the social sciences. RCT can function as either a 'positive' (i.e. descriptive/explanatory) or 'normative' (i.e. prescriptive) theory, although normative uses are rare outside economics. When used normatively, a rational choice analysis may provide guidance to those who depart from rationality as to how they should change their course of action. If, however, such recommendation is respected then the analyst usually assume that the model is inaccurate and will often adjust their assumptions about the actors' preferences/utilities.

RCT is often subject of both formal and informal criticism. Prospect theory, supported by experimental evidence, has detected widespread departures from EUT (e.g. framing effects and simplification of complex problems, asymmetric impact upon utility of equivalent losses and gains). These can sometimes be accommodated by introducing search and calculation costs. This leads to ideas about rational rule (norm) following and copying (mimetics).

PETER ABELL
LONDON SCHOOL OF ECONOMICS AND POLITICAL SCIENCE

Further reading

Abell, P. (1991) Rational Choice Theory, Aldershot.
Axelrod, R. (1984) The Evolution of Cooperation, New York.
Coleman, J.S. (1986) 'Social theory and social research and a theory of action', American Journal of Sociology 91: 1,309–35.
Coleman, J.S. and Fararo, T. (1992) Rational Choice Theory: Advocacy and Critique, Newbury Park, CA.
Cook, K.S. and Levi, M. (1990) The Limits of Rationality, Chicago.
De Vos, H. (1989) Nuts and Bolts for the Social Sciences, Cambridge.
Kahneman, D. and Tversky, A. (1979) 'Prospect theory: An analysis of decisions under risk', Econometrica 47: 263–91.
Kreps, D.M. (1990) Game Theory and Economic Modelling, Oxford.
Moser, P.K. (ed.) (1990) Rationality in Action, Cambridge.
Olson, M. (1965) The Logic of Collective Action, Cambridge, MA.
Ordeshook, P.C. (1986) Game Theory and Political Theory, Cambridge, UK.
Simon, H. (1982) Models of Bounded Rationality, Cambridge, MA.

SEE ALSO: economic man; game theory; optimization; prisoners' dilemma; rational expectations

RATIONAL EXPECTATIONS

Expectations of the future play an important part in economics. Investment is affected by expectations of demand and costs. The foreign exchange rate is affected by expectations of inflation, interest rates and future movements of exchange rates. The price of shares depends on expectations of future dividends and share prices. The rational expectations hypothesis embodies the assumption that people do not make systematic errors in using the information that they have to predict the future. Some errors in prediction are generally inevitable due to lack of information and the inherent uncertainties of economic affairs. The rational expectations hypothesis postulates that, given the information used, the prediction errors are random and unavoidable.

Rational expectations are on average self-fulfilling. The term rational expectations equilibrium is used to describe situations in which expectations lead to actions that confirm the original expectations. The absence of systematic predictions errors in a rational expectations equilibrium suggests that people have no incentive to change the way they make predictions, and hence that the equilibrium is likely to persist unless disturbed by outside events.

The concept of a rational expectations equilibrium has been applied extensively, particularly in finance and macroeconomics. The demand and therefore the price of financial assets depends upon investors' expectations of their future value. Thus the price itself is a source of information about the asset. In a simple model, where investors are risk-neutral price takers, with no limits on borrowing or arbitrage, the price of an asset is the expected present discounted value of its future payoffs. In the rational expectations equilibrium of such a model, all the information relevant to the investment decision is fully incorporated into the price. Investors have no need to seek any information that is already available to some investor in the market. The market is in a very strong sense informationally efficient. However, if the assumptions of the model are relaxed, for example by allowing risk aversion, and introducing a random asset supply, as in Grossman and Stiglitz (1980), the market price no longer aggregates information efficiently, and investors have an incentive to obtain costly information. The Grossman–Stiglitz model, and the related literature, works within the framework of a rational expectations equilibrium, which has proved to be an important analytical tool.

The use of rational expectations equilibria in macroeconomics follows from the Lucas critique of econometric models (Lucas 1976). This influential paper argued that the estimated relationships in Keynesian macroeconometric models are likely to break down when policy changes, because they fail to take account of the effect of the policy changes on the expectations and actions of optimizing agents. This led to the emergence of the 'new-classical' or 'rational expectations' school of macroeconomics, which developed rational expectations equilibrium models incorporating the hypothesis that, in the absence of unanticipated inflation, there is a unique 'natural rate' of unemployment. If monetary policy is systematic and predictable, then inflation surprises are due to uncontrollable random factors in the economy. The conjunction of the natural rate and rational expectations hypothesis is the basis for the claim of policy neutrality, that monetary policy can have no systematic effect on output and employment, and hence that there is no long-term trade-off between inflation and unemployment.

Rational expectations are difficult to test directly. With the benefit of hindsight it may seem clear that shares in Internet and telecommunications companies were overvalued in early 2000. Investors may have been acting on the best available evidence at the time, or they may have succumbed to irrational exuberance. There are firm believers in both hypotheses. Appeals to the data have not produced a consensus. Models invariably embody both the rational expectations hypothesis and other hypotheses such as the impact of inflation shocks, the functional form of production functions or the nature of market competition. Econometric tests are necessarily tests of joint hypotheses. The debate on rational expectations is largely a discussion of the plausibility and applicability of the hypothesis.

The rational expectations hypothesis is seen by some economists, including Muth (1961), who coined the term rational expectations, as the extension to expectation formation of the assumption that people act rationally in pursuit of their own self-interest, an expectation that forms the basis of neo-classical economics. However, there are some difficulties. Certain models have multiple rational expectations equilibria. In these models, some mechanism outside the model is needed to co-ordinate expectations in order to select a particular equilibrium. A similar issue arises in game theory, particularly in the context of repeated games. Some rational expectations equilibria involve 'sunspots'. These are variables that matter only because people think they matter. If everyone believed that the sunspot variable was irrelevant to things they are trying to predict, the sunspots would indeed be irrelevant. But if people believe that sunspots have an effect, then they do indeed have an effect.

A rational expectations equilibrium requires that agents are not only rational, in the sense of acting optimally given their own beliefs, but also that their beliefs are correct. Agents in a rational expectations equilibrium act as if they knew both the structural form, and the numerical values of the parameters, of the model that describes the economy in which they operate. The formula agents use in making predictions may be a reduced form of the model, which can be stated in terms of a small number of parameters. In rational expectations equilibrium, agents need to know only the parameters of the reduced form. Nevertheless they act as if they knew the entire model. This raises the question of where agents get the necessary knowledge of either the entire model, or its reduced form. There are two possibilities. One is that agents are somehow endowed with the knowledge of the structure and parameter values they need to know to form rational expectations. This could be knowledge of the reduced form, or it could be knowledge and understanding of the entire model and its rational expectations equilibrium. This requirement can be demanding. Solving for the forecasting rule in a rational expectations model can be a technical challenge, even for a research economist who knows the structure and parameters of the full model. This is particularly so in a dynamic setting.

The other possibility is that agents learn about the model by some process of statistical inference, in which case a rational expectations equilibrium makes most sense in the context of a long-run stationary state. Learning about the parameters of the model may be a straightforward and standard econometric exercise for a single agent who has a negligible influence on the outcome of the model. The situation is wholly different if a significant proportion of agents are trying to learn about the model econometrically.

In this case, the expectations of agents who are learning affects the outcome of the model. The way in which agents learn affects the data they observe, and standard results on the asymptotic properties of estimators do not apply. One approach to modelling the learning process is to assume that agents estimate the model using ordinary least squares with a specification that would be appropriate were the economy in a rational expectations equilibrium. The model is mis-specified because the economy is not in a rational expectations equilibrium, and the resulting dynamics involve a highly non-linear stochastic difference equation. However, the analysis of learning is rendered tractable by the notion of e-stability, which involves the behaviour of an ordinary differential equation in the neighbourhood of a rational expectations equilibrium. Essentially a rational expectations equilibrium is e-stable if the new data point, generated by estimators based on past data, on average pushes beliefs closer to the rational expectations equilibrium. Evans and Honkapohja (2001) use e-stability to explore the stability under learning of a wide variety of models. In some models requiring e-stability eliminates sunspot equilibria, or reduces the number of rational expectations equilibria.

The concept of a rational expectations equilibrium continues to be an extremely important benchmark in economic modelling. It provides a relatively simple and plausible description of expectation formation in a long-run steady state. Rational expectations models have provided a very important vehicle for exploring the impact of phenomena such as risk aversion, asymmetric information and money. However, there is increasing interest in non-rational expectations models, such as those involving learning, or the wider departures from full rationality encountered in research on behavioural economics and finance.

MARGARET BRAY
LONDON SCHOOL OF ECONOMICS
AND POLITICAL SCIENCE

References

Evans, G.W. and Honkapohja, S. (2001) *Learning and Expectations in Macroeconomics*, Princeton, NJ.
Grossman, S.J. and Stiglitz, J.E. (1980) 'On the impossibility of informationally efficient markets', *American Economic Review* 70.
Lucas, R.E. (1976) 'Econometric policy evaluation: A critique', in K. Brunner and A.H. Melzer (eds) *The Phillips Curve and Labor Markets*, Amsterdam.
Muth, J.F. (1961) 'Rational expectations and the theory of price movements', *Econometrica* 29.

Further reading

Miller, P.J. (1994) *The Rational Expectations Revolution*, Cambridge, MA.
Pesaran, M.H. (1987) *The Limits to Rational Expectations*, Oxford.

SEE ALSO: game theory; macroeconomic theory; optimization; rational choice (action) theory

RAWLS, JOHN (1921–2002)

John Rawls was born in Baltimore and educated at Princeton. He interrupted his studies in 1943 to serve as an infantryman in New Guinea and the Philippines. After the war, he completed his doctorate at Princeton and in 1962, after spells at Cornell and MIT, took up a position at Harvard where he remained for the rest of his career.

Rawls's claim to being the most important and influential political philosopher of the twentieth century rests on his 1971 masterpiece, *A Theory of Justice*. At the time of its publication, Anglophone moral and political philosophy was largely moribund as a result of logical positivism, the philosophy of language and Marxism, which in their various ways had undermined belief in the possibility of substantive engagement with moral questions. In resurrecting political philosophy Rawls turned to the social contract tradition of Locke, Rousseau and Kant. The object of so doing was to give an account of justice as 'the first virtue of social institutions' (Rawls 1999: 3). Principles of justice are needed because persons – conceived of as free, equal, rational and possessed of a sense of justice – are led by the free use of their reason to have different conceptions of the good, and in pursuing these conceptions they make conflicting demands on the scarce resources that are the outcome of their co-operation.

In Rawls's contract argument we are to ask what principles would be chosen by people in an 'original position' deliberating within constraints that it is reasonable to impose. These constraints take the form of a 'veil of ignorance' from behind which the people in the original position choose principles of justice. The veil of ignorance captures a vision of fairness and included within it (that is, included in the things that the deliberators do not know) are their race, gender, social position, personal characteristics (including their natural talents and abilities) and conception of the good. The social contract argument is not, then, an attempt to derive morality from rationality, but gives expression to a substantive moral conception of justice (one that many commentators think superior to the social contract argument that gives it form). People's fates, Rawls thinks, should not depend on factors that are arbitrary from a moral point of view. Particularly controversial is Rawls's belief that one such factor is genetic inheritance.

Although the contracting parties behind the veil of ignorance do not know anything that might individuate them, they must know enough to choose principles of justice. They are thus aware of general facts about economics, psychology, sociology and so on, and they know that they would prefer more rather than fewer primary social goods – income, wealth, rights, liberties, opportunities and powers, and the social basis of self-respect – which are the things it is rational to want no matter what else one wants (no matter what conception of the good they turn out to have once the veil is lifted).

Controversially, Rawls believes that in such conditions it is rational to maximize the minimum (maximin) so as to ensure that the representative worst-off position is as good as it can be. Further, Rawls argues that the persons in the original position would accord priority to equal liberty over gains in economic and social goods. The persons in the original position thus choose two principles:

1 Each person has an equal right to a fully adequate scheme of equal basic rights and liberties compatible with a similar scheme for everyone [the equal liberty principle].
2 Social and economic inequalities are to be arranged so that they are:

a attached to positions and offices open to all under conditions of fair equality of opportunity [the fair equality of opportunity principle];
b to the greatest benefit of the least advantaged [the difference principle].

These principles are then checked against our most deeply held considered convictions. If they match, then a state of 'reflective equilibrium'

obtains. However, a question remains: Why should we give priority to justice when its demands conflict with the pursuit of our other aims? This is what Rawls calls the problem of stability.

In Part III of A Theory of Justice, Rawls argues that a society regulated by his principles of justice – a 'well-ordered society' – will be stable because people in such a society will develop a settled disposition to act justly. Moreover, he goes on to argue that acting justly is 'congruent' with each person's good. In addressing this question Rawls calls on an account of human nature and on the Kantian interpretation of his theory. It is this that motivates some of the changes in his work after A Theory of Justice.

The problem with the congruence argument in A Theory of Justice is that it is incompatible with the pluralism about the good that characterizes modern societies. In his writings after A Theory of Justice, and in particular in his second book, Political Liberalism, Rawls reformulates the theory as 'freestanding' or 'political'. His aim is to provide a justification for the principles of justice that could be accepted by all reasonable citizens in a well-ordered society. Such a justification must appeal not to a comprehensive (or 'metaphysical') argument, but to ideas latent in the public political culture of a modern democracy. It must, therefore, be expressed in terms of 'public reason'; that is, reasons that all reasonable people can endorse.

The stability of political liberalism depends on an 'overlapping consensus' that obtains when citizens endorse the principles of justice as true or reasonable on grounds connected to their own particular conceptions of the good. Rawls argues that each reasonable comprehensive view – Kantian, utilitarian, religious – can endorse political liberalism and so stability is possible without recourse to controversial comprehensive or metaphysical doctrines.

In his third significant book, The Law of Peoples, Rawls extends political liberalism to international justice. Refusing simply to extend his principles of justice to the international realm, Rawls's argument concerns relations between entire peoples. His vision of the international sphere is thus less egalitarian and cosmopolitan than might be expected. Moreover, although the requirements of equal respect do not extend to societies that violate basic human rights, Rawls allows that there can be 'decent hierarchical' societies.

Rawls was largely incapacitated by a series of strokes beginning in 1995. Nevertheless, he completed *The Law of Peoples*. In addition, his *Lectures on the History of Moral Philosophy* and *Justice as Fairness: A Restatement* were published in 2000 and 2001.

MATT MATRAVERS
UNIVERSITY OF YORK, UK

References

Rawls, J. (1971) *A Theory of Justice*, Cambridge, MA (rev. edn 1999).
—— (1993) *Political Liberalism*, New York.
—— (1999) *The Law of Peoples*, Cambridge, MA.
—— (2000) *Lectures on the History of Moral Philosophy*, Cambridge, MA.
—— (2001) *Justice as Fairness: A Restatement*, ed. E. Kelly, Cambridge, MA.

Further reading

Barry, B. (1989) *Theories of Justice: Volume 1 of A Treatise on Social Justice*, Berkeley and Los Angeles.
—— (1995) 'John Rawls and the search for stability', *Ethics* 105.
Daniels, N. (ed.) (1975) *Reading Rawls: Critical Studies of A Theory of Justice*, Oxford.
Freeman, S. (ed.) (2001) *The Cambridge Companion to John Rawls*, Cambridge, UK.
Mendus, S. (1999) 'The importance of love in Rawls's theory of justice', *British Journal of Political Science* 29.
Rawls, J. (1999) *Collected Papers*, ed. S. Freeman, Cambridge, MA.

SEE ALSO: equality; human rights; justice, distributive; social contract

REASON, RATIONALITY AND RATIONALISM

Rationality is a problem shared by the social sciences and philosophy. Before considering the various issues it raises, it is best to offer provisional definitions of the three related notions of reason, rationality and rationalism.

Reason is the name of an alleged human faculty capable of discerning, recognizing, formulating and criticizing truths. Philosophic disputes about reason concern its very existence (extreme irrationalism may deny that any such faculty exists at all); the nature of its operations (for example, can it actually secure data, or can it only make inferences; how powerful are the inferences it can make; can it make discoveries or can it only check discoveries made by other means?); the areas of its operations (is it restricted to deductive reasoning, or to science; can it be applied to moral, aesthetic, political issues; can it initiate conduct?).

Rationality is a trait that individuals or collectivities display in their thought, conduct or social institutions. Various features can be seen, singly or jointly, as marks or defining features of rationality:

1 A tendency to act only after deliberating and calculation, as opposed to acting impulsively or in obedience to unexamined intimations.
2 A tendency to act in accordance with a long-term plan.
3 A control of conduct by abstract and general rules.
4 Instrumental efficiency – the selection of means purely by their effectiveness in bringing about a clearly specified aim, as opposed to allowing means to be selected by custom or impulse.
5 A tendency to choose actions, institutions and so on in terms of their contribution to a single and clearly specified criterion, rather than by evaluating them by multiple, diffuse and unclear criteria, or accepting them in virtue of their customariness.
6 A propensity to systematize convictions and/or values in a single coherent system.
7 An inclination to find human fulfilment in the exercise or satisfaction of intellectual faculties rather than in emotion or sensuality.

Rationalism is the name of a number of doctrines or attitudes:

1 The insistence of the authority of individual, independent, cognitive activity, as opposed to authority of some extraneous privileged sources (Revelation, Church).
2 The higher valuation of thought or inference as against sensation, observation or experiment, within cognitive activity.
3 The view that collectivities, or individuals, should best conduct their lives in accordance with explicit and intellectually chosen plans, rather than by custom, trial and error, or under guidance of either authority or sentiment.

It should be noted that doctrine (1) opposes the partisans of human reason, assumed to be fairly universally or evenly distributed among all people, to followers of privileged Authority. In other words, rationalists in sense (1) include *both* sides of dispute (2), that is, both adherents of thinking and adherents of sensing as the main source of knowledge. In other words, issues (1) and (2) cut across each other. As 'rationalism' is widely used in both senses, and the issues are cross-related in complex ways, failure to see this ambiguity leads to confusion. A key figure in Western rationalism was Descartes, who was a rationalist in both senses. On the one hand, he recommended that all traditional, inherited ideas be subjected to doubt, a kind of intellectual quarantine, and be awarded certificates of clearance only if they were found logically compelling to the enquiring mind. Though Descartes, when applying this method, did in fact eventually award just such a certificate to the theism of the faith of his birth, the sheer fact of making inner reason the first and last Court of Appeal in effect constituted and encouraged rationalism in sense (1). But he was also a rationalist in the second sense, and considered innate rational powers to be far more important than sensory information. His view of the human mind has been powerfully revived by the contemporary linguist, Noam Chomsky, notably in *Cartesian Linguistics* (1966), and supported by the argument that the amazing range of linguistic competence of most humans cannot be explained without the assumption of an innate grammatical structure present in all minds, which thus corresponds to one aspect of the old 'reason'.

In the seventeenth and eighteenth centuries, the programme of Descartes's rationalism (sense 1) was implemented, among others, by the school of 'British empiricists', of whom the greatest was probably David Hume. However, at the same time they repudiated rationalism (sense 2). Hume (1976 [1739–40]), for instance, basically considered thinking to be nothing but the aftertaste of sensations: thinking about a given object was like having an aftertaste of a dish when one is no longer eating.

The eighteenth century is often said to have been the Age of Reason; in philosophy, however, it was also the age of the Crisis of Reason. This was most manifest in the work of Hume. His main discovery was this: if rationalism (1), the subjection of all belief to evidence available to the individual, is combined with empiricism, the view that the senses alone supply the database at the individual's disposal, we end with an impasse: the database supplied by the senses simply is not strong enough to warrant our endorsement of certain convictions that seem essential for the conduct of life – notably, the presence of causal order in the world, or continuous objects, or of moral obligation. Hume's solution for this problem was that these crucial human tendencies, such as inferring from the past to the future, or feeling morally constrained, not being warranted by the only database available to us, were simply rooted in and justified by habit, a kind of Customary Law of the mind.

Immanuel Kant (1929 [1781]) tried to provide a stronger and less precarious refutation to Hume's scepticism. His solution was, in substance, that the human mind has a rigid and universal structure, which compels humans (among other things) to think in terms of cause and effect, to feel obliged to respect a certain kind of ethic (a morality of rule-observance and impartiality, in essence), and so on. So the inner logical compulsions on which Descartes relied as judges of culturally inherited ideas were valid after all, but they were only valid for the world as experienced by beings with our kind of mind; they were not rooted in the nature of things, as they were 'in themselves'. They were rooted in *us*.

It is among Kant's numerous intellectual progeny that the problem of reason becomes sociological. The two most important ones in sociology were Emile Durkheim and Max Weber. Each of them very obviously inherits the Kantian problem, but they apply it to society and to the diversity of human cultures in radically different, indeed almost diametrically opposed, ways. Durkheim followed Kant in being concerned with our conceptual compulsions, in holding conceptual compulsion to be central to our humanity. But where Kant was content to explain it by invoking an allegedly universal structure of the human mind, operating behind the scenes in each individual mind, Durkheim sought the roots of compulsion in the visible life of distinct communities and above all in ritual. The core of religion is ritual, and the function of ritual is to endow us with shared concepts, and to endow those concepts with a compelling authority for all members of a given community. This is the central argument of his *The Elementary Forms of*

Religious Life (1915 [1912]). For Durkheim, all humans are rational, rationality manifests itself in conceptual compulsion, but the form that rationality takes varies from society to society. Sharing the same compulsions makes humans members of a social community.

If for Durkheim all humans are rational, for Weber some humans are more rational than others. He notes that the kind of rationality that Kant analysed – orderly rule-bound conduct and thought – is specially characteristic of one particular tradition, namely the one that engendered the modern capitalist and industrial society. (Weber is less explicitly concerned with Kant than is Durkheim, but the connection is nevertheless obvious.) Weber's problem is not why all humans are rational (all humans think in concepts and are constrained by them), but why some humans are *specially* rational, quite particularly respectful of rules and capable of selecting means for their effectiveness rather than for their congruence with custom, thereby becoming apt at establishing modern capitalist and bureaucratic institutions.

Weber (1961 [1924], 1968 [1922]) noted that the kind of world codified by the great philosophers of the Age of Reason, a world amenable to rational orderly investigation and manipulation rather than propitiation, was not a world inhabited by all humankind, but only by the participants of the historical tradition that had engendered capitalism and large-scale bureaucracy. He believed that this kind of rational mentality was an essential precondition of a capitalist or bureaucratic civilization, and was *not* the necessary corollary of the other preconditions of that civilization: in other words, in opposition to historical materialism, he did not believe that the emergence of that civilization could be explained in terms of its material preconditions alone. One further and independent necessary factor was also required. (He modified rather than inverted the materialist position, in so far as he did not claim or believe that the non-material necessary condition, or any set of such conditions, could ever be sufficient.) Hence in his hands the philosophical problem of rationality becomes a sociological one – how did rationality come to dominate one particular civilization and eventually, through it, the entire world?

The Durkheimian and Weberian traditions are not the only ones through which the philosophers' concern with Reason reaches the social sciences. There are at least two others.

In Kant, the attribution of rationality to a rigid and universal structure of the human mind, but *not* to the material which that mind (or those minds) handled, led to a tense and uncomfortable dualism: the world was a blind, amoral machine, and the intrusion of either cognitive rationality or moral conduct into it was a mysterious imposition by our minds of order on to material indifferent and alien to that order. At the core of the philosophy of Hegel lay the supposition that Reason was not merely (as Kant thought) responsible for the individual striving for consistent behaviour and explanations, but that it was also a kind of grand and impersonal Puppet Master of History. In other words, the pattern of history had an underlying principle that was not alien to the rational strivings within us, but, on the contrary, provided a kind of guarantee for them. The idea is attractive, inherently and inescapably speculative, but it did seem to receive some support from the vision of history as Progress, which had become fashionable at about the same time. Marxism, while disavowing the mystical elements in Hegel, nevertheless took over the underlying intuition of a rational historic design. People who continue to uphold some version of this view are not normally called rationalists, but nevertheless their ideas are relevant to the debate about the relation of reason to life.

The other relevant tradition, in addition to the Marxist–Hegelian one, is associated with the great names of Schopenhauer, Nietzsche and Freud. Kant had identified Reason with all that was best in humankind. Schopenhauer (1958 [1819]) taught that humans were dominated by a blind irrational Will, whose power they could not combat in the world, though they could at best occasionally escape it through aesthetic contemplation and compassion. Nietzsche (1909–13) shared Schopenhauer's views, but inverted his values: why should the Will be condemned, in the name of a morality that was really the fruit of resentment, of a twisted and devious manifestation of that very Will which was being damned? Freud (1930) took over the insights of both thinkers (though not Nietzsche's values), provided them with an elaborate setting in the context of clinical practice and psychiatry, invented a technique purporting to alleviate at least some of the more pathological manifestations of irrational forces and set up an organization for the application and supervision of that technique. In so far as he did not applaud the dominance of irrational forces but on the contrary sought to mitigate them, he cannot (unlike Nietzsche) be accused of irrationalism, but his views of the devious and hidden control of seeming reason by hidden unreason closely resemble Nietzsche's, though as stated they are elaborated in what seems to be a far more specific form, and are linked to clinical practice.

The social scientist is likely to encounter the problem of Reason and Rationality (under a diversity of formulations) in connection with the various traditions and problems that have been specified. The main problem areas are:

1 Innate reason versus experience as a source of cognition, the debate opposing thinkers such as Descartes and Chomsky to empiricists and behaviourists.
2 The anchoring of inner logical compulsions either to an allegedly universal human mental equipment, or to the specific culture – in other words the opposition of (say) Kant and Durkheim.
3 The question of a historically specific form of rationality, its roots and its role in engendering modern civilization – what might be called the Weberian problem.
4 The feasibility, in principle or in particular cases, of locating a rational plan in history.
5 The debate as to whether the real driving force, and the location of genuine satisfaction, within the human psyche is to be sought in irrational drives or in rational aim, calculation, insight or restraint (or in what proportion).
6 Rationality in the sense of explicit criteria and conscious plan, as opposed to respect for tradition and continuity in the management of a polity.
7 Rationalism in the sense of favouring free enquiry as against the authority of either Revolution or Tradition.

These various issues are of course interrelated, although by no means identical, but they are often confused, and the lack of terminological consistency frequently furthers this confusion.

ERNEST GELLNER
formerly UNIVERSITY OF CAMBRIDGE
CENTRAL EUROPEAN UNIVERSITY

References

Chomsky, N. (1966) *Cartesian Linguistics: A Chapter in the History of Rationalist Thought*, New York.
Durkheim, E. (1915 [1912]) *The Elementary Forms of Religious Life*, London.
Freud, S. (1930) *Civilization and its Discontents*, London.
Hume, D. (1976 [1739–40]) *A Treatise on Human Nature*, 2 vols, London.
Kant, I. (1929 [1781]) *Immanuel Kant's Critique of Pure Reason*, Riga.
Nietzsche, F. (1909–13) *Beyond Good and Evil and The Genealogy of Morals*, in O. Levy (ed.) *The Complete Works of Friedrich Nietzsche*, vols 12 and 13, Edinburgh.
Schopenhauer, A. (1958 [1819]) *The World as Will and Representation*, New York.
Weber, M. (1961 [1924]) *General Economic History*, London.
—— (1968 [1922]) *Economy and Society*, New York.

Further reading

Bartley, W.W. (1962) *The Retreat to Commitment*, New York.
Elster, J. (1978) *Logic and Society: Contradictions and Possible Worlds*, Chichester.
Hollis, M. and Lukes, S. (1982) *Rationality and Relativism*, Oxford.
MacIntyre, A.C. and Emmet, D. (1970) *Sociological Theory and Philosophical Analysis*, London.
Magee, B. (1963) *The Philosophy of Schopenhauer*, Oxford.
Wilson, B. (ed.) (1970) *Rationality*, Oxford.

SEE ALSO: Durkheim; Hume; philosophy of the social sciences; rational choice (action) theory; relativism; science, sociology of; Weber

REFERENCE GROUPS

Reference group refers to an individual or social grouping that either sets or maintains standards for the individual, or which acts as a frame of comparison relative to which individuals compare themselves.

Reference group theory and research developed out of the symbolic interactionist tradition within US social science. It was related to Charles Cooley's view that the self arises out of the ideas that others entertain of the given individual. The idea is also present in G.H. Mead's analysis of the differences between role-taking, the 'significant other' in the play stage, and the 'generalized other' in the game stage of human development. Being able to take on the role of the generalized other means that individuals are able to develop fully human characteristics, of effective selves able to look at, assess, control and direct their actions. The existence of the generalized other means that individuals can be the object of their own reflexive consciousnesses. Furthermore, Mead's discussion implies that it is because humans are able through symbols to take on the role of the other that they can refer their attitudes and behaviour to social groups with which they are not directly involved. Reference group analysis thus developed to take cognizance of the fact that people may refer for judgement to groups of which they are not and perhaps cannot be members.

H.H. Hyman first coined the term reference group in 1942 (Hyman and Singer 1968). He distinguished two different orientations that might be taken to such a group – the *identificatory* and the *judgemental*. In the former case, this produces a normative commitment to the group in question; in the latter, it entails actors evaluating themselves with respect to income, status, education and so on by comparison with the achievements of the other group. This distinction was clarified by H.H. Kelly who distinguished between the normative and comparative function of any reference group; this in turn developed into the now commonplace distinction between the normative reference group and the comparative reference group.

Four other points should be noted. First, we should distinguish between different forms of the social object to which reference is made, that is, whether it is an individual, a group, a collectivity or a social category. Second, reference to any such social object should be viewed as either positive or negative, as in the case of the normative reference group involving respectively identification with or separation from the given social object. Third, we should also distinguish audience reference groups, namely those social objects that function as a source of evaluation and appraisal for the social actor but which are not bases of normative identification or social comparison. Fourth, there are highly complex and variable relations possible between an individual and a given group, ranging from formal membership, psychological membership, regular interaction, intermittent interaction, to no contact at all (Merton 1957).

There have been a number of attempts to identify universalistic explanations of the *selection* of normative reference groups. Some writers suggest that the acceptance of a reference group depends upon the ease with which satisfactory interpersonal contacts can be made. Others argue that the choice of normative references depends upon an individual's status-image and the function of the reference group in a process of status conferral. Others again argue that the selection of normative references will depend upon the degree of perceived interdependence between the individual and the group in question. And, finally, it is suggested that individuals are more likely to refer to a given group the more that the individuals are perceived to be socially valuable to the group in question. However, although these are all useful hypotheses, none has been seen to be universally valid.

The best known examination of the *consequences* of normative reference group selection is Theodore Newcomb's study of Bennington College (Hyman and Singer 1968). He observed that during 4 successive years, junior and senior students were markedly less conservative than freshmen in terms of a number of public issues; a cohort study over the same period showed the same trend. Moreover, non-conservatism was associated with high participation, involvement and status within the college. Hence, where the college acted as a normative reference group then the student's attitudes became less conservative; where this was not the case and the home and family remained as significant normative reference groups, then attitudes stayed more conservative. However, there are difficulties in this and related studies. First, it is often difficult to avoid circular argument, since the change of attitude both constitutes the explicandum *and* provides evidence for the patterning of normative group selection. Second, it is necessary to analyse an actor's *interpretation* of competing normative reference groups rather than assume that particular consequences necessarily follow. Third, changing patterns of reference group selection have to be related to the temporal development of the self and especially to changes in the life-cycle – hence reference group choices may be historically dependent one upon the other, as in Merton's (1957) analysis of anticipatory socialization.

Comparative reference group analysis is based on the argument that once clear physiological needs have been satisfied, then human beings require other bases by which to assess their achievements and satisfactions. In particular, it is argued, humans derive such assessments by comparing themselves with others. Many social philosophers from Aristotle onwards have noted these processes (Urry 1973). De Tocqueville analysed how the mass of the citizenry began to compare themselves with the newly emergent middle class who 'have no conspicuous privileges, and even their wealth...is impalpable and, as it were, *invisible*'. Marx in turn disputed this, arguing that 'although the pleasures of the labourer have increased, the social gratification which they afford has fallen in comparison with the increased pleasures of the capitalist'. He concludes that since our wants and pleasures 'are of a social nature, they are of a relative nature'. And, from a different tradition, Max Scheler maintained that

> The medieval peasant prior to the thirteenth century does not compare himself to the feudal lord, nor does the artisan compare himself to the knight...every comparison took place within a strictly circumscribed frame of reference....In the 'system of free-competition', on the other hand...aspirations are intrinsically *boundless*, for they are no longer tied to any particular object or quality.

A version of this can be found in the famous intepretation of the 'promotion finding' in the *American Soldier* study, which established that those units where there was a high rate of promotion expressed *more* dissatisfaction about future promotion chances than units where promotion rates were lower. Hence, Robert Merton (1957) argued that higher mobility rates induced excessive hopes and expectations for further promotion, and more widespread comparisons were made. This view was amplified by W.G. Runciman (1972) who also, on the basis of a national sample survey, concluded that manual workers in the UK had fairly restricted comparative reference groups, especially with regard to class dimensions of inequality. Certain non-manual workers made wider and more class-conscious comparisons. An important reason for this was that there generally has to be some kind of basis or similarity along other dimensions of social inequality, apart from the one where the comparison is occurring, in order that wideranging comparisons can be made. For example, the Amba in East Africa were willing to work for Europeans at a much lower price than for employers from another tribe, because 'a European is on a much higher social plane, and therefore comparisons are out of the question'. There was no other similarity or basis for the comparison.

Most research indicates that actors normally operate in terms of fairly restricted patterns of social comparison. It is only in periods of rapid social change that these established patterns may be upset. John Urry (1973) distinguished between 'conventional comparisons', those used in everyday life and structured in terms of the actor's social network, and 'structural comparisons', those feasibly made when that everyday world is disrupted, and comparisons are structured by the environing patterns of social stratification. Urry also emphasized that relative deprivation involves a number of distinct stages of development, in particular, that there are varied conditions under which revealed deprivations are deemed unjust, and blame may be attributed to the dominant groups or the wider society. Ted Gurr (1970) has likewise elaborated an integrated theory of political violence, in which the first stage, the development of discontent, stems from the perception of relative deprivation between people's value expectations and value capabilities.

Overall, there is nothing that we might term 'reference group theory'. The term is, as Runciman argues, useful in describing certain processes of attitude formation within an individualistic social science, based on related notions of self, identity and role. The key idea is, as Thoreau puts it, 'If a man does not keep pace with his companions perhaps it is because he hears a different drummer.'

JOHN URRY
UNIVERSITY OF LANCASTER

References

Gurr, T. (1970) *Why Men Rebel*, Princeton, NJ.

Hyman, H.H. and Singer, E. (eds) (1968) *Readings in Reference Group Theory and Research*, New York.

Merton, R.K. (1957) *Social Theory and Social Structure*, New York.

Runciman, W.G. (1972) *Relative Deprivation and Social Justice*, Harmondsworth.

Urry, J. (1973) *Reference Groups and the Theory of Revolution*, London.

SEE ALSO: deprivation and relative deprivation; symbolic interactionism

REFLEXIVITY

Reflexivity is a term used in a wide variety of senses. Two main tendencies can be discerned. First, reflexivity is used to characterize general features of (modern) social life. Second, reflexivity is used more specifically to refer to certain characteristics of social scientists' attempts to explain social life. It is not clear how these uses are interrelated: the definitively reflexive history of the term is yet to be written.

An example of the first usage is Beck's (1992) discussion of reflexive modernity. Here reflexivity refers to the fact that modern societies are now reaping the negative results of their mishandling of the environment, and to humankind's increasing awareness of these negative consequences. The supposed virtue of human dominance of nature is increasingly called into question. Beck also suggests that this leads to a form of personal reflexivity whereby members of mature modern societies question established patterns of life and social mores.

Arguably, what is missing from Beck's account is attention to the second main usage of reflexivity. What are the reflexive consequences of Beck's account? Does increasing personal reflexivity also mean that different forms of social science account are now appropriate (or necessary)? This second sense of reflexivity connotes the idea that the claims and arguments made by social science in some sense refer back to social science itself.

Classically, the second usage of reflexivity is associated with a species of philosophical paradox, the most well known of which is the Liar's Paradox. Thus, the statement that All Cretans Are Liars, when uttered by a Cretan, generates both false and true conditions for its evaluation: if the statement is true then it is false; if it is false, then it is true.

Notwithstanding the negative connotations associated with such aporia, reflexivity is sometimes encouraged as an aid to improved analysis. This form of reflexivity is benign introspection. Social scientists are encouraged to reflect upon the social circumstances of the production of their knowledge, either as a methodological corrective (often consigned to the appendix of research reports), or as part of a general injunction towards healthy awareness of the social and political context within which they operate.

In Garfinkel's (1967) discussion of ethno-methodology, reflexivity refers to the intimate interdependence between surface appearances (documents or accounts) and the associated underlying reality (a distinction that is characteristic of the documentary method of interpretation). The sense of the former is elaborated by drawing on knowledge of the latter, while, at the same time, the sense of the latter is elaborated by what is known about the former. Accounts are thus 'constituent features of the settings they make observable'. Constitutive reflexivity has radical implications for social science's pretensions to causal argument, since it casts considerable doubt on the extent to which explanans and explanandum can be considered distinct elements in an explanation.

Reflexivity is often said to be engendered by all social science with relativizing tendencies. Any claim about the influence of social circumstances on a particular situation can be understood as also referring to the claim itself. This aspect of reflexivity comes into particular focus in work in the sociology of scientific knowledge. Whereas it has been convincingly demonstrated that natural scientific knowledge is a product of social, cultural, historical and political processes, rather little attention has been given to the fact that social science itself is an activity generated by these same forces. Sociology of science treats scientific knowledge in broadly relativist terms, but often continues to practise its own craft in realist terms. This has led to criticisms of inconsistency, especially from objectivist philosophers of science. The recommended solution from this latter quarter is to abandon relativism. By contrast, a body of work has arisen that takes the opposite tack and upholds the principle of consistency by exploring ways of abandoning realist methods in the social study of science.

One source of antipathy to this reflexive project is the assumption that such work is incompatible with good (serious) research practice because of its self-regarding quality or because it leads to a regress of meta-studies. Such assumptions have led researchers interested in reflexivity to develop a practice in which the interrogation of the methods proceeds simultaneously with, and as an integral part of, the investigation of the object. This has led to a variety of experimental textual forms ranging from the use of dialogue to the visible display of various material constraints on form, such as (following Ashmore 1989) the 750 word limit of this.

STEVE WOOLGAR
OXFORD UNIVERSITY

References

Ashmore, M. (1989) *The Reflexive Thesis: Wrighting Sociology of Scientific Knowledge*, Chicago.
Beck, U. (1992) *Risk Society: Towards a New Modernity*, London.
Garfinkel, H. (1967) *Studies in Ethnomethodology*, Englewood Cliffs, NJ.

Further reading

Bartlett, S.J. and Suber, P. (eds) (1987) *Self-Reference: Reflections on Reflexivity*, Dordrecht, The Netherlands.
Woolgar, S. (ed.) (1988) *Knowledge and Reflexivity: New Frontiers in the Sociology of Knowledge*, London.

SEE ALSO: ethnomethodology; postmodernism; science, sociology of

REFUGEES

Refugees are heterogeneous populations found across the world that have been singled out from ordinary migrants as an object of study for all social science disciplines. As a label applied to individuals, 'refugee' carries with it not only specific legal and cultural connotations, but also a great deal of analytical baggage (Indra 1999; Zetter 1991).

Legal and political dimensions

Refugees became a matter of international concern in the twentieth century (Marrus 1985; Zolberg *et al.* 1989). The technical meaning grew out of the experiences of the First World War, distinguishing those groups who had lost the protection of their own state, i.e. refugees, from other types of migrants. Refugees were people forced to cross international boundaries under particular conditions of political duress. The 1933 Refugee Convention allocated this status to specific nationalities, e.g. Russians, Armenians, Assyrians and Turks, and obliged receiving states to provide assistance and protection. A separate category of people in need of international protection, 'denationalised' Germans, mainly Jews, was identified by the 1938 Refugee Convention (Skran 1995). These definitions identified refugees in terms of nationality and the political situation that led to their flight.

The main international legal instrument – the 1951 UN Convention Relating to the Status of Refugees – emerged as a result of the European experience of the Second World War. The drafters of the Convention, thirty-five primarily Western countries defined refugees as individuals who had a 'well-founded fear of persecution for reasons of race, religion, nationality, membership of a particular social group or political opinion'. (See Weis 1994 for details of the drafting process. Jackson 1999 demonstrates how the 1951 Convention has also been applied to groups.) It was limited to people fleeing events occurring in Europe before 1 January 1951. Governments were supposed to apply this definition to all asylum seekers in a neutral manner, and the Office of the UN High Commissioner for Refugees (UNHCR) was to be entirely non-political, but, because of the politics of the Cold War, people fleeing communist countries were nearly always granted asylum for ideological reasons.

In the aftermath of decolonization, refugees became an international problem and the 1967 Protocol to the 1951 Convention extended the definition of a refugee beyond European boundaries. The Organization of African Unity's 1969 Convention on refugees expanded the definition of a refugee to include those who fled their countries 'owing to external aggression, occupation, foreign domination or events seriously disturbing public order'. The Cartagena Declaration of 1984 makes similar provisions for Latin America, emphasizing massive human rights violations as a cause of flight. An important feature of these conventions is a negative stricture (the condition of *non-refoulement*, i.e. no forced return), which does not, however, oblige the signatory states to grant asylum. (It is arguable that under Islamic law the state has a duty to grant asylum; see Elmadmad 2002.)

The UN Relief and Works Agency for Palestinian Refugees in the Near East (UNRWA) was created under UN General Assembly Resolution 194 (III) to assist Palestinian refugees who were expelled in 1948. UNRWA registered Palestinians as refugees if they had lost *both* home *and* livelihood, and had taken refuge in places where this organization was providing relief. At the behest of Arab states, Article 1D of the 1951 Convention excludes any group of refugees who receive protection or assistance from another UN body. Since UNRWA only operates in Jordan, Lebanon, Syria, West Bank and Gaza, UNHCR is responsible for Palestinian refugees elsewhere (UNHCR 2002).

The evolution of the 'refugee problem'

Five main phases in the evolution of the 'refugee problem' can be identified. Each phase is characterized by both a particular conceptualization of the refugee and a corresponding policy solution (Tuitt 1996; Voutira and Harrell-Bond 2000).

PHASE I

The interwar period was dominated by the spirit of nationalism, understood as one nation for each state and one state for every nation. Refugees were defined in terms of their membership of a nation without a state, in need of international protection. In response, passports (travel documents for Russian refugees) and livelihood support (jobs for Armenian refugees) were provided by the host states (Skran 1995). In some cases, settlement sponsorship schemes were supported for nation-states trying to absorb those refugees who had an ethnic claim (e.g. Turkish refugees from Greece and Greek refugees from Turkey). The dominant solution in the interwar years was 'assimilation' in the host state.

PHASE II

In the period following the Second World War, resettlement was to be a *permanent* solution, involving the *assimilation* of the newcomers into the host society (Kunz 1981).

PHASE III

By the 1970s, refugees became mostly identified as a 'Third World' problem – one to be resolved in these regions (Zolberg et al. 1989). Asylum was perceived as temporary, as was (and still remains) the solution devised to address it: the refugee camp. The refugee camp was both a strategy of political containment (Karadawi 1999; Chimni 2002), and an efficient mechanism for the delivery of humanitarian relief supposedly leading to economic self-sufficiency (Harrell-Bond 1986). None of these objectives was, in fact, achieved. Refugee camps became hothouses of activism, and, for the most part, people living in refugee camps have been systematically im-poverished, surviving only through international aid (Crisp 2002; Harrell-Bond 1986).

PHASE IV

From the early 1980s, increasingly restrictionist policies in Western countries promoted the idea that refugees were not victims of human rights violations, but rather opportunists (Tuitt 1996: 144–7). With the increasing poverty and instability in the South, such beliefs were further reinforced by the general unwillingness to recognize the degree to which human rights abuses underlie the diverse economic, environmental and political issues that cause refugee movements. The promotion of voluntary repatriation became the preferred solution (Harrell–Bond 1989), although many observers criticized the coercion that often accompanied the implementation of these programmes (Allen and Morsink 1994; Black and Koser 1999). Even repatriation back into conflict situations may be seen as legitimate (Cuny et al. 1992), and *refoulement* is legitimized by the concept of 'safe' countries (EXCOM 1991; Amnesty International 1992).

PHASE V

War in the former Yugoslavia made refugees a European problem once again. 'Preventative protection' and 'safe havens', reinterpreted as the 'right not to be uprooted', became policy (Jaeger 1993). Threatened people were actively prevented from accessing asylum on the territory of Western states (e.g. Pallis 2002).

At the end of the twentieth century, the 'crisis of asylum' was confounded with the 'migration crisis' (Weiner 1995), both construed as a common economic burden for the receiving states that had to be addressed as part of 'global solidarity' (van Selm 2003). A common strategy of Northern states in response to the two crises has been to further classify refugees (*convention, prima facie, in orbit, sur place, de facto, 'humanitarian'*), and to distinguish them from the internally displaced (IDPs), who remain under the ostensible protection of their own state (Deng and Cohen 1999; Tuitt 1996). The tension between 'harmonization' of asylum procedures and migration containment has led to the progressive erosion of human rights protection for refugees (Tuitt 1996).

On a regional level, approaches to refugee protection are defined by the relative political and economic priorities. New international instruments for the implementation of refugee protection standards have been put in place (Okoth-Obbo *et al.* 2003: 31–43). The Afghan refugee crisis and the events of 11 September 2001 have caused a backlash towards refugees and migrants on a global scale (FMR 2002). Regional responses have included the closing of borders in most Central Asian states, publicly equating the war against terrorism with the fight against 'illegal' immigration, and trying to control human trafficking, now construed as a 'crime against humanity' (Crépeau 2003).

Media images of refugees, often reinforced by charity fundraising, focus on depictions of misery, destitution, helplessness and dependency (Benthall 1993). These familiar images of the 'global culture' are far removed from anthropological analyses of the refugee experience. Accordingly, we need to identify the degree to which the technical meanings of the legal terms discussed above vary with respect to different ideologies and local practices concerning strangers, foreigners and guests (Voutira 2003).

In conclusion, refugees are people who have undergone a violent 'rite of separation', and unless they are 'incorporated' into their host state (or returned to their state of origin), they find themselves in a perpetual state of 'liminality' or 'between and betwixt'. Incorporation is an interactive process involving the adaptation of both refugees and their hosts. A number of anthropologists have documented these processes, as well as the strategies of survival people use in times of crisis. (See, e.g., Cernea and Guggenheim 1993; Frechette 2002; Harrell-Bond 1986; Hirschon 1998; Loïzos 1981; McDowell 1996.) Coming to terms with the different dimensions of human suffering that are encapsulated in the refugee experience has functioned as a corrective device for theory. The study of dispossessed populations has also established social science more firmly within public affairs.

EFTIHIA VOUTIRA
UNIVERSITY OF MAKEDONIA,
THESSALONIKI, GREECE
BARBARA HARRELL-BOND
AMERICAN UNIVERSITY IN CAIRO

References

Allen, T. and Morsink, H. (eds) (1994) *When Refugees Go Home*, London.

Amnesty International (1992) *Europe: Harmonization of Asylum Policy. Accelerated Procedures for 'Manifestly Unfounded' Asylum Claims and the 'Safe Country' Concept*, London.

Benthall, J. (1993) *Disasters, Relief and the Media*, London.

Black, R. and Koser, K. (eds) (1999) *The End of the Refugee Cycle? Refugee Repatriation and Reconstruction*, Oxford.

Cernea, M. and Guggenheim, S. (eds) (1993) *Anthropological Approaches to Resettlement: Policy, Practice, and Theory*, Boulder, CO.

Chimni, B.S. (2002) *Aid, Relief, and Containment: The First Asylum Country and Beyond*, Centre for Development Research, Copenhagen (http://www.cdr.dk).

Crépeau, F. (2003) 'The fight against migrant smuggling: Migration containment over refugee protection', in J. van Selm *et al.* (eds) *The Refugee Convention at Fifty: A View from Forced Migration Studies*, Lanham, MD.

Crisp, J. (2002) *No Solution in Sight: The Problem of Protracted Refugee Situations in Africa*, EPAU, UNHCR, Geneva (http://www.unhcr.ch).

Cuny, F., Stein, B. and Reed, P. (1992) *Repatriation during Conflict in Asia and Africa*, Dallas.

Deng, F. and Cohen, R. (1999) *The Forsaken People: Case Studies of the Internally Displaced*, Washington, DC.

Elmadmad, K. (2002) *L'Asile et réfugiés dans les pays afro-arabes*, Casablanca.

EXCOM (UNHCR Executive Committee) (1991) *Background Note on the 'Safe Country' Concept and Refugee Status* (EC/SCP/68 GE.91-02095).

FMR (2002) 'September 11: Has anything changed?' *Forced Migration Review* 13.

Frechette, A. (2002) *Tibetans in Nepal: The Dynamics of International Assistance among a Community in Exile*, New York.

Harrell-Bond, B.E. (1986) *Imposing Aid: Emergency Assistance to Refugees*, Oxford.

—— (1989) 'Repatriation: Under what conditions is it the most desirable solution for refugees? An agenda for research', *African Studies Review* 32.

Hirschon, R. (1998) *Heirs of the Greek Catastrophe: The Social Life of Asia Minor Refugees in Piraeus*, Oxford.

Indra, D. (1999) *Engendering Forced Migration: Theory and Practice*, New York.

Jackson, I. (1999) *The Refugee Concept in Group Situations*, Amsterdam.

Jaeger, G. (1993) 'The recent concept of preventative protection', *Refugee Participation Network* 15.

Karadawi, A. (1999) *Refugee Policy in Sudan, 1967–1984*, Oxford.

Kunz, E.F. (1981) 'Exile and resettlement refugee theory', *International Migration Review* 5.

Loïzos, P. (1981) *The Heart Grown Bitter: A Chronicle of Cypriot War Refugees*, Cambridge.

McDowell, C. (1996) *A Tamil Asylum Diaspora: Sri Lankan Migration, Settlement and Politics in Switzerland*, Oxford.

Marrus, M.R. (1985) *The Unwanted European Refugees in the Twentieth Century*, New York.

Okoth-Obbo, G., O'Connor, C.M., Kjaerum, M. and

Chantavanich, S. (2003) 'Regional approaches to forced migration', in J. van Selm *et al.* (eds) *The Refugee Convention at Fifty: A View from Forced Migration Studies*, Lanham, MD.

Pallis, M. (2002) 'Obligations of states towards asylum seekers at sea: Interactions and conflicts between legal regimes', *International Journal of Refugee Law* 14.

Skran, C. (1995) *Refugees in Inter-War Europe: The Emergence of a Regime*, Oxford.

Tuitt, P. (1996) *False Images: The Law's Construction of the Refugee*, London.

UNHCR (2002) 'Note on the applicability of Article 1D of the 1951 Convention relating to the status of refugees to Palestinian refugees', *International Journal of Refugee Law* 14.

van Selm, J. (2003) 'Global solidarity: Report of a plenary session', in J. van Selm *et al.* (eds) *The Refugee Convention at Fifty: A View from Forced Migration Studies*, Lanham, MD.

Voutira, E. (2003) 'Refugees: Whose term is it anyway?: *Emic* and *etic* constructions of "refugees" in modern Greek', in J. van Selm *et al.* (eds) *The Refugee Convention at Fifty: A View from Forced Migration Studies*, Lanham, MD.

Voutira, E. and Harrell-Bond, B.E. (2000) 'Successful refugee settlement: Are past experiences relevant?' in M. Cernea and C. McDowell (eds) *Risks and Reconstruction: Experiences of Resettlers and Refugees*, Washington, DC.

Weiner, M. (1995) *The Global Migration Crisis: Challenge to State and to Human Rights*, New York.

Weis, P. (1994) *Commentary on the Convention Relating to the Status of Refugees*, Cambridge.

Zetter, R. (1991) 'Labeling refugees: Forming and transforming an identity', *Journal of Refugee Studies* 4.

Zolberg, A., Suhrke, A. and Aguayo, S. (1989) *Escape from Violence: Conflict and the Refugee Crisis in the Developing World*, New York.

Further reading

Ager, A. (ed.) (1999) *Refugees: Perspectives on the Experience of Forced Migration*, London.

Hathaway, J. (1991) *The Law of Refugee Status*, Toronto.

Loescher, G. (2001) *The UNHCR and World Politics: A Perilous Path*, Oxford.

van Selm, J. *et al.* (eds) (2003) *The Refugee Convention at Fifty: A View from Forced Migration Studies*, Lanham, MD.

SEE ALSO: human rights; migration

REGION

A region is an area of the earth's surface that is relatively homogeneous, and differs from its neighbours, on certain criteria. The definition and description of regional mosaics at a range of spatial scales (from the global to the very local) was the predominant concern of geographers during the central decades of the twentieth century, who interpreted their role within the academic division of labour as accounting for the areal differentiation that characterizes the earth's surface. For several decades regional geography was at the discipline's core: 'regional geography is at least a vital and indispensable part of the subject...for the general reader it is and always has been geography *par excellence*' (Wooldridge and East 1958: 141).

The practice of regional geography involved selecting the scale and criteria on which regional delimitation was to be based, applying the criteria (usually deploying cartographic methods), and then describing the assemblage within each region. The latter involved synthesizing the results of systematic investigations of the different phenomena that make up the contents of a region, and Wooldridge saw the geographer's task as gathering up 'the disparate strands of the systematic studies, the geographical aspects of other disciplines, into a coherent and focused unity, to see nature and nurture, physique and personality as closely related and interdependent elements in specific regions' (1956: 53). This defined geography as a synthesizing discipline, dependent on many others for much of its raw material.

The criteria for regional definition, and the form that their synthesis should take in regional description, engendered substantial debate. Many authors identified the physical environment as the key to regional understanding, with their regional definitions and descriptions strongly underpinned by (implicit) notions of environmental determinism – human activities are strongly conditioned, if not determined, by their physical context. Some authors distinguished between a 'natural region', for which physical characteristics alone were the defining criteria, and a 'geographical region', whose character reflected human response to the environment. Others went further, and likened the region to an organism.

Regional geography was structured on the concept of the region as a homogeneous spatial unit, and as the core of the discipline it was presented as the study of how parts of the world vary because of the uneven distribution of natural and human phenomena (including their interactions). Different types of phenomena cluster in different areas, creating regions, so the study of regions both illuminates the reasons for the clustering and illustrates the unique features of the different parts of the world.

The region was perceived as an entity that was an important pedagogic device, and much published geographical work portrayed spatial variations through regional descriptions: this included substantial textbooks covering areas of continental or subcontinental scale. Others criticized such study, however, as 'trying to put boundaries that do not exist around areas that do not matter' (Kimble 1951: 159). This latter view gained increased acceptance by the late 1950s, and regional geography's dominance of geographical practice was challenged by those attracted to an alternative view of the discipline as spatial science. Regional geography was attacked as ill defined and poorly done, and rapidly fell into disrepute, although the concept of the region was retained in the new task of defining homogeneous areas for the practice of spatial analysis.

Paralleling the declining interest in 'formal regions', however, was increased attention on 'functional regions', areas whose homogeneity was defined by common flow patterns – as between a port and its hinterland, a town and the tributary area it serviced, and a shopping centre and its customers' homes. Definition of such functional regions formed a link between 'old' and 'new' geographical practices, with some advancing the argument that they should be used to define metropolitan regions around major nodes – perhaps as the basis for major regional or more local units of local government and administration.

Although it is now extremely rare for regional geography as a research activity to be promoted, it retains supporters among those who identify a pedagogic role for the description of regions as a means of transmitting knowledge about areal differentiation, which task is 'popular and educational rather than practical or narrowly professional' (Paterson 1974: 21); indeed, one eminent US geographer has claimed that regional geography is 'the highest form of the geographer's art', involving the production of 'evocative descriptions that facilitate an understanding and appreciation of places' (Hart 1982: 2).

This siren call has attracted few disciples. Nevertheless, the increased focus on place (locale, locality, region) within geographical work has led to some calls for the study of regions, if not of regional geography as traditionally practised. Regions in that context are changing milieux within which social relations are forged and reforged, and individuals are socialized and resocialized: they are the local settings (or arenas) within which global processes are played out, and whose particular characteristics interact with those processes to generate spatial variability in place characteristics.

R.J. JOHNSTON
UNIVERSITY OF BRISTOL

References

Hart, J.F. (1982) 'The highest form of the geographer's art', *Annals of the Association of American Geographers* 72.

Kimble, G.H.T. (1951) 'The inadequacy of the region', in L.D. Stamp and S.W. Wooldridge (eds) *London Essays in Geography*, London.

Paterson, J.L. (1974) 'Writing regional geography', in C. Board, R.J. Chorley, P. Haggett and D.R. Stoddart (eds) *Progress in Geography*, Vol. 6, London.

Wooldridge, S.W. (1956) *The Geographer as Scientist*, London.

Wooldridge, S.W. and East, W.G. (1958) *The Spirit and Purpose of Geography*, 2nd edn, London.

Further reading

Clout, H. (2003) 'Place description, regional geography and area studies: The chorographic inheritance', in R.J. Johnston and M. Williams (eds) *A Century of British Geography*, Oxford.

Johnston, R.J., Hauer, J. and Hoekveld, G.A. (eds) *The Challenge of Regional Geography*, London.

Paassi, A. (1991) 'Deconstructing regions: Notes on the scales of social life', *Environment and Planning A* 23.

SEE ALSO: place; spatial analysis

REGULATION

Regulation, here defined as any rule laid down by the government that affects the activities of other agents in the economy, takes many forms, but in general the types of activities concerned and the methods of control vary together. Three broad areas can be identified.

The first is legislation: this approach is commonest for issues such as safety. Most countries have regulations concerning health and safety at work, such as protection for workers against dangerous machinery; other examples include speed limits and the wearing of seatbelts in cars. Enforcement may be carried out by the normal police authorities or by special agencies such as factory inspectors.

The second category is the regulation of monopolies. A monopoly will charge higher prices than a competitive industry, so consumers' interests need some protection. It is useful to distinguish the general case, where action is infrequent, from the particular case of natural monopoly typified by public utilities, where regulation is more continuous.

General competition law operates when a company either has, or is about to acquire, a significant share of the market; then a body such as the Competition Commission in the UK would determine whether a proposed merger or take-over should go ahead. However, the benefits of monopoly can also be gained by a group of firms acting collusively, and the threat of this has led to anti-trust legislation such as the Sherman Act in the USA.

The second area of monopoly regulation is that applied to industries where competition is not feasible for structural reasons; this includes much of the transport, communication, water and energy sectors. Here a regulator may be needed more or less permanently, although the extent of regulation may well decrease if competition can be increased. The difficulty then is to control the monopoly sufficiently tightly without removing all its incentive to cut costs and develop new products. Two main methods have been used: the traditional US method of rate-of-return regulation, where the firm may not exceed a given percentage return on its capital assets, and the price-capping approach pioneered in the UK, which controls prices directly. The latter's success can be measured by the fact that it has displaced rate-of-return regulation for many utilities in the USA.

The final method of regulation is self-regulation, where an industry polices itself. This seems to occur where the problem is incomplete knowledge on the part of consumers. In areas such as medicine or the law, consumers depend on the doctor or lawyer making the right decision on their behalf. Some control of practitioners is therefore needed, and licensing is delegated to their professional bodies: someone 'struck off' their registers can no longer practise. Financial services markets are often self-regulatory, too, requiring membership of the appropriate organization to work in the market, although the banking system is usually regulated by the government's central bank as part of its general responsibility for the stability of the financial system.

In conclusion, two features of regulation in the UK in the last decade or so are worth noting here. One is the extent to which regulation is now done at the European level, so that it is Brussels rather than London which is the driving force (although much of the implementation often remains at the national level). The other is the tendency for regulators to be restructured in response to changes in technology and the markets they control; the obvious examples here are the merger of the gas and electricity regulators during 1999 and 2000, and the coming together of telecommunications and broadcasting regulation in the Office of Communications (Ofcom) at the end of 2003.

STEPHEN TROTTER
UNIVERSITY OF HULL

Further reading

Baldwin, R. and Cave, M. (1999) *Understanding Regulation: Theory, Strategy and Practice*, Oxford.

Crew, M.A. and Kleindorfer, P.R. (1986) *The Economics of Public Utility Regulation*, Basingstoke.

Francis, J.G. (1993) *The Politics of Regulation: A Comparative Perspective*, Oxford.

Goodhart, C., Hartman, P., Llewellyn, D., Rojas-Suarez, L. and Weisbrod, S. (1998) *Financial Regulation: Why, How and Where Now?* London.

Helm, D. and Jenkinson, T. (1998) *Competition in Regulated Industries*, Oxford.

Henry, C., Matheu, M. and Jeunemaitre, A. (eds) (2001) *Regulation of Network Utilities: The European Experience*, Oxford.

Robinson, C. (ed.) (2003) *Competition and Regulation in Utility Markets*, Cheltenham.

Young, A. (2001) *The Politics of Regulation: Privatized Utilities in Britain*, Basingstoke.

SEE ALSO: competition policy; financial regulation; industrial organization; markets; mixed economy; monopoly; privatization

RELATIVISM

The root of relativism is the thought that there are multiple frameworks of thought and judgement, and that there is no independent way of determining which is superior to another or others, since such a determination can only be made from within.

From this root an abundance of contemporary relativisms has bloomed. They can be divided into two broad varieties: cognitive and moral.

Cognitive relativism, in turn, comprises various distinguishable claims, namely:

1 that truth (i.e. what counts as true and false) is relative;
2 that there are alternative logics;
3 ontological relativism – the idea that there are or can be alternative true accounts of the basic structure and components of the world;
4 epistemological relativism – the idea that there are alternative conceptual schemes and no way of deciding between or among them, other than from within one or another of them;
5 relativism about rationality – the idea that there is no single standard of rationality to which all human beings must assent.

Moral relativism, likewise, embraces several distinct claims, namely:

6 descriptive relativism – that is, the factual existence of fundamental moral diversity, within societies and across the world;
7 normative relativism – the claim that moral judgements (as to what is right and wrong, just and unjust, etc.) can only be relative to some framework that limits the scope of their application – that moral principles always come with a 'relativising clause', such as '*For Americans* head hunting is wrong' (see Cook 1999: 14);
8 meta-ethical relativism – a philosophical thesis about the meaning of moral statements which asserts that, however absolute their formulation may be, they can only be understood as relative to a given framework.

Furthermore, there are significant disagreements over what the framework is to which what is relative relates. Among the favoured candidates have been: languages, conceptual schemes, scientific paradigms, cultures and communities.

Anti-relativists typically seek to trap relativists into several allegedly self-refuting paradoxes that reduce to the question: 'To what framework is your statement of relativism itself relative?' but relativists typically find ways of escaping or ignoring this charge. Others correctly observe that relativists often veer between two mutually contradictory assertions: that the constituents of alternative frameworks are equally valid and that they are incommensurable. Some are convinced by an argument of the philosopher Donald Davidson (Davidson 1984 [1973–4]) that the very idea of alternative frameworks or conceptual schemes makes no sense, since, if radically different, they could not be recognized as such. They could only be so recognized if they were already sufficiently similar to our own. Others are less convinced. Some doubt that rationality itself can be relative, since, without presupposing a common core of standards of rationality, we could have no bridgehead into alternative frameworks, so that differences could never show up. Others deny that there must be any single such core. Some suppose that relativism would be refuted by the discovery of so-called 'cultural universals', but others point out that 'relative' contrasts with 'absolute', and 'universal' with 'particular', and that what is in fact common to all may still be relative to the framework they happen to share. In short, relativism is resilient and the debates about its cogency are live and well.

Though philosophers will continue to argue about these and other such matters, the social sciences have been primarily concerned with versions (4), (5), (6) and (7) above, and primarily in relation to language, culture and community.

Among cognitive relativists, linguistic relativism was classically formulated in the so-called 'Sapir–Whorf hypothesis', according to which we 'dissect nature along lines laid down by our native languages' (Whorf 1954: 213). This doctrine has not survived subsequent language–cognition research and developments in linguistic theory. An influential school of sociologists of science advocates the so-called 'strong programme', which abstains from making 'external' judgements of the cognitive worth of the ideas it seeks to explain by reference to the interests of scientific communities, drawing on Wittgensteinian philosophy, anthropological studies of classification systems and the idea, notoriously advanced by Thomas Kuhn, that after a scientific revolution, generating a new 'paradigm', the scientist 'works in a different world' (Kuhn 1964: 120) (but Kuhn himself came to resist the relativist implications of his earlier writings). Within anthropology, debates about relativism and rationality have been endemic, ever since Lucien Lévy-Bruhl and Emile Durkheim clashed over whether 'primitives' moved within a 'prelogical' and mystical thought-world. E.E.

Evans-Pritchard's early work on witchcraft and magic (Evans-Pritchard 1937) took a strongly anti-relativist position, distinguishing 'mystical' from 'scientific beliefs', and deeming Zande witchcraft beliefs unscientific and contradictory, and their magic futile, but he was criticized for this by the Wittgensteinian philosopher Peter Winch, whose essay 'Understanding a primitive society' argued that standards of rationality could vary from culture to culture (Winch 1970 [1964]). Winch generated a wide-ranging debate pitting relativist against rationalist arguments. Most recently, Marshall Sahlins (Sahlins 1995) and Gananath Obeyesekere (Obeyesekere 1997 [1992]) have revived these issues in their dispute over whether or not the Hawai'ians who killed Captain Cook thought he was a god. Sahlins says yes, because 'Different cultures, different rationalities'; Obeyesekere says no, because such an imputation of irrationality is a typical piece of 'European myth-making.'

Moral relativism has ancestors in Michel de Montaigne, who, though ambivalent, cites Pindar's saying that custom is 'the Queen and Empress of the world' (Montaigne 1993 [1580]: 129), J.G. Herder, who powerfully expressed the idea of incommensurable cultural diversity (Herder 1989), and W.G. Sumner, for whom 'immoral' simply meant contrary to the mores of the time and place (Sumner 1934 [1906]). This elision of *mores* or custom and *morality* is inherent in moral relativist views, as is an insistence on the centrality of *enculturation* to the learning of moral standards and principles. Both of these ideas are basic to the school of cultural relativist anthropologists who were followers of Franz Boas (though Boas himself explicitly disclaimed being a relativist), notably Ruth Benedict, Melville Herskovits and Margaret Mead. Thus Benedict's widely read *Patterns of Culture* portrayed contrasting tribal societies in New Mexico, Melanesia and Northwest America as exemplifying 'co-existing and equally valid patterns of life which mankind has created for itself from the raw materials of existence' (Benedict 1935 [1934]: 201). Benedict, Mead and others took such studies to show the errors of ethnocentrism: the assumption that 'Western' or 'American' assumptions and practices (concerning childrearing, sexual relations, etc.) were 'correct' or 'superior'. But their own assumptions were, in turn, subsequently undermined, within anthropology and elsewhere, by the critical deconstruction of their holistic conception of 'cultures', which have increasingly come to be viewed as porous, hybrid and sites of contestation. However, the claims of descriptive and normative moral relativism remain influential among social anthropologists and sociologists who study beliefs and practices, not least because of the pervasive impact of the notion of 'social construction' within these branches of social scientific enquiry and beyond.

Relativism's root idea is, of course, at least as old as the Greek philosopher Protagoras, but it has found ever more fertile ground in which to flourish since the early twentieth century and, indeed, with the spread of 'postmodernist' thinking, it has become rampant in Western culture, taking extreme and sometimes exotic forms. It has also, in turn, generated passionate controversy and resistance, often allied to political contention, though the alliances have changed over time. Thus the early twentieth-century cultural relativists were combating racism and widespread assumptions about the contemporary West as the culmination of civilizational progress. This apparently progressive attitude received a setback with the rise of Fascism and Nazism (Were these not cultures too? If not, why not?), as evidenced in the failure of the American Anthropological Association to convince the framers of the United Nations Declaration of Human Rights to make that document 'a statement of the rights of men [sic] to live in terms of their own traditions' (quoted in Cook 1999: 39). The growing human rights movement since then has, indeed, taken a robustly anti-relativist stance, proclaiming principles held to be applicable everywhere on the planet, and resisting arguments that, for example, 'Asian values' show such principles to be internal to 'Western' culture. On the other hand, the increasing concern to protect minority cultures, the growth of identity politics and of multiculturalist policies has returned moral relativist thinking to the progressive segment of the political spectrum. The so-called 'politics of recognition', focusing on the harms of Eurocentrism and orientalism (Said 1978), and, in general, what are taken to be misrecognition and denigration of other cultures, at home and abroad, has led many to argue that the defence of liberal values can no longer rest content with toleration of others and their practices but must move to a recognition of the cultural specificity of liberal principles *vis-à-vis* other culturally embedded principles. Others maintain, in contrast, the robust view that liberalism is a fighting creed, which, although Western in provenance, is, if it is taken seriously, universal in its scope, If optimistic, they may nurse the hope that the norms, rights and freedoms liberalism proclaims and defends can secure agreement within an 'overlapping consensus', finding alternative justifications from within other cultural and religious traditions.

STEVEN LUKES
NEW YORK UNIVERSITY

References

Benedict, R. (1935 [1934]) *Patterns of Culture*, London.

Cook, J.W. (1999) *Morality and Cultural Differences*, New York and Oxford.

Davidson, D. (1984 [1973–4]) 'On the very idea of a conceptual scheme', in *Inquiries into Truth and Interpretation*, Oxford.

Evans-Pritchard, E.E. (1937) *Witchcraft, Oracles and Magic among the Azande*, Oxford.

Herder, J.G. (1989) *J.G. Herder on Social and Political Culture*, trans., ed. and with an introduction by F.M. Barnard, London.

Kuhn, T. (1964) *The Structure of Scientific Revolutions*, Chicago.

Montaigne, M. de (1993 [1580]) *The Complete Essays*, trans. M.A. Screech, London.

Obeyesekere, G. (1997 [1992]) *The Apotheosis of Captain Cook: European Mythmaking in the Pacific*, 2nd edn with new afterword by the author, Princeton, NJ.

Sahlins, M. (1995) *How 'Natives' Think: About Captain Cook, for Example*, Chicago.

Said, E. (1978) *Orientalism*, New York.

Sumner, W.G. (1934 [1906]) *Folkways: A Study of the Sociological Importance of Usages, Manners, Customs, Mores and Morals*, Boston.

Whorf, B.L. (1954) *Language, Thought and Reality*, Boston and New York.

Winch, P. (1970 [1964]) 'Understanding a primitive society', in B.R. Wilson (ed.) *Rationality*, Oxford.

Further reading

Cook, J.W. (1999) *Morality and Cultural Differences*, New York and Oxford.

Hatch, E. (1983) *Culture and Morality: The Relativity of Values in Anthropology*, New York.

Hollis, M. and Lukes, S. (eds) (1982) *Rationality and Relativism*, Oxford and Cambridge, MA.

Levy, N. (2002) *Moral Relativism: A Short Introduction*, Oxford.

Meiland, J.W. and Krausz, M. (eds) (1982) *Relativism: Cognitive and Moral*, Notre Dame.

Moody-Adams, M.M. (1997) *Fieldwork in Familiar Places*, Cambridge, MA.

Moser, P.K. and Carson, T.L. (eds) (2001) *Moral Relativism: A Reader*, New York.

O'Grady, P. (2002) *Relativism*, Chesham.

SEE ALSO: human rights; philosophy of the social sciences; reason, rationality and rationalism; science, sociology of; social construction

RELIGION

As with many key terms in the social sciences, 'religion' cannot be given a definition that is both precise and universally accepted. In some societies people distinguish between natural and supernatural worlds, or between sacred and profane domains, and in others they do not. Sorcery may be associated with gods or demons, or it may be understood in terms of biological theories of causation (Evans-Pritchard 1937). Should the former class of instances be included in the study of religion and the latter be excluded? To do so would seem inappropriately arbitrary. The modern European differentiation of society into 'economy', 'religion', 'family' and so forth is only one of many ways to draw lines of social demarcation, and in any case it hardly makes the problem any easier, as many Europeans would deny that life outside of churches, temples and mosques is devoid of religious significance. Furthermore, definitions proposed by social scientists rarely are politically neutral. Governments may define 'religion' for purposes of taxation or toleration, and religious institutions may do so for purposes of enforcing orthodoxy. These definitions are sure to collide with those proposed by anthropologists or sociologists for the very different purpose of facilitating cross-cultural comparisons.

Given, then, that any analytically precise definition of 'religion' would arbitrarily eliminate certain social phenomena from the category and would favour some political positions (and theoretical stances) over others, anthropologists generally pursue a two-pronged strategy, combining a broad cross-cultural definition with more precise accounts of the ideas and practices found in each society. The broad definition will be overly inclusive in nearly all cases. For example, religion defined as 'ideas, practices, and institutions that postulate or imply reality beyond that which is immediately available to the senses' – not a bad starting-point – would include certain elements of theoretical physics. At this point the anthropologist or sociologist studying religion in, say, France will point to the particular constellation of ideas and practices surrounding the terms 'religion', 'science', 'medicine', 'astrology' and so forth as providing a framework for religion in France. (He or she also will note the French debates about those domain boundaries, concerning for example the status of Scientology as a religion, astrology as a science, or homeopathy as medicine.)

Most anthropological and sociological studies of religion focus on the logic of religious phenomena within a society or on the geneses and transformations of religious ideas and practices. Nineteenth-century evolutionary theorists did both, analysing the logic of religious beliefs as if they revealed a historical progression. E.B. Tylor (1970 [1871]), for example, pointed out that one finds similar ideas about souls and spirits in many societies, and suggested how humans might first have arrived at these ideas by reflecting on the experiences of sleep, dreams and death. These similarities do exist, and researchers continue to ask why it is that humans posit certain features of gods but not other ones: gods think about the same things we do, for example, and they do not randomly appear and disappear. Research that combines ethnography and experimental psychology (Boyer 2001) suggests that people have been most likely to create and transmit ideas about gods that have direct social implications – that gods will reward and punish morally relevant acts, for example.

Religion does indeed have to do with social norms and institutions, an insight usually traced to Émile Durkheim's sociology, although Aristotle had said that 'men create the gods after their own image', and the same idea runs throughout Scottish social theory. Durkheim (1995 [1912]) complained that Tylor's focus on spirit beliefs missed the point about religion, and argued that religion refers not falsely to a set of beliefs but truly to an emotionally charged sense of a spiritual and moral force. He believed to have found evidence for the origins of that force in the Australian ethnography of the day, where dance-suffused assemblies of small subgroups created the sense of powers outside the individual, but associated with the group. This religious idea is the source of all our modern religious institutions and of our knowledge, he

argued, because it provides a social grounding for norms and for ideas.

Shorn of their evolutionary component, Durkheim's emphasis on the embedded quality of religion (and of other knowledge domains) in society has been particularly influential in the social sciences. It directs scholars to look for ways in which religion, social organization, economy and so forth interconnect. Differences among anthropologists arise over the precise nature of these connections. Durkheim's nephew Marcel Mauss (1990 [1923–4]) analysed phenomena of exchange and competition as 'total social facts', and emphasized the logical interconnections of religion, authority and economics in Northwest Coast potlatch or Melanesian exchange. The subsequent work of E.E. Evans-Pritchard (1956) on Nuer religious ideas, Claude Lévi-Strauss (1964 [1962]) on totemic classification, and Marshall Sahlins (1985) on structures of authority have made it clear that people in all societies engage in intense intellectual speculation about life, fertility, time and space in ways that are not simply projections of social forms but provide complex commentaries on social relations.

A functionalist interpretation of these connections was developed by a wide range of anthropologists. Mary Douglas (1966) drew on her African ethnography and a reading of biblical prohibitions to support Durkheim's contention that religion had to do with separating things and people into sacred and profane categories, but she also argued that these distinctions performed specific social functions, such as preventing undesired intermarriage. Marvin Harris (1974) formulated logically similar arguments about the ecological consequences of religious prohibitions. Drawing on psychoanalysis, Clyde Kluckhohn (1967 [1944]) claimed that witchcraft beliefs served the function of releasing tensions in Navaho society. In general, a socially functionalist logic – that a practice can be explained in terms of the social end it achieves – found support in a Durkheimian approach to religion, even if Durkheim himself stressed the importance of causal-historical accounts.

Durkheim's focus on the simultaneous classification of people, practices and objects along religiously charged lines (his meaning of 'church') remains an analytically attractive starting-point for studying religion in a wide range of settings. Religious institutions often operate by separating and forbidding. Judaism and Islam do so by emphasizing the fundamental devotional importance of distinguishing between followers and non-followers of God, and between forbidden and permitted things. Judaism's ethnic interpretation of membership (with consequent impediments to conversion) contrasts with Islam's practice-oriented openness to conversion. Christian religions generally place still more emphasis on conversion than does Islam, but many of these religions also defend strong moral boundaries between members and non-members of a church (Ammerman 1987). Definition through mechanisms of exclusion and inclusion are found in all societies, from Melanesian secret societies, with their multistage initiation rituals and transmission of secrets, to Hindu regulations of eating and worship between caste groups.

Although some Marxist views of religion reduce it to a reflection of the economically 'real', Karl Marx and Friedrich Engels (1965 [1846]) argued most emphatically for the historically shaped role of religious (or any other) set of institutions and beliefs, against a notion that religion was a simple projection of human, or even social, realities. Marx's writings underlie the contemporary idea that religious knowledge may be seen as one of the forms of socially refracted knowledge through which we 'misrecognize' social forces and institutions (Bourdieu 1977 [1972]). Even the widely shared religious idea of a time beyond human time and transcending death may be analysed as a mechanism through which social actors are deflected from perceiving the relations of control in their own society (Bloch 1992).

The comparative study of large-scale, 'world' religions draws most importantly from the work of Max Weber (1958 [1904–5]), who asked how particular religious orientations develop in interaction with sociopolitical and economic structures. In writing about European religion, Weber acknowledged the shaping force of politics and economics on religion, but argued for the independent causal role played by a religious orientation or ethos, such as the ascetic Protestant's desire to succeed in this world in order to allay doubts concerning eternal election.

Weber's framework highlights the individual actor's orientation towards authority and doctrines, and the possibility of multiple religious orientations within a single religious tradition. Disputes about the sources and workings of

authority underlie many, if not most, of the many fissions and schisms in Christianity (consider the issues of congregational authority, national churches and whether individuals can override scripture), but they also underlie the division between the 'Sunni' mainstream and the Shi'i followers of 'Ali in Islam, and the distinction between the Theravada and the Mahayana approaches within Buddhism. These divisions concerning authority often are at one and the same time divisions concerning salvation or access to divinity – after all, what is religious authority for?

Weber developed a typology of authority, but also, and more interestingly, described the historical processes by which authority structures change. Religious movements may arise from the work of a prophet, who attracts followers based on his charismatic authority, but as the movement develops or the prophet dies, followers must develop other bases for authority. As Weber observed, one solution is to create rule-based or rationalized forms of authority. This type of authority is dominant in modern society, not because of an inevitable process of 'modernization', as sociologists once claimed, but for two distinct reasons: because in the absence of a prophet or a traditional leader, agreement on rules provide a workable source of authority, and because some governments reward religions that have clear, controllable hierarchies. Nonetheless, contemporary ethnographies show not a smooth movement towards rationalized religions, but contradictions and agonies as religious women and men struggle between a search for authentic religious experience and voice, and pressures to regulate and rationalize (Bauman 1983; Geertz 1968; Peacock and Tyson 1989).

Most anthropological and sociological studies of religion approach their topic by studying specific practices: how people pray, give speeches or sermons, consult oracles, shun miscreants, enter trances, or call on the ancestors to help in the birth of a baby (Evans-Pritchard 1937; Tambiah 1970). This methodological emphasis usually is traced to Bronislaw Malinowski's (1954 [1925]) ethnographic writings, which emphasized the differences between social norms and how things worked out in everyday life. Malinowski also emphasized that individuals in all societies act on the basis of rational calculation, but that these calculations made use of magical and religious ideas. This approach, emphasizing socially embedded practices of reasoning, has inspired studies of the instrumental dimensions of religion, such as sorcery, religious law and curing, and remains one of anthropology's major contributions to cross-cultural understanding. But reasoning is not all there is to experience; spells and prayer can serve to allay anxiety and provide hope. This pragmatic approach to religion was advocated by the psychologist William James (1972 [1901–2]) and was underscored by Malinowski. Of particular recent interest to anthropologists has been the role of religion in healing; narratives that invoke the travails of spirits and the designs of gods may produce pain-reducing endorphins and strengthen the immune system as well as yielding a sense of order and empowerment (Laderman 1983).

These studies of individuals' practices also highlight the complex relations of gender and religion. Women often occupy key roles in practices related to healing, birthing and possession, such as the cults of mediumship and possession found throughout East Africa that provide women with channels to express their perceptions of social life (Sharp 1993). Certain practices are notoriously difficult to 'decode', such as wearing 'Islamic dress'. Here the ethnographic focus on specific practices and motives underscores the multitude of meanings that can be conveyed to wearers and observers by a choice of dress. Religions contain traditions of interpretive practices, and partisans of gender equality and toleration of other religions draw on those traditions to advance their positions, as is particularly evident in contemporary internal debates among Muslims (Bowen 2003).

The ethnographic focus on practices has provided new ways of understanding the dynamics of large-scale ('world') religions. In studying a Christian religion, for example, anthropologists and sociologists derive propositions about ideas or themes by examining the ways in which practitioners give sermons, sing hymns, eat together and resolve disputes – much in the spirit of Weber, who constructed his ideal types of Protestant religious orientations from diaries and sermons (Bauman 1983; Harding 2000). The self-designated Primitive Baptists of the southeastern USA, for example, carefully choose sermons and hymns that fit with their adherence to the doctrine of divine election – singing 'Amazing Grace' but avoiding the overly confident 'Blessed Assurance, Jesus is Mine' (Peacock and Tyson 1989).

The anthropology of colonialism and postcolonialism has highlighted the role of religious movements and religious ideology in creating the modern world. Christian missions created models for 'civilizing' the objects of colonial dominion (Comaroff and Comaroff 1991), and colonialism also objectified religion as a feature of a social collectivity. The very idea of a population defined primarily by its membership in a religion is a modern idea; indeed, most names for the large-scale ('world') religions were invented by outside observers (Smith 1978 [1962]). Although it may be an overstatement to claim that religious nationalism was created by colonialism, it clearly was promoted by colonial community-based policies (van der Veer 1994). Once religious affiliation had become a principal way through which one identified with a community, political leaders could mobilize religious sentiments for constructive or genocidal purposes, as in South Asia, the Balkans and Northern Ireland. However, in these and other cases, religious differences are hardly the cause or reason for conflict, as if theology drove politics. Rather, religions have become signs of affiliation with communities, and thereby can be made into signs of fears or hatred based on past or imagined future dangers to one's own autonomy, resources, life or safety.

JOHN R. BOWEN
WASHINGTON UNIVERSITY, ST LOUIS

References

Ammerman, N.T. (1987) *Bible Believers: Fundamentalists in the Modern World*, New Brunswick, NJ.

Bauman, R. (1983) *Let Your Words Be Few: Symbolism of Speaking and Silence among Seventeenth-Century Quakers*, Cambridge, UK.

Bloch, M. (1992) *Prey into Hunter: The Politics of Religious Experience*, Cambridge, UK.

Bourdieu, P. (1977 [1972]) *Outline of a Theory of Practice*, Cambridge, UK.

Bowen, J. (2003) *Islam, Law and Equality in Indonesia: An Anthropology of Public Reasoning*, Cambridge, UK.

Boyer, P. (2001) *Religion Explained*, New York.

Comaroff, J. and Comaroff, J. (1991) *Of Revelation and Revolution: Christianity, Colonialism, and Consciousness in South Africa*, Chicago.

Douglas, M. (1966) *Purity and Danger*, London.

Durkheim, É. (1995 [1912]) *The Elementary Forms of the Religious Life*, New York.

Evans-Pritchard, E.E. (1937) *Witchcraft, Oracles and Magic among the Azande*, Oxford.
—— (1956) *Nuer Religion*, Oxford.
Geertz, C. (1968) *Islam Observed: Religious Development in Morocco and Indonesia*, Chicago.
Harding, S.F. (2000) *The Book of Jerry Falwell: Fundamentalist Language and Politics*, Princeton, NJ.
Harris, M. (1974) *Cows, Pigs, Wars and Witches*, New York.
James, W. (1972 [1901–2]) *Varieties of Religious Experience*, London.
Kluckhohn, C. (1967 [1944]) *Navaho Witchcraft*, Boston.
Laderman, C. (1983) *Wives and Midwives: Childbirth and Nutrition in Rural Malaysia*, Berkeley.
Lévi-Strauss, C. (1964 [1962]) *Totemism*, London.
Malinowski, B. (1954 [1925]) *Magic, Science, and Religion and Other Essays*, Garden City, NY.
Marx, K. and Engels, F. (1965 [1846]) *The German Ideology*, London.
Mauss, M. (1990 [1923–4]) *The Gift: The Form and Reason for Exchange in Archaic Societies*, New York.
Peacock, J.L. and Tyson, R.W., Jr (1989) *Pilgrims of Paradox: Calvinism and Experience among the Primitive Baptists of the Blue Ridge*, Washington, DC.
Sahlins, M. (1985) *Islands of History*, Chicago.
Sharp, L.A. (1993) *The Possessed and the Dispossessed: Spirits, Identity, and Power in a Madagascar Migrant Town*, Berkeley, CA.
Smith, W.C. (1978 [1962]) *The Meaning and End of Religion*, San Francisco.
Tambiah, S.J. (1970) *Buddhism and Spirit Cults in North-East Thailand*, Cambridge.
Tylor, E.B. (1970 [1871]) *Primitive Culture*, 2 vols, London.
van der Veer, P. (1994) *Religious Nationalisms: Hindus and Muslims in India*, Berkeley, CA.
Weber, M. (1958 [1904–5] *The Protestant Ethic and the Spirit of Capitalism*, New York.

SEE ALSO: Durkheim; fundamentalism; James; ritual; sects and cults; shamanism; syncretism; taboo; Weber

REPRESENTATION, POLITICAL

The history of political representation is that of the rise of European parliaments, through the transformation of the sovereign's councillors into a sovereign assembly.

The medieval monarch used to seek advice from persons chosen at his discretion for their competence and trust. But since he wanted them to report from all the land and then to convey his orders and tax demands back to 'their' people, he tended to pattern his selection after the actual social hierarchy, choosing those in the nobility

and high clergy, whose fiefs and dioceses constituted his kingdom, plus (as early as the thirteenth century in England) important commoners.

During crises, when the king most needed their co-operation, the councillors demanded and obtained the right to be convened periodically and to be masters of their agenda. Also, instead of answering individually to the king for their particular community (which was soon to be reapportioned into electoral districts), they deliberated collectively and rendered their decisions obligatory and compelling. They were now acting as one single assembly (whose number, election, immunity and so on had to be formalized) and speaking for the people as a whole. In consequence, the king, who had been seen as the head and also the natural representative of his people, implicitly began to speak only for himself.

Not only political legitimacy but also power had shifted in their favour. Their rule was established in the name of political representativeness. However, the troubling fact soon became obvious that no method could guarantee the selection of genuine representatives of a population, or of aggregating the votes of the representatives who had been selected. Whether representatives were grouped into one chamber or two (the classical formula of bicameralism), or indeed several (providing assemblies for special territories, or for ethnocultural or religious minorities, or for socioeconomic categories), it would inevitably be protested that some right or interest had no appropriate representation. Another conspicuous weakness is that every electoral system benefits some groups or territories or interests to the detriment of others. Furthermore, even if there were such a thing as a faultless representation of the citizenry, this does not automatically translate into a democratic political will capable of producing a legitimate leadership for the polity. Indeed, representative government is an awkward proposition because the more faithful, i.e. accurate and exhaustive, the representation, the less the ability to rule, that is, to make choices or compromises, or even to employ coercion.

The demands of modern politics have brought about the rise everywhere of the executive branch. This has diminished the role of parliaments based on territorial representation, while elections have often become geared to the nomination of a government rather than to the selection of representatives. Moreover, barely had the citizenry successfully imposed the principle 'one man, one vote' than they realized that one vote is too little to guarantee full representation. They felt the need to mobilize specific spokesmen or organizations in order to bring their multifarious interests to the notice of decision-makers. This was, in effect, to counter the suppressions, amalgamations and distortions that territorial representation implies in each electoral district and then at the legislative level. By practising functional representation, voters implicitly criticize parliaments for disregarding the concrete demands of the people, and for imposing their idea of the common interest. It was in much the same way that the kings had been criticized as unrepresentative.

And while governments surround themselves more or less formally with 'councillors' who are drawn from the most important interest groups in the country, and whose 'advice' tends to become obligatory and compelling, discontented or emergent groups keep knocking at the gate. One might speak of the three gates that bar the way to political power: the first opens to allow entrance to the constitutional or socially constitutive structure; the second admits only those who will be seated in representative bodies at all levels of politics and administration; and the third guards the doors that open to the lobbies of the executive branch.

JEAN TOURNON
UNIVERSITY OF GRENOBLE

Further reading

Graham, B. (1993) *Representation and Party Politics. A Comparative Perspective*, Oxford.

Hoggart, K. and Clark, T. (2000) *Citizen Responsive Government*, Amsterdam.

International Commission for the History of Representative and Parliamentary Institutions (1984) *Assemblee di Stati e istituzioni rappresentative nella storia del pensiero politico moderno (secoli XV–XX)*, Rimini.

Morgan, E.S. (1989) *Inventing the People: The Rise of Popular Sovereignty in England and America*, New York.

Phillips, A. (1995) *The Politics of Presence*, Oxford.

Pitkin, H. (1967) *The Concept of Representation*, Berkeley, CA.

Ryden, D. (1996) *Representation in Crisis*, Albany, NY.

Warley, A. and Fairbrass, J. (2002) *Influence and Interests in the European Union. The New Politics of Persuasion and Advocacy*, London.

Williams, M. (1998) *Voice, Trust and Memory. Marginalized Groups and the Failings of Liberal Representation*, Princeton, NJ.

SEE ALSO: citizenship; democracy; elections; interest groups and lobbying; parties, political; voting

RESEARCH AND DEVELOPMENT (R&D)

Research and development activity lies at the heart of economic growth, even though spending on R&D on its own accounts for only a small percentage of national income, and R&D is important for other reasons besides growth. Putting research together with development is, however, to group two rather different activities. Basic research produces new scientific knowledge, hypotheses and theories that are expressed in research papers and memoranda, while inventive work drawing on this basic research produces patentable inventions. These are important whether or not commercial developments follow from these inventions. Development work takes this stock of knowledge and patentable inventions as its raw materials and develops blueprints, specifications and samples for new and improved products and processes (Freeman and Soete 1997; Nelson 1959). Grouping R and D together also hides the fact that most corporate spending on R&D should properly be described as D rather than R, and most R is done in the public sector (Dasgupta and David 1994; Geuna et al. 2003; Pavitt 2001; Rosenberg and Nelson 1994; Stephan 1996).

Allied with this is Schumpeter's distinction between 'invention' and 'innovation' (Freeman and Soete 1997). Inventions are the culmination of research activity and are ideas, sketches or models for a new product or process that may often be patented. An innovation in the economic sense takes place when a new product is marketed or a new process is put to commercial use, and as such represents the culmination of development, production and marketing. Many inventions never turn into innovations, and that need not imply they are of no value. Moreover, for those that do, there can be a long and complex chain of events between invention and innovation.

R&D is often used as a measure of comparative innovative activity (OECD 1981), but it is an input measure rather than an output measure.

For that reason, some prefer to measure innovative activity by counting innovations, though this is a very labour-intensive activity (Townsend *et al.* 1981).

As an intermediate measure of innovative activity, many researchers have made use of patent data (Griliches 1990). The patent gives a firm a monopoly right to commercial use of a particular invention (embodied in a product or process) for a given period. The rationale for this is that, in the absence of a patent, some inventions might be copied comparatively freely by many firms other than the originator, and the inventor would not recoup the costs of invention. Hence, the aim of the patent is to sustain the incentive to innovate. It is recognized, however, that the value of different patents is highly variable, with a large majority having little or no economic value – whatever their technological merit – while a few are of huge value. For that reason, counting patents is not a very reliable measure of inventive or innovative activity.

The economic importance of R&D is not to be judged simply in terms of the inventions and innovations to which it gives rise. First, as Cohen and Levinthal (1989) argue, there are two sides to R&D: the first is generation of inventive output, while the second is learning. Much R&D may be carried out to learn from the R&D efforts of others.

Second, patents can have important implications for the competitive environment, even if they do not always translate into innovative outputs. Patents can act as a barrier to entry, although they can sometimes be invented around. If, however, firms hold patents that they do not use, this may constitute 'pre-emptive patenting', and anti-trust authorities may call for compulsory licensing of these patents.

Third, research activity can have significant implications for the competitive environment, even if its outputs are not registered as patents. Firms may announce how much R&D resources they are committing to a particular area as a signal to potential entrants. In these circumstances, accumulated R&D activity can be a deterrent to entry, and hence influence the competitive environment, even if the firm is not actually selling any products currently that use this accumulated technological knowledge.

Finally, it is often argued that the fruits of R&D efforts spill over outside the originating firm (Jaffe 1986; Griliches 1992). As is well known from the basic economic analysis of externalities, this may mean that the private incentive for firms to invest in R&D is less than the social value of that R&D, because some of the benefit is not captured by the investor. This is a part of the rationale for favourable tax treatment of R&D (Stoneman 1987). However, Geroski (1994) has cast doubt on how serious this problem is in practice.

G.M.P. SWANN
UNIVERSITY OF NOTTINGHAM

References

Cohen, W.M. and Levinthal, D.A. (1989) 'Innovation and learning: The two faces of R&D', *Economic Journal* 99.

Dasgupta, P. and David, P.A. (1994) 'Towards a new economics of science', *Research Policy* 23(5): 487–521.

Freeman, C. and Soete, L. (1997) *The Economics of Industrial Innovation*, 3rd edn, London.

Geroski, P.A. (1994) 'Markets for technology: knowledge, innovation and appropriability', in P. Stoneman (ed.) *Handbook of the Economics of Innovation and Technical Change*, Oxford.

Geuna, A., Salter, A.J. and Steinmueller, W.E. (eds) (2003) *Science and Innovation: Rethinking the Rationales for Funding and Governance*, Cheltenham.

Griliches, Z. (1990) 'Patent statistics as economic indicators: A survey', *Journal of Economic Literature* 28.

—— (1992) 'The search for R&D spillovers', *Scandinavian Journal of Economics* 94 (3, supplement): 529–47.

Jaffe, A. (1986) 'Technological opportunity and spillovers of R&D: Evidence from firms' patents, profits and market value', *American Economic Review* 76.

Nelson, R.R. (1959) 'The simple economics of basic research', *Journal of Political Economy* 67.

OECD (1981) *The Measurement of Scientific and Technical Activities: Proposed Standard Practice for Surveys of Research and Experimental Development (The 'Frascati' Manual)*, Paris.

Pavitt, K. (2001) 'Public policies to support basic research: What can the rest of the world learn from US theory and practice? (and what they should not learn)', *Industrial and Corporate Change* 10(3): 761–79.

Rosenberg, N. and Nelson, R.R. (1994) 'American universities and technical advance in industry', *Research Policy* 23(3): 323–48.

Stephan, P.E. (1996) 'The economics of science', *Journal of Economic Literature* 34(3): 1,199–235

Stoneman, P. (1987) *The Economic Analysis of Technology Policy*, Oxford.

Townsend, J., Henwood, F., Thomas, G., Pavitt, K. and Wyatt, S. (1981) *Innovations in Britain since 1945*, Occasional Paper 16, University of Sussex.

SEE ALSO: economies of scale; investment; productivity

REVOLUTIONS

A revolutionary crisis, or revolution, is any political crisis propelled by illegal (usually violent) actions by subordinate groups that threatens to change the political institutions or social structure of a society.

Some revolutionary crises result in great changes in politics and society, as the Russian and Chinese Revolutions; some result in great political changes but few changes in social life outside of politics, as the English Revolution; some result in hardly any change at all and are hence considered unsuccessful revolutions, as the revolutions of 1848 in Germany.

The word revolution first appeared in political writing in fourteenth-century Italy and denoted any overturning of a government; such events were seen as part of a cycle in the transfer of power between competing parties, with no great changes in institutions implied. However, since the French Revolution, revolution has become associated with sudden and far-reaching change. It is this particular sense of the word that has been carried to fields other than politics, as in the Industrial Revolution or scientific revolutions.

Revolutions have causes, participants, processes of development and outcomes. No two revolutions are exactly alike in all these respects, thus no general theory of revolutions has proven satisfactory. Understanding revolutions requires theories of causes, of participants, of processes and of outcomes of revolutions that stress the variations in each element and how they combine in specific historical cases.

Many of the key issues in studies of revolution were set out in the nineteenth century by Marx and Engels (1968 [1848]). Marx viewed Europe's history since the Middle Ages as a progression through various modes of production, each one more fruitful than the last. Transitions between different modes of production took place through revolutions, in which new elites overthrew and replaced the old dominant class. Bourgeois revolutions, exemplified by the French Revolution of 1789, were necessary to destroy the privileged feudal aristocracy and the agrarian society over which it presided. However, Marx argued that under the succeeding capitalist society workers would still be oppressed by big-business owners; thus a further revolution in the name of labourers remained necessary to extend self-determination and the material benefits of modern industrial technology to all. The major elements of this view – that revolution is a necessary agent of change; that such change is progressive and beneficial; and that revolutions, in both cause and effect, are intimately related to great historical transitions – pose the articles of faith for practising revolutionaries and the chief research problems for academic analysis.

Yet many of Marx's predictions have not come true. Revolutions have not always brought progress towards greater freedom or prosperity. Thus the work of Tocqueville (1998 [1856]) has assumed increasing importance. Tocqueville's analysis of the French Revolution stressed the continuity of the old regime and the post-revolutionary state, and the greater centralization of state power that followed from the revolution. Similar continuities have occurred elsewhere: the Russian imperial bureaucracy and secret police, the Chinese imperial bureaucracy and the Iranian personal authoritarian state have been replaced by similar, albeit more powerful, post-revolutionary versions. Thus the extent of the historical transformation associated with revolutions appears less striking in practice than in Marxist theory.

Since the 1970s, modern social scientists seeking the causes of revolutions first focused on changes in people's expectations and attitudes, but later moved to an emphasis on institutions and the resources of states. Tilly's (1978) 'resource mobilization' view argued that popular protest depended chiefly on whether regime opponents had sufficient resources – manpower, arms and organization – to effectively challenge the power of the state. Skocpol (1979) further developed the view of revolutions as a consequence of state weakness, pointing to a combination of losses in international competition, plus resources and organization that provided leverage to elites and popular groups, as the critical factors that created major revolutions. Goldstone (1991) demonstrated that it was often sustained population growth in traditional economies, which by producing a combination of stresses on state budgets, conflict among those seeking elite positions and hardship for popular groups, produced revolutionary conjunctures. It is such conjunctures, involving defeat in war or a financial crisis, revolts by politically or economically powerful elites, and mass uprisings by peasant villages or urban crowds, that underlay major social revolutions, such as those in England in 1640, France in 1789, Mexico in 1910, China in 1911, Russia in 1917 or Iran in 1979.

In modern revolutions, peasant organization has often been supplied by a revolutionary party, rather than autonomous village organization. This functional substitution has led to different, characteristically peasant-party-based, revolutions: China 1949; Cuba 1958; Vietnam 1972; Nicaragua 1979 (Wolf 1969).

A military or fiscal crisis in an institutionally vulnerable state may begin a revolution; however, the process of revolution and the roles of various participants vary greatly. Certain processes appear to be, if not universal, extremely common: an initial alliance between moderates seeking reform and radicals seeking far-reaching change; involvement in international war (in part because nearby states fear the revolution spreading, in part because revolutionary leaders find the nationalist fervour generated by external wars useful); a gradual fission between moderates and radicals, with the latter triumphing; a civil war as leaders of the revolutionary parties seek to extend their control throughout the nation and eliminate opposition; the emergence of authoritarian rule by a single dominant leader. Other variables – the extent and autonomy of popular participation, the extent of civil war, the degree and permanence of radical triumph, and the duration of autocratic rule – range from high to low across revolutions, depending on the resources available to various groups, the skills of individuals, and the luck of political and military battles.

The outcomes of revolutions are equally diverse. These depend not only on the factors that caused the revolution, but also on the vagaries of the revolutionary process, the influence wielded by external countries and the problems and resources faced by the eventual victors in the revolutionary struggle. The French and English revolutions, though differing greatly in the level of popular uprisings, resulted eventually in similar regimes: monarchies in which possession of private property was the key to political participation and social status (Moore 1966). By contrast, the Russian and Chinese (1949) revolutions, the former with a level of autonomous popular participation, both rural and

urban, akin to that of France, the latter with a chiefly rural peasant-party revolution, both resulted eventually in socialist party-states, in which membership and rank in the state party are the keys to political participation and social status. Mexico's revolution led to a hybrid capitalist party-state, in which political participation is directed by and through the state party, but private wealth is the chief criterion of social status. The postcommunist revolutions in Eastern Europe, the Soviet Union and Central Asia in 1989–91 have produced a diverse array of outcomes, ranging from dictatorships such as that of Tajikistan to shaky democracies dominated by strong leaders such as that of the Ukraine, to stable capitalist democracies such as those of Hungary or the Czech Republic.

Evaluations of the material progress made under post-revolutionary regimes are also mixed. There are cases of great progress in health and literacy, such as Cuba, but the ability of post-revolutionary regimes to provide a generally higher material standard of living than similarly situated non-revolutionary regimes is yet to be demonstrated (Eckstein 1982). Indeed, the overthrow of communism in Eastern Europe and the USSR in 1989–91 demonstrated widespread unhappiness that communist states had failed to provide a material living standard comparable to that of Western nations.

Revolutions have also varied in their outcomes with regard to gender roles and rights. Some revolutions have liberated women and created greater equality, as in Russia in 1917 and China in 1949. Yet other revolutions have been conservative and reinforced male-domination in their societies, as in Mexico 1910, or Iran in 1979 (Moghadam 1997).

The role of ideological changes in causing revolutions and shaping their outcomes is hotly debated (Parsa 2000; Selbin 1993). Most revolutionaries have proven quite pragmatic in modifying revolutionary programmes as seemed necessary; Russia under the New Economic Plan of the 1920s, and China in the 1980s, have embarked on such pragmatic paths. At other times ideological fervour has taken precedence, as in the Jacobin years of the French Revolution, and the Great Leap Forward and Cultural Revolution in China. Ideological programmes are thus a rather unpredictable, if far from dominant, element in shaping revolutions.

Ideology in a broader sense, as an overall cultural perspective, has been a more uniformly important factor. Eisenstadt (1978) has noted that the key to revolution lies in the coalescence, in a time of political crisis, of diverse movements – peasant uprisings, elite political revolts, religious heterodoxies – into a widespread attack on the institutions of the old regime. Thus the main role of ideologies in revolutions has been to bring together diverse grievances and interests under a simple and appealing set of symbols of opposition. For this purpose, any ideology that features a strong tension between good and evil, emphasizes the importance of combating evil in this world through active remaking of the world, and sees politics as simply one more battlefield between good and evil, may serve as the foundation for a revolutionary ideology. Thus Puritanism, liberalism, communism, anti-colonialism and Islam have all proved adaptable to providing symbols for revolutions. Studies of peasants' and workers' revolts have stressed that traditional ideologies – the communal ideology of 'members' against 'outsiders' of the peasant village and the craft guild – can also motivate actors in revolutionary crises. None of these ideologies of themselves brought down governments; but they were crucial in providing a basis for uniting diverse existing grievances under one banner and encouraging their active resolution.

Revolutions have occurred in a remarkably varied range of societies. Preindustrial monarchies, Third World colonies of industrialized states, modernizing dictatorships and totalitarian party-states have had their governments suddenly overturned by popularly backed movements for change. What most regimes that have fallen to revolutions had in common – from colonial regimes, to military dictatorships, to community party-states – was a closed state with limited elite access to power and few channels for the populace to influence changes in leadership (Goodwin 2001). If this pattern holds, the arena for future revolutions will be the remaining authoritarian states of Africa, the Middle East, Latin America and Southeast Asia, and the party-dictatorships of communist China and Cuba. The advanced industrial democracies may see strikes and demonstrations, but are unlikely to witness revolutions.

The degree of violence in revolutions is also highly variable, and this seems rooted in the diverse nature of the societies in which revolutions have occurred. Societies with higher levels of industrialization and education, and with less influential conservative and counter-revolutionary forces, seem to be able to sustain popular revolutions without descending into mass violence and terror. This is the basis for positive results from the revolutions in the Czech Republic, Poland and Hungary. However, societies with large agricultural populations, low-to-moderate levels of literacy, or a large proportion of powerful conservative or counter-revolutionary elites, tend to fall into revolutionary spirals of struggles for power and internal violence, sometimes escalating to civil war. This suggests that new crises may be anticipated in parts of Africa, Latin America, the Middle East and Asia. Even in parts of Eastern Europe, including many of the successor states to the Soviet Union, the clash between reformers and still powerful conservatives may ignite new explosions. Revolutions are thus likely to continue to shape, and reshape, world politics for years to come.

JACK A. GOLDSTONE
GEORGE MASON UNIVERSITY

References

Eckstein, S. (1982) 'The impact of revolution on social welfare in Latin America', *Theory and Society* 11.

Eisenstadt, S.N. (1978) *Revolution and the Transformation of Societies*, New York.

Goldstone, J.A. (1991) *Revolution and Rebellion in the Early Modern World*, Berkeley.

Goodwin, J. (2001) *No Other Way Out: States and Revolutionary Movements 1945–1991*, Cambridge, UK.

Marx, K. and Engels, F. (1968 [1848]) *The Communist Manifesto*, London.

Moghadam, V.M. (1997) *Gender and Revolutions*, in J. Foran (ed.) *Theorizing Revolutions*, London, pp. 137–67.

Moore, B., Jr (1966) *Social Origins of Dictatorship and Democracy*, Boston, MA.

Parsa, M. (2000) *States, Ideologies, and Social Revolutions: A Comparative Analysis of Iran, Nicaragua, and the Philippines*, Cambridge, UK.

Selbin, E. (1993) *Modern Latin American Revolutions*, Boulder, CO.

Skocpol, T. (1979) *States and Social Revolutions*, Cambridge, UK.

Tilly, C. (1978) *From Mobilization to Revolutions*, Reading, MA.

Tocqueville, A. de (1998 [1856]) *The Old Regime and the French Revolution*, Chicago.

Wolf, E.R. (1969) *Peasant Wars of the Twentieth Century*, New York.

Further reading

Foran, J. (ed.) (1997) *Theorizing Revolutions*, London.
Goldstone, J.A. (ed.) (2003) *Revolutions: Theoretical, Comparative, and Historical Studies*, Fort Worth, TX.

SEE ALSO: radicalism; terrorism

RICARDIAN ECONOMICS

David Ricardo (1772–1823) is one of the few (political) economists whose name has been recognized as part of the English language. The *Oxford English Dictionary* (OED) lists two usages of 'Ricardian', viz. 'Of, pertaining to, or accepting the doctrines of...David Ricardo', and 'A follower of Ricardo'. 'Ricardian' indeed may be used to refer to the doctrines of Ricardo himself, but it has been more usually employed in the second of the two senses, as it will be hereafter.

The *OED* traces the second usage of 'Ricardian' to the year 1886, although one of the first references in the English-language literature to a 'Ricardian' *qua* follower of Ricardo may be found in an 1827 edition of *Blackwood's Edinburgh Magazine*. However, for at least the period 1820–50 it is more common to encounter references to members of the 'Ricardo school' or, synonymously, to members of the 'new school' or 'Ricardoite school'. The first such printed reference appears to have been made in 1820, 3 years before Ricardo's death.

The identification of a 'new school' in 1820 is evidence of the impact that Ricardo's ideas were having at that early time and, more particularly, of the *perception* that he had attracted a following of like-minded enthusiasts who were disseminating a new and distinctive brand of political economy. That his ideas had made an impact, both positively and negatively, is indisputable: his work was reviewed in the leading periodicals of the day and, as a Member of Parliament (from 1819), Ricardo was prominent in disseminating the 'truths' of political economy as he saw them. He had also been fortunate in attracting one follower, James Ramsay McCulloch, who was to prove tireless over several decades in his efforts to promote a brand of Ricardo's economics (as he understood them, it should be added) through the pages of the influential *Edinburgh Review*, newspapers, pamphlets, serial monographs and,

in a singular coup for the 'new school', in the prestigious *Encyclopaedia Britannica*.

One follower scarcely amounts to a 'school'. Yet, it is a remarkable fact that Ricardo's close followers were very few in number. According to James Mill (the father of J.S. Mill), writing in correspondence soon after Ricardo's death, he and McCulloch had been Ricardo's 'two and only genuine disciples' (which was notably to exclude Robert Torrens, who had worn two hats both as a supporter and critic of Ricardo). Subsequently, J.S. Mill, sundry writers in the Benthamite *Westminster Review* and Thomas De Quincey have all been identified as 'core' Ricardians, albeit to varying degrees, but even the addition of these recruits does not amount to a significant head-count in Ricardo's favour. Rather, what appears to have bolstered the impression of a 'school' was the unparalleled enthusiasm and self-promoting efforts of Ricardo's would-be followers, especially McCulloch, J.S. Mill and the *Westminster* reviewers, and the absence of anything approaching a unified opposition. As many historians have commented, the importance of the 'new school' was out of all proportion to its membership.

What the 'school' stood for is debatable. With the untimely demise of Ricardo in 1823 his followers were left free to expound, develop or (as with the case of Ricardo's 'pure' labour theory of value and his search for the perfect 'invariable measure') even abandon elements of his teaching without the benefit of his counsel. Least controversially, perhaps, the 'school' accepted a version of the theory of differential rent (according to which rent is the differential surplus of produce between the 'worst' land, which pays no rent, and the 'best' land), upheld a notion of an inverse relationship between wages and profits, regarded the conditions of producing wage-goods, especially food, as the dominant influence on wages and (inversely) on profits, and contended that the attempt to expand agricultural production in a 'closed' economy would encounter diminishing returns, in turn responsible for a higher price of corn, higher money wages, increased (differential) rent and a lower general rate of profit. To varying degrees they also endorsed Malthusian population theory, the law of markets (the doctrine that 'supply creates its own demand') and a theory of value that emphasized conditions of production – rather than the forces of 'supply and demand' – in the determination of competitive prices. In terms of economic policy they stood for free trade in general and the abolition of agricultural protection in particular while, at the political level, some (principally James and J.S. Mill, but not McCulloch) married the political economy with the Benthamite utilitarian programme for political reform.

Internally heterogeneous as the 'school' undoubtedly was, it had a profound impact on political economy and on public opinion more generally, although at no stage did it triumph victoriously over all opposition. During Ricardo's lifetime, he and his school were reviled by some for their alleged stress on class conflict, their perceived bias against agriculture and their 'heartlessness' in promoting the values of the market economy over a paternalistic order under the benevolent guidance of the landed aristocracy. Answering in kind, the *Westminster Review* was equally forthright in condemning the 'old school' and their friends (as they referred to critics of Ricardo and his school) as sinister, bigoted reactionaries who were too 'interested', dull, or both, to appreciate the new 'truths' (which, for the *Westminster*, included the Ricardo-inspired 'truth' that the country was governed by an unelected class of landlords whose interest was directly opposed to the interests of everyone else). Exchanges of this nature were to continue throughout the 1820s and 1830s, and were to be given a new lease of life through the publications of the (misnamed) 'Ricardian socialists': a quite separate tendency that argued, more in the spirit of Adam Smith than Ricardo, that labour produced everything and therefore had a right to its entire produce without any deductions for rent or profit.

The more ideological debates were not conducted independently of theoretical issues. Those who opposed the political messages of the 'new school' were invariably to be found promoting some vague version of supply and demand analysis as the perfect antidote to noxious Ricardian influences. For example, supply and demand was enlisted in support of the proposition that profits, wages and rent were each determined *independently*, so dissolving the perception of an immutable, economically based conflict of interest between the three great social classes of capitalists, labourers and landlords. At its crudest, the very mention of supply and demand was thought by some to invalidate virtually every doctrine of Ricardo and his followers.

However, it is by no means true that those who upheld supply and demand were universally opposed either to the policy proposals, the political programme or even to some of the theoretical positions of Ricardo and his school. To take a prominent example, Nassau Senior, the first Oxford University Professor of Political Economy and, like Ricardo, a vigorous supporter of free trade and minimal government, used supply and demand to arrive at many of Ricardo's own conclusions by a different route (including the central conclusion that the rate of profit is determined by the conditions of producing wage-goods). T.R. Malthus also came to absorb elements of Ricardo's economics within his own supply and demand system (such as the proposition that profits depend on the 'proportions' of produce allocated between capitalists and labourers) and others followed his example. More pervasively, the once much-abused Ricardo and Ricardian versions of the theory of differential rent were to receive widespread acceptance after their supply and demand reformulations. In a sense, therefore, the Ricardo school had scored some notable victories. Ironically, it is this very success that may be at least partly responsible for the widely held perception of the school's early demise.

The thesis of the early fall (around 1830) of Ricardianism was advanced from very different theoretical perspectives by Karl Marx and Joseph Schumpeter. While it is true that the doctrinal and polemical debates were to lose much of their vigour in the 1830s, Ricardian ideas continued to survive in more or less explicit form both in the writings of the avowed supporters and, of no lesser importance, in the writings of the critics. Thus, although the debates were to become less intense, it can be argued that this was not so much a sign of the defeat of the Ricardians as an indication of their relative success, taken against the backdrop of an increasingly fragmented opposition. The lines of demarcation between the 'new' and the 'old' schools had become blurred.

What is true, however, is that the Ricardian which survived and later prospered with the publication in 1848 of J.S. Mill's highly acclaimed *Principles of Political Economy* was by no means identical with the work of Ricardo himself. Yet, if we insist on a strict correspondence between *true* Ricardianism and Ricardo's own teaching, we must conclude (effectively as

Marx did) that Ricardianism was on the wane from its very inception, especially with regard to the subsequent uninterest in the labour theory of value and those problems associated with it that preoccupied Ricardo to the end of his life. Ricardo's economics and Ricardian economics are distinct but related entities. The latter owed its existence to the former but was to develop its own multiple identities of which, historically, the most influential was to be J.S. Mill's.

TERRY PEACH
UNIVERSITY OF MANCHESTER

Further reading

Blaug, M. (1958) *Ricardian Economics*, New Haven, CT.
Marx, K. ([1863] (1971)] *Theories of Surplus Value Part III*, London.
Peach, T. (2003) 'Introduction', in *David Ricardo: Critical Assessments*, London.
Schumpeter, J.A. (1954) *History of Economic Analysis*, London.

SEE ALSO: classical economics; Malthus; Mill; Ricardo

RICARDO, DAVID (1772–1823)

David Ricardo was born in London on 18 April 1772, the third son of Abraham Israel Ricardo, a Sephardic Jew who had moved from Amsterdam to London around 1760. The young Ricardo was groomed to follow his father on the London Stock Exchange. Although his education was by no means negligible, it appears to have been somewhat narrow, perhaps explaining in part his later outbursts of despair over his literary ability.

Ricardo worked with his father for 7 years until, at the age of 21, he married a Quaker and disavowed the Jewish faith. Estranged from his parents, Ricardo pursued a brilliant career as a jobber and loan contractor. Through a combination of fine judgement and good luck he soon amassed a considerable fortune and began a gradual retirement from business in 1814.

It was in 1799 that his interest in political economy was aroused by a chance perusal of Adam Smith's (1981 [1776]) *The Wealth of Nations*. His first rash of publications came 10 years later with letters and pamphlets addressed to the 'Bullion Controversy'. Ricardo, always a strict quantity theorist, sought to expose the inflationary consequences of the Bank Restriction

Act 1797, which had suspended the free convertibility of paper currency into gold. He argued that the government had been mistaken in suspending convertibility and even more wayward in trusting ignorant Bank of England officials with monetary control. The remedy for inflation was a return to convertibility, ideally accompanied by the establishment of an independent authority to oversee monetary management.

Following the Bullion Controversy, Ricardo's next important publication, *An Essay on the Influence of a Low Price of Corn on the Profits of Stock* (1815), was one of many pamphlets spawned by the Tory government's controversial proposal to impose a new scale of duties on the importation of foreign corn. Borrowing and adapting the theory of differential rent, rediscovered by his contemporary and friend, Thomas Robert Malthus, Ricardo inveighed against protection. His principal argument was that a protection-induced expansion of domestic cultivation would tend to run up against diminishing returns, thus resulting in a rising corn price, higher money wages, a falling general rate of profit and a slackening pace of capital accumulation. The only true gainers would be the landlords, whose rents would increase as general profitability declined.

Ricardo's major work, *The Principles of Political Economy and Taxation* (three editions: 1817, 1819, 1821), was initially conceived as an expanded *Essay* and, although its scope was broader, the contents of the core theoretical chapters reflect that early conception. In particular, Ricardo now sought to demonstrate beyond logical doubt that diminishing agricultural returns *must* (permanently) depress general profitability in the absence of technological advances and the free importation of foreign grain. Since, as far as he was concerned, rising corn prices posed the sole empirical threat of permanently declining profitability, the clear message of his work was that the newly revised corn law should be scrapped.

Prominent among the theoretical innovations in the *Principles* was the development of a pure labour theory of value according to which permanent changes in exchange relationships between most commodities result from alterations in direct or indirect *quantities* of labour expended on their production. At the same time, Ricardo had discovered various limitations to the theory, later reduced by him to differences in the 'time profiles' of labour inputs. Pressed by Malthus to justify a theory that he had himself undermined, Ricardo embarked on his futile quest for a perfect measure of value that would magically restrict (permanent) variations in exchange relationships to those resulting from altered expenditures of labour-time, and this *without* assuming identical time profiles of labour inputs. That bizarre line of enquiry found expression in an extensively rewritten chapter 'On value' for the third edition of the *Principles*, in which Ricardo also asserted the empirical relevance of the 'pure' labour theory. The complexities of value continued to trouble him until his death, not least because of his muddled attempt to reconcile 'value' in the sense of expended labour with 'value' in the more conventional sense of cost-of-production.

Adumbration of a theory of comparative advantage in international trade, the treatment of profit as a residual or 'surplus', consideration of the possibility of labour displacement following the introduction of new machinery (in the third edition of the *Principles*) and a strict adherence to the 'law of markets' (in short, the doctrine that 'supply creates its own demand'), all count among the distinctive features of the *Principles*. Mention should also be made of Ricardo's austere, logico-deductive style of reasoning, for which he has been often condemned as an ultra-abstractionist. Despite superficial appearances, however, Ricardo's political economy was mostly addressed to the concrete issues of his time; with the partial exception of his later deliberations on 'value', his was not an interest in theory for its own sake.

The success of the *Principles* was decisive in persuading Ricardo that he should follow the advice of his mentor, James Mill, to enter Parliament. So it was that in 1819 he took his seat as the member for the small pocket borough of Portarlington in Ireland. From the floor of the Commons, Ricardo was untiring in his efforts to disseminate the scientific truths of political economy, as he saw them. With an almost fanatical belief in the efficiency and wealth-generating potential of competitive capitalism, he campaigned vigorously against monopolies, international trade restrictions, the poor laws, relief works and government borrowing generally (he boldly proposed that the national debt should be paid off over a 2- or 3-year period by the imposition of a property tax). As a convert to the Bentham–Mill cause of parliamentary reform, though always remaining a moderate reformer, he also argued for a (very) limited extension of the electoral franchise, triennial parliaments and, most important of all in his view, the introduction of a secret ballot. He apparently believed, and certainly hoped, that those reforms would bring about a Parliament free from party and factional interest: a legislative environment that would promote the greatest happiness of the greatest number. When, at some future point in time, the working class came to appreciate the unique benefits of *laissez-faire* capitalism, they too could be trusted with democratic participation.

Ricardo's 'political economy' has attracted and repelled, both in his lifetime and subsequently. Nor is there any consensus over his location in the history of economic thought: some have claimed him for the neo-classical school, others for the Marxian, others still for a neo-Ricardian (or Sraffian) school. Part of the reason for the seemingly endless debate over his doctrinal home can be traced to the presence of a confusion and ambiguity in his writings that facilitates contradictory readings. But it is also the fate, perhaps even the hallmark, of great historical figures that they should be enlisted in support of causes held dear by subsequent generations. By that criterion, David Ricardo is one of the greatest political economists ever.

TERRY PEACH
UNIVERSITY OF MANCHESTER

References

Ricardo, D. (1951–73) *The Works and Correspondence of David Ricardo*, ed. P. Sraffa with M.H. Dobb, 10 vols, Cambridge, UK.

Smith, A. (1981 [1776]) *An Inquiry into the Nature and Cause of the Wealth of Nations*, eds R. Campbell and A. Skinner, Indianapolis, IN.

Further reading

Blaug, M. (1958) *Ricardian Economics: A Historical Study*, New Haven, CT.

Hollander, J.H. (1910) *David Ricardo: A Centenary Estimate*, Baltimore, MD.

Hollander, S. (1979) *The Economics of David Ricardo*, Toronto.

Peach, T. (1993) *Interpreting Ricardo*, Cambridge, UK.

Sraffa, P. (1951) 'Introduction', in *The Works and Correspondence of David Ricardo*, Vol. 1, Cambridge, UK.

SEE ALSO: Ricardian economics

RISK ANALYSIS

The field of risk analysis has assumed increasing importance in recent years given the concern by both the public and private sectors in safety, health and environmental problems. The tragic attacks of 11 September 2001 have raised an additional set of issues regarding how we deal with events where there is considerable ambiguity and uncertainty on the likelihood of their occurrence and their potential consequences.

Risk analysis encompasses three interrelated elements: risk assessment, risk perception and risk management. It is also recognized that both public and private sectors must be involved in the determination of the nature of the risk, and then in developing strategies for risk management.

Risk assessment

Risk assessment encompasses studies that estimate the chances of a specific set of events occurring and/or their potential consequences. Scientists and engineers need to provide the users of these data with a picture of what we know regarding the nature of a particular risk and the degree of uncertainty surrounding these estimates. They also have to be sensitive to their role as assessors of these estimates (Haimes 1998).

It is not uncommon for the public to hear Expert 1 say that there is 'nothing to worry about regarding a particular risk' while at the same time learning from Expert 2 that 'this risk should be on your radar screen'. There may be many different reactions to these conflicting reports. One lay-person may decide that they cannot rely on the judgement of any expert. Another individual may decide to focus on the expert supporting his or her own view of the risk. Someone else may seek out the views of other experts to see if there is a degree of consensus on the nature of the risk.

One way to capture what experts know and do not know about a particular risk is to construct an exceedance probability (EP) curve. An EP curve specifies the probabilities that certain level of losses will be exceeded. The losses can be measured in terms of dollars of damage, fatalities, illness or some other unit of analysis (Grossi and Kunreuther 2004).

Suppose one was interested in constructing an EP curve for dollar losses to homes in Los Angeles from an earthquake. Using probabilistic risk assessment, one combines the set of events that could produce a given dollar loss and then determines the resulting probabilities of exceeding losses of different magnitudes. Based on these estimates, one can construct the mean EP depicted in Figure 10. By its nature, the EP curve inherently incorporates uncertainty associated with the probability of an event occurring and the magnitude of dollar losses. This uncertainty is reflected in the 5 per cent and 95 per cent confidence interval curves in the figure.

A key question that needs to be addressed in constructing an EP curve is the degree of uncertainty regarding both probability and outcomes. It is a lot easier to construct such a curve for natural disasters and chemical accidents than it is for terrorist activities. But even for these more predictable accidents or disasters, there may be considerable uncertainty regarding both the likelihood of the occurrence of certain risks and the resulting damage. For low-probability–high-consequence risks, the spread between the three curves depicted in Figure 10 shows the degree of indeterminacy of these events. Providing information on the degree of uncertainty associated with risk assessments should increase the credibility of the experts producing these figures.

The EP curve is an important element for evaluating risk management tools. It puts pressure on experts to state the assumptions on which they are basing their estimates of the likelihood of certain events occurring and the resulting consequences. In fact, EP curves, such as those depicted in Figure 10, supplemented by a discussion of the nature of these assumptions, should enable the general public to gain a clearer picture as to why there is so much ambiguity surrounding estimates of some risks and much less uncertainty on others.

Risk perception

Traditional risk assessment focuses on losses that are often measured in monetary units. Risk perception is concerned with the psychological and emotional factors that have been shown to have an enormous impact on behaviour. (For a comprehensive summary of recent work, see Slovic 2000.) In a set of pathbreaking studies begun in the 1970s, Paul Slovic, Baruch Fischhoff and other psychologists began measuring laypersons' concerns about different types of risks.

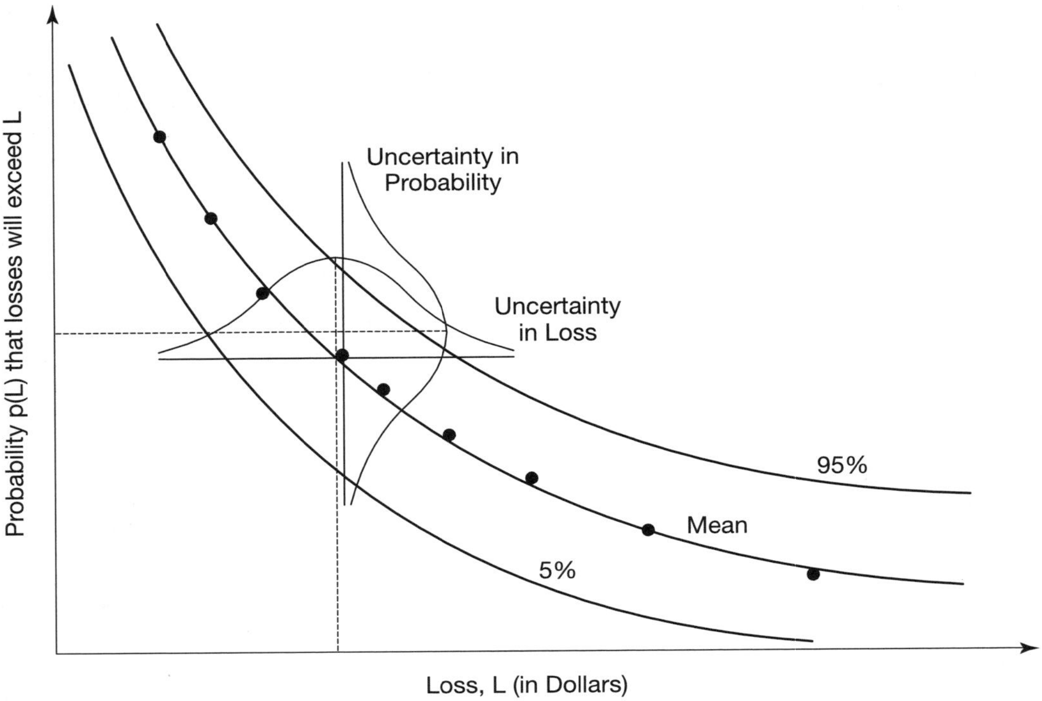

Figure 10 Example of exceedance probability (EP) curves

These studies showed that those hazards for which the person had little knowledge and were also greatly dreaded were perceived as being the most risky. For some technologies, such as nuclear power, and activities such as storing radioactive waste, there was a wide disparity between the general citizenry and the experts' view of the risk. The general finding that lay-persons see the world differently from the scientific community also raised a set of questions as to the nature of the decision-making process for dealing with risks. For a long time the scientific community felt it was appropriate to ignore the public's perception of the risk if it differed significantly from their own estimates. The public did not believe the experts' figures because they were not communicated very well, the assumptions on which they were based were not well stated, and there was little understanding as to why experts disagreed with each other.

The situation has changed in recent years, and there is now more sympathy for including these psychological and emotional factors as part of the risk assessment process. Recent studies have confirmed this view by showing that the public

will avoid certain activities because they are perceived to be unduly dangerous. More specifically, there is a *stigma* associated with technologies, places and products because the public perceives them to be hazardous. In many of these situations the scientific evidence suggests that there is no reason to be concerned about these risks (Flynn *et al.* 2001).

Risk management

In developing risk management strategies for reducing future losses there is a need to incorporate the data from risk assessment studies and the factors that have been shown to influence risk perception. Since a number of studies indicate that people have difficulty processing data regarding uncertain events, this poses challenges as to how one can effectively communicate information on the risk to the public (see Morgan *et al.* 2002). The use of exceedance probability curves, such as those shown in Figure 10, can indicate the uncertainties surrounding a particular risk. However, as pointed out above, lay-persons are not likely to process these data in ways that scientists and engineers would like them to. Risk management approaches must recognize the difficulties that individuals have in collecting and analysing data from experts.

One can utilize both positive and negative economic incentives to encourage individuals to take protective measures to reduce their losses. Fines coupled with specific regulations or standards can also be used to encourage protective measures but there has to be a sufficiently high probability that the negligent individual or firm will get caught. Otherwise the person or manager is likely to play a different game than intended – ignore the regulation. If the probability is sufficiently low and/or the fine is not very large, then it may pay in the long run not to take protective action. The behaviour in such cases is not all that different from the decision not to put a quarter into the parking meter because one feels that there is a small chance of getting a ticket and if one does the amount one has to pay is not that high.

There is a need to bring together interested parties from the private sector, representatives from public interest and citizen groups, and leaders from governmental organizations to develop risk management strategies. This type of private–public partnership is likely to be more successful than working independently with each of these groups. When a building collapses it may break a pipeline and cause a major fire that could damage other property not affected by the earthquake. Losses from these and other externalities would not be covered by the firm's insurance policy. A well-enforced building code that requires cost-effective mitigation measures would help reduce these risks and obviate the need for financial assistance to those who would otherwise suffer uninsured losses.

If the private sector feels that it cannot provide insurance protection against losses from catastrophic events, then one may need some type of government pooling arrangement to cover these losses. The Florida Hurricane Catastrophe Fund was established by the state following Hurricane Andrew when a number of insurers claimed that they could not include windstorm in the future as part of the standard homeowners' coverage. After the 1994 California Northridge earthquake insurers had a similar reaction to providing earthquake coverage in California. In 1996 the state formed the California Earthquake Authority that offers homeowners in the state earthquake coverage as a separate policy.

Finally let us turn to the question that has been preoccupying the USA since 11 September 2001 and is likely to be high on the agenda for the coming months: What is the appropriate role of the public and private sectors in dealing with terrorism? Prior to the collapse of the World Trade Center towers, there was certainly a concern with terrorism but also a feeling that 'it will not happen in my backyard'. The private sector was expected to finance protective measures rather than relying on government for any assistance.

The terrorist attacks provide an opportunity to reassess the role of the public and private sectors with respect to providing protection. One needs to recognize that for many situations there may be a need for the public sector to take the leading role with respect to providing protective measures because the private sector may have few economic incentives to take these steps on their own. More specifically one can show that there is a much lower incentive for individuals and firms to undertake protection when they know that others have not invested in these measures and they could be contaminated by them. In other words these interdependencies lead to underinvestment and thus may require the involvement of the public sector (see Kunreuther and Heal 2002).

To illustrate this point, suppose we have an airline, Airline A, considering whether to institute a system to check their incoming bags on flights to detect the possibility of an explosive that could damage or destroy the plane. It knows that none of the other airlines have instituted such a system. Hence there is some chance that an unchecked bag that is contaminated could be transferred from Airlines B, C, D or E to one of Airline A's planes. The economic incentive for Airline A to undertake this protective measure under the current liability and insurance systems is somewhat lower than if all the airlines had checked-baggage systems.

This result applies to any situation where those who do not take protective measures and are not financially responsible for the damage they cause to others can contaminate a responsible individual or firm. In these cases, one may need government regulations and standards to provide adequate protection against extreme events in ways that provide substantial benefits to the affected individuals and firms.

The same logic applies to the incentive of divisions of firms to invest in protection against a catastrophic accident that could bankrupt the entire organization. The actions of Nick Leeson and the traders he hired at the Barings Futures Singapore office were primarily responsible for bringing down Barings Bank. Arthur Anderson was sent into bankruptcy by the actions of its Houston branch. Both of these examples illustrate this type of contamination. If a division knows that other divisions in the firm are not investing in protection, then it has less incentive to incur these costs than if the other units were investing in safety measures. There may thus be a need for centralized organizational controls or third-party inspections from outside the firm to deal with this situation.

Conclusions

We have always faced many challenges in dealing with safety, health and environmental risks. Recent terrorist activities have brought these issues to the fore in very graphic ways. Successful risk analyses require scientists and engineers to undertake assessments to characterize the nature and uncertainties surrounding a particular risk. One also needs social scientists to characterize the factors that influence the perception of a risk by individuals, groups and organizations. Finally there is a need to develop strategies that involve risk communication, economic incentives, standards and regulations for managing these risks. Given the challenges in processing information on these risks as well as the interdependencies between individuals and firms that create negative externalities, public–private partnerships are necessary for developing risk management strategies that will reduce future losses efficiently while satisfying the needs of the affected stakeholders.

HOWARD KUNREUTHER
THE WHARTON SCHOOL,
UNIVERSITY OF PENNSYLVANIA

References

Flynn, J., Slovic, P. and Kunreuther, H. (eds) (2001) *Risk Media and Stigma*, London.
Grossi, P. and Kunreuther, H. (2004) *New Approaches to Managing Risks from Natural Hazards*, Boston.
Haimes, Y. (1998) *Risk Modeling, Assessment and Management*, New York.
Kunreuther, H. and Heal, G. (2002) 'Interdependent security', *Journal of Risk and Uncertainty* 26: 231–49.
Morgan, G., Fischhoff, B., Bostrom, A. and Atman, C.J. (2002) *Risk Communication: A Mental Models Approach*, New York.
Slovic, P. (2000) *The Perception of Risk*, London.

SEE ALSO: risk society

RISK SOCIETY

'This concept describes a phase of development of modern society in which the social, political, ecological and individual risks created by the momentum of innovation increasingly elude the control and protective institutions of industrial society' (Beck 1996: 27).

As Lash and Wynne note in their introduction to the English translation of *Risk Society* (Beck 1992a), few contemporary social science books have enjoyed the influence – or the sales – achieved by Ulrich Beck's account of a 'new modernity'. Given even greater weight by the overlap and congruity with Anthony Giddens's exploration of 'self and society in the Late Modern Age' (Giddens 1991), Beck's analysis of the changing conditions of modernity and the rise of risk anxieties has attracted substantial academic and political attention. Although risk has a longer-standing social scientific pedigree (see Douglas and Wildavsky 1982; Perrow 1984), Beck's publications since the late 1980s have helped place the treatment of risk and uncertainty at the very core of contemporary social theory. High-profile risk and environmental problems during this period have also sustained the topicality and relevance of Beck's key themes (notably, the 1986 Chernobyl accident and continued uncertainty since the 1990s over such cases as 'mad cow disease' (BSE), global warming and genetically modified foods).

The theory of the risk society can be presented in many different ways, but central to Beck's various formulations is the notion that two lines of historical and cognitive development are converging in late twentieth-/early twenty-first-century societies. On the one hand, science and modernity have produced new forms of innovation, new institutions and new ways of life. On the other, a new generation of hazards and uncertainties – created largely by the very science and technology that has brought relative wealth and personal freedom – threatens to undermine the overall sense of progress. 'Classical' (or nineteenth-century) modernity promised a considerable step forwards from premodern existence. 'Late' modernity offers doubt where once there was certainty and generates anxieties and insecurities that threaten our existence and well-being. Importantly, these doubts should be seen as a consequence of the *success* of modernity rather than its failure. Equally, and although the discussion of environmental and physical risk has dominated the response to Beck, the uncertainties also encompass individual and family matters (as, for example, we are liberated from prescribed gender roles but struggle to find new ways of living).

Taking nuclear power as one symbol of life in the risk society, Beck portrays the new risks as being both invisible and ubiquitous. Existing institutions struggle to cope with the demands of risks that are as impossible to specify as they are to insure against: 'the injured of Chernobyl are today, years after the catastrophe, not even all *born* yet' (Beck 1996: 31). Crucially, science and technology both create the risks and become the means of treating them. Meanwhile, new forms of 'subpolitics' emerge based on direct action and extra-parliamentary movements. Citizens who engage in criticism and protest find themselves battling *against* the technical experts while simultaneously depending upon science as a 'sensory organ' (what Beck describes as 'arm-wrestling against oneself'). Presented in this fashion, hazards possess 'a social as well as a physical explosiveness' (Beck 1992b: 104). Equally, and as the case of nuclear power serves to emphasize, risks are *global* in character. In what Beck has increasingly come to call a 'world risk society' (Beck 1999), national state structures begin to disintegrate and conventional democratic institutions find themselves undermined or else irrelevant. The point is not that contemporary society has become objectively riskier: instead there has been a qualitative shift in the kinds of risk being generated and in our institutional and cognitive abilities to cope with them.

Beck employs the term 'reflexive modernisation' to describe the current state of societal development. The shift from 'classical' to 'late' modernity (or the risk society) represents a process whereby what were once seen simply as side effects and unintended consequences of technical and scientific advances (e.g. scientifically generated risks to health) have seemingly come to predominate. Put differently, the 'bads' of modernity have begun to overwhelm the 'goods'. At the same time, new possibilities are created for individual and collective action. Beck is not nostalgic for classical modernity. Rather he identifies a possible reshaping of politics and a redirection of technological change.

This use of the term 'reflexive' has been the focus of substantial discussion among sociologists – especially given its dual meaning in English of 'reflex-like' (i.e. involuntary and unintended) and 'reflection' (i.e. involving conscious deliberation and choice). Beck suggests in his later work that reflexive modernization is precisely concerned with the unintentional and unpredicted (i.e. reflex-like) consequences of modernity, since the current changes were never planned or chosen. Somewhat confusingly, however, Beck notes that this structural change gives further rise to personal reflection as, for example, we become ever more individualized and detraditionalized. Consequently, each citizen is forced to make personal choices about how to live. Beck's theory therefore both addresses the structural dimensions of reflexive modernization and the consequences for individuals and institutions as they are freed from old social roles but strive to find meaning and purpose. At this point, there are very close parallels with Giddens's discussion of 'ontological security and existential anxiety' (Giddens 1991).

One important aspect of Beck's account is its treatment of science and technical expertise. Certainly, the social critique of expertise has emerged as a major theme within European and North American society since the late 1980s. In areas such as food safety and environmental degradation, a problematic relationship has developed between science, institutions and the wider publics (Irwin and Wynne 1996). In line with the notion of reflexive modernization, Beck presents science as being increasingly confronted with its own products, limitations and problems. In this situation, the previous faith in science and technology as offering 'progress' breaks down and science is seen to become 'demystified'. Beck is especially critical of the tendency of experts to regard lay-people as ignorant and uninformed. Instead, he views social criticism of science and technology as the possible beginning of a more open and productive relationship between what would become the '*coproducers* of socially valid "knowledge"' (Beck 1992a: 172).

Finally, Beck has much to say about the relationship between society, environmental problems and the natural world. Whilst at times Beck makes great play of the rise of risks and environmental threats, he also argues that the categories of 'nature' and 'society' are no longer separable: 'nature can no longer be understood *outside of* society, or society *outside of* nature' (1992a: 80). For scientific analysis this means that the social conditions and context of environmental issues must be properly recognized rather than being dismissed as irrelevant. For the environmental movement it suggests that what might be presented as external or natural problems would be better seen as social and political questions of 'how we are to live'. Faced with this array of problems, institutions tend to offer 'organized irresponsibility' (Beck 1995) rather than a more thorough analysis and self-appraisal. However, the problem of how to take potentially far-reaching decisions in a context of 'manufactured uncertainty' remains both pressing and deeply problematic (as emerging issues in the biosciences, information technology and nanotechnology strongly suggest).

Inevitably, the notion of the risk society has been challenged for its overabstraction (Beck is no empiricist), slipperiness and, perhaps most tellingly, its bias towards Western (some would say German) society. In its suggestion that risk has replaced class as a 'master concept' Beck has also attracted the ire of certain Marxists. Meanwhile, the term 'risk society' is regularly employed simply as shorthand for the social phenomenon of risk controversy. From a historical point of view, the presentation of classical (or primary) modernity is certainly open to question: consensus over the direction of progress in the nineteenth century seems not to have been so complete. Doubt can also be shed on Beck's generalizations about the character of contemporary life. Beck's broad response to these challenges is to note that '(w)e do not *yet* live in a risk society, but we also no longer live *only* within the distribution conflicts of scarcity societies' (Beck 1992a: 20). In that sense, risk society is as much about projecting forwards as it is about mapping changes that have already taken place. Nevertheless, perhaps the main limitation of the risk society perspective is its relentless focus on risk itself. Beck acknowledges that 'risk' may largely be a projection of wider social concerns but cannot entirely avoid the inherent limitations of viewing risk as the central issue of our time.

In the end, Beck is best seen as an essayist and committed commentator rather than as a systematic thinker or empirical social scientist. As Goldblatt notes, his work is intended to be provocative and stimulating rather than comprehensive and strictly analytical (Goldblatt 1996). The main strength of the risk society thesis is in pointing to the full character of the environmental, political and epistemological challenges being faced in the new century. It is for this rather than for any precise sociological framework, that it should be drawn upon, engaged with and debated.

ALAN IRWIN
BRUNEL UNIVERSITY

References

Beck, U. (1992a) *Risk Society: Towards a New Modernity*, London (original, German, edn, 1986).
—— (1992b) 'From industrial society to the risk society: Questions of survival, social structure and ecological enlightenment', in M. Featherstone (ed.) *Cultural Theory and Cultural Change*, London.
—— (1995) *Ecological Politics in an Age of Risk*, Cambridge.
—— (1996) 'Risk society and the provident state', in S. Lash, B. Szerszynski and B. Wynne (eds) *Risk, Environment and Modernity: Towards a New Ecology*, London, Thousand Oaks, New Delhi.
—— (1999) *World Risk Society*, Cambridge.
Douglas, M. and Wildavsky, A. (1982) *Risk and Culture: An Essay on the Selection of Technological and Environmental Dangers*, Berkeley and London.
Giddens, A. (1991) *Modernity and Self-Identity: Self and Society in the Late Modern Age*, Cambridge.
Goldblatt, D. (1996) *Social Theory and the Environment*, Cambridge.
Irwin, A. and Wynne, B. (eds) (1996) *Misunderstanding Science? The Public Reconstruction of Science and Technology*, Cambridge.
Perrow, C. (1984) *Normal Accidents: Living with High-Risk Technologies*, New York.

Further reading

Adam, B., Beck, U. and van Loon, J. (eds) (2000) *The Risk Society and Beyond: Critical Issues for Social Theory*, London.
Allan, S. (2002) *Media, Risk and Science*, Buckingham.
Irwin, A. (1995) *Citizen Science*, London and New York.
Lupton, D. (1999) *Risk*, London and New York.

RITES OF PASSAGE

'The life of an individual in any society is a series of passages from one age to another and from one occupation to another' (Van Gennep 1960 [1909]). Since the publication in 1909 of Arnold Van Gennep's *Les Rites de passage*, this term has been used primarily to refer to life-crisis rituals, such as those accompanying birth and death, puberty, marriage, initiation into adulthood or entry to priestly or political and other secular offices. Also included are those individual or collective rites that mark changes in the season or calendar. The common element in such rites, Van Gennep argued, is that they effect a transition from one social condition to another and, as a consequence, display a definite three-phase structure, with *rites of separation, transition* and *aggregation*. This pattern, though discernible to some extent in all, tends to be most fully realized in initiation rites where it may be given added force in the symbolism of death and rebirth. The *rites of separation* thus enact a symbolic death that removes individuals from society and their old social status before they are transformed in the subsequent *rites of transition* and, finally, reborn into a new social position and back into the community in the culminating *rites of aggregation*.

For Van Gennep the theme of passage provided the clue to the diverse symbolic devices employed in such rites. For example, the ritual movements may be represented in spatial terms, by exits and entrances, crossings and journeys, and in the general significance attached to crossroads, boundaries and thresholds. Of continuing interest is Van Gennep's identification of the mid- or transitional period as one of marginality or liminality (from the Latin, *limen*, meaning threshold). It represents, he writes, the point of inertia for the novices between contrary ritual movements; they are regarded as outside society, untouchable and dangerous, sacred as opposed to profane. Sharing with Van Gennep a similar concern with social classification and the cultural imposition of order on natural and social affairs, structuralist anthropologists such as Mary Douglas (1966) and Edmund Leach (1976) have argued that ideas of danger attach to any situation or object that transgresses or cannot be placed within the dominant system of social classification. Novices, betwixt-and-between defined social positions, are inherently anomalous and thus likely to be regarded as both polluted and polluting. Outside and opposed to normal social life, liminality is also given ritual expression in licence, disorder and role reversal.

From a functionalist perspective, Max Gluckman (1963) saw such inversional elements as motivated by underlying conflicts in the structure of social relations. Proposing the idea of 'rituals of rebellion', he argued that they give a voice to those usually held inferior and oppressed. For example, Zulu women, never full citizens in the villages of their husbands, dressed up as men in a first sowing rite and were given licence to behave obscenely and ape the ways of their menfolk. This interpretation has been influential but meets with difficulties in dealing with ritual situations where superiors assume the style and behaviour of inferiors. By contrast, Victor Turner (1969), associated also with the Manchester School of anthropology, explored the experiential implications of liminality. He identified the key process in initiations as one of ritual levelling, with the person stripped of social insignia and signs of secular status, reduced to nakedness and subject to humiliation by ordeal, test and trauma. Socially invisible, dead to the normal world, the initiate is at the same time united with fellow initiates. This humbling process, he suggests, contains a revitalizing element, 'giving recognition to an essential and generic human bond, without which there could be *no* society' (Turner 1969). In this context he asks us to consider two modalities of social experience, of 'structure' where people are differentiated by social role and position, as opposed to 'communitas' as an undifferentiated community of equals able to recognize each other in an immediate and total way. 'Communitas emerges where social structure is not,' says Turner, reaffirming the bonds of essential unity upon which the social order ultimately rests. While he feels that communitas finds its most characteristic expression in the liminal period of *rites de passage* where the individual is divested of normal social attributes, he argues that it may be engendered also in role reversals in seasonal rites and be an attribute more generally of structural marginality and inferiority, exemplified by such figures as sacred clowns and holy beggars.

In contrast to psychoanalytic accounts, anthropological theory has made relatively little of the dramatic ordeals and mutilations that are commonly found in association with initiations. For example, circumcision for Van Gennep is best explained as a separation rite, while for Turner it is an aspect of ritual levelling. Such symbolism is seen as essentially arbitrary – Van Gennep (1960

[1909]) writes, 'The human body has been treated like a simple piece of wood which each has cut and trimmed to suit him.' Psychoanalytic accounts of initiation tend to take the opposed view that genital mutilation is central to the development and purpose of such rites. Neo-Freudian explanations diverge, with some regarding circumcision as a symbolic castration, while Bettelheim (1954) has suggested that it is best regarded as a mimetic menstruation, representing male envy of female reproductive powers. Seen as a response to universal problems, such explanations fail to account for the cross-cultural variability in incidence and type of such ordeals. However, a more psychologically informed anthropology seems to be developing, aiming to explore the subjective experience of initiation as this is encoded in different cultural idioms. It is perhaps no accident that interesting work here is coming from New Guinea societies with their plethora of explicit sexual symbolism (see Herdt 1982; Gillison 1994).

Critically concerned with transformations in social identity, the concepts stemming from Van Gennep and developed by Turner have been influential for much social and ethnographic analysis. Both inside and outside anthropology, they have been applied in a wide range of social settings from leisure activities, sport and shopping, to medical and healing practices in both Western and non-Western settings. Of note here is Kapferer's (1991) study of the elaborate aesthetic forms of demonic exorcism rituals in Sri Lanka and the worlds of experience that they construct and deconstruct. Current postmodernist concerns with the marginal and hybrid have given the ideas yet further currency. Nevertheless, two broad approaches to the study of *rites de passage* can still usefully be distinguished. The first looks to social classification and, with Van Gennep, gives primacy to the idea of transition. This gives a unity to the category but, in so far as it portrays rituals as static dramas of form, tends to underplay the creative intent of such rites in preindustrial society and the culturally specific ways in which this is conceived and realized. As Turner reminds us, many *rites de passage* intend an active transformation of the person. The second approach looks to the subjective effects of ritual and the concepts of personhood mediated by the ritual process. To some extent this harks back to earlier functionalist concerns with the efficacy of ritual (prefigured, for example, in Richards 1982 [1956]), but it is a far more eclectic venture, drawing freely upon other disciplines.

SUZETTE HEALD
BRUNEL UNIVERSITY

References

Bettelheim, B. (1954) *Symbolic Wounds*, Glencoe, IL.
Douglas, M. (1966) *Purity and Danger: An Analysis of Concepts of Pollution and Taboo*, London.
Gillison, G. (1994) 'Symbolic homosexuality and cultural theory: The unconscious meaning of sister exchange among the Gimi of Highland New Guinea', in S. Heald and A. Deluz (eds) *Anthropology and Psychoanalysis: An Encounter through Culture*, London.
Gluckman, M. (1963) *Order and Rebellion in Tribal Africa*, London.
Herdt, G.H. (1982) *Rituals of Manhood: Male Initiation in Papua New Guinea*, Berkeley, CA.
Kapferer, B. (1991) *A Celebration of Demons: Exorcism and the Aesthetics of Healing in Sri Lanka*, Oxford and Washington, DC.
Leach, E. (1976) *Culture and Communication: The Logic by which Symbols are Connected*, Cambridge, UK.
Richards, A.I. (1982 [1956]) *Chisungu: A Girl's Initiation among the Bemba of Northern Rhodesia*, London.
Turner, V.W. (1969) *The Ritual Process*, London.
Van Gennep, A. (1960 [1909]) *The Rites of Passage*, London (original edn, *Les Rites de passage*, Paris).

SEE ALSO: life-span development; ritual

RITUAL

In all societies, significant changes in the composition of the social group and in the individual's life cycle are marked by rituals. The birth and death of members of the community, succession to office, the setting up of an independent household and the coming of age of young men and women are either effected by or given social recognition by cultural performances. These 'rites of passage', as A. Van Gennep (1960 [1909]) called them, give symbolic form to transitions that may be either natural or conventional. Thus, a boy grows to physical maturity, but the capacities and rights of an adult male are socially defined and are conferred or engendered in ritual.

It is sometimes said that all rituals are rites of passage in that they bring about a transformation in participants within a scheme of social relations, enacting the changes by moving actors through ritually marked spaces. However, in acts of worship and blessing, as in agricultural and curing rites, the element of transition may be absent. What is it, then, that identifies these varying performances as similar kinds of events? What have sacrifice, baptism, the Eucharist, exorcism and domestic Hindu offerings in common? Do they form a class of acts distinct from ordinary, non-ritual behaviour? And what distinguishes rituals from other formal activities such as games, drama and etiquette, or, more broadly, from custom and convention?

Definitions matter since they direct our attention to particular features and facilitate comparison, but none of its commonly adduced attributes applies exclusively to ritual. Thus, ritual is formal, but so are table manners; it is rule-bound, but so is voting in elections; it is standardized and repetitive, as is factory work; it has to do with a society's core values, but so, in the industrialized West, do shopping and hospital medicine; and it is symbolic, as is signing a cheque. Successive anthropological schools – functionalist, semiotic, interpretive, practice-oriented – have placed the emphasis differently. But the fact that a category equivalent to ritual is absent from many languages – especially in those non-literate traditions where what we call 'ritual' appears most abundant – should cause us some disquiet. For if 'ritual' is a product of modern European, specifically Christian, history (Asad 1993), its use in cross-cultural analysis may be as misleading as those other standard analytical concepts – economy, religion, kinship – have often proved. Ethnographers seeking an indigenous equivalent have often been presented with terms that mean something like 'service', 'doing' or 'work'. The Tikopia of Polynesia describe their cycle of offerings and sacrifices as 'the work of the gods'. And their ethnographer emphasizes the interweaving of economic with ritual activities and the fact that the ritual cycle co-ordinates and motivates production and redistribution (Firth 1967). Nevertheless such rituals are not simply 'work' like any other. They are directed to the spirit world and they mobilize various means – stylized gestures, changes of voice, dramatization, etc. – to achieve ends that need have no obvious practical outcome.

Recent studies have focused on the fact that actors in ritual stand in a peculiar relation to their actions. Participants in ritual are performing actions 'scripted' authoritatively by others (the ancestors, prophets, tradition). Hence their intentions, beliefs and feelings may be irrelevant to the ritual's efficacy, meaning and correct performance (Humphrey and Laidlaw 1994; Rappaport 1999; Tambiah 1985). This may partly explain why anthropologists in the field – whether at a healer's seance or in a church or temple – are often faced with divergent accounts or expressions of ignorance when they ask participants in rituals to explain what they are doing. The temptation for the observer is to assume that meanings have been lost, or to dig deeper, or ask the experts; but to insist on a single, definitive meaning, or indeed any meaning, is to belie the nature of ritual (Lewis 1980). To be sure, rituals may express or encode meanings, but it is not this property that identifies them as rituals.

Arguments over definitions will go on. But – to turn to substantive analyses – two approaches have proved both productive and popular: those that treat rituals as symbolic and those that analyse them as performances. Of the thinkers who have favoured a symbolic approach, the most influential has been Durkheim. Defining 'rites' as 'the rules of conduct which prescribe how a man should comport himself in the presence of...sacred objects', Durkheim (1915 [1912]) saw the sacred as symbolizing the social. Indeed, he made ritual fundamental to the constitution of society and believed that he had proved his case with the example of the Australian Aborigines. By coming together in ritual, we (at any rate the Australians) discover the bonds that connect us as individuals; or rather we create those bonds and realize our nature as social beings. And in the collective emotion generated in ritual we feel transported outside of ourselves and subject to a greater power. That power may appear to us as supernatural, but it is socially produced: it is a projection and sacralization of society. Durkheim argued that ritual is not merely an element of religion; ritual *creates* religion (i.e. a congregation, beliefs, practices). This functionalist insight has been repeated in different terms by most major thinkers on the subject, though the opposite view – that ritual *enacts* beliefs – has also had important adherents, among them Firth (1967): 'What we term ritual is in part a formal expression of beliefs and translation of them into social action.'

The symbolist approach has been taken furthest by Victor Turner for whom symbols are the 'smallest units' of ritual. Turner showed how rituals achieve their emotive and transformative effects by linking a group's primary social concepts and values to symbols of natural processes (birth, death, sex, body products, growth, decay). Through symbolism, the humanly invented social order becomes naturalized; and through the ritual process it is internalized (Turner 1969). Geertz (1973) has similarly emphasized the emotive power of ritual symbols and their capacity to shape cognition and direct moods.

Once the symbolic character of ritual is granted, however, there arises the problem of whose meanings are the correct ones. Like Durkheim, many social scientists have looked beyond indigenous explanation, seeking an authoritative meaning that transcends actors' interpretations. For those working in the Durkheimian tradition, society – or the 'social system' – has remained the ultimate reference for ritual symbolism. Hence, for Leach (1954), 'ritual action and belief are alike to be understood as forms of symbolic statement about the social order'. When the Kachins of Highland Burma perform sacrifices to the spirits, they are, in effect, making symbolic statements about the system of intermarrying lineages handed down by the ancestors. Whether or not such sociological reductionism is defensible – few would now state the case so simply – there are several objections to the view of rituals as symbolic action: (1) It fudges the problem of interpretation, even to the extent of implying that meanings, congealed in symbols, can exist independently of actors' understandings. (2) It assumes the observer knows best – a political as well as epistemological error. (3) It privileges symbolism over actors' practical aims and thus denies their agency. In fact, a ritual in whose end the observer disbelieves is likely to seem symbolic rather than practical, or else – as for the Victorians – it must be irrational. (4) It underplays differences of perspective and class position. (Do men and women, rich and poor, leaders and led, young and old all perceive a single unitary meaning? Who, in practice, is authorized to pronounce on meaning?) (5) It assumes a communicative function when rituals are often obscure to participants.

Marxist-influenced approaches, which circumvent some of these objections, see ritual as a legitimation of authority that cloaks or 'mystifies' the true sources of power. (The observer, of course, is not mystified.) Inequality is justified by the symbolic representation of the social order as divinely or ancestrally given, an immutable system that is part of – or, in some versions, transcends – the 'natural' order of things. Bloch (1989) argues that ritual is especially apt to this ideological purpose since its formality permits neither challenge nor discussion. To take part is to accept the axioms ritual expresses. For Rappaport, in contrast, this acceptance is more than a submission to power. In bringing together actors in a standardized performance – which owes its form to no individual intentions – ritual models social co-operation and thus constitutes 'the basic social act'. As such, human rituals may have had social evolutionary significance and may, indeed, build upon a substrate of ritualization common to other animals (Watanabe and Smuts 1999). For Rappaport, co-operation in ritual is made possible because its standardized speech and action exclude the possibility of difference and duplicity inherent in ordinary speech. However, work on rituals in complex societies has shown that a measure of solidarity can be achieved despite – or even by means of – the divergent meanings attributed to shared symbols. For example, Javanese prayer-meals bring together villagers of diverse ideologies in a shared format. An explicit commentary on the symbolic offerings masks rival interpretations that, though privately expressed, remain conventional, the common property of constituent groups (Beatty 1999). In similar fashion, large-scale public events such as state ceremonies and national festivals can become the common focus of rival constituencies, each proclaiming its own interpretation. The Mexican national patroness, the Virgin of Guadalupe, whose holy day is celebrated on 12 December, has been promoted variously as a symbol of the triumph of Christianity, the resilience of native tradition (she is dark-skinned and first appeared to an indigenous convert) and as a symbol of Mexican – as opposed to Spanish-colonial – identity (Wolf 2002). She has been claimed as the champion of indigenous-rights groups, presidential candidates and the conservative Catholic hierarchy.

In recent years attention has shifted from ritual's communicative aspects to its pragmatic functions: from an interest in what people say by doing things to what people do by saying things. The operative question then becomes (for example): How does a spell achieve its ends through verbal and gestural forms specific to, or at least characteristic of, ritual? One source of inspiration, from linguistic philosophy, has been the study of speech acts and performative utterances (Tambiah 1985). Just as promises and declarations are performed in the saying (to say 'I apologize' or 'I curse' is to *make* an apology or curse), so ritual ends are accomplished in the saying or acting. This is evident enough in weddings, initiations and other rites of passage where candidates are transformed into different social beings through performative utterances and the manipulation of symbols. But it is less clear in 'magical' acts where some objective change in circumstances – a cure, rain, the death of an enemy – is intended. In such cases the supposed efficacy may not simply depend upon the intrinsic form of the rite (no one is cured by an analogy) but upon some power or external agency to which the practitioner – through priestly office or ancestral blessing – has access. Anyone may learn the liturgy of the Catholic mass, but only a priest, as God's mandatory, is qualified to turn the wafer into the body of Christ. Where no spiritual agency is explicitly invoked, the force of a performative utterance may derive from the authority of tradition: the power of the ancestors or gods is implicit in the choice of language.

An emphasis on rituals as performances has been valuable in drawing attention to the historical circumstances of their staging, the media of gesture, sound and colour employed, the logic by which they bring about their effects, and the complex relations among actors and actions. It has also restored a sense of the subjective aspect of action, the fact that, although a rite may be rule-bound and conventional, it is performed by particular persons to a particular audience. In this tension between personal and public aspects – the performer's condition, circumstances and biography on the one hand, and the scripted, external frame of the performance on the other – lies a clue to the singularity of ritual.

ANDREW BEATTY
BRUNEL UNIVERSITY

References

Asad, T. (1993) *Genealogies of Religion: Discipline and Reasons of Power in Christianity and Islam*, Baltimore and London.
Beatty, A. (1999) *Varieties of Javanese Religion: An Anthropological Account*, Cambridge.
Bloch, M. (1989) *Ritual, History, and Power*, London.
Durkheim, E. (1915 [1912]) *The Elementary Forms of the Religious Life*, London.
Firth, R. (1967) *The Work of the Gods in Tikopia*, 2nd edn, London.
Geertz, C. (1973) *The Interpretation of Cultures*, New York.
Humphrey, C. and Laidlaw, J. (1994) *The Archetypal Actions of Ritual*, Oxford.
Leach, E. (1954) *Political Systems of Highland Burma*, London.
Lewis, G. (1980) *Day of Shining Red: An Essay on Understanding Ritual*, Cambridge.
Rappaport, R. (1999) *Ritual and Religion in the Making of Humanity*, Cambridge.
Tambiah, S. (1985) *Culture, Thought, and Social Action: An Anthropological Perspective*, Cambridge, MA.
Turner, V. (1969) *The Ritual Process*, Chicago.
Van Gennep, A. (1960 [1909]) *The Rites of Passage*, London.
Watanabe, J.M. and Smuts, B.B. (1999) 'Explaining religion without explaining it away: Trust, truth, and the evolution of co-operation in Roy A. Rappaport's "The obvious aspects of ritual"', *American Anthropologist* 101(1): 98–112.
Wolf, E. (2002) 'The Virgin of Guadalupe: A Mexican national symbol', in M. Lambek (ed.) *A Reader in the Anthropology of Religion*, Oxford.

Further reading

Bell, C. (1992) *Ritual Theory, Ritual Practice*, Oxford.
Coppet, D. de (ed.) (1992) *Understanding Rituals*, London.
Kertzer, D. (1988) *Ritual, Politics, and Power*, New Haven and London.
Skorupski, J. (1976) *Symbol and Theory: A Philosophical Study of Theories of Religion in Social Anthropology*, Cambridge.

SEE ALSO: religion; rites of passage; shamanism; symbolism

ROLE

A role is the expected behaviour associated with a social position. People from Outer Mongolia visiting the courts of justice in Britain and observing a series of criminal trials would not understand what they saw until they appreciated that people in court proceedings have to play particular roles: judge, prosecutor, defence advocate, accused, witness, juror, usher, spectator and so on. The interpretation of behaviour in a courtroom provides a good example of the utility, indeed the necessity, of a concept of role. Its positive features will be discussed first before considering whether the selection of some other example might not cast doubt upon the value of the concept.

Were they able to overhear conversations in various parts of the court building, the visitors would be able to discover the number and names of the positions that have to be occupied if the proceedings are to be lawful; the names of the individuals occupying these positions on particular occasions; and how well particular individuals were thought to perform their roles. Over a long period of time, the visitors could watch particular barristers pleading before various judges and taking different kinds of cases; some would advance their careers more rapidly than others.

Watching individual lawyers after they had become judges, the observers might conclude that they had taken certain of the other judges as models of what to emulate and what to avoid. In such ways the observers could ascertain the processes by which individuals learn to play roles according to the satisfaction or dissatisfaction of others. The observers would also learn about the processes by which individuals come to occupy the various positions.

To start with, the observers might be surprised to notice that the barrister who had spoken for the prosecution in a case that had just been completed was appearing for the defence in the next case. They would learn that it is the role of barristers to speak for whichever client they are engaged (by a solicitor) to represent; their personal opinions of their clients' moral merits are irrelevant, while the uniform they wear (wig, gown and standardized costume) reinforce the message that their personality is subordinated to their role. Observation would also show that barristers are punished for infringing the rules (one who asks leading or irrelevant questions will be rebuked by the judge) and rewarded for doing well (by being asked to take more cases, and cases bringing higher fees). Every now and again an unusual event would reveal some other kind of rule showing that two roles may not be held by the same person if there is any suspicion that their obligations may conflict. Judges may not preside over a case in which they have a personal interest. A barrister may be unable to represent both of two people jointly charged with an offence, since the two may dispute with each other as to their relative culpability. Judges and barristers would be criticized were they, in their leisure time, to associate with known criminals.

The roles of judge and barrister are assumed willingly, while that of the accused is usually not.

Sometimes accused persons deny the authority of the court to try them, but they are still tried. However reluctant people may be to feature as accused persons, once they have been arraigned it is usually in their interest to play the expected role in the hope that they may be able to utilize it in a manner that will enable them either to escape conviction or to secure a lighter sentence. Thus it may be possible to obtain a better understanding of the way such people behave if it is assumed that they comprehend what is expected of them and are seeking to turn those expectations to their advantage.

Court proceedings illustrate the utility of the role concept for the additional reason that they can be given a historical dimension that reveals the steady differentiation and sharper definition of the roles involved. In many societies at one stage of their history, cases were settled by *kadi*-justice (to use an expression of Arabic origin employed by Max Weber). In *kadi*-justice a politically powerful person makes an informal decision according to ethical or practical values, rather than by reference to previous decisions or to statute law. In such circumstances political and judicial roles are not distinguished. Even in the mid-seventeenth century, English criminal trials were, by modern standards, very brief: the Surrey assizes tried on average per day fourteen defendants charged with serious offences. Nowadays the proceedings are more complex. The evidence of each witness can be examined at length; there is time to evaluate the evidence in terms of the roles the witnesses were playing; while everyone in court will be conscious that the judge, the lawyers and the witnesses are taking part in a drama and interpreting their roles in a way that can be compared with actors on a stage. A higher material standard of living permits people to be more self-conscious about their behaviour.

In *Games People Play*, Eric Berne (1964) describes and assigns names to the various characteristic disputes arising in families. One of them is 'Uproar', occurring most frequently between a domineering father and an adolescent daughter bidding for greater freedom. It has sexual undertones. It derives its name from the fact that the dispute is often terminated by one or both parties shouting angrily, retiring to a bedroom and slamming the door. It is possible to see Uproar as a game in which two people play distinctive roles (even though these roles are not defined by rights and obligations, which has been the traditional way of conceptualizing role in anthropology and much of sociology). If, however, the players have read an analysis of the game, they are much more likely to recognize what is happening if they themselves are drawn into a dispute of this kind. They will have an insight into the dynamics of the relationship and the way in which they are contributing to it. Not only may they find themselves playing a role but also they will be conscious of themselves as doing so, and in some circumstances they may even distance themselves from their role by signalling that their behaviour is not completely serious. This awareness is facilitated by the use of the word 'role' in ordinary language and by the availability of books analysing behaviour in role terms, a feature of European and North American culture in the second half of the twentieth century.

'Father' and 'adolescent daughter' can both be considered social positions, but the behaviour expected of people occupying these positions is much less well defined than in the case of the judge and the barrister. Until relatively recently in Britain (and in many parts of Europe), adolescent daughters were constrained much more narrowly than their brothers. When they reached marriageable age, middle-class young women put their hair up to indicate their change of status. The dressing of their hair was a role sign; the alteration in it was a minor ceremonial of role-changing (as a wedding is a major ceremonial of it). An unmarried woman was not supposed to meet a man unless a chaperone was present. These role expectations have since changed, along with other changes in the social structure, but the speed and extent of their change in particular households will have been an outcome of a conflict between fathers and daughters, each seeking to impose their own definitions of expected behaviour. Indeed, changing expectations with respect to gender roles have been an occasion for intense discussion. What the sociologist or social psychologist can do is to ascertain the expectations of a role such as 'adolescent daughter' held by people in other, related positions. An examination of these expectations and their determinants could contribute to an analysis of the more general problem and indicate ways in which it could most easily be resolved. This could be particularly relevant to the domestic problems of immigrant Muslim groups in European cities. In the father–daughter relationship within these groups, the conflicts between two value systems are brought to a head.

The various senses of the word 'expect' in English conceal a particular difficulty. Someone may expect a doctor to be male and a nurse to be female simply because most people in these two positions are of those genders. This is a purely *statistical* expectation. Someone else may expect a doctor to be male and a nurse female because of a belief that this is right and proper (just as the office of priest in the Catholic Church is limited to males). This is a *normative* expectation. The two kinds of expectations go together in the sense that someone growing up in a society in which all doctors are male may come to believe that all doctors should be male. Anyone who makes use of the concept of role may need to explain whether the expectations associated with a position are of the one kind or the other; both can be comprehended in role analysis.

Role as a concept in social science cannot be compared to an elementary particle in physics. It is not possible to list all the roles in a particular society, because there are no clear principles for deciding what is a social position: in the end it is a question of discovering whether it is useful in given circumstances to regard, say, pedestrian as a role. In so far as people are conscious of themselves and others as occupying positions with generally known rights and duties, then their behaviour cannot be understood without reference to their expectations about how they should behave and others should behave towards them. The research worker may ask them what their expectations are; the researcher may observe their behaviour and deduce their expectations from it; or the researcher may do both and find out that when their stated expectations are not met they do not necessarily do anything about it (a serious breach will be another matter). In order to analyse actual behaviour, the concept of role is only a beginning that must be supplemented by a battery of related concepts which give it greater utility. Biddle (1979) defines 334 such concepts.

Biddle also comments upon research work showing that boys and girls are treated somewhat differently in the classroom. In the USA, boys (who are taught mostly by women teachers) do less well in reading than girls, whereas in Germany (where the teachers are more likely to be male) boys do better than girls. One possible explanation of this finding is that schoolchildren take teachers as role models. Female pupils can identify with female teachers, but male pupils experience a conflict between their masculinity and their relationship to a female role model. This conflict can stimulate them to behave in ways that the school system defines as deviant. A similar argument is heard in societies like the USA and Britain, in which black people constitute a minority of the population. The poor performance in examinations by black children may be ascribed to the dearth of suitable role models, such as black teachers, black newsreaders on television and black popular heroes. This kind of hypothesis can be tested by the methods of social science. Evidence also suggests that the absence of good male and female role models in the home can have a negative effect upon the personality development of children.

Writers who are concerned about social harmony are readily drawn to a conception of society as a unit in which everyone has a series of roles to play and where all the main roles are clearly defined. For them the concept of role helps describe the relation between the individual and society. But for those who see society as an arena in which groups with opposed interests clash with one another, such a view is regarded as suspect; they are most inclined to picture individuals as coerced by unjustifiable role expectations that exact compliance, or to maintain that the very concept of role is redundant. These are criticisms of an unimaginitive use of the concept of role (seen as a representation of social relations) rather than of a problem-solving approach to role that seeks to elucidate a particular pattern of behaviour. When social scientists start from a set of observations and seek to account for what people do, they regularly have to explain behaviour in terms of people's conforming with rules. The barrister does not ask a leading question in circumstances where it is forbidden. Any explanation of why people follow rules implies a concept of role, because the rules apply to those who occupy particular social positions. Depending on the nature of the problem, it then becomes necessary to make use of other concepts from the vocabulary of role analysis particularly as it has been developed by social psychologists. By discovering which formulations are most effective in providing explanations, the present confusion about alternative definitions will eventually be dispelled.

MICHAEL BANTON
UNIVERSITY OF BRISTOL

References

Berne, E. (1964) *Games People Play*, Harmondsworth.
Biddle, B.J. (1979) *Role Theory: Expectations, Identities and Behaviour*, London.

Further reading

Banton, M. (1965) *Roles: An Introduction to the Study of Social Behaviour*, London.
Goffman, E. (1959) *The Presentation of Self in Everyday Life*, New York.
Jacksons, J.A. (ed.) (1972) *Role*, Cambridge, UK.
Turner, R.H. (1990) 'Role change', *Annual Review of Sociology* 16: 87–110.

SEE ALSO: identity; person; self-concept

ROUSSEAU, JEAN-JACQUES (1712–78)

One of the central figures of the Enlightenment and also its most formidable critic, Rousseau addressed a great variety of subjects in works regarded as classics of Western literature and philosophy. His *New Heloïse* was the most widely read French novel of the period, his *Emile* the most significant work on education after Plato's *Republic*, his *Confessions* the most notable autobiography after that of Saint Augustine, and his unfinished *Reveries* the most influential of all eighteenth-century contributions to what came to be termed *romanticism*. Much of his life was devoted to music, which he both composed and copied as his only reliable source of income, and in 1767 he produced a learned *Dictionary of Music* following, around a decade earlier, his *Letter on the Theatre*, which occasioned more controversy than any of his other writings. It is, however, as a moralist and political thinker that he achieved his greatest renown.

Born in Geneva, then an independent republic, Rousseau always identified with the constitution of his native state, often proclaiming himself *citizen of Geneva* on the title-page of his works, as distinct from progressive contemporaries who advocated what was already in the late eighteenth century known as *enlightened despotism*. His mother died giving birth to him, but inspired by his father's love of books he completed his education under the guidance of a Swiss baroness, Madame de Warens, who also became his lover when he was 15 and who as a devout Catholic kindled in him an intense religiosity at odds both with the austere Calvinism of his compatriots and the scepticism of most of his colleagues in the republic of letters.

After a brief period as secretary to the French Ambassador in Venice he came, in 1745, to live mainly in Paris with Thérèse Levasseur, whom he eventually married long after she bore him five children he abandoned as orphans, protesting that he could not afford to care for them. *Emile* was partly conceived as a work of atonement, and to this day, especially in France, his detractors hold his treatment of his own children to be his chief crime against humanity. In the winter of 1750–1, following the publication of other works that attracted scant notice, he became a celebrity on the appearance of his first *Discourse on the Arts and Sciences*, initially drafted with the encouragement of his friend Diderot as a prize essay for a competition that he won. Our intellectual progress had generated moral decay, Rousseau claimed, spread 'like garlands of flowers round the iron chains by which mankind is weighed down'. The whole of his subsequent philosophy of history elaborates that proposition, which anticipates a Marxist conception of the ideology of the ruling class and foreshadows Michel Foucault's postmodernist account of the links between *savoir* and *pouvoir*, and therefore the disciplines of knowledge and punishment.

In 1755 Rousseau published his second *Discourse on Inequality*, in which he offered a conjectural history of the human race with reference no longer to the trappings of culture but, as with Engels later, to private property, the family and the state. In reconstructing what he supposed must have been the evolutionary metamorphosis of human nature and the genesis of social institutions, he challenged the tradition of modern natural jurisprudence according to which governments must have come to be established through the agreement of their subjects to overcome or avert the defects of their natural condition. Contrary to Grotius, Hobbes, Pufendorf and Locke, Rousseau claimed that the establishment of states, even if apparently through consent, had not secured mankind's passage from barbarism to civilization. It had instead ensured

only that the rule of law protected the property of the rich at the expense of the poor, so that in civil society our forebears would have 'run headlong into their chains thinking themselves free'. Our morality, he insisted, stems from our denaturation in society rather than from our original nature, so that savage man must really have been closer to animals than to civilized man, whose identity is shaped by the opinions of others. The *Discourse on Inequality*, in which the term *perfectibility* is employed in print for the first time in any European language, provides an alternative reading to the Book of Genesis by ascribing sin to human history rather than to human nature. Adam Smith conceived his *Theory of Moral Sentiments* in part as a reply and probably drew from this work the expression 'the invisible hand' that was to figure there as well as in his *Wealth of Nations*. With reference to it but also other writings Claude Lévi-Strauss has described Rousseau as the 'founder' of anthropology.

In 1762, in the *Social Contract*, he articulated more comprehensively than in any earlier work the principles of his republican political philosophy that drew the constitutions of ancient Rome and modern Geneva together in opposition both to royal absolutism, as in France, and to mixed or parliamentary sovereignty, as in England. Only when a state's subjects also formed its sovereign could the people, acting in accordance with their *general will*, be said to enjoy civil and moral liberty, different in kind from the unregulated natural liberty of our forebears. Rousseau's conception of moral liberty as obedience to laws we prescribe to ourselves was to serve as one of the main sources of Kant's notion of autonomy, while his account of unmediated popular sovereignty and his insistence that civil liberty excludes political representation would come to be described as ancient or direct democracy as distinct from the indirect democracy deemed by others to be necessary in modern commercial societies and large states.

In both the *Social Contract* and *Emile*, published at almost the same time, he portrayed all revealed religions, and especially Christianity, as inimical to the authority of the state as well as to the liberties of its subjects, Such pronouncements occasioned political and theological censorship of his works in both France and Geneva, forcing his banishment from each state. In 1766 David Hume came to his rescue, but in England Rousseau imagined himself the victim of an international conspiracy to discredit him, and returning to France virtually incognito he spent the last decade of his life mainly botanizing in communion with nature and completing his *Confessions*. Always loath to engage in politics and convinced that revolutions were worse than the disease they were intended to cure, he had nevertheless accepted invitations to prepare constitutions for the fledgling state of Corsica in 1764 and the endangered state of Poland in 1770. With the advent of the French Revolution of 1789 his posthumous authority as prophet and legislator would be invoked more than that of any other figure of the *ancien régime*. In 1794, two years after France became a republic, his ashes were transported from their grave at Ermenonville where he had died 16 years earlier to the Panthéon in Paris, where they still lie, opposite the remains of Voltaire, whose embrace of civilization, science, commerce, scepticism, English empiricism and the glories of French monarchical culture encapsulate virtually everything in the age of Enlightenment that Rousseau despised.

ROBERT WOKLER
YALE UNIVERSITY

References

Rousseau, J.J. (1997) *Discourses and other Early Political Writings*, ed. G. Gourevitch, Cambridge, UK.
—— (1997) *The Social Contract and other Later Political Writings*, ed. G. Gourevitch, Cambridge, UK.

Further reading

Cranston, M. (1983–97) *Rousseau*, 3 vols, London.
Dent, N.J.H. (1992) *A Rousseau Dictionary*, Oxford.
Hendel, C.W. (1962) *Jean-Jacques Rousseau: Moralist*, 2nd edn, Indianapolis, IN.
Hope Mason, J. (1979) *The Indispensable Rousseau*, London.
Masters, R. (1968) *The Political Philosophy of Rousseau*, Princeton.
Shklar, J. (1985) *Men and Citizens: A Study of Rousseau's Social Theory*, 2nd edn, Cambridge.
Wokler, R. (2001) *Rousseau*, 2nd edn, Oxford.

SEE ALSO: freedom; social contract

S

SAMPLE SURVEYS

The modern sample survey evolved from the Victorian social survey movement, which assembled facts about urban poverty. Other origins were the development of the statistical theory of probability, and early attempts to carry out straw polls before elections. Early in the twentieth century, Bowley and others began to use samples in preference to attempts (on the model of Charles Booth) to survey entire populations. Gradually, and particularly in the USA, surveys broadened scope to include questions about attitudes as well as about facts. Respondents on surveys may be questioned about their own lives or asked about the society around them. The range of applications of the method is vast. The common denominator is that information is elicited by answers to questions ordered in a consistent structure having uniform wording, response choices, etc. These reports may be combined with various kinds of additional information. For example, in a survey of office workers, administrative data on productivity might be spliced with attitudinal data on issues such as employee's morale. Survey data can be collected face-to-face, by telephone, through the mail, or over the Internet. Whatever the mode of contact, or combination of modes, the resulting body of variables (the items of information) classified by respondents is arranged into a matrix amenable to statistical analysis. Unstructured interviews, in which a data matrix is not the outcome, do not constitute a survey even if interviewees are selected at random. The unit of analysis in a survey is not always the individual, but the unit of observation is. If persons, for example, provide information about a larger

entity such as business firms, that is still a survey. In contrast, a data set tabulating, say, United Nations aggregate social indicators for nation-states is not a survey as most researchers would use the term, even if such data have the same matrix format characteristic of surveys.

Sample surveys are intended to provide information about a larger population. The probable accuracy of generalizations from a sample survey to its population can be calculated using the mathematics of significance testing, so long as certain conditions are met. Sampling must be random, so that every member of the population sampled stands an equal chance of selection into the sample. In a 'stratified sample', the probabilities may vary across strata, but can be made equal via a weighting adjustment; the key point is that the probability of selection into the sample for each member of the population be known. For some populations, students enrolled in a school for instance, random selection poses no obstacle, but for more diverse constituencies true random sampling is virtually impossible. In a national population, which changes constantly as individuals are born, age and die, a sampling frame (a list of all members of the population from which to sample) becomes outdated before it can be used, and requires a massive effort to compile in the first place. Short-cut approximations to random sampling often are employed, especially in the large samples collected by national statistical agencies serving government. Special procedures must then be used to correct for 'design effect', so that standard errors remain accurate.

Human subjects not only complicate sampling by ageing, changing social characteristics and shifting residence, but also are often not available or not willing to respond to a survey. The study of this non-response preoccupies many survey methodologists, and is motivated by both technical and ethical considerations. Technically, non-response is only a minor inconvenience so long as the erosion of the sample case base occurs at random. Much evidence, however, shows that non-response to surveys follows predictable lines such as a tendency for low response from the lower socioeconomic strata. Even if non-response derives from a simple availability factor, such as the difficulty of contacting night-shift workers at home during the conventional leisure hours, the resulting uncompleted questionnaires or interview schedules constitute a form of sampling error not accommodated in standard significance testing. The large literature on survey response is a dynamic field of research because non-response issues and patterns change as societies change. For example, in the 1970s many books and articles explored the feasibility of surveying by telephone. In the 2000s, the same attention turned to Internet surveys.

Ethically, if people ignore calls by interviewers or solicitations through the mail or Web, should their wishes be respected? This depends in part on their motives for non-response. Some researchers regard considered, philosophically grounded, principled refusal as rare, implying that survey workers are justified in employing 'compliance' tactics gleaned from social psychology. Sensitivity, however, to the rights of the citizen to privacy and confidentiality has increased since the mid-twentieth-century period in which the sample survey took its modern form, influenced perhaps by a trend of eroding response rates. Many of the granting agencies that fund survey research now require projects involving human subjects to undergo ethical vetting.

Survey researchers have accommodated over time to both the technical and the ethical issues. Much technical knowledge has accumulated around optimal doorstep or telephone approaches for fieldworkers, the effect of cash incentives or other inducements, best design for Internet-based surveys, the importance of topic, sponsorship and the interaction between some of these factors. Alert survey fieldwork agencies update procedures to fit the times. For example, as reaching people at home becomes more difficult, the standard number of 'callbacks' will be increased. On the ethical front, some form of 'informed consent' is built into most government and academic surveys, even if not so much in the commercial-sector ones.

The sample survey has developed into a key method of research for the social sciences, but not all methodologists applaud this development, and some prefer such alternatives as participant observation. In market research, the qualitative approach known as the focus group (a discussion among nine or so people, run by a moderator) has grown in importance. Often it is fruitful to use qualitative research as a supplement to a sample survey, either prior to the survey for working out questions and issues, or afterwards, for interpretation of survey findings. It has been suggested recurrently over the years that to collect a sample survey alone is somehow to impose or assume a model of social life. There may be a liberal democracy presupposition to surveys, a naïve and overly individual-centred view which assumes that every person is an independent agent. *Realpolitik* and power brokering are not well reflected in a random survey. Survey respondents may be echoing views absorbed from the mass media, sometimes making the study of these attitudes and opinions a rather vacuous exercise. Governments may commission a survey of attitudes towards some problem such as pollution simply to give the impression that action is being taken. It may be easier to ask people if they think a problem is indeed a problem than to fix that problem. At one time surveys were faulted for giving only one-time snapshots instead of a sense of process in social life. This criticism has waned as government statistical agencies mounted increasingly ambitious longitudinal surveys in which panels of respondents are tracked for re-interviews at several different times spread over months or years. But a qualitatively-oriented social scientist might still criticize the structure-over-process bias within the sample survey. Catherine Marsh (1982) addressed these epistemological criticisms of the sample survey and concluded that the flexibility of the method should not be underestimated.

The survey is especially useful in the collection of comprehensive information about naturally occurring (as distinguished from laboratory) social phenomena, generalizing from relatively small samples to represent larger populations. The resulting data may be used either for description or for multivariate analysis. In the latter, statistical techniques are used to weigh the influence of different factors on the dependent (to be explained) variable. Techniques for such modelling have increased greatly in sophistication over the past several decades, benefiting from the explosion of computer power.

The survey attracts many social scientists because it satisfies some key conditions for scientific procedure. The procedures used in a sample survey can be codified, scrutinized and replicated with a precision denied to less formal methods. The rules for reaching conclusions about the association between variables measured in a survey can be specified in advance (as, for example, when a significance level upon which an hypothesis test will hinge is selected). Social scientists who place importance on the second word of their title tend to be drawn to sample surveys.

JOHN GOYDER
UNIVERSITY OF WATERLOO

Reference

Marsh, C. (1982) *The Survey Method: The Contribution of Surveys to Sociological Explanation*, London.

Further reading

Converse, J.M. (1986) *Survey Research in the United States: Roots and Emergence 1890–1960*, Berkeley, CA.
Dillman, D.A. (2000) *Mail and Internet Surveys: The Tailored Design Method*, 2nd edn, New York.
Goyder, J. (1987), *The Silent Minority: Nonrespondents on Sample Surveys*, Cambridge, UK.
Groves, R.M. and Couper, M.P. (1998) *Nonresponse in Household Interview Surveys*, New York.
Groves, R.M., Dillman, D.A., Eltinge, J.L. and Little, R.J.A. (2002) *Survey Nonresponse*, New York.
Lohr, S. (1999) *Sampling Design and Analysis*, Pacific Grove, CA.

SEE ALSO: methods of social research; public opinion polls; questionnaires

SAUSSURE, FERDINAND DE (1857–1913)

Although linguistics existed as a science as early as the beginning of the nineteenth century, Ferdinand de Saussure, born in 1857 in Geneva, son of an eminent Swiss naturalist, is generally regarded as the founder of modern linguistics. Saussure's *Cours de linguistique générale* (1959 [1916], *Course in General Linguistics*) is the most important of all linguistic works written in Western Europe in the twentieth century. Yet it was first published only after his death and was an edited version of notes taken by his students of lectures he gave in Geneva between 1907 and 1911. After *having* spent 10 productive years (1881–91) teaching in Paris (before returning to a chair at Geneva, where he remained until his death), Saussure became increasingly perfectionist, and this prevented him from presenting any treatment of linguistics in the form of a book, since he found it impossible to write anything at all, on such a difficult subject, which he regarded as worthy of publication. This combination of modesty and painful consciousness may explain why he produced only two books in his lifetime, both of them when he was still young, and both in comparative and Indo-European grammar, and not in theoretical linguistics. His first book, published in 1879 when he was only 21, was written in Leipzig while he was attending the lectures of two important neo-grammarians, Leskien and Curtius. His brilliant insights into the vexed question of the Indo-European resonants brought him immediate fame. The second book was his doctoral dissertation (1880), and was concerned with the absolute genitive in Sanskrit.

Saussure's major contribution is to theoretical linguistics. Yet his writings on the subject are confined to the *Cours*, and then only in the introduction, in Part 1, 'Principes généraux', and in Part 2, 'Linguistique synchronique', the remainder of the book, albeit suggestive, not having enjoyed equivalent fame. His theory is characterized by the famous distinctions he introduced, which were adopted later by all linguists, and by his conception of the linguistic sign.

After distinguishing the study of all social institutions from semiology, as the study of sign systems, then semiology itself from linguistics, and finally the study of language in general from the study of specific human languages, Saussure arrives at the three distinctions that have deeply influenced all linguistic thinking and practice in the twentieth century.

The first was *langue* versus *parole*, that is, a distinction between, on the one hand, language as a social resource and inherited system made up of units and rules combining them at all levels, and, on the other hand, speech as the concrete activity by which language is manifested and put to use by individuals in specific circumstances.

Saussure states that linguistics proper is linguistics of *langue*, even though we may speak of a linguistics of *parole* and despite the fact that the use of speech alters language systems themselves in the course of history. In fact, he considers only linguistics of *langue* in the *Cours*.

The second is *synchrony* versus *diachrony*: Saussure repeatedly emphasizes that linguistics, like any other science dealing with values (see below), must embrace two perspectives. A synchronic study is conducted without consideration of the past and it deals with the system of relationships that is reflected in a language as a collective construct. A diachronic study deals mostly with unconscious historical change from one state to another.

The third is *syntagmatic* versus *associative* relationships: a syntagm is defined as a combination of words in the speech chain, and it ties together elements that are effectively present, whereas the relationships called *associative* by Saussure (and, later, paradigmatic by Hjelmslev) unite absent terms belonging to a virtual mnemonic series. Thus, the word *teaching* has an associative relationship with the words *education*, *training*, *instruction* and so on, but a syntagmatic relationship with the word *his* in the syntagm *his teaching*. Saussure adds that the very best type of syntagm is the sentence, but he says that sentences belong to *parole* and not to *langue*, so that they are excluded from consideration. This attitude, although consistent, was to have serious consequences for structural linguistics, as it is the reason for its almost total neglect of syntax.

Saussure defines the linguistic sign as a double-faced psychic entity that comprises the concept and the acoustical image. These he calls the *signifié* and the *signifiant*. The sign has two fundamental material characteristics. First, it is arbitrary. There is no internal and necessary relationship between the signifié and the signifiant; if there were any, then, to take an example, [ks] would be the only possible signifiant for the meaning 'ox'. Thus different languages would not exist in the world. Second, the signifiant is linear: it is uttered along the time dimension, which is a line, and it is not possible to utter more than one sign at the same time. Saussure adds that the whole mechanism of language relies on this essential principle.

Saussure then goes on to treat the notion of *value* (*valeur*), which is the status of a linguistic unit in relation to other units, from the very existence of which it draws its definition, so that value and identity are two notions that can be equated. Therefore, in language, as Saussure says in a formula that was to become very famous, 'there are only differences'. For example, since English *sheep* coexists, in the language, with *mutton*, whereas there is nothing comparable as far as the French *mouton* is concerned, *sheep*, although meaning *mouton*, has a different value.

Saussure's theory, despite its uncompleted form, has been very influential. The phonology of the Prague School and Hjelmslevian glossematics, to mention only two examples, owe much to it. Even some of the gaps have been indirectly useful. Thus, the absence of the sentence has been compensated for by transformational syntax, and the non-treatment of the linguistics of *parole* by the development of pragmatics.

CLAUDE HAGÈGE
ECOLE PRATIQUE DES HAUTES ETUDES

References

Saussure, F. de (1879) *Mémoire sur le système primitif des voyelles dans les langues indo-européennes*, Leipzig.
—— (1880) *De l'emploi du génitif absolu en sanscrit*, Geneva.
—— (1959 [1916]) *Course in General Linguistics*, New York.

Further reading

Amacker, R. (1975) *Linguistique saussurienne*, Paris.
Culler, J. (1976) *Saussure*, Glasgow.
Engler, R. (ed.) (1968–74) *Ferdinand de Saussure, Cours de linguistique générale*, Wiesbaden.
Harris, R. (2002) *Saussure and His Interpreters*, New York.
Holdcroft, D. (1991) *Saussure: Signs, System and Arbitrariness*, Cambridge, UK.

SEE ALSO: linguistics; semiotics; structural linguistics

SCIENCE, SOCIOLOGY OF

The sociology of science comprises a broad church of approaches concerned to discern the nature and consequences of the social relations associated with the practice and culture of science. Since the early 1970s the sociology of science has acquired a special significance arising from its particular attention to the content of scientific knowledge. By contrast with earlier modes of sociological analysis of science (such as those championed by Merton 1973), the more recent variants have not only examined the sets of institutional and other social relations between those who happen to be scientists, but also attempted to articulate the consequences of these relations for the nature, direction, content and truth status of scientific knowledge itself. The shift in focus from the social relations between those who just happened to be scientists to the character of the knowledge itself marked a significant metamorphosis in the field. The sociology of science (which was more exactly a sociology of scientists) became the 'sociology of scientific knowledge' (SSK).

The claim that the truth-value of the content of scientific knowledge is dependent on (or, less strongly, associated with) the social circumstances of its production is of course highly controversial. This form of relativist claim is most famously associated with the 'strong programme in the sociology of knowledge' (Bloor 1976). Under this rubric sociologists were enjoined to adopt a symmetrical approach to explaining the emergence of scientific knowledge: the occurrence of both true and false scientific knowledge, it was suggested, could be explained by invoking the same kinds of sociological factors. Moreover, the strong programme argued that this sociological approach could be extended to the heartland of rationality, namely to logic and mathematics. Whereas true scientific and mathematical knowledge is traditionally defined in terms of the absence of social factors, this approach argues that science is constitutively social. Unsurprisingly, this and the related work of other British sociologists of science engendered considerable debate between sociologists and philosophers of science throughout the 1970s and early 1980s. Sociology was intruding upon philosophers' turf: philosophers were no longer the (sole) arbiters of which standards and practices could ensure reliable scientific knowledge.

The work of this period both contributed to and derived from earlier debates in the history of science about the relative merits of internalist and externalist explanations of the genesis of scientific knowledge. In particular, the arguments of SSK resonated with the more radical interpretations of Thomas Kuhn's (1970) general description of the dynamics of scientific change,

although these were subsequently largely disavowed by their author.

Until this point, SSK was largely based on detailed historical case studies of specific episodes in science: famous experiments, controversies over the interpretation of observations and so on. Social studies of science depended largely on interviews with scientists who were themselves public spokesmen or women on behalf of science. In line with Kuhn's adage about the problems of rational reconstruction in the history of science, the accounts resulting from this work often embodied confusions between historical and logical accuracy. In the context of injunctions that sociology should take the 'content' of scientific argument into account, a further formidable barrier to understanding the social basis of science was the fact that its practitioners enjoyed lengthy and intensive specialized technical training. The move by sociologists to study science 'naturalistically' turned this barrier to advantage. Science was studied 'ethnographically': sociologists adopted the stance of an anthropologist joining a strange tribe, engaging in prolonged participant observation of the day-to-day activities of the scientific laboratory (Knorr-Cetina 1981; Latour and Woolgar 1986; Lynch 1985). This afforded the possibility of being deliberately sceptical about just those knowledge claims that seemed most evident and obvious to members of the tribe.

It was evident from the first moment that sociology of science embraced a form of relativism, that significant questions of reflexivity were implicated: in its simplest form, if the claim of sociology of science was that knowledge depended on social factors, then this also applied to the claims of the sociology of science. Many philosophers (incorrectly) seized upon this argument from reflexivity as the basis for the charge that relativistic sociology of science is inconsistent and self-refuting. But, of course, refutation follows only if the presence of social factors entails falsehood and distortion, and it was just this asymmetric approach to the sociology of science that its proponents were at pains to disavow. The point they insisted upon was that social circumstances were implicated in the genesis of scientific knowledge whether it subsequently be designated true or false.

Since the 1980s the sociology of science has both derived from and contributed to several parallel intellectual movements, including poststructuralism, constructivism, feminism, discourse analysis, ethnomethodology and postmodernism. Against this background the further significance of the sociology of science has become evident. The strategic value of SSK is that in demonstrating the relativist basis of scientific knowledge – a particularly hard case of knowledge production – it makes more plausible arguments for the social basis of other forms of knowledge (Collins 1985). However, over and above its epistemologically contentious claims about the social basis for scientific knowledge, the sociology of science (and technology) has relevance for broader questions in social theory. This arises directly from the growing emphasis on 'epistemic' questions, from its attention to the reflexive implications of arguments about the social basis of explanatory adequacy, and from the basic point that 'science' is conventionally defined in opposition to the 'social'. As a result, sociology of science is no longer concerned merely to convey substantive findings about the nature of science, but instead finds itself involved in attempts to respecify key notions such as 'social', 'society' and 'agency'. One example of the last derives from the movement known as 'actor network theory' or the 'sociology of translation' (Callon 1986; Latour 1987, 1991; Law 1991).

Actor network theory posits a description of scientific (and technological) process whereby an array of heterogeneous elements are defined, identified and aligned into a network. In this view successful scientists are those able to enrol the best and most elements into a network. In particular, successful scientists are no longer necessarily those who follow (or, as recommended by Feyerabend, deliberately flout) the rules of scientific method prescribed by philosophers. Instead, in this view, scientists strive to provide effective representation – in a way that conflates the epistemological and political meanings of the term – of an endless variety of esoteric elements: electrons, microbes, scallops and so on. The fidelity of these allies is what holds the network together; the strength of the network is the direct correlate of the robustness of the scientific fact. Scientific and technical facts are not, in this view, derived from adherence to special or superior methodology. The 'hardness' of a fact is a reflection of subsequent usage rather than of its correspondence to a pre-existing nature; hardness is simply a measure of the work required to unpack and dissolve the network. People are not convinced because something is a fact; rather, a claim becomes a fact in virtue of the conviction of sufficient numbers of allies.

Developments like actor network theory suggest that sociology of science is an important source of new ideas for social theory. Given the basic premise of liberal intellectual enquiry that 'it could be otherwise', sociology of science explores the possibility and problems of a form of relativist enquiry that urges a reconsideration of the nature and scope of social theory. In particular, it provokes an examination of a form of social theory that includes non-human elements as part of an extended conceptualization of the social. What would a social theory look like that attempts to revise basic preconceptions about the nature of 'social' and of 'agency' (Woolgar 1995)?

Whereas the sociology of science in the 1970s and 1980s exhibited considerable solidarity in its antipathy to 'realist' and 'objectivist' philosophies of science, controversy over the later developments has exposed significant fissions in the post-Kuhnian relativist bloc. For example, there is debate over the ways in which Wittgensteinian philosophy can be used as a progenitor of a sceptical sociological programme of enquiry (Lynch 1993); about the extent to which reflexivity and actor network theory take relativism too far (see contributions to Pickering 1992); about whether and to what extent SSK's engagement with relativism and constructivism prevents it from having relevance for moral, political and policy questions.

These questions both underscore the pertinence of sociology of science for theoretical issues beyond the substantive focus upon science, and promise increasing engagement with related intellectual movements – constructivism, feminism, postmodernism and so on. Over a relatively short space of time sociology of science has undergone several major transformations. This trajectory has involved the successive questioning of a series of asymmetric assumptions about the nature of scientific knowledge and the scope of social study: Merton (1973) problematized the asymmetric notion that science could not be understood as a social institution on a par with others; the strong programme criticized the assumption that truth and false knowledge could not be treated symmetrically; the reflexive project purveys symmetrical treatments of author and object; and actor network theory attempts to redress asymmetries between human and non-human objects.

It is entirely consistent with its relativist commitment that no one of these trends in the brief history of the sociology of science can claim to be the ultimate social perspective on science. Rather, the value of the endeavour is constantly to provoke, re-energize and question accepted views.

STEVE WOOLGAR
OXFORD UNIVERSITY

References

Bloor, D. (1976) *Knowledge and Social Imagery*, London.

Callon, M. (1986) 'Some elements of a sociology of translation: Domestication of the scallops; and The fishermen of St. Brieuc Bay', in J. Law (ed.) *Power, Action and Belief: A New Sociology of Knowledge?* Sociological Review Monograph 32, London, pp. 196–233

Collins, H. (1985) *Changing Order*, Chicago, IL.

Knorr-Cetina, K.D. (1981) *The Manufacture of Knowledge: An Essay on the Constructivist and Contextual Nature of Science*, Oxford.

Kuhn, T.S. (1970) *The Structure of Scientific Revolutions*, Chicago.

Latour, B. (1987) *Science in Action*, Milton Keynes.

—— (1991) 'Technology is society made durable', in J. Law (ed.) *A Sociology of Monsters: Essays on Power, Technology and Domination*, London.

Latour, B. and Woolgar, S. (1986) *Laboratory Life: The Construction of Scientific Facts*, Princeton, NJ.

Law, J. (ed.) (1991) *A Sociology of Monsters: Essays on Power, Technology and Domination*, London.

Lynch, M. (1985) *Art and Artefact in Laboratory Science: A Study of Shop Work and Shop Talk in a Research Laboratory*, London.

—— (1993) *Scientific Practice and Ordinary Action: Ethnomethodology and Social Studies of Science*, Cambridge, UK.

Merton, R.K. (1973) *The Sociology of Science: Theoretical and Empirical Investigations*, Chicago.

Pickering, A. (ed.) (1992) *Science as Practice and Culture*, Chicago.

Woolgar, S. (1995) 'Science and technology studies and the renewal of social theory', in S. Turner (ed.) *Social Theory at the End of the Century*, Oxford.

Further reading

Latour, B. and Weiber, P. (eds) (2002) *Iconoclash: Beyond the Image Wars in Science, Religion and Art*, Cambridge, MA.

Lynch, M. and Woolgar, S. (eds) (1990) *Representation in Scientific Practice*, Cambridge, MA.

Woolgar, S. (1988) *Science: The Very Idea*, London.

SEE ALSO: positivism; reflexivity; relativism; technology, sociology of

SECESSION

Secession involves a national community severing what it sees as its territory from a state in order to form a new state or to join a neighbouring state. In the latter case, secession is combined with irredentism. Secessionism, like separatism, or what communist China calls 'splittism', implies a negative act. It is a term more often used by academics and state representatives than by those who are engaged in the act themselves. The latter prefer positive terms, such as, in Quebec, 'sovereigntist', 'nationalist' or 'independentist'.

Secession should be distinguished from related terms with which it is sometimes confused. It is not the same as national 'self-determination', but merely one form that self-determination might take. It is different from 'partition', which involves an outside force dividing what a national community perceives as its homeland (O'Leary 2001). The Irish Free State seceded from the UK in 1921, but the latter partitioned Ireland. Secession, particularly as understood by states and multistate organizations, is distinct from 'decolonization', the act of imperial withdrawal from colonies separated by salt water from their metropoles and whose people lack metropolitan citizenship rights. Secession implies the break-up of states, the territories of which are fairly contiguous and where extreme disparities in citizenship rights are absent. While colonies (peoples) have a right to self-determination under international law, there is no equivalent right of secession.

Generally, states and the international states system strongly resist secession, which explains why it is rare. Between the end of the Second World War in 1945 and the end of the Cold War in 1990, there was only one act of secession, Bangladesh from Pakistan in 1971. To succeed, secessionists must accomplish two difficult feats: (1) they must defeat or persuade the state to which they are attached, and (2) they must win recognition from other states, for without this they cannot be members of the international states system, a prerequisite for joining crucial international agreements, on such things as trade, travel and investment. Negotiated secessions, such as Norway's in 1905, Ireland's in 1921 and the dual secessions in Czechoslovakia in 1993, lead unproblematically to international acceptance, as they do not create awkward precedents. The collapse of states, such as the Soviet Union in 1991 and Yugoslavia in 1991–2, also facilitate secession. Here there is no strong centre capable of defeating the secessionists or of rallying the international community to withhold recognition. The prospects for an uncontested secession are enhanced if the breakaway region is homogeneous (McGarry 1998).

Military victory over the central government's forces does not lead straightforwardly to international recognition. There are several parts of the world today that have achieved the former, but not the latter: they exist in a grey world between *de facto* and *de jure* independence. The regions include Abkhazia, Nagorno-Karabakh, Trans-Dniestria, Somaliland, and Kosovo (Bahcheli and Bartman 2004).

All successful secessions have occurred in territories that previously existed as separate administrative units. This condition appears to enhance the prospects for both international recognition and group mobilization. The standing of the administrative unit also seems to matter. Thus, Kosovo's current failure to achieve recognition is owed largely to the fact that, while it was a self-governing unit within the former Yugoslavia, it was not a full federal republic, like Croatia or Macedonia. Still, Kosovo is likely to be recognized as independent in the long term, as there is virtually no prospect of its successful reintegration into what is now Serbia and Montenegro.

There are divergent views in liberal philosophy on the legitimacy of secession. As liberals are committed to the idea of a legitimate state, it is difficult for them to rule out secession under any circumstances, although some suggest the priority should be to make the state legitimate, not to break it up. The two main schools of thought are based on 'just-cause' and 'choice' theories (Moore 1998). Just-cause theorists have traditionally taken a restrictive view of secession, arguing that a right to secede exists only when the state has been egregiously abusive. One of their most prominent representatives has recently offered a softer version of this: minorities can secede if they are denied autonomy (Buchanan 2003). Choice theorists, using democratic arguments based on consent, draw an analogy between marital and political divorce: minorities should be able to leave if they want to and not just if they have been abused or not accommodated (e.g. Beran 1984).

Some scholars believe that states, particularly Western states, are becoming less resistant to secession (Kymlicka 2001: 387–93). Canada now has a constitutional process by which its provinces may secede. Under the recent Good Friday Agreement, Northern Ireland can join the Republic of Ireland as soon as a majority wants to, and a British prime minister is on record as saying Scotland can leave also. Even Indonesia recently allowed East Timor to secede after a referendum, and Papua New Guinea is committed to providing the same privilege to Bougainville. From the other side, one academic has noted that national minorities, at least within the European Union, are becoming less insistent on their own states, provided they are given autonomy and permitted access to international institutions (Keating 2001). It must be said, however, that these trends are far from universal: outside the West, and even, indeed, inside it (e.g. France and Greece), there are plenty of states that continue to insist on their 'territorial integrity' and resist autonomy for minorities lest it facilitate secession, and a number of minorities respond by demanding a state of their own.

JOHN MCGARRY
QUEEN'S UNIVERSITY, KINGSTON, CANADA

References

Bahcheli, T. and Bartman, B. (2004) *De Facto States: The Quest for Sovereignty?* London.

Beran, H. (1984) 'A liberal theory of secession', *Political Studies* 32: 21–31.

Buchanan, A. (2003) *Justice, Legitimacy, and Self-Determination: A Moral Theory of International Law*, Oxford.

Keating, M. (2001) 'Nations without states: The accommodation of nationalism in the new state order', in M. Keating and J. McGarry (eds) *Minority Nationalism and the Changing International Order*, Oxford, pp. 19–43.

Kymlicka, W. (2001) 'Reply and conclusion', in W. Kymlicka and M. Opalski (eds) *Can Liberal Pluralism be Exported? Western Political Theory and Ethnic Relations in Eastern Europe*, Oxford.

McGarry, J. (1998) 'Orphans of secession: National pluralism in secessionist regions and post-secession states', in M. Moore (ed.) *National Self-Determination and Secession*, Oxford, pp. 215–32.

Moore, M. (1998) 'The self-determination principle and the ethics of secession', in M. Moore (ed.) *National Self-Determination and Secession*, Oxford, pp. 1–13.

O'Leary, B. (2001) 'The elements of right-sizing and right-peopling the state', in B. O'Leary, I.S. Lustick and T. Callaghy (eds) *Right-Sizing the State: The Politics of Moving Borders*, Oxford.

SEE ALSO: consociation; federalism and federation; partition; state

SECTS AND CULTS

The sociological concepts of sect and cult usually refer to religious groups or quasi-groups – which may be large or small, with complex or simple forms of organization – which are regarded, by members and non-members alike, as deviant in relation to a wider cultural or doctrinal context. The deviance in question has negative connotations for non-adherents and positive connotations for adherents. It is necessary in this stipulation to mention quasi-groups as well as groups: groups regarded as sectarian tend to promote intragroup solidarity and personal identification with the group, while cultic quasi-groups do not systematically encourage group cohesion and explicit sharing of ideas.

Sects have been more frequently studied than cults, for two reasons. First, for some purposes, it has often been found unnecessary to make a distinction between the two forms, and the more generic 'sect' has in that case been used by social scientists. Second, even though sect has a clear history as a pejorative term, for long used within Christendom to denote heretical departures from official doctrine, sociologists in the twentieth century have used the term more or less non-judgementally. That orientation has arisen from the scholarly view that the history of Christianity (and perhaps other major religious traditions) has been characterized by an interplay between *sectarian heterodoxy* and *churchly orthodoxy*, and from the argument that certain kinds of sectarian movements have been crucial in the development of Western conceptions of individualism, voluntary organization and democracy – notably Protestant sects of the seventeenth century.

In contrast, cults have not as such had an innovative impact on the wider society. They tend not to be solidary groups. Cults have typically offered particular, concrete benefits to their adherents rather than the comprehensive world-views and conceptions of salvation typical of religious sects. A complication in distinguishing between sects and cults became particularly evident in the 1970s, with the proliferation in a number of societies of controversial 'new religious movements' (many of them inspired by non-Western ideas or leaders). These became labelled as cults by journalists and leaders of anti-cult movements that developed for the purpose of stimulating legal control of their activities, most notably their conversion techniques and methods of retaining recruits. But many of these new movements are, more accurately, described as sects from a sociological standpoint.

Yet the term *cultus* is probably much older than words linked to sect. That status derives from the fact that the traditional connotation of words linked to cult has focused upon religious rituals and practices (often of a magical, instrumental rather than a religious, celebratory kind), while sect has a shorter, clear-cut history because of its primary reference to deviant religious doctrines. The history of religious doctrines, i.e. intellectually systematized bodies of knowledge elaborated by religious specialists as orthodoxies, is confined to the period since the rise of the great world-religious traditions, such as Judaism, Christianity, Islam and Buddhism; while in periods and areas relatively untouched by the major religions of world significance, the more typical form of orientation to the superempirical world has taken the form of an emphasis on ritual practice and concrete religious action – within the context of, or in relation to, mythologies that have tended not to emphasize the notion of the salvation of the individual. In the mythological, as opposed to the doctrinal, context a variety of different rituals and practices – including magical ones directed at the obtaining of immediate, concrete (rather than long-term salvational) benefits – have typically arisen.

This does not mean that cultic phenomena have not appeared outside the relatively primitive contexts of predoctrinal mythology and orthopraxis. In fact we may illuminate an important aspect of the difference between sects and cults by pointing to the fact that while in medieval Christianity sect was used as a condemnatory way of talking about movements that were regarded officially as heretic (displaying undesirable heterodoxical tendencies), the Church could at the same time tolerate and even encourage cults devoted to the veneration of individuals who had been sanctified, often posthumously, as saints. Indeed the problem of heterodoxy (sectarian departure from official doctrine) was alleviated in the traditional Catholic Church by the carefully monitored sanctioning of cultic practices – often of a more-or-less magical character – in such a way as to institutionalize heteropraxis, the latter meaning departure from official conceptions of religious ritual and concrete action. However, within the Christian Church of that time and within Catholicism since the Protestant Reformation of the sixteenth century, the tolerance of orders of priests and monks has constituted a form of institutionalized sectarianism – specifically, their incorporation within the official conception of variations on and departures from doctrinal orthodoxy.

In the wake of the Reformation – and most particularly in those societies that became strongly influenced by Protestantism – social and cultural circumstances arose that encouraged the flowering of a great variety of religious beliefs and practices, notably because those societies witnessed a considerable growth of religious individualism. Thus, whereas the notion of sect had developed almost entirely for the purpose of depicting violation of the dominant, official religious beliefs and values of the Church, in societies extensively affected by Protestantism the relevance of a distinction between sect and church was greatly reduced, most notably in the USA after that country achieved independence from Britain in the late eighteenth century and established a 'wall' separating religion from the state. As a consequence, the idea of 'Church' lost most of its sociological significance in the USA, *except* in the important sense that the relationship between 'religion' and 'politics' has become of *greater* significance in the period from the mid-twentieth century until now. In other words, the original distinction between Church and state has become increasingly contested.

The modern study of deviant religious groups was initiated in Germany early in the twentieth century by Max Weber (1930 [1922]) and Ernst Troeltsch (1931 [1908–11]). Weber, as a historical sociologist, was interested in the contribution of sectarian Christian movements to the development of modern conceptions of rationality and economic individualism; Troeltsch was, as a sociologically informed theologian, particularly interested in the interplay in Christian history between churchly orthodoxy and sectarian heterodoxy, with particular reference to the ways in which religion had in the past and could continue to have an impact on secular institutions. In spite of frequent references to Weber and/or Troeltsch, the typical student of religious movements since the mid-twentieth century has been interested in different kinds of questions.

Much of the modern perspective can be traced to the influence of Richard Niebuhr (a student of Troeltsch) whose book, *The Social Sources of Denominationalism* (1929), crystallized interest in the kinds of social and economic circumstances that constrained individuals to join deviant religious movements, and in the degree to and manner in which religious sects moved away from a deviant to a more mainstream position within the wider society. Under Niebuhr's influence, and with particular reference to North American and British societies, this position has been characterized in terms of religious organizations of the *denominational* type. In this perspective denominations are seen as standing midway between the sect, which demands a great deal of involvement from its participants and stands in a negative relationship to the wider society, and the Church, which is more central to the society and therefore does not typically demand that its members discipline themselves strongly against the culture and lifestyles of the wider society. Sociologists have concluded that sects which seek to convert as many members as possible are most likely to relinquish their original commitments, while those that emphasize strict, and sometimes esoteric, doctrines are much less likely to do so, for which they 'pay' by remaining relatively small.

More recently, however, the study of sects has taken a new turn, while the study of cults – including the circumstances under which cults may become transformed into sects – has been revived. Sociological focus upon sects and cults now tends to be less directly concerned with the conceptual identification of sects and/or cults as distinctive types of religious organizations than with the ways in which new religious movements arise, their methods of organizing their memberships, and the critiques that they frequently offer with respect to modern societies, as well as to the global situation. More specifically, whereas until recently the major sociological interest in sects and cults centred upon their esoteric nature and the conditions of their persistence or demise, the proliferation of many new religious movements in the early 1970s, and the rise to prominence of what are often, and problematically, called 'fundamentalist' religious movements since the late 1970s, has given rise to a much broader set of sociological concerns about the nature and direction of change of modern societies, indeed of the world as a whole. Among those concerns have been the relationship between religious movements and the modern state, not least because in some societies the state has sought to regulate the activities of new movements, and the extent to which the proliferation of new religious movements (and the revival of older ones) signals a *global* resurgence of religiosity, a resurgence much related to the very complex and 'chaotic' global circumstance.

The pejorative meaning often attached to the term sect and, more particularly, cult has largely resulted from the controversial nature of many of these movements' practices. Some of them have been charged with 'brainwashing' their converts and/or engaging in deviant sexual behaviour. Such movements have on occasion become involved in dramatic incidents of physical violence perpetrated on their own members, among the most notable recent cases in the Western world being the suicide, or murder, of more than 900 adherents to the People's Temple in Jonestown, Guyana, in 1978; the deaths of seventy-eight members of the Branch Davidians in Waco, Texas, in 1993; and the demise of about fifty members of the Solar Temple in Chiery, Switzerland, in 1993. However, the even more significant trend has been for violent new movements to address their doctrines and practices to the *global* situation and to broaden both the scope and the potential impact of their symbolic and/or strategic activities via repeated, ongoing or uniquely traumatic events, increasingly of a political nature (Juergensmeyer 1993, 2000). An example of this is the Aum Shinrikyo movement which began in part as a Buddhist sect and later, in 1995, released sarin, a deadly nerve gas, in a crowded Japanese subway – a kind of symbolic attack on the contemporary world as a whole. This is, undoubtedly, a trend that is embedded within the comprehensive process of globalization (Robertson 1992).

Indeed, it is not too much to say that the whole theme of 'sects and cults' cannot now be satisfactorily addressed without attention to the global human condition (Robertson 1992). Increasingly, new movements, including religious or politico-religious ones, arise in response to that condition, as it is differentially perceived and experienced (Guidry *et al.* 2000). The most dramatic example of this to date has been the combined attack on the World Trade Center in New York and the Pentagon in Washington, DC, in September 2001 by the Islamic al Qa'ida.

ROLAND ROBERTSON
UNIVERSITY OF ABERDEEN

References

Guidry, J.A., Kennedy, M.D. and Zald, M.N. (eds) (2000) *Globalizations and Social Movements: Culture, Power and the Transnational Public Sphere*, Ann Arbor, MI.
Juergensmeyer, M. (1993) *The New Cold War? Religious Nationalism Confronts the Secular State*, Berkeley and Los Angeles, CA.
—— (2000) *Terror in the Mind of God: The Global Rise of Religious Violence*, Berkeley and Los Angeles, CA.
Niebuhr, H.R. (1929) *The Social Sources of Denominationalism*, New York.
Robertson, R. (1992) *Globalization: Social Theory and Global Change*, London.
Troeltsch, E. (1931 [1908–11]) *The Social Teachings of the Christian Churches*, London.
Weber, M. (1930 [1922]) *The Protestant Ethic and the Spirit of Capitalism*, London.

Further reading

Beckford, J.A. (1985) *Cult Controversies*, London.
Bromley, D.G. and Hadden, J.K. (eds) (1993) *The Handbook of Cults and Sects*, 2 vols, Greenwich, CT.
Juergensmeyer, M. (ed.) (2003) *Global Religions: An Introduction*, Oxford.
Minkenberg, M. and Willems, U. (eds) (2003) *Politik und Religion*, Wiesbaden.
Robbins, T. (1988) *Cults, Converts and Charisma*, London.
Robbins, T. and Anthony, D. (eds) (1990) *In Gods We Trust*, New Brunswick, NJ.
Robertson, R. (1970) *The Sociological Interpretation of Religion*, Oxford.
Robertson, R. and White, K.E. (eds) (2003) *Globalization: Critical Concepts in Sociology, Vol. V: Religion, Nature and the Built Environment*, London.

SEE ALSO: cargo cults; fundamentalism; religion; syncretism

SECURITIZATION

Asset-backed securitization is a technique of asset and liability management for banks. It is a well-established and important technique in the USA and, to a lesser extent, the UK, although to date it is less well established in other European countries. In addition to being a technique of asset and liability management, it has also become an alternative means of funding bank lending.

Asset-backed securitization involves a bank transforming a portfolio of loans that it currently holds on the balance sheet into tradable securities issued by a bankruptcy-remote Special Purpose Vehicle (SPV). It offers many opportunities for banks to manage their assets and liabilities, and to shift risks. There are many dimensions to this. In essence, it raises the liquidity of bank loan portfolios, and transforms illiquid loans on the balance sheet into tradable securities. It thereby transforms non-marketable into marketable assets. In addition, by removing assets from the balance sheet, it is a technique for managing risks and shifting risks to other institutions and to the market. Dependent upon how the securitization is undertaken, it can release capital for the bank and can therefore also be regarded as a technique for managing capital. It can also lower a bank's cost of funding both because it taps new sources of funds (and from lenders who would not normally offer deposits), and because new (marginal) funds can be raised without raising the general level of interest rates.

A perspective can be offered by briefly considering the two main alternative financial intermediation mechanisms (i.e. how funds are made available to those who need to borrow). In *market financing* (e.g. when a company issues securities) funds are made available to the borrower by investors on the basis of publicly available information. As the debt that is issued is traded in a secondary market, the lender is not locked into an exposure to the borrower for the full maturity of the loan. Market participants and rating agencies monitor the behaviour of the borrower and, on the basis of this monitoring, there is a constant market repricing of the securities based on the market's perceptions of risk.

On the other hand, *intermediated financing* (e.g. when banks make loans to borrowers) is based on inside information held by the bank, and the assets created (loans) are not liquid or marketable and there is no constant market repricing of loans. The bank undertakes the monitoring of the borrower, and it is effectively committed until the loan matures. In other words, the bank makes loans that are held to maturity on the balance sheet and that are funded by a mix of capital and deposits.

A central characteristic of securitization is that this strict dichotomy need not apply: the distinction between *market* and *intermediated* finance is not as strong as has traditionally been the case. This is because while the bank conducts some of the processes involved in making loans (origination etc.), and the loans are initially placed on the balance sheet, the ultimate financing and holding of the asset is undertaken elsewhere. Securitization involves splitting the different functions involved in making loans. While banks continue to make loans (and are remunerated for doing so), they do not necessarily hold the assets permanently on the balance sheet.

Securitization makes previously non-marketable debt marketable and thereby increases the liquidity of bank assets. Two alternative definitions of the concept are summarized as follows:

> Securitization is a technique that transforms or repackages a pool of assets on the balance sheet of a bank into securities that can be resold to investors in the capital market.

> Securitization involves the conversion of cash flows from a portfolio of assets into negotiable instruments or assignable debts that are sold to investors, are secured on the underlying assets and carry a variety of credit enhancements.

In essence, securitization involves the transfer of receivables into securities.

The most common securitized assets in the USA and UK are home mortgages, credit card receivables, personal or consumer loans, and car loans. A bank constructs a portfolio of assets it wishes to sell and move off the balance sheet. This will be a portfolio of a large number of small loans. The financing can be undertaken in one of two ways. An existing institution (such as an insurance company) issues securities in the market and uses the proceeds to buy the portfolio being sold by the bank. More commonly, the bank itself establishes an SPV on a bankruptcy-remote basis. This means that the SPV is fully protected from the bankruptcy of the bank (because the bank has no claim on the assets sold to the SPV). It also means that the bank is fully protected from the bankruptcy of the SPV. Thus, if the loans in the portfolio decline in value (because they are not serviced or repaid) and the credit enhancement is insufficient, the SPV may itself default on its securities.

An SPV of the securitization institution issues asset-backed securities that are bought by investors in the market either on an open basis or through a private placement. The cash received is used to purchase a portfolio of assets assembled by the selling bank. The bank continues to receive interest on the assets during their remaining maturity and this is passed to the SPV, which now effectively owns the assets. The securities are serviced and eventually repaid by the SPV through the cash flow produced by the portfolio of assets.

Providing the transfer of assets is conducted in a particular way, securitization transfers credit risk to others and hence the bank gains economies in the use of capital. The objective of securitization is to transfer a portfolio of assets to another party such that the risks are separated from the seller. It protects the seller from the risks of the assets, and protects the investor (the buyer of the securities issued by the SPV) from the risks of the bank.

Even though the assets are sold to another party, the selling bank continues to administer the loans in the portfolio. The SPV pays administration fees to the selling bank. In addition, the bank maintains the relationship with the customer. Thus securitization enables the bank to maintain its customer relationships, and to provide customers with the full range of services as in the past, but without the necessity of holding assets permanently on the balance sheet.

A key feature of securitization is that it differentiates between the process of making loans and the holding of assets on the balance sheet of the originator. The purchasers of the securities have a more specific risk than would be the case if they made loans (offered deposits) to the bank itself. Investors in asset-backed securities choose a specific risk (e.g. mortgages) rather than share in the overall portfolio risk of the selling bank. If a bank issues more equity and debt to fund an expansion of the balance sheet, investors and depositors acquire a claim on the whole portfolio of the bank. The lender is exposed to the bank as a whole and the debt acquired is serviced by the bank from its overall earnings. On the other hand, if an investor purchases securities issued by an SPV it acquires a claim on the specific assets behind the securities. Some investors would be prepared to purchase asset-backed securities issued by an SPV (with the funds being used to buy assets from a bank) but would not normally make funds directly available to the bank itself. From the bank's point of view there are two particular funding attractions: (1) it widens the source of funding, and (2) it is usually a cheaper form of funding.

DAVID T. LLEWELLYN
LOUGHBOROUGH UNIVERSITY

Further reading

Eisenbeis, R. (1990) 'The impact of securitisation', in E. Gardener (ed.) *The Future of Financial Systems*, London.
Feeney, P. (1993) *The Economics of Securitisation*, London.

SEE ALSO: banking; capital, credit and money markets

SELF-CONCEPT

At its core, the idea of self-concept is based on the human capacity for reflexivity, frequently considered the quintessential feature of the human condition. Reflexivity, or self-awareness, the ability of human beings to be both subjects and objects to themselves, can be conceptualized as the dialogue between the 'I' (the self-as-subject) and the 'me' (the self-as-object), an internal conversation that emerges (at both the ontogenetic and the phylogenetic levels) with the emergence of language – an argument extensively developed by G.H. Mead (1934). Language requires us to take the role of the other with whom we are communicating, and in the process enables us to see ourselves from the other's perspective.

This process of reflexivity refers to the concept of self. The *self-concept*, on the other hand, is the *product* of this reflexive activity. It is the conception that individuals have of themselves as physical, social, moral and existential beings. The self-concept is the sum total of individuals' thoughts and feelings about themselves as objects (Rosenberg 1979). It involves a sense of spatial and temporal continuity of personal identity, a distinction of 'essential' self from mere appearance and behaviour, and is composed of the various attitudes, beliefs, values and experiences, along with their evaluative and affective components, in terms of which individuals define themselves.

The concept of *identity* focuses on the meanings constituting the self as an object, gives structure and content to the self-concept, and anchors the self to social systems. 'Identity' has had its own interesting and complex history in the social sciences. In general, it refers to who or what one is, to the various meanings attached to oneself by self and others. Within sociology, identity refers both to the structural features of group membership that individuals internalize and to which they become committed (for example various social roles, memberships and categories) and to the various character traits that individuals display and that others attribute to actors on the basis of their conduct in particular social settings. The structure of the self-concept can be viewed as the hierarchical organization of a person's identities, reflecting in large part the social and cultural systems within which it exists (Stryker 1980).

The concept of identity has been a major focus of theory and research on self-concept, from Erikson's (1959) developmental theory of identity struggles during adolescence, to Goffman's (1963) ethnographic analyses of 'stigmatized identities' and identity negotiations, to the work of processual symbolic interactionists on identity maintenance in social situations, and structural symbolic interactionists on 'role-identities' linking individuals and social systems (Gecas and Burke 1995), and to the 'social identity theory' of cognitive psychologists (Tyler *et al.* 1999) focusing on identities based on group memberships and their consequences for group conflict. Identity has also become a central concept in the 'identity politics' of the 'new' social movements, based on gender, ethnic, religious or lifestyle identities (Britt and Heise 2000).

Self-evaluation (or self-esteem) can occur with regard to specific identities that an individual holds, or with regard to an overall evaluation of self. People tend to make self-evaluations on the basis of two broad criteria: their sense of competence or efficacy, and their sense of virtue or moral worth (Gecas and Schwalbe 1983). Self-esteem has been, and continues to be, the major focus of theory and research on self-concept, mainly because of its perceived motivational consequences for individual functioning and well-being (Wylie 1979; Gecas and Burke 1995).

Several processes have been identified as important to the development of self-concepts: reflected appraisals, social comparisons, self-attributions and role-playing. The most important of these in sociology is 'reflected appraisals'. Based on Cooley's (1902) influential concept of the 'looking-glass self' and Mead's (1934) theory of role-taking as a product of symbolic interaction, the reflected appraisals proposition suggests that our self-conceptions reflect the appraisals and perceptions of others, especially significant others, in our environments. The process of reflected appraisals is the basis of the 'labelling theory' of deviance in sociology, and of self-fulfilling processes in social psychology. Much research on the development of self-esteem, as well as programmes to enhance self-esteem (see Hewitt 1998), are based on the reflected appraisals proposition. It should be noted, however, that the influence of this process, as well as the other developmental processes, is muted and distorted by the agency of the self (discussed below), which protects the self-concept from damaging information by means of various defence mechanisms, including selective perception, denial, rationalizations, excuses, etc. (Rosenberg 1979).

Social comparison and self-attribution are processes more likely to be emphasized by psychologically oriented social psychologists. Social comparison is the process by which individuals assess their own abilities and virtues by comparing them to those of others. Local reference groups or persons are most likely to be used as a frame of reference for these comparisons, especially under conditions of competition, such as athletic contests or classroom performance. Such comparisons have consequences, especially for self-esteem. If the comparison with regard to some attribute or performance is favourable, one's self-esteem increases, if unfavourable, it decreases (but not always, due to the self's defence mechanisms).

Self-attributions refer to the tendency to make inferences about ourselves from direct observation of our behaviour. Bem's (1972) 'self-perception theory' proposes that individuals determine what they are feeling and thinking by making inferences based on observing their own overt behaviour, just as they make inferences about other people's motives and dispositions from observations of their behaviour. Role-playing as a process of self-concept formation is most evident in studies of socialization. It emphasizes the development of self-concepts through the learning and internalizing of various social roles (for example age and sex roles, family roles, occupation roles). An important manifestation of this process is role-modelling.

The self-concept is both a product of social forces and, to a large extent, an agent of its own creation. Along with the capacity for self-reflexivity discussed earlier, the self's agency is most evident in discussions of self-motives (that is, the self-concept as a source of motivation). By virtue of having a self, and consequently a self-concept, we are motivated to maintain and enhance it, to think of ourselves as consequential and efficacious, and to experience ourselves as meaningful and real. This motivational core of the self can be stated as self-esteem, self-efficacy and authenticity (Gecas 1991). The *self-esteem motive* refers to the motivation of individuals to maintain or to enhance their self-esteem. It is manifest in the general tendency of persons to distort reality in the service of maintaining a positive self-conception, through such strategies as selective perception, reconstruction of memory, biased attributions for behavioural outcomes, and some of the classic ego-defence mechanisms. It is a central process in numerous self theories in social psychology. The *self-efficacy motive* refers to the importance of *experiencing* the self as a causal agent, that is, to the motivation to perceive and experience oneself as being efficacious, competent and consequential. The suppression or inhibition of this motive has been associated with such negative consequences as alienation, learned helplessness and the tendency to view oneself as a pawn or victim of circumstances (Gecas and Schwalbe 1983). The *authenticity motive* (which is also conceptualized as 'self-consistency', 'self-verification' and 'self-affirmation') refers to the motivation to act in congruence or consistency with one's central values and identities, thereby providing individuals with a sense of ontological grounding, that is, a sense of 'realness' and meaningfulness. We are most likely to invoke the authenticity motive when the self-concept is viewed primarily as an organization of identities, or as a configuration of values and beliefs.

Much of what we do is guided by, and has implications for, our self-esteem, self-efficacy and self-authenticity. We may go to great lengths to protect our self-concepts, because of the power of these self-motives, by structuring our social environments, managing our self-presentations and selectively perceiving and processing information that either supports or challenges our self-concepts. Actions and reactions that support our self-concepts typically give rise to feelings of pride and other positive emotions; those that challenge or threaten our self-views may give rise to shame, guilt or other negative emotions. The emotional consequences of these self-motives are motivational in their own right and have increasingly become the focus of social psychological enquiry (Tangney 2003).

In the past, the bulk of research on the self-concept has focused on self-esteem, specifically, on the antecedents of self-esteem, the consequences of self-esteem and the relationships between self-esteem and almost every other aspect of personality and behaviour. Much of this research focus continues to be evident. But there are noticeable trends in other directions as well. Self-efficacy has increased in prominence because of its perceived consequences for mental and physical health (Bandura 1997) and its association with self-determination. The emergence and proliferation of identity-based (e.g. gender, ethnicity, race, religion, lifestyle) social movements has increased the political relevance of this aspect of self-concept and highlights its importance for social change. In general, there is greater interest in the social sciences in the interconnections between macro-structures and forces and self-concepts – for example postmodern or postindustrial society, information and computer technology, globalization, virtual reality and the Internet; and the very rapidity of social change has major consequences for our self-conceptions.

VIKTOR GECAS
PURDUE UNIVERSITY

References

Bandura, A. (1997) *Self-Efficacy: The Exercise of Control*, New York.

Bem, D.J. (1972) 'Self-perception theory', in L. Berkowitz (ed.) *Advances in Experimental Social Psychology*, Vol. 6, New York.

Britt, L. and Heise, D. (2000) 'From shame to pride in identity politics', in S. Stryker, T. Owens and R. White (eds) *Self, Identity, and Social Movements*, Minneapolis, MN.

Cooley, C.H. (1902) *Human Nature and the Social Order*, New York.

Erikson, E.H. (1959) *Identity and the Life Cycle*, New York.

Gecas, V. (1991) 'The self-concept as a basis for a theory of motivation', in J.A. Howard and P.L. Callero (eds) *The Self-Society Dynamic*, Cambridge, UK.

Gecas, V. and Burke, P.J. (1995) 'Self and identity', in K.S. Cook, G.A. Fine, and J.S. House (eds) *Sociological Perspectives on Social Psychology*, Boston.

Gecas, V. and Schwalbe, M.L. (1983) 'Beyond the looking-glass self: Social structure and efficacy-based self-esteem', *Social Psychological Quarterly* 46.

Goffman, E. (1963) *Stigma*, Englewood Cliffs, NJ.

Hewitt, J.P. (1998) *The Myth of Self-Esteem*, New York.

Mead, G.H. (1934) *Mind, Self and Society*, Chicago.

Rosenberg, M. (1979) *Conceiving the Self*, New York.

Stryker, S. (1980) *Symbolic Interactionism: A Social Structural Version*, Menlo Park, CA.

Tangney, J.A. (2003) 'Self-relevant emotions', in M. Leary and J.P. Tangney (eds) *Handbook of Self and Identity*, New York.

Tyler, T.R., Kramer, R.M. and John, O.P. (1999) *The Psychology of the Social Self*, Mahwah, NJ.

Wylie, R.C. (1979) *The Self-Concept*, Lincoln, NB.

Further reading

Gecas, V. (1982) 'The self-concept', *Annual Review of Sociology* 8.

Rosenberg, M. (1979) *Conceiving the Self*, New York.

SEE ALSO: identity; labelling theory; person; role

SEMANTICS

Any system used to convey information must be characterized syntactically, defining its well-formed or grammatical expressions, and semantically, defining how their content is determined by the content of their constituent expressions in context. Its syntax and semantics are distinguished in addition from its phonology, the sound structure a system may have, and from its pragmatics, including the rules of social interaction between its users. The interfaces between the syntax, semantics, phonology and pragmatics of an information system constitute a core concern of theoretical research in linguistics.

A very strict view of the relation between syntax and semantics is based on the principle of 'compositionality', stemming from Gottlob Frege's (1960 [1892]) work, according to which the meaning of an expression is a function derived from the meaning of its parts and the way they are put together. Logicians adopted it as a methodological principle in the late 1960s to characterize the syntax and semantics of a fragment of English in a logically precise way. Several other assumptions were inherited from Frege, including the view that clauses refer to truth-values, that the substitution of logically equivalent expressions preserves truth-value in extensional contexts, but in intensional contexts substitution of expressions with the same meaning, not merely co-reference, is required to preserve truth-value. A flourishing research programme ensued on the logical semantics of

natural language with a categorial syntax and a truth-conditional semantics. Interpretation was considered a structure preserving mapping from a syntactic tree of a clause to its truth-conditions in a set-theoretic possible worlds model. The central notion of logical entailment was characterized by truth-preserving operations on the 'logical form' of the premises. Logical entailments disregard context, for no matter what additional information is obtained, they are always preserved. Key questions in this research programme were scope ambiguities, binding of pronouns and the interpretation of noun phrases as higher-order generalized quantifiers.

First, scope ambiguities: quantificational expressions can be found in various linguistic categories. Noun phrases (NPs) contain 'universal quantifiers', *every student* or *all books*, and 'existential quantifiers', *a student* or *three books*. 'Modal quantification' is expressed in adverbials, *possibly*, *necessarily*, *allegedly*, *hypothetically*, and modal auxiliary verbs, *may*, *must*, *can*, *might*, or attitude verbs with clausal complements, *doubt that*, *believe that*, *consider that* and *know that*. Any clause that contains at least one universal and one existential quantificational expression exhibits a scope ambiguity, requiring disambiguation by systematically permuting their order in the logical form. To obtain different orders in a compositional semantics the technique of 'quantifying in' combines the quantifier Q_1 to occur first with an expression containing the other quantifiers $Q_2, \ldots, Q_{11}$ and a free variable, to be bound by Q_1. This proved to be widely applicable not only to linguistic quantification, but also to relative clauses and bound pronouns.

Second, binding of pronouns: a pronoun may refer to different referents, depending on the linguistic context in which it occurs. The inviting analogy between free variables in logic and pronouns in natural language constituted a very fruitful heuristic, despite its obvious shortcomings, e.g. a proper name binds a pronoun in *John loves his mother*, but an individual constant cannot bind a free variable in logical systems. If an NP is quantified in, it binds all free occurrences of the same variable, expressing co-reference. However, scope conflicts may arise, for instance, in the interpretation of *Every student who read a book liked it*. When *a book* is quantified into *Every student who read it liked it* to bind both occurrences of *it*, *a book* cannot refer to different books depending on which student is meant, but implies that all students who read a book, read the same one and liked it. Similar problems arise in expressing co-reference of individuals across intensional contexts, as in *A student believed he read a novel, but John thought it was a short story*. Furthermore, pronouns can be bound only by existential NPs or proper names across clauses, but in logic no quantifier can bind a variable in another formula. These three kinds of problems facing truth-conditional semantics lead eventually to the dynamic semantic systems, defining interpretation as a process of incremental updates of information.

Third, generalized quantifiers: initiated by R. Montague, all NPs are interpreted by sets of sets of individuals. The universal quantifier *every student* requires a set containing all sets that include all students, the existential *a student* requires a set containing all sets that include at least one (possibly different) student, and a proper name *John* requires a set of all sets that have John as an element. All kinds of natural, non-logical determiners lend themselves to such set-theoretic interpretation, enriching our understanding of the variety of quantification in natural languages and allowing a universal account of binding of variables by any kind of NP antecedent.

After two decades the truth-conditional approach proved to face insuperable technical difficulties in accounting for the linguistic principles binding pronouns within a clause as well as between clauses and for the variable meaning of any context-sensitive expressions as demonstratives and indexicals. To remedy this, the concept of interpretation had to be changed fundamentally, argued some semanticists in the early 1980s, including J. Barwise, I. Heim, H. Kamp and B. Partee. Rather than consider it a static relation between a syntactic analysis of an isolated expression and its truth-conditions in a model, interpretation should be viewed as a dynamic process updating the information available at a certain stage, using connected discourse or texts. The reference of a pronoun and, in general, the content of an expression often depend on the current context, the information available and the external situation in which it is used. Various logical systems, designed for dynamic interpretation, broadened the concerns of semantics beyond co-reference of pronouns,

scope ambiguities and logical entailments, to include new topics on how context is affected by interpretation. Core issues in this research programme of dynamic semantics are dynamic binding of pronouns across sentences in discourse, context shifts and hybrid forms of reasoning that need not be monotonic as pure logical deduction is.

First, dynamic binding of pronouns: co-reference of pronouns within a clause as well as between clauses in discourse motivated the development of dynamic semantics. Some systems require a pronoun to co-refer with a definite description in which the information about the intended referent is accumulated. Other systems design structured representations of the information available so that only some of the descriptive conditions determine the referent. This constitutes a very lively area of research, combining logical and computational techniques with linguistic data.

Second, context shifts: a dynamic semantics must determine how information is preserved while the interpretation proceeds, requiring a precise understanding of how the presuppositions of expressions (conditions that must be satisfied for the expression to be evaluated) are projected in a clause, and preserved or lost during the interpretation of discourse. This issue was raised originally in linguistic theory by L. Karttunen and S. Peters in the 1970s, as a pragmatic issue, but resurfaced in dynamic semantics. The interpretation of indefinites, and tense and aspect also gives rise to specific rules for shifting contexts when descriptive information is given about different individuals or events.

Third, hybrid forms of reasoning: reasoning may mix descriptive information with assumptions on what the words mean, how causal correlations are structured, what we see or hear and our private information. To design logical systems that model such hybrid forms of inference constitutes a major challenge for dynamic semantics. This concept of inference must be sensitive to various forms of context-change, for different conclusions are drawn at different times depending on what information is available. Though logical entailments are immune to changes in context, our reasoning is not, even if linguistic means exist to immunize information against context-sensitivity.

In dynamic semantics the old boundary disputes between syntax, phonology, semantics and pragmatics have turned into more fruitful collaborations on representational interfaces of the modular system. The information one expresses in using language may also depend on intonation, social status and power, on traditions and cultural values. Ultimately, a comprehensive semantic theory of meaning and interpretation should encompass all such issues and yet represent a precise system of inference.

ALICE G.B. TER MEULEN
UNIVERSITY OF GRONINGEN, THE NETHERLANDS

Reference

Frege, G. (1960 [1892]) 'On sense and reference', in P. Geach and M. Black (eds) *Translations from the Philosophical Writings of Gottlob Frege*, Oxford.

Further reading

Barwise, J. and Perry, J. (1983) *Situations and Attitudes*, Cambridge, MA.
Benthem, J. van (1986) *Essays in Logical Semantics*, Dordrecht, The Netherlands.
Davidson, D. and Harman, G. (1972) *Semantics of Natural Language*, Dordrecht, The Netherlands.
Gårdenfors, P. (ed.) (1987) *Generalized Quantifiers: Linguistic and Logical Approaches*, Dordrecht, The Netherlands.
Kamp, H. and Reyle, U. (1993) *From Discourse to Logic*, Dordrecht, The Netherlands.
Keenan, E. and Faltz, L. (1985) *Boolean Semantics of Natural Language*, Dordrecht, The Netherlands.
Meulen, A. ter (1994) *The Representation of Time in Natural Language: The Dynamic Interpretation of Tense and Aspect*, Cambridge, MA.
Montague, R. (1972) *Formal Philosophy*, ed. R. Thomason, New Haven, CT.
Oehrle, R., Bach, E. and Wheeler, D. (eds) (1988) *Categorial Grammars and Natural Language Structures*, Dordrecht, The Netherlands.
Partee, B., Meulen, A. ter and Wall, R. (1990) *Mathematical Methods in Linguistics*, Dordrecht, The Netherlands.

SEE ALSO: pragmatics; semiotics

SEMIOTICS

Semiotics is an ancient mode of enquiry that incorporates all forms and systems of communication as its domain. The development of semiotic theory and methods took place within specific fields, first in medicine, then in philosophy and, in the twentieth century, in linguistics. The rapid development of semiotics since 1950 spans several fields, including sociology, anthropology, literary and cultural criticism, linguistics and psychoanalysis.

The central idea in semiotics is a particular conception of the structure of the *sign* that is defined as a bond between a signifier and a signified: for example the bond that exists between a series of sounds (signifier) and their meaning (signified) in a given language, or the social convention that the colour red stands for danger. Semiotic research involves the study of conventions, codes, syntactical and semantic elements, and logic: in short, all the mechanisms that serve both to produce and obscure meanings, and to change meanings in sign systems. As such, semiotics is uniquely adapted to research on several questions that fall in the domain of the social sciences: communication conduct, myth, ritual, ideology and sociocultural evolution and change. Major contributions to sociosemiotic research include Erving Goffman's studies of face-to-face interaction, Roland Barthes's critique of modern material culture, Lévi-Strauss's research on Native American myths, and Jacques Lacan's psychoanalytic investigations.

Historical origins

The first known synthesis of semiotic principles was accomplished in classical Greek medicine, a branch of which dealt with the symptoms and signs of illness. It was in this applied context that the Greeks made explicit the *principle of the arbitrariness of the relationship of the signifier to the signified* that became the basis for the first accurate diagnosis of disease. The Greeks noted, for example, that a pain in the wrist may indicate a problem with the vital organs, not the wrist, and began to base their diagnosis on the pattern of *relationship between signs*. The combination of arm pains, pale skin and difficult breathing was given a more nearly correct medical meaning in the place of the incorrect array of meanings they might have for someone operating within the primitive framework of a concrete, analogical connection between signifiers and signified. This effected a transfer of phenomena that formerly could be understood only within a religious framework into the scientific domain.

Semiotics flourishes during times, such as the present, when there is general anxiety about the capacity of Western science to solve important problems, or when there is widespread questioning of the ultimate validity of Western cultural and philosophical values. When there is an intellectual crisis, the problematical relationship of the signifier to the signified is not a secret buried deep in the heart of the sign and social consensus. Rather the signifier/signified relationship appears to almost everyone as a series of discontinuities between events and their meanings.

Peirce's typology of signs

The intellectual base of current semiotic activity is mainly the writings of the Swiss linguist, Ferdinand de Saussure, and the US pragmatist philosopher, Charles S. Peirce. Following Peirce's synthesis of semiotic principles, there are three major types of signs based on the structure of the relationship of the signifier to the signified: icons, indices and symbols. An *iconic* sign depends on a bond of resemblance between the signifier and the signified, and requires social and legal arrangements and agreements concerning authenticity and originality. *Indices* are produced by the direct action of that which they represent, such as the line left at high tide, and they engage scientific, historical and other forms of curiosity and detective work. *Symbols* are arbitrary and conventional (such as the words in a language) and they require community consensus on proper meanings. Since any object or idea can be represented by each of the three types of signs, the mode of representation implies the form of interpretation and specific social arrangements as well. In short, every mode of scientific and other discourse is the result of (unconscious) decisions that reflect basic, often unstated, social values. Semiotics can function as a meta-language by analysing the ways the various fields and disciplines represent their subject matter, for example the frame of mind and form of social relationship that is implicit in experimental science or in Marxist theory.

The semiotic critique of 'rational' science

Semioticians often make a claim to be both more rigorous and more politically engaged than their colleagues in disciplines that base their methods on Cartesian rationalism. The source of this seemingly paradoxical claim is found in the contrast of the *signifier/signified* relationship that is the basis of semiotics, and the *subject/object* relationship that is the basis of rational science.

According to the semiotic critique of rationalism (and its offspring, positivism), the *subject/object* opposition takes the form of an imperative to establish a hierarchy in which scientific subjectivity dominates its empirical object. This originally innocent formulation, which unleashed enormous intellectual energy, contains no safeguards against excesses and abuse. Specifically, the subject/object split is the ultimate philosophical justification for one group or class (for example the 'West' or the 'East') to claim the right to dominate others, to assert that the *meanings* they provide are the only correct meanings from the range of possible meanings. Of course it is possible to advance scientific understanding and social thought within this paradigm by policing deviant intellectual tendencies and precisely calibrating social ideology to scientific theory, but the successes of this approach should not render it less suspect. From the perspective provided by the signifier/signified relationship, it appears more a moral or political *position* than a rigorous analytical mode.

DEAN MACCANNELL
UNIVERSITY OF CALIFORNIA, DAVIS

Further reading

Barthes, R. (1972 [1957]) *Mythologies*, New York.
Baudrillard, J. (1981) *For a Critique of the Political Economy of the Sign*, St Louis, MO.
Burke, K. (1973 [1941]) *The Philosophy of Literary Form: Studies in Symbolic Action*, Berkeley, CA.
Chandler, D. (2001) *Semiotics: The Basics*, London.
Eco, U. (1976) *A Theory of Semiotics*, Bloomington, IN.
Goffman, E. (1974) *Frame Analysis: An Essay on the Organization of Experience*, New York.
Greimas, A.J. and Courtèes, J. (1979) *Sémiotique: dictionnaire raisonné de la théorie du langage*, Paris.
Lacan, J. (1977 [1966]) *Ecrits*, London.
Lévi-Strauss, C. (1976 [1958–73]) 'The scope of anthropology', in *Structural Anthropology, vol. II*, New York.
MacCannell, D. and MacCannell, J.F. (1982) *The Time of the Sign: A Semiotic Interpretation of Modern Culture*, Bloomington, IN.
Peirce, C.S. (1940, 1955) *Selected Writings*, selected and ed. J. Buchler, New York.
Saussure, F. de (1959 [1916]) *Course in General Linguistics*, New York.
Sebeok, T.A. (ed.) (1978) *Sight, Sound and Sense*, Bloomington, IN.

SEE ALSO: Saussure; semantics; symbolism

SENSATION AND PERCEPTION

The terms 'sensation' and 'perception' have been confused and conflated for centuries. Many textbooks are still entitled *Sensation and Perception* (e.g. Coren *et al.* 1999; Goldstein 2002; Matlin and Foley 1997), but the two are rarely distinguished adequately from one another. In his comprehensive history, Boring (1942) maintained that sensation and perception were at the heart of experimental psychology. The term 'sensory' is typically used to describe those areas concerned with the early stages of processing (as in sensory physiology) and the term 'perceptual' is applied to those dealing with later stages (as in space perception). Both sensation and perception are obviously dependent upon the stimulation of the senses, and both are concerned with guiding action. The perceptual process commences with stimulation of the senses. The electrochemical activities initiated in the sensory receptors trigger nerve impulses in the sensory nerves that are relayed to the brain. Behaviour can, and usually does, result from this sequence of events, and we use behaviour to make inferences about the underlying processes.

The senses have evolved to make and maintain adaptive contact with the environment. Receptors for sources of environmental energy that have proved beneficial for survival have emerged and become more specialized for the needs of each species. Through the action of the senses an organism seeks sustenance, shelter and sex in order to survive and reproduce. The senses of all species have become adapted to the demands of their survival and reproduction, and there is a great variety in the ways in which senses have evolved. In addition, the senses are linked to an intricately organized brain, which has evolved to extract more than the elements of material sustenance. It furnishes us with intellectual sustenance, too, and extracts links to language and thought from the patterns of sensory stimulation. Humans not only use their senses, they also muse about them, too.

Most of the musing has been conducted by philosophers. Aristotle restricted the number of senses to five. (However, he added 'common sensibles': 'movement, rest, number, figure, magnitude; these are not peculiar to any one sense, but are common to all' (Ross 1931).) Aristotle's categories were retained for 2,000 years. In the eighteenth century, Reid (1764, 1785) proposed that perception is distinct from sensation, and that neither involves cognition. For example, redness and roundness may be sensations produced by an apple, but its perception includes an appreciation of the object itself. Perceptions also involve projective aspects that are not present in sensations: the apple is perceived as being out there, but the sensations can be internal. Finally, perception is immediate and not a consequence of reasoning. The confusion between the two was appreciated by Reid (1785):

> Almost all our perceptions have corresponding sensations which constantly accompany them, and, on that account, are very apt to be confounded with them. Neither ought we to expect that the sensation, and its corresponding perception, should be distinguished in common language, because the purposes of common life do not require it.

Reid's distinction has had far-reaching consequences; it has pervaded our language and it even defines the categories of our enquiries.

Reid's severance of sensation from perception has been used principally by empiricist philosophers, and by those psychologists following in this line. For example, Helmholtz summarized his position succinctly: 'The fundamental thesis of the empirical theory is: *The sensations of the senses are tokens for our consciousness, it being left to our intelligence to learn how to comprehend their meaning*' (2000 [1867]). Sensation provided fragments that were assembled, on the basis of our past experience, to yield perception. Perception was considered to be both indirect and a consequence of learning. By adopting such a starkly empiricist interpretation of perception, and by contrasting it so sharply with nativism, Helmholtz reopened a debate that has reverberated ever since, engaging in a conflict with Hering in which the main battlegrounds were colour vision and stereoscopic depth perception (see Turner 1994).

The debate took a fresh turn in the late twentieth century, in which indirect, or cognitive, theorists of perception were ranged against direct theorists, like Gibson. Although Gibson is considered by many to be a philosophical realist he argued, like Reid, against making a distinction between sensation and perception. Gibson essentially abolished the senses when he replaced them by perceptual systems. That is, the terms sensation and perception were abandoned by him, and perceptual systems afforded useful information for interaction with the external world (Gibson 1966):

> We shall have to conceive the external senses in a new way, as active rather than passive, as systems rather than channels, and as interrelated rather than mutually exclusive. If they function to pick up information, not simply to arouse sensations, this function should be denoted by a different term. They will here be called *perceptual systems*.

Moreover, Gibson considered that there is a perfect correlation between the stimulus and its perception; no stages of representation need be involved. The doctrine of specific nerve energies that had informed almost all studies of the senses since the time of Müller (2003 [1840]) emphasized the indirectness of perception. The brain had access only to the nerve signals initiated by external objects, not to the objects themselves. Gibson cast aside this tradition in favour of direct perception. However, Gibson retained separate perceptual systems that he called orienting, auditory, haptic-somatic, tasting and smelling, and visual.

A radical revision of Gibson's theory has been advanced first by Stoffregen and Riccio (1988) and more recently by Stoffregen and Bardy (2001). Stoffregen and Riccio attacked the traditional view that information from the otolith organs of the vestibular system is involved in perception of force direction. Stoffregen and Bardy went much further:

> We will attempt to redefine perception, not as a process of picking up information through a group of disparate 'channels', and not as a set of interactions among discrete modalities, but as the pick-up of information that exists in irreducible patterns across different forms of energy.

In order to sustain this redefinition, they required first to dismantle the edifice of separate senses. They proposed that there is a global array that 'consists of spatiotemporal structures that extend across multiple forms of ambient energy. These patterns are higher-order in the sense that they are superordinate to (and qualitatively different from) the patterns that exist within single energy arrays.' Most examples they use to support this

view are from the maintenance of balance during motion.

Stoffregen and Bardy seem to be advocating a theory of Aristotle's 'common sensibles' rather than of perception generally. They do not refute Aristotle's statements about the special objects of sense. In this context, it is surprising that they did not cite the work of the 'common-sense' philosopher mentioned above – Reid. He made the distinction that Stoffregen and Bardy are trying to sustain, but, unlike Gibson, Reid maintained that, while it is not influenced by reasoning, there are representational stages in perception and that it is indirect. Reid wrote: 'Although there is no reasoning in perception, yet there are certain means and instruments, which, by the appointment of nature, must intervene between the object and our perception of it; and by these our perceptions are limited and regulated' (1764).

On the one hand, those psychologists who retain the terms sensation and perception conceive of the latter as an indirect process, in which information provided by the senses is augmented by the brain, on the basis of past experience. On the other hand, those who abandon the distinction tend to consider that perception is direct, without the involvement of any representational stages. The expanding knowledge of neurophysiology, with increasing evidence of centrifugal fibres, is blurring the distinction between sensation and perception further.

NICHOLAS J. WADE
UNIVERSITY OF DUNDEE

References

Boring, E.G. (1942) *Sensation and Perception in the History of Experimental Psychology*, New York.

Coren, S., Ward, L.M. and Enns, J.T. (1999) *Sensation and Perception*, 5th edn, London.

Gibson, J.J. (1966) *The Senses Considered as Perceptual Systems*, Boston.

Goldstein, E.B. (2002) *Sensation and Perception*, 6th edn, Pacific Grove, CA.

Helmholtz, H. (2000 [1867]) *Helmholtz's Treatise on Physiological Optics*, Bristol.

Matlin, M.W. and Foley, H.J. (1997) *Sensation and Perception*, 4th edn, Boston.

Müller, J. (2003 [1840]) *Müller's Elements of Physiology*, trans. W. Baly, Bristol.

Reid, T. (1764) *An Inquiry into the Human Mind, On the Principles of Common Sense*, Edinburgh.

—— (1785). *Essays on the Intellectual Powers of Man*, Edinburgh.

Ross, W.D. (ed.) (1931). *The Works of Aristotle*, Vol. 3, Oxford.

Stoffregen, T.A. and Bardy, B.G. (2001) 'On specification and the senses', *Behavioral and Brain Sciences* 24: 195–261.

Stoffregen, T.A. and Riccio, G.E. (1988) 'An ecological theory of orientation and the vestibular system', *Psychological Review* 95: 3–14.

Turner, R.S. (1994) *In the Eye's Mind. Vision and the Helmholtz–Hering Controversy*, Princeton, NJ.

Further reading

Gordon, I.E. (1997) *Theories of Visual Perception*, Chichester.

Schwartz, R. (ed.) (2004) *Perception*, Oxford.

Wade, N.J. (1998) *A Natural History of Vision*, Cambridge, MA.

SEE ALSO: cognitive neuroscience; mental imagery; vision

SEXUAL BEHAVIOUR

Among humans sexual behaviour extends far beyond the mere act of copulation between male and female resulting in offspring. An elaborate superstructure has evolved out of the basic facts of female capacity to bear children, and the necessity, until the merest moment ago in historical time, for male impregnation. Sexual intercourse in humans may occur throughout the female ovulatory cycle. Usually described as continuous female receptivity, this may equally well be considered a highly atypical manifestation of continuous sexual interest (irrespective of female readiness for impregnation) on the part of the human male.

While a great deal of sexual behaviour must have gone on throughout history, since without it there would have been no human species today, it is by no means easy either to define or to quantify it. The occurrence of pregnancy may indicate that some kind of sexual activity has occurred, but its absence hardly indicates the converse. Quantification of the extent of same-sex erotic practices, and of non-coital heterosexual behaviour, is extremely difficult. Abortion and infanticide, and various forms of contraception, render recorded birth rates a dubious guide to the extent of sexual activity.

Activities involving the genital, and secondary sexual, areas may serve social and personal purposes that have no necessary connection with the primary reproductive purpose of such acts: economic survival, the assertion of power, and pleasure. Within all known human societies, sexual activity has been subjected to various restrictions and taboos, such as who constitutes an appropriate partner, defined by factors such as gender, race, relative social status, age and degree of kinship, what are acceptable sexual acts, and where and when these may take place.

It is relatively easy to establish attitudes recorded in legal codes, and texts of moral and religious prescription, but whether these have been representative of the views of more than an articulate and literate elite (usually ruling-class males) is much more questionable, and their relation to actual practice even more so. Certain acts or relationships being outlawed, however, does not mean their absence: the very existence of overt proscription or deprecation of certain types of conduct indicates that a possibility, if no more, was felt to exist. Contemporary descriptions of a society's mores tend to exaggerate either the degree to which it adhered to accepted standards of sexual propriety, or, conversely, flouted them, to make a moral point.

Sex in the human has been a site of constant speculation, taboo, stigma and controversy, and the work of scholars in a wide variety of disciplines has failed to produce a clearly descriptive whole. It has been much easier to describe phenomena conceivable as 'other', either among non-human animals, remote tribes or traditional enemy nations, or to define particular manifestations as pathological or exceptional, than to attempt to study, instead of make assumptions about, normal conduct.

It is practically impossible to establish a baseline of 'normal', 'natural' human sexual behaviour, given how widely this has varied between cultures and throughout history. Has there been roughly the same amount of all kinds of sexual behaviour going on at all times and all places, or has behaviour been determined by current ideologies and assumptions? We may perhaps assume that neither of these positions is entirely the case, although historical evidence, except for that relating to occurrence of pregnancy or sexually transmitted disease, will seldom reveal much about ordinary, rather than exceptional, sexual activity. Anecdotal evidence and prescriptive agendas have beset attempts at clarification. Extremely specific local conditions have been assumed to represent a universal norm. To become visible certain forms of sexual conduct have generally had to be practised by high-status figures within society; or else perceived as transgressive and the domain of legal action, as in sodomy trials or the divorce court, or seen as constituting a menace to health.

Human sexuality was a latecomer to the nineteenth-century physiological mapping of the human body, and social sciences were equally reluctant to grapple with it. Early investigators, if they did not fall foul of the legal system, found that interest in the subject excluded them from professional rewards. The study was thus sporadic and unco-ordinated, with individual researchers considering different problems and asking different questions, and therefore producing results not comparable. Accounts of human sexual activity have suffered from male bias. Although Herschberger (1948) made an early (and witty) assault on the sexism of their language and assumptions, recent writers (Tiefer 1995; Kaschak and Tiefer 2001) point out the continuing hegemony of a male-defined model of sexual activity.

Attempts to interpret sexual mores among humans by the use of the somewhat less sensitive, and more readily observable, behaviour of animals of a variety of species must raise serious questions of validity. There is little reliable evidence available (even in contemporary society) about what people are actually doing sexually, and the very attempt to find out is often branded as unacceptable, however necessary such findings may be for urgent questions of health. The researchers contributing to *Researching Sexual Behavior: Methodological Issues* (Bancroft 1998) point out that such investigations as do take place are driven by perceived problems and crises (e.g. the spread of STDs, unacceptable levels of teenage pregnancy), which may not favour the elucidation of data about 'normal' or apparently unproblematic behaviours, however helpful this might be to the enterprise. Even within these narrow parameters, researchers constantly encounter significant methodological problems and the difficulty of producing comparable sets of data, even within the same or similar societies.

The uncoupling of sexual responsiveness in both sexes from the reproductive cycle of the female has had profound consequences for human social arrangements. However, throughout history, and even in the late twentieth century, in spite of occasional reports of scientific advances in bringing about 'male pregnancy', it has been women who have physically undergone pregnancy and childbirth, and who, in the social arrangements of most cultures, are primarily responsible for their rearing. The male contribution, physically, is fleeting and need have no further repercussions for the individual male. It has been argued that men are continuously manufacturing sperm (and ejaculate a vastly redundant number during the sexual act), while women are born with a finite number of ova, and therefore men are biologically programmed to maximize the promiscuous scattering of their genetic potential. The aim of women, conversely, is to obtain the support of a (genetically superior) partner during childrearing, thus they are innately monogamous. It has, however, been hypothesized that, given the impossibility of reliable ascription of paternity for most of history, women have made their contribution to maintaining sexual diversity and obtaining superior paternal genes for their children through clandestine adultery. But it is hard to disentangle the innate dispositions of the two sexes at different historical periods, and in diverse cultures, and subject to a variety of environmental and social factors. Consequently the concept of some innately 'natural' sexual behaviour is exceedingly problematic.

Attempts to establish an explanatory model for sexual behaviour either heterosexual or homosexual on the basis of biological factors, be these hormonal or genetic, or differences in brain structure, operate in the face of a lack of any reliable generally valid picture of what constitutes 'normal' human sexual behaviour. That such attempts continue, and generate massive media attention, suggests enormous bewilderment, and continuing curiosity, about the entire subject.

LESLEY A. HALL
WELLCOME LIBRARY FOR THE HISTORY AND UNDERSTANDING OF MEDICINE, LONDON

References

Bancroft, J. (1998) *Researching Sexual Behavior: Methodological Issues*, Bloomington, IN.
Herschberger, R. (1948) *Adam's Rib*, New York.
Kaschak, E. and Tiefer, L. (2001) *A New View of Women's Sexual Problems*, New York.
Tiefer, L. (1995) *Sex is Not a Natural Act, and Other Essays*, Boulder, CO.

Further reading

Altman, D. (2001) *Global Sex*, Chicago.

SEE ALSO: homosexualities; incest; queer theory

SHAMANISM

In his *Shamanism: Archaic Techniques of Ecstasy* (1951) Mircea Eliade characterized the shaman as someone who entered a state of 'ecstasy' in order to interact with spirits on behalf of the community, and he pointed to remarkable similarities in these spiritual and community healing practices around the world. Shamans typically engage the entire local community in all-night ceremonies. The shaman's dancing, drumming and chanting is accompanied by a dramatic recounting of mythological themes and struggles with the spirits. The shaman's ecstasy involves an out-of-body experience that is typically characterized as a 'soul journey' during which an aspect of the person leaves the body and travels to other worlds. The shaman communicates with animal allies and guardians that are acquired in a guardian vision quest, arduous experiences that bring the shaman into contact with spirits and the powers they can provide. These spirit world encounters are basic to shamanism and they characterize the cosmology, hunting practices, healing, and ecological and community relations of societies in which shamanism is practised.

Later research has established various cross-cultural features of shamanism, including: an altered state of consciousness induced by fasting, chanting, drumming and dancing; soul journeys, vision quests and initiatory death-and-rebirth experiences; divination, diagnosis and prophecy; control of animal spirits, transformation into animals, and hunting magic; belief in illnesses that are caused by object-intrusion and attacks by spirits and sorcerers; healing activities involving soul recovery; charismatic group leadership; and the potential for malevolent acts such as sorcery (Winkelman 2000).

Winkelman (2000, 2002a, 2002b) suggests that some universal features of shamanism have neurological foundations. The altered states of consciousness produced through drumming, chanting and dancing activate the autonomic nervous system to the point of collapse into a parasympathetic dominant phase, producing a physiological response like sleep, and evoking the body's relaxation response and natural recuperative processes. This brain activation is manifested in coherent slow-wave brain patterns (theta and alpha) that propagate up the neuraxis and synchronize levels of the brain and hemispheres of the frontal cortex. Music also helps to induce these states. Hunt (1995) suggests that there are parallels with the psychophysiology of dreaming.

Some archaeologists have argued that shamanic themes are central to the cultural productions of the Middle/Upper Palaeolithic transition that gave rise to culturally modern humans some 40,000 years ago. The visual symbolism in cave art may refer to a shamanic cosmology, and depict shamanic rituals (Clottes and Lewis-Williams 1998; Ryan 1999; Lewis-Williams 2002), and it has been hypothesized that shamanic practices facilitated adaptation to changing ecological and social conditions, promoting group bonding through rituals that enhanced symbolic identity formation. The ancient biological foundation of shamanism and its role in cognitive evolution has led some scholars to suggest that shamanism was humanity's first spiritual practice (Winkelman 2002a, 2002b).

MICHAEL WINKELMAN
ARIZONA STATE UNIVERSITY

References

Clottes, J. and Lewis-Williams, D. (1998) *The Shamans of Prehistory: Trance and Magic in the Painted Caves*, New York.

Eliade, M. (1951) *Shamanism: Archaic Techniques of Ecstasy*, New York.

Hunt, H. (1995) *On the Nature of Consciousness*, New Haven and London.

Lewis-Williams, D. (2002) *The Mind in the Cave: Consciousness and the Origins of Art*, London.

Ryan, R. (1999) *The Strong Eye of Shamanism: A Journey into the Caves of Consciousness*, Rochester, NY.

Winkelman, M. (2000) *Shamanism: The Neural Ecology of Consciousness and Healing*, Westport, CT.

—— (2002a) 'Shamanism and cognitive evolution', *Cambridge Archaeological Journal* 12(1):71–101.

—— (2002b) 'Shamanism as neurotheology and evolutionary psychology', *American Behavioral Scientist* 45(12): 1,875–87.

Further reading

McClennon, J. (2002) *Wondrous Healing Shamanism, Human Evolution and the Origin of Religion*, DeKalb, IL.

Mithen, S. (1996) *The Prehistory of the Mind: A Search for the Origins of Art, Religion and Science*, London.

Vitebsky, P. (2001) *Shamanism*, Norman, OK.

SEE ALSO: religion; ritual

SLAVERY

The definitions of slavery are as numerous as the societies in which slavery was to be found, and for good reason. The rights that owners had over their slaves and the duties by which they were bound constituted a bundle whose composition varied from society to society, although the slave's rights were always heavily circumscribed. Nevertheless, certain elements can probably be considered part of all these bundles. First, the slaves were initially outsiders, brought by force to serve their new master, or they were in some way expelled from full membership of their society, for instance because of debt or as the result of a criminal trial. They might of course be the descendants of such individuals, depending on the degree to which a given society was prepared to assimilate slaves and their offspring to full membership. Second, at least in the first generation, slaves were marketable commodities, at any rate where commercialization was present in any recognizable form. In other words, they were a species of property and it was this which distinguished slaves from other forms of forced labour. Third, slaves had specific, generally inferior, occupations within the total division of labour. Finally, slaves were held in their status only by force or the threat of it, and in many ways the ending of the necessity for this marked a slave's full assimilation into the society.

Within this broad framework, the variations were enormous. This is to be expected from an institution which, in its various forms, existed all over the world – Australia is the only large and inhabited land mass where slavery never occurred – and from the beginnings of recorded human history until the twentieth century. Indeed, vestiges still survive, particularly in parts of the Islamic world and in various prostitution rackets. Nevertheless, the various slave systems may perhaps be distinguished according to two criteria, namely the degree of openness and the extent to which the system of production was organized around it.

As regards the former question, particularly in societies whose social systems were organized around kinship groups, slavery could be a valued means of expanding the size of that group and the number of dependants an important individual had beyond the limits set by the natural processes of reproduction. Since slaves were by definition outsiders, and thus people without kin of their own, they and their descendants could be incorporated into their owners' group, albeit often in an inferior position. Where there was no premium on the number of kin an individual might have, or where the rules for the division of property made it advantageous to cut down the number of co-sharers, then slaves and their descendants could rarely gain admission to the higher ranks of society. In such circumstances, slaves would be freed only as a result of a formal act of manumission, and the likelihood that slavery would be racialized increased very considerably. These might occur with greater or lesser frequency, but in all such cases the ex-slave began his or her life of freedom in a lowly status, often still formally dependent on his or her former owner.

With regard to the second criterion, while slavery as such has existed in an enormous number of societies, the number in which it has been crucial to the organization of production has been relatively few. Ancient Greece, ancient Rome and, in modern times, the southern USA, the Caribbean and parts of Brazil are the best known of these, although there were a number of other parts of the world, such as seventh-century Iraq, eighteenth-century colonial South Africa, Zanzibar in the nineteenth century, and parts of the western and central Sudan in the same period, for which a convincing case could be made. The emergence of economies based on slave labour depended on at least three conditions: first, private-property rights, above all land, had to be established, and concentrated to the extent that extra-familial labour was required. Second, internal labour had to be insufficiently available, often as the result of the emancipation of earlier labourers, whether they were bonded peasants as in ancient Greece or indentured servants as in colonial America – in other words, large-scale slavery was a consequence of large-scale freedom. Third, since slaves generally had to be bought, commercial market production had to be sufficiently developed. Although the demand for slaves on a grand scale may well have been logically prior to their supply, the continued existence of a slave society required the regular importation of new slaves, almost invariably through an organized slave trade, as – with the exception of the USA – slave populations were unable to reproduce themselves naturally.

In those cases where slavery was an integral part of the organization of labour, it tended to be rather towards the closed pole of the assimilation continuum, even though the distinction between slave and free was nowhere as harsh as in the USA. For this reason, it was only in these societies (and not always even there) that a genuine slave culture was able to develop, as something distinct from that of the owners. Therefore, it was only in such societies that slaves were able to organize sufficiently for a large-scale rebellion to be possible, although individual acts of resistance were to be found wherever slavery existed. Very often, the major revolts were nonetheless the work of newly imported slaves, as the efficacy of repression tended to persuade second-generation slaves of the futility of a rising, and led them to adopt an ambivalent attitude, which combined outwards acquiescence with the effort to create a way of life for themselves that was as free and as comfortable as the circumstances permitted. In this way they tended to confirm the paternalist ideology of their masters, although this would then be rudely shattered by the general refusal of ex-slaves to remain in their former owners' service when, after the abolition of the institution, there was no longer legal compulsion for them to do so.

ROBERT ROSS
UNIVERSITY OF LEIDEN

Further reading

Finkelman, P. and Miller, J.C. (1998) *Macmillan Encyclopedia of World Slavery*, New York.
Miller, J.C. (1999) *Slavery and Slaving in World History: A Bibliography*, Armonk, NY.
Patterson, O. (1982) *Slavery and Social Death: A Comparative Study*, Cambridge, MA.

SLEEP

Sleep is an area of human behaviour, which occupies one-third of the total life-span and occurs throughout all societies and all of history. Despite its pervasiveness it was largely ignored by social scientists until the mid-twentieth century. As laboratory-based studies began in earnest in the early 1950s to describe the nature and dimensions of sleep as a regularly recurring behaviour (Aserinsky and Kleitman 1953; Dement and Kleitman 1957), it became clear that this period was far from a passive state of quiescence or non-behaviour. By recording the electroencephalogram (EEG), electro-oculogram (EOG) and electromyogram (EMG) continuously throughout the time period from waking into sleep until the final reawakening, it was found that there were regular cyclic changes within sleep itself. The discovery that sleep consists of two distinct types, rapid eye movement (REM) sleep and non-rapid eye movement (NREM) sleep, which differed as much from each other as each did from wakefulness, led to a series of studies detailing the properties of these two states and their interactions within the context of the whole circadian (sleep–wake) rhythm. Each hour and a half the shift from a synchronized, physiologically quiescent, NREM sleep in which motor activity is intact, to the desynchronized, physiologically active, REM state accompanied by motor paralysis, became known as the 'ultradian rhythm'. Within NREM sleep, variations in EEG pattern were further differentiated by convention into numerical sleep stages 1, 2, 3, 4. This laid the basis for the descriptive mapping of a night's sleep by the number of minutes spent in each sleep stage across the hours of the night and by the length of the ultradian cycle. This plot is referred to as 'sleep architecture'. Once these conventions were established (Rechtschaffen and Kales 1968) age norms for these sleep characteristics were also established (Williams *et al.* 1974). Study of these developmental changes provided insight into sleep–wake relations. Individual differences in sleep parameters were also explored and related to variations in intelligence, personality and lifestyle. For example, although it is still a matter of some debate, long sleepers (those sleeping in excess of 9 hours per night) were found to differ reliably from short sleepers (who sleep less than 6 hours per night) in psychological make-up, with long sleepers being more introverted, with lower energy and aggressive drive than short sleepers. It is clear that there is a selective difference in the stage of sleep that is increased for these people. Long and short sleepers have the same proportion of stages 3 and 4, but long sleepers have twice the per cent of REM sleep and their REM sleep has increased eye movement density. Thus it is in the area of REM function that the need of long sleepers for more sleep must be explored. Other variations also occur, for example, in depth of sleep. These have been studied using the degree of auditory stimulation needed to produce an arousal as the measurement. This procedure has established that all sleep stages become progressively lighter with age, making sleep more fragile in the elderly, and with more frequent awakenings.

Beyond the descriptive and correlational studies there has been the continuing challenge concerning the question of sleep function. This question has been approached most often by looking into the effects on waking behaviour of sleep deprivation, either total or selective. Until recently these studies have been hampered by the limits to which human subjects could be subjected. Short studies of sleep loss have produced only small and equivocal results. These have been summed up ironically as: the effects of sleep deprivation are to make one more sleepy. However, the effects on subsequent sleep are clear. After total sleep loss, sleep architecture is changed. REM sleep is postponed in favour of a prolonged period of stages 3 and 4 sleep. It appears that this synchronized sleep is pre-emptive and is recouped first. In fact, if the degree of sleep loss has been more than a night or two, the first night of recovery sleep may contain no REM sleep at all. This may not reappear until a second recovery night. The opposite is true of the recovery following a period of selective REM sleep deprivation. On the first night of *ad lib* sleep, REM sleep appears earlier in the architectural plot and the total amount may be increased above the usual proportion when total sleep time is controlled. In other words, both NREM stages 3 and 4 and REM sleep act as if they have the properties of needs requiring they be kept in homeostatic balance. A long-term sleep deprivation study using rats and employing yoked non-sleep-deprived animals as controls established that extreme sleep loss results in debilitative organic changes and death (Rechtschaffen *et al.* 1983). This is the first study to establish that sleep is necessary to sustain life. How much sleep of what kind is necessary at the human level to ensure well-being will probably be determined not from experimental studies, but may come from the many clinical studies being carried out of patients suffering from various disorders of sleep and of sleep–wake relations.

Against the background knowledge of normative sleep architecture, for each sex across the whole life-span, significant deviations in amount and type of sleep can now be identified, as well as differences in the distribution of sleep across the circadian cycle. Studies that have sought to relate waking psychopathology to sleep pathology have been most productive in the area of depression. Although it has been well known that most persons suffering from affective disorders also suffer from insufficient and poor-quality sleep, the detailed laboratory monitoring has revealed the nature of this dysfunction to be largely related to REM sleep. This is found to be significantly displaced in the overall architecture. The first REM sleep often occurs too soon, can be abnormally prolonged on first occurrence, from a norm of 10 to as much as 40 minutes, and shows an increase in the density of eye movements within this time period and a change in total time distribution. Instead of REM being predominant in the second half night, as in normal individuals, in the depressed the distribution in the first and second halves of the night is equal (Kupfer *et al.* 1983). Since REM deprivation is known to increase waking appetite and sexual activity in cats and depression is associated with reduction of these behaviours, the finding of a specific REM dysfunction in these patients hints that this sleep stage is implicated in the regulation of appetitive behaviours, and mood.

Studies of sleep under time-free conditions have established that the normal human circadian rhythm is not 24 hours but slightly greater. This finding suggests that social learning has played a part in entraining sleep to a 24-hour cycle. Loss of these social cues (*Zeitgebers*) during vacation time or when unemployed, for example, often leads to later sleep onset time and longer sleep periods leading to later arousal hours. Most normal individuals have little trouble becoming re-entrained. However, some individuals with withdrawn schizoid personalities, or perhaps some neurological deficit, have no established sleep–wake rhythm. These people suffer from an inability to function in regular occupations due to the unpredictability of their time periods for active pro-social behaviours.

Clinical sleep studies of persons whose waking life is interrupted by uncontrollable episodes of sleep have revealed several different types of sleep disturbance that are responsible for these intrusions, including narcolepsy and sleep apnoea syndromes. The study of sleep and its interaction with waking behaviour has enlarged the capacity of the social and behavioural scientist to account for some aspects of human behaviour previously poorly understood and has changed the time frame of observation to one including the full circadian cycle.

The two-process model of sleep regulation proposed by Borbely has advanced the understanding of the mechanisms behind fatigue and sleep propensity. These are called process S and process C. The first refers to the need for sleep that builds up a result of the length of time awake, i.e. time since the last sleep period. The second is a circadian component, which is independent of process S, and is indexed by core body temperature. This becomes most obvious during periods of extended waking (sleep deprivation), when the pressure to sleep shows a waxing and waning rhythm that is experienced as drowsiness followed by 'getting a second wind'. This model of the sleep/wake control mechanism has contributed to an understanding of the variability of performance under extended duty hours of long-haul truckers, pilots, train engineers and medical personnel. Sleep is now being studied with increased technical sophistication: spectral analysis and brain imaging have both proven fruitful in further explaining pathologies of sleep and their waking consequences.

ROSALIND D. CARTWRIGHT
RUSH-PRESBYTERIAN-ST LUKE'S MEDICAL CENTER, CHICAGO

References

Aserinsky, E. and Kleitman, N. (1953) 'Regularly occurring periods of eye motility and concomitant phenomena during sleep', *Science* 118.
Dement, W. and Kleitman, N. (1957) 'Cyclic variations in EEG during sleep and their relation to eye movements, body motility and dreaming', *Electroencephalography and Clinical Neurophysiology 9*.
Kupfer, D., Spiker, D., Rossi, A., Coble, P., Ulrich, R. and Shaw, D. (1983) 'Recent diagnostic treatment advances in REM sleep and depression', in P.J. Clayton and J.E. Barretts (eds) *Treatment of Depression: Old Controversies and New Approaches*, New York.
Rechtschaffen, A. and Kales, A. (eds) (1968) *A Manual of Standardized Terminology, Techniques and Scoring System for Sleep Stages of Human Subjects*, Los Angeles, CA.
Rechtschaffen, A., Gilliland, M., Bergmann, B. and Winter, J. (1983) 'Physiological correlates of prolonged sleep deprivation in rats', *Science* 221.
Williams, R., Karacan, I. and Hursch, C. (1974) *Electroencephalography (EEG) of Human Sleep: Clinical Applications*, New York.

Further reading

Borbely, A. (1986) *Secrets of Sleep*, New York.
Pace-Schott, E., Solms, M., Blagrove, M. and Harnad, S. (2003) *Sleep and Dreaming*, Cambridge, UK.
Kryger, M., Roth, T. and Dement, W. (2000) *Principles and Practice of Sleep Medicine*, 3rd edn, Philadelphia, PA.

SEE ALSO: dreams

SMITH, ADAM (1723–90)

Adam Smith was born in the town of Kirkcaldy on the east coast of Scotland, the son of another Adam Smith and of Margaret Douglas of Strathendry. After attending the Burgh School, Smith proceeded to Glasgow University (1737–40) where he was most influenced by Francis Hutcheson, the second Professor of Moral Philosophy. Thereafter Smith took up the Snell Exhibition to Balliol College Oxford (1740–6). He found the period to be uncongenial but derived great benefit from access to the excellent library.

In 1748 Henry Home (Lord Kames), the eminent jurist, together with Robert Craigie of Glendoick, later Lord President of the Court of Session, and an old boyhood friend, James Oswald of Dunnikier, helped to establish a course of lectures on rhetoric. These lectures were of an 'extra-mural' kind and delivered in the city (as distinct from the University) of Edinburgh.

The success of the course led directly to Smith's appointment to the Chair of Logic and Rhetoric in Glasgow University in 1751. The following year he was translated to the Chair of Moral Philosophy (1752–63). During his tenure of the Chair Smith continued to lecture on rhetoric, but extended the scope of the course to include ethics, jurisprudence and political economy.

Smith's most important publications in this period, apart from two contributions to the *Edinburgh Review* (1755–6), were the *Theory of Moral Sentiments* (1759, later editions 1761, 1767, 1774, 1781, 1790) and the *Considerations Concerning the First Formation of Languages* (1761).

The *Theory of Moral Sentiments* served to draw Smith to the attention of Charles Townshend, of Stamp Act fame, and was to lead to his appointment as tutor to the young Duke of Buccleuch, and his younger brother, Hew Scott.

The appointment was confirmed, and Smith duly resigned his Chair in February 1764, by which time he was already in France. After a tour through France that involved, for Smith, an exciting meeting with Voltaire in Geneva, the party settled in Paris in February 1766 where Smith met the leading philosophers and especially the economists (or physiocrats), notably Quesnay and Turgot, who had already developed a sophisticated model of a macro-model for a capital-using system. Since Smith's lectures in Glasgow were innocent of such a model, it is plausible to suggest that a person so interested in intellectual systems would have had little difficulty in appreciating the significance of the contribution. Smith's charges were taken ill in 1766: the Duke recovered but his young brother died. Smith returned to London early in November 1766 and never travelled abroad again.

Smith returned to his maternal home in 1767 and spent the next 6 years working on his major study. He left for London in 1773 to see to the publication of his manuscript but did not complete the book until much later; a delay that his friend David Hume attributed to his preoccupation with the unfolding crisis with the American colonies. The *Inquiry* was published on 9 March 1776 (the year of Hume's death) and went through a number of editions, of which the third is the most important: in 1778, 1784, 1786 and 1789.

In 1778 Smith was appointed Commissioner of Customs and of the Salt Duties, posts that brought an additional income of £600 per annum (to be added to the continuing pension of £300 from Buccleuch) and that caused Smith to remove his household to Edinburgh (where his mother died in 1784). Adam Smith died, unmarried, on 17 July 1790 after ensuring that his literary executors, Joseph Black and James Hutton, had burned all his manuscripts with the exception of those that were published under the title of *Essays on Philosophical Subjects* (1795). He did not complete his intended account of 'the general principles of law and government', although generous traces of the argument survive in the lecture notes.

The broad structure of the argument on which Smith based his system of social sciences may be established by following the order of Smith's lectures from the chair of moral philosophy. The ethical argument is contained in *Theory of Moral Sentiments* and stands in the broad tradition of Hutcheson and Hume. Smith was concerned, in large measure, to explain the way in which the mind forms judgements as to what is fit and proper to be done or to be avoided. He argued that people form such judgements by visualizing how they would behave in the circumstances confronting another person or how an imagined or 'ideal' spectator might react to their actions or expressions of feeling in a given situation. A capacity to form judgements on *particular* occasions leads in turn to the emergence of *general rules* of conduct that correct the natural partiality for self. In particular Smith argued that those rules of behaviour that related to justice constitute the 'main pillar which upholds the whole edifice' of society.

Smith recognized that rules of behaviour would vary in different communities at the same point in time as well as over time, and addressed himself to this problem in the lectures on jurisprudence. In dealing with 'private law' such as that which relates to life, liberty or poverty, Smith deployed the analysis of the *Theory of Moral Sentiments* in explaining the origin of particular rules in the context of four socioeconomic stages – those of hunting, pasture, agriculture and commerce. In the lectures on 'public' jurisprudence he paid particular attention to the transition from the feudal-agrarian state to that of commerce; that is, to the emergence of the exchange economy and the substitution of a cash for a service nexus.

The economic analysis that completed the sequence and which culminated in the *Wealth of Nations* is predicated upon a system of justice and takes as given the point that self-regarding actions have a social reference. In fact the most complete statement of the psychology on which the *Wealth of Nations* relies is to be found in Part VI of the *Theory of Moral Sentiments* that was added in 1790.

The formal analysis of the *Wealth of Nations* begins with an account of the division of labour and of the phenomenon of economic interdependence, and then proceeds to the analysis of price, the allocation of resources and the treatment of distribution. Building on the equilibrium analysis of Book I, the second book develops a version of the Physiocratic model of the circular flow of income and output before proceeding to the analysis of the consequences of individual activity and leads directly to the policy prescriptions with which Smith is most commonly associated:

namely, the call for economic liberty and the dismantling of all impediments, especially mercantilist impediments, to individual effort. Yet Smith's liberalism can be exaggerated. In addition to such necessary functions as the provision of defence, justice and public works, Jacob Viner (1928) has shown that Smith envisioned a wide and elastic range of governmental activity.

The generally optimistic tone that Smith uses in discussing the performance of the modern economy has also to be qualified by reference to further links with the ethical and historical analyses. Smith gave a great deal of attention to the social consequences of the division of labour, emphasizing the problem of isolation, the breakdown of the family unit and the mental mutilation (affecting the capacity for moral judgement) that follows from concentrating the mind on a restricted range of activities. If the government has to act in this, as in other spheres, Smith noted that it would be constrained by the habits and prejudices of the governed. He observed further that the type of government often found in conjunction with the exchange or commercial economy would be subject to pressure from particular economic interests, thus limiting its efficiency, and, also, that the political sphere like the economic was a focus for the competitive pursuit of power and status. He was aware of the phenomenon of market *and* of government failure.

ANDREW SKINNER
GLASGOW UNIVERSITY

References

Smith, A. (1976 [1759]) *Theory of Moral Sentiments*, ed. D.D. Raphael and A.L. Macfie, Oxford.
Smith, A. (1976 [1776]) *Wealth of Nations*, eds R.H. Campbell, A.S. Skinner and W.B. Todd, Oxford.
Smith, A. (1980 [1795]) *Essays on Philosophical Subjects*, ed. W.P.D. Wightman, Oxford.
Viner, J. (1928) 'Adam Smith and Laisser-Faire', in J.M. Clark, P. Douglas, J.H. Hollander, G.R. Morrow, M. Palyi and J. Viner, *Adam Smith, 1776–1926: Lectures to Commemorate the Sesquicentennial of the Publication of The Wealth of Nations*, Chicago.

Further reading

Brown, V. (1994) *Adam Smith's Discourse*, London.
Campbell, T.D. (1971) *Adam Smith's Science of Morals*, London.
Haakonssen, K. (1981) *The Science of the Legislator*, Cambridge.
Hollander, S. (1973) *The Economics of Adam Smith*, Toronto.
Lindren, R. (1975) *The Social Philosophy of Adam Smith*, The Hague.
Macfie, A.L. (1967) *The Individual in Society: Papers on Adam Smith*, London.
Rae, J. (1985) *Life of Adam Smith*, London.
Ross, I.S. (1995) *The Life of Adam Smith*, Oxford.
Rothschild, E. (2001) *Economic Sentiments*, London.
Skinner, A.S. (1996) *A System of Social Science: Papers Relating to Adam Smith*, Oxford.
Smith, A. (1977) *Correspondence of Adam Smith*, eds E.C. Mossner and I.S. Ross, Oxford.
—— (1978) *Lectures on Jurisprudence*, eds R.L. Meek, D.D. Raphael and P.G. Stein, Oxford.
—— (1983) *Lectures on Rhetoric and Belles Lettres*, ed. J.C. Bryce, Oxford.
Werhane, P.H. (1991) *Adam Smith and His Legacy for Modern Capitalism*, Oxford.
Wood, J.C. (1984) *Adam Smith: Critical Assessments*, Beckenham.

SOCIAL ANTHROPOLOGY

The term 'social anthropology' refers to that part of anthropology which has a mainly sociological basis, and the discipline was once defined by Leach (1982) as a kind of comparative microsociology.

Although the term had been used slightly earlier (James Frazer was appointed professor in 'social anthropology' in 1910), it is generally agreed that the discipline was founded in the early interwar period, through the methodological revolution associated with Bronislaw Malinowski's meticulous ethnographic fieldwork in Melanesia (1915–18) and A.R. Radcliffe-Brown's ambitious theoretical programme for a rigidly scientific discipline based on fieldwork, comparison and Durkheim's sociology. In the space of a couple of decades, 'The British School', actually two rival factions led by the two men (Kuper 1996), produced a number of highly influential monographs, some of them seen as canonical today. In spite of the differences between the Malinowskians and the structural-functionalist students of Radcliffe-Brown, there was enough common ground in the work of these scholars to establish an identity that was distinct from US cultural anthropology and also from earlier European approaches in what was commonly termed ethnology or, more broadly, anthropology, although that term began to be restricted in Europe to biological anthropology. Although there were strong affinities with French anthropology as it was being developed by Marcel

Mauss and his students, British social anthropology was at the time more of an empiricist enterprise, seeing itself as being inductive rather than deductive.

As it developed through the work of Malinowksi, Radcliffe-Brown and their leading students, amongst others E.E. Evans-Pritchard, Meyer Fortes, Raymond Firth, Audrey Richards and Isaac Schapera, the social anthropological approach was characterized by six features:

1 A synchronic perspective was preferred, and speculative historical reconstructions were rejected.
2 Field studies generally focused on small-scale, non-literate societies.
3 The main research interests were in the fields of local politics, law and conflict, religion (seen largely as a socially integrating institution) and, above all, kinship.
4 Ethnographies were based on long-term, intensive fieldwork.
5 The goal was to make wide-ranging comparison leading to general insights (or even laws) about society.
6 Finally, unlike their predecessors, the social anthropologists were not evolutionists. They did not search for underlying principles of social evolution, and most did not believe that societies evolved along certain, prescribed lines.

After the Second World War, the initially very small network of people who practised social anthropology grew rapidly. The discipline became more diverse and geographically less centralized, although it remained associated with the British Empire (later Commonwealth) for some time still. However, the principles of structural-functionalism, the dominant theoretical orientation, were soon challenged. Firth argued that social practices emerged from individual choices. Accordingly, one should look for discrepancies between norms and actual behaviour. Leach claimed that models of society, whether constructed by actors or observers, had little to do with the ways in which actual societies operated. Evans-Pritchard, who succeeded Radcliffe-Brown at Oxford in 1946, dissociated himself from his old mentor by arguing that social anthropology would never arrive at general laws like those of the natural sciences, but should instead devote itself to interpretation and translation. Although

some later social anthropologists have defended causal explanations and systematic comparison, and so retain the ambition to build a cumulative, scientific body of knowledge, the discipline has become closer to history and qualitative sociology than to the natural sciences.

The 1950s and 1960s saw other important developments in addition to the break with orthodox structural-functionalism. Important studies of social change and urbanization were carried out in Southern Africa, and network analysis entered the methodological portfolio as a method appropriate for the study of complex urban settings. At the same time a political anthropology was developed that focused not on questions of stability and social integration but on individual strategies and resource competition. The influence of Claude Lévi-Strauss's structuralism was making itself felt and, although structuralism made few converts in Britain, it set new agendas for research and theoretical debate, inspiring research on phenomena such as ritual, classification and knowledge systems. Some of the major achievements of the period, such as Mary Douglas's original merging of structural-functionalism with structuralist theory, and Victor Turner's sophisticated analyses of rituals and their associated symbols, were indebted both to British empiricism and continental rationalism, while Fredrik Barth's transactionalism and modelling of ethnic boundaries represented attempts to break with structural-functionalism without abandoning the empiricist foundations of social anthropology.

In spite of this new breadth of theoretical and empirical approaches, matched by increasing geographical scope, the discipline retained its main defining characteristics. No longer a Commonwealth speciality, social anthropology was now established in many European countries, and largely thanks to structuralism, contact with French *ethnologie* was increasing. It also had a major impact on anthropology as practised in Latin America.

By the last quarter of the twentieth century, it became increasingly difficult to draw the boundary between a European 'social anthropology' and a US 'cultural anthropology'. Neo-Marxist approaches were adopted by many anthropologists on both sides of the Atlantic, feminism led to a reconsideration of fundamental assumptions everywhere, Foucauldian discourse analysis entered anthropology, and postcolonial critiques as well as postmodernism undermined scientific pretensions and led to what is often called 'a crisis of representation' in the discipline of anthropology as a whole. Interpretive and symbolic anthropology, originating in the USA, made a major impact in Europe. In addition, many US anthropologists, whether influenced by Marxism or not, carried out research on social relations, political power and traditional economics. It often seemed as if the divisions within social anthropology were more pronounced than the differences between social and cultural anthropology.

The changes in social anthropology in the 1960s and 1970s were due to two, partly overlapping, influences. First, the student movement of the late 1960s had lasting effects. Feminism made gender a core theme on a par with kinship and peasant economics. Political radicalism and the popularity of academic Marxism led to a fundamental critique of the earlier tendency to study single societies as if they were isolated and unchanging. Whereas the Marxist terminology would soon disappear, this critique has had enduring consequences, and contemporary social anthropology is concerned with both systemic connections and historical change. In addition, decolonization in the Third World gave impetus to a critique of anthropology as a 'colonial discipline' that exoticized 'the others' rather than understanding them as equals. Postcolonial theory, as typified in Edward Said's work on orientalism, raised issues of symbolic power concerning who had the right to represent whom, quite explicitly accusing anthropologists (and historians) of constructing ideologically motivated misrepresentations of 'Orientals'.

Second, the new philosophical scepticism usually called postmodernism, which proclaimed 'the end of the great narratives', anti-scientific relativism and 'deconstruction' made inroads into anthropology – first in the USA, later in Europe – from the early 1980s. Seemingly compatible with the traditional anthropological emphasis on local knowledges and methodological relativism, postmodernism nevertheless led to a widespread insecurity concerning the soundness of ethnographic method and representation. The reason was that not only did the postmodernists relativize cultural knowledge. They also relativized scientific truth and argued that language itself could not be context-independent. If taken literally, this would imply the end of social anthropology not only as a science, but also as a descriptive endeavour.

In spite of, or perhaps because of, these upheavals, social anthropology was a vibrant and diverse discipline at the turn of the millennium. European social anthropology also became increasingly integrated with the foundation of the European Association of Social Anthropologists in 1989, which led to many long-term collaborations and exchanges of views between traditions of social anthropology that had formerly been unaware of each other. Significantly, large numbers of Central and East European social anthropologists, relatively intellectually isolated under socialism, entered into lively networks with West European colleagues. Contacts were also made with Latin American anthropologists, although the language problem has restricted these exchanges somewhat.

With hindsight, it is clear that what may have seemed major intellectual revolutions at the time – Marxism, feminism, postcolonialism, postmodernism – effectively led to adjustments rather than to radical shifts in mainstream social anthropology. The subject had nevertheless come a long way since the heady days of the 1920s. Social anthropology no longer concentrated exclusively on small-scale societies. The historical division of labour between social anthropology and sociology, whereby sociologists studied 'us' (industrial societies) while anthropologists studied 'them', collapsed as social anthropologists increasingly did fieldwork 'at home'. Moreover, the methodology of social anthropology became more catholic due to the need to look beyond the village snapshot. What was, and is, left of the original project of social anthropology nevertheless remains substantial. The discipline still bases its intellectual legitimacy on its ability to represent other life worlds in their proper context. It retains a perspective 'from below', that is from the perspective of local social life – whether the locality in question is a stock exchange or a fishing community. Finally, social anthropology remains committed to comparison. This does not usually entail grand, global schemes aiming at establishing universal laws, but comparison – anecdotal or systematic, explicit or implicit – nevertheless remains an important technique in the production of anthropological knowledge.

A summary of some of the central current research areas in social anthropology may indicate where the discipline is going, and indicates both continuity and change.

Ethnicity, nationalism and identity politics

These phenomena, associated with modernity and social change, involve the politicization of culture and engage a classic social anthropological contrast between the instrumental and the emotional poles of symbols. Studies of these large-scale phenomena can also draw on earlier work on community integration and the political role of myth, as well as – in many cases – earlier ethnographic work among the same or neighbouring peoples.

The body, including medical anthropology

Pioneered by Mauss in the 1930s, the widespread study of the body as a social phenomenon is nevertheless recent. Important work on reproductive technologies and reconceptualizations of kinship due to these and other changes can draw extensively on detailed extant knowledge of kinship in all parts of the world. Medical anthropology, also a relatively new speciality, relates to a range of classical issues, from indigenous cosmologies to questions of cultural translation and power in intergroup relationships.

Material culture and consumption

The material was for many years marginal in social anthropology, which emphasized social relations. The recent interest in consumption and the symbolic qualities of objects, more often than not focused on modern complex societies, is nevertheless directly connected to classic economic anthropology as evident in the work of Mauss on gift exchange, of Malinowski on the *kula* ring, or of Barth on cultural norms regulating economic flows.

Globalization, movement and hybridity

At first glance, the most radical of the new empirical foci of social anthropology, the study of transnational flows, challenges several key assumptions from classic anthropology. It does not treat social life as spatially bounded, and makes it difficult if not impossible to delineate the boundaries of any society; it depicts cultural meaning as negotiable, changing and only par-

tially shared by people. It also reintroduces diffusionist thought, a tradition that was abandoned by the first generation of social anthropologists proper. Yet it can be shown that the questions raised in the anthropology of transnational flows arise from classic research, such as: What are the possibilities for stable collective identities and functioning social communities under circumstances of migration and cultural change? To which extent can societies be integrated given increasing ethnic and cultural complexity? How is cultural retention combined with change and outside influence in a migrant group? And which social boundaries remain operative in increasingly complex settings? The research methodologies used in studies of globalization are often network studies and participant observation, and social anthropologists always emphasize that globalization is in effect *globalocalization*: it is just as much a local as it is a global phenomenon.

Other contemporary tendencies might equally have been mentioned. Some social anthropologists are engaged in cognitive science, others in cultural history. Some study refugee issues, while others do research on local politics. Some theorize about constructions of nature, while others are busy creating a social anthropology of urbanism. Whatever the current research concerns, what keeps this diverse discipline together is its continuing commitment to seeing the world through the lens of local life.

THOMAS HYLLAND ERIKSEN
UNIVERSITY OF OSLO

References

Kuper, A. (1996) *Anthropology and Anthropologists: The Modern British School*, 3rd edn, London.
Leach, E. (1982) *Social Anthropology*, Glasgow.

Further reading

Barnard, A. (2000) *History and Theory in Anthropology*, Cambridge.
Eriksen, T.H. and Nielsen, F.S. (2001) *A History of Anthropology*, London.
Goody, J. (1995) *The Expansive Moment: The Rise of Social Anthropology in Britain and Africa, 1918–1970*, Cambridge.
Stocking, G.W. (1995) *After Tylor: British Social Anthropology, 1888–1951*, Madison, WI.
Vermeulen, H.F. and Roldan, A.A. (eds) (1995) *Fieldwork and Footnotes: Studies in the History of European Anthropology*, London.

SEE ALSO: anthropology; economic anthropology; ethnography; political anthropology

SOCIAL CHOICE

Social choice is concerned with the selection of options made by a group of individuals (for example members of a committee, members of a parliament or voters). An individual choice, where there are several criteria, may be considered as equivalent to social choice, the set of criteria replacing the set of individuals.

Social choice theory developed rapidly after the publication of works by Kenneth J. Arrow and Duncan Black at the end of the 1940s. However, its origin can be traced back to the analysis of voting by Condorcet and Borda a few years before the French Revolution (though Condorcet and Borda had medieval precursors), and to Bentham's utilitarianism.

The so-called *Condorcet paradox* can be easily described. Suppose that three persons, Ann, Brigitte and Charlotte, want to have dinner together in a restaurant. They have the choice of selecting one of three restaurants: a pizzeria, a Chinese restaurant and an Indian restaurant. They decide that they will select the restaurant on the basis of the following rule (hereafter *majority rule*): if the number of those who prefer restaurant A to restaurant B is greater than the number of those who prefer restaurant B to restaurant A, then restaurant A will be ranked before restaurant B. Ann prefers the pizzeria to the Chinese restaurant, and the Chinese restaurant to the Indian restaurant, and, since she is rational – as are her two friends – she also prefers the pizzeria to the Indian restaurant. Brigitte prefers the Chinese to the Indian restaurant, and the Indian to the pizzeria. Charlotte prefers the Indian restaurant to the pizzeria, and the pizzeria to the Chinese. Since two of them prefer the pizzeria to the Chinese restaurant, the pizzeria is ranked above the Chinese restaurant. Two of them prefer the Chinese restaurant to the Indian, so it is ranked above the Indian restaurant. But two of them prefer the Indian restaurant to the pizzeria, so the Indian restaurant is ranked above the pizzeria. The upshot is that the three women cannot find any restaurant that is ranked above the other two, and therefore fail to select a restaurant. One must remark that the

(possible) selection of an option is based upon the construction of a collective (social) ranking. The famous *Arrow's impossibility theorem* (1963) can be considered as a generalization of this paradox.

To simplify the presentation of Arrow's theorem, consider a finite set of options and a finite set of individuals. Each individual ranks the options from the best to the worst (with possible ties). A social welfare function associates a social ranking to a list of the individuals' rankings (a ranking for each individual). A first condition (call it *universality*) stipulates that all the possible individual rankings are admissible. With three options and three individuals, a classical combinatorial result is that, in this case, there are 13^{2197} social welfare functions. The following conditions will drastically reduce this number, in fact reduce it to 0. The condition of *independence of irrelevant alternatives* requires that the information used to socially rank two options is restricted to the individuals' rankings of these two options. For instance, if there are ten options, the fact that an individual ranks some option A first and another option B tenth is not relevant. Only the fact that A is ranked above B should be taken into account. The obtained social ranking between A and B would have been identical if this individual had ranked, say, A first and B second. The *weak Pareto principle* asserts that a unanimous ranking of two options must be reflected by the social ranking of these two options. The last condition requires that there is no *dictator*, i.e. no individual such that, for any option X and Y, X is socially ranked above Y whenever this individual ranks X above Y. If there are at least two individuals and three options, there is no social welfare function that satisfies these four conditions. Most of the results in modern social choice stem from Arrow's analysis.

Black's analysis (1958) was developed independently, at about the same time. In a kind of geometrical approach, Black proved that if the individuals' rankings are suitably restricted, majority rule selected a best option. More precisely, he assumes that the set of options is an interval of the real line and that the preference of each individual can be represented by a curve with a unique peak. As one moves away from the peak to the left and to the right (where this is possible) the preference decreases. The further one moves from the peak, the less preferred is the option.

(This condition is called *single-peakedness*.) He demonstrates that, given some mild restriction on the number of individuals, majority rule yields a transitive social preference, and that the best option is the point corresponding to the median peak among all the individuals' peaks. This is the basis of what is now called the median voter theorem, and Black's work is at the origin of most of the developments in mathematical politics. Arrow proposed a discrete version of single-peakedness and this discrete approach was the source of the analysis of domain restrictions (Gaertner 2001). Then, given single-peakedness, majority rule is a social welfare function satisfying independence of irrelevant alternatives and the weak Pareto principle (and, of course, non-dictatorship).

Among the main sources of other recent developments, one may consider Sen's (1970) result on the conflict between the weak Pareto principle and *assignments of rights to individuals*. He considers a function slightly more general than the Arrovian social welfare function – but assumes, to simplify, that it is a social welfare function – and showed that such a function does not exist if it must satisfy the weak Pareto principle and also the following condition: there are at least two individuals and, for each of them, two options such that the social ranking of the respective two options exactly reflects the respective individual's rankings of these two options. These two options could be options that differ only about characteristics specific to the respective individual (Mill's personal sphere). Sen's work is the first example of the introduction of concepts not related to preference or utility in social choice theory. Rights and freedom studies are now a very active domain within the subject.

Another major result due to Gibbard and Satterthwaite demonstrates that there is no social choice function – a function associating a unique option to the individuals' rankings – immune to individual strategic behaviour. An individual is said to *manipulate* the function for a given list of individuals' rankings if, in revealing ranking other than the one he or she has in the list, the function selects an option that he or she prefers to the one that the function would have initially selected. As an example of group manipulation (rather than individual manipulation as described above) consider a US presidential election in a given state with three candidates. A Republican

gains 49 per cent of the vote, a Democrat 48 per cent and a Green 3 per cent. The Republican wins. Now, assume that the Green voters prefer the Democrat to the Republican. Then if the Green voters had voted Democrat rather than Green, the Democrat would have 51 per cent of the votes and would have won. Gibbard–Satterthwaite stipulates that with at least three options, the only social choice function that cannot be manipulated is dictatorship (where a dictator is an individual whose first ranked option is systematically selected by the function).

Sen (1970) also pioneered an analysis based on a richer information about individuals' rankings than that permitted by Arrow's condition of independence of irrelevant alternatives. This approach (together with Harsanyi's work (Harsanyi 1977)) has been crucial in the axiomatic analysis of various concepts of moral philosophy including utilitarianism and Rawlsian principles.

It should be emphasized that social choice theory is strongly related to game theory (non-co-operative as in Gibbard–Satterthwaite's theorem) as well as co-operative game theory as in voting (or simple games) through solution concepts, bargaining theory – stemming from Nash's famous paper (1950) – fairness analysis and power measurement.

Finally, a major recent research programme deals with the scoring of voting rules. A scoring rule is based on scores attributed to options (candidates) on the basis of their rankings. These scores are added to determine the social ranking. The plurality rule used in the USA and in Great Britain provides that where a candidate is ranked first by an individual he gets one point and the other candidates get 0. Borda's rule, with k options and no ties, is the voting rule where the candidate ranked first gets $k-1$ points, the second $k-2$...and the last 0. Major contributions on scoring rules are due to Saari (see Saari 1995).

MAURICE SALLES
UNIVERSITÉ DE CAEN

References

Arrow, K.J. (1963) *Social Choice and Individual Values*, 2nd edn, New York.
Black, D. (1958) *Theory of Committees and Elections*, Cambridge, UK.
Gaertner, W. (2001) *Domain Conditions in Social Choice Theory*, Cambridge.
Gibbard, A. (1973) 'Manipulation of voting schemes: A general result', *Econometrica* 41: 587–602.

Harsanyi, J.C. (1977) *Rational Behavior and Bargaining Equilibrium in Games and Social Situations*, Cambridge, UK.

Nash, J. (1950) 'The bargaining problem', *Econometrica* 28: 155–62.

Saari, D.G. (1995) *Basic Geometry of Voting*, Heidelberg.

Satterthwaite, M.A. (1975) 'Strategy-proofness and Arrow's conditions: Existence and correspondence theorems for voting procedures and social wefare functions', *Journal of Economic Theory* 10: 187–217.

Sen, A.K. (1970) *Collective Choice and Social Welfare*, San Francisco.

Further reading

Arrow, K.J., Sen, A.K. and Suzumura, K. (2002) *Handbook of Social Choice and Welfare, Volume 1*, Amsterdam.

—— (2004) *Handbook of Social Choice and Welfare, Volume 2*, Amsterdam.

Dummett, M. (1984) *Voting Procedures*, Oxford.

Fleurbaey, M. (1996) *Théories économiques de la justice*, Paris.

Moulin, H. (2003) *Fair Division and Collective Welfare*, Cambridge, MA.

Roemer, J. (1996) *Theories of Distributive Justice*, Cambridge, MA.

SEE ALSO: bargaining; justice, distributive; Pareto efficiency; voting

SOCIAL CONSTRUCTION

The idea of social construction is fundamental to sociology and social anthropology, and has heavily influenced social psychology. It may be among social science's most enduring contributions to modern thought.

The expression itself is relatively novel, deriving from Berger and Luckmann (1967). Its intellectual origins can be found, *inter alia*, in Marx's arguments that consciousness is the product of social being, and that the ruling ideas are the ideas of the ruling class; in Durkheim's focus on 'social facts' as distinct from other kinds of facts; in Mannheim's writings on ideology; in European phenomenology and Schutz's concept of the 'life world'; and in Wittgenstein's arguments about language and knowledge. Perhaps the clearest early articulation of the idea can be found in the Chicago School of the 1920s, when W.I. Thomas insisted that if something is believed to be real it is real in its consequences, and is therefore socially real. People act in terms of what they know and believe.

Matters other than social theory have been at stake, however. The post-1945 assault on biological determinism – the women's movement, the emergence of a notion of human rights, anti-racism and anti-colonialism, the disability rights movement – has given impetus to, and derived intellectual sustenance from, the social constructionist perspective.

So, what does the notion of 'social construction' mean? Various things, is the answer. Epistemologically, for example, it may mean that our knowledge of the universe is dependent on our language and concepts. Reality as we know it is thus socially constructed. The less ambitious epistemological lesson is that social facts are not like natural facts, 'out there' to be discovered. Since they are produced and reproduced in the course of human interaction, a different approach is needed to understand them. With a different emphasis, social construction means that biology and nature have no part to play in our explanation and understanding of human behaviour. Human lives do not have to be the way they are, and the realities of human life are not biologically determined.

Perhaps the most common use of the expression, sociologically and otherwise, draws on all of the above. It is short on explicit conceptual rigour, and the impact of political debates about women, disability, sexuality and 'race' is clear. It says that human social phenomena are neither universal nor natural: they are historically, culturally and locally relative and contingent, and can be changed. Hacking (1999) calls this *strong constructionism*. It can be taken further to imply either that what is being described is not really real (i.e. *only* a social construction) or that human behaviour is definitively plastic (and perhaps infinitely so).

Each of these meanings of social construction is predicated upon one or both of two key assumptions. The first of these is that an absolute difference of kind exists between the 'natural world' and the 'human world', the distinct sphere of human experience and destiny. Searle offers a sophisticated version and critique of this position (1995), distinguishing between *brute facts* (an antelope, for example) and *social facts* (such as leather, cured meat or a bone knife-handle). Social facts he further divides into *functional facts* (the uses of which depend on their brute properties) and *institutional facts* (which are useful only because of collective and arbitrary definition, e.g. money or wedding rings). The distinction between the natural and the human world is established –

brute facts and social facts are differentiated – only to have to have the external discipline of brute properties reappear in the distinction between functional and institutional facts.

The second assumption is that all things human are contingent and relative in one way or another: there are no universal human truths. Hacking (1999) observes that this assumption often leads to *relativity of meaning* being confused with *lack of substance* or reality. He argues for the sharpest possible distinction between behaviour and the ideas and concepts used to name and understand it: between *reality* and *discourse about reality*. While some adult humans have, for example, always committed acts of violence, sexual or otherwise, on prepubertal humans, 'child abuse' as a notion is a recent phenomenon with a specific history. Hacking argues that since all discourse is, by definition, 'social', the expression 'social construction' is redundant. Although he emphasizes historical and local contingency and context, Hacking prefers to talk about 'making and moulding' rather than 'social construction'.

Arguably, however, neither of these assumptions is strictly necessary to social constructionism. Nor is it necessary to abandon the centrality of social construction for our understanding of the human world if we want to do more sociologically with biology than simply define it out of court. Rejecting the categorical distinction between the natural world and the human world, Jenkins argued that patriarchy, for instance, cannot be understood as a historical and thoroughly constructed institution without admitting the facts of human reproduction, fertility and sexuality, and gender dimorphism (males being bigger and stronger than females) (Jenkins 2002: 111–38). This is in broad sympathy with the 'corporeal feminist' argument, which points out that acknowledging the organic embodiment of sex does not necessarily mean that the social construction of gender should be neglected (Lovell 2000).

Although Hacking's logic may be impeccable, the notion of social construction, and the expression itself, remains vital to social science for two reasons. First, it reminds us that the complexities of human experience are not 'just there', they do not 'just happen'. The human world exists because of work and co-ordination: it is constructed and *requires* construction. Second, it reminds us of the enormous historical, cultural and local variability of the human world. Some

kind of anthropological relativism is epistemologically and ethically necessary if we are to deal with this. And, while most social scientists may not need reminding of these facts of human existence, much of the rest of the world, at one time or another, does.

RICHARD JENKINS
UNIVERSITY OF SHEFFIELD

References

Berger, P.L. and Luckmann, T. (1967) *The Social Construction of Reality*, London.
Hacking, I. (1999) *The Social Construction of What?* Cambridge, MA.
Jenkins, R. (2002) *Foundations of Sociology: Towards a Better Understanding of the Human World*, Basingstoke.
Lovell, T. (2000) 'Feminisms transformed?' in B.S. Turner (ed.) *The Blackwell Companion to Social Theory*, 2nd edn, Oxford.
Searle, J.R. (1995) *The Construction of Social Reality*, London.

Further reading

Gergen, K.J. (1999) *An Invitation to Social Construction*, London.
Sarbin, T.R. and Kitsuse, J.I. (eds) (1994) *Constructing the Social*, London.

SEE ALSO: relativism; science, sociology of

SOCIAL CONTRACT

Prefigured in the biblical account of God's covenants with Moses and Abraham that gave birth to the Jewish people, followed by intimations in Plato's *Republic* and then a number of medieval texts, the idea of a social contract came into prominence in the late sixteenth century, when it was invoked to justify resistance to tyranny. French Huguenot writers of the period, such as Philippe du Plessis Mornay in his *Vindiciae contra Tyrannos* of 1579, argued that the people's covenant to obey the word of God granted to their magistrates both the religious duty and the political right to oppose despots who broke their own oath of office to protect the subjects of their kingdoms. In Scotland, George Buchanan and others envisaged that this right of resistance in fact belonged to the people as a whole, who in exercising it gave warrant to the deposition of the Catholic Queen Mary. From its inception in this period of religious schism, the idea of a social contract was put forward by its advocates principally to check the abuse of royal power when it interfered in matters of faith and conscience. In circumstances when Catholics felt persecuted, Jesuit thinkers such as Juan de Mariana and Francisco Suárez also began around the same time to justify opposition to despotism, in portraying civil authority as restricted by the will of those over whom it was exercised. Through their notions of association that imposed constraints upon the powers of the state, advocates of the idea of a social contract around the end of the sixteenth century thus devised a political principle in a theological idiom, in the light of which it appeared that communities could be bound by governments of their own creation with constitutionally limited powers.

In the course of the seventeenth century, this idea came to be employed, especially by Hugo Grotius, Thomas Hobbes and Samuel Pufendorf, for precisely the opposite purpose – that is, as a justification for absolute sovereignty. In his *De jure belli ac pacis* of 1625, Grotius claimed that a whole people could agree to obey a king in the same manner that an individual might freely enslave himself, by alienating or transferring its freedom in perpetuity to a master. Pufendorf, in his *De jure naturae et gentium* of 1672, likewise derived his notion of the legitimacy of an absolutist monarchical state through the people's voluntary subjection to their ruler, while Hobbes had in the sixteenth chapter of his *Leviathan*, dating from 1651, meanwhile put this thesis somewhat differently. The people, he argued, were the real authors of the state, who, in transferring their rights to the sovereign and entrusting him to act on their behalf, made him their representative and the public impersonator of their will. Each of these writers portrayed the state's sovereign as established by the consent of its subjects through a covenant that created an unlimited power, without which, as Hobbes insisted, mankind would find itself in a state of nature that was in fact a state of war.

The chief critic of this theory of the social contract in the seventeenth century, John Locke, argued in his *Second Treatise on Government* of 1690 that the absolute and arbitrary power it legitimated was worse than the disease it was meant to avert. Not only would the protection of private property, which he took to be the main reason for men's entering civil society, be imperilled by a power that could expropriate it, but also the idea of liberty actually excluded such a pact of voluntary servitude, since slavery was always incompatible with freedom. Because men's bodies belonged only to God, they could not dispose of a right of life and death over themselves that they did not originally possess. Locke's own notion of a social contract thus reverted largely to that of the Huguenots a century earlier, radicalized by his introducing a conception of government based upon trust and a right of revolution against tyrants that would come to be regarded as a justification of the Glorious Revolution of 1688, although he had in fact completed his text some years earlier.

The most notable social contract theory of the eighteenth century was that of Jean-Jacques Rousseau in the work of 1762 that he entitled the *Social Contract*, where he contrived to draw its absolutist and liberal strains together. Rousseau agreed with Hobbes that sovereignty must be indivisible and inalienable if a state's public order was to be maintained. But he also agreed with Locke and contended against Grotius, in particular, that the notion of voluntary subjection was incompatible with freedom. Through the social contract, properly understood, the people gained rather than lost their liberty in civil society, he argued, by exercising sovereignty for themselves. With this doctrine of popular sovereignty Rousseau transformed a theory of resistance into a theory of supremacy; more than any thinker of the age of Enlightenment it made him appear the prophet of the French Revolution of 1789. The chief mistake of his absolutist precursors had been to confuse sovereignty, which was always general, with government, which always dealt with particulars. Unlike sovereignty, government was not formed by contract; his forerunners had confused a pact of association with a pact of submission.

In his *Discourse on the Origins of Inequality* of 1755, his principal contribution to the philosophy of history, Rousseau had drawn an altogether different portrait of the original contract from which the rule of law in civil society was derived. He there depicted Locke's argument – that such a contract was devised to render private property secure – as superficially plausible, but only because it was a hoax perpetrated in society by the rich upon the poor. To avoid society's degeneration into war when property was scarce, the rich would have persuaded the poor to repudiate their right to share the wealth that men of property enjoyed, so that in exchange for peace and protection of their lives, everyone would have run 'headlong into their chains, believing they had secured their liberty'. Rousseau's critique of civilization, no less than his image of popular sovereignty, was thus drawn around an image of the social contract.

In virtually all its formulations the idea of a social contract envisaged that through popular consent mankind's passage out of the state of nature was made possible, thereby contradicting Aristotle's notion that politics was itself natural to man. Robert Filmer had in his *Patriarcha* of 1680 claimed that the idea of a prepolitical natural state was a fiction, and from different perspectives numerous eighteenth-century philosophers such as Montesquieu, Hume and Smith agreed, challenging the whole social contract tradition for its spurious supposition of a non-existent world prior to society. Although the idea of the social contract became unfashionable in the nineteenth century, John Rawls's various formulations of a theory of justice whose principles could be framed behind a veil of ignorance have transported some of its elements to contemporary political thought. In 1974 the British Labour Party's pact with the unions that helped return it to power was described as a social contract.

ROBERT WOKLER
YALE UNIVERSITY

References

Hobbes, T. (1996 [1651]) *Leviathan*, ed. R. Tuck, New York.
Locke, J. (1967 [1690]) *The Two Treatises of Government*, ed. P. Laslett, Cambridge.
Rousseau, J.J. (1997 [1762]) *The Social Contract and other Later Political Writings*, ed. G. Gourevitch, Cambridge.

Further reading

Allen, J.W. (1957 [1928]) *A History of Political Thought in the Sixteenth Century*, London.
Gough. J.W. (1978 [1936]) *The Social Contract: A Critical Study of Its Development*, 2nd edn, Westport, CT.
Plamenatz, J. (1992) *Man and Society*, Vol. I: *From the Middle Ages to Locke*, 2nd edn, London.
Skinner, Q. (1978) *The Foundations of Modern Political Thought*, Vol. 2: *The Age of the Reformation*, Cambridge.
Tuck, R. (1979) *Natural Rights Theories: Their Origin and Development*, Cambridge.

SEE ALSO: equality; Hobbes; human rights; justice, distributive; Locke; Rawls; Rousseau

SOCIAL CONTROL

The concept of social control is widely and variously used in the social sciences. In sociology and anthropology it is used as a generic term to describe the processes that help produce and maintain orderly social life. In the specialist field of criminology, it usually carries a narrower meaning, referring to the management of deviance by criminal justice, social welfare and mental health agencies. Sometimes the term takes on a critical sense, for example in social history and women's studies, where the notion of social control has been used to describe the subtle constraints and forms of domination exercised by institutions such as the family or the welfare state.

The expansiveness of the social control concept has meant that it has tended to work as an orienting device for thinkers and researchers, rather than as an explanatory tool of any refinement or precision. Sociologists in the early twentieth century developed the concept to explore the problem of social order in the industrialized, urbanized societies then emerging. Criminologists in the 1960s used the term to redirect attention away from an exclusive focus upon the individual criminal and to stress the role that social rules and reactions play in the process of criminalizing particular behaviours and persons. Social historians in the 1970s employed the notion of social control as a means of subverting and revising orthodox accounts of social reform that had tended to overlook the hidden class-control aspects of many reform programmes.

Once such reorientations have been achieved, however, the concept of social control often ceases to be useful and gives way to more specific questions about the different forms, objectives, supports and effects of the control practices under scrutiny. Like many sociological concepts, social control is a subject of continuing contestation, either by those who deny the appropriateness of this approach to particular phenomena, or else by those who find the term insufficiently precise to do the analytical and critical work required. That the concept is also and inevitably tied into political debates – either as part of a conservative quest for social order, or else in support of a radical critique of social institutions – serves to deepen the controversy surrounding its use. So too does the semantic proximity of the term to cognate concepts such as socialization, regulation, domination, power and culture. Social scientists who use this concept are obliged to define it for their own purposes or else invite misunderstanding.

Given this conceptual state of affairs, the most illuminating way of understanding the term is to summarize its intellectual history (Coser 1982; Janowitz 1975a) bearing in mind that contemporary usage draws upon many of these past conceptions, and often reinvents under a different name many of the ideas and distinctions that earlier writers first established.

The classical social theorists of the nineteenth and early twentieth centuries – Comte, Marx, Durkheim, Weber, Simmel, etc. – did not employ the term social control, although their work certainly dealt with issues of social regulation, enforcement of norms and class domination that social control theorists were later to address. The concept was first explicitly developed by the sociologists of the early-twentieth-century USA, particularly E.A. Ross and W.G. Sumner, who sought to identify the myriad ways in which the group exerts its influence upon the conduct of the individual. Ross's (1901) *Social Control* took as its starting-point the shift from small-scale, agrarian, face-to-face communities to dense, industrialized urban societies, and argued that this shift entailed a qualitative transformation in the bonds that made social order possible. Whereas the earlier *Gemeinschaft* communities had been held together by what Ross regarded as a 'living tissue' of natural controls such as sympathy, sociability and a shared sense of justice, social control in the newer *Gesellschaft* societies was a matter of 'rivets and screws' that had to be consciously created and maintained if order was to be achieved within these complex and conflictual social settings. Ross's work catalogued and anatomized these foundations of order, dealing in turn with public opinion, law, belief, education, religion, art and social ceremony. In much the same way, Sumner's (1906) *Folkways* described how usages, manners, customs and morals provided the basic underpinning of social regulation, upon which the more formal system of law was built.

Underlying this early work is a Hobbesian conception of individual human nature as disruptive and anti-social, to be reined in by the imposition of group controls and sanctions – as well as an anxiety that deliberate social control was more than ever necessary in burgeoning metropolises such as Chicago and New York, with their masses of newly arrived immigrants and diverse ethnic groups. Later work, by writers such as G.H. Mead (1925) and C.H. Cooley (1920), developed a different conception of the individual's relation to society in which social control was accomplished not by the suppression of individuality but rather in its very creation. For these writers, the self emerges through a process of interaction with others, out of which develops the individual's capacity to take the point of view of other people. To the extent that this socialization process is successful, individuals are constituted as social actors, internalizing the norms of the wider society ('the generalized other'), and adapting their conduct to the various roles demanded by social interaction. Thus the social control that permits co-ordination and integration operates in and through the individual, rather than over against individuality, and the internal self-control of the individual is as much a social matter as the rules and regulations that constrain individuals from the outside. (In somewhat different language, and from somewhat different premises, Durkheim, Freud and Piaget had come to similar conclusions: see Coser (1982). See also Elias's (1979; 1981 [1939]) *The Civilizing Process*, which sets out a sociohistorical account of how social controls and self-controls evolve over time.)

For Chicago sociologists such as Park and Burgess (1925), 'all social problems turn out finally to be problems of social control'. By this they meant that the practical problems of administering social institutions and governing populations, as well as the theoretical problems of understanding the dynamics of social organizations, turn on the ability of the analyst or policymaker to comprehend the mechanisms that permit groups to regulate their own activities without recourse to violence and in accordance with specified moral ideals. In this conception, social control is contrasted with coercive control (and, indeed, with minority or class domination) and is viewed as an integral part of purposive social planning and the rationalization of social institutions. Social controls of this kind can take either positive and negative forms, operating to elicit and evoke action in individuals through rewards, persuasion or education, or else to restrain and repress by means of gossip, satire, laughter and criticism (see Lumley 1925). For the early US Pragmatists and Progressives – and, indeed, for a few later sociologists such as Janowitz (1975b) and Melossi (1990) – social control was thus an ideal to strive after. (One version of this ideal was the welfare state, which utilized controls such as Keynesian demand management, insurance-based protections, personal social services, and processes of democratic opinion formation, in order to govern in accordance with an ethic of solidarity and security.) By the 1970s, many writers had come to regard the history of twentieth-century rationalization and social engineering in a much more negative light, with the consequence that social control came to be regarded by some as a regrettable feature of social organization and a subject for critical attack.

In anthropology, the issue of social control was first explicitly addressed as part of a controversy about the social organization of 'primitive' societies. In his account of *Crime and Custom in Savage Society* (1926) Malinowski attacked the then orthodox view that small-scale, preindustrial societies were held together by virtue of the 'spontaneous obedience' of group members, whose individuality was stifled by the operation of a harshly conformist *conscience collective* (cf. Durkheim 1984 [1893]). Against this view, Malinowski argued that social control was embedded in the reciprocity of routine social relations, and was supported by the self-interest of each individual in maintaining his or her place in the system of exchange and reputation, as well as by the ceremonial enactment of social obligations that ensured that individual deviance was made visible to others. Social control involved not only the individual internalization of social norms but also the active pursuit of self-interest and the occasional deployment of coercive sanctions. As Etzioni (1961) later pointed out, social organizations can be distinguished in terms of the three modes of control that Malinowski identifies. Thus prisons, mental hospitals and concentration camps are founded primarily (though not exclusively: see Sykes 1958) on *coercive* controls; organizations such as the workplace depend upon the *utilitarian* controls of remuneration; while others – such as religious, voluntary and political associations – maintain their cohesion

primarily through the *normative* commitment of their members.

In the 1950s Parsons (1951) defined the theory of social control as 'the analysis of those processes in the social system which tend to counteract...deviant tendencies'. Social control here refers to a subsystem or, at most, a special remedial aspect of social relations, rather than the patterning effect of social relations as such. This narrower usage has tended to prevail in the specialist field of criminology, where it has spawned a large literature analysing the effects – especially the unintended effects – of the actions of 'agencies of social control' such as the police, prisons, psychiatrists, etc. (Though Hirschi's (1969) influential control theory of crime utilizes the term in its older sociological sense to argue that the key variable in explaining offending is the strength of the social bonds that tie individuals into patterns of conformity.) In the 1960s, Lemert (1967) and Becker (1963) transformed that field by arguing that 'social control leads to deviance' rather than the reverse, and by stimulating research on the ways in which the 'labelling' and 'stigmatizing' of deviant conduct by officials tends to reinforce and amplify deviant identities and behaviour.

In the 1970s, this critical attitude towards the practices of social control came to take a more radical form, partly under the influence of Marxist theories of the state, and partly as a result of the new social history that argued that the emergence of modern institutions such as the reformatory prison, the asylum and the social welfare system ought to be seen not as humane and progressive reforms but instead as strategic measures to consolidate the subordination and control of the lower classes (Donajgrodzki 1977). In the 1980s there emerged a new specialism, the sociology of social control, focused upon the developmental forms and functioning of the 'control apparatus' (Cohen 1985; Cohen and Scull 1983). An influential thesis that has emerged from this work – and which resonates with the dystopian themes of Orwell's (1949) *Nineteen Eighty-Four* and Huxley's (1932) *Brave New World* – asserts that, since the 1960s, there has been an 'increasing expansion, widening, dispersal, and invisibility' of the 'net of social control' (Cohen 1985: 14). The assumption underlying this thesis is that modern society is increasingly governed by reference to expert knowledge, classification systems and professional specialists in the administration of deviance. Styles of social control may change (e.g. the shift from reliance upon closed institutions to greater use of community-based provision for mentally ill people), as may the ideologies that gloss these practices (e.g. the decline of 'rehabilitative' philosophies in the penal system), but the build-up of the control apparatus is viewed as a secular trend.

Critics of this version of the social control concept (see Miller and Rose 1986) object to the implication that diverse strategies and practices of governance – operating in different social sites, involving different personnel, different techniques and different objectives – can somehow be said to share a common source (usually the state or the ruling class) and a common purpose (integration or domination). To lump all of these together as social control is to impart a spurious unity to a variety of problems and practices that may have little in common. Others (e.g. Thompson 1981; van Krieken 1991) object to the implication that social controls are *imposed upon* the subordinate classes, rather than negotiated or even embraced by the groups concerned, and to the frequently made assumption that the social control objectives implicit in a reform programme are automatically realized just because laws are passed or agencies set up. A closer attention to the origins and operation of the 'control' practices in question, and to the actors and agencies involved, suggests a more complex and dynamic process, in which specific regulatory practices are sites of competing interests and strategic struggles, rather than blunt controls imposed by one group upon another. Donzelot's (1979) *The Policing of Families*, which traces the emergence of modern welfare institutions in nineteenth-century France, is exemplary in this respect (see also Rose 1999: Ch.7 and Garland 2001).

DAVID GARLAND
NEW YORK UNIVERSITY

References

Becker, H. (1963) *Outsiders*, New York.
Cohen, S. (1985) *Visions of Social Control*, Cambridge, UK.
Cohen, S. and Scull, A. (eds) (1983) *Social Control and the State*, Oxford.
Cooley, C.H. (1920) *Social Process*, New York.
Coser, L.A. (1982) 'The notion of control in sociological theory', in J.P. Gibbs (ed.) *Social Control: Views from the Social Sciences*, Beverly Hills, CA.
Donajgrodzki, A.P. (ed.) (1977) *Social Control in Nineteenth Century Britain*, London.
Donzelot, J. (1979) *The Policing of Families*, London.
Durkheim, E. (1984 [1893]) *The Division of Labour in Society*, trans. W.D. Halls, London.
Elias, N. (1979; 1981 [1939]) *The Civilizing Process*, 2 vols, London.
Etzioni, A. (1961) *A Comparative Analysis of Complex Organisations*, New York.
Garland, D. (2001) *The Culture of Control: Crime and Social Order in Contemporary Society*, Oxford.
Hirschi, T. (1969) *Causes of Delinquency*, Berkeley, CA.
Huxley, A. (1932) *Brave New World*, London.
Janowitz, M. (1975a) 'Sociological theory and social control', *American Journal of Sociology* 81.
—— (1975b) *Social Control of the Welfare State*, Chicago.
Lemert, E. (1967) *Human Deviance, Social Problems and Social Control*, Englewood Cliffs, NJ.
Lumley, F.E. (1925) *Means of Social Control*, New York.
Malinowski, B. (1926) *Crime and Custom in Savage Society*, London.
Mead, G. H. (1925) 'The genesis of the self and social control', *International Journal of Ethics* 35.
Melossi, D. (1990) *The State of Social Control*, Cambridge, UK.
Miller, P. and Rose, N. (eds) (1986) *The Power of Psychiatry*, Cambridge, UK.
Orwell, G. (1949) *Nineteen Eighty-Four*, London.
Park, R.E. and Burgess, E.W. (1925) *Introduction to the Science of Sociology*, Chicago.
Parsons, T. (1951) *The Social System*, London.
Rose, N. (1999) *Powers of Freedom*, Cambridge.
Ross, E.A. (1901) *Social Control*, New York.
Sumner, W.G. (1906) *Folkways*, Boston, MA.
Sykes, G. (1958) *The Society of Captives*, Princeton, NJ.
Thompson, F.M.L. (1981) 'Social control in Victorian Britain', *Economic History Review* 34.
van Krieken, R. (1991) 'The poverty of social control: Explaining power in the historical sociology of the welfare state', *Sociological Review* 39.

SEE ALSO: criminology; penology; police and policing; power

SOCIAL DEMOCRACY

Social democracy is a party-based political movement, inspired by socialism, which has held different meanings in different times and places. Not all social democratic parties have adopted the name, the most common alternatives being Socialist Party (France) and Labour Party (Holland, Great Britain and Norway).

Three historical phases can be distinguished: from 1875 when the German Social Democratic Party (SPD) was founded to 1914; between the World Wars; and the period since 1945.

The first period, one of expansion and consolidation, coincided with European industrialization and the formation of a large proletariat. Social democrats (or socialists – the terms were then interchangeable) were then members of centralized and nationally based parties, loosely organized under the banner of the Second International (1889) supporting a form of Marxism popularized by Friedrich Engels, August Bebel and Karl Kautsky. This held that capitalist relations of production would dominate the whole of society, eliminating small producers until only two antagonistic classes, capitalists and workers, would face each other. A major economic crisis would eventually open the way to socialism and common ownership of the means of production. Meanwhile, social democrats, in alliance with trade unions, would fight for democratic goals such as universal suffrage and a welfare state, and traditional workers' demands such as a shorter working day. It was assumed that in democratic countries power could be achieved peacefully, though participation in bourgeois governments was ruled out. Some (e.g. Rosa Luxemburg) proposed the mass general strike as the best revolutionary weapon.

The SPD provided the main organizational and ideological model though its influence was less pronounced in Southern Europe. In Britain the powerful trade unions tried to influence the Liberals rather than forming a separate working-class party until, in 1900, they created a Labour Party that was never Marxist and adopted a socialist programme (defined as the common ownership of the means of production, distribution and exchange) only in 1918.

The First World War and the October Revolution divided the movement, setting the supporters of Lenin's Bolsheviks against the reformist social democrats, most of whom had backed their national governments during the war. Thereafter the rivalry of social democrats and communists was interrupted only occasionally, as in the mid-1930s, in order to unite against fascism. Between the wars socialists and social democrats formed governments in various countries including Britain, Belgium and Germany. In Sweden, where social democrats have been more successful than elsewhere, they governed uninterruptedly from 1932 to 1976.

After 1945, while in Northern Europe socialists called themselves social democrats, in other countries, notably in Britain, France and Italy,

social democrat was the label given to right-wing socialists who sided with the USA in the Cold War, objected to extensive nationalization and were hostile to Marxism. In practice the differences between various tendencies were never as significant as internal doctrinal debates suggest. Eventually all social democratic parties discarded Marxism, accepted the mixed economy, loosened their links with the trade unions and abandoned the idea of an ever-expanding nationalized sector. In the 1970s and 1980s they adopted some of the concerns of middle-class radicals, such as feminism and environmentalism. Socialism was no longer a goal at the end of a process of social transformation but the process itself, in which power and wealth would gradually be redistributed according to principles of social justice and equality – a position advocated by Eduard Bernstein (1993 [1899]) in the 1890s. The success of capitalism in the 1950s favoured such revisionism, enshrined in the SPD at its Bad Godesberg Conference in 1959 and popularized in Britain by Anthony Crosland (1956). All social democrats assumed that continuous economic growth would sustain a thriving public sector, assure full employment and fund a burgeoning welfare state. These assumptions corresponded so closely to the actual development of European societies that the period 1945–73 has sometimes been referred as the era of 'social democratic consensus'. Significantly, it coincided with the 'golden age' of capitalism.

Since 1973, left-wing parties obtained power where they had never held it before, in Portugal, Spain, Greece and France (except briefly in 1936–7). But social democracy faced a major crisis of ideas. Contributing factors were the end of continuous economic growth, massive unemployment (which made the welfare state more difficult to fund), global economic interdependence (which made national macroeconomic management inadequate), popular resistance against high levels of taxation, a sharp fall in the size of the factory-based proletariat, and the challenge of neo-liberal and anti-statist ideas of deregulation and privatization. The collapse of communism and the transformation of communist parties into social democratic ones provided little comfort for social democrats when the ideology of the free market appeared stronger than ever before.

Strong social democratic parties have remained substantially confined to Europe or to countries whose population is or was mainly of European extraction such as Australia, New Zealand and Israel. The USA is the main exception to this rule – something that has often puzzled socialist theorists who wrongly assumed that industrialization would always be associated with a strong socialist movement. The Japanese Social Democratic Party has always been in opposition except in 1993 when it led, albeit briefly, a governing coalition. In Indonesia, after gaining independence from the Dutch, there was a relatively strong left that included both socialists and communists, but this was annihilated in 1965 following the anti-communist military take-over led by Suharto. No socialist tradition remained to take advantage of the return to democracy in the 1990s. In Latin America only Chile produced a significant socialist party, strong enough to survive underground after the military takeover of 1973 and be elected to power after the end of the dictatorship. In 1990s Brazil, after years of military dominance, Fernando Henrique Cardoso's new social democratic party won the presidential election, but his social democratic credentials were in dispute as he found himself veering between neo-liberalism and social reforms. His more radical successor, Luis Inácio Lula da Silva, generally known as Lula, won the presidential elections in 2002 at the head of a recently created Workers Party. Lula himself was a trade union leader and his new party has considerable support from organized labour. This is not a necessary sign of leftism, especially in Latin America where the most important political movement supported by the trade unions was Argentina's right-wing populist party founded by Juan Perón, whose influence outlasted its creator.

Socialist ideas, though they seldom led to the formation of significant social democratic parties on the European pattern, greatly influenced independence and anti-colonial movements, notably the National Congress Party in India, the African National Congress in South Africa and other postcolonial regimes. When in power African socialist parties concentrated on nation-building and social reform often at the expense of democratic rule and civil rights. Several parties in Southeast Asia have been influenced by social democracy, particularly after the economic crisis of the late 1990s. Notable examples of Asian parties and leaders that might be defined as social democrat have been Kim Dae Jung, elected president of South Korea in 1998, and Chen Shui-bian, the leader of the Progressive People's Party of Taiwan elected president in 2000.

The collapse of communism in the Soviet Union and in Eastern and Central Europe led to the transformation of many of the former communist parties into social democratic parties. Their supporters were increasingly concerned that the spread of neo-liberal ideas would seriously impair public services, health care and education.

The defence of the welfare state and its reform, rather than its expansion – let alone the establishment of a vast public sector – is now the trait uniting social democratic parties. A considerable part of their previous ideological commitments has been abandoned. Though it was widely claimed, in the wake of the collapse of communism, that social democratic parties were in crisis too, they returned to power in unprecedented number. By the end of the 1990s they were in power in almost all member states of the European Union. In the first few years of the millennium the situation has become more fluid and permits fewer generalizations.

Differences between various parties and leaders of the left are often emphasized by the media. In reality comparisons are difficult. Political parties are constrained by national traditions, economic circumstances and, above all, by the institutional system. Important policy differences have always divided the left throughout the world, even in Western Europe, in spite of a common past and inherited traditions. Some socialist parties have been strongly pro-USA, while others kept themselves and their countries out of the Atlantic Alliance; some were enthusiastically pro-European, while others remained sceptical about the benefits of an integrated Europe. Nevertheless a remarkable convergence of the European left has occurred over the last 15 years under a new moderate leadership advocating broadly centrist policies known in Britain as 'the Third Way', *la Gauche plurielle* in France, *Neue Mitte* in Germany and the *Polder Model* in the Netherlands. The new line is that inflation is more dangerous than unemployment and that socialists should be pro-business. If one looks beyond the vicissitudes of electoral politics and the constant passages from opposition to government and vice-versa, there is much to support the view that social democracy is moribund. Socialism – as represented by the social democratic parties – has not only lost its original anti-capitalist outlook but is also coming to terms, albeit painfully, with accepting that, in the age of globalization, capitalism could not be adequately controlled, let alone abolished, in individual countries.

DONALD SASSOON
QUEEN MARY COLLEGE,
UNIVERSITY OF LONDON

References

Bernstein, E. (1993 [1899]) *The Preconditions of Socialism*, ed. H. Tudor, Cambridge, UK.
Crosland, A. (1956) *The Future of Socialism*, London.

Further reading

Anderson, P. and Camiller, P. (eds) (1994) *Mapping the West European Left*, London.
Eley, G. (2002) *Forging Democracy: The History of the Left in Europe, 1850–2000*, Oxford.
Glyn, A. (ed.) (2001) *Social Democracy in Neoliberal Times: The Left and Economic Policy since 1980*, Oxford.
Sassoon, D. (1997) *One Hundred Years of Socialism*, London.
Schorske, C. (1972) *German Social Democracy 1905–1917: The Development of the Great Schism*, New York.

SEE ALSO: communism; socialism

SOCIAL EXCLUSION

The problem of social exclusion is a central concern within the European Union, it is a key term in the policies of New Labour and, although less frequently used in North America, parallel discourses are present in the major arenas of social policy. It is a term that is flexible and somewhat amorphous in use, yet there are core features that separate it out from previous notions such as poverty or marginalization. First, it is multidimensional: social exclusion can involve economic, political and spatial exclusion as well as lack of access to specific areas such as information, medical provision, housing, policing, security, etc. These dimensions are seen to interrelate and reinforce each other: overall they involve exclusion in what are seen as the 'normal' areas of participation of full citizenship (Percy-Smith 2000). Second, social exclusion is conceived as a social not an individual problem. It contrasts with earlier postwar notions that treated marginality as a problem of isolated

dysfunctional individuals. Rather it is a collective phenomenon, hence its association with a posited underclass that recalls the discourse about the dangerous classes of Victorian times rather than the debates of the 1950s and 1960s about the dysfunctional families of the welfare state. Third, social exclusion is regarded not as a particular local problem, but as a development that has global roots. It is a function of the impact of the rapid changes in the labour market, the decline of manufacturing industries, the rise in a more fragmented service sector, and the creation of structural unemployment in particular areas where industry has shut down. It is thus a systemic problem: global in its causes, local in its impact (see Byrne 1999). Fourth, the concept of social exclusion suggests the imperative of inclusion. Those who use it do not wish the excluded to languish outside the sphere of citizenship, and they seek to generate opportunities for the excluded, whether by changing their motivation and capacity or by making new openings available to them.

This being said there are important differences and political divergent interpretations of social exclusion. There would seem to be three basic positions on agency:

1   That which blames the individuals concerned for their lack of motivation and their self-exclusion from society as a whole, although the ultimate responsibility for this exclusion is placed at the doors of the welfare state, which is seen as engendering a state of 'dependency' where, for example, even if the jobs are available out there the underclass does not want to take them. The classic example of this position is the work of Charles Murray (1984).

2   That which sees the problems as a sort of hydraulic failure of the system to provide jobs, a failure that leads to a situation of social isolation in which people lose not the motive to work but the capacity to find work because of lack of positive role models. Direct exclusion (for example, because of racism) is explicitly ruled out as a primary reason for social exclusion. The classic texts here are the work of William Julius Wilson: *The Truly Disadvantaged* (1987) and *When Work Disappears* (1996).

3   Finally there is a commentary that stresses the active rejection of the underclass by

society: through the downsizing of industry, the stigmatization of the workless and the stereotyping of an underclass that is criminogenic and drug ridden. The images evoked in this discourse are frequently racialized and prejudiced.

The inclusionary policies of parties such as New Labour tend to be constructed around a fusion of the first two positions (see Social Exclusion Unit 1999, 2001; cf. Young and Matthews 2003). However, the first position smacks of the ideology of blaming the poor for their poverty (see Bauman 2000; Colley and Hodgkinson 2001), while the second ignores the active process of exclusion inherent in late modern societies (see Young 2003).

Substantially, the concept of social exclusion has been criticized for its dualistic nature and for the loss of the dimension of class. Thus, the discourse of social exclusion has encapsulated within it a notion of a dualism of the included over and against the excluded. The chief flaws of this conception are:

1   *Homogeneity* – it suggests a homogenous group of people in the category of the excluded, whereas the term could be loosely applied to young and old, the temporarily poor, etc. (Gans 1995).

2   *Social immobility* – the presumption of a fairly static underclass is misleading. There is in fact a great deal of social mobility across categories (see Hills *et al.* 2002).

3   *Fixed locality and separate morality* – the concept gives the impression that there is a group of people who are effectively outcasts, spatially cut off from the rest of society, and perhaps with different values and motivations. In fact, no such spatial segregation occurs (physical mobility in and out of the ghetto, for example, is frequent) and values are shared with the wider society (see Young 1999; Nightingale 1993). Most urban areas have a mixed population, many of whom are in work (Hagedorn 1991; Newman 1999).

4   *Focus on poverty and deprivation* – the notion of a socially excluded underclass conveys the false idea that the majority of social problems are located in particular urban areas. In fact, problems exist across the city. Most of the socially excluded do not live in the poorest areas (Mooney and Danson 1997). If, then, a rough estimate of say 20 per cent of the population is said to be excluded and segregated, while the rest of the population is assumed to be happily integrated, this massively underestimates the economic and social problems of those in the wider society. It also suggests that if only the socially excluded would make the transition from the zones of exclusion to the inclusive world of mainstream society, the rest of their problems would vanish. Most importantly, the notion of social exclusion carries with it the implication that the problem is a Durkheimian one of a failure of integration, rather than one that requires a socialist approach that would emphasize problems of class. That is, globalization is seen as having resulted in problems of social cohesion – the issue being those left behind by change – rather than exacerbating previously existing class divisions (Levitas 1996).

John Andersen argues that this notion of social exclusion involves a major conceptual transformation:

> a change of focus in the poverty and inequality discourse from a vertical to a horizontal perspective. The shift of focus can to some extent also be described as a shift from Marxist and Weberian tradition of class and status analysis to a Durkheimian 'anomie-integration' discourse.
>
> (1999: 129)

This widely accepted assertion is incorrect on two levels. First, it exaggerates the extent to which class-oriented redistributive policies are absent in official policy documents (see, e.g., Social Exclusion Unit 2001). Second, it is unwise to dismiss a concern for integration and citizenship. This has formed the basis of French social inclusion policies (see Pitts 2003) and is directly aimed at reducing the problems of racism, 'othering' and active social exclusion both within civil society and by the criminal justice system. These issues are neglected in the majority of accounts of social exclusion. What is needed are policies that address both the problems of economic exclusion, on the one hand, and social and political exclusion, on the other (Young and Matthews 2003).

JOCK YOUNG
MIDDLESEX UNIVERSITY

References

Andersen, J. (1999) 'Social and system integration and the underclass', in I. Gough and G. Olofsson (eds) *Capitalism and Social Cohesion*, New York.

Bauman, Z. (2000) 'Social uses of law and order', in D. Garland and R. Sparks (eds) *Criminology and Social Theory*, Oxford.

Byrne, D. (1999) *Social Exclusion*, Buckingham.

Colley, H. and Hodgkinson, P. (2001) 'Problems with "Bridging the Gap": The reversal of structure and agency in addressing social exclusion', *Critical Social Policy* 21(3): 335–59.

Gans, H. (1995) *The War against the Poor*, New York.

Hagedorn, J. (1991) 'Gangs, neighborhoods and public policy', *Social Problems* 38(4): 429–42.

Hills, J., LeGrand, J. and Pichaud, D. (eds) (2002) *Understanding Social Exclusion*, Oxford.

Levitas, R. (1996) 'The concept of social exclusion and the new Durkheimian hegemony', *Critical Social Policy* 16(46): 5–20.

Mooney, G. and Danson, M. (1997) 'Beyond culture city: Glasgow as a dual city', in N. Jewson and S. Macgregor (eds) *Transforming Cities*, New York.

Murray, C. (1984) *Losing Ground*, New York.

Newman, K. (1999) *No Shame in My Game*, New York.

Nightingale, C. (1993) *On the Edge*, New York.

Percy-Smith, J. (2000) 'The contours of social exclusion', in J. Percy-Smith (ed.) *Policy Responses to Social Exclusion*, Buckingham.

Pitts, J. (2003) *The New Politics of Youth and Crime*, Lyme Regis, Dorset.

Social Exclusion Unit (1999) *Bringing Britain Together*, London.

—— (2001) *Preventing Social Exclusion*, London.

Wilson, W.J. (1987) *The Truly Disadvantaged*, Chicago.

—— (1996) *When Work Disappears*, New York.

Young, J (1999) *The Exclusive Society*, London.

—— (2003) 'Merton with energy, Katz with structure', *Theoretical Criminology* 7(3): 389–414.

Young, J. and Matthews, R. (2003) 'New Labour, crime control and social exclusion', in R. Matthews and J. Young (eds) *The New Politics of Crime and Punishment*, Cullompton, Devon.

SEE ALSO: deviance; disability; poverty; social problems; stigma

SOCIAL HISTORY

The most famous definition of social history is attributed to G.M. Trevelyan: 'history with the politics left out'. Like many often repeated quotes it is a misquotation. What Trevelyan (1942) actually wrote in the introduction to his *English Social History* was not so silly: 'Social history might be defined negatively as the history of a people with the politics left out.' He went on to suggest that this was an inadequate definition, but since so many works of history had consisted of politics with society left out there was a case for redressing the balance, for 'without social history, economic history is barren and political history is unintelligible'. He went on:

> social history does not merely provide the required link between economic and political history. Its scope may be defined as the daily life of the inhabitants of the land in past ages: this includes the human as well as the economic relation of different classes to one another, the character of family and household life, the conditions of labour and leisure, the attitude of man to nature, the culture of each age as it arose out of these general conditions of life and took ever-changing forms in religion, literature and music, architecture, learning and thought.

Trevelyan sought in his survey of six centuries to retrieve what he could of the lives of rich and poor, women and men, children and parents, to analyse as well as to tell a story, seeking to define and to celebrate the characteristics of Englishness as a contribution to wartime morale-building. He was preoccupied with the problems of coherence and periodization in social history that 'cannot like the web of political history be held together by the framework of well-known names of kings, Parliaments and wars'; aware that important changes in attitudes and practices (towards childrearing for example) occurred gradually, the old surviving alongside, and interacting with, the new. These preoccupations have endured.

Although, as Trevelyan indicated, the writing of history had previously been dominated by political narrative, alternative strands had emerged. First, in Britain social history developed along with economic history. The first generation of classics in economic history written in the interwar years, a striking number of them by women, including Eileen Power, professor of economic history at the London School of Economics (to whom Trevelyan dedicated his *Social History*), were as much concerned with social as with strictly economic history, for example

Power's (1922) *Medieval English Nunneries* (Berg 1992).

Second, intellectuals associated with the early Labour Party sought to analyse social inequality and institutions historically to suggest how they might be changed, in particular Barbara and J.L. Hammond's books on the impact of industrialization on the labouring poor (Hammond and Hammond 1911, 1917, 1919) and Beatrice and Sidney Webb's histories of trade unionism and of local government (Webb and Webb 1894, 1929).

Around the same time in France a similar reaction against history as the history of political events gave birth to the journal *Annales d'histoire économique et sociale* in 1929. The *Annalistes* had a definite programme not merely to explore societies and the economies of the past but also to integrate the study of society, economy, politics, intellectual life, geography and demography all in their broadest sense, ideally over long time periods (if sometimes of very small places) in order to understand, as they put it, 'civilization', the complex network of interactions that constitutes a society. In 1946 the title of the journal was changed to *Annales: économies, sociétés, civilisations* (as it remains). This aspiration to total history was an influential stimulus internationally for many decades – especially under the direction of Braudel (1949) in the 1950s and 1960s – reminding historians that they could be bold, though relatively few took up the challenge and fewer still could match practice with ambition. But it provided a new rigour both in the definition of social history and its methods. Above all it was systematic. French historians were the first to apply quantitative techniques to the study of politics, social structure and demography. They were strongly positivist in rarely questioning how the structures that they studied or their data were constructed. Driven by *Annales*, social history acquired greater and earlier legitimacy and prominence in French academic life than elsewhere (Prost 1992).

British social history did not advance so tidily. After 1945 the tradition of Labour intellectuals writing the history of the labour movement and of the working class, notably G.D.H. Cole (1948), and later Asa Briggs (1991), continued as did the close association of economic and social history, though they moved apart from the 1960s.

A new and important stimulus was the Communist Party History Group, several of whom achieved a remarkable international eminence: Hilton (1987), Kiernan (1988), Hill (1986), Hobsbawm (1978, 1987), E.P. Thompson (1992) and Dorothy Thompson. All had interests in the history of radical ideas, social protest and subordinate groups, and a preference for literary over quantitative sources.

The liberal strand, to which Trevelyan and G.M. Young (1936) belonged, carried on. One of its important products, G. Kitson Clark's (1962) *The Making of Victorian England*, was dedicated to Trevelyan. Clark was 'primarily a political historian', but 'anxious to write what might be called "history in depth"', combining demographic, economic and political history with the study of socioeconomic groups at all levels and central aspects of culture such as religion. This he felt 'quite sure...is the right line of development for historiography'. H.J. Perkin (1969) was already working on his study of *The Origins of Modern English Society 1780–1880* and defining social history as a 'vertebrate discipline' built around the theme of the history of social structure (Perkin 1962), rather than as the 'shapeless container for everything from changes in human physique to symbol and ritual' that some perceived (Hobsbawm 1980). Perkin (1992) sought to analyse how a 'viable class society' emerged amid the change of industrialization, while others emphasized conflict. Social history was stronger and more varied in Britain by the early 1960s than subsequent commentators have suggested.

The expansion of the social sciences in the postwar period, especially sociology, influenced historical work. A successful example was the work of the Cambridge Group for the History of Population and Social Structure, formed in 1964 by Peter Laslett and E.A. Wrigley. This set out to apply quantitative techniques developed in France and questions and concepts previously largely confined to sociologists and anthropologists to the study of demography and social structure over long time periods (Laslett 1965, 1988). The outcome has transformed our understanding of the process of population change (Wrigley and Schofield 1981) and household structure (Laslett and Wall 1972) in Britain over several centuries and has been widely influential elsewhere. This work has raised important general questions about the relationship between economic and social change especially during the process of industrialization (Wrigley 1988), and more specific ones, such as about the relative roles of family and welfare agencies in support for the poor in European societies. In the USA quantitative historical sociology particularly influenced studies of social mobility (Thernstrom 1964) and of social protest (Tilly and Shorter 1974).

Also important from the mid-1960s was the growing oppositional culture in sections of the academy. This attracted historians in Britain and elsewhere to social history, especially 'history from below', also much influenced by the publication of E.P. Thompson's (1963) *The Making of the English Working Class*.

Social history in the 1960s, from whatever perspective it was written, was centrally organized around a conception of society as hierarchically structured, with class as the primary organizing category. In the 1970s and 1980s more historians became aware that behaviour and beliefs (about politics for example) could not be explained as satisfactorily in terms of socioeconomic position as had been thought. Growing attention to women's history made it clear that gender was as important a social category as class. Changing ideological preoccupations, combined with a wider academic challenge to structuralism in all its forms, made social historians more sensitive to the variety of divisions within societies and the variety of identities each individual possessed related to race, nation, age group and religion as well as gender and class.

This greatly complicated the writing of social history, leading some to fear that it was about to collapse into random empiricism. Others turned to anthropology for help in understanding social complexity, in particular to the cultural ethnography of Geertz and the insights of Mary Douglas. The task was further complicated by the growing influence in the academy of Foucault and of sociolinguistics, semiotics and literary theory: Saussure, Derrida, Bakhtin, Baudrillard and Bourdieu pre-eminently. The impacts of these very different theorists were controversial (Jenkins 1991; Evans 1997; Jordanova 2000). At their best they challenged historians to recognize that the objects of their investigation – social groups, madness, sexuality, the state or any other – are not givens as they had implicitly supposed but constructs whose construction in time must be interpreted; so also are the languages of written sources, which contributed to the construction of, and are not merely the expression of, feeling and action. And they could provide a richer range of resources for interpreting the wide range of sources used by social historians, oral, visual and material as well as documentary.

Under these influences, historians (more in some countries than in others, more slowly in the UK than the USA or Australia, slower still in Germany, at different paces among historians of different time periods: medievalists, for example, often practised cultural history without defining it as such; Rubin 2002) began to talk of studying 'culture' rather than 'society' (Hunt 1989) or in France '*mentalités*' (Chartier 1982). In Britain the Social History Society (founded 1973) is launching in 2004 an academic journal called *Cultural and Social History*, which suggests a significant shift. The value of this approach is that it enables historians to conceptualize values, beliefs, language, political organization, economic activity and much else as interacting elements of the same system rather than as isolated features of human activity. The danger is that, like 'total history', it becomes so inclusive that specificity is lost. But it can remain a desirable aspiration within which social historians can continue to pursue a variety of themes, and social and cultural history can develop independent theories and concepts that learn from but are not parasitic upon other disciplines; and can provide the historian's indispensable contribution to the social sciences: analysis over time, long-run as well as short-run time.

PAT THANE
UNIVERSITY OF SUSSEX

References

Berg, M. (1992) 'The first women economic historians', *Economic History Review* 2.

Braudel, F. (1949) *La Méditerranée et le monde méditerranéen à l'époque de Philippe II*, Paris.

Briggs, A. (1991) 'Videotaped interview with J. Harris', *Interviews with Historians*, Institute of Historical Research, London.

Chartier, R. (1982) 'Intellectual history or sociocultural history? The French trajectories', in D. LaCapra and S. Kaplan (eds) *Modern European Intellectual History: Reappraisals and New Perspectives*, Ithaca, NY.

Clark, G.K. (1962) *The Making of Victorian England*, London.

Cole, G.D.H. (1948) *A Short History of the British Working Class Movement, 1789–1947*, London.

Evans, R.J. (1997) *In Defence of History*, London.

Hammond, B. and Hammond, J.L. (1911) *The Village Labourer*, London.

—— (1917) *The Town Labourer*, London.

—— (1919) *The Skilled Labourer*, London.

Hill, C. (1986) 'Videotaped interview with P.J. Corfield', *Interviews with Historians*, Institute of Historical Research, London.

Hilton, R. (1987) 'Videotaped interview with J. Hatcher', *Interviews with Historians*, Institute of Historical Research, London.

Hobsbawm, E. (1978) 'The Historians Group of the Communist Party', in M. Cornforth (ed.) *Rebels and Their Causes*, London.

—— (1980) 'The revival of narrative: Some comments', *Past and Present* 86.

—— (1987) 'Videotaped interview with P. Thane', *Interviews with Historians*, Institute of Historical Research, London.

Hunt, L. (ed.) (1989) *The New Cultural History*, Berkeley, CA.

Jenkins, K. (1991) *Re-Thinking History*, London.

Jordanova, L (2000) *History in Practice*, London.

Kiernan, V.G. (1988) *The Duel in European History: Honour and the Reign of Aristocracy*, Oxford.

Laslett, P. (1965) *The World We Have Lost*, London.

—— (1988) 'Videotaped interview with K. Wrightson', *Interviews with Historians*, Institute of Historical Research, London.

Laslett, P. and Wall, R. (1972) *Household and Family in Past Time*, Cambridge, UK.

Perkin, H. (1962) 'What is social history?' in H. Finberg (ed.) *Approaches to History*, London.

—— (1969) *The Origins of Modern English Society*, London.

—— (1992) 'Videotaped interview with P. Thane', *Interviews with Historians*, Institute of Historical Research, London.

Power, E. (1922) *Medieval English Nunneries, c.1275–1535*, Cambridge, UK.

Prost, A. (1992) 'What has happened to French social history?' *Historical Journal* 35(2).

Rubin, M. (2002) 'What is cultural history now?' in D. Cannadine (ed.) *What is History Now?* London, pp. 80–94.

Thernstrom, S. (1964) *Poverty and Progress: Social Mobility in a Nineteenth Century City*, Cambridge, MA.

Thompson, E.P. (1963) *The Making of the English Working Class*, London.

—— (1992) 'Videotaped interview with P.J. Corfield', *Interviews with Historians*, Institute of Historical Research, London.

Tilly, C. and Shorter, E. (1974) *Strikes in France, 1830–1848*, Cambridge, UK.

Trevelyan, G.M. (1942) *English Social History: A Survey of Six Centuries*, London.

Webb, B. and Webb, S. (1894) *The History of Trade Unionism, 1666–1920*, London.

—— (1929) *English Local Government*, London.

Wrigley, E. (1988) *Continuity, Chance and Change: The Character of the Industrial Revolution in England*, Cambridge, UK.

Wrigley, E. and Schofield, R. (1981) *The Population History of England*, London.

Young, G.M. (1936) *Victorian England: Portrait of an Age*, London.

Further reading

Cannadine, D. (ed.) (2002) *What is History Now?* London.

Fulbrook, M. (2002) *Historical Theory*, London.

SEE ALSO: cultural history; history; Marx's theory of history and society; Marxist history; oral history

SOCIAL MOVEMENTS

For Lorenz von Stein (1855: vi), the social movement of the nineteenth century was the working class. Scholarship and social change in the twentieth century have pluralized the term, loosening it from its historical bounds and applying it to a variety of phenomena, from unstructured collective behaviour to cults and religious sects to issue-oriented protest movements all the way to organized coups, rebellions and revolutions. Recently, some scholars have complicated the lives of readers by taking as their purview all of what they call 'contentious politics' (McAdam *et al.* 2001). The only common denominators in the variety of definitions that have resulted is that social movements are seen as uninstitutionalized groups of unrepresented constituents engaged in sequences of contentious interaction with elites or opponents (Tilly 1978, 1986, 1995).

With so broad a focus and so unconstrained a definition, empirical richness has been gained at the cost of agreed upon methodological canons. Although organizational analyses and survey studies are employed more and more often, the typical approach remains the configurational case study, often of a movement with which the author has had a personal relationship. The resulting mass of case studies has fed the urge to typologize, based in part on the empirical properties of groups and in part on their relation to existing society. Following the Tillys' lead, a number of scholars have experimented with protest-event analysis over more or less long time periods (Tilly *et al.* 1975; Kriesi *et al.* 1995). More recently, some have taken the cultural turn, interpreting movements according to their collective action frames (Snow *et al.* 1986), their ideological discourses (Gamson 1990) or their collective identities (Melucci 1989).

Theoretically, the field has focused on three major questions.

First, what kind of people are recruited into social movements? In the past, these were often seen as fanatics or social isolates in search of new collective identities, but since the mid-1970s research has shown that movement activists come from almost any sector of the population. They are most often recruited out of social networks and tend to stay active in one form or another of movement activity after their initial recruitment experience (McAdam 1988). Women have emerged more and more centrally as social movement actors (Katzenstein 1998).

Second, how does the emergence of a movement relate to cycles in economic growth and changes in class relations? It used to be thought that economic deprivation was the main source of movement formation, but the movements of the 1960s led to the opposite hypothesis – that movements are the result of 'postmaterial' attitudes that grow out of affluence (Inglehart 1977). With the decline of Marxism, analysts have become wary of ascribing causal priority to such macrostructural factors as economic cycles, and have been increasingly turning to the changes in political opportunities that lower the costs of collective action (Eisinger 1973; Tarrow 1998). In recent years, both opportunities and threats have been seen as the dual sources of social movement activism (Goldstone and Tilly 2001).

Third, how do relations between leaders and followers affect the outcomes of movement activity and the careers of social movements? Here the classical Michelsian insight about the displacement of group goals by leaders has been a guiding star, but research since the 1960s suggests that such institutionalization is far from preordained (Zald and Ash 1966). The problem of leader–follower relations has been recast in the form of the now-familiar problem of the free rider (Olson 1968). But since people do, increasingly, engage in contentious collective action, even the most stalwart rationalists cast doubt on the applicability of Olson's theory to social movements.

Social movement theory and research have had two main historical sources: first, the conservative reaction to the French and the Industrial revolutions (see Oberschall 1973 for sources); and, second, the rise of the socialist movements of the late nineteenth century. After the decline of anarchism and the rise of reformist movements, a slow-growing belief in the rationality of collective action combated the earlier presumption of irrationality. The great cataclysms of the twenti-

eth century – fascism and the Russian Revolution – revived the earlier view of movements as catchment areas for people seeking new identities, but in newer, post-Freudian forms (Fromm 1969). This was particularly the case in the USA. Influenced by a generation of exiles who brought with them nightmarish memories of the 'mob', and lacking the strong Marxist matrix of European theorists, North American social movement researchers were particularly vulnerable to the persuasion that social movements are an expression of dysfunctions in society (Smelser 1963).

The decade of the 1960s contested this vision and revivified a field that had been sinking into marginality. As the student, anti-war, women's and environmental movements developed concrete and purposive critiques of elites and authorities, the result for social movement research in both Europe and the USA was the 'normalization' of collective action (Piven and Cloward 1992). There was a growing tendency to see movements as the outcome of the instrumental mobilization of resources and collective action as one element – albeit a turbulent and uncivil one – in the political process (McAdam 1982; McCarthy and Zald 1977).

The analytical gains brought by these new models have been enlightening, but have been purchased at the cost of obscuring the special character of social movement activity. Europeans, in particular, have criticized North American approaches for neglecting the ideological projects of movements and for becoming insensitive to their impact on culture. Americans themselves criticized the lack of attention to emotions in their models (Aminzade and McAdam 2001). The response of some scholars has been to revive social psychological approaches to movements and, of others, to pay greater attention to how movements construct meaning (Klandermans 1992).

The impact of the movements of the 1960s was somewhat different in Europe, where the structuralist persuasion, stripped of its Marxist integument, led to the theory of 'new' social movements. This had French (Touraine 1988), German (Offe 1987) and Italian (Melucci 1989) variants, with somewhat less impact on British researchers, many of whom continued to beat a Marxist drum. More recently, the rise of the 'ugly movements' of the extreme right took some of the bloom off the 'new social movement' rose.

The spread of extremist religious movements in the Muslim world and elsewhere pointed to the Western, reformist bias of much social movement research.

An important heritage of the 1960s movements was to underscore the remarkable diffusion of contentious collective action among a variety of social groups and nation-states in broad cycles of protest that appeared to follow a dynamic that was not predictable from either macrosocietal trends or from state policies (Tarrow 1998). Analysts have also observed a growing appearance of hybrid forms of interest group/ social movement-type organizations that combine a capacity for contentious collective action with more traditional lobbying and educational activities.

McCarthy and Zald (1977) called these new forms of movement 'professional movement organizations', but they often encompass part-time and amateur activists using the widely diffused organizational skills and communication resources available to quite ordinary people in today's societies. The capacity of these groups to overcome their paucity of resources, to use innovative forms of collective action, and to gain access to the media differentiates them from earlier forms of social movement (Klandermans 1992). The Internet and other forms of personal communication reinforce this trend away from professionalization and towards decentralized movement mobilization.

Two pairs of contradictory trends mark social movements today. On the one hand, there has been so great a diffusion of movement activity that the world may be entering a stage in which collective action has become an accepted part of routine politics; on the other hand, there has been a spread of violent, intolerant and mutually exclusive movements like Islamic fundamentalism, ethnic violence in Eastern Europe and anti-immigrant and racist movements in the West. Second, as grassroots forms of participation compete with ever more declining electoral turnout, transnational movements rise above the national state, targeting international institutions, foreign states and inchoate objects like 'globalization'. While the last phase of social movement research took its cues from the largely civil, national and purposive movements of the 1960s, the next phase will have to come to grips with these contradictory aspects of a movement society.

SIDNEY TARROW
CORNELL UNIVERSITY

References

Aminzade, R. and McAdam, D. (2001) 'Emotions and contentious politics', in R. Aminzade, J.A. Goldstone and D. McAdam (eds) *Silence and Voice in the Study of Contentious Politics*, Cambridge.

Eisinger, P.K. (1973) 'The conditions of protest behavior in American cities', *American Political Science Review* 67.

Fromm, E. (1969) *Escape from Freedom*, New York.

Gamson, W. (1990) *The Strategy of Protest*, 2nd edn, Belmont, CA.

Goldstone, J. and Tilly, C. (2001) 'Threat (and opportunity)', in R. Aminzade, J.A. Goldstone and D. McAdam (eds) *Silence and Voice in the Study of Contentious Politics*, Cambridge.

Inglehart, R. (1977) *The Silent Revolution: Changing Values and Political Styles among Western Publics*, Princeton, NJ.

Katzenstein, Mary F. (1998) *Faithful and Fearless*, Princeton, NJ.

Klandermans, B. (1992) 'The social construction of protest and multiorganizational fields', in A. Morris and C. McClurg Mueller (eds) *Frontiers in Social Movement Theory*, New Haven, CT.

Kriesi, H.P. *et al.* (1995) *The Politics of New Social Movements in Western Europe*, Minneapolis, MN.

McAdam, D. (1982) *The Political Process and the Development of Black Insurgency*, Chicago.

—— (1988) *Freedom Summer*, New York.

McAdam, D., Tarrow, S. and Tilly, C. (2001) *Dynamics of Contention*, Cambridge.

McCarthy, J. and Zald, M. (1977) 'Resource mobilization and social movements: A partial theory', *American Journal of Sociology* 82.

Melucci, A. (1989) *Nomads of the Present: Social Movements and Individual Needs in Contemporary Society*, Philadelphia, PA.

Oberschall, A. (1973) *Social Conflict and Social Movements*, Englewood Cliffs, NJ.

Offe, C. (1987) 'New social movements: Challenging the boundaries of institutional politics', *Social Research* 52.

Olson, M. (1968) *The Logic of Collective Action*, Cambridge, MA.

Piven, F.F. and Cloward, R. (1992) 'Normalizing collective protest', in A.D. Morris and C. Mueller (eds) *Frontiers in Social Movement Theory*, New Haven, CT.

Smelser, N. (1963) *The Theory of Collective Behavior*, New York.

Snow, D., Rochford, E.B., Warden, S. and Benford, R. (1986) 'Frame alignment process, micromobilization and movement participation', *American Sociological Review* 51.

Stein, L. von (1855) *Geschichte der socialen Bewegung Frankreichs von 1789 bis auf unsere Tage*, Berlin.

Tarrow, S. (1998) *Power in Movement: Social Movements and Contentious Politics*, Cambridge.

Tilly, C. (1978) *From Mobilization to Revolution*, Reading, MA.

—— (1986) *The Contentious French*, Cambridge, MA.

—— (1995) *Contentious Politics in Great Britain, 1758–1834*, Cambridge, MA.

Tilly, C., Tilly, L. and Tilly, R. (1975) *The Rebellious Century, 1830–1930*, Cambridge, MA.

Touraine, A. (1988) *Return of the Actor: Social Theory in Postindustrial Society*, Minneapolis, MN.

Zald, M. and Ash, R. (1966) 'Social movement organizations: Growth, decay and change', *Social Forces* 44.

Further reading

Aminzade, R., Goldstone, J.A. and McAdam, D. (eds) (2001) *Silence and Voice in the Study of Contentious Politics*, Cambridge.

Gurr, T.R. (ed.) (1980) *Handbook of Political Conflict: Theory and Research*, New York.

Marx, G.T. and Wood, J.L. (1975) 'Strands of theory and research in collective behavior', *Annual Review of Sociology* 1: 21–42.

Zald, M. and McCarthy, J. (1987) *Social Movements in an Organizational Society*, New Brunswick, NJ.

SEE ALSO: collective action; radicalism

SOCIAL PROBLEMS

The study of social problems has undergone a shift since the 1970s. The field was once dominated by approaches that treated social problems as objective and observable conditions that are undesirable, unjust, offensive or in some way threatening to the smooth functioning of society. The primary concern for those adopting an objectivist approach was to identify such conditions and to get at their root causes, often with a view to recommending a remedy.

Since the 1970s an alternative perspective has emerged. Social constructionism, as it is called, begins with the premise that what gets viewed as a social problem is a matter of definition. Many conditions that are now regarded as social problems were not always considered problematic. Parents once had the right to discipline their children as they saw fit. We now regard many forms of discipline as child abuse. Date rape, drunk driving, sexual harassment and AIDS have all become an integral part of public consciousness and debate, yet until recently were unnamed or unnoticed. Other conditions such as interracial marriages might have been considered social problems in the past but are now less likely to be viewed in these terms. These examples show that our experiences and interpretations of conditions change and that what constitutes a social problem is essentially a subjective judgement. If this is the case, how can social problems be studied?

Rather than focusing on objective conditions, constructionists direct attention to the social process by which conditions come to be seen as problems. In *Constructing Social Problems*, a book that has been described as a 'watershed in the development of the contemporary sociology of social problems' (Miller and Holstein 1989: 2), Spector and Kitsuse (1977) encourage sociologists to abandon the notion of social problems as conditions and suggest a conception of social problems as an activity. They define social problems as the activities of groups expressing grievances and making claims about putative conditions. The task for sociologists of social problems, they suggest, is not to evaluate or assess such claims but to account for claims-making activity and its consequences. Indeed, to guard against the tendency to slip back into an analysis of conditions, Spector and Kitsuse insist that all assumptions about the objective conditions, including assumptions about their very existence, be suspended. To the extent that sociologists address the conditions themselves they become participants in, rather than analysts of, the process they should be studying. This orientation to the study of social problems and especially the concept of claims-making have become the heart of the constructionist approach. In contrast to objectivists, then, who look at social conditions, their causes and solutions, constructionists are interested in the claims-making about conditions, the ways in which meanings concerning undesirable conditions are produced and the responses that these activities generate.

The significance of the constructionist thrust in the study of social problems is that it has given sociologists and other social scientists a way to deal with the subjective nature of social problems. In so doing, it has provided a distinctive subject matter for the field. The traditional objectivist approaches produced analyses of social conditions bound together by nothing more than the analyst's assessment of these conditions as undesirable. The conditions themselves had little in common so that an understanding of any one condition contributed little to an understanding of others. In conceptualizing the field in terms of claims-making, constructionism provides a separate focus, a specific set of questions to guide research and a framework for building a theory of social problems that is distinct from theories about undesirable conditions (Best 1995: 5; Schneider 1985: 210).

Since its emergence, the constructionist perspective has become the leading theoretical approach in the study of social problems. It has generated an enormous body of empirical research examining claims-making efforts around issues ranging from prostitution, missing children, smoking, fathers' rights and toxic work environments to AIDS, hate crimes, factory farming and child, spousal and elderly abuse. The literature covers not only contemporary issues but also historical efforts such as the early eugenics campaigns against impoverished women. It covers successful claims-making efforts as well as those – like the movement to focus public attention on the risk of earthquakes (Stallings 1995) – that have met with limited success. Increasingly there are studies that look at the social problems process in cross-cultural contexts (Best 1995). A prominent theme is the medicalization of social problems. Medicalization refers to the tendency to view undesirable conditions and behaviours as medical problems and/or to seek medical solutions or controls (Conrad and Schneider 1980). Constructionists have examined the medicalization of such conditions as alcoholism, drug addiction, cult membership, academic underachievement, crime control, compulsive gambling, homelessness, transsexualism and premenstrual syndrome. They have also studied efforts to demedicalize conditions such as hermaphroditism, obesity and homosexuality. (Most of these studies have been published in the journal *Social Problems*; see also the JAI research annual *Perspectives on Social Problems*; Best 1995; Loseke and Best 2003.)

The ever-growing number of case studies provide the field with a strong foundation for theorizing about the underlying processes involved in social problems work. How is it that some conditions are accorded the status of social problems while others are not? Who are the people and what are the tasks involved in constructing social problems? What difference does it make how claims are constructed and what rhetorical devices or strategies for pressing those claims are used? In what ways does claims-making construct people (as victims or villains),

conditions and solutions? When competitions erupt between groups over how to view a problem or what remedy to pursue, how does one group gain ownership over the problem or the institutionalized procedures for dealing with the problem (Loseke 1999)? These are the types of questions increasingly guiding social problems research.

The constructionist approach has also generated lively theoretical debates. Many of these have centred around whether there is a place for objective conditions in the study of social problems. Some sociologists feel strongly that analyses ought to be restricted to the definitional activities of claims-makers. Others do not see the need for such a strict interpretation and allow themselves to consider objective conditions, often using them to challenge the truth of claims they 'know' to be false (Gusfield 1985). There are disagreements about whether the radically subjectivist position that Spector and Kitsuse call for is desirable or even possible (Best 1995; Woolgar and Pawluch l985). From those working outside of a constructionist perspective there are still questions about the real social problems that have an existence independent from how they might be seen and the moral obligation social scientists have to speak out and even to act against conditions they consider to be unjust (Eitzen 1984). Despite these debates, what remains clear is that the constructionist approach has been and will probably continue to be a productive source of social problems theorizing and research for many years to come.

DOROTHY PAWLUCH
MCMASTER UNIVERSITY, CANADA

References

Best, J. (ed.) (1995) *Images of Issues: Typifying Contemporary Social Problems*, 2nd edn, Hawthorne, NY.

Conrad, P. and Schneider, J.W. (1980) *Deviance and Medicalization: From Badness to Sickness*, St Louis.

Eitzen, S. (1984) 'Teaching social problems', *Society for the Study of Social Problems Newsletter* 16.

Gusfield, J.R. (1985) 'Theories and hobgoblins', *Society for the Study of Social Problems Newsletter* 17.

Loseke, D. (1999) *Thinking about Social Problems: An Introduction to Constructionist Perspectives*, Hawthorne, NY.

Loseke, D. and Best, J. (eds) (2003) *Social Problems: Constructionist Readings*, Hawthorne, NY.

Miller, G. and Holstein, J.A. (1989) 'On the sociology of social problems', in J.A. Holstein and G. Miller (eds) *Perspectives on Social Problems*, Vol. 1, Greenwich, CT.

Schneider, J.W. (1985) 'Social problems theory: The constructionist view', *Annual Review of Sociology* 11.

Spector, M. and Kitsuse, J.I. (1977) *Constructing Social Problems*, New York.

Stallings, R.A. (1995) *Promoting Risk: Constructing the Earthquake Threat*, Hawthorne, NY.

Woolgar, S. and Pawluch, D. (1985) 'Ontological gerrymandering: The anatomy of social problems explanations', *Social Problems* 32.

Further reading

Best, J. (ed.) (2001) *How Claims Spread: Cross-National Diffusion of Social Problems*, Hawthorne, NY.

Holstein, J.A. and Miller, G. (eds) (1993) *Reconsidering Constructionism: Debates in Social Problems Theory*, Hawthorne, NY.

SEE ALSO: alcoholism and alcohol abuse; crime and delinquency; deviance; domestic violence; drug use; mental health; poverty; social exclusion; social work; suicide; violence

SOCIAL PSYCHOLOGY

Social psychology is the study of the nature, functions and phenomena of social behaviour and of the mental experience of individuals in social contexts. It includes the study of social effects on aspects of behaviour and mental experience that are studied more generally in other branches of psychology. It also includes a number of psychological phenomena that do not arise, or in some cases cannot even be delineated, in individuals outside of their social contexts. Among these distinctively social psychological phenomena are aggression and anger, altruism and helping behaviour, social attitudes and persuasion, attraction and social relationships, attribution and social cognition, bargaining and negotiation, conformity and social influence processes, co-operation and competition, group decision-making, group dynamics, language and speech, leadership and group performance, non-verbal communication and body language, obedience to authority, prejudice and intergroup conflict, self-presentation and impression management, sex roles, sexual behaviour, social learning and socialization.

Most authorities agree that social psychology is the biochemistry of the social sciences, a field lying between sociology and individual psychology. The field is in this sense interstitial, and it plays a pivotal role as a major social science discipline. In its theories and research, social psychology provides vital information about how social factors influence individual thoughts, feelings and actions.

Although there remain a number of highly resonant pockets of overlapping interest in sociology, most of the research literature and most of the recent texts in social psychology have been written by psychologists. It is also the case that the early development of social psychology was dominated by theories and research generated in the USA. Many of the seminal figures behind this array of contributions did, however, emigrate from Europe in the 1930s: they included Brunswik, Heider, Katona, Lazarsfeld and Lewin. Under the stimulus of the European Association of Experimental Social Psychology (founded in 1967), there has been considerable momentum towards redressing the imbalance represented by the pre-eminence of the USA. The European tradition of social psychology has tended to place more emphasis on such non-experimental approaches as discourse analysis, social representations research and various qualitative research methodologies, in addition to experimental social psychology.

Social psychology evolved out of a recognition of human diversity within cultural uniformity. It focuses on choices and behavioural decisions among the competing options that confront us all in complex contemporary societies, and on the rich complexity of human social life. It has become a field that, more than any other, deals with the psychology of everyday life.

Historical outline

In the mid-1950s, Gordon Allport (1954) argued that most of the major problems of concern to contemporary social psychologists were recognized as problems by social philosophers long before psychological questions were joined to scientific methodology. Perhaps the most fundamental question was posed by Comte: How can people simultaneously be the cause and the consequence of society? Although many textbook authors conveniently identify the birth date of social psychology as 1908, when two influential early texts by McDougall and Ross were published, in a very real sense the field began to cohere and develop its own identity only in the mid-1930s and did not really take on momentum until after the Second World War. This coherence and subsequent momentum depended largely on the development of genuinely social theories and methods, the most influential early examples of which were the contributions of Kurt Lewin in the late 1930s and early 1940s.

Partly through sustained advocacy and partly through example, Lewin championed the possibilities of experimentation in social psychology. His experimental studies of autocratic, democratic and *laissez-faire* leadership atmospheres (with Lippitt and White in 1939) showed how complex situational variables could be manipulated, validated and shown to produce distinctive but orderly consequences. Lewin hoped to solve the problems of generalizing from the laboratory to the 'real world' by advocating not only the linkage of experimentation to theory but also the parallel conduct of laboratory and field experimentation on conceptually cognate problems.

Although there would be wide agreement that Kurt Lewin deserves the title of the father of *experimental* social psychology, there were many other influences gathering under the social psychology umbrella during the 1920s and 1930s in the USA. These included a sustained series of empirical studies on group problem-solving, the invention by Thurstone and Chave (1929) and Likert (1932) of ingenious attitude measurement techniques, and the development of respondent sampling and survey research methodologies.

The central identity of social psychology was to remain anchored in the experimental approach. One of Lewin's students, Leon Festinger, exemplified Lewin's emphasis on going back and forth between the laboratory and the field, and showed in particular how experimentation made sense only when it was wedded to theory. Between the mid-1940s and the mid-1960s, when he was active as a social psychologist, Festinger (1954, 1957) developed two theories that had a profound impact on the field. The first was a theory of 'social comparison processes', a detailed set of postulates and propositions concerning the consequences for social interaction of people's need for the kinds of information about themselves and the outer world that only other people could provide. The second was a theory of 'cognitive dissonance', which portrayed the various mental and behavioural manœuvres by which people attempt to maintain and restore cognitive consistency. The power of this theory was greatly enhanced by Festinger's recognition

that some cognitions are more resistant to change than others, and that behavioural commitment is a potent source of such resistance. This recognition permitted rather precise predictions to be made concerning the form that dissonance reduction would take in different situations, in particular that changes would usually be observed in the least resistant cognition. The ideas informing both of these theories remain important in much current social psychological thinking and have become a part of our cultural wisdom. Equally important, perhaps, the voluminous research generated by the theory of cognitive dissonance provided a clear example of coherent progress through experimental research in social science, research yielding cumulative insights that helped to refine and amplify the theory that inspired it.

Just as enthusiasm for investigating dissonance phenomena began to wane in the late 1960s, a very different kind of theoretical orientation became prominent in social psychology. This was the 'attributional approach' to social cognition, an approach pioneered by Fritz Heider and identified with his seminal treatment of *The Psychology of Interpersonal Relations* (1958). The basic premise of the attributional approach is that people are motivated to understand behaviour, and readily do so by viewing it within a meaningful causal context. Our responses to others, in other words, are a function of the causes we attribute to explain their behaviour. Although initially the focus of attribution theory was almost exclusively on the perception of other people, Kelley (1967) and Bem (1967) extended the attributional orientation to include self-perception. The perception of our own inner dispositions and emotions may sometimes be mediated by our causal evaluations of our own behaviour, taking into account relevant features of the situational context.

As the attributional orientation flourished in the early 1970s, it fed and was fed by a broad revival of interest in *social cognition*. Social psychology (at least since the subjectivism championed by W.I. Thomas) has always been interested in the ways in which people interpret their social environments, but an emphasis on detailed analyses of information processing and social cognition has become more dominant since the late 1980s (see e.g. Fiske and Taylor 1991). The influence of the attributional approach has been reflected in a concern with attributional biases and errors in the application of inference strategies (Nisbett and Ross 1980; Schneider 1994).

While these developments in social cognition were occurring within the mainstream of experimental social psychology, some social psychologists continued to concentrate on the traditional problems of social influence and group processes. Asch's (1956) classic studies of conformity and Milgram's (1974) research into obedience to authority have become standard textbook topics. In different ways, their findings showed the remarkable sensitivity of normal adults to social influence pressures. The nature of group processes was especially informed by Thibaut and Kelley's (1959) analysis of outcome exchanges in dyads and larger groups. This analysis capitalized on the contingency matrices of game theory, as well as building on both reinforcement and social comparison theories within psychology. It provided a rich and provocative framework for dealing with power relations, roles and the development of norms, and it also influenced the development of the distinctively European social identity theory of intergroup relations. Many publications since the 1960s have dealt with complex interpersonal conflict situations that might be resolved through bargaining and negotiation. Throughout this period, also, a series of articles dealt with such social phenomena as aggression, helping behaviour, attitude change, jury decision-making, crowding, social discrimination, sex-role stereotypes, the impact of television and a variety of other applied topics. More comprehensive historical overviews – both general and within specific content areas – may be found in the *Handbook of Social Psychology* (Lindzey and Aronson 1985) and *Advances in Experimental Social Psychology* (Zanna 1990–9).

Current status of the field

Any brief characterization of such a complex discipline must be arbitrary and selective in many respects. It is nevertheless possible to venture a few generalizations on the current status of the field that would probably recruit a reasonable consensus among social psychologists. The emphasis on experimentation has been buffeted by critical winds from several directions. Some critics have concluded that the problem of generalizing from artificial laboratory situations is insurmountable, and that there is no way to extrapolate meaningfully from the historical and

contextual particularities of any given experiment. Other critics have been concerned with the ethics of those deceptive cover stories that used to be common in social psychological experiments but have become much less so with the tightening up in the USA, Britain and elsewhere of ethical guidelines for the conduct of research with human subjects. Still others are bothered by the treatment of research subjects as manipulable objects rather than autonomous agents with whom one negotiates appropriate explanations for behaviour. Finally, there are those who feel that experimentation implies a highly restrictive form of one-way causation, misrepresenting the normal processes of situation selection and movement through complex feedback loops in which the behaviour of actors is both causal and caused.

Although many of these criticisms raise vital concerns, neither singly nor in combination are they likely to relegate the experimental approach to a secondary position in the armamentarium of social psychology. The viability of the experimental approach may be even more assured as its practitioners more clearly realize its particular strengths and its limitations. Even if the generalization problem seems insurmountable, on occasion, the design of experiments is often useful in facilitating and disciplining conceptual thought. There is no doubt, however, that non-experimental approaches will continue to make important contributions to social psychology.

The current flowering of cognitive social psychology seems to be producing new intellectual alliances and breaking down old boundaries between general experimental and social psychology. Certainly social psychologists are borrowing paradigms from the traditions of general research on attention, memory and thinking; cognitive psychologists in turn are showing greater sensitivity to the influences of social factors. In a similar fashion, social psychological theory has shed light on such clinical phenomena as depression, alcohol and drug abuse, obesity, and a range of problems associated with symptom labelling. Although social psychology may in some respects play the role of a gadfly within the social sciences, borrowing here and lending there, it is not likely to lose its special identity as the one field especially concerned with the details of interpersonal influence. During the 1980s, the pendulum seemed to swing away from a concern with social interdependence and group phenomena towards a concern with individual information processing, but at the end of the twentieth century many cognitive psychologists moved away from the entirely non-social implications of the information-processing metaphor. Here there seems to be some divergence between the more 'individualistic' Americans and the more 'groupie' Europeans. It would be interesting if the more blatantly *social* psychology of the Europeans influenced a US revival of interest in groups. This seems to be an old story in social psychology: the study of individuals must be informed by a clear understanding of the matrices of social interdependence within which they function; the study of groups must comprehend the cognitive and motivational processes of group members. The tension between these two foci, in the long run, may be what keeps the field on its relatively straight track, in spite of temporary deviations in course.

EDWARD E. JONES
formerly PRINCETON UNIVERSITY
ANDREW M. COLMAN
UNIVERSITY OF LEICESTER

References

Allport, G.W. (1954) 'The historical background of modern social psychology', in G.E. Lindzey (ed.) *Handbook of Social Psychology*, 1st edn, Vol. 1, Cambridge, MA.

Asch, S.E. (1956) 'Studies of independence and conformity: A minority of one against a unanimous majority', *Psychological Monographs* 70.

Bem, D.J. (1967) 'Self-perception: An alternative interpretation of cognitive dissonance phenomena', *Psychological Review* 74.

Festinger, L. (1954) 'A theory of social comparison processes', *Human Relations* 7.

—— (1957) *A Theory of Cognitive Dissonance*, Evanston, IL.

Fiske, S.T. and Taylor, S.E. (1991) *Social Cognition*, 2nd edn, New York.

Heider, F. (1958) *The Psychology of Interpersonal Relations*, New York.

Kelley, H.H. (1967) 'Attribution theory in social psychology', *Nebraska Symposium on Motivation* 14.

Lewin, K., Lippitt, R. and White, R.K. (1939) 'Patterns of aggressive behavior in experimentally created "social climates"', *Journal of Social Psychology* 10.

Likert, R. (1932) 'A technique for the measurement of attitudes', *Archives of Psychology* 140.

Lindzey, G.E. and Aronson, E. (eds) (1985) *Handbook of Social Psychology*, 3rd edn, 2 vols, New York.

McDougall, W. (1908) *An Introduction to Social Psychology*, London.

Milgram, S. (1974) *Obedience to Authority: An Experimental View*, New York.

Nisbett, R.E. and Ross, L. (1980) *Human Inference: Strategies and Shortcomings of Social Judgment*, Englewood Cliffs, NJ.

Ross, E.A. (1908) *Social Psychology: An Outline and a Source Book*, New York.

Schneider, D.J. (1994) 'Attribution and social cognition', in A.M. Colman (ed.) *Companion Encyclopedia of Psychology*, Vol. 2, London.

Thibaut, J.W. and Kelley, H.H. (1959) *The Social Psychology of Groups*, New York.

Thurstone, L.L. and Chave, E.J. (1929) *The Measurement of Attitude*, Chicago, IL.

Zanna, M.P. (ed.) (1990–9) *Advances in Experimental Social Psychology*, Vols 23–31, San Diego, CA.

Further reading

Hogg, M.A. and Cooper, J. (eds) (2003) *The Sage Handbook of Social Psychology*, New York.

SEE ALSO: altruism and co-operation; anger, hostility and aggression; attitudes; cross-cultural psychology; discourse analysis; group dynamics; identity; labelling theory; leadership; personality; prejudice; psychological anthropology; psychology; self-concept; social construction; sociolinguistics; stigma; stereotypes

SOCIAL SCIENCE

The idea of social science is distinctively modern. Four developments set the stage for its emergence between the seventeenth and nineteenth centuries.

First, the seventeenth-century revolution in science was pivotal. It generated the notion of science as a cumulative empirical project, and complemented this with an ethos favouring the public sharing of knowledge and the foundation of social institutions to further both enquiry and publication. Science, in this new sense, combined inductive enquiry with explicit testing of propositions and formulation of theories based on empirical evidence.

Second, the rise of the modern state (in both its domestic and colonial forms) gave social science both a topic and a client. States sought knowledge as the basis for policy. And the state itself could be an important object of science, as scholars sought to understand which policies worked and which did not, what factors made for better rule, and what organization of the state advanced human liberty. Closely related, the notion of nation as a prepolitical definition of the people who rightly belonged in a given state helped frame 'society' as bounded, integrated and developing through history.

Third, the dramatic expansion of trade, division of labour, industry and capital accumulation that marked the modern era provided both an impetus to study society and a basis for differentiating directly societal sources of change and self-organization from the effects of political rule. If the idea of nation suggested seeing society as a culturally unified entity with its own history, the modern idea of economy added the notion that society could develop on its own through material transformations in its productive capacity as well as through knowledge.

Fourth, Europeans in the early modern era undertook projects of exploration and eventually empire on a scale the world had never seen before. These paved the way for social science by making manifest the enormous diversity of human cultural forms and practices. Missionaries, administrators and, eventually, anthropologists sought to understand kinship, family, the organization of household economies, hierarchies of power, specialization of religious responsibilities and approaches to educating the young. Knowledge of human diversity helped to break the assumption that locally observable social organization needed no explanation.

From classical philosophy to modern social science

From the Renaissance through the eighteenth century, scholarship on political and social subjects remained largely commentary on ancient texts. Thomas Hobbes's *Leviathan* (1996 [1651]) drew in important ways on classical sources, but also marked a transition to modern social science. It presented a theory of the state formulated through what Hobbes claimed were strict deductions from empirical bases. To be sure, the notion of social contract at its centre was either a thought experiment or a metaphor, not a statement of factual history. But Hobbes based his arguments about the legitimacy of government on reasoning from what he took to be facts and logical necessity, not tradition or divine inspiration. Criticism and revision could (and did) focus on both the putative facts and the reasoning without (always) going back to first principles.

John Locke made political theory depend more on an idea of society (and the benefits that language and money as well as government could bring). Among the first great works of comparative social science was Montesquieu's *Spirit of the Laws* (1989 [1748]). Montesquieu made a more systematic effort than Locke to account for the differences in legal and governmental systems by differences in environmental context, social organization and culture. Adam Ferguson developed the notion of 'civil society' as a counterpart to government (and indeed to the derivation of social laws from theology). In 1767, Ferguson presented the history of civil society in a series of stages, prefiguring nineteenth-century evolutionary thought. Much less empirical, Jean-Jacques Rousseau nonetheless contributed to social science a theory of learning from experience, a strong idea of the social whole, the idea of alienation, a scepticism about progress, and an alternative construction of the social contract to that of Hobbes and Locke.

The Physiocrats in eighteenth-century France introduced the powerful notion of system, suggesting that the accumulation of wealth was based on circulation in society, not the action of the state. At least in its economic aspect, society could therefore be largely self-regulating. This paved the way for Adam Smith's (1998 [1776]) suggestion that a market ordered 'as though by an invisible hand' could be a model for social self-organization with minimal government interference. But Smith importantly rejected the Physiocrats' notion that all wealth derived from nature, especially agriculture, insisted that human labour was itself productive, and that the social organization of production, as through the division of labour, could make it more so.

Smith used the notions of division of labour and market to theorize the ways in which interactions among individuals could produce a self-regulating system. The behaviour of each conditioned that of all. The capacity of the market to turn private greed into motivation for publicly useful work was testimony to the extent to which civil society could organize itself outside the control of the state – in non-economic as well as economic dimensions. Thomas Malthus (1992 [1798]) gave the idea of system a different twist, arguing that the growth of population followed 'natural' laws that would periodically result in social catastrophe. Like the proto-evolutionary analyses of Ferguson and other Scots, that of Malthus influenced Charles Darwin and the formulation of a theory of biological evolution.

Indeed, in the nineteenth century, biological and sociological thought were not altogether distinct, as the career of Herbert Spencer (1820–1903) reveals. Spencer contributed the phrase 'survival of the fittest' to an evolutionary theory he thought equally applicable to biological and social life.

In every European country, the state had become a dramatically larger set of institutions, and had begun to penetrate much more basically into the daily lives of its citizens. This was among the pivotal occasions for the development of social science, not only because the state demanded knowledge to guide its actions but because the state's very efficacy suggested the potential for remaking society. At the same time, thinking in terms of the state, rather than simply the ruler (as in Machiavelli's *Prince* [1513]), not only emphasized the extent to which the government was a complex social organization, but also drew attention to the way in which a public, political order defined a whole country. This is the sense in which the state, not the government of that state, enjoyed sovereignty.

The American and French revolutions symbolized this. Alexis de Tocqueville combined the influences of the two, studying the interrelationship of an individualistic culture and an egalitarian political economy in *Democracy in America* (2000 [1835–40]), and of the nature of politics itself in *The Old Regime and the French Revolution* (1998 [1856]). His work formed part of the lineage of both liberal political theory and of sociology. John Stuart Mill integrated Tocqueville's insights with Jeremy Bentham's more systematic approach in his account of utilitarianism (Mill 1985 [1848], 1998 [1861]). The starting-point was the identification of the social good as the greatest good of the greatest number. Social science was essentially an enquiry into how best to achieve that end. But while Mill and Bentham approached society as aggregation of individuals, other social scientists stressed the importance of social structure.

The idea of structure received a dramatic articulation in Karl Marx's theory of capitalism (Marx 1993 [1867]). This centred both on a view of history as class struggle and on an analysis of modern society as grounded in an economic structure that transformed the production and accumulation of value, more or less independently of the intentions of individuals. Marx's theory was not only more social, in the sense that it emphasized the analysis of an emergent whole, not the individuals who made it up, it was also more systemic, in seeking to grasp how the complex patterns of that whole could be traced to certain fundamental causal influences and their interrelationships. Marx relied on a labour theory of value and agreed with Smith about the importance of social organization to making labour more productive, but following Rousseau he was much less willing to accept private property as a given. He insisted both that capitalism (like all earlier economic formations) was a system of constraints, not the achievement of freedom that Smith had extolled, and also that it was unstable, prone to crises but also transcendable. The socialism that would follow could rely much more directly on social science (than on inefficient and unfair markets) to guide production and distribution. Building on the classical political economists, thus, Marx insisted that capitalism was a historical stage, not simply an expression of timeless natural laws.

In this, Marx shared much with other evolutionary thinkers of the nineteenth century (and, indeed, he praised Darwin warmly). In Herbert Spencer's evolutionary theory, individualism itself would be seen as an outcome of evolutionary change in social structure. Some social scientists, like the American William Graham Sumner, would however develop Spencer's thought into 'social Darwinism', a rationalization for unfettered competition in capitalism, since only the fittest would survive (and in unDarwinian fashion, they equated fitness with virtue) (Sumner 1906).

Disciplines

The differentiation of social science into a set of distinct intellectual disciplines dates only from the nineteenth century. This involved, first, a growing distinction of the social sciences from the natural and physical sciences, on the one hand, and what came to be called the humanities, on the other. Second, particular social sciences evolved distinct disciplinary identities.

Increasingly economics was defined by the study of market (and related) phenomena that could in principle operate independently of direct government intervention (whether or not a specific intervention might be beneficial, as economists sometimes argued). Economics included studies of the relative merits of organization through markets and through hierarchical power, of non-market allocation of goods, of regulative action and of macroeconomic factors shaped by governments on non-market bases. It also addressed questions of the nature of rationality and purposive action, and of the relations among different factors of production. Nonetheless, market exchange was definitive; non-market phenomena were on the frontier between economics and other fields. Economics is distinctive for much greater use of mathematics than the other social sciences, a development made possible by the development of a concept of utility (pioneered by Jeremy Bentham and made more operational by W.S. Jevons). This allowed for the modelling of otherwise disparate market phenomena, involving seemingly incommensurable goods, in terms of units of 'good' as such. The very success of mathematical modelling, however, has been the occasion for recurrent debates over the trade-offs between theoretical elegance and empirical veracity.

Political science matured as a field studying, and sometimes advising, modern states. It developed out of a much older tradition of advice to rulers and philosophical consideration of themes like justice. Machiavelli is often taken to mark a turning point, as the first modern political theorist, though his modernity (like that of the Italian city-states in which he lived) is ambiguous. Hobbes was more decisively modern. At least as important, however, was the late nineteenth- and early twentieth-century redefinition of the field in terms of the empirical study of states (and sometimes power more generally). A further 'behavioural revolution' (mainly after the Second World War) refined this idea of an empirical science of politics, and the distinction from older fields like normative political theory and diplomatic history, but the discipline retains a hybrid character. Unlike economics or sociology, it is united more by a concern for certain 'dependent variables' – political outcomes – than by a focus on the effects of certain sorts of independent variables (such as supply and demand, population structure or group dynamics).

The term sociology was coined by Auguste Comte in the 1840s, though like other social sciences sociology can claim an older ancestry. It was shaped by the growth of industrial organization, studies of population change, patterns of immigration, changes in family structure and concern for the 'social question' of how the poor would fare economically in modern societies and inequality would shape modern political systems. Never altogether distinct from economics and political science, sociology nonetheless developed a focus on the dimensions of social life that were organized at least largely on bases other than market relations and governmental dictates. Significantly engaged with empirical data collection from its origins – for example in the studies of working-class families by Frédéric Le Play – sociology increasingly developed a distinctive body of theory addressing questions of social structure, orientations to social action and processes of social change.

If economics, politics and sociology constituted the core of the social sciences, this is not because they were larger or more important intellectual fields, but because they fit more squarely and completely into the social sciences, overlapping less with the natural sciences and the humanities. Most of the time, they were also more closely related to each other than to the rest of the social sciences. Anthropology, psychology, geography, history and statistics have also been central to the growth and improvement of the social sciences. But, cultural anthropology and archaeology have always been closely linked to the humanities while physical anthropology (and certain versions of archaeology) has been more centrally involved in natural science. Social psychology has always been among the social sciences, but the extent of emphasis on the social dimensions of human mental and emotional life in the rest of psychology has varied. In the decades after the Second World War, an effort to integrate psychology and social sciences in the paradigm of 'behavioural sciences' flourished. More recently, much of psychology has tended away from social science and towards the natural sciences and cybernetics. Similarly, geography has always been divided between an emphasis on social and cultural dimensions and on physical dimensions (with the two partially joined in work made possible by technologies like satellite imaging). History is part of the older intellectual tradition out of which social science emerged, and most often understood as part of the humanities; at the same time, several branches of historical research have been transformed by social science and historical research remains central to social science. Not least, though last for this list, statistics grew up in significant part as a social science – for example in the pioneering social statistics of the Belgian, Adolphe Quetelet, who invented the notion of the 'average man' – and the work of many social science disciplines is organized largely in terms of statistics. Statistics remains, however, a partially autonomous discipline and heavily influenced by biological and medical statistics, and models from the physical sciences.

Into the academy

Each of the social sciences was shaped importantly by the ways in which it was institutionalized during this period, and by the contrasts used to distinguish it from others. Crossing all the social sciences was a struggle over methods, or *Methodenstreit*, which pitted more objectivist, universalizing sciences against more subjectivist, particularizing humanities, dividing the social sciences between the two. Economics and psychology have been the most universalizing, while politics, sociology and anthropology have been internally divided.

National contexts also mattered. In France, for example, Emile Durkheim fought to distinguish sociology from psychology, following Comte in claiming that each science needed its own distinct subject matter and arguing that sociology should study 'social facts' that were irreducible to more individual level phenomena. In the USA, economics was the more influential counterpart discipline (and remains so to this day). Sociology was initially organized as an interest area within the American Economic Association, and then split off to form the American Sociological Association in 1905. In Germany, sociology was commonly taught in faculties of law and the distinction between normative and empirical theory was especially salient. But the most important founder of German sociology, Max Weber, was keenly interested in maintaining the relationship between economics and sociology, and approached both using a comparative-historical method that remained a hallmark of German sociology. Great Britain was strong in economics but particularly weak in sociology.

German anthropology (and that of countries influenced especially by Germany) was more closely tied to historical ethnology, linguistics and folklore than most other national variants of the discipline. Both French and British anthropology were closely linked to exploration and colonial rule. The French emphasized cultural

and psychological enquiries – including questions about whether 'savages' were mentally equipped to assimilate immediately to 'civilization'. The British, by contrast, placed greater emphasis on problems of colonial administration and 'native' political and legal systems, partly because of the strategy of 'indirect rule'; accordingly they produced a more social anthropology. In the USA, overseas colonies figured less but the effort to 'salvage' a record of the rapidly vanishing diversity of Native American 'Indians' shaped the dominance of a 'four fields' approach in which physical anthropology, archaeology, linguistics and cultural anthropology were combined (with the last heavily influenced by German ethnology).

Other social sciences were similarly shaped by the contexts in which they matured. Economics was stronger in relation to neighbouring disciplines, but heavily influenced by expectations that it would deliver immediately useful advice to governments and businessmen. The world depicted by neo-classical economic theory is generally devoid of historical specificity and political action. Nevertheless, from the late nineteenth-century introduction of marginal utility theory, economics has been closely linked to policy-making. It became particularly influential through the efforts of John Maynard Keynes and others to address the great Depression, and remained so on into the development of monetarism.

Political science had if anything a greater difficulty emancipating itself from political commentary and history, and in some national settings from law. Indeed, the very name of the discipline was contested – with some calling it politics, some government, and others political science. Though its origins are old, the last of these grew in popularity in the mid-twentieth century as many leaders in the field sought to stress the objective, especially quantitative, study of political 'behaviour' rather than more interpretative or normative relations to or preparations for politics as such.

Quantification and comparison

Across the social sciences the second half of the twentieth century was an era of growing emphasis on quantification. This accompanied efforts to make the social sciences more scientific, a project understood largely in terms of an objectivistic orientation to knowledge and a belief in the accumulation of truth. There were innovations in techniques of empirical data collection, perhaps most prominently in sample surveys, but also in censuses, experimental research (especially in psychology) and secondary analysis of data produced as by-products of market transactions, elections and other processes. And there were new approaches to both analytical statistics and mathematical modelling. While certain multivariate methods, like regression and path analysis, form a sort of centrepiece to this process, becoming standard in the 1960s and 1970s, the overall pattern is not only advancement but proliferation of different techniques, often linked to different theoretical assumptions (but also to different empirical challenges, like handling the massive data of censuses and global surveys versus the smaller populations more common studied in psychology). Network analysis and non-linear models have grown in importance, sometimes in competition with conventional multivariate methods.

In economics, and to a much lesser extent in other social sciences, empirical quantification was complemented (or even overridden) by theoretical mathematicization. Both trends reflected the computational power made available by the increasing improvement of electronic computers. But the competition between them represented also a return of the eighteenth-century opposition between empiricists and deductive theorizers. The distinction, though never hard and fast, was always significant. Econometric statistics made major advances in the mid-twentieth century. Theory, in the form of mathematical models, dominated from the 1970s to early 1990s. In economics a recent trend has been the renewed prestige of empirical enquiry, especially where this examines whether important basic assumptions are in fact valid, or perhaps operate only under restricted conditions. Behavioural economics, produced largely by economists drawing explicitly on psychological research, but also by researchers in new fields like 'decision sciences', has proved especially fertile in this regard.

Quantification and mathematics introduced a greater division among social science disciplines (and within disciplines between lines of work in which quantitative methods figured more or less). It sharply reduced the connections between anthropology and the other social sciences, for

example, reinforcing closer links between cultural anthropology and the humanities.

Qualitative research methods also underwent continual improvement. Among the most significant was the development of 'ethnography' within anthropology and to a lesser extent sociology. This signified efforts, usually based on long-term 'participant-observation' fieldwork, to document the different aspects of a way of life and how they fit together. Ethnography integrated cultural and social organizational analysis, and was typically a strongly integrative, holistic perspective. Later developments included both a growing reflexivity about the location and perspective of the ethnographer within the field site, and attention to the limits of what could be known through first-hand observation and conversation (as for example ethnography tended to explore the local thoroughly but state-level structures minimally).

The predominantly qualitative fields of international and comparative research also became significant in the postwar period. The most visible institutionalizations of this new emphasis on international knowledge were the 'area studies' fields – African Studies, Latin American Studies, South Asian Studies, and so forth. These were organized in varying degree on notions of ancient civilizational roots, contemporary political concerns, linguistic commonalties and artefacts of history such as the way the USA divided the world into regions for military organization in the Second World War. The demand for such knowledge was itself stimulated by the simultaneous processes of decolonization and the intensification of the Cold War.

The area studies fields were distinctively interdisciplinary, combining not only different social science disciplines but also history, literature and other humanistic inquiries as well. Though the area studies fields flourished and produced major and influential research, they developed in tension with the 'core' social science disciplines. To some extent, the terms of this tension replayed the early twentieth-century *Methodenstreit*. The area studies fields were seen by many social scientists as producing particularistic knowledge while the disciplines sought universal truths. To a very large extent, mainstream economics withdrew from the area studies project. Political science and sociology were split, but by the last third of the century the non-context-specific approaches had the upper hand.

Struggle and renewal

If the growth and spread of social science looked smooth in the 1950s and early 1960s, it suffered a shock in the late 1960s and early 1970s. Each of the fundamental premises that had sustained the social science project came under threat. The idea of an objective social science was challenged by complaints about the hubris of those who believed knowledge was more perfect than the freedom of human beings or the complexity of culture and society allowed. There was accordingly a renewal of interest in interpretative approaches, in critical theories that sought to avoid generalizing from what currently existed, and in reflexivity, especially the ways in which the sociocultural location of the researcher shaped his or her perspective.

The close relationship of many social scientists to their states was also criticized. The most visible version of this was the implication of some social scientists in US government counter-insurgency programmes, but there was also a more international wave of critique of the way anthropologists had served colonial states, of how political scientists were embedded in domestic power structures, and so forth. But the debate was vigorous, for at the same time certain links of social scientists to states were challenged, there were also calls for social science to be more 'relevant', less abstractly academic and more directly engaged in efforts to solve social problems. In some cases this meant that social scientists allied themselves more with social movements and less with states. In economic affairs, too, while social scientists were increasingly engaged in market research and other work done specifically on behalf of for-profit clients, there was also a renewal of interest in Marxism and more generally in social science that challenged existing political and economic arrangements.

Not least of all, the independence struggles of former European colonies occasioned a rethinking of the relationships between power and culture. This included a critique of the ways in which Europeans had viewed the cultures of non-Western societies and constructed evolutionary schemes that implied that there was only one form of advancement – and that it called for non-Western societies to become more like the dominant countries of the West. Even the idea of modernity came under attack, partly because unilinear evolutionary ideas had been incorpo-

rated into the notion of modernization. In the 1960s and 1970s, this critique came often in the framework of Marxism or other alternative modernist programmes. Soon, though, postmodern thought (rooted more in the humanities) criticized the mainstream social sciences as embodiments of a modernity that was built around notions of unidirectional progress, reductions of diversity, and the imposition of power even through the forms in which knowledge was produced. False universalisms were challenged by social scientists writing from the perspectives not of the ivory tower or what Karl Mannheim had called the 'free-floating intelligentsia' but of different social locations: women, people of colour, postcolonial subjects; or of engagement in one or another movement or struggle.

This struggle was played out against the background of more material transformations in the social sciences. The postwar era was marked by dramatic growth in higher education generally and in the social sciences in particular. This came sooner and was more pronounced in the USA, and that accelerated a second trend which was a growing prominence of US social science on the global scene. Where the roots of social science lay mostly in Europe, new developments came increasingly from the USA. Without comparable resources, there was nonetheless also a growth of social science outside the Euro-American countries. India was perhaps the single most influential setting for the growth of non-Western social science, and by the late twentieth century fields like Subaltern Studies had become influential throughout the world. International social science associations were founded (often under the auspices of UNESCO) to complement the national societies. International social science was also significantly influenced by the major ideological and political economic struggles of the era, from the Cold War and decolonization through the non-aligned and non-proliferation movements to the intensification of capitalist globalization and opposition to it in the 1990s and early twenty-first century.

Even while the social sciences were most engaged in political disputes in the 1960s and 1970s, the seeds were being laid for another material change that would change their engagement with practical affairs and political policy-making. This was the growth of professional schools, and with them new fields of social science organized outside the traditional disciplines, and usually with a more 'applied' orientation. Business schools, for example, have departments of finance that have largely supplanted one of the core fields of economics. Sociology and psychology figure prominently in both organizational behaviour and marketing programmes, but each of these fields now offers its own PhD programmes, making for a greater distance from the 'parent' disciplines. Schools of education, public health, medicine, nursing, engineering and communications have also both employed social scientists in large numbers and in varying degree produced parallel fields of social science focused on their specific professional domains.

Conclusion

The social sciences have expanded enormously since their early modern origins. They have become impressively international, though in all countries they are still (with the partial exception of anthropology) disproportionately domestic in focus. They have been at once part of the spread of a dominant version of Western culture, and one of the resources for developing critical analyses of that culture – as indeed of other dominant cultural and institutional formations.

The social sciences have also become a great deal more methodologically sophisticated, and now use a variety of both quantitative and qualitative techniques to advance knowledge. Theory too has advanced from several early contending grand systems to a range of middle-range theories and several theoretical frameworks with different strengths and weaknesses, and potential for mutual engagement. Most importantly, substantive knowledge of different problems and empirical topics has grown exponentially. From inequality and organizational processes through market structures, voting procedures and behaviour, decision-making, to kinship, family dynamics, and migration, social scientists have created numerous fields of cumulative research and scholarship. Social scientists are now centrally involved in projects such as the creation or the reform of modern health care or welfare systems, business organizations or trade unions, humanitarian assistance or peacekeeping operations, and the monitoring and regulation of the mass media.

CRAIG CALHOUN
NEW YORK UNIVERSITY AND PRESIDENT OF THE
SOCIAL SCIENCE RESEARCH COUNCIL, NEW YORK

References

Ferguson, A. (1995 [1767]) *An Essay on the History of Civil Society*, ed. F. Oz-Salzberger, Cambridge, UK.
Hobbes, T. (1996 [1651]) *Leviathan*, ed. R. Tuck, Cambridge, UK.
Malthus, T. (1992 [1798]) *An Essay on the Principle of Population*, ed. D. Winch, Cambridge, UK.
Marx, K. (1993 [1867]) *Capital*, Harmondsworth.
Mill, J.S. (1985 [1848]) *Principles of Political Economy*, ed. D. Winch, Harmondsworth.
—— (1998 [1861]) *Utilitarianism*, ed. R. Crisp, Oxford.
Montesquieu, C. de (1989 [1748]) *Spirit of the Laws*, eds B.C. Miller, H.S. Stone and A.M. Cohler, Cambridge, UK.
Rousseau, J.J. (1997 [1762]) *The Social Contract and other Later Political Writings*, ed. G. Gourevitch, Cambridge, UK.
Smith, A. (1998 [1776]) *Wealth of Nations*, ed. K. Sunderland, Oxford.
Sumner, W.G. (1906) *Folkways*, Boston.
Tocqueville, A. de (2000 [1835–40]) *Democracy in America*, eds H.C. Mansfield and D. Winthrop, Chicago.
—— (1998 [1856]) *The Old Regime and the French Revolution*, Chicago.

Further reading

Anderson, L. (2003) *Pursuing Truth, Exercising Power: Social Science and Public Policy in the Twenty-first Century*, New York.
Flyvberg, B. (2001) *Making Social Science Matter*, Cambridge, UK.
Haskell, T.L. (2001) *The Emergence of Professional Social Science*, Baltimore, MD.
Hollis, M. (1994) *The Philosophy of Social Science*, Cambridge, UK.
Hughes, H.S. (1976) *Consciousness and Society: The Reorientation of European Social Thought, 1890–1930*, New York.
Porter, T. and Ross, D. (eds) (2003) *The Modern Social Sciences*, Vol. 7 of The Cambridge History of Science, Cambridge, UK.
Ross, D. (1992) *The Origins of American Social Science*, Cambridge, UK.

SOCIAL WORK

Social work emerged as a profession more than a century ago in the UK, but here, as in most parts of the world, it is only now coming of age as a professional activity guided by degree-level training for all future social workers, professional standards and accreditation, a code of practice, as well as, which may be more important, the beginnings of an evidence-based knowledge to inform its activities.

The International Federation of Social Workers agreed upon the following definition of social work at its meeting in Montreal July 2000:

> The social work profession promotes social change, problem solving in human relationships and the empowerment and liberation of people to enhance well being. Utilising theories of human behaviour and social system, social work intervenes at the points where people interact with their environments. Principles of human rights and social justice are fundamental to Social Work.
> (IFSW 2000; http://www.ifsw.org/ publications/4.6e.pub.html)

The practice of social work is continually evolving, and varies from country to country, depending on the cultural, historical and socioeconomic conditions, but professional training and collective statements still appeal to its early humanitarian, democratic ideals and values, which are based on the respect for equality, worth and the dignity of all people. The range of the services that social workers provide has, however, greatly expanded. In the early twenty-first century, social workers are seen in hospitals, in statutory welfare departments, in communities and in non-governmental organizations all around the world. At times of need and crisis, social workers work with children and their parents, the troubled adolescents, the mentally distressed, the sick, the homeless, the disabled, the elderly and those incarcerated in prisons or hospitals. Much of their work is with the vulnerable and oppressed, and it is directed to alleviating suffering and promoting social inclusion.

Social work can trace its origins back to the Elizabethan Poor Law of 1601, but owes much to the work of the early nineteenth-century pioneers in England (Young 1956). Octavia Hill is credited with the founding of social work when she set up the Charity Organisation Society in 1869. Her pragmatic approach was to control begging and thoughtless almsgiving by dividing the needy into the 'deserving' and the 'undeserving'. In 1870, Dr Barnardo opened his first home in Stepney for children, regardless of whether their parents were 'deserving' or 'undeserving'. His promise was that 'No destitute child would ever be refused admission'. Other pioneers, such as Canon Barnett, who founded Toynbee Hall in London, and the Fabian Society,

supported this more structural approach. Studies on poverty by Booth in London in the 1890s and Rowntree in 1899 showed that some social problems were caused by 'primary poverty' – families did not have enough money to survive. The Royal Commission on the Poor Laws 1905 in England fuelled the rush of welfare legislation, which continued up to the First World War.

The history of social work is inextricably bound up in politics and development of social reforms, but, in general, periods of rapid growth in social work have been informed by growing knowledge about the causes of social problems, which in turn has led to welfare reform. In line with the prevailing beliefs about the underlying causes of social problems, the early twentieth century saw a shift from a focus on individual pathology to a focus on the structural problems in society. The coming of the welfare state heralded the second great flurry of social work activity, in Britain as elsewhere in Europe. An army of social workers, most of whom were untrained, were employed in large numbers by local authorities to support those who fell through the welfare net.

The heyday of the welfare state was the high point of this tendency. More recently, the profession was influenced by the new individualism of the Reagan–Thatcher years, when the individual and the family were held accountable for the social problems of their members. Social workers moved in the public mind from being the 'good guys' who supported the needy and vulnerable to becoming social policemen who pried on vulnerable families. In the UK, under Blair and New Labour, a third great reforming period began in the late 1990s. Community interventions in England and Wales are now targeted at areas of disadvantage with the aim of 'including' those at risk of 'social exclusion'. A range of programmes 'zoned' on these communities are intended to tackle the more intransigent health, education and employment problems in these areas. Linked programmes, such as Sure Start for the 0–4s (modelled on the US Head Start programme), the Children's Fund for the 5–13s and Connexions for the 13–19-year-olds, are targeted at both communities and the intergenerational cycle of disadvantaged. These programmes involve large numbers of both semi-qualified social care workers and professionally trained social workers.

The professionalization of social work has always created problems. At various points in the history of social work, there have been the two positions. On the one hand, there is the popular view that all we need to solve the social problems in our societies is experience, good will and common sense. On the other hand, particularly when tragedies occur, featuring children in the care of public services, or under their surveillance, there is a realization that the work is highly complex and needs training of the highest order.

ANN BUCHANAN
UNIVERSITY OF OXFORD

Reference

Young, A.F. (1956) *British Social Work in the Nineteenth Century*, London.

Further reading

Barker, R.L. (2003) *The Social Work Dictionary*, 5th edn, Washington, DC.
Grobman, L.M. (ed.) (1999) *Days in the Lives of Social Workers*, Harrisburg, PA.
Roof, M. (1972) *A Hundred Years of Family Welfare*, London.

SEE ALSO: social problems

SOCIALISM

Socialism is a political theory the central tenets of which are that the means of production should be taken into collective or common ownership and that, as far as possible, market exchange should be replaced by other forms of distribution based on social needs. Socialism was brought into existence by the Industrial Revolution and it was designed to appeal to the mass working class of the new factory towns created by machine production. Before the development of modern industry, radical conceptions of the reorganization of society were predominantly egalitarian and democratic republican, committed to empowering artisans and peasants. Socialism aimed to solve the problems of modern industry and a competitive market society, and was thus a new departure in political ideas.

Socialist ideas and political movements began to develop in the early nineteenth century in England and France. The period between the 1820s and the 1850s was marked by a plethora of diverse socialist systems proposed by Saint-Simon, Fourier, Owen, Blanc, Proudhon, Marx and Engels, and many lesser thinkers. Most of these systems were Utopian and many of their advocates were middle-class philanthropists committed to improving the lot of the workers. Most socialists sought a more organized society that would replace the anarchy of the market-place and the mass poverty of the urban masses.

Socialist solutions varied enormously: some were strongly in favour of state ownership while others favoured co-operative and mutual ownership, some favoured a decentralized and mutualist economy while others supported centralized economic planning. Socialism in this period did not develop strong political movements; rather it relied on the formation of model communities by wealthy patrons like Robert Owen, on winning established elites to reform, as with the Saint-Simonians in France, or with proposing projects for state action, as with Louis Blanc's National Warshops after the 1848 revolution in France.

The radical and revolutionary mass movements in this period were not socialist. Rather they were nationalist in countries like Hungary or Poland, or Italy under foreign domination; in England and France they were popular-radical, committed to democratic republican reform. Between 1848 and 1871 the popular democratic and revolutionary traditions exhausted themselves in the European countries in a series of political defeats, at the barricades in countries like France, or through less violent political containment by the established parties and classes, as was the case with the Chartists in England.

In the period between 1848 and 1871 Marx and Engels in particular attempted radically to recast socialist theory. They attacked the Utopianism of their predecessors, refusing to promulgate schemes of social reform. In essence they argued that the class struggle arising from the system of capitalist production is the objective basis of socialist victory, socialism is to be identified with the cause of the proletariat, and its aim is to overthrow the ruling class and create a new society without economic exploitation or state domination. Marx and Engels consistently advocated revolution and the seizure of power by the working class, but they did recognize that universal suffrage might facilitate the downfall of capitalism.

Actually, it did nothing of the sort. Between 1870 and 1914 the institutional foundations of modern socialism were developed in Britain and Germany. Universal suffrage created the modern political party – a permanent machine with paid officials whose task was to mobilize the mass electorate. The Social Democratic Party (SPD) became the dominant force in German socialism, not primarily because it adopted Marxism party orthodoxy, but because it started early and was effectively competing for votes in national elections. In Britain and Germany large-scale industrialism was accompanied by the growth of trade unionism, The British Labour Party was created to facilitate the parliamentary representation of the trade unions, and the links between the SPD and the unions were similarly close.

As a mass electoral party and the political representative of unionized labour, any socialist movement in an advanced industrial country had to relegate to virtual impotence the popular insurrectionary politics of the old European 'left'. Even Engels conceded as much, and one of Marx's disciples, Eduard Bernstein, did no more than carry the conclusion to its logical extreme. Bernstein's (1993 [1899]) *The Preconditions of Socialism* represented the first articulate advocacy of 'social democracy' as against revolutionary socialism. It displaced the goal of 'revolution' in favour of a never-ending struggle for attainable reforms. Others, like Karl Kautsky, orthodox but politically cautious, argued that by parliamentary and acceptable political means the workers could engineer a revolutionary change in the social system.

To the mass party and the labour union must be added as a key institutional support of modern socialist movements the rise of big government. In the period 1870–1914 in Britain and Germany, governments came to provide, administer and organize an increasing range of activities, mass schooling, social insurance, public health, public utilities, etc. This provided another base for socialist advocacy and practice. British Fabian socialism sought to intervene in shaping central and local government's provision, aiming to provide an organizing core of the practical intellectuals. The success of Fabianism stands in stark contrast to the failure of its competitors, such as the anti-statist and decentralist doctrines of the Guild Socialists. For all the forceful advocacy by able thinkers like G.D.H. Cole (1953–61), the Guild Socialist movement was dead by the early 1920s. Likewise, British labour syndicalism (strong in the run-up to 1914

and during the First World War) perished at the same time, while conventional institutional trade unionism survived and continued to flourish.

Western European socialism was exported to the periphery, and to rapidly industrializing Russia in particular. Russian socialists adopted Marxism. Some like the Mensheviks remained faithful to German social democratic models, emphasizing an evolutionary strategy and cooperation with capitalistic modernization. Lenin and the Bolshevik faction came to favour an immediate revolutionary overthrow of tsarism and capitalism, and aimed to build a socialist society rapidly without long intermediary stages. Lenin's seizure of power in the Russian Revolution was a victory over social democrats and agrarian socialists as much as anything else. It was condemned by many Western socialists, notably both the parliamentarist Kautsky and the revolutionary Rosa Luxemburg, as leading to authoritarian rule that would betray the interests of the workers.

These criticisms proved prescient. Before 1914 the socialist movement was essentially, despite differences, one enterprise. The First World War produced a split in socialism and a communist regime implacably opposed to European democratic socialism. European communist parties created after 1918 were under Soviet tutelage. Communist parties in the 1920s and early 1930s emphasized insurrectionary politics, going so far as to stigmatize democratic socialist parties like the SPD as 'social fascist'. The aftermath of the Second World War, with the consolidation of Soviet rule in Eastern Europe and the restoration of parliamentary democracy in Western Europe, led to a radical change in communist parties. In France and Germany they became mass electoral parties and sought to participate in government. The split between communism and socialism in Europe, bitter into the 1950s, ceased to have much meaning with the rise of Eurocommunism in the 1970s.

After 1945 social democratic parties in Europe participated in government to a hitherto unprecedented degree. The post-1945 boom was a period of intensification of big government and welfarism. In Scandinavia, the UK and Germany, socialist parties became accepted parties of government. Radical socialist ideas declined in favour of social democratic objectives of redistribution and welfare in a state-managed full-employment capitalist system. For example,

Anthony Crosland's *The Future of Socialism* (1956) advocated a basic change in Labour Party doctrine.

In the 1970s Western European social democracy entered a period of profound crisis from which it has failed to emerge. Socialists had become dependent on Keynesian national economic management to deliver the growth and full employment necessary to make their welfare and redistribution strategies possible. With the oil crisis of 1973 and the collapse of the long postwar boom, Western economies entered into a period of economic turbulence, uncertain growth, and the internationalization of major markets that made social democrats little more than crisis managers. For a period the fashionable monetarist and free-market doctrines seemed to threaten to wipe out socialism or social democracy completely. These new doctrines have failed in large measure too and their destructive social consequences have provoked a renewed concern for social justice. Nevertheless the socialist parties in Western societies still have no coherent strategies. This is not only due to the absence of an alternative economic programme, but also because social changes have fatally undermined the constituency to which reformist and revolutionary socialists alike appeal, a large and relatively homogenous manual working class. The occupational structure has diversified, and with it the socialist claim to represent the majority has lost its force.

The spectacular collapse of communism after 1989 has further undermined Western socialism. Even if most socialists in Europe rejected the Soviet model, it always remained the one 'actually existing' socialism that had replaced the market by planning and it was repellent to most free people. Its collapse makes the idea of a fundamental social change to a non-market system seem unsustainable. The future of socialism is thus uncertain.

PAUL HIRST
FORMERLY UNIVERSITY OF LONDON

References

Bernstein, E. (1993 [1899]) *The Preconditions of Socialism*, ed. H. Tudor, Cambridge, UK.
Cole, G.D.H. (1953–61) *A History of Socialist Thought*, 5 vols, London.
Crosland, A. (1956) *The Future of Socialism*, London.

Further reading

Lichtheim, G. (1970) *A Short History of Socialism*, London.
Sassoon, D. (1998) *One Hundred Years of Socialism: The West European Left in the Twentieth Century*, New York.
Wright, A.W. (1986) *Socialisms: Theories and Practices*, Oxford.

SEE ALSO: communism; social democracy

SOCIOLEGAL STUDIES

Sociolegal studies is both a body of knowledge and a set of institutions, and it has different significance in the USA and UK. Many commentators have explicitly declined to define the discipline that they acknowledge sociolegal studies to be (see Economic and Social Research Council (ESRC) 1994; Genn and Partington 1993). Definitions that are offered tend to be highly abstracted formulations such as 'the study of the law and legal institutions from the perspectives of the social sciences' (Harris 1983) or work bearing on 'the relationship between society and the legal process' (Law and Society Review 1994). Institutionally sociolegal studies reflects the work that is carried on by members of the Law and Society Association (LSA) in the USA and the Socio-Legal Studies Association (SLSA) in the UK. Although the discipline has roots both in law faculties and social science departments, it tends not to encompass scholars who are not affiliated with the LSA or SLSA even though they work on the social underpinnings and consequences of law. Thus researchers who do law and economics in the USA and criminology and conventional sociology of law in the UK are not likely to label themselves as sociolegal scholars.

For many years US scholars interested in the interactions between law and its social environment considered themselves to be affiliated with the law and society movement. The leading journal in both the USA and UK has 'law' and 'society' in its title. However, law and society is problematic as a description of the field on two accounts. It carries the unfortunate implication that law is distinct from, rather than a constitutive part of, society; historically it has implied a research strategy involving positivist assumptions and normal science models. In the USA sociolegal studies has then become a term of refuge for scholars who wish to emphasize the interpenetration of law and society and to make clear their tolerance of, even commitment to, interpretative and other forms of postpositivist enquiry. In addition, for these scholars sociolegal studies has become self-referential: their professional references and affiliations are to other sociolegal scholars and sociolegal studies rather than to the disciplines in which they were trained and generally teach. In the UK, sociolegal studies described the discipline from the start and was accorded the definitive imprimatur in the 1970s when Oxford's ESRC-supported programme was labelled the Centre for Socio-Legal Studies.

The traditional concerns of sociolegal scholars can be characterized as either peeling back law's façade or filling in its blanks. The first focus has directed attention to the differences between prescription and behaviour, commonly denominated the gap between 'law on the books' and 'law in action'. The second concern has produced empirical descriptions and analyses of areas of legal life that have not been systematically studied. These traditional interests have led to important research on fields such as the social structure of the legal profession, access to justice and the tolerance of inequality, the level and direction of discretion exercised by legal authorities, historical and cultural variation in legal practices, doctrines and ideologies, the consumers' perspective of law, the indirect and unanticipated consequences of regulation, the transformation of disputes over time, and the symbolic dimensions of social problems.

While there is no reason to believe that interest and productivity in traditional concerns will diminish, a new set of questions about theory, methods and politics are increasingly debated. The new theoretical issues arise from the engagement of sociolegal scholars with the ideas of continental social theorists such as Foucault, Habermas, Bourdieu and Luhmann, the work of feminist and race theorists, and the various strands of 'new institutionalism' in organizational sociology, economics and political science. While the impact of each of these currents is different, all prompt a serious reconsideration of accepted sociolegal assumptions about law. More specifically, two important emergent issues concern the 'constitutive' approach and the 'globalization' perspective (the proliferation of world-level rule systems to regulate transnational social, economic and political relations). The constitu-

tive perspective has been developed in studies of lower courts, welfare and education law, and the role law plays in the everyday lives of ordinary people. Its lesson is that law is not simply applied to people, but is to a large degree 'constituted' or made meaningful within citizens' encounters with law and their use of it. This insight has led to an analysis of the plurality of meanings people attribute to law and of the ways people resist the taken-for-granted reality promoted by formal legal institutions. The globalization perspective encourages an examination of the expansion of regulatory structures developed to co-ordinate global and regional economic relations and to deal with the transnational dimensions of crime, business disputes, the environment and social and ethnic conflict. Moreover, the globalization perspective has focused attention on the ways transnational social and legal institutions, in turn, affect the development of national and subnational identities and legal cultures (Darian-Smith 1999).

Second, although methodological pluralism has always been a hallmark of sociolegal work, questions of method have increasingly come to occupy a central point of discussion within the field. This development is best understood as an outgrowth of the movement towards interpretative forms of enquiry occurring throughout the social sciences, including a philosophical critique of empiricism. The traditional view had led sociolegal analysts to examine the objective features of law, such as its formal structures, and to explain such structures by identifying objective non-legal 'social factors' that are correlated with them. Interpretivist approaches, on the other hand, rest upon the idea that law cannot be understood solely in terms of its material manifestations. Thus, interpretivist sociolegal scholars are fundamentally concerned with questions of meaning. In their view even the 'obejctive' manifestations of law are symbolically constructed. The task of the sociolegal investigator then is to examine the range of meanings found in law and the consequences of those meanings for the constitution of law's subjects.

The final issue is that of politics. Because sociolegal studies represent a 'second kind of learning about law and legal institutions' (Galanter 1985) – distinct from the professional image of law – and because critical legal studies and Marxist sociology of law have been a strong presence, questions of politics have always been an important part of the field. But an increasingly large component of the sociolegal community is reluctant to engage unreflectively in the politics inherent in policy work and legal reform campaigns. Scholars involved in such work often must accept official criteria and definitions of legal problems. These efforts also have historically been confounded with 'liberal legalism' – the unequivocal acceptance of the desirability of enhancing the effectiveness of law. To many contemporary sociolegal scholars these connections create impediments to developing truly critical appraisals of the operation of law in society.

W.L.F. FELSTINER
UNIVERSITY OF CALIFORNIA, SANTA BARBARA,
AND CARDIFF UNIVERSITY
RYKEN GRATTET
UNIVERSITY OF CALIFORNIA, DAVIS

References

Darian-Smith, Eve (1999) *Bridging Divides: The Channel Tunnel and English Legal Identity in the New Europe*, Berkeley.

Economic and Social Research Council (ESRC) (1994) *A Review of Socio Legal Studies*, London.

Galanter, M. (1985) 'The legal malaise or justice observed', *Law and Society Review* 537.

Genn, H. and Partington, M. (1993) *Socio-Legal Studies: A Review by the ESRC*, London.

Harris, D. (1983), 'The development of socio-legal studies in the United Kingdom', *Legal Studies* 547.

Law and Society Review (1994) 'Policy', *Law and Society Review*.

Further reading

Cotterell, R. (1984) *The Sociology of Law*, London.

Hunt, A. (1993) *Explorations in Law and Society*, New York.

Lempert, R.O. and Sanders, J. (1986) *An Invitation to Law and Social Science*, New York.

Tamanaha, B.Z. (2001) *A General Jurisprudence of Law and Society*, Oxford.

SEE ALSO: criminology; judicial process; law

SOCIOLINGUISTICS

The field of sociolinguistics started in the early 1970s (see Fishman 1971; Hymes 1973). This new linguistic paradigm endorsed the view that language could not be adequately studied without taking the social context into account, be it the situational context of utterances, the origin of the speakers, the region/city/country where the speakers come from, their age, gender, social class, ethnicity and so on. The fundamental framing question is: Who speaks where, in which way, why and with what kind of impact?

Of course, such a perspective on language was not entirely new. The philosopher Ludwig Wittgenstein had already proposed the notion of 'language game' several decades before (Wittgenstein 1953). 'Language games' (*Sprachspiele*) are defined as situated verbal and non-verbal actions that follow conventionalized rules and are acquired during socialization. Sociolinguistics also has roots in anthropology, in symbolic interactionism and in dialectology. Anthropologists had already recognized long ago that specific functions of language are related to rituals and other social practices (Malinowski 1938). Erving Goffman and other qualitative sociologists had started to study language in context, though lacking the linguistic expertise required for the detailed analysis of language in use. Dialectologists investigated specific dialects, vernaculars and registers, doing fieldwork and interviewing speakers, but their research was often unsystematic.

One of the triggers for a 'different' linguistics was the conflict between Chomskyan Transformational Grammar Theory and other views on language and meaning. The linguistic 'competence' studied by Transformational Grammarians involves isolated sentences, sometimes even artificially constructed sentences. Jürgen Habermas and other critics proposed a different approach. Language should be viewed as social practice and studied in use. They proposed the concept of 'language as action'. What should be studied are authentic verbal utterances in context, be it oral conversations or written documents. (See the famous debate in Habermas and Luhmann 1971.) The approach taken by Habermas is closely related to 'speech act theory' in the tradition of John Austin and John Searle. Wittgenstein's theory of meaning (i.e. 'meaning is constantly created in use') was also taken up by another theory of grammar: functional systemic linguistics, created by M.A.K. Halliday (1985), in the tradition of Firth (1968 [1957]). Hallidayan Linguistics (specifically his 'sociological semantics') was very close to a sociolinguistic view of 'language in/and society'.

Chomsky (1965) labelled 'language in use' 'performance'. In his view it was unsystematic and irrelevant for scientific investigation. Sociolinguists hold the contrary view. Conversations and everyday interactions have their own systems and rules, and are predictably dependent on social variables, on all levels of language (from phonetics and phonology up to syntax and discourse/text).

Because of their roots in the social sciences and in empirical research, sociologists differ from formal linguists, dealing with different data sets and applying different methods of quantitative and qualitative methods, ethnography and so on (see Titscher *et al.* 2000). The basic aim is to uncover systematic relationships between language, language change/shifts and social phenomena. Language in use can manifest social phenomena, but language in use can also produce and reproduce social phenomena. This fundamental dialectic is to be regarded as a central characteristic of sociolinguistics.

Several different objects of investigation and levels of analysis were developed in the 1970s. The main subjects of interest were language planning, diglossia and bilingualism. The scientific debate featured two theoretical approaches on a micro-level. The 'deficit hypothesis' put forward by Basil Bernstein (1960) claimed that working-class children in the UK were discriminated against because of their different linguistic 'code', for which he coined the term 'restrictive code'. Middle-class children, in contrast, were socialized differently and acquired an 'elaborated code' that enabled them to succeed much better in schools and also in other socially relevant institutions. Coming from the field of education, Bernstein integrated theoretical approaches from pedagogy, sociology (the systems theory of Talcott Parsons) and linguistics. He also proposed an educational programme ('compensatory education') that would enable working-class children to compete with children from other social milieux.

'Difference theory' was put forward by William Labov in his seminal research on linguistic variation in New York City, 1966. Labov proved that language change (on the phonological level) was directly connected to the age and social class of the speakers. He was also able to show that speakers of non-standard English were just as elaborate in their usage as standard speakers of English. Language use was shown to be related to the setting and to the interviewer. Thus, an African American interviewer was able to chat and talk quite elaborately with African American children, although the children remained almost totally silent when a white interviewer asked questions. Labov was therefore able to refute the deficit theory. Difference theory also had implications for social practice. Labov and others were consulted officially on issues of language education in the USA, and Labov himself won several court cases that enabled African American children to use their own vernacular in school. The 'ebonics-controversy' is another aspect of such applications and debates (Baugh 2001).

The Bernsteinian approach was developed by Bernstein himself and by other linguists. The concept of 'recontextualisation', defined as one of the most relevant processes of transfer of knowledge in educational discourses, became an important concept in studies of organizational discourse and in critical discourse analysis (Iedema and Wodak 1999).

It is important today to distinguish between macro- and micro-sociolinguistics. Macro-sociolinguists deals with language planning, languages in contact, diglossia and bilingualism, intercultural communication, and language policies. Micro-sociolinguistics focuses on the study of conversations, narratives and language use in everyday life and institutions (see Wodak 1996; Phillipson 2003). Empirical research reveals fundamental differences between lanuage use in institutional, formal contexts, and in everyday life. A number of variables were found to be important in the choice of specific codes, registers, styles and variants, such as gender, 'belonging' (in the sense of group membership), local and regional identities, and ethnicity. These are termed 'static variables', because they are presupposed at the outset without taking a specific setting or context into account. More recent theoretical approaches propose different units of investigation, such as 'communities of practice' or 'networks', where interaction modes and language in use are viewed as more important than static variables. 'Communities of practice' are defined by similar socialization modes and social practices of groups. 'Networks' cover the frequency and quality of interactions in groups or larger communities (Eckert and McConnell-Ginet 1992; Milroy and Milroy 1978; Trudgill 1978).

Micro-sociolinguistics has shifted from the phonological level to the level of texts. Conversations and narratives are analysed while focusing on gender-specific or class-specific differences. (Labov and Waletzky (1967) proposed a theory of 'narratives' that remains influential.) Institutional discourses are correlated with sociological approaches: doctor–patient communication, therapeutic communication, communication in business, and so on (Wodak 1986; Sarangi and Roberts 1999). Often enough, the macro- and micro-levels overlap. For example, intercultural communication can be studied in institutional contexts. Language planning for educational purposes has to consider many different genres and also include spontaneous conversations. And so forth.

In the twenty-first century, new challenges confront sociolinguistics: new media, new technologies of communication and new social issues, such as the impact of globalization, the fluidity of borders and mobility as well as migration. Visual communication is gaining rapidly in importance. All these new and very complex issues demand more interdisciplinary research in sociolinguistics and the development of new methodologies and new tools for language analysis.

R. WODAK
UNIVERSITY OF VIENNA

References

Baugh, J. (2001) 'American parallels: Racial conflict and the ebonics controversy. Ethnolinguistic conflict and the quest for educational enhancement', in R. de Cillia, H.-J. Krumm and R. Wodak (eds) *Kommunikationsverlust im Informationszeitalter/Loss of Communication in the Information Age*, Vienna, pp. 9–17.

Bernstein, B. (1960) 'Language and social class', *British Journal of Sociology* 2: 271–6.

Chomsky, N. (1965) *Aspects of the Theory of Syntax*, Cambridge, MA.

Eckert, P. and McConnell-Ginet, S. (1992) 'Communications of practice: Where language, gender, and power all live', in K. Hall, M. Buchholtz and B. Moonwomon (eds) *Locating Power: Proceedings of the Second Berkeley Women and Language Conference*, Berkeley, CA, pp. 89–99.

Firth, C.R. (1968 [1957]) 'A new approach to grammar', in F.R. Palmer (ed.) *Selected Papers of J.R. Firth, 1952–1959*, London, pp. 114–25.

Fishman, J. (1971) *Sociolinguistics. A Brief Introduction*, Rowley, MA.

Habermas, J. and Luhmann, N. (eds) (1971) *Theorie der Gesellschaft oder Sozialtechnologie – Was leistet die Systemforschung?* Frankfurt/M.

Halliday, M.A.K. (1985) *An Introduction to Functional Grammar*, London.

Hymes, D. (1973) 'The scope of sociolinguistics', in R.W. Shuy (ed.) *Report of the Twenty-third Annual Round Table Meeting on Linguistics and Language Studies*, Washington, DC, pp. 313–33.

Iedema, R. and Wodak, R. (1999) 'Introduction: Organizational discourse and practices', *Discourse and Society* 10: S1–20.

Labov, W. and Waletzky, J. (1967) 'Narrative analysis: Oral versions of personal experience', in J. Helms (ed.) *Essays on the Verbal and Visual Arts*, Seattle, WA, pp. 12–44.

Malinowski, B. (1938) 'The problem of meaning in primitive languages', in C. Ogden and I.A. Richards (eds) *The Meaning of Meaning*, London, pp. 297–336.

Milroy, J. and Milroy, L. (1978) 'Belfast: Change and variation in an urban vernacular', in P. Trudgill (ed.) *Sociolinguistic Patterns in British English*, London, pp. 19–36.

Phillipson, R. (2003) 'English for the globe, or only for globe-trotters?' in R. de Cillia, H.-J. Krumm and R. Wodak (eds) *Die Kosten der Mehrsprachigkeit – Globalisierung und sprachliche Vielfalt*, Vienna, pp. 93–100.

Sarangi, S. and Roberts, C. (1999) *Talk, Work and Institutional Order*, Berlin.

Titscher, St., Wodak, R., Meyer, M. and Vetter, E. (2000) *Methods of Text and Discourse Analysis*, London.

Trudgill, P. (ed.) (1978) *Sociolinguistic Patterns in British English*, London.

Wittgenstein, L. (1953) *Philosophical Investigations*, Oxford.

Wodak, R. (1986) *Language Behaviour in Therapy Groups*, Los Angeles.

—— (1996) *Disorders of Discourse*, London.

Further reading

Wodak, R. and Dressler, W.U. (1982) 'Sociophonological methods in the study of sociolinguistics variation in Viennese German', *Language in Society*, Cambridge, pp. 339–70.

SEE ALSO: discourse analysis; language; language and culture; pragmatics

SOCIOLOGY

More intimately than any other discipline that investigates the patterns of human interaction, sociology is associated with the advent of modernity, and this for several reasons.

First, perhaps the only common denominator of the great number of schools of thought and research strategies that claim sociological provenance is their focus on *society*. This focus may take one of two forms. Some sociologists have taken as their subject those structures and processes that can properly be conceived only as the attributes of a 'totality' (that is, shown not to be reducible to the traits of the individuals or associations whose interlocking and mutually dependent actions form that totality). Others have been concerned rather with the difference that is made to the condition and the conduct of individuals and groups of individuals by virtue of the fact that they form part of such a totality, called 'society'. But society, understood as the supra-individual, *anonymous* and not immediately visible site of powerful forces that shape individual fates and prompt or constrain individual actions, is a *modern* creation (distinct both from the *polis*, the site of articulated intentions, open debate, decision-making and explicit legislation, and the *household*, the sphere of free exercise of individual will, both of which are rooted in premodern history). Within society, actions tend to take the form of conditioned and determined (and thus more or less predictable) modes of conduct, shaped as they are by a constant pressure towards uniformity. But because society is 'the rule of nobody' with no fixed address, the mechanisms underlying this conditioning, the source of pressures towards uniformity, are far from evident. They are not represented in the awareness of the actors whose behaviour they shape. They must first be discovered in order to be grasped. Only once statistics had been developed did it become possible to set apart society as an autonomous object of study, as an entity distinct from individual, motivated actions, since statistics allowed for the uniform representation of a mass of actions, stripped of individuality.

Second, another typically modern phenomenon is the constant tension between humans uprooted from their traditional and communal settings, transformed into 'individuals' and cast into the position of autonomous subjects of action, and 'society', experienced as a daily constraint upon, and ultimately the outer limit to, the action of individual will. The paradox is that the modern individual neither can be fully at home and at peace with society, nor can he or she exist (indeed, come into being as an *individual*) outside society. In consequence, the study of society, and of the tension between its capacity both to constrain and to enable, has been prompted throughout modern history by two diverse though connected interests, in principle contradictory to each other in their practical applications and consequences. On the one hand, there is an interest in manipulating social conditions in such a way as to elicit more uniform behaviour of the kind desired by those in positions of power. The central question here is one of *discipline*, that is of coercing people to behave in certain ways even if they do not share, or even reject, the goals set by the designing and controlling agencies. On the other hand, there is an interest in understanding the mechanisms of social regulation so that, ideally, their enabling capacity can be revealed, allowing people better to resist constraints and pressures towards uniformity.

It goes without saying that these two interests are at cross-purposes. One aims to limit the very human freedom that the other is designed to promote. More precisely, there is a clash between the two kinds of freedom that the respective interests require, and in the end they undermine each other. The pursuit of enhanced uniformity is conducted in the name of improving human control over nature, that is, in the name of a *collective* freedom to shape the world in conformity with a vision of human needs or human nature. Yet the objective of controlling nature also inevitably entails the control of *human* nature (in practice, of human *individuals*), that is, of imposing patterns of conduct that would not necessarily be followed if matters were left to take what we call their natural course.

The inherent ambivalence of the modern human condition, situated in a society that simultaneously constrains and enables, was reflected in the self-definition of sociology as *the scientific study of society and of the aspects of human life that derive from 'living in society'*. Much sociological work has been inspired by a variety of controlling agencies, which sought precise and efficient instruments for eliciting disciplined and manageable behaviour. Above all, the modern state had to install and sustain 'law and order' through the rational design of an institutional network that would constrain individual life. Theoretical models of society constructed by sociology more often than not presented a view from the top, from, as it were, the control room. Society was perceived as an object of social engineering, while 'social problems' were depicted as in the first place problems of administration, to be met by legal rules and the redeployment of resources. On the other hand, sociology responded willy-nilly to the resentment felt against the oppression entailed in social engineering, for it inevitably exposed the artificial, arbitrary, 'man-made' and contrived character of social institutions, which according to the powers that be were objectively necessary or rational. That is why throughout its history sociology has attracted criticism from both sides of the political divide. Power-holders will go on accusing sociologists of relativizing the kind of order they are sworn to promote and defend, and so of undermining their hold over their subjects, and inciting what they see as unrest and subversion. People defending their way of life or their ideals against what they experience as oppressive, stifling constraints imposed by resourceful powers are likely to object that sociology serves as a counsellor to their adversaries. The intensity of these charges will in each case reflect not so much the condition of sociology as the nature of social conflict in which, by virtue of the very nature of its work, it is inescapably enmeshed.

Understandably, both sets of adversaries would like to delegitimize the validity of sociological knowledge and to deny its scientific authority. Such assaults make sociologists acutely sensitive about their scientific status. They prompt ever renewed, yet forever inconclusive attempts to convince both academic opinion and the lay public that the knowledge produced by sociologists, as a result of the application of sociological methods, is superior to unaided and freely formed popular opinions, and that it can even claim truth-values equivalent to those imputed to the findings of science.

The boundaries of sociological discourse

The term 'sociology' has been in use since the second quarter of the nineteenth century, following the influential work of Auguste Comte, who not only coined the name for a not-yet-practised area of study but also claimed for the future science the status of a generalized and generalizing knowledge of the laws governing the progressive yet orderly development of human society (in his terms, the laws of social dynamics and social statics) – knowledge that would be obtained by deploying universally applicable scientific methods of observation and experiment. When attempts were made in Europe and the USA in the late nineteenth and early twentieth centuries to establish sociology as a superior source of comment on human experience (as scientific knowledge in general is superior to folk beliefs), and particularly to introduce it as a separate academic discipline into a field of study already occupied by subjects that had become established and recognized at an earlier stage, the

pioneer sociologists chose to spell out the genuine or putative differences between the subject-matters or approaches of sociology and its older and established competitors. These pioneer sociologists wished to define and fence off an area of reality that none of the established disciplines had explored, and/or a type of knowledge that no discipline had hitherto provided.

Emile Durkheim, retrospectively acclaimed as one of the founding fathers of sociology as an academic discipline, followed the French positivist tradition and postulated the existence of specifically social facts, which had been left out (and by their very nature could not but be neglected) by other types of human studies, and particularly by psychology, the most obvious competitor for the job of explaining the observed regularities in human conduct. Durkheim postulated the objective status of such social facts, that is their irreducibility in principle to the data of individual, subjective experience. (By objectivity he meant the assumed independence of social facts from the self-consciousness of human actors, and also their power to coerce the conduct of individuals and to bring them into line should they veer from socially accepted standards.) This necessarily implied that such facts should be treated in the way that all respected sciences study their areas of reality: *objectively*, from the point of view of an external observer, without reference to subjectively experienced 'states of mind' and the motives of the actors.

At the same time, another founding father of academic sociology, Max Weber, inspired by the German *Geisteswissenschaften* and *Kulturlehre* traditions, attempted to set the new discipline apart by following what was virtually the opposite strategy. Sociology was to be distinguished by its approach and interpretative stance, rather than by claiming that a separate set of 'facts' constituted an exclusive domain for its study. For Max Weber, sociology was distinguished by its attempt to *understand* human conduct (always a *meaningful* – purposive – phenomenon, unlike the behaviour of inanimate bodies that can be explained, but not understood) in terms of the meanings that actors invest in their actions. Unlike the natural-scientific explanation of events with reference to external causes, sociological understanding was to be an inside job. What set apart properly sociological explanations was that they operated 'at the level of meaning'. To understand social action one had to postulate the meanings that 'made sense' of the observed conduct.

The differences between the disciplines collectively designated as social sciences (of which sociology is one, alongside psychology, anthropology, political science and various others) were, however, originally determined by the kinds of questions they posed about humans, regarded as social beings, that is, as entities whose conduct is regular, by and large predictable, and also potentially (given the availability of adequate resources) controllable, and who are for these reasons potential objects of study in the sense defined by the strategies of modern science. These questions were in turn dictated by the often practical and policy-oriented interests of the modern state and other agencies. Only later were the originally contingent differences reinforced through the progressive departmentalization of academic research and teaching, and it was then argued that each dealt with an allegedly distinct and autonomous aspect of human reality.

The core of the discourse of sociology has been relatively well defined by a distinctive written tradition, but it has been, and remains, notoriously frayed at the edges, despite the fact that for most of its history it struggled to set itself apart from related academic enterprises, and thus to demarcate the area over which it exercised exclusive sovereignty. The frontiers of sociology are porous, letting in materials formed within other interpretive traditions and other discourses. It is also far from clear (let alone universally agreed) what sort of propositions belong to sociology proper, and from which 'sites' such propositions can be formulated if they are to be accepted as being sociologically relevant. Little wonder that there are few, if any, themes, topics, questions or practical interests that may be classified as unambiguously and exclusively sociological without their assignment being contested by other discourses within the humanities or social sciences. Moreover, as commentators on human experience, sociologists share their subject-matter with countless others, not only members of other social scientific communities but also with novelists, poets, journalists, politicians, religious thinkers and the educated public in general.

There is another reason that sociology has been unable to make the transition from the status of a discourse to what Michel Foucault terms a discursive formation. It is characterized by what Anthony Giddens (1976) describes as a 'double hermeneutics'. The object of sociological commentary is always an already experienced experience, filled with meaning, interpreted and narrated even while it is still (for a sociologist) raw material. Unlike the objects dealt with by the natural sciences, which are not as a rule part of the daily practice and experience of non-specialists, the objects of the sociologists' hermeneutical efforts are the products of a competent, wide-ranging and incessant – though largely unreflective – hermeneutical activity on the part of the lay members of society.

Apart from the fact that the data of sociology are in this way secondary or second level, the interpretative operations of the sociologist do not differ in kind from the lay hermeneutic practices that are already embedded in the objects of its study – that are, indeed, responsible for the constitution of these objects. It is not immediately apparent – and must therefore be proven – that professional sociological interpretations are necessarily superior, more credible, trustworthy and otherwise privileged than the primary, lay meanings that they are intended to improve upon or to replace. Hence – again in striking contrast to the practices of most natural sciences, but in common with the experience of many human sciences – the clarification of its relationship to common sense (that is, lay sense, beliefs that have been denied the status of professional knowledge) and intensive methodological self-reflection constitute an integral, and inordinately prominent, aspect of sociological work.

The most common strategy of sociologists is to denigrate popularly held opinion, and to cast doubt upon the introspective capacity of actors. However profound the other differences between them may be, most schools of thought in sociology agree that the actors hold at best a hazy, at worst a mistaken, image of the true motives and reasons for their conduct, and that they cannot reliably represent the social forces that affect their lives, for they reason from within the confines of their own, always partial and fragmentary, life experiences. On that view, common sense is incoherent and internally contradictory, vulnerable to distorting influences, and always in need of correction. Being mere opinions, popular interpretations should be treated as *objects* of research and not as a *source* of true knowledge. This strategy of denigrating common sense is supplemented by the effort to elaborate methods of data collection and an interpretive methodology that might claim the authority of established scientific procedures, so assuring a degree of reliability of sociological knowledge to which mere opinions, which are not formed in a similarly methodical fashion, cannot aspire.

The formative interests of sociology

The projects of research and teaching that were collected under the name of 'sociology' in the USA were stimulated by concerns about the turbulence that was caused by rapid industrialization and the massive immigration in the urban areas of the US Midwest in the early twentieth century. These concerns were shared initially by politicians, journalists, social reformers and religious preachers (the first academic sociologists being drawn from their ranks). The constantly changing social world seemed to be poorly integrated, the direction of change unconstrained by shared traditions or by self-regulating communal mechanisms. Consequently the options were apparently wide open, offering a perhaps dangerous freedom for social experiment. The social setting, and therefore also human conduct, seemed to be flexible and pliable – available for rational design and for social engineering. In this context, the emerging 'science of society' regarded itself as first and foremost an instrument of policy for local governments and social workers. The policies to be designed with social scientific inspiration and assistance were intended to deal with 'deviation', 'abnormality' and 'pathology'. In short, they aimed to resolve social problems. Society was seen, indeed, as first and foremost a collection of *problems*, and the science of society was accordingly asked to deliver a theoretical guide to practical problem-solving.

A similar practical bias also characterized continental European sociology when, like its North American counterpart, it began to be assimilated into the universities at the end of the nineteenth century. However, the Europeans did not concentrate on problem-solving. Rather, the emerging social science was intended to enable rational human beings to play a conscious part in the large movements of history, movements that were believed to exhibit a direction and logic, if one that had yet to be revealed. Sociology would therefore enable people to feel more at home in an unfamiliar world, more in charge of their own

actions and – collectively and obliquely – having a measure of control over the conditions under which they were obliged to act. In other words sociology, it was hoped, would discover the historical tendency of modern society, and modify it. In the place of a spontaneous, elemental, poorly understood process, it would set an orderly, monitored development. It was also widely assumed from the start that not all modern transformations were unambiguously beneficial and desirable. Sociology therefore had to alert the public, at all levels but in particular at the level of the law-makers, to the dangers hidden in uncontrolled social processes, and it had to propose ways of preventing such undesirable processes from materializing, or to propose ways of repairing the damage.

The founders of the new discipline and their successors, whose ideas were later to be absorbed into its canon, agreed on this understanding of the calling of sociology, even if they differed in their interpretation of the crucial features and guiding factors of the historical trends that they all wished to grasp. Comte (1798–1857) identified the moving force of history in the progress of scientific knowledge and, more generally, in the 'positive spirit'. Herbert Spencer (1820–1903) envisaged the passage of modern society from the conflict-ridden military stage to a peaceful 'industrial' stage, where a multitude of products became available for distribution. He foresaw a continuous progress towards the increasing complexity of society, paired with the growing autonomy and differentiation of individuals. Karl Marx (1818–83) expected the progressive control over nature to result eventually in the complete emancipation of society from the constraints of necessity arising from want – a redemption from misery and strife, which would put an end to the alienation of products from their producers and to the transformation of those products into capital deployed to enslave and further expropriate the producers, eventually putting to an end all exploitation. Ferdinand Tönnies (1855–1936) conceived of a historical succession whereby the original *Gemeinschaft* – the natural togetherness of communities held together by mutual sympathy, solidarity and co-operation – would be replaced in modern times by *Gesellschaft* – a web of partial, purposeful, impersonal and contractual bonds. Emile Durkheim (1858–1917) focused his analysis of historical trends upon the progressive division of labour and thus the growing complexity of the social whole. He proposed a model of society integrated first by the 'mechanical' solidarity of similar segments and later by the 'organic' solidarity of functionally differentiated yet complementary classes and professional groups. Max Weber (1864–1920) represented modernity mainly in terms of an ubiquitous rationalization of all spheres of social life, thought and culture, and the increasing role played by action grounded in the calculation of means and ends at the expense of the non-rational or irrational, custom-bound or affective forms of conduct. Georg Simmel (1859–1918) emphasized the passage from qualitative and differentiated to quantitative and uniform relations, and underlined the new and growing role played by universalizing and disembodied forces, best exemplified by the institution of money and by abstract, categorical thought.

The appearance of sociology coincided in continental Europe with a wave of optimism in the creative, life-improving potential and the universal destiny of European civilization, which was identified in the public mind with civilization as such. That faith drew inspiration and apparent confirmation from the rapid and un-resisted global expansion of European rule and influence. The profusely demonstrated practical superiority of the European way of life seemed to offer the budding social science an uncontroversial model of social development in general, and a standard by which to measure other societies and to anticipate their future development. Then, as later, sociology was in tune with the general intellectual mood of the time, sharing the widespread belief in progress, the expectation of constant improvement, the conviction that all present or future problems could be solved through the advance of science and technical know-how, if the political will existed, and the expectation that rationally organized, humane societies would come to dominate the world. Sociology aimed to be a part of this progressive change, through reflecting upon the course history had taken and was likely to take in the future, and thereby supplying the standards by which practical measures might be evaluated. The identification of unsolved and potentially dangerous problems, and criticisms of misguided or ineffective ways of handling social problems, was seen as an integral constituent of the task of sociology.

At the time of the establishment of continental sociology, Britain was the centre of a worldwide empire. The principle of indirect rule in the colonies presupposed that the conquered populations were enclosed and by and large self-reproducing totalities. They were societies in their own right. Evidently different from metropolitan societies, yet viable and retaining their own distinctive traits, they put on the agenda the task of the comparative study of societies – a task undertaken by what came to be known as 'social anthropology'. Until the middle of the twentieth century, social anthropology dominated social science in Britain, thereby delaying the establishment of academic sociology. The emergence of sociology in Britain coincided with the dismantling of the empire and the concomitant concern with the study of Britain itself. The circumstance that sociology entered public debate in Britain at a time of retreat and retrenchment, rather than at a time of expansion and optimism, as had been the case in continental Europe and the USA, was to have consequences for the status and public reception of sociology in Britain for a long time to come.

The changing profile of sociology

Attempts are often made, misleadingly, to reduce the variegated and open sociological discourse to a succession of clearly demarcated periods, each distinguished by the dominance, or at least prevalence, of a single paradigm – a coherent and circumscribed body of interrelated concepts. Yet one can hardly think of sociology as a discursive formation with boundaries, let alone as characterized by the practice of 'normal science' in Thomas Kuhn's sense, focused upon a shared paradigm. Always part and parcel of the intellectual life of its time and place, the shifts in the interests of sociological discourse and in the tasks that sociology sets itself reflect more than anything else general cultural changes.

By common consent, the most radical of all shifts to which modern culture has been exposed since its inception occurred in the second part of the twentieth century. The most seminal, and the most important of its intellectual consequences, was the collapse of the hierarchy of values that had hitherto underpinned modern culture. A new scepticism became established, that put in question all modern certainties, above all the conviction that the Western type of society represents the form of civilization that will eventually achieve universal dominion, and that (notwithstanding temporary slow-downs and occasional set-backs) a continuous progress towards a more rational and accident-proof society has already been assured. Closely connected with this crisis of confidence has been the gradual yet relentless fall from grace of the ideal of an all-regulating, ubiquitous, obsessively legislating state engaged upon great enterprises of social engineering.

The most momentous consequence for the shape and status of sociology was the disappearance of the vantage point from which most of the orthodox sociological work had been done: that of the cockpit, or control room, of an administrative centre willing and resourceful enough to treat society as an object that could be closely monitored and managed, once social processes had been analysed into a series of definable and in principle resolvable problems. To be sure, much of the work done in sociology departments retains the impress of the past of the discipline, when it was sustained by demands emanating from expanding warfare and welfare bureaucracies. Nonetheless the overall trend is away from the old ways and towards new 'cognitive' perspectives. There can be no doubt that the nature and tasks of sociological work are now understood in a very different way from that taken for granted in the first half of the twentieth century.

To sum up, the focus of sociological interests is shifting from *structure* to *agency*, from society understood primarily as a set of external constraints that restrict the field of choices available to the members of society, and to a large extent determine their behaviour, to social settings that are understood primarily as pools of enabling resources from which the actors draw in order to pursue their own goals. Society is conceived of less as a self-perpetuating pattern of social positions and functions, more as an ongoing process, which in its course puts together and dismantles (always temporary) networks of dependency and stages for action. Though the category of society is not likely to vanish from sociological discourse, its meaning is undergoing fateful changes. Increasingly, the category is used in the sense of 'sociation' (actors entering into or abandoning relationships) or – yet more symptomatically – in the sense of 'sociality' (meaning the very capacity of actors to sociate). This is arguably the crucial shift: other new traits or new emphases that will be listed below, and which set contemporary

sociological discourse apart from the received tradition of modern sociology, may be represented as its manifestations or consequences.

Where once sociology was concerned above all with stability, self-reproduction and repetitiveness, and with the ways and means of securing these (the central preoccupation of the once dominant 'systems theory' of Talcott Parsons and equally of the opponents of his structural functionalism), attention moved to the study of innovation. It is understood that every action is to an extent a creative act, though it always takes account of extant, already meaningful patterns.

There was also a move away from the search for laws and regularities. These were conceived of as preceding the action, affecting its course while themselves remaining unaffected. Actions are no longer portrayed as *determined* but rather as *contingent*, each a unique creation and therefore not truly predictable. Doubt is also cast upon the predictive value of statistics. It is accepted that the most frequent or numerous phenomena will not necessarily represent the trends of the future. In consequence, there seem to be no clear-cut criteria by which to anticipate the consequences of events, their impact and durability, and thus to judge their significance. This in turn leads to the erosion of once central, privileged objects or areas of sociological study. Since sociologists no longer evoke 'basic conflicts', 'main links' or 'steering processes', it is not obvious why certain topics, actors or events ought to be given priority by the sociologist.

The attention of sociologists accordingly passed from the concerns of the control room (from issues like the impact of the state, class domination, etc.) to mundane, elementary interactions, to the grassroots level of social reality, to what actors do to one another and to themselves in the context of face-to-face interaction. Largely under the influence of Alfred Schütz's argument that the 'world within reach' supplies the archetype for the actors' model of all other 'universes of meaning' (Schütz 1982), it is assumed that the essential skills and knowledge reflectively or unreflectively deployed by actors in their daily life are ultimately responsible for what is perceived in retrospect to be a global, impersonal trend, or the persistence of objective structures.

Once actors were conceived of as knowledgeable and in principle prone to self-monitoring, the prime task of sociological investigation became the reconstruction of their knowledge. This dramatically alters the role assigned to common sense in sociological discourse. Initially conceived of as alternative, poorly informed and essentially false interpretation of social reality (to be criticized, corrected or supplanted) it now becomes the major resource for sociological interpretation. To an unprecedented degree, sociology assumed a hermeneutical stance. It emphasizes that social realities are intrinsically meaningful (endowed with meaning by the actors who produce them), and that in consequence to understand those realities one must reconstruct the actors' meanings. This does not necessarily mean that the sociologist strives to achieve empathy: to discover what is going on in the minds of the actors, to bring to light their conscious motives and explicit goals. Sociologists still tend to deny that the actors are necessarily the best judges of sociological interpretations. But the hermeneutical approach does mean that explanations or interpretations of social realities must treat the actors as meaning-driven and meaning-creating, rather than as being pushed and pulled by impersonal, objectively describable forces and constraints.

Another intimately related trend is the switch in interest from external coercion and constraint to the actor's self-construction and self-definition. Actions are meaningful, actors are knowledgeable, reflecting constantly upon their own identity and motives. One might say that if human beings were seen by orthodox sociology as driven primarily by necessity and as the target of social forces, they tend to be construed now, more often than not, as identity-driven and motivated, choosing subjects.

The most general trend is to move down the levels of social organization in search of the genuine levers of social actions. Contemporary sociologists accordingly pay particular attention to *community* at the expense of 'society' (which in modern sociology was assumed to be, for all practical purposes, identical with the nation-state). For a long time, sociologists believed that community was a relic of premodern times, bound to disappear in the course of modernization. It was restored to a central position in sociological analysis, and is regarded as the ultimate source of actors' meanings, and thus of social reality itself. Communities are considered to be the bearers of tradition, which is sustained and recreated by the actions of their members; to be the ultimate source of whatever commonality

and sharing is to be found in the actors' meanings; and to be the point of reference in the process whereby the actors define themselves and construct their identities (and so, reciprocally, sustain the community). Unlike 'society', which is identified with the nation-state, communities have no objective boundaries (that is, boundaries guarded by coercive powers). They are fluid, and the strength of the grip in which they hold their members may vary too (that grip being none other than the intensity of the actors' emotional identification with what they conceive as, or imagine to be, community).

Sociologists say that communities are *imagined*. As conceived in contemporary sociology, community is postulated – the postulate becoming reality where actions are undertaken as if it *was* a reality. There is therefore a constant interplay between actors and 'their' communities, neither being assigned priority in sociological analysis.

Alternative sociologies

The perspectival shift in contemporary sociology – the new self-awareness that admits the community-, culture-, time-bound nature of any sociological discourse and body of knowledge – is simultaneously responsible for, and a response to, the emergence of alternative sociologies that promote different interpretations of shared social realities. These insist that a plurality of interpretations is inevitable, given the difference between the experiential vantage points from which interpretive efforts are launched. To be sure, earlier social theorists sometimes argued that there was an intimate affinity between position-related experience and the style and content of sociological knowledge. Most notably, this is true of the Marxist thesis that there is an unbridgeable opposition between the 'bourgeois' and 'proletarian' view of society. The novelty consists, first, in an extension of the perspectival principle from two opposing classes to a multitude of categories distinguished by ethnic, gender or cultural characteristics, and the overt acceptance of the *interested* nature of each perspective (for each serves the needs of a group whose collective experience it claims to articulate, and each is necessary for the integration of the group and the sustenance of group tradition). Moreover, the alternative sociologies abandon the claim to objectivity and to exclusive truth, openly admitting the relativity of any interpretation. However strong the mutual interest (both approving and critical) that various alternative sociologies show in the assertions of others, little progress has been made so far towards a genuine synthesis of interpretive standpoints. Given their strategies and their understanding of the nature of sociological work, it is legitimate to doubt whether such a synthesis is a realistic objective. More likely the coexistence of alternative perspectival sociologies will be a lasting (nay constitutive) condition of sociology.

Arguably the most prolific and influential among alternative sociologies has been born of the new awareness of the specificity of gender-related experience, inspired by the feminist movement of the second half of the twentieth century. Feminist sociology, like other alternative sociologies, assumes that all knowledge is socially situated. In other words, it is related in both its subject-matter and its interpretive angle to an experience unique to a specific group or category, distinguished by the content of its life concerns. Mainstream sociology, on this view, has been situated in the essentially male context of the 'relations of ruling' (Smith 1987) – in the world of paid labour, politics and formal organizations. Emerging in this context, and serving it, the mainstream, male sociology produces 'rulership texts' that masquerade as objective knowledge. They construct and impose general identities and classifications, and deploy abstract, impersonal and anonymous categories that denigrate or exclude from the realm of the significant all real, personal life experience. The assumed objectivity of such knowledge, feminist sociologists aver, is a mere pretence; its allegedly non-partisan viewpoint can be seriously asserted only in so far as male domination itself has been exempted from the discourse, while providing its tacit premise. Once that premise is questioned, it becomes clear that mainstream sociology is but one of the many potential situated sociologies – one that focuses on a selected part of 'the social', excluding other parts. In particular it leaves out – and fails to account for – the social world as it is experienced and lived by women. For this reason, a sociology by women and for women needs to be developed to supplement the extant male sociology, and simultaneously to expose its limited scope, its situatedness and its unwarranted bid for monopoly, reflecting as it does at the level of theory the practice of male domination.

On this view, the part of the 'social' on which the new female sociology must be constructed is the sphere of daily domestic life, childcare, service-oriented activities, in which women's roles are cast and moulded. But female sociology is not set apart only by concentrating on a specific, often underplayed area of experience. The different experience of women must also be processed in a new way, steering clear of the male inclination to abstract, depersonalize and categorize. Such a sociology should aim to return to the real and the concrete. Women are immersed in the practical context of the everyday/everynight world, the world of the actual and specific, which they never leave (at least in their gender-specific capacity). This kind of experience, marginalized and declared out of court by the dominant sociological discourse, must be granted social significance so that women's lives can be brought back from the margins to which they have been exiled to the centre of social life and of the knowledge of the social.

The feminist-inspired alternative sociology takes 'gender' as the key differentiator of social situatedness and situated experience. It considers gender to be the constitutive factor of the most consequential social division and social conflict, as well as the basis of the critical dimension of social domination and oppression – that is, of patriarchal rule. Other alternative sociologies select their key differentiator differently – most often from class, ethnic or racial attributes – but on the whole they share the assumption that all knowledge of the social is position bound, situated and interested, and treat with reserve any claims of unencumbered objectivity, suspecting that behind such claims must lurk a bid for domination, and an apology for oppression.

Areas of sociological study

Sociology is a widely ramifying discipline, subdivided into numerous fields of specialized study, often united quite loosely by little more than shared hermeneutic strategies and an ambition to correct common beliefs. The demarcation of these fields follows quite closely the institutionalized, functional divisions in organized society, answering the effective or assumed demand of the established areas of management. Thus specialized bodies of knowledge have accumulated that focus on deviance and corrective or punitive policies, politics and political institutions, army and war, race and ethnicity, marriage and the family, education, the cultural media, information technologies, religion and religious institutions, industry and work, urban living and its problems, health and medicine.

Not all specific research interests, however, can be referred unambiguously to administrative demands. The endemic ambivalence of sociology, which can be traced back to the ambivalent response of the early sociologists to the rationalization project of modernity, manifests itself in the persistence of areas of study that have no direct administrative application, and are even potentially disruptive from the managerial point of view. To be sure, the distinction between the potentially stabilizing and destabilizing, overt or latent intentions and effects of sociological knowledge cuts across the thematic divisions, none of the specialized fields being entirely free from ambivalence. Still, certain areas of sociological thought address themselves more explicitly than others to individuals resisting managerial manipulation and attempting to assert control over their own lives. Relevant areas of study include social inequality (whether based on class, gender or race), identity-formation, interaction in daily life, intimacy and depersonalization, etc. In contrast to management-oriented areas of study, there is a pronounced tendency to cross-fertilize, to borrow insights, to dismantle boundaries between different areas of expertise. This is in keeping with the overall strategic aim of restoring the wholeness of life and personality, which are fragmented and separated by institutionalized divisions.

Major theoretical influences in contemporary sociology

The formative, classic ideas of Marx, Weber, Durkheim or Simmel continue to constitute the backbone of sociological discourse, providing the reference point for self-identification over the wide range of schools and styles between which sociological practice is divided. The classic works are frequently revisited, reread and reinterpreted in the light of changing experiences, interests and priorities. Given the spread of interpretations imposed upon the variety of original classical insights, revivals of classic sources may serve the integration of sociological work or sustain the division between different schools of thought. Talcott Parsons's social action and system theory,

which under the name of 'structural functionalism' dominated the sociological scene in the 1950s and 1960s, was constructed as a (highly idiosyncratic) interpretation of the classic sociological tradition. So was the opposition to Parsons – by C. Wright Mills, Ralf Dahrendorf, David Lockwood, John Rex and others – which prepared the ground for the eventual replacement of the Parsonian version of sociology by providing new insights into the classical foundations of the discipline.

The most seminal of departures that led in the course of the 1970s to widespread criticism and rejection of what Anthony Giddens termed the 'orthodox consensus' was the phenomenological revolution. Initiated by Berger and Luckmann (1966), the revolution was sustained by a spate of radical reformulations of the subject-matter and proper strategy of sociological work. The posthumously published work of Alfred Schütz served as the main theoretical inspiration and authority. It prepared the way for the influence of the continental philosophies of Husserl and Heidegger, and their hermeneutical applications in the writings of Paul Ricoeur and Hans Gadamer. The effect of the exposure to phenomenology was to shift interest from external, extra-subjective structural constraints to the interpretation of the subjective experience of actors; and from the determination to arbitrate between objective truth and prejudiced opinion to the effort to reveal the conditions of knowledge rooted in communally transmitted traditions. Harold Garfinkel's 'ethnomethodology' (which treated the social as the accomplishment of knowledgeable actors, in the course of their everyday work) added further impetus to the reorientation of sociology away from 'objective' systems and structures, and towards 'social agency', self-reflexive, intentional action and its unanticipated consequences, a move most emphatically expressed in the work of Anthony Giddens.

There has been a greater openness of sociology to developments and fashions in other disciplines, and more generally in other areas of culture. Apart from phenomenology and hermeneutics, powerful influences have been Adorno and Horkheimer's critical theory, Wittgenstein's philosophy, Lévi-Strauss's and Barthes's semiotics, Foucault's philosophy of knowledge, Braudel's historiography, Lacan's psychoanalysis and Derrida's deconstruction – to name but the most obvious instances.

Two other developments should also be noted. First, North American sociology lost the dominant position that it had gained in the years following the Second World War. It has been in retreat at home, due to the diminishing resources of its sponsoring bureaucracies, while its empirical methodology, once the source of its greatest strength and appeal, has found less application in European sociology due to its changed concerns and strategies. Second, there has been a growing interchange between national sociologies, sociological discourse acquiring increasingly a transnational character. Examples are the worldwide impact of Jürgen Habermas's (1979) 'communication theory', Niklas Luhmann's 'revised system theory', Ulrich Beck's (1992) *Risikogesellschaft*, Frederik Barth's analysis of ethnic boundaries, or Pierre Bourdieu's (1985) notions of 'cultural capital' and 'habitus'.

The postmodern controversy

Through the works of Charles Jencks, Jean-François Lyotard, Jean Baudrillard, Gianni Vattimo, Alberto Melucci, Michel Maffesoli and other writers, the twin issues of the reassessment of the current trends of modern society and of the aim and function of sociological work have moved to the centre of sociologists' concerns, expressed in what came to be called the 'postmodern debate'.

The nub of the debate concerns the thesis that the modern project has ground to a halt or exhausted itself, being displaced by 'postmodernity' – a non-systemic condition of multiple realities, of change without direction, with no prospect of being controlled. Doubts are voiced as to whether the present condition is so distinctive and novel as to warrant the description postmodern. Habermas (1979) and Giddens (1993), for instance, insist that the features described as postmodern are traits of a late or mature modernity, and that the modernist project is still far from exhausted. Others, however, argue that the demise of Utopias, of the trust in progress and in historical direction, as well as the collapse of projects to impose universal and uniform cultural standards and structural patterns, testify to a decisive break.

Both sides in the debate invoke the concept of the 'society of risk', originally introduced by Ulrich Beck (1992) and now very generally accepted. One view is that the modern forces of science and technology have further reinforced their central position, since only techno-science can locate, articulate and deal with the new, global risks. The contrary view is that present-day society is shaped by its responses to the new risks created mostly by past responses to risks previously revealed – a process that feeds postmodern fragmentation.

With respect to the micro-social level, some maintain that the notorious fluidity of individual identity, the instability of personal relationships, signals the fulfilment of the long modern development towards individual freedom. The alternative view is that the current human condition is marked above all, in characteristic postmodern fashion, by the difficulty of holding on to already acquired identities.

Finally, another hotly contested issue is the connection between the condition called 'postmodern' and the affluence of certain highly developed consumer societies. Doubts are accordingly raised as to the global significance of the postmodern condition.

The views adopted as to what are the appropriate strategies for sociology in the new circumstances are closely related to the stands taken in the debate between modernists and postmodernists. Those who argue that contemporary society is increasingly postmodern maintain that sociology ought to take stock of the multiplicity of cultures, traditions and forms of life, and thus concentrate its efforts on facilitating communication and understanding between distinct realities rather than continue the search for a unique and universally binding truth, in defiance of communally grounded and tradition-bound local, lay knowledge. Those who hold this view are ready to accept that sociology is essentially an attempt to replicate, somewhat more systematically, the interpretive activity in which all members of society are engaged, in the daily activities of sociation. Not everyone, however, is prepared to abandon the modernist ambition of social science to provide privileged knowledge, which is bound to expose the frailty of lay beliefs and eventually to replace them with scientifically grounded, objective truth, and which aspires to co-operate in political and legislative efforts to establish rational structures that will make possible and promote the replacement of lay enterprises with rational, scientific projects.

ZYGMUNT BAUMAN
UNIVERSITY OF LEEDS

References

Beck, U. (1992) *Risk Society: Towards a New Modernity*, New York.
Berger, P. and Luckmann, T. (1966) *The Social Construction of Reality*, New York.
Giddens, A. (1976) *New Rules of Sociological Method: A Positive Critique of Interpretive Sociology*, London.
Schütz, A. (1982) *Life Forms and Meaning Structure*, London.
Smith, D.E. (1987) *The Everyday World as Problematic: A Feminist Sociology*, Boston, MA.

Further reading

Bauman, Z. (1991) *Intimations of Postmodernity*, London.
Bourdieu, P. (1985) *Languages as Symbolic Power*, Oxford.
Coser, L.A. and Rosenberg, B. (1985) *Sociological Theory: Selected Readings*, New York.
Fay, B. (1975) *Social Theory and Political Practice*, London.
Giddens, A. (1993) *Sociology*, Cambridge, UK.
Habermas, J. (1979) *Communication and the Evolution of Society*, Oxford.
Heritage, J. (1984) *Garfinkel and Ethnomethodology*, Oxford.
Mestrovic, S.G. (1991) *The Coming Fin de Siècle*, London.
Turner, B.S. (1990) *Theories of Postmodernity*, New York.
Whistler, S. and Lasch, S. (1987) *Max Weber: Rationality and Modernity*, London.

SOCIOLOGY: NEW THEORETICAL DEVELOPMENTS

New theoretical movements of the 1980s

The shift from structure to agency that characterized postwar sociology led in the 1970s to a theoretical stalemate. Micro-sociologies dealing with the minutiae of social action and conversations practices were opposed to macro-sociologies that analysed the long-term changes of the world economy. In the early 1980s there were several attempts to overcome the opposition between agency and structure, micro- and macro-, the individual and society (Alexander 1988). Pierre Bourdieu initiated the series of

theoretical innovations in 1979 with the publication of *Distinction. A Social Critique of the Judgment of Taste*. Two years later Jürgen Habermas, the legitimate heir of the Frankfurt School, published *The Theory of Communicative Action*. In this two-volume book, he presented a reformulation of critical theory that grounded the emancipatory impulse of reason in the intersubjective communications of the life world, and warned against its colonization by the systemic logic of the subsystems of the economy and the administration of the state. In 1982–3, Jeffrey Alexander published *Theoretical Logic in Sociology*, an impressive meta-theoretical work in four volumes in which he proposed a systematic reconstruction of Weber, Durkheim, Marx and above all a suitably edited Talcott Parsons. In 1984, Anthony Giddens presented an outline of his structuration theory in *The Constitution of Society* that was heavily influenced by Schütz's, Goffman's and Garfinkel's theories of action. His central thesis is that action and structure are mutually implicated in the practices of everyday life. Agents routinely, but unintentionally, reproduce social systems by recursively drawing on sets of rules and resources that structure their actions. In 1987 the last of this series of groundbreaking publications appeared, Niklas Luhmann's *Social Systems*, which paved the way for his two-volume *The Society of Society*, published in 1997, a year before his death, in which he masterfully presents the main concepts of his systematic theory of world society.

During the 1990s, following the fall of the Berlin Wall, explicit political concerns began to preoccupy the most prominent of these authors. As Bourdieu's sociology of cultural production and consumption slowly gained influence internationally, he established himself in France as the main intellectual on the left since Sartre and Foucault. Habermas largely abandoned sociology and returned to philosophy and politics. Giddens wrote a series of books on the role of reflexivity and identity in late modernity and moving from sociological to political theory, he published, in 1998, *The Third Way*, in which he advocated a kind of market socialism, and established himself as the guru of Tony Blair.

From postmodernism to globalization

Sociology is a product of its time. As the revolutionary enthusiasm of the 1960s and

1970s ebbed, postmodernism emerged on the academic scene, its adherents proclaiming the end of 'grand narratives' of emancipation while denouncing reason as being inherently repressive and potentially totalitarian. During the 1980s, heated debates about postmodernism appeared in the overlapping discursive contexts of the humanities, philosophy and sociology. Analysing the growing predominance of the media and information technology, the growth of the service and knowledge sectors, and the changes in the regime of capital accumulation, (post-)Marxist authors like Offe, Harvey, Jameson, Castells, Lash and Urry advanced the claim that we now have reached a new stage in history, beyond modernity, and that we now live in a new sort of society, variously called the postmodern, postindustrial, post-Fordist, information or network society.

Since the beginning of the 1990s, debates about globalization have succeeded and increasingly displaced arguments about 'postmodernism'. Globalization refers to the social processes of 'time–space compression' in which the constraints of geography on social and cultural arrangements recede, and people become increasingly aware that they recede. Objectively, the economic, political and cultural subsystems of societies are interconnected and interdependent as never before; subjectively, we are increasingly conscious of the world as a whole. The world 'shrinks' as immense flows of capital, money, goods, services, people, information, technologies, policies, ideas, images and regulations transcend individual nation-states and dissolve their borders. Although the impact of the forces of globalization is most strongly felt in the domain of economics, it is important to consider the process of globalization as a multidimensional phenomenon and to analyse, if possible, its economic, ecological, political, juridical, military and cultural dimensions simultaneously. Globalization is not just about the expansion of free trade and competitiveness in a global market but involves a process of social change in which the local and the global are mutually implicated. In addition to the development of a capitalist world economy and a shifting system of nation-states, the rise of global culture is an especially salient feature of contemporary globalization. Global culture is ambiguous, however. It involves the worldwide diffusion of capitalist cultural products and the spread of consumerist ideology (the

'homogenization thesis', defended by critical theorists like Schiller, Gitlin, Mattelaert and Ritzer) as well as the local interpretation and indigenization of those global cultural products (the 'heterogenization' thesis, defended by anthropologists and postcolonial cultural theorists like Appadurai, Hannerz, Spivak and Bhabha). Among the major social theorists, Habermas, Bourdieu, Wacquant, Bauman, Beck, Touraine, Castells and Negri have offered critical analyses of globalization that are sympathetic to the anti-globalization movement that emerged as a transnational coalition of new social movements in the wake of the WTO-protest in Seattle in 1999.

New trends in world sociology

The effervescence of the new theoretical movement of the 1980s is largely spent, but as a direct reaction to it, competing schools with thriving research projects have emerged in France, Canada, the UK, the USA and Germany.

The most interesting developments in French sociology are post-Bourdieusian (Dosse 1998). In *De la justification* (*On Justification*), Luc Boltanski and Laurent Thévenot, two former colleagues of Bourdieu, have developed a pragmatic model of critical competence that analyses how actors justify their claims to justice in ordinary situations of dispute by invoking different axiological orders and by bringing in common objects that allow them to test the stature of the persons whose claims are in dispute. Extending the pragmatic model of the 'Cités' to analyse the transformations of contemporary network society, Boltanski and Chiapello have argued in *Le Nouvel Esprit du capitalisme* (*The New Spirit of Capitalism*) that capitalism has co-opted the postmodernist critique of the 1960s and 1970s, becoming more flexible, while its critics have been disarmed. In the field of the new sociology of science and technology, Bruno Latour and Michel Callon have creatively drawn on the work of Gilles Deleuze and Michel Serres to work out a highly original and provocative actor network theory (ANT) that introduces objects into sociology and considers them as actors or 'actants'. Redefining sociology as the science of associations of humans and non-humans, ANT analyses how micro-actors become macro-actors by enrolling humans and non-humans alike in a heterogeneous rhizomatic network. In an attempt to counter the ascent of utilitarian approaches like rational choice in the social sciences, Alain Caillé and his collaborators from the MAUSS (an acronym for Mouvement Anti-Utilitariste dans les Sciences Sociales) have worked out Marcel Mauss's classic essay on the gift into a full blown political sociology of associations that considers the triple obligation – to give, accept and return the gift – as the bedrock of social life. Meanwhile, in Francophone Canada, Michel Freitag has developed a monumental neo-dialectical critical theory of the modes of the regulation of practices and the constitution of society through the ages that culminates in a militant critique of the desymbolizing tendencies of the systemic mode of reproduction that characterizes postmodernity.

If the new sociology in France is predominantly post-Bourdieusian, the new sociology in England is post-Giddensian and poststructurationist. Triggered by the publication of Roy Bhaskar's A Realist Theory of Science in 1975, critical realism emerged in the1990s as an important movement in philosophy and the human sciences (Archer et al. 1998). Offering a third way between positivism and conventionalism, realism establishes by means of a transcendental argument that reality (out there) exists independently of our descriptions of it. Rejecting the Humean notion of causality as the constant conjunction of events, it argues that science explains empirical phenomena by positing underlying causal generative mechanisms that may escape observation. Bhaskar later transposed the realist argument from the natural to the social sciences and argued for a qualified anti-positivist naturalism. In an attempt to overcome the opposition between explanatory and interpretative sociologies, he developed a dialectical transformational model of social action that is inspired by Marx's critique of political economy. Taking up some of the main insights of Bhaskar's critical realism, Margaret Archer has worked out in a series of four books a morphogenetic theory of culture, structure and agency. Criticizing structuration theory for conflating agency and structure, she has reworked Lockwood's classic distinction between social and systems integration into a complex analytical theory that recognizes culture, structure and agency as emergent causal powers, and offers an elegant model to

conceptualize their interactions without reductionism. Rethinking the notion of government that Michel Foucault had introduced in 1978 to analyse the 'conduct of conduct', Nikolas Rose and his Anglo-Australian colleagues have produced a new approach and a new subdiscipline within the social sciences: Governmentality Studies (Rose 1999). It theorizes and empirically analyses the multiplicity of theories and vocabularies, methodologies and technologies, instruments and techniques of rule (from the layout of buildings to the statistical methods of calculation and the psychoanalytic ones of interpretation) through which a heterogeneous network of governmental and non-governmental authorities and agencies seek to control and regulate, shape and modulate the conduct of individuals that constitute a population by working on and through their aspirations and intentions. In a trilogy on modernity, the Holocaust and morality, Zygmunt Bauman continues the tradition of critical theory while bringing their philosophical arguments home to sociology. Starting with a sociological reinterpretation of Adorno's theory of the repression of non-identity, his critique of the modern world-view of intellectuals was immediately followed by an analysis of modernity and the Holocaust that reworks Hannah Arendt's thesis on the banality of evil as well as by a postmodern ethics that draws upon the ethics of Emmanuel Levinas (Bauman 1989).

In the USA, Randall Collins, a Weberian who had become known for his work on conflict sociology and micro-reduction, published The Sociology of Philosophy (1998), on which he had worked for 25 years. Covering the development of philosophical ideas in China, Japan, India, the Middle East, Europe and America over the last 2,000 years, Collins explains the development of philosophy by means of a theory that integrates a Goffmanian theory of interactional rituals that generate emotional energy with a network analysis of philosophical schools.

If English sociology is post-Giddensian, German sociology is post-Habermasian. Leaving aside the sophisticated developments and refinements of systems theory offered by followers of Luhmann (Teubner, Willke, Kneer, Nassehi), whose work remains largely untranslated, the work of Ulrich Beck, Axel Honneth, Hans Joas and Klaus Eder should be singled out for attention. Following the publication of *Risk Society* (Beck 2002 [1986]), Ulrich Beck has developed his political sociology of scientific knowledge into a full-blown theory of 'reflexive modernization'. The main idea of this influential theory is that the pursuit of industrial modernity can lead to catastrophic consequences and that the awareness of those risks undermines the systemic foundations of industrial modernity, and opens up the way to an alternative and ecologically enlightened modernity. More recently, Beck has also worked out a cosmopolitical critical theory of globalization. Axel Honneth, the successor of Habermas and director of the Institut für Sozialforschung in Frankfurt, has developed a promising theory of intersubjective recognition that draws on the phenomenology of Hegel, the pragmatism of G.H. Mead and the object relations theory of Winnicott to explain how a lack of confidence, respect and esteem lead to social pathologies that can trigger social movements which struggle for recognition and inclusion (Honneth 1995 [1991]).

FRÉDÉRIC VANDENBERGHE
UNIVERSITY FOR HUMANIST STUDIES,
THE NETHERLANDS

References

Alexander, J. (1988) 'The new theoretical movement', in N. Smelser (ed.) *Handbook of Sociology*, London, pp. 77–101.
Archer, M., Bhaskar, R., Collier, A., Lawson, T. and Norrie, A. (1998) *Critical Realism. Essential Readings*, London.
Bauman, Z. (1989) *Modernity and Holocaust*, Cambridge, UK.
Beck, U (2002 [1986]) *Risk Society. Towards a New Modernity*, London.
Dosse, F. (1998) *Empire of Meaning. The Humanization of the Social Sciences*, Minneapolis, MN.
Honneth, A. (1995 [1991]) *The Struggle for Recognition: The Moral Grammar of Social Conflicts*, Cambridge, MA.
Rose, N. (1999) *Powers of Freedom: Reframing Political Thought*, Cambridge, UK.

Further reading

Connor, S. (1996) *Postmodernist Culture: An Introduction to Theories of the Contemporary*, Oxford.
McGrew, A. (1992) 'A global society', in S. Hall, D. Held and A. McGrew (eds) *Modernity and Its Futures*, Cambridge, UK, pp. 61–153.

SEE ALSO: actor, social; Bourdieu; globalization; Habermas; information society; postmodernism; science, sociology of

SPATIAL ANALYSIS

Spatial analysis is an approach within geography and associated disciplines, such as archaeology, which uses statistical methods to describe and generalize spatial patterns. Geographers have a continuing interest in establishing correlations between phenomena that vary over space, such as rainfall amounts and crop yields. Those who see this as the prime purpose of geography conceive of it as a spatial science 'concerned with the formulation of the laws governing the spatial distribution of certain features on the surface of the earth' (Schaefer 1953: 227). There has been much technical and substantive experimentation, assisted by the rapid development of computing technology, into both the mathematical modelling strategies and the statistical procedures that can be employed in reaching such generalizations (see Johnston and Sidaway 2004).

Spatial analysis of quantitative data presents several major challenges to scholars because of the particular features of spatial data.

First, there are the difficulties constituted by the nature of spatial phenomena, their measurement and correlation. Haggett (1965) produced a pioneering classification of the phenomena into point patterns (which may or may not be hierarchically organized); line patterns; areal patterns; flow patterns; and patterns of change in all four. Some of these are relatively easy to measure (a point pattern such as the distribution of shops in a town, or stations along a railway line, for example), but others are less so, such as the amount of rainfall over an area, which has to be estimated from measurements at a sample of points. (For an introduction to these measurement methods, see O'Sullivan and Unwin 2003.)

Correlation of measurements of two or more spatial patterns is often difficult because the data have necessarily been collected within different spatial templates. Rainfall amount is usually measured at a sample of points, for example, and crop yields by areal units: how does one superimpose the one on the other and obtain a measure of their correspondence? As importantly, what are the errors involved in establishing correlations through procedures that combine different frameworks? Techniques of overlaying data sets using common spatial co-ordinate systems are at the core of geographical information systems, which comprise integrated hardware and software for the capture, storage, integration display and analysis of spatial data.

In many such studies, spatial analysts have to use aggregate data for territorial units such as counties or countries – when their real interest is the behaviour of individuals. A good example is provided by studies of migration, which may be interested in the relationship between a person's occupation and propensity to migrate, but can only analyse the relationship between the percentage of people in an area in certain occupations and the percentage of people there who migrate during a defined period. They have to infer an individual relationship (between class and migration) from an aggregate one, which can involve errors often termed 'ecological' (Alker 1969). Furthermore, the relationship between those two variables can vary according to both the scale of the areas used (in general, the larger the area and the coarser the aggregation the higher the correlation) and the actual configuration of areas (there are thousands of ways in which twenty-nine wards in a city can be combined to form six parliamentary constituencies, for example, which may well result in different election results): together these produce what is known as the 'modifiable areal unit problem' (Openshaw and Taylor 1981). Several methods have been advanced for estimating individual behaviour from aggregate data, as in the methods of ecological inference (King 1997), entropy-maximization (Johnston and Pattie 2000) and micro-simulation (Ballas et al. 2002).

A further set of difficulties involves the use of classical (parametric) statistical procedures to analyse spatial data. These may have a particular property ('spatial autocorrelation') that can introduce bias and error to statistical estimates of relationships. Spatial autocorrelation is a two-dimensional extension of a widely appreciated, and fairly readily resolved, issue in the analysis of temporal data: the value of a variable at one point in time can be strongly influenced by its value at the previous point, hence introducing an element of double-counting. With temporal data, autocorrelation extends in one direction only; with spatial data it extends in all directions. For this reason, some argue that conventional statistical procedures cannot be applied to many geographical data sets, hence the exploration of specific methods for spatial analysis (Cliff and Ord 1981).

Spatial patterns and relationships may themselves vary over space and time, and their exploration has been the focus of considerable work on *local statistics*. These include methods for identifying clusters of events in space and/or time – as with outbreaks of diseases – and of variations in the strength (and even direction) of relationships – as with that between school quality and individual student performance; they include multilevel modelling (Jones and Duncan 1996), geographically weighted regression (Fotheringham et al. 2002) and spatial econometrics (Anselin 1988).

Advances in spatial analysis have been much assisted recently by massive increases in computing power, which allows the analysis of large and complex, spatially referenced data sets. Sometimes known as *geocomputation* (Longley et al. 1998), this incorporates such topics as data visualization and transformation, representing and modelling spatial interactions, and generalization regarding spatial processes. This is but one part of a wider area of technical development termed *geoinformatics*, incorporating not only geocomputation but also geodesy, cartography, photogrammetry, global positioning systems, remote sensing, geostatistics and geographical information systems.

The near-hegemony that spatial science held over the practice of geography in some countries in the 1960s and 1970s has since been challenged by proponents of alternative views. But it continues to attract practitioners seduced by the possibility of identifying and accounting for 'spatial order' (Haggett 1990) and remains a buoyant area within contemporary geography and associated social sciences.

R.J. JOHNSTON
UNIVERSITY OF BRISTOL

References

Alker, H.R. (1969) 'A typology of ecological fallacies', in M. Dogan and S. Rokkan (eds) *Quantitative Ecological Analysis in the Social Sciences*, Cambridge, MA.

Anselin, L. (1988) *Spatial Econometrics: Methods and Models*, Dordrecht.

Ballas, D., Clarke, G.P. and Turton, I. (2002) 'A spatial microsimulation model for social policy microspatial analysis', in B. Boots, A. Okabe and R. Thomas (eds) *Modelling Geographical Systems: Statistical and Computational Applications*, Dordrecht.

Cliff, A.D. and Ord, J.K. (1981) *Spatial Process*, London.

Fotheringham, A.S., Charlton, M.E. and Brunsdon, C. (2002) *Geographically Weighted Regression: The Analysis of Spatially Varying Relationships*, Chichester.

Haggett, P. (1965) *Locational Analysis in Human Geography*, London.

—— (1990) *The Geographer's Art*, Oxford.

Johnston, R.J. and Pattie, C.J. (2000) 'Ecological inference and entropy-maximizing: An alternative estimation procedure for split-ticket voting', *Political Analysis 8*.

Johnston, R.J. and Sidaway, J.D. (2004) *Geography and Geographers: Anglo-American Human Geography since 1945*, 6th edn, London.

Jones, K. and Duncan, C. (1996) 'People and places: The multilevel model as a general framework for the quantitative analysis of geographical data', in P. Langley and M. Batty (eds) *Spacial Analysis: Modelling in a GIS Environment*, Cambridge.

King, G. (1997) *A Solution to the Ecological Inference Problem: Reconstructing Individual Data from Aggregate Behavior*, Princeton, NJ.

Longley, P.A., Brooks, S.M., MacDonnell, R. and Macmillan, B. (eds) (1998) *Geocomputation: A Primer*, Chichester.

Openshaw, S. and Taylor, P.J. (1981) 'The modifiable areal unit problem', in N. Wrigley and R.J. Bennett (eds) *Quantitative Geography: A British View*, London.

O'Sullivan, D. and Unwin, D.J. (2003) *Geographic Information Analysis*, New York.

Schaefer, F.K. (1953) 'Exceptionalism in geography: A methodological examination', *Annals of the Association of American Geographers 43*.

Further reading

Fotheringham, A.S., Charlton, M.E. and Brunsdon, C. (2001) *Quantitative Geography: Perspectives on Spatial Data Analysis*, London.

O'Sullivan, D. and Unwin, D.J. (2003) *Geographic Information Analysis*, New York.

SEE ALSO: geographical information systems; region

SPORT, SOCIOLOGY OF

The sociology of sport examines the role and meaning of sport in the lives of individuals and societies (Jarvie and Maguire 1994; Maguire and Young 2002). The first writings on the subject were published in Germany in the 1920s, but it was not until the 1960s that the discipline became institutionalized (Coakley and Dunning 2000). Today, universities in Europe, North America and Asia have prominent centres for research into the sociology of sport, and there are several important journals and national and international associations dedicated to the subject (see http://u2.u-strasbg.fr/ISSA/). It is a notably interdisciplinary field, drawing on a range of expertise in relevant areas of research.

In attempting to explain the emergence and diffusion of sport over time and across different societies – and to identify the processes of socialization into and through modern sport – the sociology of sport investigates the values and norms of dominant, emergent and residual cultures and subcultures in sport. It also studies the effects of the exercise of power and social stratification on the involvement and success of performers, officials, spectators and consumers (Maguire 1999). In seeking to debunk popular myths about sport, sociologists examine how people become involved in sport and what barriers they face; how gender, class, ethnicity and sexual relations work in sport; the ways in which sport is mediated and contoured by political economy and mass media; and the relation of sport to global identity politics (Coakley 2003). Here, consideration is given to three key issues: socialization into and through sport; sport and national identity; and sport and globalization.

Socialization into and through sports

Participation in sports is motivated by a combination of personal enjoyment and external rewards (Coakley 2003). Satisfaction is associated with opportunities for self-expression, freedom and spontaneity (Huizinga 1970 [1949]). Extrinsic rewards involve the attainment of public approval, status and material compensation for performing better than a competitor. However, access is not guaranteed. Gender, social class, age, culture, geography, ethnicity, religion and nationality can often structure the socialization processes involved in access to sport (Foley 1990), and many people in the world do not get the opportunity to participate in sports.

Play, games and sports have a crucial and quite specific role in the general socialization processes (Fine 1987). The sense of 'self' is not natural but develops through childhood socialization as a result of role taking. By learning to recognize and express symbols, individuals are able to interpret the meanings and intentions of others. Two stages have been identified in childhood socialization: a 'play stage' and a 'game stage' (Mead 1962 [1934]). In the first, the child plays roles such as those of a mother, father, firefighter or athlete. In so doing, children learn the difference between themselves and the parts they are playing. In the 'game stage', children learn to see themselves as others see them. They play positions and thereby develop a reflexive conception of self and their position in the community. Through the performance of a specific position, the player must address his or her actions to the expectations of the generalized team. Thus, through socialization with 'significant others' and with the 'generalized other', children develop their sense of identity and self.

In socialization through sports, individuals develop their self-consciousness as active social actors (Coakley and Donnelly 1999). This process of socializing young people through sport into the acceptable norms of a society has long been recognized and underpins some of the reasons for state support of physical education and sport programmes. Sport, then, is said to 'build character' – although it is more accurate to say that sport creates characters (Klein 1993). Socialization into and through sport reflects and reinforces wider societal stratification systems, which generate a variety of possible value systems and personalities (Miracle and Rees 1994).

Nationalism, identity politics and sport

By the beginning of the final decades of the nineteenth century, sports had become a form of 'patriot games' in which particular views of national identities and social codes were constructed (Bairner 2001). Both established and outsider groups used sports to represent, maintain and challenge identities. In this way, sports can both support or undermine dominant social relations (Gruneau 1999). In sporting encounters a historical legacy is invoked, past glories or traumas are emphasized, and players are faced with maintaining or challenging a set of 'invented traditions'. Some sports are seen to encompass all the qualities of national character. In the value system of upper-class Englishmen, for example, cricket embodies the qualities of fair play, valour, graceful conduct and steadfastness in the face of adversity (James 1963). Seen to represent the essence of England, it gives meaning to being 'English' by fixing 'England' as a focus of identification in the emotions of upper-class males. In a similar manner, Sumo wrestling is said to represent the indefinable nature of Japa-nese culture. Ironically, baseball also has become very important to the Japanese, though its spread is the result of the growth of US influence (Snyder and Spreitzer 1984). But while Japanese baseball is played by the same rules as its US counterpart, it has been reinterpreted and indigenized, with the values that govern the conduct of the players a reflection of the local culture (Guttmann 1994).

National culture and identity are also represented by an emphasis on origins, continuity, tradition and timelessness. Yet, the traditions associated with sport are not as deeply rooted as sometimes claimed. By spilling over into sport, foundational myths shore up the wider invention and representation of national culture and identity. The myth surrounding Abner Doubleday's role in the creation of baseball, the US 'national pastime', is a case in point. Instead of tracing the origins of the game to its English roots, Americans traditionally have sought to emphasize the unique role that Doubleday played in 'inventing' the sport (Dunning et al. 1993).

The role sport plays in the interaction of culture and identity is sometimes viewed as inherently conservative. Some believe that sport helps to consolidate not only official views of nationalism and patriotism, but that it can also act as a safety valve by functioning as an emotional outlet for frustrated peoples or nations (Dunning 1999). Others argue that in operating as an instrument of national unity and integration, sport also has contributed to popular nationalist political struggles (Bairner 2001; Jarvie and Walker 1994). In any case, sport – through its use of nostalgia, mythology, invented traditions, flags, anthems and ceremonies – contributes to a quest for identity and exciting significance (Maguire 1999). It serves to nurture, refine and further develop the image that nations and people have of themselves. Yet, in the context of global sport, this role has become increasingly contradictory. In introducing people to other societies, global sport strengthens cosmopolitanism, but it also feeds ethnic defensiveness and exclusiveness (Bairner 2001).

Globalization and sport processes

The emergence and diffusion of sports since the nineteenth century is interwoven with the broad secular process of globalization (Maguire et al. 2002). The creation of national and international sports organizations, the growth of competition between national teams, the worldwide acceptance of rules governing specific Western sports, and the establishment of global competitions such as the Olympic Games and the men's and women's soccer world cups, all are prominent examples of the globalization of sports.

As with broader globalization processes, the international development of sport has undoubtedly led to a degree of homogenization. Modern sport first emerged in England, and the spread of British/Western sports has been characterized by elements of cultural imperialism (Guttmann 1994; Maguire 1999). In the process, Westerners have been the global winners at their own games – both on and off the field and court. The tastes, codes of conduct and the sports of male members of Western societies have functioned as signs of distinction, prestige and power, producing effects similar to those of elite cultural activities within Western societies (Maguire 1999).

In the globalization of sport, several structured processes can be identified. These include the diffusion of a male-dominated ideology, content, meaning and control of global sport; the scientization, rationalization and valorization of human expressiveness; the notion of the athlete as an enhanced, efficient machine adhering to the sport ethic associated with success and the ultimate performance; the athlete and spectator as consumers of scarce resources and, in certain respects, destroyers of the environment; the emergence of a global sport power elite; and the reinforcement and enhancement of inequalities within the West and between the West and non-Western societies (Maguire et al. 2002).

While each of these processes permeates the making of modern sport, there is another side to this global process. Within the West the diffusion of 'English'/British sport has been resisted as well as embraced; more broadly, the rise of Western sport has been contested, and its pre-eminence is not inevitable. For example, there has been considerable debate regarding the extent to which Western values and capitalist marketing, advertising and consumption have influenced the ways people throughout the world use, represent and experience their bodies. Unquestionably, there is a political economy at work in the production and consumption of global sport and leisure products. It has resulted in the relative ascendancy of a narrow selection of Western media-led sport cultures and the homogenization of specific body cultures through achievement sports. This is evident through the spread of the Olympic movement and the development of standardized forms of sport science programmes.

But while there has been a long-term decline of indigenous Western and non-occidental folk body cultures, recent interest in martial arts and extreme sports, and the revival of folk games, has led to an increase in the diversity of sports and body cultures (Van Bottenburg 2001). Sports may become increasingly contested, with different constituencies challenging hegemonic masculine notions regarding the content, meaning, control, organization and ideology of sport. Moreover, global flows are increasing the varieties of body cultures and identities available to people. Global sport, then, seems to be leading to the reduction in contrasts between societies, but also to the emergence of new varieties of body cultures and identities (Maguire et al. 2002). In many ways sports can thus be examined as a barometer of wider social processes.

JOSEPH MAGUIRE
LOUGHBOROUGH UNIVERSITY

References

Bairner, A. (2001) Sport, Nationalism, and Globalization, Albany, NY.

Coakley, J. (2003) Sport in Society, 8th edn, Boston, MA.

Coakley, J. and Donnelly, P. (eds) (1999) Inside Sports, London.

Coakley, J. and Dunning, E. (eds) (2000) Handbook of Sport Studies, London.

Dunning, E. (1999) Sport Matters. Sociological Studies of Sport, Violence, and Civilization, London.

Dunning, E., Maguire, J. and Pearton, R. (eds) (1993) The Sports Process, Champaign, IL.

Fine, G.A. (1987) With the Boys: Little League Baseball and Preadolescent Culture, Chicago.

Foley, D. (1990) Learning Capitalist Culture, Philadelphia.

Gruneau, R. (1999) Class, Sports, and Social Development, Champaign, IL.

Guttmann, A. (1994) Games and Empires: Modern Sports and Cultural Imperialism, New York.

Huizinga, J. (1970 [1949]) Homo Ludens. A Study of the Play-Element in Culture, London.

James, C.L.R. (1963) Beyond a Boundary, London.

Jarvie, G. and Maguire, J. (1994) Sport and Leisure in Social Thought, London.

Jarvie, G. and Walker, G. (1994) Scottish Sport in the Making of the Nation: Substitutes and Ninety-Minute Patriots, Leicester, UK.

Klein, A. (1993) Little Big Men: Bodybuilding Subculture and Gender Construction, Albany, NY.

Maguire, J. (1999) *Global Sport: Identities, Societies, Civilisations*, Cambridge, UK.

Maguire, J., Jarvie, G., Mansfield, L. and Bradley, J. (2002) *Sport Worlds. A Sociological Perspective*, Champaign, IL.

Maguire, J. and Young, K. (eds) (2002) *Theory, Sport and Society*, Cambridge, UK.

Mead, G.H. (1962 [1934]) *Mind, Self and Society: From the Standpoint of a Social Behaviorist*, Chicago.

Miracle, A. and Rees, C.R. (1994) *Lessons of the Locker Room: The Myth of School Sports*, Amherst, MA.

Snyder, E. and Spreitzer, E. (1984) 'Baseball in Japan', in S. Eitzen (ed.) *Sports in Contemporary Society*, New York, pp. 46–50.

Van Bottenburg, M. (2001) *Global Games*, Chicago.

Further reading

Elias, N. and Dunning, E. (eds) (1986) *Quest for Excitement*, Oxford.

STAGFLATION

Stagflation is the term used to describe the coincidence of economic stagnation – high unemployment and slow-growing or falling output – and a high rate of inflation. The term is attributed to Iain Macleod, a British Conservative politician who introduced it in the House of Commons in 1965 while describing the state of the UK's economy. The term was subsequently applied to describe the USA's experience nearly a decade later by the economist Paul Samuelson.

The USA has suffered two recent episodes of stagflation: the first from 1973 to 1975 and the second from 1979 to 1980. Between 1960–72, inflation in the USA averaged 3 per cent and unemployment averaged 4.9 per cent. In the period 1973–81, inflation averaged 7.8 per cent and unemployment 6.7 per cent. This same pattern was repeated across much of Europe and around the globe as well. In the UK, for instance, average inflation rose from 5.2 per cent to 15.8 per cent and average unemployment rose from 2.8 per cent to 5.8 per cent in the same periods. Subsequent economic performance has been more mixed across countries. While average inflation and unemployment nearly returned to their pre-1970s levels in the USA from 1985 to 2002 (2.4 per cent and 5.7 per cent, respectively), similar improvement was not universal. For example, average inflation in the UK during this time fell to 4 per cent but unemployment averaged 8.1 per cent.

The advent of stagflation marked a watershed in the history of macroeconomic theory, bringing to an end the postwar ascendancy of the Keynesian school of thought. During the period 1954–69, unemployment and inflation rates moved inversely to such an extent that the Phillips curve appeared to hold, although this was disputed by Milton Friedman and Edmund Phelps. If the Phillips curve did indeed illustrate a real relationship, then policy-makers could choose to lower unemployment, but only at the cost of higher inflation (as happened as a result of spending on the Vietnam War and the 'Great Society'), and vice versa. It therefore came as quite a shock when inflation remained high while unemployment increased during a short recession in 1970, leading the Chairman of the Federal Reserve, Arthur Burns, to remark that 'the rules of the game are not working in quite the way they used to' (Burns 1978). The arrival of stagflation several years later made it even clearer that the old 'rules' no longer applied. Clearly new ideas were required. The door was opened for alternative schools of thought, notably the Monetarist, New Classical (Real Business Cycle) and New Keynesian.

Explanations for stagflation can be separated in a rough and ready way into those that emphasize supply shocks, and those that give more weight to demand conditions. If the cause of stagflation is a supply shock, this must mean that there has been an exogenous shock, i.e. one originating outside the economy, to its supply-producing capabilities. The shock either reduces capacity and causes widespread shortages (a natural disaster), or substantially raises the costs of production across a large proportion of industries in the economy (economy-wide exogenous input price increases). Several such supply shocks occurred during the 1970s: crop failures in the Soviet Union sharply increased prices in world grain markets; wage and price controls implemented by the Nixon administration to rein in inflation led to a burst of 'catch-up' inflation once they were lifted; and the Organization of Petroleum-Exporting Companies (OPEC) raised oil prices sharply in late 1973 and then again in 1979–80 (see Blinder 1982).

To illustrate how such shocks might cause stagflation, consider the specific example of an increase in the price of oil in a simple framework in which firms are monopolistically competitive and set prices infrequently due to costs of adjustment. When firms set new prices, they set them as a mark-up over their marginal costs. An increase in the price of oil will lead to rapid increases in the prices of petrol and energy. This will affect most firms, and will squeeze profits. Some firms will pass their new, higher costs on to consumers. And that leads to inflation. Firms that do not change their prices will seek to reduce costs by lowering production. Unless oil and labour are substitutes in the production process, layng off workers would lead to stagnation. Provided that the economy began with a moderate level of inflation and output equal to the natural rate, this oil price shock could precipitate a situation similar to that which the USA witnessed during the 1970s. To be sure, however, the magnitude and length of the period of stagflation would depend upon the response of policy-makers, the nature of the shock (transitory or permanent), the availability of alternative inputs, the price-setting processes of the firms, and the nature of their costs (e.g. the institutional structure of the labour market), among other things (see Blinder 1979; Bruno and Sachs 1985).

Economists today tend to doubt that stagflation is generally triggered by exogenous supply shocks. The prices of a wide range of commodities besides food and energy rose sharply in the early 1970s. This indicates that strong demand conditions were present worldwide. If so, the supply 'shocks' that caused that episode of stagflation may have had endogenous causes. Moreover, oil prices have experienced considerable spikes (in both directions) since the 1970s, without causing stagflation (although there is evidence to support the view that rises in oil price have led to recession (e.g. Hamilton 2003)). It seems that the connection between the timing of the oil price increases and the onset of stagflation in the 1970s may have been accidental.

A number of authors have blamed much of the performance of the US economy during the 1970s on various mistakes made by policy-makers at the time. For instance, one way to generate stagflation from the demand side is through 'go–stop' monetary policy. According to this theory, the monetary authority would initially increase aggregate demand through strongly expansionary monetary policy (the 'go' portion). This would lead to an expansion of output and a gradual increase in inflation. Conventional wisdom suggests that output responds more quickly than inflation to a monetary policy shock. Consequently, if the monetary authority were sharply to contract the money supply (the 'stop' portion) while inflation were still accelerating, output would then begin falling while inflation remained high. The result would be stagflation. It does appear that monetary policy was too expansionary in the late 1960s and throughout much of the 1970s, whether due to mismeasurement of the natural rate of unemployment and the extent of the productivity slowdown (Orphanides 2000), political considerations (De Long 1997), or the willingness of the monetary authority to meet the expectations of particular parties (Christiano and Gust 2000). The breakdown of the Bretton Woods system at the beginning of the 1970s is one indicator of conditions at the time. This expansionary environment, coupled with attempts to rein in inflation by periodically contracting the money supply, or curtailing government spending (as occurred in 1973), would produce a go–stop pattern that could trigger stagflation (see Barsky and Kilian 2002).

It is necessary to identify the cause of stagflation before it is possible to prescribe a remedy for it. To the extent that it is caused by mistaken economic measures, stagflation can be prevented by avoiding 'go–stop' policies. To the extent that it is caused by exogenous events beyond the control of policy-makers, stagflation becomes much more problematic. In that case, policy-makers face unhappy prospects at every turn. They might attempt to reduce unemployment by stimulating demand, but this would risk high inflation. They could hold inflation in check by contracting demand, but would then have to endure a recession. Or they might choose to ride out the period of high inflation and high unemployment, and hope the economy will eventually right itself.

ROBERT BARSKY AND EDWARD KNOTEK II
UNIVERSITY OF MICHIGAN, ANN ARBOR

References

Barsky, R. and Killian, L. (2002) 'Do we really know that oil caused the great stagflation? A monetary alternative', *NBER Macroeconomics Annual 2001* (May).

Blinder, A.S. (1979) *Economic Policy and the Great Stagflation*, New York.

—— (1982) 'The anatomy of double-digit inflation in the 1970s', in R.E. Hall (ed.) *Inflation: Causes and Effects*, Chicago.

Bruno, M. and Sachs, J.D. (1985) *Economics of World-wide Stagflation*, Cambridge, MA.

Burns, A. (1978) *Reflections of an Economic Policy Maker: Speeches and Congressional Statements, 1969–1978*, Washington.

Christiano, L.J. and Gust, C. (2000) 'The expectations trap hypothesis', *Economic Perspectives* 25(2): 21–39.

De Long, J.B. (1997) 'America's only peacetime inflation: The 1970s', in C. Romer and D. Romer (eds) *Reducing Inflation: Motivation and Strategy*, Chicago.

Hamilton, J.D. (2003) 'What is an oil shock?' *Journal of Econometrics* 113: 363–98.

Orphanides, A. (2000) 'Activist stabilization policy and inflation: The Taylor rule in the 1970s, Board of Governors of the Federal Reserve System', *Finance and Economics Discussion Series 2000*: 13.

SEE ALSO: employment and unemployment; inflation and deflation; macroeconomic policy

STATE

Passions, hopes and fears surround discussions of the state. Friends of the state regard it as a mechanism for realizing 'the common good', 'the public interest' or 'the General Will'. Mindful of the state's capacity to be manipulated for externally aggressive and internally oppressive purposes, others would 'bind', 'tame' and control what Hobbes called *Leviathan* in his memorable vision of the state as an artificial man, a giant composed from little men (Hobbes 1651). They recommend that constitutional devices should be used to make the state accountable, to divide and fragment its organizations and capacities. Those convinced the state is merely a necessary evil advocate shrinking it to its essential core – 'rolling it back' from its current aggrandizement, allowing it to 'intervene' only if private markets cannot provide particular benefits efficiently, and equipping it solely to defend its people, and their property, at home and abroad. By contrast, most contemporary social scientists regard states as ineluctable features of modernity, part of all civilizations that have evolved beyond, or at least succeeded, societies based on kinship, segmentary societies, nomadic communities or feudal ties.

Amongst other confusing definitions the state has been called 'the factor of cohesion in a social formation' by French Marxists, 'the authoritative allocator of values' by systems theorists, the possessor of 'a monopoly of legitimate violence within a given territory' by followers of Max Weber, the 'public power' by exponents of

European legal theory, and 'the *Grundnorm*', the ultimate source of normative authority, by 'legal positivists'. Here a definition of the modern state will be bluntly advanced, some confusions clarified, contrasts to the idea of the state explained, and then the definition will be defended.

A modern state may be defined as (1) a differentiated and impersonal institution that is (2) politically centralized – though not necessarily unitary; that (3) authoritatively binding rule-making (or sovereignty) over persons, groups and property (4) generally exercises an effective monopoly of publicly organized physical force; and (5) that is sufficiently recognized by a sufficient number of its subjects, and (6) of other states, that it can maintain its (7) organizational and policy-making powers within (8) a (potentially variable) territory. Each of these eight elements helps us understand what is meant by the modern state, and helps us understand the nature of state crises.

Before elaborating these elements readers may be counselled against three errors in understanding the state. These recurrent mistakes treat the state as equivalent to, first, the nation; second, the government; and, last, political entities best described as substates or as interstatal organizations.

A state is not a nation. Even if the nation-state is now the dominant form of state, or the dominant aspiration of most states, it does not exhaust the present and especially the past universe of states. There are, for example, some explicitly binational and multinational states. There are also nations that have no states, stateless nations and states that have not managed to become nation-states, even though some of their officials want to achieve that goal.

A state is not a synonym for government. In contemporary social science it is agreed that whereas all states must have governments, i.e. rulers and personnel who discharge state functions, not all governments must have states (a stateless tribe may have governance, but not be a state). States manifestly include organizations and personnel that are not directly part of the central government(s) or local government(s), e.g. armies, navies, air forces, the police, health, welfare and educational bureaucracies, and auditors. To this list most would add courts. States may have state or public sectors, through which governments may govern, but these sectors, and their representatives, are not identical with governments. In short, government is not synonymous with public administration, public management or the public sector, whereas the state encompasses governments, public administration, public management and the public sector.

States are not found below centres or above them. The least important, but still regular, confusion in these matters is the interutilization of state with what is perhaps best described as a regional unit of government. In federal systems it is common for the federating units to be known as states, e.g. the states that make up the United States of America and the Commonwealth of Australia. These states are, however, not states proper, i.e. sovereign and independent states. These entities are constitutional partners in federal systems, which, in their totality, are states in our sense, because in a federal system both the federal government and the federated regional units are parts of the state. The converse, and less frequent, confusion occurs when people take what 'international' relations specialists call a regional organization to comprise a state. Such organizations may include military alliances, such as the North Atlantic Treaty Organization (NATO), or free-trade agreements with intergovernmental arrangements, such as the North American Free Trade Agreement (NAFTA). Confederal organizations are multipurpose and multistate organizations, precisely because they are made up of states that maintain a right to withdraw from these organizations, because they grant strictly limited delegated powers to their shared confederal organizations, and because their governing structures are intergovernmental in nature. The European Union (EU) has been such a confederation; it has not, therefore, been a state; though there are Europeans who want to make the EU into a federation that would be a state.

Rectifying these confusions helpfully suggests that states have three necessary attributes: (1) the possession of independent central governments, (2) the capacity and right to opt out from intergovernmental arrangements or policies agreed with other states, and (3) the capacity and right to withdraw completely from international organizations or confederations, or, more positively, the right to make binding treaties. Our corrections of the most frequent confusions in defining the state have pointed towards some of the modern state's essential attributes – government, territory, centralization, independence, in-

ternational legal personality – but before we can elaborate our proposed definition we should further our understanding of the notion of the state by contrasting it with its antonyms: the 'non-state', 'the opposites' of the state.

What is not the state: its major antonyms

Four of these contrasts have recurred in political theory, political science and law since the sixteenth century, and illuminate the genealogy of the concept of the state: (1) the state contrasted with civil society or society; (2) the state contrasted with the individual; (3) the state or public realm contrasted with the private realm; (4) the state contrasted with statelessness.

THE STATE AND CIVIL SOCIETY

The state–civil society contrast has a seven-century history in European political thought, though its roots can be traced back to the thinking of Romans like Cicero. It has recently been given a new lease of life during and after the collapse of communist regimes in Eastern Europe. In almost all political attempts to revitalize communities previously subjected to despotic regimes, efforts are made to create or revitalize 'civil societies'. The original notion of civil society, from the Latin *civilis societas*, implied a 'civilized' society – one with cities, laws and with 'civility', i.e. pacified and predictable manners. The concept was later developed to describe social institutions (including markets, civil law, professional bodies, interest associations) separate from the state and from the family, and, in some formulations, churches. The state–civil society contrast implies that a 'good' state supports, but is separate from, its civil society; it does not and should not penetrate or control its civil society, or if it does it does so with clear limits. It suggests that a vibrant civil society checks, controls and energizes its state, but retains its own autonomy. The state is also the recipient of negative imagery in this contrast. The state is a compulsory, authoritative and coercive association, whereas civil society is voluntary, argumentative and interactive. A tacit bias in much political science and political theory assumes that to each state there is a society, and that this society is a national society – a variation on the error that a state is necessarily a nation-state.

STATE VERSUS INDIVIDUAL

For many nineteenth-century liberal thinkers, especially political economists, the state–civil society contrast was eclipsed in importance by contrasting the state (as a collective power) with individuals, or rather the individual. In this style of thinking, relations between the state and the individual may be seen as 'mediated', first by representative institutions, and then by parties and interest groups. However, the notion of civil society as a collectivity is often lost sight of in economic liberalism – as is the extent to which individuals' social identities and class may shape their political choices, interests and potentialities. Rational choice theorists may analyse the behaviour of individuals as economically rational consumers of state services, and arguably lose sight of individuals as citizens, and as members of one or more civil societies. The state–civil society contrast is more inclusive and broadening in what it highlights.

THE STATE AS PUBLIC REALM VERSUS PRIVATE REALM

The state versus civil society contrast has a legal dimension that distinguishes public and private law. Public law is the state's law of itself – the domain of constitutional, administrative, tax, welfare and criminal law; it specifies the legal powers, regulation, organization and duties of the state and its agencies. In private law, by contrast, private individuals are the parties; it is the law of civil society that the state (actually or allegedly) protects and regulates. Indeed, the differentiations of public and private law, and the expansion of the former, are seen by many as hallmarks of the emergence of the modern state. In European political thought, the state has more generally been regarded as the public domain: the word republic derives from the Latin *res publica* (things public). It is where *public* policy as well as public law are formulated, argued and made, and where their implementation is organized. By contrast, the domain of the private has been understood as that of civil society and the family. The public–private contrast therefore hides a more differentiated triad to that of state and civil society: the elements of the triad are state, civil society and family, a triad that can be seen explicitly in the political philosophy of Hegel. Much European political thought has operated with this double emphasis, in which the state is both the realm of the public and of the (allegedly) most rational human conduct – the word

'idiot' derives from the Greek word for a private person. Most European political thinkers also saw the realms of state and civil society as 'naturally' male (though not open to all males), whereas the familial domain was assumed female (though in the last instance male-governed). Feminists therefore argue that the state has been a public or male arena, excluding females from decision-making; but so too has much of civil society, operating in public view but as part of the 'private' economic sector. The fully private 'sphere' has been overwhelmingly assigned to women – the intimate and personal features of individual and household life, the burdens of child-producing, childrearing, domestic labour and emotional support.

THE STATAL VERSUS THE STATELESS

The last of our antonyms, which contrasts stateness with statelessness, is the most descriptive and least obviously morally evaluative. It highlights differences between the state as an organization with other political systems that lack statal qualities. Two important variations in this comparison exist. The first compares states with acephalous societies; the second compares modern states with the political systems that preceded them, the states of 'agraria': feudal kingdoms, city-states and agro-literate empires.

There have been, and still are, some stateless societies, segmentary tribal systems or small, isolated bands, in which rules and decisions are made collectively, or through implicit negotiation, with no specialization of government in the hands of one set of persons. These are acephalous (or headless) societies – they may have arbiters or holymen who referee disputes, but they have none of the powers of judges in states (Fortes and Evans-Pritchard 1940). The point made, rightly, by anthropologists, is that states are not essential features of the human condition; rather, they are historically and sociologically contingent; or to put it another way, states are unnatural: 'we' did not have them in our pre-histories.

The formation of the first states is likely to remain shrouded in mystery, not least because there are few cases of 'pristine' state-formation to study – though the process happened independently in six different parts of our planet (in China, the Indus Valley, Mesopotamia, Egypt, Central America and the Andes). Most of the early examples of state-creation known to historians appear to have arisen in opposition to nearby state-formations, so it is difficult to distinguish 'primary' from 'secondary' states (Claessen and Skalnik 1978).

The alternative approach to the state–acephalous society contrast distinguishes the (modern) state from all previous political systems – including entities described as states by those who emphasize the state–acephalous contrast. The first specimens of the modern state, and the modern state system, on this view, emerged in Europe in the sixteenth and seventeenth centuries, and then spread, through conquest, and protective imitation in fear of conquest, to the rest of the world (Shennan 1974). This modern state is commonly contrasted with both the personalized, weak and non-bureaucratic forms of feudal rule, and with the weaker tributary empires of the ancient world. It is, however, in one sense widely seen as a project modelled on what the Roman Empire failed to be. As the modern state emerged, so did theoretical reflection on the emergence of the statal system, and the state. The names given to this entity, of the modern state, vary, even today. Some call it 'the organic state' to emphasize its rootedness in and productive integration with its civil society, by contrast with the 'capstone' and 'predatory' forms of rule characteristic of Roman, Hindu, Islamic and Chinese imperial civilizations (Hall 1994). Others, especially Marxists, call it the capitalist state; yet others call it the nation-state. Let us call it the modern state, to avoid prejudging its organic, capitalist or national character; what is meant by modern here is little more than 'relatively recent' and 'associated with industrialized and literate peoples'. Essential to this insistence on the distinctiveness of the modern state is its organizational nature, which we have attempted to capture in our definition to which we may now return.

Elaborating the definition

(1) A modern state is *a differentiated and impersonal institution*. This definitional attribute requires the state to be different from the society or societies that it encompasses, i.e. it must not be acephalous. It must, literally and metaphorically, have at least a head of state. But the modern state must also be differentiated impersonally, i.e. it must have an existence and continuity independently of its head(s) or ruler(s).

The emergence of the modern state can be written as the history of the de-personalizing or de-dynasticizing of the mandate to rule. The medieval prince of the Renaissance 'personified' the state, inheriting lands that he governed as a landowner, as his father's property, but by the eighteenth century the prince had become a different being from the land he owned and represented. The concept of the impersonal state had emerged. In the modern constitutional monarchy, as in the modern republic, there is a clear separation between what belongs to the monarch or president as a private person and what belongs to them as head of state. 'Corruption' is the universal mark of poor performance by a modern state. The modern state is not the personal property of the head of state. Indeed, it is a mark of the non-modernity, or at least of the corruption, of a state when rulers treat its resources as his or her personal property. The modern state is not a dynasty, even though its head of state may come from a dynastic family.

(2) A modern state is *politically centralized*. The state must be organizationally unified and coherent in some respects, and have 'emergent' properties of its own. A state can be decentralized or federal but there must be a centre or a distinct set of centres where executive, legislative and judicial authority is concentrated. A state need not be a single, hierarchical pyramidal monolith. But without some centralized core capacities it will cease to be a state. When a state becomes merely an aggregation of multiple organizations and officials with rival identities, interests and preferences without any authoritative steering capacity it is in crisis. These multiple organizations, especially executives, legislatures, judiciaries and bureaucracies, may be configured in multiple ways, but a working state is ultimately *an* institution, or a hierarchy of institutions, rather than a messy bundle of disconnected institutions.

(3) A modern state exercises *authoritatively binding rule-making (or sovereignty) over persons, groups and property*. The idea of sovereignty, the possession and use of a supreme, hierarchical, integrated and implicitly homogenous law-making authority within the state's territory, has been seen as the central legal innovation of the modern state. In such a state there should be a formal sovereign – a body competent to make all final decisions, with competence to decide competences, as the

Germans put it. That there is and should be a final and absolute source of political and legal authority within a given community or territory now seems straightforward, but it was not always so. Though anticipated in the Roman Empire, it was, however, only with the emergence of the modern European state that the idea was clearly expressed: 'The emergence of the state as a form of rule is a necessary condition of the concept of sovereignty, it is not a sufficient condition of it' (Hinsley 1986: 21). The idea of sovereignty also requires the state to be an impersonal institution that exists apart from its particular rulers, and a further distinction is required between the state and its subjects (Skinner 1989).

(4) A modern state *exercises an effective monopoly of publicly organized physical force.* The agrarian predecessors of the modern state rarely possessed an effective monopoly of organized physical force. In feudal Europe a king's capacity to wage war was dependent upon a levy controlled by nobles with decentralized local power; in the Islamic political systems of North Africa and the Middle East caliphs and sultans did not generally intervene in tribal feuding, and tribes maintained autonomous military capabilities. It is for this reason that Max Weber famously defined the state as 'a human community that (successfully) claims the monopoly of the legitimate use of physical force within a given territory'. This definition, at least as it is rendered into English, will not do: no state has ever successfully claimed a monopoly of all legitimate physical force – though many have successfully claimed a monopoly of publicly organized force. One implication of feminist writing provides an amendment to Weber's and the conventional way of defining this attribution of statehood. Given that, at least in the eyes of feminists and that of their sympathizers, 'states arm men and disarm women', it might be more politically and sexually neutral to specify that the modern state has an effective monopoly of *publicly* organized physical force.

The modern European state developed from the successful struggle of absolutist rulers to disarm feudal nobilities, to defortify and demilitarize 'private' aristocratic military defensive and offensive capabilities, to decommission or dispense with mercenaries, and to crush pirates. In their place they generally sought to substitute standing armies – and later standing police

forces. European empires and their postcolonial successors likewise sought to break the military self-reliance and self-help practices of tribes without rulers. In their centralization and monopolization of publicly organized force, together with the technological innovations of the last five centuries, lie the origins of the fearsome power of modern states.

(5) A modern state *is sufficiently recognized by a sufficient number of its subjects* and (6) *by a sufficient number of other states.* In order to qualify as a state it must have both internal and external recognition; that is to say, it must have 'recognizers'. It must sustain such acknowledgements, and acknowledgers, or die. Internally, the recognizers are the subjects, sometimes the citizens, of the state. Internally, recognition means that sufficient numbers of its subjects, or sufficient numbers of the powerful and wealthy, must recognize and respect the state's authority, enough to ensure its survival. Even though they may loathe its authority, it is sufficient that they fear it, generally obey it and thereby recognize it. Some maintain in consequence that states ultimately only exist in the minds of their subjects. Such recognition need not be internalized. Those who recognize the state may do so entirely from prudential motives.

External recognition is the acknowledgement that the state is such by those who make such decisions, and those who make such decisions are the authorized personnel of other states. Externally, recognition means that the state's peers, other states, recognize it as a state, even though they may seek to deny it membership in particular approved clubs of states, such as the United 'Nations' or the EU. Again, recognition here may flow from prudence, or fear, rather than warm endorsement. In international law, this position is called a 'declaratory' rather than 'constitutive' view of recognition. In the declaratory view it is a matter of fact whether a state is recognized as an entity that has effective control of its territory and population; this fact can be created by force alone – provided, of course, other states recognize such force within the relevant delimited territory.

To be, in other words, a state requires recognition, not legitimacy. Others must recognize its brute reality, domestically, as well as those outside its jurisdiction. Those who grant this reality may not regard the state's existence as just, and indeed may wage war or insurrection with the intent to destroy its current power-holders. States die through external conquest, or through internal insurrection or collapse, or all combined. These terminal conditions mark the loss of recognition.

(7) A modern state *sustains its organizational and policy-making powers*. Modern states, whether to fight wars, organize public welfare or stimulate economic investment, require taxes, the life-blood of the state. Without taxes maintaining a monopoly over publicly organized physical force would be impossible, and bureaucrats would corrupt their offices if they are not paid, or not paid enough. Bureaucracies, professional or mass-line organizations, provide states with the capacities to intervene in, regulate and steer their societies. Any serious erosion of the fiscal bases, bureaucratic capabilities and steering capacities available to central governments signal crises of statehood that will reduce their capacities to win the trust and inspire the fear of their subjects. Much of contemporary political science and political sociology addresses these capacities of contemporary states, especially of liberal democratic states.

(8) A modern state has *a (potentially variable) territory*. On the simplest conception a state is a specific combination of a sovereign organization, a population and a place, a territory. Modern states claim a monopoly of authority over their territory – or to cede such authority in the case of confederations (Baldwin 1992).

Modern states have borders or boundaries that encompass their territories; i.e. they have precise cartographically represented lines, entrenched in bilateral and multilateral treaties, which demarcate their territories from those of other states. Sometimes these cartographic statements are physically expressed in electric fences and walls, but they are more often signified by border posts and border patrols (on land, at sea and in the air). By contrast, premodern or ancient state systems had 'frontiers' rather than 'boundaries' – i.e. their cores were surrounded by military zones in which they disputed and faced the enemy. Frontiers were 'marches', zones of conflict, rather than demarcated lines or borders. This contrast between a modern state and the ancient Chinese or Roman Empire is immediate and striking: the economic, administrative and (internal) military domains of the state are, now, in principle, identical. Within its well-bordered territory the grip of the state, and its extractive

and policy-making agencies, is supposed to be of equal and uniform capacity; and there is, in principle, no differentiation between an inner and outer military frontier. The state's sovereignty is territorially uniform; no zones are recognized in which state-sanctioned law does not apply.

These eight elements of the state are abstractions. They are not found equally intensely in all modern countries that are members of the United Nations. Some states are more statal than others; some states are more powerful than others, though in principle all states are equal in diplomatic recognition. These eight elements nevertheless represent the features that social scientists and historians say distinguish the modern state from premodern governing systems. A ninth element is sometimes suggested when it is claimed that modern states have citizens, with rights, whereas ancient states had subjects. There is some truth in this, but there are too many exceptions: many modern states have had subjects rather than citizens, especially when they have presided over empires; conversely, some ancient city-states had meaningful practices of citizenship.

The eight elements are not merely definitional: they enable us merely through deduction to define potential crises of the state. (1) Corruption repersonalizes politics, weakening the state's impersonal reputation. (2) Fundamental attacks on the central or federal governing institutions put its survival in jeopardy. (3) Challenges to the state's exclusive sovereignty (legal authority) may come from within and without its territory. (4) Its monopoly of publicly organized physical force may be challenged by paramilitaries, guerrillas, Mafiosi and militiamen. (5) A state may fail to inspire fear, let alone love, amongst its subjects, threatening it with a fundamental loss of authority. (6) A state may cease to be recognized by its peers, leaving it vulnerable to predators and devoid of the mutual services that states provide one another. (7) A state's organizational and policy-making powers may be weakened by agents within its civil society, or by external agencies and forces, including technological transformations that impair its authority. (8) Its territorial rights may also be challenged: by conquerors, who may partition it, or by secessionists, who will take away at least one of its existing internal units. Theories of the state vary in the emphases and explanations they give to these logically possible forms of state crises.

A last word on the definition of the state, elaborated here, and that has attempted to synthesize modern arguments. There is nothing obviously democratic about the state in the definition, despite the formal requirement that subjection to sovereignty applies to all individuals. Equally this definition leaves open the question of whether the state should be treated as a single, unified actor, for some purposes but not others – it is compatible with seeing states, especially in their domestic face, as the sum total of the roles and activities of the individuals in a conglomerate of suborganizations that are nevertheless legally structured.

The approach outlined here has been organizational: the modern state has been defined by its institutional and spatial characteristics. This approach facilitates debate on precisely which organizational attributes make states distinctive. By contrast, the functional approach to defining the state specifies that the performance of certain functions is distinctly state-like; the state is that which performs these functions, e.g. the administration of justice. This approach may also prompt debate on precisely which functions are statal functions. *Functional definitions* of the state can take two forms. One, *ex ante*, approach defines the state as that set of institutions which carry out particular goals, purposes or objectives. An obvious contrast with the organizational approach is that 'the state' may be empirically identified with a range of institutions not normally classified as part of the 'public' realm, because any organization whose goals or purposes overlap with 'statal functions' then automatically becomes part of the state. A second, *ex post*, approach defines the state by its consequences, e.g. the maintenance of social order. The state is then identified with those institutions or patterns of behaviour that have stabilizing effects. Again, this approach enlarges what can count as a component of 'the state'. For instance, if we say that a key function of the state is to produce social cohesion, and believe that family life achieves much the same result, we may be driven to conclude that the family as an institution is part of the state (an argument implied by some feminist thinkers).

Modern statal order is a necessary condition of most things that moderns want. Without a well-ordered state there cannot be democracy, the rule of law, functioning markets, human development, civil society or participation. Unlike Hobbes, we know that states may be lethal, often more lethal than the 'war of all against all'. States are the most powerful agencies of exclusion, governments of modern states the major killers in human history, but that does not mean that we can dispense with them: we can, however, temper, regulate and democratize them; we can share power better within them, and we may be able to make them more just.

BRENDAN O'LEARY
UNIVERSITY OF PENNSYLVANIA

References

Baldwin, T. (1992) 'The territorial state', in H. Gross and R. Harrison (eds) *Jurisprudence: Cambridge Essays*, Oxford.
Claessen, H. and Skalnik, P. (eds) (1978) *The Early State*, The Hague.
Fortes, M. and Evans-Pritchard, E.E. (eds) (1940) *African Political Systems*, Oxford.
Hall, J.A. (1994) *Coercion and Consent: Studies on the Modern State*, Oxford.
Hinsley, F.H. (1986) *Sovereignty*, 2nd edn, Cambridge, UK.
Hobbes, T. (1651) *Leviathan*, London.
Shennan, J.H. (1974) *The Origins of the Modern European State, 1450–1725*, London.
Skinner, Q. (1989) 'The state', in T. Ball, J. Farr and R.S. Hanson (eds) *Political Innovation and Conceptual Change*, Cambridge, UK.

Further reading

Brubaker, R. (1996) 'National minorities, nationalizing states, and external national homelands in the New Europe', in *Nationalism Reframed: Nationhood and the National Question in the New Europe*, Cambridge, UK.
Dunleavy, P. and O'Leary, B. (1987) *Theories of the State: The Politics of Liberal Democracy*, London.
Hegel, G.W.F. (1967 [1821]) 'The state', in T.M. Knox (ed.) *Hegel's Philosophy of Right*, Oxford.
Poggi, G. (1990) *The State: Its Nature, Development and Prospects*, Stanford, CA.
Tilly, C. (1975) 'Reflections on the history of European state-making', in C. Tilly (ed.) *The Formation of National States in Western Europe*, Princeton, NJ.

SEE ALSO: anarchism; bureaucracy; citizenship; civil society; constitutions and constitutionalism; corruption; democracy; federalism and federation; feudalism; Hobbes; law; Machiavelli; partition; political theory; privacy; public administration; public choice; public goods; secession; state, origins of

STATE, ORIGINS OF

Since the seventeenth century, much Western scholarship has focused on the origin of the state, a form of political organization in which power rests in the hands of a small governing group that monopolizes the use of coercive force to maintain internal order and cope with neighbouring peoples. This type of government is found in all large-scale societies, which are also invariably characterized (even in socialist examples) by marked political and economic disparities.

Theorizing has centred on whether states evolve primarily through consent or conflict and as a result of internal or external factors. It has also been debated keenly whether states have improved or degraded the human condition by comparison with smaller, seemingly more natural societies. 'Social contract' theorists, including Thomas Hobbes and John Locke, believed that individuals submitted willingly to the state in return for the protection it offered their persons and property. Karl Wittfogel and Julian Steward argued that the state first evolved to manage large irrigation systems in arid regions. Others see the state developing in order to regulate the production, importation and redistribution of valuable materials.

The oldest 'conflict' theories postulated that states originated as a result of conquest, especially of agricultural peoples by pastoralists. Marxists view agricultural and craft specialization as producing socioeconomic differentiation that results in class conflict and ultimately the formation of the state as a means to maintain ruling-class dominance. Robert Carneiro argues that population increase within geographically or socially circumscribed areas results in warfare over arable land and the emergence of the state. More generally, Mark Cohen maintains that population increase leads to the intensification of food production and eventually to competition for arable land, population agglomeration and the development of the state. In each of these theories, the state evolves at least in part to protect social and political inequalities.

None of these theories explains satisfactorily the origin of the state. Marxists assume that emergent classes developed prior to the state, a position that is not widely accepted. Other explanations do not appear to cover all, or even most, cases. 'Prime-mover' theories of the origins of the state have been rejected. Synthetic theories, which combine a number of causal variables, have not proved more successful. It is widely accepted that many different factors promote the development of larger and more differentiated societies that require state controls. This has led interest to shift away from explaining why the state develops to how.

Increasing use has been made of 'information theory' to account for the development of the state. It is argued that the delegation of decision-making to central authorities becomes increasingly necessary for political systems to function adequately as their size and complexity increase. Centralized control requires the collection of information from all parts of the system and the effective transmission of orders from the centre to these parts. Archaeologists have argued that the state can be equated with settlement hierarchies of at least three levels, corresponding to an equal number of levels of decision-making. This does not explain, however, why early civilizations were characterized by marked economic and status disparities rather than simply by functionally differentiated leadership roles.

A further application of information theory suggests that gossip, ridicule, accusations of witchcraft and other economic and political levelling mechanisms that are found in small, egalitarian societies work only when people are known to one another. As larger societies develop, leaders can use their newly acquired control of public information to weaken opposition and silence critics. This facilitates the concentration of political and economic power among an elite and the development of conspicuous consumption as a feature of elite lifestyles.

At the same time, it is recognized that rulers must curb the predatoriness of officials and excessive increases in the bureaucracy and distribution of state largess if exactions are to remain within limits that are acceptable to the taxpayer. This assumes that the state provides services, such as defence and internal order, which the bulk of the population accepts as essential. If exactions are kept within accepted limits, most people will continue, at least passively, to support the state.

Additional theories stress the emulation of inegalitarian behavioural patterns within extended and nuclear families, and other spheres of personal interaction. This strengthens the power of the state by making domination appear universal and natural from each person's earliest infancy. Attention is also paid to hegemonic ideologies that elites employ to naturalize inequality and enhance their own power. There is, however, disagreement about the extent to which dominated classes accept elite claims or construct counter ones. The latter position rejects theocratic explanations of state power. While the state is not coterminous with human societies, discussions of its origins remain intimately tied to an understanding of human nature.

BRUCE G. TRIGGER
MCGILL UNIVERSITY

Further reading

Clastres, P. (1977) *Society against the State*, New York.
Flannery, K.V. (1972) 'The cultural evolution of civilizations', *Annual Review of Ecology and Systematics* 3.
Hass, J. (1982) *The Evolution of the Prehistoric State*, New York.
Johnson, G.A. (1973) *Local Exchange and Early State Development in Southerwestern Iran*, Ann Arbor, MI.
Patterson, T.C. and Gailey, C.W. (eds) (1987) *Power Relations and State Formation*, Washington, DC.
Tainter, J.A. (1988) *The Collapse of Complex Societies*, Cambridge, UK.

SEE ALSO: government; political anthropology; state

STATISTICAL REASONING

Statistical reasoning (SR) is a form of reasoning with probabilistic features, applicable to inference and decision-making in the presence of an uncertainty that cannot be expressed in terms of known and agreed chance probabilities. Thus SR is not relevant to games of pure chance, such as backgammon with well-engineered dice, but is likely to be involved in guessing the voting intentions of an electorate and fixing an advantageous polling date.

Its application is usually mediated by some *statistical method* whose prestige and convenience, especially if computerized, can induce a neglect of the associated SR. Even when explicitly formulated, SR may be *plausible* (or not) in appearance and *efficacious* (or not) in its ultimate influence. The evolutionary theory of SR (Campbell 1974) postulates that, in its broadest form, it is a genetically controlled mental activity justified by survival advantage. A related black-box view of the efficacy of SR may be useful in

deciding between the claims of different SR schools that their respective nostrums are found to work in practice. We shall concentrate here, however, on the varieties of SR conventionally invoked to support a selection (in italics) of particular statistical methods and principles.

Randomly selected observations: the incorporation of an element of objective random sampling in any observations on a population of identifiable items, which ensures for each item a specified, non-negligible probability of being included in the sample.

Without the element of random sampling, it is impossible for the sampler to justify the selection of items without reference to some systematic, comprehensive theory that may be erroneous or, worse, subject to undeclared or subconscious bias.

Non-Bayesian sampling theory makes use of the random-sampling probabilities to test hypotheses about the population as a whole, or to generate unbiased estimates of population parameters, allowing for potential differences between the unobserved items and those observed.

Randomized experimentation: random manipulation of controllable independent variables in the treatment of experimental units, and the analysis of the effect of this manipulation on dependent variables.

If the effect referred to were reliably established, it could be described as *causal*, operating either directly or through the agency of other variables. The use of an isolated random manipulator – uninfluenceable, and influential only through controllable independent variables – is necessary in order to rule out the hypothesis of spurious correlation between the dependent variables and naturally occurring variation of the independent variables. As a bonus, it also rules out the possibility of the experimenter using 'inside knowledge' to produce such a correlation by unconscious or deliberate choice of the values of the control variables.

The extent to which such causal inference is possible in non-experimental investigation depends on the extent to which changes in the independent variables are induced by factors judged to be equivalent to an isolated random manipulator, as in *quasi-experimental studies*.

The non-Bayesian school (Fisher 1935) makes explicit use of the randomization probabilities for various types of inference.

Significance testing: evaluation of the achieved

significance level P *for the observed value* t *of a test statistic* T. *The evaluation is made using the distribution of* T *under a (null) hypothesis* H_0 *specified by the observer: without any allowance for selection of* T, $P = Pr(T \mid tH_0)$.

When small, *P* provides a standardized interpretation of the deviation of *t* from the values of *T* that would be expected if H_0 were true. Increasing values of *t* are encoded as decreasing values of *P* that induce increasing dissatisfaction with H_0. A small value of *P* forces the simple dichotomy: either H_0 is true and a rare event has occurred, or H_0 does not describe the actual distribution of *T*.

P is not the probability that H_0 is true, which is a probability that is not definable under H_0.

The dissatisfaction with H_0 increases smoothly: there is no critical value, 0.05 for example, at which *P* suddenly becomes scientifically important.

The *provenance* of *T* should be taken into account in the calculation of *P* when, for example, *T* has been selected as a result of a search for any interesting feature of the data, whose extreme manifestation is *data ransacking*.

The Fisherian school sees significance testing simply as a screening device that protects observers from attributing reality to chimerical features created by chance variation under some uninteresting (null) hypothesis: it does not need to be complicated by the Neyman–Pearsonan concepts of 'alternative' hypotheses and 'power'.

There are serious problems of logical coherence in any *evidential* interpretation of *P*-values, which are not designed to do more than their simple definition countenances (Stone 2003).

Confidence intervals: For data x, *the construction of a 95 per cent confidence interval* [L(x), U(x)] *for a real-valued parameter* Ø, *in a statistical model defined as a set* {Pr$_ø$} *of probability distributions of* X, *the random generic of* x.

The particular interval *[L(x), U(x)]* is regarded as relevant to inference about the true value of Ø because of its 'hoop-la' coverage property, e.g. $Pr_ø [L(X) (Ø (U(X)] (0.95$. The value 0.95 here is not the probability that Ø lies in the particular interval *[L(x), U(x)]*, which is a probability not defined in the assumed statistical model.

Can the 'relevance' of *[L(x), U(x)]* be reasonably maintained when, as may happen, the calculated interval turns out to be the whole real line, or the empty set, or when it may be logically

established that the interval contains Ø? Fortunately, such counter-examples do not arise in the commoner applications of the confidence interval method.

Decision procedures – given are:

1 *a statistical model* {Pr$_ø$} *for* X;
2 *a set* {d} *of possible decisions;*
3 *a loss function* L[d, Ø], *the loss if decision* d *is taken when* Ø *is true;*
4 *a set* {ô} *of decision rules, each of which individually specifies the decision to be taken for each data-value* x.

Deducible are the risk functions of Ø, *one for each* ô, *defined by the expectation under* Pr$_ø$ *of the randomly determined loss* L[ô (X), Ø].

The completely specified method selects a decision rule from *{ô}* that has a risk function with some optimal character. The SR of decision procedures stems from, and is clearly justifiable in, the context of industrial production where the loss *L* has a cumulative financial imperative. However, its application to statistical inference can have surprising or unintended consequences.

One example arose in connection with the widespread use of least-squares estimates. For normal models and taking risk as mean square error, it was found that improvements could be made, whatever the true values of the parameters, by means of a special estimator even when this combined the data of quite unrelated problems – by shrinking the estimates towards any common arbitrarily selected value! This phenomenon may be seen as a criticism of least-squares estimators as decision rules: a proper Bayesian approach whose prior insists that the problems are indeed unrelated will not allow any pooling of information but will also not produce least-squares estimates.

For significance testing, there are problems too. The Fisherian subjectivity in the choice of a significance test statistic, coupled with that school's lack of concern about its performance when H_0 (Ø $= Ø_0$, say) does not hold, led Neyman and Pearson to treat testing a hypothesis as a decision procedure. This has {d} = {Accept H_0, Reject H_0}, L = 0 or 1 according as the decision *d* is right or wrong, and, as a consequence, a risk function that is equivalent to a statement of the probabilities of two kinds of error: 'size' (the probability of rejecting H_0 when it is true) and '1 – power' (the probability of accepting it when it is not). A problem with this identification was discovered by Cox (1958). It can be illustrated with a simple story. Two pollsters A and B wanted to test the null hypothesis that no more than half the electors of a large city, willing to respond to a particular yes/no question, would do so affirmatively. Pollster A suggested that the poll would require only 100 randomly chosen respondents, whereas B wanted to get 10,000 responses. They agreed to toss a fair coin to decide the sample size; then to employ the 5 per cent hypothesis test that is most powerful in detecting a yes/no ratio of 2/1 (an alternative hypothesis) – with probabilities of error defined before the outcome of the toss is known. They check with a statistician that this test would have an overall power of 99 per cent for the alternative hypothesis. In the event, the sample size was 10,000 and the number of yes's was 5,678. Both A and B were astonished when advised that this number was too small to reject the hypothesis by the agreed test even though, had it been obtained in a survey with a non-random choice of the sample size 10,000, it would have delivered a *P*-value less than one in a million! The explanation for this contretemps is that the 99 per cent power is an average of two *conditional* powers, one for each of the eventuating sample size *n*. This average is maximized when the conditional 'size' is just under 10 per cent for the event $n = 100$ and just above zero for the event $n = 10,000$, with an average of 5 per cent. Neither A nor B realized that, when they optimized power for the 2/1 alternative, they would be implicitly excluding consideration of any other alternative.

So far, the examples of SR are somewhat *ad hoc* and fragmentary. Are there no general principles that can be brought to bear on any problem of statistical methodology of whatever size and shape? The answer depends very much on the extent to which the *uncertainty* in the problem has been crystallized in the form of an agreed statistical model *{Prₒ}* for the random *X* realized as data *x* in some observational set-up þ. In the abstract but powerful terminology of Dawid (1977), an *inference pattern* is a specified function *I(þ,x)* of the two arguments (where the values of *I* can be absolutely any aspiringly inferential statement). The following principles refer to the situation (not necessarily hypothetical) in which data *x* and data *x'* are realized in observational set-ups *þ* and *þ'* with possibly

different models – but models that are *indexed by the same parameter Ø taking the same (true) value*. With no essential loss of generality suppose that, for every value of Ø, *X* is discretely distributed with discrete probabilities $p_Ø(x)$.

Ancillarity principle: suppose the statistic A = f(X) *has the same probability distribution for all values of Ø (and is therefore a so-called 'ancillary statistic'). Suppose that* A = a *is its observed value in* þ. *Let* þ' *be the (conceptual) observational set-up for which the model is given by the set of probability distributions for* X *given the event* A = a. *Suppose that, if we had actually used* þ', *we would have found that* x' = x. *The ancillarity principle requires that I should satisfy the identity* I(þ', x) = I(þ, x) – *in other words, that the inference is the same whether we see the data as embedded in the original set-up or as coming afresh from a set-up that does not recognize the embedding.*

The principle is well illustrated by our story of two pollsters A and B, where it rules out their clearly indicated inference pattern: 'Whatever the set-up, use a test of size 5 per cent with maximum power for a yes/no ratio of 2/1.' For, with *X* = (coin toss, observed proportion of yes's), the coin toss is an ancillary statistic – and A and B's *P*-value 'inference' would have been very different from the one (as if for þ) that surprised them if only it had been made conditionally on the 10,000 outcome of the toss (as if for þ').

Sufficiency principle: suppose S = f(X) *is a sufficient statistic, i.e. the conditional distribution of* X *given* S = s *does not depend on Ø whatever the value of* s. *Let* þ', s) = I (þ, x) *for* s f(x).

The sufficiency principle is universally accepted: once we know the value of *S*, what value can further knowledge of *X* possibly have when its distribution can be simulated by a random device whose specification depends on *x* but not at all on the value of Ø?

Likelihood principle: for the observation X = x, *the likelihood function of Ø may be defined as* $L_x(Ø)$ ($p_Ø$ (x) *(ditto for* L', x' *and* p'). *The likelihood principle requires that* I(þ' ,x') = I(þ, x) *if* L'x'(Ø) (c(x',x)Lx(Ø), *i.e. if the two likelihood functions of Ø are proportional.*

It is relatively straightforward to check that any inference pattern which obeys the Likelihood Principle also obeys the Ancillarity and Sufficiency Principles. Statisticians were both dismayed and delighted, according to taste or prejudice, when Birnbaum (1962) proved the converse. The same holds true when Ancillarity is replaced by Censoring: we do not change our inference when we are told that we would not have been given the value of X if it had been in some other set! Nothing more then appears to be needed from the statistical model than the probabilities of the observed data for different values of $\emptyset$. Likelihood achieves the ultimate in conditioning: it conditions on the whole data – but with non-trivial consequences, e.g. the principle rules out any inferential use of the randomization probabilities in our first two examples of statistical method.

With one extra step from the Likelihood Principle – adding a prior distribution – we arrive at the door of the Bayesian school.

Bayesian method: given data x for a statistical model indexed by a parameter $\emptyset$, a posterior probability distribution for $\emptyset$ is calculated by the Bayesian formula that increases or decreases the prior probabilities of particular values of $\emptyset$ – by multiplying them by the likelihood function and rescaling the whole so that the products sum to a total probability of unity. In this way, quite reasonably, the odds on some values of $\emptyset$ are increased if they give higher probability to the observed data than other values do.

There are several nearly equivalent axiomatic formulations of the Bayesian rationale whose upshot, roughly, is that any individual willing to accept a few qualitative axioms about probability and to give expression to them in a rich enough context will discover that he or she has a subjective probability distribution $\ddot{E}$ over everything – or at least over everything related to x and $\emptyset$. When pushed further, the axioms deliver a *utility function* that, with change of sign, serves as the loss function L for the decision procedure method (Berger 1993).

The Bayesian formula is particularly convenient if the first fruits of the introspective process for determining $\ddot{E}$ are not only the assignment of probability 1 to the assertion that data x was indeed randomly generated by the 'given' statistical model, but also the (prior) probabilities of $\emptyset$. Suppose this introspective process were faithfully undertaken by a very large number of Bayesians in a range of contexts. Then, even if the statistical models to which unit probability is assigned truly generated the observed values of the corresponding data, it would be a necessary consequence that the data would, with high probability, show a conventional statistically significant departure from its associated model in a proportion of cases. This would be so even if the Bayesians were fully aware of the features of their data at the time of their probability assignments. It may therefore be necessary to defend the rights of Bayesians to use statistical models that would be rejected by other statistical methods.

The difficulty for the Bayesian approach just described may be overcome by the assignment of a probability of $1-\tilde{O}$, rather than unity, to the statistical model: awkward data could then be accommodated by reserving the prior probability $\tilde{O}$ for any *ad hoc* models. The $\tilde{O}$ here might be christened *cromwell* in honour of that regicide's plea: 'I beseech you, in the bowels of Christ, think it possible you may be mistaken.' So a 'cromwell' would be useful to override the acceptance of the one in a million deviation in the yes/no polling example, when that is formulated as a Bayesian decision procedure.

It could also be used to deal with the paradox created by data that simultaneously deviates highly significantly from what is expected under a sharp subhypothesis ($\emptyset = \emptyset_0$ say) of the model, while *increasing* the odds in favour of $\emptyset_0$ (Lindley 1957). For example, suppose that a clairvoyant correctly predicts 50,500 out of 100,000 tosses of a fair coin and that the statistical model is that the number of correct guesses is binomially distributed with probability $\emptyset$. For the prior that puts probability 1/2 at $\emptyset=$ 1/2 and probability 1/2 spread uniformly over the interval (0, 1), the posterior odds in favour of $\emptyset$ 1/2 are 1.7/1, even though the clairvoyant's extra 500 correct guesses over expectation are statistically significant at $P = 0.0008$.

Bayesians claim that all probabilities are subjective with the possible exception of the quantum theoretic sort. At best, subjective probability distributions may agree to assign unit probability to the same statistical model but posterior distributions will then differ, reflecting individual priors. There have been extensive efforts (Berger 1993) to promulgate *objective priors* in order to formalize the apparently reasonable slogan 'Let the data speak for themselves!' and give Bayesian methods an appearance of scientific objectivity.

When there is no agreed statistical model, SR runs short of mathematical support. Perhaps as a consequence, in this area – one that impinges heavily on issues of public concern – SR has not received the attention it deserves, except in books such as Gigerenzer (2003) or the occasional philosophical article (most philosophical discussions of SR are implicitly model-dependent). At this premodelling level, there is a broad consensus among the statistically minded as to what constitutes poor SR: it is much more difficult to characterize good SR. The latter is required to avoid the elementary logical pitfalls, but needs to go well beyond that in constructive directions. A paradoxical snag in statistical thinking about some problems is how to recognize that the data are inadequate to support such thinking: imaginative SR may be needed to specify the kind of data needed to support the embryonic inferences being formulated. Stone (1974, for cross-validation) and Dawid (1991, for sequential prediction) dispensed with the concept of truth for a statistical model and still found room for some SR mathematics: Dawid has even introduced a new principle – *prequentialism* – for the statistical evaluation of merely adopted models. Premodelling SR has gained much from the graphical techniques of *exploratory data analysis* (Tukey 1977), but it is also challenged by them. *Computer-intensive methods* (Diaconis and Efron 1983) powerfully extend the range of statistical activity subject to SR scrutiny. However, they also increase the risk that SR will be neglected in favour of the pyrotechnics that such techniques can display. *Caveat emptor!*

M. STONE
UNIVERSITY COLLEGE LONDON

References

Berger, J.O. (1993) *Statistical Decision Theory and Bayesian Analysis*, New York.

Birnbaum, A. (1962) 'On the foundations of statistical inference', *Journal of the American Statistical Association* 57.

Campbell, D.T. (1974) 'Evolutionary epistemology', in P.A. Schilpp (ed.) *The Philosophy of Karl Popper*, La Salle, IL.

Cox, D.R. (1958) 'Some problems connected with statistical inference', *Annals of Mathematical Statistics* 29.

Dawid, A.P. (1977) 'Conformity of inference patterns', in J.R. Barra, F. Brodeau, G. Romier and B. van Cutsem (eds) *Recent Developments in Statistics*, Amsterdam.

—— (1991) 'Fisherian inference in likelihood and prequential frames of reference', *Journal of the Royal Statistical Society B* 53.

Diaconis, P. and Efron, B. (1983) 'Computer-intensive methods in statistics', *Scientific American* 248.

Fisher, R.A. (1935) *The Design of Experiments*, Edinburgh.

Gigerenzer, G. (2003) *Reckoning with Risk*, London.

Lindley, D.V. (1957) 'A statistical paradox', *Biometrika* 44.

Stone, M. (1974) 'Cross-validatory choice and assessment of statistical predictions', *Journal of the Royal Statistical Society B* 36.

—— (2003) 'Commentary on Berkson's "Tests of significance considered as evidence"', *International Journal of Epidemiology* 32(5): 694–8.

Tukey, J.W. (1977) *Exploratory Data Analysis*, Reading, MA.

SEE ALSO: mathematical models; methods of social research

STEREOTYPES

The term 'stereotype' was first used in the printing industry where it referred to a cast iron plate used to make repeated impressions of the same image. This sense of an impression that is enduring, fixed and resistant to change was imported into the social sciences when in his book *Public Opinion* the journalist Walter Lippmann (1922) applied the term to refer to the 'pictures in the head' that people have of social groups. In a minimalist sense, a stereotype is an image or representation of a group of people that is widely known and shared within a particular community or group. However, in addition to this, within social research (as in society more generally) stereotypes are typically understood to have a number of negative features, many of which were identified in Lippmann's writing. In particular, they are seen as akin to caricatures that, as well as being resistant to change, are also biased, selective and simplistic.

Consistent with these views, a large body of social psychological research confirms that stereotypes tend to accentuate both the differences between groups and the similarities within them. Their content is often also observed to be ethnocentric in the sense that the stereotypes of groups that we belong to (in-groups) tend to be more positive than those of groups to which we do not belong (out-groups) (Tajfel 1981). For this reason, when most social scientists use the term stereotype they are implicitly referring to perceptions that are believed to be fundamentally inaccurate – representing members of out-groups as being more similar to each other, more different from other groups, and of worse character than they really are. For this reason, holding and expressing stereotypes is often seen as a form of prejudice, and this has contributed to an intertwining of research into these two phenomena.

The history of research into stereotypes and stereotyping has gone through a number of clearly defined phases. Indeed research into this topic has been a market-place for key debates in social psychology and a harbinger of major trends in the discipline as a whole. The earliest research, pioneered by Katz and Braly (1933), examined stereotype consensus and content by asking people to assign adjectives from a long list to members of a range of national and ethnic groups including their own. This research confirmed that some stereotypes were indeed widely shared and that some were very disparaging. However, against the view that stereotypes are inherently fixed and disparaging, later studies showed that stereotype content changed to reflect changes in the nature of intergroup relations. During the Second World War, for example, Americans' stereotypes of Germans and Japanese became much more negative, but these improved once the conflict was over. Later studies using the same methodology also showed that stereotypes of one group changed substantially depending on which other groups it was compared with.

In the aftermath of the Second World War a large amount of energy was focused on the question of whether people with particular personalities were more likely to exhibit 'black and white' thinking of the type associated with stereotypes. Again, though, the evidence did not support this view. So, although initially popular, research provided little support for the view that people only endorse stereotypes if they are authoritarians, or if frustration has rendered them aggressive. As a result, Allport (1954) followed Lippmann in observing that members of all groups hold and use stereotypes. Moreover, he argued that stereotyping was a normal cognitive activity that was essential for a predictable and manageable life. These insights were distilled into the view that stereotypes are a form of 'necessary evil' – the outcome of simplifying acts of categorization that are required by the cognitive impossibility of treating everyone as an individual but which also introduce distortion and bias as a result.

This latter view was given further impetus by the empirical work of Tajfel (1969), which provided evidence that cues which encouraged people to perceive objects as members of distinct categories (e.g. the labels 'A' and 'B' attached to long and short lines) led to the accentuation of intercategory difference and intraclass similarity. This fuelled a third wave of stereotyping research in which researchers cast the stereotyper as a 'cognitive miser' (Fiske and Taylor 1984) and sought to identify those normal cognitive processes that make stereotypes efficient but errorful. Work in this tradition suggested that stereotypes arise automatically from a range of energy-saving information-processing biases that beset every stage of the stereotyping process – from encoding and storage to retrieval and communication. Researchers claimed that such biases lead people to attend to novel and distinctive information, as well as to that which is consistent with their expectations and prior theories, and to emphasize the homogeneity of out-groups and the heterogeneity of in-groups. The most recent cognitive work has also sought to explore the differences between the aspects of these processes that are automatic and those that are under the perceiver's conscious control.

Although the cognitive approach to stereotypes and stereotyping remains highly influential, it has also been critiqued by researchers who argue that such research neglects the role that social context plays in shaping and structuring cognition (after Tajfel 1981). In particular, social identity and self-categorization theorists have argued that stereotypes are primarily political tools that allow groups to represent and influence the reality of intergroup relations as perceived from their particular social vantage point (Oakes et al. 1994). According to this view, stereotypes exist not to save effort but to make social and political behaviour possible. Hence, where it is observed, the error of stereotypes has its basis not in psychological deficiency but in the political positions and aspirations of the groups that hold them. Moving away from the view that stereotypes are the product of more-or-less automatic intrapsychic processes, this research has led to renewed interest in group processes (e.g. of communication and social influence) that contribute to stereotype consensus and help bring about stereotype change (Haslam et al. 2002).

S. ALEXANDER HASLAM
UNIVERSITY OF EXETER

References

Allport, G.W. (1954) *The Nature of Prejudice*, Cambridge, MA.

Fiske, S.T. and Taylor, S.E. (1984) *Social Cognition*, Reading, MA.

Haslam, S.A., Turner, J.C., Oakes, P.J., Reynolds, K.J. and Doosje, B. (2002) 'From personal pictures in the head to collective tools in the world: How shared stereotypes allow groups to represent and change social reality', in C. McGarty, V.Y. Yzerbyt and R. Spears (eds) *Stereotypes as Explanations: The Formation of Meaningful Beliefs about Social Groups*, Cambridge, UK, pp. 157–85.

Katz, D. and Braly, K. (1933) 'Racial stereotypes of one hundred college students', *Journal of Abnormal and Social Psychology* 28: 280–90.

Lippmann, W. (1922) *Public Opinion*, New York.

Oakes, P.J., Haslam, S.A. and Turner, J.C. (1994) *Stereotyping and Social Reality*, Oxford.

Tajfel, H. (1969) 'Cognitive aspects of prejudice', *Journal of Social Issues* 25: 79–97.

—— (1981) 'Social stereotypes and social groups', in J.C. Turner and H. Giles (eds) *Intergroup Behaviour*, Oxford, pp. 144–67.

Further reading

Adorno, T.W., Frenkel-Brunswik, E., Levinson, D.J. and Sanford, R.N. (1950) *The Authoritarian Personality*, New York.

SEE ALSO: labelling theory; prejudice; racism; stigma

STIGMA

The term 'stigma' derives from the Greek and Latin words for brand or mark. Indeed in Latin *stigmatae* was the name given to branded slaves – individuals who bore an outward sign of their low status. The term was introduced into the social sciences by the sociologist Erving Goffman (1963) who used it to connote the broader meaning of personal characteristics that set a person apart from others and which mark him or her out as in some sense inferior, as having what Goffman referred to as a 'spoiled identity'. Significantly too, in contemporary usage stigma more commonly refers to the *consequence* of those characteristics than to the characteristics themselves. For example, the stigma of belonging to a particular group typically refers to the feelings (e.g. of shame or embarrassment) that this engenders rather than to the group membership itself. Moreover, these consequences derive from the relationship between the person who has particular characteristics and other people who perceive and pass judgement on them. Thus greater stigma is associated with particular characteristics to the extent that relevant others (i.e. those who define and embody 'normal' identity) perceive those characteristics to be undesirable.

In his discussion of stigma, Goffman made a number of key distinctions that have served as a focal point for subsequent research. Most famously, he differentiated between (1) 'abominations of the body' (e.g. physical handicaps and disfigurement), (2) 'blemishes of individual character' (e.g. drug abuse, delinquency, homosexuality) and (3) 'tribal stigma' (e.g. associated with membership of a given religious, national or ethnic group). As it has developed, stigma research has related to key themes in sociology and social psychology concerning the nature of deviance and abnormality, the consequences of labelling, and the identity functions of stereotypes and discrimination (e.g. Crocker and Major 1989; Schmitt and Branscombe 2002). Several further distinctions in the bases of stigma have been made that bear upon these issues. In particular, researchers have distinguished between forms of stigma in terms of their visibility, their stability, their controllability and their centrality to identity (Jones *et al.* 1984).

Variations in these dimensions are found to impact both on the behaviour of the stigmatized individual and on the reactions of others towards them. For example, if stigma is associated with characteristics that are invisible and controllable (e.g. displaying hidden tattoos) this means that the individual who has those characteristics can make a political and strategic decision about whether or not to reveal them and this will be structured, amongst other things, by their social identification with relevant groups and the social identity and status of those who are monitoring their behaviour (Jetten *et al.* 2001). And if those individuals do reveal their stigmatizing characteristics, this in turn is likely to affect the attributions that others make about them. For example, these may be more hostile and internal (i.e. to the person rather than to the situation) if the stigma is perceived to be controllable rather than uncontrollable.

One of the key debates that has been stimulated by research of this form concerns the consequences of stigma for the stigmatized individual. Traditionally, researchers from symbolic interactionist and labelling perspectives have argued that these consequences are negative. This is based on evidence that those who are stigmatized tend to have lower self-esteem, lower perceived self-efficacy and poorer social and economic outcomes than those who are not. Although they may receive sympathy and charity, under certain conditions they can also be targets of hatred and abuse. In general, then, attitudes to the stigmatized are found to range from ambivalence and indifference to overt hostility.

However, the assumption that stigma has negative implications for the self has recently been challenged by Crocker and Major (1989). They argue that perceiving oneself to be a victim of others' prejudice has a self-protective function in denying personal responsibility for one's condition and feelings. Paradoxically, they suggest, this may lead those who are stigmatized to have higher self-esteem than those who are not. However, in response to this analysis, Schmitt and Branscombe (2002) have found that the positive consequences of perceiving oneself to be stigmatized tend to be confined to members of privileged high-status groups (e.g. men, white Americans) whose experience of stigma tends to be more fleeting, more controllable and more trivial than that of members of low-status groups (e.g. women, black Americans). They argue that for those whose stigma is more enduring and less escapable, stigma has very negative consequences.

Nonetheless, Schmitt et al.'s (2003) research provides support for Tajfel's (1978) hypothesis that under certain conditions stigma, or treatment based on a devalued group membership (e.g. as a foreigner studying in the USA), can provide the basis for the formation of a new more positive minority identity (e.g. as an international student). In line with Tajfel and Turner's (1979) social identity theory, Schmitt and Branscombe's (2002) rejection–identification model thus suggests that recognition of one's stigma, and identification with other members of a stigmatized group, can be one important way in which individuals attempt to cope with the pain of stigma and to bring about social change that will materially improve their conditions. Elaboration upon these ideas and exploration of links with issues of clinical well-being, stress and group mobilization is currently proving a fertile ground for research in this area.

S. ALEXANDER HASLAM
UNIVERSITY OF EXETER

References

Crocker, J. and Major, B. (1989) 'Social stigma and self-esteem: The self-protective properties of stigma', *Psychological Review* 96: 608–30.

Goffman, E. (1963) *Stigma: Notes on the Management of Spoiled Identity*, Englewood Cliffs, NJ.

Jetten, J., Branscombe, N., Schmitt, M.T. and Spears, R. (2001) 'Rebels with a cause: Group identification as a response to perceived discrimination from the mainstream', *Personality and Social Psychology Bulletin* 27: 1,204–13.

Jones, E.E., Farina, A., Hastorf, A., Marcus, H., Miller, D. and Scott, R.A. (1984) *Social Stigma: The Psychology of Marked Relationships*, New York.

Schmitt, M.T. and Branscombe, N.R. (2002) 'The meaning and consequences of perceived discrimination in disadvantaged and privileged social groups', *European Review of Social Psychology* 12: 167–99.

Schmitt, M.T., Spears, R. and Branscombe, N.R. (2003) 'Constructing a minority group identity out of shared rejection: The case of international students', *European Journal of Social Psychology* 33: 1–12.

Tajfel, H. (1978) *The Social Psychology of Minorities*, London.

Tajfel, H. and Turner, J.C. (1979) 'An integrative theory of intergroup conflict', in W.G. Austin and S. Worchel (eds) *The Social Psychology of Intergroup Relations*, Monterey, CA, pp. 33–47.

SEE ALSO: deviance; disability; labelling theory; prejudice; stereotypes

STRATEGIC MANAGEMENT

The subject of strategic management is the positioning of the firm in its broadest sense – its relationship with its customers, suppliers and competitors. Strategic management is therefore a discipline very different from those concerned with the functional activities of the firm – accounting, marketing, scheduling and control of operations, personnel and human relations – although all of these will be influenced by the firm's strategy.

Writers on strategic management commonly distinguish three phases of the process. The first is an appreciation of the internal and external environment within which the firm operates. The second is the choice of a strategy to match that environment, and the third is the implementation of the preferred strategy within the firm. This distinction is somewhat artificial; the selection of strategy must be determined by the business environment within which the company operates, and it is impossible to make sensible choices of strategy in the absence of an analysis of the means by which alternative strategies are to be implemented.

Strategic management was first recognized as a subject in the early 1960s. It originated in integrative management courses taught at the Harvard Business School, and in works such as Ansoff (1965) and Andrews (1980). Strategic management was then equated with corporate planning – the preparation of quantitative forecasts or targets for 5 or more years ahead. Scepticism about the practical value of such exercises in the face of changing economic conditions and competitive behaviour has steadily diminished the influence of such strategic plans, and the resources that firms devote to them.

In the early 1970s, new thinking in strategic management came from consulting companies such as McKinsey and the Boston Consulting Group that developed tools of market and competitor analysis. Conventional scholarship emphasizes the evolutionary nature of scientific knowledge, while the commercial orientation of strategic management has established a subject in which the dependence of new thinking on old is often concealed, and slight differences in approach are much exaggerated. This manner of evolution has seriously inhibited the establishment of an agreed structure or body of knowledge in strategic management, and calls into question the claims of the subject to be regarded as an academic discipline.

Porter (1980) is the most comprehensive exposition of strategy as competitor analysis. But since the early 1980s there have been reactions against analytic styles of strategic management. Softer approaches are in vogue, which attach greater importance to human factors in understanding the position of the firm. There is wide agreement that implementation is the most neglected of the three components of strategy. Yet the difficulties of implementing strategy are perhaps more appropriately seen as criticisms of the process of strategy formulation itself.

The most important developments on strategic management concern resource-based theories of strategy. The strategy of the firm is, in this view, dependent on the match between the unique capabilities of the firm and the external environment within which it operates. While reasserting the prescriptive focus of strategic management, this approach emphasizes the firm-specific nature of valid prescription and, by focusing on the relationships between individuals and markets, links the economic and the sociological dimensions of strategy.

JOHN KAY
LONDON SCHOOL OF ECONOMICS
AND POLITICAL SCIENCE

References

Andrews, K.R. (1980) *The Concept of Corporate Strategy*, rev. edn, Homewood, IL.

Ansoff, H.I. (1965) 'The firm of the future', *Harvard Busines Review* 43(5).

Porter, M.E. (1980) *Competitive Strategy: Techniques for Analyzing Industries and Competitors*, New York.

Further reading

Kay, J.A. (1993) *Foundations of Corporate Success*, Oxford.

Quinn, J.B., Mintzberg, H. and James, R.M. (1998) *The Strategy Process*, Englewood Cliffs, NJ.

SEE ALSO: human resource management; leadership

STRATIFICATION

Social stratification refers to the division of people into layers or strata that may be thought of as being vertically arranged, in the same way that layers of the earth are arranged above or below other layers Although the geological metaphor that sociologists use draws attention to a striking feature of many, if not most, societies, there are limits beyond which its use becomes misleading. The arrangement of persons in a society is enormously more complex than the arrangement of the layers of the earth, and social strata are not visible to the naked eye in the way that geological strata are.

When we talk of social stratification we draw attention to the unequal positions occupied by individuals in society. Sometimes the term is used very broadly to refer to every kind of inequality, although it may be useful to restrict it to inequalities between groups or categories of persons with a definite or at least a recognizable identity. Thus we speak of stratification between manual and non-manual workers or between blacks and whites, but not usually of stratification between the members of a family. The implication of this is that one may reasonably describe such simple societies as the Andaman Islanders or the !Kung

Bushmen as being unstratified although there certainly are inequalities in these societies.

There is disagreement as to whether stratification is a universal feature of all human societies (Bendix and Lipset 1967). While some of this disagreement may be traced to divergent uses of the same terms, there are also genuine differences in point of view. The so-called functional theory of stratification maintains that stratification in the broad sense not only is universally present but also performs a definite social function. Others maintain that just as there have been societies in the past where stratification in the strict sense was absent or rudimentary, so also there can be societies in the future where it will be absent or inconsequential. It is not easy to see how societies that are at present stratified will cease to be stratified in the future or to prove that stratification has a determinate social function because it is present everywhere, or nearly everywhere.

The geological metaphor of stratification tends to obscure the fact that in a given society the same individuals may be differently ranked depending upon the criteria selected. Every society uses more than one criterion of ranking, and different societies do not give prominence to the same criteria. It requires much skill and judgement to identify the significant criteria in each case and to determine their degree of consistency. While some scholars stress the consistency between the different dimensions of stratification or even the determining role of one or another among them, others argue that, though related, these dimensions are mutually irreducible (Béteille 1977).

The economic aspect or dimension of stratification is important in all societies and manifestly so in modern societies. But we see how complex the problem is as soon as we try to specify the nature of the economic dimension, for it may refer to either wealth or income, or occupation that, although closely related, are not one and the same. Wealth and income are relatively easy to measure, but, since their distribution is continuous, there is no easy way to draw lines between people on the basis of how much of the one or the other they have. Moreover, what matters is not simply how much wealth or income people have but also how it is acquired and how it is used.

In past societies, wealth in some forms, such as land, was valued more than wealth in other forms, such as money, and inherited wealth more than wealth acquired by trade or commerce. Capitalism reduces the significance of such distinctions but does not eliminate them altogether. And while the accumulation and transmission of wealth might be severely restricted in socialist societies, disparities of income are important there as well.

All industrial societies, whether of the capitalist or the socialist type, show a certain family resemblance in their occupational structure. The occupational role acquires far greater salience in these societies than in all other societies known to history. As the separation of the occupational from the domestic domain becomes more complete, more and more people come to have definite occupations, and their social identity comes increasingly to be defined in terms of these. Much of an adult's life is spent in the pursuit of an occupation in a factory or an office, and the person's early life is largely a preparation for it. The occupational structure itself becomes more differentiated and more complex.

While all occupations may in some sense be equally useful, they are not all equally esteemed by members of society. The commonsensical view of this, at least in capitalist societies, is that occupations are differentially esteemed because they are unequally paid, but this leaves unexplained why some occupations are better paid than others. The ranking of occupations is in fact a very complex phenomenon, being governed partly by considerations of scarcity and partly by the values distinctive to the society concerned (Bendix and Lipset 1967; Goldthorpe and Hope 1974). In all modern societies, occupational ranking is complicated by the variability of values among sections of the same society and by the rapid replacement of old occupations by new ones.

While there obviously is some correspondence between the esteem enjoyed by an occupation and the income it provides, this correspondence is not perfect (Cole 1955). This is partly due to the changes continuously taking place in the modern world among the various occupations in regard to both income and esteem. But there may be other, more fundamental, reasons behind the lack of perfect correspondence. Disparities of income between manual and non-manual occupations have been greatly reduced in most industrial societies, but manual occupations continue to be less esteemed than non-manual ones, sometimes even when they are better paid. This is true not only of capitalist but also of socialist societies, despite the bias for the manual worker in socialist ideology.

Occupation is closely linked with education in all industrial societies but probably more so in socialist than in capitalist ones (Cole 1955; Wesolowski 1979). Obviously, education is valued because it provides access to well-paid occupations but it is valued for other reasons as well. Education gives people access to knowledge and to the inner meaning of life both within and outside their own occupational sphere; all of this is valued for its own sake and not merely for the financial returns it provides.

Education, occupation and income enter as important ingredients in the styles of life adopted by men and women. Social stratification manifests itself typically through differences in styles of life among members of the same society (Bottomore 1965; Heller 1969). Such differences relate to both the material and the non-material sides of life, and may manifest themselves in gross or subtle ways. Habitation, dress and food all indicate differences in styles of life and, as is well known, language divides people no less than it unites them. Groups differentiated by their styles of life, particularly when they are ranked among themselves, are generally referred to as status groups.

Popular usage does not distinguish systematically between classes and status groups, but it is useful to do so. According to a famous distinction, a class is defined by its position in the system of production, whereas what characterizes a status group is its pattern of consumption (Weber 1978 [1922]). A class is conceived of as being a somewhat larger aggregate than a status group, and classes acquire their identity in opposition to each other in the political arena. Whereas the relations between classes are typically relations of conflict, the relations between status groups are relations of emulation. Emulation by inferiors of the styles of life of their superiors provides stability to the prevailing system of stratification.

Income, occupation and education are not the only things that count in regard to status or style of life, even in modern societies. Race and ethnicity have independent significance in regard to both. Although differences of race are biological in origin, how much they count in stratification depends on the value assigned to these differences in the society in question. The very existence of sharp differences of race as in South Africa and, to some extent, the USA indicates the restriction by law or custom of intermarriage between members of different races. Such restriction is usually, if not invariably, associated with feelings of superiority and inferiority between the races concerned.

Endogamy, as either a rule or a tendency, is perhaps the most effective mechanism for maintaining the boundaries between social strata (Ghurye 1969; Weber 1958 [1920]). On the whole it is more strictly practised between groups based on race, caste and ethnicity than between those that are defined solely in terms of income, occupation and education. Where boundaries are strictly maintained between racial or ethnic groups through endogamy, through residential segregation and in other ways, access to higher education and employment tends to be more difficult for members of some than of other groups. In such cases equality of opportunity can do very little to prevent the reproduction of the existing system of stratification.

Stratification by race was seen in its clearest and most extreme form in South Africa. There the segregation of races was not only a widespread social practice, but, until recently, was also accepted as a basic social principle. Segregation or apartheid – literally meaning 'apartness' – was the official norm of South African society, and it sought to regulate every sphere of social life from marriage to politics. The roots of apartheid, as of a great deal of stratification by race, go back to the experience of colonial rule. In South Africa the unequal relationship between a settler and an indigenous population was imposed by the former on the latter and perpetuated until 1994 through the principle and practice of segregation.

Power plays a part in the maintenance and reproduction of social stratification everywhere (Béteille 1977; Dahrendorf 1968). First, there is the use of the apparatus of state for enforcing the privileges and disabilities of superior and inferior strata, as in pre-1994 South Africa. But violence may also be used for the same end outside the framework of the state as in the case of lynching, whether of blacks by whites in the USA or of untouchables by caste Hindus in India. Whereas power is important everywhere in upholding the existing order, the extent to which force is openly used to the advantage of superior against inferior strata varies. The naked use of force becomes common where agreement breaks down in a society about the ranks to be occupied by its different members.

Race is often compared with caste, since both forms of stratification are marked by great rigidity. Indeed, the term caste has become a synonym for rigid social stratification. The caste system was found in its most characteristic form in traditional India among the Hindus, although divisions of a broadly similar kind were found also among other religious groups in India as well as in other South Asian countries. Until recently the divisions of caste were very elaborate among the Hindus, and they were kept in place by a variety of rules and restrictions. Each caste or subcaste had in the course of time developed its own style of life through which it maintained its social identity, and Max Weber thought that castes were best characterized as status groups.

Many changes are taking place in the caste system. The division into castes in contemporary India – like the division into races in the USA – coexists with many other divisions and inequalities whose roots lie elsewhere. An important aspect of the traditional order of Indian society was that inequalities between people not only existed in fact but also were accepted as a part of the natural scheme of things. To a large extent this was true also of medieval Europe where the hierarchical conception of society was supported by both law and religion. Things have changed considerably, and in most societies inequality or stratification exists within a legal and moral environment in which equality is the dominant value. This means that stratification in most contemporary societies is far more amorphous and fluid than the division of past societies into orders or estates or castes whose hierarchy was recognized and acknowledged by most, if not all, members of society.

ANDRÉ BÉTEILLE
UNIVERSITY OF DELHI

References

Bendix, R. and Lipset, S.M. (eds) (1967) *Class, Status and Power: Social Stratification in Comparative Perspective*, London.
Béteille, A. (1977) *Inequality among Men*, Oxford.
Bottomore, T.B. (1965) *Classes in Modern Society*, London.
Cole, G.D.H. (1955) *Studies in Class Structure*, London.
Dahrendorf, R. (1968) 'On the origin of inequality among men', in *Essays in the Theory of Society*, London.
Ghurye, G.S. (1969) *Class, Caste and Occupation*, Bombay.
Goldthorpe, J.H. and Hope, K. (1974) *The Social Grading of Occupations: A New Approach and Scale*, Oxford.
Heller, C.S. (ed.) (1969) *Structured Social Inequality: A Reader in Comparative Social Stratification*, London.
Weber, M. (1958 [1920]) *The Religion of India*, New York.
—— (1978 [1922]) *Economy and Society*, 2 vols, Berkeley, CA.
Wesolowski, W. (1979) *Classes, Strata and Power*, London.

Further reading

Jencks, C. *et al.* (1972) *Inequality*, New York.
Liecht, K.T. (ed.) (1998) *Research in Social Stratification and Mobility*, Stanford, CA.
Marshall, T.H. (1977) *Class, Citizenship and Development*, Chicago.

SEE ALSO: caste; class, social; equality; Marx's theory of history and society

STRUCTURAL LINGUISTICS

Structural linguistics, the study of languages through observation and description of their basic units and the relationships of same, may be said to have begun with the great Sanskrit grammar of Panini (*c*.300 BCE). This work was not known in the West until the end of the eighteenth century. The foundations of modern structural linguistics were laid in the later nineteenth century by Jan Baudouin de Courtenay, a Pole teaching in the Russian University of Kazan, and Ferdinand de Saussure, a Swiss. Baudouin, working closely with his Polish graduate student (and successor in the Kazan chair), Mikolaj Kruszewski, approached the notion of a system of basic units of sound ('phonology') and form ('morphology'), which derive their informative power from the fact of their opposition (or contrast) to each other. It was at Kazan that the terms *phoneme* and *morpheme* were first used in approximately their present sense. Saussure was working along the same lines, and he was acquainted with the ideas being developed at Kazan through German translations of two works by Kruszewski. Kruszewski died early and Saussure's lectures were published only after his death by devoted students. Since Baudouin de Courtenay, because of his concern for social and psychological factors in language use, came to define phonological and morphemic units as, at least in part, mental constructs, he lost touch with the main body of structuralists, who were led by Edward Sapir and Leonard Bloomfield in the USA and by N.S. Trubetzkoy, Roman Jakobson and L.V. Shcherba in Europe. Shcherba remained in the Soviet Union, while Trubetzkoy (from Vienna) and Jakobson helped to found the Prague Circle, where structural linguistics was stretched to include 'structural' studies of literature. An offshoot of the Prague Group was the Copenhagen Circle, of which the leading figures were Louis Hjelmslev and Hans Uldall.

A major difference between the formulations of the Prague School (as exemplified in the work of Jakobson) and the New World structuralists is the definition of the basic units of phonology (phonemes) as *bundles of distinctive features* by the former, and as *classes of sounds and phones* by the latter (exemplified particularly in the work of Bernard Bloch, Bloomfield's successor at Yale). An interesting development of the Prague doctrines was offered by the Frenchman André Martinet who sought, in the phonological structure of a language, the 'pressures' or impulses for future phonological development. In the Bloomfield–Sapir tradition, universals of phonological structure have been sought notably by C.F. Hockett, and of morphosyntax by J.H. Greenberg, while efforts at writing a distribution-based grammar (with minimal recourse to meaning) were made by Zellig Harris.

Much of the linguistic work accomplished in the twentieth century was a result of the efforts of Kenneth Pike, a student of Sapir's, who trained hundreds of missionary linguists at the Summer Institute of Linguistics. Thus, as a prerequisite to Bible translation, structural linguistic analysis provided excellent accounts of many languages from the preliterate world.

D.L. OLMSTED
UNIVERSITY OF CALIFORNIA, DAVIS

Further reading

Hymes, D. and Fought, J. (1981) *American Structuralism*, The Hague.

Rieger, J., Szymcak, M. and Urbanczyk, S. (eds) (1989) *Jan Niecisław Badouin de Courtenay, a Lingwistika Swiatowa* (Conference Proceedings), Warsaw.

Stankiewicz, E. (ed. and trans.) (1972) *A Baudouin de Courtenay Anthology: The Beginnings of Structural Linguistics*, Bloomington, IN.

SEE ALSO: Saussure

STRUCTURALISM

The founding figure of structuralism in the social and human sciences is normally considered to be the French anthropologist Claude Lévi-Strauss. The main theoretical inspiration for Lévi-Strauss's structuralism was structural linguistics, which itself originated in the pioneering work of the Swiss linguist Ferdinand de Saussure earlier in the century. In his *Course in General Linguistics* (1983 [1916]), Saussure distinguished between two levels of language, *langue* and *parole*. *Parole* refers to the external and contingent aspect of language production in activities such as speech and writing, while *langue* (the principal object of linguistic science) is the set of patterns or rules that precedes and makes possible the realization of language in *parole*. For Saussure *langue* is a *system*, in which it is the relations between elements and not the elements themselves that are responsible for meaning. On the semantic level, an individual word (e.g. 'car') only makes sense in terms of its *difference* from other, related concepts (e.g. 'lorry', 'train', 'bicycle', etc.). On the phonetic level, difference of meaning is generated by the substitution of minimally distinct units of sound: 'bar', 'far', 'Tsar', etc. From this differential explanation of signification follows the central postulate of Saussure's linguistic theory, the arbitrariness of the sign. Word and concept (or 'signifier' and 'signified') have no essential connection other than their habitual association within the system of *langue*. An important aspect of Saussure's distinction between *langue* and *parole* is that it also implies a distinction between the individual and the collective. Saussure emphasizes that *langue* is by nature a social construct, whereas *parole*, the contingent execution of *langue*, is individual and variable. Finally, Saussure argues that in order to achieve a properly scientific analysis of *langue*, methodologically it is necessary to bracket out the *diachronic* (historical) dimension of a language and concentrate on its *synchronic* dimension.

Saussure is generally recognized as the father of modern linguistics. Two of his continuators in the field of phonology, the Russian linguists Trubetzkoy and Jakobson, are Lévi-Strauss's main references in linguistics, apart from Saussure himself. It was a meeting with Roman Jakobson in 1942 that first inspired Lévi-Strauss to apply the methods of structural linguistics to social phenomena. In his first major book, *The Elementary Structures of Kinship* (1969 [1949]), Lévi-Strauss started from the idea that in the same way that the phonologist has reduced the diversity of sounds in natural languages to a limited set of basic sonic distinctions, so the anthropologist should be able to reduce the many different permutations of kinship relations observed in human society to a small group of elementary and invariant structures, from which the diversity of observable kinship structures might be derived. In the 1950s he went on to extend this application of the linguistic model to the field of collective representations. Already in the *Course in General Linguistics*, Saussure had indicated that linguistics dealt with only one of a number of sign systems used in human society, and for this reason suggested that the study of language should ultimately be part of a more general science of signs, *semiology*. In his turn, Lévi-Strauss argued for the *symbolic* nature of social customs and institutions. The collective constructs that mediate relationships between the different members of a community are symbolic to the extent that their construction is a matter of arbitrary convention and that they form discrete systems with their own 'grammar' or rules of operation. Collective representations such as totemism or myth could therefore be analysed in the same way as a language. In *Totemism* (1964 [1962]) and *The Savage Mind* (1966 [1962]), Lévi-Strauss argued that whereas traditional interpretations of totemism focused on the mystical link between individual and totem, the structuralist interpretation looked at totemism as a kind of 'code' based on a structural homology between natural species and social groups – differences existing in nature were mapped onto differences in society. In 'The structural study of myth' (1955), he proposed that rather than looking at a particular myth in terms of isolated elements or themes, structural analysis should look at the ensemble of its variants as a system. Just as the linguist distinguished the minimal units of language (phonemes, morphemes, etc.), so structural analysis isolated the elementary constituents of a myth (mythemes). As a system, the signification of the myth came not from any individual element or mytheme, but from the differential relations between these elements,

more precisely their mode of combination or binary opposition. As in language, this combination of elements was not arbitrary, and followed specific rules of operation. The aim of structural analysis was therefore to determine the rules of combination that would constitute the underlying *structure* of the myth. Moreover, as Lévi-Strauss argued in *Mythologiques* (1970–81 [1964–71]), the myth itself was not an isolated system. Structurally, each myth was a more or less distant transform of another myth, so that the totality of myths generated by the human mind could be said to represent a closed system.

An important feature of Lévi-Strauss's definition of structure is that, like Saussure's *langue*, it is independent of the conscious intentions and interpretations of the individual member of the social group. This does not mean that structure is unconscious in the Freudian sense, i.e. is the subject of censorship or repression; rather, it is unconscious in the same way that the implicit rules of a language are not conscious to the average speaker of the language. As Lévi-Strauss has asserted, it is not individuals that speak through myths but myths that speak through individuals. A second important feature of Lévi-Strauss's structuralism is that, again like Saussure's linguistics, it aims to be a synchronic rather than a diachronic study of systems. As with Saussure, this choice of perspective is a methodological rather than an ideological one, but inevitably it has drawn criticism from a number of quarters.

Lévi-Strauss's version of structuralism has been immensely influential in the social sciences, and in a wide spectrum of humanities disciplines. This influence was first most apparent in France, where from the mid-1950s onwards Lévi-Strauss's ideas were being adopted in a number of different disciplines. Thus, in psychoanalysis, Jacques Lacan's proposed return to Freud was combined with a theory of the unconscious based on Saussurian linguistics. In history Fernand Braudel described his analysis of long-term social and economic trends, *la longue durée*, as 'structural history'. For the philosopher Michel Foucault, structuralism announced the dissolution of 'man', a comparatively recent construct of Western philosophy and science. In the field of literary studies Roland Barthes proposed a semiology of contemporary social and cultural forms, applying structural analysis to items of popular culture. Together, this constellation of thinkers was seen in the 1960s and 1970s to constitute the structuralist movement, with Lévi-Strauss as their leading figure.

The differences between thinkers categorized as 'structuralist' were often very great, and they themselves often resisted assimilation with the movement. Lévi-Strauss was generally sceptical about what he viewed as unwarranted extensions of structural analysis to other fields. Despite this, structuralism played an important role in crystallizing the climate of reaction against the kind of philosophical humanism that had dominated intellectual debate in France since the war. Jean-Paul Sartre's version of existentialism was primarily concerned with moral questions, questions of individual choice, responsibility and commitment, and also with the individual's engagement with the historical process. Structuralism, on the other hand, was concerned with systems in which the role of individual agency was both contingent and relative. Taking its inspiration from the natural sciences, the ambition of structuralism was to arrive at structures so general as to transcend any specificities of time, place or subjective instantiation. This scientific ambition was evident in Lévi-Strauss's referencing of cybernetics, information theory and molecular biology, as well as linguistics, and as such it represented a break with traditional humanistic thought. Under the new division of intellectual labour announced by structuralism, the human sciences, as they were called, no longer needed the mediating discourse of philosophy to explain their principles and their ends, and could think for themselves.

Marxist and humanist thinkers like Sartre attacked what they perceived as the anti-humanism and anti-historicism of structuralism, but arguably the most effective critique came from a new generation of philosophers who, like Jacques Derrida, had assimilated the lessons of structuralism but were also prepared to think beyond it. While Derrida recognized the importance of the paradigm shift in which structuralism was implicated, he questioned structuralism's claim to have broken with the history of metaphysics. The discourse of structuralism and the human sciences was thoroughly determined by the discourse of Western philosophy, and to fail to recognize this determination was to fall prey to the unexamined presuppositions of that discourse.

Standard critical accounts of structuralism have often interpreted Derrida's 'deconstruction' of Lévi-Strauss as marking the beginning of a new phase of critical enquiry, that of poststructuralism. However, despite the importance of Derrida's critique of Lévi-Strauss, it should be remembered that in France the influence of structuralism was to persist for at least another decade, and that the term 'poststructuralism' was itself not a French but a US invention. Whatever the perceived limitations of structuralism – its reductionism, its scientism, its lack of critical reflexivity – nevertheless it remains an important and indispensable staging post in twentieth-century thought. In short, if terms such as difference and code, sign and signification, synchrony and diachrony have become part of the lingua franca of the humanities and social sciences, it is largely thanks to the original and essential mediation of Lévi-Strauss.

CHRISTOPHER JOHNSON
UNIVERSITY OF NOTTINGHAM

References

Derrida, J. (1978 [1967]) *Writing and Difference*, London.

Lévi-Strauss, C. (1969 [1949]) *The Elementary Structures of Kinship*, Boston.

—— (1955) 'The structural study of myth', *Journal of American Folklore* 68(270): 428–44.

—— (1964 [1962]) *Totemism*, London.

—— (1966 [1962]) *The Savage Mind*, Chicago.

—— (1970–81 [1964–71]) *Mythologiques. Introduction to a Science of Mythology*, 4 vols, London.

—— (1977 [1958]) *Structural Anthropology 1*, Harmondsworth.

Saussure, F. de (1983 [1916]) *Course in General Linguistics*, London.

Further reading

Dosse, F. (1997 [1991, 1992]) *History of Structuralism*, 2 vols, Minneapolis, MN.

Johnson, C. (2003) *Claude Lévi-Strauss: The Formative Years*, Cambridge.

Sturrock, J. (ed.) (1979) *Structuralism and Since. From Lévi-Strauss to Derrida*, Oxford.

—— (1993) *Structuralism*, London.

SEE ALSO: Lévi-Strauss; poststructuralism

STRUCTURE AND AGENCY

Specifying the relationship between 'agency' and 'structure' has proved problematic, and as yet there has been no statement of the relationship that has met with general satisfaction. It is somewhat misleading to suggest that there is a single issue here, for several different problems – all significant with respect to the fundamental nature of social thought – fall under this heading. The debate involves *at least* these persistent topics:

- Is individual action to be explained causally? If so, is it to be explained by the causal influence of social structures? What is the balance between freedom and constraint?
- Are there any such things as social structures? Is society a reality in its own right, something more than an aggregate of individuals? If so, what more is there to society than its individual members?
- Is society an objective or a subjective reality? Does it have existence outside of the consciousness of its members (unknown to them, except where they are availed of sociological theory)? Or does it exist in the minds of the individual members of society (constituted out of the consciousness and beliefs)? Should sociology be on the side of materialism or idealism?
- Who, if anyone, makes society? Is it the product of individual actions and intentions, or, on the contrary, are individuals themselves the creation of society? Is society the unintended product of individual actions? Can individuals mould their social reality at all, and if so, how far? (This is what questions about 'agency' are designed to elicit.)

The argument over these issues is still lively. Some of the more influential contemporary theorists, such as Giddens, Habermas and the critical realist school, have made resolute efforts to resolve the structure/agency problem, each in a different way.

The division within contemporary sociology can be traced back at least to those leading figures in classic sociology, Karl Marx, Emile Durkheim and Max Weber. It is the opposition between Marx and Durkheim, on the one hand, and Weber, on the other, that is often treated as the starting-point for the continuing debate. Although working with very different perspectives, Marx and Durkheim bequeathed the 'structure' lineage, while Weber, with his 'social action' approach, is the icon for 'agency'.

Marx and Durkheim stressed the value of regarding society as a reality in its own right, one that was not the conscious and intentional creation of its individual members, but that, instead, was dominant over and formative of that very consciousness and those intentions. Despite their theoretical differences, Marx and Durkheim each emphasized the value of regarding society as a 'totality', an independently existing, articulated complex whole (composed of units such as 'classes' or 'institutions' rather than individuals). Weber, however, eschewed all such conceptions and defined sociology as the study of individual actions directed towards others, those actions being conducted on the basis of the 'meanings' they had for the individuals performing them.

Two important moves were made in the 1930s and 1940s by the US sociological theorist Talcott Parsons, and the Austrian philosopher of science Karl Popper. In *The Structure of Social Action* (1937), Parsons attempted a synthesis of the ideas of Durkheim and Weber (and others) into a general theory of social action. For his part, Popper made a fierce assault on Marx (and others) in the name of individualism (especially in *The Open Society and Its Enemies*, 1943). To Popper, the idea of society as consisting of anything more than individuals was not only unsound, it was also politically dangerous. The idea of society as any kind of really existing whole was to be rejected entirely.

Parsons's efforts were to be the more consequential for the future shape of sociology, though not in the way he intended. After *The Structure of Social Action*, his thinking took a more functionalist direction. Functionalism is a strategy for analysing society as a whole, primarily in terms of the way that the conditions essential to the society's stability and persistence are met by its organizational arrangements. Questions soon arose as to whether Parsons had entirely abandoned his roots in 'action' theory and had come to place excessive emphasis upon the overall structure of the society, to the extent that individual autonomy was effectively eliminated. Whether or not this was true of Parsons, it was generally perceived to be true, and that was decisive for the reputation of his theory.

Within US sociology, hostilities began between what had temporarily become the dominant (functionalist) orthodoxy and two approaches that may reasonably be considered as falling within the 'social action' tradition, though their indebtedness to Weber himself was mainly indirect. These traditions, symbolic interaction-ism and ethnomethodology, assumed that the reality of society consists in the meaning that it has for individual members (although this capsule characterization perhaps captures more the per-ception than the reality of their respective views).

The political turbulence created in the USA by the Vietnam War and by the ballooning expan-sion of university sociology departments in the UK made Parsons a focal target of criticism in another respect: functionalism was now damned as a conservative doctrine. Symbolic interaction and ethnomethodology became increasingly in-fluential, and they were taken to constitute an effective critique of Parsons, but the alternative that these offered seemed worryingly devoid of any idea of 'structure'. Both took what some-times appeared to be a radically individualist view of society, even apparently denying that there was anything other than individuals. They were also seen as regarding 'society' as being constituted out of the meanings in the minds of those individuals: society had only subjective existence. This was a deep threat to the idea of sociology as a science (since it would have no real subject to study, if society exists only in the individual mind) and also to that of sociology as a political critique of society as a whole (Holm-wood and Stewart 1991; Jessop 1996).

In reaction to these concerns, and also partly because of the effects of the Vietnam dispute on European campuses and the associated rediscov-ery of a 'Western Marxist' tradition, the door began to open to European, and especially French, theory. Particularly influential in the 1970s was Louis Althusser, who offered an 'anti-humanist' interpretation of the late doc-trines of Marx, which he considered to represent the 'true' Marx. Marx's doctrines were not about individuals at all, they were about structures, especially those (such as Church, state, economy, etc.) that combine in an articulated way to make up 'social formations' (i.e. roughly 'society as a whole') (Althusser 1969 [1965]).

There could have been no more polarized opposition than that between the individualism/ agency of interactionism and ethnomethodology and a structuralism that excluded individuals altogether. This growing polarization led some writers to attempt a synthesis between the structure and the action traditions. It was argued that while sociologists should not deny that society is made up of individuals, this should

not be taken to imply that it is reducible to individuals. Among other influential theorists who struggled to reconcile this opposition:

- Peter Berger and Thomas Luckmann (1966) argued that society is both an objective and a subjective reality.
- Anthony Giddens (1979, 1984) dismissed the traditional idea of structure altogether. Society has no reality except as a product of the actions of individuals and the intended and unintended consequences of these actions, a process he termed 'structuration'. The society engendered by the process of structuration provides the conditions under which indivi-duals and their actions are formed.
- The critical realists (combining Roy Bhaskar's realist philosophy of science with the tradition of critical theory initiated by Marx) maintain that society and individual are both realities and that one cannot be reduced to the other (see Archer 1995).

Since the early 1970s, social theorists have been more apt to identify a 'structure' problem than an 'agency' one. Interactionism and ethno-methodology represent the usual starting-points for further discussion. What they have to say about individuals, action and interaction can be appropriated to constitute the 'agency' part of the proposed synthesis. At the same time, their alleged shortcomings are taken to indicate that a 'structure' component is required to complement them (Mouzelis 1991; Sibeon 1999).

This period of debate surely cannot be taken as a glorious moment in sociological reflection. The treatment of the individualist and interac-tionist strategies in social thought often attributes to them a simplicity that is more than naïve, and the supposed weaknesses of these approaches are greatly exaggerated. However, it is frequently concluded that the 'action' tradition, while fun-damentally flawed, must be allowed to make a substantial contribution to any general socio-logical theory. The problem is what to say about 'large-scale' social arrangements (for these are what are most commonly intended by 'struc-tures'). Disagreements persist on all these issues, especially with respect to:

- How to identify what it is that makes society 'something more' than a mere collection of individuals. (What makes it an 'objective reality'?)

- How to specify the way in which society or structure limits individual action (or imposes constraints) (see Healy 1998).
- How to understand the relationship between structure and the individual's point of view. Is structure something that can be recognized through a sociological theory, or can it be known by some members of the society by virtue of their special position (e.g. they are responsible for managing the society as a whole)? Is it recognizable to all individuals in a society?

There is, however, little sign of clarity or agreement about what the idea of 'structure' is specifically supposed to do, and how it is to play the role in sociological thought that some nevertheless consider to be indispensable (Mouzelis 1995).

WES SHARROCK
UNIVERSITY OF MANCHESTER

References

Althusser, L. (1969 [1965]) *For Marx*, London.
Archer, M. (1995) *Realist Social Theory*, Cambridge.
Berger, P.L. and Luckmann, T. (1966) *The Social Construction of Reality: A Treatise in the Sociology of Knowledge*, Garden City, NY.
Giddens, A. (1979) *Central Problems in Social Theory*, London.
—— (1984) *The Constitution of Society*, Cambridge.
Healy, K. (1998) 'Conceptualising constraint: Mouzelis, Archer and the concept of social structure', *Sociology* 32(3): 509–22.
Holmwood, J. and Stewart, A. (1991) *Explanation and Social Theory*, London.
Jessop, B. (1996) 'Interpretive sociology and the dialectic of structure and agency', *Theory, Culture and Society* 13(1): 119–28.
Mouzelis, N. (1991) *Back to Sociological Theory*, London.
—— (1995) *Sociological Theory: What Went Wrong?* London.
Parsons, T. (1937) *The Structure of Social Action*, New York.
Popper, K. (1943) *The Open Society and Its Enemies*, London.
Sibeon, R. (1999) 'Anti-reductionist sociology', *Sociology* 33(2): 317–34.

Further reading

Archer, M. (1982) 'Morphogenesis versus structuration: On combining structure and action', *British Journal of Sociology* 33: 455–83.

SEE ALSO: actor, social

SUICIDE

The concept of suicide is relatively straightforward, as it is defined by a legal judgment where there is clear evidence that the person intended to take his or her own life. Cases where clear evidence is lacking, though there is suspicion of suicide, are usually recorded as undetermined deaths but are often included in the suicide statistics. There is also non-fatal suicidal behaviour, which is more complicated because of the range of behaviours encompassed and the variety of terms used, for example 'attempted suicide' and 'deliberate self-harm'. Kreitman (1977) suggested the term 'parasuicide' to cover all deliberate but non-fatal acts of self-harm non-lethal suicidal behaviour, whatever the level of potential or actual harm. This term is useful because level of intent to die is difficult to judge from the outside, and following an episode of parasuicide people commonly report that they wanted to escape, but they may not be clear whether they meant to die or not (Williams 2001). Suicide and parasuicide are linked: between one-third and two-thirds of those who die by suicide will have had a previous episode of parasuicide. Because parasuicide is much more common than suicide, however, the vast majority of those who engage in parasuicide do not go on to kill themselves.

The suicide rate in England and Wales is about 10 per 100,000 of the population (Department of Health 2001). Rates do vary in different countries (World Health Organization (WHO) 2001). For example, rates in Northern European countries and most, but not all, former Soviet states are high (e.g. Ukraine 30/100,000) and rates in Mediterranean countries tend to be low (e.g. Greece 4/100,000). The rate in the USA is 11.3/100,000, though there are marked ethnic variations. For example, the rate for those who are white is 12.2/100,000 compared to a rate of 5.8/100,000 for black or African Americans (US Department of Health and Human Services 2000). Suicide is predominantly a male behaviour: the aggregate male/female ratio across countries is 3.5:1 (WHO 2001) and in the UK is 3:1 (Department of Health 2001). Suicide rates change over time. For example, there has been a substantial rise in suicide rates among young men in the last 20 years, the reason for which is not clear (Williams 2001). Although parasuicide is much more common than suicide, data tend to be less reliable than for suicide itself, due to the varying ways they are collected as well as different definitions of parasuicide being used in different places. A European, multicentre study found average rates of 186/100,000 (Kerkhof 2000), with rates varying from 69/100,000 in the Spanish centre to 462/100,000 in the French centre. Unlike suicide, parasuicide is more common in females: the female to male ratio in the European multicentre study was 1.5:1. Estimates have also been made from population surveys rather than hospital presentations. This has the benefit of potentially detecting non-presenting cases but the reliability of the data is unknown. Prevalence will depend on the exact question asked. A recent UK survey reported that 4.4 per cent of adults said that they had attempted suicide (Meltzer et al. 2002). The same survey found that 14.9 per cent of adults said that they had considered suicide at some point in their lives. Very similar figures have been reported in the USA where, in a recent population survey, 4.6 per cent reported having made a suicide attempt and 13.5 per cent reported having suicidal thoughts at some point in their lives (Kessler et al. 1999).

Durkheim's view was that suicide represented a breakdown in the connection between the individual and society (Williams 2001). Empirical research has focused mainly on delineating in what ways individuals who commit suicide are different from those who do not. These risk factors include: sociodemographic factors, such as gender (male), low social class and being unemployed; psychological factors, such as poor problem-solving skills and difficulty regulating emotions; and psychiatric factors, notably depression and alcohol and substance misuse. These factors are discussed in more detail by Maris et al. (1992) and Williams (2001). Depression is particularly strongly associated with suicidal behaviour. A recent study of suicides occurring in the UK found that over half of the people who committed suicide met criteria for depression (Department of Health 2001). Depression is possibly even more common in parasuicide. More recent research suggests that hopelessness about the future, particularly a lack of positive thoughts about the future rather than the presence of negative thoughts, is the key element of depression that is related to suicidality (MacLeod et al. 1997).

There are two main clinical issues in relation to suicidal behaviour: can it be predicted, and

can it be prevented? Studies have generally found that even with knowledge of all the associated risk factors described earlier it has not been possible to predict who within a large sample of high-risk individuals will commit suicide and who will not. The main problem usually lies in the fact that the vast majority (often 90 per cent and over) of those who are deemed to be at risk turn out not to have been at risk. Trying to reduce the number of these 'false positives' has the effect of increasing the chance of missing those who really are at risk. One problem is that suicidal behaviour is relatively unusual. Another is that predictive, statistical models cannot take account of the individuality and subjective nature of the experience. Predicting parasuicide has also been shown to be difficult, though one of the problems that besets suicide prediction – rarity – is less marked. The general failure of prediction has led to a reconceptualization of risk in terms of relative risk as opposed to absolute risk: someone may be at greatly elevated risk relative to the general population but their absolute level of risk might still be very low.

There is a wide range of psychological treatments aimed specifically at reducing suicidal behaviour. Treatments tend to focus on preventing repetition of parasuicide, partly because of the near impossibility of demonstrating treatment effectiveness in such a rare behaviour as completed suicide. On the whole, studies suggest that special treatments have limited success. Many studies find no difference in parasuicide rates between those given a specific treatment and those given standard treatment, though some treatments do show evidence of effectiveness (Hawton et al. 1998). There remains great room for improvement in the understanding, assessment and treatment of suicidal behaviour.

ANDREW K. MACLEOD
ROYAL HOLLOWAY COLLEGE,
UNIVERSITY OF LONDON

References

Department of Health, UK (2001) *Safety First: Five-Year Report of the National Confidential Inquiry into Suicide and Homicide by People with Mental Illness*, London.

Department of Health and Human Services, USA (2000) *Healthy People 2010*, Washington, DC.

Hawton, K. et al. (1998) 'Deliberate self-harm: Systematic review of efficacy of psychosocial and pharmacological treatments in preventing repetition', *British Medical Journal* 317: 441–7.

Kerkhof, A.J.F.M. (2000) 'Attempted suicide: Patterns and trends', in K. Hawton and K. van Heeringen (eds) *The International Handbook of Suicide and Attempted Suicide*, Chichester, pp. 49–64.

Kessler, R.C., Borges, G. and Waiters, E.E. (1999) 'Prevalence of and risk factors for lifetime suicide attempts in the national comorbidity survey', *Archives of General Psychiatry* 56: 617–26.

Kreitman, N. (1977) *Parasuicide*, London.

MacLeod, A.K., Pankhania, B., Lee, M. and Mitchell, D. (1997) 'Depression, hopelessness and future-directed thinking in parasuicide', *Psychological Medicine* 27: 973–7.

Maris, R.W., Berman, A.L., Maltsberger, J.T. and Yufit, R.I. (eds) (1992) *Assessment and Prediction of Suicide*, New York.

Meltzer, H., Lader, D., Corbin, T., Singleton, N., Jenkins, R. and Brugha, T. (2002) *Non-fatal Suicidal Behaviour among Adults Aged 16–74 in Great Britain*, London.

Williams, J.M.G. (2001) *Suicide and Attempted Suicide*, London.

World Health Organization (2001) *The World Health Report*, Geneva.

SUPPLY-SIDE ECONOMICS

The term 'supply-side economics' has both a general and a specific meaning. At its most general, the term relates to analyses that stress the importance of supply factors in determining output and economic growth in the long run. In its specific sense, the term is associated with US economic policy of the 1980s, sometimes referred to as Reaganomics, which held as one of its more extreme beliefs that tax cuts need not be matched by expenditure cuts because the tax cuts will cause enough growth to restore tax revenues. We consider these aspects in turn.

Modern supply-side economics is built on analysis of individual choice. It is fundamentally microeconomic in nature – a factor that might explain its neglect in macroeconomics until comparatively recently. Major factors in the supply-side determination of output include the effect of incentives on production, the efficiency of the labour market, the avoidance of over-regulation and the level of saving. These ideas lie at the heart of economics. Writers include Kuznets (1971) on economic development, Kendrick (1961) and Denison (1962) on growth and productivity, Mincer and Polachek (1974) on the sensitivity of women's labour supply to post-tax wages, Becker (1964) on human capital, and Schultz (1974) and Becker (1981) on the eco-

nomics of the family. Friedman's (1968) demonstration of the illusory nature of the long-run Phillips curve trade-off between unemployment and inflation also relies on supply-side (individual-choice) analysis: he showed how the curve depended on workers and firms being surprised by the current rate of inflation. Thus monetary policy could not effect a permanent reduction in unemployment, which required instead long-run policies such as improved education opportunities that would reduce the constraints faced by unemployed people. Buchanan and Tullock (1962) and the economists of the public choice school can also be said to have made a contribution to supply-side economics. Their conclusion that government intervention, rather than increasing national output and economic growth, can often have the reverse effect (governments as well as markets can fail), places an important limit on the role of government in promoting economic growth.

In macroeconomic analysis, the demand side has tended to overshadow the supply side, particularly since the Great Depression and the rise of Keynesianism. For much macroeconomic policy, aggregate demand has been viewed as the determining factor of output, with aggregate supply established in the main simply by labour supply and labour productivity trends. In this context, the long-run effect of aggregate demand management in reducing output via increased taxes and a bigger share of government in national income tends to be ignored. Higher marginal tax rates on personal and corporate incomes can impact adversely on national output and growth by lowering labour force participation, worker effort and capital accumulation. The clear failure of demand-side policies in the face of the 'stagflation' of the 1970s led academic economists such as Feldstein (1981) to reassert the need to address neglected supply-side issues.

Supply-side economics, in its more specific meaning, was developed by economists such as Arthur Laffer, Jude Wanniski, Michael Evans and Paul Craig Roberts, who worked more in the government policy arena rather than the academic arena. These economists are often referred to as 'supply-siders'. Accounts of their ideas can be found in Roberts (1984) and Bartlett and Roth (1984). The Economic Recovery Tax Act (1981) was strongly influenced by supply-sider arguments and included saving and investment incentives, reduced capital gains taxes and reductions in personal taxation. Advocacy of reduced personal taxation was associated with the supply-siders' most widely known contribution, the Laffer curve. The Laffer curve posits an inverted-U relation between the total tax revenue and marginal tax rates. With a zero tax rate, the tax yield will be zero. With a 100 per cent tax rate, the financial incentive to work will be absent and tax yield will again be zero. Between these two points tax yield will at first rise with increasing tax rates, but then fall as the incentive to work decreases. If the economy is operating beyond the maximum point of this curve, tax cuts will increase rather than decrease revenue. The supply-siders asserted that this was the case.

However, the shape of such a Laffer curve, and the position of countries upon it, is not clear empirically. Stuart (1981) examined the case of Sweden. He estimated that the maximum point of the Laffer curve occurred at a marginal tax rate of 70 per cent, whereas at the time of his study actual rates were slightly in excess of 80 per cent. He therefore concluded that Sweden was on the downward-sloping part of the curve. Lindsey (1987) analysed data for the USA and concluded that the maximum point of the curve lay at a 40 per cent marginal tax rate. Looking at the US tax rate reductions from 1982 to 1984, which involved a 23 per cent reduction of tax rates over 3 years, and a reduction of the top rate in the first year from 70 to 50 per cent, he concluded that up to a quarter of the revenue lost from these reductions that simple arithmetic would suggest would be recouped by 'changes in taxpayer behaviour'. Evidence for the UK was examined by Brown (1988). He rejected completely any view that the reduction of the UK basic rate from 27 to 25 per cent in 1988 could lead to increased revenue, but argued that it is possible that reducing the higher rate from 60 to 40 per cent could lead to more revenue. Broadly, the empirical evidence refutes the more extravagant supply-sider claims that major reductions in basic tax rates could be self-financing, but lends support to the view that this is likely to work for reductions in higher-rate taxation.

Overall, there is now more emphasis on the importance of supply-side issues in economics, and the extreme neglect of the supply side, seen in the heyday of Keynesian demand management, has decreased. However, the wilder claims of supply-siders associated with the US tax reform of 1981 have not been found to have been realized.

S. SIEBERT
P.A. WATT
UNIVERSITY OF BIRMINGHAM

References

Bartlett, B. and Roth, T.P. (1984) *The Supply-Side Solution*, London.
Becker, C. (1964) *Human Capital*, New York.
—— (1981) *A Treatise on the Family*, Cambridge, MA.
Brown, C. (1988) 'Will the 1988 income tax cuts either increase work incentives or raise more revenue?' *Fiscal Studies* 9.
Buchanan, J. and Tullock, G. (1962) *The Calculus of Consent*, Ann Arbor, MI.
Denison, E. (1962) 'Education, economic growth, and gaps in information', *Journal of Political Economy* 70.
Feldstein, M. (1981) 'The retreat from Keynesian economics', *Public Interest* 64.
Friedman, M. (1968) 'The role of monetary policy', *American Economic Review* 58.
Kendrick, J.W. (1961) *Productivity Trends in the United States*, Princeton, NJ.
Kuznets, S. (1971) *Economic Growth of Nations*, Cambridge, MA.
Lindsey, L.B. (1987) 'Individual taxpayer response to tax cuts: 1982–1984', *Journal of Public Economics* 33.
Mincer, J. and Polachek, S. (1974) 'Family investments in human capital: Earnings of women', *Journal of Political Economy* 82.
Roberts, P.C. (1984) *The Supply Side Revolution: An Insider's Account of Policymaking in Washington*, Cambridge, MA.
Schultz, T. (1974) *The Economics of the Family*, Chicago.
Stuart, C.E. (1981) 'Swedish tax rates, labour supply and tax revenues', *Journal of Political Economy* 89.

SEE ALSO: inflation and deflation; labour market analysis; microeconomics; monetary policy; public choice; regulation

SYMBOLIC INTERACTIONISM

Symbolic interactionism is the title that was awarded belatedly and retrospectively to the ideas of a group of sociologists and social psychologists originally centred on the University of Chicago. As that group evolved during the 1920s, 1930s and 1940s, its members began to scatter throughout the universities of North America, bearing interactionism with them. The critical early generation of George Mead, William James, Charles Cooley, William Thomas and Robert Park was succeeded first by that of

Herbert Blumer and Everett Hughes, and then by third and successive generations populated by such people as Erving Goffman, Howard Becker, Anselm Strauss, Eliot Freidson, Ken Plummer, Norman Denzin, Harvey Farberman and Gary Fine. There is still a Society for the Study of Symbolic Interaction and an eponymous journal.

Interactionism itself alludes to a deliberately unsystematic method of interpreting the ways in which, in Howard Becker's phrase, people do things together, a method that has flowed from the theoretical and practical work of the Chicago School (of Sociology). Because it is unsystematic, there are a number of versions of interactionism rather than a single orthodoxy, and any published account must therefore be a little partial.

Theoretically, interactionism was shaped by pragmatism and the special perspectives that the pragmatists brought to bear on the possibilities of knowledge and the limits of enquiry. It not only describes the character of social life but also suggests how it should be studied. Knowledge itself is described as belonging neither to the observing mind alone nor to the observed world alone but in a moving synthesis between them. On the one hand, interactionists contend that people's interpretations of events and things are not free because their interpretations are restrained by the capacity of phenomena to 'answer back'. On the other hand, they claim that knowledge is not a simple mirror of its objects because people actively create, shape and select their response to what is around them. Knowledge is then represented as an active process in which people, meanings and phenomena are bound together in what has been called the 'knowing–known transaction'. That transaction is exploratory, emergent and situated, lending a dialectical structure to all activity. In this sense, practical knowledge does not arise in seclusion. Rather, it addresses problems and purposes that are liable to raise questions and produce answers that will transform the original problems and purposes, and lead to yet another round of questions and interpretations. Processes of knowing thus entail an indefinite regress that will end only when exhaustion, boredom or practical satisfaction has been attained. It is evident that there cannot be a logical terminus for any investigation or activity because all knowledge is destined to be provisional, liable to reformulation with the answering of just one more question or the learning of one more fact. All knowledge is a novel and often unanticipated synthesis of what has gone before. Moreover, all knowledge is reflexively embedded in its own context and history of development. And, because it is contingent and emergent, there must be very real limits to sociological generalization and abstraction.

Chief among the problems that confront individuals is the nature of their own identity. People can never fully understand themselves, their past and their possible futures. To the contrary, fresh facts about the self are revealed with each new action and they cannot always be predicted or neatly assimilated. Yet it is vital to learn what one is and what one might become. Without that knowledge, there would be no appreciation of how one's actions will affect others and how others will affect oneself. Just as people observe those about them, so they will observe themselves, constructing a series of running conjectures about their own identity. That process of self-exploration translates the subject into two phases of activity, an examining 'I' as subject and an examined 'me' as object, the 'me' being an inference made by oneself and others. The responses of others are thus critical in another sense because they disclose something of how one appears, and one may read in them what interactionists have called a 'looking-glass self'. Over time, such responses can become relatively anonymous, generalized and aggregated to become the basis of a more abstract and stable representation called the 'generalized other'. The whole process is itself orchestrated and mediated by language, and its constituent forms have been likened by interactionists to those of a conversation. Great emphasis has been given to words in this analysis because they are seen as a means of animating, stabilizing, objectifying and recording what would otherwise be fleeting and private experiences. It is in the work done by language that people can appear to share a community of perspectives about themselves, one another and the objects that are in their environment, and conversation has become a metaphor for social interaction at large.

The prime vehicle of social action is the 'significant gesture', an expression or display that incorporates a prediction of the replies which others might make to it. In its anticipation of others' answering behaviour, the significant gesture symbolically ties people together, allowing lines of conduct to converge and unite in the imagination. By extension, society itself tends to be seen as a mosaic of little scenes and dramas in which people make indications to themselves and others, respond to those indications, align their actions, and so build identities, lines of conduct and social structures.

The task of the interactionist is to describe that activity, and it is also thought to be emergent and contextual. Enquiry is frequently tentative, open and exploratory, deploying a variety of strategies but leaning towards ethnography and participant-observation. The job of sociologists is to enter the social situations of their subjects, observe their conduct, understand their practices and the symbolic work that accompanies them, and then retire to report what has been seen. Those descriptions of conduct are frequently built up into larger portraits of social worlds, reference being made to the patterns and multiple interacting interpretations that seem to organize them, and there is interest in developing accounts of formative processes such as the career and conflict. Any resulting analysis may be tested by its plausibility or correspondence with the experience of the reader, its ability to provide scripts for behaviour that readers might test, and by the criticism supplied by the subjects themselves.

Interactionists would maintain that sociology resides in research, not in schematic treatises about society, epistemology and methodology. All argument, including interactionism itself, must be rooted in the unravelling of particular problems in specific contexts. The conventional interactionist territory has then been the small worlds of occupations, institutions and social groups, and exponents of the approach have been most conspicuous in those sectors of sociology that dwell on substantive areas such as medicine, deviance, education and religion. In the main, it has been closely identified with US scholars who are linked at first or second hand with the University of Chicago, and its greatest impact was probably achieved in the 1960s and 1970s when it changed the form of the sociology of deviance, Becker and Goffman being especially important figures.

PAUL ROCK
LONDON SCHOOL OF ECONOMICS
AND POLITICAL SCIENCE

Further reading

Becker, H. (1970) *Sociological Work*, Chicago.
Blumer, H. (1969) *Symbolic Interactionism: Perspective and Method*, Englewood Cliffs, NJ.
Denzin, N. (2000) *Handbook of Qualitative Research*, 2nd edn, London.
Goffman, E. (1959) *The Presentation of Self in Everyday Life*, New York.
Hughes, E. (1958) *Men and Their Work*, Glencoe, IL.
Plummer, K. (ed.) (1991) *Symbolic Interactionism*, Brighton.
Rock, P. (1979) *The Making of Symbolic Interactionism*, London.
Rose, A. (ed.) (1962) *Human Behavior and Social Processes*, Boston, MA.

SEE ALSO: pragmatics

SYMBOLISM

The various notions of symbolism developed in the social sciences constitute different responses to a central, perhaps inevitable, tension in a scientific description of culture. Most cultural productions seem to convey some 'meaning' yet a social science cannot readily accept these overt meanings as a sufficient explanation for those manifestations. To close this gap is the main point of developing a notion of symbolism. The point is argued forcefully by Durkheim; consider for instance his famous statement, that a human institution like religion 'cannot be founded on an error and a lie....One must know how to go underneath the symbol to the reality which it represents' (Durkheim 1947 [1915]: 14). This statement also introduces the ambiguity, to be found in most discussions of symbolism, between three different understandings of the term. Cultural manifestations are called symbolic, first, because they can be interpreted as indices of underlying social realities by social scientists, or, second, because they are expressive of particular concerns of the actors, or, finally, in the sense that they are *prima-facie* irrational. These different understandings are at the foundation of three major approaches to cultural symbolism – sociological, hermeneutic and cognitive respectively.

The first, *sociological* stance is principally associated with the name of Durkheim, although the notion of cultural productions as signs or symptoms of social relations was forcefully articulated in Hegelian and Marxist approaches to culture. In Marx in particular, the uneasy definition of ideology reflects a central ambiguity in the study of symbolism. In popular interpretations of Marxism, 'ideology' is often construed as an exercise in camouflage, as the representations whereby a social class explicitly and misleadingly portrays the social order in which it dominates as the only possible one. Although Marx himself used the term in this way, he also at times conceived of 'ideology' as the entire set of mental representations that make social interaction possible in a particular mode of production. In this sense most cultural productions are 'symbolic' and tacitly refer to their conditions of production. This is also the sense of cultural symbolism that Durkheim focused on, although from a very different perspective. The main thrust of Durkheimian accounts of symbolism was a rejection of Tylorian intellectualism (Skorupksi 1976). The contrast is particularly evident in the domain of religion, seen by Tylor as a misguided attempt at explaining the natural world, while for Durkheim it is a 'figurative expression' of social structure. In the Durkheimian system, however, symbols cannot be seen as just projections of pre-existing social forms. Religion also creates social cohesion and makes social reality more intuitively real by enforcing its ideal counterpart, conceptual cohesiveness.

One may argue that the Durkheimian symbolist tradition tends to confuse two quite different aspects of cultural symbols, namely, their use as a source of information for the sociologist and their meaning for the social actors. Consider for instance Leach's statement that 'the various *nats* [i.e. spirits] of Kachin religious mythology are, in the last analysis, nothing more than ways of describing the formal relationships that exist between real persons and real groups in ordinary human Kachin society' (Leach 1954: 182). The explanation proposed may well exhaust the sociological significance of the various spirit-notions of the Kachin. But this leaves untouched the particular meanings they articulate for Kachin actors. Such considerations found the second, *hermeneutic* stance in the approach to symbolism, in which the main problem is to translate the meanings of cultural symbols rather than explain their occurrence. For Clifford Geertz, for instance, the study of culture is 'not an experimental science in search of law but an interpretive one in search of meaning' (Geertz 1973: 5). In such authors as Victor Turner (1967, 1974) or James Fernandez (1986), the emphasis lies on the figurative power of cultural symbols, on their effects as both expressive figures and organizing principles for inchoate or unstructured feelings and thoughts.

It is possible, however, to approach meanings without taking this hermeneutic stance, and to consider the production of meaning as a psychological process, amenable to scientific investigation like any other such process. This leads us to the third, *cognitive* understanding of symbolism, intrinsically related to considerations of rationality. From Lévy-Bruhl or Rivers down to modern cognitive approaches, anthropology has tried to provide some description of the cognitive processes whereby people can be led to hold beliefs for which rational justifications seem either impossible or unavailable. So symbolism could be construed as the product of a special 'mode of thought', with particular functional properties. An echo of this conception can be found in Lévi-Strauss's notion of a *pensée sauvage*, an 'untamed' form of speculation. Here symbols are produced by the application of universal, formal operations, such as binary opposition and analogy, to a set of 'concrete' categories: nature and culture, male and female, the raw and the cooked, etc., made available by the organization of the human brain (Lévi-Strauss 1966 [1962]; see also Leach 1976). In the absence of precise psychological models, however, the idea of a particular 'mode of thought' may lead to a conception of symbolism as a residual category, justifying Ernest Gellner's comment that 'in social anthropology if a native says something sensible it is primitive technology, but if it sounds very odd then it is symbolic' (Gellner 1987: 163).

An important attempt to go beyond this characterization can be found in Sperber's (1975) cognitive account of symbolism. For Sperber, certain cultural phenomena are 'symbolic' to particular actors if their rational interpretation does not lead to a limited and predictable set of inferences. This triggers a search for possible, generally conjectural representations, which, if true, would make a rational interpretation possible. This conception has two interesting corollaries for the social scientist. First, it implies that it is futile to provide keys or translations for cultural expressions. The fact that a phenomenon is treated symbolically precisely excludes the possibility of a single, exhaustive interpretation. Second, while symbolism exists as a psychological process, there are no such things as 'symbols', as a particular class of cultural products. Any conceptual or perceptual item can become symbolic, if there is some index that a rational interpretation is unavailable or insufficient. In this framework, a proper account of cultural symbolism will be found, not in the social sciences as such, but in the empirical and theoretical developments of cognitive science.

This and other cognitive accounts of cultural symbolism substantially agree with Lévi-Strauss's assumption that the organization of the brain makes certain kinds of cultural representations more likely than others and 'better to think'. The new twist is in the much enriched database that is now available due to the spectacular development of cognitive science. The conjunction of experimental psychology and cognitive neuroscience, for instance, may explain why certain types of animal symbols, spirit concepts or mythologies are much easier than others for human minds to acquire and transmit (Boyer 2003). More generally, and this time in contrast to Lévi-Strauss, these models lead to a 'naturalization' of culture (Sperber 1996), a conception of cultural phenomena as just another manifestation of evolved human dispositions.

PASCAL BOYER
WASHINGTON UNIVERSITY IN ST LOUIS

References

Boyer, P. (2003) 'Religious thought and behaviour as by-products of brain function', *Trends in Cognitive Sciences* 7: 119–24.
Durkheim, E. (1947 [1915]) *The Elementary Forms of the Religious Life*, London.
Fernandez, J.W. (1986) *Persuasions and Performances: The Play of Tropes in Culture*, Bloomington, IN.
Geertz, C. (1973) *The Interpretation of Culture*, New York.
Gellner, E. (1987) *Culture, Identity and Politics*, Cambridge, UK.
Leach, E.R. (1954) *The Political Systems of Highland Burma: A Study of Kachin Political Systems*, London.
—— (1976) *Culture and Communication: The Logic by which Symbols Are Connected*, Cambridge, UK.
Lévi-Strauss, C. (1966 [1962]) *The Savage Mind*, London.
Skorupski, J. (1976) *Symbol and Theory: A Philosophical Study of Theories of Religion in Social Anthropology*, Cambridge, UK.
Sperber, D. (1975) *Rethinking Symbolism*, Cambridge, UK.
—— (1996) *Explaining Culture: A Naturalistic Approach*, Oxford.
Turner, V. (1967) *The Forest of Symbols: Aspects of Ndembu Ritual*, Ithaca, NY.
—— (1974) *Dramas, Fields and Metaphors*, Ithaca, NY.

SEE ALSO: cognitive psychology; ritual; semiotics

SYNCRETISM

Syncretism denotes the mixture of different religious traditions, but the term is frequently extended to describe hybridity in a number of other domains such as medicine, art or culture generally. It is important to be aware of the word's original religious associations, however, because these have not always been positive, and they have generated some uncertainty among social scientists as to whether the term can be used in a neutral, non-evaluative way.

In the seventeenth century the Catholic Church branded 'syncretists' those Protestants who wished to sink their differences with each other and with the Catholics and establish a new ecumenical Christianity (Martin 1983). Catholic theologians rejected any compromise form of Christianity as an inconsistent jumble of theological ideas – a syncretism. A negative assessment of religious mixture was perhaps to be expected from a Church interested in safeguarding the integrity of its doctrine and practice throughout the world.

Syncretism retained its negative connotations during missionary expansion. It served to excoriate unauthorized local appropriations of Catholicism or Protestantism where missionaries deemed the missionized to have distorted the truth of Scripture through the introduction of elements from indigenous religions. An example is Sundkler's (1961) characterization of Zulu Zionism as a nativistic-syncretistic bridge that carried its practitioners back from their foothold in true Christianity to 'the African animism from where they once started'. Sundkler wrote as a missionary in the service of the Church of Sweden Mission (Lutheran). For the most part, subsequent Africanist anthropologists did not contest or revise this European, Church-controlled, negative definition of syncretism. Instead they have let it stand and sought to demonstrate that Independent African Churches are not syncretic, but rather faithful translations of Christianity into African contexts.

On the other side of the Atlantic, the general attitude of social scientists towards syncretism has been more positive, perhaps because until the last quarter of the twentieth century many North and South American countries publicly espoused melting-pot ideologies as a strategy of nation-building. The melting-pot is the analogue of syncretism in the ethnopolitical domain, and it would have been difficult to criticize the one without simultaneously undermining the other. Thus, for example, the influential mid-century anthropologist Melville Herskovits (1958) considered syncretism a valuable concept for specifying the degree to which diverse cultures had integrated; it was not a bridge leading to religious relapse, but rather a stage (for African Americans and other minorities) on the road towards the ideal of cultural assimilation and integration. It becomes apparent, then, that syncretism can receive positive or negative connotations depending on the regional scholarly tradition within which one encounters it.

Historians of religion for the most part agree that *all* religions are syncretic: all have mixed with other religious traditions and incorporated exogenous features during their history. Such an observation would seem to diminish the importance of syncretism since the term says nothing new or special. This does not, however, change the manifest fact that religions constantly come into contact with each other, or break apart and reform under internal pressures, all the more so in an age of increased multiculturalism and global intercommunication. Syncretism thus furnishes a potentially useful term in the analytical vocabulary of contemporary social science alongside 'creolization', 'hybridization' and 'interculturation'. Religions should perhaps be viewed less as fixed systems, and more as traditions in a continual process of change, dynamically coping with the tensions generated by internal social developments or the challenges of alternative religious traditions. Syncretic appropriations of new forms are thus part of the very nature of religion at any point in time and may be a means of resisting domination and preserving cultural autonomy.

Although nearly every religion may be objectively characterized as syncretic, such an observation conflicts with the subjective opinion that individuals frequently have of their own religious traditions (Droogers 1989). Followers of doctrinal religions of the Book, such as Christianity and Islam, are very unlikely to regard their religions as other than authentic and even pure. Having accepted the proposition that all religious traditions are syncretic, anthropologists and sociologists are now increasingly turning to ethnographic analyses of power, rhetoric and subjectivity, which motivate people to accept or reject the description of their practice as syncretic (Stewart and Shaw 1994).

CHARLES STEWART
UNIVERSITY COLLEGE LONDON

References

Droogers, A. (1989) 'Syncretism: The problem of definition, the definition of the problem', in J. Gort, H. Vroom, R. Fernhout and A. Wessels (eds) *Dialogue and Syncretism: An Interdisciplinary Approach*, Grand Rapids, MI.

Herskovits, M. (1958) *The Myth of the Negro Past*, 2nd edn, Boston, MA.

Martin, L. (1983) 'Why Cecropian Minerva? Hellenistic religious syncretism as system', *Numen* 30: 131–45.

Stewart, C. and Shaw, R. (eds) (1994) *Syncretism/Anti-Syncretism: The Politics of Religious Synthesis*, London.

Sundkler, B. (1961) *Bantu Prophets in South Africa*, 2nd edn, London.

SEE ALSO: religion; sects and cults

T

TABOO

The term 'taboo' derives from various Polynesian languages where it has the sense of 'forbidden'. More specifically, what is forbidden and dangerous is unregulated contact between the everyday world and the sacred, which includes both the holy (for example the person of a chief) and the unclean (for example a corpse). Most modern anthropological thinking about taboo derives from Durkheim (1976 [1912]), for whom this disjunction between profane and sacred was the cornerstone of religion – the sacred being secondarily divided between the 'auspiciously' and 'inauspiciously' sacred. Taboos have the function of keeping separate what must not be joined – of policing the boundaries between sacred and profane, and between 'good' and 'bad' sacred – while rites in general recreate the solidarity of the group. Developing this second proposition, Radcliffe-Brown (1952) argued that taboo behaviour expresses and reinforces the values and sentiments essential to the maintenance of society. Other work, however, has taken as its starting-point the notion that taboos mark the boundaries between a culture's fundamental categories.

This line of thought was brilliantly exploited by Douglas (1966, 1975). Dirt, said Lord Chesterfield, is 'matter out of place'. It implies disorder and a confusion of cherished categories. Pollution behaviour and taboo focus on that which is ambiguous in terms of such categories. There is even a sense in which taboos entrench the categories by highlighting and defining the boundaries between them. Margins and boundaries tend therefore to be populated by anomalous creatures of various kinds, and if they don't exist they have to be invented. In myth, for example, the elephant-headed Hindu deity Ganesa often appears – in keeping with his physical character – as an ambivalent trickster. It is he who marks the boundaries between sacred and profane space and time, for he conventionally stands at the entrances to temples, and is worshipped at the beginning and end of major rituals.

Anomalies can be dealt with in various ways: first, they can be suppressed or eradicated. In some societies twins are destroyed for they are seen as blurring the boundary between humans (characterized by single births) and animals (characterized by multiple births). As products of the same parturition, they are mystically one but physically two; in a society that attaches much importance to the birth order of siblings they are doubly ambiguous, for there are two physical beings to occupy one structural role in the kinship system (Turner 1969). A second possibility is to regard the anomaly as filthy and unclean – as in the 'abominations' of Leviticus. Here, for example, land animals are divided into the clawed and hoofed; the latter having the linked characteristics of being ruminant and cloven-hoofed, and being rated as the only legitimate meat. Creatures like the pig (which divide the hoof but do not chew the cud), or the camel, hare and hyrax (which chew the cud but are not cloven-hoofed) are abominated and tabooed. Third, the anomaly may be welcomed as a positive mediator between, say, the sacred and the profane, or between nature and culture. Thus, in the taxonomic system of the Congolese Lele the pangolin is a highly ambiguous creature. It is an arboreal animal with the scaly body and tail of a fish, and is credited with a number of anthropomorphic qualities, the most important of which are a sense of sexual 'modesty' and the reproduction of only one offspring at a time. It therefore stands in the same kind of relationship to humans as begetters of twins stand to animals. Both mediate between nature and culture, and are the focus of cult groups that control hunting and fertility.

What the theory fails to explain, however, is why some anomalous creatures are filthy abominations while others are positive mediators. Douglas (1973) tried to solve this puzzle, though not entirely satisfactorily, by suggesting that attitudes to boundary crossing in the social sphere are reflected in attitudes towards potential mediators in other spheres (evaluation of creatures – like pigs – which straddle the Jewish insistence on endogamy, for example, going with the negative evaluation of creatures that straddle conceptual boundaries). More plausibly, she notes that that which is anomalous and marginal is not only the focus of pollution and danger, but also a source of extraordinary power. The Aghoris are a small sect of Hindu ascetics who perform austerities at, and may live on, the cremation grounds. They rub their bodies with cremation ash, use shrouds for loin-cloths, cook their food on wood pilfered from the pyres, consume it out of a human skull; and they are *supposed* to meditate while seated on top of a corpse, and to eat and drink all manner of foul substances including urine, excrement and the putrescent flesh of corpses. By such austerities ascetics are held to acquire extraordinary supernatural powers by which they can surmount the ordinary physical limitations of the mortal condition (Parry 1981). The categories are safe and orderly, but imply restriction. What lies outside is dangerous, but also highly potent.

J.P. PARRY
LONDON SCHOOL OF ECONOMICS
AND POLITICAL SCIENCE

References

Douglas, M. (1966) *Purity and Danger: An Analysis of Concepts of Pollution and Taboo*, London.
—— (1973) *Natural Symbols*, Harmondsworth.
—— (1975) *Implicit Meanings: Essays in Anthropology*, London.
Durkheim, E. (1976 [1912]) *The Elementary Forms of the Religious Life*, London.
Parry, J.P. (1981) 'Sacrificial death and the necrophagous ascetic', in M. Bloch and J. Parry (eds) *Death and the Regeneration of Life*, Cambridge, UK.
Radcliffe-Brown, A. (1952) *Structure and Function in Primitive Society*, London.
Turner, V. (1969) *The Ritual Process: Structure and Anti-Structure*, Chicago.

TECHNOLOGY, SOCIOLOGY OF

The current sociology of technology is a combination of predominantly constructivist approaches to the study of the development of technology, the relations between technology and society, and the technical shaping of society. The centre of gravity of these studies now lies within an interdisciplinary field of science, technology and society (STS) studies rather than within the discipline of sociology. Its roots lie in classical social theory, notably Marx's analysis of the impact of technology on labour relations on the shop floor and his theory of the role of technology in changing the production and power relations. The present conceptualization of technology as value-laden and socially embedded, rather than as something neutral and freely available for instrumental use, refers back to Marx's political economy. Weber's study of bureaucratization for its part has inspired the study of a social technologies.

The first self-defined sociologists of technology were William F. Ogburn and Sean C. Gilfillan. Ogburn's book on the social effects of aviation, to which Gilfillan contributed too, may be considered the first full-fledged sociological assessment of technology (Ogburn *et al.* 1946). Gilfillan's study of invention, illustrated by an account of the development of the ship, provides a very sophisticated and detailed study that stresses the internal logic of technical development processes (Gilfillan 1935). Harry Braverman's critical analysis of management literature, and his thesis that automation leads to deskilling and the degradation of jobs, has sparked a neo-Marxist line in the sociology of technology that was quite fruitful in the 1970s and 1980s (Braverman 1974; Blackburn *et al.* 1985).

In the 1980s these studies were criticized for technological determinism, a theoretical position that was associated with two propositions: (1) that technology develops autonomously, and (2) that technology has a determining influence on societal development. It was argued that technological determinism imposes a teleological, linear and one-dimensional view of technological development, impoverishing research. It was considered to be politically debilitating because technological determinism suggests that social and political interventions in the course of technology are futile, undermining any attempt to democratize the development and use of technologies.

The social construction of technology (SCOT) was one approach among several constructivist ways of studying science and technology that emerged in the 1980s. It was explicitly aimed at redressing the flaws of technological determinism. Here, 'constructivist' means that the truth of scientific facts and the working of technical artefacts are studied as accomplishments – as being constructed, rather than as intrinsic properties of those facts and machines. Historically the development of the social construction of technology is closely linked to the sociology of scientific knowledge and to the science and society movement in the 1970s. In the 1980s and 1990s it developed primarily as an academic enterprise, but subsequently also found application in the policy domain, in innovation management and in discussions about new forms of democracy.

Constructivist studies of science and technology come in more and less radical versions. Some merely stress the importance of including the social *context* when describing the development of science and technology. More radical versions argue that the *content* of science and technology is socially constructed. In other words, the truth of scientific statements and the technical working of machines are not derived from nature but are constituted in social processes (see, e.g., Callon 1987; Latour 1992; Sismondo 1993; Woolgar 2002).

Key concepts in SCOT are 'relevant social group' and 'interpretative flexibility'. An artefact is described through the eyes of relevant social groups. In describing the high-wheeled Ordinary bicycle in the 1870s, Bijker argued that such groups included bicycle producers, young athletic Ordinary users, women cyclists and anti-cyclists. Because the description of an artefact through the eyes of different relevant social groups produces different descriptions (and so different artefacts) the research revealed the 'interpretative flexibility' of the artefact. There is not one artefact, but there are many. In the case of the Ordinary bicycle: there was the *Unsafe machine* (as viewed through the eyes of women) and there was the *Macho machine* (as seen through the

eyes of the young male Ordinary users). For women the bicycle was a machine in which your skirt got entangled and from which you frequently had a steep fall. Bold young men regarded it as a machine with which to impress ladies (Bijker 1995).

The initial analytic move is the sociological deconstruction of an artefact in order to demonstrate its interpretative flexibility. The next step is the description of the artefact's social construction. The researcher shows how the interpretative flexibility diminishes, because some artefacts gain dominance over the others and meanings converge. Eventually, one artefact stabilizes in this process of social construction. Finally, this process of construction is explained in sociological terms.

Current social studies of technology comprise a rich variety of theoretical approaches in addition to SCOT. Actor network theory draws on semiotics and describes a technology and its context as a network of human and non-human *actants* (Latour 1992). The systems approach is rooted in the history of technology, and describes the development of technology in society as a sociotechnical system that is initially socially constructed, but then builds up 'momentum' and increasingly shapes society.

Current social studies of technology address the mutual shaping of technology and society. In a way, this leads to a rehabilitation of technological determinism. All current work in the social studies of technology tries to develop conceptual solutions that combine the social construction of technology with the technical shaping of society. One further example is the concept of 'domestication', which focuses on the mutual adaptation of daily-life technologies and their contexts (Lie and Sorensen 1996).

There are also new areas of empirical research in current social studies of technology, notably Internet research. It does not necessarily fall within the constructivist tradition, although most of its practitioners do use that perspective. Internet research comprises a wide array of studies, ranging from ethnographies of virtual communities to quantitative studies of the impact of the Internet on research practices (Hine 2000).

Whatever the differences between the various approaches, the concept of 'interpretative flexibility' is the *condition sine qua non* of the social studies of technology. Demonstrating the interpretative flexibility of a technology entails arguing that the identity of a technology cannot be fully understood simply by 'reading' its technical content. Because technologies have interpretative flexibility, sociologists are required to understand their development.

The development of technology is explained as a social process in which a variety of relevant social groups participate. This social process does not stop when an artefact leaves the factory, but continues when users assign to technology its specific usage and meaning. Laws of physics and economics are not irrelevant, but insufficient to characterize technology's development. Analogously, the development of social institutions in our modern society can also not be fully understood without taking into account the role of technology. This requires a view on technology's impact on society. In the social construction of technology this is done by conceptualizing the hardness or obduracy of technology.

Recent social studies of technology not only give an affirmative answer to Winner's question 'Do artefacts have politics?' but also offer ways to analyse these politics (Winner 1980; Kraft and Vig 1988). Technology is socially (and politically) constructed; society (including politics) is technically built; technological culture consists of sociotechnical ensembles. If it is accepted that a variety of social groups are involved in the social construction of technologies and that the construction processes continue through all phases of an artefact's life cycle, it makes sense to extend the set of groups involved in political deliberation about technological choices. Experiments are in train in several countries with consensus conferences, public debates and citizens' juries. One of the key issues here is the role of expertise in public debates. Constructivist studies of science and technology suggest that all relevant social groups have some form of expertise, and that no one form, for example the scientists' or engineers', has a special and a priori superiority over the others.

WIEBE E. BIJKER
UNIVERSITY OF MAASTRICHT,
THE NETHERLANDS

References

Bijker, W.E. (1995) *Of Bicycles, Bakelites and Bulbs. Toward a Theory of Sociotechnical Change, Inside Technology*, Cambridge, MA.

Blackburn, P., Coombs, R. and Green, K. (eds) (1985) *Technology, Economic Growth and the Labour Process*, London.

Braverman, H. (1974) *Labor and Monopoly Capital: The Degradation of Work in the Twentieth Century*, New York.

Callon, M. (1987) 'Society in the making: The study of technology as a tool for sociological analysis', in W.E. Bijker, T.P. Hughes and T.J. Pinch (eds) *The Social Construction of Technological Systems. New Directions in the Sociology and History of Technology*, Cambridge, MA.

Gilfillan, S.C. (1935) *The Sociology of Invention: An Essay in the Social Causes of Technic Invention and Some of its Social Results*, Chicago.

Hine, C. (2000) *Virtual Ethnography*, London.

Kraft, M.E. and Vig, N.J. (eds) (1988) *Technology and Politics*, Durham, NC.

Latour, B. (1992) *ARAMIS ou l'amour des techniques*, Paris.

Lie, M. and Sorensen, K.H. (eds) (1996) *Making Technology Our Own? Domesticating Technology into Everyday Life*, Oslo.

Ogburn, W.F., Adams, J. and Gilfillan, S.C. (1946) *The Social Effects of Aviation*, Boston.

Sismondo, S. (1993) 'Some social constructions', *Social Studies of Science* 23: 515–53.

Winner, L. (1980) 'Do artifacts have politics?' *Daedalus* 109(1): 121–33.

Woolgar, S. (2002) *Virtual Society? Technology, Cyberbole, Reality*, Oxford.

Further reading

Hughes, T.P. (1983) *Networks of Power. Electrification in Western Society, 1880–1930*, Baltimore, MD.

Latour, B. (1992) 'Where are the missing masses? The sociology of a few mundane artifacts', in W.E. Bijker and J. Law (eds) *Shaping Technology/Building Society. Studies in Sociotechnical Change*, Cambridge, MA.

Smith, M.R. and Marx, L. (eds) (1995) *Does Technology Drive History? The Dilemma of Technological Determinism*, 2nd edn, Cambridge, MA.

Summerton, J. (ed.) (1994) *Changing Large Technical Systems*, Boulder, CO.

Wouters, P. and Schröder, P. (eds) (2000) *Access to Publicly Financed Research. Background Papers to the Global Research Village III Conference*, Amsterdam.

TERRORISM

In current usage the term 'terrorism' is primarily applied to acts of clandestine political violence carried out by substate groups seeking to advertise their cause beyond the confines of one society. By the same token, a terrorist is someone who carries out such an attack or who assists it to take place. Acts with which terrorism are commonly associated include bombing, assassination, hostage-taking and hijacking. However, usage has often extended beyond these broad parameters. Further, even with these parameters, there has been considerable variation across both time and space in how these terms have been used. Thus, in the late nineteenth century the archetypal terrorist was the bomb-throwing anarchist exploiting the new invention of dynamite. To the authorities anarchism appeared to be the enemy of all government and that distinguished anarchists from rebels of other kinds. When the League of Nations addressed the issue following the assassination of the King of Yugoslavia in Marseilles in 1934, the primary focus was on outlawing attacks on heads of state. In the late 1960s and early 1970s during the onset of what has commonly been called the age of terrorism, the main distinguishing feature of the groups that were labelled as terrorist was that they used violence to attract international attention to their cause. In fact, publicity appeared to be their main objective, prompting the aphorism that what terrorism sought was a few people dead but many millions watching.

However, by the end of the twentieth century terrorism had also come to be associated with acts in which hundreds of people lost their lives in a single episode and that were not accompanied by any claim of responsibility. While the events of 11 September 2001, in which thousands died in a series of co-ordinated attacks that employed hijacked civilian jets as gigantic flying bombs, were sufficiently unprecedented to prompt the coining of new terms such as hyper-terrorism and super-terrorism, they clearly followed a trend towards increasingly lethal acts. Indeed, even before 11 September it had been widely contended that terrorists might at some stage in the future employ weapons of mass destruction. This fear has been enhanced by the events of 11 September, even though they did not actually involve the use of weapons of mass destruction, as that term was generally understood. A variety of factors influenced the escalation of numbers killed in terrorist attacks, including the capacity of societies to adjust to the existence of terrorism at low levels, blunting the shock value of killing small numbers of people. Also significant as a factor was the growth in the technical capabilities of substate groups. This issue was commonly linked to how far such groups were able to attract support from governments for their activities. Instances in which states not merely provided sanctuary but

actively supported such groups gave rise to the concept of state-sponsored terrorism. This became a major cause of concern in the 1980s, prompting the displacement of the term transnational terrorism by international terrorism. American Administrations adopted measures to punish such states, labelling them terrorist states.

The concept of the terrorist state needs to be carefully distinguished from that of state terrorism. The term state terrorism refers to cases of mass violence carried out directly and usually overtly by agents of the state. A further difference is that state terrorism is overwhelmingly associated with actions in a domestic not international context. A justification of this usage, despite the large differences between this violence and the terrorism of small groups, is that it accords with the original use of the term. Thus, the term was first used in the late eighteenth century to refer to the actions taken by the state during the Reign of Terror in revolutionary France, in particular to the guillotining of political adversaries. The addition of the suffixes -ism and -ist to the term terror was a way of conveying the horror that the actions of the revolutionaries evoked as well as their novelty. Both these connotations have continued to be important in the context of modern usages of the concept.

However, applying the term to the actions of the state remains problematic. This is because of the special role accorded to the state both in defending the society from external attack and in maintaining law and order, so that generally speaking a measure of legitimacy adheres to its actions. The issue of legitimacy is of crucial importance in the context of terrorism. The term is not only a very emotive one but it also carries the connotation of absolute illegitimacy. Thus, the effectiveness of the title of Doris Lessing's novel, *The Good Terrorist*, derives from the instant recognition that it is an oxymoron. The strength of this negative connotation is one reason why a consensus on the definition of the term has been so difficult to achieve. The problem does not derive from any lack of agreement among states that certain actions should be condemned as totally unacceptable in an international context. Thus, there has been relatively little difficulty in getting the vast majority of states to agree to Conventions through the United Nations that outlaw hijacking and other attacks on civilian airliners, attacks on diplomats and hostage-taking.

What causes difficulty is the question of when groups may legitimately use any form of violence to advance a claim of self-determination, a dispute encapsulated in the aphorism that one person's terrorist is another person's freedom fighter. Differences over this issue, particularly in the context of intractable conflicts in deeply divided societies, account for the reluctance of journalists or broadcasters addressing a global readership or audience to use the terms terrorist and terrorism without qualification or outside quotation marks in such contexts. The problem is further compounded by the tendency of governments threatened by violence from below to exploit the demonizing potential of these terms. Thus, such governments commonly seek to extend the meaning of these terms beyond the perpetration of outrages (or assistance in their commission) to a much wider category of actions. This may even encompass passive resistance or simply non-co-operation with the authorities, giving rise to such expressions as terrorist opinions, terrorist communities and even terrorist populations. The elastic nature of the concept presents an especial problem to policy-makers seeking to formulate a coherent and prudent response to particular threats. Thus, it is far easier to proclaim a war against terrorism, as President Bush did in response to the horrific events of 11 September 2001, than it is to define what would constitute victory in such a war or to limit its scope.

ADRIAN GUELKE
QUEEN'S UNIVERSITY BELFAST

Further reading

Halliday, F. (2002) *Two Hours that Shook the World – September 11, 2001: Causes and Consequences*, London.
Henderson, H. (2001) *Global Terrorism: The Complete Reference Guide*, New York.
Stern, J. (1999) *The Ultimate Terrorists*, Cambridge, MA.
Townsend, C. (2000) *Terrorism: A Very Short Introduction*, Oxford.

SEE ALSO: revolutions; violence

THINKING

The term 'thinking' refers to the mental processes whereby given information is used to generate new information. Given the reasoning task, 'If Tom had arrived at the station he would have phoned me' and 'He hasn't phoned me', we can infer the new and possibly very useful piece of information that 'Tom has not arrived at the station'. In complex problem-solving tasks, such as arise in chess, a player can choose a winning move by thinking through relatively few possible move sequences, whereas a computer might arrive at this choice only through examining millions of possible move sequences. In general, the study of thinking is concerned with the information-processing steps that people go through in a range of tasks such as solving puzzles, deciding between alternatives, applying expert knowledge to new problems, reasoning and being creative. In all these cases of *directed* thinking, a mental representation of an initial situation is transformed in a series of exploratory steps until a goal is reached (see entry on problem-solving). If a person does not have a specific pressing goal then thinking tends to be *undirected*, as we experience in daydreaming where the changes of content are free-associative and not tightly constrained. Most research has focused on directed forms of thinking and this article will outline the main historically important approaches, including the currently dominant information-processing approach.

In the late nineteenth and early twentieth century *classical introspectionism* was the major approach to the study of thinking. This approach focused on the attempted analysis of conscious experience into elementary sensations. The basic data were verbal reports by trained observers of the sensations of which they were aware while carrying out various tasks, such as free association to a word. Classical introspectionism was associated with the first laboratories for experimental psychology, set up in Leipzig by Wundt and at Cornell by Titchener (see Boring 1950). The method had various drawbacks. A major difficulty lay in reconciling divergent reports from different laboratories, such as whether thought could occur without imagery being experienced. Also, the method was restricted to trained, normal, sane, adult humans and could not be applied to the untrained, or to animals, children or the mentally disturbed. (More recently researchers following the information-processing approach have applied a 'think-aloud' method that uses normal everyday language to report what the person is aware of while tackling problems. Although this method is sometimes labelled as 'introspection' it avoids most of the drawbacks of classical introspectionism.)

Partly in reaction to the limitations of classical introspectionism, the *behaviourist* school focused on objectively observable behaviour and particularly stressed the role of learning. Problem-solving was seen to be a matter of trial-and-error learning such as was evident when cats were placed in puzzle boxes (Thorndike 1898). Initially the cat would engage in much overt trial and error before escaping; on repeated trials escape would become faster and faster as correct responses were strengthened by the reward of escape. Even if overt trial and error was not evident, as in a person solving an anagram, the behaviourists argued that covert trial and error was taking place.

A contrasting view was put forward by the *Gestalt* psychologists, between the First and Second World Wars. Gestalt psychology objected to the behaviourists' denial of any role for understanding or insight in problem-solving. The Gestalt school pointed out that some problems cause special difficulty because the ways in which people first represent them are misleading. In such cases, the representation of the problem has to be changed before solution is possible. This process of changing representation was known as '*restructuring*'. A restructuring that leads to a rapid solution was called an '*insight*'. The Gestalt psychologists gave the example of 'Young Gauss' (Wertheimer 1945). When he was a young child, the famous mathematician Gauss and his classmates were set the task of adding the numbers from 1 to 100. Gauss very rapidly produced the answer (5,050), while his classmates were still struggling to complete the sum. How had Gauss found the answer so quickly? It was not by super-rapid addition but by restructuring the problem. He noticed that the numbers to be added formed pairs (1,100), (2,99), (3,98)...and so on, in which each pair summed to 101 and that there were 50 such pairs. Hence, the answer was $50 \times 101 = 5,050$. A typical small-scale example that can be used in laboratory studies of restructuring and insight is the nine-dot problem in which people are given a square array of nine dots and are asked to connect the dots with four straight lines without lifting pen from paper. Typically, people assume that solution to the nine-dot problem must be within the square shape. The 'insight' that is

required is that solutions can go outside the square shape. Lack of insight in problem-solving can be related to factors such as 'set' (a fixation on one approach) and 'functional fixity' (difficulty in thinking of a novel use for a familiar object).

Since the 1960s, the *information-processing* approach has been dominant. This approach draws on the idea that thinking is akin to the execution of steps in a computer program. The computer metaphor offers a concrete example of a well-understood system that carries out complex information-processing tasks (playing chess, predicting weather, predicting economic developments, etc.). The programs followed by computers are likened to *strategies* followed by humans.

The information-processing approach attempts to specify the strategies used by people to solve problems, taking due account of the limitations that people must contend with such as limited working memory capacity, slow rate of transfer of information into long-term memory and so on. Much research has focused on how people tackle small-scale problems or 'puzzles' that do not require extensive background knowledge (e.g. moving three hobbits and three orcs from one side of a river to another, using a boat that can only hold two creatures, without the hobbits ever being outnumbered by the orcs). Studies of problem-solving in this tradition (which have often used a think-aloud method) indicate that people typically generate a small number of possible moves at each step and think ahead to a very limited extent; choices of moves are made on the basis of how promising each move looks in terms of similarity to the goal. This approach of 'hill-climbing' or 'following one's nose' and not looking ahead very far, however, leads to difficulties with many problems in which the apparent direction of progress has to be reversed and a move made that appears to move away from the goal. That is to say, with 'detour' problems, such as the hobbits and orcs problem, trying to go straight to the goal will not succeed. As expected, strategies observed in problem-solving reflect limitations on holding more than a small amount of newly generated information in working memory at any one time. Performance in a number of puzzles has been successfully modelled by 'production systems', i.e. collections of rules that modify the contents of working memory in response to current goals and problem conditions.

The information-processing approach has also been applied to 'insight' tasks (e.g. Ohlsson 1992). Ohlsson proposed that changing representations involved particular processes of 'elaboration' (i.e. adding information by noticing features), 're-encoding' (i.e. changing interpretation of ambiguous materials) and 'constraint relaxation' (i.e. making the goal less restricted, as in the nine-dot problem outlined above). This approach has received experimental support in recent studies (Knoblich *et al.* 1999).

Creative thinking, whereby people arrive at new and useful ideas, has also been addressed within the information-processing approach. Smith *et al.* (1995) have developed a two-stage model for tasks of combining items into new and useful combinations. They propose an initial stage of 'generation' in which new combinations are formed and a second stage of 'exploration' in which possible uses for the new combinations are developed. Typical laboratory tasks used with this approach are to combine three basic object shapes (such as sphere, hook, cross) to make some useful object or device. Best results occurred when the initial forms were produced with no specific goal in mind and only subsequently interpreted in terms of possible uses. Thus, according to this approach, 'function follows form', in contrast with the oft-stated design maxim that 'form follows function'. Creative thinking does often seem to involve a stage of 'incubation' (Wallas 1926) in which impasses are reached, the task is set aside and fruitful work follows a period away from the task. Three main views to explain incubation effects have been (1) forgetting of misleading sets, (2) spreading activation in long-term memory eventually activates some relevant knowledge above threshold (possibly aided by accidental cues from the environment) and (3) unconscious systematic exploration produces appropriate sequence of actions that then become conscious. Experimental studies have found support for the first two explanations (Smith and Blankenship 1991; Beeman and Bowden 2000) but no evidence seems to have been found in favour of systematic but unconscious search processes.

K.J. GILHOOLY
UNIVERSITY OF PAISLEY

References

Beeman, M.J. and Bowden, E.M. (2000) 'The right hemisphere maintains solution-related activation for yet-to-be-solved problems', *Memory and Cognition* 28.

Boring, E.G. (1950) *A History of Experimental Psychology*, 2nd edn, New York.

Knoblich, G., Ohlsson, S., Haider, H. and Rhenius, D. (1999) 'Constraint relaxation and chunk decomposition in insight', *Journal of Experimental Psychology: Learning, Memory and Cognition* 25.

Ohlsson, S. (1992) 'Information processing explanations of insight and related phenomena', in M.T. Keane and K.J. Gilhooly (eds) *Advances in the Psychology of Thinking*, London.

Smith, S.M. and Blankenship, S.E. (1991) 'Incubation and the persistence of fixation in problem solving', *American Journal of Psychology* 104.

Smith, S.M., Ward, T.B. and Finke, R.A. (eds) (1995) *The Creative Cognition Approach*, Cambridge, MA.

Thorndike, E.L. (1898). *Animal Intelligence*, New York.

Wallas, G. (1926) *The Art of Thought*, London.

Wertheimer, M. (1945) *Productive Thinking*, New York.

Further reading

Baron, J. (2000) *Thinking and Deciding*, 3rd edn, Cambridge, UK.

Gilhooly, K.J. (1996) *Thinking: Directed, Undirected and Creative*, 3rd edn, London.

SEE ALSO: cognitive neuroscience; cognitive psychology; memory; problem-solving

TOTAL INSTITUTIONS

The term 'total institution' was coined and employed by the sociologist Erving Goffman in reference to the apparently closed social worlds that are constituted by places of residence in which a single authority regulates all aspects of the life of the inmates. Institutions such as prisons, hospitals, boarding schools, old-age homes, monasteries, army barracks and concentration camps had been the subject of research prior to Goffman's analysis, but he was the first to suggest that a range of characteristics was inherent in and common to these establishments.

The common characteristics of total institutions derive from the coercion of inmates to conform to an internal regime. They are stripped of their former identities and obliged to accept an alternative selfhood, designed to fit the expectations of staff. This transformation is effected by procedures and practices including the breakdown of the divisions separating work, sleep and play. All activities are tightly scheduled and geared to serve institutionally set tasks. These can be carried out only by obeying rules and regulations that are sanctioned by privileges and punishments administered by staff whose authority is sustained through the maintenance of a distance from inmates. Inmates respond to the repressive forces embedded in institutional settings by developing adaptive strategies that range from acceptance through withdrawal, taking advantage of the situation, 'playing it cool' and, at the extreme, overt rebellion. The enforced split between the institutional culture, which deprives the inmate of self-expression and autonomy, and the outside culture is often managed by drawing on illicit, unregimented aspects of subjectivity furnished by previous life, or by newly acquired forbidden pastimes.

Five types of total institution are distinguished, depending on the cultural codes of exclusion and inclusion that determine the social category of their inhabitants. The first deals with persons conceived of as both harmless and helpless such as the aged, the disabled, the indigent and the orphaned. The second accommodates those felt to be helpless but who may be unintentionally harmful such as the mental patient and the leper. The third type secludes those, typically prisoners, who are deemed to warrant sequestration because they pose a straightforward and intentional threat. The fourth type deals with the trainee and the employee such as the soldier, the servant and the boarding-school student. Finally, the fifth category houses vocationally designated persons such as monks and nuns. Each institution brands its inmates. 'Mad' for instance is a label reserved for those committed to mental hospitals, 'old' for residents of old people's homes and 'criminal' for prison inmates. Institutional boundaries therefore become symbolic devices by which distinctions are made, positions are allocated and social recognition is awarded or withdrawn. The social categorization of inmates delineates institutional boundaries. These may be physically impenetrable, as in the case of some jails and concentration camps, or just symbolically and diffusely marked, as in the case of holiday retreats and general hospitals.

Other features of total institutions also vary between institutions and even within a single setting. For instance, the degree and extent of coercion wielded may vary over time, as may the differential bargaining positions of inmates and their custodians. However, since the total institution is a hybrid between organization and community, internal hierarchies may grow up, principles of stratification and tracks of mobility may develop, codes of ethics and conduct may become customary, and a local argot may evolve. In this respect the institution could be regarded as a microcosmic order, a small society in its own right. This observation undermines the ideal type constructed by Goffman, of the total institution as a quintessential social frame. If the boundary between the institution and its surroundings is unclear and arguably untenable, and since the division between staff and inmates is blurred, and at times indistinguishable, both the totality and the boundedness of the phenomenon are in doubt.

Goffman presented his model by way of sketchy illustrations while neglecting the enduring interactions that constitute institutional life. He also ignored the political economy, as well as the cultural conditions that produce such settings. Moreover, his approach was particularly relevant to the anti-psychiatric movement, which treated mental illness as a social construct, but this movement is now less influential. Nevertheless, the social context and content of asylum-like enclaves still warrants the attention of social scientists, and interest in them has been revived through the work of scholars such as Foucault, and Deleuze and Guattari. These authors set mental institutions within a wider historical context, particular attention being drawn to the interaction between knowledge systems and forms of power.

By virtue of their very existence, total institutions challenge taken-for-granted cultural assumptions. Their undifferentiated structure goes against the grain of the compartmentalized modern society. There is ample room for further research and reflection into such unsettling settings and their analytic derivatives like the meaning of selfhood in a culture of multiple identities, the possibility of engineering and manufacturing persons, and the planning and execution of projects of dehumanization. Cases of extreme subjugation such as slavery, totalitarianism and colonialism, situations of total commitment such as work or military service, submergence into addiction and suppression by stigma or self-imposed bodily regimes could all be illuminated by comparisons with what happens in total institutions.

HAIM HAZAN
UNIVERSITY OF TEL-AVIV

Further reading

Cohen, S. and Taylor, L. (1972) *Psychological Survival*, Harmondsworth.

Coser, L.A. (1974) *Greedy Institutions*, New York.

Deleuze, G. and Guattari, F. (1987 [1980]) *A Thousand Plateaus: Capitalism and Schizophrenia*, Minneapolis, MN.

Foucault, M. (1965) *Madness and Civilization: A History of Insanity in the Age of Reason*, New York.

Goffman, E. (1961) *Asylums*, New York.

Rothman, D. (1990) *The Discovery of the Asylum: Social Order and Disorder in the New Republic*, Boston.

Sykes, G.M. (1966) *The Society of Captives*, New York.

Wallace, S.F. (ed.) (1971) *Total Institutions*, New Brunswick, NJ.

TRADE UNIONS

More than a century ago, Beatrice and Sidney Webb defined a trade union as 'a continuous association of wage earners for the purpose of maintaining or improving the conditions of their employment' (1894: 1). They emphasized the variety of roles performed by unions: 'mutual insurance'; 'collective bargaining' with employers; and efforts to extend individual and collective rights via 'legal enactment'. Today's unions can still be understood on the one hand as collective organizations that rely on voluntary support by members (for instance in case of a strike), and on the other hand as corporate actors that represent the social, economic and political interests of their members *vis-à-vis* employers and the state.

Radical political theorists hoped that syndicalist worker movements would use direct industrial action to overthrow the capitalist system, while criticizing reformist unions allied to the Social Democratic party for fostering the 'embourgeoisement' of the working class. The Social Democrats themselves believed that the political and social rights of workers would be improved by a combination of electoral politics and collective bargaining. Early reformist social scientists (like the Webbs in the UK or Selig Perlman in the USA) acknowledged the contribution of the 'economism' of British and US unionism. In social science today, economists in the neoclassical tradition concentrate primarily on the impact of wage bargaining on economic performance, and the business cycle effects on union membership. Sociologists, political scientists and social historians analyse the wider role of unions in society and politics. They stress the importance of the institutionalization of class conflict that followed the integration of unions in postwar societies, the participation of trade unions in corporatist policy-making, the collective regulation of labour markets, and the promotion of social rights by organized labour.

Trade unions are collective associations; the membership base shapes their organization, resources and orientation. They are formal organizations with regular membership dues, union statutes for internal democracy, and paid union officials. In pluralist democracies, they are voluntary associations organizing primarily the dependent workforce free of employers' tutelage ('yellow' unionism) and (authoritarian) state control. Since they largely provide 'public goods' (such as wage agreements for all employees in a firm), they face the 'free-rider' problem that non-members do not contribute to collective action but benefit from it (Olson 1965). The practice of 'closed shops' (when organized workers insist that their co-workers join a union) is largely an outdated strategy limited to some industries or occupations. Many unions offer various 'club goods' to members such as mutual insurance, strike pay or legal advice, though these 'selective benefits' will rarely equal an individual's membership dues. In addition, ideological orientation, socialization and cultural factors may foster collectivist orientation conducive to union membership, particularly when unions are embedded in broader social and political movements.

Historically, trade unions together with allied political parties and co-operative self-help associations formed part of the 'labour movement', which promoted the political, social and economic rights of the working class. They demanded universal suffrage for working men and women, association and strike rights, regulation of employment and workplace conditions, and protection against social risks. In early industrializing Britain, the trade unions formed their annual congress (TUC) prior to sponsoring the Labour Party. In many other European countries, the Social Democratic party preceded and shaped the formation of an allied union confederation. In countries with syndicalist traditions, particularly in Southern Europe, unionists were reluctant to affiliate with left political parties, although this changed with the foundation of communist parties in the interwar period. In addition, Christian unionism, based on Catholic teaching of harmonious 'social partnership', emerged as a separate worker movement. During the Cold War, these political divisions were also significant at the international and European level.

There are pronounced cross-national differences in the organization of unions. Historically, craft unions emerged as successors to guilds (e.g. the printers' union), first in Britain and later elsewhere. They organized skilled workers and sought job regulation and control of apprenticeships. Unskilled and semi-skilled workers (e.g. dock and transport workers) were organized by 'general' unions from the late nineteenth century. Industrial unions were formed to organize all workers within a particular sector irrespective of occupational differences. This makes it easier to engage in bargaining with many or all employers in a particular sector, and constrains sectionalist union competition. Industrial unionism has become the dominant principle in most Nordic or continental European union movements, partly as a consequence of the more class-oriented political labour movements (Hyman 2001). White-collar workers had different political leanings and traditional status differences, and formed their separate sectoral unions, professional organizations or staff associations. Recently trade unions in many countries have sought mergers as a result of membership decline, financial problems and loss in bargaining and political power. Large 'conglomerate' unions have spread across sectoral and occupational barriers, often leading to changes in the balance of power within union confederations as these 'super' unions become increasingly influential.

Where they have sufficient membership, local unions may represent the workforce in all dealings with management, as in Anglo-American or Nordic workplaces, but in continental Europe there is often in addition to union representative structures statutory workplace representation ('works councils') with legally circumscribed rights and duties (Rogers and Streeck 1995).

Members are crucial to trade unions. They provide the dues income, non-paid activists and potential strike participants, and it is because they have sufficient members that unions can claim to represent a workforce or to speak for workers' interests more generally. While some sectional craft unions and professional organizations are capable of organizing a large proportion of people employed within a particular trade or occupation, larger general and industrial unions find it difficult to mobilize workers given the 'free-rider' problem. In general, blue-collar industrial workers, employees in the public sector, the full-time employed and men tend to be more organized than white-collar workers in the private sector, those with part-time or temporary employment contracts and women. Most union movements face increasing membership problems given the decline of the industrial workforce, the end of public-sector growth, and more precarious employment conditions.

Comparisons of advanced economies within Europe and across the OECD show considerable cross-national variations in union density (the share of union members in the dependent workforce). It is exceptionally high in most Scandinavian countries (above 80 per cent, except in Norway), thanks largely to the union-led unemployment insurance funds and the firmly institutionalized union involvement in bargaining at national and workplace level. British unions have suffered a substantial decline of membership (from above 50 per cent before 1979 to below 30 per cent in 2000) following legal changes and more confrontational employer strategies. Unionization ranges widely across continental European countries (from around 10 per cent in France to around 60 per cent in Belgium), though nearly all union movements suffer from membership losses (Ebbinghaus and Visser 2000). Union density is even lower in the USA (below 16 per cent since the 1990s) and in Japan (below 25 per cent). With the exception of some Asian and the South African unions, the proportion of organized workers in developing countries declined in the course of the 1990s (ILO 1997), and they often confront obstacles in the way of union organization, despite the right of association conventions of the International Labour Organization.

Of the three primary functions of unions, collective bargaining remains the most important in advanced Western economies. Unions have, however, faced increased difficulties in negotiating collective agreements since the end of the postwar phase of rapid economic growth, and with increased international competition. Where there is a large gap between the wages earned by union members and non-unionized labour (as in the USA and the UK), employers have a strong incentive to evade unions. Trade unions everywhere have had to adapt their organizational structure and pool their resources in order to respond to the progressive decentralization of bargaining. In their role as political lobbyists, unions have been forced on the defensive, concerned to protect the social rights they have won, and aiming to restrict the deregulation of the labour market and cuts in welfare provision (Boeri *et al.* 2001). The traditionally close relations between unions and political parties have loosened as party and unions cope with the new realities of postindustrial societies.

BERNHARD EBBINGHAUS
MAX PLANCK INSTITUTE FOR THE STUDY
OF SOCIETIES, COLOGNE, GERMANY

References

Boeri, T., Brugiavini, A. and Calmfors, L. (eds) (2001) *The Role of Unions in the Twenty-First Century*, Oxford.

Ebbinghaus, B. and Visser, J. (2000) *Trade Unions in Western Europe since 1945*, London.

Hyman, R. (2001) *Understanding European Trade Unionism*, London.

ILO (1997) *World Labour Report 1997–98*, Geneva.

Olson, M. (1965) *The Logic of Collective Action: Public Goods and the Theory of Groups*, Cambridge, MA.

Rogers, J. and Streeck, W. (eds) (1995) *Works Councils*, Chicago.

Webb, S. and Webb, B. (1894) *The History of Trade Unionism*, London.

SEE ALSO: collective bargaining; industrial relations; industrial sociology

TRANSACTION COSTS

Transaction costs represent the cost of the resources (physical as well as human) deployed to complete an exchange of goods and services between parties (individuals and/or organizations), in a way that leaves them satisfied. Such resources are not wasted: if successfully invested in smoothing transactions they keep markets, firms and the economy in general efficient. Costless transactions obtain only in an ideal world. Factors that may contribute to the cost of a transaction in the real world are the search for the 'true' price at which the sale/purchase ought to take place, since prices are never known by the agents in a complete way; discovering the 'true' quality of the good or service (their quality is often not fully known to some of the parties); checking the reputation of the partners in order

to avoid subsequent surprises; carefully crafting the contract that regulates the exchange, so as to avoid later claims; and monitoring its execution so as to pinpoint responsibilities and dues if modifications have to be added to the original contract. Resources have to be devoted both to overcome deficiencies and asymmetries in information and to maintain a reasonable perception of equity among partners who do not necessarily share the same goals or trust each other. Difficulties may arise from the lack of information, or its asymmetric distribution, and, furthermore, strategic or opportunistic behaviour may also drive up the costs of the transaction. For example, one party may be willing to exploit exclusive information about the quality of a good or its value in order to profit from the transaction, and this may lead to litigation if discovered. Hence, the higher the level of trust between the parties the lower the costs of transacting.

The imperfections that may endanger real as opposed to ideal transactions cause friction in the functioning of the economy. However, as in mechanics, friction may also enable movement and change. Institutional economists have pointed out that the failure of the market, due to excessive transaction costs, need not completely impede transactions. The exchange process may simply be transferred to other arrangements, such as the hierarchy or the clan. These 'non-price' institutions internalize market transactions by governing them through long-term, open contracts that create mutual dependence between the parties, improve reciprocal control, curb opportunism and allow for better co-operation. Specifically, one way to avoid costly litigation or disappointments that may endanger the repetition of the exchange over time is for some of the parties to internalize the supplier, that is, to transform the supplier into an internal department, so that the production of the good may be monitored more closely: a hierarchy thus obtains. In any case, costs have to be borne, either because of haggling in a malfunctioning market or through the setting up of administrative controls and the monitoring apparatus of the hierarchy.

The strength of the transaction costs perspective is that it offers a compact set of concepts and a unifying language to analyse and interpret a variety of micro- and macro-phenomena, such as vertical integration between firms; the employment contracts and the internal labour relations;

anti-trust laws and interventions; and even the emergence and failure of economic institutions. More recently, it has also proven to be an effective framework to understand and predict the impacts of information and communication technologies on markets and firms (e-commerce and e-business). Nevertheless, it has two major limitations. First, transaction costs economics is based on a more sophisticated, but still narrow view of the agent as 'economic man', who maximizes utility despite the limits of his or her rationality. Therefore altruistic behaviour, for example, is beyond its scope. Second, the approach presents a static, comparative view of why different economic institutions exist, develop or decay. Transaction costs economics indicates that for a given level of uncertainty and amount of trust between the parties there is usually a limited number of governance structures that are more efficient and will survive in the long run. When circumstances change, efficient governance structure must adapt swiftly, or it will be swept away by competition. The approach is silent, however, on the forces that make certain organizations stickier than others. In sum, transaction costs economics seems to assume an implicit notion of frictionless change. It may, however, be ignoring the widespread role of transition costs in socioeconomic organizations undergoing continuous change.

CLAUDIO CIBORRA
LONDON SCHOOL OF ECONOMICS
AND POLITICAL SCIENCE

Further reading

Ciborra, C.U. (1996) *Teams, Markets and Systems*, Cambridge, UK.
Coase, R., Buckley, P. and Michie, J. (eds) (1996) *Firms, Organizations and Contracts*, Oxford.
Williamson, O.E. (1985) *The Economic Institutions of Capitalism*, New York.

SEE ALSO: corporate enterprise; firm, theory of; institutional economics; markets

TRANSCULTURAL PSYCHIATRY

Transcultural psychiatry emerged at the beginning of the twentieth century when Emil Kraepelin, having defined the entity dementia praecox (his original term), realized that his new categorization would have much greater validity if it could be demonstrated to apply to populations remote in language and culture from his own (German). He set out for Java and examined some psychiatrically ill people there, presumably through an interpreter. He was delighted to find patients whose symptoms matched those in Germany whom he had designated as suffering from dementia praecox, a term later replaced by 'schizophrenia'. The pattern he established, of Western psychiatrists visiting 'exotic' cultures and seeking for similarities and differences between local conditions and those familiar in the West, dominated the early decades of transcultural psychiatry. The pioneers failed to appreciate their ethnocentric approach to other cultures and their efforts later earned the opprobrious label of colonial psychiatry. One of the most notorious examples is Carothers's treatise on the African mind, in which he wrote that Africans could not experience depression because they had smaller brains than Europeans.

The search for conditions that appeared to be peculiar to one cultural group became analogous to a hunt for rare butterflies. The specimens captured became known as 'culture-bound psychoses', and include *amok*, *koro* and *latah*, all of which are virtually confined to Southeast Asia, although sporadic reports have appeared in the West. Amok, as suggested by its colloquial use in English, is an indiscriminate murderous attack on innocent bystanders by a man who has been brooding on a real or imagined insult. Koro, which can occur in an epidemic form, is a panic state sparked by the belief that the genitals are disappearing into the person's abdomen and that death will ensue. It can rarely affect women, but is mostly seen in men. Latah is confined to women and is a state in which the person shouts out sexual and scatological expletives on being startled, and can be induced to imitate another's gestures. The use of the generic term 'culture-bound psychoses' for these conditions was clearly a misnomer, because the beliefs that underlay the behaviour were shared with the sufferer's cultural group and hence disqualified as delusions. Furthermore the occurrence of these conditions among native Westerners, albeit rare, casts doubt on their cultural specificity.

Their recognition provoked a debate between universalists, who claimed they were familiar Western conditions thinly disguised by local beliefs, and relativists, who asserted they were genuine cultural products. Yap (1965), for example, viewed koro as equivalent to depersonalization syndromes in Western patients. A parallel was drawn between amok and the French legal concept of *crime passionnel* (Leff 1988), while Simons (1980) viewed latah as one manifestation of a universal startle reflex. With the development of postmodernism and the concept of ethnocentrism, the awareness dawned that there were psychiatric conditions common in the West that were unknown or very rare in developing countries. The best-known example is eating disorders, anorexia nervosa and bulimia being rarely reported outside Western countries. The explanation put forward for this difference in distribution rests on the pervasive advertising propaganda, devoted to persuading women to emulate slim models and to cut down on their calorie intake. It is obvious that health farms and calorie-free food are obscene luxuries in countries where millions are living below the subsistence level.

During the 1970s it became evident that the process of making a psychiatric diagnosis was strongly influenced by the culture of the psychiatrist. Comparison of the diagnostic practices of psychiatrists in different countries in two key studies revealed major differences in the rules used to diagnose schizophrenia (Cooper *et al.* 1972; World Health Organization (WHO) 1973). This was achieved by training the psychiatrists involved to assess patients' symptoms with a semi-structured interview until they became highly reliable. The interview employed was the Present State Examination (PSE) (Wing *et al.* 1974), which was developed in English and then translated into eight other languages for the WHO study. The interview is informed by a phenomenological approach leading to a clear definition of each symptom to be rated, the definitions constituting a glossary to which raters can refer if they are in doubt. The technique of interviewing is to cross-question the patient about the nature of their experience until the rater is sure that the criteria for a symptom have been satisfied, or else that the patient's experience can be disregarded as not pathological. This approach has drawn fire from critics who object that since the interview was developed in Western cultures it inevitably excludes the experiences of people in non-Western cultures whose emotional and psychiatric disorders may manifest in ways not detected by the PSE.

In an influential article, Kleinman (1977) attacked the assumption that Western diagnostic categories were culture-free, and announced the dawn of the 'new cross-cultural psychiatry'. He argued that the depressive syndrome is 'a cultural category constructed by psychiatrists in the West to yield a homogeneous group of patients. By definition, it excludes most depressive phenomena, even in the West, because they fall outside its narrow boundaries.' A useful analogy is a chip machine, which works by forcing potatoes through a standard grid. Whatever shape the potatoes are, they all emerge as identical chips. There is an alternative to the chip machine that was pioneered by Beiser and colleagues (1972) in studying the Serer of Senegal. Instead of starting from a Western view of psychopathology, they enquired from key people, such as village headmen and traditional healers, in the society, whom they considered to be mentally disturbed. They then asked for descriptions of the individual's behaviour and the terms used for any disturbance. They found that there was a general category for illnesses of the spirit. In fact most of these could be equated with Western diagnostic classes, but there was one form of behaviour that had no obvious Western equivalent. This was earth-eating, which was considered by the Serer to be normal among children and pregnant women, but was taken to be a sign of mental disturbance if exhibited by other age and gender groups. It is clear that this would not have been detected by the PSE. Regrettably, few, if any, other researchers have replicated Beiser's approach.

The process of translating the PSE exposed complex issues stemming from culture and language. The standard procedure for checking the accuracy of a translation is known as back-translation. The text in language A is translated into language B, which is then translated back into language A by a second independent translator. Comparison between the two versions in A should reveal glitches in the translation. However, this is not foolproof, because the meaning of words can be strongly dependent on context. An example derives from the translation of the PSE into Xhosa, in which the term for emotion was translated as *inimba*. The back-translation revealed no problem, but when the Xhosa version was used it was discovered that the word *inimba* is confined to the experience of women (Swartz *et al.* 1985).

Other difficulties that emerged were that some of the languages in the WHO study seemed to lack equivalent words for English expressions. For example, the terms depression and anxiety could not be represented by a single word in Yoruba, a Nigerian language. The phrases employed for these key psychiatric terms back-translated respectively as 'the heart is weak' and 'the heart is not at rest'. This focus on the heart as the seat of emotions is widespread among the world's languages, but it is not easy to determine whether these phrases have the status of metaphors, for example the English phrase 'my heart was in my mouth', or whether they evoke the bodily experience more directly. The way in which language may shape the expression of emotional distress is at the centre of a debate about the prevalence of 'somatization' in developing countries, which has been claimed to be much more frequent than in the West.

A study under the auspices of the WHO examined the proportion of attenders at primary care facilities who presented with identifiable psychiatric illness. The proportions varied from 53 per cent in Santiago de Chile and 36 per cent in Rio de Janeiro to only 7 per cent in Shanghai and 6 per cent in Ibadan, Nigeria. A likely explanation for this dramatic variation is the presentation of distress through bodily complaints in the Chinese and Nigerian patients. There is anthropological evidence that traditional healers, who are consulted by many people in developing countries with somatic complaints of emotional origin, are adept at understanding the relationship problems that provoke them. Difficulties arise when Western-trained psychiatrists are confronted with such symptoms since they are insufficiently versed in the clients' culture to make the necessary links with sources of interpersonal stress.

Kleinman's studies in China encouraged a growth of interest in folk beliefs about the origins of psychiatric illnesses, and the conceptual distance between these and biomedical formulations. The development of urban anthropology during a similar period focused interest on Western peoples in industrial urban settings rather than tribal societies remote from the West. Helman (1978) explored the folk beliefs of white city-dwellers in Britain, a hitherto neglected topic. Both Kleinman and Helman are trained in anthropology as well as medicine, and collaboration between practitioners of these two disciplines is currently opening up fruitful areas of research in psychiatry. For example, study of the health beliefs of African Caribbeans in Britain is shedding light on their excessive rate of compulsory admission to psychiatric units.

The upheavals of world wars and civil wars in recent times and the relative ease of international travel have led to an unprecedented mass movement of peoples across the globe. Transcultural psychiatry can now be pursued at home rather than abroad by comparing migrant populations with indigenous people. As time passes, a second generation is born to the migrants and, growing up in the dominant culture, this provides opportunities to study the processes of change in both cultures as a result of their contact. This area of study is likely to generate new insights in the future, not only into 'the other' but also into ourselves as we gain awareness of our own culture that surrounds us, as imperceptible as the air we breathe.

JULIAN LEFF
INSTITUTE OF PSYCHIATRY,
KING'S COLLEGE, LONDON

References

Beiser, M., Ravel, J.-L., Collomb, H. and Engelhoff, C. (1972) 'Assessing psychiatric disorder among the Serer of Senegal', *Journal of Nervous and Mental Diseases* 154: 141–51.

Cooper, J.E., Kendell, R.E., Gurland, B.J., Sharpe, L., Copeland, J.R.M. and Simon, R. (1972) *Psychiatric Diagnostic in New York and London*, London.

Helman, C.G. (1978) '"Feed a cold; starve a fever"' – Folk models of infection in an English suburban community, and their relation to medical treatment', *Culture, Medicine and Psychiatry* 2: 107–37.

Kleinman, A. (1977) 'Depression, somatization and the new cross-cultural psychiatry', *Social Science and Medicine* 11: 3–10.

Leff, J. (1988) *Psychiatry around the Globe*, 2nd edn, London.

Simons, R.C. (1980) 'The resolution of the Latah paradox', *Journal of Nervous and Mental Diseases* 168: 195–206.

Swartz, L., Ben-Arie, O. and Teggin, A.F. (1985) 'Subcultural delusions and hallucinations: Comments on the Present State Examination in a multi-cultural context', *British Journal of Psychiatry* 146: 391–4.

Wing, J.K., Cooper, J.E. and Sartorius, N. (1974) *The Measurement and Classification of Psychiatric Symptoms*, London.

World Health Organization (1973) *The International Pilot Study of Schizophrenia*, Vol. 1, Geneva.

Yap, P.M. (1965) 'Koro – A culture-bound depersonalisation syndrome', *British Journal of Psychiatry* 111: 43–50.

SEE ALSO: cross-cultural psychology; DSM-IV; medical anthropology; mental health; psychological anthropology

TRIBE

Victorian scholars used the term 'tribe' as part of their attempt to construct a science of so-called 'primitive' societies. They laboured to identify core features of the array of indigenous societies in areas such as Africa, the Americas and Melanesia. The term 'tribe' was initially applied very generally to major social groups, but it was soon apparent that there was considerable diversity, and efforts were devoted to deciding which groups should properly be called tribes, and what their defining characteristics were. The term passed into common usage and persisted in anthropology for many years (as late as the 1960s in some cases, e.g. Lewis 1968), but it fell increasingly into disuse when it became apparent that the groups described as tribes had little in common. Moreover, intellectuals in decolonizing states argued that Western scholars, particularly anthropologists, had colluded in the colonial invention of the tribe in order to divide people and hinder nation-building.

In the 1970s many anthropologists embarked on a reflexive exercise to discover why the notion of tribe had exercised such a hold on the discipline and, indeed, on the Western imagination. Part of the answer, they decided, lay in nineteenth-century fascination with ideas of social evolution. Armchair ethnographers had not been careful empiricists, but had constructed images of primitive society through a priori inversion of supposed traits of their own society, and had then selected evidence to prove this vision.

Early ethnographers had argued that recruitment to significant groups in industrial society turned on criteria of achievement, contract and choice. They speculated that 'primitive' groups were recruited by ascription, on the basis of status. Evidence that kinship played some part in constituting these groups led them to conclude that tribes were ascriptive groups based solely on kinship. This was patently untrue, but it allowed Westerners to believe that primitive and civilized worlds were fundamentally different, and that the latter had evolved superior forms of social existence.

From the reflexive vantage of the 1970s, 'tribe' was part of an intellectual process that had imposed 'otherness' (difference *and* inferiority) on people in certain parts of the world. Imposing otherness had also been a practical process. Imbued with nineteenth-century notions of tribe, administrators had imposed tribal identities on people throughout the colonial world. It was convenient to believe that these constructions denoted natural groups that had existed since time immemorial. It was argued in the 1970s that early twentieth-century ethnography had not seriously challenged these assumptions, because its ostensibly neutral research was integral to the colonial enterprise, and to the way the West used its image of 'the Rest' to justify inequality and exploitation. A new generation of scholars now proclaimed that tribes had never existed, except in the minds of observers. This reaction, however, went too far, and was insulting to the people whose plight it sought to explain. It implied that they had passively allowed tribe, and related paraphernalia of otherness, to be imposed.

In the 1980s, scholars from various disciplines sought more nuanced analysis of the practical ways the idea of tribe was imposed by diverse agents of colonialism. This allowed exploration of how colonized people responded – by adapting new ideas and practices to old ways, transforming them while adopting them, and subverting them to their own ends. In the Comaroffs' (1991) phrase, attention was given to both the 'colonization of consciousness' and the 'consciousness of colonization'.

Recent research has revealed who led responses of adaptation, transformation and subversion, and why others followed. In doing so it has also uncovered the ambiguity of tribe. Tribe involved ideas that were new in much of the world – primordiality, ascription and absolute boundaries. But, once adopted, these ideas could not be contained at one level of society. This mode of thinking informed new perceptions of smaller and larger groups, and was used to construct images of ethnic groups and nations, and to separate difference from inferiority. People were enabled to claim, and redeem, their otherness in various contexts. Tribe was one key to a Pandora's box of claims about identities.

The repercussions are still evident, and gain significance in a postindustrial world where narratives of progress and social mobility turn sour. There is now a widespread tendency to emphasize identities and groups for which people qualify by ascription rather than achievement. Belonging to such a group is a way to assert dignity and to compete for resources in national global contexts. Tribe is only one label that may be used, and in Africa it is likely, for historical reasons, that cognate terms such as ethnic group, nation and race will be preferred. But as Maffesoli (1996 [1988]) showed recently, in part by questioning the extent to which significant social groups in industrial society have ever been based solely on achievement and contract, it would be foolhardy to proclaim the idiom of tribe dead.

JOHN SHARP
UNIVERSITY OF PRETORIA, SOUTH AFRICA

References

Comaroff, J. and Comaroff, J. (1991) *Of Revelation and Revolution: Christianity, Colonialism and Consciousness in South Africa*, Chicago.
Lewis, I.M. (1968) 'Tribal society', in D. Sills (ed.) *International Encyclopedia of the Social Sciences*, New York.
Maffesoli, M. (1996 [1988]) *The Time of the Tribes: The Decline of Individualism in Mass Society*, London.

SEE ALSO: primitive society; state, origins of

U

UNCONSCIOUS

Perhaps the single most important idea in Freud's theory is that human beings are influenced by ideas, feelings, tendencies and ways of thinking of which they are not conscious. Freud's original topography of the mind had three divisions: the conscious, the preconscious and the unconscious. His theory can be pictured as follows: the mind is like a darkened theatre, with a single spotlight to illuminate the actors on the stage. Consciousness is equivalent to the actor in the spotlight at any moment. All of the other actors who can be illuminated as the spotlight moves across the stage are equivalent to the preconscious. To complete Freud's picture we must imagine that there are many actors who are off-stage, in the unconscious. Unless they make the transition to the stage, the light of consciousness cannot illuminate them. Seen or unseen, on-stage or off, all the actors take part in the play of psychic life. The barrier between off-stage and on-stage is removed or weakened in dreams, and by free association, which is the basic technique of psychoanalysis.

Freud understood the unconscious as dynamic. Unconscious impulses were thought to be constantly active, influencing the preconscious and conscious – sometimes in discernible ways. Freud's explanation for slips of the tongue (now commonly called Freudian errors) is the substitution of an unconscious thought for what was consciously intended. By considering these unconscious influences, Freud found meaning in what others saw as trivial mistakes – for example when a man calls his wife by his mother's name. Freud's theory of humour is similarly based on the dynamic interaction between conscious and unconscious. The joke allows the pleasurable release of some repressed idea or feeling; aggressive sexual jokes are thus a classic example.

Freud's theory of the unconscious became more complex in the course of his writings. At first he assumed that everything that was unconscious had once been conscious and had been repressed. The paradigmatic example was the subject who under hypnosis could be given some posthypnotic suggestion, such as to open an umbrella indoors, but told to *forget* that he had been given that instruction. When the trance was ended, the subject would comply with the suggestions and open the umbrella indoors, but be unable to explain why he had done such a silly thing. Thus his behaviour was influenced by an idea about which he had no conscious awareness. Freud believed that his patients, like hypnotic subjects, were capable of splitting off from consciousness certain ideas and feelings by a defensive process he called repression. These repressed unconscious ideas could influence the patient's behaviour, producing neurotic symptoms without his awareness.

Freud's clinical work demonstrated that the most significant repressed ideas led back to childhood experiences. The content of the unconscious seemed to be ideas and tendencies, mainly sexual and aggressive – which he thought of as instinctual and biological – which were repressed under the moral influence of the environment. But the repressed remained active in the unconscious and continued in dynamic interaction with the conscious. Thus Freud's conception of the unconscious emphasized the continuing and irrational influence of the past on the present.

The idea of the splitting of consciousness was not original to Freud, nor was that of an instinctive unconscious. These ideas in some form go back at least as far as Plato. The German philosophers of the nineteenth century, Schopenhauer and Nietzsche, had a view of human nature that, in many ways, anticipated Freud. Freud's theory of the unconscious nonetheless met with intense philosophical criticism, even ridicule. The idea that what was mental was not identical with consciousness and that the mental might be a mystery to consciousness was problematic for certain philosophical notions. Descartes had said, 'I think therefore I exist.' He used this introspective claim as the basis of a theory of knowledge. Freud's concept of the unconscious challenged the certitude of all such introspective claims about the certainty of self-knowledge. The idea of unconscious influences also called into question the notion of free will. Perhaps because Freud emphasized the sexual aspects of the unconscious, his views were easy for philosophers to ridicule. The philosopher Sartre, who was in many ways more sympathetic than most contemporary philosophers to Freud's emphasis on the importance of sex, still found it necessary to reject Freud's fundamental concept of the unconscious. He interpreted repression as self-deception; asserting that it is impossible to lie to oneself, he described repression as bad faith.

Freud's concept of the unconscious derived from his study of dreaming. He viewed the unconscious (associated with the infantile, the primitive and the instinctual) as striving towards immediate discharge of tension. Dreaming and unconscious thinking are described as primary process thought, that is, they are unreflective, concrete, symbolic, egocentric, associative, timeless, visual, physiognomic and animistic, with memory organized about the imperative drive, in which wishes are equivalent to deeds and there is a radical departure from norms of logic – for example contradictory ideas exist side by side. Primary process thought is contrasted with the modulated and adaptive discharge of tension in secondary process. By contrast, conscious thinking is reflective or directed, abstract, specific and particular, situation oriented, logical, chronological, auditory, verbal and explanatory. Memory is organized around the conscious focus of attention; thought and actions are clearly distinguished; thinking is rational and logically oriented. Freud's view was that although the child advances from primary process to secondary process thinking, primary process does not disappear, but remains active in the unconscious. It can be revealed in dreams, in psychotic thinking and in other regressed mental states. Preconscious thinking was characterized as intermediate between these two types. The distinction between primary and secondary process is a key development in Lacan's linguistic reinterpretation of Freud.

Carl Jung, probably the greatest figure in psychoanalysis next to Freud, was an early advocate of what he called the collective unconscious. He assumed that in addition to repressed content, there was an inherited component to the unconscious shared by the human race. He based this conception on the evidence that certain symbols and complexes endlessly recur in the history of civilization. The Oedipus myth of the Greeks is the Oedipal dream of modern times. Freud and Jung took these ideas quite literally, believing that the individual was born not only with instinctual tendencies, but also with inherited complexes and symbols – for example the serpent as a phallic symbol. Despite his eventual break with Jung, Freud maintained his own version of a collective unconscious, which also included the idea that certain moral concepts such as taboos had been inherited.

Freud subsequently reconceptualized his ideas about the unconscious in terms of the ego, the superego and the id. The id and the unconscious are now often used interchangeably in the psychiatric and psychoanalytic literature. While the theory of the unconscious remains controversial even now, the intuition that consciousness does not fully grasp the deeper mystery of our mental life continues to play an important role in twentieth-century thought.

ALAN A. STONE
HARVARD UNIVERSITY

Further reading

Ellenberger, H.F. (1970) *The Discovery of the Unconscious: The History and Evolution of Dynamic Psychiatry*, New York.
Freud, S. (1953 [1900]) *The Interpretation of Dreams, Standard Edition of the Complete Psychological Works of Sigmund Freud*, ed. J. Strachey, Vol. 4, London.

SEE ALSO: dreams; Freud; Lacan; psychoanalysis

UNDERDEVELOPMENT

Although it is possible to trace ideas about underdevelopment back through history to the masterworks of antiquity, the modern sense of the term can be dated to 1949, when the US President, Harry Truman, inaugurated his Point Four Program. One feature of this Program was the provision of assistance for the transfer of scientific and industrial knowledge to impoverished nations. With the onset of the Cold War, and decolonization, there was pressure to think more systematically about the problems of these nations. The initial response took the form of modernization theory. Essentially, modernization theory posits a duality between tradition and modernity, and explains that a failure to make the leap to modernity is due to an incapacity ingrained in traditional cultures. The path towards economic take-off demands the achievement of high levels of civic participation, national integration, specialization and differentiation of roles, empathy extending beyond the family to fellow citizens, and an emphasis on individual achievement rather than status based on ascription.

According to Marxists and other critical scholars, it is wrong to give the impression that underdevelopment is a condition akin to original sin, or a fate due to chance or bad luck. In *How Europe Underdeveloped Africa* (1984), Walter Rodney stressed the causal links between the condition of underdeveloped countries and the policies of mature capitalist countries. These links are, of course, deeply rooted, going back to slavery, plunder and forced trade. According to Rodney, the transfer of resources to the metropolis fuelled capital accumulation in the advanced countries and underdeveloped the South.

On the basis of these early theoretical contributions, it becomes possible to establish a general definition. Underdevelopment refers to the blockages that forestall a rational transformation of the social structure in poor countries. What is meant by rationality in this context is that the interests and needs of the majority are increasingly dominant. And what blocks development is a constellation of internal and external power and privilege.

The blockage is multifaceted, having both subjective and objective dimensions. The subjective side of underdevelopment is expressed in terms of fatalism and defeatism, a deep frustration often conjoined to uncertainty and expressed as a reliance on faith, the expectation that nothing of significance is willed except by God. For some observers, such as V.S. Naipaul, this fatalism betrays the deficiency of reason, and is itself a cause of lack of progress (Naipaul 1979). In stark contrast is the romantic vision of Frantz Fanon, a West Indian psychiatrist turned revolutionary. Fanon understood racism as an ideological weapon accompanying domination. Decolonization is an inherently violent phenomenon. The nation is consecrated in blood, and the flame of violence purifies the creative power of revolution. Far from celebrating violence as an end, however, Fanon looked to its transcendence by a new and higher social order. His enduring legacy lies in the emphasis that he gave to the psychocultural dimensions of development, and the decolonization of the imagination (Fanon 1968 [1961]).

The objective dimensions of underdevelopment are its agents and structures. Modernization theorists believe that nation-states enjoy a great deal of autonomy, and stress the scope of leaders as well as the roles that bilateral and multilateral agencies can play in assisting them. From a different perspective, the dependency school, which originated in Latin America in the 1950s and 1960s, drew attention to features of the global economy that disadvantage the underdeveloped countries. In particular, the work of the United Nations Economic Commission for Latin America, under its first secretary general, Raúl Prebisch, highlighted the unequal terms of trade between the exporters of raw materials and the exporters of manufactured goods, which resulted in chronic balance of payments problems. Other intellectuals in Latin America, including the sociologist Fernando Henrqiue Cardoso (later president of Brazil), showed that peripheral economies face enormous obstacles in altering the basic features of production because some powerful groups in the society benefit from their ties to the centre of the global economy (Cardoso and Faletto 1979).

The economist Clive Thomas (1974) contended that due to their external linkages, underdeveloped countries produce what they do not consume and consume what they do not produce, so remaining entrenched in their subordinate positions. Marxists such as Samir Amin (1997) maintained that market imbalances are not the root of the problem of underdevelopment. The primary issue is unfolding social relations in the production system, central to the dynamics of capital accumulation. The focus thus shifted from relations between nations, as in the sphere of trade, to class conflict. Both dependency thinkers and Marxists called for a basic realignment but of a different sort, the one at the level of exchange, the other in terms of production relations. Yet they agreed that it is a matter of fundamental importance which groups control state power and how they manage it. It is not sufficient to call for a transformation in productive forces or in the social relations of production without taking political will into account.

Amartya Sen, the 1998 Nobel Laureate in economics, regards the expansion of choice as the major issue in development. He calls for eliminating 'unfreedoms' that pervade the political, economic and social spheres and that obstruct development. Ultimately, enhancing freedom is connected to the establishment of a democratic process (Sen 1999).

The real choices for underdeveloped countries in the global political economy are constrained. Most countries have opened up their markets to the global economy. A small number tried to disengage from it (for example China under Mao, Tanzania under Nyerere, and North Korea), but the strategy had dire consequences and it has been abandoned everywhere except North Korea. Dramatic changes in the global political economy portend both new opportunities and barriers for overcoming underdevelopment. With the rise of neo-liberalism (a set of ideas centring on heightened integration with the global economy and a policy framework of deregulation, liberalization and privatization), most underdeveloped countries have increasingly opened up to global capital and international institutions. Philip McMichael (2000) contends that globalizing processes have supplanted the development project. Some observers argue that these processes severely limit policy choices, and that in consequence the prospects for national development are dismal.

In sum, underdevelopment is a multilayered process culminating in the stifling of human creativity, skill and self-confidence. While underdevelopment is embedded in different historical and cultural contexts, the key question today is whether freedom from want and need can be achieved by national units or whether the scale must be enlarged to the regional or global levels.

JAMES H. MITTELMAN
AMERICAN UNIVERSITY, WASHINGTON, DC

References

Amin, S. (1997) *Capitalism in the Age of Globalization: The Management of Contemporary Society*, Atlantic Highlands, NJ.

Cardoso, F.H. and Faletto, E. (1979) *Dependency and Development in Latin America*, Berkeley, CA.

Fanon, F. (1968 [1961]) *The Wretched of the Earth*, New York.

McMichael, P. (2000) *Development and Social Change: A Global Perspective*, Thousand Oaks, CA.

Naipaul, V.S. (1979) *A Bend in the River*, New York.

Rodney, W. (1984) *How Europe Underdeveloped Africa*, Washington, DC.

Sen, A.K. (1999) *Development as Freedom*, New York.

Thomas, C.Y. (1974) *Dependence and Transformation: The Economics of the Transition to Socialism*, New York.

Further reading

Hettne, B. (1995) *Development Theory and the Three Worlds: Towards an International Political Economy of Development*, Essex, UK, and New York.

Mittelman, J.H. and Pasha, M.K. (1997) *Out from Underdevelopment: Changing Global Structures and the Remaking of the Third World*, Houndsmill, Basingstoke, UK, and New York.

SEE ALSO: modernization; reason, rationality and rationalism; world-system analysis

UTILITARIANISM

Utilitarianism is the doctrine that decisions should promote good consequences. It is a normative theory, meant to guide conduct and to serve as the basis of sound evaluations. It does not assume that actual decisions or judgements always satisfy that standard.

Like other important philosophical ideas, utilitarianism has many variations. The founders of modern utilitarianism, Bentham (1789) and J.S. Mill (1861), assumed that good consequences are, at bottom, desirable conditions of individuals (perhaps including animals other than humans). Bentham's hedonistic utilitarianism called for the promotion of pleasure and the prevention of pain. Mill, who distinguished higher and lower pleasures, seems to have held that human good consists in the free development of individuals' distinctive, and distinctively human, capacities. Ideal utilitarians believe that what is most fundamentally of value can include such things as beauty, which need not be defined in terms of human good or conscious states.

Utilitarianism in its various forms can be understood to combine a theory of intrinsic value with some notion of how stringently and directly it should be served, for example whether good consequences must be maximized or need only be promoted to a lesser degree, and whether each and every decision should be so regulated ('act' utilitarianism) or rather that acts should conform to useful patterns ('rule' utilitarianism).

Utilitarians often claim as a virtue of their theory that it bases evaluations on ascertainable facts, such as how much pleasure and pain would result from alternative courses of action. But the calculations require interpersonal comparisons of utility, of which many are sceptical. This has led some theorists to develop normative standards in terms of less demanding notions of efficiency, as in welfare economics.

Utilitarians have generally favoured social reforms (because, for example, income transfers from rich to poor are supposed to promote welfare overall), and they have championed political rights and personal liberty (because, for example, paternalistic interference is supposed to be counter-productive). Critics charge, however, that utilitarianism lacks principled commitment to all such values: it cares only how much good is produced, but not about equitable distribution, respect for personal desert, or the security of freedom and individual integrity.

Most generally, critics charge that utilitarianism distorts sound moral judgement: to promise to do something, for example, is deliberately to place oneself under an obligation, the demands of which (it is argued) are greater and more specifically directed than utilitarianism allows. They claim that utilitarianism fails to take obligations (or for that matter rights) seriously.

Utilitarianism nevertheless remains a widely accepted theory of central importance, though its status – like that of any normative principle – is uncertain. The idea that principles merely express more or less arbitrary attitudes seems largely based upon an exaggerated contrast between ethics and science, which suffers from overly simple conceptions of empirical knowledge and discovery. Developments in the theory of reference and justification, along with the decline of logical positivism, have revived interest in moral realism (or cognitivism) and in the possibility of rationally defending either utilitarianism or some competing doctrine.

DAVID LYONS
BOSTON UNIVERSITY

References

Bentham, J. (1789) *An Introduction to the Principles of Morals and Legislation*, London.
Mill, J.S. (1861) *Utilitarianism*, London.

Further reading

Brandt, R.B. (1979) *A Theory of the Good and the Right*, Oxford.
Hare, R.M. (1963) *Freedom and Reason*, Oxford.
Lyons, D. (1965) *Forms and Limits of Utilitarianism*, Oxford.
Parfit, D. (1984) *Reasons and Persons*, Oxford.
Sidgwick, H. (1874) *The Methods of Ethics*, London.
Smart, A. and Williams, B. (1973) *Utilitarianism: For and Against*, Cambridge, UK.

SEE ALSO: Bentham; Mill

UTOPIANISM

Utopianism is a form of social theory that attempts to promote certain desired values and practices by presenting them in an ideal state or society. Utopian writers do not normally think of such states as realizable, at least in anything like their perfectly portrayed form. But nor are they engaging in a merely fanciful or fantastic exercise, as the popular use of the term suggests. Often, as in Plato's *Republic*, the first true Utopia, the aim is to show something of the essential nature of a concept – justice or freedom – by painting it large, in the form of an ideal community based on such a concept. At other times, as with Sir Thomas More's *Utopia* (1516), the object is primarily critical or satirical, to scourge the vices of the writer's society by an artful contrast with the virtuous people of Utopia. Only rarely – Edward Bellamy's *Looking Backward* (1888) is a good example – do Utopian writers seek to transform society according to the blueprint painstakingly drawn in their Utopia. Essentially the function of Utopias is heuristic.

Until the seventeenth century, Utopias were generally located in geographically remote areas of the globe. The European voyages of discovery of the sixteenth and seventeenth centuries killed off this useful device by making the world too familiar. From then on Utopias were spatially displaced: to outer space – journeys to the moon begin in the seventeenth century – or beneath the sea, as in the frequent discovery of the sunken civilization of Atlantis, or deep below the earth's crust. But increasingly too the displacement was temporal rather than spatial, a move encouraged first by the seventeenth-century idea of progress and later by the vastly expanded notion of time offered by the new geology and biology of Lyell and Darwin. Instead of Utopia being the better place, it became the better time. H.G. Wells took his Time-Traveller billions of years into the future, and Olaf Stapledon in *Last and First Men* (1930) employed a timescale of 2,000 million years to show the ascent of humans to full Utopian stature.

The displacement of space by time also produced a new sociological realism in Utopias. Utopias were now placed in history and, however distant the Utopian consummation, it could at least be presented as something that humankind was tending towards, perhaps inevitably. The link with science and technology in the seventeenth century – as in Bacon's *New Atlantis* (1627) and Campanella's *City of the Sun* (1637) – strengthened this development. With the rise of nineteenth-century socialism, itself heavily Utopian, Utopianism became increasingly a debate about the possible realization of socialism. The Utopias of Bellamy and Wells (*A Modern Utopia*, 1905) were the most powerful pleas on behalf of orthodox socialism, but William Morris offered an attractive alternative version in *News from Nowhere* (1890). An alternative of a different kind came with the invention of the dystopia or anti-Utopia, an inversion and a savage critique of all Utopian hopes. Foreshadowed in Samuel Butler's anti-Darwinian *Erewhon* (1872), it reached its apogee in the 1930s and 1940s, especially with Aldous Huxley's *Brave New World* (1932) and George Orwell's *Nineteen Eighty-Four* (1949). Only B.F. Skinner's *Walden Two* (1948) kept the Utopian torch alight in these dark years, and there were many who saw in this Utopia of behavioural engineering a nightmare worse than the blackest dystopia. Utopianism, however, revived strongly in the 1960s, in such works as Herbert Marcuse's *An Essay on Liberation* (1969), and is to be found alive and flourishing in the futurological and ecological movements.

Perhaps Utopianism is inherent in the human condition, perhaps only in those cultures affected by the classical and Christian traditions, but one might well agree with Oscar Wilde that 'a map of the world that does not include Utopia is not worth even glancing at'.

KRISHAN KUMAR
UNIVERSITY OF VIRGINIA

Further reading

Kumar, K. (1987) *Utopia and Anti-Utopia in Modern Times*, Oxford.
Schaer, R., Claeys, G. and Sargent, L.T. (eds) (2000) *Utopia: The Search for the Ideal Society in the West*, New York.

SEE ALSO: futurology

V

VIOLENCE

Violence entails inflicting emotional, psychological, sexual, physical and/or material damage. It involves the exercise of force or constraint perpetrated by individuals, on their own behalf or for a collective or state-sanctioned purpose. Research on violence includes its definition, its psychological impact, its origins, its collective expressions, its cultural meanings and its relevance to law.

Definitions of violence range widely. We usually associate violence and its use with individually motivated action, although a great deal of violence is committed by individuals on behalf of others. The violence of institutions, such as within prison, or that of state-sanctioned agencies, such as the use of deadly force by police, are examples of the use of violence by the state for the constraint of its citizens. Too few definitions characterize negligent or reckless driving, or negligent deaths at work as violence, yet these actions may involve intentional disregard for the safety of others. The violence arising from war or actions of civil insurgency has dramatic impacts on the psychological and physical well-being of countless people.

Developing and developed countries often cite the lower incidence of violence as a barometer of democracy and freedom. Yet countries, such as Bosnia, previously characterized as peaceful, sometimes erupt into brutality and violence. Nationalism, cultural intolerance and fundamentalism continue to fuel political conflicts and violence. Questions linger about collective violence: under what conditions does violence serve as an agent of control or an agent of resistance to particular sets of beliefs?

Criminal violence, and the fear of it, has a particular niche within discourses of and about civility, especially within countries largely considered peaceable. Violence in such places is considered to be the actions of errant or unsocialized individuals. At the same time, such jurisdictions are characterized as safe, although research suggests that there is a great deal of violence – defined by individual acts of threat and assault – which occur in so-called peaceable societies. Physical and sexual assault of girls and women, for example, are commonplace in many societies.

In 'developed' countries, people themselves largely manage violence on their own. In effect, most violence is decriminalized, either because recipients fail to report it to authorities, such as the police, in the first place, or because they refuse to co-operate with the justice system when they or others do report. The context within which violence occurs influences how individuals define and respond to violence. Crime surveys consistently show that incidents of violence are reported far less frequently than other forms of crime. Truer data about the incidence of violence can be found in crime surveys rather than police statistics, which suggests that violent crime constitutes approximately 6 per cent of all reported serious crime.

Gender-specific differences in the nature and rate of violence and victimization are especially important in understanding violence. Generally speaking, men are the overwhelming perpetrators and recipients of violence, and are as likely to be assaulted and killed by acquaintances as they are by strangers. Women encounter physical and sexual violence most often in and around their own homes, and their assailants are typically intimates, former intimates and other acquaintances. However, both women and men cite stranger violence as that which they fear the most. Research consistently shows that the fear of violence restricts women's lives much more than men's, and that women report higher levels of fear of violence than do men, despite the much higher official statistics indicating men's experiences of violence.

Whether physical or psychological, the harm felt by the recipient of violence varies, as does the long-term impact on his or her everyday life. A recent experience of violence, or its threat, may have significant effects, altering an individual's routines and personal lifestyle or it may have little noticeable influence on daily life. Studies of posttraumatic stress disorder, for instance, often explore the impact of violence upon individuals' lives.

Typically, in law and in popular culture, the focus for explaining violence is on the behaviour of specific, criminally defined offenders. Debates continue about how to account for the violence of individuals. Biological explanations suggest that violence is rooted in hormonal imbalances, low intelligence or brain injury. Psychology provides another route to interpretations of acts of violence. Low self-esteem, feelings of inadequacy and depression are found among the explanations given for those who commit violence. Evolutionary psychology, too, provides a framework for explaining violence, suggesting that competition, status and control over reproductivity provide men with strong legacies within which contemporary, individually committed violence should be placed.

Sociological explanations, such as those that examine the links with economic deprivation, gang involvement, dominant social groups and use of violence in the informal economy, provide descriptions of the context within which violence occurs, but fail to predict which individuals within those environments will commit violence. Analysis of structural vulnerability, such as, for example, the violence towards women by men, racial attacks and homophobic violence, displays the use of violence to maintain dominance. Violence that is specifically targeted against particular groups or individuals because of their beliefs, their skin colour, their gender, their sexuality or their social class works to remind those more vulnerable that they will be constrained by those structurally advantaged. Violence does succeed in achieving dominance

through force. But violence may also be a sign of resistance as well. The violence of civil insurgents demonstrates the use of violence for this purpose.

Naming actions as violence or resistance to oppression demonstrates how explanations of violence are subjective. Resistance to violence can be on an individual basis, as in situations where battered women kill their assailants, or they can be on a collective basis, as in armed insurgencies against state regimes. Public debates, as well as criminal trial defences, revolve around the use, meaning and consequences of violent actions. Often the subjective meanings of violence, and the social and political contexts within which violence arises, are contested and contestable. The meanings of violence are socially constructed.

Violence continues to fascinate people, as the proliferation of violence on television, the cinema, in books and in the news attests. The effects of viewing violence is hotly contested among researchers. Debates continue about how much of this type of violence we should be viewing on our televisions each evening. We are now able to witness the brutality and violence that others commit, in living colour. How this affects viewers, whether and how actual experiences of violence affect individuals' future behaviour, and how violence prevention can increase the quality of life of many people are crucial debates for social scientists.

ELIZABETH A. STANKO
ROYAL HOLLOWAY COLLEGE,
UNIVERSITY OF LONDON

Further reading

Lee, R.M. and Stanko, E.A. (eds) (2003) *Researching Violence*, London.
Stanko, E.A. (ed.) (2003) *The Meanings of Violence*, London.

SEE ALSO: domestic violence; terrorism

VISION

Through visual perception, we obtain knowledge of our position and orientation within an environment consisting of light, surfaces and a transparent medium (usually air), and we are able to move, act, recognize objects and people, and identify physical properties. For those with adequate eyesight, vision effortlessly delivers a rich, compelling, immediate and informative 'reality'. To understand how this is accomplished will require the integration of diverse sciences, as well as advances in philosophical or conceptual thought.

The physiology of visual systems

Although the eye is an image-forming device like a camera, the idea that an image of a physical world is transmitted into the brain leads to an infinite regress – who or what would see and interpret the image in the brain (Gregory 1997)? On the contrary, physiological studies have shown that at successive stages along the visual pathways, there is a parallel and hierarchical process of analysis (Bruce *et al.* 2003). Early stages of the visual pathways perform spatial and temporal filtering on local patches of the retinal image, and later stages extract 'higher-order properties', that is, more complex relationships, over time and space, between these local image properties. These *relational* properties of the image stream show a progressively closer correspondence with 'valid properties' of the external world (Gibson 1979; Marr 1982).

In the retina, a two-dimensional mosaic of receptor cells (rods and cones) receives light energy and converts it to a spatio-temporal pattern of electrical activity, which is further processed by the layered neurons in the retina itself. The output of the retina passes along the optic nerves, each consisting of the axons of millions of individual retinal ganglion cells. Each cell has a 'receptive field', defined as that small patch of the visual field where visual stimulation influences the firing of the cell. The receptive fields of optic nerve fibres have two regions (centre and surround) that respond to light in opposite ways, so that they respond strongly to differences in illumination of adjacent regions (spatial contrast). Most of these fibres terminate in the lateral geniculate nucleus (LGN), which in humans and many other primates has two large cell (M cell) layers and four small cell (P cell) layers. The P pathway acts as a channel for transmitting spatial and chromatic contrast, whereas the M pathway is sensitive to motion of large, low-contrast stimuli (Merigan and Maunsell 1993). This represents the beginning of the segregation of different image properties, such as contour, movement, colour and depth, along parallel pathways and into discrete areas (Maunsell and Newsome 1987). LGN M and P cells project to different layers of primary visual cortex (V1). Hubel and Wiesel (1962, 1968) demonstrated that V1 neurons have highly distinctive stimulus preferences. Most have a preferred orientation of a bar or edge to which they will respond: additionally the location, size, colour or luminance contrast, binocular disparity and direction of motion of the stimulus must be specified. V1 projects in turn relate to higher visual areas with yet more complex receptive field properties. A dorsal pathway runs from V1 and V2 via V3 and V3a to the middle temporal area V5, MST and parietal lobe area 7a. One important function of this pathway is the analysis of motion (Culham *et al.* 2001). A ventral pathway runs from V1 via V4, and the lateral occipital complex, LOC, to the temporal lobe (PIT and AIT) and is implicated in the analysis of form and colour. Functional brain imaging (fMRI) studies in human volunteers show that early stages of the ventral stream respond equally to pictures of objects, and to scrambled mosaics of the same pictures. However, area V4v, and area LOC, further along the ventral pathway, respond much more strongly to pictures of natural objects (Grill-Spector *et al.* 1998). Furthermore, areas within LOC and temporal lobe are sensitive to specific object categories. There is a 'fusiform face area' (FFA) showing enhanced activation to face images (Kanwisher *et al.* 1997) and a 'parahippocampal place area' (PPA) sensitive to images of buildings and scenes (Aguirre *et al.* 1998; Epstein and Kanwisher 1998). It seems likely that further specific functional areas of the dorsal and ventral visual pathways will be identified by fMRI techniques. There are different patterns of visual deficits in patients with dorsal or ventral pathway damage. Ventral pathway lesions tend to impair the identification and discrimination of objects and faces (e.g. visual form agnosias), and dorsal pathway lesions can interfere with visuo-spatial localization, and the guidance of visual action (e.g. optic ataxia) (Milner and Goodale 1995).

The functions of visual perception: computational approaches

In very broad terms, therefore, vision has a dual function: knowledge of objects and their properties, and visual guidance of action (Milner and Goodale 1995). But there are no objects or locations as such in the retinal image. To derive a representation of objects in locations from the information available in retinal images, it is necessary to solve a set of *computational problems* (Marr 1982). Each and every visual submodality (motion, form, colour, etc.) itself needs to solve computational problems. For example, the direction and speed (velocity) of a moving object is ambiguous in the retinal image, which can be considered as a time-varying, two-dimensional array of points of light varying in intensity and wavelength. The derivation of object velocity from the available image data requires the solution of (at least) two computational problems.

1   Any local sample of the time-varying image will be consistent with an infinity of possible object motions. How does the visual system combine local samples in order to determine the global object motion? (Aperture Problem.)
2   How does the visual system determine which image points, sampled at different times, belong to the same moving object? (Correspondence Problem.)

Several solutions to these problems have been proposed and are discussed by Bruce *et al.* (2003).

Constructivist and ecological approaches

We have seen that retinal events in themselves are inadequate to explain how perception occurs. Constructivist approaches propose that it is prior knowledge, in some sense, that makes perception possible: for Helmholtz (1962 [1866]) perception requires *unconscious inference*, for Gregory (1997) perceptions are *hypotheses*. For Marr (1982: 104), the visual system embodies general *assumptions* that allow certain interpretations to emerge and others to be suppressed. Visual illusions are important to constructivist arguments since they demonstrate the dominance of biases, hypotheses or organizing constraints over weak or ambiguous sensory data. On the other hand, ecological theories (Gibson 1966, 1979) assert that perception does not start from static retinal images, but from a sampling of the *optic array*, that is, all the optical information potentially available to an active organism. Certain relationships in the optic array remain constant over changes in viewpoint, and these are the *invariants* that permit object recognition and other functions. Perception does not require cogitation – for example the *affordances* of an object are its directly perceived potentialities for action. Constructivist and ecological approaches may not ultimately be as contradictory as they first appear. Marr's purpose was to show *how* Gibsonian invariant relationships might be computed by the visual system (Marr 1982: 30). Gibson's approach is particularly useful in understanding visually guided actions – 'dorsal pathway' functions (see above). Gibson's emphasis on studying vision in real environments enabled a distinction to be made between *local motion signals* (specifying an object moving relative to a background) and global *optic flow* (specifying motion of the observer). However, the organism brings structure to perception, and these structuring processes can often be quantified using artificial stimuli. Constructivist approaches have been useful in understanding 'ventral pathway' functions – how vision achieves a conscious identification of objects and shapes on the basis of ambiguous retinal input. Both approaches allow an important role for learning.

Is the completeness and detail of the visual world an illusion?

Observers frequently fail to notice large changes in scenes. For example, when two pictures are presented in succession separated by a blank interval, a normally salient object such as a building or person may be removed (or added) without observers noticing it. However, when the location of the change is cued, it becomes trivially easy to detect. The blank interval prevents attention being attracted to any flicker or apparent movement caused by the local changes in the image. Eye movements (saccades) and 'mud splashes' have the same effect. Under these circumstances 'change blindness' occurs (Blackmore *et al.* 1995; Simons 1996; O'Regan *et al.* 1999). Change blindness does not require a complex scene. It can occur with 2–4 simple stimuli if attention is distributed across spatial locations (Wright *et al.* 2000). One explanation of change blindness is that attention is required for awareness of a change, and the capacity of visual attention is very limited. So, if attention is necessary for conscious perception, and if attention is very selective, why do we perceive a visual world that appears complete, stable and detailed?

Perhaps the visual world is a 'grand illusion' (Noë and O'Regan 2000). Although we experience a rich and detailed visual world, it is mistaken to suppose that vision must therefore create a detailed picture or replica of the world in the brain or mind. Noë and O'Regan (2000) propose that we are perceptually sensitive to a great deal of the visual world *without* conscious awareness. This sensitivity can, for example, guide action and, indeed, guide the way we look at the visual environment. On this view, the outside world functions as an 'external memory' (O'Regan 1992) because anything that we need to attend to and actively engage with is there to be looked at. We do not need a representation of all the detail of the world in our memory. Moreover, the detail is not all simultaneously present in awareness.

Development of visual function

An infant is born with low visual acuity and limited sensitivity to contrast, but the visual system develops very rapidly in the first 6 months of life, providing a rapid expansion of visual capacities that form the foundation for perceptual, motor, cognitive and social skills (Atkinson 2002). Early visual development in mammals spans a number of sensitive periods during which functions are adversely affected by deprivation of specific kinds of visual stimulation (Blakemore 1978). In human infants, deprivation of patterned input, for example by a cataract, can result in reduced spatial acuity even after the cataract is removed (Ellemberg *et al.* 2000). Anomalies of visual development may also give rise to high-level deficits, such as 'magnocellular' deficits in certain types of dyslexia (Stein and Walsh 1997), and anomalous processing of faces in autism (Pierce *et al.* 2001). It is unlikely that these effects are environmentally mediated.

Learning and cultural influences

Visual performance is affected by learning in many different ways (Goldstone 1998). An ecological approach would emphasize the extraction of previously unused information from the optic array (Gibson 1969). One key issue is the distinction between perceptual and cognitive learning (including that mediated by language), and their interaction (Goldstone *et al.* 2000). Many recent studies have shown that even low-level visual processes are modified by learning,

and that attention plays a role in determining the level of the visual pathway at which such modifications occur (Fahle 2002). Cultural influences on perception and categorization have been widely debated and researched. Recently the work of Berlin and Kay (1969), suggesting an underlying universality of basic colour categories across cultures, has been replicated and extended. However, these more recent studies (Davidoff *et al.* 1999) indicate a much stronger influence of language on perceptual categorization and perceptual judgements than was previously thought.

MICHAEL J. WRIGHT
BRUNEL UNIVERSITY

References

Aguirre, G.K., Zarahn, E. and D'Esposito, M. (1998) 'An area within human ventral cortex sensitive to "building" stimuli: Evidence and implications', *Neuron* 21: 373–83.

Atkinson, J. (2002) *The Developing Visual Brain*, Oxford.

Berlin, B. and Kay, P. (1969) *Basic Color Terms: Their Universality and Evolution*, Berkeley and Los Angeles.

Blackmore, S.J., Brelstaff, G., Nelson, K. and Troscianko, T. (1995) 'Is the richness of our visual world an illusion? Transsaccadic memory for complex scenes', *Perception* 24: 1,075–81.

Blakemore, C. (1978) 'Maturation and modification in the developing visual system', in R. Held, H. Liebowitz and H. Teuber (eds) *Handbook of Sensory Physiology*, Vol. 8, *Perception*, New York.

Bruce, V., Green, P.R. and Georgeson, M.A. (2003) *Visual Perception: Physiology, Psychology and Ecology*, 4th edn, Hove, UK.

Culham, J., He, S., Dukelow, S. and Verstraten, F.A.J. (2001) 'Visual motion and the human brain: What has neuroimaging told us?' *Acta Psychologica* 107: 69–94.

Davidoff, J., Davies, I. and Roberson, D. (1999) 'Colour categories of a stone-age tribe', *Nature* 398: 203–4.

Ellemberg, D., Lewis, T.L., Maurer, D. and Brent, H.P. (2000) 'Influence of monocular deprivation during infancy on the later development of spatial and temporal vision', *Vision Research* 40(23): 3,283–95.

Epstein, R. and Kanwisher, N. (1998) 'A cortical representation of the local visual environment', *Nature* 392: 598–601.

Fahle, M. (2002) 'Perceptual learning: gain without pain?' *Nature Neuroscience* 5: 923–4.

Gibson, E.J. (1969). *Perceptual Learning and Development*, New York.

Gibson, J.J. (1966) *The Senses Considered as Perceptual Systems*, Boston.

—— (1979) *The Ecological Approach to Visual Perception*, Boston.

Goldstone, R.L. (1998) 'Perceptual learning', *Annual Review of Psychology* 49: 585–612.

Goldstone, R.L., Stevyers, M., Spencer-Smith, J. and Kersten, A. (2000) 'Interactions between perceptual and conceptual learning', in E. Diettrich and A. Markman (eds) *Cognitive Dynamics: Conceptual Change in Humans and Machines*, Mahwah, NJ, pp. 191–228.

Gregory, R.L. (1997) *Eye and Brain*, 5th edn, Princeton, NJ.

Grill-Spector, K., Kushnir, T., Hendler, T., Edelman, S., Itzchak, Y. and Malach, R. (1998) 'A sequence of object-processing stages revealed by fMRI in the human occipital lobe', *Human Brain Mapping* 6: 316–28.

Helmholtz, H. Von (1962 [1866]) *Treatise on Physiological Optics*, Vol. 3, New York.

Hubel, D.H. and Wiesel, T.N. (1962) 'Receptive fields, binocular interaction and functional architecture in the cat's visual cortex', *Journal of Physiology* 166: 106–54.

—— (1968) 'Receptive fields and functional architecture of the monkey striate cortex', *Journal of Physiology* 195: 215–43.

Kanwisher, N., McDermott, J. and Chun, M. (1997) 'The fusiform face area: A module in human extrastriate cortex specialised for face perception', *Journal of Neuroscience* 17: 4,302–11.

Marr, D. (1982) *Vision*, New York.

Maunsell, J.H.R. and Newsome, W.T. (1987) 'Visual processing in monkey extrastriate cortex', *Annual Review of Neuroscience* 10: 363–401.

Merigan, W.H. and Maunsell, J.H.R. (1993) 'How parallel are the primate visual pathways?' *Annual Review of Neuroscience* 16: 369–402.

Milner, A.D. and Goodale, M.A. (1995) *The Visual Brain in Action*, Oxford.

Noë, A and O'Regan, J.K. (2000) 'Perception, attention and the grand illusion', *Psyche* 6, http://psyche.cs.-monash.edu.au/v6/psyche-6-15-noe.html.

O'Regan, J.K. (1992) 'Solving the "real" mysteries of visual perception: The world as an outside memory', *Canadian Journal of Psychology* 46: 461–88.

O'Regan, J.K., Rensink, R.A. and Clark, J.J. (1999) 'Change blindness as a result of "mud splashes"', *Nature* 398: 34.

Pierce, K., Muller, R.A., Ambrose, J., Allen, G. and Courchesne, E. (2001) 'Face processing occurs outside the fusiform "face area" in autism: Evidence from functional MRI', *Brain* 124: 2,059–73.

Simons, D.J. (1996) 'When object representations fail. In sight, out of mind: when object representations fail', *Psychological Science* 7: 301–5.

Stein, J. and Walsh, V. (1997) 'To see but not to read; The magnocellular theory of dyslexia', *Trends in Neuroscience* 20: 147–52.

Wright, M.J., Green, A. and Baker, S. (2000) 'Limitations for change detection in multiple Gabor targets', *Visual Cognition* 7: 237–52.

Further reading

Gibson, J.J. (1950) *The Perception of the Visual World*, Boston.

SEE ALSO: cognitive neuroscience; mental imagery; sensation and perception

VITAL STATISTICS

An individual's entry into or departure from life, or change in civil status, is known as a vital event. In demographic applications the term most commonly encompasses births, marriages and deaths, including stillbirths as well as live births, and divorces as well as marriages. An exhaustive list of such events would also contain annulments, adoptions, legitimations, recognitions and legal separations, but these latter vital events are less commonly the subject of demographic analysis. Vital statistics are the basic or derived data regarding vital events.

Christenings, marriages and burials were recorded in European parish registers as long ago as the sixteenth century. The first serious study of vital statistics, that of John Graunt in 1662, was based upon burial and christening records, and presented the first crude life tables. Civil registration of vital events became compulsory in Scandinavia and some of the American colonies fairly early in the seventeenth century but in England not until 1837, although England was the first country to produce regular publications of vital statistics. In contrast, most developing countries have either a defective system of vital registration, or none at all.

The information contained in a registration document includes the date and place of the vital event being registered, and the date and place of registration. The sex of the child and names and ages of parents are included on a birth certificate, and the cause of death, and age, marital status and occupation of the deceased on a death certificate. Other information on background characteristics is also obtained, the exact inventory varying with the type of event being registered, and from country to country.

Demographic data are of two types, stock and flow, the stocks being population totals at a particular moment and the flows represented by movements into and out of a population over a period of time. Information on stocks is obtained from periodic population censuses or population registers, and on flows from a system of registration of vital events. The most obvious examples of flows are births and deaths, although marriage is also a flow as it represents movement from the unmarried to the married state. The most basic demographic measures incorporate both types of information, with a flow in the numerator and a stock in the denominator. Thus, for example, the crude birth rate, the simplest fertility measure, is calculated as the ratio of births that occurred during a particular year, as obtained from registration data, to the estimated mid-year population. Similarly, the total number of deaths in a particular year is related to the mid-year population in order to estimate the crude death rate.

Such measures can be made more informative by taking into account additional attributes such as age or, depending on the background information collected on the registration forms and its comparability with census information, other characteristics as well. Some examples are life tables for different occupational groups or regional age-specific fertility rates.

Most developing countries lack a comprehensive system of vital registration. In an attempt to compensate for this deficiency, since the mid-1960s a number of techniques have been developed by which vital rates can be estimated from fairly simple questions appended to a census schedule. Vital rates are also estimated, with varying degrees of success, from specially designed sample surveys.

GIGI SANTOW
SYDNEY

Further reading

Brass, W. and Coale, A.J. (1968) 'Methods of analysis and estimation', in W. Brass, A.J. Coale, P. Demeny, D.F. Heisel, F. Lorimar, A. Romaniuk and E. van de Walle (eds) *The Demography of Tropical Africa*, Princeton, NJ.

Graunt, J. (1939) *Natural and Political Observations Made upon the Bills of Mortality*, ed. W.F. Willcox, Baltimore, MD.

Shryock, H.S., Siegel, J.S. and associates (1973) *The Methods and Materials of Demography*, Washington, DC.

Spiegelman, M. (1968) *Introduction to Demography*, Cambridge, MA.

Wrigley, E.A. and Schofield, R.S. (1983) 'English population history from family reconstitution: Summary results 1600–1799', *Population Studies* 37.

SEE ALSO: census of population; fertility; migration; mortality; population projections

VOTING

Voting is a means of expressing and aggregating a choice of party or candidate in elections. Ancient Greeks voted by placing a pebble (*psephos*) in an urn, giving rise to the term psephology, or study of elections. By the end of the nineteenth century most Western states had granted the vote to most adult males and in the first few decades of the twentieth century it was extended to women on the same terms. Free competitive elections are regarded as the key to representative democracy.

Electoral systems and constitutions prescribe the conduct of elections. They cover such features as:

1 Frequency – e.g. fixed calendar elections as in the USA or elections that have to be held within a fixed time period (e.g. Britain).
2 Occasions – for local, regional and national legislatures and head of state; they can also be held on policy questions, via referendums, or nominations, via primaries.
3 Eligibility – virtually all states confine the right to vote to adult citizens, although they may differ in their criteria for adulthood and citizenship.
4 Registration – voters have to be registered on an electoral roll or register; in the USA registration is more complex than in other states.
5 The weight of the vote – the extent to which the system approximates to one person, one vote, one value depends on the type of electoral system and size of constituencies.

The study of voting behaviour has gone through several stages and employed different approaches. There are various models, drawn from different intellectual backgrounds, including historical, aggregate data, sociological, party identification, and issue voting approaches.

First, the historical approach considers that it is easily overlooked that voters are usually presented at elections with a fixed choice of parties: these are the product of historical forces that long preceded the birth of the present-day electors. Important work by Lipset and Rokkan (1967) traced the origins of many party systems to such key historical events as the Reformation and Counter-Reformation, the Industrial Revolution, the early stages of nation-building and the French Revolution. These formative events have given rise to party systems that are variously based on religious allegiance, class interest and centre versus periphery loyalties. Once created some parties endure beyond the circumstances that gave rise to them. They adapt to new interests and issues, and socialize voters into voting for them.

Second, the aggregate data approach analyses census data for the particular unit (which may be a region, constituency or ward) to establish correlations between the dominant social factors of the population and the strength of a political party. It was well established in the USA and France in the first decades of the twentieth century and André Siegfried used it to describe the geographical division of France into political left and right regions. The approach is more useful where the unit under study has a pronounced social character (e.g. a mining or a farming community). The problem is to move from aggregate to individual data correlations.

Third, the sociological approach, using sample surveys to interview voters, was pioneered in the USA in the 1940s (Lazarsfeld *et al.* 1948) and enabled studies to be made of individual voters. This work showed that such social background factors as class, religion and residence predisposed people to vote Republican or Democrat. It was also useful in showing the extent to which the parties drew on attitudinally integrated groups of support. In Britain the pioneering study by Butler and Stokes (1969) showed the importance of social class and of religion in shaping party votes.

Fourth, the party identification approach, borrowed from psychology, was developed by Angus Campbell (1960) and his colleagues at the University of Michigan. They found that most US voters were attached to a political party; they had a party identity, often inherited from parents, and reinforced by occupation, class and neighbourhood. It was a force for continuity in voting behaviour. The party identification approach has had a major impact on electoral studies, on cross-national research and on developing typologies of elections. In the USA in the 1970s and 1980s identification declined as a predictor of party vote. Although the Democrats enjoyed a clear lead on identification over Republicans they regularly lost presidential elections. The concept is also useful in helping to construct a *normal* vote for a party.

Fifth, the issue voting approach has been inspired by Downs (1957) and applied by Himmelweit and Jaeger (1985). It emphasizes the importance of issue preferences to the voter. For Himmelweit, who terms it the *consumer model of voting*, it is issue preferences, moderated by the strength of party identification and habit of voting for one party rather than another, which shapes the vote decision. Students specify three conditions for issue voting: the voter must be aware of the issue, care about the issue, and perceive the parties as taking different stands on the issue, with one party representing their issue preference. If party identification leads to *expressive* voting, then rational choice leads to instrumental voting. Early voting studies pointed to the apathy and ignorance of many voters and suggested that only a small minority of voters were able to satisfy the conditions for issue voting. But more recent research, which allows voters to suggest their own important issues, finds that issue voting is more widespread.

Other approaches have stressed the importance of how the economy is performing. Economic-based explanations of voting have to come to terms with the fact that key indicators vary over time; unemployment, inflation, take-home pay or economic optimism differ in their salience from one election to another. Carried to extremes, models that link voting behaviour to rates of unemployment and inflation would predict that continued economic decline would lead to the demise of established political parties. But in times of economic depression voters' expectations may be scaled down, other concerns may become more significant, or alternative parties viewed as less attractive to the government of the day. In the British general election in 1997, voters' perceptions of poor Conservative economic management was important in delivering a landslide victory to the Labour party.

Scholars also differ as to whether voting is primarily *retrospective*, that is, based on the perceived record of the government, or *prospective*, in which the citizen votes on the basis of the policy proposals of the parties. A neo-Marxist or radical approach emphasizes the voter's relationship to the state as an employer or consumer of services. This approach cuts across conventional social class analysis and emphasizes the importance of employment in the private or the public sector, or dependence on public or private housing, transport, education and so on.

The concept of the *normal vote* is crucial for developing a typology of elections and interpreting the outcome of an election. If the change proves to be durable then the election has been *critical*, or realigning, inaugurating a long-term change in the strength of the parties. Thus, the Democrats became the clear majority party in the USA after Roosevelt's *critical* 1932 election, and the Labour victory in 1997 seems to have been a critical one in Britain. A *maintaining* election is one in which the great majority of voters follow their traditional party loyalties and the majority party wins. A *deviating* election is one in which the usual minority party wins, in response to short-term factors associated with the campaign (e.g. Eisenhower's victories in the 1952 and 1956 US presidential contests).

More rapid social and economic change is weakening the bases of traditional voting. In turn, this loosening of allegiance gives more scope to short-term factors such as the mass media, economic trends and the campaign and candidates. The availability of different models of voting behaviour and the development of more sophisticated techniques of data analysis have greatly enriched our knowledge of voting. On the whole, what emerges is a more complex pattern. For example, is party identification, outside of the USA, anything more than a reflection of the party vote? How does one establish the direction of influence between issue preferences and party loyalty?

DENNIS KAVANAGH
UNIVERSITY OF LIVERPOOL

References

Butler, D. and Stokes, D. (1969) *Political Change in Britain*, London.
Campbell, A. (1960) *The American Voter*, New York.
Downs, A. (1957) *An Economic Theory of Democracy*, New York.
Himmelweit, H. and Jaeger, M. (1985) *How Voters Decide*, Milton Keynes.
Lazarsfeld, P., Berelson, B. and Gaudet, H. (1948) *The People's Choice*, New York.
Lipset, S. and Rokkan, S. (1967) *Party Systems and Voter Alignments*, New York.

Further reading

DiClerico, R.E. (2004) *Voting in America: A Reference Handbook*, Santa Barbara, CA.
LeDuc, L., Niemi, R.G. and Norris, P. (eds) (2002) *Comparing Democracies: Elections and Voting in Global Perspective: New Challenges in the Study of Elections and Voting*, London.
Nie, N.H., Petrocik, J.R. and Verba, S. (1976) *The Changing American Voter*, Cambridge, MA.

SEE ALSO: democracy; elections; parties, political; public choice; representation, political

W

WAR STUDIES

The study of war is still dominated by Carl von Clausewitz's reflections based on his experience of the Napoleonic campaigns, *On War* (Clausewitz 1989 [1832]). The book was still being revised when he died in 1831 so that only the first chapters reflect his developed thought, and this has led to a debate over whether the early or later Clausewitz represents a truer or better picture. As the Napoleonic Wars were held to represent a shift in the character of war towards total confrontations involving the mobilization of whole societies, and as Clausewitz was the most influential expositor of this shift, he was often blamed for the wars that followed, especially as his early writings can be taken to legitimize a drive for a decisive battle. Yet he can also be used as a source of caution, in that the later Clausewitz became more concerned with the tension between an inherent nature of war, which can take over and push it to absolute levels of violence, and the limiting factors, of which the most important was the definition of war aims that led to his famous injunction that war is the continuation of politics by other means (Gat 1989).

While politics might provide the purposes of war, its actual conduct was a military responsibility. Some, such as the Swiss Henri de Jomini (1971 [1862]), another veteran of the Napoleonic Wars, believed that success in war was governed by the application of general principles. On a more modest scale, investigations into past campaigns were undertaken by the military so as to be able to apply any lessons when developing new doctrine and tactics. The German Hans Delbruck was almost unique as an academic military historian. He distinguished between wars of annihilation, directed largely at the decisive destruction of the enemy armies, and those of exhaustion, where resources are limited and battle has to be complemented by attempts to destroy the economic base of the opponent, for example by destroying crops or blockade (Craig 1985). Otherwise, the origins of particular wars were studied by historians but theories of war's causation were few and far between.

By the turn of the century, there was some understanding of how the combination of the revolutions in industrialization and transport were leading to a revolution in warfare. Even some military planners understood that at issue was whether the new capacity for manoeuvre could produce results before the new capacity for attrition took over. The absolute nature of the First World War transformed the study of war.

One consequence of this was that the problem of war was put at the centre of the new study of international relations and at the centre of the practice of international law. It was treated as an interstate crime. The objective was to design an international order in which disputes would be settled without resort to arms and so war could be prohibited. The study of its conduct was tantamount to endorsing its continued place in human affairs. Causation came to be understood in terms of irrational factors, such as an arms race, more than deliberate state policy.

Even those who were not convinced that war could be abolished, and pursued studies of its conduct, were profoundly influenced by the desire to avoid the carnage of the First World War. Most were veterans of the war, though they were also often disaffected or retired. There were those such as the Italian Douhet, and the American Billy Mitchell (Warner 1943), who believed that air power now offered a way to bring wars to a swift conclusion, possibly without any encounters on land, while others, such as the British writers 'Boney' Fuller and Basil Liddell Hart, believed that the key innovation was the tank (Bond 1977). The search for an 'indirect strategy', promoted by Liddell Hart, reflected a yearning for forms of military operation that could achieve decisive results without large-scale battle. Inspiration for this approach can be traced back to the ancient Chinese strategist, Sun Tzu, who encouraged the view that wars could be won through superior intelligence and guile as much as brute force (Wing 1999).

The Second World War did not conform exactly to the expectations of any prewar theorist. Moreover its finale, with the atomic destruction of Nagasaki and Hiroshima, suggested that previous types of warfare might have all been rendered obsolete. For students of war, the events of the 1930s and their consequences produced a new seriousness. International relations moved from idealist to realist mode. An interest in the theory of war was reflected in the major collection on *Makers of Modern Strategy* put together by Edward Meade Earle, almost as part of the war effort, but that served as a standard text for four decades until superseded by a new collection under the same name (Earle 1943; Paret 1985). In Chicago Quincy Wright (1942) produced his monumental *Study of War*, thereby demonstrating the importance of serious empirical analysis.

Another important feature of the Second World War was the growing relevance of science, and the scientific method, in the development of both weapons and tactics, marked by developments in radar, missiles and jet engines as well as nuclear fission. This in itself ensured that the study of the conduct of, and preparations for, war would have a distinctive civilian quality. The awesome dilemmas of the nuclear age accelerated this civilian tendency. Following the adoption of the doctrine of massive retaliation by the Eisenhower Administration in 1954, a boom in strategic studies took place. It appeared as if US security policy was going to depend on a threat to inflict terrible damage on the Soviet Union and its allies as punishment for even the smallest transgression. This was despite the declining credibility of such a threat as the Soviet capacity for counter-punishment grew.

It was initially students of history and politics who worried most as to the sense of all this. Those from this background tended to doubt whether nuclear strength could be turned into a decisive military asset when faced with an adversary of some – even if inferior – nuclear strength. But the two sides were acting and talking as if nuclear weapons had superseded all other types of weapons, and commitments to allies had been made on exactly this supposition. So the classical strategists found themselves in a conundrum for which their intellectual traditions left them unprepared (Freedman 2003).

Into the breach stepped a new breed of strategists, often from schools of economics and engineering rather than politics and history, who sought to demonstrate how a wholly novel situation might be mastered by exploiting novel methodologies. As this logic led to co-operative attempts to manage superpower antagonism through arms control negotiations, studies of strategic matters came to be seen as an almost exclusively civilian – and academic – domain.

Because of the catastrophic consequences of a superpower confrontation, there appeared to be grounds for believing that war was close to abolishing itself. Certainly, the importance of avoiding war meant that its study became overtaken by the study of deterrence. In terms of the theory of war, this could be accommodated within a realist model which assumed that great powers would pursue their interests in a rational manner (Waltz 1960).

In this context the study of war came to revolve around three distinct questions. First, was there a possibility that developments in nuclear weapons technology could produce conditions for a meaningful victory in a superpower confrontation? Second, failing that, and assuming that nuclear arsenals continued to neutralize each other, how significant were developments with conventional military forces? Third, how much was it possible to rely on rational behaviour at times of crisis, when such factors as poor information and misperception, flaws in decision-making processes and the psychology of individual leaders, as well as overdependence on automatic early warning and launch procedures, could all have catastrophic consequences?

This last question in particular encouraged detailed empirical studies on past successes and failures in deterrence (Jervis *et al.* 1985). This work raised important methodological issues concerning the possibility of generalizing from a series of distinct events in quite different historical periods and geopolitical settings. There has been since the 1960s one distinct approach to war studies marked by a rigorous empiricism (Midlarsky 1989). This has included a major investigation into the 'correlates of war' (Small and Singer 1980).

With the end of the Cold War all approaches to the study of war had to undergo some reappraisal. The Gulf War suggested that classical studies on the conduct of war still might have their place, yet the overall thrust of much analysis was to suggest that the great power encounters that had dominated the study of war since the time of Clausewitz were becoming consigned to history. If any military tradition remained relevant it was that of the irregular/guerrilla war. These had been fought in the name of anti-colonialism but, now that the processes of decolonization were all but complete, were largely bound up with conflicts within and between the newly independent, and often quite weak, states.

This tradition of writing on war tends to take large-scale land operations as the starting-point. Indeed, thinking on war has been dominated by a focus on large-scale acts of aggression and decisive battles (including the avoidance thereof). To some this also meant the end of Clausewitz's influence and the irrelevance of his intellectual schema (Creveld 1991; Keegan 1993). However, even so-called ethnic conflicts and civil wars are waged for political purposes and require some understanding of the effective manipulation of the means of violence. This aspect still ensures some continuity in the study of war, even in the light of the enormous changes in the international environment, social and economic conditions, and the advance of military technology.

The terrorist attack on the USA launched on 11 September 2001 recast the security debate in the West. Having been unsure of whether it had any interests bound up with turbulence in the poorer parts of the world, the USA became determined to root out the instigators and supporters of militant Islamic groups deemed responsible for terrorism. This led to wars against the Taliban regime in Afghanistan and then, more controversially, against Iraq. During the 1990s the key new area of interest in the study of war lay in the origins and conduct of ethnic conflict (Brown 1993), and from then on to a preoccupation with issues related to external intervention in these conflicts on humanitarian

grounds (Wheeler 2000). The twenty-first century has reinforced this agenda, adding questions on the impact of militant Islam (Laqueur 2003), the potential of attacks on civil society as a means of balancing the West's conventional military strength (so-called asymmetric warfare) (Berkowitz 2003) and the role of international institutions.

LAWRENCE FREEDMAN
KING'S COLLEGE, UNIVERSITY OF LONDON

References

Berkowitz, B. (2003) *The New Face of War: How War will be Fought in the 21st Century*, New York.
Bond, B. (1977) *Liddell Hart: A Study of His Military Thought*, London.
Brown, M. (ed.) (1993) *Ethnic Conflict and International Security*, Princeton.
Clausewitz, C. von (1989 [1832]) *On War*, Princeton, NJ.
Craig, G. (1985) 'Delbruck: The military historian', in P. Paret (ed.) *Makers of Modern Strategy*, Princeton, NJ.
Creveld, M. van (1991) *The Transformation of War*, New York.
Earle, E.M. (ed.) (1943) *Makers of Modern Strategy*, Princeton, NJ.
Freedman, L. (2003) *The Evolution of Nuclear Strategy*, 3rd edn, New York.
Gat, A. (1989) *The Origins of Military Thought*, Oxford.
Jervis, R., Lebow, R.N. and Stein, J.G. (eds) (1985) *Psychology and Deterrence*, New York.
Jomini, Baron H. de (1971 [1862]) *The Art of War*, Westport, CT.
Keegan, J. (1993) *History of Warfare*, London.
Laqueur, W. (2003) *No End to War: Terrorism in the Twenty-First Century*, New York.
Midlarsky, M. (ed.) (1989) *Handbook of War Studies*, Boston, MA.
Paret, P. (ed.) (1985) *Makers of Modern Strategy*, Princeton, NJ.
Small, M. and Singer, J.D. (1980) *Resort to Arms: International and Civil Wars, 1816–1980*, Beverly Hills, CA.
Waltz, K. (1960) *Man, the State and War: A Theoretical Analysis*, New York.
Warner, E. (1943) 'Douhet, Mitchell, Seversky: Theories of air warfare', in E.M. Earle (ed.) *Makers of Modern Strategy*, Princeton, NJ.
Wheeler, N. (2000) *Saving Strangers: Humanitarian Intervention in International Society*, Oxford.
Wing, R. (1999) *The Art of Strategy: A New Translation of Sun Tzu's 'The Art of War'*, New York.
Wright, Q. (1942) *The Study of War*, Chicago.

Further reading

Aron, R. (1968) *On War*, New York.
Blainey, G. (1988) *The Causes of War*, London.

Cowley, R. (ed.) (1992) *Experience of War*, New York.

Gilpin, R. (1983) *War and Change in World Politics*, Cambridge, UK.

Jones, A. (1987) *The Art of War in the Western World*, Oxford.

Liddell Hart, B.H. (1968) *Strategy: The Indirect Approach*, London.

Luttwak, E. (1987) *Strategy: The Logic of War and Peace*, Cambridge, MA.

McInnes, C. and Sheffield, G.D. (eds) (1988) *Warfare in the Twentieth Century: Theory and Practice*, London.

Schelling, T. (1963) *The Strategy of Conflict*, New York.

Walzer, M. (1980) *Just and Unjust Wars*, Harmondsworth.

SEE ALSO: conflict; defence economics; peace studies

WEBER, MAX (1864–1920)

Max Weber, the son of a member of the Reichstag and an activist Protestant mother, grew up in Berlin in an intellectually lively home frequently visited by the Bismarckian era's leading politicians and intellectuals. After receiving an outstanding secondary education in languages, history and the classics, he studied law, economics, history and philosophy at the Universities of Heidelberg, Strasbourg, Berlin and Göttingen. Although his first appointments, at the Universities of Freiburg (1894) and Heidelberg (1897), were in the faculty of economics, he is best known today as one of the major founders of modern sociology and as one of the intellectual giants of interdisciplinary scholarship. His studies ranged freely from the ancient Greeks to the early Hindus, from the Old Testament prophets to the Confucian literati, from the economic organization of early Near Eastern civilizations to the trading companies of the Medieval West, and from the origins of continental law to comparative analyses of the rise of the modern state. Yet notwithstanding the diversity of the themes he tackled, a grand design may be discerned in Weber's writings.

Weber and others of his generation in Germany viewed the dawning of rapid industrialization and the modern age itself with profound ambivalence rather than as a first step towards a new era of progress. While welcoming the possibilities it offered for a burgeoning of individualism and an escape from the feudal chains of the past, he saw few firm guidelines in reference to which modern persons might be able to establish a comprehensive, value-based meaning for their lives, or even their everyday action (2004). Moreover, the towering bureaucracies indispensable to the organization of industrial societies were endowed with the capacity to render persons politically powerless, to replace creative potential with stifling routine and merely functional relationships, and so to rob societies of all dynamism. If a certain openness vanishes societies will become ossified and competition between values will cease, and as values are not renewed they will no longer provide guides to action. What Weber termed practical rationalism will then expand in an unrestrained manner. These developments, he believed, would in the end preclude an anchoring of action in ethical values.

These concerns inform Weber's sociological writings, particularly those undertaken after 1903. In these studies he wished to define the uniqueness of Western civilization and to understand the manner in which persons East and West, influenced by social constellations, formulate *meaning* for their lives, a meaning that then guides action. Once he had constructed a 'mental image' of a social group, era and civilization, Weber showed an amazing capacity to enter into the minds of persons quite unlike himself. This aim to *understand* how values and actions made sense to their beholders, however foreign they may be at times to the social scientist investigating them, formed the foundation for Weber's *verstehende* sociology of 'interpretive understanding'.

Perhaps it was in part this sensitivity, as well as a sheer respect for subjective meaning formulated over centuries, which prompted him to construct one of his most famous axioms, one debated heatedly to this day. To Weber, all scientific research must be 'value-free'. Once scholars have selected their themes of enquiry by reference to their interests and values, then preferences, prejudices and values must not be allowed to interfere with the collection of empirical data and its 'objective' evaluation (1949). Persons involved in scientific work should avoid an inadvertent intermixture of their values with those of the actors being studied. To Weber, even the scientist who happened to be a puritan was duty-bound (as long as he wished to pursue science) to describe, for example, tribal sexual practices accurately and to interpret them in reference to their indigenous 'cultural significance', however repugnant they seemed to him personally. This postulate also implied a strict division between that which *exists* (the question for scientific analysis) and that which *should be* (the realm of personal values and hopes).

In explicitly circumscribing the legitimate domain of science and denying it the right to produce norms, ideals and values, Weber had a larger purpose in mind. He wished to establish an inviolable realm within which individuals would be forced to confront themselves and to formulate on their own a set of personal values capable of guiding their actions and endowing them with an ethical aspect. Nothing less was required as a counterforce in an age in that bureaucratization and the scientific world-view threatened to encroach upon decision-making, thus upsetting the already tenuous character of individualism. Weber's own adherence to a value-free science, particularly in his studies of pre-modern and non-Western societies, his insight into the diverse ways in which subjective meaning could be formed and could induce patterned action, and the universal scope of his investigations, enabled him to write a comparative historical sociology of civilizations unique in the history of sociology, however fragmented, incomplete and poorly organized (Kalberg 2004).

Even though his interest focused upon comparisons across civilizations, Weber's emphasis on meaning prevented him from taking the Hegelian Absolute Spirit, the Marxian organization of production and class struggle, or the 'social facts' of Durkheim as his point of departure and guide. Nor was he inclined to view societies as integrated wholes. Rather he emphasized the conflicts between diverse 'spheres of life' (religion, the law, political 'rulership' and the economy), and acknowledged the ubiquity of power and domination.

Weber's orientation to individuals and the subjective meaning they attach to their actions would seem to carry him dangerously close to a radical subjectivism. Two procedures guarded against this possibility. First, he focused on the patterned meaningful actions of individuals in groups, rather than individuals acting alone, insisting that only this regular action proved to be culturally significant and historically powerful. Individuals tended to become knit together into collectivities primarily in five ways: cognizance of common material interests (as occurred when classes were formed), recognition of common values (as took place when status groups arose), adherence to a broad constellation of values or 'world-view' (as occurred in the major religious groupings and nineteenth-century ideologies), acknowledgement of affectual feelings (as found in person-oriented groups, such as the family, the clan and the traditional neighbourhood), and awareness of relations of rulership (as took place in the charismatic, patriarchal, feudal, patrimonial and bureaucratic forms of rulership). However massive and enduring an organization might appear, it must not, according to Weber, be understood as more than the patterned orientations of individuals acting in common.

The second means Weber employed to avoid lapsing into a radical subjectivism involves his major methodological tool, one that reveals his indebtedness to Kant: the 'ideal type' (1949). Indeed, this heuristic construct guarded against subjectivity so effectively that a number of commentators have accused Weber of moving away, particularly in his later work, from a *verstehende* sociology and of reifying the social phenomena he studies. In part, Weber himself is to blame. He used the term 'bureaucracy', for example, rather than 'bureaucratically oriented action' and 'classes' instead of 'class-oriented action'.

Perhaps the ideal type can be best understood against the backdrop of Weber's view of reality. Basic social reality presented itself to him as a ceaseless flow of occurrences and events, very few of which, although repeatedly interwoven, seem to fall together coherently. Moreover, due to its infinite complexity, no investigator can expect exhaustively to capture reality, nor even accurately to render all its contours.

Weber adopted a nominalistic position to confront this conundrum and propounded the use of the ideal type. This purely analytic tool enables us to acquire a purchase upon social reality. Far from arbitrary, the procedures for doing so involve, first, a definition of the investigator's particular research theme, and hence a demarcated angle upon infinite social reality, and, second, from the point of view of this theme, a deliberate exaggeration of the essence of the phenomenon under study and its reconstruction in a form with greater internal unity than ever appeared in empirical reality. As a construct, the ideal type abstracts from reality and fails to define any particular phenomenon.

For example, although Weber's conceptualization of the bureaucracy or the Calvinist was empirically grounded, he never aims to portray all bureaucracies or Calvinists, but rather he calls attention only to essential aspects as they are related to his research theme (for instance, in the case of Calvinism, its view of work). Once an entire series of ideal types has been formulated that is appropriate to a theme under investigation (different organizations, status groups, classes or 'economic ethics', for example), it serves two crucial purposes. First, the ideal type allows researchers to undertake rigorous comparisons. Second, when it is used as a conceptual yardstick in comparison to which a given empirical case can be defined, and its deviation assessed, reference to the ideal type enables an investigator to isolate and conceptualize distinctive attributes. An investigation of the empirical causes for this uniqueness can then commence. The establishment of clear definitions, often also arrived at through the use of typologies, constitutes an important task for all social science enquiry, Weber insists, yet one that must be viewed as an indispensable preliminary exercise to the major endeavour: to ascertain the causal reasons for the appearance of the unique case or development.

Although he outlined a methodology that would allow him to investigate the manner in which individuals formulated subjective meaning in different social contexts, civilizations and epochs, as well as to define the uniqueness and origins of the modern West, it must be concluded that Weber's various writings constitute fragments when viewed against these broad aims. Most, including his comparative studies on the *Economic Ethics of World Religions* (*EEWR*; 1951 [1920], 1952 [1920], 1958 [1920]) and *Economy and Society* (*E&S*; 1968 [1922]), were published in incomplete form. Nonetheless, the discrete elements of the whole have become classics in their own right.

Broadly speaking, Weber's works divide into more empirical investigations on the one hand and analytical models on the other. By far his most famous, debated and readable book, *The Protestant Ethic and the Spirit of Capitalism* (2002 [1920]), falls into the former category. Weber's purpose in this study was to understand certain features of the origins of modern capitalism. For him, this type of capitalism was distinguished by a systematic organization of work, the replacement of a 'traditional economic ethic'

among workers as well as entrepreneurs by the methodical labour of the 'modern economic ethic', and a systematic search for profit. Thus, he saw a specific 'frame of mind' (*Gesinnung*) – an eighteenth-century 'spirit of capitalism' – as causally important, and denied that the influx of precious metals, technological advances, population increases, the common desire for riches, or the Herculean efforts of 'economic supermen' (Carnegie, Rockefeller, Fugger) were sufficient in themselves to explain the origin of modern capitalism.

According to Weber, this 'spirit' had religious roots, specifically in the doctrines of the ascetic Protestant sects and churches, particularly the pastoral exhortations of Calvinism. In the sixteenth and seventeenth centuries the Calvinist doctrine of Predestination induced deep anxiety about personal salvation. A few were saved but most were condemned, and no earthly good works could change this everlasting decree. Some theologians and ministers, responding to discontent in their congregations, gradually formulated new interpretations that allowed the devout to believe they were among the saved. It was here that the sources of a systematic work ethic could be located. First, the faithful knew that God expected, for His majesty and greater glory, the devout to create abundance and wealth throughout His earthly kingdom. If only to attain this goal, God ordained that all should work. Moreover, God willed that the faithful work methodically, for labour in a calling (*Beruf*) was pleasing to Him: it counteracted egocentric wishes, provided regularity to the believer's life, tamed creaturely desires (which distracted the devout from their appropriate focus on God and His commandments) and dispelled doubt and anxiety about personal salvation. Furthermore, the faithful came to believe that their intense devotion, capacity for righteous conduct and energy to work hard must have its source in God, for He is omnipotent.

In this manner faith, conduct and systematic work testified to believers and their communities that God's divine powers were active within them, and this majestic Deity, they knew, would not 'operate within' and assist just anyone. Indeed, if the faithful sought to work in a systematic manner and discovered an ability to do so, it could be concluded that a sign of God's favour had been given to them. They were (or so they could convince themselves) among the predestined elect. Work now became 'providential'; it acquired a religious value.

Finally, methodical labour became sanctified in another way. In light of God's desire for an earthly kingdom of abundance to serve His glory, the devout could logically conclude that the production of great wealth was a positive sign from God. In effect, personal riches, which were received exclusively through the favour of an omnipotent and omniscient God, became important evidence of religious virtue and a sign of salvation in the eyes of the sincere believer. Like work, wealth became sanctified, and shed the suspect character it possessed in Catholicism. Moreover, the continuous reinvestment of one's wealth, rather than its squandering on worldly pleasures, proved a further effective means to create God's kingdom of abundance. Accordingly, great success, which must have come from God's hand, also became sanctified. To Weber, the ascetic, other-worldly organization of life by medieval monks in monasteries was transformed through the Protestant ethic into an inner-worldly asceticism that organized the believer's life comprehensively and methodically around work in a calling.

In charting this monumental shift away from a traditional economic ethic, and offering a religion-based cause of modern capitalism, Weber never sought to substitute an 'idealist' for a 'materialist' explanation. Rather, he aimed only to emphasize that a comprehensive explanation of modern capitalism's origins must include consideration of the 'economic ethic' as well as the 'economic form'. Far from claiming that Calvinism led to modern capitalism in a monocausal fashion, he asserted that the rise of this type of capitalism can be explained adequately only through multidimensional causal analyses. Entire arrays of, for example, political, legal, urban and economic developments had to occur in order to create a broad social context within which the spirit of capitalism, as well as the Protestant ethic, could take hold (1961 [1927], 1968 [1922]). On the other hand, once firmly entrenched, modern capitalism perpetuates itself by way of value-based legacies of ascetic Protestantism, now fully secularized, and a variety of external constraints. It no longer requires its original spirit (Kalberg 2002).

While addressing the rise of modern capitalism in an unorthodox and heretofore unexplored manner, *The Protestant Ethic* failed to grapple with the larger comparative issue. Weber knew well that the distinctiveness of what he termed Western rationalism could be established only through a series of comparisons with non-Western civilizations. In turning in *EEWR* to China and India he again took the issue of modern capitalism as his focus, though here he posed the negative question of why this type of capitalism had failed to develop in these civilizations. However, he attempted not only to assess whether Confucian, Taoist, Hindu and Buddhist teachings introduced or inhibited methodical action oriented towards work and profit; rather, he also turned in these studies to the 'interests' side of the equation, investigating the economic ethics of non-Western world religions in the context of a whole series of legal, economic, political and status group factors, and in relation to urbanization. This comparative procedure enabled Weber to delineate the array of forces in the West that proved unique and conducive to the long-term development of modern capitalism. These empirical studies, as well as his investigation of ancient Judaism, carried him a giant step further towards his goal of understanding the manner in which social configurations in the East and West influenced the formation of subjective meaning. Chinese, Indian and Western forms of rationalism were now distinguished.

As Weber himself repeatedly emphasized, however, these studies remained incomplete, especially if examined with reference to his overall goals. They are, furthermore, too poorly organized to provide us with a distinctively Weberian approach that can be used to unlock the elusive relationship between what he termed ideas and interests. These empirical investigations must be read through the lens of the analytical categories and models he develops for the analysis of social action, East and West, in one of the genuine classics of modern social science, *E&S* (1968 [1922]).

At first glance, this three-volume tome seems to conceal Weber's larger aims. Part One is concerned primarily with the articulation of a broad series of ideal types. Although empirically based, each concept is formulated on a universal scale and so remains at a high level of abstraction. Nonetheless, each can serve as a point of reference for the definition of particular cases. The ideal types in Part Two are often less all-encompassing and relate to specific epochs and civilizations (Mommsen 1989). This section reveals on every page how its author, in considering historical examples, extracted their essence and constructed ideal types. Just this perpetual movement between the historical and ideal-typical levels, as well as Weber's unwillingness to formulate an ideal type before scrutinizing innumerable cases, accounts for the exceedingly disjointed character of *E&S*. Its readability is also diminished by his failure to discuss overriding themes in a synoptic fashion.

These problems have blinded many commentators upon this treatise to its 'analytic' of social action, which can be utilized to study even entire civilizations (Kalberg 2004). Consequently, each chapter has often been read and debated apart from its broader purposes in the Weberian corpus and in an ahistorical fashion. Nonetheless, even standing on their own, the separate chapters have attained classical status in a wide variety of sociology's subfields. In each chapter, while dealing with questions and dilemmas specific to the spheres of law, religion, the economy, 'rulership', the city, the family and the clan, Weber sets out to describe how meaningful action becomes patterned by diverse 'internal' (values and ideas) and 'external' (political and economic interests) influences, and becomes manifest in specific status groups and organizations, or 'social carriers'.

Only the typology of 'rulership' (*Herrschaft*) can be given special attention here. (This translation has been suggested by Benjamin Nelson and appears preferable to either 'domination', which captures the element of force yet weakens the notion of legitimacy, or 'authority', which conveys legitimacy but downplays the component of force.) In this voluminous section Weber wished to define the major bases conceivable for the legitimation of rulership and to articulate for each the typical relationships between rulers, administrative bodies and the ruled. *Charismatic* personalities derived a right to rule from their extraordinary personal qualities and the belief of the ruled in their superhuman inspirations; *traditional* rulership (patriarchal, feudal and patrimonial/monarchical) rested upon custom and the belief that time immemorial itself provided a justification for continued rule; and *rational-legal* (bureaucratic) rulership was legitimated through enacted laws, statutes and regulations. Crucial for the endurance of all types is at least a minimum belief on the part of the ruled that obedience to the ruler is justified. Much more is

therefore involved than sheer power, or, in Weber's classic definition, 'the likelihood that one person in a social relationship will be able to carry out his own will despite resistance' (1968 [1922]: 53; translation altered). While many interpreters have reified Weber's rulership concepts, he designed them exclusively as heuristic yardsticks to be utilized for research purposes.

A subtle and complex view of the relationships between action oriented to values, rulership, material interests, political considerations, and traditions prevails throughout *E&S* and *EEWR*. As opposed to the more empirically based *EEWR* studies, the chapters in *E&S* deal with these relationships more as models that, on the one hand, combine ideal types in relationships of 'elective affinities' and, on the other hand, chart the patterned 'relations of antagonism' across these discrete constructs. At this point, Weber's sociology moves far beyond mere concept-formation and the construction of typologies; he outlines in addition the dynamic interactions of constellations of ideal types. He also shifts back and forth across ideal types of varying range, many of which aim to articulate 'developmental sequences', namely, entire series of sphere-specific ideal types that, in reference to developmental questions and dilemmas indigenous to them on the one hand and particular empirical transformations on the other, seek to conceptualize epochal change, East and West, within the spheres of religion, law, economy and rulership (Kalberg 1994). Whether the transformations hypothesized by these research models in fact took place in the history of a particular epoch and civilization remained an empirical question for Weber, one that involved above all the strength of carrier strata, economic forces, the success of new groups and organizations in establishing their rulership, sheer power, and orientations to broad constellations of values (whether religious or ideological).

Despite his awareness of the sustaining capacity of tradition-oriented action and the manner in which millennia-long histories remained within civilizational tracks, or world-views, Weber's conviction that power and unexpected historical accidents, not to mention new beliefs and charismatic leadership, could always introduce a chain-reaction realignment of social configurations prevented him from constructing formulas that would predict the future. He held to this position even though he saw that some complex civilizations became highly bureaucratized and might remain ossified for centuries (ancient Egypt, classical China). Unforeseen developments and even major shifts may occasionally take place despite bureaucratization. Evolutionary theories (including Marxism) provided useful hypotheses rather than scientific explanations. He refused to simplify on behalf of doctrinal or ideological positions and struggled persistently with the immense complexity, unresolved paradoxes and even contradictory drifts of social reality.

This sketch of Weber's sociology has touched upon only a few of its major contours. His effort to define the constellations of meaning in major civilizations and to offer a comparative-sociological explanation for their origin and unfolding, particularly those of modern Western rationalism, constitutes perhaps his overarching theme. His massive investigations were motivated in the end by a deep-seated scepticism regarding the survival of individuals oriented to values and ethical positions amidst the impersonal exchange relationships of advanced capitalism, the functional rules and regulations of the modern bureaucracy, and the orientation towards power typical in the modern state.

STEPHEN KALBERG
BOSTON UNIVERSITY

References

Kalberg, S. (1994) *Max Weber's Comparative Historical Sociology*, Oxford.
—— (2002) 'Introduction to *The Protestant Ethic*', in M. Weber, *The Protestant Ethic and the Spirit of Capitalism*, Oxford.
—— (2004) *Max Weber's Sociology of Civilizations* (forthcoming).
Mommsen, W. (1989) 'Ideal type and pure type: Two variants of Max Weber's ideal-typical method', in *The Political and Social Theory of Max Weber*, Chicago.
Weber, M. (1949) *The Methodology of the Social Sciences*, New York.
—— (1951 [1920]) *The Religion of China*, New York.
—— (1952 [1920]) *Ancient Judaism*, New York.
—— (1958 [1920]) *The Religion of India*, New York.
—— (1961 [1927]) *General Economic History*, New York.
—— (1968 [1922]) *Economy and Society*, New York.
—— (2002 [1920]) *The Protestant Ethic and the Spirit of Capitalism*, Oxford.
—— (2004) *Max Weber: The Confrontation with Modernity*, Oxford.

Further reading

Bendix, R. and Roth, G. (1971) *Scholarship and Partisanship: Essays on Max Weber*, Berkeley, CA.
Kalberg, S. (2000) 'Max Weber', in G. Ritzer (ed.) *The Blackwell Companion to Major Social Theorists*, Oxford.
Ringer, F. (1997) *Max Weber's Methodology*, Cambridge, MA.
Roth, G. (2001) *Max Webers deutsch–englische Familiengeschichte, 1800–1950*, Tübingen.
Weber, M. (1975) *Max Weber: A Biography*, New York.

WELFARE ECONOMICS

If economics is the study of how to make the best, or optimal, use of limited resources, welfare economics is concerned with the meaning of the term 'optimal' and with the formulation of statements that permit us to say that a given policy or event has improved or reduced social welfare.

Optimality is defined in terms of maximizing social welfare, so that the focus of concern is on what comprises the latter concept. Typically, it is taken to be the sum of the welfares of all members of a defined society. By adopting the value judgement that what should count in the formulation of a measure of social welfare is the judgements that individuals make about their own welfare, we have the basis for Paretian welfare economics (named after Vilfredo Pareto). In this case, to say that individual A's welfare has improved is to say no more than that A prefers one situation to another. To say that social welfare has improved requires a further definitional statement, namely, that the improvement in A's welfare has occurred without any other individual being worse off in consequence. Thus social welfare has improved if, and only if, at least one individual's welfare has improved without causing a decrease in the welfare of somebody else. It may be noted that while the first requirement is a value judgement, the second is rather a matter of definition.

Paretian welfare economics is almost self-evidently sterile, since we can envision few situations in which no one is harmed by a policy. Some individuals gain and others lose. The sterility of the pure Paretian principle arises because of the alleged difficulty of comparing one person's gain in welfare and another's loss. This is the so-called 'fallacy of interpersonal comparisons of utility'. If this is accepted, there are obvious difficulties for the formulation of criteria for a gain in social welfare. Kaldor (1939) and Hicks (1939) argued that there is a net gain in social welfare if those who gain can use part of their gains to compensate the losers and still have something left over. In other words, if compensation occurred, those who stand to lose would be fully compensated and their welfare would accordingly be the same after the policy in question was implemented as it had been before. Gainers would still be better off, provided the required compensation is less than their gross gains. This is the Kaldor–Hicks compensation principle.

Scitovsky (1941) pointed out that a further condition is required, since a policy may alter the distribution of income in such a way that those who lose may be able to pay those who gain sufficient to induce them back to the initial situation. The requirement that this should not be the case defines the Scitovsky reversal test for a state of affairs to be defined as a (modified) Pareto-improvement. Since actual compensation mechanisms are complex, all compensation criteria are typically formulated in terms of the potential for compensation. There is no requirement for the compensation to occur. This implies a definitive departure from the Pareto principle: the compensation principle may sanction a policy that leads to a (strict) Pareto deterioration in social welfare. Scitovsky's work opened the way for an explicit treatment of the distribution of income. Little (1957) defined various alternatives whereby social welfare can be said to increase according to the fulfilment of the compensation criterion (the efficiency test) and an improvement in the distribution of income (an equity test). The seminal work of Rawls (1971), however, marked a turning point in welfare economics, since when explicit and simultaneous attention is paid to both efficiency and equity through the adoption of Rawls's 'maximin' principle of benefiting the least well off in society.

The historical oddity of welfare economics remains that it has survived as an elaborate framework in itself, and as the foundation of practical techniques such as cost–benefit analysis, despite severe and arguably fatal criticism in the 1950s notably in the work of de V. Graaf (1957). Arrow's (1963) famous 'impossibility theorem' also indicates the problems of defining any social welfare function based on the fundamental Paretian value judgement about consumer sovereignty.

The basic analysis of welfare economics has remained largely unchanged since the mid-1970s. It has formed the foundation for environmental economics as well as cost–benefit analysis. Recent work has integrated psychological concepts, notably in work on the divergence found in practice between the Hicksian concepts of *compensating and equivalent variations (CV and EV)*, two measures of consumer surplus. Theoretically, the two measures should be nearly the same. In practice, EV appears to be substantially above CV, or, in plain language, 'willingness to accept compensation' to tolerate a welfare loss greatly exceeds 'willingness to pay' for an equivalent environmental improvement. Some work speculates that these differences amount to non-reversible indifference curves, that is, consumers' valuations are heavily dependent on where they are to begin with. This is known as the theory of 'reference-dependent utility' because the valuation of a gain or loss is dependent on the initial state. If the state changes, valuations change, but not necessarily as predicted by orthodox theory. Economists and psychologists continue to debate the validity of reference-dependent utility.

DAVID W. PEARCE
UNIVERSITY COLLEGE LONDON

References

Arrow, K. (1963) *Social Choice and Individual Values*, 2nd edn, New York.
de V. Graaf, J. (1957) *Theoretical Welfare Economics*, Cambridge, UK.
Hicks, J. (1939) 'Foundations of welfare economics', *Economic Journal* 49.
Kaldor, N. (1939) 'Welfare propositions of economics and interpersonal comparisons of utility', *Economic Journal* 49.
Little, I.M.D. (1957) *A Critique of Welfare Economics*, 2nd edn, Oxford.
Rawls, J. (1971) *A Theory of Justice*, Oxford.
Scitovsky, T. (1941) 'A note on welfare propositions in economics', *Review of Economic Studies* 9: 77–88.

Further reading

Boardman, A., Greenberg, D., Vining, A. and Weimer, D. (2001) *Cost Benefit Analysis: Concepts and Practice*, Upper Saddle River, NJ.

SEE ALSO: cost–benefit analysis; Pareto efficiency; poverty; welfare state

WELFARE STATE

The term welfare state refers to the role that states have played in providing welfare services and benefits for their citizens primarily in income maintenance and health care but also in housing, education and social work. From the end of the nineteenth century, the states of most industrialized countries involved themselves, with varying degree, form and effect, in such provision. In 1884 Germany introduced the first system of compulsory national insurance against sickness. Shortly afterwards Denmark, New Zealand and Australia introduced non-contributory old-age pensions. In Britain a series of similar welfare reforms was enacted by the Liberal government between 1906 and 1914. However, the most significant developments took place in the 1930s and 1940s with, for example, the New Deal in the USA, the People's Home in Sweden, and postwar welfare reforms in Britain, France and Germany. Most of these reforms centred upon the goal of full male employment supported by family allowances and insurance benefits for sickness, unemployment and old age. They were premised upon a male breadwinner family model and eligibility by nationality. This particular historical development of what is sometimes called the Keynesian welfare state underpins the meaning of the term welfare state.

However, this general understanding of the welfare state conceals a number of important issues. First, not all welfare provision emanates from the state, nor do all citizens benefit equally. The market, the voluntary sector and the family, especially the unpaid work of women, also provide welfare. Second, the postwar welfare settlement has faced major challenges. Third, these challenges have been accompanied by different political standpoints and explanations for the role of welfare in society.

Up until the 1970s the study of welfare states was dominated by a Fabian or social democratic approach in which the extension of state-provided welfare was seen as the key to a more egalitarian and integrated socialist society (Titmuss 1958). However, not all those who favoured state welfare intervention were necessarily socialist. The architect of the British postwar settlement, Beveridge, was a Liberal who believed in state intervention to remove the warts from the face of capitalism. By the mid-1970s economic recession and a rise in unemployment along with political and intellectual challenges from right and left began to emerge.

In Britain and the USA in the 1980s New Right governments marked the articulation and practice of particular forms of neo-liberal approaches to welfare. Here, the welfare state is seen not as a solution to society's ills but as a cause: it creates high taxation; interferes with the market; acts as a disincentive to economic growth; it creates a culture of dependency (an underclass) sapping individual initiative; and is wasteful, inefficient and bureaucratic (Friedman 1962).

Critical analyses of the welfare state also emerged from the left. A political economy of welfare explains the development of the welfare state as an uneasy truce between conflicting interests: the interests of capitalism in accumulating profit and in having a healthy, cared-for and appropriately skilled workforce; the interests of the working class in improving their conditions, and the interests of the state in maintaining political stability and its own legitimacy (Gough 1979). Changes in the organization of capitalism since the 1970s, particularly the shift to post-Fordism and industrial flexibility, have fragmented the working class and undermined the rationale of the truce.

Greater emphasis is placed by other analysts on the political variations of different welfare states. One major comparative study of eighteen advanced capitalist democracies argues that their welfare systems cluster around three distinct welfare regimes: e.g. liberal (USA, Canada, Australia, Japan, Switzerland), e.g. conservative (France, Germany, Italy, Austria, Belgium) and e.g. social democratic (Sweden, Norway, Denmark, Finland, The Netherlands) (Esping-Andersen 1990, 1999). What distinguishes the three regimes most are their political histories, especially working-class mobilization and the capacity for class coalitions, the relative influence of the state and the market, and the extent to which access to social security benefits effectively cushions citizens from dependence upon the market.

Other analysts emphasize how the development of social movements around gender, race and disability exposed the 'false' universalism of the postwar welfare state. Here the development of welfare states is understood in terms of the changing conditions not just of 'work' but of 'family' and 'nation' too (Williams 1989). While welfare has the capacity to give people greater security from risk, many policies have reinforced assumptions of the dependency of women, disabled and older people, as well as the marginalization of racialized minorities, not granting them full citizenship (Oliver 1990; Lister 2000).

By the 1990s the conditions of welfare states' existence had changed further: an ageing population, changing family structure, increases in migration, poverty and class, gender and racial inequalities. Further, international organizations such as the EU (Hantrais 2000), the World Bank and IMF increased their influence over the trajectories of national welfare states (Deacon 1997). This was followed by a reshaping – or 'modernizing' – of the aims and organization of many welfare states with greater emphasis given to the three 'M's: markets, managers and the mixed economy in the organization and delivery of services. When Bill Clinton announced in the USA in 1996 that it was 'the end of welfare as we know it' he was referring to the shift from welfare to workfare programmes where eligibility to benefits becomes conditional upon participation in paid work. This has been adopted by a number of welfare states (USA, UK, Denmark, The Netherlands) in different ways. This development indicates a new twenty-first 'Third Way' century variant of the welfare state that emphasizes responsibilities over rights (Giddens 2000). It is no longer based upon the male breadwinner but upon the 'adult worker model' where all adults – men and women – are expected to be in paid work. This is already creating new contradictions for the welfare state, not least in terms of the provisions that are required in order to allow women to work, such as child and elder care, as well as problems for 'work/life' balance (Duncan and Williams 2002).

FIONA WILLIAMS
UNIVERSITY OF LEEDS

References

Deacon, B. (1997) *Global Social Policy*, London.
Duncan, S. and Williams, F. (eds) (2002) 'New cross-national perspectives on gender equality, care and paid work', Special Issue of *Critical Social Policy* 22 (1).
Esping-Andersen, G. (1990) *The Three Worlds of Welfare Capitalism*, Cambridge, UK.
—— (1999) *Social Foundations of Post-Industrial Economies*, Cambridge.
Friedman, M. (1962) *Capitalism and Freedom*, Chicago.
Giddens, A. (ed.) (2000) *The Third Way and its Critics*, Cambridge.
Gough, I. (1979) *The Political Economy of Welfare*, London.
Hantrais, L. (2000) *Social Policy in the European Union*, Basingstoke.
Lister, R. (2000) *Citizenship: Feminist Perspectives*, Basingstoke.
Oliver, M. (1990) *The Politics of Disablement*, London.
Titmuss, R.M. (1958) *Essays on the Welfare State*, London.
Williams, F. (1989) *Social Policy: A Critical Introduction. Issues of Race, Gender and Class*, Cambridge, UK.

SEE ALSO: citizenship; poverty; social work; welfare economics

WITCHCRAFT AND WITCH-CLEANSING MOVEMENTS

Europeans and North Americans often regard the belief in witchcraft as unique to the witch persecutions of the Inquisition and Reformation. Actually, witchcraft beliefs are much more widely distributed in time and place. They are encountered throughout history, in virtually all continents, and continue to be an important feature of contemporary times. In many Mediterranean societies it is believed that the envy of certain persons can bring harm to objects and other people through an 'evil eye' (Stewart 1991), and in rural France, witchcraft is invoked to explain misfortunes such as alcoholism, impotence and insanity (Favret-Saada 1980). Another recent example of witchcraft-type beliefs is the allegation that English children are sexually abused in Satanic rituals (La Fontaine 1997).

Due to their widespread distribution, witchcraft beliefs and accusations have become a staple topic of anthropological research. In his classic study among the Azande of colonial Sudan, Evans-Pritchard (1937) distinguished between 'witchcraft' and 'sorcery'. He defined witchcraft as the innate, inherited ability to cause misfortune or death. For Azande, witchcraft involved unconscious psychic powers, emanating from a black swelling, located near the liver. By contrast, Azande described as sorcery the performance of rituals, the uttering of spells and the manipulation of organic substances such as herbs, with the conscious intent of causing harm. Whilst this distinction is widespread throughout East Africa, it is not made in other parts of Africa, or elsewhere. Many contemporary authors therefore use the terms 'witch' and 'witchcraft' more broadly to denote both types of persons and modes of action. (In this essay I retain the word 'sorcery' only where used by authors in the original texts.)

In an overview of ethnographic studies, Mayer (1954) points to the recurrence of certain features in witchcraft beliefs. (1) Though human, witches incorporate non-human power. So witches may be possessed by Satan; have pythons in their bellies; work with animals such as snakes, cats, baboons and owls, which they own as familiars, or may change themselves into the shape of familiars. (2) Witches are nearly always adults who are said to inherit their destructive power. They may bear physical stigmata like a red eye, a Devil's mark or a special witchcraft substance. (3) Witches tend to become socially important in times of crisis, when all sorts of misfortune – sickness, death, drought or plague – are ascribed to them. (4) Witches harm their own kin and neighbours rather than strangers. (5) Witchcraft is motivated by envy and malice, rather than by the pursuit of material gain. (6) Witches reverse usual expectations of behaviour. They work at night, commit incest, practise cannibalism, go naked instead of clothed or may stand backwards when they knock at doors. (7) Witchcraft is nearly always immoral.

Classical anthropological theories have left open questions about the actual performance of witchcraft. Instead, they have sought to unearth the psychological and social realities underlying witchcraft beliefs, or the cultural meanings encoded by them. Fortune (1932) treated sorcery on the Dobu Island of Melanesia as a conception of mystical power. He suggests that in a political system with no titular authority, prowess in sorcery was perceived as an important component of leadership. Dobuans used sorcery 'for collecting bad debts and enforcing economic obligation, in vendetta to avenge one's own sickness or one's kinsmen's death, to wipe out serious insult' (Fortune 1932: 175). Evans-Pritchard (1937) demonstrated how witchcraft constituted an 'ideational system' amongst the Azande, offering a logical explanation of unfortunate events. He insisted, however, that the theory of witchcraft did not exclude empirical knowledge about cause and effect, but rather supplemented theories of natural causation, and answered questions about the particularity of misfortunes. He cited as an example the collapsed granary,

which injured those sitting beneath it. The Azande explained this event in empirical terms: that termites had eaten the supports. But they resorted to witchcraft to explain why particular individuals were sitting beneath the granary at the precise moment when it collapsed. Kluckhohn (1944) elaborated a psychological theory of witchcraft. He argued that among the Navaho witchcraft served as a channel for projecting emotions of guilt, desire and aggression. By investing the witch with responsibility for misfortune, Navaho absolved themselves from blame. Their forbidden desires, such as incest, also found an outlet in fantasies of witchcraft. Moreover, under stressful conditions, witches were scapegoats for hostile impulses. Through accusations of witchcraft Navaho could directly express their hostile feelings for people to whom they would otherwise be unable to show anger.

Sociological theories of conflict inspired analysis of witchcraft in the 1960s. Marwick (1965) contended that witchcraft accusations reformulate problematic social relations that are not susceptible to judicial processes. He argued that amongst the Chewa of Zambia accusations of witchcraft occurred when the matrilineage grew beyond the size that resources could sustain. As tensions over inheritance became apparent, accusations of witchcraft served as an idiom for initiating processes of fission, and enabled the accusers to break off redundant relationships.

During the 1970s neo-Marxists demonstrated the instrumentality of witchcraft beliefs and accusations in political economic struggles, whilst interpretive studies delineated the meaning of witchcraft beliefs within wider symbolic systems. In this tradition, Kelly (1976) showed that there was an analogical relationship between witchcraft and sexual intercourse amongst the Etoro of Papua New Guinea. The Etoro perceived both acts as transmitting life forces from one person to another, in pursuit of extra vigour.

Recent studies show how modernization and globalization spawn new forms of occult beliefs. Ciekawy and Geschiere (1998) contend that witchcraft is a fertile discourse for interpreting modern changes. By betraying his or her victims to outsiders, the witch forges a link between local kinship networks and global changes. Using this idiom, people can express concern about the way in which new technologies open up local communities, while providing only selective opportunities and benefits.

According to Lattas (1993), sorcery constituted a kind of political language in the New Britain area of Papua New Guinea. Discourses of sorcery incorporated European symbols, offices and commodities. People allegedly learnt and swapped sorcery skills on the plantations, and purchased sorcery substances such as powerful herbicides in the market-place. In this way a 'violent space of death' was coextensive with commodity production. Geschiere (1997) showed how discourses of witchcraft had infiltrated political life in Cameroon. Like conspiracy theories, he suggests, witchcraft rendered political processes, and the sudden accumulation of wealth, comprehensible. Villagers believed that an occult force called *djambe* was the principle behind the success of politicians. They also suspected that the newly rich had transformed their victims into zombies in order to exploit their labour. Local witches were even accused of working with the mafia to organize a worldwide zombie traffic.

Witchcraft has evoked various responses: ranging from divination, the use of protective devices and legal procedures, to the killing of witches and to the organization of witch-cleansing cults. In Greece, villagers diagnosed the evil eye by dropping oil into water, and removed its influence by saying prayers, and by dropping a cross into a glass of water (Stewart 1991). In Cameroon the state constantly experiments with new ways of containing witchcraft. Regional courts in Cameroon's East Province have even sentenced witches to imprisonment on the basis of testimony provided by certified diviners (Geschiere 1997).

Elsewhere in Africa and in Melanesia, alleged witches have been severely dealt with, and campaigns against witches could be a means of pursuing enemies. Amongst the Hewa of Papua New Guinea, the killing of witches was associated with competition for resources between different roofing and flooring parties. By executing those members of other parties who threatened their interests, the witch killers generated fear and communicated their capacity to use violence to protect these interests (Steadman 1985).

Since colonial times, regular witch-cleansing cults have occurred in a number of areas in sub-Saharan Africa. Though these cults lacked formal organizational structure, they readily crossed ethnic and national boundaries. The *kamcape*

movement of the 1930s, for instance, spread from Nyasaland into northern and southern Rhodesia, the Congo and Mozambique (Willis 1968). The organizers used hand-mirrors as a form of divination. A medicine was then administered to render the witchcraft ineffective, to protect the innocent against mystical attacks and to kill anyone who reverted to witchcraft. Self-confessed witches usually resumed their places in the community, without any hint of ostracism, and a morally regenerated life began for everyone. Willis argues that by rooting out the cause of all trouble, these cults aim to inaugurate an instant millennium – 'an age of bliss in which pain, disease, untimely death, violence, strife, war and hunger will be unknown' (1970: 131).

Witch-cleansing cults involve considerable ambiguity. They explicitly aim to restore social harmony but often the cults aim to introduce social reforms and give temporary power to younger men at the expense of elders. The younger men generally have a wider universe of interests, and are often linked to African nationalist movements. In postcolonial Africa witch-cleansing cults addressed fears by the youth that their paths to prosperity were being blocked. Auslander (1993) shows that in rural Zambia, the popular appeal of witch-cleansing lay in its promise to restore productivity. The witch-cleansing cult symbolically used tools of government surveillance – roadblocks, identity cards, numbers and rubber stamps – to detect witches.

ISAK NIEHAUS
UNIVERSITY OF PRETORIA, SOUTH AFRICA

References

Auslander, M. (1993) 'Open the wombs!': The symbolic politics of modern Ngoni witchfinding', in J. Comaroff and J. Comaroff (eds) *Modernity and Its Malcontents: Ritual and Power in Postcolonial Africa*, Chicago, pp. 167–92.

Ciekawy, D. and Geschiere, P. (1998) 'Containing witchcraft: Conflicting scenarios in postcolonial Africa', *African Studies Review* 41(3): 1–14.

Evans-Pritchard, E.E. (1937) *Witchcraft, Oracles and Magic amongst the Azande of Anglo-Egyptian Sudan*, Oxford.

Favret-Saada, J. (1980) *Deadly Words: Witchcraft in Brocage*, Cambridge.

Fortune, R. (1932) *Sorcerers of Dobu: The Social Anthropology of the Dobu Islands of the Western Pacific*, London.

Geschiere, P. (1997) *The Modernity of Witchcraft: Politics of the Occult in Postcolonial Africa*, Charlottesville, VA.

Kelly, R. (1976) 'Witchcraft and sexual relations: An exploration in the social and semantic implications of the structure of belief', in P. Brown and G. Buchbinder (eds) *Man and Woman in the New Guinea Highlands*, AAA Special Publications No. 8, Washington, DC, pp. 36–53.

Kluckhohn, C. (1944) *Navaho Witchcraft*, Boston.

La Fontaine, J. (1997) *Speak of the Devil: Tales of Satanic Abuse in Contemporary England*, Cambridge.

Lattas, A. (1993) 'Sorcery and colonialism: Illness, dreams and death as political languages in west New Britain', *Man* (n.s.) 28(2): 51–77.

Marwick, M. (1965) *Sorcery and Its Social Setting: A Study of the Northern Rhodesian Cewa*, Manchester.

Mayer, P. (1954) *Witches*, Inaugural Lecture, Grahamstown: Rhodes University.

Steadman, L. (1985) 'The killing of witches', *Oceania* 56(2): 106–23.

Stewart, C. (1991) *Demons and the Devil*, Princeton, NJ.

Willis, R. (1968) 'Kamcape: An anti-sorcery movement in S.W. Tanzania', *Africa* 38(1): 1–15.

—— (1970) 'Instant millennium: The sociology of African witch-cleansing cults', in M. Douglas (ed.) *Witchcraft Confessions and Accusations*, London, pp. 129–40.

WITTGENSTEIN, LUDWIG JOSEF JOHANN (1889–1951)

Wittgenstein was born in Vienna and though originally trained as an engineer became a pupil of Bertrand Russell at Cambridge. He returned to Austria to serve in the First World War, and in 1921 published the German edition of the *Tractatus Logico-Philosophicus*. He then became a schoolteacher in Lower Austria. In this, as in everything else, he was an intense and demanding man, and soon resigned his post. After that, he became involved in the design of a house that still stands in Vienna, a monument to the aesthetic austerity that he championed. Around this time he rejected the *Tractatus* and began to articulate his later philosophy. He returned to Cambridge in 1929 and held the chair of philosophy from 1939 to 1947.

In the *Tractatus* the essence of language is assumed to reside in its fact-stating function. This is said to rest on the capacity of sentences to 'picture' facts. Pictures consist of parts that correspond to the parts of the thing pictured. The parts of a picture stand to one another in a certain relation, and this says how the corresponding objects are arranged if the picture is true. In language the parts are names, and elementary sentences are arrangements of names.

More complicated sentences can then be built up by using the rules of Russell's logic. Wittgenstein may have based his picture theory on the way in which systems of material points have a symbolic representation in sophisticated versions of theoretical mechanics. Certainly the conclusion he drew was that the only meaningful language was the language of science. All attempts to transcend this and express what is 'higher' – namely ethics, aesthetics and the meaning of life – are doomed. Even the attempt to state the relation of language to the world tries to go beyond these limits, so the doctrines of the *Tractatus* itself are meaningless. Those who understand my propositions correctly, said Wittgenstein, will surmount them like a ladder, and then throw them away.

Is this an attack on everything non-scientific? Wittgenstein's friend, Paul Engelmann, tells us that it is the exact opposite. The aim is not to dismiss what cannot be said, the 'higher', but to *protect* it. The *Tractatus* is an ethical document that must be understood in terms of Wittgenstein's involvement with the great Viennese critic Karl Kraus and the influential architect Adolf Loos. Kraus exposed moral corruption that shows itself in the corruption of language. Loos conducted a campaign against aesthetic corruption that shows itself in the confusion of art with utility and the pollution of functional simplicity by needless decoration. The *Tractatus* likewise expressed the ethics of purity, separation, simplicity and the integrity of silence.

Why Wittgenstein became dissatisfied with this position is unclear, but some light may be shed by relating his shift of opinion to a broad cultural change in which he participated. If the *Tractatus* addressed the issues that exercised prewar Viennese intellectuals, the late philosophy addressed the problems that confronted them in the postwar years. We know that the military defeats and economic and constitutional problems in Europe were accompanied by an acute sense of cultural crisis. One symptom of this was the enormous popularity of Spengler's irrational life-philosophy with its conservative pessimism. Wittgenstein is known to have been impressed by Spengler, and the later work can be seen as a brilliant expression of this form of conservative irrationalism. All the features of this style – the priority of the concrete over the abstract, of practice over norms, life over reason and being over thought – are prominently displayed.

In his later work Wittgenstein rejected the idea that language has a single essential function. It is not structured by correspondence with objects but by its role in the stream of life. There are as many ways for words to carry meaning as there are ways of organizing action. The picture theory gave way to the idea of 'language games'. We must not theorize about language but observe its diversity as we name, count, instruct, question, promise, pray and so on. The real heart of the late philosophy, however, is the analysis of rule following. It is tempting to explain human behaviour in terms of our capacity to follow rules. In § 201 of the *Investigations* Wittgenstein argued that no course of action can be determined by rules, because any course of action could be said to accord with the rule. Any non-standard interpretation of a rule could be justified by a non-standard interpretation of the rules for following the rule. Ultimately it must be said of all rules that they are obeyed blindly. At every point, rules, and the application of the concepts in them, depend on taken-for-granted practices or customs. Wittgenstein used this insight to bring out the conventional character of all knowledge and discourse, whether it was an introspective report or a mathematical truth.

For the later Wittgenstein, then, the notion of meaning is explained in terms of *use*. Meaningless or metaphysical discourse is language 'on holiday', that is, not employed in a language game that has a genuine role in a form of life. The job of the philosopher is to inhibit our tendency to detach words from their real use. In this the philosopher is like a doctor who must bring language back to its healthy everyday life. What had to be accepted as given, said Wittgenstein, was the 'form of life'. Other than this all belief is groundless: this is the end-point of all justification. Nothing could be a clearer expression of the conservative thinker's belief in the priority of life over reason.

It is only now that this European dimension of Wittgenstein's thinking, both in its early and late phase, is beginning to emerge. This offsets the somewhat narrow readings that have been given them as forms of logical and linguistic 'analysis'. Nevertheless the full potential of the late philosophy, as the basis of a social theory of knowledge, still awaits exploitation.

DAVID BLOOR
UNIVERSITY OF EDINBURGH

Further reading

Bloor, D. (1997) *Wittgenstein. Rules and Institutions*, London.
Engelmann, P. (1967) *Letters from Ludwig Wittgenstein with a Memoir*, Oxford.
Janik, A. and Toulmin, S. (1973) *Wittgenstein's Vienna*, London.
Monk, R. (1990) *Ludwig Wittgenstein: The Duty of Genius*, London.
Specht, E.K. (1963) *The Foundations of Wittgenstein's Late Philosophy*, Manchester.
Winch, P. (1958) *The Idea of a Social Science and Its Relation to Philosophy*, London.
As Wittengstein's unpublished writings gradually appear in print, the corpus of his work now stands at over a dozen volumes. Nevertheless, the main texts of the early and late philosophy, respectively, are still:
Wittgenstein, L. (1953) *Philosophical Investigations*, Oxford.
—— (1961) *Tractatus Logico-Philosophicus*, London.

WOMEN

The definition, description and classification of women within the bounds of an autonomous and discrete category is contentious. Although the history of conceptualizing women as a social class in the West is a long one, the problem lies in its definition being relative to the category, 'men'. Women are 'the *opposite* sex', the 'feminine *other*' in a masculine/feminine paradigm dependent on the biological dichotomy male/female. Accordingly, male/man/masculine is the assumed norm against which female/woman/feminine is measured and found wanting within a heterosexual patriarchal social order. Perhaps at the very least women universally share the common and fundamental experience of being defined by their biology. They may not be genetically programmed to be nurturing, caring and emotionally literate but by virtue of their biological ability to bear children they are assigned social roles that require these skills. Child-rearing, child care and home management are overwhelmingly considered women's work the world over even when women also enjoy opportunities outside the domestic sphere. Herein then may lie the single uncontestable feature of women's experience that validates the classification 'women'.

One of the earliest dissenting voices to challenge women's secondary status was the French revolutionary, Olympe de Gouges, in her *Declaration of the Rights of Women* (1791).

However, even her rallying cry to women to 'awake' and 'unite' was a reaction to their exclusion from the French Assembly's *Declaration of the Rights of Man* (1791). Likewise Mary Wollstonecraft's *A Vindication of the Rights of Woman* (1792). Nevertheless, the latter is arguably the first person to view gender as a construct rather than an essence, thus challenging the notion of women's *natural* subordination to men. Virginia Woolf (1929) explains the differences between men and women in terms of economic inequalities and the unequal distribution of material resources. Later, Simone de Beauvoir's thesis that 'woman is made, not born' (1953 [1949]) was taken up by feminist theorists in the 1970s and 'woman' as a social construct gained currency. From now on the apparent essentialism underpinning the category 'women' was problematized within feminism. 'Woman', it was argued, is a myth born of male fantasies of desire and/or castration anxiety and is realized in and naturalized by Western cultural stereotypes. Prescribed within a virgin/whore dichotomy, women are represented as either chaste, good wives or promiscuous and sexually available.

Over the next two decades, while persistently challenging these stereotypes, the women's movement and its academic manifestation, women's studies, continued to conceptualize 'women' as a specific and identifiable constituency. Oppression and the desire for liberation was the common feature and 'sisterhood' the global phenomenon that would make liberation possible. The touchstone of feminist praxis was founded on the experience and knowledge of 'women'. Liberation would be achieved 'by women, for women, through women'. However, by the 1980s Western feminism's generalizations about women were further challenged by black women and women of colour who argued that the assumption of universality was invalid and exclusive, indeed racist, ignoring the diversity of women's experiences and so rendering invisible the inequalities and power differentials that prevail amongst women. Thus black women and women of colour argued that white Western usage of the collective 'women' excluded them and rendered them and their lived experience invisible. Age, race, sex and class as well as a myriad other variables militate against the categorical representation of women. By the 1990s, 'Third World' women's voices problematized the universalizing of women's gendered identification still further

by highlighting struggles and experiences in which the political, social and economic inequalities between North and South implicated the relationships between women across the divide. The development of late twentieth-century 'globalization' exacerbates the issue as the social and material gaps between 'First' and 'Third World' women (and men) appear to be widening.

These circumstances thus beg the questions: Must 'women' as description be discarded? Is the category 'women' a fiction? Do we validate the myth of 'woman' through usage of the plural 'women'? Notwithstanding the cultural and historical specificity of what it means to be a woman, consideration of economic, demographic and political variables across the world gives reason to talk very generally about the condition of women. Women constitute half the world's population, perform two-thirds of the world's work hours, earn one-tenth of the world's income and own less than one-hundredth of the world's property. And most of the world's poor are women. At least from the material point of view, it could be said that women do indeed constitute an identifiable social category. They are also more likely than men to be victims of rape and domestic violence. And political leadership everywhere is assumed almost exclusively by men. Finally, on every continent there is history of women mobilizing for specific social, political and/or economic objectives that are explicitly gendered.

The question of the extent to which performance of women's traditional roles draws on a feminine essence and the extent to which they must be learned may perhaps ultimately be answered by the geneticists. It remains to be seen whether current research into the connections between sex, brain and gender will be the final arbiter in the as yet unresolved contest between essentialist definitions of women and social constructionist explanations of 'woman' and 'women'. In the meantime 'women' as a political and economic social group continue to operate across time and space, more or less defined by those who are 'not-woman' whose lived experience, relative to their own, may, in general, be advantaged. However, notwithstanding the varying degrees of constraint, the diversity of experience and the inequalities of power and privilege amongst women (and between men and women), women are increasingly defining themselves, setting their own autonomous agendas and challenging and demystifying those stereotypes that underpin the myth of 'woman' through ever more confident self-representation.

MERIDY HARRIS
UNIVERSITY OF KENT

References

de Beauvoir, S. (1953 [1949]) *The Second Sex*, Harmondsworth.
Wollstonecraft, M. (1792) *A Vindication of the Rights of Woman*, London.
Woolf, V. (1929) *A Room of One's Own*, London.

Further reading

Baron-Cohen, S. (2003) *The Essential Difference*, Boulder, CO.
Butler, J. (1990) *Gender Trouble*, London.
Davis, A. (1981) *Women, Race and Class*, New York.
Evans, M. (ed.) (1994) *The Woman Question*, London.
Gilligan, C. (1982) *In a Different Voice*, Cambridge, MA.
hooks, b. (1982) *Ain't I a Woman: Black Women and Feminism*, London.
Morgan, R. (ed.) (1985) *Sisterhood is Global*, Harmondsworth.
Rich, A. (1976) *Of Woman Born*, New York.

SEE ALSO: feminist theory; gender, sociology of; women's studies

WOMEN'S STUDIES

The area of academic study that has become known as women's studies grew out of the feminist movement in the USA and Western Europe in the late 1960s and early 1970s. The movement had close intellectual and political links with the various campaigns of the time to democratize the universities, and as such one of the first targets of contemporary feminism was the sexism and misogyny of much of traditional scholarship. While feminism as a political movement campaigned around issues of sexuality (access to abortion and contraception, and the deconstruction of heterosexuality as the single permissible form of sexual practice) and unequal power relations between the sexes (in both the household and the public worlds of politics and paid work) feminism within the academy questioned the ways in which knowledge was constructed. Initially, campaigns were organized around the issue of the absence of women from the curriculum. If one subject dominated feminist critiques of the academy it was that the human

subject (in any discipline) was always, and uncontentiously, male.

The radicalism and the creativity of feminism of the early 1970s brought to academic debates and discussion profoundly innovative questions. For example, Kate Millett (1971) and Germaine Greer (1970) – both trained within the discipline of English literature – examined the ways in which official versions of culture marginalized and/or excluded women. Sheila Rowbotham's (1973) *Hidden from History* claimed the existence of another history – that of women. Across the range of disciplines taught in universities women academics turned to examine what they had been taught and found it both exclusive (in that it was largely blind to the existence of women) and informed by assumptions about the relative importance of women and men. Although feminists did uncover, and recover, a feminist tradition in which women had written about women (in the academy women such as Viola Klein, Alice Clark and Mirra Komarovsky and outside it figures such as Virginia Woolf and Simone de Beauvoir) a great deal of energy was also devoted to documenting the lives of women. The political slogan 'the personal is political' informed the studies by women of women within the household and personal relationships. As the boundaries between the public and the private started to shift, what was to emerge was public discussion of both pathological forms of male–female relationships (such as violence against women) and the more ordinary day-to-day responsibilities carried by women. Childcare, the care of sick and elderly people, and housework itself became part of the remit of the social sciences. Within the same context, feminist academics also turned to examine the ways in which information about the social world was collected. Personal experience and subjectivity were validated as legitimate forms of research data and research practice: as in previous debates about the objectivity of the social sciences, the case was made against the apparently disinterested social investigator. Thus just as the object of study shifted, so too did the subject.

This considerable and diverse project of the documentation of women's lives has continued since the late 1960s. However, as it has grown older, so two developments have become marked. The first, identifiable in the earliest days of women's studies, is debate around the issue of the theoretical systems underlying and informing the collection of information. In the early 1970s the term 'patriarchy' was widely used as an explanation for what was assumed to be the universal subordination of women. Feminist writers, within and outside the academy, used the term widely to indicate a male epistemology that inevitably led to the oppression of women. Within this theoretical stance were coined such vivid phrases as 'all men are rapists' and 'male power is the *raison d'être* of pornography'. A fundamental social and psychological distinction was assumed between women and men, from which followed an ongoing campaign by men to secure their domination.

The polarity explicit in this view has never lost its radicalizing impact, and despite the sophistication and diversity that now informs theoretical debates within women's studies the idea of a basic division between women and men still retains its intellectual as well as its political impact. But what has happened since the late 1960s in academic feminism is that the category of 'woman' has lost its initial homogeneity. Two developments in particular have been significant here: the first is the influence of psychoanalysis, the second the challenge to Western feminism by women of the South and women of minority groups within the North. The first major shift towards the integration of psychoanalysis into women's studies and feminism occurred in 1976 when Juliet Mitchell published *Psychoanalysis and Feminism*. In this she initiated a debate that still continues about the relationship between biological sex and sexuality. Written as a defence of Freud against those traditions in feminism that defined his work as misogynist, Juliet Mitchell (and subsequently numerous other women) turned to Freud in order to re-examine both the ways in which individual sexual identity is created and the construction of the symbolic order of sexuality. Both themes have remained central to women's studies. In 1980 Adrienne Rich attacked what she termed 'compulsory heterosexuality' and throughout the 1970s and 1980s French feminists, informed by Freud and Lacan, re-examined the assumed stability (and indeed existence) of femininity and the feminine.

The impact of psychoanalysis and psychoanalytically informed feminism on women's studies has been immense, and particularly so in the case of the study of literature. Whereas feminists in the early 1970s had worked to establish the existence of women writers, by the 1980s the canon of literature was to be further re-examined by feminist readings of the 'great tradition'. Women literary critics reread and reinterpreted literature, and in doing so demonstrated the diversity of interpretation made possible by feminism.

That theme of diversity has been equally significant in terms of the challenge to, and by, women's studies of ethnocentric perceptions of the social world. When Ester Boserup's *Women's Role in Economic Development* was published in 1970, the impact of the North on the South as a modernizing, and universally progressive, force was seldom questioned. 'Development' was widely read as positive. But after Boserup's intervention, anthropologists and economists were held accountable for the extent to which their understanding of other cultures was not merely ethnocentric in its conclusions but also sexist. In the 1970s feminists from cultures other than those of the white Northern middle class were to attack vehemently what they saw as the internal colonization of their cultures: imperialism was seen not only in terms of politics in subject territories but also in terms of the domination within societies of one culture over all others. In Britain and the USA in particular women of colour initiated campaigns to reclaim their past and construct their future. Another movement slogan 'finding our voice' became the organizing focus for the documentation of the lives of non-white women.

By the mid-1980s women's studies was established as an area of study in higher education throughout the North. An initial attack on the empirical absence of women as both objects of academic study and active subjects in the construction of knowledge had established the validity of each critique. While the Northern academy did not change its practices or curriculum, women academics established a space within universities for the legitimate discussion of issues affecting women and relevant to sexual difference. Nevertheless, although women now constitute about half of all students in higher education, they are still a small proportion (in all Western societies) of academics.

Despite the massive underrepresentation of women in the Western academy, women's studies (with which only some women academics identify) has made a significant impact on diverse disciplines and established new methodological and epistemological models. What has been put on the academic agenda is sexual difference, and the implications of sexual difference for the social experiences of the two sexes. In recent women's studies literature new departure can be detected in the subject matter and more particularly in the discussion of sexual difference. In terms of the first, what can be seen is a gradual development of interest in the issue of how sexual difference affects not only what we think about, but also the very processes through which knowledge in our society is collected and systematized. Women academics have turned to philosophy and the natural sciences (traditionally subjects in which the actual presence of women has been even more limited than in the social sciences and the humanities) to examine the dominating epistemologies of the West and post-Enlightenment thought. In part through the impact of postmodernism as a disempowering agency on all synthesizing 'grand theories' but equally through feminist scepticism about claims to universalism of all theoretical traditions, feminist scholars have taken to task the underlying claims to universal explanation and validity of a range of moral and methodological assumptions. For example, Sandra Harding (1986) has argued that natural science is 'gendered'; that is, that its method and its object is structured by organizing distinctions between male and female. In other contexts, a range of authors have made similar claims: that the great, supposedly abstract and objective systems of law, political science and medicine formed within a post-Enlightenment discourse are deeply gendered and founded upon an assumed, and certainly unnegotiated, distinction between female and male.

This radical attack on the very foundations of the Western academy has achieved the recognition of the impact of gender on both the questions, and the answers, of academics. The concept of 'difference' has, in this context, come to play a crucial part in discussions of the way in which people live and in the systems of knowledge that they construct. As Henrietta Moore has pointed out in *A Passion for Difference* (1994), it is one of the great ironies of the late twentieth (and now the twenty-first) century that just as the world apparently becomes more homogeneous so the idea of difference and toleration of difference is high on the political agenda. Feminists such as Moore and Judith Butler have further emphasized the theoretical (and indeed the empirical) instability of concepts such as desire and

sexual identity, an emphasis that has had a considerable impact on feminist studies of the body such as those by Kathy Davis (1995) and Susan Bordo (1993). In these, and other works, feminists have been engaged in an exercise in the deconstruction of rigid and definitive definitions of masculinity and femininity, an exercise that has both informed, and been informed by, the sexual imagination of the West. At the same time, feminists working on the study of class relations and the labour market point out the continuation of differential labour market rewards for women and men, the value of femininity as a 'form' in men but not in women and the global relationships that underpin certain forms of Western privilege.

Thus women's studies at the beginning of the twenty-first century can look back on 30 years of active engagement with the Western academy. That engagement has demonstrated that gender is a crucial element in all areas of social life. At the same time, as women's studies has become increasingly complex in its definition of gender, masculinity and femininity it has tended to move away from that essentialist position that identified biological difference as the determining form of social difference. In this, there now exists considerable distance from Western feminism – where gender differences can be construed in terms of symbolic and metaphorical differences and distinctions – and feminism outside the West, where biological difference remains for many women the crucial defining difference in social existence.

MARY EVANS
UNIVERSITY OF KENT

References

Bordo, S. (1993) *Unbearable Weight: Feminism, Western Culture, and the Body*, Berkeley, CA.

Boserup, E. (1970) *Women's Role in Economic Development*, New York.

Butler, J. (1990) *Gender Trouble*, London.

Davis, K. (1995) *Re-Shaping the Female Body*, London.

Greer, G. (1970) *The Female Eunuch*, London.

Harding, S. (1986) *The Science Question in Feminism*, Ithaca, NY.

Millett, K. (1971) *Sexual Politics*, London.

Mitchell, J. (1976) *Psychoanalysis and Feminism*, London.

Moore, H. (1994) *A Passion for Difference*, Cambridge, UK.

Rich, A. (1980) 'Compulsory heterosexuality', *Signs 5*.

Rowbotham, S. (1973) *Hidden from History*, London.

Further reading

Barrett, M. and Phillips, A. (1992) *Destabilising Theory*, Cambridge, UK.

Brown, L., Collins, H., Green, P., Humm, M. and Landells, M. (eds) (1992) *The International Handbook of Women's Studies*, Hemel Hempstead.

Humm, M. (ed.) (1992) *Feminisms: A Reader*, Hemel Hempstead.

Marks, E. and de Courtivron, I. (eds) (1981) *New French Feminisms*, Brighton.

Mitter, S. (1986) *Common Fate, Common Bond: Women in the Global Economy*, London.

Pateman, C. (1988) *The Sexual Contract*, Oxford.

Rose, J. (1986) *Sexuality in the Field of Vision*, London.

Sayers, J. (1992) *Mothering Psychoanalysis*, London.

Showalter, E. (1976) *A Literature of Their Own*, Princeton, NJ.

Stanley, L. and Wiseman, S. (1993) *Breaking Out Again*, London.

SEE ALSO: division of labour by sex; feminist theory; gender, sociology of; women

WORLD-SYSTEM ANALYSIS

Sociologist Immanuel Wallerstein developed world-system analysis in the early 1970s to explain the origins and processes of capitalism, the Industrial Revolution, and the complex interconnections of what were then labelled the First, Second and Third Worlds. He argued that the modern world-system arose in Western Europe about 500 years ago. It was based on capitalist trade networks that transcended state boundaries, hence he called it the capitalist world economy. The drive for capital accumulation via production for exchange caused increasing competition among capitalist producers for labour, materials and markets. As competition waxed and waned through repeated crises of overproduction, various regions of the world were incorporated into the unevenly expanding world economy. These cyclic processes are a fundamental property of the modern world-system.

Uneven expansion of the system differentiates it into three interrelated types of societies. First are 'core' societies that specialize in high-tech industrial production, distribution and administrative services, have relatively strong states, a strong bourgeoisie, a large wage-labour class, and are heavily involved in the affairs of non-core societies. At the other extreme, in the 'periphery', are societies that concentrate on the production of raw materials or low-tech industries, have weak states, a small bourgeoisie, a large peasant class, and are heavily influenced by core societies. The remaining societies form the semi-periphery, which shares characteristics of both the core and periphery. Semi-peripheral societies are typically rising peripheral societies, or declining core societies. The semi-periphery blocks polarization between core and periphery, and thus stabilizes the system. The economic and political interrelations of the core and periphery are the presumed sources of development in the core, and the lack of development in the periphery. A variety of network studies provides empirical validation of this tripartite division.

A key assumption of world-system analysis is that the world-system must be studied as a whole. Social change (a cover term for political, economic, cultural changes) in any component of the system – nations, states, regions, ethnic groups, classes – must begin by locating that component within the system. Conversely, changes in any component can affect the overall system. Thus world-system analysis has a dual research agenda. On the one hand research examines the consequences of changes in its components (states, regions, groups) for evolution of the system and for the movement of various components within the system. On the other hand research also examines the consequences of changes in the world-system for the internal dynamics and social structure of its various components. The key is the interplay of bottom-up and top-down processes.

World-system literature is complicated by a number of intertwined polemics including the possibility of a global democratic socialism; the degree to which underdevelopment in the periphery is a necessary consequence of core development; and the degree to which underdevelopment of peripheral areas was vital or only helpful to core development.

World-system researchers have gone far beyond Wallerstein's original agenda. In response to critics they have begun to study the roles of women, households, gender, race, ethnicity and culture in the world economy. Many case studies address these issues as well as slavery, agrarian capitalism and the incorporation of indigenous populations into the world economy. Scholars have also studied cyclical processes, labour relations, commodity chains and the collapse of the Soviet Union. Many case studies focus on how various actors have sought to limit world-systemic effects, and how those effects, in turn, have reshaped the overall system.

One burgeoning area of world-system research has been the study of precapitalist world-systems. This extension has two roots. Archaeologists and anthropologists have sought to use, albeit in modified form, world-systems analysis to study intersocietal interaction processes in the archaeological record and among precapitalist and non-state societies. Among world-system analysts debates centre on whether there has been one sporadically growing world-system since the origin of states some five millennia ago or several types of world-systems, of which the modern world-system is only one. Other evolutionary studies examine prestate world-systems. This extension of world-system analysis has led to re-examination of many of its founding assumptions, derived from the study of the modern world-system, and to refinement of its terminology. For instance, the word 'world' in world-system analysis does *not* mean 'global', but means a self-contained system, a world. It is only with the modern world-system that it became truly planetary. These re-examinations have been empirical, historically grounded and often conducted with an eye to foreseeing possible future transformations of the contemporary system.

These studies, in turn, also linked to discussions of globalization. Key points from a world-system perspective are that globalization processes are actually quite old. What is new in the last two centuries is that they have now become truly planetary and far more intense. Indeed, in a world-system perspective globalization is not so much a new social process or processes, as the logical culmination of the spread and intensification of capitalist practices. As with the study of precapitalist world-systems, the point is that careful, nuanced and critical use of studies of older systems can be useful to gain insights into the contemporary world-system. This requires careful attention to historical contexts in order to avoid either mechanically reading the past into the future or uncritically projecting current processes into the past.

The major enduring contribution of world-system studies has been to push social scientists to embed their research in global and historical contexts. Another contribution has been to make sense of the often confounding observation that social processes have one set of effects in core areas and other, often opposite, effects in peripheral areas. Furthermore, these effects often vary significantly among different peripheral regions. Studies of gender and households have been most enlightening in this regard. Development has generally led to improved status and social conditions for women in core areas, but frequently lowered status and worse social conditions in peripheral areas. The latter, however, is riddled with a great deal of variation and significant exceptions. Researchers have discovered similar differences in labour processes, ethnic conflict, social movements, and relations with indigenous peoples to name only a few.

World-system studies use techniques of and have been conducted from bases in all the social sciences. Studies have been published in many books and a wide range of journals. Because world-system research requires careful attention to historical and global contexts, much of its best work is presented in books rather than journals. Journal articles are often summaries of longer, more nuanced treatments, and thus sometimes appear to be overly deterministic and mechanical. Still, two journals are devoted to world-system issues. *Review* is published by the Fernand Braudel Center [FBC] at the Binghamton University in New York. The *Journal of World-Systems Research* is sponsored by the Institute for Research on World-Systems [IR-OWS] at the University of California, Riverside. The American Sociology Association sponsors a section on the Political Economy of the World-System [PEWS] devoted to world-system research. All of these have websites with extensive links to other Internet sites on world-system analysis.

THOMAS D. HALL
DEPAUW UNIVERSITY

Further reading

Chase-Dunn, C. (2001) 'World-systems theorizing', in J. Turner (ed.) *Handbook of Sociological Theory*, New York, pp. 589–612.

Hall, T. (ed.) (2000) *A World-Systems Reader*, Lanham, MD.

Shannon, T. (1996) *An Introduction to the World-System Perspective*, 2nd edn, Boulder, CO.

Wallerstein, I.M. (2000) *The Essential Wallerstein*, New York.

SEE ALSO: globalization; imperialism; underdevelopment

WORLD TRADE ORGANIZATION

Established in 1995 in Geneva, Switzerland, the World Trade Organization (WTO) is an international organization that deals with the rules of trade between its member countries. Its primary functions include serving as a forum for negotiations aimed at lowering barriers to trade, administering the subsequent agreements, monitoring trade policies, and arbitrating trade disputes between its members.

The Bretton Woods Conference of 1944 had proposed the creation of just such a multilateral institution, the International Trade Organization (ITO), which was expected to oversee international commerce and work together with the World Bank and the International Monetary Fund in enabling international economic co-operation and the smooth functioning of the international economy. However, ratification by national legislatures proved difficult to obtain (most notably in the USA) and the ITO was aborted. Instead, the multilateral trade system in the postwar period was largely based on the General Agreement on Tariffs and Trade (GATT), a provisional treaty that had by then emerged under which states undertook to adhere to specific rules and principles relating to goods trade and to participate in periodic rounds of multilateral trade negotiations to lower trade barriers. In its early years, GATT achieved enormous success in lowering trade barriers and increasing the volume of international goods trade. However, the evident weaknesses of its dispute settlement mechanisms, the exclusion of important sectors of the economy (agriculture, textiles and the increasingly important services sector) from its ambit, and the proliferation of new and more complex instruments of trade protection (such as anti-dumping procedures) that enabled countries to effectively sidestep GATT agreements led, by the 1980s, to numerous calls for the extension and reinforcement of the system.

The GATT's Uruguay round of trade negotiations, concluded in 1994, created the WTO and the GATT itself, now expanded to include agriculture and textiles, *inter alia*, was folded into the WTO's mandate. The Uruguay round also gave the WTO two other agreements to oversee: the General Agreements on Trade in Services (GATS), which achieved some (limited) market access commitments in this area from WTO members but broader agreement on mod-alities for future negotiations on service liberalization, and the agreement on Trade Related Intellectual Property Rights (TRIPS), which obliged WTO members to agree to grant minimum periods of protection to copyrights, patents and trademarks. Important changes to strengthen the dispute settlement process and to make it more efficient were also implemented.

The primary WTO agreements (GATT, GATS and TRIPS) reflect its essential principles, the most central of which is that of *non-discrimination* among members. This is itself expressed in the joint principles of *most-favoured-nation* (implying that no member country may be discriminated against and any special favour granted to one member must be granted to all) and *national treatment* (which requires that imported and locally produced goods will be treated in the same way after the imports have entered the home market), which are explicitly stated in all three agreements. A further guiding principle underlying WTO agreements is predictability in trade policy, to be achieved through binding commitments and the use of simple and transparent policies (tariffs rather than non-tariff measures, for instance) that are publicly disclosed.

Important and much debated exceptions to the prescription of non-discrimination do, however, exist. The WTO permits countries to enter into preferential trade agreements (in the form of *free-trade areas* and *customs unions*) with one another. This is subject to the requirement that trade restrictions imposed by the members of the preferential agreement on non-member countries will not be more restrictive than before. A further restriction (itself controversial) is that the member countries eliminate barriers to 'substantially' all trade between themselves. However, violations of these restrictions are common, and the WTO has shown limited ability to enforce its rules. The recent proliferation of such preferential treaties among WTO members has led to concerns regarding the future shape of the world trading system and calls to strengthen its non-discriminatory disciplines. Separately, developing countries benefit from *special and differential status*, which gives them considerable leeway in using trade barriers to protect their 'infant industries' and balance of payments, and allows them to receive preferential market access (granted separately by individual industrialized countries on specific commodities of their choice) under the *general-*

ized system of preferences (which was developed by UNCTAD and incorporated into the GATT through an enabling clause introduced in its Tokyo round). Whether such exceptions have benefited developing countries or have acted to their detriment by encouraging egregiously protective regimes remains a subject of debate.

Ever-expanding membership (currently over 140 countries) and the increasing range of international economic activity under its jurisdiction mark the success of the WTO. A newly launched round of trade talks was launched in Doha, Qatar, in 2001, placing a special emphasis on developing countries (the Doha Development Agenda).

P. KRISHNA
BROWN UNIVERSITY

Further reading

Bhagwati, J. (1991) *The World Trading System at Risk*, Princeton, NJ.

Bhagwati, J., Krishna, P. and Panagariya, A. (1999) *Trade Blocs: Alternate Analyses of Preferential Trade Agreements*, Cambridge, MA.

Hoekman, B., Mattoo, A. and English, P. (2002) *Development, Trade, and the WTO: A Handbook*, Oxford.

Jackson, J. (1997) *The World Trading System: Law and Policy of International Economic Relations*, 2nd edn, Cambridge, MA.

SEE ALSO: free trade; globalization; international institutions; international monetary system; international trade

INDEX

Note: where headings are followed by more than six page references major treatments appear in **bold type**.